FUNDAMENTALS
   OF CRIMINAL LAW

EDITORIAL ADVISORY BOARD
Little, Brown and Company
Law Book Division

Richard A. Epstein
James Parker Hall Distinguished Service Professor of Law
University of Chicago

E. Allan Farnsworth
Alfred McCormack Professor of Law
Columbia University

Ronald J. Gilson
Charles J. Meyers Professor of Law and Business
Stanford University
Marc and Eva Stern Professor of Law and Business
Columbia University

Geoffrey C. Hazard, Jr.
Sterling Professor of Law
Yale University

James E. Krier
Earl Warren DeLano Professor of Law
University of Michigan

Elizabeth Warren
William A. Schnader Professor of Commercial Law
University of Pennsylvania

Bernard Wolfman
Fessenden Professor of Law
Harvard University

FUNDAMENTALS OF CRIMINAL LAW

Second Edition

PAUL H. ROBINSON
Professor of Law
Northwestern University School of Law

LITTLE, BROWN AND COMPANY
Boston   New York   Toronto   London

Copyright © 1995 by Paul H. Robinson.
All rights reserved. No part of this book may be reproduced in any form or by any electronic or mechanical means including information storage and retrieval systems without permission in writing from the publisher, except by a reviewer who may quote brief passages in a review.

Library of Congress Catalog Card No. 94-77905
ISBN 0-316-75111-1

EB-M

Published simultaneously in Canada
by Little, Brown & Company (Canada) Limited

Printed in the United States of America

*To
Sarah
—friend, exemplar, spouse*

SUMMARY OF CONTENTS

Contents	ix
Preface	xxv
Acknowledgments	xxvii
Preliminaries: The Criminal Justice Process	1

I / The Nature of Criminal Law — 21

Chapter 1.	The Criminal-Civil Distinction	23
Chapter 2.	Justification and Distribution of Liability and Punishment	31
Chapter 3.	The Structure and Sources of Criminal Law: An Overview	53
Chapter 4.	An Offense Illustration: Homicide	65
Chapter 5.	The Legality Principle	117
Chapter 6.	Proving Crimes	143

II / Defining Criminal Offenses — 175

Chapter 7.	Defining Offenses: A Closer Look	177
Chapter 8.	Inchoate Offenses	249

III / Imputing Offense Elements — 341

Chapter 9.	Introduction to Imputation	343
Chapter 10.	Complicity and Causing Crime by an Innocent	

		353
Chapter 11.	Imputing Culpability	389
Chapter 12.	Voluntary Intoxication and Causing One's Own Defense	395
Chapter 13.	Omission Liability	413
Chapter 14.	Corporate Criminality	429

IV / General Principles of Defense   453

Chapter 15.	Justifications	455
Chapter 16.	Excuses	525
Chapter 17.	Nonexculpatory Defenses	603

V / Changing Notions of Crime   625

Chapter 18.	Sexual Offenses	627
Chapter 19.	Racketeer Influenced and Corrupt Organizations (RICO)	655
Chapter 20.	Hate Crimes	675

VI / A Final Overview   685

Chapter 21.	Functions of Criminal Law	687

Appendix: Model Penal Code   699

CONTENTS

Preface	xxv
Acknowledgments	xxvii

Preliminaries: The Criminal Justice Process — 1

An Overview of the Criminal Justice Process: The Steps in the Process, W. LaFave and J. Israel, Criminal Procedure — 1
Chart: An Overview of the Criminal Justice System, The President's Commission on Law Enforcement and Administration of Justice, Task Force Report: Science and Technology — 17
Notes on a Statistical Overview of the Criminal Justice System — 18

I / THE NATURE OF CRIMINAL LAW — 21

Chapter 1. The Criminal-Civil Distinction — 23

Fear, Pain, and Bubble Gum	23
Notes on the Nature of Criminal Law	25
Questions	28

Chapter 2. Justification and Distribution of Liability and Punishment — 31

Daughters' Mustard	31

K. R. Greenawalt, Moral Justifications and Legal Punishment	32
Notes on Justificatory Purposes and Distributive Principles	39
Questions	43
Model Penal Code §1.02(1), The Purposes of the Provisions Governing the Definition of Offenses	45
P. Robinson, Hybrid Principles for the Distribution of Criminal Sanctions	45
Questions	47

Chapter 3. The Structure and Sources of Criminal Law: An Overview   53

Fear of the Daggers	53
Notes on the Operational Structure of Criminal Law	54
Notes on the Sources of Criminal Law	60

Chapter 4. An Offense Illustration: Homicide   65

4.1 Homicide Statutes	65
California Penal Code §§187, 188, 189, 192, Homicide Offenses	65
New York Penal Law §§125.00, 125.10, 125.15, 125.20, 125.25, 125.27, Homicide Offenses	67
Model Penal Code, Article 210, Criminal Homicide	70
4.2 Culpability Requirements	72
Babies and Ditches	72
Model Penal Code §§1.13(9)(a), 2.02(1)-(2), (5)-(7), Culpability Requirements	73
Notes on Modern Offense Culpability Requirements	74
Chart: Model Penal Code §2.02(2), Culpability Definitions	79
Questions	80
4.3 Doctrines of Aggravation: Premeditation, Specified Means, Reckless Murder, Felony Murder	81
"Meurtre" and Its Aggravations, J. F. Stephen, A History of the Criminal Law	81
Commonwealth v. Malone	*81*
Model Penal Code §210.2, Comment 6 (1980), Felony Murder	84
Questions	87
4.4 The Death Penalty	88

Model Penal Code §210.6, Sentence of Death for Murder; Further Proceedings to Determine Sentence	88
H. A. Bedau, Arguments For and Against Capital Punishment	91
Questions	95
4.5 Doctrines of Mitigation: Extreme Emotional Disturbance, Provocation, Mental Illness Negating an Element, "Diminished Capacity"	96
The Pot Boils	96
State v. Ott	*97*
New Zealand Crimes Act of 1961, §169(1), (2)	107
Questions	108
Beating Moles	109
United States v. Brawner	*109*
Model Penal Code §4.02(1), Evidence of Mental Disease or Defect Admissible When Relevant to Element of the Offense	113
Questions	114
People v. Mentry: "Mother Says She Was Told to Sit on Child, Who Died"	115
Questions	116

Chapter 5. The Legality Principle   117

The CG-PLA at the UN	118
Model Penal Code §1.05(1), All Offenses Defined by Statute	119
Calder v. Bull	*119*
Papachristou v. City of Jacksonville	*120*
Axis War Criminals Prosecution Report	126
Questions	129
Propping Up Ed	130
Model Penal Code §§1.02(3) & 2.12(2) & (3), Principles of Construction	131
Notes on the Interpretation of Criminal Statutes	131
United States v. Gray, Problem Case	139
Questions	140

Chapter 6. Proving Crimes   143

Burdens of Pleading, Production, and Persuasion, P. Robinson, Criminal Law Defenses	143

Model Penal Code §1.12 Proof Beyond A Reasonable Doubt; Affirmative Defenses; Burden of Proving Fact When Not an Element of an Offense; Presumptions	147
Patterson v. New York	*148*
Questions	156
Jackson v. Virginia	*157*
Questions	166
County Court of Ulster County v. Allen	*166*
Questions	172

II/DEFINING CRIMINAL OFFENSES 175

Chapter 7. Defining Offenses: A Closer Look 177

7.1 Determining Culpability Requirements	177
Regina v. Prince	*178*
Questions	181
Jake Sets a Record	182
Model Penal Code §2.02(3), Culpability Required Unless Otherwise Provided	183
Model Penal Code §2.02(4), Prescribed Culpability Requirement Applies to All Material Elements	183
Notes on Determining Offense Culpability Requirements	183
Questions	199
7.2 Minimum Culpability Requirements: The Debate over Recklessness, Negligence, and Strict Liability	199
Oatmeal For Ian	200
State v. Williams	*200*
Reasons for Punishing Negligence, G. Williams, Criminal Law: The General Part	204
Questions	205
Criticism of Practical Grounds of Strict Liability, J. Hall, General Principles of Criminal Law	207
Model Penal Code §2.05, When Culpability Requirements Are Inapplicable to Violations and to Offenses Defined by Other Statutes; Effect of Absolute Liability in Reducing Grade of Offense to Violation	211
State v. Buttrey	*211*
Questions	219

7.3 Culpability Requirements and Mistake Defenses	219
Model Penal Code §2.04(1), Ignorance or Mistake	220
Alaska Stat. §11.41.410(a)(1)	221
Alaska Stat. §11.81.610(b)	221
Laseter v. State	*221*
Chart: Culpability Requirements and Mistake Defenses	226
Questions	226
Vt. Pub. L. §8602, The Blanket Act	227
State v. Woods	*227*
Model Penal Code §2.02(9), Culpability as to Illegality of Conduct	229
Questions	229
7.4 Causation	229
Manny the Master	230
State v. Wood	*231*
Questions	233
Notes on Multiple Causes	234
Commonwealth v. Root	*237*
Questions	242
Jones v. Commonwealth	*243*
Questions	245
Model Penal Code §2.03, Causal Relationship Between Conduct and Result; Divergence Between Result Designed or Contemplated and Actual Result or Between Probable and Actual Result	245
Questions	246

Chapter 8. Inchoate Offenses   249

8.1 The Act Requirement	250
Cat in the Box	250
Model Penal Code §2.01(1), Requirement of Voluntary Act	250
Model Penal Code §1.13(2), Definition of "Act"	251
The Necessity for an Act, G. Williams, Criminal Law: The General Part	251
Conduct as a Prerequisite, H. Packer, The Limits of the Criminal Sanction	252
Robinson v. California	*253*
Powell v. Texas	*256*
Questions	260
Model Penal Code §2.01(4), Possession as an Act	261

Model Penal Code §5.06(1), Possessing Instruments of Crime	261
Questions	261
8.2 Attempt	262
A Plan to Kill	262
Model Penal Code §5.01, Comment	263
Model Penal Code §5.01(1) & (2), Criminal Attempt	268
Questions	269
Gambling Life	270
People v. Trinkle	*270*
State v. Maestas	*273*
Questions	275
8.3 Impossibility	277
The Smuggler's Deceit	278
People v. Rollino	*279*
Model Penal Code §5.01(1), Criminal Attempt	285
Questions	285
Notes on the Requirements for Attempt Liability	287
Notes on Impossibility Defenses that Continue to Exist Even in Modern Codes	287
Model Penal Code §5.05(2), Mitigation in Cases of Lesser Danger	289
H. Wechsler, W. K. Jones, and H. L. Korn, The Treatment of Inchoate Crimes in the Model Penal Code of the American Law Institute: Attempt, Solicitation, and Conspiracy	289
Questions	290
In re "The Nose . . ."	290
Questions	291
8.4 Grading of Inchoate Offenses	292
Model Penal Code §5.05(1), Grading of Criminal Attempt, Solicitation, and Conspiracy	292
S. Schulhofer, Harm and Punishment: A Critique of Emphasis on the Results of Conduct in the Criminal Law	292
G. Fletcher, A Crime of Self-Defense: Bernhard Goetz and the Law on Trial	294
Questions	297
8.5 Conspiracy and Solicitation	298
Selling Death	298
Archbold v. State	*299*
Model Penal Code §5.03(1) & (5), Criminal Conspiracy	302
Model Penal Code §§1.07(1)(b) & 5.05(3), Prosecution for Multiple Offenses; Limitation on Convictions	302

Questions	303
United States v. Feola	*304*
Model Penal Code §5.03 Comment	308
Questions	311
Gebardi v. United States	*312*
Model Penal Code §5.04, Incapacity, Irresponsibility, or Immunity of Party to Solicitation or Conspiracy	315
Model Penal Code §2.06(5) & (6), Special Defenses to Complicity	315
United States v. Lester, Problem Case	316
Questions	318
Notes on the Requirements for Conspiracy Liability	319
Bank Robbery with a Sub	320
Notes on Scope, Duration, and Collateral Consequences of Conspiracy	321
Questions	326
Bongo Sam Blows It	326
Model Penal Code §5.02, Criminal Solicitation	327
Questions	327
8.6 Termination and Renunciation	328
The Crays Go to Church	329
People v. Kimball	*330*
Model Penal Code §5.01(4), Renunciation of Attempt	337
Model Penal Code §5.02(3), Renunciation of Solicitation	337
Model Penal Code §5.03(6), Renunciation of Conspiracy	338
Model Penal Code §2.06(6)(C), Termination of Complicity	338
Questions	338

III / IMPUTING OFFENSE ELEMENTS 341

Chapter 9. Introduction to Imputation 343

Notes on the Imputation of Offense Elements 343

Chapter 10. Complicity and Causing Crime by an Innocent 353

10.1 Complicity 353

Bib Tries to Help	353
Model Penal Code §2.06(1)-(4), Liability for Conduct of Another; Complicity	354
State ex rel. Martin. Atty. Gen. v. Tally, Judge	*355*
Questions	358
Backun v. United States	*358*
Model Penal Code §2.04(3)(b), Complicity (Tent. Draft No. 1)	361
New York Penal Law §115.00, Criminal Facilitation in the Second Degree	362
Questions	362
N.H. Rev. Stat. Ann. §626.8, Criminal Liability for Conduct of Another	363
State v. Etzweiler	*364*
Questions	369
Notes on the Requirements for Complicity Liability	370
Questions	371
10.2 Causing Crime by an Innocent	372
The Egg Hunt	372
Bailey v. Commonwealth	*373*
Model Penal Code §2.06(1)-(2)(a), Liability for the Conduct of Another	377
Questions	377
Notes on the Requirements for Liability for Causing Crime by an Innocent	378
Questions	379
10.3 Defenses to Imputation of Another's Conduct	379
Chucky Backs Out	379
Regina v. Cogan, Regina v. Leak	*380*
People v. Anonymous	*384*
Model Penal Code §2.06(5), (6)(a) & (b), Qualified Rejection of Offense Exemption Defenses to Complicity	386
Model Penal Code §2.06(7), Rejection of Unconvictable Perpetrator Defense	386
Model Penal Code §5.01(3), Conduct Designed to Aid Another in Commission of a Crime	386
Questions	386

Chapter 11. Imputing Culpability   389

11.1 Divergence Between Intended and Actual Result	389
An Accidental Kidnapping	389

Model Penal Code §2.03(2)(a) & (3)(a), Divergence Between Result Designed or Contemplated and Actual Result or Between Probable and Actual Result	390
Questions	390
11.2 Inculpatory Mistakes	391
Impossible Incest?	391
Model Penal Code §2.04(2), Ignorance or Mistake	392
Questions	392

Chapter 12. Voluntary Intoxication and Causing One's Own Defense — 395

12.1 Voluntary Intoxication Negating an Offense Element	395
Food For Thought	395
Model Penal Code §§2.08(1), (2) & (5)(b), Intoxication Negating an Offense Element	396
Director of Public Prosecutions v. Majewski	*397*
P. Robinson, Causing the Conditions of One's Own Defense: A Study in the Limits of Theory in Criminal Law Doctrine	404
Questions	407
12.2 Causing the Conditions of One's Own Defense	408
Trading Corn for People	409
Model Penal Code §220.3, Criminal Mischief	410
Model Penal Code §§3.02(1)(a) & (2) Justification Generally: Choice of Evils	411
Model Penal Code §§2.09(1) & (2), Duress	411
Questions	411

Chapter 13. Omission Liability — 413

Dunning's Deal	414
Pa. Stat. Ann. Title 18, §2504, Involuntary Manslaughter	414
Model Penal Code §2.01(1) & (3), Liability for an Omission	414
Jones v. United States	*415*
Questions	418
"37 Who Saw Murder Didn't Call Police," N.Y. Times	418

A Penal Code Prepared by the Indian Law Commissioners	422
R.I. Gen. Laws §11-56-1, Duty to Assist	424
Wis. Stat. Ann. §940.34(1), (2), Duty to Aid Endangered Crime Victim	424
Questions	425
State v. Adelson	*425*
Questions	428

Chapter 14. Corporate Criminality   429

14.1 Liability of Corporate Officials	429
Collapse at Kalahoo No. 3	429
Model Penal Code §2.07(6), Liability of Person Acting, or Under a Duty to Act, in Behalf of a Corporation or Unincorporated Association	430
United States v. Park	*430*
Questions	437
14.2 Liability of Corporations	438
Evergreen Greenbacks	438
State v. Christy Pontiac-GMC, Inc.	*440*
Model Penal Code §2.07(1)-(5), Liability of Corporations and Unincorporated Associations	444
Questions	445
Model Penal Code §2.07, Comment	446
A New Form of Corporate Liability?, A. Ashworth, Principles of Criminal Law	448
Questions	450

IV/GENERAL PRINCIPLES OF DEFENSE   453

Chapter 15. Justifications   455

15.1 The Nature of Justifications	455
Notes on the Nature of Justifications	455
15.2 Lesser Evils	458
A Life-Saving Break-in	458
Model Penal Code §3.02(1), Justification Generally: Choice of Evils	459
The Queen v. Dudley and Stephens	*459*

	State v. Green	*463*
	Questions	467
	State v. Dorsey	*467*
	Questions	469
15.3	Public Authority	470
	Docker's Box	470
	Model Penal Code §3.03, Execution of Public Duty	471
	Model Penal Code §3.08, Use of Force by Persons with Special Responsibility for Care, Discipline or Safety of Others	472
	Questions	474
	Tennessee v. Garner	*474*
	Model Penal Code §3.07(1)-(3), (5), Use of Force in Law Enforcement	480
	Questions	481
15.4	Defensive Force	482
	Rosie's Homerun	482
	Model Penal Code §§3.04, 3.05, 3.06, 3.10, 3.11(2) & (3), Defensive Force Justifications	483
	Judgement of the German Supreme Court	*488*
	Questions	490
	United States ex rel. Means v. Solem	*490*
	Questions	496
15.5	Mistake as to a Justification	497
	Moro's Mistake	497
	Model Penal Code §3.11(1), Definition of "Unlawful Force"	498
	Model Penal Code §3.09, Mistake of Law as to Unlawfulness of Force or Legality of Arrest; Reckless or Negligent Use of Otherwise Justifiable Force; Reckless or Negligent Injury or Risk of Injury to Innocent Persons	499
	Questions	499
	North Dakota Cent. Code §§12.1-05-03, -04, -07, -08, -12 Defensive Force Justifications; Excuse for Mistake	500
	Questions	501
	People v. Goetz	*502*
	Questions	510
	State v. Kelly	*511*
	Questions	517
	United States v. Calley, Problem	517
	Questions	519
	Model Penal Code §2.10, Military Orders	520
15.6	Unknowingly Justified Actor	520

Biker's Break	520
Notes on the Unknowingly Justified Actor	521
Questions	523

Chapter 16. Excuses   525

16.1 The Nature of Excuses	525
The Brothers' Brawl	525
Notes on the Nature of Excuses	526
Questions	536
16.2 Insanity and Involuntary Intoxication	536
Michael's Madness	537
Parson's v. State	*538*
Model Penal Code §4.01, Mental Disease or Defect Excluding Responsibility	543
United States v. Brawner	*543*
United States Code, Title 18, §17, Insanity Defense	551
Questions	551
Model Penal Code §2.08(4) & (5), Defense of Involuntary Intoxication	552
Questions	553
State v. Rodriques, Problem	553
Questions	555
Jones v. United States	*555*
Questions	561
16.3 Duress, Immaturity, and the Voluntary Act Requirement	562
Arthur's Adventure	562
State v. Toscano	*563*
Model Penal Code §2.09, Duress	569
Questions	569
Model Penal Code §4.10, Immaturity Excluding Criminal Convictions; Transfer of Proceedings to Juvenile Court	570
Questions	571
Hypnotizing Bunny	572
Automatism: Nature of the Defence, G. Williams, Textbook on Criminal Law	572
Model Penal Code §2.01(1) & (2), Requirement of Voluntary Act	574
Questions	575
16.4 Mistake Excuses	576
Sophie's Stand	576

United States v. Anthony	*577*
United States v. Barker, United States v. Martinez	*578*
Model Penal Code §2.04(3) & (4), Ignorance or Mistake of Law Defense	585
N.J. Stat. Ann. §2C:2-4(c)(3)	586
Questions	586
16.5 Problematic Excuses	587
Who Is Edward Drum?	587
R. Delgado, Ascription of Criminal States of Mind: Toward a Defense Theory for the Coercively Persuaded ("Brainwashed") Defendant	588
United States v. Alexander	*591*
Questions	599
People v. Kimura: "A 'Cultural Defense' at Issue in Trial"	600
Questions	601

Chapter 17. Nonexculpatory Defenses — 603

17.1 The Nature of Nonexculpatory Defenses	603
Farnsworth v. Zerbst, Warden	*603*
Notes on the Nature of Nonexculpatory Defenses	605
Questions	609
17.2 Entrapment	610
JJ's Out	610
Del. Code Ann. Title 11, §432 Entrapment as Affirmative Defense; Defense Unavailable in Certain Situations	611
Harrison v. State	*611*
Model Penal Code §2.13, Entrapment	618
Questions	619
United States v. Perl	*619*
Questions	622

V/CHANGING NOTIONS OF CRIME — 625

Chapter 18. Sexual Offenses — 627

Bob and Linda	627
Model Penal Code §213.1, Rape and Related Offenses	628

Questions	629
Model Penal Code §213.1, Comment 8(c), The Spousal Exclusion	635
Questions	637
Model Penal Code §213.3, Corruption of Minors and Seduction	638
Model Penal Code §213.6(3), Sexually Promiscuous Complainants	639
Model Penal Code §213.3, Comment 2, Statutory Rape	639
Questions	641
Model Penal Code §213.6(1), Mistake as to Age	643
Model Penal Code §213.6, Comment 2, Mistake as to Age	643
Questions	645
Model Penal Code §213.1, Comment 8(a), Limitation of Liability to Males for Offenses Against Females	646
Questions	647
Model Penal Code §213.2, Comment 2, Decriminalization of Deviate Sexual Intercourse Between Consenting Adults	650
Questions	653

Chapter 19. Racketeer Influenced and Corrupt Organizations (RICO)   655

Statement of Findings and Purpose, Organized Crime Control Act of 1970	655
18 U.S.C. §§1961-1962, Racketeer Influenced and Corrupt Organization Act	656
United States v. Masters, Corbitt, and Keating	*657*
Questions	661
G. Lynch, RICO: The Crime of Being a Criminal	662
Questions	667
National Organization for Women, Inc. v. Scheidler	*668*
Questions	673

Chapter 20. Hate Crimes   675

Recurring Nightmare of Hate Crimes, National Journal	675

Wisconsin Criminal Code §939.645, Crimes Committed Against Certain People or Property	676
State v. Mitchell	*677*
Questions	682

VI/A FINAL OVERVIEW   685

Chapter 21. Functions of Criminal Law   687

Your Basement Burglar	687
Notes on the Functions of Criminal Law Doctrine	688

Appendix: Model Penal Code   699

Table of Cases	797
Table of Statutes	801
Index	809

PREFACE

This edition continues with the philosophy of the first, that the primary goal of a basic text ought to be the development of a sophisticated understanding of the fundamentals. The book seeks to assure that students will come away with an understanding of the basic rules of criminal liability, their underlying rationales, and the larger conceptual framework that defines their interrelation. In the process of presenting the fundamentals, the book aims at developing the skills of case reading, statutory interpretation, and theoretical analysis.

This edition significantly modifies the format of the previous, building upon those aspects of the first edition that proved most successful in my teaching and in others'. The use of case problems has been expanded; most of the 48 sections now begin with a hypothetical or real fact pattern that focuses attention on the primary issues of the section. Experience suggests that putting the theoretical issues in a factual setting piques interest and focuses attention.

The streamlined style of the previous edition is taken further by substituting notes and questions for some of the material previously presented through excerpts. This shortening created room in this edition for new material on such topics as sexual offenses, RICO, hate crimes, the death penalty, and burdens of proof and presumptions. Yet, even with the addition of these topics, the resulting volume is the shortest criminal law coursebook available. This means that students can read and carefully consider all of the material assigned, and instructors realistically can expect students to do this. Despite its brevity, most instructors of a three-credit course will have to be selective in the sections they assign.

My hope is that you will find that this edition retains the rigor and challenge of the first while providing an even more rewarding experience for both student and teacher.

Paul H. Robinson

October 1994

ACKNOWLEDGMENTS

I am indebted to many people for their contributions to the Second Edition: to several anonymous reviewers and many not so anonymous colleagues and friends who offered comments and criticisms on the First Edition, to three excellent secretaries—Robert Dennis, Dreama King, and Valerie Mercurio—who cheerfully labored through many drafts, and to Dean Roger Dennis of Rutgers University School of Law at Camden and Dean Robert Bennett of Northwestern University School of Law for their support. My greatest debt, for reasons obvious to anyone who knows me, is to my spouse, Sarah McAlpine Robinson.

Thanks are also in order for permission to reprint material, granted by:

American Law Institute, Model Penal Code Parts I-II. Copyright © 1985 by the American Law Institute, as Adopted at the 1962 Annual Meeting of the American Law Institute. Reprinted with permission of the American Law Institute.

Ashworth, A., Principles of Criminal Law, 86-88 (1991). Reprinted with permission of Oxford University Press.

Bedau, H. A., Arguments For and Against Capital Punishment, Encyclopedia of Crime and Justice, 139-141 (S. Kadish ed. 1983). Reprinted with permission of MacMillan and Free Press.

Delgado, R., Ascription of the Criminal States of Mind: Toward a Defense Theory for the Coercively Persuaded ("Brainwashed") Defendant, 63 Minn. L. Rev. 1, 1-11 (1978). Reprinted by permission of the author and Minnesota Law Review.

Fletcher, G., A Crime of Self-Defense: Bernhard Goetz and the Law on Trial, 64-67 (1988). Reprinted with the permission of The Free Press, an imprint of Simon & Schuster. Copyright © 1988 by George P. Fletcher.

Fletcher, G., Translation of Judgment of the German Supreme Court, 55 Decision of the Supreme Court in Criminal Matters 82 (unpublished). Reprinted by permission of the author.

Gansberg, M., "37 Who Saw Murder Didn't Call Police," The New

York Times. Copyright © 1964 by The New York Times Company. Reprinted by permission.

Greenawalt, K. R., Punishment: Moral Justifications and Legal Punishment. Reprinted with permission of Macmillan, Inc. from Encyclopedia of Crime and Justice, Sanford H. Kadish, Editor in Chief, Volume IV, 1337-1342 (1983). Copyright © 1983 by The Free Press, a Division of Macmillan, Inc.

Hall, J., General Principles of Criminal Law 342-351 (2d ed. 1960). Reprinted by permission of the author and The Michie Co.

LaFave, W. and Israel, J., Criminal Procedure §1.4 (1984). Reprinted by permission of West Publishing Co.

Landers, A., "The Nose Knows in Arizona," The Philadelphia Inquirer. Copyright © Los Angeles Times Syndicate. Reprinted by permission of Ann Landers and Los Angeles Times Syndicate.

Lynch, G., RICO: The Crime of Being a Criminal, 87 Colum. L. Rev. 661, 920, 932-953 (1987). Reprinted by permission of the Columbia Law Review.

MacKinnon, C., "Rape: On Coercion and Consent," in Toward a Feminist Theory of the State, 175-176 (1989). Reprinted by permission of the publisher, Harvard University Press, Cambridge, Mass. Copyright © 1989 by Catherine A. MacKinnon.

National Journal, Recurring Nightmare of Hate Crimes, Dec. 15, 1990, v. 22, no. 50, p.3045. Reprinted by permission.

National Law Journal, "Mother Says She Was Told To Sit on Child, Who Died," Ellison, K., March 14, 1983, at 4. Copyright © 1983 by New York Law Publishing Company. Reprinted by permission.

Olsen, F., Statutory Rape: A Feminist Critique of Rights Analysis, 63 Texas L. Rev. 387, 390. Copyright © 1984 by the Texas Law Review Association. Reprinted by permission.

Packer, H., The Limits of the Criminal Sanction 73-75 (1968). Copyright © 1968 by Herbert L. Packer. Reprinted with the permission of the publishers, Stanford University Press.

Philadelphia Inquirer, A "Cultural Defense" at Issue in Trial, Sept. 1, 1985. Reprinted by permission of the Philadelphia Inquirer, Copyright.

Robinson, Causing the Conditions of One's Own Defense: A Study in the Limits of Theory in Criminal Law Doctrine, 71 Va. L. Rev. 1, 14-17, 27-36, 51 (1985). Reprinted by permission of Virginia Law Review Association and Fred B. Rothman & Co.

Robinson, P., Criminal Law Defenses, Vol. 1 §3 (1984). Reprinted with permission of West Publishing Company.

Robinson, P., Hate Crimes: Crimes of Motive, Character, or Group Terror?, 1992/93 Ann. Surv. Am. L. 605, 615. Reprinted by permission of Annual Survey of American Law, New York University School of Law.

Acknowledgments

Robinson, P., Hybrid Principles for the Distribution of Criminal Sanctions, 82 Northwestern University Law Review, 19-22, 28-35 (1987). Reprinted by permission of the Northwestern University Law School.

Robinson, P., and Grall, J., Element Analysis in Defining Criminal Liability: The Model Penal Code and Beyond, 35 Stan. L. Rev. 681, 728 (1983). Reprinted by permission of the authors.

Russell, D., Rape in Marriage 198-199 (1982). Reprinted by permission of Indiana University Press.

Schulhofer, S., Harm and Punishment: A Critique of Emphasis on the Results of Conduct in the Criminal Law, 122 U. Pa. L. Rev. 1497, 1514-1516 (1974). Reprinted by permission of the author and University of Pennsylvania Law Review.

Stephen, J. F., A History of the Criminal Law of England, Volume 3, p. 94 (1883). Reprinted by permission of Macmillan, Inc.

Wechsler, H., Jones, W. K., and Korn, H. L., The Treatment of Inchoate Crimes in the Model Code of the American Law Institute: Attempt, Solicitation, and Conspiracy, 61 Colum. L. Rev. 571, 584-585 (1961). Copyright © 1961 by the Directors of the Columbia Law Review Association, Inc. All rights reserved. Reprinted by permission.

Wiener, R., Shifting the Communication Burden: A Meaningful Consent Standard in Rape, 6 Harv. Women's L.J. 143, 147-148. Copyright © 1983 by the President and Fellows of Harvard College and Harv. W.L.J.

Williams, G., Criminal Law: The General Part 1-2, 122-124 (2d ed. 1961). Reprinted by permission of the author and Sweet and Maxwell, Ltd.

Williams, G., Textbook on Criminal Law 608-611 (1979). Reprinted by permission of Sweet & Maxwell, Ltd.

FUNDAMENTALS
OF CRIMINAL LAW

PRELIMINARIES: THE CRIMINAL JUSTICE PROCESS

An Overview of the Criminal Justice Process: The Steps in the Process
W. LaFave and J. Israel, Criminal Procedure, §1.4 (1985)

[W]e will describe briefly the major steps taken in the processing of a criminal case. Our focus . . . is on the processing of a "typical case" in a "typical jurisdiction." This means that our description basically is limited to those procedures employed by most states in processing most of their felony and misdemeanor cases. Where no single procedural pattern is followed by a substantial majority of the states, we will note the major alternatives followed by significant groups of states. However, variations adopted by only a few states, or variations applied only to a limited class of cases, are largely ignored. . . .

(a) Step 1: The Report of the Crime. The criminal justice process usually starts when the police receive information concerning the possible commission of a crime. The police may obtain that information either through their own observations or from the reports of interested citizens. In either case, if it appears likely that a crime was committed, the offense will be recorded in the police files as a "reported" crime (and will be listed statistically as an offense "known to the police").

Surprisingly, we have somewhat limited data on the exact distribution of reported crimes in this country. The data is adequate, however, to provide a rough estimate of the likely distribution of reported offenses in a typical industrial state. Approximately 60 percent of all reported crimes will relate to the taking or destruction of property. The major offenses in this group will include the various forms of theft (perhaps 50 percent of all property offenses), burglary (15 percent), and vandalism (15 percent). Assaults of all varieties, ranging from assaults with weapons to simple assaults, may provide an additional 10 percent of the reported crimes. Offenses relating to the use of alcohol and drugs (e.g., public drunkenness, possession of drugs, and driving under the influence) are likely to constitute another 10 percent of the reported offenses. The remaining 20 percent of the reported crimes will be spread over a variety of offenses. Included in this group are the most serious violent felonies, such as robbery (likely to constitute 2 to 4 percent of all reported offenses), and murder and forcible rape (each likely to fall below one-half of one percent).

(b) Step 2: Pre-arrest Investigation. Once the police become aware of the possible commission of a crime, they must determine (1) whether the crime actually was committed and (2) if it was, whether there is sufficient information pointing to the guilt of a particular person to justify arresting and charging him. Pre-arrest investigative procedures are designed to answer these questions and to collect evidence that may be helpful in establishing guilt at trial. The particular procedures used will vary with the circumstances of the crime. In some instances, a police officer will observe a crime being committed in his presence and will make an arrest "on the spot." In such cases, the pre-arrest investigation consists of no more than the officer's initial observation. In other cases, the officer will observe activity that is suspicious, though not necessarily criminal, and will seek further information to determine whether to make an arrest. Where an alleged offense has been called to the officer's attention by an interested citizen, the officer also is likely to seek further information.

Where additional information is sought, the officer may utilize a variety of investigatory techniques to gather that information. Perhaps the most common is to question the suspect. Pre-arrest questioning may be accompanied by the temporary detention of the suspect on the street or at home, but does not involve taking him into custody, as occurs with an arrest. The scope of the officer's questioning may range from merely asking the suspect to identify himself to asking him to respond to an accusation made by others. Where the crime investigated involved violence, or there is some other reason to believe the suspect could be armed, the officer may undertake some sort of search of the temporarily detained suspect (usually a pat-down or "frisk" of the suspect's outer clothing). In a small percentage of these police-suspect encounters, the officer also may search the car of a suspect who was stopped while driving.

Along with the police-suspect encounter, the other common pre-arrest investigatory techniques are the interviewing of witnesses (including the victim) and the examination of the scene of the crime. In certain types of cases (e.g., homicides and burglaries) that examination may include the collection of physical evidence (e.g., fingerprints) that will be subjected to scientific analysis. For other offenses, commonly those committed by specialized professional criminals, police informants may be contacted for information concerning possible offenders. Thorough searches of homes and offices, and electronic eavesdropping through wiretaps and similar devices, are also used in certain types of investigations. These procedures, however, commonly require prior judicial authorization through the issuance of a search warrant.

(c) Step 3: The Arrest. Once the officer has acquired sufficient information to justify arresting a suspect, the arrest ordinarily is the next step in the criminal justice process. An arrest generally occurs when the officer takes the suspect into custody for the purpose of transporting him to the station and there charging him with a crime.[3] Although an arrest may be authorized in advance by a judicially issued warrant, the vast majority of all arrests are made on the officer's own initiative, without a warrant.

As with reported crimes, arrests will be distributed over a variety of offenses. The distribution of arrests will differ substantially from distribution of reported crimes, however, because some reported crimes are more likely to lead to arrests than others.[4] While the exact distribution will vary with the individual jurisdiction, a general pattern emerges that roughly fits most jurisdictions. Typically, only 20 to 30 percent of the arrests will be for felonies, with the remainder being for misdemeanors. Though the theft group of offenses constitutes the number one category of reported crimes, it often ranks behind the alcohol/drug offenses as a basis for arrests. In those jurisdictions that continue to treat public drunkenness as a crime, that offense alone, even where not enforced with full vigor, can account for 20 percent of all arrests. When that 20 percent is added to arrests for driving under the influence and possession or sale of drugs, over one-third of all arrests are likely to be attributable to alcohol/drug offenses. The theft offenses are then likely to account for 25 to 30 percent of the arrests. A substantial percentage of the arrests, perhaps as high as 20 percent, will be for public disorder misdemeanors, such as simple assaults, vandalism, and disorderly conduct. Less than 10 percent will be for serious felony offenses against the person, with aggravated assault and robbery likely to account for 2 percent each and forcible rape and murder for less than one-half of one percent each. The remaining arrests, approximately 10 percent,

---

3. As an alternative to the traditional "custodial arrest," many jurisdictions grant the officer discretion to briefly detain a person subject to arrest and to then release him upon issuance of a citation (sometimes called an "appearance ticket"). This alternative is most commonly authorized for misdemeanor offenses, and sometimes is limited to particular types of misdemeanors.

4. The "arrest-clearance" rate for reported crimes (which is basically the percentage of reported offenses resulting in the arrest of a suspected offender) varies from over 90 percent for some offenses to less than 20 percent for others. Those crimes that tend to come to the attention of a police officer through his personal observation of the crime usually have the highest arrest-clearance rates. Substantially lower rates are found for offenses that become known to the police primarily through victim reports. Here, the most significant factor will be the victim's ability to identify the offender. Thus, the arrest-clearance rate for burglary (20 percent) is far less than that for aggravated assault (over 60 percent).

will be spread over a wide variety of offenses, including arson, nonviolent sex offenses, and possession of weapons.

A substantial percentage of the persons arrested, typically 20 to 30 percent, will be within the age limit for juvenile court jurisdiction. Ordinarily, juvenile arrestees will be separated from the adult arrestees shortly after their arrest. From this point on, we will assume that we are dealing only with the adult arrestees.

(d) Step 4: Booking. Immediately after making an arrest, the arresting officer usually will search the arrestee's person and remove any weapons, contraband, or evidence relating to a crime. He then will arrange for the transportation of the arrestee to the police station, a centrally located jail, or some similar "holding" facility. It is at this facility that the arrestee will be taken through a process known as "booking." Initially, the arrestee's name, the time of his arrival, and the offense for which he was arrested are noted in the police "blotter" or "log." The arrestee then will be photographed and fingerprinted. Typically, he also will be informed of the charge on which he has been booked and will be allowed to make at least one telephone call. When booked on a minor offense, he may be able to obtain his release on "stationhouse bail," that is, by posting cash as a security payment and promising to appear before a magistrate at a specified date. Persons arrested on serious offenses, and those arrested on minor offenses but unable to gain their release, will remain at the holding facility until ready to be presented before a magistrate (see step 8). Ordinarily, they will be placed in a "lockup," which usually is some kind of cell. Before entering the lockup, they will be subjected to another search, more thorough than that conducted at the point of arrest. This search is designed primarily to inventory the arrestee's personal belongings and to prevent the introduction of contraband into the lockup.

(e) Step 5: Post-Arrest Investigation. The extent of the post-arrest investigation will vary with the fact situation. In some situations, such as where the arrestee was caught "red-handed," there will be little left to be done. In other situations, police will utilize many of the same kinds of investigative procedures as are used before arrest (e.g., interviewing witnesses, searching the suspect's home, and viewing the scene of the crime). Post-arrest investigation does offer one important investigative source, however, that ordinarily is not available prior to the arrest—the person of the arrestee. Thus, the arrestee may be placed in a lineup or simply taken to a place where a witness can view him individually (a "showup"). He may be required to provide handwriting or hair samples that can be compared with evidence the police have found at the scene of the crime. He also may be questioned at length about the crime for which he was arrested and any other crime thought to be related. Although we do not have precise data on these post-arrest procedures involving the arrestee, the best available estimates indicate they are not

applied to the vast majority of arrestees. In most communities, they are used almost exclusively in the investigation of felony cases and even then not in most of those investigations.

(f) Step 6: The Decision to Charge. Sometime between the booking of the arrestee and his presentation before a magistrate, there will be a review of the decision to file charges. Initially, the police officer making the arrest fills out an arrest report, which is reviewed by a higher ranking police officer. That officer may conclude either that charges should not be brought or that they should be based on a lower level offense than that for which the arrestee was booked. The decision not to charge may be based upon the officer's conclusion that there is insufficient evidence or that the particular offense can more appropriately be handled by a "stationhouse adjustment" (e.g., in the case of a fight among acquaintances, a warning and lecture may be deemed sufficient). If the officer decides against prosecution, the arrestee may be released from the lockup on the officer's direction (although some departments follow the practice of seeking prosecutor approval before releasing felony arrestees). In some jurisdictions, the police will drop as many as 10 to 15 percent of their arrests (predominantly misdemeanor arrests) at this point.

The second review of the decision to charge is usually the review of the case by a prosecuting attorney. Prosecutor offices vary considerably, however, both as to the timing and extent of their review. In some jurisdictions, prosecutors regularly screen all felony and misdemeanor cases before charges are filed with the court. In other jurisdictions, pre-charge prosecutorial review is limited to exceptional cases, primarily those in which the police seek the prosecutor's advice. Here, the primary prosecutorial screening occurs sometime after charges have been filed. In the case of felonies, the prosecutor may not review the case until he is required to present it at a preliminary hearing or a grand jury screening. In misdemeanor cases, the prosecutor may not review the case until it goes to trial (and thus he may never screen misdemeanor charges to which the defendant pleads guilty). Still other jurisdictions prefer a midway position, with prosecutors undertaking a pre-charge screening for all felony cases, but utilizing a post-charge review for all but the most serious misdemeanors.

The timing of the screening is likely to have an impact upon the scope of the screening, as prosecutors tend to have less information available to them the earlier their review is undertaken. However, even among prosecutors utilizing the most prompt post-arrest screening, there is considerable variation in the sources considered in deciding whether to charge. The practice ranges from prosecutors who read only the police reports to those who regularly interview the police officer and often the victim of the crime as well.

Prosecutor offices also vary in the weight that will be given to a particular factor in determining whether to prosecute. The most significant factor, of course, is the strength of the evidence. If the evidence clearly is insufficient to gain a conviction, the case will be dropped. Similarly, if the evidence will support only a lesser offense than that suggested by the police, the charge will be reduced. Where the evidence arguably is sufficient to support the requested charge, the prosecutor will then turn to other factors that might suggest the case is inappropriate for prosecution in light of the equities of the situation and the overall caseload of the prosecutor's office. Such factors include the harm caused by the offense, the victim's attitude toward pressing the case, the arrestee's criminal record, and the adequacy of alternative remedies.[5] It is in the consideration of these factors that differences between prosecutors are most likely to be significant.

Though we can hardly characterize any particular pre-charge screening program as typical of most jurisdictions, a fairly common pattern is found in the eventual results of the overall screening carried on through the entire criminal justice process. In the end, at least as to felonies, the cases against 30 to 60 percent of all arrestees will be dropped as a result of such screening.[6] If only a small percentage of the felony cases are rejected at pre-charge screening, then there will be a much higher percentage rejected at subsequent stages when the prosecutor engages in more thorough screening.

To some extent, the prosecutor's post-charge screening will give greater weight to the sufficiency of the evidence, but the prosecutor is still free to consider all of the factors that are considered in pre-charge screening. If the prosecutor decides in his post-charge screening that the case does not merit prosecution, he will file a motion to terminate the prosecution (a *nolle prosequi* motion), which will be granted almost automatically by the court. In jurisdictions in which pre-charge screening is not extensive, post-charge screening may account for the disposition of more charges than any other step in the criminal justice process.

---

5. Many prosecutor offices have developed pre-charge "diversion programs" that provide a formal structure for the prosecutor's refusal to charge notwithstanding sufficient evidence. Under these programs, certain types of charges (usually misdemeanors) will not be prosecuted if the arrestee agrees to comply with specified "rehabilitative conditions" (e.g., making restitution to the victim, maintaining regular employment, etc.). Other prosecutors prefer not to tie the decision to charge to such conditions. They will bring charges and then seek to have the rehabilitative conditions imposed as conditions of probation following conviction.

6. The limited data available on the disposition of misdemeanor arrests indicates that a high percentage of misdemeanor cases also are rejected as a result of prosecutorial screening, but those figures are much more difficult to evaluate. In some jurisdictions, for example, post-charge dismissals may include situations in which defendants charged with offenses such as public drunkenness are allowed to forfeit their bail, with the charges against them then being dismissed—a practice that amounts, in effect, to imposing a fine without a conviction record.

In New York City, for example, where only one percent of all felony arrestees are rejected for prosecution at the pre-charge stage, approximately 40 percent of all charges are subsequently rejected through post-charge screening, usually before the cases reach the trial court. Secondary screening also can be quite significant in jurisdictions with extensive pre-charge screening. In the District of Columbia, for example, the cases against 21 percent of the arrestees are rejected by an initial decision not to charge, but then an additional 29 percent are dismissed after charges are brought, on *nolle prosequi* motions.[7]

Statistics on charge reductions reflect a less consistent pattern than that characterizing dismissals. The percentage of reductions attributable to the screening process varies considerably, but prosecutors have been known to reduce the offense from that designated in the police booking in as many as 30 percent of the felony cases subjected to pre-charge screening. In many jurisdictions, certain types of felony arrests, most notably those involving non-professional thefts, are almost automatically reduced to misdemeanors (e.g., first-offense shoplifting reduced to petty theft). While most reductions occur before the initial charge is filed, a substantial number of reductions often occur later in the proceedings on the prosecutor's motion. Where plea bargaining takes the form of a charge bargain rather than a sentence bargain (see step 12), most of the later reductions are likely to be attributable to plea bargaining rather than post-charge prosecutorial screening.

(g) Step 7: Filing the Complaint. Assuming that the pre-charge screening results in a decision to prosecute, the next step in the criminal justice process is the filing of charges with the magistrate court. Typically, the initial charging instrument will be called a "complaint." In misdemeanor cases, which may be tried before the magistrate court, the complaint will serve as the charging instrument throughout the proceedings. In felony cases, on the other hand, the complaint serves to set forth the charges only before the magistrate court; an information or indictment will replace the complaint as the charging instrument when the case reaches the general trial court. The complaint ordinarily includes a brief description of the offense and is sworn to by a complainant. The complainant usually will be either the victim or the investigating officer. When an officer-complainant did not observe the offense being committed, but relied on information received from the victim or other witnesses, he will note that the facts alleged in the complaint are based on "information and belief."

In most jurisdictions, at some point between the filing of the com-

---

7. One factor that often leads to the dismissal of a case that was approved at pre-charge screening is a "change of heart" by the victim. This factor is especially significant for those cases in which the victim is likely to have had a previous acquaintance with the arrestee (a common situation, for example, in aggravated assault cases).

plaint and the first appearance (see step 8), the magistrate will conduct an ex parte review of the case. The purpose of this review is to ensure that the arrest and complaint are supported by sufficient incriminating information to establish probable cause to believe the defendant committed the crime charged. The magistrate's review may be based on the complaint itself where the complaint alleges the facts establishing probable cause (e.g., that the complainant observed the offense). In other cases, it may be based on a police officer's affidavit setting forth available information establishing probable cause. In some jurisdictions, the magistrate also may base his determination upon a brief oral statement presented by the complainant. If the magistrate finds that probable cause has not been established, he will direct the prosecution to promptly produce more information or release the arrested person. Such instances tend to be quite rare, however.[8]

(h) Step 8: The First Appearance. After the complaint has been filed and reviewed, the arrestee (who is now formally a defendant) is presented before the magistrate. This proceeding before the magistrate usually is described as the "first appearance," although some jurisdictions call it the "initial presentment" or the "arraignment on the warrant." Where the arrested person was released by police on a citation or stationhouse bail, the first appearance will not be scheduled until several days after the arrest. In most instances, however, the arrestee will still be in custody, and state law will require that he be brought before the magistrate without unnecessary delay. Ordinarily, the time consumed in booking, transportation, reviewing the decision to charge, and limited post-arrest investigation makes it unlikely that the arrestee will be presented before the magistrate until at least several hours after his arrest. Thus, if the magistrate court does not have an evening session, a person arrested in the afternoon or evening will not be presented before the magistrate until the next day. If arrested on a Friday, or a weekend, he will not be presented until the next Monday, unless the magistrate court has a special weekend session.

The first appearance often is a quite brief proceeding. Initially, the magistrate will make certain that the person before him is the person named in the complaint. The magistrate then will inform the defendant of the charge in the complaint and will note various rights that the defendant may have in further proceedings. The range of rights men-

---

8. In many states, if the defendant was arrested without a warrant (as is usually the case), the magistrate will issue an arrest warrant after finding probable cause. Since the defendant has already been arrested, the warrant is not being used here for its traditional function of obtaining prior judicial approval for the arrest. Instead, the post-arrest warrant serves simply to provide judicial authorization for continuing to hold the arrestee in custody. In most jurisdictions, the post-arrest issuance of a warrant is viewed as an unnecessary formality, and the magistrate's finding of probable cause will combine with the complaint to authorize continuing custody.

tioned will vary from one jurisdiction to another. Commonly, the magistrate will inform the defendant of his right to remain silent and warn him that anything he says in court or to the police may be used against him at trial. The magistrate also will inform the defendant of his right to be represented by counsel and his right to appointed counsel if he is indigent. Although the timing varies, most jurisdictions at least initiate the process of providing counsel for the indigent at the first appearance. The magistrate first will determine that the defendant is indigent and desires the assistance of appointed counsel. The magistrate then will either himself arrange for representation by the public defender or appointed private counsel or notify the judge in charge of appointments.

Other aspects of the first appearance are likely to depend upon whether the defendant is charged with a felony or misdemeanor. In the felony case, the magistrate will advise the defendant of the next step in the process, the preliminary hearing, and will set a date for that hearing unless the defendant desires to waive it. If the defendant is charged with a misdemeanor, he will not be entitled to a preliminary hearing (or a subsequent grand jury review). The misdemeanor charge is triable to the magistrate, and the magistrate therefore can proceed with the misdemeanor case in the same fashion as a general trial court receiving a felony case. For the misdemeanor, the first appearance becomes an arraignment on the complaint, equivalent to the arraignment on the information or indictment in a felony case (see step 12).[9]

The final function of the magistrate at the first appearance is to set bail (i.e., set the conditions under which the defendant can obtain his release from custody pending the final disposition of his case). If the defendant obtained his release previously by posting stationhouse bail, the magistrate will merely review that bail. In felony cases, the defendant ordinarily will still be in custody and the magistrate will be making the initial decision on bail. At one time, bail was limited almost entirely to the posting of cash or a secured bond, purchased from a professional bondsman. Today, the defendant may also be able to obtain

---

9. The initial step in the magistrate's arraignment of the misdemeanor defendant involves an explanation of available pleas to the charge stated in the complaint and an entry of a plea to that charge. While most misdemeanor defendants eventually plead guilty, many will not to so at the first appearance since they have not yet had the opportunity to consult with counsel or others (e.g., relatives) whose advice might be sought. They will plead not guilty or will be allowed to defer entry of their plea to a later day. In a jurisdiction relying primarily on post-charge screening, a substantial percentage of the misdemeanor cases will be reviewed by the prosecutor and dismissed on his motion prior to the defendant's next scheduled court appearance. For the cases that survive this screening, the rate of guilty pleas is likely to be between 80 and 95 percent. For these defendants, the next step in the process is sentencing (see step 15). For the 5 to 20 percent of the surviving cases that go to trial, the next step will be the filing of pretrial motions (see step 13).

his release by depositing with the court cash equal to 10 percent of the amount of the bond set by the magistrate. Indeed, several states make such extensive use of the 10 percent alternative that they have effectively eliminated the role of the professional bondsman. In addition, courts today are more frequently authorizing release upon the defendant's unsecured promise to appear (commonly called "release on personal recognizance" or "personal bond"). In some jurisdictions, as many as one-third of all defendants are released under this procedure. Overall, however, even in jurisdictions that make liberal use of the various bail alternatives, as many as 30 percent of all felony defendants are unable to make bail and therefore remain in jail pending the disposition of their case. In misdemeanor cases, the percentage remaining in custody will be much lower, very often less than 10 percent.

(i) *Step 9: Preliminary Hearing.* Following the first appearance, the next scheduled step in a felony case ordinarily is the preliminary hearing. In many jurisdictions, however, a substantial portion of the felony caseload will be disposed of during the period (usually one or two weeks) between the first appearance and the scheduled preliminary examination. As mentioned previously, where the primary screening by the prosecutor occurs after charges are filed, a substantial number of felony charges are likely to be dismissed or reduced to a misdemeanor during this period. Even for those felony charges that remain, a preliminary hearing will not necessarily be held. The defendant ordinarily may waive his right to a preliminary hearing, and it is not unusual for a substantial percentage (e.g., 20-30 percent) to waive, usually because they intend to plead guilty. Also, even if the defendant desires a preliminary hearing, state law allows the prosecutor to bypass the hearing in a significant number of states.[10]

Where the preliminary hearing is held it will provide, like grand jury review, a screening of the decision to charge by a neutral body. In the preliminary hearing, that neutral body is the magistrate, who must determine whether, on the evidence presented, there is probable cause to believe that [the] defendant committed the crime charged. Ordinarily, the magistrate will already have determined that probable cause exists as part of the ex parte screening of the complaint (see step 7). The preliminary hearing, however, provides screening in an adversary

---

10. In almost all of the "indictment jurisdictions," (see step 10), the prosecutor can bypass the preliminary hearing by taking the case directly before the grand jury. In the federal courts, this route is taken so frequently that preliminary hearings are a rarity in many districts. In the typical indictment jurisdiction, however, preliminary hearings are bypassed only in a limited class of cases (e.g., murder prosecutions), and most felony cases go through both a preliminary hearing and grand jury screening. In several indictment states, almost all cases are given this double review. In information states (see step 11), since alternative screening by the grand jury is not utilized, the felony defendant commonly has a right to a preliminary hearing.

proceeding in which both sides are represented by counsel. Jurisdictions vary in the evidentiary rules applicable to the preliminary hearing, but most require that the parties rely primarily on live witnesses rather than affidavits. Typically, the prosecution will present its key witnesses and the defense will limit its response to the cross-examination of those witnesses. The defendant has the right to present his own evidence at the hearing, but traditional defense strategy advises against subjecting defense witnesses to prosecution cross-examination in any pretrial proceeding.

If the magistrate concludes that the evidence presented establishes probable cause, he will "bind the case over" to the next stage in the proceedings. In an indictment jurisdiction (see step 10), the case is bound over to the grand jury, and in a jurisdiction that permits the direct filing of an information (see step 11), the case is bound over directly to the general trial court. If the magistrate finds that the probable cause supports only a misdemeanor charge, he will reject the felony charge and allow the prosecutor to substitute the lower charge, which will then be set for trial in the magistrate court. If the magistrate finds that the prosecution's evidence does not support any charge, he will order that the defendant be released. The rate of dismissals at the preliminary hearing quite naturally varies with the degree of previous screening exercised by the prosecutor. In a jurisdiction with fairly extensive screening, the percentage of dismissals is likely to fall in the range of 5 to 15 percent of the cases heard.

(j) Step 10: Grand Jury Review. Although all American jurisdictions still have provisions authorizing grand jury screening of felony charges, such screening is mandated only in those states requiring felony prosecutions to be instituted by an indictment, a charging instrument issued by the grand jury. About half of the states currently require grand jury indictments for at least some classes of felony prosecutions. In several of these "indictment states," prosecution by indictment is required only for felonies subject to the most severe punishment (life imprisonment and capital punishment). In the remaining indictment jurisdictions, including the federal system, a grand jury indictment is required in all felony prosecutions (unless waived by the defendant). If there has been a preliminary hearing, the magistrate's decision at that hearing is not binding on the grand jury. It can reject prosecution notwithstanding a preliminary hearing bindover, or reinstitute prosecution even though the magistrate concluded that the prosecution's evidence was inadequate.

The grand jury is composed of a group of private citizens who are selected to review cases over a term that may range from one to several months. Traditionally the grand jury consisted of 23 persons with the favorable vote of a majority needed to indict. Today, many states use a somewhat smaller grand jury (e.g., 12) and some require more than a simple majority to indict. As in the case of the magistrate at the preliminary hearing, the primary function of the grand jury is to determine whether there is sufficient evidence to justify a trial on the charge sought by the prosecution. The grand jury, however, participates in a screening process quite different from the preliminary hearing. It meets in a closed session and hears only the evidence presented by the prosecution. The defendant has no right to offer his own evidence or to be present during grand jury proceedings. If a majority of the grand jurors conclude that the prosecution's evidence is sufficient, the grand jury will issue the indictment requested by the prosecutor. The indictment will set forth a brief description of the offense charged, and the grand jury's approval of that charge will be indicated by its designation of the indictment as a "true bill." If the grand jury majority refuses to approve a proposed indictment, the charges against the defendant will be dismissed. In most indictment jurisdictions, grand juries refuse to indict in only a small percentage (e.g., 3 to 8 percent) of the cases presented before them.

(k) Step 11: The Filing of the Indictment or Information. If an indictment is issued, it will be filed with the general trial court and will replace the complaint as the accusatory instrument in the case. Where grand jury review either is not required or has been waived in the particular case, an information will be filed with the trial court. Like the indictment, the information is a charging instrument which replaces the complaint, but it is issued by the prosecutor rather than the grand jury. Approximately half of the states do not require prosecution by indictment, and prosecutors in these jurisdictions proceed by information in the vast majority of their prosecutions. In these "information states," the charge in the information ordinarily must be supported by a preliminary hearing bindover (unless the preliminary hearing was waived).

(l) Step 12: Arraignment on the Information or Indictment. After the indictment or information has been filed, the defendant is arraigned—i.e., he is brought before the trial court, informed of the charges against him, and asked to enter a plea of guilty, not guilty, or, as is permitted under some circumstances, *nolo contendere*. Most of the cases that reach the arraignment stage will not go to trial. Depending upon the quality of pre-arraignment screening, anywhere from 10 to 30 percent of the cases will be dismissed as a result of a *nolle prosequi* or a successful defense motion. Of the remaining felony cases, 70 to 90 percent will be resolved by a guilty plea in most jurisdictions. Whether the guilty plea rate in a particular jurisdiction is closer to 70 percent or 90 percent depends upon several factors. One very significant variable may be the extent to which the prosecutor is willing to plea bargain—i.e., grant concessions in return for a guilty plea. While the vast majority of prosecutors make substantial use of plea bargaining, they vary markedly both as to the type of cases in which they will grant major concessions and

as to the nature of those concessions. One of the most common concessions is the reduction of the offense charged in return for a guilty plea to a lesser offense. Thus, in a jurisdiction with extensive plea bargaining, it is not unusual to find that only a small percentage of the defendants plead guilty to the original charge. In other jurisdictions, prosecutors will offer concessions that deal directly with the sentence as opposed to the level of the charge. Such sentencing concessions often take the form of a prosecution recommendation for a lenient sentence (which will be given great weight by the sentencing judge) or a promise of a specific sentence agreed to by the judge.

(m) Step 13: Pretrial Motions. In most jurisdictions, a broad range of objections must be raised by a pretrial motion. Those motions commonly present challenges to the institution of the prosecution (e.g., claims regarding the grand jury), attacks upon the sufficiency of the charging instrument, requests for discovery of the prosecution's evidence, and motions to suppress evidence obtained in violation of the federal Constitution. While some pretrial motions are made only by defendants who intend to go to trial, other motions are advanced almost as frequently by defendants expecting to plead guilty even if the motion succeeds. Nevertheless, pretrial motions are likely to be made in no more than 10 percent of all felony cases that reach the trial court. In misdemeanor cases, pretrial motions may be made in less than one percent of the cases before the magistrate court. The use of pretrial motions varies, of course, with the nature of the case. In narcotics cases, for example, motions to suppress are quite common. In the typical forgery case, on the other hand, pretrial motions of any type are quite rare.

As a group, pretrial motions are likely to result in the dismissal of not substantially more than 5 percent of all of the felony cases before the trial judge (and they are likely to have even less impact on the misdemeanor docket). The pretrial motion most likely to produce a dismissal is the motion to suppress. Quite frequently, if the defendant gains suppression of unconstitutionally obtained evidence, there will be insufficient remaining evidence to continue with the prosecution.

(n) Step 14: The Trial. As noted previously, most felony and misdemeanor cases are likely to be disposed of either by a guilty plea or by a dismissal. Quite commonly, only 10 to 15 percent of the felony cases that reach the trial court actually will go to trial. Misdemeanor cases tend to have an even lower trial rate. Magistrate courts often have trials in less than 5 percent of the cases presented before them. Most trials will not be lengthy affairs. Misdemeanor trials typically last less than one day. Felony trials may occupy somewhat more time, particularly when tried to a jury, but most will be completed within a few days.

In all jurisdictions, the defendant will have a right to a jury trial for all felony offenses and for misdemeanors punishable by more than 6 months imprisonment (although the jury trial right in the misdemeanor cases may exist only through a trial *de novo*). Most states also provide a jury trial for lesser misdemeanors as well. Juries traditionally were composed of 12 persons, but many states now utilize 6 person juries in misdemeanor cases and several use the smaller juries in non-capital felony cases as well. Of course, the right to a jury trial can be waived, and in most jurisdictions, a significant number of defendants will waive the jury in favor of a bench trial. Over the country as a whole, however, a clear majority (perhaps 60-65 percent) of all felony trials are tried to a jury. In several jurisdictions, the percentage of jury trials comes close to 80 percent, although in at least one state, it is as low as 13 percent. In misdemeanor cases, bench trials often are in the majority even in jurisdictions that extend the defendant's jury trial right to all misdemeanors. In all but a few jurisdictions, the jury verdict in misdemeanor and felony cases, whether for acquittal or conviction, must be unanimous. Where the jurors cannot agree, no verdict is entered and the case may be retried. Such "hung juries" occur in a small percentage of the cases (e.g., 3-6 percent).

The criminal trial resembles the civil trial in many respects. There are, however, several distinguishing features that are either unique to criminal trials or of special importance in such trials. These include (1) the presumption of defendant's innocence, (2) the requirement of proof beyond a reasonable doubt, (3) the right of the defendant not to take the stand, (4) the exclusion of evidence obtained by the state in an illegal manner, and (5) the more frequent use of incriminating statements of defendants. In most jurisdictions, the misdemeanor trial will be almost indistinguishable from a felony trial. In some jurisdictions, however, misdemeanor trials tend to be less formal, with rules of evidence applied in a rather loose fashion.

Whether a criminal case is tried to the bench or to a jury, the odds favor conviction over acquittal. The acquittal rate for felonies generally does not exceed one-third. At the misdemeanor level, the rate of acquittals often is somewhat lower. A substantial variation exists, however, among the different types of crimes. Acquittal rates for rape and robbery tend to be considerably higher, for example, than acquittal rates for forgery or assault. Where the offense is one that is not likely to produce either an offender caught "red-handed," more than one eyewitness, or contraband discovered in the defendant's possession, the acquittal rate for the offense is likely to be higher than the average for offenses generally.

(o) Step 15: Sentencing. If the defendant pleads guilty or is found guilty at trial, the judge will enter a judgment of conviction and set the case for sentencing. The structure of the sentence and the discretion of the judge in choosing among sentencing alternatives will be controlled by statute. For misdemeanors a judge ordinarily has discretion

to impose a fine, probation, suspended sentence, or fixed jail term not to exceed a statutorily prescribed maximum. For felony offenses, the choice ordinarily is between imprisonment and probation although the legislature is likely to have prohibited probation for some offenses. When imprisonment is imposed, a majority of the states require that the sentence be indeterminate, i.e., the court sets a minimum and maximum term, with the parole board determining the actual release date between the minimum and maximum. State law will set the highest maximum sentence permissible for the particular crime and will also require that the minimum be no greater than a certain percentage (e.g., one-half) of the maximum. Some jurisdictions also impose other restrictions upon the court (e.g., sentencing guidelines) in its setting of the maximum and minimum terms. In recent years, many states have moved from indeterminate to determinate prison sentences for most felonies. Under determinate sentencing, the judge sets a single fixed term of imprisonment, which must fall within a fairly narrow range set by the legislature for the particular crime. This sentencing structure eliminates earlier parole release except for limited good-behavior credits.

Among misdemeanor convictions, there often is a substantial difference in the pattern of sentences for those cases that were originally filed as misdemeanors and those that started as felonies but were reduced to misdemeanors as part of a plea bargain. In the former group, the vast majority of the defendants will be fined, placed on probation, or receive a suspended sentence. Where the initial charge was at a felony level, the defendant convicted of a misdemeanor is more likely to receive a jail sentence (often combined with probation). Defendants convicted on felony charges also are likely to be incarcerated for at least a short period. Prison sentences usually are imposed in anywhere from one-third to one-half of the felony convictions. Many jurisdictions also make extensive use of short jail sentences, combined with probation, in felony cases. Of course, the likelihood of incarceration and the length of incarceration will vary with the seriousness of the offense for which conviction was obtained (and, in guilty plea cases, often the seriousness of the original charge).

(p) Step 16: Appeals. In felony cases, initial appeals will be taken to the intermediate appellate court or to the state supreme court if there is no intermediate appellate court. Initial appeals in misdemeanor cases will be taken to the general trial court, and in some jurisdictions will consist of a trial de novo. Although all convicted defendants are entitled to appeal their convictions, appeals are taken predominantly by those defendants who were sentenced to imprisonment. In several states, a fairly substantial portion of felony appeals (perhaps as many as 20 percent) come from imprisoned defendants who pled guilty and are challenging their pleas. Most felony appeals, however, are taken by

imprisoned defendants who are seeking review of a trial conviction. In some jurisdictions, as many as 90 percent of the defendants who were convicted after trial and sentenced to imprisonment will appeal their convictions. Even with almost automatic appeals by this group of defendants, however, the total number of felony appeals is still not likely to exceed 15 percent of all felony convictions. In misdemeanor cases, the appeal rate is much lower.

The rate of reversals on appeal varies with the particular appellate court, but tends to fall within the range of 10 to 20 percent of the cases heard. In many jurisdictions, the most common objection raised on appeal is the trial court's admission of evidence obtained through an allegedly unconstitutional search. That objection also provides the most common basis for reversal. Other grounds raised quite frequently (but with much less success) are the insufficiency of the evidence, the incompetency of counsel, constitutional violations in identification procedures, and challenges to the admission of defendant's incriminating statements made to the police.

(q) Step 17: Postconviction Remedies. After the appellate process is exhausted, imprisoned defendants may be able to use post-conviction remedies to challenge their convictions on limited grounds. In particular, federal post-conviction remedies allow state as well as federal prisoners to challenge their convictions in the federal courts on certain constitutional grounds. The federal district courts receive roughly 9,000 such post-conviction applications each year. Relief is granted on less than 4 percent of these petitions, however, and the relief often is limited to requiring a further hearing. In the state systems, post-conviction remedies are used far less frequently.

(r) The Criminal Justice Funnel. If one drew a diagram of the criminal justice process, charting the numbers of persons processed at each stage, the shape of the diagram would be roughly that of a funnel. A great number of persons are subjected to the process at its initial stage (pre-arrest investigation), and at each subsequent stage, fewer and fewer persons are involved. There are more persons investigated as suspects than arrested, more persons arrested than charged, more persons charged than finally brought to adjudication, more persons adjudicated than found guilty, and more persons found guilty than subjected to incarceration. As the caseload moves through it, the criminal justice process sifts out individual cases in much the same manner as a sieve. This "sieve effect" or "funnel analogy" is aptly illustrated by a rough model of the distribution of a cross-section of felony cases in a typical jurisdiction. While our model probably is not duplicated in any particular jurisdiction, available figures suggest it is roughly approximated in many urban communities.

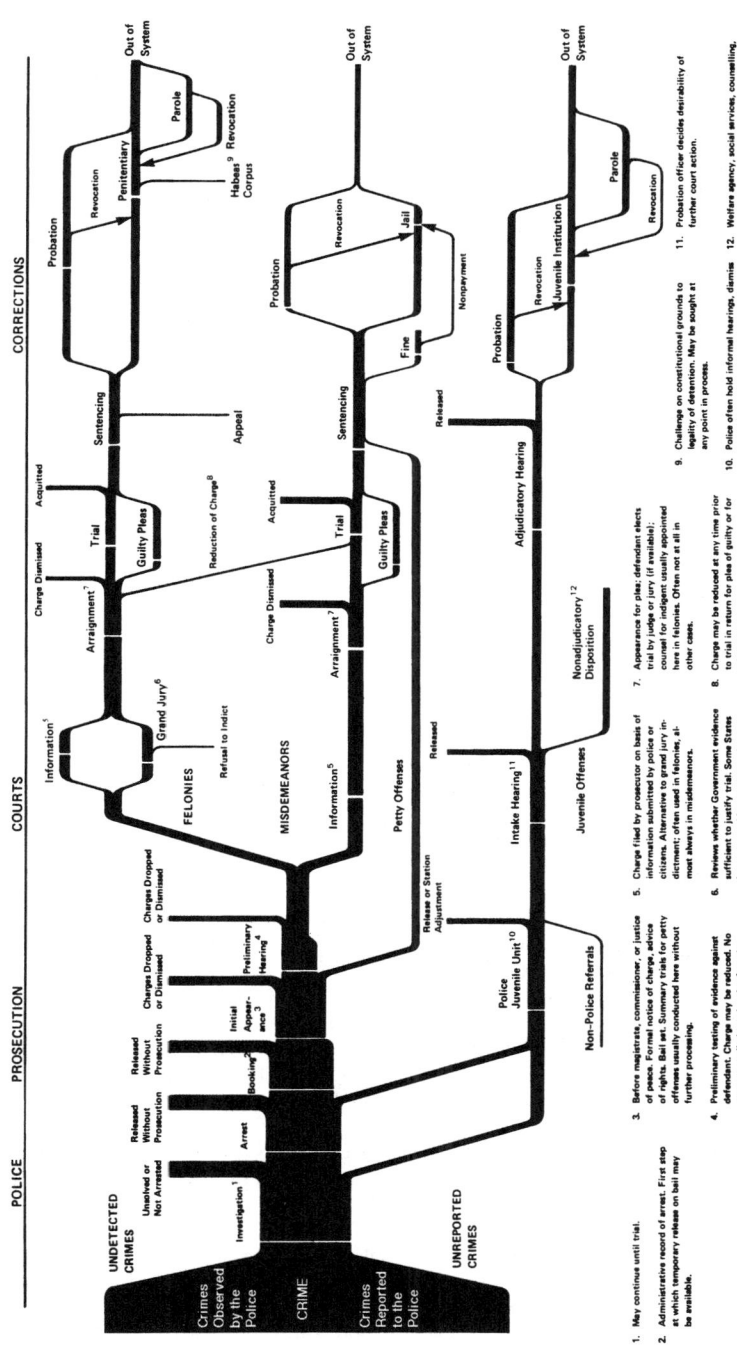

Chart: An Overview of the Criminal Justice System
The President's Commission on Law Enforcement and Administration of Justice Task Force Report: Science and Technology 58-59 (1967)

Notes on a Statistical Overview of the Criminal Justice System

The chart above gives a visual picture of how cases drop out or are disposed of by the criminal justice system. The table below gives a statistical snapshot of the system for the year 1990, including information on sentencing practice.*

---

*The source of the data is as follows:

Column (a): Table 1, Personal and household crimes, 1990, 1990 Criminal Victimization in the United States 16 (1992).

Column (b): Table 3.122, Estimated number and rate of offenses known to police, 1990, 1992 Sourcebook of Criminal Justice Statistics 357 (1993).

Column (c): Table 4.2, Number and rate of arrests, 1990, 1991 Sourcebook of Criminal Justice Statistics 433 (1992).

Column (d): Federal figures from Table 5.15, Defendants convicted in U.S. District Courts, 1990, 1992 Sourcebook of Criminal Justice Statistics 486 (1993); State figures from Table 5.50. Most serious offense of felony offenders convicted in State courts, 1990, 1992 Sourcebook of Criminal Justice Statistics 528 (1993).

Column (e): Federal figures from Table 5.19, Offenders sentenced to prison in U.S. District Courts, 1990, 1992 Sourcebook of Criminal Justice Statistics 490 (1993); State figures from Table 5.52, Felony sentences imposed by State courts, 1990, 1992 Sourcebook of Criminal Justice Statistics 529 (1993) (figures determined by converting percentage incarcerated back to totals through Table 5.50 supra).

Column (f): Federal figures from Table 5.20, Average length of prison sentences imposed for offenders convicted in U.S. District Courts, 1990, 1992 Sourcebook of Criminal Justice Statistics 491 (1993); State statistics from Table 5.53, Average length of felony sentences imposed by State courts, 1990, 1992 Sourcebook of Criminal Justice Statistics 529 (1993).

Column (g): Federal statistics from Table 5.22, Average time served until first release for offenders sentenced to prison in U.S. District Courts, 1989, 1992 Sourcebook of Criminal Justice Statistics 493 (1993); State statistics from Table 6.108, First releases from prisons in 34 states, 1990, 1992 Sourcebook of Criminal Justice Statistics 655 (1993).

PRELIMINARIES: THE CRIMINAL JUSTICE PROCESS

Type of offense	(a) Number committed	(b) Number reported	(c) Number arrests	(d) Number convictions	(e) Prison sentence	(f) (Months) Sentence imposed	(g) (Months) Time served
Total	26,122,820	14,475,630 55.4%	2,313,247 8.9%	379,292 1.5%	279,909 1.1%	Fed = 61.4 State = 91.0	Fed = 36.23 State = 35.9
Murder and Non-Negligent Manslaughter	NA	23,440 —	18,298 78.1%	Fed = 133 State = 10,895 47%	Fed = 124 State = 10,350 44.7%	Fed = 134.7 State = 233.0	Fed = 53.3 State = 83.0 (6.9 years)
Rape	130,260	102,560 78.7%	30,966 23.8%	Fed = 149 State = 18,024 14.0%	Fed = 120 State = 15,500 12.0%	Fed = 78.9 State = 128.0	Fed = NA State = 55.0 (4.6 years)
Robbery	1,149,710	639,270 55.6%	136,300 11.9%	Fed = 1,337 State = 47,446 4.2%	Fed = 1,313 State = 42,701 3.8%	Fed = 100.7 State = 97.0	Fed = 58.6 State = 41.0 (3.4 years)
Assault	4,728,810	1,054,860 22.3%	376,917 8.0%	Fed = 455 State = 53,861 1.1%	Fed = 282 State = 38,780 0.8%	Fed = 34.8 State = 52.0	Fed = 41.9 State = 23.0 (1.9 years)
Burglary	5,147,740	3,073,900 59.7%	341,192 6.6%	Fed = 99 State = 109,250 2.1%	Fed = 83 State = 82,313 1.6%	Fed = 34.4 State = 61.0	Fed = 26.0 State = 22.0 (1.8 years)
Larceny-Theft	12,975,320	7,945,700 61.2%	1,241,236 9.6%	Fed = 2,709 State = 113,094 0.9%	Fed = 940 State = 73,511 0.6%	Fed = 18.8 State = 33.0	Fed = 16.3 State = 14.0 (1.2 years)
Motor-Vehicle Theft	1,967,540	1,635,900 83.1%	168,338 8.6%	Fed = 275 State = 21,065 1.1%	Fed = 200 State = 13,692 0.7%	Fed = 27.6 State = 33.0	Fed = 21.3 State = 13.0 (1.1 years)

I/THE NATURE OF CRIMINAL LAW

Chapter 1. THE CRIMINAL-CIVIL DISTINCTION

Our legal system distinguishes *criminal* law from civil law and *criminal* commitment from civil commitment. We speak of a "crime" rather than a "violation" or a "breach," and "punishment" rather than "sanction" or "liability." Why is criminal law kept distinct? A system in which no distinction between criminal and civil law exists is conceivable. An actor who commits a *violation of the legal rules of conduct* (not a "crime") would have *jurisdiction* taken over him (not "convicted") during which time he would be *corrected* or *sanctioned* (but not "punished"). What is now dealt with as criminal law could be treated as just another aspect of civil law, perhaps even using the same procedures now used in criminal law; different aspects of civil law commonly have different procedures, depending upon the interests at stake. Some academics have proposed just such a system,[1] although I know of no society in which such a system currently operates. Why are societies persistent in maintaining a distinct "criminal" system? How is criminal law different from other bodies of law?

Fear, Pain, and Bubble Gum

Ike has decided to join ΔBT fraternity. During "hell week" the aspiring "pledges" are on call at all times to provide labor, entertainment, or anything else that a brother of ΔBT might desire. School policy prevents skipping classes during hell week, a god-send for the pledges. Classes provide the only opportunity to sleep. With the altered function of classes, books are unnecessary. Instead, pledges carry hardwood pledge paddles and the favorite candy of each brother. After a very restful hour of thermodynamics, Ike meets Brother Constin. "Cherry bubble gum, pledge." Ike's mouth drops and his heart stops. "Aaaah

---

1. See, e.g., Barbara Wootton, Crime and the Criminal Law, chs. 2-3 (1963); Jay Campbell, A Strict Accountability Approach to Criminal Responsibility, 29 Fed. Probation 33 (1965); Sheldon Glueck, Law and Psychiatry, ch. 4 (1963).

. . . I thought you liked strawberry, Mr. Constin." "You have five minutes to compensate for your incompetence, pledge." Ike scrambles. He spots Ed Begley, another ΔBT pledge, 100 yards away. "Ed, have you got cherry bubble gum for Constin?" Ed's eyebrows pop up. "I thought he liked strawberry." Ike bolts for the local convenience store, with Ed close behind. He spots cherry in the bubble gum box. "Yes!" The moment sours as they realize that neither has any money. Ike grabs two pieces and heads for the door. "I'll be back later to pay for this," he shouts over his shoulder to the shopkeeper, who is unimpressed. "Come back here. You can't take that without paying for it."

Ed explains their situation to the shopkeeper. After some discussion, the shopkeeper lets Ed have two pieces free, but notes that he still considers Ike a thief. Ed dashes out the front and around the back of the store. He thinks he can make up for lost time by taking a shortcut that he knows. But as he squeezes between two cars parked in the alley behind the store, he loses his footing. As he falls, he cuts his leg badly and becomes wedged between the two cars. His struggles only wedge him tighter and his cries for help go unheard. He feels himself getting faint from loss of blood and decides that he must break the window of one of the cars to get maneuvering room to extricate himself. He gets free and limps back into the store, where the owner calls an ambulance and puts a tourniquet on his bleeding leg.

Ike wonders where Ed is and concludes that Ed may be having second thoughts about pledging ΔBT. Brother Constin is waiting at the edge of campus. "That was six minutes, pledge." Ike's watch says four minutes but he decides protestation would not be useful. Brother Constin pronounces sentence. "Three whacks." Ike hands Brother Constin his paddle and bends over. All three are stingers. He responds, "Thank you sir, you have helped me in my quest to reach the perfection of brotherhood." "You are welcome." Ike expects to have permanent scarring, as do all of the current brothers of ΔBT.

The incident at the convenience store provokes a University investigation. The fraternity's pledge privileges are suspended for a year. To show its concern for lawless conduct during pledge week, the University insists that both civil and criminal charges be filed against Brother Constin for assault, against Ike for theft of the bubble gum, and against Ed for damage to the car. The civil assault charges against Constin are dismissed on the ground that Ike consented, he knew the effects of the paddling he was consenting to, and he is an adult who can make an informed decision to consent to the injury. In the civil action for taking the gum without permission, Ike concedes his civil liability and pays the minor damages sought by the store owner. Ed similarly concedes and compensates the car owner. What result on the criminal charges against Constin, Ike, and Ed?

Notes on the Nature of Criminal Law

Criminal-Civil Similarities Criminal law is not unique in the conduct it punishes; some conduct violates criminal and civil law.[1] Striking another person without her consent may be both a crime and a tort. Nor is criminal law unique in the deprivations that it imposes; civil commitment, tort law, and a variety of other civil measures can deprive a person of his or her liberty, put restrictions on what a person can do, and compel the payment of money. Criminal cases typically do have procedural characteristics that are different from civil cases. Crimes are prosecuted by the state rather than by the victim, while civil cases have a private "plaintiff" who brings the action. On the other hand, state prosecution is not unique to criminal actions; civil actions sometimes are brought by the state, as when the state sues for breach of a contract. If criminal law is not unique in either the conduct it prohibits, the deprivations it dispenses, or the party that brings the action, why is it kept distinct? Its existence must have an explanation apart from its prohibitions, deprivations, or procedures.

Criminal Conviction as Moral Condemnation Conventional lay wisdom holds that criminal liability and criminal commitment are different from civil liability and civil commitment in that the former generally are thought to reflect moral blameworthiness deserving condemnation and punishment. "An act or omission and its accompanying state of mind which, if duly proven to have taken place, will incur a formal and solemn pronouncement of the moral condemnation of the community."[2] This notion that the distinctiveness of criminal law is its focus on moral blameworthiness is supported by the traditional requirements for criminal liability, which as a group are not characteristic of civil liability.

De Minimis Defense Criminal law addresses only harms of a sufficient seriousness; situations analogous to civil law's liability-with-nominal-damages typically do not support criminal liability. Under the Model Penal Code's "de minimis infraction" defense, for example, "The Court shall dismiss a prosecution if . . . it finds that the defendant's conduct . . . did not actually cause or threaten the harm or evil sought to be prevented by the law defining the offense or did so only

---

1. The phrase "civil law" is used here to refer to all law that is not criminal. That is, the criminal-civil distinction is taken to be comprehensive in its coverage. Other definitions of "civil law" are possible, of course.
2. Hart, The Aims of the Criminal Law, 23 Law & Contemp. Probs. 401, 405 (1958).

to an extent *too trivial to warrant the condemnation of conviction*. . . ."[3] Consider the person who leaves a restaurant with an apple from a buffet, after paying for the buffet, but in violation of the establishment's rule against removal of food. This violates the terms of the theft prohibition—taking property of another without consent—yet one might conclude, as the court did, that such a violation is too trivial to generate community condemnation and therefore is not properly dealt with by the criminal law.[4] At civil law, in contrast, the extent of the harm is important to assessment of the amount of the award, but generally does not affect liability. Thus, the shopkeeper from whom Ike took the gum will not recover much in tort, but he does have a right to liability and compensation from Ike for the extent of his injury. Criminal law, on the other hand, generally limits liability to cases where the conduct is sufficiently serious to merit the condemnation of criminal conviction.

Crimes vs. Violations In the same vein, the Code distinguishes "crimes" from "violations": "A violation does not constitute a crime and conviction of a violation shall not give rise to any disability or legal disadvantage based on conviction of a criminal offense."[5] (Thus, violations of parking, motor vehicle, and other such prohibitions generally are not "crimes," although they are enforced by the same officers who enforce the criminal law.)

Consent as a Defense Consent similarly has a different effect in the criminal and civil context. It generally is a complete defense to a civil action. A plaintiff generally has no right to recover for a harm that he or she has consented to. It was for this reason that Brother Constin was able to successfully defend the civil suit for assault. In contrast, a victim's consent is rarely a defense to a criminal charge. It is allowed as a defense only if it *vitiates the harm or evil of the offense.* That is, consent is a defense to criminal liability only if the presence of consent means that there no longer is a harm. That Ed got the shopkeeper's permission to take the bubble gum without paying for it means that the taking is not theft. Similarly, where valid consent is present, sexual intercourse is not rape.

Denying Consent Defense to Crime In most criminal offenses, however, consent is not a defense. Assault occurs if one "purposely, knowingly, or recklessly causes bodily injury to another."[6] The criminal law generally does not allow consent of the victim to bodily injury as a

---

3. Model Penal Code §2.12(2) (1962) (emphasis added). Where the damage is minor under civil law, in contrast, liability nonetheless is imposed, but only nominal damages are awarded.
4. See State v. Nevens, 197 N.J. Super. 531, 485 A.2d 345 (1984) (conviction reversed and complaint dismissed as a de minimis infraction).
5. Model Penal Code §1.04(5). For a definition of what constitutes a "violation," see id.
6. Model Penal Code §211.1(1)(a).

defense.[7] Criminal conduct is seen as a harm against the community. While it may be an individual who suffers the immediate injury, it is the breach of the society's rules of conduct prohibiting the act that serves to justify punishment. If the law prohibits the conduct without exception, it is not within the power of an individual to revoke the law's prohibition. The law may give an individual the authority to consent to minor injury,[8] just as it gives individuals the authority to give away their property, as the shopkeeper gave Ed free bubble gum. But causing more than minor injury is an offense, no matter that the victim consents.

Culpability Requirement Also characteristic of criminal law is a requirement that the actor have a culpable state of mind. Bringing about a prohibited harm or evil, even wrongfully, is not itself sufficient for criminal liability. Generally, a minimum culpability of recklessness is required as to every offense element;[9] that is, an actor must have some degree of awareness of the facts that make his or her conduct criminal. Still higher culpability levels, knowledge or purpose, commonly are required as to one or more offense elements. Lower culpability than recklessness, criminal negligence, is used infrequently; strict liability, liability in the absence of culpability, generally is limited to "violations"[10] (which, you recall, are distinguished from "crimes"). Civil liability, in contrast, frequently requires no culpable state of mind. When culpability is required, commonly only negligence need be shown.

Justification and Excuse Defenses Even if the actor has the required culpable state of mind for the offense, criminal liability is barred if the actor's conduct is justified because it avoids a greater societal harm. Such an actor is exculpated under a justification defense. Thus, one has a justification defense to theft if one breaks into a cabin to avoid

---

7. See, e.g., Model Penal Code §2.11(1). As is common in civil law, assent might not necessarily provide effective consent. See Model Penal Code §2.11(3).

8. See, e.g., Foster v. People, 1 Colo. 293 (1871) (consent of parties to a fight was defense to charge of mayhem where the victim had his ear bitten off); cf. People v. Samuels, 250 Cal. App. 2d 501, 53 Cal. Rptr. 439 (1967) (stating in dicta that consent is generally no defense to assault or battery but may be in situations involving ordinary physical contact or injuries incident to sports such as boxing, wrestling, or football); Model Penal Code §2.11(2) (victim's consent to injury or risk of injury a defense if minor or a foreseeable hazard of participation in lawful sport).

9. Model Penal Code §2.02(3).

10. Id. §2.05(2). The most notorious exception to this is the common law's use of strict liability in statutory rape, a serious offense. Modern codes commonly recognize two forms of statutory rape. The first punishes intercourse with a person under 16 (or similar age). Here, criminal negligence is required. A second offense punishes intercourse with a person under 10 (or similar age). Here, strict liability is imposed, but typically in the belief that no one in good faith could mistake a person under 10 for a person over 16. Where someone does, they no doubt will be exculpated from criminal liability under an excuse defense, such as insanity. See, e.g., Model Penal Code §§213.1(1)(d), 213.3(1)(a), 213.6(1); id., comment to §213.6(1) (1980).

starvation and exposure while lost in the woods. Even if the actor is not justified, criminal liability also is barred if the person commits the offense because of circumstances or conditions that render the person blameless for the offense, as is frequently the case with one who is insane or who commits the offense because coerced to do so by another. Such an actor is exculpated under an excuse defense. Criminal codes recognize a wide range of justification and excuse defenses, such as lesser evils, law enforcement authority, insanity, immaturity, involuntary intoxication, duress, or reasonable mistake as to a justification.[11] Civil liability, such as tort, typically recognizes neither justification nor excuse defenses. If you tie up to my dock in a storm in order to save your ship and those aboard, you will have a justification defense to criminal liability but nonetheless may be liable in tort to pay me for the damage you caused to my dock. Similarly, an insane person may gain an insanity defense to criminal liability but the person or his guardian nonetheless must compensate another for harm caused. The difference logically follows from the difference in the criteria for criminal and civil liability. Rather than the moral blameworthiness of the actor, the criterion for civil liability is frequently said to be the fair or efficient allocation of the loss, or some other non-blameworthiness criteria.

Condemnation as Criminal Some aspects of civil law may recognize some doctrines similar to these but criminal law is unique in reliance upon such a collection of doctrines: the requirement of conscious culpability, rejection of consent as a general defense, recognition of a defense for de minimis violations, justification, and excuse. This is as one would expect. For, taken together, these doctrines serve "to safeguard conduct that is without fault from condemnation as criminal,"[12] and it is moral condemnation that distinguishes criminal law from all other law.

Questions

1. *Consent Defense.* Brother Constin escapes civil liability because Ike readily consented to the injury. Will he similarly have a defense to the criminal charges for the same conduct? What Model Penal Code sections are relevant? If he is criminally liable, why does the criminal law come to a different result than the civil law?

2. *De Minimis Defense.* Ike is civilly liable for the bubble gum theft.

---

11. E.g., Model Penal Code §§2.08(4), 2.09, 3.02, 3.07, 4.01, 4.10.
12. Id. §1.02(1)(c).

Will he similarly be liable at criminal law?* What Model Penal Code sections apply? If he is not criminally liable, why does the criminal law come to a different result than the civil law?

3. *Justification and Excuse Defenses.* Ed is civilly liable for the damage to the car. Will he similarly be held liable at criminal law? What Model Penal Code sections apply? If he is not criminally liable, why does the criminal law come to a different result than the civil law?

4. *"Punishment" as the Distinguishing Characteristic of Criminal Law.*

> The best candidate for a conceptual proposition about the criminal law is that the infliction of "punishment" is sufficient to render a legal process criminal in nature. In the United States, the labelling of a process as "criminal" triggers certain basic constitutional guarantees, such as the right to counsel and the right to a jury trial.[1] As a test for when processes are criminal, the Supreme Court unhesitatingly invokes the concept of "punishment" as the relevant criterion.[2] That a sanction is inflicted in the criminal courts for a violation of the criminal code is sufficient to classify the sanction as "punitive," but there are recurrent problems in assessing the punitive nature of other sanctions, such as administrative commitment, expatriation, deportation, fines for custom violations and the deprivation of social security benefits. That the legislature has identified these sanctions as civil in nature does not control the constitutional issue, for if the sanction is "punitive," if it constitutes "punishment," then regardless of the legislative label, the process is criminal and the constitutional guarantees apply.

George Fletcher, Rethinking Criminal Law 408-409 (1978). Assume "punishment" were defined as follows:

(1) Punishment must be imposed for the sake of inflicting pain or other consequences normally considered unpleasant.
(2) It must be for a violation of legal rules.
(3) It must be of an actual or supposed offender for his offense.

---

*In State v. Smith, 195 N.J. Super. 468, 480 A.2d 236 (1984), the court reversed a conviction for the theft of three pieces of bubble gum as de minimis:

> In the milieu of bubble gum pilferage, the only cases more trivial are those involving two pieces or one. It is difficult to conclude the lawmakers would have intended the dividing line be drawn at three. It would seem the larceny of a single piece of bubble gum would fall within the statutory intendment of a trivial offense. Does then the theft of three pieces remove the actor's conduct from the scope discretionary protection afforded [by the de minimis defense]? In a case involving substantially different conduct and attending circumstances perhaps it would; in this case it does not.

480 A.2d at 240.

1. U.S. Const. amend. VI.
2. Kennedy v. Mendoza-Martinez, 372 U.S. 144 (1963); Helvering v. Mitchell, 303 U.S. 391 (1938).

(4) It must be intentionally administered by human beings other than the offender.
(5) It must be imposed and administered by an authority constituted by a legal system against which the offense is committed.

See H. L. A. Hart, Prolegomenon to the Principles of Punishment, in Punishment and Responsibility 4-6 (1968); G. Fletcher, id., at 409-411. Which, if any, of the following would be "punishment":

(a) Voluntary payment of restitution by one who has unlawfully injured another?
(b) Use of force against a person who is attacking with deadly force without provocation?
(c) Involuntary quarantine of a person who has contracted a contagious disease?
(d) Deportation from the United States of persons who were former nazi prison camp guards?
(e) Imprisonment of an aggravated assault defendant prior to trial to prevent him from committing further assaults?
(f) Commitment of a "sexual psychopath" to a mental hospital for treatment that would help avoid future acts of molesting children?
(g) Impeaching a President for misbehavior in office?

Additional issues concerning the nature of criminal law and the purpose of punishment are taken up in the next chapter.

Chapter 2. JUSTIFICATION AND DISTRIBUTION OF LIABILITY AND PUNISHMENT

Why punish? The materials below give a variety of arguments for why we should have a criminal justice system in order to punish those who violate society's announced rules of conduct. For the most part, the justification of punishment is an issue for moral philosophers. But the arguments used are also relevant to a question more directly relevant to lawyers and judges: If we are to have a criminal justice system to impose punishment, by what principles should liability and punishment be distributed within that system? That is, who should be held criminally liable? And, how is the amount of punishment to be determined?

Daughters' Mustard

Benine receives a call from the doctor who has been caring for her mother and her sister, Iota, back home. The doctor asks Benine to return home as soon as possible, explaining that the effects of Iota's mental illness have become more severe and have made her difficult to handle. The doctor strongly recommends civil commitment. Mother has been painfully ill for several years and as a result has been unable to care for troubled Iota. Benine takes the first train home. She is met at the station by Penne, her other sister, who also was called by the doctor. Benine considers Penne deceitful and untrustworthy. She believes Penne's primary interest in the family is in trying to get as much inheritance as possible from her mother's sizeable fortune.

Soon after they arrive at the house, it becomes apparent why Iota's condition has worsened. Mother is in constant pain, unabated by the massive doses of pain killers prescribed by the doctor. She is frequently screaming and crying, asking to be killed. Benine feels that it is her mother's condition, rather than Iota's, that presents the emergency. The nurse who cares for both Mother and Iota reveals that, in her demented form, Iota has concluded that screaming Mother is a wild dog, which will kill her if she does not kill it first. Iota has tried to poison Mother several times, but to date has given her harmless substances—peanut butter, chicken bones—that she thinks may kill what she thinks is a dog.

After a week at the house, Benine can no longer bear her mother's suffering. She concludes that Mother's death would be a blessing. Iota's constant mumblings indicate that she next intends to poison Mother with the "yellow poison," by which she aprently means the hot mustard in the refrigerator. Benine throws out the mustard and substitutes a jar laced with arsenic. Iota feeds it to Mother and Mother dies within hours. Both Benine and Iota are taken into custody after investigators piece together what happened. To Benine's surprise, Penne also is taken into custody. It turns out that, in order to inherit her share of the estate more quickly, Penne came up with the same mustard-substitution plan. When Benine threw away the mustard jar in the refrigerator, she was throwing away a jar that Penne had laced with arsenic. What liability for whom?

K. Greenawalt, Moral Justifications and Legal Punishment
Encyclopedia of Crime and Justice
1337-1342 (S. Kadish, ed. 1983)

Since punishment involves pain or deprivation that people wish to avoid, its intentional imposition by the state requires justification. The difficulties of justification cannot be avoided by the view that punishment is an inevitable adjunct of a system of criminal law. If criminal law is defined to include punishment, the central question remains whether society should have a system of mandatory rules enforced by penalties. Relatively small associations of like-minded people may be able to operate with rules that are not backed by sanctions, and a choice by the larger society against authorizing legal punishment is at least theoretically possible. . . .

The dominant approaches to justification are retributive and utilitarian. Briefly stated, a retributivist claims that punishment is justified because people deserve it; a utilitarian believes that justification lies in the useful purposes that punishment serves. Many actual theories of punishment do not fit unambiguously and exclusively into one of these two categories. Satisfying both retributive and utilitarian criteria may be thought necessary to warrant punishment; or utilitarian criteria may be thought crucial for one question (for example, whether there should be a system of punishment) and retributive criteria for another (for example, who should be punished);

or the use of retributive sorts of approaches may be thought appropriate on utilitarian grounds. Beginning from rather straightforward versions of retributive and utilitarian theory, the analysis proceeds to positions that are more complex.

Retributive Justification

Why should wrongdoers be punished? Most people might respond simply that they deserve it or that they should suffer in return for the harm they have done. Such feelings are deeply ingrained, at least in many cultures, and are often supported by notions of divine punishment for those who disobey God's laws. A simple retributivist justification provides a philosophical account corresponding to these feelings; someone who has violated the rights of others should be penalized, and punishment restores the moral order that has been breached by the original wrongful act. The idea is strikingly captured by Immanuel Kant's claim that an island society about to disband should still execute its last murderer. Society not only has a right to punish a person who deserves punishment, but it has a duty to do so. In Kant's view, a failure to punish those who deserve it leaves guilt upon the society; according to G. W. F. Hegel, punishment honors the criminal as a rational being and gives him what it is his right to have. In simple retributivist theory, practices of punishment are justified because society should render harm to wrongdoers; only those who are guilty of wrongdoing should be punished; and the severity of punishment should be proportional to the degree of wrongdoing, an approach crudely reflected in the idea of "an eye for an eye, a tooth for a tooth."

Close examination of this theory dispels much of its apparent simplicity, reveals some of the tensions between its implications and the practices of actual societies, and exposes its vulnerability to powerful objections. Taken as claiming an intimate connection between moral guilt and justified legal punishment, the retributive theory raises troubling questions about the proper purposes of a state and about any human attempts to equate reward and punishment to moral deserts.

Moral Guilt and Social Judgment

One fundamental question is whether people are ever morally guilty in the way that basic retributive theory seems to suppose. If all our acts are consequences of preceding causes over which we ultimately have had no control, causes that were set in motion before we were born—if, in other words, philosophical determinism is true—then the thief or murderer is, in the last analysis, more a victim of misfortune than a villain on the comic stage. Although he may be evil in some sense and able to control his actions, his character has been formed by forces outside himself, and that ultimately determines the choices he makes. From this perspective, assertions that a vicious person should be punished simply because he deserves to be seem as anomalous as assertions that a vicious dog should be punished simply because he deserves to be. Unless one wishes to take the paradoxical position, analogous to certain religious doctrines of predestination, that people are guilty for qualities and acts they cannot help, the simple retributive theory is incompatible with determinism. It requires some notion of free will that attributes to humans responsibility for doing wrong in a way that is not attributed to other animals.

Acceptance of free will, which is certainly the undergirding for the ordinary sense of morality, does not remove all the obstacles to acceptance of retributivism. One human can rarely judge with confidence the moral guilt of others, and few doubt that among persons who commit similar wrongful acts, vast differences in moral guilt exist. Many of those who commit very serious crimes have suffered extreme psychological or social deprivation. Moreover, a penalty supposed to redress a moral imbalance should perhaps depend upon an offender's overall moral record and how the good and bad fortunes of his life compare with that record; yet making such an evaluation with any accuracy is even more beyond human capacities than judging the moral guilt attaching to a particular act.

Finally, not all acts that reflect serious moral guilt are the subject of criminal punishment in a liberal society. Personal wrongs that members of families and acquaintances do to one another may be of greater magnitude morally than some petty crimes, even though they do not carry publicly imposed penalties. If the purpose of punishment were truly to redress moral guilt, justifying this variance in treatment would be difficult, but few people believe that a liberal society should make the punishment of all serious moral wrongs its business. To some, the very idea that pain should be inflicted on a person simply because he has committed an earlier moral wrong may seem indefensible, whether the agent inflicting the pain is human or divine. Even if one believes that a just God would strike some such balance, he may think that restoring the moral order is not an appropriate human purpose, and is certainly not a proper purpose of the state, limited as the state should be in its capacities to learn about events and to dispose of people's lives.

The retributivist may resist this conclusion and maintain that the infliction of legal penalties for moral transgressions is a legitimate public purpose, one that happens to be outweighed by other values in certain circumstances. He can argue that the severity of an offense provides at least a rough indication of the magnitude of moral wrong and that a punishment proportioned to the offense, and perhaps tailored to some extent to other factors of moral relevance, can give the offender approximately what he deserves. These responses may save retributive theory from the attack of total irrelevance, but they do not provide a complete justification for practices of legal punishment as they exist or might exist.

Violations of Social Norms and Fairness

A rather different retributive approach is that criminals deserve punishment because they violate norms established by society, the magnitude of the violation being measured by the seriousness with which society treats the offense. In this form, the theory sidesteps the objection that correcting moral wrongs is not the business of the criminal law, and it does not impose upon officials the impossible burden of ascertaining subtle degrees of moral guilt. This version of the theory fits better with existing (and conceivable) practices of criminal punishment, but in doing so, it no longer connects moral guilt so strongly to justifiable punishment and does not resolve the question of why morality demands that society punish those who violate its norms simply for the sake of punishing them.

One answer to this question is that fairness to citizens who make sacrifices by obeying the law requires that violators be punished rather than reap benefits for disregarding legal standards. What is crucial and debatable about this view is the claim that law-abiding members of the community will suffer an actual injustice if the guilty go unpunished. The position is most persuasive in respect to crimes whose commission actually increase the overall burden on those who obey. Given steady revenue needs, a sufficient amount of tax evasion will increase the burdens of those who pay in full. Demanding that the evader pay back taxes does redress an injustice, but whether failure to send him to jail, if that is the only possible penalty, would be unfair to honest taxpayers is less clear. The unjust loss to the honest will not be made up in any event, but the jail term will at least offset the evader's unfair advantage. Some criminal activities, such as speeding and theft, would be engaged in more widely if it were not for the law's prohibition, but their commission does not increase general burdens as directly as does tax evasion. Because the ordinary law-abiding person has foregone some possible gain, the criminal may still be perceived as having attained an unfair advantage that should be offset by punishment. The claim about fairness to law-abiding citizens is least persuasive in respect to criminal activities (such as rape) that very few citizens would wish to undertake, no matter what the law said about them. For these crimes, as well as others directed at individuals, fairness to victims, rather than (or as well as) fairness to all law-abiding citizens, might be thought to justify punishment. Fairness to victims undoubtedly requires redress of their injuries to whatever extent that can be effected, but whether it requires harsh treatment of criminals that does not benefit victims is doubtful.

The general normative question about both fairness arguments is this: If someone has achieved a comparative advantage over another by an unjust act, does fairness to the person suffering a comparative disadvantage require stripping the offender of his advantage, even when that would do nothing to improve the position of the disadvantaged person? So understood, the fundamental question about the fairness argument is close to the question about the intrinsic value of punishing wrongdoing, although emphasizing a comparative dimension. Many of those who believe that inflicting pain on the morally guilty is not worthwhile for its own sake will also conclude that such pain cannot be supported simply because it nullifies some comparative advantage.

Utilitarian Justification

Utilitarian theories of punishment have dominated American jurisprudence during most of the twentieth century. According to Jeremy Bentham's classical utilitarianism, whether an act or social practice is morally desirable depends upon whether it promotes human happiness better than possible alternatives. Since punishment involves pain, it can be justified only if it accomplishes enough good consequences to outweigh this harm. A theory of punishment may make the balance of likely consequences central to justification without asserting, as Bentham did, that all relevant consequences are reducible to happiness and unhappiness. It may even claim that reducing future instances of immoral violations of right is itself an appropriate goal independent to the effect of those violations on the people involved. In modern usage, utilitarianism is often employed to refer broadly to theories that likely consequences determine the morality of action, and this usage is followed here.

The catalogs of beneficial consequences that utilitarians have thought can be realized by punishment have varied, but the following have generally been regarded as most important.

1. *General deterrence.* Knowledge that punishment will follow crime deters people from committing the unhappiness and insecurity they would cause. The person who has already committed a crime cannot, of course, be deterred from committing that crime, but his punishment may help to deter others. In Bentham's view, general deterrence was very much a matter of affording rational self-interested persons good reasons not to commit crimes. With a properly developed penal code, the benefits to be gained from criminal activity would be outweighed by the harms of punishment, even when those harms were discounted

by the probability of avoiding detection. Accordingly, the greater the temptation to commit a particular crime and the smaller the chance of detection, the more severe the penalty should be.

Punishment can also deter in ways more subtle than adding a relevant negative factor for cool calculation. Seeing others punished for certain behavior can create in people a sense of association between punishment and act that may constrain them even when they are sure they will not get caught. Adults, as well as children, may subconsciously fear punishment even though rationally they are confident it will not occur.

2. *Norm reinforcement.* For young children, the line may be very thin between believing that behavior is wrong and fearing punishment. Adults draw the distinction more plainly, but seeing others punished can still contribute to their sense that actions are wrong, helping them to internalize the norms society has set. Practices of punishment can thus reinforce community norms by affecting the dictates of individual consciences. Serious criminal punishment represents society's strong condemnation of what the offender has done, and performs a significant role in moral education.

A person's feeling of moral obligation to obey rules may depend considerably on his sense that he is treated fairly under them. If others profit with impunity from violations of the law, a law-abiding person may develop a sense of unfairness, wondering if he too should break the law to obtain similar advantages. Punishment helps assure citizens that the laws as administered deal fairly with their interests. Whether or not the law-abiding citizen actually has some individualized moral claim to have wrongdoers punished, punishment will probably contribute to his willing acceptance of legal constraints. This consideration constitutes the utilitarian side of the fairness argument for punishment.

3. *Individual deterrence.* The actual imposition of punishment creates fear in the offender that if he repeats his act, he will be punished again. Adults are more able than small children to draw conclusions from the punishment of others, but having a harm befall oneself is almost always a sharper lesson than seeing the same harm occur to others. To deter an offender from repeating his actions, a penalty should be severe enough to outweigh in his mind the benefits of the crime. For the utilitarian, more severe punishment of repeat offenders is warranted partly because the first penalty has shown itself ineffective from the standpoint of individual deterrence.

4. *Incapacitation.* Imprisonment puts convicted criminals out of general circulation temporarily, and the death penalty does so permanently. These punishments physically prevent persons of dangerous disposition from acting upon their destructive tendencies.

5. *Reform.* Punishment may help to reform the criminal so that his wish to commit crimes will be lessened, and perhaps so that he can be

a happier, more useful person. Conviction and simple imposition of a penalty might themselves be thought to contribute to reform if they help an offender become aware that he has acted wrongly. However, reform is usually conceived as involving more positive steps to alter basic character or improve skills, in order to make offenders less antisocial. Various psychological therapies, and more drastic interventions such as psychosurgery, are designed to curb destructive tendencies. Educational and training programs can render legitimate employment a more attractive alternative to criminal endeavors. These may indirectly help enhance self-respect, but their primary purpose is to alter the options that the released convict will face.

6. *Vengeance.* The utilitarian, in contrast to the retributivist, does not suppose that wrongful acts intrinsically deserve a harsh response, but he recognizes that victims, their families and friends, and some members of the public will feel frustrated if no such response is forthcoming. Satisfying these desires that punishment be imposed is seen as one legitimate aim in punishing the offender. In part, the point is straightforwardly to increase the happiness, or reduce the unhappiness, of those who want the offender punished, but formal punishment can also help increase their sense of respect for the law and deflect unchanneled acts of private vengeance.

Unlike a basic retributive theory, the utilitarian approach to punishment is compatible with philosophical determinism. Whether or not human acts are completely determined by prior causes, punishment can be an efficacious prior cause. A determinist can support even the "condemnation" component of punishment on utilitarian grounds, believing that condemnation and feelings of guilt are useful instruments in guiding human behavior.

From the utilitarian perspective, the acts for which criminal punishment should be authorized are those with respect to which the good consequences of punishment can outweigh the bad; the persons who should be punished are those whom it is useful to punish; and the severity of punishment should be determined not by some abstract notion of deserts but by marginal usefulness. Each extra ingredient of punishment is warranted only if its added benefits outweigh its added harms. (Of course, in real life such a fine scale cannot be developed, but legislators and those administering punishment should be guided by this principle.) The utilitarian does not start with the premise that penalties of equal severity should go to those with equal blame. For general deterrence, roughly equal penalties for the same offenses may be appropriate, but goals relating to individual offenders may support individuation of treatment, leading, for example, to long confinement for those judged irredeemably antisocial, and to rehabilitation and prompt release for those whose character can be positively transformed. . . .

The most fundamental objection [to utilitarianism] is to treating the criminal as a means to satisfy social purposes rather than as an end in himself. This objection bears on why, and how, guilty offenders may be punished; but the most damaging aspect of the attack is that utilitarianism admits the possibility of justified punishment of the innocent. The retributivist asserts that such punishment is morally wrong even when it would produce a balance of favorable consequences.

Many people will feel that none of [the] utilitarian responses adequately accounts for the unacceptability of punishing the innocent, which is regarded as inherently wrongful. Similarly, many regard it as intrinsically unfair and morally wrong to impose severe punishment on those who commit minor crimes, however useful that might be; to give widely variant punishments to those who have committed identical offenses with similar degrees of moral guilt; or to count the interests of an offender as having as much intrinsic weight as the interests of a victim or ordinary law-abiding person.

Notes on Justificatory Purposes and Distributive Principles

Unanimity of Justificatory Purposes One need not decide whether a utilitarian or a just desert (retributive) justification is the correct or the most attractive justification of punishment in order to answer the question of whether society should impose punishment. Each of these justifications leads to the same conclusion: We ought to have a system of criminal justice that punishes offenders. The imposition of sanctions on offenders can serve each of the purposes noted. It can prevent crime by deterring the offender or others, by encouraging the law-abiding, and by incapacitating or rehabilitating a potential offender. The same conviction can give punishment the offender deserves, take away any unfair advantage gained over the law-abiding, and reaffirm the offender's status as a rational being whose freedom to make decisions must be acknowledged through punishment.

Justificatory Purposes vs. Distributive Principles The differences among the theories, especially between utilitarian and just desert theories, are important in answering a different question: If punishment is to be inflicted, *how should it be distributed?*[1] The issue of *justifying* punishment—whether to have a criminal justice system that imposes sanctions—is distinct from the issue of how punishment should be

---

1. See H. L. A. Hart, Punishment and Responsibility 3-13 (1968). Hart distinguishes between theories for justifying punishment and for distributing punishment.

distributed within such a system. The above discussions of each of the theories of punishment touch on both justificatory and distributive issues. It is the distributive issue to which the doctrines of criminal law address themselves. They answer the question, who should be punished for what and how much punishment should be imposed for a given violation by a given offender?

Different Distribution Patterns of Different Theories While both utilitarian and nonconsequentialist (retributivist) rationales justify having a criminal justice system, within such a system they each would distribute liability and punishment in a different manner. Each utilitarian theory, when used as the principle for the distribution of punishment, would distribute punishment differently from each other utilitarian theory. More important, a distribution that would most effectively deter or incapacitate or rehabilitate potential offenders is not the distribution that would provide punishment to offenders who deserve it in an amount that they deserve.[2] That the different theories distribute liability and punishment differently logically follows from the fact each theory has a different purpose and thus different criteria.

Utilitarian Distribution in Conflict with Desert A utilitarian distribution has the potential to conflict with a distribution of punishment according to desert. Some of the points of conflict are noted above. Deterrence as a distributive principle might justify punishment of an innocent person if the deterrent benefit of such punishment was greater than the cost of the punishment. Less dramatic but more likely is a deterrence principle's infliction of punishment that is disproportionately high in relation to the seriousness of the offense or the moral accountability of the offender. That is, it may well be cost-effective in preventing crime to impose more or less punishment than is deserved. Incapacitation and rehabilitation have a similar potential for conflict with desert. Even if an offender's crime is minor, a long term of imprisonment might be justified under an incapacitation or rehabilitation theory if the offender is seen as likely to commit another offense in the future. Indeed, at the extreme, distributive principles based upon either incapacitation or rehabilitation do not require commission of an offense. If reliable predictive judgments could be made as to an offender's future dangerousness, a criminal justice system under these distributive principles could "convict" an "offender" who has not, but who is

---

2. Of course, different utilitarian theories will conflict. A distribution that maximizes deterrence will not maximize incapacitation of dangerous offenders. But because utilitarian theories seek the same end—avoiding future crime—it seems likely that one can combine utilitarian theories to maximize this end by giving prominence to the theory that will have greatest effectiveness toward that end in the given situation. See P. Robinson, Hybrid Principles for the Distribution of Criminal Sanctions, 82 Nw. U.L. Rev. 19-42 (1987).

predicted to commit, an offense and "punish" him in order to incapacitate or rehabilitate him. While some writers have proposed something close to this,[3] no purely utilitarian system for the distribution of liability and punishment has ever been adopted. This is the case, in all likelihood, because such a system, built upon purely utilitarian distributive principles, would generate results too inconsistent with society's notions of just punishment and thus would run afoul of the popular desire to impose punishment proportionate to an offender's blameworthiness.

Absolute and Relative Assessments of Desert Some writers suggest that desert theory gives only broad ranges of punishment, outside of which a sanction will be seen as *un*just.[4] Admittedly, it is difficult to establish the amount of punishment an offender might deserve, as an absolute matter. It has been observed however, that it is possible to establish the *relative* blameworthiness of offenders.[5] And, given the natural ceiling for punishment—the death penalty or life imprisonment—the rank ordering of offenders ultimately sets each on a specific point or within a narrow range on the continuum of punishment. Because the utilitarian distributive principles look to factors extraneous to an actor's blameworthiness—e.g., the newsworthiness of a case, which may increase the general deterrent effect of punishment; the reliability or lack thereof of the device predicting future dangerousness; the clinical success or failure of a particular rehabilitative program for a particular kind of offender—offenders committing similar offenses and having similar blameworthiness can receive different punishments under a utilitarian system. Thus, utilitarian distributive principles can create not only absolute but also relative injustices.

Disutility of Desert Distribution On the other hand, a desert distribution of liability and punishment can be criticized for failing to avoid avoidable crimes. Such a distribution fails to maximize the crime reduction potential of the criminal justice system, as could be achieved by the utilitarian mechanisms of deterrence, norm reinforcement, incapacitation, and rehabilitation. While citizens might prefer that justice be done, it is argued, there is nothing so compelling as being hit over the head by a mugger or having one's house burglarized or vandalized to clarify one's priorities. Preventing crime continues to be one of the most important, if not the most important function that a citizen asks of government. Therefore, it would not be surprising if citizens might

---

3. See, e.g., B. Wootton, Crime and the Criminal Law 40-57 (1963) (suggesting that the objective of the criminal law should be prevention rather than punishment; among other things, this justifies use of strict liability crimes).

4. See, e.g., N. Morris, The Future of Imprisonment 73-76 (1974); Morris & Miller, Predictions of Dangerousness, G. Crim & Just. 1 (1985).

5. See, e.g., Andrew von Hirsch, Past or Future Crimes: Deservedness and Dangerousness in the Sentencing of Criminals ch. 4 (1985).

compromise their demand for a just distribution of liability and punishment if, by doing so, they could reduce crime.

Crime Reduction Through Other Mechanisms Where a desert distribution of liability is seen as ineffective crime control, nondesert distributive principles are attractive. This is especially so where people see an intolerable and dangerously increasing rate of crime. While the desire to reduce crime is understandable, it is not true that manipulation of the rules governing assignment of criminal liability and punishment is the only means or even the most efficient means of reducing crime. If another systemic reform can reduce crime more effectively or has the same crime reduction effect but without the resulting injustice that comes with deviation from a distributive principle of just desert, then such a reform ought to be implemented instead of, or at least before, deviation from just desert. For example, one might argue that a relaxation of the rules limiting search and seizure by police might hurt privacy interests, but it also might both reduce crime and increase the just distribution of punishment.[6] Given the choice, a community might trade less privacy for less crime and more justice. The larger point is that in the utilitarian calculus for reducing crime, there are many systemic changes possible other than deviating from a distribution of liability based upon just desert. The utility of any unjust distribution must be judged from the larger perspective, taking account of both the cost of the injustice and the comparative benefit of alternative crime control reforms.

Utility of Desert One interesting aspect of the conflict between desert and utilitarian crime control is the recent claim that there is no conflict, that even a utilitarian analysis suggests a distribution of liability according to just deserts. The utility of desert is said to arise from the efficiency of the system in gaining compliance with the criminal law and the criminal justice process. First, the perceived "justice" of the system is crucial to gaining the cooperation and acquiescence of those persons involved in the process (offenders, potential offenders, witnesses, jurors, etc.). Greatest cooperation will be elicited where the criminal law's liability rules and the community's views of justice generate identical results. Conflict between the two undercuts the moral credibility of the system and thereby engenders resistance and subversion.[7]

Moral Condemnation as Deterrence In addition, moral condemna-

---

6. For example, broader search and seizure power by police might improve the truth finding process of trials and permit more successful prosecutions.

7. See, e.g., Seidman, Soldiers, Martyrs, and Criminals: Utilitarian Theory and the Problem of Crime Control, 94 Yale L.J. 315, 319 (1984); S.M. Kassin & L.S. Wrightsman, The American Jury on Trial, 158-159 (1988); Scheflin & Van Dyke, Jury Nullification: The contours of a controversy, 43 Law & Contemporary Problems 52 (1980); M.R. Kadish & S.H. Kadish, Discretion to Disobey (1973).

tion is an inexpensive yet powerful form of deterrent threat. It demands none of the costs that attend imprisonment or even supervised probation, yet, for many persons, it is a sanction to be very much avoided. The more important social acceptance is to the person, the more terrible this threatened sanction. This marvelously cost-efficient sanction is available, however, only if the system retains its moral credibility. Each time the system is seen to convict where no community condemnation is appropriate, the condemnation for subsequent convictions is weakened.

Boosting Law's Moral Authority More importantly, recent empirical evidence suggests that criminal law's most effective mechanism of compliance is not the deterrent threat (of punishment or condemnation) but rather is law's capacity to authoritatively describe the moral rules of conduct, which people will then follow, not out of fear but because they see themselves as good and law-abiding people who are inclined to obey the law because it is the right thing to do. Further, and most importantly, the compliance power of the criminal law is directly proportional to its moral credibility.[8] If the criminal law is seen as unjust in one instance, its moral credibility and its concomitant power to gain future compliance is incrementally reduced.

Interaction of Law and Societal Norms Boosting the law's moral authority, as a utilitarian crime control mechanism, is similar to norm reinforcement in some respects but different in important ways. Norm reinforcement uses the law's liability and punishment decisions to teach the public what is and is not wrong. Law is seen as creating or reinforcing societal norms. Boosting the law's moral authority, as a utilitarian crime control mechanism, focuses on the opposite dynamic between law and societal norms. It is law that is under the influence of community views here, not vice versa. The extent to which people will comply with the law is a function of the law's existing moral credibility, which is in turn a function of the perceived justice of its past adjudications. Under this view, maximum compliance is achieved by law that reflects the community's shared intuitions of justice.[9]

Questions

1. *Mind Games with Distributive Principles.* For each daughter, consider whether liability would be imposed if each of the goals discussed

---

8. See, e.g., T. Tyler, Why People Obey the Law (1990); Sarat, Studying American Legal Cultures: An Assessment of Survey Evidence, 11 Law & Soc. Rev. 427 (1977); C.R. Tittle, Sanction and Social Deviance: A Question of Deterrence (1980).

9. See generally P. Robinson & J. Darley, Justice, Liability, and Blame: Community Views and the Criminal Law (1994).

above, in turn, were considered the *sole* distributive principle for liability: (1) just deserts (retribution), (2) general deterrence, (3) individual (special) deterrence, (4) incapacitation of the dangerous, (5) reform/ rehabilitation, (6) reinforcing societal norms, (7) avoiding vengeance, (8) increasing the community's perception of the criminal law as a moral authority.

2. *More Games.* Alternative distributive principles can be used not only to assess liability in a given case but to analyze the propriety of liability rules and policies. What would each of the above goals, used as the sole distributive principle, suggest for each of the following:

(a) *Predictions of Future Criminality.* If a test could correctly identify future rapists with 95 percent accuracy,* should the test be used as the grounds for assigning criminal liability? Should it be used as the basis for committing those predicted to commit rape?
(b) *Prior Criminal Record.* Is an offender's prior criminal record relevant to determining the degree of liability and punishment for the present offense?
(c) *Death Penalty.* Should the death penalty be available as a sanction? What information would you want to know in making this decision? Under which distributive principles, if any, would it be useful to know the strength of community feeling on the morality of the death penalty?
(d) *Necessity Defense.* Assume that two men and a boy have been adrift at sea without food or water for sometime and that, in order to survive a few days longer, the two men kill the boy, who is almost dead, and drink his blood. As they are about to expire, they are spotted by a passing ship and rescued. Both men are charged with the murder of the boy.† Should they be liable?

3. *Liability for the Daughters?* Taking account of what you have learned above, what degree of liability and punishment, if any, should Iota receive? Benine? Penne? Because different distributive principles suggest different liability conclusions for each of the sisters, as per Question 1, whatever liability answer you give will be consistent with some principles and inconsistent with others. In reaching your liability conclusion for each sister, how did you decide which principles to follow and which to ignore? Did you follow the same system or formula in deciding among conflicting principles for each of the three cases, Iota, Benine, and Penne?

---

*For example, a "penile plethysmograph" test has been developed to make such predictions. (Results from such a test, which "measures a man's sexual response to photographs and audio tapes of sexual activity, including heterosexual and homosexual acts and sex with children," have been offered (by the defense) and admitted as evidence in at least one court.)

†Based upon the *Dudley and Stephens* case excerpted in Section 15.2.

4. *Punishment Theories Meet the Real World.* Re-examine the statistical table at the end of the section on Preliminaries: The Criminal Justice Process. What is the significance of this data for theories for the distribution of liability and punishment? For example, what is the effect on each of the alternative distributive principles of the low rate of conviction for many offenses? Can changes in grading and sentencing of offenses affect potential offenders if those persons see the chance of being convicted as so low as to be irrelevant to them?

Model Penal Code §1.02(1)
The Purposes of the Provisions Governing the Definition of Offenses

The general purposes of the provisions governing the definition of offenses are:

(a) to forbid and prevent conduct that unjustifiably and inexcusably inflicts or threatens substantial harm to individual or public interests;

(b) to subject to public control persons whose conduct indicates that they are disposed to commit crimes;

(c) to safeguard conduct that is without fault from condemnation as criminal;

(d) to give fair warning of the nature of the conduct declared to constitute an offense;

(e) to differentiate on reasonable grounds between serious and minor offenses.

P. Robinson, Hybrid Principles for the Distribution of Criminal Sanctions
82 Nw. U.L. Rev. 19, 19-22, 28-35 (1987)

Most criminal codes, and criminal law courses, begin with the "familiar litany" of the purposes of criminal law sanctions—just punishment, deterrence, incapacitation of the dangerous, and rehabilitation. We train and direct our lawyers, judges, and legislators to use these purposes as guiding principles for the distribution of criminal sanctions. The purposes are thus to guide both the drafting and interpretation of criminal statutes and the imposition of criminal sanctions in individual cases.

The purposes frequently conflict, however, ... Conflicts arise because each purpose requires consideration of different criteria; in some cases a particular fact suggests different sentences or statutory formulations under different purposes. Ultimately, a choice must be made to follow one purpose at the expense of another. Yet, when faced with conflicting purposes, judges, legislators, and sentencing-guideline drafters have no principle to guide that decision.

In the absence of a guiding principle, the choices made are at best inconsistent. For example, most state criminal codes maintain an insanity defense because it exculpates the blameless (and thus furthers just punishment), even though abolishing the defense might more effectively incapacitate the dangerous. Yet, the same codes sacrifice just punishment, in favor of increasing deterrence, when they recognize strict liability. At the same time, rather than increasing the threatened sanction when the temptation or inclination is greater, as a deterrence principle suggests, the same codes frequently decrease the deterrent threat—as, for example, in cases of provocation—because of the offender's reduced blameworthiness. Code drafters are choosing to further different purposes in different contexts.

At worst, the absence of a guiding principle fosters arbitrariness or prejudice. This happens when the inconsistency in choice of distributive principles occurs in individual sentencing decisions. For instance, while rehabilitation might be the best means of avoiding future crime by a young addict who is caught selling drugs to support his habit, a judge rationally might decide to impose a long prison term in order to further general deterrent interests. When faced with a young bank teller who embezzled money from her cash drawer, the same judge might decide to sacrifice the general deterrent value of a long prison term and put the offender on probation, under an incapacitative theory—she is no longer dangerous because she will never again be placed in a position of trust. The judge has chosen to follow one distributive principle in one case but another principle in another case, but we do not know the grounds for the selection. Such unguided and hidden discretion creates the opportunity for arbitrary or biased decision making, although each of the sentences will appear to have a social justification. Without a principle governing when one sentencing purpose is to be followed at the expense of another, judges and guideline drafters are free to choose whatever purpose justifies the sentence that they may desire for other, unspoken, reasons.

Why do we not insist that code and sentencing-guideline drafters adopt, and that judges follow, a statement of the interrelation among purposes that will guide the choice among conflicting purposes? A cynic may conclude that the use of "the purposes" to justify a particular code formulation or sentence is a convenient means of rationalizing results for which the decision maker has another undisclosed reason. This suspicion—that "the purposes" are popular as a method of justification precisely *because* they offer hidden flexibility—is fueled by the almost universal failure to articulate a guiding principle. The Model Penal Code, for example, lists the traditional purposes, directs judges to use them in interpreting the provisions of the Code and in fashioning sentences under the Code; but the Code provides no more guidance in cases of conflict than to urge, in commentary, that the purposes be "just[ly] harmonize[d]." Other writers suggest that the competing interests are to be "balance[d]," "blend[ed]," "accommodate[d]," "taken account of," or "deal[t] with [such that] the public interest will be served."

Is it, as some suggest, simply a failure of the theorists? That is, "we would love to articulate a governing principle, but we cannot figure out how one feasibly can be fashioned." If so, then all will be greatly heartened by . . . this essay, which demonstrates several mechanisms for constructing a workable distributive principle embodying multiple purposes (a "hybrid distributive principle"), and . . . which illustrates how several of these mechanisms can be combined, creating hundreds of possible hybrid distributive principles, one of which is likely to be suitable to every decision maker. On the other hand, [this essay] may be bad news to some. Identification of a principled basis for fashioning sentences and statutes will underscore the arbitrariness and personal bias of those who continue to adhere to ad hoc decision making.

Whether the flexibility of rationalization offered by "the purposes" has been used for conscious manipulation or is the result of inadvertent vagueness, a rational and principled system for the distribution of criminal sanctions is needed. If multiple principles are to be relied upon, a principled system must define the interrelation among the principles; that is, it must fully articulate a hybrid distributive principle.

Questions

1. *Hybrid Distributive Principles.* If different distributive principles suggest different conclusions on an issue, how can one decide among or in some other way resolve the conflicting advice given by the different distributive principles? Is the conflict between retributivist and utilitarian principles different in nature from the conflict among different utilitarian principles?

2. *Alternative Approaches to Constructing a Hybrid Distributive Principle.* If you were to construct a hybrid distributive principle that embodied your own views, what would it look like? Here are several general approaches that one might use:

Establishing Priorities

Under what might be called a "simple priority" approach, whenever Purpose *A* (the purpose of highest priority) supports a doctrine or sentence different from that supported by another purpose, Purpose *A* shall govern. To the extent that Purpose *A* is different as to which of two doctrines or sentences is adopted, but Purpose *B* supports one and Purpose *C* the other, then Purpose *B* (the second highest priority purpose) shall be followed, and so on. Under such an approach, the purpose selected as primary is given greater weight than in any other approach described below. The primary purpose controls whenever it would make a difference.

Somewhat more sophisticated is a "contingent priority" approach. It sets priorities, as in a simple priority approach, but it also sets conditions assuring that a purpose is given priority only in those cases where a defined level of reliability or effectiveness is present. Thus, for example, incapacitation might be given first priority, but that priority can [be] exercised only if, for example, the empirical data for the given situation shows that the reliability of the prediction of dangerousness exceeds a minimum level. Or, general deterrence might be given first priority, contingent upon, for example, empirical data projecting a deterrence effectiveness of a minimum rate. Under this approach, the decision maker would follow the purpose with the highest priority that satisfies its contingent criteria. The virtue of such an approach is that it permits a purpose to control only to the extent that the assumptions underlying the effectiveness or accurateness of the purpose are true. . . .

Combining Purposes

Both of the approaches described above are priority systems of a sort, in which one purpose is furthered at the expense of another. One could formulate, however, an approach by which purposes are combined to give a result influenced in part by all purposes, rather than choosing among purposes. Such an approach seems ideal; it seems to further all and sacrifice none.

Unfortunately, while the concept seems perfect, the extent of its realization is limited. The combination of purposes is feasible only if the purposes to be combined share certain characteristics. First, all purposes considered must share the same ultimate goal, for example, efficient crime prevention. Second, they must be measurable in a common currency, for example, the "costs" in monetary terms of avoiding or not avoiding certain crimes.

Consider, for example, the combination of deterrence and incapacitation. Assume that from a general deterrence perspective, doctrinal formulation or sentence *A* costs 10 units to gain a benefit of 15 units for a net societal benefit of 5, while formulation *B* costs 15 to save 15, for a net benefit of 0. In this situation, general deterrence as a distributive principle would prefer formulation *A*. Assume that incapacitation finds that formulation *A* costs 20 in order to avoid a harm of 15, for a net loss of 5, while formulation *B* costs 10 to avoid an injury of 15, for a net gain of 5. Thus, incapacitation as the distributive principle prefers formulation *B*. This would be an instance where the two purposes conflict.

One might have a system that simply gave priority to one utilitarian mechanism over another. But the better approach would be to take account of the effect on both mechanisms. Because the two purposes have the same goal (efficient crime prevention) and a single currency, the costs and benefits of each formulation for both mechanisms may be determined and these totals for each formulation may be compared to select the best formulation. Thus, if the incapacitation mechanism is significantly increased in effectiveness by a formulation that only minimally hurts the general deterrence mechanism in comparison to the alternative formulation, that difference in magnitude of effect might be enough to justify following the formulation that the incapacitation mechanism prefers. The example above generates the following combined analysis:

	Formulation A	**Formulation B**	
Deterrence	−10	−15	
	+15	+15	
	+5	0	Deterrence prefers Formulation *A*
Incapacitation	−20	−10	
	+15	+15	
	−5	+5	Incapacitation prefers Formulation *B*
Combined Assessment	0	+5	Combined purposes prefer Formulation *B*

Thus, by combining the costs and benefits of both purposes one can determine that formulation *B* will best further the common goal of efficient crime prevention.

The difficulty, of course, is that not all purposes of sentencing share a common goal of crime prevention or a common currency of monetary cost and benefit. As the Model Penal Code commentary suggests:

> It is also recognized that not even crime prevention can be said to be the only end involved. The correction and rehabilitation of offenders is a social value in itself, as well as a preventive instrument. Basic considerations of justice demand, moreover, that penal law safeguard offenders against excessive, disproportionate, or arbitrary punishment. . . .

Others may disagree. Some may suggest that the ultimate purpose of rehabilitation is the same as that of deterrence and incapacitation of the dangerous—that is, crime prevention. On the other hand, some may state the difference between the utilitarian goals and desert in even stronger terms than the commentary does; justice not only bars "excessive, disproportionate, or arbitrary punishment" but also requires specific formulations for rules, doctrines, offenses, and sentences. Whatever view one takes, the important point is that the combined approach cannot be used to amalgamize purposes that do not share a common currency and goal. . . .

Distinguishing the Assignment and Amount from the Method of Sanction

The traditional purposes are used to resolve a range of distinguishable issues in the distribution of sanctions: Who should be sanctioned? How much sanction should they receive? How should the sanction be imposed? The first issue is essentially one of liability assignment—who should be held criminally liable? The second issue—how much sanction?—goes to both liability rules (that is, what grade or degree of offense is appropriate for certain conduct) and sentencing practice (for example, how long a sentence or how great a fine is appropriate in a particular case). Together, these two issues govern the quantitative distribution of sanction—who will receive how much. The third issue, concerning the method of sanction, is distinguishable from the distribution of amount. Two offenders may merit the same *amount* of sanction yet different *methods* of sanctioning may be suitable for imposing that amount. These two issues—how much for whom and what method—are not only functionally distinguishable but also may be properly subject to different distributive principles.

Each of the distributive purposes may treat the different issues differently. Effective crime control can be furthered through a variety of mechanisms—by setting the amount or the method of sanction (as well as by setting enforcement and prosecution patterns and expenditures). Satisfaction of desert concerns, in contrast, depends almost exclusively on the amount issue—who receives how much; the method issue (as well as the resource allocation issues) is generally not relevant.

The desert requirement of a proper ordinal ranking of offenders by overall blameworthiness, for example, concerns the ranking of *amounts* of sanctions. As long as the ordinal ranking is correct, the *method* by which each amount is imposed is not relevant to desert. If one month in the state prison is the punitive equivalent to 5 months of weekends in the local jail, then desert is satisfied even if the more blameworthy offender gets probation, with a condition of 7 months of weekends in jail, while the less blameworthy offender goes to prison for one month. It is critical, of course, that the sanction equivalencies be properly set. Some empirical research has been done on perceptions of relative seriousness of sanctions, but the work is still in its infancy.

With an estimate of equivalencies, one could construct a sentencing system that allows independent determination of the amount and method issues. The principles governing the "amount" issue can generate total "sanction units" for each offender, which can then be allocated to a particular sanctioning method or combination of methods according to a different set of "method" principles. As long as the issues can be effectively segregated in practice, one can develop a different hybrid distributive principle for governing amount of sanction that is different from the principle used to determine method of sanction. One could, for example, emphasize desert in determining the amount of sanction but ignore it in determining the method. The selection of method could be made to maximize pure utilitarian concerns with no infringement of desert interests—a precious no-loss, all-win opportunity.

P. Robinson, Hybrid Principles for the Distribution of Criminal Sanctions, 82 Nw. U.L. Rev. 19, 19-22, 28-35 (1987) (other approaches to creating hybrid principles are also discussed, such as distinguishing determining from limiting principles and relying upon the principle that gives the greatest sanction).

3. *Conflicts, Hybrids, and the Utility of Desert.* If one took the view that a desert distribution had greatest utility in avoiding future crime, what kind of distributive principle would one adopt? Would it be a hybrid? Would the distribution of liability be guided by moral philosophy or community intuitions of justice? In other words, in drafting a rule, would one ask moral philosophers what formulation of the rule best reflects just deserts? Or, would one ask social psychologists what formulation best reflects the community's shared intuitions of justice on the issue?

Chapter 3. THE STRUCTURE AND SOURCES OF CRIMINAL LAW: AN OVERVIEW

This section provides an overview of criminal law doctrine's operation. In working through the hypothetical below, you will be introduced to the great variety of issues that this course will examine in some detail. Note that there is a structure to the analysis, which you may find useful in analyzing other cases. It is not the only way to broadly conceptualize the issues.

You may find it useful to look at the specific statutes relating to each of the issues. You will see each of the statutes again. The footnotes give a citation to the relevant Model Penal Code section, which can be found in the Appendix. The Model Penal Code, its history, and significance, are discussed at the end of this chapter.

Fear of the Daggers

Box lives next door to the Golden Daggers' clubhouse. As he walks by on this morning, on his way home from his night shift at the Tower Grill, two gang members grab him and drag him inside. "I hear you're friendly with Pet Peppe," one spits, with his face an inch from Box's. "No, not really," Box says, shaking. "I used to see her around, hanging with you guys. I'm not really a friend of hers." The man responds, "Then you won't mind doing me a favor. You'll cut her face for me." Box isn't thrilled about the idea. He says nothing. "Look, it's either your face or hers," the man says as he pricks a knife in Box's face an inch below his eye. "OK. OK. I'll do it." The Dagger stares. "If I don't see scars on her face tomorrow, we'll be looking for you."

Box goes to his apartment and pours himself a drink, spilling much of it because his hands are shaking. Yes, he is scared of those guys, he admits to himself. Hurting Pet would be a bad thing, but what's the alternative, especially if the Daggers find out that he and Pet have been dating? After several more hours of anxious drinking, Box gets a butcher knife from the kitchen and heads for Pet's, bottle in hand. By the time he gets there, he is staggering badly and barely coherent. Pet opens the door. "Hi Box." Box lurches forward, stumbling into the back of the sofa. "What's wrong with you?" Box does not respond. He staggers around the apartment, knocking over furniture. "This is your own fault," he screams at her, and babbles on about blood, knives, and eyes. When he has worked himself into a frenzy, he pulls his knife and begins flailing at everything around him, curtains, lamps, pictures on the wall. Pet gets caught by several of his swings and is badly cut. She runs from the apartment, screaming for the police. Box also runs. He takes the subway to his brother's place on the other side of town where he spends the night.

After reflecting on his situation, Box decides not to return to his apartment but rather to take a job in a small town in the southern part of the state. Unaware that Box has left town, Pet does not disclose his identity to the police for fear of reprisals by Box. Pet's shoulder heals but a cut to her hand has permanently damaged the muscles. She is no longer able to write with that hand and becomes increasingly bitter about the episode.

Several years later Box returns to town. Pet chances to see him on the subway one day and, after much stewing, decides to report him to the police. His arrest comes three years after the incident.

Is Box liable for aggravated assault?

Notes on the Operational Structure of Criminal Law

Operational structure Let us use Box's case to examine how the doctrines of criminal law operate. Each rule typically does one of three things. A doctrine may define what constitutes an *offense*. A doctrine may define the conditions under which an actor will be acquitted even though he satisfies the elements of an offense. Such a doctrine commonly is termed a *defense*. Or, a doctrine may define the conditions under which an actor will be held liable even though he does not satisfy the elements of an offense. Such a doctrine may be called a doctrine of *imputation*. This coursebook is organized around this three-part doctrinal structure.

Offense Definitions The definition of an offense typically is comprised of objective elements—for example, conduct, its attendant circumstances, or its results—and culpability elements—for example, purpose, knowledge, recklessness, or negligence—as to each objective element. Thus, the objective elements of murder might require that an actor engage in *conduct* that causes the *death* of *another human being*. The culpability elements might require that the actor *know* the nature of his conduct, that it will cause a death, and that the death caused is that of a human being (e.g., not that of an inviable fetus). The culpability requirements may be different for different elements of the same offense. A jurisdiction might, for example, require that an actor *know* the nature of his conduct and that it will cause a death, but only require that the actor be *reckless* as to whether the death is that of a human being.

Special vs. General Part of Code Chapter 7 examines the general principles governing objective and culpability elements of the offense definitions. Chapter 4 examines the elements of the most important offense, homicide. The definition of specific offenses makes up what is called the Special Part of a criminal code. The general rules governing the definition of offenses, together with the doctrines of imputation and defense, make up the General Part of a code and typically apply to many or all specific offenses. Look at the Table of Contents of the Model Penal Code in the Appendix to see the distinction between General Part and Special Part in the organization of a criminal code.

Box and Elements of Aggravated Assault In Box's case, aggravated assault might be defined to require, as objective elements, that an actor engage in conduct that causes serious bodily injury to another.[1] Box has done that. The offense also might require, as culpability elements, that the actor be at least reckless as to causing such injury, at the time of his conduct. It is unclear that Box satisfies this requirement. Recklessness as to causing an injury is defined to require that the actor is aware of a risk that his conduct will cause such injury.[2] Because of his grossly intoxicated state, it may well be that, at the time he cut Pet, Box was simply flailing madly at the world around him, with no specific intention or awareness that he might cut Pet with his swings. If he were sober, he certainly would realize the potential effect of such knife-swinging but he is not sober. If Box is not aware of this risk of harm to Pet at the time of his flailing, he does not satisfy the requirements of the offense definition of aggravated assault. As we shall see, he nonetheless may be liable for the offense.

Imputing Objective Elements An actor may be held liable for an offense, even if he does not satisfy an element of the offense definition, if he satisfies the requirements of a doctrine of imputation that will impute to him the missing element. For example, an actor may participate in a bank robbery in which it is planned that one of the other participants will kill the bank guard if the guard resists. Although the accomplice does the killing, the robber may be liable for murder. This is true even if the offense of murder is defined to require that the actor engage in the conduct that causes the death. While the robber did not

---

1. Model Penal Code §§210.0(3), 211.1(2).
2. Model Penal Code §2.02(2)(c).

engage in the conduct that caused the death, the killer's conduct will be imputed to him under the doctrine of complicity. That is, the doctrine of complicity allows him to be treated *as if* he had engaged in the conduct.

Imputing Culpability Elements Just as the doctrine of complicity can impute to the defendant an objective element another's conduct, the doctrine of voluntary intoxication can impute a culpability element. An actor who voluntarily intoxicates herself and in that drunken state strikes and kills a pedestrian with her car in fact may lack the culpability required for the offense of manslaughter—that is, an awareness of a substantial risk that her conduct will cause the death of another human being. Yet, such awareness of a risk of causing a death (i.e., recklessness as to causing death) may be imputed to the actor under the doctrine of voluntary intoxication. That is, because of her voluntary intoxication, she may be treated *as if* she satisfies the required element of recklessness as to causing death, and therefore may be convicted of manslaughter. Box would fall under the application of this doctrine. Because his intoxication was voluntary, recklessness as to causing serious bodily injury, required for aggravated assault liability, will be imputed to him.[3] Part III of this book takes up the doctrines of imputation.

Doctrines of Defense Where an actor satisfies all of the elements of an offense, actually or through imputation, he nonetheless may be acquitted of the offense if he satisfies the conditions of a defense. Box has several claims of defense that he might make, although some are more promising than others. He might claim that his conduct was justified by his need to protect himself from the Golden Daggers. He might claim that he should be excused because the Daggers coerced him into doing what he did. Or, he might claim that the period of limitation has run and that he can no longer be prosecuted for the offense.

Failure of Proof Defenses Some doctrines that are called "defenses" are nothing more than the absence of a required offense element. When I take your umbrella believing it to be my own, I may claim a *mistake defense*. Yet my defense derives not from a special defense doctrine about mistake as to ownership but rather derives from the elements of the theft offense. The definition of theft includes a requirement that the actor know that the property taken is property owned by another. If I mistakenly believe that the umbrella I take is my own, I do not satisfy that required element of knowledge. Such a mistake "defense" is called a *failure of proof defense* because it derives from the inability of the state to prove a required element. When Box claimed that he did not have the required recklessness as to causing serious bodily injury to Pet, he is claiming such a failure of proof defense. He is claiming

---

3. Model Penal Code §2.08(2).

that the prosecution cannot prove all of the elements of the offense. In causal usage, such claims are called "defenses," but they are simply another way of talking about the requirements of an offense definition.

Offense Modification Defenses Some defenses are indeed independent of the offense elements, but in fact, concern criminalization issues closely related to the definition of the offense. They typically refine or qualify the definition of a particular offense or group of offenses. Voluntary renunciation, for example, can provide a defense to inchoate offenses like attempt or conspiracy. Consent is recognized as a defense to some kinds of assault. The consent defense helps to define what we mean by the offense of assault, (as including minor injury when it is not consented to), just as renunciation helps refine the definition of inchoate offenses (as including only unrenounced criminal plans). Indeed, assault frequently is defined as an *unconsented to* touching. That is, the absence of consent sometimes is included as an element of the offense. As the practice illustrates, the difference between failure of proof defenses and offense modification defenses is one of form more than substance. An offense modification *defense* can as easily be drafted as a *negative element* of the offense.

Criminalization Defenses vs. General Defenses Because both failure of proof and offense modification defenses serve to refine the offense definition, (and therefore might be called "criminalization" defenses), they tend to apply to a single offense or group of offenses. Justifications, excuses, and nonexculpatory defenses, in contrast, are unrelated to a particular offense; they theoretically apply to all offenses and therefore are called *general defenses*. The recognition of each general defense rests upon reasons extraneous to the criminalization goals and policies of the offense. A general defense is provided, not because there is no criminal wrong, but rather despite the occurrence of a legally-recognized harm or evil. The offense harm or evil may have occurred but the special conditions establishing the defense suggest that the violator ought not be punished for the offense harm or evil.

Justification Defenses An actor may satisfy all of the elements of an offense and his or her conduct may clearly be a legally-recognized harm or evil of the sort that generally is prohibited, yet the circumstances of the offense may suggest that, because of the justifying circumstances, this particular offense conduct ought to be tolerated or even encouraged. An unconsented to striking of another constitutes assault and generally is prohibited, yet it ought not result in liability if done in self-defense against an aggressor to protect one's life. Burning another's farm constitutes arson, yet it ought to be tolerated and even encouraged if it creates a firebreak that saves a town from a raging forest fire. Providing a justification defense in such cases is not meant to lessen the general prohibition against assault and arson but only to recognize that the harm or evil of even such serious offenses as these can be outweighed by a greater good that flows from the commission of the offense under the special justifying circumstances.

Justification for Box? Box might claim a justification defense, arguing that the cuts to Pet were a less serious harm than the injury he was likely to suffer at the hands of the Daggers. But his conduct is not likely to be deemed justified. The defensive force justifications authorize injury to aggressors but Pet is an innocent person.[4] Justification defenses also typically require that no other less harmful means of avoiding the harm be available.[5] Box could have reported the incident to police, gone into hiding as he did, or both. Cutting Pet was not the least harmful means of avoiding the harm. Justification defenses are examined in Chapter 15.

Excuse Defenses Even if an actor's conduct is harmful or evil in itself and is not justified by special circumstances, an acquittal nonetheless may be appropriate. The criminal law has a special commitment to punishing only the blameworthy. An actor who is acting involuntarily, who is insane, involuntarily intoxicated, or immature, or who is acting under duress or under a reasonable mistake of law or mistake as to a justification may be blameless. That is, we may feel that such an actor in such a situation could not reasonably have been expected to remain law-abiding. The excuse defenses are designed to exculpate such blameless offenders. Excuse defenses are the subject of Chapter 16.

Excuse for Box? Box might claim an excuse of some sort. Because his intoxication was voluntary, the law does not permit it to be the basis for an excuse.[6] He might do better to claim a duress defense based upon the coercion from the Daggers. But many states make the duress defense unavailable for offenses of violence against another person. And, where it is not expressly barred in such cases, as in the Model Penal Code, a duress defense is available only where a person of reasonable firmness would have been unable to resist the coercion to commit the offense.[7] It seems unlikely that a jury could be persuaded that, faced with threats like those from the Daggers, a person of reasonable firmness would slash Pet as Box did. In other words, a jury is likely to find that, despite the Daggers' threats, Box is blameworthy and ought to be held liable for his offense.

Nonexculpatory Defenses Even blameworthy actors may be acquitted if they satisfy the requirements of a nonexculpatory defense. Such defenses are disfavored yet recognized because they each further an important societal interest, judged to be more important than punishing the offender at hand. Diplomatic immunity, for example, is allowed to

---

4. Model Penal Code §3.04.
5. See, e.g., Model Penal Code §3.02.
6. Model Penal Code §2.08(4).
7. Model Penal Code §2.09.

shield criminal offenders because by recognizing such a defense we protect our diplomats abroad, and this in turn allows the establishment of diplomatic relations between nations. That a societal benefit is derived from the defense may seem to make nonexculpatory defenses similar to justifications, but note that the benefit in nonexculpatory offenses flows not from the actor's offense conduct, as is the case with justifications, but rather from foregoing his conviction despite the undesirability of his conduct and his blameworthiness.

Nonexculpatory Defense for Box? Box may claim a nonexculpatory defense in the statute of limitations.[8] The passage of three years, during which he has been in the jurisdiction, may well bar his prosecution for the offense. The defense is not based upon any lack of harm or blame but rather is recognized, despite the presence of both, because such a limitation period is said to avoid a counterproductive preoccupation with the past. At some point, the argument goes, society is better off letting go of the past and moving ahead to deal with the problems and challenges of today. In most jurisdictions, if the arrest warrant for Box is issued more than three years after the assault, prosecution will be barred. Chapter 17 examines nonexculpatory defenses.[9]

Liability Assignment vs. Sentencing All of these criminal law doctrines—offense definitions, doctrines of imputation, and general defenses—serve only to assign criminal liability. Such liability suggests that some punishment is appropriate and gives a general classification of the offense—for example, third degree felony, first degree misdemeanor—that serves as a starting point for determining how much punishment is appropriate. The specific amount and nature of the punishment, however, is determined during the sentencing process, which frequently is entirely discretionary with the sentencing judge. In that sense, the criminal law, for all its intricacy and for all the resources devoted to its adjudication of an individual case, has a limited effect in determining the ultimate sanction. It has the important role of determining *who* shall be punished but it leaves to the sentencing process most of the determination of *how much* or *what kind* of punishment will be imposed.

Criminal Law Principles in Sentencing This state of affairs may seem peculiar. The criminal law is drafted with great care to make the assignment of liability a matter of rules rather than discretion. As Chapter 5 details, this commitment to the articulation of liability rules, called the principle of legality, has always been a foundation of Anglo-American criminal law. Yet the highly articulated criminal law has a limited effect in

---

8. Model Penal Code §1.06.
9. For a more detailed discussion of the differences among the groups of defenses and their implications, see Paul H. Robinson, Criminal Law Defenses: A Systematic Analysis, 82 Colum. L. Rev. 199, 204-243 (1982).

determining the punishment imposed. Instead, the highly discretionary sentencing process determines the punishment. If unguided discretion is carefully avoided in the liability assignment process, why is it tolerated in sentencing, where the punishment is in large part determined? In part because of legality concerns, the trend in modern sentencing systems is toward more articulated sentencing rules.[10] As one might expect, these articulations typically draw upon and extend principles of criminal law. Thus, while the rules of liability assignment are only a stop on the way to determining punishment, the principles behind those rules are likely to play an increasingly larger role in the formulation of sentencing rules and guidelines.

Practical Importance of Criminal Law Theory The articulation of sentencing rules is but one example of the value of understanding the principles behind criminal law and not just its rules. The effective advocate and the informed judge are at their best when they understand the theory of the rules, why the doctrine is the way it is. Only then can they interpret code provisions to give them proper effect or criticize interpretations that would frustrate the purpose of a provision. In addition, lawyers inevitably play a large role in the law-making process, in which criminal codes are drafted and enacted. Therefore, a rational, effective, and just criminal law depends upon an informed bar. The conceptual structure for criminal law described above is an example of a conceptualization that can have significant practical value. Lawyers and judges, not just academics, benefit from a sense of this larger conceptual framework of criminal law, for it is through such a structure that they can appreciate the role that each doctrine plays within the larger whole.

Notes on the Sources of Criminal Law

Two hundred years ago in England, criminal law was generally uncodified. This "common law" was developed by and embodied in judicial opinions. The American colonies adopted this common law of England as it existed at the time of independence. The most popular treatise of the time, Blackstone's Commentaries on the Laws of England, became a highly influential work in America, not because of anything

---

10. For a description and critique of some current structured sentencing systems, see D. Parent, Structuring Criminal Sentences: The Evolution of Minnesota's Sentencing Guidelines (1988); A. von Hirsch, K. Knapp & M. Tonry, The Sentencing Commission and its Guidelines (1987); Tonry, Criminal Law: The Missing Element in Sentencing Reform, 35 Vand. L. Rev. 607 (1982).

particularly distinguished about the four volumes but rather because its popularity coincided with American independence. Volume 4 provided a useful summary of then-existing English common law criminal law.[11] American courts then took on the role of further refining and developing the law, thereby creating differences with English law. Today, courts generally no longer have this role with respect to criminal law. The function has been taken over by the legislatures. Nearly every state has a criminal code as its primary source of criminal law. Courts interpret the code but generally have no authority to create new crimes or change the definition of existing crimes. The reasons for the shift from common law's judicially defined offenses to criminal codes are found chiefly in the rationales for what is called the Legality Principle, the subject of Chapter 5. Even with codification, the power of courts to interpret criminal statutes can have significant effect.

Common Law Defined When lawyers speak of "common law," they may mean either the law as it existed during the Common Law period in England or law that is derived from a process of judicial development. The intended meaning frequently is evident from the context. For example, the "common law *process*" typically refers to the process of judicial law-making, whether or not it occurs during the Common Law *period*. "*The* Common Law rule" usually refers to the legal rule that existed in England during the Eighteenth Century. On the other hand, a minority of states continue to rely upon judicially-modified variations of the original Common Law rule. Such rules may be referred to as "common law" rules even if they are significantly different from the rule described by Blackstone.[12]

Current Role of Common Law While no state continues to permit judges to create crimes, the common law continues to be important for several reasons. Some state criminal codes incorporate common law offenses by name, without defining them. Under so-called "reception" statutes, judicial decisions must be relied upon to determine the requirements of a common law offense.[13] In addition, because some codes are simply codifications of the previously-existing common law doctrine, ambiguity in code language that calls for an examination of the drafters' intent may require review of the cases in which the doctrine was developed. Similarly, the common law cases may be referred to because they tend to explain the rationale behind the original rule, where the codification of the rule frequently does not.

---

11. W. Blackstone, Commentaries on the Laws of England (1803, reprinted 1969).

12. If "Common Law" is capitalized it typically is meant to refer to the Common Law period, but most writers, including this one, are not consistent in following this convention.

13. For a discussion of the difficulties and potential unconstitutionality of such statutes, see Chapter 5.

An attorney seeking to persuade a court of the wisdom, or folly, of the policy behind a particular interpretation of a statute may look to common law cases to establish and explain the policy. The rules and techniques of statutory interpretation are discussed further in Chapter 5, covering The Legality Principle.

Modern Criminal Code Reform While there were some heroic efforts,[14] little criminal code reform occurred in the United States before the 1960s. Most codes were less a code and more a collection of ad hoc statutory enactments, each enactment triggered by a crime or a crime problem that gained public interest for a time.[15] The major contribution of early codifiers frequently was to put the offenses in alphabetical order. The greatest catalyst of modern American criminal law codification has been the Model Penal Code, which was promulgated by the American Law Institute. Beginning even before its formal adoption in 1962, the Model Penal Code served and continues to serve as a basis for wholesale replacement of existing criminal codes in over two-thirds of the states.[16] Some states have adopted the Code with only minor revision, while others, especially those that adopted it early, tended to redraft their existing doctrine, borrowing only parts of the Model Penal Code's style and form.

The Model Penal Code The American Law Institute, which drafted the Code, is a nongovernmental broad-based highly-regarded group of lawyers, judges, professors, and others that undertakes research and drafting projects designed to bring rationality and enlightenment to American law. The Institute's Restatements of the Law have been influential in bringing clarity and uniformity to many fields. When a criminal law project was undertaken in 1953,[17] it was concluded that the criminal law of the various states had become too disparate to permit a "restatement" and, in any case, the existing law was seen as too unsound and ill-considered to merit restating. What was needed instead was a model criminal code. After nine years of work and a series of Tentative Drafts, the Institute approved an Official Draft in 1962. The original

---

14. See Kadish, Codifiers of the Criminal Law: Wechsler's Predecessors, 78 Colum. L. Rev. 1098 (1978) (describing the statutory reform efforts of Edward Livingston and David Dudley Field in Louisiana and New York, respectively).

15. See, e.g., 18 U.S.C. §§1201-1202 (the so-called Lindbergh Law) enacted in 1932 making kidnapping a federal crime when the victim is transported across state lines. The statute was an immediate response to the kidnapping of Charles Lindbergh, Jr. on March 1, 1932.

16. For a list of states that have replaced their criminal codes since promulgation of the Model Penal Code, see American Law Institute, Annual Report 21 (1984).

17. A proposal for a Model Penal Code was advanced in 1931, but the project lacked funding. In 1950 after a grant from the Rockefeller Foundation, an advisory committee was assembled by the ALI to undertake the reformation of American criminal law. See McClain, "Criminal Law Reform: Historical Development in the United States," Encyclopedia of Crime and Justice 510 (S. Kadish, ed. 1983).

commentary, which was contained in the various Tentative Drafts, was consolidated, revised, and republished with the 1962 text in 1980 and 1985 as a six volume set.[18]

Federal Criminal Code Reform Of the third or less of the jurisdictions that have not yet adopted a modern criminal code, the federal system is the most unfortunate example of frustrated reform. The Congress has been engaged in an effort to reform the federal criminal code since 1966.[19] A modern code bill passed the Senate but did not pass the House.[20] Criminal code reform is always difficult because it touches highly political issues, but the lack of a modern federal criminal code is a matter of some embarrassment in a country whose states lead the world in enlightened criminal codification. The present federal criminal code is not significantly different in form from the alphabetical listing of offenses that was typical of the original American codes in the 1800s.[21]

Format of Modern Codes Modern criminal codes have several hallmarks. All have a General Part that contains general provisions, affecting all or many of the specific offenses defined in the Special Part of the code. General provisions include such things as the general rules concerning omission liability, complicity, and voluntary intoxication, general defenses such as self-defense, insanity, and time limitations, general rules for the definition and interpretation of offenses, and a collection of definitions for commonly used terms. In the Special Part of a code, offenses are defined and organized as conceptually related groups and are consolidated and revised to avoid overlaps and gaps. The offenses against property work together to define all prohibited harms involving property, for example. A significant practical effect of reform is that code sections can no

---

18. Three volumes containing Part II of the Model Penal Code, Definition of Specific Crimes, with revised comments were published in 1980. Three additional volumes containing Part I of the Code, General Provisions, with revised Comments, were published in 1985. An official version of the completed text of the Model Penal Code was published in 1985.

19. These efforts began with the establishment of the "Brown Commission" (Act of Nov. 8, 1966, Pub. L. No. 89-801, 80 Stat. 1516) followed by that Commission's Final Report on Reform of Federal Criminal Laws presented in 1971. See also Gainer, Report to the Attorney General on Federal Criminal Code Reform, 1 Crim. L. Forum 99 (1989) (a comprehensive critique of the federal criminal code).

20. S.1437 "The Criminal Code Reform Act of 1977," 95th Cong., 2d Sess. (1978) (Senate vote 72 for; 15 against), 1 Congressional Index, 23,049 95th Cong. January 30, 1978. A criminal code bill was actively considered in two earlier Congresses. S.1, 93d. Cong., 1st Sess. (1973); S.1, 94th Cong., 1st Sess. (1975).

21. For a review of federal criminal code reform efforts and a discussion of the need for reform, see Gainer, Report to the Attorney General on Federal Criminal Code Reform, 1 Crim. L. Forum 99 (1989).

longer be read in isolation. To fully understand each offense definition in the Special Part, several General Part provisions must be consulted. The largely successful goal of modern criminal code reform is a code that provides clarity in defining a sophisticated and rational set of rules for distributing liability and punishment.

Chapter 4. AN OFFENSE ILLUSTRATION: HOMICIDE

To give us a point of reference in our discussions, let us examine the details of an offense. Homicide is useful as an illustration because, as the most serious offense, it is particularly interesting and well-developed and raises many, if not most, of the issues that can arise in criminal offenses. For these same reasons, however, it is not a typical offense and it would be wrong to assume that other offense definitions will be as elaborate as homicide.

SECTION 4.1 HOMICIDE STATUTES

Below are three statutory homicide schemes. California comes close to being a codification of the common law scheme. New York is heavily influenced by the Model Penal Code but retains some common law forms and introduces some variations of its own. Many modern jurisdictions adopt the bulk of the Model Penal Code scheme. The remainder of the chapter requires your familiarity with these provisions.

California Penal Code §§187, 188, 189, 192
Homicide Offenses

§187. Murder Defined; Death of Fetus

(a) Murder is the unlawful killing of a human being, or a fetus, with malice aforethought. . . .

§188. Malice, Express Malice, and Implied Malice Defined

Such malice may be express or implied. It is express when there is manifested a deliberate intention unlawfully to take away the life of a fellow creature. It is implied, when no considerable provocation appears, or when the circumstances attending the killing show an abandoned and malignant heart.

When it is shown that the killing resulted from the intentional doing of an act with express or implied malice as defined above, no other mental state need be shown to establish the mental state of malice aforethought. Neither an awareness of the obligation to act within the general body of laws regulating society nor acting despite such awareness is included within the definition of malice.

§189. Murder; Degrees

All murder which is perpetrated by means of a destructive device or explosive, knowing use of ammunition designed primarily to penetrate metal or armor, poison, lying in wait, torture, or by any other kind of willful, deliberate, and premeditated killing, or which is committed in the perpetration of, or attempt to perpetrate, arson, rape, robbery, burglary, mayhem, or any act punishable under Section 288 [lewd or lascivious acts with child under age 14], is murder of the first degree; and all other kinds of murders are of the second degree.

As used in this section, "destructive device" shall mean any destructive device as defined in Section 12301, and "explosive" shall mean any explosive as defined in Section 12000 of the Health and Safety Code.

To prove the killing was "deliberate and premeditated," it shall not be necessary to prove the defendant maturely and meaningfully reflected upon the gravity of his or her act.

§192. Manslaughter; Voluntary, Involuntary, and Vehicular, Construction of Section

Manslaughter is the unlawful killing of a human being without malice. It is of three kinds:

1. Voluntary—upon a sudden quarrel or heat of passion.
2. Involuntary—in the commission of an unlawful act, not amounting to felony; or in the commission of a lawful act which might produce death, in an unlawful manner, or without due caution and circumspection; provided that this subdivision shall not apply to acts committed in the driving of a vehicle. . . .
3. Vehicular—[omitted].

New York Penal Law §§125.00, 125.10, 125.15, 125.20, 125.25, 125.27
Homicide Offenses

Section 125.00 Homicide Defined

Homicide means conduct which causes the death of a person or an unborn child with which a female has been pregnant for more than twenty-four weeks under circumstances constituting murder, manslaughter in the first degree, manslaughter in the second degree, criminally negligent homicide, . . .

Section 125.10 Criminally Negligent Homicide

A person is guilty of criminally negligent homicide when, with criminal negligence, he causes the death of another person.
Criminally negligent homicide is a class E felony.

Section 125.15 Manslaughter in the Second Degree

A person is guilty of manslaughter in the second degree when:
 1. He recklessly causes the death of another person; or
 2. He commits upon a female an abortional act which causes her death, unless such abortional act is justifiable pursuant to subdivision three of section 125.05; or
 3. He intentionally causes or aids another person to commit suicide.
Manslaughter in the second degree is a class C felony.

Section 125.20 Manslaughter in the First Degree

A person is guilty of manslaughter in the first degree when:
 1. With intent to cause serious physical injury to another person, he causes the death of such person or of a third person; or
 2. With intent to cause the death of another person, he causes the death of such person or of a third person under circumstances which do not constitute murder because he acts under the influence of extreme emotional disturbance, as defined in paragraph (a) of subdivision one of section 125.25. The fact that homicide was commit-

ted under the influence of extreme emotional disturbance constitutes a mitigating circumstance reducing murder to manslaughter in the first degree and need not be proved in any prosecution initiated under this subdivision; or

3. He commits upon a female pregnant for more than twenty-four weeks an abortional act which causes her death, unless such abortional act is justifiable pursuant to subdivision three of section 125.05.

Manslaughter in the first degree is a class B felony.

Section 125.25 Murder in the Second Degree

A person is guilty of murder in the second degree when:

1. With intent to cause the death of another person, he causes the death of such person or of a third person; except that in any prosecution under this subdivision, it is an affirmative defense that:

(a) The defendant acted under the influence of extreme emotional disturbance for which there was a reasonable explanation or excuse, the reasonableness of which is to be determined from the viewpoint of a person in the defendant's situation under the circumstances as the defendant believed them to be. Nothing contained in this paragraph shall constitute a defense to a prosecution for, or preclude a conviction of, manslaughter in the first degree or any other crime; or

(b) The defendant's conduct consisted of causing or aiding, without the use of duress or deception, another person to commit suicide. Nothing contained in this paragraph shall constitute a defense to a prosecution for, or preclude a conviction of, manslaughter in the second degree or any other crime; or

2. Under circumstances evincing a depraved indifference to human life, he recklessly engages in conduct which creates a grave risk of death to another person, and thereby causes the death of another person; or

3. Acting either alone or with one or more other persons, he commits or attempts to commit robbery, burglary, kidnapping, arson, rape in the first degree, sodomy in the first degree, sexual abuse in the first degree, escape in the first degree, or escape in the second degree, and, in the course of and in furtherance of such crime or of immediate flight therefrom, he, or another participant, if there be any, causes the death of a person other than one of the participants; except that in any prosecution under this subdivision, in which the defendant was not the only participant in the underlying crime, it is an affirmative defense that the defendant:

(a) Did not commit the homicidal act or in any way solicit, request, command, importune, cause or aid the commission thereof; and

CHAPTER 4   AN OFFENSE ILLUSTRATION: HOMICIDE

(b) Was not armed with a deadly weapon, or any instrument, article or substance readily capable of causing death or serious physical injury and of a sort not ordinarily carried in public places by law-abiding persons; and

(c) Had no reasonable ground to believe that any other participant was armed with such a weapon, instrument, article or substance; and

(d) Had no reasonable ground to believe that any other participant intended to engage in conduct likely to result in death or serious physical injury.

Murder in the second degree is a class A-I felony.

Section 125.27 Murder in the First Degree

A person is guilty of murder in the first degree when:

1. With intent to cause the death of another person, he causes the death of such person; and

(a) Either:

(i) the victim was a police officer as defined in subdivision 34 of section 1.20 of the criminal procedure law who was killed in the course of performing his official duties, and the defendant knew or reasonably should have known that the victim was a police officer; or

(ii) the victim was an employee of a state correctional institution or was an employee of a local correctional facility as defined in subdivision two of section forty of the correction law, who was killed in the course of performing his official duties, and the defendant knew or reasonably should have known that the victim was an employee of a state correctional institution or a local correctional facility; or

(iii) at the time of the commission of the crime, the defendant was confined in a state correctional institution, or was otherwise in custody upon a sentence for the term of his natural life, or upon a sentence commuted to one of natural life, or upon a sentence for an indeterminate term the minimum of which was at least fifteen years and the maximum of which was natural life, or at the time of the commission of the crime, the defendant had escaped from such confinement or custody and had not yet been returned to such confinement or custody; and

(b) The defendant was more than eighteen years old at the time of the commission of the crime.

2. In any prosecution under subdivision one, it is an affirmative defense that:

(a) The defendant acted under the influence of extreme emotional disturbance for which there was a reasonable explanation or excuse, the reasonableness of which is to be determined from the viewpoint of a person in the defendant's situation under the circumstances as the defendant believed them to be. Nothing contained in this paragraph shall constitute a defense to a prosecution for, or preclude a conviction of, manslaughter in the first degree or any other crime except murder in the second degree; or

    (b) The defendant's conduct consisted of causing or aiding, without the use of duress or deception, another person to commit suicide. Nothing contained in this paragraph shall constitute a defense to a prosecution for, or preclude a conviction of, manslaughter in the second degree or any other crime except murder in the second degree.

Murder in the first degree is a class A-I felony.

Model Penal Code, Article 210
Criminal Homicide

Section 210.0 Definitions

    In Articles 210-213, unless a different meaning plainly is required:
    (1) "human being" means a person who has been born and is alive;
    (2) "bodily injury" means physical pain, illness or any impairment of physical condition;
    (3) "serious bodily injury" means bodily injury which creates a substantial risk of death or which causes serious, permanent disfigurement, or protracted loss or impairment of the function of any bodily member or organ;
    (4) "deadly weapon" means any firearm, or other weapon, device, instrument, material or substance, whether animate or inanimate, which in the manner it is used or is intended to be used is known to be capable of producing death or serious bodily injury.

Section 210.1 Criminal Homicide

    (1) A person is guilty of criminal homicide if he purposely, knowingly, recklessly or negligently causes the death of another human being.
    (2) Criminal homicide is murder, manslaughter or negligent homicide.

Section 210.2 Murder

(1) Except as provided in Section 210.3(1)(b), criminal homicide constitutes murder when:
    (a) it is committed purposely or knowingly; or
    (b) it is committed recklessly under circumstances manifesting extreme indifference to the value of human life. Such recklessness and indifference are presumed if the actor is engaged or is an accomplice in the commission of, or an attempt to commit, or flight after committing or attempting to commit robbery, rape or deviate sexual intercourse by force or threat of force, arson, burglary, kidnapping or felonious escape.
(2) Murder is a felony of the first degree [but a person convicted of murder may be sentenced to death, as provided in Section 210.6].

Section 210.3 Manslaughter

(1) Criminal homicide constitutes manslaughter when:
    (a) it is committed recklessly; or
    (b) a homicide which would otherwise be murder is committed under the influence of extreme mental or emotional disturbance for which there is reasonable explanation or excuse. The reasonableness of such explanation or excuse shall be determined from the viewpoint of a person in the actor's situation under the circumstances as he believes them to be.
(2) Manslaughter is a felony of the second degree.

Section 210.4 Negligent Homicide

(1) Criminal homicide constitutes negligent homicide when it is committed negligently.
(2) Negligent homicide is a felony of the third degree.

Section 210.5 Causing or Aiding Suicide

(1) *Causing Suicide as Criminal Homicide.* A person may be convicted of criminal homicide for causing another to commit suicide only if he purposely causes such suicide by force, duress or deception.
(2) *Aiding or Soliciting Suicide as an Independent Offense.* A person who purposely aids or solicits another to commit suicide is guilty of a

felony of the second degree if his conduct causes such suicide or an attempted suicide, and otherwise of a misdemeanor.

SECTION 4.2 CULPABILITY REQUIREMENTS

Babies and Ditches

Geets and Carrie find Anver intolerable. He struts about the club, being pompous beyond belief, expecting that he will be elected the next president. They concoct a practical joke to bring him down to earth. A winding road leading down the hill from the club runs by a playground. They plan to buy a baby carriage and two life-like dolls and to place them in the middle of the road near the playground. As Anver comes around the turn, he will be surprised by the carriage. If he pulls his precious Jaguar off the road into the high grass, he may get stuck in the soft ground. If he fails to pull off, he will blast through the carriage and the "babies." Either way, Geets and Carrie will have a tale to tell, either about Anver's humorous slide or his apparent indifference to killing babies. Either one will serve Carrie's purpose.

Geets has a slightly different goal in playing the practical joke: to kill Anver. While he jokes with Carrie about what a buffoon Anver is, the truth is Anver is likely to be elected the next president, a position that Geets covets. He knows that the tall grass adjacent to the stretch of road by the playground hides a drainage ditch. If Anver swerves to miss the baby carriage, and if he is unable to keep his car on the road, and if he slides in the direction of the ditch, he may get injured and possibly even killed. Geets sees the chances of successfully killing Anver through this scheme as something less than 10 percent but he is hoping for the best. Carrie is unaware that their joke creates any risk of killing Anver.

The next day is perfect for the scheme, overcast with a light rain. Geets and Carrie put the carriage and dolls in the road just before Anver is scheduled to leave the club. Without telling Carrie about the ditch, Geets selects the location that he thinks maximizes the chance that Anver will slide into it. Anver's car approaches, swerves before hitting the carriage, hits the ditch, and sends Anver through the windshield. When he sees Anver's serious injuries, Geets has second thoughts about whether his scheme was such a good idea. He feels bad about Anver's injuries and hopes he will survive. Unfortunately, Anver dies two days later from injuries sustained in

CHAPTER 4 AN OFFENSE ILLUSTRATION: HOMICIDE 73

the accident. Are Geets and Carrie liable for homicide? If so, for which homicide offense?

Model Penal Code §§1.13(9)(a), 2.02(1)-(2), (5)-(7)
Culpability Requirements

Section 1.13. General Definitions.

In this Code, unless a different meaning plainly is required: . . .
(9) "element of an offense" means (i) such conduct or (ii) such attendant circumstances or (iii) such a result of conduct as
   (a) is included in the description of the forbidden conduct in the definition of the offense. . . .

Section 2.02. General Requirements of Culpability.

(1) *Minimum Requirements of Culpability.* Except as provided in Section 2.05, a person is not guilty of an offense unless he acted purposely, knowingly, recklessly or negligently, as the law may require, with respect to each material element of the offense.
(2) *Kinds of Culpability Defined.*
   (a) *Purposely.* A person acts purposely with respect to a material element of an offense when:
      (i) if the element involves the nature of his conduct or a result thereof, it is his conscious object to engage in conduct of that nature or to cause such a result; and
      (ii) if the element involves the attendant circumstances, he is aware of the existence of such circumstances or he believes or hopes that they exist.
   (b) *Knowingly.* A person acts knowingly with respect to a material element of an offense when:
      (i) if the element involves the nature of his conduct or the attendant circumstances, he is aware that his conduct is of that nature or that such circumstances exist; and
      (ii) if the element involves a result of his conduct, he is aware that it is practically certain that his conduct will cause such a result.
   (c) *Recklessly.* A person acts recklessly with respect to a material element of an offense when he consciously disregards a substantial and unjustifiable risk that the material element exists or will result from his conduct. The risk must be of such a nature and degree that,

considering the nature and purpose of the actor's conduct and the circumstances known to him, its disregard involves a gross deviation from the standard of conduct that a law-abiding person would observe in the actor's situation.

(d) *Negligently.* A person acts negligently with respect to a material element of an offense when he should be aware of a substantial and unjustifiable risk that the material element exists or will result from his conduct. The risk must be of such a nature and degree that the actor's failure to perceive it, considering the nature and purpose of his conduct and the circumstances known to him, involves a gross deviation from the standard of care that a reasonable person would observe in the actor's situation. . . .

(5) *Substitutes for Negligence, Recklessness and Knowledge.* When the law provides that negligence suffices to establish an element of an offense, such element also is established if a person acts purposely, knowingly or recklessly. When recklessness suffices to establish an element, such element also is established if a person acts purposely or knowingly. When acting knowingly suffices to establish an element, such element also is established if a person acts purposely.

(6) *Requirement of Purpose Satisfied if Purpose Is Conditional.* When a particular purpose is an element of an offense, the element is established although such purpose is conditional, unless the condition negatives the harm or evil sought to be prevented by the law defining the offense.

(7) *Requirement of Knowledge Satisfied by Knowledge of High Probability.* When knowledge of the existence of a particular fact is an element of an offense, such knowledge is established if a person is aware of a high probability of its existence, unless he actually believes that it does not exist.

Notes on Modern Offense Culpability Requirements

Culpability Levels Under Model Penal Code Many writers have suggested that the Model Penal Code drafters' greatest single contribution is their use of a limited number of defined culpability terms. In place of the plethora of common law terms—wantonly, heedlessly, maliciously, and so on—the Code defines four levels of culpability: purposely, knowingly, recklessly, and negligently. Ideally, all offenses are defined by designating one of these four levels of culpability as to each objective element. If the objective elements of an offense require that an actor take property of another, the culpability elements might require, for example, that the actor know that he is taking property and that he be at least reckless as to it being someone else's property. Each of the four culpability levels is specifically defined.

Purposely vs. Knowingly To use an actor's culpability as to causing a result as an example, a person acts "purposely" with respect to a result, under the Code, if his conscious object is to cause such a result. A person acts "knowingly" with respect to a result if it is not his conscious object yet he is practically certain that his conduct will cause that result. The antiwar activist who sets a bomb to destroy the draft board offices may be practically certain that the bomb will kill the night watchman but may wish that the watchman would go on a coffee break so that he will not be killed. The essence of the narrow distinction between these two culpability levels is the presence or absence of a *positive desire* to cause the result; purpose requires a culpability beyond the knowledge of a result's near certainty. In the broader sense, this distinction divides the vague notion of "callousness" from the more offensive "maliciousness" or "viciousness." The latter may be simply an aggressively ruthless form of the former.

Knowingly vs. Recklessly A person acts "knowingly" with respect to a result if he is nearly certain that his conduct will cause the result. If he is aware only of a substantial risk, he acts "recklessly" with respect to the result. The narrow distinction between knowledge and recklessness lies in the *degree of risk*—"practically certain" versus "substantial risk"—of which the actor is aware. The distinction between recklessness (and lower levels of culpability) and the two higher levels of culpability (purposely and knowingly) is that we tend to scold a reckless actor for being "careless," while an offender who falls within one of the higher culpability categories is condemned for "intentional" conduct.

Purpose as Independent of Likelihood Was Geets purposeful as to killing Anver? While knowing and reckless culpability focus upon the likelihood of causing the result—"practically certain" vs. "substantial risk"—purposeful culpability pays no regard to the likelihood of the result. This characteristic of the purpose reflects an instinct that *trying* to cause the harm, whatever the likelihood, is more condemnable than acting with the belief that the harm will or might result without desiring it. The practical effect of this is that reckless conduct, as manifested in risk-taking, can be elevated to purposeful conduct if the actor hopes that the risk will come to fruition. This characteristic of the purpose requirement also illustrates how specially demanding it is. A requirement of a particular belief is something a jury might logically deduce from other facts: the actor "must have known" the certainty or the risk of harm if he knew this fact or that. A purpose requirement requires the jury to determine an actor's object or goal, a somewhat more complex psychological issue. To find this, a jury may have to dig deeper into the actor's psyche, his general wants and motivations, to reach a conclusion. If a jury is conscientious in adhering to the proof-beyond-a-reasonable-doubt standard constitutionally required for offense elements, a finding of an actor's "purpose" may be a difficult conclusion to reach.

Recklessly vs. Negligently A person acts "recklessly" with respect to a result if he consciously disregards a substantial risk that his conduct will cause the result; he acts only "negligently" if he is unaware of the substantial risk but he should have perceived it. If it is true that it never occurred to Carrie that their joke created any risk of death to Anver, then she cannot be held reckless as to the death. Nor is it adequate that Carrie might have been aware of a risk of minor injury. If manslaughter requires recklessness as to causing the death of another, Carrie cannot be liable for the offense unless she was aware of a substantial risk of Anver's death. The recklessness issue focuses not on whether she should have been aware of the risk but on whether, in fact, she was aware (and, as we shall see in Chapter 7, whether it was culpable for her to disregard such a risk).

Recklessness as Conscious Wrongdoing The narrow distinction between recklessness and negligence lies in the actor's *awareness of risk*. The distinction between negligence and the three higher levels of culpability is one of the most critical to criminal law. A person who acts purposely, knowingly, or recklessly is aware of the circumstances that make his conduct criminal or is aware that harmful consequences may result and is therefore both blameworthy and deterrable. A defendant who acts negligently, in contrast, is unaware of the circumstances or consequences and therefore, some writers argue, is neither blameworthy nor deterrable.[1] While writers disagree over whether negligence ought to be adequate to support criminal liability, it is agreed that negligence represents a lower level of culpability than, and is qualitatively different from, recklessness, in that the negligent actor fails to recognize rather than consciously disregards the risk. For this reason, recklessness is considered the norm for criminal culpability, while negligence is punished only in exceptional situations, as where a death is caused.[2]

Negligence as a Normative Assessment A person who fails to appreciate the risk that his conduct will cause a result is "negligent" as to the result if the failure "involves a gross deviation from the standard of care that a reasonable person would observe in the actor's situation."[3]

---

1. See, e.g., J. Hall, General Principles of Criminal Law 128 (2d ed. 1960).

2. Some jurisdictions do not even punish negligently caused homicide. See, e.g., N.J. Stat. Ann. §2C:11-5 (negligent homicide an offense only if committed by auto).

3. Model Penal Code §2.02(2)(d). Parallel language appears in the definition of recklessness, in §2.02(2)(c). In the context, however, the language concerns whether a "law-abiding" person would have consciously disregarded the risk that the actor disregarded.

Thus, unless he grossly deviates from the standard of care that a reasonable person would observe, an actor is not negligent and, at least in the eyes of the criminal law, is without cognizable fault. If Carrie was not aware of the risk of death created by their joke, should she have been? Would a reasonable person in her situation have been aware that a risk of death existed? Was her failure to perceive the risk a gross deviation from the attentiveness to the possibility of risk that the reasonable person in her situation would have had? These are the issues that the jury would consider in assessing whether Carrie ought to be liable for negligent homicide. They are not factual but normative issues, calling for an expression of the community's shared intuitive notions of blame. The jury is asked to judge whether Carrie's failure to perceive the risk was, under the circumstances, a blameworthy failure.

Negligently vs. Faultlessly Liability imposed for faultless conduct is termed "absolute" or "strict" liability. The narrow distinction between negligence and strict liability focuses on whether the defendant's unawareness of the risk is *a failure to meet the standard of the reasonable person*. The broader distinction between the four categories of culpability and faultlessness is the distinction between a blameworthy and a blameless actor. Theoretical objections to strict liability understandably stem from a reluctance to punish conduct that is not unreasonable. The dispute over the use of negligence and strict liability in criminal law is taken up in Section 7.2.

Negligence and Omissions One might think that "negligence" has something to do with omissions; one "neglects" to act. Older cases sometimes suggested or assumed such a connection but it has long since been agreed that "negligence," when used to refer to a level of culpability, can as easily apply to a commission as to an omission. With regard to Carrie, for example, the issue is whether, in her *conduct* in putting the carriage and dolls in the road, she was negligent as to causing Anver's death. The crux of negligent culpability is the failure to perceive a risk that one should be aware of, a risk that can be either from an act or an omission. It is equally clear that one can have any level of culpability, not just negligence, as to an omission. Where a parent fails to obtain needed medical care for a child and as a result the child dies, the actor may have been purposeful, knowing, reckless, negligent, or faultless as to causing the death. The parent may have failed to get medical care because he desired to cause the child's death; or, he may not have desired to cause the death but he may have been practically certain that his omission would cause the death; or, he may have been aware of a substantial risk that his omission would cause the death; or, he may have been unaware of a substantial risk but should have been aware (the reasonable person would have been aware); or, he may have been unaware and a reasonable person similarly would have been unaware. The culpability requirements apply to omissions in the same way that they do to commissions.

Concurrence Requirement When an offense definition requires a particular level of culpability as to a particular element, it means that the required culpability as to the element must exist at the time of the conduct constituting the offense. This required concurrence between act and culpability, which is implicit in the Model Penal Code culpability definitions in §2.02(2), is carried over from common law. In *State v. Hopple,* for example, Hopple took possession of a neighbor's sheep in order to protect his land from their unauthorized trampling of his cattle feed. Without the neighbor's permission, he subsequently attempted to sell the sheep.[4] Citing the "concurrence requirement," the court held that if the defendant had not formed his intention to permanently deprive the owner of the sheep until after gaining possession, there was no concurrence between the taking and the intent to permanently deprive, as is required for theft.[5] Note that the concurrence requirement applies to the time of the offensive conduct, not to its result. It is neither necessary nor sufficient that the culpability exists at the later time of the result of the conduct. Changing one's mind after setting a bomb does not bar liability for deaths caused by the blast, even if the intent to kill no longer exists at the time the bomb explodes or the victims die.[6] The concurrence requirement stems from the criminal law's interest in determining whether the actor's *conduct* constituting the offense is blameworthy, not whether he or she generally is a good or bad person. That is, the criminal law is a system for condemning and punishing types of conduct, not types of persons.

Subverting the Concurrence Requirement In Thabo Meli and Others v. The Queen, the defendants struck the victim over the head, intending to kill him. They believed they were successful and rolled his body off a cliff to make the killing appear to be an accident. In fact, the victim was alive after the beating but died when they rolled him off the cliff.[7] Strict application of the concurrence requirement would find liability for attempted murder for the beating and reckless or negligent homicide for rolling the body off the cliff (assuming it is reckless or negligent as to causing death to treat apparently dead bodies in this way). However, the court chose to treat the two events as one "transaction" and, therefore, affirmed the conviction for murder.[8]

---

4. 357 P.2d 656 (Idaho 1960).
5. Id. at 659. Such an actor could be liable for another offense, however, perhaps unlawful conversion.
6. See People v. Claborn, 224 Cal. App. 2d 38, 36 Cal. Rptr. 132 (1964) (defendant's conviction of assault with an automobile affirmed despite existence of 21 feet of skid marks leading up to the victim's vehicle which defendant argued indicated a change of intent at the last moment).
7. 1 W.L.R. 228, 1 All E.R. 373 [1954].
8. Id. at 230, 1 All E.R. at 374.

Dangers of "Transaction" Analysis Even if one finds the result in *Thabo Meli* to be intuitively satisfying, such "transaction" analysis has the potential to undermine the concurrence requirement. There seems little to distinguish the events in *Thabo Meli* from many other instances of related but distinct acts. Would it matter if the attackers went home and celebrated and happen upon the apparently-dead body two days later and then thought it prudent to shove it off the cliff? Still one transaction? What if the victim had recovered during the intervening two days and, when his "body" is found, is simply lying in a drunken stupor? If a transaction approach is to be taken, as in *Thabo Meli*, it is unclear how the law is to define the bounds of such an analysis.

Culpability with Respect to Each Kind of Objective Element The description of culpability levels at the beginning of these notes uses culpability as to causing a result to illustrate the differences between levels. In fact, Model Penal Code §2.02(2) defines each of the four kinds of culpability in relation to each of the three kinds of objective elements: conduct, circumstance, and result. The chart below gives the §2.02(2) definition for each variation.

CHART: Model Penal Code §2.02(2) Culpability Definitions

A person acts [culpability level] with respect to [type of objective element] when:

		Type of Objective Element		
		Result	**Circumstance**	**Conduct**
Culpability Level	**Purposely**	"it is his conscious object. . . to cause such a result"	"he is aware of such circumstances or hopes that they exist"	"it is his conscious object to engage in conduct of that nature"
	Knowingly	"he is aware that it is practically certain that his conduct will cause such a result"	"he is aware . . . that such circumstances exist"	"he is aware his conduct is of that nature"

(chart, continued)
Type of Objective Element

Culpability Level		Result	Circumstance	Conduct
	Recklessly	"he consciously disregards a substantial and unjustifiable risk that the material element . . . will result from his conduct"	"he consciously disregards a substantial and unjustifiable risk that the material element exists"	—
	Negligently	"he should be aware of a substantial and unjustifiable risk that the material element . . . will result from his conduct"	"he should be aware of a substantial and unjustifiable risk that the material element exists"	—

Questions

1. *Geets' Culpability With Regard to Anver's Death.* Was Geets negligent as to Anver's death? That is, does he satisfy the requirements of the definition of negligence as to causing a result? Was Geets reckless as to Anver's death? Was he knowing? Purposeful? What is the significance of the fact that at the time of Anver's death, Geets genuinely hopes that he (Anver) will survive? What would be Geets' liability under the Model Penal Code? Under the California homicide statutes?

2. *Carries Culpability With Regard to Anver's Death.* Was Carrie negligent as to Anver's death? Reckless? Knowing? Purposeful? What would be Carrie's liability under the Model Penal Code? Under the California homicide statutes?

3. *Why Defined Culpability Levels?* It may be too early for you to give a full answer to these questions, but ask yourself: Why should the criminal law want to have such distinctions in levels of "culpability"? Why is it not sufficient to show that some minimum level of culpability is satisfied? (Chapter 21, Functions of Criminal Law, looks more carefully at the issue of grading.) Why should the law go to such lengths to have

culpability requirements defined so carefully and precisely? Why not simply leave it to the jury to decide whether they see the actor as sufficiently blameworthy? (Chapter 5, The Legality Principle, will make the answer clear.) Why should the law insist on a concurrence of the culpability and the conduct constituting the offense? (Chapter 16, Excuses, will help with this.)

4. *Homicide Schemes.* To what extent does the Model Penal Code rely upon culpability distinctions—purpose, knowledge, recklessness, and negligence—to grade criminal homicide? To what extent does the New York scheme rely upon these distinctions? To what extent does the California scheme?

SECTION 4.3 DOCTRINES OF AGGRAVATION: PREMEDITATION, SPECIFIED MEANS, RECKLESS MURDER, FELONY MURDER

"Meurtre" and Its Aggravations
3 J. F. Stephen, A History of the Criminal Law of England 94 (1883)

As much cruelty, as much indifference to the life of others, a disposition at least as dangerous to society, probably even more dangerous, is shown by sudden as by premeditated murders. The following cases appear to me to set this in a clear light. *A*, passing along the road, sees a boy sitting on a bridge over a deep river and, out of mere wanton barbarity, pushes him into it and so drowns him. A man makes advances to a girl who repels him. He deliberately but instantly cuts her throat. A man civilly asked to pay a just debt pretends to get the money, loads a rifle, and blows out his creditor's brains. In none of these cases is there premeditation unless the word is used in a sense as unnatural, as "aforethought" in "malice aforethought," but each represents even more diabolical cruelty and ferocity than that which is involved in murders premeditated in the natural sense of the word.

Commonwealth v. Malone
Supreme Court of Pennsylvania
354 Pa. 180, 47 A.2d 445 (1946)

MAXEY, Chief Justice.
This is an appeal from the judgment and sentence under a conviction of murder in the second degree. William H. Long, age 13 years,

was killed by a shot from a 32-caliber revolver held against his right side by the defendant, then age 17 years. These youths were on friendly terms at the time of the homicide. The defendant and his mother, while his father and brother were in the U.S. Armed Forces, were residing in Lancaster, Pa., with the family of William H. Long, whose son was the victim of the shooting.

On the evening of February 26th, 1945, when the defendant went to a moving picture theater, he carried in the pocket of his raincoat a revolver which he had obtained at the home of his uncle on the preceding day. In the afternoon preceding the shooting, the decedent procured a cartridge from his father's room and he and the defendant placed it in the revolver.

After leaving the theater, the defendant went to a dairy store and there met the decedent. Both youths sat in the rear of the store ten minutes, during which period the defendant took the gun out of his pocket and loaded the chamber to the right of the firing pin and then closed the gun. A few minutes later, both youths sat on stools in front of the lunch counter and ate some food. The defendant suggested to the decedent that they play "Russian Poker."[1] Long replied: "I don't care; go ahead." The defendant then placed the revolver against the right side of Long and pulled the trigger three times. The third pull resulted in a fatal wound to Long. The latter jumped off the stool and cried: "Oh! Oh! Oh!" and Malone said: "Did I hit you, Billy? Gee, Kid, I'm sorry." Long died from the wounds two days later.

The defendant testified that the gun chamber he loaded was the first one to the right of the firing chamber and that when he pulled the trigger he did not "expect to have the gun go off." He declared he had no intention of harming Long, who was his friend and companion. The defendant was indicted for murder, tried and found guilty of murder in the second degree and sentenced to a term in the penitentiary for a period not less than five years and not exceeding ten years. A new trial was refused and after sentence was imposed, an appeal was taken. Appellant alleges certain errors in the charge of the court and also contends that the facts did not justify a conviction for any form of homicide except involuntary manslaughter. This contention we over-rule. A specific intent to take life is, under our law, an essential ingredient of murder in the first degree. At common law, the "grand criterion" which "distinguished murder from other killing" was malice on the part of the killer and this malice was not necessarily "malevolent to the deceased particularly" but "any evil design in general; the dictate of a wicked, depraved and malignant heart"; 4

---

1. It has been explained that "Russian Poker" is a game in which the participants, in turn, place a single cartridge in one of the five chambers of a revolver cylinder, give the latter a quick twirl, place the muzzle of the gun against the temple and pull the trigger, leaving it to chance whether or not death results to the trigger puller.

CHAPTER 4 AN OFFENSE ILLUSTRATION: HOMICIDE   83

Blackstone 199. Among the examples that Blackstone cites of murder is "coolly discharging a gun among a multitude of people," causing the death of someone of the multitude.

. . . When an individual commits an act of gross recklessness for which he must reasonably anticipate that death to another is likely to result, he exhibits that "wickedness of disposition, hardness of heart, cruelty, recklessness of consequences, and a mind regardless of social duty" which proved that there was at that time in him "the state or frame of mind termed malice." This court has declared that if a driver "wantonly, recklessly, and in disregard of consequences" hurls "his car against another, or into a crowd" and death results from that act "he ought . . . to face the same consequences that would be meted out to him if he had accomplished death by wantonly and wickedly firing a gun."

Appellant has assigned for error certain excerpts from the charge of the court. The charge in its entirety affords no grounds for the reversal of the judgment and sentence. . . . Defendant's rights were fully protected by the charge in its totality.

However, the charge was in several respects prejudicial to the Commonwealth. For example, the trial judge said: "It is the duty of the Commonwealth to prove that the killing was unlawful and intentional, and if the evidence taken as a whole raises reasonable doubt in the minds of the jury as to whether the killing was accidental or intentional, you must acquit the accused, for the reason that the Commonwealth has failed to sustain its case." This instruction was tantamount to saying that the Commonwealth in order to obtain the conviction of the defendant of any crime included in the indictment had to prove him guilty of murder in the first degree, for if the killing was intentional, it would have been murder in the first degree. The alternative presented to the jury by the instructions was limited to an intentional killing or to an accidental killing. The jury found that the killing was neither intentional nor accidental but that it was a malicious killing though without a specific intent in the killer to take life, and that, therefore, it was murder in the second degree.

The trial judge also erred in charging that "A person on trial for murder cannot be convicted of any offense if the testimony shows that the death was accidental." Death may be accidental though it resulted from a malicious act intentionally committed. In such a case the means were not accidental; the result was. In the instant case if the defendant had by some negligent, unintentional act, caused Long to fall off the stool at which he was sitting in the store and if, as a result of that fall, Long had sustained a fatal injury, both the initial act and the death might be correctly characterized as accidental. But when the defendant knowing that a revolver had at least one loaded cartridge in it, pressed the muzzle of that revolver to the side of Long and pulled the trigger three times, his act cannot be characterized as accidental, even if his statement that he had no intention to kill Long is accepted (as the jury accepted it). The way the trial judge used the word "accidental" throughout the charge must have been confusing to the jury and might easily have misled it into acquitting the accused on the theory that since the death of Long was accidental, "the defendant cannot be convicted of any offense" (as the trial judge said). The latter should have made it clear to the jury that even though Long's death might have been unintended and, therefore, accidental, the evidence showed that the act which caused the victim's death was not accidental. This was the view the jury took of the case despite the court's instructions. . . .

The killing of William H. Long by this defendant resulted from an act intentionally done by the latter, in reckless and wanton disregard of the consequences which were at least sixty percent certain from his thrice attempted discharge of a gun known to contain one bullet and aimed at a vital part of Long's body. This killing was, therefore, murder, for malice in the sense of a wicked disposition is evidenced by the intentional doing of an uncalled-for act in callous disregard of its likely harmful effects on others. The fact that there was no motive for this homicide does not exculpate the accused. In a trial for murder proof of motive is always relevant but never necessary.

All the assignments of error are overruled and the judgment is affirmed. The record is remitted to the court below so that the sentence imposed may be carried out.

Model Penal Code §210.2, Comment 6 (1980)
Felony Murder

The presumption [provided in Model Penal Code §210.2(1)(b), quoted at the beginning of this chapter] operates in the following manner. It applies only to the culpability for murder and in particular to the establishment of the extreme indifference required by Subsection (1)(b). In any circumstance, the actor must cause the death of another, except as general complicity principles provide otherwise. As Section 1.12(5) specifies, the presumption has the effect of leaving on the prosecution the burden of persuasion beyond a reasonable doubt that the defendant acted recklessly and with extreme indifference. The jury may, however, regard the facts giving rise to the presumption as sufficient evidence of the required culpability unless the court determines that the evidence as a whole clearly negatives that conclusion. The presumption may, of course, be rebutted by the defendant or may simply not be followed by the jury. In either of these cases, the defendant may be liable for manslaughter or negligent homicide, as these crimes are defined in Sections 210.3 and 210.4. If the presumption is not rebutted and if the jury finds, with or without its aid, that the requisite extreme indifference in fact existed beyond a reasonable doubt, then the appropriate conviction is murder. The effect of the Model Code, therefore, is to abandon felony murder as a separate basis for establishing liability for homicide and to retain the presumption described above as a concession to the facilitation of proof.

The classic formulation of the felony-murder doctrine declares that one is guilty of murder if a death results from conduct during the commission or attempted commission of any felony. Some courts have made no effort to qualify the application of this doctrine, and a number of earlier English writers also articulated an unqualified rule. At the time the Model Code was drafted, a number of American legislatures, moreover, perpetuated the original statement of the rule by statute. As thus conceived, the rule operated to impose liability for murder based on the culpability required for the underlying felony without separate proof of any culpability with regard to the death. The homicide, as distinct from the underlying felony, was thus an offense of strict liability. This rule may have made sense under the conception of *mens rea* as something approaching a general criminal disposition rather than as a specific attitude of the defendant towards each element of a specific offense. Furthermore, it was hard to claim that the doctrine worked injustice in an age that recognized only a few felonies and that punished each as a capital offense.

In modern times, however, legislatures have created a wide range of statutory felonies. Many of these crimes concern relatively minor misconduct not inherently dangerous to life and carry maximum penalties far less severe than those authorized for murder. Application of the ancient rigor of the felony-murder rule to such crimes will yield startling results. For example, a seller of liquor in violation of a statutory felony becomes a murderer if his purchaser falls asleep on the way home and dies of exposure. And a person who communicates disease during felonious sexual intercourse is guilty of murder if his partner subsequently dies of the infection.

The prospect of such consequences has led to a demand for limitations on the felony-murder rule. American legislatures had responded to these demands at the time the Model Code was drafted primarily by dividing felony-homicides into two or more grades or by lowering the degree of murder for felony homicide. Only Ohio had abandoned the rule completely.

In addition, the courts had imposed restrictions, both overt and covert, on the reach of the felony-murder doctrine. . . .

These limitations confine the scope of the felony-murder rule, but they do not resolve its essential illogic. This doctrine aside, the criminal law does not predicate liability simply on conduct causing the death of another. Punishment for homicide obtains only when the deed is done with a state of mind that makes it reprehensible as well as unfortunate. Murder is invariably punished as a heinous offense and is the principal crime for which the death penalty is authorized. Sanctions of such gravity demand justification, and their imposition must be premised on the confluence of conduct and culpability. Thus, under the Model Code, as at common law, murder occurs if a person kills purposely, knowingly, or with extreme recklessness. Lesser culpability yields lesser liability, and a person who inadvertently kills another under circumstances not amounting to negligence is guilty of no crime at all. The felony-murder rule contradicts this scheme. It bases conviction of murder not on any proven culpability with respect to homicide but on liability for another crime. The underlying felony carries its own penalty and the additional punishment for murder is therefore gratuitous—gratuitous, at least, in terms of what must have been proved at trial in a court of law.

It is true, of course, that the felony-murder rule is often invoked where liability for murder exists on another ground. One who kills in the course of armed robbery is almost certainly guilty of murder in the form of intentional or extremely reckless homicide without any need of special doctrine. Similarly, a man who burns another's house will scarcely be heard to complain that he lacks the culpability for murder if the blaze kills a sleeping occupant. For the vast majority of cases it is probably true that homicide occurring during the commission or attempted commission of a felony is murder independent of the felony-murder rule. At bottom, continued adherence to the doctrine may rest on assessments of this sort.

The problem is that criminal liability attaches to individuals, not generalities. It is a weak rejoinder to a complaint of unjust conviction to say that for most persons in the defendant's situation the result would have been appropriate. To be sure, limiting the rule to specified felonies increases the probability that conviction in a particular case will be warranted. Criminal punishment should be premised, however, on something more than a probability of guilt. Requiring that the defendant's conduct in committing the underlying felony create a foreseeable risk to human life is a roundabout way of limiting felony murder to cases of negligent homicide. This is a worthwhile reform, for it effectively excludes extreme applications of the rule to instances in which the actor would not otherwise be guilty of any homicide offense. Yet murder and negligent homicide are not interchangeable; they carry vastly different sanctions. Punishment for the greater offense, on proof that should suffice only for conviction of the lesser, works within reduced compass the same essential violence to the general principles of criminal liability as does the unqualified rule.

Principled argument in favor of the felony-murder doctrine is hard to find. The defense reduces to the explanation that Holmes gave for finding the law "intelligible as it stands":

[I]f experience shows, or is deemed by the law-maker to show, that somehow or other deaths which the evidence makes accidental happen disproportionately often in connection with other felonies, or with resistance to officers, or if any other ground of policy it is deemed desirable to make special efforts for the prevention of such deaths, the law-maker may consistently treat acts which, under the known circumstances, are felonious, or constitute resistance to officers, as having a sufficiently dangerous tendency to be put under a special ban. The law may, therefore, throw on the actor the peril, not only of the consequences foreseen by him, but also of consequences which, although not predicted by common experience, the legislator apprehends.

The answer to such argument is twofold. First, there is no basis in experience for thinking that homicides *which the evidence makes accidental* occur with disproportionate frequency in connection with specified felonies. Second, it remains indefensible in principle to use the sanctions that the law employs to deal with murder unless there is at least a finding that the actor's conduct manifested an extreme indifference to the value of human life. The fact that the actor was engaged in a crime of the kind that is included in the usual first degree felony-murder enumeration or was an accomplice in such crime, as has been observed, will frequently justify such a finding. Indeed, the probability that such a finding will be justified seems high enough to warrant the presumption of extreme indifference that Subsection (1)(b) creates. But liability depends, as plainly it should, upon the crucial finding. The result may not differ often under such a formulation from that which would be reached under some form of the felony-murder rule. But what is more important is that a conviction on this basis rests solidly upon principle.

Given a finding of extreme indifference, the fact that the actor was engaged in the commission of another crime of the kind enumerated will have relevance, along with other factors, to the issue of capital punishment in jurisdictions where a sentence of death may be imposed. Section 210.6(3)(e) so provides.

Questions

1. *Premeditation and Related Provisions.* Which of the statutory schemes—California, New York, and the Model Penal Code—uses a premeditation requirement? Are the specified means of causing death that you see in the California provisions generally situations that suggest a premeditated killing? Why might it have been dropped in some modern homicide schemes?

2. *"Malignant Heart" and Extreme Indifference to the Value of Human Life.* The reckless murder provision applied in the *Malone* case—

requiring "a wicked, depraved and malignant heart"—is similar to that of the California statute—requiring "an abandoned and malignant heart." On what grounds might one criticize this aggravation? How is the "malignant heart" aggravation similar to and different from the "extreme indifference to the value of human life" aggravation found in the Model Penal Code and the "grave indifference to human life" aggravation found in the New York scheme? For what, if anything, would Malone have been liable under the Model Penal Code?

3. *Felony Murder.* If the killing occurs in the course of a robbery, what must a California prosecutor prove to the jury beyond a reasonable doubt? A New York prosecutor? A prosecutor under the Model Penal Code? Does a New York felony-murder defendant have the opportunity to escape murder liability by rebutting the presence of the normal (i.e., non-felony murder) culpability requirements for murder? A defendant under the Model Penal Code? If the killing occurs during an enumerated felony, does a New York defendant have any means of escaping murder liability (other than through general defenses)? What arguments can you make for and against each of the three statutory treatments of felony murder?

SECTION 4.4 THE DEATH PENALTY

First degree murder typically is distinguished from second degree murder in order to define the cases in which the death penalty is available. The United States Supreme Court has upheld the death penalty against constitutional challenge as cruel and unusual punishment in violation of the eighth amendment but, under the fifth amendment due process clause, has restricted the way in which the death penalty decision may be made. While the A.L.I. did not take a position for or against the death penalty in drafting the Model Penal Code, it did include a provision to govern its use by those jurisdictions that do impose it. The Code's approach generally is consistent with the Court's current constitutional requirements and has been used as a model by many jurisdictions.

Model Penal Code §210.6
Sentence of Death for Murder; Further Proceedings to Determine Sentence

(1) *Death Sentence Excluded.* When a defendant is found guilty of murder, the Court shall impose sentence for a felony of the first degree if it is satisfied that:

(a) none of the aggravating circumstances enumerated in Subsection (3) of this Section was established by the evidence at the trial or will be established if further proceedings are initiated under Subsection (2) of this Section; or

(b) substantial mitigating circumstances, established by the evidence at the trial, call for leniency; or

(c) the defendant, with the consent of the prosecuting attorney and the approval of the Court, pleaded guilty to murder as a felony of the first degree; or

(d) the defendant was under 18 years of age at the time of the commission of the crime; or

(e) the defendant's physical or mental condition calls for leniency; or

(f) although the evidence suffices to sustain the verdict, it does not foreclose all doubt respecting the defendant's guilt.

(2) *Determination by Court or by Court and Jury.* Unless the Court imposes sentence under Subsection (1) of this Section, it shall conduct a separate proceeding to determine whether the defendant should be sentenced for a felony of the first degree or sentenced to death. The proceeding shall be conducted before the Court alone if the defendant was convicted by a Court sitting without a jury or upon his plea of guilty or if the prosecuting attorney and the defendant waive a jury with respect to sentence. In other cases it shall be conducted before the Court sitting with the jury which determined the defendant's guilt or, if the Court for good cause shown discharges that jury, with a new jury empaneled for the purpose.

In the proceeding, evidence may be presented as to any matter that the Court deems relevant to sentence, including but not limited to the nature and circumstances of the crime, the defendant's character, background, history, mental and physical condition and any of the aggravating or mitigating circumstances enumerated in Subsections (3) and (4) of this Section. Any such evidence, not legally privileged, which the Court deems to have probative force, may be received, regardless of its admissibility under the exclusionary rules of evidence, provided that the defendant's counsel is accorded a fair opportunity to rebut such evidence. The prosecuting attorney and the defendant or his counsel shall be permitted to present argument for or against sentence of death.

The determination whether sentence of death shall be imposed shall be in the discretion of the Court, except that when the proceeding is conducted before the Court sitting with a jury, the Court shall not impose sentence of death unless it submits to the jury the issue whether the defendant should be sentenced to death or to imprisonment and the jury returns a verdict that the sentence should be death. If the jury is unable to reach a unanimous verdict, the Court shall dismiss the jury and impose sentence for a felony of the first degree.

The Court, in exercising its discretion as to sentence, and the jury, in determining upon its verdict, shall take into account the aggravating and mitigating circumstances enumerated in Subsections (3) and (4) and any other facts that it deems relevant, but it shall not impose or recommend sentence of death unless it finds one of the aggravating circumstances enumerated in Subsection (3) and further finds that there are no mitigating circumstances sufficiently substantial to call for leniency. When the issue is submitted to the jury, the Court shall so instruct and also shall inform the jury of the nature of the sentence of imprisonment that may be imposed, including its implication with respect to possible release upon parole, if the jury verdict is against sentence of death.*

(3) *Aggravating Circumstances.*

(a) The murder was committed by a convict under sentence of imprisonment.

(b) The defendant was previously convicted of another murder or of a felony involving the use or threat of violence to the person.

(c) At the time the murder was committed the defendant also committed another murder.

(d) The defendant knowingly created a great risk of death to many persons.

(e) The murder was committed while the defendant was engaged or was an accomplice in the commission of, or an attempt to commit, or flight after committing or attempting to commit robbery, rape or deviate sexual intercourse by force or threat of force, arson, burglary or kidnapping.

(f) The murder was committed for the purpose of avoiding or preventing a lawful arrest or effecting an escape from lawful custody.

(g) The murder was committed for pecuniary gain.

(h) The murder was especially heinous, atrocious or cruel, manifesting exceptional depravity.

(4) *Mitigating Circumstances.*

(a) The defendant has no significant history of prior criminal activity.

(b) The murder was committed while the defendant was under the influence of extreme mental or emotional disturbance.

(c) The victim was a participant in the defendant's homicidal conduct or consented to the homicidal act.

(d) The murder was committed under circumstances which the defendant believed to provide a moral justification or extenuation for his conduct.

---

*The Code's alternative formulation of Subsection (2) is omitted.

(e) The defendant was an accomplice in a murder committed by another person and his participation in the homicidal act was relatively minor.

(f) The defendant acted under duress or under the domination of another person.

(g) At the time of the murder, the capacity of the defendant to appreciate the criminality [wrongfulness] of his conduct or to conform his conduct to the requirements of law was impaired as a result of mental disease or defect or intoxication.

(h) The youth of the defendant at the time of the crime.

H. A. Bedau, Arguments For and Against Capital Punishment
Encyclopedia of Crime and Justice
133-141 (S. Kadish, ed. 1983)

With the rise of rationalist thought in European culture during the Renaissance and Enlightenment (1550-1750), and the concurrent decline in an exclusively religious foundation for moral principles, philosophers and jurists increasingly lent their support to the doctrine of "the rights of man" as the foundation for constitutional law and public morality. The most influential continental, British, and American Enlightenment thinkers—John Locke, Jean-Jacques Rousseau, Cesare Beccaria, William Blackstone, Immanuel Kant, and Thomas Jefferson—all agreed that the first and foremost of these rights is "the right to life." Few of these thinkers, however, opposed the death penalty (Beccaria was the notable exception); most endorsed it explicitly. They argued, typically, that since each person is born with a "natural" right to life, murder must be viewed as a violation of that right; accordingly, executing the murderer is not wrong since the murderer has forfeited his own right to life by virtue of his crime.

Modern thinkers, under the influence of the human rights provisions advocated by the United Nations in various resolutions, declarations, and covenants, have sought to appeal to a more complex line of considerations embedded in other human rights, as well as in the idea of the right to life. This view was advocated most prominently in the 1970s by Amnesty International, the human rights organization awarded the Nobel Peace Prize in 1978 for its worldwide campaign against torture. On this view, the death penalty violates human rights because (1) its administration is inevitably surrounded by arbitrary practices and unreliable procedures that violate offenders' rights; (2) erroneous executions are an irrevocable and irremediable violation of the right to life; and (3) there are less severe and equally effective alternatives—notably, long-term imprisonment.

In the United States since the 1960s, these themes have been argued most vigorously by the American Civil Liberties Union and by attorneys for the NAACP Legal Defense and Educational Fund and the Southern Poverty Law Center on behalf of nonwhite and indigent clients accused of murder. Their basic argument has been that the death penalty as it is actually used in contemporary American criminal justice systems is inherently and irredeemably class- and race-biased, so that a self-respecting civilized society cannot afford to employ it.

Racism

The central evidence for the main criticism—racist administration of the death penalty—comes from research conducted in several states, particularly in the South, in which it has been shown that a person is more likely to be sentenced to death if the victim is white than if nonwhite. These results are consistent with the generally acknowledged results of earlier research on the death penalty for rape, in which it was shown that the overwhelming preponderance of death penalties for black offenders could be explained only by the race of the offender taken in conjunction with that of the victim: the death penalty was highly probable only if the victim was white.

Defenders of the death penalty have, or could have, replied as follows: (1) all current capital laws are colorblind and impose equal liability on all persons regardless of race, color, class, or sex of offender or of victim; (2) racism in the current administration of the death penalty cannot be inferred from evidence relating to the admittedly racist practices of the distant past; (3) the evidence tending to show that the race of the victim is the chief explanation for whether an offender is sentenced to death (white victim) or to prison (non-white victim) is incomplete and inconclusive; (4) since justice requires that all murderers be sentenced to death and executed, some racial bias (if there is any) in the day-to-day administration of capital punishment is merely another case of the regrettable but tolerable imperfect enforcement of a just law; and (5) the deterrent and incapacitating effects of executions provided by even a somewhat racially biased death penalty are better for society than are the results of a less potent (even if less biased racially) alternative mode of punishment.

Retribution

Many defenders of the death penalty rest their position on principles of retributive justice and the appropriateness of moral indignation at murder, which they believe can be expressed adequately only by punishing that crime (and others, if any, no less heinous) by death. Whether such retributive reasoning has its origins in a passion for vengeance is less important than whether the principles to which it appeals are sound. Most opponents of the death penalty do not dispute (1) the principle that convicted offenders deserve to be punished; (2) the principle that a suitable punishment is, like a crime itself, some form of harsh treatment; and (3) the principle that the severity of the punishment should be proportional to the gravity of the offense. What is disputed is whether the third principle *requires* the death penalty for murder (and other crimes) or whether this principle is merely *consistent* with such a punishment, so that the further step in favor of death as the ideally fitting penalty must be taken by reference to other (perhaps nonretributive) considerations. Making the punishment fit the crime in any literal sense is either impossible or morally unacceptable, given the horrible nature of many murders. Interpreting the third principle so that it entails "a life for a life" thus verges on begging the question. As a result, the focus of controversy between proponents and opponents of the death penalty who agree in arguing the issue primarily on grounds of retributive justice is on how closely it is necessary and desirable to model a punishment on the crime for which it is meted out. It is perhaps noteworthy that the most influential proponents of the "new retributivism" do not advocate capital punishment for any crimes.

Utility and the Prevention of Crime

Quite apart from considerations rooted in principles of retributive justice or of constitutional law, arguments for and against the death penalty often proceed by reference to essentially utilitarian considerations, in which the consequences for overall social welfare—especially as this involves the reduction of crime—are the criteria to which both sides appeal. For example, defenders of the death penalty have argued that executions are a far less costly mode of punishment than any alternative. Abolitionists have replied that this is untrue if one takes into account the enormous cost to society of the extremely complex and lengthy litigation that surrounds a capital case, beginning with the search for an acceptable jury and culminating in postsentencing appeals and hearings in both state and federal courts. The chief issue of utilitarian concern, however, has always been whether the death penalty is an effective means of preventing crime and whether it is more effective than the alternative of imprisonment.

Incapacitation

Both sides concede that execution is a perfectly incapacitative punishment and that in this respect it is preferable to imprisonment. How much difference this makes to the crime rate is a matter of sharp dispute: the issue turns on (1) whether persons who have been executed would have committed further capital (or other) offenses if they had not been executed, and (2) whether persons convicted and imprisoned for capital crimes but not executed will commit further capital offenses when and if released. There is no direct evidence available regarding the first question. Evidence relevant to the second question from parole and recidivism records indicates that a very small number of capital offenders commit subsequent crimes. Roughly one convicted homicide offender out of every 340 such persons released from prison commits another homicide within the first year after release. Defenders of the death penalty often argue that it is inexcusable for society not to take measures guaranteeing that a convicted murderer is incapable of repeating his crime. Abolitionists argue that the alternatives open to society, if it abandons the present system of parole and release practices, are even worse: either society must execute *all* convicted murderers, at intolerable moral cost (these thousands of executions are unnecessary, since so few murderers recidivate), or society must imprison *all* convicted murderers until their natural death, also intolerable because of the prison management problems that such a policy would create.

General Deterrence

Still more important and controversial is the adequacy of the death penalty as a general deterrent. During the 1950s, evidence based on several different comparisons convinced most criminologists that there was no superior deterrent effect associated with the death penalty. The comparisons were between homicide rates in given states before, during, and after abolition; homicide rates in given jurisdictions before and after executions; homicide rates in adjacent states, some with and others without the use of capital punishment; and rates of police killings in abolitionist and death-penalty jurisdictions. In the 1970s, this conclusion was challenged by research which used new methods borrowed from econometrics and which asserted that each execution in the United States between 1930 and 1969 prevented between eight and twenty murders. Subsequent investigators, however, soon showed that the alleged deterrent effect was an artifact of arbitrary if not dubious statistical methods. A panel of the National Academy of Science (NAS) went even further and expressed extreme skepticism about the results of all available research studies; none, the panel said, provided any useful evidence on the deterrent effect of capital punishment. No reliable scientific investigations support the common sense inference that since the death penalty is more severe than long-term imprisonment, the death penalty must be a better deterrent.

It is difficult to say whether skepticism (as recommended by the NAS panel) or a more positive conclusion against the deterrent efficacy of the death penalty is justified by the totality of all research. Some research, based on the study of executions and homicides in New York, has even suggested the initially implausible hypothesis that executions may actually exert a "brutalizing" effect upon society and that instead of deterring murders, it incites them. What does seem true is that any argument for the death penalty based primarily on the claim of its superior deterrent efficacy is untenable. It is worth noting that the Supreme Court, in its series of death-penalty decisions during the 1970s, skirted this controversy and never spoke with a clear and unanimous voice one way or the other. (The sole exception is its decision in *Gregg*, where the majority of the Court conjectured that in such cases as "calculated murders," for example, terrorist attacks, sanctions less severe than death may not be adequate.) How much evidence proponents of the death penalty should be expected to produce in favor of the superior deterrent power of executions is also unclear, and perhaps imponderable.

Burden of Proof

It seems reasonable to many observers for the proponents to have the burden of proof, since they advocate the more severe and irreversible penalty. Some defenders of the death penalty counter by claiming that it is better to put to death someone convicted of murder, on the chance that doing so will prevent (either by incapacitation or by general deterrence) a future murder, than it is to risk the lives of the innocent by using some less severe punishment. Others argue that the proper foundation for the death penalty is not its deterrent efficacy—or, indeed, any other essentially utilitarian consideration—but reasons rooted in retributive justice. Both of these responses by advocates of the death penalty imply that burden-of-proof considerations really fall on the other side, or else should play no role in a moral and rational evaluation of the entire question.

Questions

1. *Aggravating Circumstances and First Degree Murder.* Are some of the first degree murder aggravations of other codes found in the Model Penal Code's list of aggravating circumstances? The most common modification of the Code's murder provision is the addition of an aggravating circumstance for the knowing killing of a police officer, fireman, or prison guard. Is this factor found in first degree murder definitions? If a jurisdiction adopts the Model Penal Code's death penalty provision,

is there less reason to have two degrees of murder? Does the Mo₍ ₁l Penal Code have two degrees of murder?

2. *Mitigating Circumstances.* How are the mitigating circumstances similar to and different from the mitigations contained in homicide offense definitions (discussed in the next section)? How are the mitigating circumstances similar to and different from excuse defenses contained in Articles 2 and 4 of the Model Penal Code (discussed in Chapter 16)?

3. *Retributivism and Utilitarianism.* Recalling the discussions in Chapter 2, Justification and Distribution of Liability and Punishment, what retributivist arguments can you make for and against the death penalty? What utilitarian arguments can you make, for and against?

SECTION 4.5 DOCTRINES OF MITIGATION: EXTREME EMOTIONAL DISTURBANCE, PROVOCATION, MENTAL ILLNESS NEGATING AN ELEMENT, "DIMINISHED CAPACITY"

The Pot Boils

Conran and Lester live in a small mining town and have known each other all their lives. Conran is tough and aggressive, and is something of a leader of the pack. Lester cheerfully follows. They frequently drink with the same crowd at the local bar. On this particular night, everyone is slightly drunk. Conran becomes very abusive toward Lester, to the chuckles of the rest of the group. Conran mocks Lester's slight stutter in a louder and louder voice until Lester decides to leave. Conran follows him from the bar, making stuttering sounds as he goes. As Lester turns down an alley headed toward his flat, Conran grabs him from behind and throws him to the ground. He forcibly pulls down Lester's pants and sodomizes him. Lester's struggles and screams are useless. Conran is 90 pounds heavier and very strong. When he is finished, Conran pushes Lester into the gutter and heads back to the bar. Lester is still drunk but manages to stand up and stumble after Conran. He is humiliated and angry. He arrives back at the bar a few minutes after Conran. As he enters the side door, he sees Conran talking to the usual crowd and hears his name mentioned several times. The group is howling with laughter. Lester feels completely humiliated. He slips back out the side door without being spotted.

At home, Lester can think of nothing except how much he hates Conran. He thinks of killing him but each time he tells himself that he couldn't do that, that he shouldn't do that. But he feels that he has to do something. After two days of brooding, Lester's anger boils over into action. He goes to the bar to confront Conran. Conran is not there but the other patrons are all smirking at Lester. "I heard he squealed like a pig," one says to another in a loud voice. "Yeah, Con says Les really enjoyed it." All laugh. Lester is apoplectic with rage. "I'm going to kill him. I'm going to kill him." He reaches behind the bar where he knows a gun is kept, grabs it, and heads for Conran's house. As he goes, his fast walk turns into a run and his muttering to himself turns into shouting. As he nears the house he sees a figure through the first floor window. He begins shooting wildly at the figure. The first four shots miss but the fifth catches Conran in the head. The sixth hits Conran's daughter, who is playing in the room. Both are killed instantly.

Lester runs off but is captured and charged with murder.* At trial he introduces, among other things, evidence that the members of his family, for many generations, typically are very docile until provoked, but then become very violent. For what degree of homicide liability is Lester liable, if any?

State v. Ott
Supreme Court of Oregon
297 Or. 375, 686 P.2d 1001 (1984)

LENT, Justice.

The primary issue is how a jury is to be instructed on "extreme emotional disturbance" for the purpose of determining whether a criminal homicide is murder or manslaughter. The defendant was charged with murder for killing his wife in April, 1980. It is undisputed that the defendant killed her intentionally; the dispute is whether he was under the influence of extreme emotional disturbance. If he was, he would be guilty of manslaughter rather than murder.

At that time ORS 63.115 provided:

(1) . . . [C]riminal homicide constitutes murder when:
  (a) It is committed intentionally by a person who is not under the influence of an extreme emotional disturbance. . . .
(2) For the purposes of paragraph (a) of subsection (1) of this section, a homicide which would otherwise be murder is committed under the

---

*Loosely based on the facts of State v. Gounagias, 88 Wash. 304, 153 P. 9 (1915).

influence of extreme emotional disturbance when . . . there is a reasonable explanation [for such disturbance]. The reasonableness of the explanation for the disturbance shall be determined from the standpoint of an ordinary person in the actor's situation under the circumstances as the actor reasonably believes them to be.

At the time of this homicide the state, in order to convict a killer of murder, had to prove beyond a reasonable doubt that the defendant was not under the influence of extreme emotional disturbance.

The defendant was convicted of murdering his wife. At trial he did not contest the accusation that he killed her intentionally. Instead, he adduced evidence to mitigate the charge of murder to that of manslaughter by showing that he was under the influence of an extreme emotional disturbance during the killing.

The Evidence

. . . There was evidence of the following:

The defendant exhibited instability after his discharge from the Air Force in 1972. He "drifted in various parts of the United States" and put "very little order to his life." In 1975 he returned to his mother's home in Grants Pass and stayed there intermittently.

At some point after his return to Grants Pass, he began to cohabit with a woman who had three children. This lasted for a little over a year. The woman then asked the defendant to move out because of his drinking and unannounced disappearances. She was three months' pregnant by him at the time.

The defendant then enrolled at Rogue Community College at Grants Pass. There he met the now deceased Stephanie Elaine Brinkley, whom he married three weeks after their initial meeting. Some months after their marriage, they had a fight over "money matters" and separated. They were soon together again; however, not long thereafter welfare authorities threatened to cut off Stephanie's assistance unless they separated. The defendant moved out, joined a mining operation and made a small amount of money.

Defendant attempted to return to his wife; however, she had begun seeing someone else. Defendant attempted to fight Stephanie's new lover. Stephanie intervened, sent her new lover away and promised that her conduct would not be repeated.

There were other separations, and the defendant, upon his return from each separation and his learning of more infidelities, became progressively more upset. This was especially so after the birth of their first child.

At one point, upon Stephanie's invitation to resume living together, the defendant returned home to find his wife engaged in sex with another man. A fight ensued. The police were called, and the defendant was arrested for the crime of menacing. Upon arraignment, the court in that case observed that defendant appeared to be emotionally disturbed.

After his conviction in that case, the court ordered a presentence report. The report contained a psychological evaluation which indicated the possibility that defendant could exhibit psychotic behavior under stress and recommended that the defendant be treated with therapy and medication. Defendant was given a three-year suspended sentence and was released from jail subject to the condition that he receive counseling from the county mental health department. Although he received counseling, he never received any medication.

He had been warned by the "authorities" to stay away from Stephanie. She apparently caused him to be placed under a judicial restraining order; however, despite her obtaining the order, Stephanie telephoned him regarding their divorce. They engaged in an apparently protracted series of arguments on the telephone over child custody, which eventuated in the defendant's arrest and jailing for harassment. Even though they engaged in arguments and fights, they continued to associate. Defendant could not stay away from Stephanie and Stephanie did not always discourage his attentions. In 1980 Stephanie began to live with another man. This conduct affected the defendant, as before, with tension and "stress." The defendant's reaction was even more intense than before, and he threatened to kill Stephanie on several occasions.

In early April, 1980, Stephanie's son, Jonathan (defendant's stepson), broke his arm and was in the hospital. The defendant and Stephanie met each other at the hospital in order to visit with the child on three occasions. It was arranged that on the third occasion the defendant was to drive Stephanie home after hospital visiting hours were over. Defendant had the impression from their first two meetings at the hospital that the relationship was improving. He was thus angered and disappointed when his wife's new lover appeared at the hospital on their third meeting to take her home. Defendant left the hospital in a state of agitation. He retrieved a .22 rifle that he had stored at the home of a friend, caught up with his wife and her lover, ran their truck off the road and shot his wife three times.

We emphasize that the foregoing paragraphs are not findings of fact by this court; they are a set of facts which could be found from the evidence. There was other evidence, which was in some respects contradictory.

History of Mitigating Factor

Before addressing how a jury should be charged in a case where the influence of extreme emotional disturbance may reduce an intentional criminal homicide from murder to manslaughter, we pause to examine the history of the mitigating factor.

The defense of extreme emotional disturbance is a modification of the defense of provocation or heat of passion. The provocation defense is very old. The distinction between a slaying in cold blood and one in the heat of passion existed in Anglo-Saxon criminal law and survived the Norman Conquest of 1066. The "Doctrine of Provocation" became firmly established in the law in 1628 when Coke adopted the distinction between homicide committed after deliberation and homicide committed in the course of a sudden quarrel. Coke defined murder as necessitating "malice aforethought," as distinguished from manslaughter, which he understood occurs "upon a sudden occasion" and was, therefore, called "chance-medley." Then, as now, manslaughter, understood as chance-medley, depended on the presence of heat of passion caused by adequate provocation.

As originally conceived, the only adequate provocation for heat of passion was mutual combat. Hence, heat of passion was difficult to distinguish from self defense. Other provocations were gradually recognized as legally adequate, including assault and adultery. In some jurisdictions, illegal arrest, injuries to third parties, and words conveying information of the occurrence of a legally sufficient ground have also been recognized.

In the mid-nineteenth century, the judgment as to whether a provocation was adequate for the heat of passion defense was made by the judge as a determination of law; however, judges gradually began to leave borderline cases to the jury. The reasonable man standard of review for provocation was devised as a manner of instructing the jury on marginal cases. It was also a device for enabling the jury to serve as community conscience or standard of measure for reasonable behavior.

The reasonable man test for provocation contained four elements: (1) there had to be a provocation that would arouse a reasonable man to the heat of passion; (2) the defendant must actually have been aroused to the heat of passion; (3) a reasonable man would not have cooled off; and (4) the defendant did not, in fact, cool off. This has been said to be an objective test, meaning that neither the mental nor physical peculiarities of the accused are evaluated in determining whether his loss of self-control was reasonable.

Criticism of the "Ordinary" or "Reasonable" Man Test

As originally developed, the provocation defense represented the concept that the mental state of the accused was the test for moral culpability; however, the objective test does not focus on the individual's mental state. The anomaly has been noted by several scholars.

The reasonable man test, being objective in nature, is antithetical to the concept of mens rea. Like all objective standards, it is an external standard of general application that does not focus on an individual accused's mental state. Thus, from the point of view of traditional Anglo-American jurisprudence, a paradox is inherent in the use of the reasonable man standard to test criminal responsibility: the presence or absence of criminal intent is determined by a standard which ignores the mental state of the individual accused.

The common law heat of passion or provocation defense placed the jury in the conceptually awkward (to put it kindly) position of having to determine when it is reasonable for a reasonable man to act unreasonably. In an article on the subject, Glanville Williams explained:

> In the law of contract and tort, and elsewhere in the criminal law, the test of the reasonable man indicates an ethical standard; but it seems absurd to say that the reasonable man will commit a felony the possible punishment for which is imprisonment for life. To say that the "ordinary" man will commit this felony is hardly less absurd. The reason why provoked homicide is punished is to deter people from committing the offence; and it is a curious confession of failure on the part of the law to suppose that, notwithstanding the possibility of heavy punishment, an ordinary person will commit it. If the assertion were correct, it would raise serious doubts whether the offence should continue to be punished.
>
> Surely the true view of provocation is that it is a concession to the "frailty of human nature" in those exceptional cases where the legal prohibition fails of effect. It is a compromise, neither conceding the propriety of the act nor exacting the full penalty for it. This being so, how can it be that that paragon of virtue, the reasonable man, gives way to provocation?

Williams, Provocation and the Reasonable Man, 1954 Crim. L. Rev. 740, 742. . . .

The Model Penal Code

The drafters of the Model Penal Code were aware of the anomaly and pointed out that harsh and unjust results were obtained from applying the objective test for provocation. They cited State v. Gounagias, 88 Wash. 304, 153 P. 9 (1915), as a model of an unjust result achieved through application of the objective test for provocation. That case may serve as an illustration of the test for provocation and also, by negative implication, of the object of modifying that defense.

[The Court then reviewed the facts and reasoning of State v. Gounagias, which is similar in many respects to the hypothetical at the beginning of this section.]

The drafters of the Model Penal Code found it "shocking" to disregard that the passage of time served only to increase rather than diminish Gounagias' outrage as the story [of his rape] became known. Model Penal Code Tentative Draft No. 9 §210.3 at 48. They said:

> Though it is difficult to state a middle ground between a standard which ignores all individual peculiarities and one which makes emotional distress decisive regardless of the nature of its cause, we think that such a statement is essential. For surely if the actor had just suffered a traumatic injury, if he were blind or were distraught with grief, if he were experiencing an unanticipated reaction to a therapeutic drug, it would be deemed atrocious to appraise his crime for purposes of sentence without reference to any of these matters. They are material because they bear upon the inference as to the actor's character that it is fair to draw upon the basis of his act. So too in such a situation as *Gounagias,* where lapse of time increased rather than diminished the extent of the outrage perpetrated on the actor, as he became aware that his disgrace was known, it was shocking in our view to hold this vital fact to be irrelevant.

The Oregon Criminal Law Revision Commission

Prior to 1971 Oregon law employed the concept of adequate provocation/heat of passion to distinguish murder from manslaughter. Section 506 of Deady's Code provided:

> If any person shall, without malice express or implied, and without deliberation upon a sudden heat of passion, caused by a provocation, apparently sufficient to make the passion irresistible, voluntarily kill another, such person shall be deemed guilty of manslaughter. . . .

In its consideration of this aspect of the substantive law of criminal homicide, the Criminal Law Revision Commission (Commission) was greatly influenced by the work of the drafters of the Model Penal Code. The language of the Model Penal Code drafters that we have quoted just above was cited with approval by the Commission in its Commentary.

The Commission recognized, however, as Justice Holmes had argued, that there is a need for establishing a standard to fix an average conduct to protect the general welfare. A purely subjective test would subtract from incentive to maintain self-control. The Commission [like the Drafters of the Model Penal Code] chose an intermediate position:

> The draft section also introduces a larger element of subjectivity, though it is only the actor's "situation" and "the circumstances as he believes them to be," not the defendant's scheme of moral values, that are thus to be considered. The ultimate test, however, is objective; there must be

"reasonable" explanation or excuse for the actor's disturbance. Thus, the draft retains a certain degree of the objective standard but turns away from the present Oregon law which apparently gauges the accused's acts on a purely reasonable man test without reference to the accused's circumstances or relevant personal characteristics.

Legislative Modification

The Commission presented to the legislature the following subsection:

> (1) Criminal homicide constitutes manslaughter when:
> (b) A homicide which would otherwise be murder is committed under the influence of extreme mental or emotional disturbance for which there is a reasonable explanation and excuse. The reasonableness of such explanation and excuse shall be determined from the standpoint of a person in the actor's situation under the circumstances as he believes them to be.

Early on, members of the legislature and witnesses questioned whether this approach was too subjective. . . .

By March 5, 1971, controversy over whether the test was too subjective led to amendment of the section so as to read essentially as it now does [i.e., the evaluation must be from the standpoint of an "ordinary" person in the actor's situation]. We must conclude from this legislative history that the legislature, as distinguished from the Commission, intended to present a test to be used by court and jury that would measure the reasonableness of the explanation for the disturbance more objectively than that proposed by the Commission.

The Trial Court's Instruction

[The court quotes the trial court's instruction, which included the following:]

> I instruct you that the reasonableness of the explanation for the extreme emotional disturbance shall be determined from the standpoint of an ordinary person in the Defendant's situation under the circumstances as the Defendant reasonably believes them to be. You are further instructed that when you consider the reasonableness of the explanation for an extreme emotional disturbance and its resulting homicidal act, you are not to use the Defendant's scheme of moral values or the Defendant's personality characteristics. You may only use the scheme of moral values and personality characteristics which would be possessed by an ordinary

person in our society today, and fifth, the prosecution must prove the nonexistence of any extreme emotional disturbance beyond a reasonable doubt.

Extreme emotional disturbance simply means, in the end, that an actor's loss of self control can be understood by a jury in terms that arouse the jury's sympathy to such an extent that the jury feels that the criminal consequence of murder ought, under all the circumstances, to be mitigated to manslaughter in the first degree. . . .

Extreme emotional disturbance is not to be measured in point of time. In other words, extreme emotional disturbance is not necessarily created in a sudden heat of passion or triggered by a sudden or provocative event. It may be created over an extended period of time. In order to be a mitigating factor in a homicide, however, it must exist at the same time as the homicidal event.

The defendant duly excepted to the instruction. . . .

The trial judge employed an explanation drawn from the decision of the Court of Appeals in State v. Ackridge, 23 Or. App. 633, 635, 543, P.2d 1073 (1975), in which a dictionary definition of "extreme" was given and approved: "I instruct you that the term [extreme] means the outermost or furthest; most remote in any direction; final; or last." . . .

We agree with the defendant that the jury should be instructed on the meaning of the whole term rather than singling out the word "extreme" for amplification. The point of the extreme emotional disturbance defense is to provide a basis for mitigation that differs from a finding of mental defect or disease to such an extent as altogether to preclude criminal responsibility.

The *Ackridge* definition of the word "extreme" and the implication that definition is the key to the meaning of the term "extreme emotional disturbance" derogates from the aim of providing a mitigating circumstance short of temporary derangement. The notion of "extreme" provided for the jury by the *Ackridge* court is consonant with an understanding of emotional disturbance that might preclude criminal responsibility. The words "outermost or furthest, most remote in any direction, final or last," as used by the court to define "extreme," would seem to require a state of mind so far from the norm as to be characteristic of a mental illness. The defense was meant to be understood in more relative terms as referring to a loss of self-control due to intense feelings.

Furthermore, the *Ackridge* definition may also be evocative of the old heat of passion defense. The *Ackridge* definition contains no hint of the possibility that "a significant mental trauma" could have "affected a defendant's mind for a substantial period of time, simmering in the unknowing subconscious and then inexplicably coming to the fore." Instead, the *Ackridge* definition implies that the disturbance must be visibly manifest in all of its compelling intensity.

... The *Ackridge* instruction fails to take into account the matrix of ideas and concerns from which the whole term takes its significance. An explanation of the term "extreme emotional disturbance" which reflects the situational or relative character of the concept was given in People v. Shelton, 88 Misc. 2d 136, 149, 385 N.Y.S.2d 708, 717 (1976), as follows:

> That extreme emotional disturbance is the emotional state of an individual who: . . . (b) is exposed to an extremely unusual and overwhelming stress; and (c) has an extreme emotional reaction to it, as a result of which there is a loss of self-control and reason is overborne by intense feelings, such as passion, anger, distress, grief, excessive agitation or other similar emotions." . . .

We conclude that in instructing a jury on the meaning of the term "extreme emotional disturbance" a trial court, after proper instruction as to the burden of persuasion, should pose the issue in terms of whether defendant was under the influence of an emotional disturbance to the extent that he lost his self-control that would have otherwise prevented his committing the homicide.

We have still to determine how a jury is to determine whether there was a reasonable explanation for the emotional disturbance. This is a sensitive task because the Oregon statute requires that the "reasonableness of the explanation for the disturbance shall be determined from the standpoint of an ordinary person," ORS 163.135(1). On the other hand, the statute requires that the reasonableness of the interpretation must be judged from the standpoint of "the actor's situation under the circumstances as the actor reasonably believes them to be." The juxtaposition of these two requirements for determining the adequacy of the explanation prevents the adequacy from being determined on either wholly objective or subjective grounds. The words "ordinary person" and "reasonableness of the explanation" recall the reasonable man standard of the heat of passion defense, which is an objective test, while the requirement of taking into account the actor's situation suggests a more subjective analysis.

This legislative mix of the "ordinary" person's views and the subjective belief of the defendant as to the reasonableness of his conduct in what the defendant believes the circumstances to be revives the grounds for the criticism of judicial analysis of the former adequate provocation/heat of passion defense, to which we have already referred. Under that former defense, personal characteristics of the defendant were not important. An example is found in Bedder v. Director of Public Prosecutions, W.L.R. 1119, 2 All. E.R. 801 (1954).

> Just as mental peculiarities do not give a privileged position in the law of provocation, so neither do physical peculiarities. This was decided

by the House of Lords in *Bedder* [1954] 1 W.L.R. 1119; [1954] Crim. L.R. 721. The appellant was a youth of eighteen who was sexually impotent but who attempted to have sexual intercourse with a prostitute. Discovering his impotence she jeered at him and attempted to get away; he tried still to hold her, but (according to his evidence) she slapped him in the face, punched him in the stomach, and (when he pushed her back) kicked him in the private parts. The appellant thereupon stabbed her twice with a pocket knife, causing her death. The judge directed the jury in terms of what the reasonable or ordinary person would have done, and an appeal against a conviction of murder was dismissed both by the Court of Criminal Appeal and by the House of Lords. If the provocation was insufficient for a normal man, it could not help the accused that he was conscious of his impotence and therefore liable to be more excited if "twitted" or attacked on the subject of that particular infirmity. In applying the test of the reasonable man, it could not be supposed that this hypothetical reasonable man in the position of the accused was himself impotent.

Williams, Provocation and the Reasonable Man, 1954 Criminal L. Rev. 740, 747. Similarly, Donovan and Wildman in their article, Is the Reasonable Man Obsolete? A Critical Perspective on Self-Defense and Provocation, hypothesize the following example:

> An Asian-American man, Harold Sato, who had been interned in a detention camp for Japanese during World War II, faces repeated racial prejudice at his job. One day after repeated racial slurs from a co-worker he kills the co-worker.

The authors observe:

> The anomaly of a purely objective standard of provocation is underlined by Mr. Sato's case. . . . A reasonable man, viewed in the abstract, is not likely to be roused to the heat of passion by a verbal insult. However, an Asian-American who had been interned in a concentration camp is likely to be roused to the heat of passion by racial slurs. To the extent that a jury is not allowed to consider Mr. Sato's racial background and previous experience of racial discrimination in determining his moral culpability, Mr. Sato is more likely to be convicted of murder . . . than of voluntary manslaughter.

By requiring the factfinder to focus on a person in the defendant's "situation," the drafters of the Model Penal Code sought to work change. One writer, relying upon the Model Penal Code commentary, has put it:

> [I]t makes the test more, although not entirely, subjective, by requiring the jury to test the reasonableness of the actor's conduct, "from the

viewpoint of a person in the actor's situation." Thus, the actor's sex, sexual preference, pregnancy, physical deformities, and similar characteristics are apt to be taken into consideration in evaluating the reasonableness of the defendant's behavior.

Dressler, Rethinking Heat of Passion: A Defense in Search of a Rationale, 73 Journal of Criminal Law and Criminology 421, 431 (1982).

In this case the trial court instructed that the jury was not to consider the defendant's "personality characteristics" but only the "personality characteristics which would be possessed by an ordinary person in our society today" in determining the reasonableness of the explanation for extreme emotional disturbance. Defendant argued that "personality characteristics" are a part of the actor's personal characteristics and thus of the actor's "situation" that must be taken into account in determining reasonableness.

The state answered that there is nothing in the legislative history, at either the Commission level or the legislative level, to suggest that personality traits are properly to be considered. . . .

. . . The 1971 statute, originally and now, makes the test depend upon the actor's situation. We have found nothing to indicate that this does not include those "personal" characteristics noted by the drafters of the Model Penal Code. . . .

In the case at bar, the trial court erred in instructing the jury in the terms of *Ackridge*. An adequate exception was duly taken. The error went to the heart of the case. The error was not harmless. Defendant is entitled to a new trial.

Reversed and remanded for a new trial.

New Zealand Crimes Act of 1961, §169(1), (2)
Provocation

(1) Culpable homicide that would otherwise be murder may be reduced to manslaughter if the person who caused the death did so under provocation.

(2) Anything done or said may be provocation if—

(a) In the circumstances of the case it was sufficient to deprive a person having the power of self-control of an ordinary person, but otherwise having the characteristics of the offender, of the power of self-control; and

(b) It did in fact deprive the offender of the power of self-control and thereby induced him to commit the act of homicide.

Questions

1. *Common Law Provocation.* If Lester were charged with Conran's murder under the California homicide statutes, would he be liable? (Assume "heat of passion" is similar to the common law provocation defense described in *Ott.*) Which facts would be relevant to this determination and which would not be relevant? If Lester were charged with the killing of Conran's daughter, would he be liable in California? If so, for what?

2. *Extreme Emotional Disturbance.* If Lester were charged with Conran's murder under the Model Penal Code, would he be liable? Which facts would be relevant and which would not be relevant? What is the practical effect, if any, of Oregon's revision of the Model Penal Code formulation of the extreme emotional disturbance formulation? If Lester were charged with the murder of Conran's daughter, would he be liable under the Model Penal Code? If so, for what?

3. *Individualizing the Objective Standard.* What arguments can you make against using a purely objective standard in judging an actor's reaction to provocation or other possible causes of extreme emotional disturbance? Why not have a purely subjective standard? What approach does the Model Penal Code take? If the objective standard is to be individualized with some conditions or characteristics of the actor, how can a judge determine which conditions or characteristics should be used and which should not be used? At trial, Lester seems to claim a genetic predisposition toward being provoked to violence. If the evidence supported this claim, should the objective standard be individualized to take account of this? (This issue is raised again in Chapter 7, in relation to the objective standard used for assessing negligence and recklessness.)

4. *A Bad Temper.* Assume that a personal "characteristic" of actor *A* is that he has a certifiably bad temper. If *A* intentionally kills someone while in a rage from his bad temper, would he be liable for murder in California? What arguments can you make that the actor could get a mitigation under the Model Penal Code? Would the actor be likely to get a mitigation under the New Zealand statute quoted above?

5. *A Fourth-Generation Terrorist.* Actor *B* is good-tempered in her personal relationships but has grown up in a family, indeed a community, of terrorists. As a fourth-generation terrorist, *B* has a firmly instilled moral code that not only permits but encourages, as acts of valor, conduct that most of the world considers to be immoral acts of terror. If *B* intentionally kills as a result of her "terrorist" philosophy, would she be liable for murder in California? Under the Model Penal Code? Under the New Zealand statute quoted above?

Beating Moles

During a recent camping trip, Jeanne Cogdon became separated from her group and was lost in the woods for six days. When she was found, she was suffering from exposure, disorientation, and severe depression. Since that time, she has been seeing a psychiatrist, who is treating her for post-traumatic stress disorder. On this particular night, she goes to bed at 10:30 PM as usual. At 1:30 AM she awakes and goes to check on her daughter, Pat. She sees little things moving in the shadows on Pat's bed. She turns on the light. Hundreds of furry rat-like creatures are crawling all over Pat. "Pat," she screams, "Moles! They're eating your face!" She picks up Pat's field hockey stick and begins beating the moles. "Pat! Get your other stick! Kill them! Kill them!" When her husband Frank arrives, he finds his wife striking at different parts of Pat's bed. "Hit them over here, Pat!" He can see nothing on the bed except Pat, who has been knocked unconscious by a blow to the head. Pat dies two days later from her head injuries. Psychiatrists testify that, as a result of a psychotic episode triggered by her post-traumatic stress disorder, Mrs. Cogdon was hallucinating at the time she struck and injured her daughter. She did not realize that she was hitting her daughter, but rather believed that both of them were beating the creatures on Pat's bed.* Does Mrs. Cogdon satisfy the offense elements of homicide? If so, for what grade of homicide?

United States v. Brawner
United States Court of Appeals for the District of Columbia Circuit
471 F.2d 969 (1972)

LEVENTHAL, Circuit Judge:

The principal issues raised on this appeal from a conviction for second degree murder and carrying a dangerous weapon relate to appellant's defense of insanity. After the case was argued to a division of the court, the court *sua sponte* ordered rehearing en banc. We identified our intention to reconsider the appropriate standard for the insanity defense. . . .

---

*Based loosely on the facts of King v. Cogdon, Supreme Court of Victoria, 1950, reported in Morris, Somnambulistic Homicide: Ghosts, Spiders, and North Koreans, 5 Res Judicata 29 (1951).

The Trial Record

Passing by various minor disagreements among the witnesses, the record permits us to reconstruct the events of September 8, 1967, as follows: After a morning and afternoon of wine-drinking, appellant Archie W. Brawner, Jr. and his uncle Aaron Ross, went to a party at the home of three acquaintances. During the evening, several fights broke out. In one of them, Brawner's jaw was injured when he was struck or pushed to the ground. The time of the fight was approximately 10:30 PM. After the fight, Brawner left the party. He told Mr. Ross that some boys had jumped him. Mr. Ross testified that Brawner "looked like he was out of his mind." Other witnesses who saw him after the fight testified that Brawner's mouth was bleeding and that his speech was unclear (but the same witness added, "I heard every word he said"); that he was staggering and angry; and that he pounded on a mailbox with his fist. One witness testified that Brawner said, "[I'm] going to get my boys" and come back, and that "someone is going to die tonight."

Half an hour later, at about eleven PM, Brawner was on his way back to the party with a gun. One witness testified that Brawner said he was going up there to kill his attackers or be killed.

Upon his arrival at the address, Brawner fired a shot into the ground and entered the building. He proceeded to the apartment where the party was in progress and fired five shots through the closed metal hallway door. Two of the shots struck Billy Ford, killing him. Brawner was arrested a few minutes later, several blocks away. The arresting officer testified that Brawner appeared normal, and did not appear to be drunk, that he spoke clearly, and had no odor of alcohol about him.

After the Government had presented the evidence of its non-expert witnesses, the trial judge ruled that there was insufficient evidence on "deliberation" to go to the jury: Accordingly, a verdict of acquittal was directed on first degree murder.

The expert witnesses, called by both defense and prosecution, all agreed that Brawner was suffering from an abnormality of a psychiatric or neurological nature. The medical labels were variously given as "epileptic personality disorder," "psychologic brain syndrome associated with a convulsive disorder," "personality disorder associated with epilepsy," or, more simply, "an explosive personality." There was no disagreement that the epileptic condition would be exacerbated by alcohol, leading to more frequent episodes and episodes of greater intensity, and would also be exacerbated by a physical blow to the head. The experts agreed that epilepsy *per se* is not a mental disease or defect, but a neurological disease which is often associated with a mental disease or defect. They further agreed that Brawner had a mental, as well as a neurological, disease. . . .

Mental Condition, Though Insufficient to Exonerate, May Be Relevant to Specific Mental Element of Certain Crimes or Degrees of Crime

Our decision [holds] that expert testimony as to a defendant's abnormal mental condition may be received and considered, as tending to show, in a responsible way, that defendant did not have the specific mental state required for a particular crime or degree of crime—even though he was aware that his act was wrongful and was able to control it, and hence was not entitled to complete exoneration.

Some of the cases following this doctrine use the term "diminished responsibility," but we prefer the example of the cases that avoid this term, for its convenience is outweighed by its confusion: Our doctrine has nothing to do with "diminishing" responsibility of a defendant because of his impaired mental condition, but rather with determining whether the defendant had the mental state that must be proved as to all defendants.

Procedurally, the issue of abnormal mental condition negativing a person's intent may arise in different ways: For example, the defendant may offer evidence of mental condition not qualifying as mental disease under *McDonald*.* Or he may tender evidence that qualifies under *McDonald*, yet the jury may conclude from all the evidence that defendant has knowledge and control capacity sufficient for responsibility under the ALI rule.

The issue often arises with respect to mental condition tendered as negativing the element of premeditation in a charge of first degree premeditated murder. As we noted in Austin v. United States, 127 U.S. App. D.C. 180, 382 F.2d 129 (1967), when the legislature modified the common law crime of murder so as to establish degrees, murder in the first degree was reserved for intentional homicide done deliberately and with premeditation, and homicide that is intentional but "impulsive," not done after "reflection and meditation," was made murder only in the second degree.

An offense like deliberated and premeditated murder requires a specific intent that cannot be satisfied merely by showing that defendant failed to conform to an objective standard. This is plainly established by the defense of voluntary intoxication. In Hopt v. Utah, 104 U.S. 631, 634, 26 L. Ed. 873 (1881), the Court, after stating the familiar rule that voluntary intoxication is no excuse for crime, said:

> [W]hen a statute establishing different degrees of murder requires deliberate premeditation in order to constitute murder in the first degree,

---

*Editor's Note—In McDonald v. United States, 312 F.2d 847, 983-984 (D.C. Cir. 1962) (en banc), the Court of Appeals defined mental disease or defect to include: "any abnormal condition of the mind which substantially affects mental or emotional processes and substantially affects behavior controls."

the question of whether the accused is in such a condition of mind, by reason of drunkenness or otherwise, as to be capable of deliberate premeditation, necessarily becomes a material subject of consideration by the jury. . . .

Neither logic nor justice can tolerate a jurisprudence that defines the elements of an offense as requiring a mental state such that one defendant can properly argue that his voluntary drunkenness removed his capacity to form the specific intent but another defendant is inhibited from a submission of his contention that an abnormal mental condition, for which he was in no way responsible, negated his capacity to form a particular specific intent, even though the condition did not exonerate him from all criminal responsibility.

In Fisher v. United States, 80 U.S. App. D.C. 96, 149 F.2d 28 (1946), the court upheld the trial court's refusal to instruct the jury that on issues of premeditation and deliberation "it should consider the entire personality of the defendant, his mental, nervous, emotional and physical characteristics as developed by the evidence in the case." Justice Arnold's abbreviated opinion was evidently premised on two factors: (1) that the instruction confused the issue of insanity with the issue of deliberation; (2) that "To give an instruction like the above is to tell the jury they are at liberty to acquit one who commits a brutal crime because he has the abnormal tendencies of persons capable of such crimes." . . .

. . . [W]e deem it appropriate to change the rule of *Fisher* on a prospective basis, and to accept the approach which . . . has been adopted by the overwhelming majority of courts that have recently faced the question. We are convinced by the analysis set forth in the recent opinions of the highest courts of California, Colorado, New Jersey, Iowa, Ohio, Idaho, Connecticut, Nebraska, New Mexico and Nevada. They have joined the states that spoke out before *Fisher*—New York, Rhode Island, Utah, Wisconsin and Wyoming.

The pertinent reasoning was succinctly stated by the Colorado Supreme Court as follows:

> The question to be determined is not whether defendant was insane, but whether the homicidal act was committed with deliberation and premeditation. The evidence offered as to insanity may or may not be relevant to that issue. . . . "A claim of insanity cannot be used for the purpose of reducing a crime of murder in the first degree to murder in the second degree or from murder to manslaughter. If the perpetrator is responsible at all in this respect, he is responsible in the same degree as a sane man; and if he is not responsible at all, he is entitled to an acquittal in both degrees. However, . . . *evidence of the condition of the mind* of the accused at the time of the crime, together with the surrounding circumstances, may be introduced, not for the purpose of establishing insanity, but to prove that the situation was such that a specific intent

was not entertained—that is, *to show absence of any deliberate or premeditated design.*" (Emphasis in original.)

On the other side of the coin, very few jurisdictions which have recently considered this question have held to the contrary position.

Intervening developments within our own jurisdiction underscore the soundness of a doctrine for consideration of abnormal mental condition on the issue of specific intent. In the *Fisher* opinion of 1946, the court was concerned lest such a doctrine "tell the jury that they are at liberty to acquit one who commits a brutal crime because he has the abnormal tendencies of persons capable of such crimes." That a man's abnormal mental condition short of legal insanity may be material as negativing premeditation and deliberation does not set him "at liberty" but reduces the degree of the criminal homicide. . . .

There has also been a material legislative development since . . . *Fisher.* . . . In 1964, after extensive hearings, Congress enacted the Hospitalization of the Mentally Ill Act, which provides civil commitment for the "mentally ill" who are dangerous to themselves or others. . . . These statutory provisions provide a shield against danger from persons with abnormal mental condition. . . .

Our rule permits the introduction of expert testimony as to abnormal condition if it is relevant to negative, or establish, the specific mental condition that is an element of the crime. The receipt of this expert testimony to negative the mental condition of specific intent requires careful administration by the trial judge. Where the proof is not offered in the first instance as evidence of exonerating mental disease or defect within the ALI rule the judge may, and ordinarily would, require counsel first to make a proffer of the proof to be adduced outside the presence of the jury. The judge will then determine whether the testimony is grounded in sufficient scientific support to warrant use in the courtroom, and whether it would aid the jury in reaching a decision on the ultimate issues.

The case is remanded for further consideration by the District Court in accordance with this opinion.

So ordered.

Model Penal Code §4.02(1)
Evidence of Mental Disease or Defect Admissible When Relevant to Element of the Offense

Evidence that the defendant suffered from a mental disease or defect is admissible whenever it is relevant to prove that the defendant did or did not have a state of mind which is an element of the offense.

Questions

1. *Mental Illness Negating an Element.* In many jurisdictions, the doctrine of "diminished capacity" or "diminished responsibility" allowed evidence of mental disease or defect to be introduced to negate only certain culpability requirements (typically only the higher requirements, such as intent or "specific intent" requirements). Some jurisdictions barred introduction of such evidence altogether. Would Mrs. Cogdon be held to satisfy the elements of the offense in either of these jurisdictions? Would Mrs. Cogdon have been held to satisfy the elements of the offense under the Model Penal Code? (If a jurisdiction has an insanity defense, Mrs. Cogdon also may be eligible for that defense. The insanity defense is discussed in Section 16.2.)

2. *Model Penal Code §4.02(1).* Assume a jurisdiction has a provision like Model Penal Code §2.02(1), Minimum Requirements of Culpability, as most have:

> [A] person is not guilty of an offense unless he acted purposely, knowingly, recklessly or negligently, as the law may require, with respect to each material element of the offense.

Assume it also has a provision like Model Penal Code §1.12(1), Proof Beyond a Reasonable Doubt, as all have:

> No person may be convicted of an offense unless each element of such offense is proved beyond a reasonable doubt. In the absence of such proof, the innocence of the defendant is assumed.

These appear to require the state to prove the actor's culpability as to all elements. If, as a result of an actor's mental illness or anything else, the actor does not have the culpable state of mind required by the offense definition, he would seem to be free of liability for the offense. Why, then, does a jurisdiction, like the Model Penal Code, need a provision like §4.02(1) quoted above?

3. *Extreme Mental Disturbance.* Assume that Mrs. Cogdon is aware that she is hitting her daughter and aware that her conduct is likely to cause her death. She just had a nightmare in which she relived her traumatic episode in the woods and attacks her daughter in the belief that her daughter caused her to be lost, although she is confused about why she thinks this is true. The experts testify that her belief and her conduct are manifestations of her mental disturbance, which they call post-traumatic stress syndrome. (Assume the jurisdiction does not have an insanity defense, as some do not.) Is Mrs. Cogdon liable for murder?

People v. Mentry:
"Mother Says She Was Told to Sit on Child, Who Died"

San Jose, Calif.—A jury trial began last week over whether a 200-pound woman was grossly negligent or reckless in following a counselor's alleged advice to discipline her 8-year old son by sitting on him.

Betty Mentry, 45, an electronics worker here, was charged with involuntary manslaughter after her son, Stephen, died last May 31 when she sat on him for the fourth time. People v. Mentry, 84637 (Santa Clara County Superior Court).

Meantime, Ms. Mentry is suing the Alum Rock Communications Center, a San Jose counseling service funded by the county with state money, for allegedly advising her to sit on her son. Her malpractice suit seeks $2.5 million. Mentry v. Alum Rock Communications Inc., 517164 (Santa Clara County Superior Court).

Police had suggested to Ms. Mentry to take her son to Alum Rock to break him of a stealing habit, said local lawyer Cyril R. Ash Jr., who represents her in both the civil and the criminal cases.

Mr. Ash claims that center counselor Jorge Sousa "insisted" that Ms. Mentry use a technique developed in the 1960s by Dr. Milton H. Erickson of New York. Mr. Sousa, the attorney said, threatened to advise the courts to remove Stephen from her custody if she refused to follow his advice.

The technique consisted, literally, of sitting on the child to make him understand who was in charge. Mr. Ash said Dr. Erickson detailed the case of a 27-year-old woman with an 8-year-old son who "refused to respond to punishment" until, as advised, his mother "threw him quickly to the floor on his stomach and sat her full weight upon him."

"I was to eat in front of him and I was to talk on the telephone [while sitting on Stephen]," Ms. Mentry testified at a preliminary examination in the criminal case last August. "I was supposed to act like I was having a gay old time. [Mr. Sousa] assured me that Stephen would yell, scream and cuss and carry on, and I was to ignore him. And when it was over, he said he was positive that Stephen would have the message that I was in charge.

Counselor's 'Assurances'

The woman said she sat her "full weight" on her son for eight hours the first time she used the technique. On the next two occasions, she said, she sat on him for a half hour and for 1½ hours. The last time, she sat on him for two hours before she noticed he had stopped breathing. He died nine days later.

Mr. Ash claims the counselor failed in his duty to warn her of any danger. In fact, he said, "the counselor assured her no harm would come to the boy." And Ms. Mentry, he said, "is the type of individual who tends to follow such instructions explicitly."

The counselor's threat to strip her of custody, he said, also is enough to absolve her of any crime.

But the person is responsible for exercising a certain amount of common sense, said John F. Marshall, a Santa Clara County deputy district attorney.

"Even somebody who's less intelligent than normal, when a kid says, 'I can't breathe,' you do something about it," he said. "And if you don't, that's gross negligence."

Ms. Mentry's 11-year-old daughter, Sherry, testified at the preliminary hearing that she walked into the room and heard her brother say he couldn't breathe. Lawyers were expected to use her preliminary hearing testimony rather than bring her back to the stand at trial.

Alum Rock's director, George Doub, denied Ms. Mentry's allegations, saying his counselors never advised her to sit on her son. He called her claim a "unique shift of blame."

Mr. Sousa has been unavailable for comment.

Questions

Sitting on a Child. Is Ms. Mentry liable for a homicide offense under the Model Penal Code? If so, for which offense? Would it change the result if Ms. Mentry honestly believed that she would lose custody of her son if she did not follow the counselor's directions and that everything she did was pursuant to those directions? Would it change the result if it were determined that Ms. Mentry is mentally retarded?

Chapter 5. THE LEGALITY PRINCIPLE

In addition to its unique focus upon moral blameworthiness, introduced in Chapter 1, criminal law is unique in its adherence to what is called the "legality principle." The principle advances interests different from either the retributivist or the utilitarian goals discussed in Chapter 2. In its original latin dress, it was stated as "nullum crimen sine lege, nulla poena sine lege," meaning roughly: no crime without law, nor punishment without law. In its modern form it means that criminal liability and punishment can be based only upon a prior legislative enactment of a prohibition expressed with adequate precision and clarity. The principle is not a legal rule but rather a concept embodied in a series of legal rules and doctrines. In addition to the nearly universal modern prohibition against judicial creation of new offenses and the strong trend toward abolition of common law offenses (offenses defined in a case rather than in a statute), the legality principle is expressed in the constitutional prohibition against vague statutes, the constitutional prohibition against ex post facto laws, and the rule requiring strict construction of penal statutes.

The last doctrine has come under attack, with many modern codes rejecting the rule of strict construction in favor of what is called the rule of fair import. The reasons for this shift illustrate the tensions inherent in the legality principle, which are the subject of this chapter. The shift also illustrates the special role that statutory interpretation plays in application of the legality principle. Most provisions implementing the principle exclude the possibility for judicial in favor of legislative criminalization decisions. But, eventually, all legislative statutes must be subject to judicial interpretation when they are applied. Thus, in setting the rules of interpretation, we define the extent of the judicial role in criminalization that we will continue to permit even under the legality principle.

The CG-PLA at the UN

Growing United Nations involvement in peace-keeping military activities has spawned a rash of terroristic acts against United Nation representatives and employees in New York. The Command Group of the Popular Liberation Army (CG-PLA) is suspected of much of the violence and is alleged to have received help in selecting targets and coordinating attacks from the United Nations representatives of several countries that oppose the United Nations involvement and that see terrorism as a legitimate political device. In response to this wave of violence, a United Nations resolution is proposed that would call upon the United States to enact legislation to criminalize entering United Nations headquarters in New York City with a terroristic purpose.* No such offense currently exists. Also recommended are increased penalties for all existing violent offenses when those offenses are against UN delegates or employees, and the withdrawal of diplomatic immunity as a defense for all violent offenses against such persons. The United States Congress unanimously passes a resolution in support of the UN proposal and begins processing a bill that would implement the resolution's call for new offenses and penalties. At the direction of the President, the United States delegate votes in support of the resolution, as do the delegates of nearly all member states.

To show its defiance of the United Nations and its recent resolution, the CG-PLA undertakes a new campaign of terror against United Nations delegates and employees in New York. Surveillance set in place because of earlier suspicions of Ahmed Modafi, the Libyan representative to the United Nations, reveals that he is helping the CG-PLA in its campaign. The CG-PLA times its campaign to end just minutes before the President signs into law the United States legislation implementing the resolution, "The United Nations Personnel Protection Act" (UNPPA). One week later, federal and state prosecutors in New York indict Modafi and others for acts and threats of violence against UN victims under both UNPPA and previously-existing statutes. The evidence of his involvement in the terror campaign is overwhelming. Can Modafi be convicted of anything?

---

*More specifically, the proposal creates an offense of leaving United States property around the United Nations to enter United Nations property with a terroristic purpose. The drafters do not wish to create United States jurisdiction over United Nations property.

Model Penal Code §1.05(1)
All Offenses Defined by Statute

No conduct constitutes an offense unless it is a crime or violation under this Code or another statute of this State.

Calder v. Bull
Supreme Court of the United States
3 U.S. (3 Dall.) 386, 1 L. Ed. 648 (1798)

All the restrictions contained in the Constitution of the United States on the power of the state legislatures were provided in favor of the authority of the federal government. The prohibition against their making any *ex post facto* laws was introduced for greater caution, and very probably arose from the knowledge that the parliament of Great Britain claimed and exercised a power to pass such laws, under the denomination of bills of attainder, or bills of pains and penalties; the first inflicting capital, and the other less punishment. These acts were legislative judgments; and an exercise of judicial power. Sometimes, they respected the crime, by declaring acts to be treason, which were not treason, when committed; at other times, they violated the rules of evidence (to supply a deficiency of legal proof) by admitting one witness, when the existing law required two; by receiving evidence without oath; or the oath of the wife against the husband; or other testimony, which the courts of justice would not admit; at other times, they inflicted punishments, where the party was not, by law, liable to any punishment; and in other cases, they inflicted greater punishment, than the law annexed to the offence. The ground for the exercise of such legislative power was this, that the safety of the kingdom depended on the death, or other punishment, of the offender: as if traitors, when discovered, could be so formidable, or the government so insecure! With very few exceptions, the advocates of such laws were stimulated by ambition, or personal resentment and vindictive malice. To prevent such and similar acts of violence and injustice, I believe, the federal and state legislatures were prohibited from passing any bill of attainder, or any *ex post facto* law.

The constitution of the United States, article I., section 9, prohibits the legislature of the United States from passing any *ex post facto* law; and, in §10, lays several restrictions on the authority of the legislatures of the several states; and, among them, "that no state shall pass any *ex post facto* law." . . .

I will state what laws I consider *ex post facto* laws, within the words and the intent of the prohibition. 1st. Every law that makes an action done before the passing of the law, and which was innocent when done, criminal; and punishes such action. 2d. Every law that aggravates a crime, or makes it greater than it was, when committed. 3d. Every law that changes the punishment, and inflicts a greater punishment, than the law annexed to the crime, when committed. 4th. Every law that alters the legal rules of evidence, and receives less, or different testimony, than the law required at the time of the commission of the offence, in order to convict the offender. All these, and similar laws, are manifestly unjust and oppressive. . . . But I do not consider any law *ex post facto*, within the prohibition, that mollifies the rigor of the criminal law: but only those that create or aggravate the crime; or increase the punishment, or change the rules of evidence, for the purpose of conviction. . . .

[The Court concludes that the prohibition against *ex post facto* laws applies only to criminal laws and has no effect with respect to civil laws.]

Papachristou v. City of Jacksonville
Supreme Court of the United States
405 U.S. 156, 92 S. Ct. 839, 31 L. Ed. 2d 110 (1972)

This case involves eight defendants who were convicted in a Florida municipal court of violating a Jacksonville, Florida, vagrancy ordinance.[1] . . .

At issue are five consolidated cases. Margaret Papachristou, Betty Calloway, Eugene Eddie Melton, and Leonard Johnson were all arrested early on a Sunday morning, and charged with vagrancy—"prowling by auto."

Jimmy Lee Smith and Milton Henry were charged with vagrancy—"vagabonds."

---

1. Jacksonville Ordinance Code §26-57 provided at the time of these arrests and convictions as follows: "Rogues and vagabonds, or dissolute persons who go about begging, common gamblers, persons who use juggling or unlawful games or plays, common drunkards, common night walkers, thieves, pilferers or pickpockets, traders in stolen property, lewd, wanton and lascivious persons, keepers of gambling places, common railers and brawlers, persons wandering or strolling around from place to place without any lawful purpose or object, habitual loafers, disorderly persons, persons neglecting all lawful business and habitually spending their time by frequenting houses of ill fame, gaming houses, or places where alcoholic beverages are sold or served, persons able to work but habitually living upon the earnings of their wives or minor children shall be deemed vagrants and, upon conviction in the Municipal Court shall be punished as provided for Class D offenses." . . .

CHAPTER 5 THE LEGALITY PRINCIPLE 121

Henry Edward Heath and a codefendant were arrested for vagrancy—"loitering" and "common thief."

Thomas Owen Campbell was charged with vagrancy—"common thief."

Hugh Brown was charged with vagrancy—"disorderly loitering on street" and "disorderly conduct—resisting arrest with violence."

The facts are stipulated. Papachristou and Calloway are white females. Melton and Johnson are black males. Papachristou was enrolled in a job-training program sponsored by the State Employment Service at Florida Junior College in Jacksonville. Calloway was a typing and shorthand teacher at a state mental institution located near Jacksonville. She was the owner of the automobile in which the four defendants were arrested. Melton was a Vietnam war veteran who had been released from the Navy after nine months in a veterans' hospital. On the date of his arrest he was a part-time computer helper while attending college as a full-time student in Jacksonville. Johnson was a tow-motor operator in a grocery chain warehouse and was a lifelong resident of Jacksonville.

At the time of their arrest the four of them were riding in Calloway's car on the main thoroughfare in Jacksonville. They had left a restaurant owned by Johnson's uncle where they had eaten and were on their way to a nightclub. The arresting officers denied that the racial mixture in the car played any part in the decision to make the arrest. The arrest, they said, was made because the defendants had stopped near a used-car lot which had been broken into several times. There was, however, no evidence of any breaking and entering on the night in question.

Of these four charged with "prowling by auto" none had been previously arrested except Papachristou who had once been convicted of a municipal offense.

Jimmy Lee Smith and Milton Henry (who is not a petitioner) were arrested between 9 and 10 A.M. on a weekday in downtown Jacksonville, while waiting for a friend who was to lend them a car so they could apply for a job at a produce company. Smith was a part-time produce worker and part-time organizer for a Negro political group. He had a common-law wife and three children supported by him and his wife. He had been arrested several times but convicted only once. Smith's companion, Henry, was an 18-year-old high school student with no previous record of arrest.

This morning it was cold, and Smith had no jacket, so they went briefly into a dry cleaning shop to wait, but left when requested to do so. They thereafter walked back and forth two or three times over a two-block stretch looking for their friend. The store owners, who apparently were wary of Smith and his companion, summoned two police officers who searched the men and found neither had a weapon. But they were arrested because the officers said they had no identification and because the officers did not believe their story.

Heath and a codefendant were arrested for "loitering" and for "common thief." Both were residents of Jacksonville, Heath having lived there all his life and being employed at an automobile body shop. Heath had previously been arrested but his codefendant had no arrest record. Heath and his companion were arrested when they drove up to a residence shared by Heath's girlfriend and some other girls. Some police officers were already there in the process of arresting another man. When Heath and his companion started backing out of the driveway, the officers signaled to them to stop and asked them to get out of the car, which they did. Thereupon they and the automobile were searched. Although no contraband or incriminating evidence was found, they were both arrested, Heath being charged with being a "common thief" because he was reputed to be a thief. The codefendant was charged with "loitering" because he was standing in the driveway, an act which the officers admitted was done only at their command.

Campbell was arrested as he reached his home very early one morning and was charged with "common thief." He was stopped by officers because he was traveling at a high rate of speed, yet no speeding charge was placed against him.

Brown was arrested when he was observed leaving a downtown Jacksonville hotel by a police officer seated in a cruiser. The police testified he was reputed to be a thief, narcotics pusher, and generally opprobrious character. The officer called Brown over to the car, intending at that time to arrest him unless he had a good explanation for being on the street. Brown walked over to the police cruiser, as commanded, and the officer began to search him, apparently preparatory to placing him in the car. In the process of the search he came on two small packets which were later found to contain heroin. When the officer touched the pocket where the packets were, Brown began to resist. He was charged with "disorderly loitering on street" and "disorderly conduct—resisting arrest with violence." While he was also charged with a narcotics violation, that charge was *nolled*.

Jacksonville's ordinance and Florida's statute were "derived from early English law," and employ "archaic language" in their definitions of vagrants. The history is an oftentold tale. The breakup of feudal estates in England led to labor shortages which in turn resulted in the Statutes of Laborers, designed to stabilize the labor force by prohibiting increases in wages and prohibiting the movement of workers from their home areas in search of improved conditions. Later vagrancy laws became criminal aspects of the poor laws. The series of laws passed in England on the subject became increasingly severe. But "the theory of the Elizabethan poor laws no longer fits the facts." . . . The conditions which spawned these laws may be gone, but the archaic classifications remain.

This ordinance is void for vagueness, both in the sense that it "fails to give a person of ordinary intelligence fair notice that his contem-

CHAPTER 5 THE LEGALITY PRINCIPLE 123

plated conduct is forbidden by the statute,"... and because it encourages arbitrary and erratic arrests and convictions. . . .

Living under a rule of law entails various suppositions, one of which is that "[all persons] are entitled to be informed as to what the State commands or forbids." Lanzetta v. New Jersey, 306 U.S. 451, 453.

Lanzetta is one of a well-recognized group of cases insisting that the law give fair notice of the offending conduct. . . .

The Jacksonville ordinance makes criminal activities which by modern standards are normally innocent. "Nightwalking" is one. Florida construes the ordinance not to make criminal one night's wandering, only the "habitual" wanderer or, as the ordinance describes it, "common night walkers." We know, however, from experience that sleepless people often walk at night, perhaps hopeful that sleep-inducing relaxation will result.

"[P]ersons able to work but habitually living upon the earnings of their wives or minor children"—like habitually living "without visible means of support"—might implicate unemployed pillars of the community who have married rich wives.

"[P]ersons able to work but habitually living upon the earnings of their wives or minor children" may also embrace unemployed people out of the labor market, by reason of a recession or disemployed by reason of technological or so-called structural displacements.

Persons "wandering or strolling" from place to place have been extolled by Walt Whitman and Vachel Lindsay. The qualification "without any lawful purpose or object" may be a trap for innocent acts. Persons "neglecting all lawful business and habitually spending their time by frequenting . . . places where alcoholic beverages are sold or served" would literally embrace many members of golf clubs and city clubs.

Walkers and strollers and wanderers may be going to or coming from a burglary. Loafers or loiterers may be "casing" a place for a holdup. Letting one's wife support him is an intra-family matter, and normally of no concern to the police. Yet it may, of course, be the setting for numerous crimes.

The difficulty is that these activities are historically part of the amenities of life as we have known them. They are not mentioned in the Constitution or in the Bill of Rights. These unwritten amenities have been in part responsible for giving our people the feeling of independence and self-confidence, the feeling of creativity. These amenities have dignified the right of dissent and have honored the right to be nonconformists and the right to defy submissiveness. They have encouraged lives of high spirits rather than hushed, suffocating silence.

They are embedded in Walt Whitman's writings, especially in his "Song of the Open Road." They are reflected, too, in the spirit of Vachel Lindsay's "I Want to Go Wandering," and by Henry D. Thoreau.

This aspect of the vagrancy ordinance before us is suggested by what this Court said in 1876 about a broad criminal statute enacted by Congress: "It would certainly be dangerous if the legislature could set a net large enough to catch all possible offenders, and leave it to the courts to step inside and say who could be rightfully detained, and who should be set at large." United States v. Reese, 92 U.S. 214, 221.

While that was a federal case, the due process implications are equally applicable to the States and to this vagrancy ordinance. Here the net cast is large, not to give the courts the power to pick and choose but to increase the arsenal of the police. In Winters v. New York, 333 U.S. 507, the Court struck down a New York statute that made criminal the distribution of a magazine made up principally of items of criminal deeds of bloodshed or lust so massed as to become vehicles for inciting violent and depraved crimes against the person. The infirmity the Court found was vagueness—the absence of "ascertainable standards of guilt" in the sensitive First Amendment area. Mr. Justice Frankfurter dissented. But concerned as he, and many others, had been over the vagrancy laws, he added:

> Only a word needs to be said regarding Lanzetta v. New Jersey, 306 U.S. 451. The case involved a New Jersey statute of the type that seek to control "vagrancy." These statutes are in a class by themselves, in view of the familiar abuses to which they are put. . . . Definiteness is designedly avoided so as to allow the net to be cast at large, to enable men to be caught who are vaguely undesirable in the eyes of police and prosecution, although not chargeable with any particular offense. In short, these "vagrancy statutes" and laws against "gangs" are not fenced in by the text of the statute or by the subject matter so as to give notice of conduct to be avoided.

Where the list of crimes is so all-inclusive and generalized as the one in this ordinance, those convicted may be punished for no more than vindicating affronts to police authority:

> The common ground which brings such a motley assortment of human troubles before the magistrates in vagrancy-type proceedings is the procedural laxity which permits "conviction" for almost any kind of conduct and the existence of the House of Correction as an easy and convenient dumping-ground for problems that appear to have no other immediate solution.

Foote, Vagrancy-Type Law and Its Administration, 104 U. Pa. L. Rev. 603, 631.

Another aspect of the ordinance's vagueness appears when we focus, not on the lack of notice given a potential offender, but on the effect of the unfettered discretion it places in the hands of the Jacksonville police. Caleb Foote, an early student of this subject, has called the vagrancy-type as offering "punishment by analogy." Such crimes, though long common in Russia, are not compatible with our constitutional system. We allow our police to make arrests only on "probable cause," a Fourth and Fourteenth Amendment standard applicable to the States as well as to the Federal Government. Arresting a person on suspicion, like arresting a person for investigation, is foreign to our system, even when the arrest is for past criminality. Future criminality, however, is the common justification for the presence of vagrancy statutes. . . .

A direction by a legislature to the police to arrest all "suspicious" persons would not pass constitutional muster. A vagrancy prosecution may be merely the cloak for a conviction which could not be obtained on the real but undisclosed grounds for the arrest. . . .

Those generally implicated by the imprecise terms of the ordinance—poor people, nonconformists, dissenters, idlers—may be required to comport themselves according to the lifestyle deemed appropriate by the Jacksonville police and the courts. Where, as here, there are no standards governing the exercise of the discretion granted by the ordinance, the scheme permits and encourages an arbitrary and discriminatory enforcement of the law. It furnishes a convenient tool for "harsh and discriminatory enforcement by local prosecuting officials, against particular groups deemed to merit their displeasure." Thornhill v. Alabama, 310 U.S. 88, 97-98. It results in a regime in which the poor and the unpopular are permitted to "stand on a public sidewalk . . . only at the whim of any police officer." Shuttlesworth v. Birmingham, 382 U.S. 87, 90. Under this ordinance,

> [I]f some carefree type of fellow is satisfied to work just so much, and no more, as will pay for one square meal, some wine, and a flophouse daily, but a court thinks this kind of living subhuman, the fellow can be forced to raise his sights or go to jail as a vagrant.

Amsterdam, Federal Constitutional Restrictions on the Punishment of Crimes of Status, Crimes of General Obnoxiousness, Crimes of Displeasing Police Officers, and the Like, 3 Crim. L. Bull. 205, 226 (1967).

A presumption that people who might walk or loaf or loiter or stroll or frequent houses where liquor is sold, or who are supported by their wives or who look suspicious to the police are to become future criminals is too precarious for a rule of law. The implicit presumption in these generalized vagrancy standards—that crime is being nipped in the bud—is too extravagant to deserve extended treatment. Of course, vagrancy statutes are useful to the police. Of course, they are nets making easy the roundup of so-called undesirables. But the rule of law implies equality and justice in its application. Vagrancy laws of the Jacksonville type teach that the scales of justice are so tipped that even-handed administration of the law is not possible. The rule of law, evenly applied to minorities as well as majorities, to the poor as well as the rich, is the great mucilage that holds society together.

The Jacksonville ordinance cannot be squared with our constitutional standards and is plainly unconstitutional.

Reversed.

Report to the President from Justice Robert H. Jackson, Chief of Counsel for the United States in the Prosecution of Axis War Criminals
Reprinted in 39 Am. J. Intl. L. 178-190 (Supp. 1945)

My dear Mr. President:

I have the honor to report accomplishments during the month since you named me as Chief of Counsel for the United States in prosecuting the principal Axis War Criminals. . . .

. . . What specifically are the crimes with which these individuals and organizations should be charged, and what marks their conduct as criminal?

There is, of course, real danger that trials of this character will become enmeshed in voluminous particulars of wrongs committed by individual Germans throughout the course of the war, and in the multitude of doctrinal disputes which are part of a lawyer's paraphernalia. We can save ourselves from those pitfalls if our test of what legally is crime gives recognition to those things which fundamentally outraged the conscience of the American people and brought them finally to the conviction that their own liberty and civilization could not persist in the same world with the Nazi power.

Those acts which offended the conscience of our people were criminal by standards generally accepted in all civilized countries, and I believe that we may proceed to punish those responsible in full accord with both our own traditions of fairness and with standards of just conduct which have been internationally accepted. I think also that through these trials we should be able to establish that a process of retribution by law awaits those who in the future similarly attack civilization. . . .

I believe that those instincts of our people [, that the Nazis were a "band of brigands,"] were right and that they should guide us as the fundamental tests of criminality. We propose to punish acts which have been regarded as criminal since the time of Cain. . . .

In arranging these trials we must also bear in mind the aspirations with which our people have faced the sacrifices of war. After we entered the war, and as we expended our men and our wealth to stamp out these wrongs, it was the universal feeling of our people that out of this war should come unmistakable rules and workable machinery from which any who might contemplate another era of brigandage would know that they would be held personally responsible and would be personally punished. Our people have been waiting for these trials in the spirit of Woodrow Wilson, who hoped to "give to international law the kind of vitality which it can only have if it is a real expression of our moral judgment."

Against this background it may be useful to restate in more technical lawyer's terms the legal charges against the top Nazi leaders and those voluntary associations such as the S.S. and Gestapo which clustered about them and were ever the prime instrumentalities, first, in capturing the German state, and then, in directing the German state to its spoliations against the rest of the world:

(a) Atrocities and offenses against persons or property constituting violations of International Law, including the laws, rules, and customs of land and naval warfare. The rules of warfare are well established and generally accepted by the nations. They make offenses of such conduct as killing of the wounded, refusal of quarter, ill treatment of prisoners of war, firing on undefended localities, poisoning of wells and streams, pillage and wanton destruction, and ill treatment of inhabitants in occupied territory.

(b) Atrocities and offenses, including atrocities and persecutions on racial or religious grounds, committed since 1933. This is only to recognize the principles of criminal law as they are generally observed in civilized states. These principles have been assimilated as a part of International Law at least since 1907. The Fourth Hague Convention provided that inhabitants and belligerents shall remain under the protection and the rule of "the principles of the law of nations, as they result from the usage established among civilized peoples, from the laws of humanity and the dictates of the public conscience."

(c) Invasions of other countries and initiation of wars of aggression in violation of International Law or treaties.

The persons to be reached by these charges will be determined by the rule of liability, common to all legal systems, that all who participate in the formulation or execution of a criminal plan involving multiple crimes are liable for each of the offenses committed and responsible for the acts of each other. All are liable who have incited, ordered, procured, or counselled the commission of such acts, or who have taken what the Moscow Declaration describes as "a consenting part" therein.

The legal position which the United States will maintain, being thus based on the common sense of justice, is relatively simple and nontechnical. We must not permit it to be complicated or obscured by sterile legalisms developed in the age of imperialism to make war respectable.

Doubtless what appeals to men of good will and common sense as the crime which comprehends all lesser crimes, is the crime of making unjustifiable war. War necessarily is a calculated series of killings, of destructions of property, or oppressions. Such acts unquestionably would be criminal except that International Law throws a mantle of protection around acts which otherwise would be crimes when committed in pursuit of legitimate warfare. In this they are distinguished from the same acts in the pursuit of piracy or brigandage which have been considered punishable wherever and by whomever the guilty are caught. But International Law as taught in the Nineteenth and the early part of the Twentieth Century generally declared that war-making was not illegal and is no crime at law. Summarized by a standard authority, its attitude was that "both parties to every war are regarded as being in an identical legal position, and consequently as being possessed of equal rights." This, however, was a departure from the doctrine taught by Grotius, the father of International Law, that there is a distinction between the just and the unjust war—the war of defense and the war of aggression.

International law is more than a scholarly collection of abstract and immutable principles. It is an outgrowth of treaties or agreements between nations and of accepted customs. But every custom has its origin in some single act, and every agreement has to be initiated by the action of some state. Unless we are prepared to abandon every principle of growth for International Law, we cannot deny that our own day has its right to institute customs and to conclude agreements that will themselves become sources of a newer and strengthened International Law. International Law is not capable of development by legislation, for there is no continuously sitting international legislature. Innovations and revisions in International Law are brought about by the action of governments designed to meet a change in circumstances. It grows, as did the Common-law, through decisions reached from time to time in adapting settled principles to new situations. Hence I am not disturbed by the lack of precedent for the inquiry we propose to conduct. After the shock to civilization of the last World War, however, a marked reversion to the earlier and sounder doctrines of International Law took place. By the time the Nazis came to power it was thoroughly established that launching an aggressive war or the institution of war by treachery was illegal and that the defense of legitimate warfare was no longer available to those who engaged in

CHAPTER 5   THE LEGALITY PRINCIPLE   129

such an enterprise. It is high time that we act on the juridical principle that aggressive war-making is illegal and criminal. . . .

Respectfully yours,

(s) *Robert H. Jackson**

Questions

1. *Legality Principle Doctrines.* Give authority—statutory, constitutional, or caselaw—for each of the five doctrines listed in the introduction to this chapter that embody the legality principle. (See Model Penal Code §1.02(3) quoted below.)

2. *Legality Virtues.* Why adhere to the legality principle? Specifically, what are the reasons for, the societal benefits from, such a practice? What virtues do cases like *Papachristou* suggest? Presumably Modafi and his confederates know that their conduct is prohibited by the UNPPA. Will this undercut their legality principle claims? If not, why not?

3. *Legality Vices.* Are there disadvantages to adhering to the legality principle? If so, what? What alternative principle might one suggest? Does the prosecution of the Axis War Criminals satisfy the requirements of the legality principle? Does the "Propping Up Ed" hypothetical, below, suggest disadvantages to following the principle?

4. *Modafi's Liability.* Can Modafi be held liable for the new offenses created by the UNPPA? Can he be held liable for previously existing offenses and punished at the higher punishment levels provided by the UNPPA? If he claims diplomatic immunity from prosecution, should he get the defense? (Assume that the UNPPA provision in this regard is binding on all member states, including Modafi's.)

5. *Interpreting the UNPPA.* What is a "terroristic purpose," as required by the UNPPA? If Modafi gives a UN speech opposing a resolution calling for a crack-down on terrorists, has he entered for a

---

*Editor's Note.—In his closing argument for the Nazi war crime trials, Justice Jackson argued that the principle of analogy was one of the mechanisms that the Nazis used to seize power.

> The doctrine of punishment by analogy was introduced to enable conviction for acts which no statute forbade. [They] considered every violation of the goals of life which the community set up for itself to be a wrong per se, and that the act could be punished even though it was not contrary to existing "formal law."

Jackson, Closing Arguments for Conviction of Nazi War Criminals, 20 Temp. L.Q. 85-87 (1946).

"terroristic purpose"? If, in going to the UN to perform his duties, Modafi hopes to learn information about other delegates that will be useful in planning subsequent attacks against them, is he going to the UN for a "terroristic purpose"?

Propping Up Ed

Ella Trucker cares for several elderly people who are on public assistance. They pay for their room, board, and care during the preceding month by signing over to Mrs. Trucker their government check, which arrives at the end of the month. Her friend Canna Baker, who provides a similar service in another state, recently had a resident die during the month and, it appeared, would not be paid for the resident's month of room, board, and care.

On May 27th one of Mrs. Tucker's residents, Ed Raymond, dies. Mrs. Trucker is determined that she will not suffer an unfair loss. She drags Ed's body into the parlor and props it up near the window, where Ed frequently sat and where passers-by can see it. At regular intervals, she shifts his body to other locations in a pattern that simulates Ed's routine. When Ed's check arrives on the 30th, she makes Ed's "mark" as endorsement and takes it immediately to the bank. Upon her return, she decides to "keep Ed alive" until the next day to throw off any suspicion that might arise from the timing of his death. The next morning she calls the doctor and the undertaker to report that one of her residents has passed away. Upon examining the body, the doctor and undertaker are aghast at its decomposed condition. A brief police inquiry reveals what has happened.*

Mrs. Trucker is held liable for the forged check endorsement but the authorities consider her mistreatment of the corpse the more serious violation. The only relevant offense in the jurisdiction, "Abuse of Corpse," has been recently modified. Its prior form used language from Model Penal Code section 250.10—treatment of a corpse in a way that "would outrage ordinary family sensibilities." That formulation was invalidated as unconstitutionally vague in a prosecution of satanic cult members for using human body parts taken from morgues, funeral parlors, and cemeteries in cult rituals. The legislature has enacted the following, more specific offense that it expects will pass constitutional tests for vagueness:

---

* The case is based loosely on the facts of Baker v. State, 215 Ark. 851, 223 S.W.2d 809 (1949).

CHAPTER 5 THE LEGALITY PRINCIPLE 131

Abuse of Corpse. A person commits a misdemeanor if, knowing others would be offended by his conduct, he dismembers, disfigures, injures, or otherwise abuses any corpse, or he disturbs a buried corpse in any way.

Is Mrs. Trucker liable for Abuse of Corpse under this provision?

Model Penal Code §§1.02(3), 2.12(2) & (3)
Principles of Construction

Section 1.02. Principles of Construction

(3) The provisions of the Code shall be construed according to the fair import of their terms but when the language is susceptible of differing constructions it shall be interpreted to further the general purposes stated in this Section* and the special purposes of the particular provision involved. The discretionary powers conferred by the Code shall be exercised in accordance with the criteria stated in the Code and, insofar as such criteria are not decisive, to further the general purposes stated in this Section.

Section 2.12. De Minimis Infractions

The Court shall dismiss a prosecution if, having regard to the nature of the conduct charged to constitute an offense and the nature of the attendant circumstances, it finds that the defendant's conduct: . . .
 (2) did not actually cause or threaten the harm or evil sought to be prevented by the law defining the offense or did so only to an extent too trivial to warrant the condemnation of conviction; or
 (3) presents such other extenuations that it cannot reasonably be regarded as envisaged by the legislature in forbidding the offense. The Court shall not dismiss a prosecution under Subsection (3) of this Section without filing a written statement of its reasons.

Notes on the Interpretation of Criminal Statutes

Vagueness, Ambiguity, and Conflict Because words are not perfect representations of ideas and because unanticipated situations inevitably

---

 * Editor's Note.—These "general purposes" are contained in Model Penal Code §1.02(1), which is quoted and discussed in Chapter 2.

arise, criminal statutes, like all other statutes, frequently are unclear. As previously noted, vague language may invalidate a statute. If a statute's language is ambiguous, that is, if it is subject to two or more meanings, a court will be required to "interpret" the statute, to decide which of the possible meanings should be adopted. Interpretation problems also may arise where two or more statutes give conflicting directions, in which case the court must determine which of the two statutes is controlling.

Legislative Intent, Notice, and Analogy In such situations, courts are not free to choose the interpretation that they think results in the best rule or result. Recall that a central rationale of the legality principle is to reserve the criminalization decision to the legislative branch. It follows that a court's role in interpreting a criminal statute is to determine and follow the legislative intent. On the other hand, the legality principle also carries a concern for fair notice. If the legislative meaning is not obvious from the language of the statute, how can persons be expected to know the meaning? Further, the legislature frequently will not have addressed, or even thought about, some of the issues that give rise to an ambiguity. It may be complete speculation as to what the legislative view on the issue would have been. Finally, the principle of legality has its limitations. The contrasting principle of analogy offers greater flexibility and avoids artificial and unwise "technicalities" in the application of law. What, then, should a court do when faced with an ambiguous statute? Several rules of construction have been developed as guides.

Plain Meaning Rule Reaffirming the limited role of courts in interpreting statutes is the *plain meaning rule*. It provides that the inquiry into legislative intent and related interpretive strategies are to be used only if a clear ambiguity exists in the statutory language. No inquiry beyond the face of the statute is appropriate "[w]here the language is plain and admits of no more than one meaning."[1] Even the limited discretion inherent in some rules of construction is not available if a statute is unambiguous. The court must apply the plain meaning of the statute even if it strongly doubts the wisdom of the underlying policy.

Drafting Errors and Implied Exceptions On the other hand, it is said that a court need not mindlessly follow the literal language of a statute that clearly does not represent the legislative intent. A court may take note of an obvious drafting error.[2] A court may recognize logically

---

1. Caminetti v. United States, 242 U.S. 470, 485, 37 S. Ct. 192, 194, 61 L. Ed. 442, 453 (1917) (Mann Act prohibits transportation of female from one state to another "for the purpose of prostitution, debauchery or for other *immoral* purpose;" defendant transported willing girl to another state to have sexual relations with her; majority held that his purpose plainly fell within the intended meaning of "other immoral purpose").

2. See e.g., United States v. Gray, 633 F. Supp. 1311 (D. Mont. 1986) (construing statute that prohibited threats against judges' family members to apply also to threats against judges themselves; illogical for Congress to have intended to exclude judges themselves from the statute's protection).

implied exceptions.³ But in each case, the court must conclude that *the legislature* would see the statute as obviously containing a drafting error or implied exception. And the conclusion that the legislature would want to correct the obviously mistaken language cannot come simply from the fact that *the court* strongly believes the language as written reflects a bad policy.

Rules of Construction The abuse of corpse statute quoted above arguably is ambiguous when applied to Mrs. Trucker's conduct.⁴ She did not disturb a buried corpse, nor did she dismember or disfigure a corpse. Might her conduct nonetheless be construed as "abuse" of a corpse? Some standard rules have been recognized by courts as being useful in resolving ambiguous language. The rules are of three sorts: rules for interpreting the language within a statute, rules directing where a court may look outside of the statutory language, and, in criminal cases, a special rule setting the standard of interpretation, usually either the rule of strict construction or the rule of fair import.

Interpreting the Language of a Statute At least five rules have been recognized for interpreting ambiguous language on the face of a statute:

Different language implies a different meaning. Where a document uses different language in different parts, there is a presumption that the legislature intended different meanings by the different language.⁵

A catch-all phrase is limited by the common factor of the items in the list. Where a list of things ends in a catch-all phrase, such as "or other . . . ," the phrase must be interpreted to be limited to the theme or common factor of the specific entries in the list. This is called the rule of *ejusdem generis*.⁶

---

3. E.g., United States v. Kirby, 74 U.S. (7 Wall.) 482, 19 L. Ed. 278 (1869). The Supreme Court held that a policeman with a warrant for the arrest of a mail carrier for murder could not be found guilty of "knowingly and willfully" obstructing the passage of mail when arresting the carrier during his deliveries. Similarly, a policeman in reasonable pursuit of a fleeing criminal may not be charged with speeding. State v. Graham, 110 Wash. 330, 188 P. 457 (1920).

4. It may even be vague to a degree.

5. E.g., State v. Bradley, 215 Kan. 642, 527 P.2d 988 (1974) (the court, in construing a statute prohibiting interference with a uniformed police officer in performance of his duties, read the statute in light of one similar which dealt with firefighters and concluded that, because "knowingly" was included in the firefighter statute, absence of some such term in the police officer statute indicated that the legislature intended that scienter was not an element of a violation).

6. E.g., United States v. Powell, 423 U.S. 87, 96 S. Ct. 316, 46 L. Ed. 2d 228 (1975) (defendant should have known that her mailing of a 22-inch sawed-off shotgun was a violation of 18 U.S.C. §1715, proscribing the mailing of "pistols and revolvers and other firearms capable of being concealed on the person"); McBoyle v. United States, 283 U.S. 25, 51 S. Ct. 340, 75 L. Ed. 816 (1931) (the statute defined "vehicle" by listing automobiles, trucks, wagons, motorcycles, or any other self-propelled vehicle not designed to run on rails; defendant's conviction for transporting an airplane he knew to

The expression of one thing excludes implication of another. Where a statute sets forth a list of exceptions, for example, other exceptions are by implication excluded. This is the rule of *expressio unius; exclusio alterius.*[7]

The special controls the general. Two statutes may each apply to the same fact situation and may generate different results. Where this occurs, the rules of construction provide that the more specific statute has priority over the more general.[8]

The later controls the earlier. Where two statutes enacted at different times conflict, the rules of construction give priority to the later enactment over the earlier.[9]

Going Beyond the Language of the Statute If a conflict or ambiguity remains unresolved after applying these rules to the language on the face of a statute, a court may look beyond the literal language of the statute. Legislatures sometimes keep records, even transcripts, of their deliberations and sometimes even the deliberations of their committees. The United States Congress is particularly good in this regard. Some state legislatures are particularly bad. These records of the *legislative history* of a statute may be examined to see whether they reveal the interpretation intended by the legislature.[10] Where the statute was borrowed from another jurisdiction, the legislative history of that jurisdiction may be enlightening, although not as persuasive as that of the home jurisdiction itself. It is in this regard that the extensive Model Penal Code commentaries are particularly important and influential. Because the Code has been so widely adopted, its commentaries provide what is sometimes the only source of legislative history for many state

---

be stolen across state lines reversed because the statute was read only to apply to vehicles which moved on land).

7. E.g., People v. Nichols, 3 Cal. 3d 150, 89 Cal. Rptr. 721, 474 P.2d 673 (1970) (felony-murder statute inapplicable where death resulted from the malicious burning of a car because the arson statute included only "trailer coaches" and therefore did not extend to other vehicles).

8. E.g., State v. Collins, 55 Wash. 2d 469, 348 P.2d 214 (1960) (defendant had killed a pedestrian with his motor vehicle and was charged with manslaughter; Court held that the information was properly dismissed because the state's negligent homicide by means of a motor vehicle statute more specifically applies and controls over the general manslaughter statute).

9. E.g., Ex parte Chiapetto, 93 Cal. App. 2d 497, 209 P.2d 154 (1949) (petitioner for writ of habeas corpus discharged from jail after serving one year of a twenty-one month sentence because a recent general statute fixed the maximum sentence for misdemeanors at one year in county jail, impliedly repealing the earlier special statute applicable to petitioner, which had set the maximum sentence for the misdemeanor of contributing to the delinquency of a minor at two years; therefore, petitioner had served the maximum sentence).

10. For a discussion of how to find and use this history, see M. Cohen & R. Berring, How to Find the Law, ch. 10 (8th ed. 1983); G. Folsom, Legislative History (1972).

code provisions. Finally, an authoritative interpretation of a statute sometimes may be available from an agency or official empowered by the legislature to issue such interpretations. The legislative history of the abuse of corpse statute, which is likely to be thin, might focus primarily on the satanic cult problem with little anticipation of conduct like Mrs. Trucker's.

Special Status of Criminal Statutes Criminal statutes are subject to special rules of statutory interpretation, being held to a higher standard of precision and clarity than civil statutes. One might argue that, if the rules of construction described above must be brought to bear to determine the proper interpretation of a criminal statute, the goals of the legality principle already have been frustrated. Only lawyers and judges are likely to know these rules for interpreting ambiguous language on the face of a statute or to have access to legislative history and authoritative agency interpretations. Thus, while the general rules for construction of statutes described above are adequate for civil statutes, they sometimes are ignored in favor of a special rule of construction for criminal statutes, the rule of strict construction. Some writers, however, suggest that the special rule of strict construction should be applied only if an ambiguity is not resolved by one of the standard rules of construction described above.[11] Many modern codes reject the rule of strict construction altogether, preferring the rule of fair import discussed below.

Rule of Strict Construction Under the rule of strict construction, "ambiguity concerning the ambit of criminal statutes should be resolved in favor of lenity."[12] This Rule of Lenity, as it also is called, suggests that while the terms of a prohibition are to be strictly construed, the same does not apply to the terms of a defense. In this respect the "rule of strict construction" label is potentially misleading, and the "rule of lenity" is preferable. The former label survives because many courts refuse to apply the rule to defenses. Their reluctance here, and with the rule generally, may stem from the potential of the rule to give absurd results if too literally applied.

Strengths and Weaknesses of Strict Construction Given that the rule of strict construction is one aspect of the legality principle, it should be no surprise that it shares the virtues and vices of the principle. Most important, it furthers the interest of fair notice by barring application of an offense provision against a defendant if, under one interpretation of the provision, the defendant's conduct is not in violation. The rule

---

11. See, e.g., A. Ashworth, Principles of Criminal Law 69 (1991); see also State v. Muller, 365 So. 2d 464, 467 (La. 1978) ("criminal statutes found ambiguous even after being construed in accordance with the [rule of fair import are to] be construed strictly in favor of the defendant and lenity").

12. Bell v. United States, 349 U.S. 81, 83, 75 S. Ct. 620, 99 L. Ed. 905 (1955).

also serves to preserve the criminalization authority to the legislature by preventing a court from expanding an offense by adopting a broad interpretation of its language. On the other hand, the rule can frustrate a legislature's obvious intent on what can be an important issue and risks bringing the criminal justice system into disrepute, as a game governed by technicalities having little relation to fairness or justice. A literal application of the rule of strict construction to the abuse of corpse statute would leave people free to do anything to or with a dead body except literally dismember, disfigure, injure, or abuse it (in the narrow, physical harm sense). Dead bodies as hood ornaments would be legal as long as the restraining device was adequate.

Rule of Fair Import Because of the dangers of the rule of strict construction and in recognition of the greater attention that has been given to clarity and precision when modern criminal codes are drafted, most current codes abrogate the rule of strict construction and adopt instead a rule of fair import.

> The rule of the common law, that penal statutes are to be strictly construed, has no application to this Code. All its provisions are to be construed according to the fair import of their terms, with a view to effect its objects and to promote justice.[13]

The fair import rule gives courts the authority to interpret statutes in a way that does not frustrate the legislative purpose yet, by relying upon the *fair import of the terms,* seeks to assure that some reasonable notice of the offense is possible. In that sense, the rule of fair import attempts a compromise between the virtues of legality and its countervailing interests (as found in the principle of analogy).

Judicial Discretion Under the Rule of Strict Construction Despite appearances, it is unclear just how different the two rules are in application. An appearance of difference may come from the tendency to overestimate the literalness with which judges apply the rule of strict construction. If the rule of strict construction were applied literally, it would require no exercise of discretion: If an interpretation more favorable to the defendant is offered it must be adopted. But courts rarely apply the rule in mindless disregard for the intended meaning of its language. First, the rule of strict construction only applies if there is an ambiguity, and it is for the court to decide whether an ambiguity exists. An absurd and farfetched interpretation may simply be ignored by a court as not raising an ambiguity. Where an interpretation is opposed by the defendant as constituting a judicial expansion of criminal liability in violation of the prohibition against judicial legislation, it can be defended on the ground that it simply represents the first-

---

13. Calif. Penal Code §4.

time application of previously-existing legislative criminalization. Would liability for Mrs. Trucker "extend" the prohibition of the abuse-of-corpse statute or simply mark the first time that body-propping has been brought to the attention of the authorities? It is the court that is to decide which characterization to adopt, even under a rule of strict construction.

Exceptions to Strict Construction Further, the rule of strict construction has been tempered with the exception that a statute is "not to be construed so strictly as to defeat the obvious intention of the legislature"[14] or "to override common sense."[15] Nor is it necessary that a statute be given its "narrowest meaning"[16] or a "forced, narrow or overstrict construction."[17] In other words, in practice, courts exercise considerable discretion in determining whether a "legitimate" ambiguity exists and in choosing among interpretations, even under the apparently mechanical rule of strict construction.

Practical Significance of Strict Construction vs. Fair Import Once it is admitted that strict construction admits judicial discretion in interpretation, much as the fair import test more explicitly calls for discretion, it is less clear that the rules generate a significant difference in application. In judging whether to recognize a defendant's claimed alternative interpretation under a rule of strict construction, a court is likely to look at such things as the common or fair meaning of the terms and the legislative purpose of the provision. Of course, this is precisely what a court is directed to consider under the fair import test. One might argue that the tests retain a significant difference in application because a fair import rule is more likely to induce a court to follow legislative

---

14. Barrett v. United States, 423 U.S. 212, 218, 96 S. Ct. 498, 502, 46 L. Ed. 2d 450, 455 (1976), quoting American Fur Co. v. United States, 2 Pet. 358, 367, 7 L. Ed. 450 (1829) (conviction for illegal possession of a firearm which had been transported in interstate commerce prior to and independently of defendant's intrastate purchase of the firearm affirmed because the Court held that Congress would have explicitly confined the scope of the statute to direct interstate receipt had it intended such a limitation).

15. United States v. Moore, 423 U.S. 122, 145, 96 S. Ct. 335, 347, 46 L. Ed. 2d 333, 349 (1975), quoting United States v. Brown, 333 U.S. 18, 25, 68 S. Ct. 376, 380, 92 L. Ed. 442 (1948) (physician's conviction for unlawful distribution of methadone reinstated where such distribution fell outside the usual course of his practice; the Court declined to construe the statute strictly to establish a separate penalty system for physicians because Congress' concern was with the nature of the drug transaction rather than with the status of the parties to the transaction).

16. Id. at 145, 96 S. Ct. at 347, 46 L. Ed. 2d at 349; Dover, 664 P.2d at 540.

17. State v. Carter, 89 Wash. 2d 236, 242, 570 P.2d 1218, 1221 (1977) (strict construction of a statute which prohibited pimping resulted in holding that a particular subsection of the statute did not require "actual procurement of another and placement in a house of prostitution" even though other subsections of the statute did require actual results); United States v. Gray, 633 F. Supp. 1311 (D. Mont. 1986) (under rule of strict construction, threat to federal judge held prohibited by statute criminalizing threats to family of a federal judge).

intent that conflicts with a literal reading. That is, judges will be more hesitant to deviate from a strict reading under a rule of strict construction that does not on its face appear to permit such deviation. But the validity of such psychological speculations are difficult to assess. The primary difference between the tests may be the *admission* that judicial discretion is at work under fair import and the apparent denial of such discretion under strict construction.[18] Some courts may prefer the strict construction test for just this reason. The rule permits discretion yet appears mechanical and thereby leaves the court's decision less open to criticism.

Effect of De Minimis Defense In addition to explicitly adopting a rule of fair import, many modern codes follow the lead of the Model Penal Code in providing a defense for what it calls "de minimis infractions." In reality, the provision has a broader effect than simply providing a defense for trivial harms, such as taking a piece of bubble gum. It directs a court to exempt from liability conduct that, for any of a variety of reasons, was not meant to be covered by the offense. It calls upon a judge to dismiss a prosecution if the defendant's conduct did not cause or threaten "the harm or evil sought to be prevented by the law defining the offense" or if it occurred under such conditions that "it cannot reasonably be regarded as envisaged by the legislature in forbidding the offense."[19] The provision explicitly directs the court to do what the rules of construction are designed to achieve: to dismiss a prosecution if, in the judge's view, the case at hand was not intended by the legislature to be punished by conviction for the offense charged. For the sake of clarity, these two distinct aspects of the "de minimis" defense might best be segregated, into a defense for trivial harms and a defense for "conduct not envisioned by the offense."

An Unresolvable Tension? In the end, none of these rules of construction gives a clear or easy answer to the range of ambiguities that can arise. Is Mrs. Trucker's conduct within the statute or not? Presumably the legislature would prohibit it if asked; such a prohibition makes good sense. On the other hand, are our notions of procedural fairness satisfied if we punish Mrs. Trucker's conduct in displaying Ed, under a statute that punishes "dismembering, disfiguring, injuring, or other abuse"? The absence of clear rules with clean results may be inevitable. In one sense, ambiguities in statutes create an unresolvable conflict

---

18. For a more detailed analysis of the differences, see Hall, Strict or Liberal Construction of Penal Statutes, 48 Harv. L. Rev. 748, 756-762 (1935); Jeffries, Legality, Vagueness, and the Construction of Penal Statutes, 71 Va. L. Rev. 189 (1985).

19. See Model Penal Code §2.12. The section also directs the court to dismiss the prosecution if the conduct is within customary license or tolerance, not inconsistent with the purpose of the law, another instance in which the legislature presumably would not intend the offense to apply.

among interests that are each important to us; they are the points of tension within the legality principle and between that principle and the principle of analogy. We prefer to apply statutes as they read, for this is the best way to assure fair notice. We also prefer to interpret statutes to give rational results consistent with the legislative intent. But, in reality, applying a statute as written can give irrational results contrary to the legislative intent. We prefer that the legislature rather than judges make the criminalization decisions. Yet, if a statute is ambiguous, we must either turn to judges to fix it or suffer the legislative purpose to be frustrated. There is no obvious means of resolving the conflict among these interests—rational and effective criminalization, fair notice, and preservation of the legislative criminalization power. The conflict does not arise if every statute is perfectly clear and anticipates every possible form of violation but, even if legislative drafting is perfect, language is not. There seems little alternative other than to have judges continue to balance the competing interests as each case arises.

United States v. Gray
Problem Case

Defendant James Edward Gray was tried before a jury on March 24, 1986 and convicted of knowingly and willfully threatening to murder a United States district judge with the intent to intimidate or retaliate against such judicial officer on account of the performance of his official duties. Defendant subsequently filed a timely motion renewing his motion for judgement of acquittal, which he made at the commencement of trial, immediately following impaneling of the jury. The pending motion does not appear to challenge the sufficiency of the evidence. Rather, defendant contends the indictment filed against him does not charge an offense. . . .

The indictment charges:

> That on or about the 12th day of August 1985, at Deer Lodge, in the state and District of Montana, James Edward Gray did knowingly and willfully threaten to murder the Honorable Paul G. Hatfield, a duly appointed United States District Judge for the District of Montana, with intent to intimidate or retaliate against Judge Hatfield on account of the performance of his official duties, in violation of Title 18 U.S.C. §115(a). . . .

. . . Section 115 provides in part:

> Whoever assaults, kidnaps, or murders, or attempts to kidnap or murder, or threatens to assault, kidnap or murder a member of the immediate

family of a United States official, judge or law enforcement officer while he is engaged in, or on account of, the performance of his official duties, shall be punished as provided in subsection (b).

[Defendant interprets the statute as making it a crime to threaten only family members of federal officials, not the federal officials themselves.]
   . . . Section 1114 provides in part:

Whoever kills or attempts to kill any judge of the United States, . . . shall be punished as provided under Sections 1111 and 1112 of this title, except that any such person who is found guilty of attempted murder shall be imprisoned for not more than twenty years.

[On its face the statute does not appear to punish mere threats to a federal judge.]

Questions

1. *Abuse of Corpse.* Is Mrs. Trucker liable under the Abuse of Corpse statute quoted above? Is the statute vague? Is it ambiguous? Do the five interpretation rules described in the Notes clarify the meaning of the statute? If not, what does a court do to resolve the case? If the Rule of Strict Construction is applied to the Abuse of Corpse statute, what result for Mrs. Trucker? Would human body hood ornaments be permissible under the statute, as long as they are fastened on securely? If the Rule of Fair Import is applied, what result for Mrs. Trucker?

2. *Strict Construction vs. Fair Import.* If defense counsel comes up with a narrow interpretation of the offense charged that would not include the defendant's conduct and the jurisdiction uses the Rule of Strict Construction, must the judge adopt that interpretation even if she thinks the interpretation is silly or bizarre? If not, what kind of factors is a judge likely to take into account in judging whether the offered interpretation is "legitimate" rather than silly or bizarre? How do these factors differ from the factors that a judge is likely to take into account in applying the Rule of Fair Import?

3. *Is a Judge a Member of His or Her Family?* Is the statute in *Gray* clear on its face? If not, what is the ambiguous language? The prosecutor in *Gray* may argue that the statute contains an obvious drafting error: It would be absurd to prohibit threats to immediate family members and not to judges themselves. There is some authority for allowing a court to correct an obvious drafting error. Is that the case here? What if defense counsel offers a policy argument in support of the statute's

CHAPTER 5 THE LEGALITY PRINCIPLE 141

language as written? (Family members need greater protection under the statute because federal security cannot hope to cover so many people. *Threats* against public officials, including judges, are not prohibited because the legislature was concerned about infringing free speech. No similar free speech concern exists for threats against family members.) Is Gray liable under the offense?

Chapter 6. PROVING CRIMES

The "burden of proof" for an issue may refer to any one of at least three distinct evidentiary burdens: the burden of pleading (or "burden of going forward"), the burden of production, and the burden of persuasion. After a brief description of each of these burdens and how they differ from one another, the chapter examines the constitutional limitations on how the burdens may be allocated and defined.

The Burdens of Pleading, Production, and Persuasion
P. Robinson, 1 Criminal Law Defenses §3 (1984)

(a) The Burden of Pleading

The burden of introducing an issue for consideration is comparable to the "burden of pleading" in a civil trial; it means simply that if a party wants to raise an issue it must say so. The party bearing the burden of pleading on a matter is the party who will benefit from raising the issue. For elements of the offense, that party is the state; for criminal law defenses, that party generally is the defendant. The defenses of insanity or duress, for example, will not be discussed in a case unless the defendant indicates his interest in raising the issue. If he says nothing, there is little reason for a court to assume anything other than that the defendant was neither insane nor coerced.

The burden of pleading is not exactly a "burden," and certainly not a true "burden of proof." There is no significant quantum of evidence that the defendant must produce to satisfy the burden. Any evidence, even a bare claim, will be sufficient to raise the issue.

The burden of pleading frequently has no independent significance in criminal cases for two reasons. First in every case, the state must plead every element of the offense charged. If a "defense" simply negates a required element of an offense, the existence of the element will be an issue even if the defendant does not raise it. The judge is always obliged to instruct the jury on all required elements of the offense charged. Thus, the burden of pleading for such a defense is only important if the defendant has a special theory for arguing the absence of the required element that requires a special instruction beyond the requirement of the element itself. In such a case, he may bear the burden of pleading that special theory. For example, if the defendant wishes the jury to consider the effect of his intoxication at the time of the crime on his ability to form a required intent, he will have to raise the issue of intoxication in order to have that fact considered in evaluating the issue of intent. But for most simple failure of proof defenses—"I did not do it" or "it was an accident"—no special instruction is necessary.

A second reason the burden of pleading may not be significant is that the defendant frequently will have the *burden of production* on most defenses other than those negating a required element; this is the case with the defenses of insanity and duress, for example. As discussed in subsection (b) of this section, the burden of production requires that the defendant produce a certain amount of evidence supporting the defense in order to have it presented to the jury. Thus, where the burden of production is imposed on the defendant, the burden of pleading is subsumed in that requirement and thus has no independent significance.

The burden of pleading retains independent significance only for special theories negating a required element and for those defenses that do not negate an element for which the defendant does not have the burden of production. In perjury, for example, retraction may be a defense, yet the prosecution, not the defense, frequently bears the burden of production on that issue. Thus, the burden of pleading has practical significance, as it should. It would be unnecessary and wasteful if the issue of whether the defendant satisfies the requirements of a retraction defense were considered where the defendant did not seek to raise that claim. Indeed, it would be difficult, if not impossible, for the prosecution to show the absence of a retraction unless the defendant first alleged when and how he made a retraction. The defendant, then, is properly required to plead the defense of retraction.

(b) The Burden of Production

The "burden of production" serves to exclude legal issues that are not sufficiently supported by the evidence from consideration by the jury, and thus seeks to avoid verdicts based on conjecture. The burden demands a legal assessment of the sufficiency of the evidence. The party bearing the burden of production must adduce sufficient evidence to either support or negate, as the case may be, the presence of an offense element or a defense. The general rule is that the party benefiting from having the issue presented to the jury must carry the burden of production on that issue. The prosecution has the burden of production for all elements of the offense. But the prosecution also is sometimes given the burden of producing evidence of the absence of a defense.

If the prosecution fails to meet its burden of production for an offense element, the case is dismissed (on the theory that, if the prosecution cannot meet its burden of production, it would be unable to meet its higher burden of persuasion). As to a defense, if the defendant successfully meets his burden of production, or if the prosecution fails to meet its burden to show the absence of the defense, the defense will be presented to the jury. Conversely, if the defendant fails to carry his burden for the defense, or the prosecution successfully carries its burden against the defense, the defense will not be presented to the jury. . . .

The burden of production must be distinguished from the *burden of pleading*, discussed above. The latter simply imposes an obligation on the burdened party to raise the issue. The former imposes a standard of evidence that must be met if the burdened party is to be successful in having the issue presented to or withheld from the jury, as the case may be. The burden of pleading is simply the first step in the evidentiary battle. Where the defendant meets his burden of pleading for a defense, for example, subsequent evidence by the prosecution may so discredit the defendant's initial claim as to leave the defendant in the same position with regard to the burden of production as before he presented his initial evidence. Unless he presents further evidence supporting the defense, he will not satisfy his burden of production, and the defense will not be presented to the jury.

(c) The Burden of Persuasion

The "burden of persuasion" seeks to guide a trier of fact who is in doubt, and indicates the decision that must be reached in the presence of a given degree of doubt. The party bearing the burden of persuasion with respect to an issue is at a disadvantage. Where the trier of fact entertains a sufficient degree of doubt, the issue must be decided in favor of the opposing party. Thus the burden of persuasion is said to define and allocate the "risk of nonpersuasion."

The term "affirmative defense" sometimes is used to indicate that the defendant bears the burden of production and sometimes to indicate that the defendant bears both the burden of production and the burden of persuasion. . . .

(d) Burden of Production vs. Burden of
    Persuasion—Allocation of the Burden

The burdens of production and persuasion may be placed on the same party. The prosecution has both the burden of production and persuasion for all elements of an offense. As to a defense, the prosecution may have the duty to introduce evidence disproving a defense in order to avoid a directed verdict, and later, having reached the jury, to persuade the jury of the defense's nonexistence. Or, the defendant may be obliged to introduce sufficient evidence supporting a defense in order to have the jury instructed on the defense, and, having done so, may have the burden of convincing the jury of its existence. Commonly, however, the burden of proving a criminal defense is divided: the defendant shouldering the burden of production and the prosecution shouldering the burden of persuasion. There are, however, many exceptions to this.

(e) Burden of Production vs. Burden of Persuasion—The
    Standard

The standards for satisfying the burden of production and the burden of persuasion address very different issues, each closely related to the function of the respective burdens. The standard of the burden of production establishes the minimum quantum of evidence sufficient to allow a reasonable trier of fact to decide the issue. The standard of the burden of persuasion establishes a permissible degree of doubt and identifies the party who must lose where the doubt is too great.

The standard of the burden of persuasion in a criminal trial commonly varies depending upon the party bearing the burden. Generally, where the prosecution bears the burden of persuasion, the trier of fact must be convinced "beyond a reasonable doubt"; where the defendant bears the burden, the fact finder need be convinced only by "a preponderance of the evidence." In contrast, the burden of production generally does not vary with the party burdened. However, some have argued that the burden of production should vary with the standard set for the burden of persuasion, and that standard may well vary with the party burdened.

(f) Burden of Production vs. Burden of Persuasion—The
    Tribunal

The tribunal entrusted with determining whether the burden of production has been met is always the judge. The determination is, after all, a legal one, the legal sufficiency of the evidence. With some

CHAPTER 6 PROVING CRIMES

important exceptions, the jury typically determines whether a party has met its burden of persuasion. The exceptions include instances where a jury trial has been waived and where a defense is specially designated as one for the court to grant or deny. Where the judge sits as the trier of fact, the burden of production is, as a practical matter, of diminished significance because that burden, recall, serves simply to control the issues that will be presented to the trier of fact.

Model Penal Code §1.12
Proof Beyond a Reasonable Doubt; Affirmative Defenses; Burden of Proving Fact When Not an Element of an Offense; Presumptions

(1) No person may be convicted of an offense unless each element of such offense is proved beyond a reasonable doubt. In the absence of such proof, the innocence of the defendant is assumed.

(2) Subsection (1) of this Section does not:

(a) require the disproof of an affirmative defense unless and until there is evidence supporting such defense; or

(b) apply to any defense which the Code or another statute plainly requires the defendant to prove by a preponderance of evidence.

(3) A ground of defense is affirmative, within the meaning of Subsection (2)(a) of this Section, when:

(a) it arises under a section of the Code which so provides; or

(b) it relates to an offense defined by a statute other than the Code and such statute so provides; or

(c) it involves a matter of excuse or justification peculiarly within the knowledge of the defendant on which he can fairly be required to adduce supporting evidence.

(4) When the application of the Code depends upon the finding of a fact which is not an element of an offense, unless the Code otherwise provides:

(a) the burden of proving the fact is on the prosecution or defendant, depending on whose interest or contention will be furthered if the finding should be made; and

(b) the fact must be proved to the satisfaction of the Court or jury, as the case may be.

(5) When the Code establishes a presumption with respect to any fact which is an element of an offense, it has the following consequences:

(a) when there is evidence of the facts which give rise to the presumption, the issue of the existence of the presumed fact must be submitted to the jury, unless the Court is satisfied that the evidence as a whole clearly negatives the presumed fact; and

(b) when the issue of the existence of the presumed fact is submitted to the jury, the Court shall charge that while the presumed fact must, on all the evidence, be proved beyond a reasonable doubt, the law declares that the jury may regard the facts giving rise to the presumption as sufficient evidence of the presumed fact.

(6) A presumption not established by the Code or inconsistent with it has the consequences otherwise accorded it by law.

Patterson v. New York
Supreme Court of the United States
432 U.S. 197, 97 S. Ct. 2319, 53 L. Ed. 2d 281 (1977)

Mr. Justice WHITE delivered the opinion of the Court.

The question here is the constitutionality under the Fourteenth Amendment's Due Process Clause of burdening the defendant in a New York State murder trial with proving the affirmative defense of extreme emotional disturbance as defined by New York law.

I

After a brief and unstable marriage, the appellant, Gordon Patterson, Jr., became estranged from his wife, Roberta. Roberta resumed an association with John Northrup, a neighbor to whom she had been engaged prior to her marriage to appellant. On December 27, 1970, Patterson borrowed a rifle from an acquaintance and went to the residence of his father-in-law. There, he observed his wife through a window in a state of semiundress in the presence of John Northrup. He entered the house and killed Northrup by shooting him twice in the head.

Patterson was charged with second-degree murder. In New York there are two elements of this crime: (1) "intent to cause the death of another person"; and (2) "caus[ing] the death of such person or of a third person." N.Y. Penal Law §125.25 (McKinney 1975). Malice aforethought is not an element of the crime. In addition, the State permits a person accused of murder to raise an affirmative defense that he "acted under the influence of extreme emotional disturbance for which there was a reasonable explanation or excuse."*

New York also recognizes the crime of manslaughter. A person is guilty of manslaughter if he intentionally kills another person "under circumstances which do not constitute murder because he acts under

---

*Editor's Note.—Section 125.25 is reproduced in Section 4.1.

the influence of extreme emotional disturbance."† Appellant confessed before trial to killing Northrup, but at trial he raised the defense of extreme emotional disturbance.

The jury was instructed as to the elements of the crime of murder. Focusing on the element of intent, the trial court charged:

> Before you, considering all of the evidence, can convict this defendant or anyone of murder, you must believe and decide that the People have established beyond a reasonable doubt that he intended, in firing the gun, to kill either the victim himself or some other human being. . . .
>
> Always remember that you must not expect or require the defendant to prove to your satisfaction that his acts were done without the intent to kill. Whatever proof he may have attempted, however far he may have gone in an effort to convince you of his innocence or guiltlessness, he is not obliged, he is not obligated to prove anything. It is always the People's burden to prove his guilt, and to prove that he intended to kill in this instance beyond a reasonable doubt.

The jury was further instructed, consistently with New York law, that the defendant had the burden of proving his affirmative defense by a preponderance of the evidence. The jury was told that if it found beyond a reasonable doubt that appellant had intentionally killed Northrup but that appellant had demonstrated by a preponderance of the evidence that he had acted under the influence of extreme emotional disturbance, it had to find appellant guilty of manslaughter instead of murder.

The jury found appellant guilty of murder. Judgment was entered on the verdict, and the Appellate Division affirmed. While appeal to the New York Court of Appeals was pending, this Court decided Mullaney v. Wilbur, 421 U.S. 684 (1975), in which the Court declared Maine's murder statute unconstitutional. Under the Maine statute, a person accused of murder could rebut the statutory presumption that he committed the offense with "malice aforethought" by proving that he acted in the heat of passion on sudden provocation. The Court held that this scheme improperly shifted the burden of persuasion from the prosecutor to the defendant and was therefore a violation of due process. In the Court of Appeals appellant urged that New York's murder statute is functionally equivalent to the one struck down in *Mullaney* and that therefore his conviction should be reversed.

The Court of Appeals rejected appellant's argument, holding that the New York murder statute is consistent with due process. The Court distinguished *Mullaney* on the ground that the New York statute involved no shifting of the burden to the defendant to disprove any fact essential

---

†Editor's Note.—Section 125.20(2) is reproduced in Section 4.1.

to the offense charged since the New York affirmative defense of extreme emotional disturbance bears no direct relationship to any element of murder. This appeal ensued, and we noted probable jurisdiction. We affirm.

II

It goes without saying that preventing and dealing with crime is much more the business of the States than it is of the Federal Government, and that we should not lightly construe the Constitution so as to intrude upon the administration of justice by the individual States. Among other things, it is normally "within the power of the State to regulate procedures under which its laws are carried out, including the burden of producing evidence and the burden of persuasion," and its decision in this regard is not subject to proscription under the Due Process Clause unless "it offends some principle of justice so rooted in the traditions and conscience of our people as to be ranked as fundamental." Leland v. Oregon, 343 U.S. 790, 798 (1952).

In determining whether New York's allocation to the defendant of proving the mitigating circumstances of severe emotional disturbance is consistent with due process, it is therefore relevant to note that this defense is a considerably expanded version of the common-law defense of heat of passion on sudden provocation and that at common law the burden of proving the latter, as well as other affirmative defenses—indeed, "all . . . circumstances of justification, excuse or alleviation"—rested on the defendant. This was the rule when the Fifth Amendment was adopted, and it was the American rule when the Fourteenth Amendment was ratified.

In 1895 the common-law view was abandoned with respect to the insanity defense in federal prosecutions. Davis v. United States, 160 U.S. 469 (1895). This ruling had wide impact on the practice in the federal courts with respect to the burden of proving various affirmative defenses, and the prosecution in a majority of jurisdictions in this country sooner or later came to shoulder the burden of proving the sanity of the accused and of disproving the facts constituting other affirmative defenses, including provocation. *Davis* was not a constitutional ruling, however, as Leland v. Oregon made clear.

At issue in Leland v. Oregon was the constitutionality under the Due Process Clause of the Oregon rule that the defense of insanity must be proved by the defendant beyond a reasonable doubt. Noting that *Davis* "obviously establish[ed] no constitutional doctrine," the Court refused to strike down the Oregon scheme, saying that the burden of proving all elements of the crime beyond reasonable doubt, including the elements of premeditation and deliberation, was placed on the

State under Oregon procedures and remained there throughout the trial. To convict, the jury was required to find each element of the crime beyond a reasonable doubt, based on all the evidence, including the evidence going to the issue of insanity. Only then was the jury "to consider separately the issue of legal sanity *per se*. . . ." This practice did not offend the Due Process Clause even though among the 20 States then placing the burden of proving his insanity on the defendant, Oregon was alone in requiring him to convince the jury beyond a reasonable doubt.

In 1970, the Court declared that the Due Process Clause "protects the accused against conviction except upon proof beyond a reasonable doubt of every fact necessary to constitute the crime with which he is charged." In re Winship, 397 U.S. 358, 364 (1970). Five years later, in Mullaney v. Wilbur, 421 U.S. 684 (1975), the Court further announced that under the Maine law of homicide, the burden could not constitutionally be placed on the defendant of proving by a preponderance of the evidence that the killing had occurred in the heat of passion on sudden provocation. The Chief Justice and Mr. Justice Rehnquist, concurring, expressed their understanding that the *Mullaney* decision did not call into question the ruling in Leland v. Oregon, with respect to the proof of insanity.

Subsequently, the Court confirmed that it remained constitutional to burden the defendant with proving his insanity defense when it dismissed, as not raising a substantial federal question, a case in which the appellant specifically challenged the continuing validity of Leland v. Oregon. This occurred in Rivera v. Delaware, 429 U.S. 877 (1976), an appeal from a Delaware conviction which, in reliance on *Leland*, had been affirmed by the Delaware Supreme Court over the claim that the Delaware statute was unconstitutional because it burdened the defendant with proving his affirmative defense of insanity by a preponderance of the evidence. The claim in this Court was that *Leland* had been overruled by *Winship* and *Mullaney*. We dismissed the appeal as not presenting a substantial federal question.

III

We cannot conclude that Patterson's conviction under the New York law deprived him of due process of law. The crime of murder is defined by the statute, which represents a recent revision of the state criminal code, as causing the death of another person with intent to do so. The death, the intent to kill, and causation are the facts that the State is required to prove beyond a reasonable doubt if a person is to be convicted of murder. No further facts are either presumed or inferred in order to constitute the crime. The statute does provide an affirmative defense—that the defendant acted under the influence of extreme emotional disturbance for which there was a reasonable explanation—which, if proved by a preponderance of the evidence, would reduce the crime to manslaughter, an offense defined in a separate section of the statute. It is plain enough that if the intentional killing is shown, the State intends to deal with the defendant as a murderer unless he demonstrates the mitigating circumstances.

Here, the jury was instructed in accordance with the statute, and the guilty verdict confirms that the State successfully carried its burden of proving the facts of the crime beyond a reasonable doubt. Nothing in the evidence, including any evidence that might have been offered with respect to Patterson's mental state at the time of the crime, raised a reasonable doubt about his guilt as a murderer; and clearly the evidence failed to convince the jury that Patterson's affirmative defense had been made out. It seems to us that the State satisfied the mandate of *Winship* that it prove beyond a reasonable doubt "every fact necessary to constitute the crime with which [Patterson was] charged."

In convicting Patterson under its murder statute, New York did no more than *Leland* and *Rivera* permitted it to do without violating the Due Process Clause. Under those cases, once the facts constituting a crime are established beyond a reasonable doubt, based on all the evidence including the evidence of the defendant's mental state, the State may refuse to sustain the affirmative defense of insanity unless demonstrated by a preponderance of the evidence.

The New York law on extreme emotional disturbance follows this pattern. This affirmative defense, which the Court of Appeals described as permitting "the defendant to show that his actions were caused by a mental infirmity not arising to the level of insanity, and that he is less culpable for having committed them," does not serve to negative any facts of the crime which the State is to prove in order to convict of murder. It constitutes a separate issue on which the defendant is required to carry the burden of persuasion; and unless we are to overturn *Leland* and *Rivera,* New York has not violated the Due Process Clause, and Patterson's conviction must be sustained.

We are unwilling to reconsider *Leland* and *Rivera*. But even if we were to hold that a State must prove sanity to convict once that fact is put in issue, it would not necessarily follow that a State must prove beyond a reasonable doubt every fact, the existence or nonexistence of which it is willing to recognize as an exculpatory or mitigating circumstance affecting the degree of culpability or the severity of the punishment. Here, in revising its criminal code, New York provided the affirmative defense of extreme emotional disturbance, a substantially expanded version of the older heat-of-passion concept; but it was willing to do so only if the facts making out the defense were established by the defendant with sufficient certainty. The State was itself unwilling to undertake to establish the absence of those facts beyond a reasonable doubt, perhaps fearing that proof would be too difficult and that too many persons deserving treatment as murderers would escape that punishment if the evidence need merely raise a reasonable doubt about the defendant's emotional state. It has been said that the new criminal code of New York contains some 25 affirmative defenses which exculpate or mitigate but which must be established by the defendant to be operative. The Due Process Clause, as we see it, does not put New York to the choice of abandoning those defenses or undertaking to disprove their existence in order to convict of a crime which otherwise is within its constitutional powers to sanction by substantial punishment.

The requirement of proof beyond a reasonable doubt in a criminal case is "bottomed on a fundamental value determination of our society that it is far worse to convict an innocent man than to let a guilty man go free." *Winship*, 397 U.S., at 372 (Harlan, J., concurring). The social cost of placing the burden on the prosecution to prove guilt beyond a reasonable doubt is thus an increased risk that the guilty will go free. While it is clear that our society has willingly chosen to bear a substantial burden in order to protect the innocent, it is equally clear that the risk it must bear is not without limits; and Mr. Justice Harlan's aphorism provides little guidance for determining what those limits are. Due process does not require that every conceivable step be taken, at whatever cost, to eliminate the possibility of convicting an innocent person. Punishment of those found guilty by a jury, for example, is not forbidden merely because there is a remote possibility in some instances that an innocent person might go to jail.

It is said that the common-law rule permits a State to punish one as a murderer when it is as likely as not that he acted in the heat of passion or under severe emotional distress and when, if he did, he is guilty only of manslaughter. But this has always been the case in those jurisdictions adhering to the traditional rule. It is also very likely true that fewer convictions of murder would occur if New York were required to negative the affirmative defense at issue here. But in each instance of a murder conviction under the present law, New York will have proved beyond a reasonable doubt that the defendant has intentionally killed another person, an act which it is not disputed the State may constitutionally criminalize and punish. If the State nevertheless chooses to recognize a factor that mitigates the degree of criminality or punishment, we think the State may assure itself that the fact has been established with reasonable certainty. To recognize at all a mitigating circumstance does not require the State to prove its nonexistence in each case in which the fact is put in issue, if in its judgment this would be too cumbersome, too expensive, and too inaccurate.

We thus decline to adopt as a constitutional imperative, operative countrywide, that a State must disprove beyond a reasonable doubt every fact constituting any and all affirmative defenses related to the culpability of an accused. Traditionally, due process has required that only the most basic procedural safeguards be observed; more subtle balancing of society's interests against those of the accused have been left to the legislative branch. We therefore will not disturb the balance struck in previous cases holding that the Due Process Clause requires the prosecution to prove beyond a reasonable doubt all of the elements included in the definition of the offense of which the defendant is charged. Proof of the nonexistence of all affirmative defenses has never been constitutionally required; and we perceive no reason to fashion such a rule in this case and apply it to the statutory defense at issue here.

This view may seem to permit state legislatures to reallocate burdens of proof by labeling as affirmative defenses at least some elements of the crimes now defined in their statutes. But there are obviously constitutional limits beyond which the States may not go in this regard. "[I]t is not within the province of a legislature to declare an individual guilty or presumptively guilty of a crime." McFarland v. American Sugar Rfg. Co., 241 U.S. 79, 86 (1916). The legislature cannot "validly command that the finding of an indictment, or mere proof of the identity of the accused, should create a presumption of the existence of all the facts essential to guilt." Tot v. United States, 319 U.S. 463, 469 (1943).

Long before *Winship,* the universal rule in this county was that the prosecution must prove guilt beyond a reasonable doubt. At the same time, the long-accepted rule was that it was constitutionally permissible to provide that various affirmative defenses were to be proved by the defendant. This did not lead to such abuses or to such widespread redefinition of crime and reduction of the prosecution's burden that a new constitutional rule was required. This was not the problem to which *Winship* was addressed. Nor does the fact that a majority of the States have now assumed the burden of disproving affirmative defenses—for whatever reasons—mean that those States that strike a different balance are in violation of the Constitution.

It is urged that Mullaney v. Wilbur necessarily invalidates Patterson's convictions. In *Mullaney* the charge was murder, which the Maine statute defined as the unlawful killing of a human being "with malice aforethought, either express or implied." The trial court instructed the jury that the words "malice aforethought" were most important because "malice aforethought is an essential and indispensable element of the crime of murder." Malice, as the statute indicated and as the court instructed, could be implied and *(was to be implied)* from "*any deliberate, cruel act* committed by one person against another suddenly . . . or *without a considerable provocation,*" in which event an intentional killing was murder unless by a preponderance of the evidence it was shown that the act was committed "in the heat of passion, on sudden provocation." The instructions emphasized that " 'malice aforethought and heat of passion on sudden provocation are two inconsistent things'; thus, by proving the latter the defendant would negate the former."

Wilbur's conviction, which followed, was affirmed. The Maine Supreme Judicial Court held that murder and manslaughter were varying degrees of the crime of felonious homicide and that the presumption of malice arising from the unlawful killing was a mere policy presumption operating to cast on the defendant the burden of proving provocation if he was to be found guilty of manslaughter rather than murder—a burden which the Maine law had allocated to him at least since the mid-1800s.

The Court of Appeals for the First Circuit then ordered that a writ of habeas corpus issue, holding that the presumption unconstitutionally shifted to the defendant the burden of proof with respect to an essential element of the crime. The Maine Supreme Judicial Court disputed this interpretation of Maine law in State v. Lafferty, 309 A.2d 647 (1973), declaring that malice aforethought, in the sense of premeditation, was not an element of the crime of murder and that the federal court had erroneously equated the presumption of malice with a presumption of premeditation.

> Maine law does not rely on a presumption of 'premeditation' (as Wilbur v. Mullaney assumed) to prove an essential element of unlawful homicide punishable as murder. . . .

Mullaney's holding, it is argued, is that the State may not permit the blameworthiness of an act or the severity of punishment authorized for its commission to depend on the presence or absence of an identified fact without assuming the burden of proving the presence or absence of that fact, as the case may be, beyond a reasonable doubt.[15] In our view, the *Mullaney* holding should not be so broadly read. The concurrence of two Justices in *Mullaney* was necessarily contrary to such a reading; and a majority of the Court refused to so understand and apply *Mullaney* when *Rivera* was dismissed for want of a substantial federal question.

---

15. There is some language in *Mullaney* that has been understood as perhaps construing the Due Process Clause to require the prosecution to prove beyond a reasonable doubt any fact affecting "the degree of criminal culpability." It is said that such a rule would deprive legislatures of any discretion whatsoever in allocating the burden of proof, the practical effect of which might be to undermine legislative reform of our criminal justice system. Carried to its logical extreme, such a reading of *Mullaney* might also, for example, discourage Congress from enacting pending legislation to change the felony-murder rule by permitting the accused to prove by a preponderance of the evidence the affirmative defense that the homicide committed was neither a necessary nor a reasonably foreseeable consequence of the underlying felony. The Court did not intend *Mullaney* to have such far-reaching effect.

Mullaney surely held that a State must prove every ingredient of an offense beyond a reasonable doubt, and that it may not shift the burden of proof to the defendant by presuming that ingredient upon proof of the other elements of the offense. This is true even though the State's practice, as in Maine, had been traditionally to the contrary. Such shifting of the burden of persuasion with respect to a fact which the State deems so important that it must be either proved or presumed is impermissible under the Due Process Clause.

It was unnecessary to go further in *Mullaney*. The Maine Supreme Judicial Court made it clear that malice aforethought, which was mentioned in the statutory definition of the crime, was not equivalent to premeditation and that the presumption of malice traditionally arising in intentional homicide cases carried no factual meaning insofar as premeditation was concerned. Even so, a killing became murder in Maine when it resulted from a deliberate, cruel act committed by one person against another, "suddenly without any, or without a considerable provocation." State v. Lafferty, at 665. Premeditation was not within the definition of murder; but malice, in the sense of the absence of provocation, was part of the definition of that crime. Yet malice, i.e., lack of provocation, was presumed and could be rebutted by the defendant only by proving by a preponderance of the evidence that he acted with heat of passion upon sudden provocation. In *Mullaney* we held that however traditional this mode of proceeding might have been, it is contrary to the Due Process Clause as construed in *Winship*.

As we have explained, nothing was presumed or implied against Patterson; and his conviction is not invalid under any of our prior cases. The judgment of the New York Court of Appeals is

Affirmed.

[The dissenting opinion of Justice Powell, with whom Justices Brennan and Marshall joined, is omitted.]

Questions

1. *Burden of Pleading.* In a murder prosecution, who has the burden of pleading intent to kill or malice aforethought, as the case may be, the defendant or the state? Who is most likely to have the burden of pleading on the issue of extreme emotional disturbance in New York, Patterson or the state? Who is most likely to have the burden of pleading on the issue of heat of passion upon sudden provocation in Maine, Mullaney or the state? What, if anything, does the burdened party have to prove to satisfy its burden?

2. *Burden of Persuasion.* Typically, which party has the burden of persuasion on which issues? What standard of evidence is required to satisfy the burden? Who decides whether the burden has been satisfied?

3. *Failure to Satisfy the Burden of Persuasion.* Assume that the jury concludes that the state has satisfied its burden of persuasion for all elements of the offense charged but has failed to meet its burden of persuasion on the absence of a defense (for which the state has been given the burden). What verdict should the jury return? Assume that the jury concludes that the defense has failed to meets its burden of persuasion on the conditions of a defense. What verdict should the jury return?

4. *Constitutionalization of the Burden of Persuasion.* Which of the rules relating to the burden of persuasion, if any, are constitutionally required? What is the rationale of the constitutional requirement? Could the state constitutionally be given the burden of persuasion for all offense elements and for the absence of all defenses pled by the defense? Could the defense constitutionally be given the burden of persuasion for an offense element? for a defense?

5. *Distinguishing Heat of Passion and Extreme Emotional Disturbance.* How is Maine's "heat of passion on sudden provocation" defense, for which the state constitutionally must bear the burden of persuasion, different from New York's "extreme emotional disturbance" defense, for which the burden of persuasion may be constitutionally shifted to the defendant? State a general rule describing the kinds of defenses for which the burden of persuasion may be allocated to the defense. Could the defendant be given the burden of persuasion for duress (e.g., Model Penal Code §2.09)? for mistake negating an offense element (e.g., Model Penal Code §2.04(1))? for renunciation of an inchoate offense (e.g., Model Penal Code §5.01(4))?

Jackson v. Virginia
Supreme Court of the United States
443 U.S. 307, 99 S. Ct. 2781, 61 L. Ed. 2d 560 (1979)

Mr. Justice STEWART delivered the opinion of the Court.

The Constitution prohibits the criminal conviction of any person except upon proof of guilt beyond a reasonable doubt. In re Winship, 397 U.S. 358. The question in this case is what standard is to be applied in a federal habeas corpus proceeding when the claim is made that a person has been convicted in a state court upon insufficient evidence.

I

The petitioner was convicted after a bench trial in the Circuit Court of Chesterfield County, Va., of the first degree murder of a woman named Mary Houston Cole. Under Virginia law, murder is defined as "the unlawful killing of another with malice aforethought." Premeditation, or specific intent to kill, distinguishes murder in the first from murder in the second degree; proof of this element is essential to conviction of the former offense, and the burden of proving it clearly rests with the prosecution.

That the petitioner had shot and killed Mrs. Cole was not in dispute at the trial. The State's evidence established that she had been a member of the staff at the local county jail, that she had befriended him while he was imprisoned there on a disorderly conduct charge, and that when he was released she had arranged for him to live in the home of her son and daughter-in-law. Testimony by her relatives indicated that on the day of the killing the petitioner had been drinking and had spent a great deal of time shooting at targets with his revolver. Late in the afternoon, according to their testimony, he had unsuccessfully attempted to talk the victim into driving him to North Carolina. She did drive the petitioner to a local diner. There the two were observed by several police officers, who testified that both the petitioner and the victim had been drinking. The two were observed by a deputy sheriff as they were preparing to leave the diner in her car. The petitioner was then in possession of his revolver, and the sheriff also observed a kitchen knife in the automobile. The sheriff testified that he had offered to keep the revolver until the petitioner sobered up, but that the latter had indicated that this would be unnecessary since he and the victim were about to engage in sexual activity.

Her body was found in a secluded church parking lot a day and a half later, naked from the waist down, her slacks beneath her body. Uncontradicted medical and expert evidence established that she had been shot twice at close range with the petitioner's gun. She appeared not to have been sexually molested. Six cartridge cases identified as having been fired from the petitioner's gun were found near the body.

After shooting Mrs. Cole, the petitioner drove her car to North Carolina, where, after a short trip to Florida, he was arrested several days later. In a postarrest statement, introduced in evidence by the prosecution, the petitioner admitted that he had shot the victim. He contended, however, that the shooting had been accidental. When asked to describe his condition at the time of the shooting, he indicated that he had not been drunk, but had been "pretty high." His story was that the victim had attacked him with a knife when he resisted her sexual advances. He said that he had defended himself by firing a number of warning shots into the ground, and had then reloaded his revolver. The victim, he said, then attempted to take the gun from him, and the gun "went off" in the ensuing struggle. He said that he fled without seeking help for the victim because he was afraid. At the trial, his position was that he had acted in self-defense. Alternatively, he claimed that in any event the State's own evidence showed that he had been too intoxicated to form the specific intent necessary under Virginia law to sustain a conviction of murder in the first degree.[2]

The trial judge, declaring himself convinced beyond a reasonable doubt that the petitioner had committed first-degree murder, found him guilty of that offense. The petitioner's motion to set aside the judgment as contrary to the evidence was denied, and he was sentenced to serve a term of 30 years in the Virginia state penitentiary. A petition for writ of error to the Virginia Supreme Court on the ground that the evidence was insufficient to support the conviction was denied.

The petitioner then commenced this habeas corpus proceeding in the United States District Court for the Eastern District of Virginia, raising the same basic claim. Applying the "no evidence" criterion of Thompson v. Louisville, 362 U.S. 199, the District Court found the record devoid of evidence of premeditation and granted the writ. The Court of Appeals for the Fourth Circuit reversed the judgment. The court noted that a dissent from the denial of certiorari in a case in this Court had exposed the question whether the constitutional rule of In re Winship, 397 U.S. 358, might compel a new criterion by which the validity of a state criminal conviction must be tested in a federal habeas corpus proceeding. But the appellate court held that in the absence of further guidance from this Court it would apply the same "no evidence" criterion of Thompson v. Louisville that the District Court had adopted. The court was of the view that some evidence that the petitioner had intended to kill the victim could be found in the facts that the petitioner had reloaded his gun after firing warning shots, that he had had time to do so, and that the victim was then shot not once but twice. The court also concluded that the state trial judge could have found that the petitioner was not so intoxicated as to be incapable of premeditation.

We granted certiorari to consider the petitioner's claim that under In re Winship, supra, a federal habeas corpus court must consider not whether there was *any* evidence to support a state-court conviction, but whether there was sufficient evidence to justify a rational trier of the facts to find guilt beyond a reasonable doubt.

---

2. Under Virginia law, voluntary intoxication—although not an affirmative defense to second-degree murder—is material to the element of a premeditation and may be found to have negated it. Hatcher v. Commonwealth, 218 Va. 811, 241 S.E.2d 756 (1978).

II

Our inquiry in this case is narrow. The petitioner has not seriously questioned any aspect of Virginia law governing the allocation of the burden of production or persuasion in a murder trial. See Mullaney v. Wilbur, 421 U.S. 684; Patterson v. New York, 432 U.S. 197. As the record demonstrates, the judge sitting as factfinder in the petitioner's trial was aware that the State bore the burden of establishing the element of premeditation, and stated that he was applying the reasonable-doubt standard in his appraisal of the State's evidence. The petitioner, moreover, does not contest the conclusion of the Court of Appeals that under the "no evidence" rule of Thompson v. Louisville, supra, his conviction of first-degree murder is sustainable. And he has not attacked the sufficiency of the evidence to support a conviction of second-degree murder. His sole constitutional claim, based squarely upon *Winship,* is that the District Court and the Court of Appeals were in error in not recognizing that the question to be decided in this case is whether any rational factfinder could have concluded beyond a reasonable doubt that the killing for which the petitioner was convicted was premeditated. The question thus raised goes to the basic nature of the constitutional right recognized in the *Winship* opinion.

III

A

This is the first of our cases to expressly consider the question whether the due process standard recognized in *Winship* constitutionally protects an accused against conviction except upon evidence that is sufficient fairly to support a conclusion that every element of the crime has been established beyond a reasonable doubt. Upon examination of the fundamental differences between the constitutional underpinnings of Thompson v. Louisville, supra, and In re Winship, supra, the answer to that question, we think, is clear.

It is axiomatic that a conviction upon a charge not made or upon a charge not tried constitutes a denial of due process. These standards no more than reflect a broader premise that has never been doubted in our constitutional system: that a person cannot incur the loss of liberty for an offense without notice and a meaningful opportunity to defend. A meaningful opportunity to defend, if not the right to a trial itself, presumes as well that a total want of evidence to support a charge will conclude the case in favor of the accused. Accordingly, we held in the *Thompson* case that a conviction based upon a record wholly devoid of any relevant evidence of a crucial element of the offense charged is constitutionally infirm. The "no evidence" doctrine of Thompson v. Louisville thus secures to an accused the most elemental of due process rights: freedom from a wholly arbitrary deprivation of liberty.

The Court in *Thompson* explicitly stated that the due process right at issue did not concern a question of evidentiary "sufficiency." The right established in In re Winship, however, clearly stands on a different footing. *Winship* involved an adjudication of juvenile delinquency made by a judge under a state statute providing that the prosecution must prove the conduct charged as delinquent—which in *Winship* would have been a criminal offense if engaged in by an adult—by a preponderance of the evidence. Applying that standard, the judge was satisfied that the juvenile was "guilty," but he noted that the result might well have been different under a standard of proof beyond a reasonable doubt. In short, the record in *Winship* was not totally devoid of evidence of guilt.

The constitutional problem addressed in *Winship* was thus distinct from the stark problem of arbitrariness presented in Thompson v. Louisville. In *Winship,* the Court held for the first time that the Due Process Clause of the Fourteenth Amendment protects a defendant in a criminal case against conviction "except upon proof beyond a reasonable doubt of every fact necessary to constitute the crime with which he is charged." In so holding, the Court emphasized that proof beyond a reasonable doubt has traditionally been regarded as the decisive difference between criminal culpability and civil liability. The standard of proof beyond a reasonable doubt, said the Court, "plays a vital role in the American scheme of criminal procedure," because it operates to give "concrete substance" to the presumption of innocence, to ensure against unjust convictions, and to reduce the risk of factual error in a criminal proceeding. At the same time, by impressing upon the factfinder the need to reach a subjective state of near certitude of the guilt of the accused, the standard symbolizes the significance that our society attaches to the criminal sanction and thus to liberty itself.

The constitutional standard recognized in the *Winship* case was expressly phrased as one that protects an accused against a conviction except on "proof beyond a reasonable doubt. . . ." In subsequent cases discussing the reasonable doubt standard, we have never departed from this definition of the rule or from the *Winship* understanding of the central purposes it serves. In short, *Winship* presupposes as an essential of the due process guaranteed by the Fourteenth Amendment that no person shall be made to suffer the onus of a criminal conviction except upon sufficient proof—defined as evidence necessary to convince a trier of fact beyond a reasonable doubt of the existence of every element of the offense.

B

Although several of our cases have intimated that the factfinder's application of the reasonable doubt standard to the evidence may present a federal question when a state conviction is challenged, the Federal Courts of Appeals have generally assumed that so long as the reasonable doubt instruction has been given at trial, the no-evidence doctrine of Thompson v. Louisville remains the appropriate guide for a federal habeas corpus court to apply in assessing a state prisoner's challenge to his conviction as founded upon insufficient evidence. We cannot agree.

The *Winship* doctrine requires more than simply a trial ritual. A doctrine establishing so fundamental a substantive constitutional standard must also require the factfinder will rationally apply that standard to the fact in evidence.[8] A "reasonable doubt," at a minimum, is one based upon "reason." Yet a properly instructed jury may occasionally convict even when it can be said that no rational trier of fact could find guilt beyond a reasonable doubt, and the same may be said of a trial judge sitting as a jury. In a federal trial, such an occurrence has traditionally been deemed to require reversal of the conviction. Under *Winship,* which established proof beyond a reasonable doubt as an essential of Fourteenth Amendment due process, it follows that when such a conviction occurs in a state trial, it cannot constitutionally stand. . . .

After *Winship* the critical inquiry on review of the sufficiency of the evidence to support a criminal conviction must be not simply to determine whether the jury was properly instructed, but to determine whether the record evidence could reasonably support a finding of guilt beyond a reasonable doubt. But this inquiry does not require a court to "ask itself whether *it* believes that the evidence at the trial established guilt beyond a reasonable doubt." Instead, the relevant question is whether, after viewing the evidence in the light most favorable to the prosecution, *any* rational trier of fact could have found the essential elements of the crime beyond a reasonable doubt. This familiar standard gives full play to the responsibility of the trier of fact fairly to resolve conflicts in the testimony, to weigh the evidence, and to draw reasonable inferences from basic facts to ultimate facts. Once a defendant has been found guilty of the crime charged, the factfinder's role as weigher of the evidence is preserved through a legal conclusion that upon judicial review *all of the evidence* is to be considered in the light most favorable to the prosecution. The criterion thus impinges upon

---

8. The trier of fact in this case was a judge and not a jury. But this is of no constitutional significance. The record makes clear that the judge deemed himself "properly instructed."

"jury" discretion only to the extent necessary to guarantee the fundamental protection of due process of law.

That the *Thompson* "no evidence" rule is simply inadequate to protect against misapplications of the constitutional standard of reasonable doubt is readily apparent. "[A] mere modicum of evidence may satisfy a 'no evidence' standard. . . ." Any evidence that is relevant—that has any tendency to make the existence of an element of a crime slightly more probable than it would be without the evidence, cf. Fed. Rule Evid. 401—could be deemed a "mere modicum." But it could not seriously be argued that such a "modicum" of evidence could by itself rationally support a conviction beyond a reasonable doubt. The *Thompson* doctrine simply fails to supply a workable or even a predictable standard for determining whether the due process command of *Winship* has been honored.[14] . . .

We hold that in a challenge to a state criminal conviction brought under 28 U.S.C. §2254—if the settled procedural prerequisites for such a claim have otherwise been satisfied—the applicant is entitled to habeas corpus relief if it is found that upon the record evidence adduced at the trial no rational trier of fact could have found proof of guilt beyond a reasonable doubt.[16]

IV

Turning finally to the specific facts of this case, we reject the petitioner's claim that under the constitutional standard dictated by *Winship* his conviction of first degree murder cannot stand. A review of the record in the light most favorable to the prosecution convinces us that

---

14. Application of the *Thompson* standard to assess the validity of a criminal conviction after *Winship* could lead to absurdly unjust results. Our cases have indicated that failure to instruct a jury on the necessity of proof of guilt beyond a reasonable doubt can never be harmless error. Thus, a defendant whose guilt was actually proved by overwhelming evidence would be denied due process if the jury was instructed that he could be found guilty on a mere preponderance of the evidence. Yet a defendant against whom there was but one slender bit of evidence would not be denied due process so long as the jury has been properly instructed on the prosecution's burden of proof beyond a reasonable doubt. Such results would be wholly faithless to the constitutional rationale of *Winship*.

16. The respondents have suggested that this constitutional standard will invite intrusions upon the power of the States to define criminal offenses. Quite to the contrary, the standard must be applied with explicit reference to the substantive elements of the criminal offense as defined by state law. Whether the State could constitutionally make the conduct at issue criminal at all is, of course, a distinct question. See Papachristou v. Jacksonville, 405 U.S. 156; Robinson v. California, 370 U.S. 660.

a rational factfinder could readily have found the petitioner guilty beyond a reasonable doubt of first degree murder under Virginia law.

There was no question at the trial that the petitioner had fatally shot Mary Cole. The crucial factual dispute went to the sufficiency of the evidence to support a finding that he had specifically intended to kill her. This question, as the Court of Appeals recognized, must be gauged in the light of applicable Virginia law defining the element of premeditation. Under that law it is well settled that premeditation need not exist for any particular length of time, and that an intent to kill may be formed at the moment of the commission of the unlawful act. Commonwealth v. Brown, 90 Va. 671, 19 S.E. 447. From the circumstantial evidence in the record, it is clear that the trial judge could reasonably have found beyond a reasonable doubt that the petitioner did possess the necessary intent at or before the time of the killing.

The prosecution's uncontradicted evidence established that the petitioner shot the victim not once but twice. The petitioner himself admitted that the fatal shooting had occurred only after he had first fired several shots into the ground and then reloaded his gun. The evidence was clear that the two shots that killed the victim were fired at close, and thus predictably fatal, range by a person who was experienced in the use of the murder weapon. Immediately after the shooting, the petitioner drove without mishap from Virginia to North Carolina, a fact quite at odds with his story of extreme intoxication. Shortly before the fatal episode, he had publicly expressed an intention to have sexual relations with the victim. Her body was found partially unclothed. From these uncontradicted circumstances, a rational factfinder readily could have inferred beyond a reasonable doubt that the petitioner, notwithstanding evidence that he had been drinking on the day of the killing, did have the capacity to form and had in fact formed an intent to kill the victim.

The petitioner's calculated behavior both before and after the killing demonstrated that he was fully capable of committing premeditated murder. His claim of self defense would have required the trial judge to draw a series of improbable inferences from the basic facts, prime among them the inference that he was wholly uninterested in sexual activity with the victim but that she was so interested as to have willingly removed part of her clothing and then attacked him with a knife when he resisted her advances, even though he was armed with a loaded revolver that he had just demonstrated he knew how to use. It is evident from the record that the trial judge found this story, including the petitioner's belated contention that he had been so intoxicated as to be incapable of premeditation, incredible.

Only under a theory that the prosecution was under an affirmative duty to rule out every hypothesis except that of guilt beyond a reasonable doubt could this petitioner's challenge be sustained. That theory the Court has rejected in the past. We decline to adopt it today. Under the standard established in this opinion as necessary to preserve the due process protection recognized in *Winship,* a federal habeas corpus court faced with a record of historical facts that supports conflicting inferences must presume—even if it does not affirmatively appear in the record—that the trier of fact resolved any such conflicts in favor of the prosecution, and must defer to that resolution. Applying these criteria, we hold that a rationale trier of fact could reasonably have found that the petitioner committed murder in the first degree under Virginia law.

For these reasons, the judgment of the Court of Appeals is affirmed.

It is so ordered.

Mr. Justice STEVENS, with whom The Chief Justice and Mr. Justice REHNQUIST join, concurring in the judgment.

The Constitution prohibits the criminal conviction of any person except upon proof *sufficient to convince the trier of fact* of guilt beyond a reasonable doubt. Cf. ante, at 309. This rule has prevailed in our courts "at least from our early years as a Nation." In re Winship, 397 U.S. 358, 361.

Today the Court creates a new rule of law—one that has never prevailed in our jurisprudence. According to the Court, the Constitution now prohibits the criminal conviction of any person—including, apparently, a person against whom the facts have already been found beyond a reasonable doubt by a jury, a trial judge, and one or more levels of state appellate judges—except upon proof sufficient to convince a *federal judge* that a "rationale trier of fact could have found the essential elements of the crime beyond a reasonable doubt."

The adoption of this novel constitutional rule is not necessary to the decision of the case. Moreover, I believe it is an unwise act of lawmaking. Despite its chimerical appeal as a new counterpart to the venerable principle recognized in *Winship,* I am persuaded that its precipitous adoption will adversely affect the quality of justice administered by federal judges. For that reason I shall analyze this new brainchild with some care.

I shall begin by explaining why neither the record in this case, nor general experience with challenges to the sufficiency of the evidence supporting criminal convictions, supports, much less compels, the conclusion that there is *any* need for this new constitutional precept. I shall next show that it is not logically compelled by either the holding or the analysis in In re Winship, supra. Finally, I shall try to demonstrate why the Court's new rule—if it is not just a meaningless shibboleth—threatens serious harm to the quality of our judicial system. . . .

Questions

1. *Burden of Production.* Which party has the burden of production? What standard of evidence is required to satisfy the burden? Who decides whether the burden has been satisfied?
2. *Prosecution Failure to Satisfy its Burden of Production.* Assume that at the close of the presentation of evidence, the defense moves for a judgment of acquittal. The court determines that the state has met its burden of production on all elements of the offense but has failed to meet its burden of production on the absence of a defense (for which the state has been given the burden). What should the court do?
3. *Defense Failure to Satisfy its Burden of Production.* Assume that at the close of the evidence, the court determines that the state has met its burden of production on all issues for which it has the burden of production but that the defense has failed to meet its burden for all of the defenses that it has pled. What can the state request with regard to a directed verdict and jury instructions? What should the court do?
4. Jackson *and the Constitutional Requirements for the Burden of Production.* The *Jackson* case does not expressly address the burden of production issue. Is it relevant to the burden? If so, how and why? Assume that upon a motion for a directed verdict a judge concludes that, considering all of the evidence in the light most favorable to the prosecution, no rational jury could find that all of the offense elements have been proven beyond a reasonable doubt. He nevertheless denies the motion because the jurisdiction's long-standing rules of criminal procedure set a lower burden of production than this for the state. Would the defense have grounds for a constitutional challenge under *Jackson?*
5. *Constitutionalization of the Burden of Production.* Which of the rules governing the burden of production, if any, are constitutionally required? What is the rationale of the constitutional requirement? Could the state constitutionally be given the burden of production for all offense elements and for the absence of all defenses pled by the defense? Could the defense constitutionally be given the burden of production for an offense element? for a defense?

County Court of Ulster County v. Allen
Supreme Court of the United States
442 U.S. 140, 99 S. Ct. 2213, 60 L. Ed. 2d 777 (1979)

Mr. Justice STEVENS delivered the opinion of the Court.

A New York statute provides that, with certain exceptions, the presence of a firearm in an automobile is presumptive evidence of its illegal possession by all persons then occupying the vehicle.[1] The United States Court of Appeals for the Second Circuit held that respondents may challenge the constitutionality of this statute in a federal habeas corpus proceeding and that the statute is "unconstitutional on its face." We granted certiorari to review these holdings and also to consider whether the statute is constitutional in its application to respondents.

Four persons, three adult males (respondents) and a 16-year-old girl (Jane Doe, who is not a respondent here), were jointly tried on charges that they possessed two loaded handguns, a loaded machinegun, and over a pound of heroin found in a Chevrolet in which they were riding when it was stopped for speeding on the New York Thruway shortly after noon on March 28, 1973. The two large-caliber handguns, which together with their ammunition weighed approximately six pounds, were seen through the window of the car by the investigating police officer. They were positioned crosswise in an open handbag on either the front floor or the front seat of the car on the passenger side where Jane Doe was sitting. Jane Doe admitted that the handbag was hers. The machinegun and the heroin were discovered in the trunk after the police pried it open. The car had been borrowed from the driver's brother earlier that day; the key to the trunk could not be found in the car or on the person of any of its occupants, although there was testimony that two of the occupants had placed something in the trunk before embarking in the borrowed car. The jury convicted all four of possession of the handguns and acquitted them of possession of the contents of the trunk.

Counsel for all four defendants objected to the introduction into evidence of the two handguns, the machinegun, and the drugs, arguing

---

1. New York Penal Law §265.15(3) (McKinney 1967):

The presence in an automobile, other than a stolen one or a public omnibus, of any firearm, defaced firearm, firearm silence, bomb, bombshell, gravity knife, switchblade knife, dagger dirk, stiletto, billy, blackjack, metal knuckles, sandbag, sandclub or slingshot is presumptive evidence of its possession by all persons occupying such automobile at the time such weapon, instrument if found, except under the following circumstances: (a) if such weapon, instrument or appliance is found upon the person of one of the occupants therein; (b) if such weapon, instrument or appliance is found in an automobile which is being operated for hire by a duly licensed driver in the due, lawful and proper pursuit of his trade, then such presumption shall not apply to the driver; or (c) if the weapon so found is a pistol or revolver and one of the occupants, not present under duress, has in his possession a valid license to have and carry concealed the same.

In addition to the three exceptions delineated in §265.15(3)(a)-(c) above as well as the stolen-vehicle and public-omnibus exception in §265.15(3) itself, §265.20 contains various exceptions that apply when weapons are present in an automobile pursuant to certain military, law enforcement, recreational, and commercial endeavors.

that the State had not adequately demonstrated a connection between their clients and the contraband. The trial court overruled the objection, relying on the presumption of possession created by the New York statute. Because that presumption does not apply if a weapon is found "upon the person" of one of the occupants of the car, the three male defendants also moved to dismiss the charges relating to the handguns on the ground that the guns were found on the person of Jane Doe. Respondents made this motion both at the close of the prosecution's case and at the close of all evidence. The trial judge twice denied it, concluding that the applicability of the "upon the person" exception was a question of fact for the jury.

At the close of the trial, the judge instructed the jurors that they were entitled to infer possession from the defendants' presence in the car. He did not make any reference to the "upon the person" exception in his explanation of the statutory presumption, nor did any of the defendants object to his omission or request alternative or additional instructions on the subject.

Defendants filed a post-trial motion in which they challenged the constitutionality of the New York statute as applied in this case. The challenge was made in support of their argument that the evidence, apart from the presumption, was insufficient to sustain the convictions. The motion was denied and the convictions were affirmed by the Appellate Division without opinion. . . .

The petition for a writ of certiorari presented [the question of] whether the application of the presumption in this case is unconstitutional. We answer the [question] in the negative. We accordingly reverse. . . .

Inferences and presumptions are a staple of our adversary system of factfinding. It is often necessary for the trier of fact to determine the existence of an element of the crime—that is, an "ultimate" or "elemental" fact—from the existence of one or more "evidentiary" or "basic" facts. The value of these evidentiary devices, and their validity under the Due Process Clause, vary from case to case, however, depending on the strength of the connection between the particular basic and elemental facts involved and on the degree to which the device curtails the factfinder's freedom to assess the evidence independently. Nonetheless, in criminal cases, the ultimate test of any device's constitutional validity in a given case remains constant: the device must not undermine the factfinder's responsibility at trial, based on evidence adduced by the State, to find the ultimate facts beyond a reasonable doubt. See In re Winship, 397 U.S. 358, 364; Mullaney v. Wilbur, 421 U.S., at 702-703, n.31.

The most common evidentiary device is the entirely permissive inference or presumption, which allows—but does not require—the trier of fact to infer the elemental fact from proof by the prosecutor of the basic one and which places no burden of any kind on the defendant. In that situation the basic fact may constitute prima facie evidence of the elemental fact. When reviewing this type of device, the Court has required the party challenging it to demonstrate its invalidity as applied to him. Because this permissive presumption leaves the trier of fact free to credit or reject the inference and does not shift the burden of proof, it affects the application of the "beyond a reasonable doubt" standard only if, under the facts of the case, there is no rational way the trier could make the connection permitted by the inference. For only in that situation is there any risk that an explanation of the permissible inference to jury, or its use by a jury has caused the presumptively rational factfinder to make an erroneous factual determination.

A mandatory presumption is a far more troublesome evidentiary device. For it may affect not only the strength of the "no reasonable doubt" burden but also the placement of that burden; it tells the trier that he or they must find the elemental fact upon proof of the basic fact, at least unless the defendant has come forward with some evidence to rebut the presumed connection between the two facts.[16] In this situation, the Court has generally examined the presumption on its face to determine the extent to which the basic and elemental facts coincide. To the extent that the trier of fact is forced to abide by the presumption, and may not reject it based on an independent evaluation of the particular facts presented by the State, the analysis of the presumption's constitutional validity is logically divorced from those facts and based on the presumption's accuracy in the run of cases. It is for this reason that the Court has held it irrelevant in analyzing a mandatory presumption, but not in analyzing a purely permissive one, that there is ample evidence in the record other than the presumption to support a conviction.

Without determining whether the presumption in this case was mandatory, the Court of Appeals analyzed it on its face as if it were. In fact, it was not, as the New York Court of Appeals had earlier pointed out.

---

16. This class of more or less mandatory presumptions can be subdivided into two parts: presumptions that merely shift the burden of production to the defendant, following the satisfaction of which the ultimate burden of persuasion returns to the prosecution; and presumptions that entirely shift the burden of proof to the defendant. The mandatory presumptions examined by our cases have almost uniformly fit into the former subclass, in that they never totally removed the ultimate burden of proof beyond a reasonable doubt from the prosecution. To the extent that a presumption imposes an extremely low burden of production—e.g., being satisfied by "any" evidence—it may well be that its impact is no greater than that of a permissive inference, and it may be proper to analyze it as such. See generally Mullaney v. Wilbur, 421 U.S. 684, 703 n.31. In deciding what type of inference or presumption is involved in a case, the jury instructions will generally be controlling, although their interpretation may require recourse to the statute involved and the cases decided under it. . . .

The trial judge's instructions make it clear that the presumption was merely a part of the prosecution's case, that it gave rise to a permissive inference available only in certain circumstances, rather than a mandatory conclusion of possession, and that it could be ignored by the jury even if there was no affirmative proof offered by defendants in rebuttal. The judge explained that possession could be actual or constructive, but that constructive possession could not exist without the intent and ability to exercise control or dominion over the weapons. He also carefully instructed the jury that there is a mandatory presumption of innocence in favor of the defendants that controls unless it, as the exclusive trier of fact, is satisfied beyond a reasonable doubt that the defendants possessed the handguns in the manner described by the judge. In short, the instructions plainly directed the jury to consider all the circumstances tending to support or contradict the inference that all four occupants of the car had possession of the two loaded handguns and to decide the matter for itself without regard to how much evidence the defendants introduced.[23]

Our cases considering the validity of permissive statutory presumptions such as the one involved here have rested on an evaluation of the presumption as applied to the record before the Court. None suggests that a court should pass on the constitutionality of this kind of statute "on its face." It was error for the Court of Appeals to make such a determination in this case.

As applied to the facts of this case, the presumption of possession is entirely rational. Notwithstanding the Court of Appeals' analysis, respondents were not "hitchhikers or other casual passengers," and the guns were neither "a few inches in length" nor "out of [respondents'] sight." The argument against possession by any of the respondents was predicated solely on the fact that the guns were in Jane Doe's pocketbook. But several circumstances—which, not surprisingly, her counsel repeatedly emphasized in his questions and his argument—made it highly improbable that she was the sole custodian of those weapons.

Even if it was reasonable to conclude that she had placed the guns in her purse before the car was stopped by police, the facts strongly suggest that Jane Doe was not the only person able to exercise dominion over them. The two guns were too large to be concealed in her handbag. The bag was consequently open, and part of one of the guns was in

---

23. The verdict announced by the jury clearly indicates that it understood its duty to evaluate the presumption independently and to reject it if it was not supported in the record. Despite receiving almost identical instructions on the applicability of the presumption of possession to the contraband found in the front seat and in the trunk, the jury convicted all four defendants of possession of the former but acquitted all of them of possession of the latter. . . .

plain view, within easy access of the driver of the car and even, perhaps, of the other two respondents who were riding in the rear seat.

Moreover, it is highly improbable that the loaded guns belonged to Jane Doe or that she was solely responsible for their being in her purse. As a 16-year-old girl in the company of three adult men she was the least likely of the four to be carrying one, let alone two, heavy handguns. It is far more probable that she relied on the pocketknife found in her brassiere for any necessary self-protection. Under these circumstances, it was not unreasonable for her counsel to argue and for the jury to infer that when the car was halted for speeding, the other passengers in the car anticipated the risk of a search and attempted to conceal their weapons in a pocketbook in the front seat. The inference is surely more likely than the notion that these weapons were the sole property of the 16-year-old girl.

Under these circumstances, the jury would have been entirely responsible in rejecting the suggestion—which, incidentally, defense counsel did not even advance in their closing arguments to the jury—that the handguns were in the sole possession of Jane Doe. Assuming that the jury did reject it, the case is tantamount to one in which the guns were lying on the floor or the seat of the car in the plain view of the three other occupants of the automobile. In such a case, it is surely rational to infer that each of the respondents was fully aware of the presence of the guns and had both the ability and the intent to exercise dominion and control over the weapons. The application of the statutory presumption in this case therefore comports with the standard laid down in Tot v. United States, 319 U.S., at 467, and restated in Leary v. United States, 395 U.S., at 36. For there is a "rational connection" between the basic facts that the prosecution proved and the ultimate fact presumed, and the latter is "more likely than not to flow from" the former.

Respondents argue, however, that the validity of the New York presumption must be judged by a "reasonable doubt" test rather than the "more likely than not" standard employed in *Leary*. Under the more stringent test, it is argued that a statutory presumption must be rejected unless the evidence necessary to invoke the inference is sufficient for a rational jury to find the inferred fact beyond a reasonable doubt. Respondents' argument again overlooks the distinction between a permissive presumption on which the prosecution is entitled to rely as one not necessarily sufficient part of its proof and a mandatory presumption which the jury must accept even if it is the sole evidence of an element of the offense.

In the latter situation, since the prosecution bears the burden of establishing guilt, it may not rest its case entirely on a presumption unless the fact proved is sufficient to support the inference of guilt beyond a reasonable doubt. But in the former situation, the prosecution may rely on all of the evidence in the record to meet the reasonable doubt standard. There is no more reason to require a permissive statutory presumption to meet a reasonable doubt standard before it may be permitted to play any part in a trial than there is to require that degree of probative force for other relevant evidence before it may be admitted. As long as it is clear that the presumption is not the sole and sufficient basis for a finding of guilt, it need only satisfy the test described in *Leary*.

The permissive presumption, as used in this case, satisfied the *Leary* test. And, as already noted, the New York Court of Appeals has concluded that the record as a whole was sufficient to establish guilt beyond a reasonable doubt.

The judgment is reversed.

So ordered.

[The dissenting opinion of Justice Powell, with whom Justices Brennan, Stewart, and Marshall joined, is omitted.]

Questions

1. *Permissive Inference vs. Mandatory Presumption.* What is the difference between a "permissive inference" and a "mandatory presumption," as described in *Allen*? Give a sample jury instruction for each. What is the effect of each kind of presumption on the allocation of the burden of persuasion? What kinds of presumptions are unconstitutional? How are the constitutional limitations on presumptions similar and different from the constitutional limitations on burdens of proof?

2. *Presumptions and the Burden of Production. Allen* discusses presumptions that have the practical effect of altering the burden of persuasion. Might a presumption have an effect of altering the burden of production? (See footnote 16 of the Court's opinion.) Would it be constitutional for a presumption to shift the burden of production on an issue to the defendant?

3. *Model Penal Code's Presumptions.* The Model Penal Code contains many statutory presumptions. Chapter 4 discusses the presumption of recklessness and extreme indifference to the value of human life that arises when a death is caused in the course of one of certain enumerated felonies. See Model Penal Code §210.2(1)(b). The effect of the Code's presumptions is governed by Model Penal Code §1.12(5). How is this presumption similar and different from that of the New York presumption constitutionally approved in *Allen*? What is the effect of the presumption on the burden of persuasion, if any? On the burden of production, if any?

4. *Rebuttable, Conclusive, and "Codified" Presumptions.* Assume a state has a presumption analogous to that of Model Penal Code §210.2(1)(b), which presumes the recklessness and extreme indifference required for murder when a killing occurs during certain enumerated felonies. If the state makes this into a mandatory presumption but allows the defendant to rebut the presumption—that is, if the state requires the jury to presume recklessness and indifference absent defense evidence to the contrary—would the presumption be constitutional? If they made the presumption mandatory and conclusive—that is, irrebuttable—would it be constitutional? If they redrafted that part of their murder definition to require only proof of a killing in the course of one of the enumerated felonies, would that be constitutional? Which would be preferable from a defendant's point of view: such a rewritten murder definition or a mandatory but rebuttable presumption?

II / DEFINING CRIMINAL OFFENSES

This coursebook is structured around the operational distinctions described in Chapter 3: offense definitions, doctrines of imputation, and general defenses. This part takes up the first kind of criminal law doctrine, the definition of specific offenses. You have already had a glimpse of these kinds of doctrines in Chapter 4's examination of homicide. Chapter 7 looks at general principles for defining offenses. Chapter 8 examines the special and revealing case of inchoate offenses, that is, offenses that punish conduct short of the intended offense. Finally, Part V reviews some specific modern offenses that have changed traditional patterns of criminalization.

Chapter 7. DEFINING OFFENSES: A CLOSER LOOK

This chapter looks more closely at several important issues that apply to many or most offenses. Culpability requirements are of central importance in defining crimes. Recall from Chapter 1 that criminal law's demanding culpability requirements are an important aspect of criminal law's distinction from civil law. We shall look at the sometimes complex way in which culpability requirements are determined under modern statutes, the debate over what should be the minimum culpability level for criminal liability, and the problem of mistake as it relates to culpability requirements. The causation requirement presents another general issue, relating to objective offense elements. Specifically, it concerns the required relation between the actor's conduct and a prohibited result, and whether the actor is to be held accountable for the result. Again, you will see that the criminal law's definition and treatment of the causation requirement is very different from that which is found in civil law, such as in torts, where causation also is an issue.

SECTION 7.1 DETERMINING CULPABILITY REQUIREMENTS

The definition of culpability requirements under current codes is examined in Section 4.2. It may be useful to review that section. Given the central importance of culpability requirements to criminal law and given the demands for precision by the legality principle, it should be no surprise that modern codes try to provide a concise statement of the culpability required for liability for any given offense. Determine the culpability required by the offense charged in the following hypothetical and apply the requirements to the facts of the case.

Regina v. Prince
Court of Crown Cases Reserved
13 Cox's Crim. Cases 138 (1875)

. . . Henry Prince was tried before me upon the charge of having unlawfully taken one Annie Phillips, an unmarried girl, being under the age of sixteen years, out of the possession, and against the will of her father. . . .

He was found guilty, but judgment was respited in order that the opinion of the Court for Crown Cases Reserved might be taken upon the following case.

All the facts necessary to support a conviction existed, and were found by the jury to have existed, unless the following facts constitute a defence. The girl Annie Phillips, though proved by her father to be fourteen years old on the 6th April following, looked very much older than sixteen; and the jury found upon reasonable evidence, that before the defendant took her away she had told him that she was eighteen, and that the defendant *bona fide* believed that statement and that such belief was reasonable.

If the Court is of opinion that under these circumstances a conviction was right, the defendant is to appear for judgment at the next Assizes for Surrey, otherwise the conviction is to be quashed. . . .

BRAMWELL, B., delivered the following judgment, to which the Lord Chief Baron Kelly, Cleasby, B., Grove, J., Pollock, B., and Amphlett, B., assented—The question in the case depends on the construction of the statute under which the prisoner was indicted. That enacts that "whosoever shall unlawfully take any unmarried girl under the age of sixteen out of the possession, and against the will of her father, or mother, or any other person having the lawful care or charge of her, shall be guilty of a misdemeanor." Now the word "unlawfully" means "not lawfully," "otherwise than lawfully," "without lawful cause"—such as would exist for instance on a taking by a police officer on a charge of felony, or a taking by a father of his child from her school. The statute, therefore, may be read thus: "whosoever shall take, &c., without lawful cause." Now the prisoner had no such cause, and consequently except in so far as it helps the construction of the statute, the word "unlawfully" may, in the present case, be left out, and then the question is, has the prisoner taken an unmarried girl under the age of sixteen out of the possession of, and against the will of her father? In fact he has; but it is said not within the meaning of the statute, and that that must be read as though the word "knowingly" or some equivalent word was in, and the reason given is, that as a rule the *mens rea* is necessary to make any act a crime or offence, and that if the facts necessary to constitute an offence are not known to the alleged offender, there can be no *mens rea.* I have used the word "knowingly," but it will perhaps be said, that here the prisoner not only did not do the act knowingly, but knew, as he would have said or believed, that the fact was otherwise than such as would have made his act a crime; that here the prisoner did not say to himself, "I do not know how the fact is, whether she is under sixteen or not, and will take the chance," but acted on the reasonable belief that she was over sixteen: and that though, if he had done what he did, knowing or believing neither way, but hazarding it, there would be a *mens rea,* there is not one when he believes he knows that she is over sixteen. It is impossible to suppose that a person taking a girl out of her father's possession against his will is guilty of no offence within the statute unless he, the taker, knows she is under sixteen—that he would not be guilty if the jury were of opinion he knew either one way nor the other. Let it be, then, that the question is whether he is guilty where he knows, as he thinks, that she is over sixteen. This introduces the necessity for reading the statute with some strange words introduced; as thus: "Whosoever shall take any unmarried girl being under the age of sixteen, and not believing her to be over the age of sixteen, out of the possession," &c. Those words are not there, and the question is whether we are bound to construe the statute as though they were, on account of the rule that the *mens rea* is necessary to make an act a crime. I am of opinion that we are not, nor as though the word "knowingly" was there, and for the following reasons. The act forbidden is wrong in itself, if without lawful cause. I do not say illegal, but wrong. I have not lost sight of this, that though the statute probably principally aims at seduction for carnal purposes, the taking may be by a female, with a good motive. Nevertheless, though there may be cases which are not immoral in one sense, I say that the act forbidden is wrong. Let us remember what is the case supposed by the statute. It supposes that there is a girl,—it does not say a woman, but a girl something between a child and a woman—it supposes she is in the possession of her father, or mother, or other person having lawful care and charge of her, and it supposes there is a taking, and that that taking is against the will of the person in whose possession she is. It is then a taking of a girl in the possession of someone, against his will. I say that done without lawful cause is wrong. . . . I do not say that taking a woman of fifty from her brother's or even father's house is wrong. She is at an age when she has a right to choose for herself, she is not a girl, nor of such tender age that she can be said to be in the possession of or under the care or charge of anyone. If I am asked where I draw the line, I answer at when the female is no longer a girl in anyone's possession. But what the statute contemplates, and what I say is wrong, is the taking of a female of such tender years that she is properly called a girl, and can be said to be in another's possession, and in that other's care or charge. No argument is necessary to prove this; it is enough to state the case.

The Legislature has enacted that if anyone does this wrong act he does it at the risk of her turning out to be under sixteen. This opinion gives full scope to the doctrine of the *mens rea*. . . . [T]he act is intrinsically wrong. For the statute says if "unlawfully" done. Could a prisoner say "I did take away the child to steal its clothes, but I believed it to be over fourteen?" If not, then neither could he say "I did take the child with intent to deprive the parent of its possession, but I believed it over fourteen." . . . The same principle applies in these cases. A man was held liable for assaulting a police officer in the execution of his duty, though he did not know he was a police officer. Why? Because the act was wrong in itself. So also in the case of burglary; could a person charged claim an acquittal on the ground that he believed it was past 6 a.m. when he entered, or in housebreaking that he did not know the place broken into was a house. . . . Take also the case of libel where the publisher thought the occasion privileged, or that he had a defence under Lord Campbell's Act, but was wrong. He would not be entitled to be acquitted, because there was no *mens rea*. Why? Because the act of publishing written defamation is wrong where there is no lawful cause. . . . I say it is a question of construction of this particular statute, no doubt bringing thereto the common law doctrine of *mens rea* being a necessary ingredient of crime. It seems to me impossible to say that, where a person takes a girl out of her father's possession, not knowing whether she is or is not under sixteen, that he is not guilty, and equally impossible when he believes, but erroneously, that she is old enough for him to do a wrong act with safety. I think the conviction should be affirmed. . . .

BRETT, J. [dissenting]—In this case the prisoner was indicted under 24 & 25 Vict. c. 100, s. 55, for that he did unlawfully take an unmarried girl, being under the age of sixteen years, out of the possession, and against the will of her father. And according to the statement of the case, we are to assume that it was proved on the trial that he did take an unmarried girl out of the possession, and against the will of her father, and that when he did so the girl was under the age of sixteen years. But the jury found that the girl went with the prisoner willingly, that she told the prisoner that she was eighteen years of age, that he believed that she was eighteen years of age, and that he had reasonable grounds for so believing. The question is whether upon such proof and such findings of the jury, the prisoner ought or ought not, in point of law, to be pronounced guilty of the offence with which he was charged. . . .

. . . "*Actus non facit reum nisi mens sit rea*" is the foundation of all criminal procedure. The ordinary principle that there must be a guilty mind to constitute a guilty act applies to this case, and must be imported into this statute. . . . It is true that the statute says nothing about knowledge, but this must be imported into the statute." . . . Upon all the cases I think it is proved that there can be no conviction for crime in England in the absence of a criminal mind or *mens rea*. Then comes the question, what is the true meaning of the phrase [*mens rea*]? [T]he maxim as to *mens rea* applies whenever the facts which are present to the prisoner's mind, and which he has reasonable ground to believe, and does believe to be the facts, would, if true, make his act no criminal offence at all. . . . I come to the conclusion that . . . to the extent that, if the facts were as believed, the acts of the prisoner would make him guilty of no criminal offence at all, is an excuse, and that such excuse is implied in every criminal charge and every criminal enactment in England. I agree with Lord Kenyon that "such is our law," and with Cockburn, C.J., that such is the foundation of all criminal procedure.

DENMAN, J.—I agree in the judgments delivered by Bramwell, B., and Blackburn, J. I also think that the conviction is right on the following grounds: . . . The belief that she was eighteen [is] no justification to the defendant for taking her out of [her father's] possession and against his will. By taking her, even with her own consent, he must at least have been guilty of aiding and abetting her in doing an unlawful act—viz., in escaping against the will of her natural guardian from his lawful care and charge. This, in my opinion, leaves him wholly without lawful excuse or justification for the act he did, even though he believed that the girl was eighteen; and, therefore, unable to allege what he had done was not unlawfully done within the meaning of the clause. In other words, having knowingly done a wrongful act, viz., in taking the girl away from the lawful possession of her father against her will, and in violation of his rights as guardian by nature, he cannot be heard to say that he thought the girl was of an age beyond that limited by the statute for the offence charged against him. He had wrongfully done the very thing contemplated by the Legislature. He had wrongfully and knowingly violated the father's rights against the father's will, and he cannot set up a legal defence by merely proving that he thought he was committing a different kind of wrong from that which in fact he was committing.

Conviction affirmed.

Questions

Changing Notions of Mens Rea. How would each of the judges in *Prince* define the *mens rea* requirement of the criminal law? Is their conception different from that of the Model Penal Code drafters, as reflected in the Model Penal Code culpability definitions examined in Section 4.2?

Jake Sets a Record

Jake works in the office of the university registrar to help pay his tuition. Anna, a student, asks for a copy of her official file. The photocopying machine in the office is not working at the moment, so Anna asks if she can take the file to copy it on another machine. Because Jake is new, he is unsure of the office policy. He thinks it probably is all right and that he probably has the authority to let her do it. When Bob, another student who works in the office, returns from his coffee break and learns that Jake has allowed Ann to take her file, he berates Jake for what he says is Jake's irresponsibility and his insensitivity to the importance of proper handling of the files. This is a serious matter, he explains, and shows Jake a copy of the following criminal statute:

> *Tampering with Records.* A person commits a misdemeanor if, knowing that he has no privilege to do so, he falsifies, destroys, removes or conceals any writing or record, with purpose to deceive or injure anyone or to conceal any wrongdoing.*

Bob is usually pleasant so Jake is taken aback by Bob's sternness and haughty tone. To lighten the mood, Jake looks up Bob's official grade file and changes two *A*'s in criminal law and advanced criminal law to *F*'s. He shows Bob the new criminal law grade, and Bob launches into another lecture, including a description of how hard he worked to get his *B*'s in those criminal law courses. He insists that Jake change the grade back, which Jake does. Jake decides not to show Bob the advanced criminal law change he made. After Bob leaves the room, Jake changes it back as well. Jake assumes that Bob knows what grades he got, especially given what an issue it apparently is with him. He concludes that the original *A*'s probably were an error and changes the joke *F* grades back to *B*'s.

A few moments later, Anna returns, very upset. She was on her way to photocopy her official file when a sudden gust of wind blew it out of her hand. She chased down as many sheets as she could but was only able to catch two and a half letters of recommendation. Jake is concerned about losing his job. He asks Anna her grades but she is able to remember only some of them. He nonetheless prepares a new

---

*Model Penal Code §224.4.

file that will look like the old one, making up the grades that Anna cannot remember. Later that afternoon, Bob, who has taken to reviewing all of Jake's work, notices the half letter of recommendation in Anna's file. Further investigation by the registrar, including questioning of Anna, reveals the full story of Anna's file and Bob's criminal law grades. (In fact, Bob had gotten an *A* in criminal law and advanced criminal law; Jake simply misunderstood Bob.) Jake is dismissed from his job and charged with four counts of violating the Tampering with Records statute: for causing Anna's file to be removed without authority; for altering Bob's criminal law grades, as a joke; for changing Bob's criminal law grades "back" to a *B;* and for fabricating a file for Anna. Is he liable?

Model Penal Code §2.02(3)
Culpability Required Unless Otherwise Provided

When the culpability sufficient to establish a material element of an offense is not prescribed by law, such element is established if a person acts purposely, knowingly or recklessly with respect thereto.

Model Penal Code §2.02(4)
Prescribed Culpability Requirement Applies to All Material Elements

When the law defining an offense prescribes the kind of culpability that is sufficient for the commission of an offense, without distinguishing among the material elements thereof, such provision shall apply to all the material elements of the offense, unless a contrary purpose plainly appears.

Notes on Determining Offense Culpability Requirements

Modern Requirement of Culpability Model Penal Code section 1.13(9) describes the objective element "building blocks" of offenses as: conduct, circumstance, and result elements. Modern codes typically follow Model Penal Code section 2.02(1) in providing that "a person is not guilty of an offense unless he acted purposely, knowingly, recklessly, or negligently, as the law may require, with respect to each material element of the offense." The provision reflects the criminal law's commitment to requiring not only a breach of society's objective rules of conduct but also an actor's culpability as to the conditions that make the conduct a breach.

Significance of Mens Rea The requirement of culpability distinguishes the criminal law from other bodies of law. Without such "mens rea," the common law expression, there is little justification for condemning or punishing an actor. An actor's conduct may be harmful; the victim may have a claim in tort; and fairness and utility both may suggest that the actor rather than the victim should bear the loss from the injury. But without culpability in the actor, the injury may be seen as "accidental," perhaps unavoidable, and therefore insufficient to suggest that the actor deserves condemnation and reprobation criminal conviction.

Early Notions of Mens Rea The law did not always require culpability of an actor. Early Germanic tribes, it is suggested, imposed liability upon the causing of an injury, without regard to culpability. But this was a period before tort law and criminal law divided. It seems likely that as the distinction between tort and crime appeared—that is, as the function of compensating victims became distinguished from the function of imposing deserved punishment—the requirement of culpability took on increasing importance. Early notions of mens rea are seen in Regina v. Prince.[1] The defendant had taken an underage girl "out of the possession" of her father, reasonably believing she was over the age of consent. That the defendant's conduct was generally immoral, was sufficient for Baron Bramwell to find that the defendant had the mens rea necessary for the crime.[2] Judge Brett, on the other hand, would require that Prince at least have intended to do something (anything) that was criminal, not just immoral.[3] A somewhat more demanding requirement is expressed in Regina v. Faulkner.[4] In the process of stealing rum from the hold of a ship, Faulkner accidentally sets the ship afire, destroying it. Judges Fitzgerald and Palles conclude that the mens rea requirement means that Faulkner at least must have intended to do something criminal that reasonably might have been expected to have led to the actual harm caused and charged.[5] Thus, Faulkner ought not be liable for the offense of burning a ship when he intended only to steal rum from it and could not reasonably have foreseen its destruction.

From Mens Rea to Mentes Reae This last shift in the notion of

---

1. 13 Cox's Crim. Cases 138 (1875).
2. Id. at 141-42.
3. Id. at 146.
4. 13 Cox's Crim. Cases 550 (1877).
5. Id. at 557, 561.

mens rea meant not only a dramatic increase in the demand of the requirement but also meant a significant qualitative change. No longer did there exist a single mens rea requirement for all offenses—the intention to do something immoral or, later, something criminal. Now each offense had a different mens rea requirement. An actor had to intend to do something that reasonably might have been expected to lead to the harm of the particular offense. As some have expressed it, there was no longer a *mens rea* for criminal liability but rather *mentes reae*.[6]

From Offense Analysis to Element Analysis The Model Penal Code carries this refinement another step. As section 2.02(1) quoted above makes clear, the Code requires culpability "with respect to each material element of the offense."[7] Even the notion of mentes reae conceives of each offense as having a single culpability requirement. Indeed, legal doctrine of that day grouped offenses according to the type of culpability that the offense required: general intent offenses, specific intent offenses, and offenses of strict liability.[8] In what may be described as a shift from *offense analysis* to *element analysis*,[9] the Model Penal Code introduced the requirement of culpability as to each element of an offense. The Code also permits the level of culpability to be different for different elements of the same offense. This element analysis approach provides, for the first time, a fully comprehensive statement of the culpability required. As becomes clear later in this chapter, the early conceptions of mens rea were not simply undemanding; they were hopelessly vague. They failed to tell courts enough about the required culpability for an offense to enable courts to resolve the cases that commonly arose. The vague conceptualizations left it for courts to "fill in" the culpability requirements that the statues did not provide.[10] Thus, element analysis permits legislatures to reclaim from the courts the authority to define the conditions of criminal liability, a result that the legality principle would be pleased with.

Misconceptions that Permitted Offense Analysis The shift to element analysis did not come from a determination by the Model Penal Code drafters to change the traditional offense requirements. Rather, the drafters believed that element analysis was necessary to accurately represent the offense requirements that had been imposed, even during the

---

6. Sayre, The Present Significance of Mens Rea in the Criminal Law, Harv. Legal Essays 399, 404 (1934).

7. Model Penal Code §2.02(1).

8. For an attempt to define and illustrate these distinctions, see Linehan v. State, 442 So. 2d 244 (1983).

9. See generally Robinson & Grall, Element Analysis in Defining Criminal Liability: The Model Penal Code and Beyond, 35 Stan. L. Rev. 681 (1983).

10. This occurs most commonly in determining whether an actor's mistake should provide a defense, taken up later in this chapter (Culpability Requirements and Mistake Defenses).

Common Law period. That is, common law lawyers and judges were wrong to think that their offense-analysis view of offense culpability requirements was adequate to describe the culpability that the common law required. Their misconception stemmed in part from their conceptualization of an independent "law of mistake," which they saw as supplementing the culpability requirements of an offense definition. Thus, an actor might satisfy the requirements of theft but might have a defense if the law of mistake allowed a defense in his situation. The Model Penal Code drafters, in contrast, recognized that a mistake defense and a culpability requirement generally are one and the same, simply two ways of describing the same thing. The Code provides that mistake provides a defense if it negates an offense culpability requirement.[11] Mistakes negating an offense element are taken up later in this chapter.

Assuming Strict Liability from Absence of Culpability Requirement The absence of a specified culpability requirement in an offense definition does *not* mean that culpability is not required.[12] Modern codes permit strict liability in very limited instances, generally only for the least serious offenses, such as traffic violations. Model Penal Code §§2.02(1) and 2.05, and similar provisions in state codes, are meant to require culpability for all elements of all offenses other than offenses classified as mere "violations." In some jurisdictions, when the drafters intend that culpability is not to be required, a phrase such as "in fact" is inserted at the appropriate place in the offense definition to signal the absence of a culpability requirement.[13]

Culpability Requirements Supplied by General Provisions Where the offense definition does not explicitly provide a culpability requirement, Model Penal Code §2.02(3) supplies one. Section 2.02(3) reads in a requirement of "recklessness" with respect to all circumstance and result elements and, because of the Code's failure to define recklessness as to conduct, it is frequently referred to read in "knowing" with respect to all conduct elements. More on this later. Consider, for example, the Model Penal Code's indecent exposure offense:

> A person commits a misdemeanor if, for the purpose of arousing or gratifying sexual desire . . . , he exposes his genitals under circumstances in which he knows his conduct is likely to cause affront or alarm.[14]

---

11. See Model Penal Code §2.04(1).

12. Morrisette v. United States, 342 U.S. 246, [263], 72 S. Ct. 240, 96 L. Ed. 288 (1952) (omission from statute, prohibiting illegal conversion of U.S. property, of any mention of intent not to be construed as eliminating that element from the crime denounced).

13. "Having intercourse with a person who is in fact under 14 years of age," indicates that no culpability is required as to the fact that the sexual partner is under 14.

14. Model Penal Code §213.5 (1980).

An application of §2.02(3), reading in culpability requirements, results in the following complete offense definition:

> A person commits a misdemeanor if, for the *purpose* of arousing or gratifying sexual desire . . . , he [*knowingly* engages in conduct by which he *recklessly* causes the exposure of what he is aware of a substantial risk are (i.e., *reckless* as to the exposed parts being)] his genitals under circumstances in which he *knows* his conduct is likely to cause affront or alarm.

Reading in Recklessness Obviously, such an explicit statement generates a grammatically awkward definition. A general provision that reads in a fixed culpability can provide the necessary guidance yet leave offense definitions readable.[15] Such a general read-in-reckless provision also is useful because, as discussed in the next section, recklessness generally is the minimum culpability required for criminal liability. Reading in "recklessness" when no culpability is stated gives voice to this norm. Special circumstances may lead code drafters to use a higher or a lower level in particular instances but, absent special reasons, recklessness will be the minimum culpability required. Thus, a general provision such as Model Penal Code §2.02(3) at once provides a comprehensive statement of all culpability requirements, a readable offense definition, and recklessness as the standard minimum culpability.

Providing Culpability Other than Recklessness Legislatures are free to deviate from the norm of recklessness in either of two ways. First, the legislature can explicitly provide a culpability requirement other than recklessness for a specific element of an offense definition. This is what the legislature has done in requiring "a purpose to arouse" and "knows . . . is likely to affront" in the indecent exposure offense. In addition, a legislature can provide that a stated culpability requirement applies to more than a single element of the offense. This second alternative is provided in the Model Penal Code by §2.02(4), which codifies a general rule of statutory construction requiring that a stated culpability term, which does not distinguish among the elements, be applied to all elements of the offense. Thus, where the offense of causing a suicide is defined to punish one who "purposely causes such suicide by force,"[16] the actor must be purposeful as to using force and as to the result of causing the suicide. Normal rules of statutory construction would no doubt generate the same result.

Conflict and Inconsistency in the Model Penal Code The Model Penal Code culpability scheme is a great improvement over "the variety, dispar-

---

15. The practice seems particularly appropriate given that the culpability requirements read in to complete an offense definition frequently are less significant—e.g., less frequently at issue—than are the explicitly stated culpability elements.

16. Model Penal Code §210.5(1) (1980).

ity, and confusion" of judicial definitions of "the requisite but elusive mental element" that existed prior to the Code's advent.[17] As is frequently the case with reform, however, while the Code makes great advances it inevitably has shortcomings. All jurisdictions that follow the Model Penal Code's culpability scheme face a variety of common difficulties. Some states have changed the Code's provisions to avoid some of the problems. Others have created additional difficulties by tinkering with the scheme's provisions without fully understanding the implications of their changes.

Failure to Define Recklessness and Negligence with Respect to Conduct The Code's precision does much to bring clarity to what previously had been a troublesome area, but some peculiarities in the definitional scheme leave several ambiguities remaining. Recall the chart summarizing definitions that appears in Section 4.2. Note that the Code does not expressly define recklessness and negligence with respect to a conduct element. One explanation for this failure is that the drafters determined that, as a practical matter, neither recklessness nor negligence as to conduct is likely to arise. The Model Penal Code commentary notes that "[w]ith respect to each of [the] three types of elements, the draft attempts to define each of the kinds of culpability *that may arise.*"[18] Other sections of the commentary, however, might be interpreted to suggest that the drafters did contemplate the possibility of recklessness or negligence as to conduct. Indeed, certain Code offenses appear specifically to proscribe reckless conduct. For example, one who "recklessly tampers with tangible property of another so as to endanger person or property" commits criminal mischief.[19] Similarly, one who "purposely or recklessly . . . kills or injures any animal" is guilty of cruelty to animals.[20]

Interpretations of Culpability as to "Conduct" One might resolve this ambiguity in the Code's definitional scheme by reasoning that, because some culpability is required as to each element of an offense and "recklessness" and "negligence" as to conduct are not defined, at least "knowledge" should be required as to a conduct element, for it is the minimum culpability that is defined with respect to conduct.[21] Some jurisdictions specifically provide that "knowing" is to be read in with

---

17. Morrisette v. United States, supra, note [20], at 252, 72 S. Ct. at 244, 96 L. Ed. at 294.
18. Model Penal Code §2.02 comment 2, 124 (Tent. Draft No. 4, 1955).
19. Model Penal Code §220.3(1)(b) (1980).
20. Id. at §250.11.
21. This argument can be buttressed by referring to §2.02(5), which states that: "When recklessness suffices to establish an element, such element also is established if a person acts purposely or knowingly."

respect to a conduct element.[22] Another approach may be for a court to define "recklessness" and "negligence" with respect to conduct by extrapolating from the definition of those terms with respect to circumstance and result elements.

A Narrow Interpretation of "Conduct" This ambiguity may be insignificant if "conduct" elements are defined narrowly to include only literally the *conduct* (muscular movement) of the actor.[23] Under this approach, culpability as to an actor's "conduct" is relevant in the rare case that he does not know that he is engaging in the muscular movement and these instances are likely to be exempt from liability under the involuntary act defense.[24] Culpability as to the *nature* of one's conduct is more accurately described as culpability as to the circumstances and the results of one's conduct and "recklessness" and "negligence" are defined with respect to circumstance and result elements. Thus, this narrow interpretation of what constitutes a "conduct" element not only gives a clear definition, without need for judicial extrapolation, but also has the important advantage of maximizing the legislature's ability to provide a different culpability level for different elements of a single offense. That is, to treat "conduct" as including the circumstances and results of one's conduct, would be to treat the conduct (narrow sense) and the circumstances and results of the conduct as a single element. This would require that a single culpability level apply to all. To strip the circumstances and results of conduct from the "conduct" element and to treat them as independent "circumstance" and "result" elements is to create several elements and thereby allow different culpability as to different elements. These issues are discussed further below.

Asymmetry in the Definition of "Purposely" Another asymmetry revealed by the culpability definition chart in Section 4.2 is found in the definition of "purposely." Recall that the hallmark of purposeful culpability in the context of a result element is the actor's *conscious object* to cause that result; "knowing" as to a result requires only that the actor be aware that his conduct will cause the result, not that he desires or hopes that it will. "Purposely" as to a conduct element has an analogous meaning: It must be the actor's conscious object to engage in conduct of that nature. It is not enough that he is aware that his conduct is of that nature ("knowing" as to conduct). In the context

---

22. See, e.g., S.1437, 95th Cong., 2d Sess. §§302(c), 303(b)(1) (1978) (recklessness as to conduct undefined; minimum state of mind that must be proved with respect to conduct is knowledge). See Alaska Stat. §§11.81.610(b), .900(a)(2)-(4) (Supp. 1984). "conduct" to mean an "*action* or omission" and defines "action" to mean "a bodily movement."

24. See Section 16.3.

of a circumstance element, however, "purposely" requires only that the actor "is *aware* of such circumstance or hopes that it exists." In other words, "purpose" as to a circumstance can be shown by proving no more than is required to show "knowing" as to a circumstance. The distinction between "purposely" and "knowingly" is thereby eliminated for circumstance elements. The commentary gives no explanation and, indeed, does not acknowledge the variation. One can only speculate that the drafters did not think the purposeful-knowing distinction to be relevant in the context of culpability as to a circumstance.[25] As we shall see, these and other ambiguities can create significant difficulties in the operation of the Model Penal Code culpability scheme.

Distinguishing Conduct, Circumstance, or Result Elements Another defect of the Code is its failure to define the three categories of objective elements—that is, to distinguish conduct, circumstance, and result elements. For example, is "obstructs" a conduct or a result element? Does "insults another in a manner likely to provoke violent response" consist of a single conduct element or of one conduct element and one or more circumstance elements? Does "the death of another human being" consist of a single result element or of a result element and a circumstance element? The definition of the three categories of objective elements is important because such categories are used as terms of art in many places in the Code. Where an offense contains a "result" element, for example, the causation requirements in §2.03 of the Code apply.[26]

Objective Element Categories and Culpability Requirements Perhaps even more important, a precise definition of the objective-element categories is essential for proper application of the defined culpability terms. Recall the asymmetries in the Code's culpability definitions, noted above. To act "purposely" with respect to "conduct" or in causing "a result," an actor must have such conduct or result as his conscious object; but to act "purposely" with respect to "an attendant circumstance," an actor need only be aware of such circumstance. Recall also that "recklessness" and "negligence" are defined as to circumstance

---

25. Knowledge that the requisite external circumstances exist is a common element of [purpose and knowledge]. But action is not purposive with respect to the nature or result of the actor's conduct unless it was his conscious object to perform an action of that nature or to cause such a result.

Model Penal Code §2.02, comment 2 at 233 (1985).

26. See Model Penal Code §2.03 (Proposed Official Draft 1962) (defining the necessary causal relationship between conduct and result elements. In addition, see id. §5.01(1)(b) (providing special culpability requirements as to a result element where attempt is charged), id. §1.03(1)(a) (providing jurisdiction over an offense if "the result which is an element [of the offense] occurs within this state"), id. §1.03(2) (excepting from (1)(a), supra, cases where "the result occurs . . . only in another jurisdiction" where the conduct is not an offense).

and result elements but not as to conduct elements. Thus, while a recklessness requirement as to a circumstance or result element will be applied as defined, if an element is a conduct element, there is some ambiguity as to what is to be required. Some jurisdictions would require that "knowing" be proven. Because of these asymmetries, the classification of an element becomes critical.

The Failure to Define Categories For these reasons, the precise requirements of an offense sometimes cannot be determined until the objective elements of an offense definition are properly characterized as either "conduct," "an attendant circumstance," or "a result." The Code does not define "result" or "circumstance." It defines "conduct," but uses seemingly contradictory forms of that term in different Code provisions. Section 1.13 takes a narrow view, suggesting that "conduct" simply refers to an actor's bodily movement.[27] In other places, however, especially where the phrase "conduct constituting the offense" appears, "conduct" seems to be used in a broad sense to mean bodily movement and all its relevant characteristics, such as the circumstances and results of the conduct.

Resulting Ambiguities Consider the offense of theft by deception, which entails purposely obtaining another's property through deceit. A person "deceives" if he purposely "[c]reates or reinforces a false impression [as to value]."[28] One might argue that this requirement is a single elaborate conduct requirement: "creates or reinforces a false impression as to value." Or, the prohibited conduct element might be "creates" or "reinforces" and the proscribed result might be interpreted as either (a) a false impression as to value (with no "attendant circumstance"), (b) a false impression (with value as a "circumstance"), or (c) an impression (with both falsity and value as "circumstances"). To select the proper interpretation requires a definition of what constitutes a "conduct," "circumstance," or "result." And the interpretation selected will determine the culpability required.

Implications of Ambiguities Assume that a court applies §2.02(4) to require that the stated culpability requirement, "purposely," applies to all elements of the offense of theft by deception. The actor's *conscious object* must then encompass all required conduct and results, but because of the way "purposeful" as to a circumstance is defined, the actor need only be *aware* of the existence of a circumstance element. If the court applies interpretation (a) described above, the actor's *conscious object* need encompass every element of the offense because all elements are either conduct or results. If interpretation (b) is applied, however, the actor's *conscious object* must encompass only "creating" and a "false impression"; it need not be the actor's conscious object or hope—he

---

27. Model Penal Code §1.13(2) & (5).
28. Model Penal Code §223.3(a).

need only be aware—that the false impression concerns "value." Finally, if the court applies interpretation (c), the actor's *conscious object* need only encompass "creating an impression"; he need be only *aware* of the fact that the impression is "false" and concerns "value." These differences create the potential to manipulate improperly a defendant's liability by altering the content of the categories "conduct," "result," and "circumstance," thereby altering the applicable culpability requirement.

Combining Conduct and Result or Conduct and Circumstance Elements Difficulties in distinguishing conduct, circumstance, and result elements also arise because most modern codes, including the Model Penal Code, use terms that combine conduct and a result as a single element or conduct and an attendant circumstance. Verbs like "damages," "obstructs," "destroys," "falsifies," "kills," and "desecrates" all combine both an act and a result of that act. Verbs like "compels,"[29] "agrees," and "removes"[30] all combine both conduct and circumstance elements as a single element. Such combinations create ambiguities and undermine consistency in the operation of the Code.

Implications of Combined Elements Consider a statute that forbids "recklessly obstructing any highway."[31] What culpability should be required as to "obstructing"? A court might take any of three approaches. Because "obstructing" appears to be a conduct element and "recklessly" is not defined with respect to conduct, the court might determine that "knowing" is the appropriate culpability as to "obstructing" because it is the minimum culpability defined with respect to conduct. Instead, a court might attempt to define recklessness as to conduct and require that newly-defined culpability. Given the enactment of a comprehensive culpability scheme, such a definition of culpability seems a legislative task. A third and perhaps the best approach might be for a court to observe that the verb "obstructing" is a combination of separate conduct and result elements. The term " 'obstructs' means to *render impassable* without unreasonable inconvenience or hazard."[32] In essence, the offense imposes liability when an actor engages in conduct by which he causes—i.e., "renders"—any highway to be impassable. The culpability term "recklessly," under this approach, can be meaningfully read to apply to the result element of causing the highway to be impassable. The separate conduct element may be interpreted as requiring

---

29. Id. §213.1(1)(a) (defining the offense of rape). The term "compels" implies an unstated yet required circumstance element: lack of consent.

30. Model Penal Code §212.1 (1980) (defining kidnapping). The actor must "remove" his victim from the victim's residence or place of business. Like the term "compels," the term "removes" implies the absence of consent.

31. See, e.g., Model Penal Code §250.7.

32. Id.

"knowing" conduct because that is the minimum culpability defined as to conduct.

Proposed Revisions It has been suggested that the difficulties with the Model Penal Code scheme—the failure to define the categories of objective elements and the use of terms that combine elements of different categories—can be avoided with a few revisions, most of which may be done through judicial interpretation of existing provisions.[33] With revision, the Code's scheme can be made workable and can realize the full benefits of the insights and advances of the drafters. Here are some of the reforms that are claimed to be helpful.

Define Conduct Narrowly First, define "conduct" elements literally, that is, narrowly, to mean pure conduct: bodily movement of the actor, as Model Penal Code §1.13 defines it. Thus, objective elements of an offense definition that might otherwise be classified as conduct elements, but which actually describe *characteristics* of the conduct would be treated as separate circumstance or result elements. For example, the definition of harassment makes it an offense if an actor "insults . . . another in a manner likely to provoke violent . . . response." Under a narrow view of the conduct element, the required conduct is the simple act of speaking. The conduct's characteristics—its insulting character, its likelihood of provoking a violent response—would be treated as circumstance or result elements. Under this narrow view of conduct, the conduct element emerges as a relatively unspecific and unimportant aspect of an offense definition. In homicide, for example, the particular conduct that the actor engages in to cause the death of another human being does not matter. What matters is that the actor's conduct, of whatever nature, did cause the prohibited result. The most significant elements of an offense definition, then, typically are the circumstance and result elements.

Narrow Conduct Element as Act Requirement Such a narrowly defined conduct element continues to adequately serve the important purposes of the act requirement: to distinguish fantasizing from intention and to thereby exclude from liability intentions too irresolute to ever be carried out, to provide some minimal objective evidence confirming mens rea, and to set a minimal objective limit on the government's criminalization power. This can be useful in applying doctrines that require such a point of reference, such as the concurrence requirement, statutes of limitations, and jurisdiction and venue. Moreover, because it provides a more definite and specific point of reference, this narrow definition of conduct, which excludes results of the conduct, more clearly provides a single time and place of the offense than would a broader definition of conduct.

Distinguish Combined Elements In a corollary to this first revision,

---

33. See Robinson & Grall, supra, note 9.

whenever a single verb compounds a conduct element with a result element or with a circumstance element, the legislature should redraft the language or, absent such redrafting, courts should distinguish the two aspects of the element in determining the culpability requirements. By more clearly identifying the existence of a result element, this approach also more clearly identifies where the special requirements of causation apply.

Proposed Distinction Between Circumstance and Result Elements The Model Penal Code provides no definition to distinguish circumstance elements from result elements. Is causing the "obstruction of a public highway" a single result element? Or is it a result element of causing an "obstruction" and a circumstance element of "a public highway"? To resolve such problems, a third proposal would define a result as a *circumstance changed by the actor.* All elements that did not fit this definition would be independent circumstance elements. In the short hypothetical above, the actor creates only the obstruction; he cannot create or alter the road's legal status as a "public highway." Thus, causing the "obstruction" would be a result element and "public highway" would be a circumstance element. To summarize, in each offense, the conduct element, although perhaps linguistically merged with other elements, is segregated. It simply performs the function of the act requirement. Result elements are easy to identify, as circumstances changed by the actor. All other elements are circumstance elements.

Culpability as to Conduct Similarly Narrow Another corollary to the narrow scope of the conduct element is to give the culpability requirement accompanying the conduct element a similarly narrow meaning. If the conduct element encompasses only an actor's act, not the characteristics of the accompanying circumstances or the results of the act, the required culpability as to the conduct encompasses only the actor's mental state as to engaging in the bare act itself and not his mental state as to the circumstances or results of the conduct. As noted previously, any broader interpretation of conduct would make the culpability as to the conduct element all encompassing. A requirement of "knowing" as to conduct, which would most frequently be required, would set "knowing" as the required culpability as to the pertinent attendant circumstances and the pertinent results of his conduct. But to assume that the culpability required as to "conduct" controls the culpability as to the circumstances and results of the conduct as well, as the broader interpretation of conduct would do, is to undermine element analysis generally. Such an approach would short-circuit the Code's attempt to allow separate and sometimes different culpability requirements with respect to the circumstances and results of one's conduct.

Culpability as to Conduct Rarely an Issue Absent Abnormal Disability Under the narrow definition, an actor's culpability as to his conduct—for example, being aware of the nature of one's conduct—rarely will be a matter of dispute; his culpability as to the circumstances and result of his conduct will be of primary practical importance. Culpability as to conduct simply requires, for example, that an actor be aware that he is moving his trigger finger or swinging his arm. The only cases that would present an issue under the narrowly-defined conduct element would involve an actor suffering a considerable and abnormal disability. Such abnormalities typically are given more detailed consideration under provisions such as those governing the voluntariness requirement or excuse defenses. The culpability requirements of an offense definition, in contrast, operate primarily to assess the culpability of normal persons. The normal person typically desires to move his body in the way that he moves it, thus satisfies the narrow culpability-as-to-conduct requirement. The narrow interpretation of conduct is consistent with and avoids the problems inherent in the drafters' failure to define recklessness and negligence as to conduct. An actor who is only "aware of a substantial risk" or is "unaware of a substantial risk" that he is moving his trigger finger or arm, is an actor who will have an excuse defense. Thus, no definitions of recklessness or negligence as to conduct are needed.

Model Penal Code §2.02(4): Applying a Stated Culpability to All Elements One final but important difficulty with the Model Penal Code scheme is found in too broad a reading of §2.02(4), quoted before these notes. The commentary describes this provision as one that will embody the most probable legislative intent.[34] The provision may well go too far, however, in allowing what may be an exceptional culpability requirement, such as purposeful, which is meant by the legislature to apply only to one element of the offense, to govern the culpability requirements of all other offense elements. In other instances, the provision may have the equally undesirable effect of having an unusually low culpability requirement, such as negligence, apply to all elements, when it was meant only to apply to one.

Too Literal a Reading of §2.02(4) Consider, for example, the offense of burglary. An actor commits burglary when he "enters a building or occupied structure . . . with purpose to commit a crime therein, unless the premises are at the time open to the public or the actor is licensed or privileged to enter."[35] As "purpose" is the only culpability element prescribed and as no contrary legislative purpose plainly appears, a provision like Model Penal Code §2.02(4) might be interpreted to require that, to be liable for burglary, an actor must not only have the purpose to commit a crime within but also must be purposeful with respect to each element. In other words, the actor must be aware of or

---

34. Model Penal Code §2.02 comment 6, 129 (Tent. Draft No. 4, 1955).
35. Model Penal Code §221.1 (1980).

believe or hope that *all the required circumstance* elements for burglary exist. He would escape liability if he thought it likely, but was not certain and did not necessarily hope, that he is not "licensed or privileged to enter" or that he is entering a "building or occupied structure."[36] But burglary typically is understood to require purpose only as to the "intent to commit a crime therein." "Purpose" is an unusually stringent culpability requirement.[37] There are few areas where legislature want so demanding a requirement. Too broad a reading of §2.02(4) allows the exceptional case, where purpose is required, to become the standard for all elements of the offense. An analogous difficulty arises with the use of negligence. Where only negligence is required as to an offense element, strict application of §2.02(4) applies this stated culpability term to all elements,[38] although recklessness normally is the minimum culpability required.[39]

A Workable Interpretation of §2.02(4) A better reading of §2.02(4) would apply its rule only to that part of the offense definition within the grammatical clause in which the stated term appears. This is consistent with the provision's direction that the rule applies only where the offense definition prescribes culpability, "without distinguishing among the material elements thereof." That is, grammatical structure may provide such distinction among elements. In the context of burglary, this interpretation would apply "purpose" only to "to commit a crime therein." The other elements of the offense would be governed by the other rules of construction; the culpability requirements would be desired either from other stated culpability terms or from §2.02(3) reading in the standard "recklessness."

Interaction of §§2.02(3) vs. 2.02(4) This discussion gives some guidance in suggesting rules for how Model Penal Code §§2.02(3) and 2.02(4) ought to interact. Consider the definition of harassment:

> A person commits a petty misdemeanor if, with purpose to harass another, he . . . insults . . . another in a manner likely to provoke violent or disorderly response.[40]

---

36. "Purposely" as to a circumstance requires either a hope *or* awareness, as required for "knowingly." See §4.1, "Asymmetry in the definition of 'purposely.' " Thus, "knowledge" as to a circumstance element—"aware of high probability of its existence," §2.02(7)—satisfies the requirement but "recklessness"—"aware of a substantial risk," §2.20(2)(c)—does not.

37. "Acting knowingly is ordinarily sufficient." Model Penal Code §2.02 comment 3, 125 (Tent. Draft No. 4, 1955).

38. See, e.g., Model Penal Code §210.4 ("Criminal homicide constitutes negligent homicide when it is committed negligently"); Model Penal Code §211.1(1)(b) (a person commits simple assault if he "negligently causes bodily injury to another with a deadly weapon; . . .").

39. This is the point of having a section like Model Penal Code §2.02(3) read in recklessness where no culpability is stated. See supra, "Reading in recklessness."

40. Model Penal Code §250.4(2) (1980).

CHAPTER 7   DEFINING OFFENSES: A CLOSER LOOK   197

Model Penal Code §2.02(3) requires recklessness whenever an offense definition fails to specify the culpability with respect to a particular element. On the other hand, when the offense definition specifies a culpability element, without distinguishing among elements, §2.02(4) requires that the stated culpability apply to all elements, unless a contrary purpose appears.

If §2.02(4) were applied to require the stated culpability of "purpose" as to all elements, even those elements outside of its grammatical clause, the actor would have to be purposeful with respect to all elements—for example, it must be his conscious object to "insult another" and his conscious object that the insult be "likely to provoke violent or disorderly response." Yet, as noted above, purpose is a special and a very demanding culpability requirement, while recklessness is well-established as the "norm" for criminal liability. If §2.02(3) is applied to all elements outside the grammatical clause in which "purpose" appears, the defendant must be purposeful only as to harassing another, and need be only reckless with respect to all other elements.

Proposed Interpretation of §§2.02(3) and 2.02(4)   It has been suggested that the §2.02(3) recklessness requirement should be preferred. Section 2.02(4) admittedly should apply to the entire grammatical clause in which it appears but should apply outside that clause only when the placement and effect of the stated culpability term suggest that it is intended to govern culpability requirements outside of the clause. This means, for example, that in the absence of legislative direction to the contrary, recklessness would be required as to the circumstance element of "an unlicensed or unprivileged entry" in burglary. This interpretation of §2.02(4) is not inconsistent with its language, which requires application of stated culpability only when such culpability is provided "without distinguishing among the material elements thereof." The interpretation rests upon an assumption that, when a stated culpability is placed within a grammatical clause, such placement distinguishes the elements within the clause from those without. The use of §2.02(3) here, to fill in any gaps after application of §2.02(4), is consistent with the Model Penal Code's view that the culpability level of recklessness should be applied when the required culpability is unstated, a view that is supported by the fact that recklessness generally is accepted as the appropriate norm for imposing criminal liability.

Application to Homicide   In many offenses, §2.02(3) will have no application. Consider homicide, for example.

> A person is guilty of criminal homicide if he purposely, knowingly, recklessly or negligently causes the death of another human being.

The different degrees of homicide are then identified as dependent upon the actor's level of culpability: purposefully or knowingly causing the death is murder, recklessly is manslaughter, and negligently is negligent homicide.[41] The more limited application of §2.02(4) nonetheless would mean that the culpability stated in the offense would apply to all elements, both culpability as to causing death and culpability as to the victim being a "human being." Because the offense is defined in a single clause, the stated culpability requirement would apply to all elements of the offense, including the circumstance element of "human being."[42] Thus, if "human being" were defined for homicide purposes to include a "viable fetus," the doctor who purposely kills a fetus and is reckless as to it being a viable fetus, would be liable for manslaughter but not murder.[43]

Proposals as Setting Drafting Technique Not Dictating Content Note that the proposed interpretations described here are not designed to either raise or lower the culpability requirements of offense definitions. They are, rather, designed to create a system in which the legislature can effectively, easily, and clearly define the culpability requirements as it desires. If a culpability requirement other than recklessness is to apply to a particular element, the legislature need only state such culpability requirement in the offense definition. If the legislature desires the stated requirement to apply to more than one element, it can achieve this by its choice of placement of the stated culpability term within the offense definition. The legislature can provide an explicit culpability requirement to apply to particular elements (those within the clause) without fear that the requirement will be interpreted to apply more broadly than it is intended.[44]

---

41. See Model Penal Code §§210.2, 210.3, and 210.4.

42. That this is the intended reading of the homicide statute is supported by Model Penal Code §2.02(10), which provides that where the grade or degree of an offense depends upon its culpability level, the grade or degree shall be that for the lowest culpability for any element. Thus, if §2.02(3) were applied to require reckless as to "human being" in homicide, one could be purposeful as to the killing and reckless as to "human being" yet still be liable only for manslaughter, under §2.02(10).

43. One might argue that, while this application of §2.02(4) is not inappropriate in homicide, it generates improper results in other instances. Under Model Penal Code §211.1(1)(b), for example, it is an assault if the actor "negligently causes bodily injury to another with a deadly weapon." Is it clear that the negligence requirement ought to apply both to "causing bodily injury" *and* to "with a deadly weapon"? Should an actor be liable for assault if he has no awareness of even a risk that what he has is a "deadly weapon"?

44. The conflict between §§2.02(3) and 2.02(4) mirrors the two competing forms of the definition of offenses—element analysis and offense analysis—described previously. In providing that any stated culpability level applies to all elements of the offense, §2.02(4) is characteristic of an offense-analysis model of offense definition. Section 2.02(3), on the other hand, reflects the element analysis approach adopted in §§2.02(1) and 2.02(2), which allow and facilitate the application of different culpability requirements to different elements of the same offense. Section 2.02(3), of course, is central to the implementation of element analysis. It assures that each objective element has

Questions

1. *Objective Requirements.* What are the objective requirements of the offense of Tampering with Records with which Jake is charged? Is "falsifies or removes, etc., a record" one element or more than one? Because "falsifies" is a single word, is it fair to say it must be a single element? Is it necessary that Jake "deceive or injure anyone"? In other words, is such a deception or injury an objective requirement of the offense?

2. *Culpability Requirements.* What are the culpability requirements of the "Tampering with Records" statute excerpted above? For example, what is the culpability required as to "falsifies"? as to having "no privilege"?

3. *Jake's Liability.* (a) As to Count One of the indictment against Jake—for causing the removal of Anna's record—what result? Does he satisfy the required culpability as to "no privilege"?

(b) As to Count Two—changing Bob's grades to *F*'s—what result?

(c) As to Count Three—changing Bob's grades back to *B*'s—what result? How many different interpretations can you give of the culpability required as to "falsifies"? Do §§2.02(3) and 2.02(4) give potentially different results?

(d) As to Count Four—fabricating Anna's file to conceal his earlier error in allowing the file to be removed—what result? Would it matter if Bob had made all lucky guesses and gotten Anna's grades all correct?

SECTION 7.2 MINIMUM CULPABILITY REQUIREMENTS: THE DEBATE OVER RECKLESSNESS, NEGLIGENCE, AND STRICT LIABILITY

Previous sections have outlined the basic requirements for a finding of recklessness or negligence. The former requires some awareness of the facts that make the conduct criminal. The latter requires no such awareness, but does require culpable inattention to such facts. Strict liability does not require either form of culpability. Should the criminal law require at least recklessness as the basis for liability? Is the use of negligence appropriate? Is strict liability ever justified in the criminal context? To help us address these questions, let us look more closely at the precise requirements of recklessness and negligence in their modern form.

---

an accompanying culpability requirement, but does not assume that such culpability is the same for each element of an offense.

Oatmeal for Ian

Dad usually leaves for work before two-year-old Ian is up but today Mom has an early meeting and Dad has none until 9:15 AM. He will feed Ian his breakfast of choice, cooked oatmeal with applesauce, drop him at day care, and make it to work just in time for his 9:15 meeting. Dad puts the oatmeal on the stove while he gets dressed. Several minutes later, Ian comes screaming into the bedroom with a burned hand. The burn looks horrible and Dad is very upset. He knows that ointment and bandages must be in the house somewhere but he cannot find them so he puts Ian into the car and drives to the pharmacy. He drives too quickly, however; he fails to keep an eye on his speedometer and is stopped and ticketed for speeding. The ointment seems to work well and the pharmacist assures him that the burn is not as serious as he thought. Ian will be fine.

Dad has missed his 9:15 meeting but nonetheless is relieved, until he arrives back at the apartment to find the fire department at work and angry neighbors in pajamas and robes. Apparently he left the stove on, the oatmeal caught fire, set the kitchen on fire, and the fire spread to the adjoining apartments, destroying that part of the building and the personal effects of his neighbors. Luckily, no one was injured, but his neighbors are demanding that Dad be criminally charged for his carelessness in starting the fire. Criminal liability for Dad for property destruction? For speeding? The answer depends on the level of culpability required by these offenses as compared to Dad's culpability. What is Dad's level of culpability with respect to causing the property destruction? With respect to exceeding the speed limit?

State v. Williams
Court of Appeals of Washington
4 Wash. App. 908, 484 P.2d 1167 (1971)

HOROWITZ, Chief Judge.

Defendants, husband and wife, were charged by information filed October 3, 1968, with the crime of manslaughter for negligently failing to supply their 17-month-old child with necessary medical attention, as a result of which he died on September 12, 1968. Upon entry of findings, conclusions and judgment of guilty, sentences were imposed on April 22, 1969. Defendants appeal.

The defendant husband, Walter Williams, is a 24-year-old full-blooded Shoshoni Indian with a sixth-grade education. His sole occupation is that of laborer. The defendant wife, Bernice Williams, is a 20-year-old Indian with an 11th grade education. At the time of the marriage, the wife had two children, the younger of whom was a 14-month-old son. Both parents worked and the children were cared for by the 85-year-old mother of the defendant husband. The defendant husband assumed parental responsibility with the defendant wife to provide clothing, care, and medical attention for the child. Both defendants possessed a great deal of love and affection for the defendant wife's young son.

The court expressly found:

> That both defendants were aware that William Joseph Tabafunda was ill during the period September 1, 1968 to September 12, 1968. The defendants were ignorant. They did not realize how sick the baby was. They thought that the baby had a toothache and no layman regards a toothache as dangerous to life. They loved the baby and gave it aspirin in hopes of improving its condition. . . . They knew that medical help was available because of previous experience. They had no excuse that the law will recognize for not taking the baby to a doctor.
>
> The defendants Walter L. Williams and Bernice J. Williams were negligent in not seeking medical attention for William Joseph Tabafunda.
>
> That as a proximate result of this negligence, William Joseph Tabafunda died.

From these and other findings, the court concluded that the defendants were each guilty of the crime of manslaughter as charged.

Defendants take no exception to findings but contend that the findings do not support the conclusion that the defendants are guilty of manslaughter as charged. The contentions raise two basic issues, (1) the existence of the duty to furnish medical aid charged by the information to be violated and the seriousness of the breach required; and (2) the issue of proximate cause, i.e., whether defendants were put on notice, in time to save the child's life, that medical care was required. Because the nature of the duty and the quality or seriousness of the breach are closely interrelated, our discussion of the first issue involved will embrace both matters.

Parental duty to provide medical care for a dependent minor child was recognized at common law and characterized as a natural duty. . . . On the question of the quality or seriousness of breach of the duty, at common law, in the case of involuntary manslaughter, the breach had to amount to more than mere ordinary or simple negligence—gross negligence was essential. . . . Under [the Washington manslaughter statutes, however,] the crime is deemed committed even though the death of the victim is the proximate result of only simple or ordinary negligence.

The concept of simple or ordinary negligence describes a failure to exercise the "ordinary caution" necessary to make out the defense of excusable homicide. RCW 9.48.150. Ordinary caution is the kind of caution that a man of reasonable prudence would exercise under the same or similar conditions. If, therefore, the conduct of a defendant, regardless of his ignorance, good intentions and good faith, fails to measure up to the conduct required of a man of reasonable prudence, he is guilty of ordinary negligence because of his failure to use "ordinary caution." If such negligence proximately causes the death of the victim, the defendant, as pointed out above, is guilty of statutory manslaughter. . . .

. . . The information charged the violation of "the legal duty of providing necessary . . . medical attention to said . . . minor child. . . ." This general language permits reliance upon the existence of the legal duty no matter from what source derived. We have already pointed out that such a parental duty is recognized in the decisions of this state and has been characterized as a natural duty existing independently of statutes. . . . We therefore hold that the violation of the parental duty to furnish medical care to a minor dependent child, the other elements of manslaughter being present, is a sufficient basis on which to rest a conviction of the crime of manslaughter under RCW 9.48.060 and 9.48.150.

In the instant case, however, the defendant husband is not the father of the minor child, nor has he adopted that child. Nevertheless, the evidence shows that he had assumed responsibility with his wife for the care and maintenance of the child, whom he greatly loved. Such assumption of responsibility, characterized in the information as that required of a "guardian and custodian," is sufficient to impose upon him the duty to furnish necessary medical care. . . .

The remaining issue of proximate cause requires consideration of the question of when the duty to furnish medical care became activated. If the duty to furnish such care was not activated until after it was too late to save the life of the child, failure to furnish medical care could not be said to have proximately caused the child's death. Timeliness in the furnishing of medical care also must be considered in terms of "ordinary caution." The law does not mandatorily require that a doctor be called for a child at the first sign of any indisposition or illness. The indisposition or illness may appear to be of a minor or very temporary kind, such as a toothache or cold. If one in the exercise of ordinary caution fails to recognize that his child's symptoms require medical attention, it cannot be said that the failure to obtain such medical attention is a breach of the duty owed. In our opinion, the duty as formulated in People v. Pierson, 176 N.Y. 201, 68 N.E. 243 (1903) . . . properly defines the duty contemplated by our manslaughter statutes RCW 9.48.060 and RCW 9.48.150. The court there said:

CHAPTER 7 DEFINING OFFENSES: A CLOSER LOOK   203

> We quite agree that the Code does not contemplate the necessity of calling a physician for every trifling complaint with which the child may be afflicted, which in most instances may be overcome by the ordinary household nursing by members of the family; that a reasonable amount of discretion is vested in parents, charged with the duty of maintaining and bringing up infant children; and that the standard is at what time would an ordinarily prudent person, solicitous for the welfare of his child and anxious to promote its recovery, deem it necessary to call in the services of a physician. . . .

It remains to apply the law discussed to the facts of the instant case.

Defendants have not assigned error to the findings either on the ground that the evidence is insufficient to prove negligence or proximate cause, or that the state has failed to prove the facts found by failing to apply the required standard of proof beyond a reasonable doubt. . . . They contended below and on appeal that they are not guilty of the crime charged. Because of the serious nature of the charge against the parent and step-parent of a well-loved child, and out of our concern for the protection of the constitutional rights of the defendants, we have made an independent examination of the evidence to determine whether it substantially supports the court's express finding on proximate cause and its implied finding that the duty to furnish medical care became activated in time to prevent death of the child.

Dr. Gale Wilson, the autopsy surgeon and chief pathologist for the King County Coroner, testified that the child died because an abscessed tooth had been allowed to develop into an infection of the mouth and cheeks, eventually becoming gangrenous. This condition, accompanied by the child's inability to eat, brought about malnutrition, lowering the child's resistance and eventually producing pneumonia, causing the death. Dr. Wilson testified that in his opinion the infection had lasted for approximately two weeks, and that the odor generally associated with gangrene would have been present for approximately 10 days before death. He also expressed the opinion that had medical care been first obtained in the last week before the baby's death, such care would have been obtained too late to have saved the baby's life. Accordingly, the baby's apparent condition between September 1 and September 5, 1968 became the critical period for the purpose of determining whether in the exercise of ordinary caution defendants should have provided medical care for the minor child.

The testimony concerning the child's apparent condition during the critical period is not crystal clear, but is sufficient to warrant the following statement of the matter. The defendant husband testified that he noticed the baby was sick about 2 weeks before the baby died. The defendant wife testified that she noticed the baby was ill about a week and a half or two weeks before the baby died. The evidence showed that in the critical period the baby was fussy; that he could not keep his food down; and that a cheek started swelling up. The swelling went up and down, but did not disappear. In that same period, the cheek turned "a bluish color like." The defendants, not realizing that the baby was as ill as it was or that the baby was in danger of dying, attempted to provide some relief to the baby by giving the baby aspirin during the critical period and continued to do so until the night before the baby died. The defendants thought the swelling would go down and were waiting for it to do so; and defendant husband testified, that from what he had heard, neither doctors nor dentists pull out a tooth "when it's all swollen up like that." There was an additional explanation for not calling a doctor given by each defendant. Defendant husband testified that "the way the cheek looked, . . . and that stuff on his hair, they would think we were neglecting him and take him away from us and not give him back." Defendant wife testified that the defendants were "waiting for the swelling to go down." . . . The evidence showed that the defendants did not understand the significance or seriousness of the baby's symptoms. However, there is no evidence that the defendants were physically or financially unable to obtain a doctor, or that they did not know an available doctor, or that the symptoms did not continue to be a matter of concern during the critical period. Indeed, the evidence shows that in April 1968 defendant husband had taken the child to a doctor for medical attention.

In our opinion, there is sufficient evidence from which the court could find, as it necessarily did, that applying the standard of ordinary caution, i.e., the caution exercisable by a man of reasonable prudence under the same or similar conditions, defendants were sufficiently put on notice concerning the symptoms of the baby's illness and lack of improvement in the baby's apparent condition in the period from September 1 to September 5, 1968 to have required them to have obtained medical care for the child. The failure so to do in this case is ordinary or simple negligence, and such negligence is sufficient to support a conviction of statutory manslaughter.

The judgment is affirmed.

Reasons for Punishing Negligence
G. Williams, Criminal Law: The General Part
122-124 (2d ed. 1961)

The use of the criminal law to punish negligence has been challenged. An American writer expressed the objection as follows:

If the defendant, being mistaken as to material facts, is to be punished because his mistake is one which an average man would not make, punishment will sometimes be inflicted when the criminal mind does not exist. Such a result is contrary to fundamental principles, and is plainly unjust, for a man should not be held criminal because of lack of intelligence.

The retributive theory of punishment is open to many objections, which are of even greater force when applied to inadvertent negligence than in crimes requiring *mens rea*. Some people are born reckless, clumsy, thoughtless, inattentive, irresponsible, with a bad memory and a slow "reaction time." With the best will in the world, we all of us at some times in our lives make negligent mistakes. It is hard to see how justice (as distinct from some utilitarian reason) requires mistakes to be punished.

Again, the deterrent theory, which is normally accepted as a justification for criminal punishment, finds itself in some difficulty when applied to negligence. At best the deterrent effect of the legal sanction is a matter of faith rather than of proved scientific fact; but there is no department in which this faith is less firmly grounded than that of negligence. . . . Even if a person admits that he occasionally makes a negligent mistake, how, in the nature of things, can punishment for inadvertence serve to deter? . . .

The argument in favour of punishment is that, just as it is possible for punishment to cause a person to exercise greater control over his acts in view of the known dangers, so it is possible for punishment to bring about greater foresight, by causing the subject to stop and think before committing himself to a course of conduct. . . .

[T]he law acts wisely in making such punishment exceptional. Even where punishment is imposed, it best takes the form of a fine, operating as a warning for the future rather than as a substantial punishment for the past. Loss of liberty is not a necessary measure for those who cause harm inadvertently. If the offender is so incompetent as to be a social danger in his present occupation, the remedy is not to incarcerate him but (if milder methods of correction fail) to exclude him from the activity in which he is a danger.

Questions

1. *Dad's Culpability.* Was Dad reckless as to speeding? causing property damage? Under the approach of the *Williams* case, was Dad at least negligent in exceeding the speed limit? in causing the property damage? Might he be found negligent as to one but non-negligent as to the

other? Would your answers be different under the Model Penal Code's definition of negligence?

2. *Individualizing the Reasonable Person Standard in Negligence.* Recall that in discussing homicide mitigation for extreme emotional disturbance (see *Ott* in Section 4.5) we saw the Model Penal Code drafters use the phrase "in the actor's situation" as a mechanism to invite a court to individualize the objective standard in judging the reasonableness of the actor's explanation or excuse for the killing. The same phrase is used by the Code in the definition of negligence (and recklessness) and for a similar reason. As before, however, the drafters are less than clear on what conditions or characteristics may be used to modify the objective standard.

> A further point in the Code's concept of negligence merits attention. The standard for ultimate judgement invites consideration of the "care that a reasonable person would observe in the actor's situation." There is an inevitable ambiguity in "situation." If the actor were blind or if he had just suffered a blow or experienced a heart attack, these would certainly be facts to be considered in a judgement involving criminal liability, as they would be under traditional law. But the heredity, intelligence or temperament of the actor would not be held material in judging negligence, and could not be without depriving the criterion of all its objectivity. The Code is not intended to displace discriminations of this kind, but rather to leave the issue to the courts.

Model Penal Code §2.02 comment 4 at 242 (1985). Is Dad's upset relevant in assessing whether he is negligent? Would it be significant that his wife would not have committed either violation if faced with the same situation? Would it matter if he had never taken care of the child before? Would it matter if his 9:15 appointment was with his brain-injury support group? a training class he was taking for mentally retarded people? with his psychiatrist, who was treating an illness manifested by low self-esteem and a corresponding belief in an inability to handle emergency situations?

3. *Individualizing the Reasonable Person Standard in Recklessness.* If Dad were aware of a risk that he was exceeding the speed limit or of a risk of burning the apartment building, would he be reckless as to those facts? Would any of the factors listed in the question above be relevant in determining whether he was reckless as to speeding or as to causing the property destruction? How is the reasonable person standard used differently in negligence than in recklessness? Specifically, what does the actor have to be reasonable about in negligence? in recklessness?

4. *Individualization and Racism.* The court in *Williams* notes in its recitation of the facts that the defendants are both Native American Indians. Of what relevance is this? What are the situations, if any, in

which a court should individualize the objective standard in negligence (or recklessness) with the race of the defendant? In other words, when might a defendant's race matter, if ever, in judging the blameworthiness of his or her failure to perceive a risk (or of his or her disregard of a known risk)?

5. *Negligence as a Basis for Criminal Liability.* What arguments can you make against the use of negligence as the basis for criminal liability? What arguments can you make in support of its use?

6. *Negligence and Omissions.* In *Williams,* the defendants are charged with causing the death of their child through their omission to get timely medical care. Is negligence an issue only in cases of omission, or might it also be an issue in a commission case? Dad failed to keep an eye on his speedometer and failed to take the oatmeal off the stove. Is his liability based upon an omission theory, as in *Williams?* (Omission liability is examined in detail in Chapter 13.)

Criticism of Practical Grounds of Strict Liability
J. Hall, General Principles of Criminal Law
342-351 (2d ed. 1960)

In appraising the practical arguments that have been made in support of strict liability, little time need be devoted to the emphasis on the slightness of the penalty. Quite apart from the outrageous exceptions met in reference to various major crimes, that explanation is patently apologetic. One can understand how it influenced the judges to ignore established principles; but it is certainly no justification of strict liability. Slight penalties may in some circumstances suggest the need for a simplified procedure and even warrant the removal of procedural safeguards normally insisted on. They cannot be relied on to discard rational penal liability.

More persuasive is the argument that in many of the cases where only the external facts need be proved, it is very probable that there was *mens rea,* e.g., the race tout in possession of lottery tickets, of whose character he was "innocent," or the crafty restaurateur in possession of forbidden liquor. In other cases, despite the "at peril" dogma, the courts have required proof of certain knowledge, e.g., that a bottle (of liquor) was known to be on the premises and was not simply "planted"; and presumably no court would convict a psychotic person or a somnambulist of any offense. It may accordingly be maintained that, despite the avowals of strict liability, intent and negligence actually play some essential part in such offenses. The key to understanding the public welfare offenses, therefore, it may be urged, is that they are designed to catch the willful and the negligent; they are not intended to penalize those who were faultless. But the statutes are so phrased as to include the innocent, and these are caught occasionally as a result of incompetent administration.

But the above arguments are untenable. Beyond indicating that behavior subjected to strict liability is sometimes distinguished from sheer accident, they merely imply that some of the offenses which are declared to be within the scope of strict liability are actually treated as requiring *mens rea*. That offers no justification of strict liability even if *mens rea* is proved. For the argument is plainly a *petitio principii* [begging the question]. It amounts not to any defense of strict liability, but rests instead on the assumption that a wise administration of these statutes avoids their admitted evil. No one would think of maintaining such a position regarding any major crime—e.g., a statute which provided that anyone who killed a human being must be held guilty of murder—on the ground that the statute would be enforced only against those who killed with malice aforethought. Nor can the assumption that strict liability is always invoked only against culpable or negligent offenders be admitted on either logical or empirical grounds. There are few facts to support such an optimistic interpretation and numerous cases oppose it. On the other hand, if enforcement is actually directed only against the culpable, there is no warrant for retaining strict liability. The fact that prosecutors often or even usually enforce strict regulations only against culpable offenders does not support strict liability. Instead, it implies that they have the evidence to prove *mens rea* and that the argument of extraordinary difficulty in that regard is unsound.

Another argument in support of strict liability is the claim that it serves as a prod to stimulate increased care and efficiency—even by those who are already careful and efficient. The assumption is that, e.g., the officials of a corporation, knowing about strict liability or having it imposed upon them, will take precautionary measures beyond what they would otherwise employ. It seems probable that most persons and businesses within the potential orbit of strict liability can improve their methods of operation. Strict liability is the gadfly which stimulates the greater effort; this redounds to the public good. The objective is unassailable; the sanctions are so slight that there is no serious ground for concern even though the "wrong" persons are occasionally subjected to them—hence criticism of strict liability from the viewpoint of the principles of penal law is merely academic. There is already a consensus that strict liability is not penal law; let us call it "economic law" or "administrative regulation," if such tagging is preferred. But let us retain it "as is"—that is the ultimate conclusion of the above justification of strict liability.

But that argument, like certain myths, is just too good to be true. It rests wholly on assumptions that have never been established. That

CHAPTER 7   DEFINING OFFENSES: A CLOSER LOOK   209

there is always room for improvement of business operations is at best a very loose generalization; frequently it is quite fallacious. The cost of operation is one serious limitation. Only "in the abstract" is it possible to employ chemists, bacteriologists, etc., etc., to analyze every can of food shipped from all the factories in America. Actually such care and efficiency are incompatible with operating a business at all. Thus an elementary discrimination of what is possible takes the form of what is reasonable—else we merely indulge in exhortation, not actual problem-solving.

If it be conceded that there are margins for improvement of business methods which are reasonably available but not yet tapped, there remains the question: Is strict liability a suitable means to implementation of that end? It need not, of course, be the whole means or the most effective of the various controls. But defense of it surely implies that it has some merit, that it does appreciably increase the social good sufficiently above its various costs to justify its continuance. There are several impelling reasons for doubting this hypothesis.

There is, first, the opinion of highly qualified experts that the present rules are regarded by unscrupulous persons merely "as a license fee for doing an illegitimate business." Such persons are not deterred by the imposition of nominal fines. To let off with a petty fine those who intentionally or recklessly violate such laws as the Pure Food Act is to encourage them to persist in their malevolence; as suggested, it is merely to impose a nominal tax on illegal enterprise. It seems only slightly less probable that the facile practice of imposing such sanctions handicaps the imposition of penalties that are commensurate with the gravity of willful adulteration of food and the like. The legislature is lulled into complacency by "passing a law"; prosecutors are content with the bulge of statistics on "convictions"; and the general public is grossly uninformed. There can hardly be any doubt that strict liability is a futile gesture so far as unscrupulous persons are concerned, i.e., as regards the very ones who are the proper targets of punitive sanctions. Regarding such individuals, it is necessary to put real teeth in the law. Not the least effect would be the elevation of the mores towards a wider appreciation of the gravity of those offenses.

Is it likely that strict liability stimulates care and efficiency on the part of reputable businessmen? That it does so in some cases may be granted, especially perhaps in individually owned businesses where the publicity following a conviction may be far-reaching and possibly disastrous to the future operation of the business. The pertinent question is whether this kind of influence is desirable. Moreover, for large corporations, the probability is that their own standards of service as well as competition for the market are the principal determinants of their business conduct. That they are to any appreciable extent further conditioned by the fear or the imposition of nominal fines is unlikely. Paramount in any realistic appraisal is that the stigma ordinarily attached to a conviction is vitiated by the knowledge that neither moral culpability nor negligence is implied. . . .

It is not very likely that improvement of either business conduct or public opinion is advanced by maintaining an attendant antagonism with the deeply rooted conviction that only the blameworthy should be punished. . . . Penal law implies moral culpability. Corrective law implies that defects exist and that they can be removed. These implications are irrelevant, indeed antithetical, to strict liability. For, since that liability is meaningful only in its complete exclusion of fault, it is patently inconsistent to assert, e.g., that a businessman is honest, exercises care and skill, and also, if a misbranded or adulterated package of food somehow, unknown to anyone, is shipped from his establishment, that he should be punished or coercively educated to increase his efficiency.

Thus, as one probes for some rational ground of strict liability (outside of torts), it becomes increasingly like the proverbial search in the dark room for the black cat that isn't there. For any attempt to supply a rational base in support of strict liability is itself unsuited to, indeed, is antithetical to, what is sought to be justified. Inasmuch as strict liability means that regardless of lack of intent, recklessness, negligence, the use of superior knowledge and skill, etc., penal liability must nonetheless be imposed, it is impossible to defend strict liability in terms of or by reference to the only criteria that are available to evaluate the influence of legal controls on human conduct. What then remains but the myth that through devious, unknown ways some good results from strict liability in "penal" law?

An important clue to what is actually the principal support of strict liability is provided by the fact that from the very beginning of the public welfare offenses to the present time, there has been an unvarying insistence on the difficulty of proving *mens rea;* e.g., "to permit such a defense would be to allow every violator to avoid liability merely by pleading lack of knowledge and thus, practically, nullify the statute. . . ." This argument implies that even though *mens rea* exists, it is impossible to prove it, presumably because there are distinctive features in such cases that make this proof peculiarly difficult. But if we appraise the actual situation in this respect, without prejudging it, it is impossible to attach any great weight to that argument. It amounts to no more than a bare assertion or a mere guess. . . .

 . . . It was statistics, not any distinctive feature of [strict liability] offenses, that suggested the argument that proof of *mens rea* would be onerous and that to insist upon it would nullify the statutes. Judged on its merits, this argument is hardly more than an admission that what ought to be adjudicated is not adjudicated, and a rationalization of that on the ground of necessity. That is the *ratio ultima* of strict liability.

Model Penal Code §2.05
When Culpability Requirements Are Inapplicable to Violations and to Offenses Defined by Other Statutes; Effect of Absolute Liability in Reducing Grade of Offense to Violation

(1) The requirements of culpability prescribed by Sections 2.01 and 2.02 do not apply to:

    (a) offenses which constitute violations, unless the requirement involved is included in the definition of the offense or the Court determines that its application is consistent with effective enforcement of the law defining the offense; or

    (b) offenses defined by statutes other than the Code, insofar as a legislative purpose to impose absolute liability for such offenses or with respect to any material element thereof plainly appears.

(2) Notwithstanding any other provision of existing law and unless a subsequent statute otherwise provides:

    (a) when absolute liability is imposed with respect to any material element of an offense defined by a statute other than the Code and a conviction is based upon such liability, the offense constitutes a violation; and

    (b) although absolute liability is imposed by law with respect to one or more of the material elements of an offense defined by a statute other than the Code, the culpable commission of the offense may be charged and proved, in which event negligence with respect to such elements constitutes sufficient culpability and the classification of the offense and the sentence that may be imposed therefor upon conviction are determined by Section 1.04 and Article 6 of the Code.

State v. Buttrey
Supreme Court of Oregon
651 P.2d 1075 (1982)

PETERSON, Justice . . .

1. In a prosecution for driving while suspended, do Oregon statutes require the state to prove a culpable mental state, i.e., that the defendant, at the time of the offense, had actual or constructive knowledge that her license had been suspended?

2. Was defendant denied Fourteenth Amendment due process ei-

ther because she was convicted absent any showing of mens rea or because ORS 482.560 unconstitutionally shifts the burden of disproving an element of the crime, knowledge, to the defendant? . . .

The case was tried to the court without a jury. The defendant stipulated that she was driving upon a highway. A copy of the order suspending her driver's license was received in evidence. The driving occurred during the suspension period. Appended to the suspension order was a certificate that the copy of the suspension order was correct and that the order "was mailed to the official address of record as recorded on the Motor Vehicles Division record." No return receipt was offered in evidence and there was no evidence, other than the suspension order itself and the certificate thereon, that the defendant had received the notice of suspension. The exhibit was received without objection.

The defendant moved for acquittal asserting that there was no proof of mens rea and that the "shifting of the burden" under ORS 487.560(2) (set forth below) was unconstitutional. The trial court denied the motion and found the defendant guilty of a class C felony, stating:

> The Court: I find that the Plaintiff, the State, has proven the elements of the offense beyond a reasonable doubt—driving by the defendant on the date alleged on a public street or road in Multnomah County and at a time when the Defendant's license to drive was suspended as a result of a conviction for driving under the influence of intoxicating liquor, and therefore I will find the Defendant guilty of felony driving while suspended.

The court suspended imposition of sentence and placed the defendant on five years' probation and required her to serve one year in the county jail. The Court of Appeals affirmed the conviction from the bench.

A Culpable Mental State Is Not An Element Of Driving
While Suspended. ORS 487.560

Historically, criminal liability has required both an act and a culpable mental state. In the past century, legislatures have passed numerous statutes which have imposed criminal liability unaccustomed by fault. Strict liability statutes have been passed because of the difficulty in proving intent, knowledge, recklessness or negligence, and because of a legislative perception that evil should be eradicated, even at the risk of convicting blameless defendants. Oregon has enacted such statutes.

The defendant claims that there are three elements to the crime

CHAPTER 7 DEFINING OFFENSES: A CLOSER LOOK 213

of driving while suspended, (1) driving a vehicle upon a highway, (2) with a suspended license, (3) with knowledge of the suspension. For the purposes of this opinion we will assume that there is no evidence that the defendant had actual or constructive knowledge that her license has been suspended. The decision turns on an analysis of the statute defining the crime, ORS 487.560 (which was enacted in 1975 as part of a comprehensive motor vehicle code reform), and general provisions in the Oregon Criminal Code of 1971, ORS chapter 161.

The Oregon Criminal Code was revised in 1971. The drafters of the law and the legislature were very much aware of "strict liability" crimes. In the "purposes" section of the code, ORS 161.025(1)(d), this legislative purpose is stated:

> (1) The general purposes of chapter 743, Oregon Laws 1971, are: . . .
> (d) To define the act or omission and the accompanying mental state that constitute each offense and limit the condemnation of conduct as criminal when it is without fault.

The Criminal Code sought to create a uniform system for determining offense classifications and culpability requirements. The Criminal Code includes provisions defining a "culpable mental state," ORS 161.085, and describing when a culpable mental state must be proved, ORS 161.095, ORS 161.115, and ORS 161.105. ORS 161.085 lists and defines four culpable mental states—intentionally, knowingly, recklessly and criminal negligence—each of which require a form of awareness or failure to be aware as a requirement of criminal liability.

A culpable mental state is generally required for criminal liability to be imposed. ORS 161.095 (2) provides:

> (2) except as provided in ORS 161.105, a person is not guilty of an offense unless he acts with a culpable mental state with respect to each material element of the offense that necessarily requires a culpable mental state.

ORS 161.115(2) provides:

> (2) Except as provided in ORS 161.105, if a statute defining an offense does not prescribe a culpable mental state, culpability is nonetheless required and is established only if a person acts intentionally, knowingly, recklessly or with criminal negligence.

ORS 161.105(1)(b), the "exception" statute referred to in ORS 161.095(2) and ORS 161.115(2), states:

> (1) Notwithstanding ORS 161.095, a culpable mental state is not required if:
> (b) An offense defined by a statute outside the Oregon Criminal

Code clearly indicates a legislative intent to dispense with any culpable mental state requirement for the offense or for any material element thereof.

The criminal statute under which the defendant was charged and convicted, ORS 487.560, is outside the Criminal Code. It provided:

> (1) A person commits the crime of driving while suspended if he drives a motor vehicle upon a highway during a period when his license or permit to drive a motor vehicle or his right to apply for a license to drive a motor vehicle in this state has been suspended by a court or by the division or revoked by the division or if he drives a motor vehicle outside the restrictions of a license issued under ORS 482.475 or 482.477.
>
> (2) In a prosecution under subsection (1) of this section, it is an affirmative defense that:
>
> (a) An injury or immediate threat of injury to human or animal life and the urgency of the circumstances made it necessary for the defendant to drive a motor vehicle at the time and place in question; or
>
> (b) The defendant had not received notice of his suspension or revocation as required by ORS 482.570 or in the manner provided in paragraph (c) of subsection (3) of this section.
>
> (3) The affirmative defense under paragraph (b) of subsection (2) of this section shall not be available to the defendant if:
>
> (a) The defendant refused to sign a receipt for the certified mail containing the notice; or
>
> (b) The notice could not be delivered to the defendant because he had not notified the division of his address or a change in his residence as required by subsection (3) of ORS 482.290; or
>
> (c) At a previous court appearance, the defendant had been informed by a trial judge that the judge was ordering a suspension of the defendant's license, permit or right to apply; or
>
> (d) The defendant had actual knowledge of the suspension or revocation by any means prior to the time he was stopped on the current charge. . . . ; [or]
>
> (f) Driving while under the influence of intoxicants.

Although the parties agree that ORS 487.560 is "an offense defined by a statute outside the Oregon Criminal Code," they do not agree that the statute "clearly indicates a legislative intent to dispense with any culpable mental state requirement for the offense or for any material element thereof." Our conclusion is that the language of ORS 487.560 itself clearly indicates a legislative intent to dispense with a culpable mental state requirement, and the legislative history puts the matter beyond question.

The key provisions, insofar as the question before us is concerned, are subsections (1), (2) and (3). Subsection (1) defines the crime. Two elements are stated. Driving a motor vehicle upon a highway. During a period when the license has been suspended. Subsection (1) does not prescribe a culpable mental state, but suggests that if the two elements are shown, proof of those elements alone is sufficient to convict. Subsection (1), by itself, does not "clearly [indicate] a legislative intent to dispense with any culpable mental state requirement." Doubt is dispelled, however, by subsections (2) and (3). Subsection (2) lists two possible "affirmative defenses," one in the nature of a choice of evils defense, section (2)(a), the other relating to the lack of receipt of notice of the suspension, section (2)(b).

The term "affirmative defense" is defined in the Criminal Code as follows:

> When a defense, declared to be an 'affirmative defense' by chapter 743, Oregon Laws 1971, is raised at a trial, the defendant has the burden of proving the defense by a preponderance of the evidence.

The legislative intent is clear: The state makes a prima facie case upon proof of the two elements in ORS 487.560(1), without proof of a culpable mental state, i.e., without proof of any knowledge by the defendant of the license suspension. The defendant can avoid liability by establishing the affirmative defense by a preponderance of the evidence. The state, in turn, can avoid the effect of the notice defense afforded by ORS 487.560(2)(b) by establishing beyond any reasonable doubt that the defendant "refused to sign a receipt for the certified mail containing the notice," ORS 487.560(3)(a), or that "[t]he notice could not be delivered . . . because he had not notified the division of his address or a change in his residence as required by subsection (3) or ORS 482.290," ORS 487.560(3)(b), or that the defendant had been informed by a trial judge that the judge was ordering a suspension of the license, ORS 487.560(3)(c), or that the defendant had actual knowledge of the suspension, ORS 487.560(3)(d).

Subsections (1), (2) and (3) of ORS 487.560, considered together and with ORS 161.055(2) (which defines an affirmative defense), set forth a procedure for the blameless defendant to establish a defense. The statutes clearly indicate that the legislature intended that the state, in its case in chief, need not prove any culpable mental state, but that the defendant might avoid conviction for conduct which is otherwise criminal by establishing one of the defenses enumerated in ORS 487.560(2)(b). As discussed below, if the state is required to prove a culpable mental state as an element of the crime, then subsections (2)(b) and (3)(d) of the statue are surplusage.

The legislative history confirms this analysis. It reveals that the legislature was concerned with a massive social problem. Suspended drivers constituted a dangerous class of drivers, causing carnage on the highway and clogged courts. Prosecutions were difficult. The legislature believed that this class of drivers caused unnecessary human suffering and constituted, as a class, a disproportionate danger. The legislature was so concerned with the risk to person and property that it wanted to make certain conduct punishable as a crime, without fault. . . .

The dissenters assert that *knowledge* of the suspension is an element of the crime; that the defendant can establish a defense if he or she can provide that he or she had not received proper *notice;* and that the driver loses this affirmative defense if the state proves that he or she had knowledge of the suspension. If, as claimed by the dissent, some form of *knowledge* is an element of the crime, then the application of the notice subsections, (2)(b) and (3)(d), results in a circuity. . . .

ORS 487.560 Does Not Violate The Due Process Clause
Of The Fourteenth Amendment

Defendant makes two Fourteenth Amendment contentions. First, she cites Lambert v. California, 355 U.S. 225 (1957), asserting that "as a matter of due process . . . proof of knowledge is a necessary element of the crime." In *Lambert,* the court held that a city ordinance which, *inter alia,* made it a crime for any convicted felon to be or remain in Los Angeles for more than five days without registering with the police department, was invalid under the Fourteenth Amendment. The opinion contains little explanation of the holding, and other Supreme Court opinions, some of which are referred to below, make it clear that the holding is limited to the facts there presented.

The Supreme Court of the United States, in applying the federal Constitution, has generally refused to interfere with the historical state power to create strict liability crimes.

> . . . The doctrines of *actus reus, mens rea,* insanity, mistake, justification and duress have historically provided the tools for a constantly shifting adjustment of the tension between the evolving aims of the criminal law and changing religious, moral, philosophical, and medical view of the nature of man. This process of adjustment has always been thought to be the province of the States. Powell v. Texas, 392 U.S. 514 (1968) (plurality opinion).
>
> . . . The legislatures have always been allowed wide freedom to determine the extent to which moral culpability should be a prerequisite to conviction of a crime. Id. 392 U.S. at 545 (Black, J., concurring).

See United States v. Balint, 258 U.S. 250 (1922) (affirming conviction for selling narcotics with no evidence that defendants knew they were selling narcotics); United States v. Dotterweich, 320 U.S. 277 (1943) (affirming conviction for shipping misbranded and adulterated drugs

CHAPTER 7   DEFINING OFFENSES: A CLOSER LOOK

absent any showing that he intentionally or negligently engaged in the proscribed conduct). . . . Other post-*Lambert* decisions have upheld convictions based upon strict liability statutes. In United States v. Freed, 401 U.S. 601 (1971), the court upheld the constitutionality of a statute which made it unlawful for any person to possess a firearm that has not been registered to him by the transferor. Observing that *Lambert* represented an "extreme" view, the court upheld the statute as "a regulatory measure in the interest of the public safety," 401 U.S. at 609 (citing *Dotterweich*).

In January, 1982, the court indicated that Lambert's application had been "limited." In Texaco, Inc. v. Short, 454 U.S. 516, 537, 102 S. Ct. 781, 796 (1982), the court stated:

> *Lambert* concerns the *mens rea* that is necessary before the State may convict an individual of crime. See United States v. Freed, 401 U.S. 601; United States v. International Minerals & Chemical Corp., 402 U.S. 558. Its application has been limited, lending some credence to Justice Frankfurter's colorful prediction in dissent that the case would stand as "an isolated deviation from the strong current of precedents—a derelict on the waters of the law." 335 U.S. at 232.

Given the legislative power to create crimes in which a culpable mental state need not be shown, *Powell, Dotterweich, Smith,* and *Balint* indicate that the creation of criminal strict liability for driving while suspended is constitutionally permitted.

Defendant's second Fourteenth Amendment contention is that the affirmative defense provisions of ORS 487.560(2)(b) unconstitutionally shift to her the burden to produce, as part of her affirmative defense, an element of the state's case. This case does not involve the shifting of proof of any element of the crime, for as we held above, knowledge of the suspension is not an element of the crime. In State v. Stroup, supra, this court rejected a similar claim. . . .

In *Patterson* the Supreme Court recognized initially that:

> . . . it is normally "within the power of the State to regulate procedures under which its laws are carried out, including the burden of producing evidence and the burden of persuasion," and its decision in this regard is not subject to proscription under the Due Process Clause unless "it offends some principle of justice so rooted in the traditions and conscience of our people as to be ranked as fundamental." (Citations omitted) (432 U.S. at 201-202).

The Supreme Court also made it clear in *Patterson* that just because a statute provides that proof of a certain fact constitutes an affirmative defense, it does not follow that those facts are an element of the crime with the burden of proof upon the state.

There is no constitutional bar to the creation of a strict liability offense while at the same time providing for excuse or mitigating factor by way of an affirmative defense. It was within the legislature's power to create this strict liability crime with no affirmative defense. The inclusion of the ORS 487.560(2) affirmative defense does not operate to thwart the goal the legislature clearly sought to achieve. We therefore affirm.

The Court of Appeals is affirmed.

LINDE, J., filed a dissenting opinion in which LENT, C. J., and ROBERTS, J., joined.

LINDE, Justice, dissenting.

The majority holds that the Oregon legislature made a felon of a person who drives a motor vehicle on an Oregon highway when his or her license to do so has been suspended, whether the driver knows of the suspension or not. According to the majority, if unknown to Mrs. Buttrey someone in the Motor Vehicles Division suspended or revoked her driver's license, even by an error, she nevertheless engaged in a crime that might send her to a prison if she drove her car in the good faith belief that she had a valid license.

The legislature did no such thing. The legislature did something very different: It rearranged the burdens of litigating in a subsequent trial whether the driver had notice or otherwise knew of the suspension. The statutes do not say that the driver's knowledge of the suspension is not material to her guilt at the time she actually drives the car, in other words when the alleged crime is committed. The rearrangement of the burden at trial does not make the act of driving under such circumstances a crime that involves no culpable mental state, a crime that is committed in ignorance of a license suspension. Yet this is what the majority would have us believe.

It is crucial not to confuse two different questions: one, whether knowledge of the suspension is an element of the crime at the time of its commission, and the other, whether this knowledge is an element of the state's proof at the time of trial. The majority opinion goes to elaborate lengths to show that the legislature intended to free the prosecution from having to prove that a defendant knew of the suspension. The demonstration is misdirected; it is not disputed that the state wished to free itself from that burden in prosecutions for "driving while suspended" and persuaded the legislature to shift the burden by making failure to notify the defendant an affirmative defense. The only issue is what retaining ignorance of the suspension as a defense, in other words, retaining the material element of knowledge at the time of driving, means for the application of the Oregon Criminal Code of 1971 and its constitutionality. . . .

CHAPTER 7   DEFINING OFFENSES: A CLOSER LOOK

Questions

1. *Strict Liability.* What arguments can you make against the use of strict liability in criminal law? What arguments can you make in support of its use?

2. *Dad's Liability.* Using these arguments, should the legislature make speeding, as in Dad's case, a strict offense? Property destruction? Should the two offenses be treated differently? If so, why?

3. *Strict Liability and Affirmative Defenses.* Is the driving while suspended offense in *Buttrey* a strict liability offense or just an offense for which the burden of proof on culpability has been shifted to the defendant? Does it matter? Is it constitutionally permissible for the Oregon legislature to create an offense of strict liability for driving while suspended? Would it be constitutional under *Mullaney* and *Patterson* (see Chapter 6) to make knowledge of suspension an element of the offense but to shift the burden of persuasion to the defendant to disprove knowledge of suspension? Is the Oregon statute, as written, constitutional under *Patterson?* Does it matter whether the prior formulation of the offense in Oregon required the state to prove culpability or imposed strict liability?

SECTION 7.3   CULPABILITY REQUIREMENTS AND MISTAKE DEFENSES

When leaving a restaurant, you take the wrong umbrella from the coatroom by mistake. While you may satisfy the objective elements of theft (an unlicensed taking of the property of another), your mistake (i.e., your mistaken belief that the umbrella you took is yours) means that you do not have the culpable state of mind required for theft; you did not intend to take the "property of another."

Your mistake concerns what earlier in this chapter we called a "circumstance" element—the ownership of the umbrella. One can also make mistakes as to result elements. Under common language usage, we call these "accidents." After you realize that you were *mistaken* as to who's umbrella you took, you *accidentally* drop it into a trash compactor (that is, you claim you have no culpability as to the result element in property destruction). Mistaken results were discussed in Chapter 4, concerning homicide, the most serious result-element offense.

Mistaken umbrella thefts and mistaken killings are both instances of an actor mistakenly believing that he is not committing an offense. The reverse sort of mistakes also are possible. An actor may believe that he *is* committing an offense when, because of a mistake, he really is not. A downpour starts just as you are leaving the restaurant. Because you lost your umbrella last week, you steal someone else's from the coatroom. When you get outside you find that the umbrella you have "stolen" is your own, apparently "lost" in the coatroom the week before. You satisfy the culpability elements of theft (you have the intention to take the property of another) but you do not satisfy the objective elements (you did not take the property of another). Such instances of mistaken belief that one *is* committing an offense are frequently punished, as *attempts* to commit an offense, and are discussed in Section 8.3, concerning impossible attempts.

This section concerns those mistakes that provide a defense by negating a culpability element—e.g., because you mistakenly believe that the umbrella you take is your own, you do not have the required intention to take property of another. A mistake can provide a defense in other ways as well. If you assault another person because you mistakenly believe that he is about to attack you with his umbrella, you may have a defense to your assault. Your mistake does not negate a culpability element; you *do* intend to hit the other person. Rather, your mistake is, or may be, a defense because it satisfies the conditions of a general defense of mistaken self defense. (Defenses for a mistake as to a justification are discussed in Section 15.5.) Or, you may commit an offense by taking your umbrella on an airplane, unaware that your conduct is criminal, because you relied upon an official misstatement of the law that you violated or because the law was not reasonably made available. Again, such ignorance or mistake of law does not negate an offense element; such mistakes provide a defense because they satisfy the conditions of one of the general mistake defenses. (General mistake defenses are the subject of Section 16.4.)

Model Penal Code §2.04(1)
Ignorance or Mistake

(1) Ignorance or mistake as to a matter of fact or law is a defense if:

    (a) the ignorance or mistake negatives the purpose, knowledge, belief, recklessness or negligence required to establish a material element of the offense; or

CHAPTER 7 DEFINING OFFENSES: A CLOSER LOOK 221

(b) the law provides that the state of mind established by such ignorance or mistake constitutes a defense.

Alaska Stat. §11.41.410(a)(1)
Sexual Assault in the First Degree

A person commits the crime of sexual assault in the first degree if,
  (1) being any age, he engages in sexual penetration with another person without consent of that person; . . .

Alaska Stat. §11.81.610(b)
Construction of Statutes With Respect to Culpability

Except as provided [otherwise], if a provision of law defining an offense does not prescribe a culpable mental state, the culpable mental state that must be proved with respect to:
  (1) conduct is "knowing"; and
  (2) a circumstance or a result is "recklessly."

Laseter v. State
Court of Appeals of Alaska
684 P.2d 139 (1984)

COATS, Judge.

Thomas Laseter was convicted, following a jury trial, of attempted sexual assault in the first degree and kidnapping. AS 11.41.410(a)(1); and AS 11.31.100(a); and AS 11.41.300(a)(1)(C). He appeals his convictions to this court, raising several specifications of error. We conclude that the trial judge improperly instructed the jury and reverse Laseter's convictions.

On April 18, 1982, Thomas J. Laseter, a twenty-one-year old career soldier stationed at Ft. Wainwright, went to the French Quarter, a local bar, where he met L.P. Because their accounts as to what happened differ significantly, they are given separately.

L.P.'s Account

Shortly before midnight L.P. went to the French Quarter to have a few drinks and to see a girlfriend who worked there. L.P. drank a few beers and played several games of pool with her friend. Laseter came in, joined them at the pool table, and played a game of pool with L.P. Laseter asked L.P. several times if she wanted to go somewhere else to have a drink with him, but she refused. When the French Quarter closed at 2:00 AM, L.P. decided to walk over to the Stampede, another bar. Shortly after she arrived there, Laseter walked in and sat down next to L.P. at the bar. Laseter bought L.P. several beers. They sat and talked until about 5:00 AM L.P. left the bar, intending to go to the Northward Building where she planned to spend the night in a friend's apartment. Although Laseter offered to drive her home several times that evening, she did not accept. L.P. saw Laseter again as he was driving out of the Stampede's parking lot. He stopped and asked if she was sure she did not want a ride home. This time L.P. accepted. After she got in the car Laseter asked for directions to her home. She gave him complete directions. Due to the amount of alcohol she had consumed, L.P. blacked out at this point. However, she remembers telling Laseter that they were going in the wrong direction. Laseter said he would turn around.

The next thing L.P. remembered was being in Hamilton Acres by the D & L Bike Shop. She told Laseter he was going the wrong way, but Laseter kept on going. L.P. became scared and told him to either turn around or stop the car so she could get out. Laseter kept on driving. At one point, when Laseter was stopped at a stop sign, L.P. tried to get out of the car. Laseter grabbed her arm and hair and pulled her back into the car. He told her she was not going anywhere. L.P. started to cry. She was so frightened that she blacked out again.

L.P. next remembered "being slapped, punched around, having her hair pulled." Laseter was muttering that since he had bought her some beer and offered her a ride home she owed it to him to go to bed with him. She told him "no way." Laseter got upset and began to hit her with his hand and with what she thought was a bottle. L.P. started to scream and yell. Laseter pushed her down onto the front seat of the car. Although she tried to fight her way back up and get out of the car, Laseter forced her to engage in fellatio. He then pulled down her pants and had intercourse with her for a few minutes. He then attempted unsuccessfully to put his penis in her rectum. L.P. did not know whether Laseter ever ejaculated. He then got up off her and she "scrambled" out of the car. L.P. ran to a nearby apartment building. The outside door was locked so she started beating on it. A woman answered and let her in when she asked for help. The next thing L.P. remembered was being examined by a doctor at the hospital.

Laseter's Account

After Laseter arrived at the French Quarter, he had a few beers and watched L.P. and the bartender play pool. After they finished, Laseter started to play. He played one game of pool with L.P. and bought her four or five drinks. When Laseter first asked L.P. if she wanted to go someplace else she refused; later she went with him to the Stampede.

Laseter and L.P. stayed at the Stampede for about an hour. Laseter bought L.P. a screwdriver. They sat and listened to the jukebox until the bartender turned it off. Then they went next door to the Arctic Bar where they stayed until 4:00 or 4:30 AM Laseter told L.P. that he had to leave so that he could take her home and still be back at the base in time to get ready for field exercises. L.P. did not want to leave so they danced a couple of times and finished their drinks. L.P. had three or four screwdrivers at the Arctic Bar. Laseter had between ten and fifteen beers that evening. Laseter finally got up, told L.P. that he was going to leave, and asked her if she wanted a ride. L.P. did not say anything, so Laseter walked out the door. As he turned around to unlock the car, he saw L.P. walking up to the passenger door. Laseter asked her if she wanted a ride, and she said yes.

Laseter asked L.P. for directions to her home. Laseter did not know the Fairbanks streets very well because he had only had an operable car since February and did not spend much time downtown. L.P. gave Laseter directions, but he told her she would have to guide him step by step. However, L.P. either fell asleep or passed out. Although Laseter tried to follow her directions, he got lost. L.P. lived on Goldstream Road but Laseter ended up in Hamilton Acres. Laseter tried to wake L.P. up. He reached over and was shaking her when he hit some ice and drove into a fence.

Laseter then drove around trying to find the way to L.P.'s home. L.P. still seemed to be asleep or passed out. While he was trying to figure out where he was, Laseter got stuck in a breakup puddle in an alley near the D & L Bike Shop. After trying for about fifteen or twenty minutes to get out, Laseter asked Bill Hoople, who was arriving for work at a nearby office, to help him. Hoople was unable to help Laseter but suggested that he wait until someone else got there.

Laseter then went back to the car to wake L.P. and tell her that they were stuck. L.P. did not say anything, but just sat up and looked around. Laseter testified that he sat there for a few minutes, then leaned over and kissed her. She responded and kissed him back. He continued to kiss her and then started kissing her breast. L.P. did not say anything but seemed to be enjoying it. When Laseter asked her if she wanted to get in the back seat, L.P. did so. Laseter continued to kiss her and then started to remove her clothing. As Laseter was pulling down his own pants, he prematurely ejaculated on the side of L.P.'s leg and on the back seat. Embarrassed, Laseter pulled his pants back up and got out of the car. As he was dressing, L.P. moved her hand up over her face. Nothing was said.

Laseter went back across the street where he found someone with a tow rope who agreed to pull him out of the puddle. When Laseter got back to the car, L.P. was gone. He looked around but he did not see her. The police arrived as Laseter was hooking up the tow strap to his car.

Jury Instructions

This court has held that "[i]n order to prove a violation of AS 11.41.410(a)(1) [sexual assault in the first degree], the state must prove that the defendant knowingly engaged in sexual intercourse and *recklessly disregarded his victim's lack of consent*," Reynolds v. State, 664 P.2d 621, 625 (Alaska App. 1983) (emphasis added). The issue before this court is whether the trial court committed reversible error when it refused to instruct the jury on subjective awareness of nonconsent as an element of sexual assault in the first degree. . . .

Prior to trial, Laseter proposed two instructions which read:

> "Without Consent." In order to find the defendant guilty of sexual assault in the first degree, you must find that he was subjectively aware that [L.P.] did not consent to sexual penetration. If from all the evidence you have a reasonable doubt as to the question whether the defendant believed that [L.P.] consented to sexual penetration, you must give the defendant the benefit of that doubt and find him not guilty.
>
> "Recklessly." With respect to the circumstance of consent, a person acts recklessly with respect to a circumstance described by the law when he is aware of and consciously disregards a substantial and unjustifiable risk that the circumstance exists. The risk must be of such a nature and such a degree that disregard of it constitutes a gross deviation from the standard of conduct that a reasonable person would observe in the situation. . . .

The state objected to both instructions, and the court did not give them. In their place, the court substituted the following instruction as to "reasonable belief."[2]

---

2. As *Laseter* notes, this instruction is similar to the "reasonable belief" instruction approved in People v. Mayberry, 15 Cal.3d 143, 125 Cal. Rptr. 745, 542 P.2d 1337, 1344-46 (Cal. 1975), and reviewed by this court in Reynolds v. State, 664 P.2d 621, 624 (Alaska

> If from all the evidence you find that the defendant had a reasonable belief that L.P. consented to sexual penetration, you shall find the defendant not guilty as to the crime of sexual assault in the first degree. . . .

It is clear that the instruction which the trial court gave is erroneous in light of *Reynolds*. . . . Looking at the instructions in their entirety, we believe that there is at least a substantial likelihood that if the jurors thought that the case turned on whether Laseter either negligently or recklessly disregarded whether L.P. consented to sexual penetration, the jury would follow the instruction which specifically dealt with consent. Since that instruction was erroneous, we do not find harmless error.

The state also contends that the erroneous instruction was harmless in light of the evidence at trial. Essentially, the state argues that if the jury believed the alleged victim, L.P., then Laseter clearly had forcible intercourse with her; if the jury believed Laseter, then L.P. consented to intercourse. We have reviewed the record and do not see the case as that clear-cut. L.P. testified that Laseter definitely sexually penetrated her, yet the jury acquitted Laseter of first degree sexual assault. The jury must have had a reasonable doubt as to whether Laseter achieved penetration. Testimony was presented at trial which indicated that L.P. was intoxicated to the point where she had multiple black-outs. We note that the prosecutor cross-examined Laseter on whether it ever occurred to him that L.P. might not be capable, because of intoxication, of being able to communicate that she did not want to have intercourse. Given the facts of this case, we believe that the jury could have convicted Laseter if it found that Laseter subjectively believed that L.P. consented to intercourse but that his subjective belief was unreasonable. Had the jury been instructed that Laseter could only be convicted if he was reckless in his belief that L.P. consented, the jury might have reached a different verdict. We therefore cannot conclude that the erroneous jury instruction was not harmless, and we reverse Laseter's convictions.

The convictions are reversed.

App. 1983). This court concluded that the Alaska Code requires the state to demonstrate greater culpability in a first degree sexual assault case than is required by this instruction. Id. at 625. [The *Reynolds* court reasoned as follows: (1) The Alaska sexual assault offense does not specify a particular culpability that is required as to lack of consent; (2) a general provision of the Code requires recklessness where no culpability is specified; (3) the *Mayberry* instruction requires only negligence as to lack of consent; (4) because the test for recklessness is a "subjective one"—requiring actual awareness of a risk—while the test for negligence is "objective"—requiring only a "failure to perceive the risk"—the "Alaska rule is more favorable" to the defendant; it is "easier for the defendant to argue *mistake* of fact" (emphasis added).]

CHART: Culpability Requirements and Mistake Defenses Element Analysis in Defining Criminal Liability: The Model Penal Code and Beyond
35 Stanford L. Rev. 681, 728 (1983)

1. Culpability Requirement	2. Will be negated by (i.e., actor will get defense for):	3. In language of "reasonable" and "unreasonable" mistake, will be negated by (i.e., actor will get defense for):
"purposely"	any mistake	any mistake
"knowingly"	any mistake (i.e., reckless negligent, or faultless)	any mistake (i.e., reasonable or unreasonable)
"recklessly"	a negligent or faultless mistake	an unreasonable (in the sense of a "negligent"*) or a reasonable mistake
"negligently"	a faultless mistake	a reasonable mistake
absolute liability	no mistake (not even faultless)	no mistake (not even reasonable)

*There is no defense, however, for an unreasonable, in the sense of a "reckless," mistake. It is this point at which the reasonable-unreasonable terminology breaks down in its translation of modern culpability terms. This is a particularly serious error given the fact that "recklessly" is the norm, the most common culpability required as to circumstance elements.

Questions

1. *Culpability Requirements.* What are the culpability requirements of the offense of Sexual Assault in the First Degree charged in *Laseter*? In particular, what culpability is required as to the victim's lack of consent?

2. *Mistake Defenses.* What kind of mistake as to consent, if any, provides a defense to Sexual Assault in the First Degree? What kind of mistake defense did the defendant want the jury instructions to describe? What mistake defense did the trial court give in its instructions? Which of these is the better view?

CHAPTER 7 DEFINING OFFENSES: A CLOSER LOOK   227

Vt. Pub. L. §8602 (1933)
The Blanket Act

A man with another man's wife, or a woman with another woman's husband, found in bed together, under circumstances affording presumption of an illicit intention, shall each be imprisoned in the state prison not more than three years or fined not more than one thousand dollars.

State v. Woods
Supreme Court of Vermont
107 Vt. 354, 179 A. 1 (1935)

BUTTLES, Superior Judge.

The respondent was convicted in Orleans county court of a violation of P.L. 8602, commonly known as the Blanket Act.

A transcript of the evidence has not been furnished, but from the respondent's amended exceptions it appears: "That the respondent, a single woman, with her three children, in company with one Leo Shufelt, of Lowell, Vermont, and of one John Ellis, motored in the summer of 1933 to Reno, Nevada, . . . where the said Leo Shufelt, who was a married man, instituted divorce proceedings against his wife, then living in Vermont; that process in said divorce proceedings was served upon the said wife; that she never accepted service of same, did not go to Nevada, and had no appearance entered in her behalf in said cause."

It further appears that after hearing, a decree was granted which purported to be a decree of divorce to the said Shufelt, and thereupon he and the respondent went through a marriage ceremony in Reno, which was performed by the same judge who granted the decree, and thereupon the respondent entered into marital relations with the said Shufelt, and after a week or so went with him to Connecticut, whence he subsequently went to Lowell, Vt., where the respondent later joined him and where the offense herein charged is alleged to have been committed.

The respondent does not challenge, by her exceptions, the submission to the jury of the questions of fact upon which the determination below of the invalidity of the attempted Nevada divorce for the purposes of this case was based. Neither does she challenge the manner in which those questions were submitted nor the determination by the court below that said attempted divorce is, for the purposes of this case, invalid. The verdict of the jury and the rulings of the trial court as to the invalidity of the attempted Nevada divorce are therefore conclusive upon the rights of the respondent in this case.

Thus there is no question of the validity or invalidity of the attempted Nevada divorce in the case. . . .

The respondent has saved one exception to the charge as given, and four to the failure of the court to comply with requests to charge. The real question involved in all of these exceptions is the same, and we will consider them together, as the respondent has done in her brief.

The respondent contends, by these exceptions, that an honest belief in the validity of the Reno divorce and of her subsequent marriage to Shufelt would be a defense to this prosecution. There is much diversity of view as to whether a mistaken belief as to a fact, based upon reasonable grounds, may or may not constitute a defense in a criminal action of a nature similar to this one. In State v. Ackerly, 79 Vt. 69, 64 A. 450, 118 Am. St. Rep. 940, 8 Ann. Cas. 1103, this court held that an honest belief that his wife was dead was not a defense in a prosecution for bigamy, the respondent having attempted to remarry.

But in State v. Audette, 81 Vt. 400, 70 A. 833, 18 L.R.A. (N.S.) 527, 130 Am. St. Rep. 1061, it was held that, under the circumstances of that case, ignorance of the fact that the woman whom the respondent attempted to marry had a husband living was available as a defense in a prosecution for adultery, he having been misled by her false statements as to that fact.

Here the respondent relies upon a mistake of law rather than of fact. Her presence in Reno and her marriage to Shufelt immediately after the supposed divorce was granted by the judge who granted the decree indicate that she must have known all about the facts and circumstances of that proceeding. No claim is made that she did not know the facts. Her mistake, if one she made, was as to the legal effect in Vermont of the Nevada decree. The maxim, "Ignorantia legis non excusat," and the corresponding presumption that every one is conclusively presumed to know the law, are of unquestioned application in Vermont as elsewhere, both in civil and in criminal cases.

This presumption applies as well in prosecutions for adultery as in other criminal prosecutions. . . .

It remains to consider whether this presumption is applicable in this case in view of the phraseology of P.L. 8602, under which the respondent was prosecuted. Clearly it does apply if the words "under circumstances affording presumption of an illicit intention" mean that the act which the respondent intends to do is forbidden and not that the respondent must have acted with a guilty mind. . . .

Judgment that there is no error in the record. Exceptions overruled. Let execution be done.

CHAPTER 7   DEFINING OFFENSES: A CLOSER LOOK   229

Model Penal Code §2.02(9)
Culpability as to Illegality of Conduct

Neither knowledge nor recklessness or negligence as to whether conduct constitutes an offense or as to the existence, meaning or application of the law determining the elements of an offense is an element of such offense, unless the definition of the offense or the Code so provides.

Questions

1. *Culpability Requirements.* What are the culpability requirements of the offense charged in *Woods?* Under the Model Penal Code, what kind of mistake by Woods would provide a defense?

2. *Mistake of Law Defense.* Is a mistake of law less likely to provide a defense under the Model Penal Code than a mistake of fact? If so, why? Did the defendant in *Woods* make a mistake with respect to "the existence, meaning or application of the law determining the elements of [the] offense"?

3. *Knowledge of Criminality as an Offense Element.* Assume that Ms. Woods knew that the Nevada divorce was invalid in Vermont and, therefore, knew that she was in bed with "another woman's husband." She claims, however, that she knew nothing about the "Blanket Act," and indeed was shocked to find out that her adultery was actually a criminal offense. Would she have a defense under the Model Penal Code? Assume that a reasonable person in her situation also would have been unaware that such adultery was a criminal offense. Would she then have a defense to her Blanket Act violation? What is the significance, if any, of Model Penal Code §2.02(9) to this case?

SECTION 7.4   CAUSATION

Where a result is an element of an offense, the defendant's conduct must be shown to be the cause of the result. While causation typically is treated as a basic issue of liability, it is less a liability issue than a grading issue. Where causation is not found, the defendant may be liable nonetheless for an attempt to commit the offense, which is typically punished at a reduced level. Thus, the fundamental issues in this section and in the next chapter, on inchoate offenses, are the same: Should an actor receive a greater punishment when his conduct causes a prohibited result than when, upon the same acts with the same culpable state of mind, his conduct does not cause the result? In other words, is resulting harm significant, or should punishment depend only upon an actor's acts and accompanying state of mind? If resulting harm is significant, why is it significant and when is it significant?

Most codes distinguish cause-in-fact issues from proximity issues. The former issue, "factual cause," is essentially a hypothetical scientific inquiry: Would the result have occurred in the absence of the defendant's conduct? The latter issue, "proximate (or legal) cause," is more akin to a general blameworthiness question. As the Model Penal Code expresses the issue, the jury must determine whether the result is "too remote or accidental in its manner of occurrence to have a [just] bearing on the actor's liability or on the gravity of his offense." Do these two requirements of causation properly describe the cases in which an actor ought to be punished more severely for being accountable for a resulting harm?

Manny the Master

An informant in the police department reports that Prosecutor Baylor is being investigated for taking bribes to forgo prosecutions. Tuoro "The Hat," the local underworld boss, suspects that if Baylor is arrested he will reveal all to the authorities. He decides to have him killed. To be sure that the job gets done, he gives contracts to both Squeeze and Manny. Squeeze, who is somewhat brighter and more experienced than her competitor Manny, arranges to poison Prosecutor Baylor at the corner hot dog stand where he frequently eats. Manny is tailing Baylor looking for an opportunity. When he sees Squeeze at the hot dog stand he suspects he has been outdone. Squeeze glides over with a smile. "He ate enough to kill an elephant," she tells Manny. "He'll be dead in 45 minutes. Better luck next time." Manny is not giving up so easily. He scurries after Baylor, who has finished his hot dog and headed down to the subway. Manny spots him at the edge of the platform and positions himself several feet behind Baylor in the crowd. As the train approaches, he pushes another waiting passenger into Baylor, so that Baylor will be pushed in front of the train and killed instantly. But as Manny pushes, the crowd surges and his push sends the wrong person off the platform. His push is also much too early. The fallen passenger scrambles back onto the platform before the train arrives. Manny turns to leave, angry and humiliated. Maybe he should go to computer school, he thinks, recalling an ad he saw on a matchbook cover. Screams from the track make him turn. People are milling about, peering under the train. He learns from others that a man straining to see the fallen passenger leaned out too far and was hit by the oncoming train. He presses forward to see the dead man. Could he be so lucky? They pull Prosecutor Baylor from under the train. Manny turns and heads for the exit, full of himself. Squeeze won't be making fun of him today.

Assume that the following statute is in force:

Section 11A-2-2 Causal Relationship Between Conduct and Result*

Conduct is the cause of a result if:
(1) the conduct is an antecedent but for which the result in question would not have occurred; and
(2) the result is not too remote or too accidental in its manner of occurrence or too dependent upon another's volitional act to have a just bearing on the actor's liability or on the gravity of his offense; and
(3) the relationship between the conduct and result satisfies any additional causal requirements imposed by the Code or by the law defining the offense.
(4) Simultaneous Causes. Where the conduct of two or more actors each simultaneously contributes to the result and each alone would have been sufficient to cause the result, the requirement of Subsection (1) of this section shall be held to be satisfied.

Manny (and Squeeze and Tuoro "The Hat") intended that Prosecutor Baylor be killed and acted upon that intention. Liability for at least attempted murder seems clear. Is Manny criminally liable for causing the death, thus liability for murder? Is Squeeze? Is Tuoro "The Hat"?

State v. Wood
Supreme Court of Vermont
53 Vt. 558 (1881)

This case was tried at the September Term, 1880, PIERPOINT, C. J., presiding. It was an indictment charging the respondents jointly with the murder of one Luman A. Smith, at Williston, in said county, on the

---

*Proposed Rhode Island Criminal Code §11A-2-2, constructed with language from a number of state code causation provisions.

23rd day of October, 1879. [Defendant Wood shot Smith in the abdomen, inflicting a mortal wound. Before Smith died from the wound, Alma, acting independently, shot and killed Smith.] Plea, not guilty, and trial by jury.

. . . The [jury instruction] request made by the respondent's counsel is as follows: "That if the jury find that respondent Wood assaulted Smith even with intent to kill him, with or without malice, and inflicted upon him the wound in the abdomen of which he did not die, still if they find there was no previous understanding or concert between him and respondent Alma to assault and kill Smith, and that they acted independently and without any previous understanding or concert, and the acts of each were without the procurement or request of the other, each are only responsible for their own acts, and Wood cannot be convicted of murder, manslaughter. . . ." [The request was denied and counsel took exception to the charge given.]

VEAZEY, J.

. . . We think the exception to the charge of the court to the jury in response to the [respondent's] request must be sustained. The evidence on the part of the State showed that Luman A. died from the effects of the wound inflicted by Alma, and not from that inflicted by Wood; and their evidence tended to show that there was no concert between them, but that each acted independently.

The court instructed the jury in substance that although Luman A. died of the wound inflicted by Alma and not from that inflicted by Wood, and although there was no concert between them, and each acted independently, and they were therefore only responsible for their own acts respectively, still if the wound inflicted by Wood was mortal, and would in course of time have killed Luman A., if he had not previously died from the wound inflicted by Alma, and although he did not die of the wound by Wood, yet the latter could be convicted of murder.

The court was in error in the assumption that a man can be convicted of murder although his act does not cause the death. The question does not turn upon the moral aspect of the case. The intent to murder may be never so plain, yet if something intervenes to prevent the consummation of the intent, if death does not follow from the act of the accused, he is not in law a murderer. All of the definitions of murder found in the books involve the idea and fact of a killing. This must have reference, when a man is on trial, to a killing by him. If one inflicts a mortal wound, but before death ensues, another kills the same person by an independent act, without concert with, or procurement of, the first man, how can he be said to have done the killing? The second person could be convicted of murder, if he killed with malice aforethought, and to convict the first man would be assuming that he killed the same person at another time.

Upon the supposition contained in the request and charge, and upon the showing made by the State that Luman A. died from the shot given by Alma and not by that given by Wood, the latter could not be convicted of any crime under this indictment. The statute providing that a person put on trial for murder may be acquitted of that, and found guilty of manslaughter, would not apply to Wood's case, because upon the supposition stated, there was no death from this act. The evidence on the part of the State, as assumed in the supposition, tends to show that Wood is guilty of an assault with intent to kill, being armed with a dangerous weapon. The statute does not provide that a person may be found guilty of this crime under an indictment for murder. . . .

Verdict set aside and new trial granted.

Questions

1. *Factual Cause.* Is Manny's conduct a "but for" (factual cause) of Baylor's death? In other words, would Baylor have died when he did if Manny had not done what he did? Is Squeeze's conduct in poisoning Baylor a "but for" cause of his death? Is her conduct in telling Manny about the poisoning a "but for" cause of Baylor's death? Is Tuoro's conduct a "but for" cause? As to which of these defendants, if any, is the *Wood* case relevant?

2. *Proximate Cause.* Is Manny's conduct a proximate cause of Baylor's death? In other words, is Baylor's death too remote or accidental with respect to Manny's conduct to have a just bearing on Manny's liability? Is Squeeze's conduct a proximate cause? Is Tuoro's?

3. *Complicity as Accountability for Another's Conduct.* The court in *Woods* was careful to say that Wood could not be held accountable for Smith's death "if [the jury] find there was no previous understanding or concert between [Wood] and respondent Alma to assault and kill Smith, and that they acted independently and without previous understanding or concert, and the acts of each were without the procurement or request of the other." This qualification is required because accomplices in an offense are generally held accountable for each other's conduct. (And, at common law, co-conspirators were similarly held accountable, under the so-called "Pinkerton Rule" in the United States.) Thus, if Wood and Alma had been accomplices, Wood could have been held liable for murder because Alma's conduct causing Smith's death would have been imputed to him. Is this

relevant to Manny's liability? Squeeze's? Tuoro "The Hat's"? We shall examine complicity in Chapter 10.

Notes on Multiple Causes

We may tend to think that the number of possible causes depends upon the facts of the case. Where the actor shoots the victim in the head, we say the gun shot is the cause of death. In the more complicated case of Baylor's death, we may say that the cause is either Manny's push or Baylor's curiosity or possibly both. Thus, more complicated cases like Baylor's seem to raise the issue of multiple causes. In fact, every result is necessarily the product of many causes, some acting immediately upon and some acting long before the present result. The train was as necessary as Baylor's curiosity to bring about the death. If the local bar had not closed early, there would not have been as many people on the platform at the time and Baylor would not have had to lean out as he did to see and would not have been hit. By closing early, the bar owner caused the death, then, in a factual cause sense. Technically, every causation case is a multiple cause case. It is not an academic question to ask how the doctrine is to determine the causal accountability of one particular cause among multiple causes of a result. The proximate cause requirement is highly useful in this effort. The bar owner's conduct is closing early is clearly so remote from Baylor's death that it ought not to be seen as a proximate cause, and the owner ought not be liable for murder even if he somehow hoped that closing early might cause Baylor's death.[1]

Imputing Another's Causal Conduct It should be noted that the doctrine sometimes avoids the problem of determining which of multiple causes is accountable for a result by treating the multiple causes as a single cause. This occurs most often where the two causes spring from accomplices or co-conspirators who are legally accountable for each

---

1. Or consider the actor who shoots at but misses his intended victim, who flees to escape the attack and four blocks later is struck and killed by a falling piano that breaks loose from its rope as it is being hoisted to a third floor apartment. The actor's shot is a "but for" cause of the death; the deceased would not have been under the piano at the moment it fell but for the shot, which caused him to flee. But the actor's missed shot would be judged by most people to be too remote and accidental a cause to have a just bearing on the actor's liability for the death caused by the piano. The actor's shot in the falling piano hypothetical creates no injury that by itself would cause death. Rather, the effect of the actor's shot in the piano hypothetical is to trigger another action (flight of the intended victim), which in turn leads to the death. It is this serial effect of the causes that creates the potential proximate-cause remoteness issues.

other's conduct, as noted previously. In Henderson v. State, for example, the defendant father stabbed the deceased during a struggle. The son then shot and killed the victim.[2] The father might argue that, even if the stab wound was lethal, his conduct was not a but-for cause of the resulting death, that the victim would have died when he did from the gun shot even without the father's stab wound. But if the father and son were accomplices, the court observes, the father is legally accountable for the conduct of the son and it does not matter whether the father's conduct alone was a necessary cause.[3]

"Combined Effect" Analysis Some jurisdictions recognize a second kind of situation in which the conduct of two actors may be combined and treated as one. In *Henderson,* for example, the court concluded that, even if the father and son were not accomplices, their independent conduct ought to be treated as one causal force if the two forces combined in their effect. Thus, the father was to be held for the death if the stab wound that he inflicted had combined in effect with the gun shot by his son.[4] If this doctrine were simply an application of the but-for test, it would be unobjectionable. That is, if the two causes were said to combine and were to be treated as one whenever neither alone would have been lethal, then each in fact is necessary for the result and therefore is a but-for cause.

Dangers of "Combined Effect" Unfortunately, by thinking in terms of "combined effects," courts sometimes apply the doctrine too broadly. In *Henderson,* for example, if the father's stabbing of the victim were *not* necessary for the resulting death, then the father's conduct should not be taken to be a factual cause of the death, even if its effect combined in some way with that of the son's shooting of the victim. For another example, assume that Squeeze's poison had caused Baylor to become dizzy and thus made it that much surer that Manny would be successful in pushing Baylor in front of the train. If Baylor had been killed at the same time, even without the dizziness from Squeeze's poison, then Squeeze's conduct is not a but-for cause, even though a court might say that its effect combined with Manny's push. "Combined effect" analysis tends to be used by courts when it is unclear whether the defendant's cause was necessary for the result or was just a contributing but non-necessary factor. Would the son have successfully shot the victim even without the father's stabbing? Would Manny's push have made Baylor fall even without the dizziness from Squeeze's poison? These may be difficult factual questions for a jury to resolve. But if a necessary cause really is a requirement for establishing causation, then the state should have to prove this element beyond a reasonable doubt, as the

---

2. 11 Ala. App. 37, 41-42, 65 So. 721, 722-23 (1914).
3. Id. at 42-43, 65 So. at 722.
4. Id.

state must prove every other offense element. To resort to "combined effect" analysis is to release the state from this burden and to substitute a lesser requirement of showing merely that the defendant's conduct contributed in some way to the result.

Serial vs. Intersecting Causes Multiple causes may interact with one another in any number of ways. The train, Manny's push, Baylor's curiosity, the early closing of the local bar, and many other circumstances came together at the moment before Baylor's death. Each represents an independent chain of events that intersects at that moment. And each of these intersecting chains of events has many links, a serial dimension in which each link has a causal connection with the links before and after.[5] Tuoro "The Hat" is a cause of Baylor's death, it might be said, by motivating Manny to do his pushing. Tuoro's contract is not an independent cause from Manny's push, in the same way that the train and Manny's push are independent. The contract stands in serial relation to Manny's push; the train intersects with the push. (There is nothing in the legal doctrine that requires this conceptualization of causation problems but many students find it useful to think about the problem in this way.) In sorting out which causes will come within the realm of legal causal accountability, the doctrine must address two distinguishable questions. Which intersecting causal chains are eligible for causal accountability? And how far back along a causal chain, the serial dimension, should accountability extend?

Assessing Serial Dimension with Proximate Cause Test The proximate cause test is the law's device for assessing the reach of accountability along the serial dimension. If Manny had successfully pushed Baylor in front of the train, his push clearly would be judged a proximate cause of the death. Tuoro's contract, which motivated Manny, probably would be considered a sufficiently proximate cause as well. But the informant's report of the investigation, which motivated Tuoro's contract, might be judged too remote to be a proximate cause, even if it were given with the intention that it would cause Tuoro to have Baylor killed. The problem of serial causes is particularly troublesome when one of the links in the causal chain is another person. *Root* and *Lassiter*, discussed below, illustrate the difficulties.

Assessing Accountability Among Intersecting Causes In addition to the issue of how far causal accountability travels down the chain of serial causes, the law must identify which among the many intersecting causal chains are eligible for being held accountable for the result. The law does this through the factual cause requirement, most commonly by using the necessary-cause test. Only those conditions that are necessary for the result are judged to be a factual cause of the result. The necessary-

---

5. In reality, each link has many causal connections, connecting with the corresponding temporal point on other causal chains.

cause test is as clear and precise in application as the proximate cause test is judgmental and vague. A different sort of difficulty attends it: It tends to exclude from causal accountability at least two kinds of cases that some people think ought to be included. They are simultaneous sufficient causes, as in *Jones* below, and intervening sufficient causes, as in *Wood* above.

Commonwealth v. Root
Supreme Court of Pennsylvania
403 Pa. 571, 170 A.2d 310 (1961)

CHARLES ALVIN JONES, Chief Justice.

The appellant was found guilty of involuntary manslaughter for the death of his competitor in the course of an automobile race between them on a highway. The trial court overruled the defendant's demurrer to the Commonwealth's evidence and, after verdict, denied his motion in arrest of judgment. On appeal from the judgment of sentence entered on the jury's verdict, the Superior Court affirmed. We granted allocatur because of the important question present as to whether the defendant's unlawful and reckless conduct was a sufficiently direct cause of the death to warrant his being charged with criminal homicide.

The testimony, which is uncontradicted in material part, discloses that, on the night of the fatal accident, the defendant accepted the deceased's challenge to engage in an automobile race; that the racing took place on a rural three-lane highway; that the night was clear and dry, and traffic [was] light; that the speed limit on the highway was 50 miles per hour; that, immediately prior to the accident, the two automobiles were being operated at varying speeds of from 70 to 90 miles per hour; that the accident occurred in a no-passing zone on the approach to a bridge where the highway narrowed to two directionally-opposite lanes; that, at the time of the accident, the defendant was in the lead and was proceeding in his right hand lane of travel; that the deceased, in an attempt to pass the defendant's automobile, when a truck was closely approaching from the opposite direction, swerved his car to the left, crossed the highway's white dividing line and drove his automobile on the wrong side of the highway head-on into the oncoming truck with resultant fatal effect to himself.

This evidence would of course amply support a conviction of the defendant for speeding, reckless driving and, perhaps, other violations of The Vehicle Code. . . . [However,] unlawful or reckless conduct is only one ingredient of the crime of involuntary manslaughter. Another essential and distinctly separate element of the crime is that the unlawful or reckless conduct charged to the defendant was the *direct* cause of the death in issue. The first ingredient is obviously present in this case but, just as plainly, the second is not.

While precedent is to be found for application of the tort law concept of "proximate cause" in fixing responsibility for criminal homicide, the want of any rational basis for its use in determining criminal liability can no longer be properly disregarded. When proximate cause was first borrowed from the field of tort law and applied to homicide prosecutions in Pennsylvania, the concept connoted a much more direct causal relation in producing the alleged culpable result than it does today. Proximate cause, as an essential element of a tort founded in negligence, has undergone in recent times, and is still undergoing, a marked extension. More specifically, this area of civil law has been progressively liberalized in favor of claims for damages for personal injuries to which careless conduct of others can in some way be associated. To persist in applying the tort liability concept of proximate cause to prosecutions for criminal homicide after the marked expansion of *civil* liability of defendants in tort actions for negligence would be to extend possible *criminal* liability to persons chargeable with unlawful or reckless conduct in circumstances not generally considered to present the likelihood of a resultant death. . . .

The instant case is one of first impression in this State; and our research has not disclosed a single instance where a district attorney has ever before attempted to prosecute for involuntary manslaughter on facts similar to those established by the record now before us. The closest case, factually, would seem to be Commonwealth v. Levin, 1957, 184 Pa. Super. 436, 135 A.2d 764, which affirmed the defendant's conviction of involuntary manslaughter. In the *Levin* case two cars were racing on the streets of Philadelphia at speeds estimated at from 85 to 95 miles per hour. The defendant's car, in the left hand lane, was racing alongside of the car in which the deceased was a passenger when the defendant turned his automobile sharply to the right in front of the other car thereby causing the driver of the latter car to lose control and smash into a tree, the passenger being thrown to the road and killed as a result of the impact. It is readily apparent that the elements of causation in the *Levin* case were fundamentally different from those in the present case. Levin's act of cutting his automobile sharply in front of the car in which the deceased was riding directly forced that car off the road and into the tree. The defendant's reckless and unlawful maneuver was the direct cause of the crucial fatality. In the instant case, the defendant's conduct was not even remotely comparable. Here, the action of the deceased driver in recklessly and suicidally swerving his car to the left lane of a 2-lane highway into the path of an oncoming truck was not forced upon him by any act of the defendant; it was done by the deceased and by him alone, who thus directly brought about his own demise.

The *Levin* case was properly decided but it cannot, by any ratiocination, be utilized to justify a conviction in the present case.

Legal theory which makes guilt or innocence of criminal homicide depend upon such accidental and fortuitous circumstances as are now embraced by modern tort law's encompassing concept of proximate cause is too harsh to be just. . . .

Even if the tort liability concept of proximate cause were to be deemed applicable, the defendant's conviction of involuntary manslaughter in the instant case could not be sustained under the evidence. The operative effect of a supervening cause would have to be taken into consideration. But, the trial judge refused the defendant's point for charge to such effect and erroneously instructed the jury that "negligence or want of care on the part of [the deceased] is no defense to the criminal responsibility of the defendant. . . ."

The Superior Court, in affirming the defendant's conviction in this case, approved the charge above mentioned, despite a number of decisions in involuntary manslaughter cases holding that the conduct of the deceased victim must be considered in order to determine whether the defendant's reckless acts were the proximate (i.e., sufficiently direct) cause of his death. The Superior Court dispensed with this decisional authority by expressly overruling Commonwealth v. Amecca, and by impliedly overruling each of the other cases immediately above cited. It did so on the ground that there can be more than one proximate cause of death. The point is wholly irrelevant. Of course there can be more than one proximate cause of death just as there can also be more than one *direct* cause of death. For example, in the so-called "shield" cases where a felon interposes the person of an innocent victim between himself and a pursuing officer, if the officer should fire his gun at the felon to prevent his escape and fatally wound the person used as a shield, the different acts of the policeman and the felon would each be a direct cause of the victim's death.

If the tort liability concept of proximate cause were to be applied in a criminal homicide prosecution, then the conduct of the person whose death is the basis of the indictment would have to be considered, not to prove that it was merely an *additional* proximate cause of death, but to determine, under fundamental and long recognized law applicable to proximate cause, whether the subsequent wrongful act *superseded* the original conduct chargeable to the defendant. If it did in fact supervene, then the original act is so insulated from the ensuing death as not to be its proximate cause.

Under the uncontradicted evidence in this case, the conduct of the defendant was not the proximate cause of the decedent's death as a matter of law. In Kline v. Moyer and Albert, 1937, 325 Pa. 357, 364, 191 A. 43, 46, 111 A.L.R. 406, the rule is stated as follows: "Where a second actor has become aware of the existence of a potential danger created by the negligence of an original tort-feasor, and thereafter, by an independent act of negligence, brings about an accident, the first tort-feasor is relieved of liability, because the condition created by him was merely a circumstance of the accident and not its proximate cause." . . .

In the case now before us, the deceased was aware of the dangerous condition created by the defendant's reckless conduct in driving his automobile at an excessive rate of speed along the highway but, despite such knowledge, he recklessly chose to swerve his car to the left and into the path of an oncoming truck, thereby bringing about the head-on collision which caused his own death.

To summarize, the tort liability concept of proximate cause has no proper place in prosecutions for criminal homicide and more direct causal connection is required for conviction. In the instant case, the defendant's reckless conduct was not a sufficient direct cause of the competing driver's death to make him criminally liable therefor.

The judgment of sentence is reversed and the defendant's motion in arrest of judgment granted.

EAGEN, Justice (dissenting).

The opinion of the learned Chief Justice admits, under the uncontradicted facts, that the defendant, at the time of the fatal accident involved, was engaged in an unlawful and reckless course of conduct. Racing an automobile at 90 miles per hour, trying to prevent another automobile going in the same direction from passing him, in a no-passing zone on a two-lane public highway, is certainly all of that. Admittedly also, there can be more than one direct cause of an unlawful death. To me, this is self-evident. But, says the majority opinion, the defendant's recklessness was not a direct cause of the death. With this, I cannot agree.

If the defendant did not engage in the unlawful race and so operate his automobile in such a reckless manner, this accident would never have occurred. He helped create the dangerous event. He was a vital part of it. The victim's acts were a natural reaction to the stimulus of the situation. The race, the attempt to pass the other car and forge ahead, the reckless speed, all of these factors the defendant himself helped create. He was part and parcel of them. That the victim's response was normal under the circumstances, that his reaction should have been expected and was clearly foreseeable, is to me beyond argument. That the defendant's recklessness was a substantial factor is obvious. All of this, in my opinion, makes his unlawful conduct a direct cause of the resulting collision. . . .

The majority opinion states, "Legal theory which makes guilt or innocence of criminal homicide depend upon such *accidental and fortuitous circumstances* as are now embraced by modern tort law's encompassing concept . . . is too harsh to be just." If the resulting death had been dependent upon "accidental and fortuitous circumstances" or, as the majority also say, "in circumstances not generally considered to present the likelihood of a resultant death," we would agree that the defendant is not criminally responsible. However, acts should be judged by their tendency under the known circumstances, not by the actual intent which accompanies their performance. Every day of the year, we read that some teenagers, or young adults, somewhere in this country, have been killed or have killed others, while racing their automobiles. Hair-raising, death-defying, law-breaking rides, which encompass "racing" are the rule rather than the exception, and endanger not only the participants, but also every motorist and passenger on the road. To call such resulting accidents "accidental and fortuitous," or unlikely to result in death, is to ignore the cold and harsh reality of everyday occurrences. Root's actions were as direct a cause of Hall's death as those in the "shield" cases. Root's shield was his high speed and any approaching traffic in his quest to prevent Hall from passing, which he knew Hall would undertake to do, the first time he thought he had the least opportunity.

. . . "When homicide is predicated upon the negligence of the defendant, it must be shown that his negligence was the proximate cause or a contributing cause of the victim's death. It must appear that the death was not the result of misadventure, but the natural and probable result of a reckless or culpably negligent act. To render a person criminally liable for negligent homicide, the duty omitted or improperly performed must have been his personal duty, and the negligent act from which death resulted must have been his personal act, and not the act of another. But he is not excused because the negligence of someone else contributed to the result, when his act was the primary or proximate cause and the negligence of the other did not intervene between his act and the result."

Professor Joseph Beale, late renowned member of the Harvard Law School faculty, said, "Though there is an active force intervening after defendant's act, the result will nevertheless be proximate if the defendant's act actually caused the intervening force. In such a case the defendant's force is really continuing in active operation *by means of the force it stimulated into activity.*" . . .

But, says the majority opinion, these are principles of tort law and should not in these days be applied to the criminal law. But such has been the case since the time of Blackstone. These same principles have always been germane to both crimes and tort. . . . Certainly, under [the majority's] reasoning, if the truck driver met death under the circumstances the case at hand presents, the defendant would not be legally responsible. Again with this conclusion, I cannot agree.

While the victim's foolhardiness in this case contributed to his own death, he was not the only one responsible and it is not he alone with whom we are concerned. It is the people of the Commonwealth who are harmed by the kind of conduct the defendant pursued. Their interests must be kept in mind.

I, therefore, dissent and would accordingly affirm the judgment of conviction.

Questions

1. *Commonwealth v. Root.* Was Root's conduct the "but for" cause of his competitor's death? Was it the proximate cause? If not, why not?

2. *State v. Lassiter,* 197 N.J. Super. 2, 484 A.2d 13 (1984):

> According to the State's evidence, Josephine Branch worked for defendant as a prostitute. She had apparently determined to leave him and on Friday, July 16, 1982 he was engaged in a search for her whereabouts in the City of Newark. He visited the Shalimar Hair Salon where he told Byron Richards that Branch had run off again, that he had too much invested in her and that when he caught her he was going to "kill the bitch." Defendant found Branch at 4:00 the following morning, Saturday, July 17, 1982, sharing the bed of a male companion in the latter's apartment. Defendant seized Branch, punched her and ordered her to get dressed. She put on her clothes and defendant then dragged her out into the hallway where he beat her with a shovel, leaving her blood on the floor of the hallway as they left the building. Branch was later admitted to the Harlem Hospital in New York City where she reported that she had suffered her injuries in a "mugging."
>
> At around 5:00 or 6:00 PM of the same day defendant picked up Branch from the hospital where her head and leg had been sutured and bandages had been placed on her head, arm and leg. He then delivered her to her apartment on Elizabeth Avenue in Newark where he left her in the company of Towanda Whitfield. Whitfield had also been formerly employed by defendant. Defendant then left the apartment and returned the following morning, Sunday, July 18 at about 6:00 AM Whitfield testified that Branch's physical ordeal had weakened her to the point where she required assistance even to reach the bathroom.
>
> When defendant returned to the apartment, Branch, who was a narcotics user, was in considerable pain and was asking for drugs. An argument developed between Branch and defendant, and Whitfield was ordered into another room of the apartment.
>
> The events of the following period of approximately fifteen minutes were then recounted not only by Whitfield, but by a number of neighbors in the building. The words "bumping" and "thumping" were used to describe the sounds of a body repeatedly hitting the bedroom wall. In the melee, Branch's voice was heard screaming for help. She called for

her mother, screaming that she could not take it any more and that she was going to jump. The apartment was on the eleventh floor of the building. One witness, a retired Newark police officer, testified that she heard a voice from the Branch apartment saying, "help me, somebody help me. He is killing me. Call the police. Please make him stop." Another witness, whose apartment was directly above Branch's, heard the girl crying and saying, "you don't love me no more; I am going to jump," and a man's voice answering "go ahead and jump." Branch then threw herself out the window and her life ended on the ground below. . . .

Was pimp Lassiter's conduct a "but for" cause of Branch's death from jumping out of the window? Was it a proximate cause? How are the facts in *Lassiter* similar and different from those in *Root*? Should the cases have the same result?

3. *Third Party Intervenors. Root* and *Lassiter* are both cases where the victim acts to bring about his or her own death, in response to the defendant's actions. Would it make a difference if it was not the victim but a third party that contributes? Assume, for example, that while the victim is being treated for the injury caused by the defendant, a doctor provides negligent treatment or a court orders a feeding tube to be disconnected. Is this conduct a "but for" cause? Is it a proximate cause? If you need more facts to make a judgement, what kind of facts do you need?

Jones v. Commonwealth
Court of Appeals of Kentucky
281 S.W.2d 920 (1955)

MONTGOMERY, Justice.

Ben Dewey Jones was convicted of willful murder and his punishment fixed at life imprisonment. He was jointly indicted with George Taylor, but tried separately. The indictment charged the willful murder of Leander Gibson in the first count. . . .

On this appeal, he seeks a reversal of the judgment on several grounds, the most serious of which [is] erroneous instructions. . . .

Deceased, Leander Gibson, thirty-six years old, and his wife lived in Jellico, Tennessee. He had operated a grocery store there for about a year. Prior to that time, he had lived in Bell County on Highway 92, running from Williamsburg to Pineville, and had been a coal miner in Knox County. On the Sunday that Gibson was killed, he, his wife and four-year-old child left Jellico in their truck for a visit to her father's home on Greasy Creek in Whitley County. When they reached Poplar Creek, her husband drove off Highway 92 and up a hollow known as

"Bullskin Branch" or "Hollow" for the purpose of trying out a pistol he had recently acquired. Bullskin Hollow is thickly wooded, with high hills on either side, and appears to have been used for various dubious purposes, both day and night. No one lived nearby.

Mrs. Gibson testified that her husband got the pistol out of the dashboard of the truck and that both fired it at a small tree growing on the bank of the mountainside. One of the shots fired hit the tree. They went down the bank and examined the place where the bullet had hit the tree.

These shots were heard by appellant Jones and his co-defendant, George Taylor. Jones had qualified as a constable on July 28, 1951, but had never renewed his bond. Taylor had been deputized by Jones that day. Jones testified that he considered this firing of shots by Gibson a misdemeanor. He and Taylor left their car and walked to where Gibson and his wife were. Neither of them knew Gibson, nor saw the shots fired.

Apparently, the first words spoken were when appellant inquired, "Don't you know it is against the law to shoot on Sunday?" The evidence is in conflict as to what took place next. Edith Gibson, wife of the dead man, said that her husband replied, "Buddy, I just got my gun and I wanted to try it out." Appellant then pulled his gun and Taylor jabbed his gun in her husband's back. When he jumped back, Taylor and Jones started shooting. . . .

Dr. H. W. Clinton removed from the body of the dead man two bullets, one a .45 caliber and the other a .38. He stated that the wound made by the .38 bullet was sufficient to produce death and that the wound made by the .45 bullet also was sufficient to produce death. Jones testified that the gun fired by him was a .38. . . .

The court gave twelve instructions designed to cover all phases of the case. Appellant complains of various errors therein.

In Instructions I and II, on murder and voluntary manslaughter, appellant contends that the use of the phrase "so as to cause or hasten his death" was error, claiming that there was no evidence which positively established that the bullet from appellant's gun killed Gibson. The testimony of Dr. Clinton was to the effect that the .38 bullet was sufficient to produce death, and Jones testified that he fired the .38. In Bennett v. Commonwealth, 150 Ky. 604, 150 S.W. 806, 808, deceased was shot by two brothers, one or both of which shots wounded him and one was necessarily fatal and the other possibly not. The Court held:

> [These brothers, according to the testimony, both shot Lawson in the one encounter. The law will not stop, in such a case, to measure which wound is the more serious, and to speculate upon which actually caused the death. In many such cases the commonwealth would be helpless; for

each defendant would go free because it could not be proven against him that his wound was the fatal one. Whether one actually inflicts the fatal wound, or contributes to or hastens the death in some minor way, he is guilty of the crime. And whether he hastens the death must be for the jury. The instruction was right.]

. . . The other grounds urged for reversal have been considered but have been found without merit. Judgment affirmed.

Questions

1. *Simultaneous Causes and the "But For" Test.* Is Constable Jones' conduct a "but for" cause of Gibson's death? Is his deputy's conduct a "but for" cause of Gibson's death? What argument can be made, if any, against causal accountability in such a case of two simultaneous causes both of which are sufficient alone to cause death? If the evidence showed that the two shots, from Jones and from his deputy, were each in themselves nonlethal, would each be a "but for" cause of Gibson's death? What is peculiar about this result, as compared to the result where the two shots are each lethal in themselves? Is causation in such a case established under the causation provision quoted at the beginning of this section?

2. *"But For" and the Sufficiency of Other Cause(s).* Looking back to the *Wood* case, in determining whether Wood's shot is a "but for" cause of Smith's death, does it matter whether his shot is itself lethal or nonlethal? In determining whether Wood's shot is a "but for" cause of Smith's death, does it matter whether Alma's subsequent shot is itself lethal or nonlethal? What conclusions do you draw from this comparison?

Model Penal Code §2.03
Causal Relationship Between Conduct and Result; Divergence Between Result Designed or Contemplated and Actual Result or Between Probable and Actual Result

(1) Conduct is the cause of a result when:
    (a) it is an antecedent but for which the result in question would not have occurred; and
    (b) the relationship between the conduct and result satisfies any

additional causal requirements imposed by the Code or by the law defining the offense.

(2) When purposely or knowingly causing a particular result is an element of an offense, the element is not established if the actual result is not within the purpose or the contemplation of the actor unless:

(a) the actual result differs from that designed or contemplated, as the case may be, only in the respect that a different person or different property is injured or affected or that the injury or harm designed or contemplated would have been more serious or more extensive than that caused; or

(b) the actual result involves the same kind of injury or harm as that designed or contemplated and is not too remote or accidental in its occurrence to have a [just] bearing on the actor's liability or on the gravity of his offense.

(3) When recklessly or negligently causing a particular result is an element of an offense, the element is not established if the actual result is not within the risk of which the actor is aware or, in the case of negligence, of which he should be aware unless:

(a) the actual result differs from the probable result only in the respect that a different person or different property is injured or affected or that the probable injury or harm would have been more serious or more extensive than that caused; or

(b) the actual result involves the same kind of injury or harm as the probable result and is not too remote or accidental in its occurrence to have a [just] bearing on the actor's liability or on the gravity of his offense.

(4) When causing a particular result is a material element of an offense for which absolute liability is imposed by law, the element is not established unless the actual result is a probable consequence of the actor's conduct.

Questions

1. *Factual Cause.* Does the Model Penal Code provision have a "but for" cause requirement similar to that of the causation provision quoted at the beginning of this section? Would the two provisions give similar results for Squeeze and for Wood?

2. *Simultaneous Causes.* Do the Model Penal Code and the quoted provision give similar results in simultaneous cause cases? What result in *Jones* under each provision?

3. *Proximate Cause.* Do the Model Penal Code and the quoted provision both give a defense if the result is "too remote or accidental in

its occurrence to have a just bearing on the actor's liability or on the gravity of his offense"? What result under each for Manny? What result in the falling piano hypothetical?

4. *Drafting Causation Provisions.* How are the Model Penal Code and the quoted provision different? In what ways, if any, do they give different results? Why might one provision be preferred over the other?

5. *Causing a "Result" Under the Model Penal Code.* Model Penal Code §2.03(2) & (3) distinguishes the "actual result" from "that designed or contemplated." In Manny's case, the drafters appear to mean the "actual result" to be *death from being hit by the train while leaning out to see the commotion that Manny had created by pushing another person on the track.* The drafters appear to mean that the result "designed or contemplated," in contrast, is *death from being hit by the train after being pushed on the track by Manny.* What is there, if anything, in the definition of murder or elsewhere in the Code that would suggest that the actual manner of causing the death is relevant to the elements of murder? If the Code is interpreted as the drafters apparently intended, to require not only "death of another human being" but also that the death caused in a particular way, how can one determine the particular cause-and-effect chain that is required in a given case? Is it the required chain of events that the actor expected to occur? What if the actor had not given any thought to the intermediate causal events? If we must look beyond the result required on the face of the statute, for example, death of a human being, to what level of detail must we look? death by bullet? death by bullet in the stomach? death by bullet in the stomach that causes massive bleeding? Why should the intermediate events that an actor expects be relevant, so long as he has the required culpability as to the particular result set out in the offense definition?

6. *Confusion in the Culpability Required with Respect to a Result.* The Model Penal Code proximate cause language ("not too remote or accidental . . .") is couched in terms of imputing a missing culpability requirement rather than in terms of giving a defense:

> When purposely or knowingly causing a particular result is an element of an offense, *the element is not established* if the actual result is not within the purpose or the contemplation of the actor *unless:* . . .

Why do the Model Penal Code drafters think that the required culpability element might be missing in cases like Manny or the falling piano hypothetical? Murder is defined as "purposely or knowingly causing the death of another human being." Model Penal Code §§210.1(1), 210.2(1)(a). The Code's culpability definitions in §2.02(2) would seem to require that, at the time of his conduct constituting a factual ("but for") cause, it is Manny's "conscious object" to cause or he is "practically certain" that his conduct will cause *"the death of another human being."*

Manny would seem to have this required culpability, as would the shooter in the falling piano hypothetical and the actor in most proximate cause problems. What in the Code, if anything, suggests that some culpability more than or different from this is required? What in the Code, if anything, would suggest that the actor must be purposeful or knowing as to *how* the required result ("death of another human being") came about?

7. *"Remoteness" as a Defense or as an Imputation Issue?* Assume for a moment that Manny and the actor in the falling piano hypothetical satisfy the required culpability as to causing the "death of another human being." They rather clearly satisfy the "but for" factual cause requirement. Presumably, we would want the jury to have an opportunity to decide whether the "remoteness" of the deaths from their conduct is such that they ought not be causally accountable for the deaths. Is the Model Penal Code causation provision effective at doing this? It has the "not too remote . . ." language in §2.03(2)(b) but that clause is reached only "if the actual result is not within the purpose or the contemplation of the actor" (introductory language of §2.03(2)). And, even if the "remoteness" language is reached, its effect is to *impute a missing culpability* as to causation. Is there anything in the Code's provision that gives a *defense* for conduct that is a "but for" cause but is too remote or accidental? Would the drafters argue with the initial assumption, that Manny and the actor in the falling piano hypothetical satisfy the culpability as to causing death required for homicide?

Chapter 8. INCHOATE OFFENSES

The previous section on causation introduces the notion that the occurrence of results sometimes makes a difference to criminal liability. The causation requirements assure that a defendant's liability and punishment are increased because of results only if the results are attributable to the defendant. This chapter continues the inquiry into the significance of results. In the context of attempts, an actor who unsuccessfully attempts murder might be as dangerous (and as much in need of deterrence and rehabilitation) as an identical actor who succeeds in the killing, but the successful actor, the murderer, is nonetheless assigned greater liability and punishment than the attempter.

While causing tangible harms may increase liability, it is not a necessary condition for liability. The criminal law's punishment of risk creation illustrates a willingness to punish in the absence of a tangible harm. Further, many of the "evils" that the criminal law prohibits and punishes are, or cause, primarily *intangible* evils, such as cheating, incest among adults, or gambling. The distributive principles discussed in Chapter 2 all support liability for proscribed conduct under defined circumstances even though the conduct does not cause harmful results. It should be no surprise, then, to find that the criminal law punishes inchoate offenses—that is, incomplete or unsuccessful offenses. Actors who plan or attempt offenses may well be blameworthy and dangerous and in need of deterrence and rehabilitation.

Inchoate offenses may be consistent with the idea that liability commonly is imposed in the absence of harmful results but, in one sense, inchoate offenses are unique. They are by definition instances where the harm or evil of the substantive offense has not come about. That is, they punish even in the absence of the prohibited evil. One can be liable for attempted cheating, attempted incest, and attempted gambling. It is the definition of inchoate offenses, then, that defines the borderline of criminal conduct, the minimum that one can do to be criminally liable.

Defining the borderline of criminal liability is, in part, what makes inchoate offenses so important and so interesting. Deciding on the minimum requirements for liability forces hard decisions, and the choices we make reveal much about our views of the nature of criminal liability generally. Principles and dilemmas that are part of the criminal liability landscape in many other areas come into sharp focus in this chapter. If criminal liability does not require completed offense conduct, what does it require? If an intention to commit an offense is the gravamen of inchoate offenses, why require any act at all? It is in the definition of the borderline that the rationales underlying the criminal law's traditional requirement of an act become directly relevant.

SECTION 8.1 THE ACT REQUIREMENT

With the exception of the special case of liability for an omission, the criminal law requires an act before liability may be imposed. Why, exactly, is an act required? And what, exactly, is required by this act requirement?

Cat in the Box

Brock is angry with her busy-body neighbor who insists on spying on her. While day dreaming in class she hits upon what she thinks is a brilliant idea. She will put her cat in her mailbox and, when her neighbor tries to check Brock's mail, the neighbor will get her eyes scratched out. Brock tells her friend of her flash of genius.

Brock returns from school early the next day so she will be home when the mailman comes. She plans to sneak the cat into the box as soon as the mailman leaves. Before the mailman comes, however, she hears from the building superintendent that her elderly neighbor died the previous evening. Can Brock be held criminally liable for an offense, perhaps attempted assault or attempted maiming?

Model Penal Code §2.01(1)
Requirement of Voluntary Act

A person is not guilty of an offense unless his liability is based on conduct which includes a voluntary act. . . .[1]

---

[1]. The Code goes on to permit, as an alternative, the actor's failure to perform a legal duty of which he is physically capable. See Model Penal Code §§2.01(1) & (3). The special case of liability for an omission is the subject of Chapter 13.

Model Penal Code §1.13(2)
Definition of "Act"

"Act" or "action" means a bodily movement whether voluntary or involuntary.

The Necessity for an Act
G. Williams, Criminal Law: The General Part
1-2 (2d ed. 1961)

That crime requires an act is invariably true if the proposition be read as meaning that a private thought is not sufficient to found responsibility. Shakespeare's lines express sound legal doctrine:

> His acts did not o'ertake his bad intent
> And must be buried but as an intent
> That perish'd by the way; thoughts are no subjects,
> Intents but merely thoughts.

"So long as an act rests in bare intention," said Lord Mansfield, "it is not punishable by our laws"; and this is so even though the intention be abundantly proved by the confession of the accused.

It is worth pausing to inquire into the reason for this rule. A reason commonly given is the supposed impossibility of proving a mental state. "A tribunal," said Blackstone, "cannot punish for what it cannot know." So also Brian, C.J.: "The thought of man is not triable, for the devil himself knoweth not the thought of man." But Brian was speaking of an intent not declared in words or conduct, and on another occasion he recognized that intent can be inferred from acts. Similarly, it can be inferred from a confession. Hence it is not true to say that intent cannot be tried. Better reasons for the rule would be (1) the difficulty of distinguishing between day dreams and fixed intention in the absence of behavior tending toward the crime intended, and (2) the undesirability of spreading the criminal law so wide as to cover a mental state that the accused might be too irresolute even to begin to translate into action. There can hardly be anyone who has never thought evil. When a desire is inhibited it may find expression in fantasy; but it would be absurd to condemn this natural psychological mechanism as illegal.

Conduct as a Prerequisite
H. Packer, The Limits of the Criminal Sanction
73-75 (1968)

It may hardly seem a startling notion that criminal law, or law in general for that matter, is concerned with conduct—people's actions (including their verbal and other expressive actions) and their failures to act. Yet there is nothing in the nature of things that compels this focus. The criminal law could be concerned with people's thoughts and emotions, with their personality patterns and character structures. It is true that if this rather than conduct was the focus, it would still be expedient in most cases to ascertain these essentially internal characteristics through inquiry into conduct. But if these internal characteristics were the focus, conduct would simply be evidence of what we are interested in rather than the thing itself; and we would not hesitate to use other evidence to the extent that it became available. If, for example, we could determine through projective tests like the Rorschach or through other and more sophisticated forms of psychological testing that a given individual was likely to inflict serious physical injury on someone, someday, somewhere, . . . we would presumably not hesitate to inflict punishment on that person for his propensities, or, as the old cliché has it, for thinking evil thoughts. . . .

Why do we not do so? The obvious historical answer is that, aside from a few antiquarian anomalies such as the offense of imagining the King's death, we have not been sufficiently stirred by the danger presented or sufficiently confident of our ability to discern propensities in the absence of conduct to use the instruments of the criminal law in this fashion. For some it may be enough to rejoice that historically this was so and to rest on that historical accident for the present and the future, but I think that a further answer is required. This answer turns, in my view, on the idea of culpability. . . .

Among the notions associated with the concept of "culpability" are those of free will and human autonomy. I do not mean this in any deep philosophical sense but in a contingent and practical social sense. It is important, especially in a society that likes to describe itself as "free" and "open," that a government should be empowered to coerce people only for what they do and not for what they are.

If this is important for law generally, it is *a fortiori* important for that most coercive of legal instruments, the criminal law. Now, this self-denying ordinance can be and often is attacked as being inconsistent with the facts of human nature. People may in fact have little if any greater capacity to control their conduct . . . than their emotions or their thoughts. It is therefore either unrealistic or hypocritical, so the argument runs, to deal with conduct as willed or to treat it differently from personality and character.

This attack is, however, misconceived. Neither philosophic concepts nor psychological realities are actually at issue in the criminal law. The idea of free will in relation to conduct is not, in the legal system, a statement of fact, but rather a value preference having very little to do with the metaphysics of determinism and free will. . . . Very simply, the law treats man's conduct as autonomous and willed, not because it is, but because it is desirable to proceed as if it were. It is desirable because the capacity of the individual human being to live his life in reasonable freedom from socially imposed external constraints (the only kind with which the law is concerned) would be fatally impaired unless the law provided a *locus poenitentiae*, a point of no return beyond which external constraints may be imposed but before which the individual is free—not free of whatever compulsions determinists tell us he labors under but free of the very specific social compulsions of the law. . . .

Robinson v. California
Supreme Court of the United States
370 U.S. 660, 82 S. Ct. 1417, 8 L. Ed. 2d 758 (1962)

Mr. Justice STEWART delivered the opinion of the Court.

A California statute makes it a criminal offense for a person to "be addicted to the use of narcotics." This appeal draws into question the constitutionality of that provision of the state law, as construed by the California courts in the present case.

The appellant was convicted after a jury trial in the Municipal Court of Los Angeles. . . .

The trial judge instructed the jury that the statute made it a misdemeanor for a person "either to use narcotics, or to be addicted to the use of narcotics. . . . That portion of the statute referring to the 'use' of narcotics is based upon the 'act' of using. That portion of the statute referring to 'addicted to the use' of narcotics is based upon a condition or status. They are not identical. . . . To be addicted to the use of narcotics is said to be a status or condition and not an act. It is a continuing offense and differs from most other offenses in the fact that [it] is chronic rather than acute; that it continues after it is complete and subjects the offender to arrest at any time before he reforms. . . ."

The judge further instructed the jury that the appellant could be convicted under a general verdict if the jury agreed *either* that he was of the "status" or had committed the "act" denounced by the statute. "All that the People must show is either that the defendant did use a narcotic in Los Angeles County, or that while in the City of Los Angeles he was addicted to the use of narcotics. . . ."

Under these instructions the jury returned a verdict finding the appellant "guilty of the offense charged." . . .

The broad power of a State to regulate the narcotic drugs traffic within its borders is not here in issue. . . .

Such regulation, it can be assumed, could take a variety of valid forms. A State might impose criminal sanctions, for example, against the unauthorized manufacture, prescription, sale, purchase, or possession of narcotics within its borders. . . .

It would be possible to construe the statute under which the appellant was convicted as one which is operative only upon proof of the actual use of narcotics within the State's jurisdiction. But the California courts have not so construed this law. Although there was evidence in the present case that the appellant had used narcotics in Los Angeles, the jury were instructed that they could convict him even if they disbelieved that evidence. The appellant could be convicted, they were told, if they found simply that the appellant's "status" or "chronic condition" was that of being "addicted to the use of narcotics." And it is impossible to know from the jury's verdict that the defendant was not convicted upon precisely such a finding. . . .

. . . This statute, therefore, is not one which punishes a person for the use of narcotics, for their purchase, sale or possession, or for antisocial or disorderly behavior resulting from their administration. It is not a law which even purports to provide or require medical treatment. Rather, we deal with a statute which makes the "status" of narcotic addiction a criminal offense, for which the offender may be prosecuted "at any time before he reforms." California has said that a person can be continuously guilty of this offense, whether or not he has ever used or possessed any narcotics within the state, and whether or not he has been guilty of any antisocial behavior there.

It is unlikely that any State at this moment in history would attempt to make it a criminal offense for a person to be mentally ill, or a leper, or to be afflicted with a venereal disease. A State might determine that the general health and welfare require that the victims of these and other human afflictions be dealt with by compulsory treatment, involving quarantine, confinement, or sequestration. But, in the light of contemporary human knowledge, a law which made a criminal offense of such a disease would doubtless be universally thought to be an infliction of cruel and unusual punishment in violation of the Eighth and Fourteenth Amendments. . . .

We cannot but consider the statute before us as of the same category. In this Court counsel for the State recognized that narcotic addiction is an illness. Indeed, it is apparently an illness which may be contracted innocently or involuntarily. We hold that a state law which imprisons a person thus afflicted as a criminal, even though he has never touched any narcotic drug within the State or been guilty of any irregular behavior there, inflicts a cruel and unusual punishment in violation of the Fourteenth Amendment. To be sure, imprisonment for ninety days is not, in the abstract, a punishment which is either cruel or unusual. But the question cannot be considered in the abstract. Even one day in prison would be a cruel and unusual punishment for the "crime" of having a common cold. . . .

Reversed. . . .

Mr. Justice HARLAN, concurring.

I am not prepared to hold that on the present state of medical knowledge it is completely irrational and hence unconstitutional for a State to conclude that narcotics addiction is something other than an illness nor that it amounts to cruel and unusual punishment for the State to subject narcotics addicts to its criminal law. Insofar as addiction may be identified with the use or possession of narcotics within the State (or, I would suppose, without the State), in violation of local statutes prohibiting such acts, it may surely be reached by the State's criminal law. But in this case the trial court's instructions permitted the jury to find the appellant guilty on no more proof than that he was present in California while he was addicted to narcotics. Since addiction alone cannot reasonably be thought to amount to more than a compelling propensity to use narcotics, the effect of this instruction was to authorize criminal punishment for a bare desire to commit a criminal act.

If the California statute reaches this type of conduct, and for present purposes we must accept the trial court's construction as binding, . . . it is an arbitrary imposition which exceeds the power that a State may exercise in enacting its criminal law. Accordingly, I agree that the application of the California statute was unconstitutional in this case and join the judgment of reversal. . . .

Mr. Justice WHITE, dissenting.

If appellant's conviction rested upon sheer status, condition or illness or if he was convicted for being an addict who had lost his power of self-control, I would have other thoughts about this case. . . .

. . . I do not consider appellant's conviction to be a punishment for having an illness or for simply being in some status or condition, but rather a conviction for the regular, repeated or habitual use of narcotics immediately prior to his arrest and in violation of the California law. As defined by the trial court, addiction is the regular use of narcotics and can be proved only by evidence of such use. To find addiction in this case the jury had to believe that appellant had frequently used narcotics in the recent past. California is entitled to have its statute and the record so read, particularly where the State's only purpose in allowing prosecutions for addiction was to supersede its own venue requirements applicable to prosecutions for the use of narcotics and in effect to allow convictions for use where there is no precise evidence of the county where the use took place. . . .

. . . The Fourteenth Amendment is today held to bar any prosecution for addiction regardless of the degree or frequency of use, and the Court's opinion bristles with indications of further consequences. If it is "cruel and unusual punishment" to convict appellant for addiction, it is difficult to understand why it would be any less offensive to the Fourteenth Amendment to convict him for use on the same evidence of use which proved he was an addict. It is significant that in purporting to reaffirm the power of the States to deal with the narcotics traffic, the Court does not include among the obvious powers of the State the power to punish for the use of narcotics. I cannot think that the omission was inadvertent.

The Court has not merely tidied up California's law by removing some irritating vestige of an outmoded approach to the control of narcotics. At the very least, it has effectively removed California's power to deal effectively with the recurring case under the statute where there is ample evidence of use but no evidence of the precise location of use. Beyond this it has cast serious doubt upon the power of any State to forbid the use of narcotics under threat of criminal punishment. I cannot believe that the Court would forbid the application of the criminal laws to the use of narcotics under any circumstances. But the States, as well as the Federal Government, are now on notice. They will have to await a final answer in another case. . . .

I respectfully dissent.

Powell v. Texas
Supreme Court of the United States
392 U.S. 514, 88 S. Ct. 2145, 20 L. Ed. 1254 (1968)

Mr. Justice MARSHALL announced the judgment of the Court and delivered an opinion in which The Chief Justice, Mr. Justice BLACK, and Mr. Justice HARLAN join.

In late December 1966, appellant was arrested and charged with being found in a state of intoxication in a public place, in violation of Texas Penal Code, Art. 477 (1952), which reads as follows:

> Whoever shall get drunk or be found in a state of intoxication in any public place, or at any private house except his own, shall be fined not exceeding one hundred dollars.

Appellant was tried in the Corporation Court of Austin, Texas, found guilty, and fined $20. He appealed to the County Court at Law No. 1 of Travis County, Texas, where a trial *de novo* was held. His counsel urged that appellant was "afflicted with the disease of chronic alcoholism," that "his appearance in public [while drunk was] . . . not of his volition," and therefore that to punish him criminally for that conduct would be cruel and unusual, in violation of the Eighth and Fourteenth Amendments to the United States Constitution.

The trial judge in the county court, sitting without a jury, made certain findings of fact . . . but ruled as a matter of law that chronic alcoholism was not a defense to the charge. He found appellant guilty, and fined him $50. There being no further right to appeal within the Texas judicial system, appellant appealed to this Court; we noted probable jurisdiction.

The principal testimony was that of Dr. David Wade, a Fellow of the American Medical Association, duly certificated in psychiatry. . . . Dr. Wade sketched the outlines of the "disease" concept of alcoholism; noted that there is no generally accepted definition of "alcoholism"; alluded to the ongoing debate within the medical profession over whether alcohol is actually physically "addicting" or merely psychologically "habituating"; and concluded that in either case a "chronic alcoholic" is an "involuntary drinker," who is "powerless not to drink," and who "loses his self-control over his drinking." He testified that he had examined appellant, and that appellant is a "chronic alcoholic," who "by the time he has reached [the state of intoxication] . . . is not able to control his behavior, and [who] . . . has reached this point because he has an uncontrollable compulsion to drink." Dr. Wade also responded in the negative to the question whether appellant has "the willpower to resist the constant excessive consumption of alcohol." He added that in his opinion jailing appellant without medical attention would operate neither to rehabilitate him nor to lessen his desire for alcohol.

On cross-examination, Dr. Wade admitted that when appellant was sober he knew the difference between right and wrong, and he responded affirmatively to the question whether appellant's act of taking the first drink in any given instance when he was sober was a "voluntary exercise of his will." Qualifying his answer, Dr. Wade stated that "these individuals have a compulsion, and this compulsion, while not completely overpowering, is a very strong influence, an exceedingly strong influence, and this compulsion coupled with the firm belief in their mind that they are going to be able to handle it from now on causes their judgment to be somewhat clouded."

Appellant testified concerning the history of his drinking problem. He reviewed his many arrests for drunkenness; testified that he was unable to stop drinking; stated that when he was intoxicated he had no control over his actions and could not remember them later, but that he did not become violent; and admitted that he did not remember his arrest on the occasion for which he was being tried. On cross-examination, appellant admitted that he had had one drink on the morning of the trial and had been able to discontinue drinking. . . .

Evidence in the case then closed. The State made no effort to obtain expert psychiatric testimony of its own, or even to explore with appellant's witness the question of appellant's power to control the frequency, timing, and location of his drinking bouts, or the substantial disagreement within the medical profession concerning the nature of the disease, the efficacy of treatment and the prerequisites for effective treatment. . . .

[T]he State contented itself with a brief argument that appellant had no defense to the charge because he "is legally sane and knows the difference between right and wrong."

Following this abbreviated exposition of the problem before it, the trial court indicated its intention to disallow appellant's claimed defense of "chronic alcoholism." Thereupon defense counsel submitted, and the trial court entered, the following "findings of fact":

(1) That chronic alcoholism is a disease which destroys the afflicted person's will power to resist the constant, excessive consumption of alcohol.
(2) That a chronic alcoholic does not appear in public by his own volition but under a compulsion symptomatic of the disease of chronic alcoholism.
(3) That Leroy Powell, defendant herein, is a chronic alcoholic who is afflicted with the disease of chronic alcoholism.

Whatever else may be said of them, those are not "findings of fact" in any recognizable, traditional sense in which that term has been used in a court of law; they are the premises of a syllogism transparently designed to bring this case within the scope of this Court's opinion in Robinson v. California, 370 U.S. 660 (1962). Nonetheless, the dissent would have us adopt these "findings" without critical examination; it would use them as the basis for a constitutional holding that "a person may not be punished if the condition essential to constitute the defined crime is part of the pattern of his disease and is occasioned by a compulsion symptomatic of the disease." . . .

On its face the present case does not fall within the holding announced in Robinson v. California, 370 U.S 660 (1962), since appellant was convicted, not for being a chronic alcoholic, but for being in public while drunk on a particular occasion. The State of Texas thus has not sought to punish a mere status, as California did in *Robinson;* nor has it attempted to regulate appellant's behavior in the privacy of his own home. Rather, it has imposed upon appellant a criminal sanction for public behavior which may create substantial health and safety hazards, both for appellant and for members of the general public, and which offends the moral and aesthetic sensibilities of a large segment of the community. This seems a far cry from convicting one for being an addict, being a chronic alcoholic, being "mentally ill, or a leper. . . ." Id., at 666. . . .

Likewise, as the dissent acknowledges, there is a substantial definitional distinction between a "status," as in *Robinson,* and a "condition," which is said to be involved in this case. Whatever may be the merits of an attempt to distinguish between behavior and a condition, it is perfectly clear that the crucial element in this case, so far as the dissent is concerned, is whether or not appellant can legally be held responsible for his appearance in public in a state of intoxication. The only relevance of *Robinson* to this issue is that because the Court interpreted the statute there involved as making a "status" criminal, it was able to suggest that the statute would cover even a situation in which addiction had been acquired involuntarily. That this factor was not determinative in the case is shown by the fact that there was no indication of how Robinson himself had become an addict. . . .

Affirmed.

Mr. Justice FORTAS, with whom Mr. Justice DOUGLAS, Mr. Justice BRENNAN, and Mr. Justice STEWART join, dissenting. . . .

Robinson stands upon a principle which, despite its subtlety, must be simply stated and respectfully applied because it is the foundation of individual liberty and the cornerstone of the relations between a civilized state and its citizens: Criminal penalties may not be inflicted upon a person for being in a condition he is powerless to change. In all probability, Robinson at some time before his conviction elected to take narcotics. But the crime as defined did not punish this conduct. The statute imposed a penalty for the offense of "addiction"—a condition which Robinson could not control. Once Robinson had become an addict, he was utterly powerless to avoid criminal guilt. He was powerless to choose not to violate the law.

In the present case, appellant is charged with a crime composed of two elements—being intoxicated and being found in a public place while in that condition. The crime, so defined, differs from that in *Robinson.* The statute covers more than a mere status. But the essential constitutional defect here is the same as in *Robinson,* for in both cases the particular defendant was accused of being in a condition which he had no capacity to change or avoid. The trial judge sitting as trier of fact found, upon the medical and other relevant testimony, that Powell is a "chronic alcoholic." He defined appellant's "chronic alcoholism" as "a disease which destroys the afflicted person's will power to resist the constant, excessive consumption of alcohol." He also found that "a chronic alcoholic does not appear in public by his own volition but under a compulsion symptomatic of the disease of chronic alcoholism." I read these findings to mean that appellant was powerless to avoid drinking; that having taken his first drink, he had "an uncontrollable compulsion to drink" to the point of intoxication; and that, once intoxicated, he could not prevent himself from appearing in public places.

The findings in this case, read against the background of the medical and sociological data to which I have referred, compel the conclusion that the infliction upon appellant of a criminal penalty for being intoxicated in a public place would be "cruel and inhuman punishment" within the prohibition of the Eighth Amendment. This conclusion follows because appellant is a "chronic alcoholic" who, according to the trier of fact, cannot resist the "constant excessive consumption of alcohol" and does not appear in public by his own volition but under a "compulsion" which is part of his condition.

I would reverse the judgment below.

Questions

1. *Rationales.* Why have an act requirement?
2. *Liability for One's Thoughts.* The act requirement is said to prevent liability for thoughts alone. Is it possible that otherwise innocent conduct can be made criminal solely by the actor's thoughts? If so, is this contrary to the goals of the act requirement?
3. *Finding a Voluntary Act.* Does Brock satisfy the act requirement? That is, does her conduct "*include* a voluntary act"? Is her returning from school a voluntary act? Did Robinson's being addicted come about through a voluntary act at some point in the process, such as voluntarily taking drugs at some point? If so, does it seem that the act requirement, as set out in Model Penal Code §2.02(1), is of little effect in serving the purposes that Williams and Packer describe?
4. *Defining Offenses vs. Adjudicating Violations.* Is the "act requirement" that Williams and Packer refer to a limitation directed primarily to judges and juries or to criminal code drafters? Can you find an offense in the Model Penal Code that does not contain in its definition the requirement of an act (or a legal duty to act)? Check the doctrines of borderline liability, such as attempt in §5.01(1), conspiracy in §5.03(1), and complicity liability in §2.06(3).
5. *The Voluntariness Requirement.* Is it possible that the key term in Model Penal Code §2.01(1) is not the requirement of "a voluntary *act*" but rather its requirement of "a *voluntary* act"? In other words, might the more important role of the provision be to provide a defense for

involuntariness? (The voluntariness requirement is discussed in Section 16.3.) Could the "act requirement" be dropped altogether if the "voluntariness requirement" were provided?

6. *Failure to Satisfy the Act Requirement as a Trigger for the Rules Governing Possession and Omission Liability.* What are the special requirements for possession and for omission liability? When do these special requirements apply? (See Model Penal Code §2.01(4), quoted below, and Model Penal Code §2.01(1) & (3).) Is it possible that the act requirement's primary significance is to provide a point of contrast for liability based upon possession or an omission, that is, to trigger the special requirements for liability that apply in such cases?

Model Penal Code §2.01(4)
Possession as an Act

Possession is an act, within the meaning of this Section [stating the requirement of a voluntary act], if the possessor knowingly procured or received the thing possessed or was aware of his control thereof for a sufficient period to have been able to terminate his possession.

Model Penal Code §5.06(1)
Possessing Instruments of Crime

Criminal Instruments Generally. A person commits a misdemeanor if he possesses any instrument of crime with purpose to employ it criminally. "Instrument of crime" means:

(a) anything specially made or specially adapted for criminal use; or

(b) anything commonly used for criminal purposes and possessed by the actor under circumstances which do not negative unlawful purpose.

Questions

1. *Possession.* Is possession of an instrument of crime (or contraband) an "act" as defined by Model Penal Code §1.13(2)? Is it an "act" for the purposes of §2.01(1)?

2. *Possession and the Voluntary Act Requirement.* When the special conditions set out in Model Penal Code §2.01(4) are satisfied—"was aware of his control thereof for a sufficient period to have been able to terminate his possession"—does the possession satisfy the reasons that are traditionally given for requiring a voluntary act?

SECTION 8.2 ATTEMPT

Here we examine the objective elements and the culpability requirements for attempt liability. The objective requirements attempt to define the point in the process, from thinking about an offense to completing it, at which the actor's conduct becomes criminal. It is only at this point that police are authorized to step in and that liability may be imposed. The culpability requirements of attempt are particularly important because, by definition, the substantive harm or evil of the offense has not occurred. It is the actor's culpability that makes what is otherwise innocent conduct criminal.

A Plan to Kill

Marsden has had enough of the President's unfair trade policies toward his homeland. To save the hundreds of people who are suffering under the bad economic conditions there, he decides to kill the President. The Vice President is on record as supporting a change in policy that Marsden prefers.

Marsden knows several patriots who feel as he does and he believes they would be willing to help if asked. He works out a plan to assassinate the President as he leaves his hotel after a local speech scheduled for next week. After studying the layout each day as he passes it on his way to work, Marsden decides that for the plot to be successful one of his friends must feign an attack from the opposite direction to divert Secret Service attention. Before he is able to raise the issue with his friends or to collect any of the needed material, his nosy cleaning lady finds his notes about his plan and reports him to police. The evidence of his intention is overwhelming. He is charged with attempted murder.

Marsden's defense counsel does not deny Marsden's intention but argues that Marsden has done nothing toward actual commission of the offense and therefore cannot be held liable for an attempt. Is counsel correct?

Model Penal Code §5.01 Comment
38-48 (Tent. Draft No. 10, 1960)

The "Last Proximate Act." There is general agreement that, where the actor has done all that [is] necessary to cause the particular result which is an element of the crime, he has committed an attempt. . . . This formulation [of the objective requirement for attempt] covers not only instances in which the actor's efforts must succeed or miscarry independently of the actor's will—as where the contemplated victim is fired upon, but the shots miss or the victim does not die—but also those cases in which the actor has the power to prevent the completion of the crime but need do no further acts towards its commission—as where a bomb is planted which will not explode for some time and can be rendered harmless by timely intervention. . . .

It is clear, of course, that while the "last proximate act" is sufficient to constitute an attempt it is not *necessary* to a finding of attempt. No jurisdiction operating within the framework of Anglo-American law requires that the last proximate act occur before an attempt can be charged. . . .

The General Distinction between Preparation and Attempt. . . . If the "last proximate act" is not required in order for there to be an attempt, and if—as is generally assumed—every act done with intent to commit a crime is not to be made criminal, it becomes necessary to establish a means of inclusion and exclusion. Some of the approaches which have been tried or suggested are as follows:

(a) *The physical proximity doctrine.* Some courts purport to be guided by principles which state in general terms that the overt act required for an attempt must be proximate to the completed crime, or that the act must be one directly tending toward the completion of the crime, or that the act must amount to the commencement of the consummation. Such opinions often admit that each case must be decided on its own facts and examine in detail the act's remoteness from the completed crime, emphasizing time, distance and the number of necessary acts as yet undone.* A stringent view of the physical proximity test holds that

---

*Editor's Note.—In People v. Rizzo, 246 N.Y. 334, 158 N.E. 888 (1927), the defendant and his confederates were arrested as they were driving through the streets of New York looking for a Mr. Rao, who the defendants thought would be delivering a payroll. They intended to rob Rao, and two of the four men were armed for that purpose. New York's high court reversed the defendant's conviction for attempted robbery on the following reasoning:

> . . . To constitute the crime of robbery the money must have been taken from Rao by means of force or violence, or through fear. . . . Rao was not found; the

the actor's conduct does not proceed beyond preparation until the actor has the power—or at least the apparent power—to complete the crime forthwith. . . .

(b) *The dangerous proximity doctrine.* A test which incorporates the physical proximity approach within it, but which proceeds beyond it, is the doctrine given impetus by the writings and opinions of Mr. Justice Holmes. In order to determine whether a given act constitutes an attempt the following factors are considered: the gravity of the offense intended, the nearness of the act to completion of the crime, and the probability that the conduct will result in the offense intended. The greater the gravity and probability, and the nearer the act to the crime, the stronger is the case for calling the act an attempt. The test is based on the assumption that the purpose of punishing attempts is to deter undesirable behavior and that until the actor's conduct becomes sufficiently dangerous there is not adequate reason for deterring it.[87] . . .

(c) *The indispensable element approach.* One variation of the several proximity tests emphasizes any indispensable aspect of the criminal endeavor over which the actor has not yet acquired control. Some decisions seem to stand for the proposition that, if the successful completion of a crime requires the assent or action of some third person, that assent or action must be forthcoming before the actor can be guilty of an attempt. Thus if *A* and *B* plan to defraud a life insurance company

---

defendants were still looking for him; no attempt to rob him could be made, at least until he came in sight; he was not in the building [outside of which the defendants were arrested]. . . . In a word, these defendants had planned to commit a crime and were looking around the city for an opportunity to commit it, but the opportunity fortunately never came. . . .

87. See the writings of Holmes.

Editor's Note.—In Commonwealth v. Peaslee, 177 Mass. 267, 59 N.E. 55 (1901), Holmes, C.J., stated the facts and issue as follows:

The evidence was that the defendant had constructed and arranged combustibles in the building in such a way that they were ready to be lighted, and if lighted would have set fire to the building and its contents. To be exact, the plan would have required a candle which was standing on a shelf six feet away to be placed on a piece of wood in a pan of turpentine and lighted. The defendant offered to pay a younger man in his employment if he would go to the building, seemingly some miles from the place of the dialogue, and carry out the plan. This was refused. Later the defendant and the young man drove towards the building, but when within a quarter of a mile the defendant said that he had changed his mind, and drove away. This is as near as he ever came to accomplishing what he had in contemplation.

The question on the evidence . . . is whether the defendant's acts come near enough to the accomplishment of the substantive offense to be punishable [as an attempt].

177 Mass. at 271, 59 N.E. at 58. Defendant's conviction was reversed. (The act of solicitation could not be used to satisfy the objective element of attempt.)

by pretending that A, the insured, is dead, and if C, the beneficiary, must file a formal claim before any proceeds can be paid, it has been held that the acts of A and B cannot amount to an attempt to defraud the insurance company until C files a claim or agrees to file a claim. And one court has held that giving counterfeit matter to another, in order that he may "pass" it, does not constitute an attempt to "pass" on the giver's part until the other makes an effort to pass the counterfeit matter to an innocent third party. If the actor seeks to influence a juror by asking a third party to approach the juror, the cases split on whether the actor has attempted to corrupt a juror. The reasoning of the courts which refuse to find an attempt here because of the need for the third party's cooperation is similar to that applied in cases which hold that solicitation does not constitute an attempt because completion of the crime requires action by the party solicited.

An analogous group of cases supports the view that a person cannot be guilty of an attempt if he lacks a means essential to completion of the offense. Thus it has been held that one cannot be guilty of an attempt to introduce whiskey into a forbidden territory until he acquires the whiskey; that a person cannot attempt an assault with a dangerous weapon until he acquires the weapon; that one cannot attempt to illegally manufacture whiskey until he acquires the necessary apparatus; and that one cannot attempt to vote illegally until he obtains a ballot. . . .

(d) *The probable desistance test.* [An alternative test] provides that the actor's conduct constitutes an attempt if, in the ordinary and natural course of events, without interruption from an outside source, it will result in the crime intended.[96] [T]his test seems to require, in order for there to be an attempt, a judgment in each case that the actor had reached a point where it was unlikely that he would have voluntarily desisted from his efforts to commit the crime. But in cases applying this test no inquiry is made into the personality of the particular offender

---

96. . . . State v. Schwarzbach, 84 N.J.L. 268, 86 A. 423 (Ct. Err. & App. 1913).
Editor's Note.—The defendant in *Schwarzbach* was charged with attempted adultery. The Court stated the facts as follows:

> The point seriously made on behalf of the defendant is that the acts of the defendant did not constitute an attempt, but only preparation to commit the offense. The facts were these: The defendant Schwarzbach repaired to the house of one Liehr during his absence, knowing him to be absent, and was surprised by Liehr in the bedroom with his wife after midnight. Mrs. Liehr was sitting on the bed in her nightgown. Alongside of the bed was Schwarzbach disrobing. He had his hat, coat, and shoes off, and his left suspenderstrap hung down, and he was evidently about to remove his trousers. There is no question but that Mrs. Liehr was a willing party. In fact, she was jointly indicted and convicted with Schwarzbach.

84 N.J.L. at 269, 86 A. 424. The conviction for attempted adultery was affirmed.

before the court. The question is whether *anyone* who went so far would stop short of the final step. . . .

. . . The opinion has been voiced that one who undertakes a criminal endeavor and performs an act pursuant to that purpose is not likely to stop short of the final step. And in actual operation the probable desistance test is linked entirely to the nearness of the actor's conduct to completion, this being the sole basis of unsubstantiated judicial appraisals of the probabilities of desistance. The test as applied appears to be little more than the physical proximity approach.

(e) *The abnormal step approach.* One commentator . . . defines an attempt as a step toward crime which goes beyond the point where the normal citizen would think better of his conduct and desist. . . .

(f) *The res ipsa loquitur test.* Taking an entirely different approach to the preparation-attempt problem is the view which holds that an attempt is committed when the actor's conduct manifests an intent to commit a crime. The conduct would be considered in relation to all the surrounding circumstances exclusive of representations made by the actor about his intentions; but presumably representations of the actor which negative a criminal intent would be admissible to disprove the intention imputed. The object of this approach is to subject to attempt liability conduct which unequivocally demonstrates that the actor is being guided by a criminal purpose.* . . .

. . . The assumption underlying [support of the *res ipsa test*] is that there is some relationship between the actor's state of mind and the external appearance of his acts. While the actor's behavior is externally equivocal the criminal purpose in his mind is likely to be unfixed—a subjective equivocality. But once the actor must desist or perform acts which he realizes would incriminate him if all external facts were known,

---

*Editor's Note.—The facts of People v. Gibson, 94 Cal. App. 2d 468, 210 P.2d 747 (1949), illustrate what might satisfy this test:

> About 12:30 o'clock of a January morning appellant crossed an alley extending easterly from San Fernando Road, the principal thoroughfare of Burbank. He carried a 14-foot wooden ladder which he placed horizontally by the fence in the rear of a department store. The darkness of the night was marred only by the street lights which were reflected into the alley. Having deposited his burden he stood erect, looked upward and walked along the edge of the building. Having reconnoitered the premises back to the point from which police officer Wooten had witnessed the prowler's movements he then proceeded easterly for 120 feet when commanded to halt. . . . Wooten then observing that this denizen of darkness wore brown cotton gloves, placed him under arrest. . . . [H]e found a burlap sack which contained various tools and burglars' equipment, including an eight pound sledge hammer, bits, braces, flashlights, gloves and 30 feet of quarter-inch, white rope ladder of about 15 steps. In addition to the contents of the sack appellant had in his pockets two flashlights, wire cutters and a coil of small brown copper wire. Wooten took also from the man's possession the keys to his automobile which was found two blocks east of the department store. . . .

then in all probability a firmer state of mind exists. Subjective equivocality seems inconsistent with an act which unequivocally demonstrates a criminal purpose. A hunter might buy extra supplies to facilitate an escape in the event he resolves to kill his companion, a question as yet unsettled in his mind. But when he buys poison which has no reasonable use under the circumstances other than the murder of his companion, the chances are that the debate has been resolved and the actor's purpose is fixed on murder. . . .

(g) *Substantiality and corroboration.* [The Model Penal Code] sets forth two requirements which distinguish attempt from preparation: (1) the act must be "a *substantial* step in a course of conduct" planned to accomplish the criminal result, and (2) the act must be "strongly corroborative" of criminal purpose in order for it to constitute such a "substantial step."

Whether a particular act is a substantial step is obviously a matter of degree. To this extent the present paragraph [of the proposed code] retains the element of imprecision found in most of the other approaches to the preparation-attempt problem. There are, however, several differences to be noted:

First, this formulation shifts the emphasis from what remains to be done—the chief concern of the proximity tests—to what the actor *has already done.* The fact that further major steps must be taken before the crime can be completed does not preclude a finding that the steps already undertaken are substantial. It is expected, in the normal case, that this approach will broaden the scope of attempt liability.

Second, although it is intended that the requirement of a substantial step will result in the imposition of attempt liability only in those instances in which some firmness of criminal purpose is shown, no finding is required as to whether the actor would probably have desisted prior to completing the crime. Potentially the probable desistance test could reach very early steps toward crime—depending upon how one assesses the probabilities of desistance—but since in practice this test follows closely the proximity approaches, rejection of probable desistance will not narrow the scope of attempt liability.

Finally, the requirement of proving a substantial step generally will prove less of a hurdle for the prosecution than the *res ipsa loquitur* approach, which requires that the actor's conduct must itself manifest the criminal purpose. The difference will be illustrated in connection with the present section's requirement of corroboration. Here it should be noted that, in the present formulation, the two purposes to be served by the *res ipsa loquitur* test are, to a large extent, treated separately. Firmness of criminal purpose is intended to be shown by requiring a substantial step, while problems of proof are dealt with by the requirement of corroboration (although, under the reasoning previously expressed, the latter will also tend to establish firmness of purpose).

In addition to assuring firmness of purpose, the requirement of a substantial step will remove very remote preparatory acts from the ambit of attempt liability and the relatively stringent sanctions imposed for attempts. On the other hand, by broadening liability to the extent suggested, apprehension of dangerous persons will be facilitated and law enforcement officials and others will be able to stop the criminal effort at an earlier stage—thereby minimizing the risk of substantive harm—without providing immunity for the offender.

In order to give greater content to the concept of the substantial step, Subsection 5.01(2) provides illustrations of certain common types of behavior which may be held to constitute substantial steps.*

Model Penal Code §5.01(1) & (2)
Criminal Attempt

(1) *Definition of Attempt*. A person is guilty of an attempt to commit a crime if, acting with the kind of culpability otherwise required for commission of the crime, he:

    (a) purposely engages in conduct which would constitute the crime if the attendant circumstances were as he believes them to be; or

    (b) when causing a particular result is an element of the crime, does or omits to do anything with the purpose of causing or with the belief that it will cause such result without further conduct on his part; or

---

*Editor's Note.—The substantial step test's potential to impose attempt liability at an early stage is illustrated by Commonwealth v. Melnyczenko, 619 A.2d 719 (Sup. Ct. Pa. 1992):

> On April 21, 1987, at 7:47 p.m., defendant left his home in West Reading, Pennsylvania, and drove approximately twenty miles to the Borough of Ephrata, in Lancaster County. . . . After driving slowly down several residential streets, he parked his car at an apartment complex, turning his lights out. . . . Mr. Melnyczenko then walked a short distance and disappeared from police view into the yards of a row of houses, reappearing some six or seven minutes later. Mr. Melnyczenko was then startled when [a police car] pulled out of a nearby driveway. . . . Mr. Melnyczenko began running behind a group of homes. Shortly thereafter he was arrested. . . . No direct evidence of an attempted break-in of any of the houses was found.

Id. at 720. The Court found the "substantial step" test to be satisfied on these facts. Note that Model Penal Code §5.01(2)(c), quoted in the text following, expressly provides that "reconnoitering the place contemplated for commission of the crime" cannot be held insufficient as a matter of law to constitute a substantial step. (Of course, the State also must prove the actor's intention to commit the offense beyond a reasonable doubt.)

(c) purposely does or omits to do anything which, under the circumstances as he believes them to be, is an act or omission constituting a substantial step in a course of conduct planned to culminate in his commission of the crime.

(2) *Conduct Which May Be Held Substantial Step Under Subsection (1)(c).* Conduct shall not be held to constitute a substantial step under Subsection (1)(c) of this Section unless it is strongly corroborative of the actor's criminal purpose. Without negativing the sufficiency of other conduct, the following, if strongly corroborative of the actor's criminal purpose, shall not be held insufficient as a matter of law:

(a) lying in wait, searching for or following the contemplated victim of the crime;

(b) enticing or seeking to entice the contemplated victim of the crime to go to the place contemplated for its commission;

(c) reconnoitering the place contemplated for the commission of the crime;

(d) unlawful entry of a structure, vehicle or enclosure in which it is contemplated that the crime will be committed;

(e) possession of materials to be employed in the commission of the crime, which are specially designed for such unlawful use or which can serve no lawful purpose of the actor under the circumstances;

(f) possession, collection or fabrication of materials to be employed in the commission of the crime, at or near the place contemplated for its commission, where such possession, collection or fabrication serves no lawful purpose of the actor under the circumstances;

(g) soliciting an innocent agent to engage in conduct constituting an element of the crime.

Questions

1. *Marsden's Liability.* Consider Marsden's liability under each of the alternative tests to distinguish noncriminal preparation from criminal attempt. Will Marsden's liability depend upon whether a common law test or the Model Penal Code test for attempt is in force?

2. *Proximity vs. Res Ipsa vs. Substantial Step.* How are the common law proximity and related tests, as a group, different from the res ipsa loquitur test? How are the proximity tests different from the Model Penal Code's "substantial step" test? How are res ipsa loquitur and "substantial step" tests different?

Gambling Life

Bertie Graham works at a convalescent hospital for cardiac patients. She has recently learned that her friend Iva, who also works at the hospital, made some extra money by selling the heart medication of the patient she cares for, substituting aspirin. Bertie would like to do the same but is concerned that she might get caught and held criminally liable if her patient dies from an attack because the medication is not immediately available. Iva explains that on many occasions when patients take the medication, they are not really having an attack. Bertie decides to make the substitution.

After Bertie acquires the aspirin that she plans to substitute and changes the label to look like heart medicine, but before she can make the switch, a patient dies from an attack and the authorities discover that the patient's medication had been switched. The offending employee, Jenkins, is found and charged with manslaughter (reckless homicide). Later that day, Iva's patient dies from a heart attack. All medication bottles are seized and a review uncovers several more medication switches. To Iva's surprise and confusion, her patient's medication is found to be heart medication, not the aspirin she thought she had substituted. Those employees who made medication switches are charged with endangerment (recklessly creating a risk of death to another). In the hopes of getting better treatment from prosecutors, Iva turns in Bertie, who admits to investigators that she planned to make the switch later that day. What, if anything, are Iva and Bertie liable for?

People v. Trinkle
Supreme Court of Illinois
68 Ill. 2d 198, 369 N.E. 2d 888 (1977)

DOOLEY, Justice.

Here the issue is whether a specific intent is requisite for the crime of attempted murder under the Criminal Code of 1961.

On February 28, 1974, the defendant drank 20 to 30 glasses of beer in Suppan's Tavern. The bartender, believing defendant to be intoxicated, refused him further service. After consuming more drinks in another bar, defendant purchased a .357 handgun. He returned to the area of Suppan's Tavern, fired a shot at the building, and wounded a patron within. He was indicted and convicted of the crime of attempted murder. The appellate court held that a specific intent is an indispensable element to this crime, and hence the indictment and instructions

relating to this crime were fatally erroneous. . . .
The indictment charged:

> David Francis Trinkle committed the offense of Attempt (murder) in that said defendant did perform a substantial step toward the commission of that offense in that he did without lawful justification shoot Gayle Lane with a gun knowing that such act created a strong probability of death or great bodily harm to Gayle Lane or another. . . .

The jury was instructed:

> A person commits the crime of attempt who, with intent to commit the crime of murder, does any act which constitutes a substantial step toward the commission of the crime of murder. . . .
>
> A person commits the crime of murder who kills an individual if, in performing the acts which cause the death he knows that such acts create a strong possibility of death or great bodily harm to that individual or another.
>
> To sustain the charge of attempted murder, the State must prove the following propositions:
>
> First: That the defendant performed the acts which caused the injury of Gayle E. Lane;
>
> Second: That when the defendant did so, he knew that his act created a strong probability of causing death or great bodily harm to Gayle E. Lane, or another;
>
> Third: That the defendant was then capable of acting knowingly and intentionally. . . .

The contradiction between the instructions is patent. Only the first exacts the "intent" to commit the crime of murder. The other two define the offense as performing an act with the knowledge that such "created a strong possibility of death or great bodily harm." The first is admittedly correct; it is at loggerheads with the other two.

The Criminal Code of 1961 provides:

> A person commits an attempt when, *with intent to commit a specific offense he does* any act which constitutes a substantial step toward the commission of that offense.

The Code's definition of murder provides:

> (a) A person who kills an individual without lawful justification commits murder if, in performing the acts which cause the death: . . .
>
> (2) He *knows that such acts create a strong probability of death or great bodily harm to that individual or another;* . . .

The State would urge that actual intention to kill is not a requisite mental state for attempted murder, and [the requisite mental state is satisfied if] the accused acted with such disregard of human life knowing his conduct created a strong probability of bodily harm.

. . . It must be remembered that "[t]here is no such criminal offense as an attempt to achieve an unintended result." People v. Viser (1975), 62 Ill. 2d 568, 581, 343 N.E.2d 903, 910.

In Thacker v. Commonwealth (1992), 134 Va. 767, 114 S.E. 504, defendant and two companions were standing outside a tent which was, as defendant knew, occupied by a woman. Stating that he wanted to shoot out a lamp which was burning inside, defendant fired a gun into the tent, narrowly missing the occupant. Defendant's conviction for attempted murder was reversed for lack of proof of specific intent to kill. The court said: "And where it takes a particular intent to constitute a crime, that particular intent must be proved either by direct or circumstantial evidence. . . ." The court also went on to quote from 1 Bishop, Criminal Law sec. 730 (8th ed.), as follows: " '. . . Thus . . . to commit murder, one need not intend to take life, but to be guilty of an attempt to murder, he must so intend. . . .' " There the facts are, of course, stronger against the defendant than here, where there is no evidence that this defendant knew someone was standing behind the door to the bar.

LaFave and Scott point out how in the crime of attempted murder there must be a specific intent to commit the specific offense, unlike the crime of murder, which does not exact that specific intent:

> Some crimes, such as murder, are defined in terms of acts causing a particular result plus some mental state which need not be an intent to bring about that result. Thus, if *A, B,* and *C* have each taken the life of another, *A* acting with intent to kill, *B* with an intent to do serious bodily injury, and *C* with a reckless disregard of human life, all three are guilty of murder because the crime of murder is defined in such a way that any one of these mental states will suffice. However, if the victims do not die from their injuries, then only *A* is guilty of attempted murder; on a charge of attempted murder it is not sufficient to show that the defendant intended to do serious bodily harm or that he acted in reckless disregard for human life. Again, this is because intent is needed for the crime of attempt, so that attempted murder requires an intent to bring about that result described by the crime or murder (i.e., the death of another).

To obtain a conviction on the charge of attempted murder, the indictment must charge a specific intent to commit the specific offense, and the jury must be accordingly instructed.

For the reasons expressed here, the judgment of the appellate court is affirmed.

Judgment affirmed.

State v. Maestas
Supreme Court of Utah
652 P.2d 903 (1982)

HALL, Chief Justice:

The state appeals from an order by the trial court dismissing a charge of attempted murder against defendant in spite of a jury verdict finding him guilty. The state seeks reinstatement of the jury verdict.

On February 20, 1980, defendant allegedly robbed a bank and attempted to escape in a black van. As defendant drove south on State Street at about 650 South, he passed Sergeant Cecil Throckmorton of the Salt Lake City Police Department, who had stationed his car on the island in the center of the street and was standing beside the car awaiting defendant's approach. As defendant's van passed him, Sergeant Throckmorton fired a shot with his shotgun into the front of the van in an unsuccessful attempt to disable it. A few seconds later, as he drove away from Sergeant Throckmorton, defendant allegedly leaned out of the van window holding a 38-caliber revolver and fired it at the officer. Defendant drove several blocks further before crashing into a parked car, at which time he was apprehended by other police officers.

Defendant was charged with attempted first degree murder. At the conclusion of his trial, he filed a motion to dismiss, which the court denied. The jury then deliberated, returning a verdict of guilty. On the date set for defendant's sentencing, he renewed his motion to dismiss. The court granted defendant's motion on the ground that "specific intent to kill could not properly be inferred from the evidence."

U.C.A., 1953, 76-5-202(1) describes the elements of first degree murder:

> Criminal homicide constitutes murder in the first degree if the actor *intentionally or knowingly* causes the death of another under any of the following circumstances: . . .
>
> (d) The homicide was committed while the actor was engaged in the commission of, or an attempt to commit, or flight after committing or attempting to commit, aggravated robbery, robbery, rape, forcible arson, aggravated burglary, burglary, aggravated kidnapping or kidnapping.
>
> (e) The homicide was committed for the purpose of avoiding or preventing an arrest by a peace officer acting under color of legal authority or for the purpose of effecting an escape from lawful custody. [Emphasis added.]

Thus, in order to find defendant guilty of attempted first degree murder, the jury was required to determine beyond a reasonable doubt that he "intentionally or knowingly" attempted to kill Sergeant Throckmorton under one of the circumstances listed above.

Defendant founds his argument for dismissal on the theory that the crime of attempted murder requires a stronger showing of intent than does the crime of murder itself. This theory derives from the common law rule that intent is a necessary element of every "attempt" crime even where the corresponding completed crime does not require intent as an element. As an example, defendant cites cases which discuss the common law rule that there is no crime of "attempted felony murder" because of the fact that felony murder requires no specific intent to kill, while an "attempt" crime must always consist of an intent to commit the corresponding completed crime accompanied by a substantial step toward realization of that crime. Defendant then attempts to carry this rule one step further by asserting that the crime of attempted first degree murder with which he is charged requires a "specific intent" beyond that which would have been required in order to prove first degree murder itself if an actual death had occurred. Defendant does not argue that the evidence concerning intent would have failed to support a first degree murder conviction in the event of actual death, but rather that such evidence fell short of establishing the stronger "specific intent" allegedly required for the crime of attempted first degree murder.

Defendant's argument ignores the fact that common law definitions of criminal behavior have no application in this jurisdiction. The criminal code of this state explicitly abolishes all common law crimes and our legislature has expressed its intention that its statutes be construed liberally even when they conflict with the common law. U.C.A., 1953, 76-4-101(1) defines the crime of "attempt" as follows:

> For purposes of this part a person is guilty of an attempt to commit a crime if, acting *with the kind of culpability otherwise required for the commission of the offense,* he engages in conduct constituting a substantial step toward commission of the offense. [Emphasis added.]

The above statute makes it clear that regardless of any requirements which the common law may impose concerning "attempt" crimes, Utah law requires only "the kind of culpability otherwise required for the commission of the [completed] offense." Thus, there can be no difference between the intent required as an element of the crime of attempted first degree murder and that required for first degree murder itself. . . .

. . . Because substantial evidence supported the jury's guilty verdict, the trial court erred in interfering with the jury's exercise of its factfinding role. We order that the verdict be reinstated.

Reversed.

CHAPTER 8 INCHOATE OFFENSES   275

Questions

1. *Elevation of Culpability Requirements for Attempt.* (a) What culpability is required for murder in *Trinkle*? If Trinkle had in fact killed someone, would he have been liable for murder? What culpability is required in *Trinkle* for the offense of attempted murder? Does Trinkle satisfy this culpability? (The rule in *Trinkle* is typical of common law cases.) What is the rationale for a rule that requires a higher level of culpability for an attempt to commit an offense that is required for the substantive offense itself? (b) What culpability is required for attempted murder in *Maestas*? Is it more than is required for the substantive offense of murder? Why might Utah, in *Maestas,* have adopted a different rule than Illinois, in *Trinkle?*

2. *The Demands of the "Purpose" Requirement.* In April, 1992, four Los Angeles police officers were acquitted of assault charges for their role in severely beating Rodney King during his arrest. The acquittals sparked riots. As the *New York Times* described it:

> A videotape taken by a television news crew in a helicopter shows Mr. Williams rearing back, hurling a brick at the head of Mr. Denny, who lies bloodied on the ground, then raising one arm and one leg in a dance of victory. He is also shown on amateur videotape racing about the intersection . . . directing rioters toward nonblack motorists and beating and kicking several victims.
>
> Mr. Watson is shown on the news videotape holding down Mr. Denny's neck with his foot as other rioters, including Mr. Williams, take turns kicking him and smashing objects onto his head.

What was referred to as a "brick" in fact was a cinder block. Reginald Denny suffered 20 skull fractures but his life was saved by a brain operation.

According to the *Times,* another victim, Takao Hirata, "was dragged from his truck, beaten, and robbed"; Fidel Lopez "was beaten unconscious and then had his face, belly, and genitals spray painted with black paint."

Damian Williams was subsequently charged with ten offenses against seven victims, male and female, white, asian, and hispanic. Henry Watson was charged with five offenses against four victims. The 15 offenses consisted of attempted murder, aggravated mayhem, assault with a deadly weapon, and robbery. The trial provoked strong feelings on both sides of the issue and Los Angeles braced for the possibility of more riots if the defendants were convicted.

As to the most serious offense, attempted murder, the defense argued that Williams ought not be convicted because he lacked the purpose to kill Denny. If Williams had intended to kill Denny, they argued, he would have continued to hit him until he was dead. The prosecution argued that Williams, and anyone else, could well have thought that Williams already had done enough to kill Denny. In any case, it argued, killing Denny was not and need not have been Williams's only purpose that day. Williams wanted to beat and rob other people as well, and moved on from Denny for that purpose.

Given the Model Penal Code definition, did Williams have the "purpose" to kill Denny? (The jury rejected the attempted murder charge. It acquitted or hung on all counts charged, returning guilty verdicts only for the lesser included offenses of simple assault and simple mayhem.)

There is little dispute that Williams's conduct suggests at least "knowing" as to causing death, which would have been enough for murder liability if Denny had died as expected. Why should attempt liability hinge on whether Williams, when he smashed the cinder block into Denny's head, actually wanted to kill Denny or just didn't care whether or not he killed Denny?

3. *Punishing Risk Creation that Leads to Harm.* Assume that manslaughter requires (a) that an actor's conduct create a substantial and unjustified risk of causing death and that a death in fact results, and (b) that the actor be reckless as to causing death (that is, that he or she consciously disregards a substantial risk that his or her conduct may cause death). Is Jenkins, whose patient died from the medication switch, liable for manslaughter? Is Iva, whose patient also died, liable for manslaughter?

4. *Punishing Risk Creation.* Assume that reckless endangerment is similar to manslaughter, except that, instead of causing a death, it requires only that the actor's conduct create a substantial and unjustified risk of death. That is, assume that reckless endangerment requires (a) that an actor's conduct to create a substantial and unjustified risk of causing death, which need not come to fruition, and (b) that the actor be reckless as to causing death (that is, he or she consciously disregards a substantial risk that his or her conduct may cause death). Are the other employees who made medication switches, but whose patients did not die, liable for reckless endangerment? Is Iva liable for reckless endangerment?

5. *Punishing Attempted Risk Creation.* Is Iva liable for attempted reckless endangerment? Does the answer depend upon whether the law in force is the common law, the Model Penal Code, or a statute like the Utah provision applied in *Maestas*? Is Bertie liable for attempted reckless endangerment? Should attempt liability depend upon whether an actor has completed the conduct that is needed for the offense? Why or why not?

6. *Punishing Attempted Risk-Taking.* Assume the defendant is about

to have intercourse with a person under 16 years old and is aware of a substantial risk that the person is under age. The person's parents rush in and intervene to prevent the intercourse. Can the defendant be held liable for attempted statutory rape? (Assume that statutory rape requires only negligence as to the partner being under age.) Is the answer different at common law than under the Model Penal Code? To help in answering this question (and the questions above) consider the following excerpt from the Model Penal Code commentary:

> In all three [subsections of the attempt provision] the mens rea is purpose, with two exceptions: with respect to the circumstances under which a crime must be committed, the culpability otherwise required for commission of the crime is also applicable to the attempt; and with respect to offenses where causing a result is an element, a belief that the result will occur without further conduct on the actor's part will suffice.

Model Penal Code §5.01 comment 297 (1985).

SECTION 8.3 IMPOSSIBILITY

Most of the discussion in the previous section concerns cases where an attempt is unsuccessful because of some intervening event (e.g., detection by authorities, abandonment because of changed conditions). Two other reasons for failure of an attempt are impossibility of completion and voluntary renunciation, each of which presents special issues and reveals important characteristics about attempt liability and criminal liability generally. Renunciation is taken up in Section 8.6. Impossibility is the topic of this section. Both issues arise in all inchoate offenses—attempt, conspiracy, and solicitation—although the impossibility issue most frequently appears, and is traditionally taught, in the context of attempts.

The failure to complete an offense because of intervention or resistance generally does not bar liability altogether, but results in inchoate liability rather than full liability for the object offense. Where an actor fails to complete an offense because it is impossible of completion, on the other hand, he may have a complete defense in some jurisdictions, even a defense to inchoate liability. This result may seem reasonable in a sense: In impossibility cases, not only is the harm or evil of the offense absent, neither is there a real danger that the harm or evil of the offense could occur. On the other hand, the cases of impossibility frequently are cases where the actor's conduct is complete. That is, we need not speculate as to whether the actor would have carried the offense through to completion, a question that is present whenever an attempt is stopped short by another's intervention or resistance. In many cases the actor may actually believe for a time that his conduct constitutes the completed offense. The strength of the actor's culpability might suggest that liability is appropriate in impossibility cases. Indeed, it might be argued that such cases provide a stronger argument for liability than do the cases of incomplete (possible) attempts.

Impossibility of completion of the contemplated offense is of special importance because, to determine whether or how such impossibility should affect liability, we are forced to determine precisely why we punish attempts. If it is the danger of completion that justifies attempt liability—that is, *coming close* to committing the offense—then impossibility would seem to undercut the justification. If it is the actor's intention to commit the offense and his demonstrated willingness to carry out that intention that justifies attempt liability, then such justification is not undercut by impossibility of completion that is unknown to the actor.

The Smuggler's Deceit

Watson and So are surprised and pleased to find each other on the same flight from Panama to London. They are classmates from reform school and have years of stories to trade during the flight, most of which concern their criminal exploits during and since school. After an hour of catching up, the conversation turns to their current activities. To neither's surprise, each is on the flight to smuggle something into England. It is 1974, and Watson is smuggling in sugar concentrate, a profitable business because of England's current sugar shortage. So compliments Watson on his plan and explains with some pride that his trip is part of a just developing drug-smuggling business operating with the unofficial help of certain Panamanian officials. Watson is deflated by the conversation. As was always the case in school, So has the better scheme and stands to make over 20 times as much for smuggling in a shipment of the same size. But Watson has become somewhat more crafty since his school days and, when So gets up to go to the bathroom, Watson switches their cases, which are similar in appearance. So does not notice until they are in line at customs. Instead of being angry with Watson, So just laughs.

Apparently having second thoughts about drug-smuggling, which he knows carries high penalties, Watson moves forward in the customs line without bringing his bag with him. So, who is further back in the same line speaks up helpfully, "Don't forget your bag, sir." Each man is stopped by the customs officers and taken with his bag for questioning. Each is at first cagey but when things look bad, each turns the other in to ingratiate himself and then, under further questioning, confesses his own wrongdoing. Their accounts are somewhat different, however, for So was really on the plane to smuggle sugar and had only made up the story about the drugs to impress Watson.

It turns out that smuggling sugar is not in fact a crime, although it was widely thought to be so at the time.* What liability for Watson and So, if any?

People v. Rollino
Supreme Court of New York, Criminal Term, Queens County
37 Misc. 2d 14, 233 N.Y.S. 2d 580 (1962)

J. IRWIN SHAPIRO, Justice.

At the conclusion of his trial without a jury, under an indictment charging him with Grand Larceny, Second Degree, defendant has moved for its dismissal and thereby revived the question whether a would-be thief can be guilty of either a consummated or an attempted larceny when the coveted property is turned over to him with the knowledge and consent of the owner, by one of its agents, by pre-arrangement with the police, in order to supply a basis for the miscreant's criminal prosecution. . . .

. . . [T]he question of "impossibility" was raised for the first time in Regina v. McPherson, Dears. & B. 197, 201 (1857), when Baron Bramwell said:

> . . . The argument that a man putting his hand into an empty pocket might be convicted of an attempt to steal, appeared to me at first plausible; but suppose a man, believing a block of wood to be a man who was his deadly enemy, struck it a blow intending to murder, could he be convicted of attempting to murder the man he took it to be?

Subsequently, in Regina v. Collins, 9 Cox C.C. 497, 169 Eng. Rep. 1477 (1864), the Court expressly held that attempted larceny was not made out by proof that the defendant pickpocket actually inserted his hand into the victim's empty pocket with intent to steal, Chief Justice Cockburn declaring:

---

*"Travellers trying to beat Britain's sugar shortage are smuggling more and more of it into [that] country. They do not know that importing sugar is legal. A woman filled a shoebox with sugar and wrapped it like a gift, with fancy ribbons and bright paper. Another woman had sugar in a can marked 'face powder.'" N.Y. Herald Tribune, Oct. 22, 1974, reprinted in Glanville Williams, Textbook of Criminal Law 398 (1978).

We think that an attempt to commit a felony can only be made out when, if no interruption had taken place, the attempt could have been carried out successfully, and the felony completed of the attempt to commit which the party is charged.

This very broad language, encompassing as it did all forms of "impossibility," was subsequently rejected by the English courts and it was held that the inability of the pickpocket to steal from an empty pocket did not preclude his conviction of an attempted larceny. Regina v. Ring, 17 Cox C.C 491, 66 L.T. (N.S.) 300 (1892). The determination in that case, generally speaking, represents the existing state of the law in the United States.

In this country it is generally held that a defendant may be charged with an attempt where the crime was not completed because of "physical or factual impossibility" whereas a "legal impossibility" in the completion of the crime precludes prosecution for an attempt.

What is a "legal impossibility" as distinguished from a "physical or factual impossibility" has over a long period of time perplexed our courts and has resulted in many irreconcilable decisions and much philosophical discussion by legal scholars in numerous articles and papers in law school publications and by text-writers.

The reason for the "impossibility" of completing the substantive crime ordinarily falls into one of two categories: (1) where the act if completed would not be criminal, a situation which is usually described as a "legal impossibility" and (2) where the basic or substantive crime is impossible of completion, simply because of some physical or factual condition unknown to the defendant, a situation which is usually described as a "factual impossibility."

The authorities in the various States and the text-writers are in general agreement that where there is a "legal impossibility" of completing the substantive crime, the accused cannot be successfully charged with an attempt, whereas in those cases in which the "factual impossibility" situation is involved, the accused may be convicted of an attempt. Detailed discussion of the subject is unnecessary to make it clear that it is frequently most difficult to compartmentalize a particular set of facts as coming within one of the categories rather than the other. Examples of the so-called "legal impossibility" situations are:

(a) A person accepting goods which he believes to have been stolen, but which were not in fact stolen goods, is not guilty of an attempt to receive stolen goods. (People v. Jaffe, 185 N.Y. 497, 78 N.E. 169, 9 L.R.A., N.S., 263).
(b) It is not an attempt to commit subornation of perjury where the false testimony solicited, if given, would have been immaterial to the case at hand and hence not perjurious.

(c) An accused who offers a bribe to a person believed to be a juror, but who is not a juror, is not guilty of an attempt to bribe a juror.
(d) An official who contracts a debt which is unauthorized and a nullity, but which he believes to be valid, is not guilty of an attempt to illegally contract a valid debt.
(e) A hunter who shoots a stuffed deer believing it to be alive is not guilty of an attempt to shoot a deer out of season.
(f) [An attempt to unlawfully buy what one mistakenly believes is a controlled drug is an instance of legal impossibility.]†

Examples of cases in which *attempt* convictions have been sustained on the theory that all that prevented the consummation of the completed crime was a "factual impossibility" are:

(a) The picking of an empty pocket.
(b) An attempt to steal from an empty receptacle or an empty house.
(c) Where defendant shoots into the intended victim's bed, believing he is there, when in fact he is elsewhere.
(d) Where the defendant erroneously believing that the gun is loaded points it at his wife's head and pulls the trigger.
(e) Where the woman upon whom the abortion operation is performed is not in fact pregnant. . . .

The foregoing lines of demarcation laid down in the cases and by text writers as to when an attempt may and may not be successfully charged has been roundly criticized. Thus in Hall, General Principles of Criminal Law, the writer says:

> . . . There are no degrees of impossibility and no sound basis for distinguishing among the conditions necessary for commission of the intended harm.

And we find Judge Thurman W. Arnold saying, with regard to the artificiality of the distinctions attempted to be made, the following:

The distinctions . . . are ingenious, but . . . they lead us either to absurd results or else to no results.

In an exhaustive and extremely well considered opinion on this subject in United States v. Thomas and McClellan, we find the United States Court of Military Appeals dealing with this subject and saying:

The lack of logic between some of the holdings; the inherent difficulty in assigning a given set of facts to a proper classification; the criticism

---

†Editor's Note.—See, e.g., United States v. Everett, 700 F.2d 900 (1983); People v. Rosencrants, 89 Misc. 2d 721, 392 N.Y.S.2d 808 (1977).

of existing positions in this area; and, most importantly, the denial of true and substantial justice by these artificial holdings have led, quite naturally, to proposals for reform in the civilian legal concepts of criminal attempts. . . .

Some Courts have by "heroic efforts" taken what I consider to be a progressive and more modern view on the subject than is permitted by the decisional law in this State. Thus, California has now abandoned the People v. Jaffe rationale that "a person accepting goods which he believes to have been stolen, but which [were] not in fact stolen goods, is not guilty of an attempt to receive stolen goods and imposes liability for the attempt."

Returning now from the discussion of "attempts" to the facts in this case which I find to be as follows:

Prior to and at the time of the occurrences resulting in this prosecution, one Edwin Martinez was an employee of Long Island Drug Company, a division of the Ketcham Company, Inc., with a stock of drugs and drug products in its wholesale business establishment on New York Boulevard in Queens County. A short time before the date charged in the indictment defendant Rollino proposed that Martinez should steal from his employer certain of the products that it stocked, as opportunity permitted, and for which the defendant would pay Martinez. Although the latter pretended to agree to the proposal he promptly reported the matter to an official of Long Island Drug Company and he in turn called in a private detective agency. At the suggestion of one of the agency's operators a responsible official of the Long Island Drug Company gave Martinez a package containing drug products having a wholesale value of $187.00, with instructions to bring it to the defendant in ostensible pursuance of the latter's criminal plan. When informed of the availability of the merchandise, Rollino directed Martinez to meet him at a specified time in a designated parking lot in Queens County.

Martinez went to the parking lot in his Nash automobile. There he was joined by the defendant, who entered the car and received the package, for which Martinez asked $25.00. Rollino offered—and his pseudo-accomplice accepted—$15.00 in payment therefor with defendant promising that he would do better the next time. Fearful that they were being watched, defendant told Martinez to leave the package in the Nash, lock it, hand over the keys and leave the lot. When Martinez complied, Rollino also left the parking lot but returned in his own car about a half-hour later and stopped directly behind the Nash. He then got out, walked over to the Nash, reached in and picked up the package but, after a period of indecision in which he looked about the parking lot with evident apprehension, he put the package down again, closed the door and started to walk away. At that point the police, who had been called in by the detective agency, moved in and apprehended the defendant. Of course, he had been under their surveillance the whole time. When questioned, Rollino said that he had been sent to pick up the package by a man whom he knew only as James Dunne. When asked why, if that was the case, he didn't take it, his only explanation was that he was scared and changed his mind about picking it up. His explanation of his status in the matter, as Dunne's messenger, was, of course, untrue.

The evidence convinces me, beyond reasonable doubt, that defendant intended and endeavored to steal drugs or drug products from Long Island Drug Company by counseling and, as he thought, inducing and procuring its employee to do so and that, on the date of the crime for which he was tried before me, acted directly and overtly to realize, as he hoped, the gain contemplated by his previous incitement. The discretion that he gave his pretended accomplice as to what would be stolen, and when, would not, of course, create any uncertainty of Rollino's criminal liability had Martinez really acted corruptly, in advancement of defendant's plan. But the employee had remained faithful to his employer and what defendant assumed to be the fruit of his crime had, in fact, been brought to him with the owner's knowledge and consent.

Although it has been said that "(i)t is . . . no longer necessary, to constitute larceny, that the property should have been taken from the possession of the owner by a trespass" the idea remains basic to the concept of what has come to be known as "common law larceny," that "(i)f an individual owner voluntarily delivers his property to one who wishes to steal it, there is no trespass" and consequently "no crime committed by the defendant . . . because it was with the full consent." A taking without consent is the *sine quo non* of that form of larceny and the charge is insupportable if the owner or his authorized agent voluntarily consents to the taking, even if it is done only for the purpose of catching the thief and even though neither of them otherwise encouraged the evil-doer to adopt and execute the criminal plan:

> An essential element of common law larceny is the taking of the property of another without his consent and against his will.

Having determined that the defendant in this case may not be found guilty of the completed act of larceny because the drugs were not in fact taken from the owner without its consent, the next question is whether, under such circumstances, he may be found guilty of an attempt to commit larceny.

The answer would seem to be "no" for the very fact that prevents a conviction for the completed crime of larceny also precludes a conviction of an attempted larceny. "(I)n the present case, the act, which it was doubtless the intent of the defendant to commit, would not have been a crime if it had been consummated" (People v. Jaffe, 185 N.Y. 497, 500, 78 N.E. 169) and "an unsuccessful attempt to do that which is not a crime, when effectuated, cannot be held to be an attempt to commit the crime specified." When the owner's agent offered the drugs to Rollino, to entrap him, defendant "succeeded in what he attempted, but what he did was not criminal." Since the completed act did not and could not as a *matter of law* constitute a larceny, it is *legally impossible* for defendant to be guilty of an attempted larceny.

The *Jaffe* [case] has been the subject of analytic discussion and much criticism. . . , but that rule of law has never been modified or overruled in this state and it must, accordingly, be accepted and enforced by this Court.

The defendant's moral guilt is unquestionable. He intended to commit the crime of grand larceny and did everything that he could to implement and effectuate his criminal purpose and intent. That he cannot be adjudged legally guilty is due entirely to the existing state of the decisional and statutory law on the subject [in New York]. Clearly a modification of the law in this regard, to make it less favorable to criminal elements, is called for but this Court may only adjudicate; it may not legislate.

In this connection, attention is called to the proposal of The American Law Institute for the adoption of a "Model Penal Code" which in Article 5.01 defines "Criminal Attempts."**

Tentative Draft No. 10 of the Model Penal Code makes obvious the reason and necessity for the adoption of the proposed Article 5.01 when it says:

> . . . It should suffice, therefore, to indicate at this stage what we deem to be the major results of the draft. They are:
> (a) to extend the criminality of attempts by sweeping aside the defense of impossibility (including the distinction between so-called factual and legal impossibility) and by drawing the line between attempt and non-criminal preparation further away from the final act; the crime becomes essentially one of criminal purpose implemented by an overt act strongly corroborative of such purpose. . . .

The motion to dismiss the indictment is granted since an element essential to defendant's legal guilt of either a larceny or an attempted larceny of the kind here charged is entirely lacking.

Short form order signed and entered.

**Editor's Note.—The complete text of Model Penal Code §5.01 is reproduced at pp. 268-269.

Model Penal Code §5.01(1)
Criminal Attempt

A person is guilty of an attempt to commit a crime if . . . he:
   (a) . . . engages in conduct which would constitute the crime *if the attendant circumstances were as he believes them to be;* or
   (b) . . . does or omits to do anything . . . *with the belief* that it will cause [a criminal result]; or
   (c) . . . does or omits to do anything which, *under the circumstances as he believes them to be,* is an act or omission constituting a substantial step [toward the offense].

Questions

1. *Watson's Liability.* Watson believes that he is smuggling in drugs but his case actually contains sugar. What, if anything, can he be convicted of? Is the answer different at common law than under the Model Penal Code?

2. *Factual vs. Legal Impossibility.* Consider the actor who lights the fuse on what he mistakenly believes are dynamite sticks. Is it true that "the act if completed would not be criminal"? The completed conduct—lighting a fuse leading to wooden sticks—is not a substantive offense, thus one might conclude that the conduct constitutes a legally impossible attempt (for which there was a defense at common law). Yet, in another sense, the case seems to be one of factual impossibility. How is lighting the dynamite sticks that in fact are wooden different from the factual impossibility case of the actor who performs an abortion on a woman who is not pregnant?

3. *Missing a Result vs. a Circumstance Element.* The factual-legal impossibility distinction is generally criticized as being difficult to apply. Consider the following claim that the distinction's reputation may not be entirely deserved.

> The categorization in most impossibility cases can be predicted by characterizing the nature of the missing objective element: conduct, circumstance, or result. Remember, because of the absence of this objective element, the conduct is an attempt rather than a substantive offense. Where the missing element is a conduct or result element, the case is more likely to be characterized as one of factual impossibility. The actor

cannot "take" (conduct) property from an empty pocket, receptacle, or house, as required by theft. The actor cannot cause "death" (result) where the victim is not in the bed or the gun is not loaded or the womb has no fetus, as required by homicide and abortion. Where the missing element is a circumstance, the case is more likely to be characterized as legal impossibility. The goods are not "stolen," the testimony is not "material," the intended bribee is not a "juror," the debt is not "valid," and the deer that is shot at is not "alive." In each instance, the missing element is a circumstance element of the offense charged to have been attempted.[4]

This test for distinguishing factual and legal impossibility requires careful reference to the elements of the offense charged. An actor's conduct cannot be judged factually or legally impossible in the abstract. Rather, an actor's conduct is judged a factually or legally impossible attempt to commit a particular offense. Shooting a stuffed deer out of season, for example, is a legally impossible attempt because *shooting at a live deer* (conduct and circumstance) is the prohibition of the offense. If the offense were defined to prohibit *killing a deer,* the same shooting of a stuffed deer would be judged a factual impossibility because a required result, death, is missing. It is understandable, then, that before the more systematic analysis of offense elements that came with modern codes, the legal-factual impossibility distinction seemed somewhat vague and unpredictable.

Are you persuaded that the legal-factual impossibility distinction might be made more workable if it relied upon the distinction between missing a required circumstance and missing conduct or a result?

4. *Why Have a Legal Impossibility Defense?* Even if the factual-legal impossibility distinction feasibly could be applied, the more important issue is whether the distinction should be applied. Why might one want to impose attempt liability on an actor whose attempt fails because he or she cannot perform the required conduct or cause the required result, yet want to exclude from liability an actor whose attempt fails because, while he or she engages in the required conduct, a required circumstance does not exist? What explanation might a common law judge give for giving a defense for legal impossibility?

---

4. This method of distinction obviously requires definitions of what constitutes a conduct, a circumstance, and a result element. The Model Penal Code does not provide such definitions. Used here is the following distinction: Conduct is defined narrowly to include physical movement but to exclude the circumstances and results of the movement; a result is a circumstance changed by the actor's conduct.

Notes on the Requirements for Attempt Liability

The doctrinal requirements for attempt liability may be summarized as follows:

Objective Requirements	Culpability Requirements
Conduct constituting substantive offense: Not required; instead: CL‡: proximity and res ipsa loquitur tests MPC: substantial step test	*Culpability as to conduct constituting substantive offense:* CL and MPC: purposeful
Result elements of substantive offense: CL and MPC: not required (nor is factual impossibility of it occurring a defense	*Culpability as to result elements of substantive offense:* CL: elevate to purposeful MPC: elevate to purposeful, but only to knowing if conduct complete and proposed Other (e.g., Utah) and proposed: as required by substantive offense; do not elevate
Circumstance elements of substantive offense: CL: required (legal impossibility is a defense MPC: not required (legal impossibility is not a defense)	*Culpability as to circumstance elements of substantive offense:* CL: elevate to purposeful MPC: as required by substantive offense; do not elevate (per commentary)

‡CL = Common Law
MPC = Model Penal Code

Notes on Impossibility Defenses that Continue to Exist Even in Modern Codes

Even if one adopts a subjective view of criminality and denies a defense for legal impossibility, as does the Model Penal Code and most of the states following its lead, two special forms of impossibility nonetheless may be recognized as defenses: what might be called "imaginary offenses" and "inherently unlikely attempts."

Impossibility Due to Mistake as to Offense Attempted The first kind of defense is provided in instances where the impossibility arises from the absence or inapplicability of an offense prohibiting what the actor intends; that is, where the actor believes (mistakenly) that his intended conduct would be an offense. The Bulgarian visitor who takes a picture of a military base may honestly believe that he is committing an offense. Under one interpretation of Model Penal Code §5.01(1)(a), he might seem to satisfy the requirements: "If the attendant circumstances were as he believes them to be" (if taking pictures of a military installation were a crime), he has "engage[d] in conduct which would constitute the crime." From the view of subjective criminality, the Soviet has shown his intention to violate the law and his willingness to carry out that intention. One might argue, then, that liability for attempt is appropriate.

Impossibility and Legality Principle: Imaginary Offenses Yet a defense to attempt liability typically is given in such a situation,[1] even by jurisdictions that adopt a subjective view of criminality. The defense is given, despite the apparent moral blameworthiness and dangerousness of such an actor, who has demonstrated a willingness to break the law, because of the demands of the legality principle. That principle, and the legal doctrines implementing it, require a prior, written, specific statement of a prohibition before its violation can be punished. Most of the rationales of the principle do not concern matters of blameworthiness or dangerousness. They focus instead upon such matters as assuring allocation of the criminalization authority to the legislative branch, minimizing the potential for abuse of discretion in the administration of criminal justice, and satisfying the due process demands for prior notice.

Imaginary Offenses Under Model Penal Code The demands of the legality principle may be given expression even without a special defense provision for attempts to commit an imaginary offense. One need only interpret the Model Penal Code's impossibility language—"if the attendant circumstances were as he believes them to be"—to refer to "the attendant circumstances" *defined to be relevant by the definition of the offense charged*. Even absent the legality principle, this would seem the better interpretation of the Code's language, for only the circumstances noted in the offense definition are relevant to determining liability and, typically, knowledge of the criminality of one's offense is not itself an element of an offense.[2]

Inherently Unlikely Attempts The second kind of impossible attempt that may be given a defense is the inherently unlikely attempt. The defense is recognized even in jurisdictions that take the Model Penal Code's subjective view of criminality. The Model Penal Code section quoted below gives the statutory language. The Wechsler excerpt illustrates its application and describes its rationale.

---

1. See, e.g., Commonwealth v. Henley, 504 Pa. 408, 474 A.2d 1115 (1984).
2. See Model Penal Code §2.02(9).

Model Penal Code §5.05(2)
Mitigation in Cases of Lesser Danger

If the particular conduct charged to constitute a criminal attempt, solicitation or conspiracy is so inherently unlikely to result or culminate in the commission of a crime that neither such conduct nor the actor presents a public danger warranting the grading of such offense under this Section, the Court shall exercise its power under Section 6.12 to enter judgment and impose sentence for a crime of lower grade or degree or, in extreme cases, may dismiss the prosecution.

H. Wechsler, W.K. Jones, and H.L. Korn, The Treatment of Inchoate Crimes in the Model Penal Code of the American Law Institute: Attempt, Solicitation and Conspiracy
61 Colum. L. Rev. 571, 584-585 (1961)

[A consideration debated in formulating the Model Penal Code attempt, impossibility, and grading provisions] was the view that the criminal law need not take notice of conduct that is innocuous, the element of impossibility precluding any dangerous proximity to the completed crime. Since, however, the law of attempts should be concerned with manifestations of dangerous character as well as with preventative arrest, that particular conduct may not create a risk of harmful consequences should not be conclusive. The innocuous character of the particular conduct becomes relevant only if the futile endeavor itself indicates a harmless personality, so that immunizing the conduct from liability would not result in exposing society to a dangerous person.

Using impossibility as a guide to dangerousness of personality presents serious difficulties. Cases can be imagined in which it might be argued that the nature of the means selected, say black magic, substantially negates dangerousness of character. On the other hand, it is probable that one who tries to commit a crime by inadequate methods and fails will realize the futility of his conduct and seek more efficacious means. It has been suggested that the test of factual impossibility should be one of reasonableness: If the actor's failure is due to a reasonable mistake or miscalculation the error should not provide a defense; but if the error is unreasonable the actor should be exonerated. Since it cannot be affirmed that those who make unreasonable mistakes are not potentially dangerous, the test is obviously inadequate.

The approach of the Code is to eliminate the defense of impossibility in all situations. The litigated cases to date have not presented instances in which the actor's futile efforts indicate that he is not likely to succeed in the future in committing the crime contemplated or some similar offense. Nor is it likely that attempts of this nature, if they do occur, will be detected or prosecuted. Nonetheless, to provide a method of coping with any such case should one arise, article 5 provides, in its sentencing provisions, that in "extreme cases" where "neither [the] . . . conduct nor the actor presents a public danger," the court may dismiss the prosecution.

Questions

1. *So's Liability for Smuggling Sugar.* So is smuggling in sugar, believing it to be an offense. What, if anything, can he be convicted of? Is the answer different at common law than under the Model Penal Code?

2. *So's Liability for Smuggling Drugs.* Based on his conduct in line, where he does not let Watson leave his case behind, is So liable for encouraging and helping Watson to smuggle what Watson believes to be drugs (but which So knows is only sugar)?

3. *Space-Age Smuggling.* Assume that So is a drug smuggler who persuades a somewhat dim-witted Digger that he (Digger) can smuggle drugs into the country with no danger of being caught if he uses a "mind transport" technique that So has developed. Digger believes this, recalling that he saw something similar done at a recent Star Trek convention. He uses So's technique to "mind transport" drugs into the country. When he arrives to pick them up from the "materialization point" in a bus station locker, he finds that they did not arrive. Instead, he is arrested by police tipped off by So, who appropriated the drugs that Digger thought he had "mind transported." Does Digger have a defense or a mitigation to a charge of attempt to smuggle illegal drugs? What are the arguments for and against a mitigation or defense in such a case?

In re "The Nose . . ."

Dear Ann Landers:

I'm a 31-year-old bachelor, college-educated, church-going and normal in every way, except one. I love the smell of women's feet.

There is no fragrance more exciting than the sweet bouquet of an unshod feminine foot, provided it is not abnormally sweaty or just out of a tennis shoe. I have sniffed the toes of dozens of ladies and could identify any of them blindfolded.

Usually women I have dated a few times don't mind. Some even find this kinkiness amusing. Lately, however, my patience is waning and I don't care to go through the formality of getting to know a woman well before I take off her shoe and savor the heavenly aroma.

Some of these women are stunned, grossed out and afraid that I am trying to undress them. I have been called "a nut" and the evening has ended abruptly.

Questions: Could I be accused of attempted rape for suddenly taking off a woman's shoe? Am I the only man in the world who has this bizarre preference? Am I crazy? Please rush your reply.

—The Nose Knows In Arizona

Questions

1. *An Unusual View of Rape.* If "The Nose" believes that the sexual satisfaction he receives by forcibly removing a woman's shoe is rape, can he be convicted of attempted rape if he successfully gains sexual satisfaction in this fashion? Why or why not?

2. *An Unusual View of "Intimate Parts."* Assume "The Nose" took a job in a women's shoe store in order to gratify his sexual desire. Could he be held liable for sexual assault under the following offense (Model Penal Code §213.4)?

> A person who subjects another not his spouse to any sexual contact is guilty of sexual assault, a misdemeanor, if:
> (1) he knows that the contact is offensive to the other person; or . . .
> (3) he knows that the other person is unaware that a sexual act is being committed; . . .
> Sexual contact is any touching of the sexual or other intimate parts of the person of another for the purpose of arousing or gratifying sexual desire of either party.

Could he be held liable for attempted sexual assault? Does it matter whether common law or the Model Penal Code is in force?

SECTION 8.4 GRADING OF INCHOATE OFFENSES

The primary issue in the previous sections of this chapter is the minimum requirements for attempt liability. We have seen, in particular, disagreement between the common law and modern codes as to whether some minimum danger or "coming close" to the harm or evil of an offense ought to be required for criminal liability. Modern codes require no such danger of commission; an actor's purely subjective culpability toward commission of an offense is judged enough. The common law and that minority of jurisdictions that follow its lead on this issue judge purely subjective criminality to be insufficient; the potential for an offense must exist in more than just the actor's mind.

The grading of inchoate offenses raises a different kind of dispute about the significance of the harm and evil of the offense: Assuming the minimum requirements of liability have been met, should an actor's degree of liability and punishment be increased where the harm or evil of the offense comes about? On this issue, modern codes are not necessarily subjectivist. The Model Penal Code does discount the significance of the occurrence of harm and evil in increasing the offense grade. That is, it tends toward subjectivism in both instances. But a majority of modern codes takes the view that occurrence of the offense harm or evil ought to increase the offense grade. That is, while the majority takes a subjectivist view as to minimum requirements, it takes a more objectivist view as to grading.

Model Penal Code §5.05(1)
Grading of Criminal Attempt, Solicitation, and Conspiracy

Except as otherwise provided in this Section, attempt, solicitation, and conspiracy are crimes of the same grade and degree as the most serious offense which is attempted or solicited or is an object of the conspiracy. An attempt, solicitation, or conspiracy to commit a [capital crime or a] felony of the first degree is a felony of the second degree.

S. Schulhofer, Harm and Punishment: A Critique of Emphasis on the Results of Conduct in the Criminal Law
122 U. Pa. L. Rev. 1497, 1514-1516 (1974)

A number of commentators have sought to justify the law's emphasis on the occurrence of harm by arguing that moral fault, the touchstone in the retributive grading of offenses, cannot be measured exclusively by an actor's conduct and state of mind. Resort is had to the "largely intuitive judgment" that "[t]he successful criminal and the person who engaged in an unsuccessful attempt are in some sense not of equal culpability."[69]

The argument is troublesome on several levels. Not the least is its basic anti-rationality. A policy so pervasive and important as the law's emphasis upon results might reasonably be expected to stand upon some fairly weighty reasons capable of coherent explanation. Still, conceding that it might be a mistake to insist on a full articulation of the reasons for every social policy, and conceding that intuitive notions, if widely felt, could sometimes be taken as valid answers to a human problem, there nevertheless remains a major difficulty. The "intuitive judgment" as to culpability cannot claim anything approaching widespread appeal. As we attempt to fill out the fact situations upon which the judgment is made, the notion of a difference in culpability seems more and more implausible. For example, suppose that A and B both shoot their wives, intending to kill. The bullets lodge in precisely the same area of the brain in both cases, but while A's wife dies, B's wife is saved by a miraculous feat of surgery. Is A more culpable than B? More to the point, can we say with any confidence that there would be uniform and fairly widespread agreement with the intuitive proposition that A is more culpable than B? Surely not.

The example, moreover, is far too kind to existing law; we might well have supposed quite different conduct by A and B after the shooting. Suppose that A, who intended to kill at the time he shot, suddenly decides he has done a terrible thing, immediately calls a hospital for help, has the country's best neurosurgeon flown in from a great distance to perform the operation, and does all else in his power to save his wife. In spite of everything, she dies. B meanwhile does everything possible to prevent his wounded wife from being discovered or treated. But neighbors have heard the shot, the police get her to the hospital in time, and she recovers. Is A still more culpable than B? Insistence that there simply *is* a difference in culpability will not convince those who neither "feel" this difference nor comprehend the basis of this feeling in others, and this group is altogether too large to be ignored.

Doubts about the soundness of the "intuitive judgment" are in any event only half of the story. The proposition that if A is more culpable than B, he should be punished more severely than B (other things being equal), can be valid only if retribution (in the sense of condemnation of moral fault) is accepted as a legitimate function of the criminal law. And even for those who believe that moral culpability should affect the severity of punishment, it seems far from evident that

---

69. Mansfield, Hart and Honoré, Causation in the Law—A Comment, 17 Vand. L. Rev. 487, 495 (1964).

this particular moral judgment, the judgment that *A* is more culpable than *B*, is one deserving of propagation and reinforcement through the office of the criminal law.

Where we are dealing with the notion that it is wrong to steal, or the notion that it is even more wrong to steal by the use of force, it may make sense to use the criminal law for "sharpening . . . the community's sense of right and wrong." Perhaps there is a value in teaching that it is wrong to cause harm, and that those who do are blameworthy. But the proposition that *A* is more culpable than *B* says much more than this. It says that of those who commit the *same* acts, with the *same* intentions and the *same* perceptions as to the risks and consequences of their conduct, the one who actually causes harm is more culpable than the one who, for whatever reason, does not. It says, in effect, that the moral quality of an act is determined not only by factors within an actor's knowledge and control, but also by unseen and unseeable circumstances, by the invisible hand of Fate. To stress the role of an uncontrollable Fate in determining our moral accountability for the harms we cause seems an unlikely way to serve the utilitarian objective of preventing harm and the conduct that causes it. But even in strictly retributive terms, it would seem a perversion of a theory conceived out of concern for moral judgments of some moment, to use the criminal law for "teaching" the soundness of a concept of this sort.

G. Fletcher, A Crime of Self-Defense: Bernhard Goetz and the Law on Trial
64-67 (1988)

. . . Two conflicting schools of thought have emerged about the essential nature of criminal wrongdoing. A traditional approach emphasizes the victim's suffering and the actor's responsibility for bringing about irreversible damage. A modern approach to crime takes the act—the range of the actor's control over what happens—as the core of the crime. It is a matter of chance, the modernists say, whether a shot intended to kill actually hits its target. . . .

The traditionalists root their case in the way we feel about crime and suffering. Modernists hold to arguments of rational and meaningful punishment. Despite what we might feel, the modernist insists, reason demands that we limit the criminal law to those factors that are within the control of the actor. The occurrence of harm is beyond his control and therefore ought not to have weight in the definition of crime and fitting punishment. The tension between these conflicting schools infects virtually all of our decisions in designing a system of crime and punishment.

Historically, it is hard to deny the relevance of actual harm and suffering in our thinking about crime. The criminal law would never have come into being unless people actually harmed each other. Our thinking about sin and crime begins with a change in the natural order, a human act that leaves a stain on the world. The sin of Eden was not looking at the apple, not possessing it, but eating it. Oedipus's offense against the gods was not lusting, but actually fornicating with his mother. Cain's crime was not endangering Abel, but spilling his blood. The notions of sin and crime are rooted in the harms that humans inflict on each other.

The classical conception of retributive punishment, the *lex tablionis,* reenacts the crime on the person of the offender. This is expressed metaphorically in the biblical injunction to take any eye for an eye, a tooth for a tooth, and life for a life. In Discipline and Punish, the philosopher Michel Foucault argues that classically, punishment symbolically *expiated* the crime by replicating on the body of the criminal the harm he inflicted on another. It is hard even to think about punishment without perceiving the relationship between the harm wrought by the criminal and the harm he suffers in return. . . .

This is not the way many or perhaps most policy makers think about crime in the modern world. Sometime in the last two or three centuries, our scientific thinking about crime began to shift from the harm done to the act that brings about the harm. The fortuitous connection between acts and their consequences did not trouble the great jurists of the past, but today, in the thinking of the moderns, a great divide separates the actor and his deed from the impact of his act on others. "There is many a slip 'twixt the cup and the lip." And all those slips, all those matters of chance, have undermined the unity we once felt between a homicidal act and the death of the victim.

The notions of risk, probability, and chance circumscribe the modern way of thinking about action and harm. Instead of seeing harm first and the action as the means for bringing about the harm, we are now inclined to see the action first and the harm as a contingent consequence of the action. And if we see the action first and the harm second, we invite the question, Why should we consider the harm at all. . . . Many radical reformers hold that indeed the harm is totally irrelevant. If you shoot and miss, you should be punished as though you had killed someone. All that matter are the acts that you can control. And you cannot control the bullet after it leaves the barrel. Power may come from the barrel of a gun, as Chairman Mao said, but according to the modernists, you exhaust your power as soon as you fire the gun.

Modernists pride themselves on the rationality of their theory. If the purpose of punishment is *either* to punish wickedness *or* to influence and guide human behavior, the criminal law should limit its sights to conduct and circumstances within human control. There is nothing wicked about the way things fortuitously turn out. The actor's personal culpability is expressed in his actions—not in the accidents of nature that determine the consequences of his actions. And so far as the purpose of punishment is to set an example and deter future offenders, the only conduct that can be deterred is that within our control. The arguments of reason seem almost unbeatable.

The shift toward arresting and prosecuting those who merely attempt crimes reflects a practical concern as well. The legal system should arguably not only react to crimes already committed, but should intervene before the harm is done. The police should arrest the would-be offender before he has a chance to realize the harm his conduct bespeaks. Crimes should be defined and jail sentences inflicted not only to expiate previous wrongs and deter future offenders, but to prevent harm from occurring. This makes a good deal of sense in a world in which we try to manage the resources of government in order to maximize the welfare of all. This approach to punishment is typically called "preventive" as opposed to the traditional "retributive" practice of punishing past crimes, measure for measure.

The rationalists have held sway over English and American criminal law for most of the period since World War II. The prevailing view is that criminal law should serve social goals, rationally determined and efficiently pursued. Punishment should serve the goal of control either by rehabilitating offenders or, when we despair of changing criminals with doses of therapy, by deterring people in the future from choosing crime as a profitable career. The modern approach to crime dismisses as subrational the argument that people simply *feel* that actually killing someone is far worse than trying to kill. The Model Penal Code, a rationalist document that reflects the attitudes of reform-minded lawyers in the 1950s, goes so far as to recommend punishing attempted murder the same way we punish murder. Yet the concern for the suffering victims is too deep-seated to be rejected simply because the reformers have so limited a conception of fair and decent punishment.

We punish convicted criminals not only because as social planners we see a need to deter crime in the future, but because we recognize the irrepressible need of victims to restore their faith in themselves and in the society in which they live. The imperative to do justice requires that we heed the suffering of the victims, that we inquire at trial whether the defendant is responsible for that suffering, and we adjudge him guilty, if the facts warrant it, not for antiseptically violating the rules of the system, but for inflicting a wrong on the body and to the dignity of the victim. . . .

Whether the defendant actually causes the harm to the victim becomes, therefore, a pivotal question in every trial responding to the fact of suffering. . . .

Questions

1. *Grading Inchoate Conduct.* Most American jurisdictions reject the Model Penal Code position that inchoate offenses generally should be graded the same as the corresponding substantive offenses. States commonly authorize a sentence for an inchoate offense at a reduced grade or some fraction of the sentence authorized for the completed substantive offense. See, e.g., Ala. Code §13A-4-2(d) (1982); Alaska Stat. §11.31.100(d) (1978); Ariz. Rev. Stat. Ann. §13-1001(C) (1978); Ark. Stat. Ann. §41-703 (1977); Cal. Penal Code §182 (West 1970); Colo. Rev. Stat. §18-2-101(4)-(8) (1978); Fla. Stat. Ann. §777.04(4) (West 1976); Ga. Code Ann. §16-4-6 (Michie 1982); Idaho Code §18-306 (1979); Ill. Ann. Stat. ch. 38, §8-4(c) (Smith-Hurd 1972); Kan. Stat. Ann. §21-3302(3) (1981); Ky. Rev. Stat. §506.010(4) (1975); La. Rev. Stat. Ann. §14:27(D) (West 1974); Me. Rev. Stat. Ann. tit. 17-A, §152(4) (1983); Mass. Gen. Laws Ann. ch. 274, §6 (West 1970); Mich. Comp. Laws Ann. §750.92 (West 1968); Minn. Stat. Ann. §609.17(Subd. 4) (West 1964); Mo. Ann. Stat. §564.016(8) (Vernon 1979); Nev. Rev. Stat. §193.330 (1981); N.M. Stat. Ann. §30-28-1 (1978); N.Y. Penal Law §110.05 (McKinney 1975); N.C. Gen. Stat. §14-2.4 (1981); N.D. Cent. Code §12.1-06-03 (1976); Ohio Rev. Code Ann. §2923.02(E) (Page 1982); Okla. Stat. Ann. tit. 21, §42 (West 1983); Or. Rev. Stat. §161.405(2), §161.435(2), §161.450(2) (1981); S.D. Codified Laws Ann. §22-4-1 (1979); Tex. Penal Code Ann. tit. 4, §§15.01(c), 15.02(d), 15.03(d) (Vernon 1974); Utah Code Ann. §76-4-102 (Cum. Supp. 1987); Vt. Stat. Ann. tit. 13, §9(2) (1974); Va. Code §18.2-22 (1982); Wash. Rev. Code Ann. §9A.28.020(3) (Cum. Supp. 1986-87); W.Va. Code §61-11-8 (1977); Wis. Stat. Ann. §939.30, §939.32(1) (West 1982); Am. Samoa Code Ann. §46.3404 (1986); P.R. Laws Ann. tit. 33, §3122 (1969); Trust Terr. Code tit. 11, §4 (1980); V.I. Code Ann. tit. 14, §331 (1964). What are the arguments in support of grading inchoate conduct the same as the substantive offense? What are the arguments in support of a reduced grade for inchoate conduct? Do retributivists and utilitarians come out differently on this issue?

2. *Minimum Requirements vs. Grading.* If one is a subjectivist as to the minimum requirements of liability, does it logically follow that one ought to be a subjectivist as to grading inchoate conduct as well?

3. *The Model Penal Code's First Degree Felony Exception.* If the Model Penal Code drafters believed that inchoate conduct generally ought to be graded the same as the substantive offense, why do they allow an exception for inchoate conduct toward a first degree felony, such as attempted murder?

4. *Appearances Matter.* If the Model Penal Code drafters believe that resulting harm generally is insignificant, why do they define offenses

with a result element (including those that are less than first degree felonies)? Why not simply define a single offense, as prohibiting conduct under certain circumstances with certain culpability, rather than defining one offense with a result element (the "substantive offense") and a second offense with the result element missing ("attempt" to commit the substantive offense), which are graded the same? Or, similarly, why is the Code so careful to distinguish complicity in a completed offense from complicity in an inchoate offense, in Model Penal Code §5.01(3), if the ultimate grade of each is the same? (Note that the Code does not bother to distinguish actual aid from attempted aid; both constitute full complicity—see Model Penal Code §2.06(3)(a)(ii).) What is going on here?

SECTION 8.5 CONSPIRACY AND SOLICITATION

Like attempt, conspiracy punishes inchoate conduct. Because the offense requires only an *agreement* to commit an offense (and sometimes an overt act by one of the conspirators in furtherance of the agreement), conspiracy may permit even earlier intervention than does attempt, before a "substantial step" toward commission.

But conspiracy has another life, beyond that as an inchoate offense. It is sometimes used as a means of aggravating a substantive offense because of the group nature of the planning and commission. The use of conspiracy to aggravate an offense because of group criminality has little to do with conspiracy as an inchoate offense; such aggravation may be appropriate in completed as well as uncompleted offenses. A lack of clarity between which of these two roles is being served in a given situation is a common source of confusion in many aspects of the law of conspiracy.

Selling Death

New national regulations requiring smoke detectors have just gone into effect. Because of anticipated enforcement difficulties, the authorities undertake a major advertising campaign announcing serious fines for any house or apartment dweller caught without the required number of detectors. Hans and Fri have seized on this as an opportunity to make some easy money. They plan to purchase several thousand unfinished smoke detectors from a scrap dealer. The detectors appear complete and the warning buzzer sounds when tested but the detection circuitry has not been installed. Hans and Fri estimate that they can make several thousand dollars each week selling their defective units door to door. When Hans calls the scrap dealer and confirms that the dealer has the units, the dealer becomes suspicious. He notifies the police, who trace the call back to Hans and Fri. Only Fri is at home when the police arrive; Hans is out purchasing a supply of the defective detectors. Under questioning Fri reveals their plan. Upon his return, Hans notices the police presence and keeps driving.

The next day Hans begins selling the faulty detectors. Business is even better than expected. Two weeks later, as a result of two nonfunctional detectors that Hans sold, a fire in a local rowhouse kills a mother and her child. The fire investigation reveals the defective detectors and ties them to the scheme by Fri and Hans. On a tip, police learn that Hans is a frequent customer at a local bar. An undercover officer approaches him and, presenting himself as a longtime con man, he suggests that Hans let him join the sales operation for half of the profit from his sales. Hans is happy to have a new partner. The next morning, Hans and the officer work together selling detectors so that Hans can show his new partner the ropes. As they work, they talk about many things including the fire deaths from earlier sales. The officer then arrests Hans. The defective detectors sold that morning are retrieved for evidence. What can Hans be held liable for? What can Fri be convicted of?

Archbold v. State
Court of Appeals of Indiana, Second District
397 N.E.2d 1071 (1979)

SHIELDS, Judge.

Appellant Keith Archbold was tried and convicted by jury of Conspiracy to Commit a Felony. He argues the offence was not committed because the named co-conspirator was an undercover law enforcement officer acting within the scope of his duties and feigning participation in the criminal enterprise. We agree, and reverse the trial court and order Archbold discharged.

The statute under which Archbold was indicted provides, in part:

> Any person or persons who shall unite or combine with any other person or persons for the purpose of committing a felony. . . . IC 35-1-111-1 (Burns Code Ed. 1975).[1]

---

1. Repealed, effective October 1, 1977 by Acts 1976, P.L. 148, §24.

The issue is whether this statutory offense requires a criminal agreement necessitating a meeting of at least two culpable minds before the offense is committed or whether the offense is completed when a single individual with a culpable mind agrees with a second individual whose culpability of mind is not in issue. . . .

[I]n Shelton v. State 259 Ind. 559, 567, 290 N.E.2d 47, 51 (1972), the Court summarized the Indiana courts' view of conspiracy:

> The Indiana conspiracy to commit a felony statute IC 1971, 35-1-111-1 (Ind. Ann. Stat. §10-1101 [1956 Repl.]) requires the uniting or combining with any person or persons for the purpose of committing a felony. *The gist of such a conspiracy is the conscious coming together of minds for the purpose of committing a felony.*
>
>> In order to be a conspiracy there must be an intelligent and deliberate agreement to commit the offense charged. It is sufficient if the minds of the parties meet understandingly to bring about an intelligent and deliberate agreement to do the acts and commit the offense, though the agreement is not manifest by any formal words. Concurrence of sentiment and cooperative conduct in the unlawful and criminal enterprise are the essential elements of criminal conspiracy. . . .
>
> (Emphasis added.)

Thus our Supreme Court has consistently held conspiracy, as defined in IC 35-1-111-1, requires the joining together of at least two persons for the purpose of committing the felony—i.e., both persons are required to have the criminal purpose (intent) when they unite or combine.

This is consistent with the purpose of criminalizing conspiracy. It ". . . is designed 'as a curb to the immoderate power to do mischief which is gained by a combination of the means.' " Conspiracy as an offense recognizes increased public harm by group action. It seeks to strike at the special dangers incident to group activity.

Therefore, conspiracy as traditionally defined and judicially interpreted requires an actual (subjective) intention in at least two persons because that is the prohibited harm. That being the case, whether the intended conduct ever results is immaterial. Thus, parties who conspire to commit the felony of burglary are not required to commit burglary before the conspiracy is a consummated offense. Rather the moment there is an agreement, a meeting of the minds, to commit the burglary the conspiracy is consummated. Therefore, it is, of course, immaterial why the felony intended in the conspiracy is not accomplished. It is of no moment whether the co-conspirators have a faint heart, a flash of honor, are interrupted by detection or apprehension, or, indeed (as in the cases cited by the dissent) cannot fulfill their goal because it is factually impossible to achieve. Again, achievement of the goal (the intended felony) is not an element of conspiracy. For this reason, impossibility in achieving the goal of the intended felony is distinguished from ". . . the impossibility . . . due to an unknown fact involving the 'co-conspirator' (e.g., no intent to consummate the offense). . . ." (Dissenting Opinion) The offense of conspiracy does not occur, a crime is not committed, until two or more persons form the intent to commit a felony. *The joint intent is the proscribed conduct.*

Other states have followed this same rationale.

Further support for this bilateral concept view of the subject statute is found in [other Indiana opinions] which, albeit *in dicta*, echoed the position that an acquittal of the alleged co-conspirator destroyed the charge as to the other. This rule is the logical extension of the proposition that one cannot conspire with another who only feigns acquiescence in the proposal because without the joint criminal intent there is no agreement and thus no conspiracy.

We reverse the trial court's judgment and order Archbold's acquittal and discharge.

BUCHANAN, Chief Judge, dissenting.

I respectfully dissent.

In interpreting Ind. Code (1971) 35-1-111-1, the majority has erroneously adopted the traditional bilateral concept of conspiracy, rejecting the better-reasoned unilateral concept. Adoption of the bilateral concept is not dictated either by the express words of the statute or by prior Indiana case law.

To recapitulate, the bilateral view of conspiracy requires two "conspirators," both with culpable intent. The unilateral view, however, focuses on the mental intent of each individual conspirator and allows a conviction even when the only "co-conspirator" was merely feigning acquiescence in the scheme (e.g., a police informant).

The basic premise of the bilateral concept is that a person cannot conspire with himself. [T]his begs the question. From one perspective, the defendant is alone in his intent to consummate the crime, but from another perspective, he is planning his criminal activity with an ally. . . .

A defendant may be convicted of conspiracy to commit an illegal abortion, even though completion of the intended crime was impossible because the intended victim was not pregnant. Similarly, a conviction for conspiracy to obtain money by forgery may stand despite undisputed evidence that consummation of the crime was impossible because the Treasury Department would not have paid out the money due to a defect in the document. Likewise, a conviction for conspiracy to commit rape is proper even though the crime was impossible because the intended victim was dead.

Factual impossibility is no defense to the crime of conspiracy. I see no reason to deviate from this rule simply when the impossibility is due to an unknown fact involving the "co-conspirator" (e.g., no intent to consummate the offense) rather than the victim (e.g., nonpregnancy, death, payment procedures).

> [T]he fact that one of them does not intend to carry out the plan, so that the purpose is incapable of fulfillment . . . is surely irrelevant, as was the fact, in the case of the conspiracy to abort, that the woman was not pregnant, so that the earlier purpose there was incapable of fulfillment. . . .

I dissent.

Model Penal Code §5.03(1) & (5)
Criminal Conspiracy

(1) *Definition of Conspiracy.* A person is guilty of conspiracy with another person or persons to commit a crime if with the purpose of promoting or facilitating its commission he:
    (a) agrees with such other person or persons that they or one or more of them will engage in conduct which constitutes such crime or an attempt or solicitation to commit such crime; or
    (b) agrees to aid such other person or persons in the planning or commission of such crime or of an attempt or solicitation to commit such crime. . . .
    (5) *Overt Act.* No person may be convicted of conspiracy to commit a crime, other than a felony of the first or second degree, unless an overt act in pursuance of such conspiracy is alleged and proved to have been done by him or by a person with whom he conspired.

Model Penal Code §§1.07(1)(b) & 5.05(3)
Prosecution for Multiple Offenses; Limitation on Convictions

Section 1.07(1):

When the same conduct of a defendant may establish the commission of more than one offense, the defendant may be prosecuted for each such offense. He may not, however, be convicted of more than one offense if: . . .

(b) one offense consists only of a conspiracy or other form of preparation to commit the other; . . .

Section 5.05(3):

A person may not be convicted of more than one offense defined by [Article 5, Inchoate Crimes] for conduct designed to commit or to culminate in the commission of the same crime.

Questions

1. *Conspiracy Offense as Liability for Group Action.* The court in *Archbold* describes "the purpose of criminalizing conspiracy" as "a curb on the immoderate power to do mischief which is gained by a combination of the means." The court goes on: "Conspiracy as an offense recognizes increased public harm by group action. It seeks to strike at the special dangers incident to group activity. With this view of conspiracy, would you expect that the jurisdiction would allow a conviction for both conspiracy and the object offense if the conspiracy were successful? (See second paragraph of the *Feala* opinion, below.) In other words, could conspiracy be used to aggravate the liability of conspirators, over the liability arising from the substantive offense, on the theory that such group criminality is itself an additional harm or danger to society? Would the Model Penal Code allow liability for both the completed offense and for conspiracy to commit the completed offense? Under the Model Penal Code, is conspiracy an independent harm from group criminality or simply a form of inchoate (preparatory) offense like attempt?

2. *Bilateral vs. Unilateral Agreement Requirement.* Would the common law hold Hans liable for a conspiracy with the undercover officer? Would the Model Penal Code? Why would a jurisdiction adopt one view rather than the other? Would it depend upon whether a jurisdiction took an objective or a subjective view of criminality?

3. *The Agreement Requirement and Impossibility.* The dissent in *Archbold* argues that, because the jurisdiction punishes conspiracies that are impossible of completion—e.g., "because the intended victim [of the abortion] was not pregnant"—it similarly should punish conspiracies that are impossible because the co-conspirator is an undercover officer who does not in fact intend his agreement that they commit an offense. Is the argument persuasive? Would it matter whether the jurisdiction punished all forms of impossibility or only factual impossibility?

United States v. Feola
Supreme Court of the United States
420 U.S. 671, 95 S. Ct. 1255, 43 L. Ed. 2d 541 (1975)

Mr. Justice BLACKMUN delivered the opinion of the Court.

This case presents the issue whether knowledge that the intended victim is a federal officer is a requisite for the crime of conspiracy, under 18 U.S.C. §371, to commit an offense violative of 18 U.S.C. §111, that is, an assault upon a federal officer while engaged in the performance of his official duties.

Respondent Feola and three others (Alsondo, Rosa, and Farr) were indicted for violations of §§371 and 111. A jury found all four defendants guilty of both charges. Feola received a sentence of four years for the conspiracy and one [to] three years, plus a $3,000 fine, for the assault. The three-year sentence, however, was suspended and he was given three years' probation "to commence at the expiration of confinement" for the conspiracy. The . . . United States Court of Appeals for the Second Circuit . . . affirmed the judgment of conviction on the substantive charges, but reversed the conspiracy convictions. Because of a conflict among the federal circuits on the scienter issue with respect to a conspiracy charge, we granted the government's petition for a writ of certiorari in Feola's case.

The facts reveal a classic narcotics "rip-off." The details are not particularly important for our present purposes. We need note only that the evidence shows that Feola and his confederates arranged for a sale of heroin to buyers who turned out to be undercover agents for the Bureau of Narcotics and Dangerous Drugs. The group planned to palm off on the purchasers, for a substantial sum, a form of sugar in place of heroin and, should that ruse fail, simply to surprise their unwitting buyers and relieve them of the cash they had brought along for payment. The plan failed when one agent, his suspicions being aroused, drew his revolver in time to counter an assault upon another agent from the rear. Instead of enjoying the rich benefits of a successful swindle, Feola and his associates found themselves charged, to their undoubted surprise, with conspiring to assault, and with assaulting, federal officers.

At the trial, the District Court, without objection from the defense, charged the jurors that, in order to find any of the defendants guilty on either the conspiracy count or the substantive one, they were not required to conclude that the defendants were aware that their quarry were federal officers.

The Court of Appeals reversed the conspiracy convictions on a ground not advanced by any of the defendants. Although it approved the trial court's instructions to the jury on the substantive charge of assaulting a federal officer, it nonetheless concluded that the failure to charge that knowledge of the victim's official identity must be proved in order to convict on the conspiracy charge amounted to plain error. The court perceived itself bound by a line of cases, commencing with Judge Learned Hand's opinion in United States v. Crimmins, 123 F.2d 271 (CA2 1941), all holding that scienter of a factual element that confers federal jurisdiction, while unnecessary for conviction of the substantive offense, is required in order to sustain a conviction for conspiracy to commit the substantive offense. . . .

The government's plea is for symmetry. It urges that since criminal liability for the offense described in 18 U.S.C. §111 does not depend on whether the assailant harbored the specific intent to assault a federal officer, no greater scienter requirement can be engrafted upon the conspiracy offense, which is merely an agreement to commit the act proscribed by §111. . . .

Our decisions establish that in order to sustain a judgment of conviction on a charge of conspiracy to violate a federal statute, the government must prove at least the degree of criminal intent necessary for the substantive offense itself. Respondent Feola urges upon us the proposition that the government must show a degree of criminal intent in the conspiracy count greater than is necessary to convict for the substantive offense; he urges that even though it is not necessary to show that he was aware of the official identity of his assaulted victims in order to find him guilty of assaulting federal officers, in violation of 18 U.S.C. §111, the government nonetheless must show that he was aware that his intended victims were undercover agents, if it is successfully to prosecute him for conspiring to assault federal agents. . . .

The general conspiracy statute, 18 U.S.C. §371,[20] offers no textual support for the proposition that to be guilty of conspiracy a defendant in effect must have known that his conduct violated federal law. The statute makes it unlawful simply to "conspire . . . to commit any offense against the United States." A natural reading of these words would be that since one can violate a criminal statute simply by engaging in the forbidden conduct, a conspiracy to commit that offense is nothing more than an agreement to engage in the prohibited conduct. Then where, as here, the substantive statute does not require that an assailant know the official status of his victim, there is nothing on the face of the

---

20. Title 18 U.S.C. §371 provides:

If two or more persons conspire either to commit any offense against the United States, or to defraud the United States, or any agency thereof in any manner or for any purpose, and one or more of such persons do any act to effect the object of the conspiracy, each shall be fined not more than $10,000 or imprisoned not more than five years, or both.

conspiracy statute that would seem to require that those agreeing to the assault have a greater degree of knowledge.

We have been unable to find any decision of this Court that lends support to the respondent. On the contrary, at least two of our cases implicitly repudiate his position. . . .

With no support on the face of the general conspiracy statute or in this Court's decisions, respondent relies solely on the line of cases commencing with United States v. Crimmins, 123 F.2d 271 (CA2 §1941), for the principle that the government must prove "antifederal" intent in order to establish liability under §371. In *Crimmins*, . . . Judge Learned Hand . . . concluded that to permit conspiratorial liability where the conspirators were ignorant of the federal implications of their acts would be to enlarge their agreement beyond its terms as they understood them. He capsulized the distinction in what has become well known as his "traffic light" analogy:

> While one may, for instance, be guilty of running past a traffic light of whose existence one is ignorant, one cannot be guilty of conspiring to run past such a light, for one cannot agree to run past a light unless one supposes that there is a light to run past.

Judge Hand's attractive, but perhaps seductive, analogy has received a mixed reception in the courts of appeals. . . . We conclude that the analogy, though effective prose, is, as applied to the facts before us, bad law.

The question posed by the traffic light analogy is not before us, just as it was not before the Second Circuit in *Crimmins*. Criminal liability, of course, may be imposed on one who runs a traffic light regardless of whether he harbored the "evil intent" of disobeying the light's command. . . . Traffic violations generally fall into that category of offenses that dispense with a *mens rea* requirement. These laws embody the social judgment that it is fair to punish one who intentionally engages in conduct that creates a risk to others, even though no risk is intended or the actor, through no fault of his own, is completely unaware of the existence of any risk. The traffic light analogy poses the question whether it is fair to punish parties to an agreement to engage intentionally in apparently innocent conduct where the unintended result of engaging in that conduct is the violation of a criminal statute.

. . . [T]he traffic light analogy, even if it were a correct statement of the law, is inapt, for the conduct proscribed by the substantive offense, here assault, is not the type outlawed without regard to the intent of the actor to accomplish the result that is made criminal. If the analogy has any vitality at all, it is to conduct of the latter variety; that, however, is a question we save for another day. We hold here only that where a substantive offense embodies only a requirement of *mens rea* as to each of its elements, the general federal conspiracy statute requires no more.

The *Crimmins* rule rests upon another foundation: that it is improper to find conspiratorial liability where the parties to the illicit agreement were not aware of the fact giving rise to federal jurisdiction, because the essence of conspiracy is agreement and persons cannot be punished for acts beyond the scope of their agreement. This "reason" states little more than a conclusion, for it is clear that one may be guilty as a conspirator for acts the precise details of which one does not know at the time of the agreement. The question is not merely whether the official status of an assaulted victim was known to the parties at the time of their agreement, but whether the acts contemplated by the conspirators are to be deemed legally different from those actually performed solely because of the official identity of the victim. Put another way, does the identity of the proposed victim alter the legal character of the acts agreed to, or is it no more germane to the nature of those acts than the color of the victim's hair?

Our analysis of the substantive offense is sufficient to convince us that for the purpose of individual guilt or innocence, awareness of the official identity of the assault victim is irrelevant. We would expect the same to obtain with respect to the conspiracy offense unless one of the policies behind the imposition of conspiratorial liability is not served where the parties to the agreement are unaware that the intended target is a federal law enforcement official.

It is well settled that the law of conspiracy serves ends different from, and complimentary to, those served by criminal prohibitions of the substantive offense. Because of this, consecutive sentences may be imposed for the conspiracy and for the underlying crime. Our decisions have identified two independent values served by the law of conspiracy. The first is protection of society from the dangers of concerted criminal activity. That individuals know that their planned joint venture violates federal as well as state law seems totally irrelevant to that purpose of conspiracy law which seeks to protect society from the dangers of concerted criminal activity. . . .

The second aspect is that conspiracy is an inchoate crime. This is to say, that, although the law generally makes criminal only antisocial conduct, at some point in the continuum between preparation and consummation, the likelihood of a commission of an act is sufficiently great and the criminal intent sufficiently well formed to justify the intervention of the criminal law. . . .

Again, we do not see how imposition of a strict "antifederal" scienter requirement would relate to this purpose of conspiracy law. Given the level of intent needed to carry out the substantive offense, we fail to see how the agreement is any less blameworthy or constitutes less of a danger to society solely because the participants are unaware which body of law they intend to violate. Therefore, we again conclude that imposition of a requirement of knowledge of those facts that serve only to establish federal jurisdiction would render it more difficult to serve the policy behind the law of conspiracy without serving any other apparent social policy.

We hold, then, that assault of a federal officer pursuant to an agreement to assault is not, even in the words of Judge Hand, "beyond the reasonable intendment of the common understanding." United States v. Crimmins, 123 F.2d, at 273. The agreement is not thereby enlarged, for knowledge of the official identity of the victim is irrelevant to the essential nature of the agreement, entrance into which is made criminal by the law of conspiracy.

Again we point out, however, that the state of knowledge of the parties to an agreement is not always irrelevant in a proceeding charging a violation of conspiracy law. [T]he knowledge of the parties is relevant to the same issues and to the same extent as it may be for conviction of the substantive offense. . . .

To summarize . . . we hold that where knowledge of the facts giving rise to federal jurisdiction is not necessary for conviction of a substantive offense embodying a *mens rea* requirement, such knowledge is equally irrelevant to questions of responsibility for conspiracy to commit that offense.

The judgment of the Court of Appeals with respect to the respondent's conspiracy conviction is reversed.

It is so ordered.

Mr. Justice STEWART, with whom Mr. Justice DOUGLAS joins, dissenting.

Does an assault on a federal officer violate 18 U.S.C. §111 [assaulting a federal officer] even when the assailant is unaware, and has no reason to know, that the victim is other than a private citizen, or indeed, a confederate in crime? . . .

. . . I believe that before there can be a violation of 18 U.S.C. §111, an assailant must know or have reason to know that the person he assaults is an officer. It follows *a fortiori* that there can be no criminal conspiracy to violate the statute in the absence of at least equivalent knowledge. Accordingly, I respectfully dissent from the opinion and judgment of the Court.

Model Penal Code §5.03 Comment
407-44 (1985)

It is worth noting . . . that in relation to those elements of substantive crimes that consist of proscribed conduct or undesirable results of conduct, the Code requires purposeful behavior for guilt of conspiracy, regardless of the state of mind required by the definition of the substantive crime. If the crime is defined in terms of prohibited conduct, such as the sale of narcotics, the actor's purpose must be to promote or facilitate the engaging in of such conduct by himself or another. If it is defined in terms of a result of conduct, such as homicide, his purpose must be to promote or facilitate the production of that result. Thus, it would not be sufficient, as it is under the attempt provision of the Code, if the actor only believed that the result would be produced but did not consciously plan or desire to produce it. For example if two persons plan to destroy a building by detonating a bomb, though they know and believe that there are inhabitants in the building who will be killed by the explosion, they are nevertheless guilty only of a conspiracy to destroy the building and not of a conspiracy to kill the inhabitants. While this result may seem unduly restrictive from the viewpoint of the completed crime, it is necessitated by the extremely preparatory behavior that may be involved in conspiracy. Had the crime been completed or had the preparation progressed even to the stage of an attempt, the result would be otherwise. As to the attempt, knowledge or belief that the inhabitants would be killed would suffice. As to the liability of one who renders aid for the completed crime, a special provision in Section 2.06 covers the matter, despite the general complicity requirement of a purpose to promote or facilitate the commission of the crime. Under that provision, when causing a particular result is an element of a crime, a person is an accomplice in the crime if he was an accomplice in the behavior that caused the result and shared the same purpose or knowledge with respect to the result that is required by the definition of the crime.

A fortiori, where recklessness or negligence suffices for the actor's culpability with respect to a result element of a substantive crime, as for example when homicide through negligence is made criminal, there could not be a conspiracy to commit that crime. This should be distinguished, however, from a crime defined in terms of conduct that creates a risk of harm, such as reckless driving or driving above a certain speed limit. In this situation the conduct rather than any result it may produce is the element of the crime, and it would suffice for guilt of conspiracy that the actor's purpose was to promote or facilitate such conduct—for example, if he urged the driver of the car to go faster and faster.

The culpability requirements of conspiracy with respect to the third class of elements of substantive crimes, those involving the attendant circumstances, have proven resistant to judicial resolution. The following discussion addresses these problems in terms of the Model Code formulation.

(ii) Culpability with Respect to Circumstance Elements. The attempt definition requires that, as to attendant circumstance elements of the substantive crime, the actor have the same kind of culpability that is

required for commission of the substantive crime. Thus, if it is a federal offense to kill an FBI agent and negligence as to the identity of the victim suffices for commission of the substantive crime, an actor who attempts to kill such an agent with negligence as to his identity would be guilty of an attempt to commit the crime.

This rule is consonant with the theories underlying inchoate criminality. If something less than knowledge—for example, recklessness, negligence, or strict liability—concerning certain circumstances suffices for a given crime, it represents a judgment that the actor's lesser awareness concerning those circumstances does not decrease his culpability of the offensiveness of his behavior below the point where criminality should be declared. Such a judgment, for example, underlies the single instance adopted by the Code of strict liability as to circumstance elements, i.e., carnal knowledge of a female less than 10 years old. If an actor sets out with . . . the lesser culpability concerning attendant circumstances that suffices for commission of the crime, and his preparation progresses to the point of a conspiracy or attempt, the reasons for reaching his behavior as an inchoate crime are in no way decreased by such lesser culpability concerning the circumstances.

The fact that conspiracy is defined in terms of an agreement produces difficulties, however, with respect to the requisite awareness by the conspirator of those circumstance elements regarding which something less than knowledge suffices for the substantive crime. The problem has arisen most often in federal cases in which some circumstance that affords a basis for federal jurisdiction such as use of the mails or crossing state lines, is made an element of the crime. Prior to the Supreme Court's apparent adoption in 1975 in United States v. Feola of the Model Code's approach, most decisions involving such offenses held that although knowledge of the jurisdictional element is unnecessary for guilt of the substantive crime, it is necessary for guilt of conspiracy to commit that crime. In a prosecution for use of the mails to defraud, for example, it is sufficient if the mails were in fact used for the purpose of furthering the scheme, while for conspiracy to commit that crime it was said that the defendants must have contemplated that the mails would be so used. . . . Federal crimes based on the transportation of stolen goods through interstate commerce were treated similarly; although strict liability as to the interstate element sufficed for the substantive crime, a conspirator had to be aware of the past or contemplate the future passage of the goods through interstate commerce. . . .

. . .[64]A decision like that in United States v. Mack, however, seemed

---

64. Thus in United States v. Crimmins, Judge Learned Hand offered the example of passing a traffic light, suggesting that though knowledge of the light may not be necessary for the substantive offense, one cannot conspire to go past the light unless he supposes that there is a light to pass.

to point the other way. The statute in that case required registration of the keeping of prostitutes who were aliens, and no mens rea was required for the substantive crime on the point of whether the prostitute was an alien. The defendants did not know that the prostitute they kept was an alien, nor were they aware that registration of alien prostitutes was required by law. The court, measuring the conspiracy's "boarders . . . with an eye to its purpose," held that the jury could find that the defendants intended to keep the affair surreptitious and understood that the chief danger of discovery was from the federal authorities. The jury could, therefore, find a conspiracy to violate the statute, since this "implied condition covered any form of disclosure" and since registration would have breached the condition of secrecy thus embraced. While the case could thus be said to stand for the proposition that awareness of the alien status of the prostitute was not a necessary element of the conspiracy, the conceptual difficulty involved in finding an agreement to fail to register an alien in the absence of any knowledge that she was an alien and that there was a duty to register aliens seems difficult to overcome.

The conspiracy provision in the Code does not attempt to solve the problem by explicit formulation, nor have the recent legislative revisions. Here, as in the section on complicity, it was believed that the matter is best left to judicial resolution as cases that present the question may arise, and that the formulations proposed afford sufficient flexibility for satisfactory decision. Under Subsection (1) of Section 5.03 it is enough that the object of the agreement is "conduct that constitutes the crime," which can be held to import no more than the mental state required for the substantive offense into the agreement to commit it. Although the agreement must be made "with the purpose of promoting or facilitating the commission of the crime," it is arguable, though by no means certain, that such a purpose may be proved although the actor did not know of the existence of a circumstance, which did exist in fact, when knowledge of the circumstance is not required for the substantive offense. Rather than press the matter further in this section, the Institute deliberately left the matter to interpretation in the context in which the issue is presented. Too many variations, many of which cannot be foreseen with any confidence, could otherwise be expected to arise and undermine any more rigid formula.

Questions

1. *Fri's Liability.* Can Fri be held liable for conspiracy to commit theft by deception based upon his agreement with Hans? Can Fri be held liable for conspiracy to endanger? Would Fri have been held liable

for the offense of endangerment (e.g., under Model Penal Code §211.2) if he had sold a detector? What arguments can be made for and against liability for Fri for conspiracy to endanger?

2. *Hans' Liability.* Can Hans be held liable for manslaughter for the two deaths that occur because of the defective detectors? Can he be held liable for endangerment for those instances where he sold defective detectors but no death has yet occurred as a result? Can be held liable for conspiracy to endanger (based on the devices he had not yet sold)? Can he be held liable for theft by deception (e.g., under Model Penal Code §223.3) for his sale of the defective detectors?

3. *Disagreement Over Multiple Offense Limitations.* Assume for the sake of argument that Fri can be held liable for conspiracy to commit theft by deception and conspiracy to endanger. If Hans were convicted of manslaughter, endangerment, and theft by deception, can he (Hans) also be convicted of conspiracy to commit theft by deception and conspiracy to endanger based upon his agreement with Fri to sell the defective detectors? Why might jurisdictions disagree about this?

4. *Disagreement Over Nature of Agreement Requirement.* If Hans can be held liable for conspiring with Fri, can he also be held liable for conspiracy with the undercover officer? Why might jurisdictions disagree about this? Where have we seen before an issue analogous to this?

Gebardi v. United States
Supreme Court of the United States
287 U.S. 112, 53 S. Ct. 35, 77 L. Ed. 206 (1932)

Mr. Justice STONE delivered the opinion of the Court.

This case is here on certiorari to review a judgment of conviction for conspiracy to violate the Mann Act. Petitioners, a man and a woman, not then husband and wife, were indicted in the District Court of Northern Illinois, for conspiring together, and with others not named, to transport the woman from one state to another for the purpose of engaging in sexual intercourse with the man. At the trial without a jury there was evidence from which the court could have found that the petitioners had engaged in illicit sexual relations in the course of each of the journeys alleged; that the man purchased the railway tickets for both petitioners for at least one journey, and that in each instance the woman, in advance of the purchase of the tickets, consented to go on the journey and did go on it voluntarily for the specified immoral purpose. There was no evidence supporting the allegation that any other person had conspired. . . .

Section 2 of the Mann Act, violation of which is charged by the indictment here as the object of the conspiracy, imposes the penalty upon "Any person who shall knowingly transport or cause to be transported, or aid or assist in obtaining transportation for, or in transporting in interstate or foreign commerce . . . any woman or girl for the purpose of prostitution or debauchery or for any other immoral purpose. . . ." . . .

The Act does not punish the woman for transporting herself; it contemplates two persons—one to transport and the woman or girl to be transported. For the woman to fall within the ban of the statute she must, at the least, "aid or assist" someone else in transporting or in procuring transportation for herself. But such aid and assistance must be more than mere agreement on her part to the transportation and its immoral purpose. For the statute is drawn to include those cases in which the woman consents to her own transportation. Yet it does not specifically impose any penalty upon her, although it deals in detail with the person by whom she is transported. In applying this criminal statute we cannot infer that the mere acquiescence of the woman transported was intended to be condemned by the general language punishing those who aid and assist the transporter, any more than it has been inferred that the purchaser of liquor was to be regarded as an abettor of the illegal sale. The penalties of the statute are too clearly directed against the acts of the transporter as distinguished from the consent of the subject of the transportation. . . . [T]his conclusion is not disputed by the government here, which contends only that the conspiracy charge will lie though the woman could not commit the substantive offense.

We come thus to the main question in the case, whether, admitting that the woman, by consenting, has not violated the Mann Act, she may be convicted of a conspiracy with the man to violate it. Section 37 of the Criminal Code punishes a conspiracy by two or more persons "to commit any offense against the United States." The offense which she is charged with conspiring to commit is that perpetrated by the man, for it is not questioned that in transporting her he contravened §2 of the Mann Act. Hence we must decide whether her concurrence, which was not criminal before the Mann Act, nor punished by it, may, without more, support a conviction under the conspiracy section, enacted many years before.

[A]n agreement to commit an offense may be criminal, though its purpose is to do what some of the conspirators may be free to do alone. Incapacity of one to commit the substantive offense does not necessarily imply that he may with impunity conspire with others who are able to commit it.[5] For it is the collective planning of criminal conduct at which

---

5. So it has been held repeatedly that one not a bankrupt may be held guilty under §37 of conspiring that a bankrupt shall conceal property from his trustee (Bankruptcy

the statute aims. The plan is itself a wrong which, if any act be done to effect its object, the state has elected to treat as criminal. And one may plan that others shall do what he cannot do himself.

But in this case we are concerned with something more than an agreement between two persons for one of them to commit an offense which the other cannot commit. There is the added element that the offense planned, the criminal object of the conspiracy, involves the agreement of the woman to her transportation by the man, which is the very conspiracy charged.

Congress set out in the Mann Act to deal with cases which frequently, if not normally, involve consent and agreement on the part of the woman to the forbidden transportation. In every case in which she is not intimidated or forced into the transportation, the statute necessarily contemplates her acquiescence. Yet this acquiescence, though an incident of a type of transportation specifically dealt with by the statute, was not made a crime under the Mann Act itself. Of this class of cases we say that the substantive offense contemplated by the statute itself involves the same combination or community of purpose of two persons only which is prosecuted here as conspiracy. . . . [W]e perceive in the failure of the Mann Act to condemn the woman's participation in those transportations which are effected with her mere consent, evidence of an affirmative legislative policy to leave her acquiescence unpunished. We think it a necessary implication of that policy that when the Mann Act and the conspiracy statute came to be construed together, as they necessarily would be, the same participation which the former contemplates as an inseparable incident of all cases in which the woman is a voluntary agent at all, but does not punish, was not automatically to be made punishable under the latter. It would contravene that policy to hold that the very passage of the Mann Act effected a withdrawal by the conspiracy statute of that immunity which the Mann Act itself confers.

It is not to be supposed that the consent of an unmarried person to adultery with a married person, where the latter alone is guilty of the substantive offense, would render the former an abettor or a conspirator or that the acquiescence of a woman under the age of consent would make her a co-conspirator with the man to commit

---

Act §29[b], 11 U.S.C., §52). In like manner, Chadwick v. United States, 141 Fed. 225, sustained the conviction of one not an officer of a national bank for conspiring with an officer to commit a crime which only he could commit.

statutory rape upon herself. The principle, determinative of this case, is the same.

On the evidence before us the woman petitioner has not violated the Mann Act and, we hold, is not guilty of a conspiracy to do so. As there is no proof that the man conspired with anyone else to bring about the transportation, the convictions of both petitioners must be
Reversed.

Model Penal Code §5.04
Incapacity, Irresponsibility, or Immunity of Party to Solicitation or Conspiracy

(1) Except as provided in Subsection (2) of this Section, it is immaterial to the liability of a person who solicits or conspires with another to commit a crime that:

    (a) he or the person who he solicits or with whom he conspires does not occupy a particular position or have a particular characteristic which is an element of such crime, if he believes that one of them does; or

    (b) the person whom he solicits or with whom he conspires is irresponsible or has an immunity to prosecution or conviction for the commission of the crime.

(2) It is a defense to a charge of solicitation or conspiracy to commit a crime that if the criminal object were achieved, the actor would not be guilty of a crime under the law defining the offense or as an accomplice under Section 2.06(5) or 2.06(6)(a) or (b).

Model Penal Code §2.06(5) & (6)
Special Defenses to Complicity

(5) A person who is legally incapable of committing a particular offense himself may be guilty thereof if it is committed by the conduct of another person for which he is legally accountable, unless such liability is inconsistent with the purpose of the provision establishing his incapacity.

(6) Unless otherwise provided by the Code or by the law defining the offense, a person is not an accomplice in an offense committed by another person if:

(a) he is a victim of that offense; or

(b) the offense is so defined that his conduct is inevitably incident to its commission.

United States v. Lester
Problem Case

[Appellants Charles E. Lester and Edward Anthony Buccieri, both private citizens, were charged in count one with conspiracy to violate the civil rights of one George W. Ratterman, under color of State law, and in count two with the substantive offense of such violation under a theory of aiding and abetting three defendant police officers who, because of their status, were acting "under color of State law."] The jury convicted both appellants of the conspiracy charged in count one, but acquitted them of the substantive offense charged in count two. All other defendants, including the three police officers, were acquitted by jury verdict of all charges—both the conspiracy and the substantive offense.

The evidence, direct and circumstantial, in the case at bar, together with the inferences which the jury could reasonably have drawn therefrom, combined to warrant the jury in finding inter alia the following facts: The Glenn-Tropicana, a combination nightclub and hotel in Newport, Kentucky, across the Ohio River from Cincinnati, had been favored for many years with somewhat-less-than-vigorous enforcement of the State laws prohibiting gambling and prostitution. In April of 1961, upon the announcement of George W. Ratterman as a "reform" candidate for sheriff, defendant Carinci, a co-proprietor of the Glenn-Tropicana, telephoned one Thomas Paisley and asked him to arrange a meeting for Carinci with Ratterman.

A few days later, on April 14, appellant Lester, attorney for the Glenn-Tropicana, telephoned a Newport photographer and asked him to talk to appellant Buccieri, another co-proprietor of the Glenn-Tropicana, about a picture. In due course, the photographer contacted Buccieri who told the photographer that his services would be needed "to take a picture of a man and a woman in a room"; and added the assurance: "Now, don't worry about anything, we will protect you." The photographer gave Buccieri a telephone number where he could be reached at night.

On May 8, 1961, Paisley came to Cincinnati and had cocktails and dinner with Ratterman, commencing at about 5:45 in the afternoon, following which they met with Carinci at a Cincinnati restaurant. After consuming several drinks in the course of the evening, Ratterman and Carinci and Paisley went over to the Glenn-Tropicana for supper. Upon their arrival about 1:30 AM, Ratterman and Paisley were ushered into Glenn-Tropicana's suite 314 on the third floor, near which an illegal gambling operation was regularly conducted. Appellant Buccieri then sent Rita Desmond, one of the club's showgirls, upstairs to suite 314 to have a drink with Paisley and Ratterman. Shortly after Rita arrived, Ratterman, who was extremely drowsy by now, left the sitting room of the suite and lay down in an adjoining bedroom.

Carinci next directed April Flowers, another of the Glenn-Tropicana's showgirls, to stop her striptease act and go at once to suite 314 without bothering to change her costume. When April arrived, she was asked by Rita to go into the bedroom and try to awaken Ratterman. April did so, but her efforts failed to arouse Ratterman. Carinci then came to suite 314 and requested Rita and Paisley to go elsewhere in the club with him, leaving April and Ratterman alone in the bedroom of suite 314.

Meanwhile, approximately ten minutes after Ratterman had arrived at the Glenn-Tropicana, someone called the photographer's home and left word for him to call Buccieri at the club. However, the photographer did not return the call. At 2:20 AM, the gambling operations on the third floor were closed substantially earlier than usual, and the patrons were asked to leave the third floor.

At 2:32 AM, an anonymous phone call was received at the Newport police station for one of the defendant police officers, who was told: "If you want to get George Ratterman, he is in Room 314 of the Glenn Hotel." The three defendant officers thereupon went to the Glenn-Tropicana at 2:35 AM, where they first arrested Carinci, and then April Flowers as she emerged from the bedroom of suite 314. That done, there followed a brief scuffle between the police officers and Ratterman, and the latter was taken into custody, wrapped in a bedspread. Testimony by the police officers that he was found with his trousers off was disputed by Ratterman, who said that his trousers had been removed from him by the officers.

Appellant Lester promptly arrived at the police station, after having called a bondsman who posted bail for April Flowers and Carinci, but refused to provide bail for Ratterman. Appellant Lester admitted that he had been up since 2:00 AM, "when the Ratterman deal broke"—well more than a half hour before the arrests occurred. At approximately 4:00 AM following the arrests, all six persons accused in the indictment—including the three police officers—were seen together at the Glenn-Tropicana, and at the Flamingo Club an hour later.

Examination of Ratterman the following day disclosed traces of from three to four grams of chloral hydrate ["knockout drops"] estimated to have been ingested between 10:00 and 11:00 PM the previous evening.

Since the jury acquitted all the accused of the substantive offense charged in count two of the indictment, it would serve no useful purpose to recount here the evidence dealing particularly with that offense; other than perhaps to record that the police-court case against Ratterman was dismissed after his attorney was able to produce the photographer, whose account of the efforts to have him take a picture of the planned bedroom scene persuaded the City Attorney of Newport that the affair was a sham.

[Appellants argue, first, that as a matter of law they cannot be liable for conspiracy to violate the civil rights "under color of State law" because they are not State officers and therefore do not fall within the prohibition of the statute. Second, appellants argue that as a matter of law they cannot be liable for conspiracy because the police officers were acquitted of both the substantive offense and of the conspiracy.]

Questions

1. Gebardi *and the Model Penal Code.* Is the holding in *Gebardi* consistent with the governing Model Penal Code rules? How is it similar or different?

2. *Statutory Exemptions.* The Mann Act makes it an offense for a person to transport a woman (other than herself) for immoral purposes. Does the woman in *Gebardi* satisfy the requirements for a substantive violation of the Mann Act? The offense charged in *Lester* makes it an offense to violate another's civil rights "under color of State law." Do the defendants in *Lester*, who are both private citizens, satisfy the requirements of the substantive offense?

3. *Statutory Exemptions and Conspiracy Liability in* Gebardi. Does the woman in *Gebardi* satisfy the requirements of conspiracy to violate the Mann Act? That is, did she agree with another (the man) that one of them would engage in conduct that would constitute a violation of the Mann Act? Under what theory might she be exempt from conspiracy liability? If the woman had conspired with the man to transport another woman (rather than herself) across a state line for the requisite purpose, could she have been held liable for conspiracy to violate the Mann Act?

4. *Statutory Exemptions and Conspiracy Liability in* Lester. Do the defendants in *Lester* satisfy the requirements of conspiracy to violate the civil rights of Ratterman under color of State law? That is, did

they agree with others that one of them (specifically the officers) would engage in conduct that would constitute the offense? Do they have available the same kind of defense arguments that the woman in *Gebardi* can make?

5. *The Unconvictable Co-conspirator.* The officers in *Lester* are acquitted of the substantive offense, violating Ratterman's civil rights under color of State law. Does this mean that the defendants, both of whom are private citizens, cannot be convicted of conspiracy to commit that offense?

6. *Gender Differences in Exempting Participants from Liability.* The Mann Act at issue in *Gebardi* criminalizes the transportation of women for immoral purposes but not men. Why do you think that the legislature limited the prohibition in this way? Although the transported woman is necessarily a participant in each violation, her conduct is not criminalized. What arguments can you give, pro and con, for why the woman transported should be liable as well as the man doing the transporting? How is this criminalization decision similar and how is it different from the decision as to whether liability should be imposed on the customer of prostitution?

Notes on the Requirements for Conspiracy Liability

The requirements for conspiracy liability may be summarized as follows:

The defendant must satisfy these requirements:

Objective Requirements	Culpability Requirements
Conduct constituting substantive offense: Not required, instead: CL and MPC: actor must agree with another that one of them will engage in the conduct that would constitute the substantive offense	*Culpability as to conduct constituting substantive offense:* CL & MPC §5.03(1): "purpose of promoting or facilitating" the offense
Result elements of substantive offense: CL and MPC: not required (nor is factual impossibility of it occurring a defense)	*Culpability as to result elements of substantive offense:* CL: elevate to purposeful MPC: elevate to purposeful Other (e.g., *Feola* reasoning): as required by substantive offense; do not elevate

Circumstance elements of substantive offense:
CL: required (legal impossibility is a defense)
MPC: not required (legal impossibility is not a defense)

Culpability as to circumstance elements of substantive offense:
CL: elevate to purposeful
MPC: perhaps do not elevate, left to "interpretation" (per commentary)
Other (e.g., *Feola*): as required by substantive offense; do not elevate

A co-conspirator must satisfy these requirements:

Objective Requirements

Agreement requirement:
CL: at least one other conspirator must actually agree (bilateral agreement: "two or more persons agree to . . .");
MPC: no conspirator need agree (unilateral agreement; defendant "agrees . . . that one of them . . .")

Overt act requirement:
CL and MPC §5.03(5): act in pursuance of conspiracy by any conspirator

Culpability Requirements

Intent to agree:
CL: bilateral requires that co-conspirator intend to agree back
MPC: unilateral does not

Unconvictable co-conspirator defense:
CL: requires that co-conspirator satisfy all elements of conspiracy and has no defense
MPC §5.04(1): rejects defense

MPC = Model Penal Code
CL = Common Law

Bank Robbery with a Sub

DeSaco, Krule, and Handler meet in New York City to plan the robbery of a bank across the river in Newark, New Jersey. It is agreed that Handler will kidnap the bank manager, bring him to the back door of the bank, where Krule will take him inside to open the vault. DeSaco is responsible for overpowering the guard, tying him up, and standing lookout during the robbery. All agree that no firearms will be used so that there will be no danger that anyone will be seriously injured.

The preparations, including a planned visit to the bank, go according to plan until Handler telephones Krule the day before to tell him that he will not be able to participate. An old girlfriend is coming to town for a few days and he wants to spend the time with her. Krule calls DeSaco and they decide to go ahead as scheduled but Krule will come up with someone to do Handler's job. Krule then calls Morris and arranges with him to sub for Handler.

When they pull the job, Morris does a fine job as a last minute replacement but DeSaco screws up. DeSaco brings a gun and shoots the guard to avoid having to wrestle with him; the guard dies from the gun shot. In this jurisdiction, the statute of limitations for bank robbery, kidnapping, and conspiracy is five years; murder has no limitation period. The three members who participated in the robbery meet annually to discuss the running of the statute of limitations and other matters relating to how best to avoid being caught. Five years and one day after the robbery they are all arrested and charged with murder, kidnapping, bank robbery, and conspiracy. Are they liable?

Notes on Scope, Duration, and Collateral Consequences of Conspiracy

Collateral Consequences In many cases, the procedural effects of a conspiracy charge are of greater importance than the penalty for a conspiracy conviction. These effects typically benefit the state more than the defendant and make conspiracy an attractive offense to prosecutors. For example, the Sixth Amendment and many state constitutions require that a defendant be tried in the district where the crime is committed. In conspiracy prosecutions, this is interpreted to mean in any district where an overt act is performed by any one of the conspirators. Especially in larger conspiracies, this gives the prosecution considerable choice in selecting a district in which to bring the prosecution. A prosecution for the conspiracy described above could be brought in either New York or Newark. While a defendant generally may request a trial separate from other offenders, defendants charged in a single conspiracy may be indicted and tried together. Such joint trials may provide judicial and prosecutorial economy but they may disadvantage defendants in several ways. Defendants may be required to share peremptory challenges of jurors, thus each defendant may have fewer to use than if tried alone. Defendants may find it more difficult to have the jury focus on the special facts and circumstances of his or her situation. Defense counsel also may be concerned about a tendency of juries to apply damaging evidence to all defendants, unless a defendant can affirmatively explain why it is inapplicable to him or her. Finally, hearsay generally is not admissible in a criminal prosecution but an exception is made for statements made by a conspirator during or in furtherance of the conspiracy. Such hearsay statements are admissible against all co-conspirators. Thus, the larger and longer the conspiracy, the more statements by more conspirators that are admissible against all conspirators.

Pinkerton Doctrine: Conspiracy as Complicity One additional collateral effect of conspiracy is the practice in some jurisdictions that allows conspiracy to be treated as a form of complicity. The Pinkerton Doctrine, as this frequently is called, holds that a conspirator is liable for substantive offenses committed by other conspirators in furtherance of the conspiracy.[1] There is no requirement that the other conspirators satisfy the culpability requirements of the offense committed; only the conspirator committing the offense need satisfy the elements of the offense. Thus, all conspirators of DeSaco at the time of the shooting of the guard would be liable with him for murder, even though they had agreed that no firearms would be used. It is this potential of the rule to hold an actor liable for crimes of another beyond those agreed to and beyond the bounds of normal complicity liability that has led to criticism of the Pinkerton Doctrine. The Model Penal Code does not adopt the rule. An actor may be held liable as an accomplice under the Code if he "aids or *agrees* . . . to aid such other person in planning or committing [an offense],"[2] but such complicity liability requires proof of the normal requirements of complicity, including "the purpose of promoting or facilitating the commission of the offense."[3]

Scope and Duration Each of these collateral consequences applies only within the time period and scope of the conspiracy. A co-conspirator's overt act, incriminating statement, or substantive offense will not trigger the relevant collateral consequences if, at the time of the act, statement, or offense, the conspiracy has ended, has not yet begun, or the actor is no longer a member or has not yet become a member. Thus, the rules governing the scope and duration of a conspiracy are critical in determining whether and to what extent these collateral consequences will have effect. The "scope" of a conspiracy concerns: Who does the conspiracy include? Is a conspiracy among many deemed one large conspiracy or two or more smaller ones? The issues relating to the "duration" of a conspiracy include: When did the conspiracy begin? When did it end?

Multiple Objectives One difficulty in determining the scope of a conspiracy arises where a conspiracy has multiple objectives. While there is some disagreement on the issue, a conspiracy with multiple objectives nonetheless is treated as a single conspiracy.[4] Thus, while the conspiracy

---

1. See Pinkerton v. United States, 328 U.S. 640, 66 S. Ct. 1180, 90 L. Ed. 1489 (1946).
2. Model Penal Code §2.06(3)(a)(ii).
3. Model Penal Code §2.06(3)(a).
4. Braverman v. United States, 317 U.S. 49, 53, 63 S. Ct. 99, 101, 87 L. Ed. 23, 28 (1942) (whether the object of a single agreement is one or several crimes, the agreement is what is prohibited and a single agreement is only one crime).

described above includes both a kidnapping and a bank robbery, under this ruling it can only be charged as one conspiracy. Such a rule is consistent with the view that conspiracy is a harm in itself, not just an inchoate form of liability. If the harm is the criminal combination or agreement, then one agreement means one harm. The rule was adopted by the Model Penal Code,[5] but its rationale in that context is less clear. The Code treats conspiracy only as an inchoate form of liability, like attempt, not as a harm in itself for group criminality. One can have two attempt convictions where a scheme involves an attempt of two different offenses—for example, the murder of two different victims or attempted murder and attempted robbery of the same victim. One may wonder why it is not similarly appropriate to have two convictions for conspiracy to murder or convictions for both conspiracy to murder and conspiracy to rob, although both offenses arise from a single agreement. Under the Code, if the conspirators are caught before commission, they cannot be convicted of both conspiracy to kidnap and conspiracy to rob the bank. Yet, it is not clear why this is the proper result. (If the hypothetical bank robbery conspirators are caught after commission, they can be convicted of both offenses. They cannot be convicted of conspiracy under the Code because, as an inchoate offense, conspiracy is subsumed in the completed offense.)

Scope of a Single Conspiracy Complications in determining the scope of a conspiracy also arise where members of the group have entered into agreements with some members but not others. For example, DeSaco has agreed with Krule (and Handler), but only Krule has agreed with Morris. Is the entire group a single large conspiracy? Or, is it a collection of smaller, overlapping conspiracies?

"Chains" and "Wheels" A single conspiracy traditionally was one in which all conspirators shared a "community of interest" or purpose. In United States v. Bruno,[6] for example, a drug distribution scheme involved smugglers, middlemen, and retailers, many of whom did not know the identity of the others in the scheme. The court held, however, that they need not know the identity of the others as long as they knew the existence of the others and the success of the conspiracy depended on all. The "chain" structure among conspirators in *Bruno* was distinguished from the "wheel" structure in Kotteakos v. United States,[7] where each conspirator dealt with a single central conspirator. Each of several applicants conspired with one Brown to obtain a fraudulent loan under the National Housing Act. Without a "rim" on the wheel, the court held, there was no "community of interest" and, thus, no

---

5. Model Penal Code §5.03(3).
6. 105 F.2d 921 (2d Cir. 1939), rev'd on other grounds, 308 U.S. 287, 50 S. Ct. 198, 84 L. Ed. 257.
7. 328 U.S. 750, 66 S. Ct. 1239, 90 L. Ed. 1557 (1946).

single conspiracy but rather multiple conspiracies between the hub and each spoke.[8] It seems likely that a court would find that DeSaco and Morris shared a "community of interest," unlike the spokes of the wheel in *Kotteakos*.

Subjective View of Scope   The Model Penal Code adopts a rule that permits a defendant to be a conspirator of another person if he knows that such other person has agreed with a person with whom the defendant has conspired.[9] This subjective view of the scope of a conspiracy means that the "scope" may be different for each member. Such is consistent with the Code's subjective view of criminality manifested in other contexts, such as attempts, impossibility, and the agreement requirement in conspiracy. Such a subjective scope does complicate the application of collateral consequences, however. A consequence may apply to one conspirator but not to another, because one may be a member of the other's conspiracy but not visa versa. From DeSaco's view Morris is a co-conspirator under the Code because he knows that a substitute for Handler was to be arranged. Whether DeSaco is a co-conspirator of Morris, from Morris's view, will depend upon whether Krule told Morris that another person was involved.

Duration   A conspiracy begins for each conspirator with that person's agreement that the object offense be committed.[10] Thus, Morris is free from the collateral consequences of conspiracy that rest upon overt acts before he joined. A conspiracy ends for a conspirator when the object of the conspiracy is completed or when the actor withdraws from the conspiracy.[11] One conspirator may end the conspiracy as to himself by withdrawing, even though the conspiracy may continue as to others who have not withdrawn.[12] Thus, Handler's withdrawal does not alter the existence or effects of the conspiracy for those remaining. Unlike renunciation, which provides a defense to conspiracy liability, withdrawal simply ends the actor's participation in the conspiracy and, thus, ends for him the collateral effects that would arise from continuing membership. For example, Handler's withdrawal bars his liability under *Pinkerton* for the subsequent substantive murder committed by DeSaco. It also triggers the running of the statute of limitations as to him but it does not trigger it for the others. He remains liable for the offense of conspiracy.

---

8. Id. at 754-55.
9. Model Penal Code §5.03(2).
10. See Model Penal Code §5.03(1)(a); 1 P. Robinson, Criminal Law Defenses §82(e)(2) (1984).
11. See Model Penal Code §5.03(7); 1 P. Robinson, Criminal Law Defenses, §81(c) (1984).
12. See Model Penal Code §5.03(7); 1 P. Robinson, Criminal Law Defenses §81(c)(4) (1984).

Requirements for Withdrawal Withdrawal, sometimes called abandonment, typically has less demanding requirements than does renunciation. Effective withdrawal traditionally required an affirmative act of disassociation; a decision and announcement that one will no longer participate may be enough if accompanied by conduct inconsistent with continued membership. To be effective, the withdrawal must be communicated to all conspirators and must be made in time for the others to abandon the conspiracy. The Model Penal Code takes a similar approach. It is adequate under the Code that the actor advise his co-conspirators of his withdrawal or that he advise law enforcement authorities of the conspiracy and his participation.[13] It seems likely that Handler's conduct is adequate to be an effective withdrawal. Thus, the statute of limitations has run out for him.

Presumed Abandonment Where conspirators do not declare withdrawal or abandonment, but simply become inactive, abandonment of the conspiracy by all members sometimes may be presumed. The Model Penal Code claims to adopt the rule of the *Grunewald* case, which provides that a conspiracy is presumed to have been abandoned after the period of limitation has passed with no overt act by any conspirator.[14] Thus, the statute of limitations has run for the hypothetical participants in the robbery, unless their meetings are taken as additional overt acts that each extend the conspiracy. But, in *Grunewald,* the Court makes clear that one cannot assume a continuing conspiracy to conceal simply from evidence that the conspiracy was kept secret.[15] Something more than mere overt acts to conceal the past offense must be shown if the original conspiracy is to be extended in duration.[16] Of course, if the jurisdiction adopts the *Pinkerton* Doctrine, all conspirators will be liable for the murder, which has no statute of limitations.

---

13. Model Penal Code §5.03(7)(c).

14. Model Penal Code §5.03(7)(b). What the Code probably means by this is not that the conspiracy is presumed abandoned at this point—after the running of the period of the statute of limitation with no overt act—for the normal rule is that the statute of limitation only begins to run at the point of abandonment. Presumably the Code means that after the period of limitation has run with no overt act, the conspiracy is retroactively presumed to have been abandoned back at the time of the last overt act. Thus, the statute of limitation already has run when the abandonment can be presumed.

15. Grunewald v. United States, 353 U.S. 391, 77 S. Ct. 963, 1 L. Ed. 2d 931 (1957).

16. The robbery conspirators may argue that their meetings, if anything, are a separate conspiracy to hide the earlier offenses. They do not extend the duration of the original conspiracy to rob. Under the Model Penal Code, however, such problems of distinguishing conspiracies to keep prior offenses secret from an extension of the original conspiracy, rarely arise because once the object is committed the conspiracy to commit that offense is subsumed by the prosecution for the object offense.

Questions

1. *Multiple Objectives.* Does the conspiracy described in the hypothetical above, which includes both a kidnapping and a bank robbery, constitute two conspiracies or a single conspiracy?

2. *Scope.* Is late-coming Morris a co-conspirator only with Krule, with whom he has discussed the job? Or is he also a co-conspirator with DeSaco, with whom he has never talked? Must the answer to these two questions be the same: Is Morris a co-conspirator of DeSaco? Is DeSaco a co-conspirator of Morris?

3. *Conspiracy as Complicity.* Does Krule's membership in the conspiracy make him liable for DeSaco's murder of the guard? Is Morris liable for it? Is Handler?

4. *Duration.* Has the statute of limitations run for Krule? For DeSaco? For Handler? Is Handler's conduct an effective withdrawal? Does it trigger the running of the statute of limitations as to him? Does it trigger it as to the other conspirators? Do the subsequent meetings of the robbery conspirators extend the duration of the original conspiracy?

Bongo Sam Blows It

Phinimin violently opposes the draft. After participating in many protests, to no avail, he decides that more direct action is needed. He searches the protest meetings for a fellow draft-opponent who has a background in chemistry and electronics. Cocker seems to fit the bill. He asks Cocker to use his expertise to build a bomb to blow up the local Selective Service Office. Cocker refuses.

Phinimin subsequently finds Bongo Sam, who also has the necessary expertise. He approaches Bongo and Bongo agrees but is unenthusiastic about the project because he does not want to kill the Office's night watchman in the process. Phinimin explains that he too would prefer that the watchman not be killed but persuades Bongo of the need to sacrifice the watchman for the greater cause.

Bongo constructs the bomb and plants it in the Selective Service Office but is surprised and disappointed when the bomb does not detonate as planned. It is found, and an investigation traces it back to Bongo. Bongo is arrested and charged with attempted murder of the night watchman and attempted arson. He confesses and reveals Phinimin's involvement. An investigation of Phinimin reveals his earlier overture to Cocker. He is arrested and charged with two counts each of solicitation to commit murder and solicitation to commit arson. Is he liable?

Model Penal Code §5.02
Criminal Solicitation

(1) *Definition of Solicitation.* A person is guilty of solicitation to commit a crime if with the purpose of promoting or facilitating its commission he commands, encourages or requests another person to engage in specific conduct which would constitute such crime or an attempt to commit such crime or which would establish his complicity in its commission or attempted commission.

(2) *Uncommunicated Solicitation.* It is immaterial under Subsection (1) of this Section that the actor fails to communicate with the person he solicits to commit a crime if his conduct was designed to effect such communication.

(3) *Renunciation of Criminal Purpose.* It is an affirmative defense that the actor, after soliciting another person to commit a crime, persuaded him not to do so or otherwise prevented the commission of the crime, under circumstances manifesting a complete and voluntary renunciation of his criminal purpose.

Questions

1. *The Elements of Solicitation.* What must a prosecutor prove to hold a defendant liable for solicitation under the Model Penal Code? As to whether an actor must be purposeful as to the circumstance elements of the object offense, the Model Penal Code commentary notes that "the matter is deliberately left open here for the reasons that the [conspiracy] comment develops." Model Penal Code §5.02 comment 3, 371 n.23 (1985). The commentary does not specifically mention the culpability required as to a result element of the substantive offense. It simply notes that "5.02 preserves the traditional requirement of 'specific intent,' " id. at 371, then quotes the provision's purpose language, which is identical to that in conspiracy: The actor must have "the purpose of promoting or facilitating commission [of the offense]."

2. *Solicitation to Commit Arson.* Based upon his approach to Cocker, can Phinimin be held liable for conspiracy to commit arson (e.g., using Model Penal Code §220.1(1)(a))? Can he be held liable for solicitation of Cocker to commit arson? Based upon his approach to Bongo Sam, can Phinimin be held liable for solicitation to commit arson? Can he be liable for conspiracy with Bongo to commit arson? Will Bongo Sam be liable for attempted arson?

3. *Solicitation to Commit Murder.* Can Phinimin be held liable for

solicitation to commit murder, based upon his approach to either Cocker or Bongo? Can Bongo be held liable for attempted murder? Can Phinimin be held liable for conspiracy to commit murder (with Bongo)?

4. *Solicitation as Complicity.* A person who solicits another or aids (or agrees or attempts to aid) another to commit an offense is liable as an accomplice if the offense is committed (Model Penal Code §2.06(3)(a)) and, thus, is liable for the full substantive offense. (As we shall see when we examine complicity in Chapter 10, complicity is a theory by which an actor is held accountable for an offense; it is not itself a separate offense.) Model Penal Code §5.01(3) provides:

> *Conduct Designed to Aid Another in Commission to a Crime.* A person who engages in conduct designed to aid another to commit a crime, which would establish his complicity under Section 2.06 if the crime were committed by such other person, is guilty of an attempt to commit the crime, although the crime is not committed or attempted by such other person.

Assume complicity liability does not require culpability greater than that required for the substantive offense, i.e., no "elevation" of culpability as to the result and circumstance elements of the substantive offense. Even if an actor could not be held liable for solicitation because the actor did not satisfy the purpose requirement as to causing a result (e.g., Phinimin's lack of liability for solicitation of murder), might the same actor nonetheless be liable for attempt to commit the offense, under §5.01(3), quoted above? Would the same actor satisfy the requirements for attempt liability contained in the definition of attempt in §5.01(1)? Isn't it always the case that solicitation of another to commit a crime would give rise to complicity liability if the crime were committed and, therefore, will always give rise to attempt liability under §5.01(3) if the offense is not committed? If so, does §5.01(3) undercut the elevation of culpability to purpose in every instance in which solicitation is charged as an inchoate offense? Could §5.01(3) be used to circumvent the elevation-to-purpose requirement in conspiracy also?

SECTION 8.6 TERMINATION AND RENUNCIATION

If you steal a classmate's notes, suffer an attack of conscience, and return the notes before your classmate discovers their absence, you are nonetheless liable for theft. Generally, once the elements of a substantive offense are satisfied, the offense cannot be "undone." Inchoate offenses, built as they are upon a different theory of liability, do permit such renunciation defenses, at least in some jurisdictions. The theory may be that the actor's presumed willingness to commit the substantive offense, which is central to the rationale for punishing inchoate offenses, is undercut by the actor's voluntary renunciation before the offense is complete. The defense also may be a means by which actors are given an incentive to stop short of commission of the offense.

The Crays Go to Church

The Cray brothers, Morse, Frear, and Dunn, have hit on a great target for a robbery: the church collection monies. After reconnoitering, they determine that security is almost nonexistent. They decide to wait until the church is empty, then two of them will stand lookout, one at each end, while the other ducks into the minister's office and jimmies open his desk drawer where the money is kept.

The brothers each disguise their appearance and go to the church after the very lucrative Easter service is over. As they are waiting for the church to clear, Morse begins to have second thoughts. He reminds the others that the church helped them when they needed it, etc., until Dunn finally blows up. "If you're chicken, just leave!" he says through clenched teeth, attempting to whisper. "I'm going to leave, but I want you guys to come too." "No way," Dunn responds. Frear speaks up, "Look, Dunn. If Morse takes off, we can't do this job without getting caught. We need three people." "If you're chicken too, Frear, just take off with Morse." Morse and Frear get up to leave. After a word whispered between them, they each grab one of Dunn's arms and drag him out of the church. Their commotion draws a good deal of attention. When they get outside, they drop Dunn and the three scatter in different directions.

Twenty minutes later, after the church is quiet again, Dunn returns. He is still steaming about what his brothers did to him. He decides to show them that he can pull off the job by himself. When he sees his chance, he slips in and steals the money and makes it safely home. But he begins to think. Perhaps Morse is right about the church money. After some thought, he decides to return the money before it is missed. He sneaks back into the church and replaces the money in the minister's drawer. As he is coming out of the office, he runs into a policeman who had been called about the original commotion. An investigation turns up witnesses to both the original fiasco and Dunn's subsequent conduct. Dunn is charged with theft of over $1,000. Morse and Frear are identified and arrested, and charged as accomplices in the theft (based upon their help in reconnoitering the scene, etc.). All three also are charged with conspiracy to commit the theft. All three plead renunciation as a defense to all charges. Will they get it?

People v. Kimball
Court of Appeals of Michigan
109 Mich. App. 273, 311 N.W. 2d 343 (1981)

MAHER, Judge.
Defendant was charged with and convicted of attempted unarmed robbery at a bench trial conducted in early August of 1979. He was sentenced to a prison term of from three to five years and appeals by leave granted.

There is really very little dispute as to what happened on May 21, 1979, at the Alpine Party Store near Suttons Bay, Michigan. Instead, the dispute at trial centered on whether what took place amounted to a criminal offense or merely a bad joke. It appears that on the day in question the defendant went to the home of a friend, Sandra Storey, where he proceeded to consume a large amount of vodka mixed with orange juice. Defendant was still suffering from insect stings acquired the previous day so he also took a pill called "Eskaleth 300," containing 300 milligrams of Lithium, which Storey had given him. After about an hour, the pair mixed a half-gallon container of their favorite drinks (vodka and orange juice, in the defendant's case), and set off down the road in Storey's '74 MGB roadster. At approximately 8:15 or 8:30 in the evening, defendant (who was driving) pulled into the parking lot of the Alpine Party Store. Although he apparently did not tell Storey why he pulled in, defendant testified that the reason for the stop was to buy a pack of cigarettes.

Concerning events inside the store, testimony was presented by Susan Stanchfield, the clerk and sole employee present at the time. She testified that defendant came in and began talking and whistling at the Doberman Pinscher guard dog on duty at the time. She gave him a "dirty look," because she didn't want him playing with the dog. Defendant then approached the cash register, where Stanchfield was stationed, and demanded money. Stanchfield testified that she thought the defendant was joking, and told him so, until he demanded money again in a "firmer tone."

Stanchfield: By his tone I knew he meant business; that he wanted the money.
Prosecution: You felt he was serious?
Stanchfield: I knew he was serious.

Stanchfield then began fumbling with the one dollar bills until defendant directed her to the "big bills." Stanchfield testified that as she was separating the checks from the twenty dollar bills defendant said "I won't do it to you; you're good looking and I won't do it to you this time, but if you're here next time, it won't matter." A woman then came in (Storey) who put a hand on defendant's shoulder and another on his stomach and directed him out of the store. Stanchfield testified that she called after the defendant, saying that she would not call the police if he would "swear never to show your face around here again." To this defendant is alleged to have responded: "You could only get me on attempted anyway." Stanchfield then directed a customer to get the license plate number on defendant's car while she phoned the owner of the store.

Defendant also testified concerning events inside the store. He stated that the first thing he noticed when he walked in the door was the Doberman Pinscher. When he whistled the dog came to him and started licking his hand. Defendant testified that while he was petting the dog Stanchfield said "[w]atch out for the dog; he's trained to protect the premises."

Defendant: Well, as soon as she told me that the dog was a watchdog and a guarddog [sic], I just walked up in front of the cash register and said to Sue [Stanchfield]—I said, "I want your money." . . .

I was really loaded and it just seemed to me like—it was kind of a cliché because of the fact that they've got this big bad watchdog there that's supposed to watch the place and there I was just petting it, and it was kind of an open door to carry it a little further and say hey, I want all your money because this dog isn't going to protect you. It just kind of happened all at once. . . .

She said—I can't quote it, but something to the effect that if this is just a joke, it's a bad joke, and I said, "Just give me your big bills." . . .

Then she started fumbling in the drawer, and before she pulled any money out of the drawer—I don't know whether she went to the ones or the twenties—I said—as soon as she went toward the drawer to actually give me the money, I said, "Hey, I'm just kidding," and something to the effect that you're too good-looking to take your money. . . .

[A]nd she said, "Well, if you leave right now and don't ever come back, I won't call the police," and I said, "Okay, okay," and I started to back up. . . .

[A]nd Sandy [Storey]—I mean I don't know if I was stumbling back or stepping back, but I know she grabbed me, my arm, and said, "Let's go," and we turned around and left, and that was it.

Both Stanchfield and the defendant testified that there were other people in the store during the time that defendant was in the store, but the testimony of these people revealed that they did not hear what was said between Stanchfield and the defendant.

Storey testified that she remained in the car while defendant went into the store but that after waiting a reasonable time she went inside to see what was happening. As she approached the defendant she heard Stanchfield say "just promise you will never do that again and I won't take your license number." She then took defendant's arm, turned around, gave Stanchfield an "apologetic smile," and took defendant back to the car. Once in the car, defendant told Storey what had happened in the store, saying "but I told her [Stanchfield] I was only kidding." Defendant and Storey then drove to a shopping center where defendant was subsequently arrested.

The general attempt statute, under which defendant was prosecuted, provides in part as follows:

> Any person who shall attempt to commit an offense prohibited by law, and in such attempt shall do any act towards the commission of such offense, but shall fail in the perpetration, or shall be intercepted or prevented in the execution of the same, when no express provision is made by law for the punishment of such attempt, shall be punished. . . .

The elements of an attempt are (1) the specific intent to commit the crime attempted and (2) an overt act going beyond mere preparation towards the commission of the crime. Considering the second element first, it is clear that in the instant case defendant committed sufficient overt acts. As the trial court noted, there was evidence on every element of an unarmed robbery except for the actual taking of money. From the evidence presented, including the evidence of defendant's intoxication, the question of whether defendant undertook these acts with the specific intent to commit an unarmed robbery is a much closer question. After hearing all the evidence, however, the trial court found that defendant possessed the requisite intent and we do not believe that finding was clearly erroneous.

Defendant raised an additional defense in the trial court. Assuming that he committed the necessary overt acts with the requisite specific intent, defendant contended that he was not guilty because he voluntarily abandoned his criminal enterprise before consummating the offense attempted. The defense was rooted in the language of the attempt statute, which refers to a person doing an act towards the commission of an offense and adds: "but shall *fail* in the perpetration, or shall be *intercepted* or *prevented* in the execution of the same." Defendant argued that, under the statute, a person who abandons a criminal scheme of his or her own volition, instead of through the intervention of outside forces, has not committed an attempt. The prosecution argued that once the defendant had committed an overt act with the requisite intent, a punishable attempt had occurred which could not subsequently be abandoned. The trial court rejected defendant's arguments, holding that an attempt may still be shown even if the defendant fails to consummate the offense attempted due to a mere lack of [perseverance]. On appeal, defendant contends that the trial court erred in rejecting the legal basis of his defense.

Regardless of what else might be said on the subject, the authorities are in agreement that it is no defense that a defendant fails to carry through to completion the crime attempted because of the intervention of outside forces, because circumstances turn out to be different than expected, or because the defendant meets more resistance than expected. On the issue of voluntary renunciation of criminal purpose after an overt act beyond preparation but before the completion of the attempted crime, however, there are few reported cases nationwide and no general consensus. . . .

Despite the lack of direction from the cases, the issue has continuously intrigued commentators and the authors of proposed criminal codes. Some commentators have espoused the traditional view that voluntary abandonment is not a defense where the elements of an attempt are already established, although it may be relevant to the issue of whether defendant possessed the requisite intent in the first place. Under this view, once a defendant has gone so far as to have committed a punishable attempt, the crime is "complete" and he or she cannot then abandon the crime and avoid liability anymore than a thief can abandon a larceny by returning the stolen goods. Other commentators, however, emphasizing the differences between attempts and other crimes and focusing on the purpose of the law of attempts, contend that a truly voluntary abandonment of the attempted offense should be recognized as a defense to the attempt as well. This view was early on expressed by Wharton: "If an attempt be voluntarily and freely abandoned before the act is put in process of final execution, there being no outside cause prompting such abandonment, then this is a defense. . . ." Perkins, while acknowledging that this was not the "accepted view" at common law, nevertheless concedes that Wharton's position "has much to commend it. . . ."

[T]he drafters of various modern criminal codes have incorporated the defense of voluntary abandonment into the law of attempts. Section 5.01(4) of the Model Penal Code recognizes as a defense to an attempt crime the abandonment of efforts to commit the crime attempted under circumstances manifesting a complete and voluntary renunciation of criminal purpose. Based on this section of the Model Penal Code, the authors of the Michigan Second Revised Criminal Code recognized voluntary renunciation of criminal purpose as an affirmative defense to a prosecution for attempt. The comments to §5.01 of the Model Penal Code (quoted extensively in the Michigan committee commentary) explain the bounds of the defense and the reasons for its recognition:

> By a "voluntary" abandonment is meant a change in the actor's purpose not influenced by outside circumstances, what may be termed repentance or change of heart. Lack of resolution or timidity may suffice. A reappraisal by the actor of the criminal sanctions hanging over his conduct would presumably be a motivation of the voluntary type as long as the actor's fear of the law is not related to a particular threat of apprehension or detection. . . .
>
> The basis for allowing the defense involves two related considerations.
>
> First, renunciation of criminal purpose tends to negative dangerousness. As previously indicated, much of the effort devoted to excluding early "preparatory" conduct from criminal attempt liability is based on the desire not to punish where there is an insufficient showing that the actor has a firm purpose to commit the crime contemplated. In cases where the actor has gone beyond the line drawn for preparation, indicating *prima facie* sufficient firmness of purpose, he should be allowed to rebut such a conclusion by showing that he has plainly demonstrated his lack of firm purpose by completely renouncing his purpose to commit the crime. . . .
>
> A second reason for allowing renunciation of criminal purpose as a defense to an attempt charge is to encourage actors to desist from pressing forward with their criminal designs, thereby diminishing the risk that the substantive crime will be committed. While, under the proposed subsection, such encouragement is held out at all stages of the criminal effort, its significance becomes greatest as the actor nears his criminal objective and the risk that the crime will be completed is correspondingly high. At the very point where abandonment least influences a judgment as to the dangerousness of the actor—where the last proximate act has been committed but the resulting crime can still be avoided—the inducement to desist stemming from the abandonment defense achieves its greatest value.
>
> It is possible, of course, that the defense of renunciation of criminal purpose may add to the incentives to take the *first* steps toward crime. Knowledge that criminal endeavors can be undone with impunity may encourage preliminary steps that would not be undertaken if liability inevitably attached to every abortive criminal undertaking that proceeded beyond preparation. But this is not a serious problem. First, any consolation the actor might draw from the abandonment defense would have to be tempered with the knowledge that the defense would be unavailable if the actor's purposes were frustrated by external forces before he had an opportunity to abandon his effort. Second, the encouragement this defense might lend to the actor taking preliminary steps would be a factor only where the actor was dubious of his plans and where, consequently, the probability of continuance was not great.
>
> On balance, it is concluded that renunciation of criminal purpose should be a defense to a criminal attempt charge because, as to the early

stages of an attempt, it significantly negatives dangerousness of character, and, as to later stages, the value of encouraging desistance outweighs the net dangerousness shown by the abandoned criminal effort.

Model Penal Code, (Tentative Draft No. 10, 1960), §5.01(4), pp. 69-73. (Footnotes omitted, emphasis in original.)

The authorities do recognize a limitation on the defense of abandonment. If a defendant has taken the last proximate step toward the completion of the attempted offense and is powerless to prevent its consummation, yet fails to actually commit the ultimate offense for other reasons, it may be too late to abandon the criminal purpose and avoid liability for the attempt. A popular example concerns a defendant who, with the intent to kill, fires a shot toward the intended victim but misses the mark altogether or succeeds only in wounding his enemy. Under such circumstances, it would not be a defense to show that the intent to kill was abandoned after the shot was fired. On the other hand, a defendant who lights the fuse of a bomb but repents and stomps out the fuse before the explosion should be allowed to assert voluntary abandonment as a defense. In this second example, the possibility of avoiding criminal liability altogether, even at the last second, encourages the defendant to prevent the greater harm from taking place. As the comments to the Model Penal Code suggest, such encouragement is most important in these final seconds.

As noted above, the issue presented is one of first impression in this state. We are persuaded by the trend of modern authority and hold that voluntary abandonment is an affirmative defense to a prosecution for criminal attempt. The burden is on the defendant to establish by a preponderance of the evidence[7] that he or she has voluntarily and completely abandoned his or her criminal purpose. Abandonment is not "voluntary" when the defendant fails to complete the attempted crime because of unanticipated difficulties, unexpected resistance, or circumstances which increase the probability of detention or apprehension. Nor is the abandonment "voluntary" when the defendant fails to consummate the attempted offense after deciding to postpone the criminal conduct until another time or to substitute another victim or another but similar objective. Such a holding is not at odds with the terms of the statute, which refer to one who "fails," is "prevented," or is "intercepted" before completion of the attempted offense. Such language lends itself to a holding that voluntary abandonment is a defense.

In the instant case, the trial court recognized that involuntary

---

7. It is not unconstitutional to place this burden on the defendant since voluntary abandonment does not negate any element of the offense.

abandonment is not a defense, but it also rejected defendant's claim that voluntary abandonment was a defense. As a result, the trial court never determined whether defendant's abandonment was voluntary or involuntary. Accordingly, defendant's conviction is reversed and this case is remanded for a new trial at which defendant may present a defense of voluntary abandonment according to the guidelines set forth in this opinion. We recognize that the judge who presided at defendant's trial was forced to decide the issue without benefit of precedent established by the appellate courts of this state. We are persuaded, however, that the defense of voluntary abandonment is in accord with the rationale of the law of attempts and that the defendant is entitled to present such a defense.

Reversed and remanded.

KALLMAN, Judge (dissenting).

I respectfully dissent. The facts clearly show the elements of an attempt in this case. There was a specific intent to commit unarmed robbery. There were overt acts that went beyond mere preparation. The clerk was getting the money out of the cash register for the defendant at his command. The attempted unarmed robbery had been completed.

The question then arises that if the attempt has been accomplished, why did the defendant suddenly discontinue the efforts necessary to complete the criminal act. We have before us a record, and that is all we can rely on. This record reflects a number of reasons why the criminal act may have been terminated:

1) The defendant's statements that he wouldn't do it to her *this time* because you're good looking.[1]
2) As defendant made this statement a woman came in and directed defendant out of the store.
3) There were other people in the store while defendant was there and the record does not reveal the effect this may have had on defendant's choosing to discontinue the crime.

The statute, as quoted in the majority opinion, reads in part: "but shall fail in the perpetration, *or*. . . ." (Emphasis added.)

One notes here that the statute is in the disjunctive. Granted, the defendant was not *intercepted* or *prevented* from completing the crime. However, under the statute he clearly *failed* in the perpetration of the crime, whatever the reason. The statute does not say that if a defendant voluntarily discontinues the criminal act the attempt fails. Nor does it say if a defendant involuntarily discontinues the criminal act the attempt

---

1. But note he said that next time he'd do it even if she were there. The criminal intent had not been abandoned.

succeeds. Where the statute, as here, says that when a defendant *shall fail* in the perpetration of a crime, that is enough to convict for an attempt. The statute is clear and unambiguous, clearly permitting, under the facts in this case, a conviction for an attempt.

In People v. Stephens, 84 Mich. App. 250, 255, 269 N.W.2d 552, Judge Beasley stated: "I would agree with the trial court that it was legally too late for defendant Stephens to abandon his criminal intent."

That is the situation in this case. The defendant had progressed too far into the crime to assert now the defense of voluntary abandonment. This was even recognized by the defendant when he told Stanchfield (unrebutted testimony): "You could only get me on attempted anyway."

I would affirm the conviction and sentence.

Model Penal Code §5.01(4)
Renunciation of Attempt

When the actor's conduct would otherwise constitute an attempt under Subsection (1)(b) or (1)(c) of this Section, it is an affirmative defense that he abandoned his effort to commit the crime or otherwise prevented its commission, under circumstances manifesting a complete and voluntary renunciation of his criminal purpose. The establishment of such defense does not, however, affect the liability of an accomplice who did not join in such abandonment or prevention.

Within the meaning of this Article, renunciation of criminal purpose is not voluntary if it is motivated, in whole or in part, by circumstances, not present or apparent at the inception of the actor's course of conduct, which increase the probability of detection or apprehension or which make more difficult the accomplishment of the criminal purpose. Renunciation is not complete if it is motivated by a decision to postpone the criminal conduct until a more advantageous time or to transfer the criminal effort to another but similar objective or victim.

Model Penal Code §5.02(3)
Renunciation of Solicitation

It is an affirmative defense that the actor, after soliciting another person to commit a crime, persuaded him not to do so or otherwise prevented the commission of the crime, under circumstances manifesting a complete and voluntary renunciation of his criminal purpose.

Model Penal Code §5.03(6)
Renunciation of Conspiracy

It is an affirmative defense that the actor, after conspiring to commit a crime, thwarted the success of the conspiracy, under circumstances manifesting a complete and voluntary renunciation of his criminal purpose.

Model Penal Code §2.06(6)(c)
Termination of Complicity

Unless otherwise provided by the Code or by the law defining the offense, a person is not an accomplice in an offense committed by another person if: . . .
    (c) he terminates his complicity prior to the commission of the offense and
        (i) wholly deprives it of effectiveness in the commission of the offense; or
        (ii) gives timely warning to the law enforcement authorities or otherwise makes proper effort to prevent the commission of the offense.

Questions

1. *Theft Defenses.* Is Dunn's renunciation and return a defense to the theft charge?

2. *Complicity Defenses and Attempt Defenses.* Do Morse and Frear have a defense to complicity in the theft? If they do have a defense to theft, are they nonetheless liable for attempted theft?

3. *Conspiracy Defenses.* Does Morse have a defense to the charge of conspiracy to commit theft? Does Frear? Does Dunn?

4. *Renunciation vs. Termination.* What are the differences in requirements of the renunciation and termination defenses to attempt, solici-

tation, conspiracy, and complicity? What are the reasons for the differences in requirements?

5. *Renunciation and Grading Inchoate Offenses.* If a jurisdiction reduces the grade of an inchoate offense from the grade that would be imposed for the completed offense, as most jurisdictions do, is it necessary to provide a renunciation defense to give an actor an incentive to stop short of an offense? If a jurisdiction rejects the Model Penal Code provision that grades inchoate conduct the same as the completed offense, would you expect it to keep or reject the Code's renunciation defense? Most keep it. Why might this be?

III/IMPUTING OFFENSE ELEMENTS

Chapter 9. INTRODUCTION TO IMPUTATION

Part II of this coursebook describes how offenses are defined. Typically, an actor is liable for an offense if and only if she satisfies the elements of an offense definition. There are two kinds of exceptions to this rule. First, an actor may be *liable* for an offense even though she does *not* satisfy all offense elements if a rule or doctrine imputes the missing element. Secondly, an actor *escapes liability* even though she *does* satisfy the elements of an offense if she satisfies the conditions of a general defense. General defenses are discussed in Part IV. This Part examines doctrines of imputation. This introductory chapter provides some examples of imputation, as well as a discussion of the imputation process generally.

Notes on the Imputation of Offense Elements

Criticisms of Imputation Some writers have suggested that the imposition of liability absent a required element of the offense is illogical and immoral. In Director of Public Prosecutions v. Majewski,[1] for example, the defendant argued that it is both illogical and unethical to impute to a defendant a culpable state of mind (for assault) that he in fact did not have (because he was voluntarily intoxicated). The defendant relies upon a passage from Lord Hailsham in Director of Prosecutions v. Morgan:

> [O]nce it be accepted that an intent of whatever description is an ingredient essential to the guilt of the accused I cannot myself see that any other direction [than requiring proof of the intent] can be logically acceptable. Otherwise a jury would in effect be told to find an intent where none existed or where none was proved to have existed. I cannot myself reconcile it with my conscience to sanction as part of the English law what I

---

1. [1976] 2 All E.R. 142.

regard as logical impossibility, and, if there were any authority which, if accepted, would compel me to do so, I would feel constrained to declare that it was not to be followed.[2]

Imputation as a Common and Accepted Basis of Liability But, just as many general defenses commonly are recognized—which exculpate despite satisfaction of the paradigm elements of the offense—many doctrines of imputation are common and well-established. That is, many traditional doctrines inculpate an actor despite the absence of a "required" element of the offense definition. If, for example, an actor causes another person to engage in illegal conduct, the actor may be liable for an offense defined to require such conduct although in fact the actor has not performed the conduct that the offense requires. The actor is held liable despite this absent element because the conduct of the other person is imputed under the doctrine of complicity or causing crime by an innocent. Similarly, a requisite culpable state of mind commonly is imputed to an actor if he would have had the culpable state of mind but for his voluntary intoxication. These familiar results follow from special rules governing complicity and voluntary intoxication. There is no suggestion that the actor in fact satisfies the required element. In each instance, the special conditions required by the doctrine of imputation are said to justify treating the actor *as if* he or she satisfies the imputed element.

Imputation Principles as Independent of Offense A legislature could conceivably include inculpatory (and exculpatory) exceptions to the offense paradigm within the offense definition.[3] Typically, this is not done, because a general provision defining the conditions of imputation (or defense) give ease and theoretical clarity. Like the general defenses, such as insanity, duress, and law enforcement authority, which are separate and apart from any offense definition, the rules of imputation represent principles of liability independent of any offense. Also like general defenses, most of the doctrines of imputed liability, at least theoretically, can impute a required element of any offense. Some may tend to apply to certain recurring factual situations: Transferred intent appears most commonly in bad-aim murder cases. But this is a factual rather than a theoretical limitation of the principles. The use of general imputation provisions also is efficient. Such general provisions can be stated once, in as much detail as is needed, yet can be applied to all offenses.

Scrutinizing Imputation Rationale Rather than Process It is not the mechanism of imputation that deserves criticism but rather those doc-

---

2. *Morgan*, [1975] 2 All E.R. 347, 360, quoted in *Majewski*, [1976] 2 All E.R. at 166.
3. Arson, for example, is defined in Tennessee to include complicity in arson: "[A]ny person who willfully and maliciously sets fire to or burns, causes to be burned,

trines of imputation in which the special conditions required do not fully justify the imputation that follows, that is, do not justify treating the actor the same as if he satisfied the missing element. Defenses—exceptions to the offense paradigm that redound to the defendant's benefit—typically are supported by articulable, rational explanations. Can one articulate sound theoretical and practical reasons to support each inculpating exception? In the description of imputation doctrines that follow, many have a sound justification. In some doctrines, however, the justification for the imputation seems weak or unpersuasive. The crucial theoretical issue in each instance is: Do the special conditions of the doctrine justify treating the actor as if he satisfies the missing element?

Doctrines Imputing Objective Elements American criminal law permits the imputation of both objective and culpability elements of an offense. While the most obvious and common instances of imputing objective elements are found in the rules governing complicity, such rules are only one of several doctrines that impose liability even though the defendant has not satisfied all of the objective elements of an offense.[4] Where an actor exercises control over an innocent person's actions, the latter's satisfaction of an objective element of an offense may be imputed to the former as an instance of "causing crime by an innocent."[5] Various statutory and judicial presumptions permit the imposition of liability even though the evidence adduced at trial would not establish all the objective elements of the offense.[6] On occasion, the doctrines of "substituted culpability" and "transferred mens rea" have been formulated in reverse, to operate as doctrines of "substituted objective elements"[7] and "transferred actus reus,"[8] which would impute a missing objective element and thereby hold the actor liable for the

---

or who aids, counsels or procures the burning of any house . . . shall be guilty of arson. . . ." Tenn. Code Ann. §39-3-202 (1982) (emphasis added).

4. See Model Penal Code §2.06(3), discussed in Section 10.1.

5. See Model Penal Code §2.06(2)(a), discussed in Section 10.2.

6. See, e.g., Tenn. Code Ann. §39-1-507 (1982) (presumption of manufacture of moonshine from assembly of still).

7. For example, assume an actor believes he is burglarizing a store while he in fact burglarizes a dwelling (a different offense), he may be convicted of the offense of burglarizing a store even though an element of the offense, "store," is not satisfied. The existence of a comparable objective element in the actual offense, "dwelling," is used as a justification for imputing the required objective element of the offense charged. This is one of the approaches originally proposed by the drafters of the Model Penal Code but ultimately rejected in favor of current Model Penal Code §2.04(2). See Model Penal Code §2.04(2) comment 2 at 137 (Tent. Draft No. 4, 1955). Kentucky and West Virginia have adopted this approach. See Ky §501.070(2); W. Va. (p) §61-2-7(b).

8. Where *A* shoots at *B* but hits *C*, the objective element of the death of *C* may be "transferred" to justify holding *A* liable for the intentional homicide of *B*, at whom he was shooting. See Mayweather v. State, 29 Ariz. 460, 462, 242 P. 864, 865 (1926).

offense intended. Thus, an actor who commits statutory rape but who, because of his mistake as to the true identity of his partner, believes he is instead committing incest, can be held liable for incest although he is not related to his partner. Modern codes more frequently adopt doctrines of "substituted culpability" and "transferred mens rea,"[9] which hold the actor liable for the offense he in fact commits, imputing to him the missing culpability requirements. Finally, the rules imposing liability for omissions, when the offense charged is defined only in terms of affirmative conduct, also may be viewed as instances of imputed conduct.[10]

Doctrines Imputing Culpability Elements Another group of doctrines impute a required culpability element. The most common of these doctrines shapes the law governing voluntary intoxication.[11] Also imputing a culpable state of mind, the doctrine of "transferred intent" imputes the required culpability to an actor who intends to harm one person but actually harms another. Imputation also is accomplished through a device that may be termed "substituted culpability." The doctrine uses an actor's culpability for the offense he thought he was committing as the basis for imputing to him the intention required for the offense that he in fact committed.[12] Courts that permit suspension of the requirement of concurrence between act and intent make a similar imputation: An actor's earlier intention to commit an act that he believes is the offense is relied upon to impute to him the required intention during his later conduct that actually constitutes the offense.[13] Finally, as with objective elements, a variety of statutory and judicial presumptions effectively impute culpability elements, upon proof of a logically related fact.

Doctrines Imputing Both Objective and Culpability Elements Other rules impute both objective and culpability elements. If *A* and *B* conspire to rob a bank and *B* purposely kills a guard, both the killing and the purposeful culpability as to killing may be imputed to *A* under the *Pinkerton* doctrine.[14] The common law's "natural and probable consequence" rule in complicity law analogously expands the liability of accomplices.[15] Similarly, the complicity aspect of the felony-murder rule

---

9. These are the subject of Chapter 11.
10. This is the subject of Chapter 13.
11. This is the subject of Chapter 12.
12. This is the subject of Chapter 11.
13. Recall the *Thabo Mali* case from the Section 4.2 discussion of the concurrence requirement.
14. The *Pinkerton* case is discussed in Section 8.5, relating to the collateral consequences of conspiracy.
15. Under this rule, "an accessory is liable for any criminal act which in the ordinary course of things was the natural or probable consequence of the crime that he advised or commanded, although such consequence may not have been intended by him." 22 C.J.S. Criminal Law §92 (1961).

imputes both objective and culpability elements to the accomplice. Finally, vicarious liability, and its special subclass governing the liability of officials of organizations, may impute offense elements to an actor because of the actor's relationship to another.[16] This is not an exhaustive list of the criminal law's instances of imputation.

Codified Doctrines of Imputation There are at least four instances of substantive if not formal imputation: the aggravation of culpability in felony murder,[17] possession offenses,[18] status offenses,[19] and strict liability offenses.[20] These are not formal instances of imputation because each offense is defined such that it does not formally require the "imputed" element. That is, liability is imposed only upon proof of all the elements of the formal definition of the offense. There is reason to believe, however, that the statutory definition itself embraces principles of imputation rather than a complete statement of the paradigm conditions for liability in such cases.

Qualifications on the Claim of Codified Imputations One may well challenge the claim that each of these four classes of offenses are designed to punish criminal conduct other than that described in their formal definition and that the elements of the *true* paradigm are im-

---

16. The liability of corporate officials is the subject of Section 14.1.
17. Felony murder is the subject of Section 4.3.
18. Possession offenses seek to prohibit and punish not possession itself, but harmful conduct, past or future, that is facilitated and evidenced by the possession. The possession of trace amounts of narcotics, for example, suggests their past use or distribution. The possession of burglar's tools suggest a planned (or past) burglary. In addition to punishing possession of narcotics and burglar's tools, many jurisdictions punish possession of counterfeiting dyes, dangerous weapons, motor vehicle master keys, or drug paraphernalia. Possession offenses are discussed in Section 8.1.
19. Status offenses are analogous to possession offenses; the definition does not represent the true paradigm of the offense. Vagrancy statutes, for example, common before they were subject to constitutional challenge, punish the conduct and culpability of attempted theft. For example, in 1547 the preamble to the "Slavery Act," a vagrancy statute, noted: "Idleness and vagabondry is the mother and root of all thefts, robberies, and all evil acts, and other mischiefs. . . ." An Act for the Punishment of Vagabonds, 1547, 1 Edw. 6, ch. 3. They frequently have been replaced by "loitering or prowling" offenses, which are designed to prohibit and punish a variety of preparatory criminal conduct. The drafters of the Model Penal Code, for example, rejected the concept of status criminality and proposed instead a "suspicious loitering" offense that punishes one whose conduct justifies suspicion that he is about to engage in criminal activity. Model Penal Code §250.12 (Tent. Draft No. 13, 1961). Section 250.12 was subsequently modified to require justifiable "alarm" for the safety of persons or property. Id. §2506 (1980). Under loitering and prowling offenses, elements of a preparatory offense are in effect imputed upon proof of loitering or prowling. Status offenses are discussed further in Section 8.1.
20. Strict liability offenses are a fourth instance of codified imputed liability, although the characterization is more tenuous here. While the definition of a strict liability offense does not formally contain a culpable state-of-mind element, a vast literature supports the normative claim that culpability should be required in all offenses. Strict liability is discussed in Section 7.2.

puted upon proof of the conditions stated in the offense's formal definition. One might argue that the definitions do accurately represent a paradigm, one that simply rejects the traditional requirements of harmful or evil conduct and personal culpability that are typical of other offense definitions. This line of argument is more successful against some claims of codified imputation than with others. It would seem difficult to argue that possession alone really is the harm or evil sought to be prohibited and punished by possession offenses. One might argue that pure status offenses and strict liability offenses define a punishable harm or evil, but this characterization is possible only if one is willing to reject the notions of act and culpability as universal requirements for criminal liability. Many would be unwilling to do so. Slightly more defensible is the claim that felony murder represents an independent harm or evil in which the traditional culpability for murder really is not relevant.

Theories and Rationales for Imputed Liability Given the variety of rules and doctrines of imputed liability, one may reasonably question whether there is any similarity in their supporting rationales. Yet four theories can be identified that commonly are used to support imputed liability. Reflecting the tensions in criminal law generally, some of these justifications adhere closely to the requirement of personal blameworthiness as a prerequisite for criminal liability, while others rely on more utilitarian concerns.[21]

Causal Theory In many instances, an actor will be held accountable despite the absence of a required offense element because he or she is causally responsible for the conduct of another or for the absence of a required state of mind in himself or another. In the case of objective conduct elements, the actor may have caused another or assisted another in performance of the required conduct. In the case of mental elements, the actor may have caused the absence of the required mental state in himself or another by external means, such as intoxicants, or through simple "deliberate blindness" to the circumstances or consequences of his own conduct or the conduct of another. This "causal theory" generally corresponds well to our collective notions of blameworthiness.

Equivalency Theory In some instances, however, while there may be a community consensus that an element should be imputed because the actor is as blameworthy as if he had in fact satisfied the element, there is no analytic theory to support the consensus. Rather, the best one can do is to restate the conclusion: The actor is as blameworthy as one who satisfies the element. The doctrine of transferred intent is illustrative. The label itself, cast in terms of transferring intention,

---

21. For a more detailed discussion, see Robinson, Imputed Criminal Liability, 93 Yale L.J. 609 (1984).

somewhat deceptively suggests an analytic process, but the best explanation of why the intent to shoot the desired victim should be "transferred" to the actual victim is that both intentions seem equally culpable. The theory is merely one of apparent equivalence. The Model Penal Code reveals its reliance upon such an "equivalency theory" when it provides that:

> Although ignorance or mistake would otherwise afford a defense to the offense charged [i.e., would negative a required culpability element], the defense is not available if the defendant would be guilty of another offense had the situation been as he supposed.[22]

The rationale for imputing the absent state of mind is simply that the actor had the intention (or other level of culpability) to commit another offense and therefore is as blameworthy, and can properly be treated, as if he had the required intention for the offense committed.

Adherence to Blameworthiness Principle Both the causal and the equivalency theory correspond to our notions of blame and are consistent with a criminal law that seeks to distribute liability in proportion to blameworthiness. Under either theory, the requirements of the imputation doctrine together with the satisfied elements of the offense, assure a degree of blameworthiness that approximates that of the offense charged. Because a causal theory both tracks blameworthiness and provides a clear analytic foundation for imputation, it may be the preferred justification for imputation. Where a strong causal theory is available, no other rationale is necessary.[23] Because of analytic shortcomings, an equivalency theory fails to provide a general principle for discovering and supporting analogous instances of imputation. Every claim of equivalency must be justified by an independent demonstration of consensus.

Evidentiary Theory A third theory eschews strictly proportioning liability to blameworthiness, primarily because of practical problems of proof. Thus, doctrines of imputation supported by this theory may generate liability disproportionate to blame. It may sometimes (even frequently) be the case that proportionate blameworthiness does exist,

---

22. Model Penal Code §2.04(2). This provision is discussed in Section 11.2.
23. In Moore v. State, 267 Ind. 270, 369 N.E.2d 628 (1977), for example, the court rejected defendant's contention that he was not guilty of burglary since he did not "break" into the victim's residence because the victim unlocked the door at gun point. But the court concluded that the defendant "was *as guilty of breaking as if* he had taken the keys from her hand and unlocked the door himself" (emphasis added). The causal argument for this type of causing crime by an innocent is so compelling that the court need not have relied upon the more vague equivalency rationale that the quoted language suggests. The actor is as culpable as if he had engaged in the prohibited conduct himself, because he caused the element to be satisfied by another.

but the prosecution need not prove requirements that would demonstrate such blame. Such proof requirements, it is argued, would allow many culpable persons to escape conviction or would make convictions too costly to obtain.[24] Such an "evidentiary theory" for imputing a required element balances the competing interests of fairness and utility. As a result, the rules and doctrines supported by this theory are the subject of considerable controversy.

Response to Practical Prosecution Concerns To accept an evidentiary rationale, one must be willing to accept potentially erroneous convictions in exchange for increased ease of prosecution. The latter interest goes beyond concern for the convenience of prosecutors. Difficulties in successful prosecutions permit dangerous criminals to escape conviction. The evidentiary advantage of such imputation can reduce the number of such dangerous acquittals. Rules relying upon evidentiary rationales are thus subject to the criticisms presented in the broader debate over evidentiary advantages for the prosecution generally. Evidentiary rationales comprise a specialized subgroup of nonculpability rationales. Rather than rejecting the validity of the blameworthiness principle, such evidentiary theories seek to approximate the desired results of the principle as closely as the problems of proof permit.

Crime Control Theory Finally, in still other instances of imputation, proportionality between liability and blameworthiness is sacrificed on utilitarian grounds to other important societal interests, most commonly crime control. Such a "crime control theory" for imputing required objective and mental elements often supports strict liability doctrines, for example. In each instance the need to reduce future crime is offered as the justification for imputing a required element even though the conditions of imputation do not suggest that the actor is (or even probably is) as blameworthy as the resulting liability normally would require. Typically, this is done because the actor, although not so blameworthy, is seen as dangerous or is seen as an effective example by which others can be deterred.[25]

Desert vs. Utilitarian Dispute Crime control rationales are the most susceptible to criticism and should be the least favored in supporting imputation. Such rationales must justify not simply the creation of an evidentiary shortcut to proving the presence of required offense elements, as in evidentiary rationales; they also must justify the injustice of liability disproportionate to blame. Crime control rationales there-

---

24. The evidentiary theory is most often employed to support imputation of mental rather than objective elements. One would expect such a pattern of application since the evidentiary rationale responds to problems of proof, and proof of mental elements is more difficult than proof of objective elements.

25. See Section 7.2 (Minimum Culpability Requirements: The Debate Over Recklessness, Negligence, and Strict Liability).

fore implicate the broader debate over whether criminal law should serve a utilitarian crime-control purpose or should punish only according to the degree of an actor's personal blameworthiness.

Overlapping Rationales These four theories—causal, equivalency, evidentiary, and crime control—do not provide categories of imputation doctrines but rather are explanations or justifications for imputing an absent element of an offense definition. It is possible, even likely, that more than one theory may justify some doctrines, while only a combination of two or more theories or rationales can adequately explain others. In each instance, examination of the underlying rationale provides a basis for assessing the legitimacy and persuasiveness of the reasons for imputation.

Summary The definition of an offense describes the elements normally required to hold an actor liable for the offense; it is that offense's paradigm for liability. Despite the absence of a required element of the definition, however, an actor may be held liable for the offense if a doctrine imputes the absent elements. Such a doctrine does not alter the definition of the offense but rather provides an alternative means of establishing the required elements, or at least an alternative means of holding the defendant liable as if the required elements were satisfied. For the most part, the principles underlying imputation reflect concerns beyond those of the offense at hand; a single doctrine of imputation may apply to a range of offenses or to all offenses. As a group, instances of imputed liability play as significant a role in criminal law theory and practice as do general defenses.

Chapter 10. COMPLICITY AND CAUSING CRIME BY AN INNOCENT

Offense definitions typically require that the actor perform certain conduct. An actor may be held liable for an offense, however, even though he or she does not satisfy its conduct requirement, if another's conduct satisfying the requirement can be imputed to the actor. It is the doctrines of complicity and causing crime by an innocent that define the conditions under which such imputation can occur. The general reasoning is as follows: Where an actor satisfies the conditions of these doctrines, the principles for distributing liability ought to apply to him the same *as if* he had engaged in the conduct himself. After reviewing the doctrinal requirements for such liability, we shall have to examine whether the requirements of these doctrines support such a conclusion.

The doctrine typically distinguishes between two kinds of instances in which another's conduct is imputed. Where the actor assists a criminal confederate, "an accomplice," in committing the offense conduct, the complicity doctrine applies. Where the actor causes an innocent or irresponsible person to perform the offense conduct, a different doctrine with different requirements is used. The following sections develop the reasons for the distinction.

SECTION 10.1 COMPLICITY

Bib Tries to Help

Having failed to pass several grades in grammar school, Muscle and Bib are 21-year-old seniors at K Street High School. Muscle is interested in dating a young freshman, Susan Rigg, but Susan's older brother, John, with whom she has lived since her parents died, has made it clear that he does not want Muscle associating with Susan. Susan nonetheless has encouraged Muscle's interest and this has resulted in several confrontations between the two men. The latest has left Muscle steaming and only more determined than ever to pursue Susan.

Muscle arranges with Susan for a rendezvous at John's house while John is away at his night job, and asks Bib to come along as a lookout. "Goin' over there's not a good idea," Bib warns. "She's probably jail bait." "Let me worry about her age. You just keep your eyes open." "Yeh, and what if big brother shows up?" "He won't give me any trouble. I'll bring my .45." Bib smiles. "You're a buster."

Muscle and Bib drive to Susan's house, where they find Susan waiting on the stoop. Muscle disappears upstairs with Susan. Bib settles in the car for a long wait but soon slips into a snooze. A rattle at the front door wakes him. John Rigg is back. Bib hits the horn to alert Muscle but it won't sound with the ignition off. As he heads for the house, he hears shouts and one shot from inside. He finds John in a pool of blood just inside the front doorway. Muscle and Bib flee but are arrested within hours. Muscle is charged and convicted of the murder of John Rigg, who dies before police arrive, and of the statutory rape of Susan Rigg, who is 14 years old. Bib is charged as an accomplice to both offenses. Is Bib liable?

Model Penal Code §2.06(1)-(4)
Liability for Conduct of Another; Complicity

(1) A person is guilty of an offense if it is committed by his own conduct or by the conduct of another person for which he is legally accountable, or both.

(2) A person is legally accountable for the conduct of another person when:

    (a) acting with the kind of culpability that is sufficient for the commission of the offense, he causes an innocent or irresponsible person to engage in such conduct; or

    (b) he is made accountable for the conduct of such other person by the Code or by the law defining the offense; or

    (c) he is an accomplice of such other person in the commission of the offense.

(3) A person is an accomplice of another person in the commission of an offense if:

    (a) with the purpose of promoting or facilitating the commission of the offense, he

        (i) solicits such other person to commit it; or

        (ii) aids or agrees or attempts to aid such other person in planning or committing it; or

(iii) having a legal duty to prevent the commission of the offense, fails to make proper effort so to do; or

(b) his conduct is expressly declared by law to establish his complicity.

(4) When causing a particular result is an element of an offense, an accomplice in the conduct causing such result is an accomplice in the commission of that offense, if he acts with the kind of culpability, if any, with respect to that result that is sufficient for the commission of the offense.

State ex rel. Martin, Atty. Gen. v. Tally, Judge
Supreme Court of Alabama
102 Ala. 25, 15 So. 722 (1894)

McCLELLAN, J. . . .

[Judge John B. Tally was charged by information with complicity in the murder of one Ross. Tally was the brother-in-law of the Skeltons, who pursued Ross to kill him because he had seduced their sister. Tally stood guard at the telegraph office in Scottsboro to prevent Ross from being warned of the pursuit of the Skeltons. When a kinsman of Ross sent him a warning telegram, Judge Tally sent another immediately after it, directing the telegraph operator at the other end, William Huddleston, "Do not let the party warned get away. Say nothing."]

. . . We [find] that John B. Tally, with full knowledge that the Skeltons were in pursuit of Ross with the intent to take his life, committed acts, namely, kept watch at Scottsboro to prevent warning of danger being sent to Ross, and, with like purpose, sent the message to Huddleston, which were calculated to aid, and were committed by him with the intent to aid, the said Skeltons to take the life of Ross under the circumstances which rendered them guilty of murder.

And we are next to consider and determine [w]hether it is essential to the guilt of Judge Tally, as charged in the second count of the information, that the said acts, thus adapted, intended and committed by him, should, in fact, have aided the said Skeltons to take the life of the said Ross,—should have, in fact, contributed to his death at their hands. . . .

. . . [Did Judge Tally] aid or abet the killing of Ross? What is meant by these terms, and what has one to do to bring himself within them? . . . [W]e have this definition of the two terms by the late Chief Justice Stone: "The words 'aid' and 'abet,' in legal phrase, are pretty much the synonyms of each other. They comprehend all assistance rendered by acts or words of encouragement or support or presence, actual or constructive, to render assistance should it become necessary. No particular acts are necessary. If encouragement be given to commit the felony, or if, giving due weight to all the testimony, the jury are convinced beyond a reasonable doubt that the defendant was present with a view to render aid should it become necessary, then that ingredient of the offense is made out." This definition was sufficient for the case then in hand, and it is in the form not infrequently found in the books. But it is incomplete. Mere presence for the purpose of rendering aid obviously is not aid, in the substantive sense of assistance by an act supplementary to the act of the principal; nor is it aid in the original sense of abetting, nor abetting in any sense, unless presence with the purpose of giving aid, if necessary, was preconcerted, or in accordance with the general plan conceived by the principal and the person charged as an aider or abettor, or, at the very least, unless the principal knew of the presence, with intent to aid, of such person; for manifestly, in such case, there being no actual, substantive assistance, and no encouragement by words, the only aid possible would be the incitement and encouragement of the fact that another was present for the purpose of assistance, and with the intent to assist if necessary; and, in the nature of things, the fact of presence and purpose to aid could not incite or encourage or embolden the principal unless he knew of the existence of that fact. That kind of aid operates solely upon the mentality of the actual perpetrator. When rendered at all, it is by way of assurance to his mind in the undertaking he is upon, and it nerves him to the deed, and helps him execute it through a consciousness—a purely mental condition—that another is standing by in a position to help him, if help becomes necessary, who will come to his aid if aid is needed. And that there could be this consciousness without any knowledge of the fact of such other's presence and purpose cannot be conceived. That one may be encouraged or incited to an act by a consideration of which he is wholly oblivious, and which has never addressed itself to his mind, is far beyond the limit of finite comprehension. The definition we have quoted is, as an abstract proposition, clearly at fault. As applied in the concrete to cases of confederacy, as it is, we undertake to say, whenever it is stated in this form, it is free from objection; but in the absence of confederacy, or, at least, of knowledge on the part of the actual perpetrator of a crime, one cannot be a principal in the second degree who is present intending to aid, and does not aid by word or deed. The definition must go further. It should appear by it that, to be an aider or abettor when no assistance is given or word uttered, the person so charged must have been present by preconcert, special or general, or at least to the knowledge of the principal, with the intent to aid him. . . .

We are therefore clear to the conclusion that, before Judge Tally can be found guilty of aiding and abetting the Skeltons to kill Ross, it must appear that his vigil at Scottsboro to prevent Ross from being warned of his danger was by preconcert with them, or at least known to them, whereby they would naturally be incited, encouraged, and emboldened—"given confidence"—to the deed, or that he aided them to kill Ross, contributed to Ross's death, in point of physical fact, by means of the telegram he sent to Huddleston. The assistance given, however, need not contribute to the criminal result in the sense that but for it the result would not have ensued. It is quite sufficient if it facilitated a result that would have transpired without it. It is quite enough if the aid merely rendered it easier for the principal actor to accomplish the end intended by him and the aider and abettor, though in all human probability the end would have been attained without it. If the aid in homicide can be shown to have put the deceased at a disadvantage, to have deprived him of a single chance of life which but for it he would have had, he who furnishes such aid is guilty, though it cannot be known or shown that the dead man, in the absence thereof, would have availed himself of that chance; as, where one counsels murder, he is guilty as an accessory before the fact, though it appears to be probable that murder would have been done without his counsel; and as, where one being present by concert to aid if necessary is guilty as a principal in the second degree, though, had he been absent murder would have been committed, so, where he who facilitates murder even by so much as destroying a single chance of life the assailed might otherwise have had, he thereby supplements the efforts of the perpetrator, and he is guilty as principal in the second degree at common law, and is principal in the first degree under our statute, notwithstanding it may be found that in all human probability the chance would not have been availed of, and death would have resulted anyway.

We have already said enough to indicate the grounds of the conclusion which we now announce that Tally's standing guard at the telegraph office in Scottsboro to prevent Ross being warned of the pursuit of the Skeltons was not by preconcert with them, and was not known to them. It is even clear and more certain that they knew neither of the occasion nor the fact of the sending of the message by him to Huddleston; and hence they were not, and could not have been, aided in the execution of their purpose to kill . . . ; and so we are come to a consideration of the effect, if any, produced upon the situation at Stevenson by the message of Judge Tally to Huddleston. Its effect upon the situation could only have been through Huddleston, and upon his action in respect of the delivery to Ross of the message of warning sent by Ed Ross. [The court finds that, because of Tally's message, Huddleston delayed in giving the warning message to Ross.]

It remains to be determined whether the unwarranted delay in the delivery of the message to Ross, or in advising him of its contents, thus caused by Judge Tally, with intent thereby to aid the Skeltons to kill Ross, did, in fact, aid them or contribute to the death of Ross, by making it easier than it would otherwise have been for the Skeltons to kill him, by depriving him of some advantage he would have had he been advised of its contents when his carriage stopped, or immediately upon his alighting from it, or by leaving him without some chance of life which would have been his had Huddleston done his duty. . . . It is inconceivable to us after the maturest consideration, reflection, and discussion, but that Ross's predicament was rendered infinitely more desperate, his escape more difficult, and his death of much more easy and certain accomplishment by the withholding from him of the message of Ed Ross. This withholding was the work of Judge Tally. An intent to aid the Skeltons to take the life of Ross actuated him to it. The intent was effectuated. They thereby were enabled to take him unaware, and to send him to his death without, we doubt not, his ever actually knowing who sought his life, or being able to raise a hand in defense, or to take an advised step in retreat. And we are impelled to find that John B. Tally aided and abetted the murder of Robert C. Ross. . . .

Questions

1. *Objective Requirements of Complicity.* Does Bib satisfy the objective requirements of complicity at common law? (*Tally* reflects the common law rule.) Does Bib satisfy the objective requirements of complicity under the Model Penal Code? How are the two requirements different?

2. *Attempt to Assist.* If Bib had not given Muscle a ride to Susan's house but rather, unknown to Muscle, had simply showed up and sat in his car outside to serve as a lookout, would he satisfy the objective requirements of complicity? (He unsuccessfully tries to honk his horn in warning, as before.) (The drafters tell us that the term "attempts" in Model Penal Code §2.06(3)(a)(ii) has the meaning given in §5.01, defining the inchoate offense of attempt.)

3. *Objective vs. Subjective Views of Criminality.* How might you explain the difference in objective requirements between the common law and the Model Penal Code? Is the difference similar in any respect to differences between the common law and the Model Penal Code that we saw in inchoate offenses?

Backun v. United States
United States Court of Appeals, Fourth Circuit
112 F.2d 635 (1940)

PARKER, Circuit Judge.

This is an appeal from a conviction and sentence under an indictment charging the appellant Backun and one Zucker with the crime of transporting stolen merchandise of a value in excess of $5,000 in interstate commerce, knowing it to have been stolen, in violation of the National Stolen Property Act. Zucker pleaded guilty and testified for the prosecution. There was evidence to the effect that he was apprehended at a pawnshop in Charlotte, N.C., in possession of a large quantity of silverware, a portion of which was shown to have been stolen a short while before. He testified that he purchased all of the silverware from Backun in New York; that the purchase was partly on credit; that Backun had the silverware concealed in a closet and in the cellar of his residence; that there was no sale for second hand silverware in New York but a good market for it in the South; that Backun knew of Zucker's custom to travel in the South and was told by Zucker that he wished to take the silverware on the road with him; and that Backun sold to him for $1,400 silverware which was shown by other witnesses to be of a much greater value. A part of the silverware was wrapped in a laundry bag which was identified by means of a laundry ticket as having been in the possession of Backun. As bearing upon Backun's knowledge that the stolen silverware was to be transported by Zucker in interstate commerce, the following quotation from the testimony of Zucker is pertinent, viz.:

Q: And you didn't discuss with him what you were going to do with it?
A: He knows I go on the road.
Q: You didn't discuss with him where you were going?
A: I told him I wanted to go on the road with it. He knew that. That is the reason he wanted to sell it to me.
Mr. Jones: I ask Your Honor to strike that out.
Q: Did you discuss with him and tell him where you were going?
A: Yes sir.

There is no serious controversy as to the evidence being sufficient to show that Backun sold the property to Zucker knowing it to have been stolen. It is contended, however, that there is no evidence that Backun had anything to do with the transportation in interstate commerce. . . .

On the question raised . . . it is to be noted that the case presented is not that of a mere seller of merchandise, who knows that the buyer intends to put it to an unlawful use, but who cannot be said in anywise to will the unlawful use by the buyer. Cf. United States v. Falcone, 2 Cir., 109 F.2d 579. It is the case of a sale of stolen property by a guilty possessor who knows that the buyer will transport it in interstate commerce in violation of law and who desires to sell it to him for that reason. The stolen property was not salable in New York. Backun knew that Zucker could dispose of it on his visits to the Southern pawnbrokers and would take it with him on his trips to the South. The sale was made at a grossly inadequate price and Zucker was credited for a part even of that. While there was no express contract that Zucker was to carry the property out of state, Backun knew that he would do so; and, by making the sale to him, caused the transportation in interstate commerce just as certainly as if that transportation had been a term of the contract of sale. As his will thus contributed to the commission of the felony by Zucker, he would have been guilty at common law as an accessory before the fact to the commission of the felony. His guilt as a principal is fixed by section 18 U.S.C.A. 550, which provides that one who "aids, abets, counsels, commands, induces, or procures" the commission of an offense is guilty as a principal, as well as by the terms of the Stolen Property Act itself which make it a crime to cause stolen property to be transported in interstate commerce.

Whether one who sells property to another knowing that the buyer intends to use it for the commission of a felony renders himself criminally liable as aiding and abetting in its commission is a question as to which there is some conflict of authority. See United States v. Falcone, supra. It must be remembered, however, that guilt as accessory before the fact has application only in cases of felony; and since it is elementary that every citizen is under moral obligation to prevent the commission of felony, if possible, and has the legal right to use force to prevent its commission and to arrest the perpetrator without warrant, it is difficult to see why in selling goods which he knows will make its perpetration possible with knowledge that they are to be used for that purpose, he is not aiding and abetting in its commission within any fair meaning of those terms. Undoubtedly he would be guilty, were he to give to the felon the goods which make the perpetration of the felony possible with knowledge that they would be used for that purpose; and we cannot see that his guilt is purged or his breach of social duty excused because he receives a price for them. In either case, he knowingly aids and assists in the perpetration of the felony.

Guilt as an accessory depends, not on [the accessory's promoting a venture himself, making it his own, and] "having a stake" in the outcome of crime, as suggested in the *Falcone* case, but on aiding and assisting the perpetrators; and those who make a profit by furnishing to criminals, whether by sale or otherwise, the means to carry on their nefarious undertakings aid them just as truly as if they were actual partners with them, having a stake in the fruits of their enterprise. To say that the sale of goods is a normally lawful transaction [and that a seller need not forego because he knows others will make an unlawful use of his property, as stated in *Falcone*], is beside the point. The seller may not ignore the purpose for which the purchase is made if he is advised of that purpose, or wash his hands of the aid that he has given the perpetrator of a felony by the plea that he has merely made a sale of merchandise. One who sells a gun to another knowing that he is buying it to commit a murder would hardly escape conviction as an accessory to the murder by showing that he received full price for the gun; and no difference in principle can be drawn between such a case and any other case of a seller who knows that the purchaser intends to use the goods which he is purchasing in the commission of felony. In any such case, not only does the act of the seller assist in the commission of the felony, but his will assents to its commission, since he could refuse to give the assistance by refusing to make the sale. This is the view taken of the matter in a number of well considered cases in the federal courts. . . .

But even if the view be taken that aiding and abetting is not to be predicated of an ordinary sale made with knowledge that the purchaser intends to use the goods purchased in the commission of felony, we think that the circumstances relied on by the government here are sufficient to establish the guilt of Backun. The sale here was not of a mere instrumentality to be used in the commission of felony, but of the very goods which were to be feloniously transported. Backun knew not only that the commission of felony was contemplated by Zucker with respect to such goods, but also that the felony could not be committed by Zucker unless the sale were made to him. The sale thus made possible the commission of the felony by Zucker; and, if Zucker is to be believed, the commission of the felony was one of the purposes which Backun had in mind in making the sale. After testifying that he had told Backun that he wished to go on the road with the silverware (i.e., transport it in interstate commerce), he says "He (Backun) knew that. That is the reason he wanted to sell it to me." There can be no question, therefore, but that the evidence sustains the view that the felony committed by Zucker flowed from the will of Backun as well as from his own will, and that Backun aided its commission by making the sale. There was thus evidence of direct participation of Backun in the criminal purpose of Zucker; and whatever view be taken as to the case of a mere sale, certainly such evidence is sufficient to establish guilt.

Reversed [on other grounds].

Model Penal Code §2.04(3)(b)
Complicity (Tent. Draft No. 1)
(subsequently revised and renumbered §2.06(3)(b))

A person is an accomplice of another person in commission of a crime if: . . .

(b) acting with knowledge that such other person was committing or had the purpose of committing the crime, he knowingly, substantially facilitated its commission; . . .

New York Penal Law §115.00
Criminal Facilitation in the Second Degree

A person is guilty of criminal facilitation in the second degree when, believing it probable that he is rendering aid to a person who intends to commit a crime, he engages in conduct which provides such person with means or opportunity for the commission thereof and which in fact aids such person to commit a felony.

Criminal facilitation in the second degree is a class A misdemeanor.

Questions

1. *Purpose vs. Knowing.* Both *Backun* and the Tentative Draft of the Model Penal Code support a "knowing" requirement for complicity, but the final draft of the Code adopts instead a "purposeful" requirement. What do you think might have been the grounds of the disagreement over the two formulations?

2. *Hypothetical: In re the Government of South Yemen.* In 1982, a combat cell of the Red Brigade hijacked an Israeli airliner bound for Panama City diverting it to South Yemen, a small marxist country on the tip of the Arabian peninsula. The government of South Yemen expressed its sympathy for the cause of the hijackers but said that it would remain neutral in the affair except to urge Israel to release its political prisoners as demanded by the hijackers, in order to save the lives of the airline passengers. After two days on the runway, an airline passenger escaped from the aircraft. The hijackers convened a "revolutionary court," convicted the passenger of antirevolutionary conduct for his escape, sentenced him to immediate death, and demanded his return by the government of South Yemen. The government publicly expressed its desire that the passenger not be killed "as a demonstration of the great compassion and humanitarianism of the revolution." The government also privately sought to avoid the "execution" because of the embarrassment that it would cause. The hijackers rejected the public and private pleas. The government returned the passenger, explaining that in order to stay neutral it could not harbor the passenger and thereby cause a change in the status quo. Immediately upon being returned, the passenger was placed kneeling in the airline doorway and shot in the head.

Would the government of South Yemen be liable as an accomplice to the killing under the Tentative Draft of the Model Penal Code? Under the final draft of the Code? In your view, should the government be liable as an accomplice?

3. *Hypothetical: State v. Whitehorse.* Jack Whitehorse, owner and operator of the High Head Shop, sells cigarette papers to approximately 60 people each week. His business is about 50 percent better than the other two "head shops" in the area because his prices are lower. He knows that essentially all of his customers buy the papers for the illegal use of marijuana.

Would Whitehorse be liable as an accomplice to unlawful drug smoking under the Tentative Draft of the Model Penal Code? Under the final draft of the Code? In your view, should Whitehorse be liable as an accomplice?

4. *South Yemen v. Whitehorse.* Assuming that the South Yemen authorities and the headshop owner are each aware of the same high probability that their conduct will aid the hijackers and a given customer, respectively, in the offenses of homicide and illegal drug use, respectively, people might nonetheless disagree that the complicity doctrine should treat South Yemen and the headshop owner the same. What are the differences between the two situations that might suggest different complicity liability conclusions? Does the extent of the accomplice's assistance matter? (See the Tentative Draft proposal.) Does the seriousness of the offense matter? (Would it matter if the shop owner was selling guns that he knew would be used in a murder?) Does the potential penalty matter? (See the New York statute.)

N.H. Rev. Stat. Ann. §626.8*
Criminal Liability for Conduct of Another

I. A person is guilty of an offense if it is committed by his own conduct or by the conduct of another person for which he is legally accountable, or both.

II. A person is legally accountable for the conduct of another person when: . . .

 (b) he is made accountable for the conduct of such other person by the law defining the offense; or

 (c) he is an accomplice of another person in the commission of the offense.

---

*Editor's Note.—This statute, which is the subject of *Etzweiler*, is modeled after Model Penal Code §2.06.

III. A person is an accomplice of another person in the commission of an offense if:

(a) with the purpose of promoting or facilitating the commission of the offense, he solicits such other person in committing it, or aids or agrees or attempts to aid such other person in planning or committing it; or

(b) his conduct is expressly declared by law to establish his complicity.

IV. When causing a particular result is an element of an offense, an accomplice in the conduct causing such result is an accomplice in the commission of that offense, if he acts with the kind of culpability, if any, with respect to that result that is sufficient for the commission of the offense.

State v. Etzweiler
Supreme Court of New Hampshire
125 N.H. 57, 480 A.2d 870 (1984)

BATCHELDER, Justice, with whom BROCK, Justice, concurs.

The issues raised in these consolidated cases involve the applicability of New Hampshire's motor vehicle laws and Criminal Code to a simple fact situation. The State and Mark A. Etzweiler, one of the defendants, have stipulated to the following facts. On July 30, 1982, the defendants, Mark Etzweiler and Ralph Bailey, arrived in Etzweiler's automobile at the plant where both were employed. Bailey had been drinking alcoholic beverages and was, allegedly, intoxicated. Etzweiler, allegedly knowing that Bailey was intoxicated, loaned his car to Bailey and proceeded into the plant to begin work. Bailey drove Etzweiler's car away. Approximately ten minutes later, Bailey, driving recklessly, collided with a car driven by Susan Beaulieu. As a result of the accident, two passengers in the Beaulieu car, Kathryn and Nathan Beaulieu, were killed.

On August 26, 1982, the grand jury handed down two indictments charging Etzweiler with negligent homicide, and two indictments charging Bailey with manslaughter. Subsequently, on April 6, 1983, the grand jury issued two additional indictments charging Etzweiler with negligent homicide as an accomplice.

Etzweiler filed motions to quash all indictments against him, and the Superior Court transferred to this court the questions of law raised by the motions. . . .

The cases were consolidated on appeal. We dismiss all indictments against Etzweiler. . . .

The superior court transferred five questions of law. We need address only the first question: whether the legislature intended to impose criminal liability upon a person who lends his automobile to an intoxicated driver but does not accompany the driver, when the driver's operation of the borrowed automobile causes death. . . .

The second indictments charge Etzweiler with the offense of negligent homicide as an accomplice.

RSA 626:8 delineates all situations in which an individual may be held criminally liable for the conduct of another. One situation is when an individual "is an accomplice of [another] in the commission of the offense." RSA 626:8, II(c). Accomplice liability under RSA 626:8, II(c) is defined in two parts, RSA 626:8, III and IV. Section III sets forth the elements which must be present above, beyond, and regardless of the substantive offense. Section IV sets forth the elements of the substantive offense that must be present in order to charge the accomplice.

RSA 626:8, III provides:

> A person is an accomplice of another person in the commission of an offense if: (a) with the purpose of promoting or facilitating the commission of the offense, he aids . . . such other person in planning or committing it. . . ."

The section sets forth the *conduct element* of accomplice liability, and the necessary accompanying mental state.

Under section III, the State has the burden of establishing that the accomplice acted with the purpose of promoting or facilitating the commission of the substantive offense. This encompasses the requirement that the accomplice's acts were designed to aid the primary actor in committing the offense, and that the accomplice had the purpose to "make the crime succeed." In other words, the accomplice must have the "purpose to advance the criminal end." Model Penal Code §5.03, comment at 107 (Tent. Draft No. 10, 1960) (RSA 626:8 is based upon the Model Penal Code).

Section IV sets forth the elements of the substantive offense that the State has the burden of establishing against the accomplice. "When causing a particular result is an element of an offense," the accomplice must act "with the kind of culpability, if any, with respect to that result that is sufficient for the commission of the offense." RSA 626:8, IV. See generally Element Analysis in Defining Criminal Liability: The Model Penal Code and Beyond, 35 Stan. L. Rev. 681, 739–41 (1983).

Our interpretation of the accomplice liability statute effectuates the policy that an accomplice's liability ought not to extend beyond the criminal purposes that he or she shares. Because accomplice liability holds an individual criminally liable for actions done by another, it is important that the prosecution fall squarely within the statute.

Applying these statutory prerequisites, we turn to the indictments charging Etzweiler as an accomplice to negligent homicide.

> Mark Etzweiler acted as an accomplice in the conduct which caused the death[s] of Kathryn [and Nathan] Beaulieu when, with a purpose to promote and facilitate the offense of driving under the influence of alcohol, he aided Ralph Bailey in the commission of that offense by lending Ralph Bailey his 1980 AMC automobile, knowing Ralph Bailey was under the influence of alcohol, and encouraging him to drive it on a public way in such condition, and Mark Etzweiler thereby acted negligently with respect to the death[s] of Kathryn [and Nathan] Beaulieu. . . .

The State has alleged that, with the purpose of promoting or facilitating the offense of driving under the influence of alcohol, Etzweiler aided Bailey in the commission of that offense. However, under our statute, the accomplice must aid the primary actor in the substantive offense with the purpose of facilitating the substantive offense—in this case, negligent homicide. Therefore, the indictments against Etzweiler must be quashed.

Even if the indictments tracked the statutory language of RSA 626:8, III and IV, Etzweiler, as a matter of law, could not be an accomplice to negligent homicide. To satisfy the requirements of RSA 626:8, III, the State must establish that Etzweiler's acts were designed to aid Bailey in committing negligent homicide. Yet under the negligent homicide statute, Bailey must be unaware of the risk of death that his conduct created. RSA 630:3, I, RSA 626:2, II(d). We cannot see how Etzweiler could intentionally aid Bailey in a crime that Bailey was unaware that he was committing. Thus, we hold, as a matter of law, that, in the present context of the Criminal Code, an individual may not be an accomplice to negligent homicide. We need not reach the question of whether the statute provides for accomplices to manslaughter or murder.

Therefore, we answer the first question posed by the superior court in the negative in regard to both RSA 630:3, I and RSA 626:8. . . . [Remanded.]

SOUTER, Justice, concurring specially:

I concur with the [result] reached by Justice Batchelder, and I join in his opinion, save in [one respect]. Although there would be no value in an extended analysis at this point, I do not read RSA 626:8, IV as my brother does. That section provides that

> [w]hen causing a particular result is an element of an offense, an accomplice in the conduct causing such result is an accomplice in the commission of that offense, if he acts with the kind of culpability, if any,

with respect to that result that is sufficient for the commission of the offense.

I read this language as an attempt to provide that a person may be criminally liable as an accomplice even if he does not act "with the purpose of promoting or facilitating the commission of an offense." RSA 626:8, III(a).

The attempt fails because the meaning of "accomplice" in section IV is unclear. Section III provides what is necessary to be an "accomplice . . . in the commission of an offense." Among other things, such an accomplice must have a "purpose" to promote or facilitate the commission of the offense. Section IV purports to determine when an accomplice in "conduct" causing a particular result is also an accomplice in the commission of the offense defined by reference to that result. Section IV does not, however, define this new sense of "accomplice" in conduct. One can guess that it means "accomplice" as used in section III minus the "purpose." This is no more than a guess, however. The confusion is probably explained historically by tracing the revisions in the Model Penal Code, on which New Hampshire's provisions are based. Compare Tent. Draft No. 1, §2.04(3)(a), (b) and (4) with final draft §2.06(3)(a) and (4); compare Tent Draft No. 1, §2.04(4) with RSA 626:8, IV. See Element Analysis in Defining Criminal Liability: The Model Penal Code and Beyond, 35 Stanford L. Rev. 681, 733 (1983). Whatever the explanation, section IV fails to give any comprehensible, let alone fair, notice of its intended effect and is thus unenforceable. It is of course open to the legislature to provide for accomplice liability more broadly than it has done in section III alone. . . .

KING, Chief Justice, dissenting in *Etzweiler* (with whom DOUGLAS, Justice, joins . . .).

For the reasons that follow, I would affirm [the] indictments against Etzweiler, as . . . an accessory to negligent homicide. . . .

In construing RSA 626:8—which imputes criminal liability to a person for the conduct of another—to determine whether the indictments in question properly state an offense under that statute, one must define the pertinent statutory language by reference to the definitions provided in the statute itself.

RSA 626:8, I and II(c) assign criminal liability to someone who is "an accomplice of another person in the commission of an offense." This phrase is defined by other provisions in the statute which designate three sets of circumstances under which a person may become "an accomplice of another person in the commission of an offense." They are:

(1) if, "with the purpose of promoting or facilitating the commission of that offense, he solicits such other person in committing

it, or aids or agrees or attempts to aid such other person in planning or committing it," RSA 626:8, III(a); or
(2) if "his conduct is expressly declared by law to establish his complicity," RSA 626:8, III(b); or
(3) if, "[w]hen causing a particular result is an element of an offense," the person is "an accomplice in the conduct causing such result" *and* "he acts with the kind of culpability, if any, with respect to that result that is sufficient for the commission of the offense."

RSA 626:8, IV.

While the statutory phrase "accomplice in the conduct causing [a particular] result" provided by RSA 626:8, IV is not explicitly defined in the statute, when viewed as part of a totality it is implicitly defined by RSA 626:8, III(a). Under section III(a), a person is an accomplice in the principal's criminal conduct causing a particular result if, with the purpose of promoting or facilitating the principal's criminal conduct, the person solicits that conduct, or aids or agrees or attempts to aid that conduct. Section III also assigns liability in those situations in which the accomplice actively seeks the criminal *result* by aiding and abetting the principal without caring precisely how the principal achieves that result.

Therefore, for a person to be criminally liable under RSA 626:8, IV for the crime of a principal, that person must act *purposefully* with respect to the principal's criminal *conduct*. However, with respect to the *result* of the principal's criminal conduct, section IV requires a showing that the person acted with the same state of mind required of the principal. See ALI, Model Penal Code and Commentaries, Tentative Draft No. 1, Comments §2.04 (4), at 34 (1953); Element Analysis in Defining Criminal Liability: The Model Penal Code and Beyond, 35 Stan. L. Rev. 681, 739-40 (1983). A showing that a person merely acquiesced in or consented to a principal's conduct is not enough to prove purposefulness under section III. Rather, it must be demonstrated that the person participated actively in the principal's conduct.

The second indictments properly allege that Etzweiler acted purposefully to "promote and facilitate" Bailey's criminal conduct—Bailey's alleged intoxicated driving—causing the deaths and "aided" Bailey by "encouraging" him in that conduct. The indictments also allege, as they must, that Etzweiler "thereby acted negligently with respect to" the resulting deaths. Of course, to obtain a conviction of Etzweiler, the State must prove each alleged act and mental state as well as the causal link between Bailey's driving and the resulting deaths. Finally, it should be noted that to find Etzweiler guilty, the jury must conclude that he was criminally negligent under RSA 626:2, II(d), a showing of culpability substantially higher than ordinary civil negligence.

While other proffered interpretations of RSA 626:8 may be plausible, they effectively give principal meaning to either section III or section IV of the statute at the expense of the other section. The majority opinion, for example, essentially reads section IV of RSA 626:8 out of the statute, notwithstanding the court's failed attempt to infuse that section with meaning. The statutory analysis herein satisfies the rule of statutory construction that all parts of a statute be read as meaningful and consistent parts of a whole. This analysis also fulfills the court's duty to interpret a statute so as to effectuate its legislative intent: here, to inculpate persons who purposely further the criminal conduct of others while [culpably] unaware of the substantial and unjustifiable risks attending that criminal conduct.

The court's holding that as a matter of law "a person may not have a purpose of having another commit negligent homicide" is problematic. First, this holding is not supported by the language of RSA 626:8. Second, the court's holding requiring purposeful conduct with respect to the result of the principal's offense, effectively precludes criminal liability for aiding any homicide other than intentional homicide. The justification, theoretical or otherwise, for such an approach to accomplice liability is imperceptible. . . .

Questions

1. *Culpability Requirements of Complicity.* What would the majority in *Etzweiler* give as a list of the culpability requirements for complicity? What would the dissent give as a list?

2. *Culpability as to Result Element of Substantive Offense.* Under the majority view in *Etzweiler,* would Bib be liable as an accomplice to the homicide offense? If so, for what degree of homicide would he be liable? Would he be liable under the dissent's view? (The Model Penal Code commentary appears to support the dissent's interpretation.)

3. *Culpability as to Circumstance Element of Substantive Offense.* Is Bib liable as an accomplice to the statutory rape? Should there be a difference in how the complicity rules operate for the homicide and statutory rape offenses? The commentary to the Model Penal Code complicity provision does not address the issue but, in explaining the phrase "purpose to promote or facilitate" in the context of conspiracy, the commentary addresses the impact of that phrase on the actor's culpability as to a circumstance element of the substantive offense. It concludes, the draft "does not attempt to solve the problem by explicit formulation but here, *as in the Section on complicity,* we believe that it affords sufficient flexibility for satisfactory decision as such cases may arise. . . . [W]e think it wise to leave the issue to interpretation." Model Penal Code

§5.03 comment 2, at 113 (Tent. Draft No. 10, 1960) (emphasis added). (See Section 8.5 for a discussion of the culpability requirements as to a circumstance element of the substantive offense in the conspiracy context.)

4. *Requirements of Perpetrator for Accomplice's Liability.* At common law, the perpetrator had to satisfy the requirements of the substantive offense if an accomplice was to be held liable. The accomplice's liability was seen as *derivative* from the perpetrator's. Model Penal Code §1.06(7) changes this:

> An accomplice may be convicted on proof of the commission of the offense and of his complicity therein, though the person claimed to have committed the offense has not been prosecuted or convicted or has been convicted of a different offense or degree of offense or has an immunity to prosecution or conviction or has been acquitted.

Under the code, what offense elements must the perpetrator satisfy for the accomplice to be liable? Section 10.3 examines these issues more closely.

Notes on the Requirements for Complicity Liability

The requirements for a defendant's liability for an offense as an accomplice may be summarized as follows:

The defendant must satisfy these requirements:

Objective Requirements	Culpability Requirements
Conduct: CL: assist (or encourage) MPC: aid or agree or attempt to aid	*Culpability as to aiding perpetrator's conduct constituting object offense:* CL and MPC: "purpose of promoting or facilitating" the offense (§2.06(3)(a)) *Culpability as to result elements of object offense:* CL: elevate to purposeful MPC: do not elevate (§2.06(4)) *Culpability as to circumstance elements of object offense:* CL: elevate to purposeful MPC: unclear; probably left to "interpretation," as in conspiracy

The perpetrator must satisfy these requirements:

Objective Requirements	Culpability Requirements
CL: objective elements of object offense	CL: culpability requirements of object offense
MPC: same? ("on proof of commission of the offense," §2.06(7))	MPC: none (§2.06(7) rejects unconvictable perpetrator defense)

MPC = Model Penal Code
CL = Common Law

Questions

1. *Strength of the Rationale for Imputation.* Does satisfaction of the requirements for complicity liability justify treating an accomplice the same as if he himself engaged in the conduct constituting the offense? That is, is it generally the case that a person who satisfies the requirements of complicity should be criminally liable? Is such a person sufficiently blameworthy to justify the condemnation of criminal conviction?

2. *Grading Complicity.* If an actor satisfies the requirements of complicity, is it generally the case that he or she ought to have the same degree of liability as the person who actually performs the conduct constituting the offense? Is the accomplice's degree of blameworthiness the same as the principal's? If not, what kinds of factors might appropriately increase or decrease the accomplice's degree of liability?

3. *United States Sentencing Commission Complicity Guidelines.* Consider the following provisions of the United States Sentencing Commission Guidelines:

§3B1.1. Aggravating Role

Based on the defendant's role in the offense, increase the offense level as follows:

(a) If the defendant was an organizer or leader of a criminal activity that involved five or more participants or was otherwise extensive, increase by 4 levels.

(b) If the defendant was a manager or supervisor (but not an organizer or leader) and the criminal activity involved five or more participants or was otherwise extensive, increase by 3 levels.

(c) If the defendant was an organizer, leader, manager, or supervisor in any criminal activity other than described in (a) or (b), increase by 2 levels.

§3B1.2. Mitigating Role

   Based on the defendant's role in the offense, decrease the offense level as follows:
       (a) If the defendant was a minimal participant in any criminal activity, decrease by 4 levels.
       (b) If the defendant was a minor participant in any criminal activity, decrease by 2 levels.
   In cases falling between (a) and (b), decrease by 3 levels.

United States Sentencing Commission, Guidelines Manual §§3B1.1 & 3B1.2 (Nov. 1993). If it is possible to articulate such rules for the grading of complicity, why is this not an aspect of the criminal code rather than an aspect of the sentencing rules?

SECTION 10.2   CAUSING CRIME BY AN INNOCENT

At common law, where the principal had to satisfy the culpability requirements of the offense, complicity liability could not be imposed where the actor caused an innocent or irresponsible person to perform the conduct constituting the offense. The perpetrator's lack of culpability would give the accomplice a defense. For this reason, the common law recognized a second kind of liability for the conduct of another, where the actor caused an innocent or responsible person to act. Typically, the defendant in these cases is the moving force in the offense, rather than simply helping another. The Model Penal Code drops the unconvictable perpetrator defense; the perpetrator's innocence or irresponsibility provides no defense to the accomplice. Yet the Code keeps the additional special form of liability for causing crime by an innocent. After reviewing the requirements for this kind of liability, we will want to ask why this doctrine survives in modern codes.

The Egg Hunt

Walker lives in an apartment at Cottage 12 of Southbury Training School. His charges are severely retarded men. "Pop," as he is called by his charges, shaves the men, helps them dress and shower, and generally supervises their activities. They are gentle people but their retardation sometimes creates difficult situations. The "boys," as the staff call them, have recently taken to collecting anything small and shiny, which they call "eggs." A recent visitor became frightened when her car was surrounded by a group of men three-deep, pressing their faces against the glass, pointing at the chrome dials on her console, and shouting "Egg! Egg!" The boys' interest in shiny objects is not accidental. Walker has cultivated it as a means of motivating them to steal silverware from the large restaurant where many of them work during the day as dishwashers.

Attie Winter, the house mother at Cottage 20, disapproves of the way Walker runs his cottage. The strip-baseball and tackle-badminton games, which Walker allows and the boys love, breed bad habits, in her view. Attie suspects Walker has the boys doing even more objectionable things but cannot prove it. Walker knows of Attie's attempts to have him fired. He decides that a little intimidation may be helpful. During lunch and again at dinner, he describes in detail to the boys Mom Winter's beautiful necklace of small silver eggs. After the boys have gone to bed, Walker leaves to meet a friend for drinks at a nearby bar, as he frequently does. The night janitor is under instructions to call the central office if any problem arises. Walker leaves the front door to the dormitory unlocked, in the expectation that the boys will take the opportunity to sneak past the sleeping night janitor, and head for Cottage 20 to find Mom Winter's necklace and no doubt scare her plenty in the process.

Half way to the bar, Walker remembers that he has forgotten to lock his room where his loaded gun is stored. He has let the boys play cops and robbers with his gun when it was unloaded. They might think to take it with them when they go to Cottage 20 on their "egg hunt." After debating with himself, he concludes that it is more likely that they will not think of it. As it happens, the boys have been calculating their attack on Cottage 20 ever since lunch. They notice immediately when Walker does not lock the dormitory door and his room. After waiting until they are sure he will not be soon returning, they take his gun and head en masse in search of the now-legendary necklace. They confront Mom Winter. When she resists turning over her necklace, they "shoot" her. To their horror, she falls to the floor bleeding. Walker is fired from his position when an investigation reveals his part in the affair. He is charged with the silverware thefts and with the murder of Attie Winter. Is Walker liable?

Bailey v. Commonwealth
Supreme Court of Virginia
229 Va. 258. 329 S.E. 2d 37 (1985)

CARRICO, Chief Justice.

Indicted for involuntary manslaughter, Joseph A. Bailey was convicted in a jury trial and sentenced in accordance with the jury's verdict to serve six months in jail and to pay a fine of $1,000. The question on appeal is whether it was proper to convict Bailey of involuntary manslaughter when, in his absence, the victim was killed by police officers responding to reports from Bailey concerning the victim's conduct.

The death of the victim, Gordon E. Murdock, occurred during the late evening of May 21, 1983, in the aftermath of an extended and vituperative conversation between Bailey and Murdock over their citizens' band radios. During the conversation, which was to be the last in a series of such violent incidents, Bailey and Murdock cursed and threatened each other repeatedly.

Bailey and Murdock lived about two miles apart in the Roanoke area. On the evening in question, each was intoxicated. Bailey had consumed a "twelve-pack" of beer and a "fifth of liquor" since midafternoon; a test of Murdock's blood made during an autopsy showed alcoholic content of ".271% . . . by weight." Murdock was also "legally blind," with vision of only 3/200 in the right eye and 2/200 in the left. Bailey knew that Murdock had "a problem with vision" and that he was intoxicated on the night in question.

Bailey also knew that Murdock owned a handgun and had boasted "about how he would use it and shoot it and scare people off with it." Bailey knew further that Murdock was easily agitated and that he became especially angry if anyone disparaged his war hero, General George S. Patton. During the conversation in question, Bailey implied that General Patton and Murdock himself were homosexuals.

Also during the conversation, Bailey persistently demanded that Murdock arm himself with his handgun and wait on his front porch for Bailey to come and injure or kill him. Murdock responded by saying he would be waiting on his front porch, and he told Bailey to "kiss (his) mother or (his) wife and children good-bye because (he would) never go back home."

Bailey then made two anonymous telephone calls to the Roanoke City Police Department. In the first, Bailey reported "a man . . . out on the porch (at Murdock's address) waving a gun around." A police car was dispatched to the address, but the officers reported they did not "see anything."

Bailey called Murdock back on the radio and chided him for not "going out on the porch." More epithets and threats were exchanged. Bailey told Murdock he was "going to come up there in a blue and white car" and demanded that Murdock "step out there on the . . . porch" with his gun "in (his) hands" because he, Bailey, would "be there in just a minute." Bailey owned a blue and white vehicle; the police vehicles were also blue and white.

Bailey telephoned the police again. This time, Bailey identified Murdock by name and told the dispatcher that Murdock had "a gun on the porch," had "threatened to shoot up the neighborhood," and was "talking about shooting anything that moves." Bailey insisted that the police "come out here and straighten this man out." Bailey refused to identify himself, explaining that he was "right next to (Murdock) out here" and feared revealing his identity.

Three uniformed police officers, Chambers, Beavers, and Turner, were dispatched to Murdock's home. None of the officers knew that Murdock was intoxicated or that he was in an agitated state of mind. Only Officer Beavers knew that Murdock's eyesight was bad, and he did not know "exactly how bad it was." Beavers also knew that Murdock would get "a little 10-96 (mental subject) occasionally" and would "curse and carry on" when he was drinking.

When the officers arrived on the scene, they found that Murdock's "porch light was on" but observed no one on the porch. After several minutes had elapsed, the officers observed Murdock come out of his house with "something shiny in his hand." Murdock sat down on the top step of the porch and placed the shiny object beside him.

Officer Chambers approached Murdock from the side of the porch and told him to "(l)eave the gun alone and walk down the stairs away from it." Murdock "just sat there." When Chambers repeated his command, Murdock cursed him. Murdock then reached for the gun, stood up, advanced in Chambers's direction, and opened fire. Chambers retreated and was not struck.

All three officers returned fire, and Murdock was struck. Lying wounded on the porch, he said several times, "I didn't know you was the police." He died from "a gunshot wound of the left side of the chest." In the investigation which followed, Bailey stated that he was "the hoss that caused the loss."

In an instruction granted below and not questioned on appeal, the trial court told the jury it should convict Bailey if it found that his negligence or reckless conduct was so gross and culpable as to indicate a callous disregard for human life and that his actions were the proximate cause or a concurring cause of Murdock's death. Bailey concedes that the evidence at trial, viewed in the light most favorable to the Commonwealth, would support a finding that his actions constituted negligence so gross and culpable as to indicate a callous disregard for human life. He contends, however, that he "did not kill Murdock."

Bailey argues that his conviction can be sustained only if he was a principal in the first degree, a principal in the second degree, or an accessory before the fact to the killing of Murdock. The Attorney General concedes that Bailey was not a principal in the second degree or an accessory before the fact, but maintains that he was a principal in the first degree.

Countering, Bailey argues he was not a principal in the first degree because only the immediate perpetrators of crime occupy that status. Here, Bailey says, the immediate perpetrators of Murdock's killing were the police officers who returned Murdock's fire. He was in his own home two miles away, Bailey asserts, and did not control the actors in the confrontation at Murdock's home or otherwise participate in the events that occurred there. Hence, Bailey concludes, he could not have been a principal in the first degree.

Bailey admits the officers acted in self defense.

We have adopted the rule in this Commonwealth . . . however, that one who effects a criminal act through an innocent or unwitting agent is a principal in the first degree. Collins v. Commonwealth, 226 Va. 223, 307 S.E.2d 884, 890 (1983) (undercover policewoman ruled innocent agent to collect fees for defendant charged with pandering); Dusenbery v. Commonwealth, 220 Va. 770, 772, 263 S.E.2d 392, 393 (1980) (person who acts through an innocent or unwitting agent is a principal in first degree, but not in rape cases). And, in State v. Benton, 276 N.C. 641, 653, 174 S.E.2d 793, 801 (1970), cited with approval in *Collins,* the court stated that the innocent-agent rule applies even though the person accused was not present at the time and place of the offense.

Bailey argues that the present case is distinguishable from *Collins.* There, Bailey says, the accused and the undercover policewoman were working in concert, pursuing a common goal of soliciting and collecting fees for sexual favors; although the policewoman was innocent of the crime of pandering because she had no intent to perform sexual acts, the accused was guilty nevertheless because the fees were collected on his behalf. Here, Bailey asserts, he and the police shared no common scheme or goal. Neither, Bailey says, did he share a common goal with Murdock; indeed, "Murdock's intent was to kill Bailey."

The question is not, however, whether Murdock was Bailey's innocent or unwitting agent but whether the police officers who responded to Bailey's calls occupied that status. And, in resolving this question, we believe it is irrelevant whether Bailey and the police shared a common scheme or goal. What is relevant is whether Bailey undertook to cause Murdock harm and used the police to accomplish that purpose, a question which we believe must be answered affirmatively. . . .

From a factual standpoint, it is clear from the sum total of Bailey's actions that his purpose in calling the police was to induce them to go to Murdock's home and unwittingly create the appearance that Bailey himself had arrived to carry out the threats he had made over the radio. And, from a legal standpoint, it is clear that, for Bailey's mischievous purpose, the police officers who went to Murdock's home and confronted him were acting as Bailey's innocent or unwitting agents.

But, Bailey argues, he cannot be held criminally liable in this case unless Murdock's death was the natural and probable result of Bailey's conduct. Bailey maintains that either Murdock's own reckless and criminal conduct in opening fire upon the police or the officers' return fire constituted an independent, intervening cause absolving Bailey of guilt.

We have held, however, that "(a)n intervening act which is reasonably foreseeable cannot be relied upon as breaking the chain of causal connection between an original act of negligence and subsequent injury." Delawder v. Commonwealth, 214 Va. 55, 58, 196 S.E.2d 913, 915 (1973) (defendant lost control of vehicle while racing and struck pedestrian; striking of defendant's vehicle by other car not intervening cause). Here, under instructions not questioned on appeal, the jury determined that the fatal consequences of Bailey's reckless conduct could reasonably have been foreseen and, accordingly, that Murdock's death was not the result of an independent, intervening cause but of Bailey's misconduct. At the least, the evidence presented a jury question on these issues. . . .

. . . According, we will affirm the conviction.

Model Penal Code §2.06(1)-(2)(a)
Liability for the Conduct of Another

(1) A person is guilty of an offense if it is committed by his own conduct or by the conduct of another person for which he is legally accountable, or both.

(2) A person is legally accountable for the conduct of another person when:

    (a) acting with the kind of culpability that is sufficient for the commission of the offense, he causes an innocent or irresponsible person to engage in such conduct; . . .

Questions

1. *Complicity.* Does Walker satisfy the requirements of complicity at common law? Does Bailey? Does Walker satisfy the requirements of complicity under the Model Penal Code? Does Bailey?

2. *Causing Crime by an Innocent.* What are the requirements for liability under the doctrine of causing crime by an innocent? What objective and culpability requirements are required of the defendant? What objective and culpability requirements are required of the person performing the offense conduct? What defenses of the person performing the conduct will provide a defense to the defendant, if any?

3. *Walker and Bailey under the Model Penal Code.* Is Walker liable for causing crime by an innocent under the Model Penal Code? What will be the points of dispute? Would Bailey be liable under the Code?

4. *Justified and Excused Innocents.* The "boys" in Walker's case will have an excuse for killing Mom Winter (see Model Penal Code §4.01(1), also see §4.02(2)). The police in *Bailey* are justified in their killing of Murdock (see Model Penal Code §§3.04(1) & (2)(b)(ii)(2) & 3.07(1)). For the purpose of determining Walker's and Bailey's liability, does it matter whether the innocent perpetrator is excused or is justified? If the police officers' conduct in *Bailey* is justified, on what theory can Bailey be held criminally liable for bringing about justified conduct?

Notes on the Requirements for Liability for Causing Crime by an Innocant

The requirements for a defendant's liability for causing crime by an innocent may be summarized as follows:

The defendant must satisfy these requirements:

Objective Requirements

Conduct:
CL and MPC: cause an innocent or irresponsible person to engage in the conduct constituting the offense (MPC §2.06(2)(a)); "cause" is defined by the normal requirements of causation

Culpability Requirements

Culpability as to causing person to perform conduct constituting object offense:
CL and MPC: unspecified; recklessness read in by MPC §2.02(3)?

Culpability as to elements of object offense:
CL and MPC: as required by the substantive offense ("acting with the kind of culpability that is sufficient for the commission of the offense," MPC §2.06(2)(a))

The "perpetrator" must satisfy these requirements:

Objective Requirements

CL and MPC: objective elements of offense

Culpability Requirements

CL and MPC: none (person performing offense conduct may be "innocent or irresponsible," MPC §2.06(2)(a))

MPC = Model Penal Code
CL = Common Law

CHAPTER 10 COMPLICITY

Questions

1. *The Rationale for Causing-Crime-by-an-Innocent Doctrine in Modern Codes.* The beginning of this section notes that modern codes keep the distinction between complicity and causing crime by an innocent even though the latter doctrine is no longer necessary to impose liability where the person performing the offense conduct is innocent or irresponsible. Why do modern codes keep this doctrine?

2. *Complicity vs. Causing Crime by an Innocent.* How are the requirements of causing crime by an innocent different from the requirements for complicity? What are the differences in objective requirements, if any? What are the differences in culpability requirements, if any? Why do these differences exist?

3. *Causing Crime by an Innocent and Causation.* Some courts found liability in cases of causing crime by an innocent without ever relying upon a special doctrine to impute the innocent perpetrator's conduct to the defendant. Instead, the court treated the innocent person as simply an instrumentality of the defendant, much as a gun or a pen might be an instrument by which one committed an offense. Why isn't this form of analysis adequate? What advantage, if any, is provided by a special doctrine of causing crime by an innocent?

SECTION 10.3 DEFENSES TO IMPUTATION OF ANOTHER'S CONDUCT

Several special defenses are available to doctrines that otherwise would impute another's conduct. The unconvictable perpetrator defense recognized at common law has been discussed above in the context of the requirements of complicity, in Section 10.1. The special statutory exemption defense first appears in the context of conspiracy, in Section 8.5. Renunciation and termination also are discussed in that context, in Section 8.6. This section examines the application of these defenses to complicity and, in the process, provides a review of previously discussed principles.

Chucky Backs Out

Chucky the Wheeze has sought to be a member of an organized crime family for some time. When Tony Bumonte, a member of a crime family in another state, approaches him for help in obtaining automatic weapons, Chucky is anxious to please. He tells Bumonte of a corrupt policeman, Dennis White, who sells automatic weapons to anyone willing to pay his price, weapons which by statute only police officers may possess. Bumonte shows interest and Chucky sets up a meeting between the two men.

Before the meeting date arrives, Chucky hears rumors that Tony Bumonte is an undercover police officer and cancels the meeting. In an attempt to insulate himself from liability, Chucky reports White and Bumonte's planned transaction to police. Having learned of Dennis White from Chucky, Tony Bumonte is able to arrange a meeting with White even without Chucky's further help. Bumonte and White meet and consummate the sale.

In fact, Tony Bumonte is an undercover police officer. Several days after the sale, Chucky and Dennis White are arrested and charged with complicity in the unlawful possession of automatic weapons by Tony Bumonte. Are they liable?*

Regina v. Cogan
Regina v. Leak
Court of Appeal, Criminal Division
[1976] 1 Q.B. 217

LAWTON, L.J. read the following judgment of the court. The defendants appeal against their conviction for rape at the Teesside Crown Court on October 25, 1974. They were sentenced by Mocatta, J. as follows: Cogan to two years' imprisonment and Leak to seven years' imprisonment. Leak was also sentenced on his [plea] of guilty . . . to three years' imprisonment for assault occasioning actual bodily harm. . . .

The indictment in the statement of offence charged Cogan with rape and Leak as "being aider and abettor to the same offence." The particulars of offence against Cogan were in common form. As against Leak they were as follows: "at the same time and place did aid and abet counsel and procure John Rodney Cogan to commit the said offence."

The victim of the conduct which the prosecution submitted was rape by both defendants was Leak's wife, a slightly built young woman in her early 20s. They had been married in 1969. There had been many quarrels and some violence. On July 9, 1974, Leak came home in the evening under the influence of alcohol. He asked his wife for money.

---

*This hypothetical is a variation of the facts of People v. Coleman, 104 A.D.2d 778, 480 N.Y.S.2d 888 (App. Div. 1984).

CHAPTER 10 COMPLICITY

She refused to give him any. Shortly afterwards he attacked her. He knocked her down and while she was on the floor he kicked her many times. She sustained numerous bruises on her back and hip. At his trial he pleaded guilty to this assault.

The next day Leak came home at about 6 PM with Cogan. Both had been drinking. Leak told his wife that Cogan wanted to have sexual intercourse with her and that he, Leak, was going to see she did. She was frightened of him and what he might do, as well she might have been. He made her go upstairs where he took her clothes off and lowered her on to a bed. Cogan then came into the room. Leak asked him twice whether he wanted sexual intercourse with her. On both occasions he said that he did not. Leak then had sexual intercourse with her in the presence of Cogan. When he had finished, Leak again asked Cogan if he wanted sexual intercourse with his wife. This time Cogan said he did. He asked Leak to leave the room but he refused to do so. Cogan then had sexual intercourse with Mrs. Leak. Her husband watched. While all this was going on for most of the time, if not all, Mrs. Leak was sobbing. She did not struggle when Cogan was on top of her but she did try to turn away from him. When he had finished, he left the room. Leak then had intercourse with her again and behaved in a revolting fashion to her. When he had finished he joined Cogan and the pair of them left the house to renew their drinking. Mrs. Leak dressed. She went to a neighbor's house and then to the police. The two defendants were arrested about three-quarters of an hour later. Both made oral and written statements. Leak did not give evidence.

Leak's statement amounted to a confession that he had procured Cogan to have sexual intercourse with his wife. He admitted that while Cogan was having sexual intercourse with her she was "sobbing on and off not all the time." There was ample evidence from the terms of his statement that she had not consented to Cogan having intercourse with her. The whole tenor of this statement was that he had procured Cogan to do what he did in order to punish her for past misconduct. He intended that she should be raped and that Cogan's body should provide the physical means to that end.

Cogan, in his written statement, admitted that he had had sexual intercourse with Mrs. Leak at Leak's suggestion and that while he was on top of her she had been upset and had cried. At the trial Cogan gave evidence that he thought Mrs. Leak had consented. The basis for his belief was what he had heard from her husband about her. The drink he had had seems to have been a reason, if not the only one, for mistaking her sobs and distress for consent.

The trial started on October 23, 1974. A few days before, namely, on October 14, press publicity had been given to the fact that the Court of Appeal in Reg. v. Morgan [1976] A.C. 182 had certified a point of law of general public importance as to whether in rape the defendant can properly be convicted notwithstanding that he in fact believed that the woman consented if such belief was not based on reasonable grounds and had given leave to appeal to the House of Lords. In the course of his summing up the trial judge stressed the need for the jury to be sure before convicting either of the defendants that the wife had not consented to sexual intercourse. He then went on to direct them in relation to Cogan's case in accordance with the decision of the Court of Appeal in Reg. v. Morgan. He prudently decided to ask the jury to make a finding as to whether any belief in consent which Cogan may have had was based upon reasonable grounds. The jury returned a verdict of guilty against Cogan thereby showing that they were sure the wife had not consented. They went on to say that Cogan had believed she was consenting but that he had had no reasonable grounds for such belief.

As to Leak he directed the jury that even if Cogan believed that the wife was consenting and had reasonable grounds for such a belief they would still be entitled to find Leak guilty as charged.

Cogan's appeal against conviction was based on the ground that the decision of the House of Lords in Reg. v. Morgan [1976] A.C. 182 applied. It did. There is nothing more to be said. It was for this reason that we allowed the appeal and quashed his conviction.

Leak's appeal against conviction was based on the proposition that he could not be found guilty of aiding and abetting Cogan to rape his wife if Cogan was acquitted of that offence as he was deemed in law to have been when his conviction was quashed. Leak's counsel, Mr. Herrod, conceded, however, that this proposition had some limitations. The law on this topic lacks clarity. . . . The only case which Mr. Herrod submitted had a direct bearing upon the problem of Leak's guilt was Walters v. Lunt [1951] 2 All E.R. 645. In that case the respondents had been charged with receiving from a child aged seven years, certain articles knowing them to have been stolen. In 1951, a child under eight years was deemed in law to be incapable of committing a crime: It followed that at the time of receipt by the respondents the articles had not been stolen and that the charge had not been proved. That case is very different from this because here one fact is clear—the wife had been raped. Cogan had had sexual intercourse with her without her consent. The fact that Cogan was innocent of rape because he believed that she was consenting does not affect the position that she was raped.

Her ravishment had come about because Leak had wanted it to happen and had taken action to see that it did by persuading Cogan to use his body as the instrument for the necessary physical act. In the language of the law the act of sexual intercourse without the wife's consent was the actus reus: It had been procured by Leak who had the appropriate mens rea, namely, his intention that Cogan should have sexual intercourse with her without her consent. In our judgment it is irrelevant that the man whom Leak had procured to do the physical act himself did not intend to have sexual intercourse with the wife without her consent. Leak was using him as a means to procure a criminal purpose. . . .

By his written statement Leak virtually admitted what he had done. As Judge Chapman said in Reg. v. Humphreys [1965] 3 All E.R. 689, 692:

> It would be anomalous if a person who admitted to a substantial part in the perpetration of a misdemeanor as aider and abettor could not be convicted on his own admission merely because the person alleged to have been aided and abetted was not or could not be convicted.

In the circumstance of this case it would be more than anomalous: It would be an affront to justice and to the common sense of ordinary folk. It was for these reasons that we dismissed the appeal against conviction.

The sentence passed upon Leak for his part in the rape was severe, but the circumstances were horrible. We can see nothing wrong with that sentence. The assault upon the wife the previous day had been brutal. The doctor found no less than 13 bruises in the middle and lower region on the left hand side of her spine. There were other bruises on her back and multiple bruises on her left hip. These bruises were consistent with punching and kicking. Men who use violence of this kind upon their wives must expect severe sentences. The sentence of three years was not too severe. . . .

Appeal against conviction dismissed.

The Court of Appeal (LAWTON and JAMES, L.JJ. and SHAW, J.) certified under section 33(2) of the Criminal Appeal Act 1968 the following point of law of general public importance, namely "Where a man has intercourse with a woman without her consent, can a person who aids and abets that act knowing that the woman does not consent be convicted of aiding and abetting rape notwithstanding that the man is acquitted on the basis that he believed the woman was consenting when in fact she has not and is the position the same where the aider and abettor is the woman's husband?"

Leave to appeal refused.

The Appeal Committee of the House of Lords (Lord WILBERFORCE, Lord KILBRANDON, and Lord SALMON) dismissed a petition by the defendant Leak for leave to appeal.

People v. Anonymous
New York Magistrate's Court
161 Misc. 379, 292 N.Y.S. 282 (1936)

RUDIH, City Magistrate.

The defendant, a male person, is charged with vagrancy under subdivision 4(f) of §887 of the Code of Criminal Procedure. The proof clearly establishes the fact that on December 3, 1936, the defendant committed an act of sexual intercourse with a prostitute, for which he paid her the sum of $1. Both were arrested in the house where the act was committed. Before the trial of this defendant the woman was arraigned in Women's Court, and she there pleaded guilty to the charge. The defendant here did not take the stand to deny the testimony against him, but he moves for a dismissal of this proceeding and for his discharge on the ground that upon the conceded facts a male person cannot be convicted of violating this law.

That part of the statute which is material to this question reads as follows:

§887. Who are Vagrants

The following persons are vagrants: . . .
    4. A person
        (a) who offers to commit prostitution, or
        (b) who offers or offers to secure another for the purpose of prostitution, or for any other lewd or indecent act; . . . or
        (e) who receives or offers or agrees to receive any person into any place, structure, house, building or conveyance for the purpose of prostitution, lewdness or assignation. . . , or
        (f) who in any way aids or abets or participates in the doing of any of the acts or things enumerated in subdivision four of section eight hundred and eighty-seven of the code of criminal procedure.

Diligent search has failed to reveal in this state any reported case in which this question was squarely presented. . . .

An analysis of subdivision 4, with its component clauses, will be helpful. It will be noted that clause (a) refers to the prostitute who merely offers to commit prostitution; clause (b) refers to the procurer, male or female; . . . clause (e) refers to the madame or keeper of the house of assignation. Comprehensive as these clauses may seem to be, there were still be some offenders, who, by a strict interpretation of the law, could not be said to be included among the foregoing; the porters, the maids, the many other henchmen, assistants, and lieutenants to procurers, prostitutes, and madames, all aiding, abetting, and participating in the business of prostitution and making their living therefrom. I hold that it was this class of persons, and not the male customer of the prostitute, that the Legislature intended to reach when it enacted clause (f). . . .

[W]e find that clause (f), which refers to those who aid, abet, or participate, was added to the statute books in 1919. In trying to arrive at the intent of the Legislature in phrasing the law in the way it did, it is not necessary to go very deeply into the highly controversial questions of the regulation, suppression, or toleration of this apparently incurable evil, if evil it be. Nor is it necessary to follow all the shifts and turns of policy adopted in this state or elsewhere in the past. They involve no new principle; they merely represent phases in the evolution of the more settled and more systematic procedure in force at the present time. However, a study of the history of prostitution from ancient times down to the present day leaves one with this underlying thought: Wherever suppressive or punitive measures were employed, they were directed against the female, not the male. I do not argue that this attitude was just or fair, or that a persistence in that attitude was best calculated to rid the vice of its cognate evils. Perhaps from the standpoint of our everchanging conception of morality, and certainly in the interest of the public health, it would have been wiser to bring the male participant, as well, under some sort of governmental supervision. But here we are not confronted with a question of morals or of public health; we are called upon to construe a statute, and it is only from the strictly legalistic standpoint that we must view the subject. By the time the year 1919 rolled around, society in these environs may have been sufficiently weaned from its ostrich-like fixation on the entire topic to consider and to discuss the advisability of a change in policy so as to include the male in our treatment of the vice. But these were still only little more than voices in the wilderness; I do not believe that they had risen to such insistence and volume as to force the Legislature to pry us loose from firmly rooted ideas by enacting a revolutionary measure making him a law violator. Before believing that our lawmaking body intended to initiate this radical departure, before concluding that it meant to class an otherwise respectable man with those "who are vagrants," I must ask for a much clearer expression of the legislative intent, for words that will leave no room for doubt. In this more enlightened day and age, when there is strong support for the movement toward lifting the stigma of criminality from the woman, I am loath to place that stamp upon the man.

Another act which is regarded as a vice rather than as a crime is gambling, and there, too, the law differentiates between participants with respect to culpability. It is now well settled that persons who bet on horse races violate no law, while the bookmaker who accepts the bets may, under certain circumstances, be guilty of a misdemeanor. The same is true of policy players as contrasted with the "banker" or manager in the policy game.

The defendant is discharged.

Model Penal Code §2.06(5)-(6)(a) & (b)
Qualified Rejection of Offense Exemption Defenses to Complicity

[Model Penal Code §2.06(5)-(6) is quoted in Section 8.5, regarding conspiracy and solicitation, at page 315.]

Model Penal Code §2.06(7)
Rejection of Unconvictable Perpetrator Defense

An accomplice may be convicted on proof of the commission of the offense and of his complicity therein, though the person claimed to have committed the offense has not been prosecuted or convicted or has been convicted of a different offense or degree of offense or has an immunity to prosecution or conviction or has been acquitted.

Model Penal Code §5.01(3)
Conduct Designed to Aid Another in Commission of a Crime

A person who engages in conduct designed to aid another to commit a crime, which would establish his complicity under Section 2.06 if the crime were committed by such other person, is guilty of an attempt to commit the crime, although the crime is not committed or attempted by such other person.

Questions

1. *An Unconvictable Perpetrator Defense for Leak?* Does Leak satisfy the requirements for complicity under the Model Penal Code? Cogan is not liable for rape, because of his mistake defense. Does this bar liability

for Leak as an accomplice to Cogan under the Model Penal Code? Would Leak have a defense at common law?

2. *An Exempted Person Defense for Leak?* The definition of rape at common law and in many modern codes excludes husbands, the "spousal exception." Does this bar liability for Leak for rape either at common law or under the Model Penal Code?

3. *An Exempted Person Defense for the Prostitution Customer?* The definition of prostitution typically does not criminalize the conduct of the customer. The customer in *Anonymous* is also held exempt from liability as an accomplice. Why? Would he be held liable as an accomplice under the Model Penal Code?

4. *An Exception to the Complicity Exception to the Exempted Person Defense.* Both Leak and the customer of prostitution can claim they are exempt from the definition of the offense. Leak is held liable nonetheless, while the customer retains his exemption from liability. Is Leak's statutory exemption different in some significant way from the customer's? Should there be different results in these two cases?

5. *Dennis White's Liability.* Is corrupt police officer Dennis White liable as an accomplice in the apparent unlawful possession of automatic weapons by undercover officer Tony Bumonte? What defense arguments can he make? What would be the law's response to each of the following arguments? (1) White cannot be liable because he, White, as a police officer, is exempt from liability under the definition of the offense prohibiting possession. (2) White cannot be liable because the person to whom he is said to be an accomplice, Tony Bumonte, is an undercover police officer and therefore obviously does not satisfy the culpability requirements for the offense, or, in any case, has a justification defense to the violation. (3) White cannot be liable because the person to whom he is said to be an accomplice, Tony Bumonte, is a police officer and therefore does not satisfy the objective elements of the offense; the offense is defined to include "not an officer" as an element.

6. *Chucky the Wheeze's Liability.* For what, if anything, is Chucky the Wheeze liable because of his complicity with Tony Bumonte in Tony's apparently unlawful possession of weapons?

7. *The Sexual Offenses in* Cogan & Leak *and* Anonymous. What arguments can you make for and against a "spousal exception" to rape? What arguments can you make for and against exempting the customer from the definition of prostitution? Many rape statutes punish only males. What arguments can you make for and against this practice? What arguments can you make for and against allowing a defense for Cogan for an unreasonable mistake as to the woman's lack of consent? How could it be that Cogan, even unreasonably, believed that the woman was consenting if she was sobbing during the attack? Is it believable that a man might think a woman was consenting under these conditions? These are among the issues taken up in Chapter 18, Sexual Offenses.

Chapter 11. IMPUTING CULPABILITY

SECTION 11.1 DIVERGENCE BETWEEN INTENDED AND ACTUAL RESULT

An Accidental Kidnapping

Ansel and Arkin are determined to prevent tomorrow's sentencing of their father on "revenuing" charges (distilling and selling alcohol, "moonshine," without the required tax stamps). They have concluded that their only option is to kill the sentencing judge, who they know is finishing a vacation in the Black Hills. Their plan is simple. They will knock him out, light a time-delay fuse to the gasoline tank of his cooking stove, and hustle back to town to have alibis twenty minutes later when the gas can explodes, sets fire to the cabin, and burns the judge to death in an apparent camping accident. Their execution of the plan is a bit shaky. When the judge sees them coming, he runs in the other direction. Although the judge is 70 years old, it takes them half an hour to corner him and knock him out and another half hour to drag his body back to the cabin. While they are preparing the "accidental" fire, they begin arguing. Ansel insists that they should have walked the judge back to the cabin, then knocked him out. Arkin responds that he might have gotten away. And so the argument continues, as they head back to town for a night of drinking at the local bar to establish alibis. It is not until the next morning that they agree to disagree and stop arguing. "Any trouble gettin' the fuse lit?," Ansel asks. Arkin responds with a blank stare. "Yo're gonna light the fuse, not me." "Hot damn. Ya screwed up agin'," Ansel insists, and so another argument begins, interrupted only briefly by the federal marshals who come to arrest the brothers. The judge regained consciousness during the night and walked to town. The sentencing of the father goes ahead as scheduled.

The brothers are charged with aggravated kidnapping, a felony of the first degree. The offense is committed if the actor unlawfully confines another for a substantial period in a place of isolation, with the purpose to interfere with the performance of any governmental or political function. What result?

Model Penal Code §2.03(2)(a) & (3)(a)
Divergence Between Result Designed or Contemplated and Actual Result or Between Probable and Actual Result

(2) When purposely or knowingly causing a particular result is an element of an offense, the element is not established if the actual result is not within the purpose or the contemplation of the actor unless:

(a) the actual result differs from that designed or contemplated, as the case may be, only in the respect that a different person or different property is injured or affected or that the injury or harm designed or contemplated would have been more serious or more extensive than that caused; or. . . .

(3) When recklessly or negligently causing a particular result is an element of an offense, the element is not established if the actual result is not within the risk of which the actor is aware or, in the case of negligence, of which he should be aware unless:

(a) the actual result differs from the probable result only in the respect that a different person or different property is injured or affected or that the probable injury or harm would have been more serious or more extensive than that caused; or. . . .

Questions

1. *Liability for Aggravated Murder or Kidnapping?* Do the brothers satisfy the objective and culpability requirements of murder? Do the brothers satisfy the objective requirements of aggravated kidnapping? Do they satisfy the culpability requirements?

2. *Divergence Between Result Intended and Actual Result.* The brothers defend the aggravated kidnapping charge by arguing that their intention was not to unlawfully confine the judge for a substantial period in a place of isolation but rather to kill him. While aggravated kidnapping is a felony of the first degree (see Model Penal Code §212.1(d)), attempted murder is only a felony of the second degree (see Model Penal Code §210.2(2), grading of murder, and §5.05(1), grading of attempt). What result under the Model Penal Code?

3. *Culpability as to Result vs. Culpability as to Circumstance.* Does aggravated kidnapping require culpability as to confinement "for a substantial period"? Presumably the brothers did not expect to confine the judge overnight, as actually occurred. If they had no culpability as to confining the judge for a "substantial period," will it be imputed to them under Model Penal Code §2.03(2)(a)? In that section, the Model Penal Code imputes culpability as to a "result . . . element of an offense." What is a result element under the Code, as distinguished from a circumstance element? Is "a substantial period" a result element or a circumstance element? Consider the following statute:

§11A-2-4. Divergence Between Consequence Intended or Risked and Actual Consequence

When the culpability as to a particular consequence is required by an offense definition and the actual consequence is not that designed, contemplated, or risked by the actor, as the case may be, the required culpability as to the consequence is nonetheless established if the actual consequence differs from the consequence intended, contemplated, or risked, as the case may be, only in the respect that:

(1) a different person or different property is injured or affected, or

(2) the consequence intended, contemplated, or risked was more serious or more extensive an injury or harm than the actual consequence.

(3) "Consequence," as used in this section, means the result element of the offense definition and the attendant circumstance elements that characterize that result.

Proposed Rhode Island Criminal Code §11A-2-4. Does this provision generate the same liability for the brothers as the Model Penal Code?

4. *Model Penal Code §2.03(2)(a) & (3)(a) vs. §2.04(2).* Does Model Penal Code §2.04(2) provide a basis for imposing liability on the brothers? (The prosecutor might argue that the brother made a mistake as to whether the fuse had been lit.) What is the intended relation between Model Penal Code §2.03(2)(a) & (3)(a) and §2.04(2)? The next section may help in answering this question.

SECTION 11.2   INCULPATORY MISTAKES

Impossible Incest?

A month after Celia and Ed Duffy are married, their daughter, Emily, is born. A year later, after one of many fights between them, Ed moves out. He occasionally sends Celia money but never stays in the same place long enough to get the mail that Celia sends him in return. Ten years later, Ed reappears and with Celia's agreement moves back in with her and Emily. After several years, the fights begin again. The primary topic has recently shifted to Celia's suspicion that Ed is having sexual intercourse with Emily, now 17 years old. With the help of a neighbor, Celia catches Ed in the act and reports him to authorities. Ed thinks it is hopeless to deny the charge and confesses to incest with his daughter.

Ed is shocked to learn from his lawyer that he is charged with statutory rape of a 15-year-old rather than incest. During pre-trial discovery he learns that "Emily" is not his daughter, who died soon after his departure, but rather the child of Celia's sister and another man, born two years after his Emily.* Ed enters a plea of not guilty to statutory rape, which requires intercourse with a female less than 16, who the actor knows or should know may be under 16. The defense accepts the prosecution's evidence that the girl is only 15 but insists that Ed reasonably believed her to be 17. Defense counsel offers Ed's confession to incest to prove that Ed thought he was having intercourse with his daughter who, everyone agrees, would have been 17. Is Ed liable for statutory rape?

Model Penal Code §2.04(2)
Ignorance or Mistake

Although ignorance or mistake would otherwise afford a defense to the offense charged, the defense is not available if the defendant would be guilty of another offense had the situation been as he supposed. In such case, however, the ignorance or mistake of the defendant shall reduce the grade and degree of the offense of which he may be convicted to those of the offense of which he would be guilty had the situation been as he supposed.

Questions

1. *Inculpatory Mistakes.* Does Ed satisfy the objective elements of statutory rape? Does he satisfy the culpability requirements? Does Ed

---

*The facts are a variation on a Scottish case reported in *The Guardian,* 6 October 1990, p. 2.

satisfy the objective requirements of incest? Does he satisfy the culpability requirements? Without Model Penal Code §2.04(2), what would Ed be liable for, if anything? If Model Penal Code §2.04(2) is relied upon, what will Ed be liable for, if anything?

2. *Imputing Culpability vs. Imputing Result.* The tentative draft of Model Penal Code §2.04(2) considered allowing the actor to be held liable for the offense he intended to commit, rather than the offense he actually committed:

> When ignorance or mistake affords a defense to the offense charged but the defendant would be guilty of another [and included] offense had the situation been as he supposed it was, he may be convicted of *that other offense.*

Model Penal Code §2.04(2) (Tent. Draft No. 4, 1955) (italics added). Thus, Ed would be held liable for incest, which he believed he was committing, rather than statutory rape. Why do you think that this approach ultimately was rejected?

3. *Imputing Culpability Between Offenses of Different Grades.* Ed thinks he is committing adult incest but in fact is committing the objective elements of statutory rape. Both are third degree felonies. See Model Penal Code §§213.3(1)(a), 230.2. Would it matter if Ed thought he was committing a much less serious offense than incest? Could he nonetheless be held liable for statutory rape? Assume, for example, that Ed knows the girl is not his daughter but rather believes (erroneously) that she is his 17-year-old niece. Thus, he thinks he is committing an offense that is a misdemeanor (a guardian having intercourse with someone under 21, Model Penal Code §213.3(1)(b)). For what offense and what grade is Ed liable when the girl turns out to be 15 years old and unrelated?

Chapter 12. VOLUNTARY INTOXICATION AND CAUSING ONE'S OWN DEFENSE

The imputation of a culpable state of mind occurs most frequently in cases of voluntary intoxication. The justification for treating the actor as if she has a culpable state of mind (usually recklessness) that she does not in fact have is said to be the actor's culpability in voluntarily becoming intoxicated. Section 12.1 examines the governing rules in this area and considers whether the justification for imputation is persuasive. Section 12.2 looks at the general problem of an actor creating the conditions of her own defense, a problem that can arise in a variety of defense situations.

SECTION 12.1 VOLUNTARY INTOXICATION NEGATING AN OFFENSE ELEMENT

Food for Thought

Sharon and Buff have become very close as they struggled together through their first year of law school. Buff is particularly appreciative of Sharon's support because Buff's husband, Peter, is so unsupportive. Buff is somewhat understanding about her husband's complaints. She knows she has been moody and, during the past exam week, even verbally and emotionally abusive. Sharon is less understanding. She thinks Peter is a worthless, whining leech who is taking gross advantage of her friend. She repeatedly urges Buff to, "Kill the pig!," only half in jest.

After their last exam, Sharon suggests that they stop at a local club for a few drinks to celebrate and unwind. Sharon's real plan is to get roaring drunk. She wants to kill Peter and knows that when she gets drunk she becomes violent toward people she does not like, the more drunk the more violent. She assumes that, while intoxicated, their conversation will turn to Peter and that he will become the focus of her drunken rage. In such a drunken state she knows she will not hesitate to kill him, but has learned from her criminal law outline that she will not be responsible for the killing because, if she is sufficiently intoxicated, she will not at the time be acting consciously. Sharon does not tell Buff of her plan. At the club Sharon orders two Bloody Marys. Buff orders a glass of white wine. Sharon wants Buff to help her in the killing and figures that white wine won't do the trick, so she adds a few pills to both of their drinks, telling Buff that the pills will give the drinks more zap. "It'll really make us fly." Buff is hesitant. She generally doesn't drink, but she has just finished a tough year, she reminds herself. She deserves to celebrate. She sips her glass of wine while Sharon has three more Bloody Marys, with additive, in quick succession. Both women are now grossly intoxicated and barely coherent. Sharon is babbling incessantly about killing "Peter-the-Pig."

A friend of Buff's sees them at the club, falling out of their chairs, and insists on taking Buff home. Sharon goes along. When they arrive, they stagger from the friend's car and sprawl on Buff's front yard. Buff discovers that she is lying on her law books, apparently thrown from the upstairs window by a disgusted Peter angry at her exam week abuse. "My books!" "The pig!," Sharon responds. They storm into the house, rip pages from the books, and stuff them into sleeping Peter's mouth. Both break into a chant of "Eat pig, eat."

The next morning, Sharon and Buff awake in bed with Peter's body. Neither woman remembers anything after the first drink at the club. Peter is found to have died of asphyxiation. From witnesses, the police piece together the events, including Sharon's plan to kill Peter by making herself grossly intoxicated. What should be the extent of Sharon's and Buff's liability, if any? What will be their liability, if any, under the Model Penal Code?

Model Penal Code §2.08(1), (2) & (5)(b)
Intoxication Negating an Offense Element

(1) Except as provided in Subsection (4) of this Section [a defense for involuntary intoxication causing dysfunction analogous to insanity], intoxication of the actor is not a defense unless it negatives an element of the offense.

(2) When recklessness establishes an element of the offense, if the actor, due to self-induced intoxication, is unaware of a risk of which he would have been aware had he been sober, such unawareness is immaterial.

(5) Definitions. In this Section unless a different meaning plainly is required: . . .

(b) "self-induced intoxication" means intoxication caused by substances which the actor knowingly introduces into his body, the tendency of which to cause intoxication he knows or ought to know, unless he introduces them pursuant to medical advice or under such circumstances as would afford a defense to a charge of crime; . . .

Director of Public Prosecutions v. Majewski
House of Lords
[1976] 2 All E.R. 142

[Each of seven Law Lords prepared an address and each reached the same conclusion. Only the address of Lord Edmund-Davies is reproduced here.]

Lord EDMUND-DAVIES. My Lords, during a brawl in a public house the appellant attacked the landlord and two others, injuring all three of them. When the police arrived, he assaulted the officer who arrested him. Another officer was struck by the appellant when he was being driven to the police station. The next morning in his cell he attacked a police inspector. As a result, he was indicted at the Chelmsford Crown Court on four counts of occasioning actual bodily harm and on three counts of assaulting a police constable in the execution of his duty. The appellant testified that he had no recollection of the greater part of what had transpired after he entered the public house, and that during the preceding 48 hours he had taken a substantial quantity of drugs and had ordered one drink at the public house. There was adduced a statement from a doctor who saw him the following morning and evidence by another doctor as to the possible effect of the ingestion of such drink and drugs as the appellant had spoken of. During the course of legal submissions, the attention of the learned judge was drawn to the short report of Bolton v. Crawley in which the Court of Appeal held that on a charge of assault occasioning actual bodily harm the consumption of drink or drugs was irrelevant to criminal responsibility. Accordingly, after telling the jury that an assault "means some blow, not something which is purely accidental," the judge directed them that—

. . . the fact that [the appellant] may have taken drink and drugs is irrelevant, provided that you are satisfied that the state which he was in was a result of those drink and drugs [*sic*] or a combination of both was self-induced. . . .

The jury convicted on six of the seven counts and the convictions were upheld by the Court of Appeal, who, however, granted leave to appeal, certifying that the following point of law of general importance was involved:

> Whether a defendant may properly be convicted of assault notwithstanding that, by reason of his self-induced intoxication, he did not intend to do the act alleged to constitute the assault.

. . . The argument advanced on behalf of the appellant can be summarized in the following propositions: (i) Save in relation to offenses of strict responsibility, no man is guilty of a crime unless he has a guilty mind. (ii) A person who, though not insane, commits what would in ordinary circumstances be a crime when he is in such a mental state (whether it be called "automatism" or by any other name) that he does not know what he is doing, lacks a guilty mind and is therefore not criminally culpable for his actions. (iii) Such freedom from culpability exists regardless of (a) whether the offence charged is one involving a "specific" (or "ulterior") intent or one involving only a "general" (or "basic") intent; and (b) whether the automatism was due to causes beyond the control of the person charged or was self-induced by the voluntary taking of drink or drugs. (iv) Assaults being crimes involving a guilty mind, a man who in a state of automatism unlawfully assaults another must be treated as free from all blame and is accordingly entitled to be wholly acquitted: The certified question therefore demands a negative answer. (v) Not only is it logically and ethically indefensible to convict such a man of assault; it also constitutes a contravention of §8 of the Criminal Justice Act 1967. (vi) There accordingly having been a fatal misdirection the appeal should be allowed.

The basic submission of the Crown, on the other hand, may be far more shortly stated thus: A rule of law has been established that self-induced intoxication can provide a defence only to offenses requiring an "ulterior" intent, and is therefore irrelevant to offenses of "basic" intent such as assaults; the direction given was accordingly right, the certified question must be answered in the affirmative, and the appeal should be dismissed. . . .

If logic is to be the sole guide, it follows that a man can never be regarded as committing an assault unless he is conscious of what he is doing. Whatever be the reason for its absence, if he in fact lacks such consciousness he cannot be said to act either intentionally or recklessly. It is submitted on the appellant's behalf that he was at all material times in a condition of "non-insane automatism resulting from pathological intoxication." In Bratty v. Attorney General for Northern Ireland Lord Kilmuir LC acceptably defined "automatism" as—

> the state of a person who, though capable of action, "is not conscious of what he is doing. . . . It means unconscious involuntary action, and it is a defence because the mind does not go with what is being done."

In strict logic it may be that a physical action performed in such a state ought never to be punished as a criminal assault, no matter how grievous the injury thereby inflicted on the person attacked.

Then is it the case that a man is always to be absolved by the criminal law from the consequences of acts performed when in a state of automatism, regardless of how that state was brought about? The law is certainly clear and commendable in relation to cases where the actor is wholly free from fault in relation to the onset of such a mental state.

But a markedly different attitude has long been taken in respect of a state of automatism brought about by the *voluntary* act of the person charged with a crime.

. . . [T]he established law then was and is now that self-induced intoxication, however gross, cannot excuse crimes of basic intent such as that giving rise to this appeal.

Of recent years there has been increasing academic criticism of this virtually uniform judicial attitude. Such criticism is understandable, being based on what is advanced as the logical necessity of acquitting an accused who acted without mens rea, whatever be the reason for its absence. Thus Professor Glanville Williams comments: "There is no reason why drunkenness should not negative a battery, if it tends to show that the accused did not intend to hit anyone." The contrary view applied in our courts certainly presents problems. So much so that counsel for the appellate denies that it is the law. He submits without qualification that legal principle requires that automatism shall constitute a complete defence to all crimes (including those having recklessness as a constituent element).

Why, then, should the trial judge have directed the jury: "You can ignore the subject of drink and drugs as being in any way a defence," even though they had reduced the appellant to an automaton? Does the law demand that he be treated differently from one who attacks another in, for example, a diabetic coma . . . simply because he had drugged himself? It seems that all the academic writers answer that question in the negative, and Professor J.C. Smith is good enough to say:

> It is time for the House of Lords to go back to first principles and to recognize that if a particular *mens rea* is an ingredient of an offence no one can be convicted of that offence if he does not have the *mens rea* in question, whether he was drunk at the time or not. . . .

The criticism by the academics of the law presently administered in this country is of a two-fold nature: (1) It is illogical and therefore inconsistent with legal principle to treat a person who of his own volition has taken drink or drugs any differently from a man suffering from some bodily or mental disorder of the kind earlier mentioned or whose beverage had, without his connivance, been "laced" with intoxicants. (2) It is unethical to convict a man of a crime requiring a guilty state of mind when, *ex hypothesi,* he lacked it. I seek to say something about each of these two criticisms.

(1) Illogicality

The appellant's counsel places strong reliance on a passage in the speech of Lord Hailsham of St. Marylebone in Director of Public Prosecutions v. Morgan in which, alluding to criminal intent, he said:

> . . . once it be accepted that an intent of whatever description is an ingredient essential to the guilt of the accused I cannot myself see that any other direction can be logically acceptable. Otherwise a jury would in effect be told to find an intent where none existed or where none was proved to have existed. I cannot myself reconcile it with my conscience to sanction as part of the English law what I regard as logical impossibility, and, if there were any authority which, if accepted, would compel me to do so, I would feel constrained to declare that it was not to be followed.

Well, I have respectfully to say that were such an attitude rigorously adopted and applied, it would involve the drastic revision of much of our established law. Many would say that this would not be a bad thing, but it is well to realize clearly that such would be the consequence, for the criminal law is unfortunately riddled with illogicalities.

So we find the Court of Appeal decision in R. v. Lipman criticized because Widgery LJ justified the conviction for manslaughter on the basis of death being caused by what was described as the unlawful act of the accused in stuffing bedclothes down his companion's throat under the delusion (induced by the drugs he had taken) that he was dealing with snakes. The criticism is that, although had the verdict been based on a finding that Lipman's act was grossly negligent, it would have been unassailable, on the other hand—

> Had (the victim) survived her "trip" and Lipman faced with any other charge based on her injuries, whether of causing grievous bodily harm with intent of an assault occasioning actual bodily harm he would, in the absence of evidence that he had realized that harm was likely to befall his fellow-tripper, have been acquitted. . . .

The undeviating application of logic leads inexorably to the conclusion that a man behaving even as Lipman unquestionably did must be completely discharged from all criminal liability for the dreadful consequences of his conduct. It was, as I recall, submissions of this startling character which led my noble and learned friend, Lord Simon of Glaisdale, to comment trenchantly to appellant's counsel: "It is all right to say 'Let justice be done though the heavens fall.' But you ask us to say 'Let logic be done even though public order be threatened,' which is something very different."

If such be the inescapable result of the strict application of logic in this branch of the law, it is indeed not surprising that illogicality has long reigned, and the prospect of its dethronement must be regarded as alarming.

(2) Lack of Ethics

It is sometimes said in such cases as the present that it is morally wrong to convict of a crime involving a certain state of mind even where it be established that the charge is based on a man's behavior when he lacked that guilty mind. Rightly or wrongly, Coke was not of that view, for although he asserted that "Actus non facit reum nisi mens sit rea" he also said that, so far from gross intoxication excusing crime, it aggravated the culpability.

Your Lordships are presently concerned with a publichouse brawl, which is said to have been due to the ingestion of drugs rather than drink. Such a plea is becoming much more common, and those acting judicially or who have otherwise acquired any knowledge of addiction are familiar with such parlance of the drug scene as "going on a trip" or "blowing the mind," the avowed intention of the taker of hallucinatory drugs being to lose contact with reality. Irrationality is in truth the very essence of drug-induced phantasies.

Illogical though the present law may be, it represents a compromise between the imposition of liability on inebriates in complete disregard of their condition (on the alleged ground that it was brought on voluntarily), and the total exculpation required by the defendant's actual state of mind at the time he committed the harm in issue. It is at this point pertinent to pause to consider why legal systems exist. The universal object of a system of law is obvious—the establishment and maintenance of order.

> The *first* aim of legal rules is to ensure that members of the community are safeguarded in their persons and property so that their energies are not exhausted by the business of self-protection.

The relevant quotations on the purpose of law are endless and they serve to explain (if, indeed, any explanation be necessary) the sense of outrage which would naturally be felt not only by the victims of such attacks as are alleged against the appellant—and still more against Lipman—were he to go scot free. And a law which permitted this would surely deserve and earn the contempt of most people. But not, it seems, of the joint authors of Smith and Hogan, who in the third edition of their valuable book write:

> While a policy of not allowing a man to escape the consequence of his voluntary drunkenness is understandable, it is submitted that the principle that a man should not be held liable for an act over which he has no control is more important and should prevail.

They add that this is not to say that such a man should in all cases escape criminal liability but that, if he is to be held liable, it should be for the voluntary act of taking the drink or drug. Such a suggestion is far from new. Thus, it appears from Hale's Pleas of the Crown that some lawyers of his day thought that the formal cause of punishment ought to be the drink and not the crime committed under its influence. Edwards expressed concern in 1965 over the possible existence of this gateway to exemption from criminal responsibility and stressed the need for urgent attention to the provision of new statutory powers under which the courts may place such offenders on probation or commit them, as the case may require, to a hospital capable of treating them for the underlying cause of their propensity to automatism. Glanville Williams anticipated in 1961 the Butler Report on Mentally Abnormal Offenders by recommending the creation of an offence of being drunk and dangerous and the committee itself proposed that a new offense of "dangerous intoxication" be punishable on indictment for one year for a first offence or for three years on a second or subsequent offence.

Such recommendations for law reform may receive Parliamentary consideration hereafter but this House is presently concerned with the law as it is. The merciful relaxation of the old rule that drunkenness was no defence appears to have worked reasonably well for 150 years. As to the complaint that it is unethical to punish a man for a crime when his physical behavior was not controlled by a conscious mind, I have long regarded as a convincing theory in support of penal liability for harms committed by voluntary inebriates, the view of Austin, who argued that a person who voluntarily became intoxicated is to be regarded as acting recklessly, for he made himself dangerous in disregard of public safety.

But, to my way of thinking, the nearest approach to a satisfactory refutation of charges of lack of both logic and ethics in punishing the most drunken man for actions which, were he sober, would call for his criminal conviction is that of Stroud, who wrote:

It has been suggested by various writers, in explanation of the doctrine respecting voluntary drunkenness as an excuse for crime, that the effect is "to make drunkenness itself an offence, which is punishable with a degree of punishment varying as the consequences of the act done." This is not exactly correct, although it is not far from the true explanation of the rule. The true explanation is, that drunkenness is not incompatible with *mens rea,* in the sense of ordinary culpable intentionality, because mere recklessness is sufficient to satisfy the definition of *mens rea,* and drunkenness is itself an act of recklessness. The law therefore establishes a conclusive presumption against the admission of proof of intoxication for the purpose of disproving *mens rea* in ordinary crimes. Where this presumption applies, it does not make "drunkenness itself" a crime, but the drunkenness is itself an integral part of the crime, as forming, together with the other unlawful conduct charged against the defendant, a complex act of criminal recklessness.

This explanation affords at once a justification of the rule of law, and a reason for its inapplicability when drunkenness is pleaded by way of showing absence of full intent, or of some exceptional form of *mens rea* essential to a particular crime, according to its definition.

Reverting to the same topic immediately after the decision in *Beard,* Stroud added:

> It would be contrary to all principle and authority to suppose that drunkenness can be a defence for crime in general on the ground that a "person cannot be convicted of a crime unless the *mens* was *rea*." By allowing himself to get drunk, and thereby putting himself in such a condition as to be no longer amenable to the law's commands, a man shows such regardlessness as amounts to *mens rea* for the purpose of all ordinary crimes *(nam crimen ebrietas et incendit et detegit).* His drunkenness can constitute a defence only in those exceptional cases where some additional mental element, of a more heinous and mischievous description than ordinary *mens rea,* is required by the definition of the crime charged against him, and is shown to have been lacking in consequence of his drunken condition.

Professor Glanville Williams would probably condemn such an approach as savoring of "judge-made fiction." While generally sharing his dislike of such fictions, in my judgment little can properly be made out of the criticisms that a law which demands the conviction of such persons who behave as the appellant did is both illogical and unethical. It may be that Parliament should look at it, and devise a new way of dealing with drunken or drugged offenders. But, until it does, the continued application of the existing law is far better calculated to preserve order than the recommendation that he and all who act similarly should leave the dock as free men. . . .

For these reasons, I concur in holding that Yes is the proper answer to the certified question and that, there having been no misdirection, the appeal should be dismissed.

P. Robinson, Causing the Conditions of One's Own Defense: A Study in the Limits of Theory in Criminal Law Doctrine
71 Va. L. Rev. 1, 14-17, 27, 30-31, 35-36, 51 (1985) (edited)

Most jurisdictions allow a defense of voluntary intoxication negating an offense element for offenses requiring purpose or knowledge but deny it for other, lesser-included offenses. Thus, a voluntarily intoxicated killer is not punished as a murderer, but neither is he given a complete defense, even if he has no culpability as to causing death. Recklessness will be imputed to him and will provide the basis for a manslaughter (reckless homicide) conviction. The most common rationale given for this rule is that the actor's culpability in becoming intoxicated is an adequate basis on which to impute recklessness as to committing the offense.

Denying a failure of proof defense for voluntary intoxication that negates the recklessness required for manslaughter is troubling, however, for a number of reasons. . . . First, the imputation of culpability—recklessness under codes following the Model Penal Code, and greater culpability under many other codes—is generally triggered by a definition of "voluntariness" in becoming intoxicated that requires only negligence. Intoxication is "self-induced" under the Model Penal Code, for example, if the actor "knows or *ought to know*" the tendency of the substance to intoxicate. Assume that X kills a pedestrian by driving at a speed that he should know risks such a death, but assume that he does not know of the risk because of his voluntary intoxication. The Model Penal Code would convict him of reckless homicide, despite his unawareness of the risk. His conviction would stand even if he had only been negligent in becoming intoxicated. Thus, he could be found guilty of reckless homicide if a neighbor gave him what he honestly but erroneously believed to be a regular cigarette if he should have known (perhaps because it was hand-rolled) that it might contain an intoxicating substance.

Second, the imputation of recklessness is objectionable because even if the actor is reckless, or even purposeful, as to *getting intoxicated*, it does not follow that he is reckless as to *causing the death of the pedestrian*. The notion that a person risks all manner of resulting harm when he voluntarily becomes intoxicated is common, but is obviously incorrect.[50]

---

50. Hawaii rejects the Model Penal Code provision for just this reason: "[The Model Penal Code] equates the defendant's becoming drunk with the reckless disregard by

Finally, the imputation of a culpable state of mind when none truly exists seems particularly strange for the Model Penal Code drafters, who opposed placing the burden of persuasion on the defendant for most defenses. Yet as to intoxication, the drafters permit what is in essence an irrebuttable presumption as to the existence of an element of the offense.

Proposal: Maintaining the Defense for the Offense
Conduct But Imposing Liability for Conduct in Causing
the Defense Conditions

As has been illustrated above, the current treatment of an actor who is culpable in causing the conditions of his defense is problematic in several respects. An alternative approach suggested here would continue to allow the actor a defense for the immediate conduct constituting the offense, but would separately impose liability on the basis of the actor's earlier conduct in culpably causing the conditions of his or her defense.

This alternative "conduct-in-causing" analysis avoids the problems arising from current law treatment and has several advantages. It avoids the improper assumption that an actor who intends to cause (or risks causing) the conditions under which an offense is committed necessarily intends to commit (or risks committing) the offense. It also properly distinguishes among levels of culpability at the time of causing one's defense in determining the level of liability to be imposed.

A General Principle of Liability for an Actor Who Culpably Causes the Conditions of His Defense

Where an actor brings about the conditions of his defense but at the time has no culpability, not even negligence, as to causing or risking the commission of the subsequent offense, it is appropriate to limit his liability to that imposed by existing statutes. If his conduct constitutes being drunk in public, then such an offense is not properly the extent of his liability. If his conduct does not constitute an offense, he faces no liability.

Where the actor is not only culpable as to causing the defense conditions, but also has a culpable state of mind *as to causing himself to engage in the conduct constituting the offense,* the state should punish him for causing the ultimate offense conduct. His punishment, however, is properly based on his initial conduct of causing the defense conditions

---

him of risks created by his subsequent conduct and thereby forecloses the issue." Hawaii Rev. Stat. §702-230 commentary (1976).

with his accompanying scheming intention, not on the offense conduct that he subsequently performs.

Under this analysis, one need simply consider whether, at the time the actor engages in his initial conduct in causing the defense conditions. . . , he has a culpable state of mind as to causing the conduct constituting the offense. [Consider an analogy in the context of justification.] If an actor sets a forest fire with the ultimate objective of creating the conditions that will justify him (or anyone else) to burn his enemy's property as a firebreak to the forest fire, he properly is held liable for intentionally causing the burning of his enemy's property. This is so even though the conduct he causes, burning the firebreak, is legally justified. His liability is based on his conduct of setting the forest fire with his accompanying intention to cause the burning of the firebreak, not on his justified burning of the firebreak. He is liable for the result that he has intentionally caused, yet all persons are still justified in burning the firebreak.

[Now consider the same analysis in the context of] a failure of proof defense where an actor's voluntary intoxication negates an offense element. Under the proposed analysis, the actor's liability for the offense may be based on his conduct at the time he becomes voluntarily intoxicated with his accompanying culpable state of mind as to the elements of the subsequent offense. If he intoxicates himself with the intention of committing a robbery while intoxicated, he would be liable for the crime even though at the time of the robbery he might not have had the required state of mind.

This analysis has several advantages. For example, it properly accounts for different levels of culpability as to causing the subsequent offense. Assume an actor knows that he always beats his wife uncontrollably after he returns from drinking with his buddies and that he knows that the severity of the beating is directly proportional to the extent of his drinking. He decides to kill his wife, goes to the bar intending to drink heavily to cause the desired beating, and returns home and uncontrollably beats his wife to death. The evidence suggests that at the time of the beating, because of his gross intoxication, he was unaware of a risk that his conduct would kill his wife. He may not even have been aware of his conduct. The Model Penal Code would permit his intoxication to negate purpose or knowledge as to the death of his wife; it would impute recklessness and thereby convict him of reckless homicide (manslaughter). It seems clear, however, that a conviction for an intentional killing (murder) would be appropriate here. The proposed conduct-in-causing analysis would hold the actor liable for murder, based on his conduct in causing his intoxication and his then-existing intention to kill his wife.

Not only does the proposed analysis avoid treating such a grand schemer too leniently, but it also protects a less-culpable actor from being treated too harshly. The Model Penal Code would impute recklessness to the drinker who at the time of his imbibing is unaware of any risk that he may kill or even beat his wife, and thus would convict him of reckless homicide. The proposed analysis would avoid such an unwarranted result. The jury would examine his state of mind as to killing his wife at the time he began to drink and would probably conclude that at that time he was at most negligent as to causing his wife's death. He would thus be liable for, at most, negligent homicide. Indeed, a jury might conclude that a *reasonable person* under the same circumstances would have been unaware of a risk of causing his wife's death; thus, the actor might escape liability even for negligent homicide. . . .

The theory developed above suggests reformulation of the doctrine governing "failure of proof" defenses. Intoxication negating an offense element is the most common such defense raising causing-one's-defense issues:

Intoxication Negating An Offense Element

(1) Evidence of intoxication, voluntary or involuntary, may be admitted into evidence to negate a culpability element of an offense.

(2) If an actor's intoxication negates a required culpability element at the time of the offense, such element is nonetheless established if:

(a) the actor satisfied such element immediately preceding or during the time that he was becoming intoxicated or at any time thereafter until commission of the offense, and

(b) the harm or evil intended, contemplated, or risked is brought about by the actor's subsequent conduct during intoxication.

(3) An actor may have a justification or excuse defense to liability under subsection (2) for his conduct in becoming intoxicated.

Thus, the translation from theory to doctrine is relatively easy. Difficulties arise, however, in guaranteeing the feasibility or workability of the resulting doctrine. . . .

Questions

1. *Conflicting Views on Voluntary Intoxication Negating an Offense Element.* The "academics," to whom the *Majewski* opinion (by Lord Edmund-Davies) responds, object to imputing to a defendant any culpable state of mind that she does not in fact possess. What are the arguments in support of this position? Some courts have taken the opposite position, holding that voluntary intoxication may not be used to negate

any required culpable state of mind (other than the deliberation and premeditation required for first degree murder). See, e.g., State v. Stasio, 78 N.J. 467, 396 A.2d 1129 (1979). Can you imagine the arguments that might be offered in support of this position? The court in *Majewski* rejects both of these positions and follows the common law compromise, allowing voluntary intoxication to negate specific intent but not a general intent. What arguments support this position? Is Lord Edmund-Davies right to concede to the academics that it is illogical to impute to an actor a culpable state of mind that she does not in fact have? To which of these three positions is the Model Penal Code closest?

2. *Sharon's and Buff's Liability.* Do Sharon and Buff have the culpable state of mind required for murder at the time they are "feeding the pig"? Do they have the culpability required for manslaughter? For negligent homicide? Assume for a moment that both women voluntarily intoxicated themselves. What culpability, if any, will the law impute to them? What will they be held liable for, if anything? Is the answer different under the common law rule, expressed in *Majewski*, than under the Model Penal Code?

3. *Culpability as to Becoming Intoxicated.* Did Sharon voluntarily intoxicate herself? Did Buff voluntarily intoxicate herself? What is the culpability level of each *as to becoming intoxicated?* What level of culpability *as to causing Peter's death* is imputed to each?

4. *The Grand Schemer and the Negligent Drinker.* What is your intuition as to the general degree of blameworthiness that Sharon has as to Peter's death? Is it closer to that of the offender in a typical murder case, a typical manslaughter case, a typical negligent homicide case, or none of the above? What is your intuition as to Buff? Should the law treat the two cases differently?

5. *An Alternative View of Voluntary Intoxication: Liability for Causing the Conditions of One's Defense.* What would be Sharon's liability, if any, under the proposal offered in the "Causing the Conditions . . ." excerpt? What would be Buff's liability? What problems of proof might a prosecutor have under this approach that would not exist under the common law approach (described in *Majewski*) or under the Model Penal Code approach?

SECTION 12.2 CAUSING THE CONDITIONS OF ONE'S OWN DEFENSE

When an actor satisfies the conditions of a general defense, but has brought about the defense conditions (e.g., by "hanging" with a gang knowing that they will coerce the actor to rob a bank or by setting

CHAPTER 12   CAUSING DEFENSE CONDITIONS   409

a forest fire which then will justify burning a neighbor's field as a firebreak), we face an apparent dilemma. On the one hand, if we focus on the circumstances at the time of the offense, the actor seems under normal rules fully excused or justified, as the case may be. On the other hand, it seems obvious that we ought not ignore the fact that the actor caused the conditions giving rise to the defense. The problem is analogous in many ways to the problem of voluntary intoxication discussed in Section 12.1, yet modern codes give this problem a different treatment than they do voluntary intoxication.

Trading Corn for People

Aaron has refused to join the local corn cooperative and has been selling his corn at a lower price, reducing the cooperative's sales. The cooperative members worry that if Aaron is not brought into line, others may follow his lead, causing the collapse of the cooperative and lower corn prices for all. None of the other members are as angry as Teppi, however, nor as clever.

Two weeks before the next harvesting date, Teppi hits on a plan to bring Aaron back into the coop. He solicits help from his good friend Bo but Bo refuses, saying Aaron ought to be left to make his own choices. They get into a fight, Teppi pulls a gun, but passers-by intervene. Teppi storms off, warning Bo that if he does not meet him at East Rock at 6 AM tomorrow, he will consider Bo a useless coward and will never speak to him again.

At 6 AM, Teppi has assembled the materials for his plan at East Rock. As predicted by the Weather Service, a strong wind is blowing out of the east. Teppi plans to pour flammable tar along a hundred yard strip, light a slow-burning fuse, and drive to Aaron's farm to discuss his joining the coop. If all goes according to plan, soon after he arrives at the farm, the fire will come raging from the east heading for the town, on a track through Aaron's cornfield. Teppi can then justifiably burn Aaron's cornfield as a firebreak, avoid any significant harm beyond this, and be a hero for saving the town. Since Aaron will be taken by surprise, it seems likely that he will resist the burning, which will provide an additional bonus. Aaron's resistance will give Teppi the opportunity to lawfully beat up Aaron and also to suggest to the townspeople that Aaron values his corn more than their lives, a useful propaganda point in pressuring Aaron into cooperation. As Teppi is congratulating himself for his clever plan, Bo appears. "I haven't changed my mind. I don't want to help. I just came to let you know." Teppi explodes and pulls his gun.

"I'm not going to fool with you, Bo. Either you start the fire here and burn the firebreak at Aaron's or I'll shoot." "Damn, I was afraid you might do something crazy like this," Bo replies. At gunpoint, Bo lays the tar and lights the fuse. Teppi helps. They both drive to Aaron's.

The scheme goes as planned except that Aaron, upon seeing the approaching fire, immediately joins in to help Bo and Teppi burn his cornfield to save the town. He is suspicious of the timing of their arrival and that of the fire, however, and insists on an investigation. Authorities track the fire back to its starting point and piece together the events. Teppi and Bo are charged with the unlawful destruction of Aaron's field, a third degree felony under Model Penal Code §220.3(1)(a) (the damage to the crop is in excess of $5,000). Teppi and Bo defend by noting that, by burning the field, they saved many lives and therefore were clearly justified. Teppi offers to plead guilty to a petty misdemeanor, accurately pointing out that the fire he and Bo set at East Rock burned nothing of value, certainly less than $100 (and created no danger to persons because of the ease of burning a firebreak). Bo offers a duress defense to both the East Rock and the cornfield burning. Are Teppi and Bo liable for burning Aaron's field?

Model Penal Code §220.3
Criminal Mischief

(1) *Offense Defined.* A person is guilty of criminal mischief if he:

(a) damages tangible property of another purposely, recklessly, or by negligence in the employment of fire, explosives, or other dangerous means . . . ; or

(b) purposely or recklessly tampers with tangible property of another so as to endanger person or property; or

(c) purposely or recklessly causes another to suffer pecuniary loss by deception or threat.

(2) *Grading.* Criminal mischief is a felony of the third degree if the actor purposely causes pecuniary loss in excess of $5,000, or a substantial interruption or impairment of public communication, transportation, supply of water, gas or power, or other public service. It is a misdemeanor if the actor purposely causes pecuniary loss in excess of $100, or a petty misdemeanor if he purposely or recklessly causes pecuniary loss in excess of $25. Otherwise criminal mischief is a violation.

Model Penal Code §3.02(1)(a) & (2)
Justification Generally: Choice of Evils

(1) Conduct which the actor believes to be necessary to avoid a harm or evil to himself or to another is justifiable, provided that:
    (a) the harm or evil sought to be avoided by such conduct is greater than that sought to be prevented by the law defining the offense charged; . . .
(2) When the actor was reckless or negligent in bringing about the situation requiring a choice of harms or evils or in appraising the necessity for his conduct, the justification afforded by this Section is unavailable in a prosecution for any offense for which recklessness or negligence, as the case may be, suffices to establish culpability.

Model Penal Code §2.09(1) & (2)
Duress

(1) It is an affirmative defense that the actor engaged in the conduct charged to constitute an offense because he was coerced to do so by the use of, or a threat to use, unlawful force against his person or the person of another, which a person of reasonable firmness in his situation would have been unable to resist.
(2) The defense provided by this Section is unavailable if the actor recklessly placed himself in a situation in which it was probable that he would be subjected to duress. The defense is also unavailable if he was negligent in placing himself in such a situation, whenever negligence suffices to establish culpability for the offense charged.

Questions

1. *Do Teppi and Bo Satisfy Offense Elements?* Presumably Teppi and Bo satisfy the elements of petty misdemeanor criminal mischief based upon their conduct at East Rock. Does their conduct in burning Aaron's cornfield satisfy the elements of third degree felony criminal mischief?

2. *Duress Defense for Bo?* If Bo had gone to East Rock suspecting nothing of Teppi's intention regarding Aaron's farm, would he have a duress defense under the Model Penal Code based upon Teppi's threat

to kill him if he does not help? Does Bo lose his duress defense if he goes to East Rock knowing of Teppi's plan and "afraid [Teppi] might do something crazy like this"? Does he lose a duress defense both to the original burning at East Rock and to burning Aaron's field?

3. *Justification Defense for Teppi and Bo?* If Teppi and Bo had not set the threatening fire, would they have a lesser evils (justification) defense to burning Aaron's field? Does the fact that they set the fire take away their defense? In other words, if the local sheriff arrived beforehand, knowing that they had set the fire and citing the relevant criminal code sections, would Teppi and Bo still try to burn Aaron's field in front of the sheriff?

4. *Resisting the Sheriff's Burning.* Would the sheriff be justified in burning Aaron's field if he (the sheriff) were present? Would Aaron have been justified in resisting Teppi and Bo's burning of his field if he had chosen to do so? (We have not yet examined defensive force justifications; assume one can lawfully resist only unjustified conduct.) Would Aaron have been justified in resisting the sheriff's burning of his field?

5. *Liability for Causing the Conditions of One's Defense.* How would questions 2, 3, and 4 be answered if the proposal of the "Causing the Conditions . . ." excerpt, in the last section, were in force in the jurisdiction? What is your own intuition of what the law should have Teppi, Bo, Aaron, and the sheriff do as they see the fire approach? What legal rules would you write to govern a lesser evil justification and a duress defense where the actor has been culpable in bringing about the conditions of either defense?

6. *Causing One's Own Involuntary Conduct.* Assume that a crane operator fails to take his anti-seizure medication, and that by doing so he risks having a seizure during work that may seriously injure others. As a result, he has a seizure and people are seriously injured. He seeks a defense under Model Penal Code §2.01(2)(a). What result?

Chapter 13. OMISSION LIABILITY

Given the good reasons for requiring an act, described in Section 8.1, one might well predict that the criminal law is always careful to avoid liability in the absence of an act. In fact, liability without an act is frequently permitted. Why? One answer offered is that, where there is no act but only an omission, the rationales of the act requirement nonetheless are satisfied if the special requirements of omission liability are present: the presence of a legal duty and a capacity to act. That is, the failure to perform a legal duty, of which one is capable, is said to be comparable to an act in satisfying the rationales. But this conclusion is something of an oversimplification. As will become apparent from the materials, the special requirements of omission liability—a legal duty and the capacity to act—serve some act-requirement rationales better than others.

A duty to act frequently arises from civil law but in some cases the criminal offense itself may create the duty by defining the offense in terms of omission. Thus, the failure to file a tax return, a motorist's failure to stop after involvement in an accident, a draftee's failure to report for induction, a parent's neglect of a sick child, and the failure to report certain communicable diseases, can all be punished without an independent showing of a duty to act. The duty is created by the statute that defines the omission to be a criminal offense. An independent duty to act is required for liability only for offenses defined in terms of affirmative conduct.

Keep in mind that liability does not necessarily follow because the special omission requirements are satisfied. If duty and capacity are shown, *the conduct* required by the offense definition may be imputed, but all other requirements of the offense definition—such as a prohibited result and all culpability requirements—still must be established.

Dunning's Deal

Dunning's expenses for school are more than he can handle so he decides to earn extra money by working as an escort. He is relatively good-looking and can be very charming as the need arises. Mrs. Harrington, an elderly widow, particularly enjoys Dunning's company and they agree that he will be an escort for her, exclusively, in exchange for a monthly salary. Both are pleased with the arrangement until Mrs. Harrington by chance sees Dunning with a young woman. When he arrives that evening at his usual time, she confronts him with her observation. "That's my girlfriend, not another customer," he insists. "We agreed that you would escort only me," she responds. They continue to argue. Concerned that Mrs. Harrington intends not to pay him what he has already earned, Dunning insists on getting paid for the past month. Mrs. Harrington snaps, "It's not due until tomorrow. Anyway, why should I pay you? You broke our agreement." She continues with a tirade on Dunning's breach of their agreement. As she gets more excited, Mrs. Harrington's face turns pale and she falls to the floor, gasping for air. She crawls toward her handbag which contains her medicine but is unable to get more than a few yards. Her breathing gets more labored and her color turns to chalk white. Dunning knows that she needs the medicine in her handbag but he turns and leaves. Mrs. Harrington dies several minutes later. Is Dunning criminally liable for his failure to aid Mrs. Harrington?

Pa. Stat. Ann. Title 18, §2504
Involuntary Manslaughter

A person is guilty of involuntary manslaughter when as a direct result of the doing of an unlawful act in a reckless or grossly negligent manner, he causes the death of another person.

Model Penal Code §2.01(1) & (3)
Liability for an Omission

(1) A person is not guilty of an offense unless his liability is based on conduct which includes a voluntary act or the omission to perform an act of which he is physically capable. . . .

CHAPTER 13 OMISSION LIABILITY 415

(3) Liability for the commission of an offense may not be based on an omission unaccompanied by action unless:
 (a) the omission is expressly made sufficient by the law defining the offense; or
 (b) a duty to perform the omitted act is otherwise imposed by law.

Jones v. United States
United States Court of Appeals, District of Columbia Circuit
308 F.2d 307, 113 U.S. App. D.C. 352 (1962)

WRIGHT, Circuit Judge.

Appellant, together with one Shirley Green, was tried on a three-count indictment charging them jointly with (1) abusing and maltreating Robert Lee Green, (2) abusing and maltreating Anthony Lee Green, and (3) involuntary manslaughter through failure to perform their legal duty of care for Anthony Lee Green, which failure resulted in his death. At the close of evidence, after trial to a jury, the first two counts were dismissed as to both defendants. On the third count, appellant was convicted of involuntary manslaughter. Shirley Green was found not guilty. . . .

. . . In late 1957, Shirley Green became pregnant, out of wedlock, with a child, Robert Lee, subsequently born August 17, 1958. Apparently to avoid the embarrassment of the presence of the child in the Green home, it was arranged that appellant, a family friend, would take the child to her home after birth. Appellant did so, and the child remained there continuously until removed by the police on August 5, 1960. Initially appellant made some motions toward the adoption of Robert Lee, but these came to nought, and shortly thereafter it was agreed that Shirley Green was to pay appellant $72 a month for his care. According to appellant, these payments were made for only five months. According to Shirley Green, they were made up to July, 1960.

Early in 1959 Shirley Green again became pregnant, this time with the child Anthony Lee, whose death is the basis of appellant's conviction. This child was born October 21, 1959. Soon after birth, Anthony Lee developed a mild jaundice condition, attributed to a blood incompatibility with his mother. The jaundice resulted in his retention in the hospital for three days beyond the usual time, or until October 26, 1959, when, on authorization signed by Shirley Green, Anthony Lee was released by the hospital to appellant's custody. Shirley Green, after a two or three day stay in the hospital, also lived with appellant for three weeks, after which she returned to her parents' home, leaving the children with appellant. She testified she did not see them again, except for one visit in March, until August 5, 1960. Consequently, though there does not seem to have been any specific monetary agreement with Shirley Green covering Anthony Lee's support, appellant had complete custody of both children until they were rescued by the police.

With regard to medical care, the evidence is undisputed. In March, 1960, appellant called a Dr. Turner to her home to treat Anthony Lee for a bronchial condition. Appellant also telephoned the doctor at various times to consult with him concerning Anthony Lee's diet and health. In early July, 1960, appellant took Anthony Lee to Dr. Turner's office where he was treated for "simple diarrhea." At this time the doctor noted the "wizened" appearance of the child and told appellant to tell the mother of the child that he should be taken to a hospital. This was not done.

On August 2, 1960, two collectors for the local gas company had occasion to go to the basement of appellant's home, and there saw the two children. Robert Lee and Anthony Lee at this time were age two years and ten months respectively. Robert Lee was in a "crib" consisting of a framework of wood, covered with a fine wire screening, including the top which was hinged. The "crib" was lined with newspaper, which was stained, apparently with feces, and crawling with roaches. Anthony Lee was lying in a bassinet and was described as having the appearance of a "small baby monkey." One collector testified to seeing roaches on Anthony Lee.

On August 5, 1960, the collectors returned to appellant's home in the company of several police officers and personnel of the Women's Bureau. At this time, Anthony Lee was upstairs in the dining room in the bassinet, but Robert Lee was still downstairs in his "crib." The officers removed the children to the D.C. General Hospital where Anthony Lee was diagnosed as suffering from severe malnutrition and lesions over large portions of his body, apparently caused by severe diaper rash. Following admission, he was fed repeatedly, apparently with no difficulty, and was described as being very hungry. His death, 34 hours after admission, was attributed without dispute to malnutrition. At birth, Anthony Lee weighed six pounds, fifteen ounces—at death at age ten months, he weighed seven pounds, thirteen ounces. Normal weight at this age would have been approximately 14 pounds.

[T]here is substantial evidence from which the jury could have found that appellant failed to obtain proper medical care for the child. Appellant relies upon the evidence showing that on one occasion she summoned a doctor for the child, on another took the child to the doctor's office, and that she telephoned the doctor on several occasions about the baby's formula. However, the last time a doctor saw the child was a month before his death, and appellant admitted that on that occasion the doctor recommended hospitalization. Appellant did not hospitalize the child, nor did she take any other steps to obtain medical care in the last crucial month. Thus there was sufficient evidence to go to the jury on the issue of medical care, as well as failure to feed.

Appellant also takes exception to the failure of the trial court to charge that the jury must find beyond a reasonable doubt, as an element of the crime, that appellant was under a legal duty to supply food and necessities to Anthony Lee. . . .

The problem of establishing the duty to take action which would preserve the life of another has not often arisen in the case law of this country. The most commonly cited statement of the rule is found in People v. Beardsley, 150 Mich. 206, 113 N.W. 1128, 1129, 13 L.R.A., N.S., 1020:

> The law recognizes that under some circumstances the omission of a duty owed by one individual to another, where such omission results in the death of the one to whom the duty is owing, will make the other chargeable with manslaughter. . . . This rule of law is always based upon the proposition that the duty neglected must be a legal duty, and not a mere moral obligation. It must be a duty imposed by law or by contract, and the omission to perform the duty must be the immediate and direct cause of death. . . .

There are at least four situations in which the failure to act may constitute breach of a legal duty. One can be held criminally liable: first, where a statute imposes a duty to care for another; second, where one stands in a certain status relationship to another; third, where one has assumed a contractual duty to care for another; and fourth, where one has voluntarily assumed the care of another and so secluded the helpless person as to prevent others from rendering aid.

It is the contention of the Government that either the third or the fourth ground is applicable here. However, it is obvious that in any of the four situations, there are critical issues of fact which must be passed on by the jury—specifically in this case, whether appellant had entered into a contract with the mother for the care of Anthony Lee or, alternatively, whether she assumed the care of the child and secluded him from the care of his mother, his natural protector. On both of these issues, the evidence is in direct conflict, appellant insisting that the mother was actually living with appellant and Anthony Lee, and hence should have been taking care of the child herself, while Shirley Green testified she was living with her parents and was paying appellant to care for both children.

In spite of this conflict, the instructions given in the case failed even to suggest the necessity for finding a legal duty of care. The only reference to duty in the instructions was the reading of the indictment which charged, inter alia, that the defendants "failed to perform their legal duty." A finding of legal duty is the critical element of the crime charged and failure to instruct the jury concerning it was plain error. . . .

Reversed and remanded.

Questions

1. *Dunning's Liability.* Does Dunning satisfy the elements of Involuntary Manslaughter, as defined in Pa. Stat. Ann. Title 18, §2504? Will Dunning be criminally liable for Mrs. Harrington's death?

2. *The Duty Requirement.* What arguments can you make that Dunning has a duty to act? What arguments can you make that he does not? Does it depend on doctrines of contract law? Does the duty requirement for omission liability satisfy the concerns of the legality principle? If it is determined that Dunning has a duty to give Mrs. Harrington her medicine, what else must be shown, if anything, to establish liability for criminal homicide?

3. *Authorization in the Model Penal Code for Omission Liability?* Recall that under Model Penal Code §210.1(1), "a person is guilty of criminal homicide if he purposely, knowingly, recklessly or negligently causes the death of another human being." Under the Model Penal Code, is criminal homicide defined to require an act causing death, as is Pa. Stat. Ann. Title 18, §2504, or can the elements of criminal homicide be satisfied by showing that an actor's omission caused the death? If the latter, must a duty to act be shown? If not, Dunning can be held liable for criminal homicide without regard to any agreement he may have had with Mrs. Harrington. This is not generally accepted to be the case. If the Code's criminal homicide is interpreted as being defined only in terms of commission, as is the Pennsylvania statute, under what authority is the required conduct imputed to the actor? That is, where does the Code expressly provide that an actor may be treated as if he engaged in the required conduct if he *fails* to perform a legal duty of which he is capable? The capacity and duty provisions in Model Penal Code §2.01(1) & (3) are stated in terms of defenses.

"37 Who Saw Murder Didn't Call Police"
N.Y. Times, March 27, 1964, col. 4, at 1

For more than half an hour thirty-eight respectable, law-abiding citizens in Queens watched a killer stalk and stab a woman in three separate attacks in Kew Gardens.

CHAPTER 13 OMISSION LIABILITY

Twice the sound of their voices and the sudden glow of their bedroom lights interrupted him and frightened him off. Each time he returned, sought her out and stabbed her again. Not one person telephoned the police during the assault; one witness called after the woman was dead.

That was two weeks ago today. But Assistant Chief Inspector Frederick M. Lussen, in charge of the borough's detectives and a veteran of twenty-five years of homicide investigations, is still shocked.

He can give a matter-of-fact recitation of many murders. But the Kew Gardens slaying baffles him—not because it is a murder, but because the "good people" failed to call the police.

"As we have reconstructed the crime," he said, "the assailant had three chances to kill this woman during a thirty-five minute period. He returned twice to complete the job. If we had been called when he first attacked, the woman might not be dead now."

This is what the police say happened beginning at 3:20 AM in the staid, middle-class, tree-lined Austin Street area:

Twenty-eight-year-old Catherine Genovese, who was called Kitty by almost everyone in the neighborhood, was returning home from her job as manager of a bar in Hollis. She parked her red Fiat in a lot adjacent to the Kew Gardens Long Island Rail Road Station, facing Mowbray Place. Like many residents of the neighborhood, she had parked there day after day since her arrival from Connecticut a year ago, although the railroad frowns on the practice.

She turned off the lights of her car, locked the door and started to walk the 100 feet to the entrance of her apartment at 82-70 Austin Street, which is in a Tudor building, with stores on the first floor and apartments on the second.

The entrance to the apartment is in the rear of the building because the front is rented to retail stores. At night the quiet neighborhood is shrouded in the slumbering darkness that marks most residential areas.

Miss Genovese noticed a man at the far end of the lot, near a seven-story apartment house at 82-40 Austin Street. She halted. Then, nervously, she headed up Austin Street toward Lefferts Boulevard, where there is a call box to the 102d Police Precinct in nearby Richmond Hill.

She got as far as a street light in front of a bookstore before the man grabbed her. She screamed. Lights went on in the ten-story apartment house at 82-67 Austin Street, which faces the bookstore. Windows slip open and voices punctured the early-morning stillness.

Miss Genovese screamed: "Oh, my God, he stabbed me! Please help me! Please help me!"

From one of the upper windows in the apartment house, a man called down: "Let that girl alone!"

The assailant looked up at him, shrugged and walked down Austin Street toward a white sedan parked a short distance away. Miss Genovese struggled to her feet.

Lights went out. The killer returned to Miss Genovese, now trying to make her way around the side of the building by the parking lot to get to her apartment. The assailant stabbed her again.

"I'm dying!" she shrieked. "I'm dying!"

Windows were opened again, and lights went on in many apartments. The assailant got into his car and drove away. Miss Genovese staggered to her feet. A city bus, Q-10, the Lefferts Boulevard line to Kennedy International Airport, passed. It was 3:35 AM.

The assailant returned. By then, Miss Genovese had crawled to the back of the building, where the freshly painted brown doors to the apartment house held out hope of safety. The killer tried the first door; she wasn't there. At the second door, 82-62 Austin Street, he saw her slumped on the floor at the foot of the stairs. He stabbed her a third time—fatally.

It was 3:50 by the time the police received their first call from a man who was a neighbor of Miss Genovese. In two minutes they were at the scene. The neighbor, a seventy-year-old woman and another woman were the only persons on the street. Nobody else came forward.

The man explained that he had called the police after much deliberation. He had phoned a friend in Nassau County for advice and then he had crossed the roof of the building to the apartment of the elderly woman to get her to make the call.

"I didn't want to get involved," he sheepishly told the police.

Six days later, the police arrested Winston Moseley, a twenty-nine-year-old business-machine operator, and charged him with the homicide. Moseley had no previous record. He is married, has two children and owns a home at 133-19 Sutter Avenue, South Ozone Park, Queens. On Wednesday, a court committed him to Kings County Hospital for psychiatric observation.

The police stressed how simple it would have been to have gotten in touch with them. "A phone call," said one of the detectives, "would have done it." The police may be reached by dialing "0" for operator or SPring 7-3100.

The question of whether the witness can be held legally responsible in any way for failure to report the crime was put to the Police Department's legal bureau. There, a spokesman said:

"There is no legal responsibility, with few exceptions, for any citizen to report a crime."

Under the statutes of the city, he said, a witness to a suspicious or violent death must report it to the medical examiner. Under state law, a witness cannot withhold information in a kidnapping.

Today witnesses from the neighborhood, which is made up of one-family homes in the $35,000 to $60,000 range with the exception of the two apartment houses near the railroad station, find it difficult to explain why they didn't call the police.

Lieut. Bernard Jacobs, who handled the investigation by the detectives, said:

"It is one of the better neighborhoods. There are few reports of crimes. You only get the usual complaints about boys playing or garbage cans being turned over."

The police said most persons had told them they had been afraid to call, but had given meaningless answers when asked what they had feared.

"We can understand the reticence of people to become involved in an area of violence," Lieutenant Jacobs said, "but where they are in their homes, near phones, why should they be afraid to call the police?"

He said his men were able to piece together what happened—and capture the suspect—because the residents furnished all the information when detectives rang doorbells during the days following the slaying.

"But why didn't someone call us that night?" he asked unbelievingly.

Witnesses—some of them unable to believe what they had allowed to happen—told a reporter why.

A housewife, knowingly if quite casually, said, "We thought it was a lover's quarrel." A husband and wife both said, "Frankly, we were afraid." They seemed aware of the fact that events might have been different. A distraught woman, wiping her hands in her apron, said, "I didn't want my husband to get involved."

One couple, now willing to talk about that night, said they heard the first screams. The husband looked thoughtfully at the bookstore where the killer first grabbed Miss Genovese.

"We went to the window to see what was happening," he said, "but the light from our bedroom made it difficult to see the street." The wife, still apprehensive, added: "I put out the light and we were able to see better."

Asked why they hadn't called the police, she shrugged and replied: "I don't know."

A man peeked out from a slight opening in the doorway to his apartment and rattled off an account of the killer's second attack. Why hadn't he called the police at the time? "I was tired," he said without emotion. "I went back to bed."

It was 4:25 AM when the ambulance arrived for the body of Miss Genovese. It drove off. "Then," a solemn police detective said, "the people came out."

A Penal Code Prepared by the Indian Law Commissioners
Note M, 53-56 (1837)

Early in the progress of the Code it became necessary for us to consider the following question: When acts are made punishable on the ground that those acts produce, or are intended to produce, or are known to be likely to produce certain evil effects, to what extent ought omissions which produce, which are intended to produce, or which are known to be likely to produce the same evil effects be made punishable?

Two things we take to be evident; first, that some of these omissions ought to be punished in exactly the same manner in which acts are punished; secondly, that all these omissions ought not to be punished. It will hardly be disputed that a gaoler who voluntarily causes the death of a prisoner by omitting to supply that prisoner with food, or a nurse who voluntarily causes the death of an infant entrusted to her care by omitting to take it out of a tub of water into which it has fallen, ought to be treated as guilty of murder. On the other hand, it will hardly be maintained that a man should be punished as a murderer because he omitted to relieve a beggar, even though there might be the clearest proof that the death of the beggar was the effect of this omission, and that the man who omitted to give the alms knew that the death of the beggar was likely to be the effect of the omission. It will hardly be maintained that a surgeon ought to be treated as a murderer for refusing to go from Calcutta to Meerut to perform an operation, although it should be absolutely certain that this surgeon was the only person in India who could perform it, and that if it were not performed the person who required it would die. It is difficult to say whether a Penal Code which should put no omissions on the same footing with acts, or a Penal Code which should put all omissions on the same footing with acts would produce consequences more absurd and revolting. There is no country in which either of these principles is adopted. Indeed, it is hard to conceive how, if either were adopted, society could be held together.

It is plain, therefore, that a middle course must be taken. But it is not easy to determine what that middle course ought to be. The absurdity of the two extremes is obvious. But there are innumerable intermediate points; and wherever the line of demarcation may be drawn it will, we fear, include some cases which we might wish to exempt, and will exempt some which we might wish to include.

Mr. Livingston's Code provides that a person shall be considered as guilty of homicide who omits to save life, which he could save "without personal danger, or pecuniary loss." This rule appears to us to be open to serious objection. There may be extreme inconvenience without the smallest personal danger, or the smallest risk of pecuniary loss, as in the case we lately put of a surgeon summoned from Calcutta to Meerut, to perform an operation. He may be offered such a fee that he would be a gainer by going. He may have no ground to apprehend that he should run any greater personal risk by journeying to the Upper Provinces than by continuing to reside in Bengal. But he is about to proceed to Europe immediately, or he expects some members of his family by the next ship, and wishes to be at the residency to receive them. He, therefore, refuses to go. Surely, he ought not, for so refusing, to be treated as a murderer. It would be somewhat inconsistent to punish one man for not staying three months in India to save the life of another, and to leave wholly unpunished the man who, enjoying ample wealth, should refuse to disburse an anna to save the life of another. Again it appears to us that it may be fit to punish a person as a murderer for causing death by omitting an act which cannot be performed without personal danger, or pecuniary loss. A parent may be unable to procure food for an infant without money. Yet the parent, if he has the means, is bound to furnish the infant with food, and if by omitting to do so he voluntarily causes its death he may with propriety be treated as a murderer. A nurse hired to attend a person suffering from an infectious disease cannot perform her duty without running some risk of infection. Yet if she deserts the sick person, and thus voluntarily causes his death, we should be disposed to treat her as a murderer.

We pronounce with confidence, therefore, that the line ought not to be drawn where Mr. Livingston has drawn it. But it is with great diffidence that we bring forward our own proposition. It is open to objections: Cases may be put in which it will operate too severely, and cases in which it will operate too leniently: But we are unable to devise a better.

What we propose is this, that where acts are made punishable on the ground that they have caused, or have been intended to cause, or have been known to be likely to cause a certain evil effect, omissions which have caused, which have been intended to cause, or which have been known to be likely to cause the same effect shall be punishable in the same manner; provided that such omissions were, on other grounds, illegal. An omission is illegal . . . if it be an offence, if it be a breach of some direction of law, or if it be such a wrong as would be a good ground for a civil action. . . .

We are sensible that in some of the cases which we have put our rule may appear too lenient. But we do not think that it can be made more severe, without disturbing the whole order of society. . . .

It is, indeed, most highly desirable that men should not merely abstain from doing harm to their neighbors, but should render active services to their neighbors. In general however the penal law must content itself with keeping men from doing positive harm, and must leave to public opinion, and to the teachers of morality and religion, the office of furnishing men with motives for doing positive good. It is evident that to attempt to punish men by law for not rendering to others all the service which it is their duty to render to others would be preposterous. We must grant impunity to the vast majority of those omissions which a benevolent morality would pronounce reprehensible, and must content ourselves with punishing such omissions only when they are distinguished from the rest by some circumstance which marks them out as peculiarly fit objects of penal legislation. Now, no circumstance appears to us so well fitted to be the mark as the circumstance which we have selected. It will generally be found in the most atrocious cases of omission: It will scarcely ever be found in a venial case of omission: And it is more clear and certain than any other mark that has occurred to us. That there are objections to the line which we propose to draw, we have admitted. But there are objections to every line which can be drawn, and some line must be drawn.

R.I. Gen. Laws §11-56-1
Duty to Assist

Any person at the scene of an emergency who knows that another person is exposed to or has suffered grave physical harm shall, to the extent that he or she can do so without danger or peril to himself or herself or to others, give reasonable assistance to the exposed person. Any person violating the provisions of this section shall be guilty of a petty misdemeanor and shall be subject to imprisonment for a term not exceeding six (6) months or by a fine of not more than five hundred dollars ($500.00), or both.

Wis. Stat. Ann. §940.34(1), (2)
Duty to Aid Endangered Crime Victim

(1) Whoever violates sub. (2) is guilty of a Class C misdemeanor.
(2) Any person who knows that a crime is being committed and that a victim is exposed to bodily harm shall summon law enforcement officers or other assistance or shall provide assistance to the victim. A person need not comply with this subsection if any of the following apply:

(a) Compliance would place him or her in danger.
(b) Compliance would interfere with duties the person owes to others.
(c) Assistance is being summoned or provided by others.

Questions

1. *For and Against a General Duty to Rescue.* What are the arguments in favor of a general duty to rescue a stranger in danger of serious bodily injury? What are the arguments against such a duty?

2. *Your Intuition on Liability for a Failure to Rescue.* Do you think that any of the 37 people in Queens who did not call the police should be criminally liable? Under what circumstances, if any, would criminal liability be appropriate, in your view?

3. *Rhode Island and Wisconsin General Duty Statutes.* Would Lord Macauley, the author of the Penal Code Prepared by the Indian Law Commissioners, find the Rhode Island statute objectionable? The Wisconsin statute? Might some of the 37 people in Queens be liable under either the Rhode Island or Wisconsin statute?

4. *"Bootstrapping" with General Duty Statutes.* Do the Rhode Island and Wisconsin statutes create a duty to act? If so, can failure to perform that duty be the basis for homicide liability, for manslaughter or negligent homicide, for example? What arguments can you make against using these statutes to impose homicide liability?

State v. Adelson
Supreme Court of New Hampshire
118 N.H. 484, 389 A.2d 1382 (1978)

GRIMES, Justice.

The issues in this criminal prosecution for nonpayment of unemployment compensation contributions are whether the defendant was physically capable of performing the act required by statute, [and] whether the defendant possessed the requisite criminal state of mind necessary for conviction. . . .

In August 1975 the defendant and several others established the AIS Corporation for the purpose of "engaging in the shoe business." The corporation acquired factories in Portsmouth and Newport, New Hampshire, and employed as many as two hundred people during some period of its existence. The defendant, who was the corporation's president and chief executive officer, contributed one hundred thousand dollars in start-up capital in return for his one-third interest. The defendant also contributed the proceeds from the sale of a racing horse and his personal automobile when the corporation first began to develop financial problems. The defendant also testified that he is personally responsible for some two hundred sixty thousand dollars that he borrowed for the corporation's benefit.

The corporation lost about three hundred thousand dollars from September 1975 to December 1975 because of unexpected costs associated with training employees. Eighty percent of these employees were unemployed stitchers referred to the corporation by the department of employment security. The corporation continually had problems in meeting its payroll and was forced to secure loans to meet these responsibilities. In August 1976 the corporation finally closed the business.

The corporation, as an employing unit, was required to file reports with the department of employment security and to pay unemployment compensation contributions for each calendar quarter. These reports and contributions are due the last day of the month following the close of the calendar quarter. The corporation filed the necessary report and paid the contributions due for the quarter ending September 30, 1975. However, the corporation's quarterly report for the period ending December 31, 1975, which was due January [30], 1976, was not filed until March 26, 1976. The quarterly report for the period ending March 31, 1976, which was due April 30, 1976, was not filed until May 24, 1976. There was no payment of contributions with either report.

The State, in attempting to show that the defendant was physically capable of making the contributions, presented evidence that the corporation paid defendant's mother one hundred twenty-five dollars a week for an unspecified period of time, that the corporation leased a Mercedes-Benz automobile for five months at a monthly cost of four hundred three dollars, and that the corporation chartered airplanes for various purposes when the use of an automobile would have been less costly. The State also presented evidence that the corporation periodically paid the utilities, telephone, furniture rental, and apartment rental for defendant. The corporation did pay the weekly payroll, an amount much in excess of that which it owed in contributions. The defendant testified that the corporation made only one or two payments on the automobile, that the use of the airplanes was a business necessity, and that any amount paid for personal bills was more than offset by the corporation's failure to pay the defendant a salary at any time during its existence.

The law requires the State to prove beyond a reasonable doubt every element of the crime charged. . . . One of the pertinent sections of the Criminal Code, RSA 626:1 I, provides: "A person is not guilty of an offense unless his criminal liability is based on conduct that includes a voluntary act or a voluntary omission to perform an act of which he is physically capable." The State therefore had the burden to prove beyond a reasonable doubt that the defendant knowingly failed or refused to make an unemployment compensation contribution of which he was physically capable of making when the obligation came due.

The State must establish that at the time the contributions were due that the corporation possessed sufficient funds to enable it to meet the statutory obligation, or that the lack of funds on such date was the result of a deliberate and intentional act without justification in view of all the financial circumstances of the corporation. The defendant argues that the State did not present evidence to establish that the corporation possessed sufficient funds to make the contributions when the contributions were due.

On review this court will consider the evidence "in the light most favorable to the State with all reasonable inferences therefrom." The evidence read in a light most favorable to the State does not establish that the corporation had the ability to make the required contributions when they became due. The evidence regarding the payments to defendant's mother before the contributions became due is irrelevant on the question whether the corporation was able to make the payments when they became due. The State made no showing that these payments were improper especially in view of the fact that defendant's salary, to which he was entitled but which was not paid, would far exceed this amount. The evidence regarding the rental of the automobile, even assuming the corporation made five payments, does not prove that the corporation had the ability to make the contributions. There was also no evidence of the amount of money spent on charter airplane services or on providing defendant with a home. Moreover, the charter and car rental were a matter of business judgment, and it was not improper for the corporation to pay the reasonable expenses of its unpaid president. Although the corporation did pay its employees weekly, it was faced with a choice of paying the contributions or paying the corporation's employees, the nonpayment of either being a crime. RSA 275:52 (Supp. 1975). We cannot say that the corporation lacked funds to pay the contributions as a result of acts that were without justification in view of all the circumstances.

In view of the result reached on the first issue, we need not reach the others.

Exceptions sustained.

Questions

1. *Causing One's Own Physical Incapacity.* Was Adelson physically able to perform the duty required by law? Would it matter to your analysis if Adelson was capable of performing at an earlier time but, at the time the payments were due, was not capable because he had spent the money on other things?

2. *Physical vs. Mental or Emotional Incapacity.* Assume a father fails to climb out on a roof to rescue his infant because he has an unreasonable fear of heights. Can he be held liable for criminal homicide under the Model Penal Code if the child subsequently falls off the roof and is killed? Assume the father fails to jump in front of an oncoming train to save his child. Is he liable for criminal homicide?

3. *Physical Capacity and Conflicting Justifications.* Adelson was physically capable of paying the required unemployment compensation contributions by using the money that was paid as wages to workers. Why is not this physical capacity adequate under the statute for liability for his failure? Assume a police officer comes upon a hold-up in progress at his local convenience store. Instead of taking his child to safety, he intervenes in the hold-up and shoots at the robber who is threatening the store owner with a gun. The robber shoots back. Is the officer criminally liable if his child is struck by the bullet?

4. *Omission Liability for the Conduct of Others.* In the case of In re Yamashita, 327 U.S. 1 (1945), the commanding general of the Japanese Army in the Philippine Islands was held liable for war crimes committed against civilians and prisoners of war, including "a deliberate plan and purpose to massacre and exterminate a large part of the civilian population of Batangas Province." The theory of the prosecution was not that the defendant had either committed or directed any of these acts, but rather that they were committed by troops of the Fourteenth Army Group of the Imperial Japanese Army that was at the time under the defendant's command. His liability for the crimes was said to lie in his failure to perform his legal duty to control the troops under his command to prevent such violations of the rules of war. Would General Yamashita have been liable for the war crimes under the omission liability rules of the Model Penal Code? What additional information, if any, do you need to know? Liability of the leader of an organization for offenses committed by members of that organization is the subject of the next section. Reconsider this question after reading that section.

Chapter 14. CORPORATE CRIMINALITY

Corporate or organizational officials sometimes seem to have the conduct or culpability of agents or employees imputed to them because of their official status. While this may be the case in some jurisdictions, it is more often the case that liability is imposed not through a special doctrine of imputation for corporate officials but rather because the official status of such officials creates certain duties to act. If they fail to perform those duties, they can be held through omission liability. In this respect, Section 14.1 presents a specialized application of the omission rules discussed in the previous chapter.

The liability of a corporation or other organization, in contrast, must be based exclusively on the imputation of all offense elements. A purely abstract legal entity cannot perform conduct or have a state of mind. If liability is to be imposed, the conduct and state of mind of officers or agents must be imputed to it. Section 14.2 examines the mechanisms and rules for this imputation. It also reviews the justifications offered for imposing criminal liability on a legal fiction that, by definition, can neither deserve nor feel the condemnation of criminal conviction.

SECTION 14.1 LIABILITY OF CORPORATE OFFICIALS

Collapse at Kalahoo No. 3

Burt Richards is operator of Kalahoo Mine, a small incorporated mining operation. Earl Single is his mining foreman. Mine inspectors frequently cite Kalahoo for safety violations but none serious enough to cause them to close the mine. On this day, Single, who is paid under a bonus system based on tonnage mined, insists on skipping the normal shoring procedures in order meet the bonus quota by the end of the month. Several of the miners object but are threatened with dismissal if they refuse to go along. Several hours later, an unshored section of Tunnel No. 3 collapses. Seven of the miners are hurt in the collapse; two are killed, one being foreman Single. Richards is charged with two counts of manslaughter, for failing to assure compliance with mining safety rules knowing that such failure created a risk of cave-in and serious injury or death. Richards argues that he always instructed Single to comply with mining safety rules and, beyond that, he left mine operations to foreman Single. Like most owner-operators, he rarely visits the mining operations himself. He points out that Single was fully qualified and certified for the position for which he was hired. Is Richards liable for two counts of manslaughter?

Model Penal Code §2.07(6)
Liability of Person Acting, or Under a Duty to Act, in Behalf of a Corporation or Unincorporated Association

(a) A person is legally accountable for any conduct he performs or causes to be performed in the name of the corporation or an unincorporated association or in its behalf to the same extent as if it were performed in his own name or behalf.

(b) Whenever a duty to act is imposed by law upon a corporation or an unincorporated association, any agent of the corporation or association having primary responsibility for the discharge of the duty is legally accountable for a reckless omission to perform the required act to the same extent as if the duty were imposed by law directly upon himself.

(c) When a person is convicted of an offense by reason of his legal accountability for the conduct of a corporation or an unincorporated association, he is subject to the sentence authorized by law when a natural person is convicted of an offense of the grade and the degree involved.

United States v. Park
Supreme Court of the United States
421 U.S. 658, 95 S. Ct. 1903, 44 L. Ed. 2d 489 (1975)

Mr. Chief Justice BURGER delivered the opinion of the Court.

We granted certiorari to consider whether the jury instructions in the prosecution of a corporate officer under the Federal Food, Drug, and Cosmetic Act, were appropriate under United States v. Dotterweich, 320 U.S. 277 (1943).

Acme Markets, Inc., is a national retail food chain with approximately 36,000 employees, 874 retail outlets, 12 general warehouses, and four special warehouses. Its headquarters, including the office of the president, respondent Park, who is chief executive officer of the corporation, are located in Philadelphia, PA. In a five-count information filed in the United States District Court for the District of Maryland, the Government charged Acme and respondent with violations of the Federal Food, Drug, and Cosmetic Act. Each count of the information alleged that the defendants had received food that had been shipped in interstate commerce and that, while the food was being held for sale in Acme's Baltimore warehouse following shipment in interstate commerce, they caused it to be held in a building accessible to rodents and to be exposed to contamination by rodents. These acts were alleged to have resulted in the food's being adulterated within the meaning of [the statute].

Acme pleaded guilty to each count of the information. Respondent pleaded not guilty. The evidence at trial demonstrated that in April 1970 the Food and Drug Administration (FDA) advised respondent by letter of insanitary conditions in Acme's Philadelphia warehouse. In 1971 the FDA found that similar conditions existed in the firm's Baltimore warehouse. An FDA consumer safety officer testified concerning evidence of rodent infestation and other insanitary conditions discovered during a 12-day inspection of the Baltimore warehouse in November and December 1971. He also related that a second inspection of the warehouse had been conducted in March 1972. On that occasion the inspectors found that there had been improvement in the sanitary conditions, but that "there was still evidence of rodent activity in the building and in the warehouses and we found some rodent-contaminated lots of food items." . . .

The Government also presented testimony by the Chief of Compliance of the FDA's Baltimore office, who informed respondent by letter of the conditions at the Baltimore warehouse after the first inspection.[6] There was testimony by Acme's Baltimore division vice president,

---

6. The letter, dated January 27, 1972, included the following:

We note with much concern that the old and new warehouse areas used for food storage were actively and extensively inhabited by live rodents. Of even more concern was the observation that such reprehensible conditions obviously existed for a prolonged period of time without any detection, or were completely ignored. . . .

We trust this letter will serve to direct your attention to the seriousness of the problem and formally advise you of the urgent need to initiate whatever measures are necessary to prevent recurrence and ensure compliance with the law. . . .

who had responded to the letter on behalf of Acme and respondent and who described the steps taken to remedy the insanitary conditions discovered by both inspections. . . .

At the close of the Government's case in chief, respondent moved for a judgment of acquittal on the ground that "the evidence in chief has shown that Mr. Park is not personally concerned in this Food and Drug violation." The trial judge denied the motion, stating that United States v. Dotterweich, 320 U.S. 277 (1943), was controlling.

Respondent was the only defense witness. He testified that, although all of Acme's employees were in a sense under his general direction, the company had an "organizational structure for responsibilities for certain functions" according to which different phases of its operation were "assigned to individuals who, in turn, have staff and departments under them." He identified those individuals responsible for sanitation, and related that upon receipt of the January 1972 FDA letter, he had conferred with the vice president for legal affairs, who informed him that the Baltimore division vice president "was investigating the situation immediately and would be taking corrective action and would be preparing a summary of the corrective action to reply to the letter." Respondent stated that he did not "believe there was anything [he] could have done more constructively than what [he] found was being done."

On cross-examination, respondent conceded that providing sanitary conditions for food offered for sale to the public was something that he was "responsible for in the entire operation of the company," and he stated that it was one of many phases of the company that he assigned to "dependable subordinates." Respondent was asked about and, over the objections of his counsel, admitted receiving, the April 1970 letter addressed to him from the FDA regarding insanitary conditions at Acme's Philadelphia warehouse. He acknowledged that, with the exception of the division vice president, the same individuals had responsibility for sanitation in both Baltimore and Philadelphia. Finally, in response to questions concerning the Philadelphia and Baltimore incidents, respondent admitted that the Baltimore problem indicated the system for handling sanitation "wasn't working perfectly" and that as Acme's chief executive officer he was responsible for "any result which occurs in our company."

At the close of the evidence, respondent's renewed motion for a judgment of acquittal was denied. The relevant portion of the trial judge's instructions to the jury challenged by respondent is set out in the margin.[9] Respondent's counsel objected to the instructions on the

---

9. In order to find the Defendant guilty on any count of the Information you must find beyond a reasonable doubt on each count. . . .

Thirdly, that John R. Park held a position of authority in the operation of the business of Acme Markets, Incorporated.

ground that they failed to reflect our decision in United States v. Dotterweich, and to define " 'responsible relationship.' " The trial judge overruled the objection. The jury found respondent guilty on all counts of the information, and he was subsequently sentenced to pay a fine of $50 on each count.

The Court of Appeals reversed the conviction and remanded for a new trial. That court viewed the Government as arguing "that the conviction may be predicated solely upon a showing that . . . [respondent] was the President of the offending corporation," and it stated that as "a general proposition, some act of commission or omission is an essential element of every crime." . . . It reasoned that, although our decision in United States v. Dotterweich had construed the statutory provisions under which respondent was tried to dispense with the traditional element of " 'awareness of some wrongdoing,' " the Court had not construed them as dispensing with the element of "wrongful action." The Court of Appeals concluded that the trial judge's instructions "might well have left the jury with the erroneous impression that Park could be found guilty in the absence of 'wrongful action' on his part," and that proof of this element was required by due process. It held, with one dissent, that the instructions did not "correctly state the law of the case," and directed that on retrial the jury be instructed as to "wrongful action," which might be "gross negligence and inattention in discharging . . . corporate duties and obligations or any of a host of other acts of commission or omission which would 'cause' the contamination of food." . . .

We granted certiorari because of an apparent conflict among the Courts of Appeals with respect to the standard of liability of corporate officers under the Federal Food, Drug, and Cosmetic Act as construed in United States v. Dotterweich and because of the

---

However, you need not concern yourselves with the first two elements of the case. The main issue for your determination is only with the third element, whether the Defendant held a position of authority and responsibility in the business of Acme Markets.

The statute makes individuals, as well as corporations, liable for violations. An individual is liable if it is clear, beyond a reasonable doubt, that the elements of the adulteration of the food as to travel in interstate commerce are present. As I have instructed you in this case, they are, and that the individual had a responsible relation to the situation, even though he may not have participated personally.

The individual is or could be liable under the statute, even if he did not consciously do wrong. However, the fact that the Defendant is pres[id]ent and is a chief executive officer of the Acme Markets does not require a finding of guilt. Though, he need not have personally participated in the situation, he must have had a responsible relationship to the issue. The issue is, in this case, whether the Defendant, John R. Park, by virtue of his position in the company, had a position of authority and responsibility in the situation out of which these charges arose.

importance of the question to the Government's enforcement program. We reverse. . . .

The rule that corporate employees who have "a responsible share in the furtherance of the transaction which the statute outlaws" are subject to the criminal provisions of the Act was not formulated in a vacuum. Cases under the Federal Food and Drugs Act of 1906 reflected the view both that knowledge or intent were not required to be proved in prosecutions under its criminal provisions, and that responsible corporate agents could be subjected to the liability thereby imposed. Moreover, the principle had been recognized that a corporate agent, through whose act, default, or omission the corporation committed a crime, was himself guilty individually of that crime. The principle had been applied whether or not the crime required "consciousness of wrongdoing," and it had been applied not only to those corporate agents who themselves committed the criminal act, but also to those who by virtue of their managerial positions or other similar relation to the actor could be deemed responsible for its commission.

In the latter class of cases, the liability of managerial officers did not depend on their knowledge of, or personal participation in, the act made criminal by the statute. Rather, where the statute under which they were prosecuted dispensed with "consciousness of wrongdoing," an omission or failure to act was deemed a sufficient basis for a responsible corporate agent's liability. It was enough in such cases that, by virtue of the relationship he bore to the corporation, the agent had the power to prevent the act complained of. . . .

. . . *Dotterweich* and the cases which have followed reveal that in providing sanctions which reach and touch the individuals who execute the corporate mission—and this is by no means necessarily confined to a single corporate agent or employee—the Act imposes not only a positive duty to seek out and remedy violations when they occur but also, and primarily, a duty to implement measures that will insure that violations will not occur. The requirements of foresight and vigilance imposed on responsible corporate agents are beyond question demanding, and perhaps onerous, but they are no more stringent than the public has a right to expect of those who voluntarily assume positions of authority in business enterprises whose services and products affect the health and well-being of the public that supports them.

The Act does not, as we observed in *Dotterweich,* make criminal liability turn on "awareness of some wrongdoing" or "conscious fraud." The duty imposed by Congress on responsible corporate agents is, we emphasize, one that requires the highest standard of foresight and vigilance, but the Act, in its criminal aspect, does not require that which is objectively impossible. The theory upon which responsible corporate agents are held criminally accountable for "causing" violations of the Act permits a claim that a defendant was "powerless" to prevent or correct the violation to "be raised defensively at a trial on the merits."

If such a claim is made, the defendant has the burden of coming forward with evidence, but this does not alter the Government's ultimate burden of proving beyond a reasonable doubt the defendant's guilt, including his power, in light of the duty imposed by the Act, to prevent or correct the prohibited condition. Congress has seen fit to enforce the accountability of responsible corporate agents dealing with products which may affect the health of consumers by penal sanctions cast in rigorous terms, and the obligation of the courts is to give them effect so long as they do not violate the Constitution.

We cannot agree with the Court of Appeals that it was incumbent upon the District Court to instruct the jury that the Government had the burden of establishing "wrongful action" in the sense in which the Court of Appeals used that phrase. The concept of a "responsible relationship" to, or a "responsible share" in, a violation of the Act indeed imports some measure of blameworthiness; but it is equally clear that the Government establishes a prima facie case when it introduces evidence sufficient to warrant a finding by the trier of the facts that the defendant had, by reason of his position in the corporation, responsibility and authority either to prevent in the first instance, or promptly to correct, the violation complained of, and that he failed to do so. The failure thus to fulfill the duty imposed by the interaction of the corporate agent's authority and the statute furnishes a sufficient causal link. The considerations which prompted the imposition of this duty, and the scope of the duty, provide the measure of culpability. . . .

Reading the entire charge satisfies us that the jury's attention was adequately focused on the issue of respondent's authority with respect to the conditions that formed the basis of the alleged violations. Viewed as a whole, the charge did not permit the jury to find guilt solely on the basis of respondent's position in the corporation; rather, it fairly advised the jury that to find guilt it must find respondent "had a responsible relation to the situation," and "by virtue of his position . . . had . . . authority and responsibility" to deal with the situation. The situation referred to could only be "food . . . held in unsanitary conditions in a warehouse with the result that it consisted, in part, of filth or . . . may have been contaminated with filth." . . .

We conclude that, viewed as a whole and in the context of the trial, the charge was not misleading and contained an adequate statement of the law to guide the jury's determination. . . .

Reversed.

Mr. Justice STEWART, with whom Mr. Justice MARSHALL and Mr. Justice POWELL join, dissenting.

Although agreeing with much of what is said in the Court's opinion, I dissent from the opinion and judgment, because the jury instructions in this case were not consistent with the law as the Court today expounds it.

As I understand the Court's opinion, it holds that in order to sustain a conviction under §301(k) of the Federal Food, Drug, and Cosmetic Act the prosecution must at least show that by reason of an individual's corporate position and responsibilities, he had a duty to use care to maintain the physical integrity of the corporation's food products. A jury may then draw the inference that when the food is found to be in such condition as to violate the statute's prohibitions, that condition was "caused" by a breach of the standard of care imposed upon the responsible official. This is the language of negligence, and I agree with it.

To affirm this conviction, however, the Court must approve the instructions given to the members of the jury who were entrusted with determining whether the respondent was innocent or guilty. Those instructions did not conform to the standards that the Court itself sets out today.

The trial judge instructed the jury to find Park guilty if it found beyond a reasonable doubt that Park "had a responsible relation to the situation. . . . The issue is, in this case, whether the Defendant, John R. Park, by virtue of his position in the company, had a position of authority and responsibility in the situation out of which these charges arose." Requiring, as it did, a verdict of guilty upon a finding of "responsibility," this instruction standing alone could have been construed as a direction to convict if the jury found Park "responsible" for the condition in the sense that his position as chief executive officer gave him formal responsibility within the structure of the corporation. But the trial judge went on specifically to caution the jury not to attach such a meaning to his instruction, saying that "the fact that the Defendant is pres[id]ent and is a chief executive officer of the Acme Markets does not require a finding of guilt." "Responsibility" as used by the trial judge therefore had whatever meaning the jury in its unguided discretion chose to give it.

The instructions, therefore, expressed nothing more than a tautology. They told the jury: "You must find the defendant guilty if you find that he is to be held accountable for this adulterated food." In other words: "You must find the defendant guilty if you conclude that he is guilty." The trial judge recognized the infirmities in these instructions, but he reluctantly concluded that he was required to give such a charge under United States v. Dotterweich, 320 U.S. 277, which, he thought, in declining to define "responsible relation" had declined to specify the minimum standard of liability for criminal guilt.[1]

---

1. In response to a request for further illumination of what he meant by "responsible relationship" the District Judge said:

> Let me say this, simply as to the definition of the "responsible relationship."
> *Dotterweich* and subsequent cases have indicated this really is a jury question. It

As the Court today recognizes, the *Dotterweich* case did not deal with what kind of conduct must be proved to support a finding of criminal guilt under the Act. *Dotterweich* was concerned, rather, with the statutory definition of "person"—with what kind of corporate employees were even "subject to the criminal provisions of the Act." The Court held that those employees with "a responsible relation" to the violative transaction or condition were subject to the Act's criminal provisions, but all that the Court had to say with respect to the kind of conduct that can constitute criminal guilt was that the Act "dispenses with the conventional requirement for criminal conduct—awareness of some wrongdoing." . . .

To be sure, "the day [is] long past when [courts] . . . parsed instructions and engaged in nice semantic distinctions." But this Court has never before abandoned the view that jury instructions must contain a statement of the applicable law sufficiently precise to enable the jury to be guided by something other than its rough notions of social justice. . . .

The *Dotterweich* case stands for two propositions, and I accept them both. First, "any person" within the meaning of 21 U.S.C. §333 may include any corporate officer or employee "standing in responsible relation" to a condition or transaction forbidden by the Act. Second, a person may be convicted of a criminal offense under the Act even in the absence of "the conventional requirement for criminal conduct—awareness of some wrongdoing." . . .

But before a person can be convicted of a criminal violation of this Act, a jury must find—and must be clearly instructed that it must find—evidence beyond a reasonable doubt that he engaged in wrongful conduct amounting at least to common-law negligence. There were no such instructions, and clearly, therefore, no such finding in this case.

For these reasons, I cannot join the Court in affirming Park's criminal conviction.

Questions

1. *Liability for Richards Based Upon Accountability for Single's Conduct?* Model Penal Code §2.07(6)(a) holds an actor accountable for any conduct that he performs or causes to be performed in the name of the corporation, but this seems to do nothing more than the normal

---

says it is not even subject to being defined by the Court. As I have indicated to counsel, I am quite candid in stating that I do not agree with the decision; therefore, I am going to stick by it.

rules of complicity or causing-crime-by-an-innocent. It essentially prevents an official from using the corporation as a shield to liability. Is Richards legally accountable for Single's conduct in creating the unsafe conditions? If so, does he satisfy the culpability requirements for manslaughter?

2. *Liability for Richards Based Upon His Failure to Perform His Duty.* Assume that the mining safety rules give the corporation a duty to shore up the mine in ways that would have prevented the collapse. Model Penal Code §2.07(6)(b) shifts any legal duty imposed on the corporation to "any agent . . . having primary responsibility for the discharge of the duty." Does this include Richards? If so, he is "legally accountable for a reckless omission to perform the required act to the same extent as if the duty were imposed by law directly upon himself." Was Richards reckless as to the failure to shore up in the way that the safety rules require? If so, can he be held liable for manslaughter or only for the penalties attached to the failure to shore up properly?

3. *Richards' Liability Under Park?* Would Richards be liable if he were charged with manslaughter in the federal system, where *Park* is applicable? Does Richards have "a responsible share in the furtherance of the transaction which the statute outlaws"? Can Richards show that he was "powerless" to prevent or correct the violation?

4. Park *as Creating General Rule vs. Confirming Demand of Specific Statute.* Does the *Park* case authorize liability whenever a corporate officer has a "responsible share" and is not "powerless" to prevent a violation by a corporate agent or employee, or does it just indicate that a statute imposing liability under such conditions is not objectionable? In other words, is it creating a rule of liability for corporate officials or simply approving one created by legislation? Do you think that Congress might provide the *Park* form of vicarious liability for Food and Drug Act violations but hesitate to provide the same for manslaughter liability? If Congress did provide for manslaughter liability under such rules of "responsible share" and not "powerless" to prevent, would the reasoning in *Park* be equally applicable, or might the court decide differently and reject such rules, as an inadequate basis for liability?

SECTION 14.2   LIABILITY OF CORPORATIONS

Evergreen Greenbacks

Garden Centers Supply, Inc. (GCS) supplies independent retailers with plants, flowers, bushes, trees, etc. During the two months before Christmas, GCS hires additional help to handle the large increase in business generated by Christmas tree sales. Bob and Chester Turner have recently been hired to tour the many small tree farms. They are authorized to buy trees for up to $2.25 per foot. If they negotiate a lower price, they receive a bonus equal to 20 percent of any amount saved. Because demand is high this year, trees are harder to find and those available are bringing higher prices. As the first three weeks of hauling close, Bob and Chester find that they are far from the bonuses that they were counting on. Indeed, they have failed to meet their quota and are concerned that they may not be hired again next year. They hit on a plan that they think will improve their situation. A state forest within their territory has suitable trees. By adding state trees to their farm purchases and doctoring their transport slips, they can both fill their quota and reduce the per-foot cost of each load. The company handbook for drivers specifically prohibits such unauthorized cuttings but they see little chance of being caught either by the state foresters or by the company. By week five, their record has improved dramatically and they are in line for big bonuses. Company officials are surprised by the dramatic improvement, especially given the poor condition of the market supply. When asked to explain their sudden success, Bob and Chester have no explanation other than, "just lucky." Officials are puzzled and suspicious but see no way to effectively pursue the matter further. They remind Bob and Chester of the company's policy against unauthorized cuttings.

A state forester in Flemington is shocked to find a Z-type Spruce on sale when she takes her children to buy their Christmas tree. Z-types are an experimental tree bred for their capacity to quickly absorb large amounts of water, an important characteristic for successful plantings in sandy soil. She relates her discovery to state investigators, who paper trace the tree to a purchase by Bob and Chester from the Elliott farm, which has no Z-types. Interviews with the Elliotts reveal alterations in the transport slips. The illegal cuttings from the state forest are discovered. Bob and Chester are charged but state officials also institute a prosecution against GCS for the actions of its employees. They cite their inability to effectively police the large stands of state evergreens found in unpopulated areas throughout the state and the special need for a high deterrent effect. By prosecuting GCS, they hope to motivate all wholesalers to more actively discourage illegal state cuttings. They also believe that the publicity surrounding the prosecution will discourage the traditional increase in state tree thefts immediately preceding Christmas. Is GCS liable for the thefts of state trees by Bob and Chester?

State v. Christy Pontiac-GMC, Inc.
Supreme Court of Minnesota
354 N.W. 2d 17 (1984)

SIMONETT, Justice.

We hold that a corporation may be convicted of theft and forgery, which are crimes requiring specific intent, and that the evidence sustains defendant corporation's guilt.

In a bench trial, defendant-appellant Christy Pontiac-GMC, Inc., was found guilty of two counts of theft by swindle and two counts of aggravated forgery, and was sentenced to a $1,000 fine on each of the two forgery convictions. Defendant argues that as a corporation it cannot, under our state statutes, be prosecuted or convicted for theft or forgery and that, in any event, the evidence fails to establish that the acts complained of were the acts of the defendant corporation.

Christy Pontiac is a Minnesota corporation, doing business as a car dealership. It is owned by James Christy, a sole stockholder, who serves also as president and as director. In the spring of 1981, General Motors offered a cash rebate program for its dealers. A customer who purchased a new car delivered during the rebate period was entitled to a cash rebate, part paid by GM and part paid by the dealership. GM would pay the entire rebate initially and later charge back, against the dealer, the dealer's portion of the rebate. Apparently it was not uncommon for the dealer to give the customer the dealer's portion of the rebate in the form of a discount on the purchase price.

At this time Phil Hesli was employed by Christy Pontiac as a salesman and fleet manager. On March 27, 1981, James Linden took delivery of a new Grand Prix for his employer, Snyder Brothers. Although the rebate period on this car had expired on March 19, the salesman told Linden that he would still try to get the $700 rebate for Linden. Later, Linden was told by a Christy Pontiac employee that GM had denied the rebate. Subsequently, it was discovered that Hesli had forged Linden's signature twice on the rebate application form submitted by Christy Pontiac to GM, and that the transaction date had been altered and backdated to March 19 on the buyer's order form. Hesli signed the order form as "Sales Manager or Officer of the Company."

On April 6, 1981, Ronald Gores purchased a new Le Mans, taking delivery the next day. The rebate period for this model car had expired on April 4, and apparently Gores was told he would not be eligible for a rebate. Subsequently, it was discovered that Christy Pontiac had submitted a $500 cash rebate application to GM and that Gores' signature had been forged twice by Hesli on the application. It was also discovered that the purchase order form had been backdated to April

CHAPTER 14   CORPORATE CRIMINALITY   441

3. This order form was signed by Gary Swandy, an officer of Christy Pontiac.

Both purchasers learned of the forged rebate applications when they received a copy of the application in the mail from Christy Pontiac. Both purchasers complained to James Christy, and in both instances the conversations ended in angry mutual recriminations. Christy did tell Gores that the rebate on his car was "a mistake" and offered half the rebate to "call it even." After the Attorney General's office made an inquiry, Christy Pontiac contacted GM and arranged for cancellation of the Gores rebate that had been allowed to Christy Pontiac. Subsequent investigation disclosed that of 50 rebate transactions, only the Linden and Gores sales involved irregularities.

In a separate trial, Phil Hesli was acquitted of three felony charges but found guilty on the count of theft for the Gores transaction and was given a misdemeanor disposition. An indictment against James Christy for theft by swindle was dismissed, as was a subsequent complaint for the same charge, for lack of probable cause. Christy Pontiac, the corporation, was also indicted, and the appeal here is from the four convictions on those indictments. Before trial, Mr. Christy was granted immunity and was then called as a prosecution witness. Phil Hesli did not testify at the corporation's trial.

I

Christy Pontiac argues on several grounds that a corporation cannot be held criminally liable for a specific intent crime. Minn. Stat. §609.52, subd. 2 (1982), says "whoever" swindles by artifice, trick or other means commits theft. Minn. Stat. §609.625, subd. 1 (1982), says "whoever" falsely makes or alters a writing with intent to defraud, commits aggravated forgery. Christy Pontiac agrees that the term "whoever" refers to persons, and it agrees that the term "persons" *may* include corporations, but it argues that when the word "persons" is used here, it should be construed to mean only natural persons. This should be so, argues defendant, because the legislature has defined a crime as "conduct which is prohibited by statute and for which the actor may be sentenced to imprisonment, with or without a fine," and a corporation cannot be imprisoned. Neither, argues defendant, can an artificial person entertain a mental state, let alone have the specific intent required for theft or forgery.

We are not persuaded by these arguments. The Criminal Code is to "be construed according to the fair import of its terms, to promote justice, and to effect its purposes." The legislature has not expressly excluded corporations from criminal liability and, therefore, we take its intent to be that corporations are to be considered persons within the meaning of the Code in the absence of any clear indication to the contrary. See, e.g., Minn. Stat. §609.055 (1982) (legislative declaration that children under the age of 14 years are incapable of committing a crime). We do not think the statutory definition of a crime was meant to exclude corporate criminal liability; rather, we construe that definition to mean conduct which is prohibited and, if committed, *may* result in imprisonment. Interestingly, the specific statutes under which the defendant corporation was convicted, §§609.52 (theft) and 609.625 (aggravated forgery), expressly state that the sentence may be either imprisonment *or* a fine.

Nor are we troubled by any anthropomorphic implications in assigning specific intent to a corporation for theft or forgery. There was a time when the law, in its logic, declared that a legal fiction could not be a person for purposes of criminal liability, at least with respect to offenses involving specific intent, but that time is gone. If a corporation can be liable in civil tort for both actual and punitive damages for libel, assault and battery, or fraud, it would seem it may also be criminally liable for conduct requiring specific intent. Most courts today recognize that corporations may be guilty of specific intent crimes. Particularly apt candidates for corporate criminality are types of crime, like theft by swindle and forgery, which often occur in a business setting.

We hold, therefore, that a corporation may be prosecuted and convicted for the crimes of theft and forgery.

II

There remains, however, the evidentiary basis on which criminal responsibility of a corporation is to be determined. Criminal liability, especially for more serious crimes, is thought of as a matter of personal, not vicarious, guilt. One should not be convicted for something one does not do. In what sense, then, does a corporation "do" something for which it can be convicted of a crime? The case law, as illustrated by the authorities above cited, takes differing approaches. If a corporation is to be criminally liable, it is clear that the crime must not be a personal aberration of an employee acting on his own; the criminal activity must, in some sense, reflect corporate policy so that it is fair to say that the activity was the activity of the corporation. There must be, as Judge Learned Hand put it, a "kinship of the act to the powers of the officials, who commit it."

We believe, first of all, the jury should be told that it must be satisfied beyond a reasonable doubt that the acts of the individual agent constitute the acts of the corporation. Secondly, as to the kind of proof required, we hold that a corporation may be guilty of a specific intent crime committed by its agent if: (1) the agent was acting within the course and scope of his or her employment, having the authority to act for the corporation with respect to the particular corporate business which was conducted criminally; (2) the agent was acting, at least in part, in furtherance of the corporation's business interests; and (3) the criminal acts were authorized, tolerated, or ratified by corporate management.

This test is not quite the same as the test for corporate vicarious liability for a civil tort of an agent. The burden of proof is different, and, unlike civil liability, criminal guilt requires that the agent be acting at least in part in furtherance of the corporation's business interests. Moreover, it must be shown that corporate management authorized, tolerated, or ratified the criminal activity. Ordinarily, this will be shown by circumstantial evidence, for it is not to be expected that management authorization of illegality would be expressly or openly stated. Indeed, there may be instances where the corporation is criminally liable even though the criminal activity has been expressly forbidden. What must be shown is that from all the facts and circumstances, those in positions of managerial authority or responsibility acted or failed to act in such a manner that the criminal activity reflects corporate policy, and it can be said, therefore, that the criminal act was authorized or tolerated or ratified by the corporation. . . .

III

This brings us, then, to the third issue, namely, whether under the proof requirements mentioned above, the evidence is sufficient to sustain the convictions. We hold that it is.

The evidence shows that Hesli, the forger, had authority and responsibility to handle new car sales and to process and sign cash rebate applications. Christy Pontiac, not Hesli, got the GM rebate money, so that Hesli was acting in furtherance of the corporation's business interests. Moreover, there was sufficient evidence of management authorization, toleration, and ratification. Hesli himself, though not an officer, had middle management responsibilities for cash rebate applications. When the customer Gores asked Mr. Benedict, a salesman, about the then discontinued rebate, Benedict referred Gores to Phil Hesli. Gary Swandy, a corporate officer, signed the backdated retail buyer's order form for the Linden sale. James Christy, the president, attempted to negotiate a settlement with Gores after Gores complained. Not until after the Attorney General's inquiry did Christy contact divisional GM headquarters. As the trial judge noted, the rebate money "was so obtained and accepted by Christy Pontiac and kept by Christy Pontiac until somebody blew the whistle. . . ." We conclude the evidence establishes that the theft by swindle and the forgeries constituted the acts of the corporation.

We wish to comment further on two aspects of the proof. First, it seems that the state attempted to prosecute both Christy Pontiac and James Christy, but its prosecution of Mr. Christy failed for lack of evidence. We can imagine a different situation where the corporation is the alter ego of its owner and it is the owner who alone commits the crime, where a double prosecution might be deemed fundamentally unfair. Secondly, it may seem incongruous that Hesli, the forger, was acquitted of three of the four criminal counts for which the corporation was convicted. Still, this is not the first time different trials have had different results. We are reviewing this record, and it sustains the convictions.

Affirmed.

Model Penal Code §2.07(1)-(5)
Liability of Corporations and Unincorporated Associations

(1) A corporation may be convicted of the commission of an offense if:

(a) the offense is a violation or the offense is defined by a statute other than the Code in which a legislative purpose to impose liability on corporations plainly appears and the conduct is performed by an agent of the corporation acting in behalf of the corporation within the scope of his office or employment, except that if the law defining the offense designates the agents for whose conduct the corporation is accountable or the circumstances under which it is accountable, such provisions shall apply; or

(b) the offense consists of an omission to discharge a specific duty of affirmative performance imposed on corporations by law; or

(c) the commission of the offense was authorized, requested, commanded, performed or recklessly tolerated by the board of directors or by a high managerial agent acting in behalf of the corporation within the scope of his office or employment.

(2) When absolute liability is imposed for the commission of an offense, a legislative purpose to impose liability on a corporation shall be assumed, unless the contrary plainly appears.

(3) An unincorporated association may be convicted of the commission of an offense if:

(a) the offense is defined by a statute other than the Code which expressly provides for the liability of such an association and the conduct is performed by an agent of the association acting in behalf of the association within the scope of his office or employment, except that if the law defining the offense designates the agents for whose conduct the association is accountable or the circumstances under which it is accountable, such provisions shall apply; or

(b) the offense consists of an omission to discharge a specific duty of affirmative performance imposed on associations by law.

(4) As used in this Section:

(a) "corporation" does not include an entity organized as or by a governmental agency for the execution of a governmental program;

(b) "agent" means any director, officer, servant, employee or other person authorized to act in behalf of the corporation or association and, in the case of an unincorporated association, a member of such association;

(c) "high managerial agent" means an officer of a corporation or an unincorporated association, or, in the case of a partnership, a partner, or any other agent of a corporation or association having duties of such responsibility that his conduct may fairly be assumed to represent the policy of the corporation or association.

(5) In any prosecution of a corporation or an unincorporated association for the commission of an offense included within the terms of Subsection (1)(a) or Subsection (3)(a) of this Section, other than an offense for which absolute liability has been imposed, it shall be a defense if the defendant proves by a preponderance of evidence that the high managerial agent having supervisory responsibility over the subject matter of the offense employed due diligence to prevent its commission. This paragraph shall not apply if it is plainly inconsistent with the legislative purpose in defining the particular offense.

Questions

1. *GCS's Liability Under* Christy Pontiac-GMC. Would GCS be liable under the rule of *Christy Pontiac-GMC*? What are the elements of proof for liability of a corporation for an offense? Were the thefts "authorized, tolerated, or ratified by corporate management"? What are the elements of theft? Must these be satisfied for GCS to be liable? Were they?

2. *GCS's Liability Under the Model Penal Code.* Would GCS be liable under the Model Penal Code? Model Penal Code §2.07(1)(a) does not appear to apply. The offense charged is theft, which is neither a violation (an offense for which no imprisonment is authorized, see Model Penal Code §1.04(5)) nor an offense defined outside of the Code.

Nor does Model Penal Code §2.07(1)(b) seem to apply. The offense charged is not an omission to perform a duty imposed upon the corporation. Does §2.07(1)(c) apply? Was the theft "recklessly tolerated" by the board of directors or by a high managerial agent? If so, does the company have a "due diligence" defense under §2.07(5)?

3. *GCS's Liability Under the Federal Rule.* Many jurisdictions, including the federal system, provide for liability of a company "for the acts of its agents in the scope of their employment," even if the offense is not recklessly tolerated, indeed, "even though contrary to general corporate policy and express instructions to the agent." United States v. Hilton Hotels Corp., 467 F.2d 1000 (9th Cir. 1972). Would GCS be liable under this rule?

4. *Different Rules for Different Offenses? Hilton Hotels* involves an antitrust prosecution under the Sherman Act. Might Congress hesitate to impose a similar rule for corporate liability for theft? Might the federal courts be less inclined to approve such conditions as a basis for liability for theft? Consider the rationales typically given in support of organizational liability summarized in the following excerpt.

Model Penal Code §2.07 Comment
332, 335-338 (1985)

The law of corporate criminal responsibility is of comparatively recent origin, the modern development having occurred almost entirely within the last century and a quarter. In the early years, the recognition of corporate responsibility was inhibited by certain procedural difficulties and certain conceptual notions. The most persistent of the latter was the idea that a corporation might not be held for a crime involving criminal intent. In recent years most of these limitations have been swept aside. The modern development, however, has proceeded largely without reference to any intelligible body of principle and the field is characterized by the absence of articulate analysis of the objectives thought to be attainable by imposing criminal fines on corporate bodies. . . .

In approaching the analysis of corporate criminal capacity it will be observed initially that the imposing of criminal penalties on corporate bodies results in a species of vicarious liability. The direct burden of a corporate fine is visited upon the shareholders of the corporation. In most cases, the shareholders have not participated in the criminal conduct and lack the practical means of supervision of corporate management to prevent misconduct by corporate agents. This is not to say, of course, that all the policy considerations at issue in imposing vicarious responsibility on a human principal are present to the same degree in the corporate cases. Two fundamental distinctions should be noted. First, the fact that the corporation is the party nominally convicted means that the individual shareholders escape the opprobrium and incidental disabilities that normally follow a personal conviction or even indictment. Second, the shareholder's loss is limited to his equity in the corporation. His personal assets are not ordinarily subject to levy and the conviction of the corporation will not result in loss of liberty to the stockholders. Nevertheless, the fact that the direct impact of corporate fines is felt by a group ordinarily innocent of criminal conduct underscores the point that such fines ought not to be authorized except where they clearly may be expected to accomplish desirable social purposes. To the extent that shareholders participate in criminal conduct, or to the extent that there are unlawful transactions involving the shareholders' holdings, they may be reached directly through application of the ordinary principles of criminal liability.

It would seem that the ultimate justification of corporate criminal responsibility must rest in large measure on an evaluation of the deterrent effects of corporate fines on the conduct of corporate agents. Is there a reason for anticipating a substantially higher degree of deterrence from fines levied on corporate bodies than can fairly be anticipated from proceeding directly against the guilty officer or agent or from other feasible sanctions of a noncriminal character?

It may be assumed that ordinarily a corporate agent is not likely to be deterred from criminal conduct by the prospect of corporate liability when, in any event, he faces the prospect of individually suffering serious criminal penalties for his own act. If the agent cannot be prevented from committing an offense by the prospect of personal liability, he ordinarily will not be prevented by the prospect of corporate liability.

Yet the problem cannot be resolved so simply. For there are probably cases in which the economic pressures within the corporate body are sufficiently potent to tempt individuals to hazard personal liability for the sake of company gain, especially where the penalties threatened are moderate and where the offense does not involve behavior condemned as highly immoral by the individual's associates. This tendency may be particularly strong where the individual knows that his guilt may be difficult to prove or where a favorable reaction to his position by a jury may be anticipated even where proof of guilt is strong. A number of appellate opinions reveal situations in which juries have held the corporate defendant criminally liable while acquitting the obviously guilty agents who committed the criminal acts.

This may reflect more than faulty or capricious judgment on the part of the juries. It may represent a recognition that the social consequences of a criminal conviction may fall with a disproportionately heavy impact on the individual defendants where the conduct involved is not of a highly immoral character. It may also reflect a shrewd belief that the violation may have been produced by pressures on the subordinates created by corporate managerial officials even though the latter may not have intended or desired the criminal behavior and even though the pressures can only be sensed rather than demonstrated. Furthermore, the great mass of legislation calling for corporate criminal liability suggests a widespread belief on the part of legislators that such liability is necessary to effectuate regulatory policy. In some cases . . . legislatures have added corporate liability to the criminal penalties in the belief, founded on experience, that such additional sanctions are necessary.

The case so made out, however, does not demonstrate the wisdom of corporate fines generally. Rather, it tends to suggest that such liability can best be justified in cases in which penalties directed to the individual are moderate and where the criminal conviction is least likely to be interpreted as a form of social moral condemnation. This indicates a general line of distinction between the "malum prohibitum" regulatory offenses, on the one hand, and more serious offenses on the other. The same distinction is suggested in dealing with the problem of jury behavior. The cases cited above involving situations in which individual defendants were acquitted are all cases of economic regulations. It may be doubted that such results would have followed had the offenses involved a more obvious moral element. In any event, it is not clear just what conclusions are to be drawn from the cited cases. In each, the jury had corporate liability available as an alternative to acquittal of all of the defendants. Conceivably, if that alternative had not been available, verdicts against the individuals in some of the cases might have been returned. Thus, it is at least possible that corporate liability encourages erratic jury behavior. It may be true that the complexities of organization characteristic of large corporate enterprise at times present real problems of identifying the guilty individual and establishing his criminal liability. It would be hoped, however, that more could be pointed to in justification of placing the pecuniary burdens of criminal fines on the innocent than the difficulties of proving the guilt of the culpable individual. Where there is concrete evidence that the difficulties are real, however, the effectuation of regulatory policy may be thought to justify the means.

A New Form of Corporate Liability?
A. Ashworth, Principles of Criminal Law
86-88 (1991)

The theoretical arguments in favor of corporate criminal liability seem strong, but developments at common law have made [such liability] possible only to a limited extent [in England]. An alternative strategy of placing the emphasis on individual liability would be unlikely to work. Any particular individual might be dispensable within a corporation (e.g., the "Company Vice-President responsible for going to goal"), allowing the company [to] continue on its course with minimal disruption; or it might be difficult to identify the individual responsible, not least because companies sometimes have convoluted lines of accountability. A further alternative strategy would be to rely even more on new offenses of strict liability to punish corporate harm-doing, but this might not be a sufficient response to some [disasters], or to other harm-doing on a broad scale.

Reasoning of this kind has led to Fisse and Braithwaite's entirely new approach to corporate criminal liability, using concepts not applicable to individuals.[25] Their strategy rests on three key elements: "enforced accountability"; a new concept of corporate fault; and a fresh approach to sanctions. The idea of "enforced accountability" is that the law should recognize the complexity of lines of accountability in some corporations, and, rather than expending prosecutorial energy and court time trying to disentangle them, should require a company which has caused or threatened a proscribed harm to take its own disciplinary and rectificatory measures. The State should order the company to activate its own private justice system, and a court should then assess the adequacy of the measures taken. As this suggests, the concept of fault would then become a *post hoc* phenomenon. Rather than struggling to establish some antecedent fault within the corporation, the prosecution would invite the court to infer fault from the nature and effectiveness of the company's remedial measures after it had been established that it was the author of a harm-causing or harm-threatening act or omission. The court would not find fault if it was persuaded that the company had taken realistic measures to prevent a recurrence, had ensured compensation to any victims, and had taken the event seriously in other respects. This "reactive corporate fault" is a far cry from the notions of *mens rea* and prior fault which dominate criminal-law doctrine. The third element in the scheme is that the courts should be able to impose new penalties, specially designed for application to companies. Under the present system, a company can hardly be imprisoned, moderate fines can be swallowed up as business overheads, and swinging fines might have such drastic side-effects on the employment and livelihoods of innocent employees as to render them inappropriate. The proposal is for a range of special penalties, some of which are rehabilitative (putting corporations on probation to supervise their

---

25. B. Fisse and J. Braithwaite, The Allocation of Responsibility for Corporate Crime: Individualism, Collectivism and Accountability, 11 Sydney L.R. 468 (1988); see also L. H. Leight, The Criminal Liability of Corporations and other Groups, 9 Ottawa L.R. 247 (1977); and J. Braithwaite, Corporate Crime in the Pharmaceutical Industry (1984).

compliance with the law), some of which are deterrent (punitive injunctions to require resources to be devoted to the development of new preventive measures), and others of which have mixed aims (e.g., community service by companies).

Fisse and Braithwaite's proposals for a radically new legal regime for corporate crime are grounded in arguments of prevention. They emphasize the enormity of the harms which corporations both cause and risk causing, and contend that the primary search should be for a regime which ensures maximum prevention. This is inconsistent with an approach to liability and punishment based on "just deserts": the authors explicitly reject the idea of holding corporations criminally liable according to their culpability in causing the harms, not merely because it is difficult in practice to make such enquiries, but also because they believe that the prevention of future harm is of greater social importance in this sphere than any abstract notion of "justice" based on past events.[26] "Desert" theory would, however, make a clearer distinction between preventive measures and conviction and sentence. In principle, punishment for corporations, no less than for individuals, should be proportioned to culpability: If that proves impossible in practice, for the reasons given by Fisse and Braithwaite, then that is an argument for legal presumptions or other special doctrines, but not for abandoning the distinctive aims of the criminal law and punishment. Broader preventive measures, perhaps through regulatory mechanisms, should be put in hand in order to reduce the risk of further harms from similar sources.

Questions

1. *Corporate Criminal Liability as a Deterrent.* What arguments can you make that criminal liability, rather than civil liability, is necessary to effectively deter crime by the agents of corporations acting on behalf of the corporation? What arguments can you make that even criminal liability is likely to be ineffective? If criminal liability can be more effective than civil liability, what are the particular instances where this is most likely to be true?

2. *"Reactive Corporate Fault" as an Alternative to Current Rules on Corporate Criminal Liability.* What arguments can you make that Fisse and Braithwaite's "reactive corporate fault" would be a more effective deterrence to crimes by corporate agents than the corporate liability

---

26. See further J. Braithwaite, Challenging Just Deserts: Punishing White Collar Criminals, 73 J. Crim. Law & Criminology 723 (1982), and the reply by A. von Hirsch, Desert and White Collar Criminality: A Reply to Dr. Braithwaite, id. at 1164.

rules of *Christy Pontiac-GMC* or the Model Penal Code or even *Hilton Hotels*? What arguments can you make that their proposed liability scheme might be less effective?

3. *Corporate Criminal Liability and Moral Condemnation of Non-Humans.* One argument in favor of criminal rather than just civil liability for corporations is that a criminal conviction, unlike a civil judgment, carries moral condemnation. Yet corporations are not moral beings. They can neither deserve nor feel condemnation. (Their officers and employees can, but if criminal liability is expressly imposed upon the corporation rather than the officers or employees, presumably it is meant to condemn the former not the latter.) What is the effect, if any, of directing the condemnation of criminal conviction to an entity for which condemnation has no meaning? Does this dilute the moral significance of criminal conviction and the strength of its condemnation?

IV / GENERAL PRINCIPLES OF DEFENSE

Many defenses and mitigations are discussed in previous chapters. Some of these "defenses" or mitigations are simply factors that prevent proof of the requirements of the offense definition, such as mistake negating a culpability element, in Section 7.3, and mental illness negating the culpability required for homicide ("diminished capacity") in Section 3.5. Other defenses and mitigations are defined in a form that is separate from an offense definition, but they apply only to a particular offense or group of offenses. This includes, for example, renunciation as a defense to inchoate liability, in Section 8.6, and "inevitably incident" conduct as a defense to complicity liability, in Section 10.3. While they are independent in form, the nature of these defenses suggests that they are, in essence, part of the definition of what constitutes the offense. That is, what we mean by complicity is assistance that is not "inevitably incident" to commission of the offense; what we mean by conspiracy is an agreement that is not renounced.

Other defenses, however, have general application to all offenses. Such "general defenses" represent general principles of defense that are not dependent upon or related to the definition of any particular offense. General defenses are of three sorts: justifications, excuses, and nonexculpatory defenses.

Justification defenses, such as lesser evils, self defense, and law enforcement authority, provide exculpation on a theory that the actor avoided a greater harm or evil. That is, while he satisfies the elements of an offense, the actor's offense conduct is tolerated or even encouraged because it does not cause a net societal harm. An actor who burns a firebreak on another's land may thereby commit arson but also may have a justification defense (of lesser evils) because the burning saves innocent lives threatened by the fire. Section 15.1 introduces these defenses. Each of the three major groups of justification defenses are examined: the lesser evils justification in Section 15.2, public authority justifications in Section 15.3, and defensive force justifications in Section 15.4.

Excuse defenses, such as insanity or duress, exculpate under a different theory. The actor has admittedly acted improperly, has caused a net societal harm or evil, but the actor is excused because he or she cannot properly be held responsible for his or her offense conduct. Note the difference in focus between justifications and excuses. An actor's *conduct* is justified; *an actor* is excused. Section 16.1 introduces the theory of excuses. Subsequent sections examine the major excuses: insanity in Section 16.2, other disability excuses in Section 16.3, and mistake excuses in Section 16.4. While there is some controversy surrounding the matter, mistaken justifications in Section 15.5 are arguably excuses, not justifications. The actor's conduct does not avoid a greater harm; if the actor is to be exculpated for his mistake it is because, as in other excuses, we conclude that the actor should not be held responsible for the admittedly undesirable conduct.

A final group of general defenses does not exculpate an actor but does provide an exemption from liability. Even though the conduct is criminal and unjustified and the actor fully responsible for it, such "nonexculpatory defenses" are provided because such furthers important societal interests. Thus, diplomatic immunity may provide a defense, without regard to the guilt or innocence of the actor, because by doing so diplomats sent abroad are protected from interference and diplomatic communications among nations can be established and maintained. Nonexculpatory defenses are the subject of Section 17.1. Section 17.2 examines the controversial entrapment defense and considers, among other things, its qualifications as a nonexculpatory defense.

Chapter 15. JUSTIFICATIONS

SECTION 15.1 THE NATURE OF JUSTIFICATIONS

Notes on the Nature of Justifications

Unlike failure of proof defenses (e.g., consent negating an offense element) and offense modification defenses (e.g., "inevitably incident" conduct and renunciation), justification defenses are not statements or alterations of the statutory definition of the harm sought to be prevented or punished by an offense. The harm caused by justified behavior remains a legally recognized harm that is to be avoided whenever possible. Under the special justifying circumstances, however, that harm is outweighed by the need to avoid an even greater harm or to further a greater societal interest.

Lesser evils defense A forest fire rages toward a town of unsuspecting inhabitants. The actor burns a field of corn located between the fire and the town; the burned field serves as a firebreak, saving lives. The actor satisfies all elements of the offense of criminal mischief by setting fire to the field with the purpose of destroying it. The immediate harm he causes—the destruction of the field—is precisely the harm that the statute seeks to prevent and punish. Yet the actor is likely to have a complete defense, because his conduct and its harmful consequences are justified. His conduct is tolerated, even encouraged, by society.

Balancing competing harms The forest fire case provides an example of the "lesser evils" or "choice of evils" justification (sometimes called "necessity" when the threat of greater harm stems from natural forces). This justification defense, though the least common in American criminal codes, most clearly reflects the general principle of justification. The defense explicitly requires that "the harm or evil sought to be avoided by such conduct is greater than that sought to be prevented by the law defining the offense charged."[1] As we shall see, the "defensive

---

1. Model Penal Code §3.02(1)(a).

force" and "public authority" justifications, described below, have no such general balancing language but nonetheless are based upon the same balancing principle. In those defenses, the legislature has undertaken to establish the balance of competing interests and has promulgated specific rules that embody their conclusions. Neither the defendant nor a jury is permitted to strike the balance differently.

Defensive force justifications A prowler attempts to steal chickens from a chicken coop. May the owner use physical force against the prowler to prevent the theft? Some limited degree of force commonly is permitted, if it is necessary to protect the property. It is not that society deems injury to a person as a less significant interest than the right of ownership of chickens. Rather, in weighing the interests at stake, the legislature considers not only the immediate physical harms—personal injury vs. loss of a chicken—but also the societal interest in maintaining a right to hold personal property. The threatened theft endangers not only the rightful possession by this owner, but also the stability and vitality of the rule of private possession generally. To state it negatively, society generally abhors unjustified aggressive takings because they undercut the rule of security and private possession. Society therefore tolerates the injury that must be inflicted to stop the aggressor. The same reasoning applies when the aggression is toward the actor himself or toward another person. Society's interest in maintaining a right to bodily integrity, when combined with the physical harm threatened, outweighs the harm that must be inflicted to block the aggression.

Defending against unlawful force Such "defensive force" justifications each are triggered by a threat of unlawful force. They are distinguished from one another by the interest that is threatened: defense of self, defense of others, defense of property. Legislatures often wish to make special alterations or exceptions to the basic principle of defensive force depending on the interest to be protected. For example, they may add a special provision to the defense of property to exclude the use of deadly force. They might permit the use of force to defend another person only if such other person would be justified in using such force.

Public authority justifications A third category of justifications, "public authority" defenses, similarly reflect a balancing of harms. When a deputy sheriff uses force in the execution of a judicial arrest warrant, his conduct may satisfy all the elements of assault. But his use of force furthers effective criminal justice, as well as the effective exercise of judicial authority. These intangible societal interests are said to justify the harm that the deputy causes in executing the warrant. Unlike defensive force defenses, public authority defenses need not be triggered by a threat from another. An actor may be justified if he or she affirmatively acts to further a legally recognized interest. For example, a bus driver might be authorized to be the aggressor in ejecting passengers who refuse to pay or who insist on playing their radio too loudly. On the other hand, the use of public authority justifications often is limited to certain persons, whose position or training makes them particularly appropriate protectors of the interest at stake, whereas defensive force justifications are generally available to all citizens.

Furthering public interests   The interests to be furthered or protected may be personal or societal. They include criminal law enforcement, child rearing and education, safety and order on public transportation vehicles or in public institutions, life or health (as in medical emergencies and suicide prevention), military operations, and effective exercise of judicial authority, to name the most prominent. In each instance, the interest gives rise to an authority for the appropriate persons to act in a way that otherwise would be criminal, if it furthers or protects the interest. Like defensive force justifications, different public authority justifications are distinguished from one another according to the interest protected. Legislatures may refine the basic principle to provide a suitably limited justification defense for each interest and authority. Thus, the restrictions on law enforcement authority may be different than the restrictions on the authority of a bus driver to maintain safety and decorum.

Common internal structure   The balancing of interests common to all justification defenses is part of the internal structure of each defense. Justifications share other characteristics as well. All justifications have the following internal structure: *Triggering conditions* permit a *necessary* and *proportional response*. Each of these requirements plays a role in assuring that the conduct justified by the defense is indeed conduct that society would encourage or at least tolerate.

Triggering conditions   *Triggering conditions* are the circumstances that must exist before an actor is eligible to act under the justification. Defensive force justifications are triggered when an aggressor threatens unjustified force against the protected interest, as by attempting to steal the defendant's chickens. Public authority justifications are triggered when the circumstances evoke the use of the public authority given to the actor. A conductor's authority to act to maintain order and safety on a train may be triggered by a passenger who refuses to stop smoking or pay for his ticket. The general justification defense, lesser evils, has the broadest triggering condition. In its purest form, the defense is available whenever any legally protected interest is threatened and the harm or evil can be avoided by defensive or offensive action.

Limitations on response conduct   The triggering conditions of a justification defense do not give the actor the privilege to act without restriction. To be justified, the conduct in response to the triggering conditions must satisfy two requirements: (1) it must be *necessary* to protect or further the interest at stake; and (2) it must cause only such harm as is *proportional* or reasonable in relation to the harm threatened or the interest to be furthered.

Necessity requirement   The *necessity requirement* demands that the defendant act only when and to the extent necessary to protect or further the interest at stake. Thus, where an aggressor announces his intention to assault the actor at noon of the next day, the threat triggers a right of self defense. But if the actor is in no danger at the time, if he can just as effectively defend himself the next morning, he is not justified in immediately using physical force against the aggressor. In addition, when an actor is threatened and must act immediately, he is privileged to use only the degree of force that is necessary for self-protection. Even if most persons would find it necessary to use greater force, the force used is not justified if the individual actor could protect himself or herself as effectively with less. Assume the actor is a karate expert who, with no risk of harm to himself, can dislodge an attacker's club with a high kick. While the average person might be justified in shooting the armed attacker, this actor may only use karate to disarm, if greater force, such as shooting, is unnecessary to protect himself.

Proportionality requirement The *proportionality requirement* places a maximum limit on the necessary force that may be used in protection or furtherance of an interest. It bars justification, even if the force used by the actor is necessary, if the force is too harmful in relation to the value of the interest at stake. Assume an actor has no other option but to use deadly force to prevent the stealing of apples from her orchard. Most jurisdictions would deny a defense for use of deadly force, even if she had tried all less harmful means of preventing the thefts. It is under this same principle that deadly force rarely, if ever, is permitted against a nonaggressor, suggesting that an innocent's life is a near absolute interest that can almost never be outweighed. It should be no surprise that there is some controversy surrounding such rules. They require the actor to stoically sacrifice a legally-recognized interest, frequently for the protection of an aggressor (e.g., in all defensive force justifications). But such commitment to proportionality—as in the valuation of human life over property, even the life of a law-breaker—is the mark of a civilized society.

SECTION 15.2 LESSER EVILS

A Life-Saving Break-In

Burke and his two roommates, Tim and Henry, have AIDS. Burke as yet has few debilitating symptoms. He remains physically and mentally strong. Tim is in very poor health and is getting worse rapidly. Henry was in the same condition several months ago until he began participating in a research study using a drug called IIR. His health, like that of many others in the study, dramatically improved upon use of the drug. While

Burke is thrilled with Henry's recovery, he is angry that the study's sponsors will not let him and Tim participate. He has urged government authorities in the Food and Drug Administration to make IIR generally available but his requests have been denied on grounds that insufficient research has been done to justify FDA approval. Burke is convinced that the only way he can save his own life and Tim's is to break into the research study's offices and steal sufficient doses of IIR for them both. He breaks into the building but trips several silent alarms and is apprehended by police as he is leaving with the drug. He is charged with burglary and offers a lesser evils justification defense. Should Burke get the defense?

Model Penal Code §3.02(1)
Justification Generally: Choice of Evils

Conduct which the actor believes to be necessary to avoid a harm or evil to himself or to another is justifiable, provided that:

(a) the harm or evil sought to be avoided by such conduct is greater than that sought to be prevented by the law defining the offense charged; and

(b) neither the Code nor other law defining the offense provides exceptions or defenses dealing with the specific situation involved; and

(c) a legislative purpose to exclude the justification claimed does not otherwise plainly appear.

The Queen v. Dudley and Stephens
Queen's Bench Division
14 Q.B.D. 273 (1884)

Lord COLERIDGE, C.J. The two prisoners, Thomas Dudley and Edwin Stephens, were indicted for the murder of Richard Parker on the high seas on the 25th of July in the present year. They were tried before my Brother Huddleston at Exeter on the 6th of November, and, under the direction of my learned Brother, the jury returned a special verdict, the legal effect of which has been argued before us, and on which we are now to pronounce judgment.

The special verdict . . . is as follows:

"That on July 5, 1884, the prisoners, Thomas Dudley and Edward Stephens, with one Brooks, all able-bodied English seamen, and the deceased, also an English boy, between seventeen and eighteen years of age, the crew of an English yacht, a registered English vessel, were cast away in a storm on the high seas 1,600 miles from the Cape of Good Hope, and were compelled to put into an open boat belonging to said yacht. That in this boat they had no supply of water and no supply of food, except two 1 lb. tins of turnips, and for three days they had nothing else to subsist upon. That on the fourth day they caught a small turtle, upon which they subsisted for a few days, and this was the only food they had up to the twentieth day when the act now in question was committed. That on the twelfth day the remains of the turtle were entirely consumed, and for the next eight days they had nothing to eat. That they had no fresh water, except such rain as they from time to time caught in their oilskin capes. That the boat was drifting on the ocean, and was probably more than 1,000 miles away from land. That on the eighteenth day, when they had been seven days without food and five without water, the prisoners spoke to Brooks as to what should be done if no succor came, and suggested that some one should be sacrificed to save the rest, but Brooks dissented, and the boy, to whom they were understood to refer, was not consulted. That on the 24th of July, the day before the act now in question, the prisoner Dudley proposed to Stephens and Brooks that lots should be cast who should be put to death to save the rest, but Brooks refused to consent, and it was not put to the boy, and in point of fact there was no drawing of lots. That on the day the prisoners spoke of their families, and suggested it would be better to kill the boy that their lives should be saved, and Dudley proposed that if there was no vessel in sight by the morrow morning the boy should be killed. That next day, the 25th of July, no vessel appearing, Dudley told Brooks that he had better go and have a sleep, and made signs to Stephens and Brooks that the boy had better be killed. The prisoner Stephens agreed to the act, but Brooks dissented from it. That the boy was then lying at the bottom of the boat quite helpless and extremely weakened by famine and by drinking sea water, and unable to make any resistance, nor did he ever assent to his being killed. The prisoner Dudley offered a prayer asking forgiveness for them all if either of them should be tempted to commit a rash act, and that their souls might be saved. That Dudley, with the assent of Stephens, went to the boy, and telling him that his time was come, put a knife into his throat and killed him then and there; that the three men fed upon the body and blood of the boy for four days; that on the fourth day after the act had been committed the boat was picked up by a passing vessel, and the prisoners were rescued, still alive, but in the lowest state of prostration. That they were carried to the port of Falmouth, and committed for trial at Exeter. That if the men had not fed upon the body of the boy they would probably not have survived to be so picked up and rescued, but would within the four days have died of famine. That the boy, being in a much weaker condition, was likely to have died before them. That at the time of the act in question there was no sail in sight, nor any reasonable prospect of relief. That under these circumstances there appeared to the prisoners every probability that unless they then fed or very soon fed upon the boy or one of themselves they would die of starvation. That there was no appreciable chance of saving life except by killing some one for the others to eat. That assuming any necessity to kill anybody, there was no greater necessity for killing the boy than any of the other three men. But whether upon the whole matter by the jurors found the killing of Richard Parker by Dudley and Stephens be felony and murder the jurors are ignorant, and pray the advice of the Court thereupon, and if upon the whole matter the Court shall be of opinion that the killing of Richard Parker be felony and murder, then the jurors say that Dudley and Stephens were each guilty of felony and murder as alleged in the indictment."

From these facts, stated with the cold precision of a special verdict, it appears sufficiently that the prisoners were subject to terrible temptation, to sufferings which might break down the bodily power of the strongest man, and try the conscience of the best. Other details yet more harrowing, facts still more loathsome and appalling, were presented to the jury, and are to be found recorded in my learned Brother's notes. But nevertheless this is clear, that the prisoners put to death a weak and unoffending boy upon the chance of preserving their own lives by feeding upon his flesh and blood after he was killed, and with the certainty of depriving *him* of any possible chance of survival. The verdict finds in terms that "if the men had not fed upon the body of the boy they would *probably* not have survived," and that "the boy being in a much weaker condition was *likely* to have died before them." They might possibly have been picked up next day by a passing ship; they might possibly not have been picked up at all; in either case it is obvious that the killing of the boy would have been an unnecessary and profitless act. It is found by the verdict that the boy was incapable of resistance, and, in fact, made none; and it is not even suggested that his death was due to any violence on his part attempted against, or even so much as feared by, those who killed him. Under these circumstances the jury say that they are ignorant whether those who killed him were guilty of murder, and have referred it to this Court to determine what is the legal consequence which follows from the facts which they have found.

[T]he real question in the case [is] whether killing under the circumstances set forth in the verdict be or not be murder. The contention that it could be anything else was, to the minds of us all, both new and strange, and we stopped the Attorney General in his negative argument in order that we might hear what could be said in support of a proposition which appeared to us to be at once dangerous, immoral, and opposed to all legal principle and analogy. . . .

Is there, then, any authority for the proposition [that this might not be murder]? Decided cases there are none. . . . The American case cited by my Brother Stephen in his Digest, from Wharton on Homicide, in which it was decided, correctly indeed, that sailors had no right to throw passengers overboard to save themselves, but on the somewhat strange ground that the proper mode of determining who was to be sacrificed was to vote upon the subject by ballot, can hardly, as my Brother Stephen says, be an authority satisfactory to a court in this country. . . .

The one real authority of former time is Lord Bacon, who, in his commentary on the maxim, "necessitas inducit privilegium quoad jura privata," lays down the law as follows:

> Necessity carrieth a privilege in itself. Necessity is of three sorts—necessity of conservation of life, necessity of obedience, and necessity of the act of God or of a stranger. First of conservation of life; if a man steal viands to satisfy his present hunger, this is no felony nor larceny. So if divers be in danger of drowning by the casting away of some boat or barge, and one of them get to some plank, or on the boat's side to keep himself above the water, and another to save his life thrust him from it, whereby he is drowned, this is neither se defendendo nor by misadventure, but justifiable.

On this it is to be observed that Lord Bacon's proposition that stealing to satisfy hunger is no larceny is hardly supported by Staundforde, whom he cites for it, and is expressly contradicted by Lord Hale in the passage already cited. And for the proposition as to the plank or boat, it is said to be derived from the canonists. At any rate he cited no authority for it, and it must stand upon his own. . . . There are many conceivable states of things in which it might possibly be true, but if Lord Bacon meant to lay down the broad proposition that a man may save his life by killing, if necessary, an innocent and unoffending neighbour, it certainly is not law at the present day. . . .

It must not be supposed that in refusing to admit temptation to be an excuse for crime it is forgotten how terrible the temptation was; how awful the suffering; how hard in such trials to keep the judgment straight and the conduct pure. We are often compelled to set up standards we cannot reach ourselves, and to lay down rules which we could not ourselves satisfy. But a man has no right to declare temptation to be an excuse, though he might himself have yielded to it, nor allow compassion for the criminal to change or weaken in any manner the legal definition of the crime. It is therefore our duty to declare that the prisoners' act in this case was wilful murder, that the facts as stated in the verdict are no legal justification of the homicide; and to say that in our unanimous opinion the prisoners are upon this special verdict guilty of murder.[1]

The Court then proceeded to pass sentence of death upon the prisoners.*

State v. Green
Supreme Court of Missouri
470 S.W. 2d 565 (1971)

HENLEY, Judge.

John Charles Green (hereinafter defendant) was charged by information with the offense of escape from a state institution in which he was lawfully confined, a felony. He waived a jury, was tried before the court, found guilty, and was sentenced to imprisonment for a term of three years. He appeals. We affirm.

Briefly, the evidence is that defendant was convicted of burglary in November, 1966, and sentenced to imprisonment for a term of three years in the custody of the Department of Corrections; that on April 14, 1967, at about 6 PM, while serving this sentence at the Training Center, he disappeared from that institution and was apprehended the next day by a State Highway Patrolman some distance from the Training Center. Defendant tacitly concedes that these are the facts and that, standing alone, they are sufficient to sustain his conviction. However, he contends that his escape was justified and that the justification constituted a legal defense to the charge of escape.

At a pretrial conference the defendant informed the court that his defense would be that prior homosexual assaults, and threats near noon on the day of his escape of a homosexual assault upon him that night by other inmates caused the conditions of his confinement to be intolerable; and, that these conditions . . . made it necessary that he escape in order to protect himself from submission to the threatened assault or the alternative of death or great bodily harm. As a result of this conference it was agreed that on trial day, and before a jury would

---

1. My brother Grove has furnished me with the following suggestion, too late to be embodied in the judgment but well worth preserving: "If the two accused men were justified in killing Parker, then if not rescued in time, two of the three survivors would be justified in killing the third, and of the two who remained the stronger would be justified in killing the weaker, so that three men might be justifiably killed to give the fourth a chance of surviving."—C.

*Editor's Note.—Their sentence was afterwards commuted by the Crown to six months' imprisonment.

be impaneled, the court would hear evidence offered by defendant in support of his defense, consider it as an offer of proof, and rule on its sufficiency as a legal defense.

The evidence offered on this issue is, in substance, that near the end of December, 1966, shortly after defendant became an inmate at the Training Center, he was attacked in his cell at night by two inmates and submitted to acts of sodomy under threat of death or great bodily harm; that immediately thereafter he feigned an attempt at suicide and was taken to the prison hospital where he told the authorities of the assaults and asked to be removed from the institution to avoid further assault; that he was told by the Center authorities to resolve his own problems and to "go back and fight it out." Approximately two weeks later, near the middle of January, 1967, he was again homosexually assaulted in his cell, this time by three inmates. He again feigned an attempt at suicide and requested that he be taken to the hospital. Instead he was placed in a disciplinary cell until the next morning when he was x-rayed and immediately thereafter taken before the Disciplinary Board and charged with attempted self-destruction. He informed this Board of the assaults, requested protection, and was moved to another wing of the Training Center. He says that he was told by a member of the Board that he would have to "fight it out, submit to the assaults, or go over the fence." Defendant declined to disclose the names of his assailants to the Training Center authorities. Approximately three months later, on April 14, 1967, during the noon hour, a group of four or five inmates told defendant that they would be at his cell that night and he would submit to their homosexual desires or they would kill or seriously harm him. He did not report this threat to anyone. He escaped at about 6 PM that evening. . . .

The court ruled that the evidence did not constitute a legal defense. Immediately after this ruling, defendant waived a jury, evidence was offered by the state on the offense charged, and, as previously noted, the court found him guilty. . . .

Defendant says he has been unable to find any Missouri cases supporting his theory of "necessity" as a defense in this case. We find none. The state refers us to People v. Richards, 269 Cal. App. 2d 768, 75 Cal. Rptr. 597 (1969), for a concise definition of the defense of necessity. The California Court of Appeal said: "The principle of justification by necessity, if applicable, involves a determination that 'the harm or evil sought to be avoided by such conduct is greater than that sought to be prevented by the law defining the offense charged.' . . . The compulsion from the harm or evil which the actor seeks to avoid, should be present and impending. . . ."

This is not a case where defendant escaped while being closely pursued by those who sought by threat of death or bodily harm to have him submit to sodomy. Moreover, the threatened consequences of his refusal to submit could have been avoided that day by reporting the threats and the names of those making the threats to the authorities in charge of the Center. Defendant had several hours in which to consider and report these threats.

The defense of "necessity" was not available to defendant and the court did not err in excluding his offer of proof. Defendant's defense resolves itself into the simple proposition that the conditions of his confinement justified his escape. Generally, conditions of confinement do not justify escape and are not a defense.

The judgment is affirmed.

SEILER, Judge (dissenting).

. . . Looking at the record in [the light most favorable to the defendant], a jury could have found the facts as follows:

Defendant was . . . nineteen years old, five feet, nine inches tall and weighed about one-hundred and fifty pounds. At the Moberly Training Center for Men, the prison population was composed of about six-hundred inmates, mostly second offenders at least twenty-five years old, and at least twenty-five inmates were serving life sentences. The inmates were confined in single cells within a residential building. The physical structure of the residential building was formed by a central rotunda with the four inmate wings radiating outward. Within each inmate wing, there were seventy-nine cells. During the day, the inmates could wander freely within the residential building. The inmates were locked in the cells at night.

There were two guards assigned to each residential building for the period of the night shift. One of these guards stayed in the rotunda. The rotunda was separated from each wing by a heavy door. The second guard walked a circuit among the four wings. There were substantial periods of time during which a wing would be without supervision.

There was a lock on the outside of each cell. The door could be unlocked with a master key. It appears that several master keys were illicitly in the hands of the inmates. These locks could easily be picked with any sharp object. There were no locks on the inside of the cell doors.

Inmate complaints could be sent to the prison administration by the use of "snitch-kites." A "snitch-kite" consisted of a written complaint transmitted through the intra-prison mail. It required several days to obtain any response to a "snitch-kite." An inmate could complain directly to a guard. Because of the physical structure of the residential buildings, it would be difficult to complain to a guard without the other inmates being aware of this action. Administrative policy was not to investigate a complaint of physical abuse unless the assailant was identified. But if an inmate "snitched"—turned in somebody's name—his life wouldn't be worth "a plugged nickel"; he (the snitch) "was as good as dead right then." Unless a guard witnessed an assault, the alleged assailant would be allowed to remain within the general population during the investigation. The victim of an assault could be removed from the general prison population. However, such an inmate would be confined to the "hole," which was the area used to discipline prisoners. The prison provided no other facilities for the protective custody of a threatened inmate.

In late December, 1966, or early January, 1967, during the night, two inmates . . . picked the lock of defendant's cell door. At knifepoint, defendant was homosexually ravaged by both inmates. Two weeks later, three inmates . . . invaded defendant's cell, knocked him unconscious as he tried to flee, and raped him. Homosexual acts including sexual assaults were matters of common knowledge among the inmates.

Following each sexual assault, the defendant injured or feigned injury to himself, in order to contact the prison administration. While hospitalized after the first attack, defendant informed the Assistant Superintendent of Treatment of the assault and requested protection. This prison official admonished the defendant to defend himself, and upon release from the hospital, defendant was returned to the same cell. After the second attack, defendant was taken before the Disciplinary Board where he informed the Board about the assaults. The Assistant Superintendent of Custody, a member of the Board, told defendant that the only protection defendant would receive was a cell change. This prison official told defendant that the alternatives were to defend himself, submit, or "go over the fence."

On April 14, 1967, defendant returned to his cell during the lunch break. Four or five . . . inmates gathered around his cell. They informed defendant of their knowledge of the previous acts of sodomy. They told him that they would return that evening to make him a "punk" (a person who plays a female role in homosexual incidents) for the remainder of his time in prison. These inmates threatened to "beat his head in" or kill defendant if he would not submit. Defendant believed it would do no good to ask the prison authorities for help, in view of what he had been told in response to his previous attempts to get help, so to avoid what he believed was inevitable, he quietly escaped about 6:00 o'clock that evening. He was found the next morning, on the side of a county highway, only a few miles from the prison and surrendered without resistance. . . .

I interpret the majority opinion to decide that the proposed defense is not available because (1) defendant did not delay his escape until his would-be assailants had him in close pursuit and (2) because he could have avoided his predicament had he only turned in their names earlier in the day.

As to the first, defendant knew from prior experience that if he waited until the band was close at hand, it would be too late. If escape were to save him, it had to be made earlier than the last minute. Five against one is hopeless odds. As to the second, this overlooks the evidence that to turn in the names to the prison authorities meant defendant was risking his life by being a "snitch."

Defendant had already been told by a high prison official that he had three alternatives: submit, defend himself, or escape. The majority opinion does not recommend submission, and as a practical matter, self defense was impossible. All that was left was escape, and under these circumstances, the coercion and necessity were not remote in time, but present and impending. Escape or submission (and I do not believe defendant was unreasonable in not being willing to submit to five-fold sodomy) were literally all this defendant had left. . . .

Questions

1. *The Proportionality Requirement and Lesser Evils.* Would Dudley and Stephens have a defense under the Model Penal Code? Could they rely upon a justification other than §3.02 (such as self defense)? What are the interests on each side of the balance? Are both tangible and intangible interests included? Is it enough that the actor *believes* that his conduct avoids a greater harm? (Section 15.5 takes up the problem of mistake as to a justification.)

2. *The Necessity Requirement.* Would Green have a defense under the Model Penal Code? Could he rely upon a justification other than §3.02? Why does the court reject his claimed defense? What arguments can you make that Green's conduct was "necessary" to protect himself?

3. *Imminent Threat vs. Immediately Necessary Conduct.* The common law frequently required that the *threat* be "imminent." Some hint of this is seen in the *Green* court's reasoning. The Model Penal Code requires only that the *actor's conduct* be "necessary" or, in some justification defenses, that it be "immediately necessary." Are these requirements different? If escape were the only way he could avoid the rape, how long would Green have to wait before escaping? Until the attackers were at his cell? Until his last chance to successfully escape?

State v. Dorsey
Supreme Court of New Hampshire
118 N.H. 844, 395 A.2d 855 (1978)

GRIMES, Justice.

The issue we decide in this criminal trespass case is whether the trial court erred in ruling that the statutory defense of competing harms, RSA 627:3, is not available to one charged with criminal trespass for occupying the construction site of a nuclear power plant. We hold that no error was committed.

Defendant was arrested during a mass occupation of the construction site of the Seabrook Nuclear Power Plant. He was charged with criminal trespass, RSA 635:2, elected to represent himself, and was tried before a jury, and convicted. His exceptions were transferred by Mullavey, J.

Prior to trial the defendant gave notice pursuant to Superior Court Rule 102 that he intended to rely upon the competing harms statute, RSA 627:3, as a defense. At trial the court ruled that the competing harms statute would not be permitted as a defense and noted defendant's exception. . . .

The trial court was correct in ruling that the competing harms defense did not apply to this case. RSA 627:3 I reads in part as follows:

> Conduct which the actor believes to be necessary to avoid harm to himself or another is justifiable if the desirability and urgency of avoiding such harm outweigh, according to ordinary standards of reasonableness, the harm sought to be prevented by the statute defining the offense charged. . . .

It establishes a statutory defense akin to the common-law defense of necessity. These and other early cases elsewhere deal with simple situations, such as killing mink out of season to protect valuable geese, and keeping a child from school without permission because of serious illness. They . . . relate to factual matters that laymen sitting as a jury have the competence to decide. They deal with dangers that the average person can recognize and about which there can be no dispute.

RSA 627:3 "is based largely on N.Y. §35.05(a) and states what the Model Penal Code calls the 'choice of evils' doctrine." The pertinent comment to the Model Penal Code states that for the defense to be available, the issue of competing values must not have been foreclosed by a deliberate legislative choice. In the context of the present dispute, however, both the legislature of the State and the Congress of the United States have made deliberate choices regarding nuclear power. RSA ch. 162-H established an Energy Facility Evaluation Committee to determine, among other things, whether any proposed site and facility will "unduly interfere with . . . the public health and safety." Section 1 of RSA ch. 162-H mandates that "undue delay in construction of any needed facilities be avoided." Having spoken so forcefully in support of nuclear power, it is inconceivable that the legislature would intend that nuclear power be considered such a harm as to justify individuals in breaking the law. We are confident that it was not intended that such matters be included within the scope of RSA 627:3.

Nor were matters of this sort contemplated under the common-law defense of necessity. The common-law defense dealt with imminent dangers from obvious and generally recognized harms. It did not deal with nonimminent or debatable harms; nor did it deal with activities that the legislative branch of government had expressly sanctioned and found not to be harms. To allow nuclear power plants to be considered a danger or harm within the meaning of that defense either at common law or under the statute would require lay jurors to determine in individual cases matters of State and national policy in a very technical field. Competing factions would produce extensive expert testimony on the danger or lack of danger of nuclear power plants, and jurors in each case would then be asked to decide issues already determined by the legislature. The competing harms statute is intended to deal only with harms that are readily apparent and recognizable to the average juror.

Defendant and others who oppose nuclear power have other lawful means of protesting nuclear power; therefore, they are not justified in breaking the law. The act of criminal trespass was a deliberate and calculated choice and not an act that was urgently necessary to avoid a clear and imminent danger. The matter of the Seabrook Nuclear Power Plant has been before the regulatory agencies and the courts of both the United States and this State with a full opportunity for the opponents of nuclear power plant construction to be heard. Opponents still have the right to try to induce the people's representatives in Congress and the legislature to change the statutes. The fact that their efforts so far have failed does not make a case of necessity. . . .

Exception overruled.

Questions

1. *Superiority of More Specific Justifications.* Could Dorsey rely on a justification other than §3.02? For example, if his claim is that the nuclear reactor was threatening him and others ought he not claim self defense under Model Penal Code §3.04(1) and defense of others under §3.05(1)? If so, what effect does this have, if any, on his lesser evils defense?

2. *Legislative Preemption.* If Dorsey relies upon the lesser evils justification in Model Penal Code §3.02, will he get a defense? What arguments can you make, pro and con, that his conduct avoided a greater harm? What arguments can you make, pro and con, that his conduct was necessary? If we conclude that his conduct was both necessary and avoided a greater harm, does it follow that he will get the defense?

3. *A Life-Saving Break-In.* In the hypothetical case at the beginning of this section, would Burke have a defense under the Model Penal

Code? Could he rely on a justification other than §3.02? Will he get a defense under Model Penal Code §3.02? What arguments can you make, pro and con, that his conduct avoided a greater harm? What arguments can you make, pro and con, that his conduct was necessary? If we conclude that his conduct was both necessary and avoided a greater harm, does it follow that he will get the defense?

SECTION 15.3 PUBLIC AUTHORITY

The lesser evils defense, in Section 15.2, calls for an ad hoc balancing of competing interests. Many situations of such competing interests are commonplace, such as a police officer's assault of a suspect during an arrest. Efficiency, as well as the legality virtues of predictability and consistency in application, suggest the use of specific defense provisions to govern such common justification situations. Such specific provisions also have the advantage of allowing the legislature to strike the balance between interests, rather than leaving it to individual judges or juries. (Recall the special lesser evils provision calling for deference to legislative balancing.)

One common and recurring justification situation is the use of force against an aggressor who threatens the personal safety or property of the actor or another. Most codes have special "defensive force" justifications to deal with such situations, examined in Section 15.4. Another common situation, the subject of this section, arises where an actor is given a special public authority and duty to act. The authority may be either to avoid a threatened harm, as is generally the case in lesser evils and defensive force justifications, or to further a societal interest if the opportunity to do so arises.

Docker's Box

Pacer (his real name is George Brooke) has been driving the same bus route for two years. He prides himself in providing safe, courteous, and on-time transportation for his riders, and believes that his service is an important part of their lives. His attitude is reflected in his nickname. Everyone calls him Pacer because, even when he is behind schedule, with bad traffic, and people standing in the aisle, he is know to "maintain an even strain." Today is one of the bad days. He fears his regulars are going to be late for work and school but is making as much progress as he can in heavy traffic. At Tenth and Locust, Docker gets on. He is carrying a huge "boom box" that takes up an entire seat. He decides to demonstrate just how high he can pump up the volume. The passengers sitting near Docker do not protest. With most of his six feet and 240 pounds covered in black leather and chrome, Docker looks intimidating and carries himself in a way that makes the point. Pacer tries to ignore the ear-splitting sound, hoping the demonstration will be brief.

After a few minutes, it becomes apparent that the sound is here to stay. The passengers grow restless. The box drowns out Pacer's yells to turn it off. After several blocks, Pacer pulls the bus over and makes his way down the aisle to confront Docker. He signals Docker to turn off the box or get off the bus but is ignored. He reaches over and flips the power switch himself. The sudden silence brings a collective sigh from the bus. "Don't touch my box, man," Docker says, staring, as he flips the power back on and the box blares again. Pacer grabs the box, wrenching it from Docker's hands, and sprints for the front of the bus with Docker a half-step behind. Docker catches up just as Pacer reaches the front. He reaches over Pacer's shoulder and gets a hand on the antenna. Pacer has been unable to find the off switch so the box is still blaring, but when he jerks it from Docker's grasp it flies down the front steps, cracks open as it bounces off the bottom step, and falls to the pavement in pieces, terribly silent. With antenna in hand, Docker slowly steps down to the box, staring in disbelief. No one breathes. Docker bends over the pile but does not touch. As he straightens, his face turns to a scowl. He fixes on Pacer. "I'm going to. . . ." His words are lost as the doors close and the engine roars. He is seen running through the exhaust, antenna outstretched and waving, but the words are muffled. No one speaks for half a block. Finally a passenger in the last row yells up to Pacer, "I think he's saying that's not his stop." Does Pacer have a justification defense for his use of force against Docker in silencing Docker's box?

Model Penal Code §3.03
Execution of Public Duty

(1) Except as provided in Subsection (2) of this Section, conduct is justifiable when it is required or authorized by:

    (a) the law defining the duties or functions of a public officer or the assistance to be rendered to such officer in the performance of his duties; or

    (b) the law governing the execution of legal process; or

    (c) the judgment or order of a competent court or tribunal; or

    (d) the law governing the armed services or the lawful conduct of war; or

    (e) any other provision of law imposing a public duty.

(2) The other sections of this Article apply to:

(a) the use of force upon or toward the person of another for any of the purposes dealt with in such sections; and

(b) the use of deadly force for any purpose, unless the use of such force is otherwise expressly authorized by law or occurs in the lawful conduct of war.

(3) The justification afforded by Subsection (1) of this Section applies:

(a) when the actor believes his conduct to be required or authorized by the judgment or direction of a competent court or tribunal or in the lawful execution of legal process, notwithstanding lack of jurisdiction of the court or defect in the legal process; and

(b) when the actor believes his conduct to be required or authorized to assist a public officer in the performance of his duties, notwithstanding that the officer exceeded his legal authority.

Model Penal Code §3.08
Use of Force by Persons with Special Responsibility for Care, Discipline or Safety of Others

The use of force upon or toward the person of another is justifiable if:

(1) the actor is the parent or guardian or other person similarly responsible for the general care and supervision of a minor or a person acting at the request of such parent, guardian or other responsible person and:

(a) the force is used for the purpose of safeguarding or promoting the welfare of the minor, including the prevention or punishment of his misconduct; and

(b) the force used is not designed to cause or known to create a substantial risk of causing death, serious bodily harm, disfigurement, extreme pain or mental distress or gross degradation; or

(2) the actor is a teacher or a person otherwise entrusted with the care or supervision for a special purpose of a minor and:

(a) the actor believes that the force used is necessary to further such special purpose, including the maintenance of reasonable discipline in a school, class or other group, and that the use of such force is consistent with the welfare of the minor; and

(b) the degree of force, if it had been used by the parent or guardian of the minor, would not be unjustifiable under Subsection (1)(b) of this Section; or

(3) the actor is the guardian or other person similarly responsible for the general care and supervision of an incompetent person; and:

(a) the force is used for the purpose of safeguarding or promoting the welfare of the incompetent person, including the prevention of his misconduct, or, when such incompetent person is in a hospital or other institution for his care and custody, for the maintenance of reasonable discipline in such institution; and

(b) the force used is not designed to cause or known to create a substantial risk of causing death, serious bodily harm, disfigurement, extreme or unnecessary pain, mental distress, or humiliation; or

(4) the actor is a doctor or other therapist or a person assisting him at his direction, and:

(a) the force is used for the purpose of administering a recognized form of treatment which the actor believes to be adapted to promoting the physical or mental health of the patient; and

(b) the treatment is administered with the consent of the patient or, if the patient is a minor or an incompetent person, with the consent of his parent or guardian or other person legally competent to consent in his behalf, or the treatment is administered in an emergency when the actor believes that no one competent to consent can be consulted and that a reasonable person, wishing to safeguard the welfare of the patient, would consent; or

(5) the actor is a warden or other authorized official of a correctional institution, and:

(a) he believes that the force used is necessary for the purpose of enforcing the lawful rules or procedures of the institution, unless his belief in the lawfulness of the rule or procedure sought to be enforced is erroneous and his error is due to ignorance or mistake as to the provisions of the Code, any other provision of the criminal law or the law governing the administration of the institution; and

(b) the nature or degree of force used is not forbidden by Article 303 or 304 of the Code; and

(c) if deadly force is used, its use is otherwise justifiable under this Article; or

(6) the actor is a person responsible for the safety of a vessel or an aircraft or a person acting at his direction, and

(a) he believes that the force used is necessary to prevent interference with the operation of the vessel or aircraft or obstruction of the execution of a lawful order, unless his belief in the lawfulness of the order is erroneous and his error is due to ignorance or mistake as to the law defining his authority; and

(b) if deadly force is used, its use is otherwise justifiable under this Article; or

(7) the actor is a person who is authorized or required by law to maintain order or decorum in a vehicle, train or other carrier or in a place where others are assembled, and:

(a) he believes that the force used is necessary for such purpose; and

(b) the force used is not designed to cause or known to create a substantial risk of causing death, bodily harm, or extreme mental distress.

Questions

Authority of Persons with Special Responsibility for Care, Discipline, or Safety of Others. Does Pacer have a defense under the Model Penal Code? What (sub)sections govern? What conditions will trigger the justification to use force? Is there a necessity requirement? Is there a proportionality requirement? In your view, should Pacer get a justification defense?

Tennessee v. Garner
Supreme Court of the United States
471 U.S. 1, 105 S. Ct. 1694, 85 L. Ed. 2d 1 (1985)

Justice WHITE delivered the opinion of the Court.

This case requires us to determine the constitutionality of the use of deadly force to prevent the escape of an apparently unarmed suspected felon. We conclude that such force may not be used unless it is necessary to prevent the escape and the officer has probable cause to believe that the suspect poses a significant threat of death or serious physical injury to the officer or others.

I

At about 10:45 PM on October 3, 1974, Memphis Police Officers Elton Hymon and Leslie Wright were dispatched to answer a "prowler inside call." Upon arriving at the scene they saw a woman standing on her porch and gesturing toward the adjacent house. She told them she had heard glass breaking and that "they" or "someone" was breaking in next door. While Wright radioed the dispatcher to say that they were on the scene, Hymon went behind the house. He heard a door slam and saw someone run across the back yard. The fleeing suspect, who was appellee-respondent's decedent, Edward Garner, stopped at a 6-feet-high chain link fence at the edge of the yard. With the aid of a flashlight, Hymon was able to see Garner's face and hands. He saw no sign of a weapon, and, though not certain, was "reasonably sure" and "figured" that Garner was unarmed. He thought Garner was 17 or 18 years old and about 5'5" or 5'7" tall. While Garner was crouched at the base of the fence, Hymon called out "police, halt" and took a few steps toward him. Garner then began to climb over the fence. Convinced that if Garner made it over the fence he would elude capture, Hymon shot him. The bullet hit Garner in the back of the head. Garner was taken by ambulance to a hospital, where he died on the operating table. Ten dollars and a purse taken from the house were found on his body.

In using deadly force to prevent the escape, Hymon was acting under the authority of a Tennessee statute and pursuant to Police Department policy. The statute provides that "[i]f, after notice of the intention to arrest the defendant, he either flee[s] or forcibly resist[s], the officer may use all the necessary means to effect the arrest." Tenn. Code Ann. 40-7-108 (1982). The Department policy was slightly more restrictive than the statute, but still allowed the use of deadly force in cases of burglary. The incident was reviewed by the Memphis Police Firearm's Review Board and presented to a grand jury. Neither took any action.

Garner's father then brought this action in the Federal District Court for the Western District of Tennessee, seeking damages under 42 U.S.C. §1983 for asserted violations of Garner's constitutional rights. The complaint alleged that the shooting violated the Fourth, Fifth, Sixth, Eighth, and Fourteenth Amendments of the United States Constitution. It named as defendants Officer Hymon, the Police Department, its Director, and the Mayor and city of Memphis. After a 3-day bench trial, the District Court entered judgment for all defendants. It dismissed the claims against the Mayor and the Director for lack of evidence. It then concluded that Hymon's actions were authorized by the Tennessee statute, which in turn was constitutional. Hymon had employed the only reasonable and practicable means of preventing Garner's escape. Garner had "recklessly and heedlessly attempted to vault over the fence to escape, thereby assuming the risk of being fired upon." . . .

The Court of Appeals reversed and remanded. It reasoned that the killing of a fleeing suspect is a "seizure" under the Fourth Amendment,[6] and is therefore constitutional only if "reasonable." The Tennessee statute failed as applied to this case because it did not adequately limit the use of deadly force by distinguishing between felonies of different magnitudes—"the facts, as found, did not justify the use of deadly force under the Fourth Amendment." Officers cannot resort to deadly force unless they "have probable cause . . . to believe that the suspect [has committed a felony and] poses a threat to the safety of the officers or a danger to the community if left at large." . . .

---

6. "The right of the people to be secure in their persons . . . against unreasonable searches and seizures, shall not be violated. . . ." U. S. Const., Amdt. 4.

II

Whenever an officer restrains the freedom of a person to walk away, he has seized that person. While it is not always clear just when minimal police interference becomes a seizure, there can be no question that apprehension by the use of deadly force is a seizure subject to the reasonableness requirement of the Fourth Amendment.

A

A police officer may arrest a person if he has probable cause to believe that person committed a crime. Petitioners and appellant argue that if this requirement is satisfied the Fourth Amendment has nothing to say about how that seizure is made. This submission ignores the many cases in which this Court, by balancing the extent of the intrusion against the need for it, has examined the reasonableness of the manner in which a search or seizure is conducted. To determine the constitutionality of a seizure "[w]e must balance the nature and quality of the intrusion on the individual's Fourth Amendment interests against the importance of the governmental interests alleged to justify the intrusion." We have described "the balancing of competing interests" as "the key principle of the Fourth Amendment." Because one of the factors is the extent of the intrusion, it is plain that reasonableness depends on not only when a seizure is made, but also how it is carried out.

B

The same balancing process . . . demonstrates that, notwithstanding probable cause to seize a suspect, an officer may not always do so by killing him. The intrusiveness of a seizure by means of deadly force is unmatched. The suspect's fundamental interest in his own life need not be elaborated upon. The use of deadly force also frustrates the interest of the individual, and of society, in judicial determination of guilt and punishment. Against these interests are ranged governmental interests in effective law enforcement. It is argued that overall violence will be reduced by encouraging the peaceful submission of suspects who know that they may be shot if they flee. Effectiveness in making arrests requires the resort to deadly force, or at least the meaningful threat thereof. "Being able to arrest such individuals is a condition precedent to the state's entire system of law enforcement."

Without in any way disparaging the importance of these goals, we are not convinced that the use of deadly force is a sufficiently productive means of accomplishing them to justify the killing of nonviolent suspects. The use of deadly force is a self-defeating way of apprehending a suspect and so setting the criminal justice mechanism in motion. If successful, it guarantees that that mechanism will not be set in motion. And while the meaningful threat of deadly force might be thought to lead to the arrest of more live suspects by discouraging escape attempts, the presently available evidence does not support this thesis. The fact is that a majority of police departments in this country have forbidden the use of deadly force against nonviolent suspects. If those charged with the enforcement of the criminal law have abjured the use of deadly force in arresting nondangerous felons, there is a substantial basis for doubting that the use of such force is an essential attribute of the arrest power in all felony cases. Petitioners and appellant have not persuaded us that shooting nondangerous fleeing suspects is so vital as to outweigh the suspect's interest in his own life.

The use of deadly force to prevent the escape of all felony suspects, whatever the circumstances, is constitutionally unreasonable. It is not better that all felony suspects die than that they escape. Where the suspect poses no immediate threat to the officer and no threat to others, the harm resulting from failing to apprehend him does not justify the use of deadly force to do so. It is no doubt unfortunate when a suspect who is in sight escapes, but the fact that the police arrive a little late or are a little slower afoot does not always justify killing the suspect. A police officer may not seize an unarmed, nondangerous suspect by shooting him dead. The Tennessee statute is unconstitutional insofar as it authorizes the use of deadly force against such fleeing suspects.

It is not, however, unconstitutional on its face. Where the officer has probable cause to believe that the suspect poses a threat of serious physical harm, either to the officer or to others, it is not constitutionally unreasonable to prevent escape, by using deadly force. Thus, if the suspect threatens the officer with a weapon or there is probable cause to believe that he has committed a crime involving the infliction or threatened infliction of serious physical harm, deadly force may be used if necessary to prevent escape and if, where feasible, some warning has been given. As applied in such circumstances, the Tennessee statute would pass constitutional muster.

III

A

It is insisted that the Fourth Amendment must be construed in light of the common-law rule, which allowed the use of whatever force was necessary to effect the arrest of a fleeing felon, though not a misdemeanant. As stated in Hale's posthumously published Pleas of the Crown:

[I]f persons that are pursued by these officers for felony or the just suspicion thereof . . . shall not yield themselves to these officers, but shall either resist or fly before they are apprehended or being apprehended shall rescue themselves and resist or fly, so that they cannot be otherwise apprehended, and are upon necessity slain therein, because they cannot be otherwise taken, it is no felony.

2 M. Hale, Historia Placitorum Coronae 85 (1736). See also 4 W. Blackstone, Commentaries 289. Most American jurisdictions also imposed a flat prohibition against the use of deadly force to stop a fleeing misdemeanant, coupled with a general privilege to use such force to stop a fleeing felon.

The State and city argue that because this was the prevailing rule at the time of the adoption of the Fourth Amendment and for some time thereafter, and is still in force in some States, use of deadly force against a fleeing felon must be "reasonable." It is true that this Court has often looked to the common law in evaluating the reasonableness, for Fourth Amendment purposes, of police activity. On the other hand, it "has not simply frozen into constitutional law those law enforcement practices that existed at the time of the Fourth Amendment's passage." Because of sweeping change in the legal and technological context, reliance on the common-law rule in this case would be a mistaken literalism that ignores the purposes of a historical inquiry.

B

It has been pointed out many times that the common-law rule is best understood in light of the fact that it arose at a time when virtually all felonies were punishable by death. "Though effected without the protections and formalities of an orderly trial and conviction, the killing of a resisting or fleeing felon resulted in no greater consequences than those authorized for punishment of the felony of which the individual was charged or suspected." American Law Institute, Model Penal Code §3.07, Comment 3, p. 56 (Tentative Draft No. 8, 1958). Courts have also justified the common-law rule by emphasizing the relative dangerousness of felons.

Neither of these justifications makes sense today. Almost all crimes formerly punishable by death no longer are or can be. And while in earlier times "the gulf between the felonies and the minor offences was broad and deep," today the distinction is minor and often arbitrary. Many crimes classified as misdemeanors, or nonexistent, at common law are now felonies. These changes have undermined the concept, which was questionable to begin with, that use of deadly force against a fleeing felon is merely a speedier execution of someone who has already forfeited his life. They have also made the assumption that a "felon" is more dangerous than a misdemeanant untenable. Indeed, numerous misdemeanors involve conduct more dangerous than many felons.

There is additional reason why the common-law rule cannot be directly translated to the present day. The common-law rule developed at a time when weapons were rudimentary. Deadly force could be inflicted almost solely in a hand-to-hand struggle during which, necessarily, the safety of the arresting officer was at risk. Handguns were not carried by police officers until the latter half of the century. Only then did it become possible to use deadly force from a distance as a means of apprehension. As a practical matter, the use of deadly force under the standard articulation of the common-law rule has an altogether different meaning—and harsher consequences—now than in the past centuries.

One other aspect of the common-law rule bears emphasis. It forbids the use of deadly force to apprehend a misdemeanant, condemning such action as disproportionately severe.

In short, though the common law pedigree of Tennessee's rule is pure on its face, changes in the legal and technological context mean the rule is distorted almost beyond recognition when literally applied. . . .

We wish to make clear what our holding means in the context of this case. The complaint has been dismissed as to all the individual defendants. The State is a party only by virtue of 28 U.S.C. 2403(b) and is not subject to liability. The possible liability of the remaining defendants—the Police Department and the city of Memphis—hinges on Monell v. New York City Dept. of Social Services, 436 U.S. 658 (1978), and is left for remand. We hold that the statute is invalid insofar as it purported to give Hymon the authority to act as he did. As for the policy of the Police Department, the absence of any discussion of this issue by the courts below, and the uncertain state of the record preclude any consideration of its validity.

The judgment of the Court of Appeals is affirmed, and the case is remanded for further proceedings consistent with this opinion.

So ordered.

Justice O'CONNOR, with whom The Chief Justice and Justice REHNQUIST join, dissenting.

The Court today holds that the Fourth Amendment prohibits a police officer from using deadly force as a last resort to apprehend a criminal suspect who refuses to halt when fleeing the scene of a nighttime burglary. This conclusion rests on the majority's balancing of the interests of the suspect and the public interest in effective law enforcement. Notwithstanding the venerable common-law rule authorizing the use of deadly force if necessary to apprehend a fleeing felon, and continued acceptance of this rule by nearly half the States, the majority concludes that Tennessee's statute is unconstitutional inasmuch as it allows the use of such force to apprehend a burglary suspect who is not obviously armed or otherwise dangerous. Although the circumstances of this case are unquestionably tragic and unfortunate, our constitutional holdings must be sensitive both to the history of the Fourth Amendment and to the general implications of the Court's reasoning. By disregarding the serious and dangerous nature of residential burglaries and the longstanding practice of many States, the Court effectively creates a Fourth Amendment right allowing a burglary suspect to flee unimpeded from a police officer who has probable cause to arrest, who has ordered the suspect to halt, and who has no means short of firing his weapon to prevent escape. I do not believe that the Fourth Amendment supports such a right, and I accordingly dissent. . . .

Model Penal Code §3.07(1)-(3), (5)
Use of Force in Law Enforcement

(1) *Use of Force Justifiable to Effect an Arrest.* Subject to the provisions of this Section and of Section 3.09, the use of force upon or toward the person of another is justifiable when the actor is making or assisting in making an arrest and the actor believes that such force is immediately necessary to effect a lawful arrest.

(2) *Limitations on the Use of Force.*

    (a) The use of force is not justifiable under this Section unless:

        (i) the actor makes known the purpose of the arrest or believes that it is otherwise known by or cannot reasonably be made known to the person to be arrested; and

        (ii) when the arrest is made under a warrant, the warrant is valid or believed by the actor to be valid.

    (b) The use of deadly force is not justifiable under this Section unless:

        (i) the arrest is for a felony; and

        (ii) the person effecting the arrest is authorized to act as a peace officer or is assisting a person whom he believes to be authorized to act as a peace officer; and

        (iii) the actor believes that the force employed creates no substantial risk of injury to innocent persons; and

        (iv) the actor believes that:

            (1) the crime for which the arrest is made involved conduct including the use or threatened use of deadly force; or

            (2) there is a substantial risk that the person to be arrested will cause death or serious bodily harm if his apprehension is delayed.

(3) *Use of Force to Prevent Escape from Custody.* The use of force to

prevent the escape of an arrested person from custody is justifiable when the force could justifiably have been employed to effect the arrest under which the person is in custody, except that a guard or other person authorized to act as a peace officer is justified in using any force, including deadly force, which he believes to be immediately necessary to prevent the escape of a person from a jail, prison, or other institution for the detention of persons charged with or convicted of a crime. . . .

(5) *Use of Force to Prevent Suicide or the Commission of a Crime.*

(a) The use of force upon or toward the person of another is justifiable when the actor believes that such force is immediately necessary to prevent such other person from committing suicide, inflicting serious bodily harm upon himself, committing or consummating the commission of a crime involving or threatening bodily harm, damage to or loss of property or a breach of the peace, except that:

(i) any limitations imposed by the other provisions of this Article on the justifiable use of force in self-protection, for the protection of others, the protection of property, the effectuation of an arrest or the prevention of an escape from custody shall apply notwithstanding the criminality of the conduct against which such force is used; and

(ii) the use of deadly force is not in any event justifiable under this Subsection unless:

(1) the actor believes that there is a substantial risk that the person whom he seeks to prevent from committing a crime will cause death or serious bodily harm to another unless the commission or the consummation of the crime is prevented and that the use of such force presents no substantial risk of injury to innocent persons; or

(2) the actor believes that the use of such force is necessary to suppress a riot or mutiny after the rioters or mutineers have been ordered to disperse and warned, in any particular manner that the law may require, that such force will be used if they do not obey.

(b) The justification afforded by this Subsection extends to the use of confinement as preventive force only if the actor takes all reasonable measures to terminate the confinement as soon as he knows that he safely can, unless the person confined has been arrested on a charge of crime.

Questions

1. *Law Enforcement Authority.* Would Officer Hymon have a justification defense under the Model Penal Code? What (sub)sections govern?

What conditions will trigger the justification to use force? Is there a necessity requirement? Is there a proportionality requirement? What are the competing interests in formulating a rule for the use of deadly force to arrest? In your view, should Officer Hymon get a justification defense?

2. *Constitutionalization of the Proportionality Requirement?* Are the Model Penal Code law enforcement provisions constitutional under the holding in *Garner*? Does *Garner* constitutionally permit more force that the Model Penal Code authorizes?

SECTION 15.4   DEFENSIVE FORCE

The most common instances of justification occur when an actor defends the personal safety or property of himself or another against an aggressor. Perhaps because of this, defensive force justifications have developed the most detailed rules of application. Throughout these rules, however, one can see the guiding hand of the necessity and proportionality requirements. For example, force is not justified if effective defense can be achieved without the use of force or with lesser force. An actor must retreat in many instances before using deadly force. Deadly force cannot be used in the protection of property alone.

The threatened harms to persons and property are obviously an important part of the balance of interests here, but it is the characteristic of the aggressor as a law-breaker that frequently has the most significant effect. It is this factor that allows an actor to take an aggressor's life to save his own. The aggressor's outlaw status tips the otherwise equal balance of one life vs. one life. On the other hand, even the life of a law-breaker is given weight and puts limits on the use of defensive force.

Rosie's Homerun

Rosie is playing ball with her friends in a vacant lot. In the bottom of the third, she hits a homerun off Spano's fastball. "I'm dangerous high and inside," she yells to Spano as she rounds first at full tilt. "I guess so," responds Spano with a smirk, "You just got Logan's window." Sure enough, the ball had caught Logan's bathroom window. Worse yet, Mr. Logan is screaming out of the window, shaking a fist with one hand and holding his eye with the other. "Game's over," Rosie yells as she rounds second and heads for her house.

As she slips through the front door, her mother and her mother's new boyfriend, Frankie, quickly sit up on the couch, clearing their throats and arranging their clothes. "How's it going, Rosie," Frankie says, a little too loudly. "Game over so soon?" "Yeah. I hit the ball through Logan's window and I don't think he's in the mood to give it back." "You leave it to me, kitten. I'll talk to the bum. I'll have you guys playing ball again in no time." "Not a good idea, Frankie, he's really pissed." "Yeah? We'll see how tough he is." He turns to Rosie's mom, "I'll take care of this for you, poopsy."

Frankie, who is six feet, 220 pounds, walks up on Logan's porch and pounds on the front door. "Let's have that ball, Logan," he bellows. Logan pulls open the door and rushes out. He is six feet, three inches tall, and 230 pounds. "Get off my f—— porch. The only way you'll get this ball back is if I stick it up your a——." Frankie, who takes two steps back in surprise when Logan rushes out, is momentarily speechless. He looks behind him to see who is watching, and catches Rosie's eye. He looks back to Logan, "Give me that ball, m—— f——, or you're dead meat." Frankie grabs the ball from Logan's hands. Logan tries to wrestle the ball away. Frankie punches Logan in the face but Logan knees Frankie in the chest and smashes him on the back of the head with his two hands cupping the ball. Frankie goes down hard, hitting his head on the cider block wall. He doesn't move. Someone calls an ambulance. Frankie dies at the hospital from head injuries suffered in the fall.[†] Logan is charged with manslaughter. Is he liable?

Model Penal Code §§3.04, 3.05, 3.06, 3.10, 3.11(2) & (3) Defensive Force Justifications

Section 3.04. Use of Force in Self-Protection

(1) *Use of Force Justifiable for Protection of the Person.* Subject to the provisions of this Section and of Section 3.09, the use of force upon or toward another person is justifiable when the actor believes that such force is immediately necessary for the purpose of protecting himself against the use of unlawful force by such other person on the present occasion.

(2) *Limitations on Justifying Necessity for Use of Force.*
   (a) The use of force is not justifiable under this Section:
      (i) to resist an arrest which the actor knows is being made by a peace officer, although the arrest is unlawful; or
      (ii) to resist force used by the occupier or possessor of

---

[†] The facts are a variation on State v. Griffith, 91 Wash. 2d 572, 589 P.2d 799 (1979).

property or by another person on his behalf, where the actor knows that the person using the force is doing so under a claim of right to protect the property, except that this limitation shall not apply if:

(1) the actor is a public officer acting in the performance of his duties or a person lawfully assisting him therein or a person making or assisting in a lawful arrest; or

(2) the actor has been unlawfully dispossessed of the property and is making a re-entry or recaption justified by Section 3.06; or

(3) the actor believes that such force is necessary to protect himself against death or serious bodily harm.

(b) The use of deadly force is not justifiable under this Section unless the actor believes that such force is necessary to protect himself against death, serious bodily harm, kidnapping or sexual intercourse compelled by force or threat; nor is it justifiable if:

(i) the actor, with the purpose of causing death or serious bodily harm, provoked the use of force against himself in the same encounter; or

(ii) the actor knows that he can avoid the necessity of using such force with complete safety by retreating or by surrendering possession of a thing to a person asserting a claim of right thereto or by complying with a demand that he abstain from any action which he has no duty to take, except that:

(1) the actor is not obliged to retreat from his dwelling or place of work, unless he was the initial aggressor or is assailed in his place of work by another person whose place of work the actor knows it to be and

(2) a public officer justified in using force in the performance of his duties or a person justified in using force in his assistance or a person justified in using force in making an arrest or preventing an escape is not obliged to desist from efforts to perform such duty, effect such arrest or prevent such escape because of resistance or threatened resistance by or on behalf of the person against whom such action is directed.

(c) Except as required by paragraphs (a) and (b) of this Subsection, a person employing protective force may estimate the necessity thereof under the circumstances as he believes them to be when the force is used, without retreating, surrendering possession, doing any other act which he has no legal duty to do or abstaining from any lawful action.

(3) *Use of Confinement as Protective Force.* The justification afforded by this Section extends to the use of confinement as protective force only if the actor takes all reasonable measures to terminate the confinement as soon as he knows that he safely can, unless the person confined has been arrested on a charge of crime.

Section 3.05. Use of Force for the Protection of Other Persons

(1) Subject to the provisions of this Section and of Section 3.09, the use of force upon or toward the person of another is justifiable to protect a third person when:
    (a) the actor would be justified under Section 3.04 in using such force to protect himself against the injury he believes to be threatened to the person whom he seeks to protect; and
    (b) under the circumstances as the actor believes them to be, the person whom he seeks to protect would be justified in using such protective force; and
    (c) the actor believes that his intervention is necessary for the protection of such other person.
(2) Notwithstanding Subsection (1) of this Section:
    (a) when the actor would be obliged under Section 3.04 to retreat, to surrender the possession of a thing or to comply with a demand before using force in self-protection, he is not obliged to do so before using force for the protection of another person, unless he knows that he can thereby secure the complete safety of such other person; and
    (b) when the person whom the actor seeks to protect would be obliged under Section 3.04 to retreat, to surrender the possession of a thing or to comply with a demand if he knew that he could obtain complete safety by so doing, the actor is obliged to try to cause him to do so before using force in his protection if the actor knows that he can obtain complete safety in that way; and
    (c) neither the actor nor the person whom he seeks to protect is obliged to retreat when in the other's dwelling or place of work to any greater extent than in his own.

Section 3.06. Use of Force for the Protection of Property

(1) *Use of Force Justifiable for Protection of Property.* Subject to the provisions of this Section and of Section 3.09, the use of force upon or toward the person of another is justifiable when the actor believes that such force is immediately necessary:
    (a) to prevent or terminate an unlawful entry or other trespass upon land or a trespass against or the unlawful carrying away of tangible, movable property, provided that such land or movable property is, or is believed by the actor to be, in his possession or in the possession of another person for whose protection he acts; or
    (b) to effect an entry or re-entry upon land or to retake tangible movable property, provided that the actor believes that he or the

person by whose authority he acts or a person from whom he or such other person derives title was unlawfully dispossessed of such land or movable property and is entitled to possession, and provided, further, that:

(i) the force is used immediately or on fresh pursuit after such dispossession; or

(ii) the actor believes that the person against whom he uses force has no claim of right to the possession of the property and, in the case of land, the circumstances, as the actor believes them to be, are of such urgency that it would be an exceptional hardship to postpone the entry or re-entry until a court order is obtained.

(2) *Meaning of Possession.* For the purposes of Subsection (1) of this Section:

(a) a person who has parted with the custody of property to another who refuses to restore it to him is no longer in possession, unless the property is movable and was and still is located on land in his possession;

(b) a person who has been dispossessed of land does not regain possession thereof merely by setting foot thereon;

(c) a person who has a license to use or occupy real property is deemed to be in possession thereof except against the licensor acting under claim of right.

(3) *Limitations on Justifiable Use of Force.*

(a) *Request to Desist.* The use of force is justifiable under this Section only if the actor first requests the person against whom such force is used to desist from his interference with the property, unless the actor believes that:

(i) such request would be useless; or

(ii) it would be dangerous to himself or another person to make the request; or

(iii) substantial harm will be done to the physical condition of the property which is sought to be protected before the request can effectively be made.

(b) *Exclusion of Trespasser.* The use of force to prevent or terminate a trespass is not justifiable under this Section if the actor knows that the exclusion of the trespasser will expose him to substantial danger of serious bodily harm.

(c) *Resistance of Lawful Re-entry or Recaption.* The use of force to prevent an entry or re-entry upon land or the recaption of movable property is not justifiable under this Section, although the actor believes that such re-entry or recaption is unlawful, if:

(i) the re-entry or recaption is made by or on behalf of a person who was actually dispossessed of the property; and

(ii) it is otherwise justifiable under paragraph (1)(b) of this Section.

(d) *Use of Deadly Force.* The use of deadly force is not justifiable under this Section unless the actor believes that:

(i) the person against whom the force is used is attempting to dispossess him of his dwelling otherwise than under a claim of right to its possession; or

(ii) the person against whom the force is used is attempting to commit or consummate arson, burglary, robbery or other felonious theft or property destruction and either:

(1) has employed or threatened deadly force against or in the presence of the actor; or

(2) the use of force other than deadly force to prevent the commission or the consummation of the crime would expose the actor or another in his presence to substantial danger of serious bodily harm.

(4) *Use of Confinement as Protective Force.* The justification afforded by this Section extends to the use of confinement as protective force only if the actor takes all reasonable measures to terminate the confinement as soon as he knows that he can do so with safety to the property, unless the person confined has been arrested on a charge of crime.

(5) *Use of Device to Protect Property.* The justification afforded by this Section extends to the use of a device for the purpose of protecting property only if:

(a) the device is not designed to cause or known to create a substantial risk of causing death or serious bodily harm; and

(b) the use of the particular device to protect the property from entry or trespass is reasonable under the circumstances, as the actor believes them to be; and

(c) the device is one customarily used for such a purpose or reasonable care is taken to make known to probable intruders the fact that it is used.

(6) *Use of Force to Pass Wrongful Obstructor.* The use of force to pass a person whom the actor believes to be purposely or knowingly and unjustifiably obstructing the actor from going to a place to which he may lawfully go is justifiable, provided that:

(a) the actor believes that the person against whom he uses force has no claim of right to obstruct the actor; and

(b) the actor is not being obstructed from entry or movement on land which he knows to be in the possession or custody of the person obstructing him, or in the possession or custody of another person by whose authority the obstructor acts, unless the circumstances, as the actor believes them to be, are of such urgency that it would not be reasonable to postpone the entry or movement on such land until a court order is obtained; and

(c) the force used is not greater than would be justifiable if the person obstructing the actor were using force against him to prevent his passage.

Section 3.10. Justification in Property Crimes

Conduct involving the appropriation, seizure or destruction of, damage to, intrusion on or interference with property is justifiable under circumstances which would establish a defense of privilege in a civil action based thereon, unless:
    (1) the Code or the law defining the offense deals with the specific situation involved; or
    (2) a legislative purpose to exclude the justification claimed otherwise plainly appears.

Section 3.11. Definitions

In this Article, unless a different meaning plainly is required: . . .
    (2) "deadly force" means force which the actor uses with the purpose of causing or which he knows to create a substantial risk of causing death or serious bodily harm. Purposely firing a firearm in the direction of another person or at a vehicle in which another person is believed to be constitutes deadly force. A threat to cause death or serious bodily harm, by the production of a weapon or otherwise, so long as the actor's purpose is limited to creating an apprehension that he will use deadly force if necessary, does not constitute deadly force;
    (3) "dwelling" means any building or structure, though movable or temporary, or a portion thereof, which is for the time being the actor's home or place of lodging.

Judgment of the German Supreme Court
September 20, 1920
55 Decisions of the Supreme Court in Criminal Matters 82

The defendant held watch during the night in a shed amidst his fruit trees; he was accompanied by his dog and armed with a loaded rifle. In the early morning, he noticed two men taking fruit from his trees. Upon hearing the defendant both took flight with the fruit that they had picked; the defendant shouted to both of them to halt and he threatened to shoot. When they did not stop, the defendant fired buckshots in their direction and injured one of them, not insignificantly.

One may surmise from the judgment below that this result was intended by the defendant. The defendant was charged with intentional battery and was acquitted on the ground that he acted in self-defense. The trial court assumed that the defendant justifiably used force to regain the fruit and that there was "no other means" except the firing of the shot to force the thieves to stop thereby to regain the property. In appealing the decision, the prosecutor argued that this was not justly to be considered a case of self-defense (*Notwehr*); for at the moment that the shot was fired the thieves had completed their attack upon the defendant's property and had begun to flee from the scene of the crime. This meant that the risk to the defendant's property was no longer "imminent." The prosecutor also argued that the defendant used excessive defensive force because the fruit in question was an insignificant interest and the defendant endangered lives and health of the fleeing persons, and thereby thought to sacrifice the higher interest to save the lower.

This appeal does not prevail [i.e., acquittal affirmed]. . . .

If the defendant fired the shot in order to protect his property and the fruit, and if the defendant had no other equally effective means to this end, then this is a case of permissible defense against an imminent attack against property and possession. The legal conclusions of the trial court are therefore unexceptionable.

The attack of the thieves had not yet ended; and this would be true even if it is assumed that the act of theft had already been completed. So long as the thieves and the property they were stealing could be reached by the defendant, the defendant's act is to be construed as a defense against a continuing attack. . . . The use of defensive force against a continuing attack against property requires only that the force be fitted to the circumstances of the case, which means that no more force be used to achieve the permitted goal than is "necessary." Whether that requirement is satisfied is a question for the trier-of-fact. . . . The opinion is occasionally expressed that the degree of permissible force should be determined not only by the severity of the attack and the available defensive means, also by the principle that to preserve a minor interest one may not force the assailant to sacrifice a valuable interest. If this were the case, defensive force involving attacks upon life and bodily integrity would simply not be available against thieves. So weighing the relative merit of competing interests could not possibly be justified where someone in the Right is locked in struggle against someone in the Wrong; it is not to be expected of the party exercising the defensive force that in protecting his rights against a *widerrechtlich* assailant, he limit the harm he causes to the amount that is threatened to him by the *rechtswidrig* [unjustified] attack. If that were the law governing the case in which one had to protect one's property or possession by threatening the life or bodily security of the assailant, the decision to fight on behalf of a relatively insignificant interest would frequently depend upon moral views, sensibilities of justice and other views held by the party under attack. Accordingly, men might frequently choose not to endanger the lives of others and suffer the loss of their rights and thereby tolerate *Unrecht* [unlawfulness]. . . . [The] statutory law does not provide any support for the view that the relative value of the conflicting interests imposes a limitation on the right of self-defense. The balancing of values may be justified where the conflict is between two rights, but not in a case in which balancing would serve to protect *Unrecht* [unlawfulness] and [would] represent a limitation on the use of defensive force against attacks upon interests of a particular sort, and thus make the degree of defensive force dependent on the harm that might occur to the *widerrechtlich* acting assailant. . . .**

Questions

1. *Proportionality of Harm Threatened and Harm Caused.* Would the defendant before the German Supreme Court have a justification defense under the Model Penal Code? What (sub)sections would govern? If we assume that the defendant had no other less harmful means to protect his fruit, might he get a defense? What should the law want an actor to do under such conditions? What does the German Supreme Court say? (The 1920 decision no longer represents the rule in Germany.)

2. *Assessing the Harm Threatened.* Should it change the result if Germany were at the time in the midst of economic chaos and the fruit trees were the only means the defendant had to feed his family? Would it change the result under the Model Penal Code?

United States ex rel. Means v. Solem
United States Court of Appeals, Eighth Circuit
646 F.2d 322 (1980)

Ross, Circuit Judge.

Ted Means was convicted of riot to obstruct justice in violation of

---

**Editor's Note.—The English language translation of this case was provided by George P. Fletcher of Columbia Law School.

SDCL section 22-10-4[1] and sentenced to thirty months imprisonment. The Supreme Court of South Dakota affirmed the conviction.

Means thereafter filed a petition for a writ of habeas corpus pursuant to 28 U.S.C. §2254. In his petition Means contended, *inter alia*, that the trial court's refusal to instruct on his theories of self-defense [and] defense of others . . . was a denial of due process, right to a trial by jury, and the right to be found guilty beyond a reasonable doubt. The district court, finding that the trial court's failure to instruct on Means' defense theories constituted error of a constitutional magnitude, granted the writ of habeas corpus and ordered that the petitioner be released from state custody.

On appeal, the state contends that the district court erred. . . . For the reasons discussed below, we affirm.

The parties have stipulated to the following facts for the purposes of this appeal.

> On April 25, 1974, a trial was in progress at the Minnehaha County Courthouse in Sioux Falls, South Dakota, in a highly publicized case, State v. Bad Heart Bull, et al. [S.D., 257 N.W.2d 715], in which several Native American persons were being prosecuted for alleged participation in a disturbance at South Dakota's Custer County Courthouse in February, 1973. The defendants were represented by one Native American attorney, Ramon Roubideaux of South Dakota, and by two white attorneys from outside South Dakota. All three attorneys refused to proceed with the *voir dire* examination on the ground that they could not conscientiously do so until a ruling was received from the South Dakota Supreme Court regarding the number of peremptory challenges available to them. The ruling was expected within twenty-four hours.
>
> When the attorneys refused to proceed, presiding Judge Bottum ordered the Native American attorney, Mr. Roubideaux, jailed for twenty-four hours and fined $100. The two white attorneys were dismissed from the case, but were not fined or jailed. Court was dismissed for the day and Mr. Roubideaux was led to jail.
>
> On April 26, 1974, attorney Roubideaux was returned from jail to court by a police officer who led him by the arm to the defense table. Roubideaux appeared disheveled and unshaven. The spectators in the courtroom rose when Roubideaux was led into the courtroom and sat when he sat. But later that morning, the Indian spectators at the trial refused to rise for Judge Bottum. Judge Bottum ordered the spectators cleared from the courtroom. The spectators were peaceably carried from

---

1. The riot to obstruct justice statute, SDCL 22-10-4, now repealed, provided: If the purpose of a riotous assembly was to resist the execution of any statute of this state or of the United States or to obstruct any public officer of this state or of the United States, in the performances of any legal duty, or in serving or executing any legal process, every person guilty of participating in the assembly is punishable by imprisonment in the state penitentiary not exceeding ten years and not less than two years.

the courtroom, one-by-one, by plainclothes police officers, detectives, and a matron. According to some defense witnesses, some of the women carried from the courtroom were fondled by some of the police.

On April 29, 1974, meetings were held among the defendants, their attorneys, and their supporters at the Van Brunt Building in downtown Sioux Falls. The prosecution presented one witness, Kenneth Dahl, concerning the contents of those meetings. Mr. Dahl testified that Russell Means told people not to stand for Judge Bottum the next day, to be "prepared to do battle" and that the signal would be "made for a broken window on the upstairs side of the courtroom for people outside to know that the fight had started inside," and that an Indian lady "agreed to drive up with a carload of debris to throw at the courthouse."

The defense's version of the events of April 29 was very different. Three defense witnesses, including one attorney, testified that at the meetings on April 29 no violence whatsoever was planned for the next day, and that the purpose of the persons in the courtroom refusing to rise for the judge was to express their protest against what they believed to be his racism and racism in the South Dakota courts against Indian people. These witnesses testified that men only were to be sent to fill the twenty seats (which Judge Bottum had announced was all he would allow to spectators) because violence by the Sioux Falls police was feared.

There was no evidence that Ted Means was present at the Van Brunt Building, or even in Sioux Falls, on April 29, or on April 25 or 26, 1974.

On April 30, a number of Indian spectators entered Judge Bottum's courtroom and refused to stand for Judge Bottum. He subsequently ordered the courtroom cleared.

Between the time that Judge Bottum entered the courtroom, which was about 9:30 AM, and the time that the Sioux Falls police Tactical Squad entered the courtroom, which was about 11:20 AM, various activities ensued in the courtroom, including discussion, negotiation, and prayer. According to the testimony of a prosecution witness, there was some communication between the Indian spectators in the courtroom and the people gathered outside. . . .

At about 11:20 AM, the Tactical Squad, equipped with jumpsuits, helmets with face shields, combat boots with steel toes, forty-inch nightsticks with steel-ball ends, gloves with metal in the knuckles, gas masks, firearms, handcuffs and mace entered the courtroom. . . .

A prosecution witness, Tactical Squad member Ideker, testified that the first violence occurred when Russell Means struck him. Ideker also testified that others in the courtroom could have perceived that Ideker himself was the aggressor in his confrontation with Russell Means.

Five defense witnesses testified that the first violence occurred when Russell Means or David Hill, a defendant in the *Bad Heart Bull* trial itself, was struck by a Tactical Squad member. Defense witness Tom Cook testified that the first Tactical Squad member in the courtroom "went into" Russell Means with his baton as though it were a hockey stick and that Russell Means put his hands up and went backwards. Cook testified that immediately after this, Ted Means was "kind of standing" and "as soon as Russell was hit . . . Ted was hit and pretty soon the next moment Ted was lying down on the ground without any more struggle." Cook testified that the spectators stood up just before the Tactical Squad got to them and stood up because the Tactical Squad was coming in at a fast gait. Cook testified that Ted Means may have grabbed an arm of a Tactical Squad member after he was struck.

Defense witness Bishop Bruno Schlachtenhaufen testified that the Tactical Squad came into the courtroom at a fast pace. He testified that it was a surprise to everyone when the Tactical Squad entered the courtroom, and that there was no opportunity for people to leave. He testified that the Tactical Squad came at the spectators with their clubs. He testified that the reaction of the Indian spectators to the Tactical Squad was a defensive reaction. He testified that the first two Tactical Squad members "attacked" David Hill, then "knocked him down and moved on." The next thing he saw was a confrontation between Russell Means and a Tactical Squad member, and immediately thereafter all the people in the first two rows of the courtroom "joined in the resistance."

Defense witness Reverend William Weber testified that the entry of the Tactical Squad was "unexpected after an hour and a half of waiting," and that it was "swift and without any reissuance of an order to stand up or to get out of the courtroom" and that "there was an almost spontaneous and simultaneous reaction on the part of everyone else in the courtroom and we simply rose instinctively." He testified that he believed that everyone who rose "was frightened and concerned about his survival." He testified that the first Tactical Squad member attempted to force Russell Means against the wall and lodged his club under Russell Means' chin. He knew Ted Means, but did not see him get struck or strike anyone. . . .

All witnesses, prosecution and defense, agree that after the initial conflicts a wild fight ensued. A Tactical Squad member, Myers, testified that he separated Ted Means from an unidentified Tactical Squad member, and that Ted Means then took one swing at him, that Myers sidestepped it and then struck Ted Means with a "butt stroke" to the left side of the head, knocking him to the ground, at which time he was arrested. Ted Means received a "goose egg" size bump on his head as a result. . . .

The events of April 30, 1974, were widely publicized throughout Minnehaha County and the State of South Dakota. It was against this background of wide publicity that Ted Means was tried for riot to obstruct justice.

Means made a timely request for several instructions relating to his theory of the case. . . .

. . . When the trial judge refused these written requests for instruction on self-defense and defense of others, Means' counsel made an oral request that South Dakota Pattern Jury Instruction Vol. II, §2-14-9h be given:

The right of self-defense exists only as against an unlawful attack. The right does not exist, even though bodily injury appears probable, as against a person who, in threatening or appearing to threaten injury, is acting [lawfully].

But the trial court had made it clear that all instructions on self-defense would be rejected. . . .

The district court concluded that the state trial court's failure to instruct the jury regarding self-defense [and] defense of others . . . denied the petitioner his "right to trial by jury and his due process right which required the prosecution to prove him guilty beyond a reasonable doubt." We agree that the trial court's failure to give instructions on self-defense and defense of others was a denial of the petitioner's right to due process.

I. The Jury Instructions—Theory of Defense

It is well established that a defendant in a criminal case is entitled to an instruction on his theory of the case if there is evidence to support it and a proper request is made. . . .

In affirming Means' conviction, the South Dakota Supreme Court made it clear that "[u]nder some fact situations, self-defense may be a valid defense to the charge of riot to obstruct justice." State v. Means, S.D., 276 N.W.2d 699, 701 (1979). That interpretation of South Dakota law clearly refutes the state's argument that "as a matter of law" Means was precluded from asserting his theory of self-defense.[3]

The state contends that the requested self-defense instructions were improper because each refers to the actions of the Tactical Squad as an unlawful attack or an assault. To the extent that the defendant's proffered instructions fail to explain that . . . a policeman's use of force becomes unlawful only when it becomes greater than that necessary for the performance of his legal duties, we agree that they are inadequate statements of the law involved in this case.

Nonetheless, we believe that the defendant's request was sufficient to alert the trial judge to an important omission in his charge going to the fundamental fairness of the trial. Being so alerted, the trial court should have given a proper instruction on the issues of self-defense.

There were facts adduced at trial from which a jury could find that the Tactical Squad used *unnecessary* force and therefore, unlawful force

---

3. South Dakota law makes no distinction among those allowed to defend themselves and coming to the defense of another. State v. Grimes, S.D., 237 N.W.2d 900, 902 (1976). Accordingly, we discuss the petitioner's requests for instructions on self defense and defense of others interchangeably.

... in attempting to remove the spectators from the courtroom. Bishop Archie Madsen testified that "it appeared to me it was like attacking a flea with a shotgun to come into the courtroom where Indians had been totally searched, had no weapons of their own with them in any way, and for a tac squad to come in with all the equipment they had, was to me an excessive use of power." The South Dakota statute provides only that the police were entitled to use *necessary* force. We believe the jury could have found, from the facts of this case, that more force than *necessary* was used, so that the defense of self-defense was available to Means. . . .

The state argues that the petitioner, by his own conduct, forfeited any right to claim self-defense [or] defense of others. . . . It urges that Means was precluded from invoking those defenses because he intentionally remained in the courtroom in disregard of the trial court's order to leave.

Under South Dakota law, the right of self-defense is not available to one who "provoke[s] an assault." Whether Means' form of protest by virtue of a peaceful sit-in the courtroom was tantamount to provoking a violent confrontation, as the state contends, is highly questionable but was a question of fact for the jury under proper instructions.

From the evidence adduced at trial, the jury could have found that the violent confrontation which ensued was not "provoked" by the Indian spectators. Only four days earlier, a number of Indian spectators had been *peacefully* carried from the courtroom, primarily by plainclothes officers, without incident, when they refused to clear the courtroom after being ordered to do so following a planned protest similar to that involved in this instance. It would have been reasonable for the Indians to assume, in planning the instant protest by again refusing to rise, that this protest might also be met with their peaceful removal and not with a violent clash with the police. . . .

> We agree with the district court that the petitioner had no right to defend himself or others from the lawful use of such force as was necessary to remove him and the other spectators from the courtroom. Such force was indeed invited by the petitioner.
>
> However, the Sioux Falls Tactical Squad was not authorized to use unlawful force in removing the spectators who remained seated in the courtroom. If the police were the aggressors in using unnecessary, unreasonable, or excessive force it was unlawful and certainly uninvited by peaceful disobedience to a court order. Therefore the fact that the petitioner and the other spectators peacefully remained in the courtroom in violation of a court order, the act which the South Dakota Supreme Court called provocation, only invited or provoked the use of lawful or necessary force by the police in performing their duty of removing the spectators. It did not remove the theory of self defense or defense of

others if there was evidence that the police were the aggressors in using unnecessary or excessive force which the petitioner reasonably believed could lead to bodily harm.

Means v. Solem, 480 F. Supp. 128, 136 (D.S.D. 1979).

. . . We simply cannot accept the state's argument that there is never any right of self-defense available to a person engaged in an obstruction of justice notwithstanding an alleged excessive use of force in effecting that person's removal pursuant to court order.

Under the circumstances involved in this case, we believe that the request for an instruction on self-defense was proper. Petitioner's requested Jury Pattern Instruction on self-defense, although misleading in the absence of an accompanying instruction regarding the necessary use of police force, was sufficient to alert the trial judge to the need to charge the jury on both of these issues. We are also satisfied that petitioner's theory of self-defense was available on these facts under South Dakota law. . . .

II. Constitutional Magnitude of the Trial Errors

Our finding that there was evidence to support instructions on self-defense and defense of others, and that a proper request for such instructions was made, is insufficient, by itself, to grant habeas corpus relief. We must also find that the error in refusing to instruct the jury in this case was of a constitutional magnitude.

We believe that the omission of the requested instruction on self-defense and defense of others, "evaluated in light of the totality of the circumstances," Kentucky v. Whorton, 441 U.S. 786, 789, 99 S. Ct. 2088, 2090, 60 L. Ed. 2d 640 (1979), so infected the "entire trial that the resulting conviction violates due process." . . .

We therefore affirm the judgment of the district court.

Questions

1. *Necessary Force and "Unlawful" Force.* Would Means get a justification defense under the Model Penal Code? What (sub)sections govern? Were the Tactical Squad members justified in using force against Means? If we assume so, was the force they used within the requirements of a justification defense? Was the Tactical Squad's use of force "unlawful"? If we assume for the sake of argument that it was, was the force Means used within the requirements of a justification defense?

2. *The Shifting Right of Justification.* Will Logan get a justification

defense under the Model Penal Code? (Assume that both Frankie and Logan have no mistaken beliefs concerning the surrounding circumstances or concerning their right to use force; mistake as to a justification is the subject of the next section.) What (sub)sections govern? At the beginning of the encounter, is Logan in "possession" of the baseball? If so, is his possession "lawful"? Would the lawfulness of his possession matter for the purposes of his justification defense? Is Frankie's grabbing the ball from Logan justified? Is Logan justified in, then, trying to wrestle the ball back from Frankie? Is Frankie justified in, then, punching Logan in the face? Is Logan justified in, then, kneeing Frankie in the chest and smashing him on the back of the head with his two hands cupping the ball? Is Logan liable for Frankie's death?

SECTION 15.5 MISTAKE AS TO A JUSTIFICATION

The previous sections on justification have focused on the rules that govern justified conduct, that is, the rules that tell actors what they can and cannot do to protect or further a legal interest that absent the justification would be an offense. It is common, however, that an actor thinks his conduct is justified but in reality it is not. His conduct in fact violates the rules of justified conduct. This is common in part because justified conduct often is undertaken under difficult circumstances, especially defensive force justifications, where the actor may be in danger and where the need to act typically is thrust upon the actor with little notice. Because of the difficult circumstances, many jurisdictions follow the Model Penal Code in giving a complete defense for a reasonable mistake as to a justification and a mitigation for an unreasonable mistake. (Many other jurisdictions give no defense for an unreasonable mistake.)

Beyond the liability of the mistaken actor, an important issue is the status of the mistaken actor's conduct. Is his mistaken conduct to be treated the same as truly justified conduct or not? Can such an actor's conduct lawfully be resisted? Is another actor entitled to assist the mistaken actor in his conduct if he does not share in the actor's mistake? These issues are examined below.

Moro's Mistake

Moro loves to play the horses. And "Snake," a local mobster, loves it when he does. Moro is so far in the hole to Snake that he can hardly cover the vig (the interest) each week. Snake has been less than happy as of late, however, because Moro has not been covering even the vig. Things have gotten out of hand. Snake has his reputation to think about. If Moro doesn't keep up, others will think they don't have to, either. To help make his point, Snake gave Moro a severe beating last week, with a warning that, if Moro missed another payment, he would be killed. Nothing personal; general deterrence and all that.

The payment is due today but Moro doesn't have the money. He borrows a gun and hangs out at Deffi's Deli, the neighborhood grocery store, in the hopes that Snake will leave him alone in public. He is shocked when Snake comes in and walks straight at him. "I won't let you get me, Snake!" he says as he pulls his gun and aims. Just before he pulls the trigger, Deffi, who is directly across the counter from him, leans over and punches him. "That's not Snake. It's his brother, you moron." Deffi, the proprietor, has made a point of learning to tell the look-alike brothers apart because Snake does not pay his bill. Deffi's punch deflects Moro's shot. Snake's brother is wounded but not killed.

At a preliminary hearing on an attempted murder charge, the court finds that, while Moro did intend to kill, he reasonably believed that he was in danger of being killed and acted in what he reasonably believed was self defense. Moro is cleared of all charges. Moro then files assault charges against Deffi. Is Deffi criminally liable for striking Moro?

Model Penal Code §3.11(1)
Definition of "Unlawful Force"

In this Article, unless a different meaning plainly is required:

"Unlawful force" means force, including confinement, which is employed without the consent of the person against whom it is directed and the employment of which constitutes an offense or actionable tort or would constitute such offense or tort except for a defense (such as the absence of intent, negligence, or mental capacity; duress; youth; or diplomatic status) not amounting to a privilege to use the force. Assent constitutes consent, within the meaning of this Section, whether or not it otherwise is legally effective, except assent to the infliction of death or serious bodily harm.

Model Penal Code §3.09
Mistake of Law as to Unlawfulness of Force or Legality of Arrest; Reckless or Negligent Use of Otherwise Justifiable Force; Reckless or Negligent Injury or Risk of Injury to Innocent Persons

(1) The justification afforded by Sections 3.04 to 3.07, inclusive, is unavailable when:

(a) the actor's belief in the unlawfulness of the force or conduct against which he employs protective force or his belief in the lawfulness of an arrest which he endeavors to effect by force is erroneous; and

(b) his error is due to ignorance or mistake as to the provisions of the Code, any other provision of the criminal law or the law governing the legality of an arrest or search.

(2) When the actor believes that the use of force upon or toward the person of another is necessary for any of the purposes for which such belief would establish a justification under Sections 3.03 to 3.08 but the actor is reckless or negligent in having such belief or in acquiring or failing to acquire any knowledge or belief which is material to the justiciability of his use of force, the justification afforded by those Sections is unavailable in a prosecution for an offense for which recklessness or negligence, as the case may be, suffices to establish culpability.

(3) When the actor is justified under Sections 3.03 to 3.08 in using force upon or toward the person of another but he recklessly or negligently injures or creates a risk of injury to innocent persons, the justification afforded by those Sections is unavailable in a prosecution for such recklessness or negligence towards innocent persons.

Questions

1. *Moro's Conduct.* Reexamine the Model Penal Code self defense provision quoted in the previous section. Is Moro's attempt to shoot Snake's brother "justified" under the Model Penal Code? If his mistake is reasonable, what would be his liability, if any?

2. *Deffi's Conduct.* Is Deffi's conduct in punching Moro "justified" under the Model Penal Code? Does he satisfy the requirements of the Model Penal Code defense-of-others provision quoted in the previous section? Would Snake's brother have had a right to use force against Moro to protect himself? If Moro has no liability for wounding Snake's

brother, is his (Moro's) use of force against Snake's brother "unlawful," as required for a defense under the Model Penal Code's self defense provision, §3.04(1)?

3. Answer Questions 1 and 2 using the following statutes rather than the Model Penal Code. What is the primary difference between the statutory schemes?

**North Dakota Cent. Code §§12.1-05-03, -04, -07, -08, -12
Defensive Force Justifications; Excuse for Mistake**[††]

12.1-05-03. Self-defense

A person is justified in using force upon another person to defend himself against danger of imminent unlawful bodily injury, sexual assault, or detention by such other person, except that:

1. A person is not justified in using force for the purpose of resisting arrest, execution of process, or other performance of duty by a public servant under color of law, but excessive force may be resisted.

2. A person is not justified in using force if:

(a) He intentionally provokes unlawful action by another person to cause bodily injury or death to such other person; or

(b) He has entered into a mutual combat with another person or is the initial aggressor unless he is resisting force which is clearly excessive in the circumstances. A person's use of defensive force after he withdraws from an encounter and indicates to the other person that he has done so is justified if the latter nevertheless continues or menaces unlawful action.

12.1-05-04. Defense of others

A person is justified in using force upon another person in order to defend anyone else if:

1. The person defended would be justified in defending himself; and

---

[††]Editor's Note.—These North Dakota statutes are modeled after those of the Final Report of the National Commission on Reform of Federal Criminal Law (1971) (see §§603, 604, 607(1), 608). A federal criminal code reform bill passed the Senate but was never passed by the House. See Chapter 3, at note 20.

CHAPTER 15 JUSTIFICATIONS

2. The person coming to the defense has not, by provocation or otherwise, forfeited the right of self-defense.

12.1-05-07. Limitations on the use of force—Excessive force

A person is not justified in using more force than is necessary and appropriate under the circumstances.

12.1-05-08. Excuse

A person's conduct is excused if he believes that the facts are such that his conduct is necessary and appropriate for any of the purposes which would establish a justification or excuse under this chapter, even though his belief is mistaken. However, if his belief is negligently or recklessly held, it is not an excuse in a prosecution for an offense for which negligence or recklessness, as the case may be, suffices to establish culpability. . . .

12.1-05-12. Definitions

In this Article, unless a different meaning plainly is required: . . .
"Unlawful" force means force that satisfies the objective elements of an offense and is not justified.***

Questions

1. *Liability for Moro and Deffi in North Dakota?* If Moro's mistake is reasonable, would he have a defense under the above provisions? If so, what kind of defense, a justification or an excuse? Would Deffi have a defense under the above provisions? If so, what kind?

2. *"Unlawful" Force vs. "Not Privileged" Force.* In its definition of "unlawful force" in §3.11(1), the Model Penal Code refers to "privileged" conduct: "unlawful force," which one lawfully may resist, is force

---

***Editor's Note.—The North Dakota Century Code does not in fact contain a definition of "unlawful" force but, given its treatment of mistake as to a justification as an excuse, it appears to logically intend such a definition.

that is not "privileged." (The Code also uses the term "privileged" in §3.10, quoted in the previous section.) What does the Code mean by "privileged" conduct?

3. *"Unlawful" Force vs. "Unjustified" Force.* Why doesn't the Code just define "unlawful force" as you see it in the §12.1-05-12: force that is not "justified"? How is the North Dakota concept of "justified" conduct different from the Model Penal Code's concept of "justified" conduct?

People v. Goetz
Court of Appeals of New York
68 N.Y. 2d 96, 497 N.E. 2d 41, 506 N.Y.S. 2d 18 (1986)

Chief Judge WACHTLER.

A Grand Jury has indicted defendant on attempted murder, assault, and other charges for having shot and wounded four youths on a New York City subway train after one or two of the youths approached him and asked for $5. The lower courts, concluding that the prosecutor's charge to the Grand Jury on the defense of justification was erroneous, have dismissed the attempted murder, assault and weapons possession charges. We now reverse and reinstate all counts of the indictment.

I

The precise circumstances of the incident giving rise to the charges against defendant are disputed, and ultimately it will be for a trial jury to determine what occurred. We feel it necessary, however, to provide some factual background to properly frame the legal issues before us. Accordingly, we have summarized the facts as they appear from the evidence before the Grand Jury. . . .

On Saturday afternoon, December 22, 1984, Troy Canty, Darryl Cabey, James Ramseur, and Barry Allen boarded an IRT express subway train in The Bronx and headed south toward lower Manhattan. The four youths rode together in the rear portion of the seventh car of the train. Two of the four, Ramseur and Cabey, had screwdrivers inside their coats, which they said were to be used to break into the coin boxes of video machines.

Defendant Bernhard Goetz boarded this subway train at 14th Street in Manhattan and sat down on a bench towards the rear section of the same car occupied by the four youths. Goetz was carrying an unlicensed .38 caliber pistol loaded with five rounds of ammunition in a waistband holster. The train left the 14th Street station and headed towards Chambers Street.

It appears from the evidence before the Grand Jury that Canty approached Goetz, possibly with Allen beside him, and stated "give me five dollars." Neither Canty nor any of the other youths displayed a weapon. Goetz responded by standing up, pulling out his handgun and firing four shots in rapid succession. The first shot hit Canty in the chest; the second struck Allen in the back; the third went through Ramseur's arm and into his left side; the fourth was fired at Cabey, who apparently was then standing in the corner of the car, but missed, deflecting instead off of a wall of the conductor's cab. After Goetz briefly surveyed the scene around him, he fired another shot at Cabey, who then was sitting on the end bench of the car. The bullet entered the rear of Cabey's side and severed his spinal cord.

All but two of the other passengers fled the car when, or immediately after, the shots were fired. The conductor, who had been in the next car, heard the shots and instructed the motorman to radio for emergency assistance. The conductor then went into the car where the shooting occurred and saw Goetz sitting on a bench, the injured youths lying on the floor or slumped against a seat, and two women who had apparently taken cover, also lying on the floor. Goetz told the conductor that the four youths had tried to rob him.

While the conductor was aiding the youths, Goetz headed towards the front of the car. The train had stopped just before the Chambers Street station and Goetz went between two of the cars, jumped onto the tracks and fled. Police and ambulance crews arrived at the scene shortly thereafter. Ramseur and Canty, initially listed in critical condition, have fully recovered. Cabey remains paralyzed, and has suffered some degree of brain damage.

On December 31, 1984, Goetz surrendered to police in Concord, New Hampshire, identifying himself as the gunman being sought for the subway shootings in New York nine days earlier. Later that day, after receiving *Miranda* warnings, he made two lengthy statements, both of which were tape recorded with his permission. In the statements, which are substantially similar, Goetz admitted that he had been illegally carrying a handgun in New York City for three years. He stated that he had first purchased a gun in 1981 after he had been injured in a mugging. Goetz also revealed that twice between 1981 and 1984 he had successfully warded off assailants simply by displaying the pistol.

According to Goetz's statement, the first contact he had with the four youths came when Canty, sitting or lying on the bench across from him, asked "how are you," to which he replied "fine." Shortly thereafter, Canty, followed by one of the other youths, walked over to the defendant and stood to his left, while the other two youths remained to his right, in the corner of the subway car. Canty then said "give me five dollars."

Goetz stated that he knew from the smile on Canty's face that they wanted to "play with me." Although he was certain that none of the youths had a gun, he had a fear, based on prior experiences, of being "maimed."

Goetz then established "a pattern of fire," deciding specifically to fire from left to right. His stated intention at that point was to "murder [the four youths], to hurt them, to make them suffer as much as possible." When Canty again requested money, Goetz stood up, drew his weapon, and began firing, aiming for the center of the body of each of the four. Goetz recalled that the first two he shot "tried to run through the crowd [but] they had nowhere to run." Goetz then turned to his right to "go after the other two." One of these two "tried to run through the wall of the train, but . . . he had nowhere to go." The other youth (Cabey) "tried pretending that he wasn't with [the others]" by standing still, holding on to one of the subway hand straps, and not looking at Goetz. Goetz nonetheless fired his fourth shot at him. He then ran back to the first two youths to make sure they had been "taken care of." Seeing that they had both been shot, he spun back to check on the latter two. Goetz noticed that the youth who had been standing still was now sitting on a bench and seemed unhurt. As Goetz told the police, "I said '[y]ou seem to be all right, here's another,' " and he then fired the shot which severed Cabey's spinal cord. Goetz added that "if I was a little more under self-control . . . I would have put the barrel against his forehead and fired." He also admitted that "if I had had more [bullets], I would have shot them again, and again, and again."

II

After waiving extradition, Goetz was brought back to New York and arraigned on a felony complaint charging him with attempted murder and criminal possession of a weapon. The matter was presented to a Grand Jury in January 1985, with the prosecutor seeking an indictment for attempted murder, assault, reckless endangerment, and criminal possession of a weapon. Neither the defendant nor any of the wounded youths testified before this Grand Jury. On January 25, 1985, the Grand Jury indicted defendant on one count of criminal possession of a weapon in the third degree (Penal Law §265.02), for possessing the gun used in the subway shootings, and two counts of criminal possession of a weapon in the fourth degree (Penal Law §265.01), for possessing two other guns in his apartment building. It dismissed, however, the attempted murder and other charges stemming from the shootings themselves.

Several weeks after the Grand Jury's action, the People, asserting that they had newly available evidence, moved for an order authorizing them to resubmit the dismissed charges to a second Grand Jury. Supreme Court, Criminal Term, after conducting an in camera inquiry, granted the motion. Presentation of the case to the second Grand Jury began on March 14, 1985. Two of the four youths, Canty and Ramseur, testified. Among the other witnesses were four passengers from the seventh car of the subway who had seen some portions of the incident. Goetz again chose not to testify, though the tapes of his two statements were played for the grand jurors, as had been done with the first Grand Jury.

On March 27, 1985, the second Grand Jury filed a 10-count indictment, containing four charges of attempted murder, four charges of assault in the first degree, one charge of reckless endangerment in the first degree, and one charge of criminal possession of a weapon in the second degree [which is possession of loaded firearm with intent to use it unlawfully against another]. Goetz was arraigned on this indictment on March 28, 1985, and it was consolidated with the earlier three count indictment.

On October 4, 1985, Goetz moved to dismiss the charges contained in the second indictment alleging, among other things, that the evidence before the second Grand Jury was not legally sufficient to establish the offenses charged, and that the prosecutor's instructions to that Grand Jury on the defense of justification were erroneous and prejudicial to the defendant so as to render its proceedings defective.

On November 25, 1985, while the motion to dismiss was pending before Criminal Term, a column appeared in the *New York Daily News* containing an interview which the columnist had conducted with Darryl Cabey the previous day in Cabey's hospital room. The columnist claimed that Cabey had told him in this interview that the other three youths had all approached Goetz with the intention of robbing him. The day after the column was published, a New York City police officer informed the prosecutor that he had been one of the first police officers to enter the subway car after the shootings, and that Canty had said to him "we were going to rob [Goetz]." The prosecutor immediately disclosed this information to the court and to defense counsel, adding that this was the first time his office had been told of this alleged statement and that none of the police reports filed on the incident contained any such information. Goetz then orally expanded his motion to dismiss, asserting that resubmission of the charges voted by the second Grand Jury was required . . . because it appeared, from this new information, that Ramseur and Canty had committed perjury.

In an order dated January 21, 1986, Criminal Term granted Goetz's motion to the extent that it dismissed all counts of the second indictment, other than the reckless endangerment charge, with leave to resubmit these charges to a third Grand Jury. The court, after inspection of the Grand Jury minutes, first rejected Goetz's contention that there was not legally sufficient evidence to support the charges. It held, however, that the prosecutor, in a supplemental charge elaborating upon the justification defense, had erroneously introduced an objective element into this defense by instructing the grand jurors to consider whether Goetz's conduct was that of a "reasonable man in [Goetz's] situation." The court . . . concluded that the statutory test for whether the use of deadly force is justified to protect a person should be wholly subjective, focusing entirely on the defendant's state of mind when he used such force. It concluded that dismissal was required for this error because the justification issue was at the heart of the case. . . .

On appeal by the People, a divided Appellate Division affirmed Criminal Term's dismissal of the charges. . . .

Justice Asch granted the People leave to appeal to this court. We agree with the dissenters that . . . the prosecutor's charge to the Grand Jury on justification [did not require] dismissal of any of the charges in the second indictment.

III

Penal Law article 35 recognizes the defense of justification, which "permits the use of force under certain circumstances." One such set of circumstances pertains to the use of force in defense of a person, encompassing both self-defense and defense of a third person. Penal Law §35.15(1) sets forth the general principles governing all such uses of force: "[a] person may . . . use physical force upon another person when and to the extent he *reasonably believes* such to be necessary to defend himself or a third person from what he *reasonably believes* to be the use or imminent use of unlawful physical force by such other person" (emphasis added).

Section 35.15(2) sets forth further limitations on these general principles with respect to the use of "deadly physical force": "A person may not use deadly physical force upon another person under circumstances specified in subdivision one unless (a) He *reasonably believes* that such other person is using or about to use deadly physical force . . . or (b) He *reasonably believes* that such other person is committing or attempting to commit a kidnapping, forcible rape, forcible sodomy or robbery" (emphasis added).

Thus, consistent with most justification provisions, Penal Law §35.15 permits the use of deadly physical force only where requirements as to triggering conditions and the necessity of a particular response are met (see, Robinson, Criminal Law Defenses §121[a], at 2). As to the triggering conditions, the statute requires that the actor "reasonably believes" that another person either is using or about to use deadly physical force or is committing or attempting to commit one of certain enumerated felonies, including robbery. As to the need for the use of deadly physical force as a response, the statute requires that the actor "reasonably believes" that such force is necessary to avert the perceived threat.

Because the evidence before the second Grand Jury included statements by Goetz that he acted to protect himself from being maimed or to avert a robbery, the prosecutor correctly chose to charge the justification defense in §35.15 to the Grand Jury. The prosecutor properly instructed the grand jurors to consider whether the use of deadly physical force was justified to prevent either serious physical injury or a robbery, and, in doing so, to separately analyze the defense with respect to each of the charges. He elaborated upon the prerequisites for the use of deadly physical force essentially by reading or paraphrasing the language in Penal Law §35.15. The defense does not contend that he committed any error in this portion of the charge.

When the prosecutor had completed his charge, one of the grand jurors asked for clarification of the term "reasonably believes." The prosecutor responded by instructing the grand jurors that they were to consider the circumstances of the incident and determine "whether the defendant's conduct was that of a reasonable man in the defendant's situation." It is this response by the prosecutor—and specifically his use of "a reasonable man"—which is the basis for the dismissal of the charges by the lower courts. As expressed repeatedly in the Appellate Division's plurality opinion, because §35.15 uses the term "*he* reasonably believes," the appropriate test, according to that court, is whether a defendant's beliefs and reactions were "reasonable *to him.*" Under that reading of the statute, a jury which believed a defendant's testimony that he felt that his own actions were warranted and were reasonable would have to acquit him, regardless of what anyone else in defendant's situation might have concluded. Such an interpretation defies the ordinary meaning and significance of the term "reasonably" in a statute, and misconstrues the clear intent of the Legislature, in enacting §35.15, to retain an objective element as part of any provision authorizing the use of deadly physical force.

Penal statutes in New York have long codified the right recognized at common law to use deadly physical force, under appropriate circumstances, in self-defense. These provisions have never required that an actor's belief as to the intention of another person to inflict serious injury be correct in order for the use of deadly force to be justified, but they have uniformly required that the belief comport with an objective notion of reasonableness. . . .

In 1961 the Legislature established a Commission to undertake a complete revision of the Penal Law and the Criminal Code. The impetus for the decision to update the Penal Law came in part from the drafting of the Model Penal Code by the American Law Institute, as well as from the fact that the existing law was poorly organized and in many aspects antiquated. Following the submission by the Commission of several reports and proposals, the Legislature approved the present Penal Law in 1965, and it became effective on September 1, 1967. The drafting of the general provisions of the new Penal Law, including the article on justification, was particularly influenced by the Model Penal Code. While using the Model Penal Code provisions on justification as general guidelines, however, the drafters of the new Penal Law did not simply adopt them verbatim.

The provisions of the Model Penal Code with respect to the use of deadly force in self-defense reflect the position of its drafters that any culpability which arises from a mistaken belief in the need to use such force should be no greater than the culpability such a mistake would give rise to if it were made with respect to an element of a crime (see ALI, Model Penal Code and Commentaries, part I, at 32, 34; Robinson, Criminal Law Defenses, op. cit., at 410). Accordingly, under Model Penal Code §3.04(2)(b), a defendant charged with murder (or attempted murder) need only show that he "*believe[d]* that [the use of deadly force] was necessary to protect himself against death, serious bodily injury, kidnapping or [forcible] sexual intercourse" to prevail on a self-defense claim (emphasis added). If the defendant's belief was wrong, and was recklessly, or negligently formed, however, he may be convicted of the type of homicide charge requiring only a reckless or negligent, as the case may be, criminal intent (see Model Penal Code §3.09[2]; MPC Commentaries, op. cit., part I, at 32, 150).

The drafters of the Model Penal Code recognized that the wholly subjective test set forth in §3.04 differed from the existing law in most States by its omission of any requirement of reasonableness. The drafters were also keenly aware that requiring that the actor have a "reasonable belief" rather than just a "belief" would alter the wholly subjective test. . . .

New York did not follow the Model Penal Code's equation of a mistake as to the need to use deadly force with a mistake negating an element of a crime, choosing instead to use a single statutory section which would provide either a complete defense or no defense at all to a defendant charged with any crime involving the use of deadly force. The drafters of the new Penal Law adopted in large part the structure and content of Model Penal Code §3.04, but, crucially, inserted the word "reasonably" before "believes."

The plurality below agreed with defendant's argument that the change in the statutory language from "reasonable ground," used prior to 1965, to "he reasonably believes" in Penal Law §35.15 evinced a legislative intent to conform to the subjective standard contained in Model Penal Code §3.04. This argument, however, ignores the plain significance of the insertion of "reasonably." Had the drafters of §35.15 wanted to adopt a subjective standard, they could have simply used the language of §3.04. "Believes" by itself requires an honest or genuine belief by a defendant as to the need to use deadly force (see, e.g., Robinson, Criminal Law Defenses, op. cit. §184(b), at 399-400). Interpreting the statute to require only that the defendant's belief was "reasonable to *him*," as done by the plurality below, would hardly be different from requiring only a genuine belief; in either case, the defendant's own perceptions could completely exonerate him from any criminal liability.

We cannot lightly impute to the Legislature an intent to fundamentally alter the principles of justification to allow the perpetrator of a serious crime to go free simply because that person believed his actions were reasonable and necessary to prevent some perceived harm. To completely exonerate such an individual, no matter how aberrational or bizarre his thought patterns, would allow citizens to set their own standards for the permissible use of force. It would also allow a legally competent defendant suffering from delusions to kill or perform acts of violence with impunity, contrary to fundamental principles of justice and criminal law.

We can only conclude that the Legislature retained a reasonableness requirement to avoid giving a license for such actions. The plurality's interpretation, as the dissenters below recognized, excises the impact of the word "reasonably." . . .

Goetz also argues that the introduction of an objective element will preclude a jury from considering factors such as the prior experiences of a given actor and thus, require it to make a determination of "reasonableness" without regard to the actual circumstances of a particular incident. This argument, however, falsely presupposes that an objective standard means that the background and other relevant characteristics of a particular actor must be ignored. To the contrary, we have frequently noted that a determination of reasonableness must be based on the "circumstances" facing a defendant or his "situation." Such terms encompass more than the physical movements of the potential assailant. As just discussed, these terms include any relevant knowledge the defendant had about that person. They also necessarily bring in the physical attributes of all persons involved, including the defendant. Furthermore, the defendant's circumstances encompass any prior experiences he had which could provide a reasonable basis for a belief that another person's intentions were to injure or rob him or that the use of deadly force was necessary under the circumstances.

Accordingly, a jury should be instructed to consider this type of evidence in weighing the defendant's actions. The jury must first determine whether the defendant had the requisite beliefs under §35.15, that is, whether he believed deadly force was necessary to avert the imminent use of deadly force or the commission of one of the felonies enumerated therein. If the People do not prove beyond a reasonable doubt that he did not have such beliefs, then the jury must also consider whether these beliefs were reasonable. The jury would have to determine, in light of all the "circumstances," as explicated above, if a reasonable person could have had these beliefs.

The prosecutor's instructions to the second Grand Jury that it had to determine whether, under the circumstances, Goetz's conduct was that of a reasonable man in his situation was thus essentially an accurate charge. It is true that the prosecutor did not elaborate on the meaning of "circumstances" or "situation" and inform the grand jurors that they could consider, for example, the prior experiences Goetz related in his statement to the police. We have held, however, that a Grand Jury need not be instructed on the law with the same degree of precision as the petit jury. This lesser standard is premised upon the different functions of the Grand Jury and the petit jury: the former determines whether sufficient evidence exists to accuse a person of a crime and thereby subject him to criminal prosecution; the latter ultimately determines the guilt or innocence of the accused, and may convict only where the People have proven his guilt beyond a reasonable doubt.

. . . The Grand Jury has indicted Goetz. It will now be for the petit jury to decide whether the prosecutor can prove beyond a reasonable doubt that Goetz's reactions were unreasonable and therefore excessive. . . .

Accordingly, the order of the Appellate Division should be reversed, and the dismissed counts of the indictment reinstated. . . .

Order reversed, etc.†††

Questions

1. *The Subjective Standard.* The New York self defense provision requires of the actor that "*he* reasonably believes" that the force is necessary. The lower court in *Goetz* interpreted this phrase to mean that the belief must be "reasonable to *him*," in part because it believed that only this interpretation would provide the opportunity to take account of such factors as the prior experiences of a given actor, which Goetz argued would help explain why he reacted the way he did. Would it be possible to take account of an actor's prior experiences and fears at the time of the encounter if the code gave a defense only if the actor's

---

†††Editor's Note.— On June 16, 1987, after trial upon remand, Goetz was acquitted by a jury of all charges except criminal possession of a weapon in the third degree.

belief was reasonable? What would be an example of an unreasonable mistake under the approach of the lower court in *Goetz*?

2. *The Model Penal Code's Individualized Objective Standard.* Under the Model Penal Code, a "reasonable belief" is defined as follows:

> In this Code, unless a different meaning plainly is required: . . . "reasonably believes" or "reasonable belief" designates a belief which the actor is not reckless or negligent in holding.

Model Penal Code §1.13(16). Does the Model Penal Code provide the decisionmaker an opportunity to take account of such factors as the prior experience of a given actor? (Recall our discussion of the individualization of the objective standard of negligence in Section 7.2.) Under the Model Penal Code approach, are there any experiences or characteristics of an actor that a judge might exclude from being presented to a jury? Under the lower court's approach in *Goetz*, what experiences or characteristics, if any, might be excluded from a jury's consideration?

3. *Effect of Culpable Mistake as to a Justification.* If Goetz's belief that he needed to use deadly force to protect himself against a threatened robbery was *un*reasonable (say negligent), what would be his liability, if any, under New York law? What would be his liability, if any, under the Model Penal Code? What objections can one make to the New York scheme for dealing with unreasonable mistakes as to a justification?

State v. Kelly
Supreme Court of New Jersey
97 N.J. 178, 478 A.2d 364 (1984)

WILENTZ, C.J.

The central issue before us is whether expert testimony about the battered-woman's syndrome is admissible to help establish a claim of self-defense in a homicide case. The question is one of first impression in this state. We hold, based on the limited record before us (the State not having had a full opportunity to prove the contrary), that the battered-woman's syndrome is an appropriate subject for expert testimony; that the experts' conclusions, despite the relative newness of the field, are sufficiently reliable under New Jersey's standards for scientific testimony; and that defendant's expert was sufficiently qualified. Accordingly, we reverse and remand for a new trial. If on retrial after a full examination of these issues the evidence continues to support these conclusions, the expert's testimony on the battered-woman's syndrome shall be admitted as relevant to the honesty and reasonableness of defendant's belief that deadly force was necessary to protect her against death or serious bodily harm.

I

On May 24, 1980, defendant, Gladys Kelly, stabbed her husband, Ernest, with a pair of scissors. He died shortly thereafter at a nearby hospital. The couple had been married for seven years, during which time Ernest had periodically attacked Gladys. According to Ms. Kelly, he assaulted her that afternoon, and she stabbed him in self-defense, fearing that he would kill her if she did not act.

Ms. Kelly was indicted for murder. At trial, she did not deny stabbing her husband, but asserted that her action was in self-defense. To establish the requisite state of mind for her self-defense claim, Ms. Kelly called Dr. Lois Veronen as an expert witness to testify about the battered-woman's syndrome. After hearing a lengthy voir dire examination of Dr. Veronen, the trial court ruled that expert testimony concerning the syndrome was inadmissible on the self-defense issue. . . . Apparently the court believed that the sole purpose of this testimony was to explain and justify defendant's perception of the danger rather than to show the objective reasonableness of that perception.

Ms. Kelly was convicted of reckless manslaughter. In an unreported decision . . . , the Appellate Division affirmed the conviction. We granted certification and now reverse. . . .

The Kellys had a stormy marriage. Some of the details of their relationship, especially the stabbing, are disputed. The following is Ms. Kelly's version of what happened—a version that the jury could have accepted and, if they had, a version that would make the proffered expert testimony not only relevant, but critical.

The day after the marriage, Mr. Kelly got drunk and knocked Ms. Kelly down. Although a period of calm followed the initial attack, the next seven years were accompanied by periodic and frequent beatings, sometimes as often as once a week. During the attacks, which generally occurred when Mr. Kelly was drunk, he threatened to kill Ms. Kelly and to cut off parts of her body if she tried to leave him. Mr. Kelly often moved out of the house after an attack, later returning with a promise that he would change his ways. Until the day of the homicide, only one of the attacks had taken place in public.

The day before the stabbing, Gladys and Ernest went shopping. They did not have enough money to buy food for the entire week, so Ernest said he would give his wife more money the next day.

The following morning he left for work. Ms. Kelly next saw her husband late that afternoon at a friend's house. She had gone there with her daughter, Annette, to ask Ernest for money to buy food. He told her to wait until they got home, and shortly thereafter the Kellys left. After walking past several houses, Mr. Kelly, who was drunk, angrily asked "What the hell did you come around here for?" He then grabbed the collar of her dress, and the two fell to the ground. He choked her by pushing his fingers against her throat, punched or hit her face, and bit her leg.

A crowd gathered on the street. Two men from the crowd separated them just as Gladys felt that she was "passing out" from being choked. Fearing that Annette had been pushed around in the crowd, Gladys then left to look for her. Upon finding Annette, defendant noticed that Annette had defendant's pocketbook. Gladys had dropped it during the fight. Annette had retrieved it and gave her mother the pocketbook.

After finding her daughter, Ms. Kelly then observed Mr. Kelly running toward her with his hands raised. Within seconds he was right next to her. Unsure of whether he had armed himself while she was looking for their daughter, and thinking that he had come back to kill her, she grabbed a pair of scissors from her pocketbook. She tried to scare him away, but instead stabbed him.[1]

The central question in this case is whether the trial court erred in its exclusion of expert testimony on the battered-woman's syndrome. That testimony was intended to explain defendant's state of mind and bolster her claim of self-defense. . . .

Whether expert testimony on the battered-woman's syndrome should be admitted in this case depends on whether it is relevant to defendant's claim of self-defense. . . .

The present rules governing the use of force in self-defense are set out in the justification section of the Code of Criminal Justice. The use of force against another in self-defense is justifiable "when the actor reasonably believes that such force is immediately necessary for the purpose of protecting himself against the use of unlawful force by such other person on the present occasion." N.J.S.A. 2C:3-4(a). Further limitations exist when deadly force is used in self-defense. The use of such deadly force is not justifiable

> unless the actor reasonably believes that such force is necessary to protect himself against death or serious bodily harm. . . . [N.J.S.A. 2C:3-4(b)(2)].

---

1. This version of the homicide—with a drunk Mr. Kelly as the aggressor both in pushing Ms. Kelly to the ground and again in rushing at her with his hands in a threatening position after the two had been separated—is sharply disputed by the State. The prosecution presented testimony intended to show that the initial scuffle was started by Gladys; that upon disentanglement, while she was restrained by bystanders, she stated that she intended to kill Ernest; that she then chased after him, and upon catching up with him stabbed him with a pair of scissors taken from her pocketbook.

These principles codify decades of prior case law development of the elements of self-defense. We focus here on the critical requirement that the actor reasonably believe deadly force to be necessary to prevent death or serious bodily harm, for the proffer of expert testimony was argued to be relevant on this point.

Self-defense exonerates a person who kills in the reasonable belief that such action was necessary to prevent his or her death or serious injury, even though this belief was later proven mistaken. "Detached reflection cannot be demanded in the presence of an uplifted knife," Justice Holmes aptly said, and the law accordingly requires only a reasonable, not necessarily a correct, judgment. . . .

[An honest belief alone] does not suffice. A defendant claiming the privilege of self-defense must also establish that her belief in the necessity to use force was reasonable. As originally proposed, the new Code of Criminal Justice would have eliminated the reasonableness requirement, allowing self-defense whenever the defendant honestly believed in the imminent need to act. This proposed change in the law was not accepted by the Legislature. N.J.S.A. 2C:3-4 as finally enacted retains the requirement that the defendant's belief be reasonable.[8]

Thus, even when the defendant's belief in the need to kill in self-defense is conceded to be sincere, if it is found to have been unreasonable under the circumstances, such a belief cannot be held to constitute complete justification for a homicide.[9] As with the determination of the existence of the defendant's belief, the question of the reasonableness of this belief "is to be determined by the jury, not the defendant, in light of the circumstances existing at the time of the homicide." It is perhaps worth emphasizing here that for defendant to prevail, the jury need not find beyond a reasonable doubt that the defendant's belief was honest and reasonable. Rather, if any evidence raising the issue of self-defense is adduced, either in the State's or the defendant's case, then the jury must be instructed that the State is required to prove beyond a reasonable doubt that the self-defense claim does not accord with the

---

8. The rejected form of §2C:3-4 was patterned after §3.04 of the Model Penal Code. The purpose of the proposed Code and M.P.C. provisions was to prevent one who killed in the honest but mistaken and unreasonable belief in the necessity of the action from being convicted of a crime like murder, which is premised on an act motivated by unlawful purpose. See Model Penal Code §3.04 commentary at 14-15 (Tent. Draft No. 8 1958); Commission report, supra, Vol. II: Commentary, at 83-84.

9. In State v. Powell, 84 N.J. 305, 419 A.2d 406 (1980), we explicitly recognized that before enactment of the Code the doctrine of imperfect self-defense could reduce murder to manslaughter when the defendant honestly but unreasonably perceived himself in such danger as to require the use of deadly force. However, we expressed no opinion on whether imperfect self-defense was available under the new Code for the purpose of reducing murder to manslaughter. The resolution of that issue is immaterial to the case at bar.

facts; acquittal is required if there remains a reasonable doubt whether the defendant acted in self-defense.

With the foregoing standards in mind, we turn to an examination of the relevance of the proffered expert testimony to Gladys Kelly's claim of self-defense.

Gladys Kelly claims that she stabbed her husband in self-defense, believing he was about to kill her. The gist of the State's case was that Gladys Kelly was the aggressor, that she consciously intended to kill her husband, and that she certainly was not acting in self-defense.

The credibility of Gladys Kelly is a critical issue in this case. If the jury does not believe Gladys Kelly's account, it cannot find she acted in self-defense. The expert testimony offered was directly relevant to one of the critical elements of that account, namely, what Gladys Kelly believed at the time of the stabbing, and was thus material to establish the honesty of her stated belief that she was in imminent danger of death. . . .

. . . Dr. Veronen would have bolstered Gladys Kelly's credibility. Specifically, by showing that her experience, although concededly difficult to comprehend, was common to that of other women who had been in similarly abusive relationships, Dr. Veronen would have helped the jury understand that Gladys Kelly could have honestly feared that she would suffer serious bodily harm from her husband's attacks, yet still remain with him. This, in turn, would support Ms. Kelly's testimony about her state of mind (that is, that she honestly feared serious bodily harm) at the time of the stabbing.

On the facts in this case, we find that the expert testimony was relevant to Gladys Kelly's state of mind, namely, it was admissible to show she *honestly* believed she was in imminent danger of death. Moreover, we find that because this testimony was central to the defendant's claim of self-defense, its exclusion, if otherwise admissible, cannot be held to be harmless error.

We also find the expert testimony relevant to the reasonableness of defendant's belief that she was in imminent danger of death or serious injury. We do not mean that the expert's testimony could be used to show that it was understandable that a battered woman might believe that her life was in danger when indeed it was not and when a reasonable person would not have so believed, for admission for that purpose would clearly violate the rule set forth in State v. Bess, supra, 53 N.J. 10, 247 A.2d 669. Expert testimony in that direction would be relevant solely to the honesty of defendant's belief, not its objective reasonableness. Rather, our conclusion is that the expert's testimony, if accepted by the jury, would have aided it in determining whether, under the circumstances, a reasonable person would have believed there was imminent danger to her life.

At the heart of the claim of self-defense was defendant's story that she had been repeatedly subjected to "beatings" over the course of her marriage. While defendant's testimony was somewhat lacking in detail, a juror could infer from the use of the word "beatings," as well as the detail given concerning some of these events (the choking, the biting, the use of fists), that these physical assaults posed a risk of serious injury or death. When that regular pattern of serious physical abuse is combined with defendant's claim that the decedent sometimes threatened to kill her, defendant's statement that on this occasion she thought she might be killed when she saw Mr. Kelly running toward her could be found to reflect a reasonable fear; that is, it could so be found if the jury believed Gladys Kelly's story of the prior beatings, if it believed her story of the prior threats, and, of course, if it believed her story of the events of that particular day.

The crucial issue of fact in which this expert's testimony would bear is why, given such allegedly severe and constant beatings, combined with threats to kill, defendant had not long ago left decedent. Whether raised by the prosecutor as a factual issue or not, our own common knowledge tells us that most of us, including the ordinary juror, would ask himself or herself just such a question. And our knowledge is bolstered by the experts' knowledge, for experts point out that one of the common myths, apparently believed by most people, is that battered wives are free to leave. To some, this misconception is followed by the observation that the battered wife is masochistic, proven by her refusal to leave despite the severe beatings; to others, however, the fact that the battered wife stays on unquestionably suggests that the "beatings" could not have been too bad for if they had been, she certainly would have left. The expert could clear up these myths, by explaining that one of the common characteristics of a battered wife is her *inability* to leave despite such constant beatings; her "learned helplessness"; her lack of anywhere to go; her feeling that if she tried to leave, she would be subjected to even more merciless treatment; her belief in the omnipotence of her battering husband; and sometimes her hope that her husband will change his ways.

Unfortunately, in this case the State reinforced the myths about battered women. On cross-examination, when discussing an occasion when Mr. Kelly temporarily moved out of the house, the State repeatedly asked Ms. Kelly: "You wanted him back, didn't you?" The implication was clear: Domestic life could not have been too bad if she wanted him back. In its closing argument, the State trivialized the severity of the beatings, saying:

> I'm not going to say they happened or they didn't happen, but life isn't pretty. Life is not a bowl of cherries. We each and every person who takes a breath has problems. Defense counsel says bruised and battered. Is there any one of us who hasn't been battered by life in some manner or means?

Even had the State not taken this approach, however, expert testimony would be essential to rebut the general misconceptions regarding battered women.

. . . Reversed and remanded for new trial.

Questions

1. *Ms. Kelly and Self Defense.* Was Ms. Kelly's use of force against her husband necessary in its timing and in its amount to defend herself? If not, did she believe that it was necessary? If her belief was reasonable, what is the extent of her liability, if any, under New Jersey law? If her belief was unreasonable (say negligent), what is the extent of her liability, if any, under New Jersey law? If her belief was unreasonable, what would be the extent of her liability, if any, under the Model Penal Code?

2. *Battered Woman's Syndrome.* Would the *Kelly* court allow the jury to take account of the defendant's prior beatings by her husband? Would it allow the jury to hear evidence not only of the beatings but also testimony from experts about the battered-woman's syndrome generally, that is, the effect of battering on others? To what issues in self defense, if any, would each of these kinds of testimony be relevant? Would such testimony be admissible under the Model Penal Code?

United States v. Calley
Problem Case

First Lieutenant Calley stands convicted of the premeditated murder of 22 infants, children, women, and old men, and of assault with intent to murder a child of about 2 years of age. All the killings and the assault took place on March 16, 1968 in the area of the village of My Lai in the Republic of South Vietnam. The Army Court of Military Review affirmed the findings of guilty and the sentence, which, as reduced by the convening authority, includes dismissal and confinement at hard labor for 20 years. . . .

Lieutenant Calley was a platoon leader in C Company, a unit that was part of an organization known as Task Force Barker, whose mission was to subdue and drive out the enemy in an area in the Republic of Vietnam known popularly as Pinkville. Before March 16, 1968, this area, which included the village of My Lai 4, was a Viet Cong stronghold. C Company had operated in the area several times. Each time the unit had entered the area it suffered casualties by sniper fire, machine gun fire, mines, and other forms of attack. Lieutenant Calley had accompanied his platoon on some of the incursions.

On March 15, 1968, a memorial service for members of the company killed in the area during the preceding weeks was held. After the service Captain Ernest L. Medina, the commanding officer of C Company, briefed the company on a mission in the Pinkville area set for the next day. C Company was to serve as the main attack formation for Task Force Barker. In that role it would assault and neutralize My Lai 4, 5, and 6 and then mass for an assault on My Lai 1. Intelligence reports indicated that the unit would be opposed by a veteran enemy battalion, and that all civilians would be absent from the area. The objective was to destroy the enemy. Disagreement exists as to the instruction on the specifics of destruction.

Captain Medina testified that he instructed his troops that they were to destroy My Lai 4 by "burning the hootches, to kill the livestock, to close the wells and to destroy the food crops." Asked if women and children were to be killed, Medina said he replied in the negative, adding that, "You must use common sense. If they have a weapon and are trying to engage you, then you can shoot back, but you must use common sense." However, Lieutenant Calley testified that Captain Medina informed the troops they were to kill every living thing—men, women, children, and animals—and under no circumstances were they to leave any Vietnamese behind them as they passed through the villages en route to their final objective. Other witnesses gave more or less support to both versions of the briefing.

On March 16, 1968, the operation began with interdicting fire. C Company was then brought to the area by helicopters. Lieutenant Calley's platoon was on the first lift. This platoon formed a defense perimeter until the remainder of the force was landed. The unit received no hostile fire from the village.

Calley's platoon passed the approaches to the village with his men firing heavily. Entering the village, the platoon encountered only unarmed, unresisting men, women, and children. The villagers, including infants held in their mothers' arms, were assembled and moved in separate groups to collection points. Calley testified that during this time he was radioed twice by Captain Medina, who demanded to know what was delaying the platoon. On being told that a large number of villagers had been detained, Calley said Medina ordered him to "waste them." Calley further testified that he obeyed the orders because he had been taught the doctrine of obedience throughout his military career. Medina denied that he gave any such order.

One of the collection points for the villagers was in the southern part of the village. There, Private First Class Paul D. Meadlo guarded a group of between 30 to 40 old men, women, and children. Lieutenant Calley approached Meadlo and told him, " 'You know what to do,' " and left. He returned shortly and asked Meadlo why the people were not yet dead. Meadlo replied he did not know that Calley had meant that they should be killed. Calley declared that he wanted them dead. He and Meadlo then opened fire on the group, until all but a few children fell. Calley then personally shot these children. He expended 4 or 5 magazines from his M-16 rifle in the incident.

Lieutenant Calley and Meadlo moved from this point to an irrigation ditch on the east side of My Lai 4. There, they encountered another group of civilians being held by several soldiers. Meadlo estimated that this group contained from 75 to 100 persons. Calley stated, " 'We got another job to do, Meadlo,' " and he ordered the group into the ditch. When all were in the ditch, Calley and Meadlo opened fire on them. Although ordered by Calley to shoot, Private First Class James J. Dursi refused to join in the killings, and Specialist Four Robert E. Maples refused to give his machine gun to Calley for use in the killings. Lieutenant Calley admitted that he fired into the ditch, with the muzzle of his weapon within five feet of people in it. He expended between 10 to 15 magazines of ammunition on this occasion.

With his radio operator, Private Charles Sledge, Calley moved to the north end of the ditch. There, he found an elderly Vietnamese monk, whom he interrogated. Calley struck the man with his rifle butt and then shot him in the head. Other testimony indicates that immediately afterwards a young child was observed running toward the village. Calley seized him by the arm, threw him into the ditch, and fired at him. Calley admitted interrogating and striking the monk, but denied shooting him. He also denied the incident involving the child.

Appellate defense counsel contend that the evidence is insufficient to establish the accused's guilt. They do not dispute Calley's participation in the homicides, but they argue that he did not act with the malice or mens rea essential to a conviction of murder; that the orders he received to kill everyone in the village were not palpably illegal; that he was acting in ignorance of the laws of war; that since he was told that only "the enemy" would be in the village, his honest belief that there were no innocent civilians in the village exonerates him of criminal responsibility for their deaths; and, finally, that his actions were in the heat of passion caused by reasonable provocation.

Questions

1. *Execution of Military Authority.* Would Lieutenant Calley's conduct be objectively justified under the Model Penal Code? What (sub)sections govern? What conditions will trigger the justification to use force under

military authority? Is there a necessity requirement? Is there a proportionality requirement? In your view, should Lieutenant Calley get a justification defense? Should emotional upset over the casualties mourned on the previous day be taken into account?

2. *The Special Case of Mistake as to Military Authority.* Assume that Calley mistakenly but honestly believed that Captain Medina had ordered all villagers killed. Assume also that he was unsure as to whether such an order was lawful. Would he have a defense under the following provision? (Note that this is not a justification defense in Article 3 of the Code but rather is in Article 2.)

Model Penal Code §2.10
Military Orders

It is an affirmative defense that the actor, in engaging in the conduct charged to constitute an offense, does no more than execute an order of his superior in the armed services which he does not know to be unlawful.

SECTION 15.6 UNKNOWINGLY JUSTIFIED ACTOR

The previous sections in this chapter have dealt with cases where the actor was motivated by a belief in the justifying circumstances (whether they actually existed or not). On occasion, an actor may engage in conduct that is in fact justified on the objective facts but the actor is unaware of those facts. While the case of the unknowingly justified actor is unusual, it is important because it forces us to reveal why we grant a justification defense. Is the defense provided to exculpate an actor who is properly motivated? Or, is the defense given to recognize the absence of a net social harm where the harm or evil of the offense is outweighed and thereby vitiated by the benefit derived from the conduct, much like the absence of an objective element of an offense definition bars liability for the substantive offense (but not liability for attempt)?

Biker's Break

Ranger Yardley, 70, retired from service several years ago but still hangs around the station. He helped lay out the fireroads that crisscross the Pine Barrens. Both crews at the station are out on small fire calls. Yardley is alone. The Southwest Tower signals: "Class 4 fire . . . burn the whole length of A-11 . . . Atsion endangered." Yardley calls the other crews but they are too far away to get to road A-11 before the blaze. He jumps in the flame truck, which is used to burn firebreaks to stop advancing forest fires, and heads out on his own. With no firefighting crews, there will be no stopping the fire if it gets across A-11. He starts at the north end, which is closest, and prepares to lay a strip of burning kerosene beside the road as he drives. But he starts to feel faint, his chest starts to hurt, he can't breath. He stops the truck, jumps to the ground gasping for air, and heads back in the direction he came, staggering and incoherent.

Jake and Spoon keep an eye out for rangers. Motorcycles aren't permitted on the Pine Barrens' fireroads but it's a great ride. They spot a flame truck up ahead and pull up in the bush. But after a few minutes they realize that no rangers are around and the truck even has its flame going! "Maybe the rangers are in the woods taking a whiz," Jake suggests. "Talk about great rides!" blurts Spoon, as she jumps off the bike and into the cab. With Jake along side on the bike watching for rangers, Spoon roars off, spreading fire as she goes. When the road ends at the state highway, Spoon dumps the truck, jumps on with Jake, and they're off down the highway. To Spoon, it was her best ride ever, and both are screaming and laughing, until a highway patrolman pulls them over and arrests them both for a third degree felony, causing a catastrophe. Jake argues the point. "Don't you know about the forest fire, man? We just saved Atsion. You should be giving us a medal." Spoon is shocked. "Are you kidding?" she says to Jake before Jake can shut her up in front of the trooper. Investigation shows that many people would have died but for Spoon and Jake's burning of A-11, that Jake realized the situation at the time they took the truck, but that Spoon did not. Do Jake and Spoon get a justification defense?

Notes on the Unknowingly Justified Actor

Current law Recall from the previous section that the Model Penal Code gives a justification defense to an actor who "believes" that her conduct is justified. Whether intended or not, such "believes" language has the effect of denying a defense to the unknowingly justified actor, because she does not "believe" her conduct is justified. On the other hand, the "believes" language may have been adopted to provide a defense for a mistaken justification, without thought to its effect on the unknowingly justified actor. Other authorities, of which there are few, are split on the issue. Some permit a defense to the unknowingly justified actor; others do not.

Objective vs. subjective justification The issue of the unknowingly justified actor is of special significance because it forces an inquiry into the basic nature of justification defenses. If the theory of a justification defense is the avoidance of a greater harm, then the defense should focus on purely objective criteria—the balance of conflicting interests—and an unknowingly justified actor, should have a justification defense to liability for the full substantive offense despite her ignorance. If the theory of justifications is an actor's blamelessness because, whatever the ultimate effect, she has tried to act in a proper way, then the defense should focus on the actor's state of mind—the purpose of her conduct. The objective theory justifies *conduct*; the subjective theory holds the *actor* justified because of her purpose.

Objective view of justification Under an objective view of justification, the primary role of justification defenses is to fill out the rules of conduct in guiding future conduct. A defense is given whenever the harm or evil of the offense charged has been outweighed by the harm avoided by the conduct. Arguing by analogy, we do not hold an actor liable for an offense simply because the person mistakenly believes that he has committed an offense. Liability and ensuing punishment for the substantive offense require that the harm or evil of the offense in fact occur. Absent this, only attempt liability is appropriate. So, too, with the unknowingly justified actor.

Impossible attempt Because an unknowingly justified actor is permitted a justification defense to the offense charged, under the objective view, it does not follow that she will escape all liability. A majority of jurisdictions follow the Model Penal Code in imposing liability upon an actor who mistakenly believes the circumstances exist that make her conduct an offense. The actor may be liable under the Model Penal Code attempt provision, for example, if she "purposely engages in conduct which would constitute the crime if the attendant circumstances were as [s]he believes them to be."[1] Attempt liability acknowledges that the harm or evil of the offense has not occurred. It bases liability instead upon the actor's demonstrated willingness to act in a

---

1. Model Penal Code §5.01(1)(a). See Section 8.3 (Impossibility). If a special attempt statute is preferred, or if the jurisdiction does not punish impossible attempts, something like the following might be used:

> *Attempt to Act Unjustifiably.* Although an actor satisfies the requirements of a justification defense, he nonetheless is guilty of an attempt to commit an offense if he:
> (a) satisfies all the elements of the definition of the offense, and
> (b) is unaware of the circumstances justifying his conduct [or does not act for the purpose of avoiding the harm or furthering the benefit that is the basis for the justification defense].

way that she believes constitutes an offense. Such attempt liability seems well suited for the unknowingly justified actor, who has not caused a net harm, but who mistakenly believes that she has.

Subjective view of justification Under a subjective view of justification, an unknowingly justified actor gets no justification defense and therefore is liable for the full offense, even though her conduct is objectively justified and in fact avoids a greater harm. Under this view, the existence of the justifying circumstances and the harm avoided is irrelevant to assessing the actor's liability. The unknowingly justified actor gets no defense because her conduct is not properly motivated. Her mistaken belief (that she is not justified) is used to support full liability for the substantive offense, not just attempt liability.

Justificatory purpose vs. knowledge One complication in the subjective theory of justification comes from the reliance upon an actor's motivation as a foundation for the offense. Fletcher, for example, claims the rule to be that "actors may avail themselves of justifications only if they act with a *justificatory intent*."[2] This rationale for the defense would seem to require that the person act for the justificatory *purpose*, not just with knowledge of the justifying circumstances. That is, not only should the unknowingly justified actor be denied a defense, so should the knowingly justified actor if it is shown that the justifying circumstances were not the *motivation* for the justified conduct. This rationale for the subjective theory is inconsistent with most subjective formulations of justification defenses, for most require only that the actor "believes" that the justifying circumstances exist. But if the defense's rationale is proper motivation, the defense should not require that the actor have acted for the justifying purpose.

Assisting and resisting unknowingly justified actor Another complication for the subjective theory is the effect it has for persons who assist or resist the unknowingly justified actor. Under an objective theory, where the unknowingly justified actor remains justified despite the absence of justificatory purpose, anyone lawfully may assist and no one lawfully may interfere with the justified conduct. Under a subjective theory, however, if the unknowingly justified actor is not justified, it would seem that the unjustified conduct may be lawfully resisted. Further, an anomalous situation arises in which, of two people engaging in the same conduct at the same time, one is justified and one is not.

Questions

1. *Knowledge of the Justifying Circumstances.* Does Jake satisfy the requirements for a lesser evils defense under Model Penal Code §3.02?

---

2. G. Fletcher, Rethinking Criminal Law 557 (1978).

Does Spoon? If Spoon is held not to have a lesser evils defense and Jake is charged not as a principal but as her accomplice, does Jake have a lesser evils defense to his complicity?

2. *Unknowingly Justified Actor and Impossible Attempt.* If Spoon is held to be justified, can she nonetheless be held liable for anything? Does she satisfy the requirements of Model Penal Code §5.01(1)(a), punishing impossible attempts?

3. *Resisting and Assisting the Unknowingly Justified Actor.* If a ranger, not knowing about the threatening forest fire, used force to try to stop Jake, would Jake have a right to defend himself? Would the ranger's use of force against Jake be "unlawful" force? If the ranger threatened Spoon, would Spoon have a right to defend herself?

4. *The Subjective Theory of Justification.* Is the justification defense provided because an actor who is properly motivated should be exculpated? If so, must avoiding the greater harm be his primary motivation? His only motivation? For example, assume that Jake knows of the justifying circumstances (the forest fire threatening Atsion) but that this information plays no part in his decision to help joyride the flame truck; he would have done exactly the same thing if there had been no fire. If his knowledge of the justifying circumstances played no role in motivating his conduct, is he less blameworthy than an actor such as Spoon, who has the same motivation and does not know of the justifying circumstances? Do the Model Penal Code justification defenses require a justificatory motivation (or purpose) or just knowledge of the justifying circumstances?

5. *The Objective Theory of Justification.* Is the justification defense given to recognize the absence of a net societal harm where the harm or evil of the offense is outweighed and thereby vitiated by the benefit derived from the conduct, much like the absence of an objective element of an offense definition bars liability for the substantive offense (but not liability for attempt)? What arguments can you make for and against the objective theory of justification?

Chapter 16. EXCUSES

SECTION 16.1 THE NATURE OF EXCUSES

Excuses, like justifications, are general defenses. That is, they are applicable to all offenses and are available even though the actor satisfies the elements of an offense. Excuses admit that the deed may be wrong, but excuse the actor because the actor's characteristics or situation suggest that the actor is not responsible for his violation. Blame sufficient for criminal liability arises not from engaging in conduct that in fact constitutes a criminal harm or evil but rather from choosing to engage in such conduct; absent a sufficient capacity to choose, there can be no blame and ought to be no liability or punishment.

The Brothers' Brawl

The Motan brothers, Acker and Ed, have a reputation for being a bit wild. Their wildness has given them near celebrity status in some quarters and they are happy to cultivate the image. They stop in at one of their favorite bars, "The Wheel," and some "fans" buy them a round of beers. After they guzzle it down, a woman in the group reveals that their drinks were spiked with a "gorilla" drug. "Watch out, everybody! You're going to get a show tonight!" she shouts to the crowd. Acker is feeling very strange, excited, and very aggressive. He starts dancing on the table. Ed joins in and before long both are kicking drinks and throwing pitchers of beer. Jote, a man in the group who usually is a fan of their antics, takes offense and begins to scream at them. As a brawl begins, the bar's bouncer moves toward the group. At 6'6" and 250 pounds, the sight of him is enough to make the Motan brothers quiet down. Jote, however, turns his anger toward the bouncer and is quickly ejected. After a few more beers, the brothers leave for another favorite bar but find Jote waiting for them outside. He is highly belligerent and vocal. His shouting draws a crowd from inside the bar. The brothers decide to beat him senseless for his remarks but then spot a patrol car across the street. They point it out to Jote but he is undeterred. When Jote begins telling the assembled "fans" that the brothers are too "wimpy" and "yellow" to fight, the brothers conclude that they have no choice but to hurt him. They take turns punching him while the other holds him but after a minute or two, the police intervene and arrest all three for their brawling.

Tired of the Motan's brothers relentless brawling, the prosecutor wants prison terms, but his case is complicated by the blood-test reports from the hospital. Acker and Jote (who mistakenly got the dose intended for Ed) had a level of Skopezine that would create uncontrollable feelings of aggression in the average person. In addition, the medical authorities explain that a belief that one has been subjected to an aggression-inducing drug, as Ed believed, could cause a loosening of psychological restraints to aggression that otherwise might prevent such conduct. Jote is tried first and acquitted, under the involuntary intoxication doctrine. Should both brothers also be excused?

Notes on the Nature of Excuses

Justifications vs. excuses Justifications and excuses may seem similar in that both are general defenses and both exculpate an actor because of his or her blamelessness. A distinction between the two was of practical importance at early common law,[1] but it fell into disuse when both kinds of defenses came to acquit a defendant in the same fashion. The distinction remains one of conceptual importance, however. Justified conduct is correct behavior that is to be encouraged (or at least tolerated) in the future. In determining whether conduct is justified, the focus is on the *act* and its circumstances, not the actor. An excuse, in contrast, represents a legal conclusion that the conduct is wrong, undesirable, but that criminal liability is inappropriate because some characteristic of the actor or his situation vitiates society's desire to punish him. Excuses do not suggest the absence of net harm, as do justifications, but rather shift blame for the harm from the actor to the disability or other cause of the excusing conditions. The focus in excuses is on the *actor.* Acts are justified; actors are excused.

Rationale for recognizing excuses Not every distributive principle for criminal liability would necessarily recognize excuses. A distributive

---

1. The excused defendant was acquitted but his property nonetheless was forfeited to the crown. See N. Hurnard, The King's Pardon for Homicide Before A.D. 1307, x-xi (Oxford 1969).

principle based upon just desert supports the recognition of excuses in order to exculpate blameless offenders. One also might argue that a utilitarian distributive principle based exclusively on special deterrence similarly would support the recognition of excuses. That is, there is little special deterrent value in sanctioning an offender if the offender is unable to appreciate the criminality of his conduct or to conform it to the requirements of law. On the other hand, there may well be *general* deterrent value—the deterrence of other potential offenders, who do not have an excuse—in sanctioning such blameless offenders. Punishing a blameless offender may be particularly effective at signaling to the general public that the law is serious about punishing such violations. Persons contemplating such an offense ought not even hope to be excused. Such an extreme form of strict liability, it might be argued, would increase the motivation to avoid such a violation. A distributive principle that looks only to incapacitation or rehabilitation of dangerous offenders similarly might deny an excuse to a blameless offender, at least where the source of the excuse continues or is likely to recur. In these cases, the criminal law would want to take jurisdiction over such offenders in order to administer required incapacitation or rehabilitation. That excuses are in fact recognized by current doctrine suggests that in this instance desert and possibly special deterrence are the guiding distributive principles rather than general deterrence, incapacitation, or rehabilitation.[2]

Common requirements of excuses Many doctrines and defenses serve as excuses: the involuntary act requirement, the defenses of insanity, subnormality, involuntary intoxication, immaturity, duress, mistake as to a justification, and certain mistake of law defenses. The common rationale of these excuses—to exculpate the blameless—gives rise to common requirements: A *disability* or *reasonable mistake* must cause an *excusing condition*. Under each doctrine, an actor is excused if, because of the special conditions of the defense, the actor could not reasonably have been expected to have avoided the violation. This conclusion may derive from either of two kinds of explanations. In all but the mistake excuses, the actor can point to abnormal circumstances or abnormal characteristics that make it too difficult for him to appreciate the criminality or wrongfulness of his conduct or too difficult to conform his conduct to the law. In the mistake excuses, no disabling abnormality exists but the actor can claim that, because of a reasonable mistake, he did not realize that his conduct violated the law or was wrongful.

Disability vs. mistake excuses The disability and mistake excuses generate the same conclusion of blamelessness in different ways. In the

---

2. Some writers have sought to argue that the recognition of excuses is not inconsistent with these utilitarian goals. See, e.g., Posner, Economic Analysis of Law 201 (3rd ed. 1986).

disability excuses, the disabling abnormality sets the actor apart from the general population. The mistake excuses seem to do the opposite: They argue that the actor should not be punished because in fact he has acted in a way that anyone else would have acted in the same situation. That is, the actor's mistake is reasonable; any reasonable person would have made the same mistake. This theory of blamelessness has complications, however, for no disabling abnormality exists to which the blame for the offense can be shifted. Further, with no disability to distinguish the actor from the general population, there is greater danger that acquitting the apparently normal actor will undercut the law's prohibition of the actor's conduct. More on this in a moment. The absence of a disabling abnormality may help explain why the law is more hesitant to recognize mistake excuses and, when they are recognized, why it severely restricts their reach. Objective appearances aside, however, the two mechanisms of excuse in fact are analogous. Both rely upon a conclusion that the actor could not reasonably have been expected to avoid the violation. Where a disabling abnormality exists, the claim of excuse is essentially a claim that the reasonable person suffering a similar disability similarly would have been unable to avoid a violation.

Disability requirement By *disability* is meant an abnormal condition of the actor at the time of the offense, such as insanity, intoxication, subnormality, or immaturity. Each such disability is a real-world condition with a variety of observable manifestations apart from the conduct constituting the offense. It may be a long term or even permanent condition, such as subnormality, or a temporary state like intoxication, somnambulism, automatism, or hypnotism. Its cause may be internal, as in insanity, or external, as in coercion from another person (duress). The disability requirement serves to distinguish the actor from the general population; it provides an object to which the blame may be shifted; and it allows the law to acquit the actor because he or she is different, while continuing to condemn and prohibit the conduct for all others. The existence of a disability also provides some evidence that a resulting excusing condition does in fact exist. These purposes confirm the need for a legal disability to have confirmable manifestations beyond the criminal conduct at hand. The Model Penal Code intoxication defense, for example, requires "a disturbance of mental or physical capacities resulting from the introduction of substances into the body."[3] The insanity defense requires that the defendant be suffering from a "mental disease or defect,"[4] which is defined to exclude "an abnormal-

---

3. Model Penal Code §2.08(5).
4. Model Penal Code §4.01(1).

ity manifested only by repeated criminal or otherwise antisocial conduct."[5]

Excusing conditions Having a recognized disability does not itself qualify an actor for an excuse, for it is not the disability that is central to the reason for exculpating the actor. An actor is not excused because he or she is intoxicated, but rather because the *effect* of the intoxication in the instant situation is to create a condition that renders the actor blameless for the conduct constituting the offense. The requirement of an *excusing condition*, then, is not an element independent of the actor's disability, but rather is a requirement that the actor's disability cause a particular result, a particular exculpating mental or emotional condition in relation to the conduct constituting the offense.

Four types of excusing conditions Society generally is willing to excuse an actor under any of four types of conditions. In descending order of severity, they include situations where:

(1) the conduct constituting the offense simply is not the product of the actor's voluntary effort or determination (e.g., the actor is having a seizure);
(2) the conduct is the product of the actor's voluntary effort or determination, but the actor does not accurately perceive the physical nature or consequences of the conduct (e.g., the actor hallucinates that what in fact is a gun is a paint brush, or accurately perceives the physical characteristics of the gun but does not know that guns shoot bullets that can injure people) and therefore does not know that the conduct is wrong or criminal;
(3) the actor accurately perceives and understands the physical nature of the conduct and its consequences, but does not know that the conduct is wrong or criminal (e.g., the actor thinks God has ordered him to sacrifice a neighbor for the good of mankind or believes, because of paranoid delusions, that the man waiting for a bus is about to attack him); or
(4) the actor accurately perceives the nature and consequences of the conduct and knows its wrongfulness and criminality, but lacks the ability to control the conduct (e.g., because of an insane compulsion or duress) to such an extent that the actor can no longer reasonably be expected to conform his or her conduct to the requirements of law.

Involuntary act The first excusing condition occurs where the conduct constituting an offense does not include a volitional act. Cases of this sort include "conduct" that is a reflex action or convulsion. This

---

5. Model Penal Code §4.01(2).

first excusing condition presents the clearest case of blamelessness. The absence of volition in the doing of a criminal act is only a step above the absence of a muscular contraction. Nearly any disability causing the excusing condition is recognized as adequate for a defense; the resulting dysfunction apparently is sufficiently gross that it establishes its own abnormality. Traditionally, such conditions bar conviction because they prevent satisfaction of the voluntary act requirement that is said to be an element of all offenses. However, there may be advantages to treating such cases as providing a general excuse defense rather than as negating a required element, as discussed later in this chapter.

Ignorance of nature of act In an excusing condition of the second sort there is, admittedly, a voluntary act but the actor is exculpated because he or she is unaware of the nature of his act, that is, unaware of its physical nature or normal immediate consequences. Such is the case of an actor who, suffering from a delusion that he is squeezing an orange, strangles his wife. The defect typically is one of perception,[6] and commonly results from insanity or intoxication or from more exotic disabilities such as automatism or somnambulism.[7] When this second excusing condition is relied upon, the law limits the excuse to specific disabilities, such as involuntary intoxication, insanity, somnambulism, one of which must be independently proved.

Ignorance of criminality or wrongfulness of act In the third category of excusing condition, the actor engages in conduct voluntarily and knows the nature of the act, but does not know that the act is wrong or criminal. The defect is one of knowledge rather than perception. It can result from a simple lack of information, or from a lack of the intelligence or cognitive function necessary to use available information to determine wrongfulness or criminality. The law seems more suspicious of these claims for excuse. A normal person's plea for excuse based on ignorance of the law proscribing the conduct generally is rejected. Because normal people can make such mistakes, presence of the excusing condition alone does little to distinguish the actor from the general population. Instances of this third excusing condition thus are more selectively excused, generally requiring either a disability with persuasive indications of abnormality or special circumstances of mistake compelling a conclusion of blamelessness. This basis for exculpating an actor underlies the disability excuses of insanity, subnormality, involuntary intoxication, and immaturity. The few mistake excuses that are recognized also use the excusing condition of this third group.

---

6. However, where the excusing condition concerns ignorance of the probable *consequences* of the actor's conduct, it can be the result of a severe defect in knowledge rather than a defect in perception.

7. The latter are sometimes treated, inaccurately, as instances of involuntary conduct.

Mistake excuses as third type of excusing condition Four types of mistakes commonly are allowed as grounds for a general excuse defense (as distinguished from mistakes that provide a "failure of proof" defense, by negating an element of the offense[8]). Reliance upon an official misstatement of law and mistake due to the unavailability of a law are two such general mistake excuses. A mistake as to whether one's conduct is justified also is commonly recognized as an excuse.[9] In the later instance, the actor does not know his conduct is wrong or criminal because, under the circumstances as he perceives and understands them, his actions are justified. A fourth commonly recognized mistake excuse, reliance upon unlawful military orders, is essentially a special subclass of a mistake as to a justification excuse, where the justification is the public authority of lawful military orders.[10]

Impairment of control The fourth excusing condition exists where an actor engages in conduct voluntarily, correctly perceives the nature of his act, and is aware that it is wrong. The act is exculpated because he or she lacks the capacity to control his or her conduct, and thus cannot fairly be held accountable for it. For this fourth excusing condition, the law generally is unwilling to excuse unless there is a clear and confirmable disability that distinguishes the actor from others, a disability that explains the criminal conduct and takes responsibility for it. A loaded .357 Magnum pointed at the actor's head, for example, may provide the objective, confirmable criteria necessary to distinguish the actor's ability to control his conduct from that of the general population. Insanity and intoxication can cause this excusing condition, as they can cause the previous two excusing conditions. The duress defense is based solely on this defect in control. Hypnotism sometimes is recognized as an excuse because it may cause this fourth excusing condition, although it often is incorrectly listed as an example of the involuntary act defense, the first excusing condition.

"Status excuses" To say that one of these excusing conditions must be satisfied is to say that a disability, by itself, will not excuse. It is not enough that the actor is intoxicated or subject to duress; his intoxication or duress must cause an excusing condition. This may seem rudimentary, especially in the case of duress or intoxication, but the implications for other excuses are dramatic. The inadequacy of a disability by itself to excuse means that there ought to be no such thing as a "status

---

8. For a discussion of these kinds of mistake defenses, see Section 7.3 (Culpability Requirements and Mistake Defenses).

9. This typically is provided by justification statutes providing that "an actor is justified if he *believes*" that justifying circumstances exist. See Section 15.5 (Mistake as to a Justification).

10. The excuse and the justification of lawful military orders commonly are treated together under the "defense of military orders." See, e.g., Model Penal Code §2.10.

excuse" as the common law recognized and some modern theorists appear to support. Being mentally ill is not itself enough. It is not that the law recognizes a class of mentally ill persons who are automatically free of criminal responsibility for whatever they might do. Rather, the insanity defense requires that the actor's mental illness be such that on this occasion it is of such a nature and effect that it excuses the offense at hand. One might well be mentally ill yet be liable for an offense, if the mental illness does not play a sufficient role in commission of the offense. In other words, the disability must cause an excusing condition *for the conduct constituting the offense charged.* If A, while preparing a knowingly false income tax return, hallucinates that a neighbor's barking dog has turned into an attacking tiger, he may be considered insane at the time of filing the false return, but he does not merit an insanity excuse if his hallucination plays no part in the preparation and filing of the return. If he kills the dog/tiger in perceived self defense, of course, he may be excused for the killing. In both cases, A may be suffering from insanity. Only in the case of the killing, however, can the disability be said to have created an excusing condition (type two) that undercuts A's responsibility for the offense.[11]

Disability as "but for" cause is insufficient The importance of the excusing condition requirement is seen in the rule that in existing liability, without an adequate excusing condition, is insufficient to excuse *even if the disability is a "but for" cause of the offense.* The effect of this rule can be dramatic. Assume an elderly male, with no prior record of child abuse, is given a drug while in the hospital and while under the influence of the drug, he goes to another room in the hospital and molests a young girl.[12] Assume further that the evidence shows conclusively that the actor would not have committed this offense if he had not been given the drug. Should he be excused? One can appreciate the appeal of the defendant's claim that it was the drug, not his own free choice, that has caused the offense. Yet, current excuse formulations might not give a defense. It is not enough that the drug created

---

11. In practice, immaturity is formulated as a "status excuse" in many jurisdictions. That is, the defense requirements look only to whether the actor fits a defined class, without regard for whether he satisfies the excusing conditions for the offense at hand. But many other jurisdictions require a showing of actual immaturity or allow the state to rebut a presumption of immaturity that arises when the defendant is under a certain age. Even where a conclusive age cut-off is used, it is offered as an effective approximation for an immaturity assessment. That is, no one claims a defendant should be excused *because he is 13* but rather because being 13 suggests that *he is immature.*

12. The facts are similar to those in State v. Mriglot, 15 Wash. App. 446, 550 P.2d 17 (1976), where the appellate court approved the trial court's denial of the defendant's requested instruction that he should be excused if the jury found that he had been "involuntarily *under the influence* or *affected* by the use of liquor or drugs" (emphasis by the appellate court).

an impulse that would not otherwise have existed or that it eroded a restraint that otherwise would have existed. Current excuses require that the compulsion be sufficiently overwhelming or that the actor's capacity to resist be sufficiently impaired that he could not reasonably have been expected to have avoided the offense. It is the excusing condition requirement that implements this normative standard in judging the adequacy of the compulsion or incapacity.

Disparate burdens to avoid crime The result of this principle may be a greater burden on one actor than on another. And the greater burden may be one for which the actor is not responsible, as is the case with the hospitalized molester. But then many people no doubt have naturally occurring greater burdens than others in conforming their conduct to the requirements of law, either because of the kind of place in which they live or grew up or the kind of genes and physiology that they have. The law generally does not take account of such differences in burden to conform unless the burden reaches a level of severity that is sufficiently gross and abnormal that compliance cannot reasonably be expected. When an actor's life circumstances or internal makeup cause a sufficiently severe burden to conform that it alters our expectations of the person's ability to avoid the offense, an excuse defense generally is available. Absent a clear abnormality causing an adequate excusing condition, each actor is obliged to resist the compulsions and overcome the incapacities tending toward crime. Thus, despite the fact that the elderly man in the hospital would not have committed the molestation but for the drug, he will not be given a defense unless the jury is persuaded that the effect of the drug was sufficiently compelling that he could not have been expected to have avoided the violation.

Objective limitation on excuses To judge whether a person has sufficient capacity to avoid a violation, the law introduces objective standards into its excuses. While we may tend to think of excuses as being very subjective, the fact is that in principle all modern excuses hold an actor to some form of objective standard in judging his or her efforts to remain law-abiding. Several excuses have explicit objective standards as part of their criteria. Mistake defenses require that the actor's mistake be reasonable. The duress defense requires that the actor meet the standard of resistance of "the person of reasonable firmness."[13] Recall that reasonableness, non-negligence, is assessed through an individualized objective standard: the reasonable person in the actor's situation.[14] Such objective limitations are what one would expect, given the fact that excuses serve a normative blaming/excusing function. It simply is not the case that we intuitively excuse every person who can show pressure or temptation or a disadvantage in resisting the same. Our

---

13. Model Penal Code §2.09(1).
14. Model Penal Code §§1.13(16) & 2.02(2)(d).

blaming/excusing judgments are more complex. We want to know: How strong was the pressure or temptation? How difficult was it for the actor to resist? Inevitably, we may try to put ourselves in the actor's situation and try to imagine whether we would have been able to resist the violation.

Presumed satisfaction of objective standard Not every excuse defense includes in its legal formulation an objective standard. Involuntary act, insanity, and involuntary intoxication have no apparent requirement of this sort. It would be a mistake, however, to assume that these defenses excuse without regard for whether the actor has met our collective normative expectations for efforts to avoid a violation. These defenses assure compliance with our normative expectations by limiting each defense in other ways that assure that the excused actor could not have been expected to have avoided the violation. In the involuntary act defense, for example, using the first excusing condition, the required dysfunction is sufficiently great that it assures that the burden of compliance was unattainable. The act constituting the offense simply was not the product of the actor's effort or determination.

Inviting normative assessment without use of objective standard The formulations of the insanity and involuntary intoxication defenses must take a somewhat different approach. A person is excused, as a result of either disability, if "he lacks *substantial* capacity either to appreciate the criminality [wrongfulness] of his conduct or to conform his conduct to the requirements of law."[15] The formulation leaves it to the jury to determine how much loss of capacity is enough to render the actor's violation blameless. Instead of explicitly providing an individualized objective standard that calls for a normative assessment, the formulation uses an openly vague term, "substantial," knowing, indeed intending,[16] that the jury will use their collective intuitive judgments in deciding whether the loss of capacity was substantial enough to excuse. It seems likely that the analysis and the result will be the same as under the individualized reasonable person test used in the mistake and duress excuses. That is, an actor's loss of capacity to appreciate or control his conduct will be judged "substantial" only if "the reasonable person in the actor's situation" could not reasonably have been expected to have avoided the offense.

---

15. Model Penal Code §§2.08(4) & 4.01(1) (emphasis added).

16. It was recognized, of course, that "substantial" is an open-ended concept, but its quantitative connotation was believed to be sufficiently precise for practical administration. The law is full of instances in which courts and juries are explicitly authorized to confront an issue of degree. Such an approach was deemed to be no less essential and appropriate in dealing with this issue. . . .

Model Penal Code §4.01 comment 3 (1985).

Mistake as to an excuse Mistaken belief that one satisfies the conditions of an excuse is not itself an excuse. Believing you are insane, even if it is a reasonable belief, does not give one an insanity defense.[17] An actor who makes a reasonable mistake as to a justification can claim that from his perspective he reasonably believed that his conduct was justified, desirable, and therefore, if not justified, at least should be excused as blameless.[18] The actor who is mistaken as to his excuse can make no similar claim. Even if he were correct in his belief that excusing conditions existed, neither his conduct nor his motivation are desirable. Excused conduct is wrongful conduct that is condemned and ought to be avoided.

Disability as distinguishing among excuses Most excuses are defined and distinguished according to the disabilities to which they apply. Where a mental disease or defect is the cause of the excusing condition, the insanity defense is applicable. Even where the results of the defendant's disability are identical to those that may result from insanity—distortion in perception, ignorance of criminality, or impairment of ability to control one's conduct—if the disability is not mental disease or defect, a defendant will not be eligible for an insanity excuse. Thus, it is the excusing condition's cause—be it intoxication, immaturity, subnormality, hypnotism, duress, or some other disability—rather than the results, that determines which excuse is applicable. This practice of defining excuses by their disability elements may have evolved because the disability is an independently observable phenomenon, while the resulting excusing condition is not.

Special rules for specific disabilities Such a disability-organized system of excuses has practical value because, as with justification defenses, it frequently is appropriate to attach special rules to particular disabilities. For example, it may be more of a concern in practice that may have voluntarily caused his or her own intoxication, then that the actor caused his or her own insanity. Thus, special rules relating to an actor's culpability in becoming intoxicated are added to the intoxication excuse. On the other hand, as a theoretical matter, it would seem that the same principles should apply, no matter what the disability. If it is appropriate to take account of an actor's causing his or her own disability, for example, there is no reason why the principle should not apply to all disabilities, whether the defendant causes his or her own intoxication, hypnotism, duress, or insanity.[19]

---

17. Such a belief could conceivably be a symptom of mental illness which, together with other symptoms, might lead to a finding of mental illness. As a legal matter, however, the belief alone, even if reasonable, does not entitle one to an insanity defense.

18. See Section 15.5 (Mistake as to a Justification).

19. For a discussion of this problem and a general solution, see Section 12.2 (Causing the Conditions of One's Own Defense). If all of the special rules now contained in the separate excuse provisions were similarly generalizable, one might conclude in the end that only a single general excuse defense is necessary.

Questions

1. *Acker's Liability.* Assume that Acker had no reason to think that his drink was spiked with Skopezine or any other drug and that he should not be held to have caused its effects on him. Do you think he should be excused for his assault on Jote? Why or why not? What information is relevant to your determination? Would it matter to you if doctors persuasively testified that, if Acker had not been given the Skopezine, he would not have attacked Jote when and as he did?

2. *Ed's Liability.* Assume that Ed had not been given any Skopezine but that he honestly and reasonably believed that he had been given the same dose that Acker received. Do you think he should be excused for his assault on Jote? Why or why not? Assume that the doctors are persuasive in their claim that Ed's belief that he had been subjected to an aggression-inducing drug could loosen psychological restraints to aggression that otherwise might have prevented the offense. Should Ed then have an excuse defense?

SECTION 16.2 INSANITY AND INVOLUNTARY INTOXICATION

An actor's mental illness may negate an element of the offense charged, may provide a general excuse defense, or may bar trial of the defendant because of his inability to adequately assist his counsel and prepare his defense. Section 4.5 examines mental illness negating an offense element (sometimes called "diminished capacity" or "diminished responsibility") in the context of homicide. Recall that, like other failure of proof defenses, it is not a true "defense" with special requirements. Like mistake negating an element, discussed in Section 7.3, the defense merely employs evidence of mental illness to refute the prosecution's claim that the actor had the culpable state of mind required for the offense. For example, an actor who, due to hallucination at the time of the offense, believes she is squeezing a lemon when she in fact is squeezing her brother's neck, does not satisfy the culpability elements of murder, which require an intention to kill a human being. Some jurisdictions attempt to limit the use of evidence of mental illness that negates an offense element.

The term "insanity defense" is typically used to describe a general excuse defense that is available even though the defendant satisfies all of the elements of the offense charged. The availability of this general defense depends not on the definition of the offense charged but on whether the actor's mental illness and its resulting effects meet the conditions of the jurisdiction's insanity defense.

Intoxication can have a similar effect, of either negating an offense element, as discussed in Section 12.1, or providing a general excuse. To provide a general excuse it must cause excusing conditions analogous to those for insanity: sufficient loss of cognitive or control function to be blameless for the offense conduct. Recall from Section 12.1 that *voluntary* intoxication is limited in the culpability elements that it is permitted to negate. Voluntary intoxication is never allowed to be the basis for a general excuse.

Mental illness *at the time of trial* also may provide a defense, one that bars trial, without regard to the defendant's blameworthiness or mental illness at the time of the offense. Such incompetency to stand trial is a nonexculpatory defense. It operates independent of the defendant's guilt or innocence. It is dependent, instead, only upon the defendant's inability to consult with and assist his attorney and to meaningfully participate in the proceedings against him.

The insanity and involuntary intoxication defenses are two of the family of disability excuses, defenses that exculpate because the actor suffers a serious dysfunction in cognition or control at the time of the offense. Several others—duress, immaturity, and a variety of conditions excused under the voluntary act requirement—are examined in the next section.

Michael's Madness

Michael Monte was discharged from the Navy at the age of 18 after a psychiatric examination concluded that he suffered from "a profound personality disorder that renders him unfit for Naval service." He now lives alone in a boarding house and, because of repeated outbursts of temper, has no close friends. He has not held a job for more than two weeks at a time and is always on the verge of being evicted from his room for his unpredictable behavior. His landlady is tolerant of his minor misconduct because she feels sorry for him, believing that he is not always in control of himself. "He is as sweet as can be for a while, then will turn to a very black mood and blow up at whoever happens to be around," she explains. "He is always very sorry immediately after and makes a nuisance of himself trying to apologize." On this particular day, when Michael leaves the building in the morning, his landlady notices that he is in one of his black moods. He seems to be even more distressed when he returns that afternoon. She asks him if he is "ok" as he passes her door. He does not respond. Twenty minutes later one of the other tenants knocks on Michael's door and demands that the music be turned down. Getting no response, he continues to pound on the door for several minutes. Michael suddenly opens the door swinging a baseball bat. He strikes the surprised tenant in the head, killing him instantly. When the landlady reaches the landing, she finds Michael standing over the body, as if frozen. She checks the body and tells Michael that the man is dead. Michael gasps and falls to his knees. "Why did I do that? I knew I shouldn't have hit him."

Court-appointed psychiatrists testify that at the time of the killing Michael knew what he was doing and knew that it was wrong, but that he suffers from a severe anger control disorder and, as a result, has great difficulty in controlling his conduct. Will Michael receive an insanity defense?

Parsons v. State
Supreme Court of Alabama
81 Ala. 577, 2 So. 854 (1887)

SOMERVILLE, J. In this case the defendants have been convicted of the murder of Bennett Parsons, by shooting him with a gun; one of the defendants being the wife and the other the daughter of the deceased. [The evidence on behalf of defendants tended to show that defendant Joe Parsons was, at the time of said killing, and had always been, an idiot; and that defendant Nancy Parsons was, at the time of the killing, insane; that the act of Nancy, assisting in the killing of deceased, was the result of an insane delusion that deceased possessed supernatural power to inflict her with disease, and power by means of a supernatural trick to take her life; that deceased by means of such supernatural power had caused said Nancy to be sick and in bad health for a long time, and that her act, at the time of said killing, in assisting therein, was under the insane delusion that she was in great danger of the loss of her life from deceased, to be effected by a supernatural trick. The defendant Nancy was the wife of deceased, and defendant Joe was his daughter. The evidence also tended to show insanity for two generations in the families of said defendants.]

The rulings of the court raise some questions of no less difficulty than of interest; for, as observed by a distinguished American judge, "of all medico-legal questions, those connected with insanity are the most difficult and perplexing." It has become of late a matter of comment among intelligent men, including the most advanced thinkers in the medical and legal professions, that the deliverances of the law courts on this branch of our jurisprudence have not heretofore been at all satisfactory, either in the soundness of their theories, or in their practical application. . . . So great a jurist as Lord Coke, in his attempted classification of madmen, laid down the legal rule of criminal responsibility to be that one should "*wholly* have lost his memory and understanding"; as to which Mr. Erskine, when defending Hadfield for shooting the king, in the year 1800, justly observed: "No such madman ever existed in the world." Lord Hale had before declared that the rule of responsibility was measured by the mental capacity possessed by a child 14 years of age; and Mr. Justice Tracy, and other judges had ventured to decide that, to be nonpunishable for alleged acts of crime, "a man must be totally deprived of his understanding and memory, so as not to know what he was doing, no more than an infant, a brute, or *a wild beast.*" Arnold's Case, 16 How. State Tr. 764. All these rules have necessarily been discarded in modern times in the light of the new scientific knowledge acquired by a more thorough study of the disease of insanity. In *Bellingham's Case*, decided in 1812, by Lord Mansfield at the Old Bailey, the test was held to consist in a knowledge that murder, the crime there committed, was "against the laws of God and nature," thus meaning an ability to distinguish between right and wrong in the abstract. This rule was not adhered to, but seems to have been modified so as to make the test rather a knowledge of right and wrong as applied to the particular act. The great leading case on this subject in England is *McNaghten's Case*, decided in 1843 before the English house of lords. It was decided by the judges in that case that, in order to entitle the accused to acquittal, it must be clearly proved that, at the time of committing the offense, he was laboring under such a defect of reason, from disease of the mind, as not to know the nature and quality of the act he was doing, or, if he did, not to know that what he was doing was wrong. This rule is commonly supposed to have heretofore been adopted by this court, and has been followed by the general current of American adjudications.

 . . . The trial court, with prudent propriety, followed the previous decisions of this court, the correctness of which, as to this subject, we are now requested to review.

We do not hesitate to say that we reopen the discussion of this subject with no little reluctance, having long hesitated to disturb our past decisions on this branch of the law. Nothing could induce us to do so except an imperious sense of duty, which has been excited by a protracted investigation and study, impressing our minds with the conviction that the law of insanity as declared by the courts on many points, and especially the rule of criminal accountability, and the assumed tests of disease, to that extent which confers legal irresponsibility, have not kept pace with the progress of thought and discovery in the present advanced stages of medical science. Though science has led the way, the courts of England have declined to follow, as shown by their adherence to the rulings in *McNaghten's Case*. . . . It is not surprising that this state of affairs has elicited from a learned law writer, who treats of this subject, the humiliating declaration that, under the influence of these ancient theories, "the memorials of our jurisprudence are written all over with cases in which those who are now understood to have been insane, have been executed as criminals." 1 Bish. Crim. Law, (7th Ed.) §390. There is good reason, both for this fact, and for the existence of unsatisfactory rules on this subject. In what we say we do not intend to give countenance to acquittals of criminals, frequent examples of which have been witnessed in modern times, based on the doctrine of moral or emotional insanity, unconnected with mental disease, which is not yet sufficiently supported by psychology, or recognized by law as an excuse for crime.

[The court reviews the progress of treatment of the insane from a period during which they were punished in jails to a period during which they were treated in "modern" asylums.] Under these new and more favorable conditions, the medical jurisprudence of insanity has assumed an entirely new phase. The nature and exciting causes of the disease have been thoroughly studied and more fully comprehended. The result is that the "right and wrong test," as it is sometimes called, which, it must be remembered, itself originated with the medical profession, in the mere dawn of the scientific knowledge of insanity, has been condemned by the great current of modern medical authorities, who believe it to be "founded on an ignorant and imperfect view of the disease." . . .

It is everywhere admitted, and as to this there can be no doubt, that an idiot, lunatic, or other person of diseased mind, who is afflicted to such extent as not to know whether he is doing right or wrong, is not punishable for any act which he may do while in that state. Can the courts justly say, however, that the only test or rule of responsibility in criminal cases is the power to distinguish right from wrong, whether in the abstract, or as applied to the particular case? Or may there not be insane persons, of a diseased brain, who, while capable of perceiving the difference between right and wrong, are, as a matter of fact, so far under *the duress of such disease* as to destroy the *power to choose* between right and wrong? Will the courts assume as a fact, not to be rebutted by any amount of evidence, or any new discoveries of medical science, that there is and can be no such state of mind as that described by a writer on psychological medicine as one "in which the reason has lost its empire over the passions, and the actions by which they are manifested, to such a degree that the individual can neither repress the former, nor abstain from the latter?" Dean, Med. Jur. 497. . . .

We first consider what is *the proper legal rule of responsibility in criminal cases*. No one can deny that there must be two constituent elements of legal responsibility in the commission of every crime, and no rule can be just and reasonable which fails to recognize either of them: (1) capacity of intellectual discrimination; and (2) freedom of will. Mr.

Wharton, after recognizing this fundamental and obvious principle, observes: "If there be either incapacity to distinguish between right and wrong as to the particular act, or delusion as to the act, or inability to refrain from doing the act, there is no responsibility." . . . If therefore, it be true, as matter of fact, that the disease of insanity can, in its action on the human brain through a shattered nervous organization, or in any other mode, so affect the mind as to subvert the freedom of will, and thereby destroy the power of the victim *to choose* between the right and wrong, although he perceive it,—by which we mean the power of volition to adhere in action to the right and abstain from the wrong,—is such a one criminally responsible for an act done under the influence of such controlling disease? We clearly think not, and such we believe to be the just, reasonable, and humane rule, towards which all the modern authorities in this country, legislation in England, and the laws of other civilized countries of the world, are gradually but surely tending, as we shall further on attempt more fully to show.

We next consider the question as to the *probable existence of such a disease*, and the *test of its presence*, in a given case. It will not do for the courts to dogmatically deny the possible existence of such *a disease*, or its pathological and psychical effects, because this is a matter of evidence, not of law, or judicial cognizance. . . . The courts could, with just as much propriety, years ago, have denied the existence of the Copernican system of the universe, the efficacy of steam and electricity as a motive power, or the possibility of communication in a few moments between the continents of Europe and America by the magnetic telegraph, or that of the instantaneous transmission of the human voice from one distant city to another by the use of the telephone. . . . The existence of such a cerebral disease as that which we have described is earnestly alleged by the superintendents of insane hospitals, and other experts, who constantly have experimental dealings with the insane, and they are permitted every day to so testify before juries. The truth of their testimony—or, what is the same thing, the existence or nonexistence of such a disease of the mind—in each particular case is necessarily a matter for the determination of the jury from the evidence. . . .

It is no satisfactory objection to say that the rule above announced by us is of difficult application. The rule in *McNaghten's Case*, supra, is equally obnoxious to a like criticism. The difficulty does not lie in the rule, but is inherent in the subject of insanity itself. The practical trouble is for the courts to determine in what particular cases the party on trial is to be transferred from the category of sane to that of insane criminals; where, in other words, the border line of punishability is adjudged to be passed. But, as has been said in reference to an every-day fact of nature, no one can say where twilight ends or begins, but there is ample distinction nevertheless between *day* and *night*. We think we can safely rely in this matter upon the intelligence of our juries, guided by the testimony of men who have practically made a study of the disease of insanity; and enlightened by a conscientious desire, on the one hand, to enforce the criminal laws of the land, and, on the other, not to deal harshly with any unfortunate victim of a diseased mind, acting without the light of reason or the power of volition.

Several rulings of the court . . . were in conflict with this view, and for these errors the judgment must be reversed. . . . It is almost needless to add that where one does not act under the duress of a diseased mind or insane delusion, but from motives of anger, revenge, or other passion, he cannot claim to be shielded from punishment for crime on the ground of insanity. Insanity proper is more or less a mental derangement, co-existing often, it is true, with a disturbance of the emotions, affections, and other moral powers. A mere moral or emotional insanity, so called, unconnected with disease of the mind, or irresistible impulse resulting from mere moral obliquity, or wicked propensities and habits, is not recognized as a defense to crime in our courts. . . .

In conclusion of this branch of the subject, that we may not be misunderstood, we think it follows very clearly from what we have said that the inquiries to be submitted to the jury, then, in every criminal trial where the defense of insanity is interposed, are these: *First.* Was the defendant at the time of the commission of the alleged crime, as matter of fact, afflicted with a *disease of the mind,* so as to be either idiotic, or otherwise insane? *Second.* If such be the case, did he know right from wrong, as applied to the particular act in question? If he did not have such knowledge, he is not legally responsible. *Third.* If he did have such knowledge, he may nevertheless not be legally responsible if the two following conditions concur: (1) If, by reason of the duress of such mental disease, he had so far lost the *power to choose* between the right and wrong, and to avoid doing the act in question, as that his free agency was at the time destroyed; (2) and if, at the same time, the alleged crime was so connected with such mental disease, in the relation of cause and effect, as to have been the product of it *solely.* . . .

The judgment is reversed, and the cause remanded. In the meanwhile the prisoners will be held in custody until discharged by due process of law.

STONE, C.J., (dissenting.) In Boswell v. State, 63 Ala. 307, . . . [t]he question presented and considered . . . was whether moral insanity was an excuse for an act otherwise punishable. We declared it was not; and in the category we included homicidal mania, irresistible impulse, and every other species of simply moral obliquity, provided the mental faculties were not shown to be unsound. . . .

I [fear] that the effect of [the majority's] ruling will be to let in many of the evils which result from allowing the defense of emotional insanity. I acquit them of all intention to alter the rule of this court on that subject. Still, I think the line cannot be too clearly and sharply drawn which separates the pitiable, unfortunate victims of diseased mental faculties from the recklessly depraved, whose chief evidence of insanity is found in the causeless atrocity of their crimes. Human life has become all too cheap; and, while we spread the mantle of mercy over the criminally irresponsible, the lawless should be made to feel that the way of the transgressor is hard. The terror of the law may thus become a minister of peace.

Model Penal Code §4.01
Mental Disease or Defect Excluding Responsibility

(1) A person is not responsible for criminal conduct if at the time of such conduct as a result of mental disease or defect he lacks substantial capacity either to appreciate the criminality [wrongfulness] of his conduct or to conform his conduct to the requirements of law.

(2) As used in this Article, the terms "mental disease or defect" do not include an abnormality manifested only by repeated criminal or otherwise anti-social conduct.

United States v. Brawner
United States Court of Appeals for the District of Columbia Circuit
471 F.2d 969 (1972) (en banc)*

LEVENTHAL, Circuit Judge:

The principal issues raised on this appeal from a conviction for second degree murder and carrying a dangerous weapon relate to appellant's defense of insanity. After the case was argued to a division of the court, the court sua sponte ordered a rehearing en banc. We identified our intention to reconsider the appropriate standard for the insanity defense. . . .

We have stretched our canvas wide; and the focal point of the landscape before us is the formulation of the American Law Institute. The ALI's primary provision is stated thus in its Model Penal Code, see §4.01(1).

---

*This is a different portion of the *Brawner* case excerpted in Section 4.5 (doctrines of mitigation relating to homicide).

Section 4.01 Mental Disease or Defect Excluding Responsibility. (1) A person is not responsible for criminal conduct if at the time of such conduct as a result of mental disease or defect he lacks substantial capacity either to appreciate the criminality [wrongfulness] of his conduct or to conform his conduct to the requirements of the law.

We have decided to adopt the ALI rule as the doctrine excluding responsibility for mental disease or defect, for application prospectively to trials begun after this date.

[The rule of Durham v. United States, 94 U.S. App. D.C. 228, 214 F.2d 862 (1954), which excused an unlawful act if it was the product of a mental disease or defect, will no longer be in effect.] [The court's review of the trial record is reproduced in Section 4.5 at pages 109-110.]

Insanity Rule in Other Circuits

The American Law Institute's Model Penal Code expressed a rule which has become the dominant force in the law pertaining to the defense of insanity. The ALI rule is eclectic in spirit, partaking of the moral focus of *McNaghten*, the practical accommodation of the "control rules" (a term more exact and less susceptible of misunderstanding than "irresistible impulse" terminology), and responsive, at the same time, to a relatively modern, forward-looking view of what is encompassed in "knowledge." . . .

The core rule of the ALI has been adopted, with variations, by all save one of the Federal circuit courts of appeals, and by all that have come to reconsider the doctrine providing exculpation for mental illness. . . .

Comments Concerning Reason for Adoption of ALI Rule
and Scope of Rule as Adopted By This Court

Need to depart from "product" formulation and undue dominance by experts.

A principal reason for our decision to depart from the *Durham* rule is the undesirable characteristic . . . of undue dominance by the experts giving testimony. . . .

The doctrine of criminal responsibility is such that there can be no doubt "of the complicated nature of the decision to be made—intertwining moral, legal, and medical judgments," see King v. United States, 125 U.S. App. D.C. 318, 324, 372 F.2d 383, 389 (1967). Hence, as *King* and other opinions have noted, jury decisions have been accorded unusual deference even when they have found responsibility in the face of a powerful record, with medical evidence uncontradicted, pointing toward exculpation. The "moral" elements of the decision are not defined exclusively by religious considerations but by the totality of underlying conceptions of ethics and justice shared by the community, as expressed by its jury surrogate. The essential feature of a jury "lies in the interposition between the accused and his accuser of the common-sense judgment of a group of laymen, and in the community participation and shared responsibility that results from that group's determination of guilt or innocence."

The expert witnesses—psychiatrists and psychologists—are called to adduce relevant information concerning what may for convenience be referred to as the "medical" component of the responsibility issue. But the difficulty . . . is that the medical expert comes, by testimony given in terms of a non-medical construct ("product"), to express conclusions that in essence embody ethical and legal conclusions. There is, indeed, irony in a situation under which the *Durham* rule, which was adopted in large part to permit experts to testify in their own terms concerning matters within their domain which the jury should know, resulted in testimony by the experts in terms not their own to reflect unexpressed judgments in a domain that is properly not theirs but the jury's. The irony is heightened when the jurymen, instructed under the esoteric "product" standard, are influenced significantly by "product" testimony of expert witnesses really reflecting ethical and legal judgments rather than a conclusion within the witnesses' particular expertise. . . .

The experts have meaningful information to impart, not only on the existence of mental illness or not, but also on its relationship to the incident charged as an offense. In the interest of justice this valued information should be available, and should not be lost or blocked by requirements that unnaturally restrict communication between the experts and the jury. The more we have pondered the problem the more convinced we have become that the sound solution lies not in further shaping of the *Durham* "product" approach in more refined molds, but in adopting the ALI's formulation as the linchpin of our jurisprudence.

The ALI's formulation retains the core requirement of a meaningful relationship between the mental illness and the incident charged. The language in the ALI rule is sufficiently in the common ken that its use in the courtroom, or in preparation for trial, permits a reasonable three-way communication—between (a) the law-trained, judges and lawyers; (b) the experts and (c) the jurymen—without insisting on a vocabulary that is either stilted or stultified, or conducive to a testimonial mystique permitting expert dominance and encroachment on the jury's function. There is no indication in the available literature that any such untoward development has attended the reasonably widespread adoption of the ALI rule in the Federal courts and a substantial number of state courts.

Consideration and rejection of other suggestions

a. Proposal to abolish insanity defense

A number of proposals in the journals recommend that the insanity defense be abolished altogether. This is advocated in the amicus brief of the National District Attorneys Association as both desirable and lawful.[17] . . .

This proposal has been put forward by responsible judges for consideration, with the objective of reserving psychiatric overview for the phase of the criminal process concerned with disposition of the person determined to have been the actor. However, we are convinced that the proposal cannot properly be imposed by judicial fiat.

The courts have emphasized over the centuries that "free will" is the postulate of responsibility under our jurisprudence. 4 Blackstone's Commentaries 27. The concept of "belief in freedom of the human will and a consequent ability and duty of the normal individual to choose between good and evil" is a core concept that is "universal and persistent in mature systems of law." Morissette v. United States, 342 U.S. 246, 250, 72 S. Ct. 240, 243, 96 L. Ed. 288 (1952). Criminal responsibility is assessed when through "free will" a man elects to do evil. And while, as noted in *Morissette*, the legislature has dispensed with mental element in some statutory offenses, in furtherance of a paramount need of the community, these instances mark the exception and not the rule, and only in the most limited instances has the mental element been omitted by the legislature as a requisite for an offense that was a crime at common law.

The concept of lack of "free will" is both the root of origin of the insanity defense and the line of its growth. This cherished principle is not undercut by difficulties, or differences of view, as to how best to express the free will concept in the light of the expansion of medical knowledge. We do not concur in the view of the National District Attorneys Association that the insanity defense should be abandoned judicially, either because it is at too great a variance with popular conceptions of guilt or fails "to show proper respect for the personality of the criminal [who] is liable to resent pathology more than punishment."

These concepts may be measured along with other ingredients in a legislative re-examination of settled doctrines of criminal responsibility, root, stock and branch. Such a reassessment, one that seeks to probe

---

17. It suggests that a mental condition be exculpatory solely as it negatives mens rea.

and appraise the society's processes and values, is for the legislative branch, assuming no constitutional bar. The judicial role is limited, in Justice Holmes's figure, to action that is molecular, with the restraint inherent in taking relatively small steps, leaving to the other branches of government whatever progress must be made with seven-league leaps. Such judicial restraint is particularly necessary when a proposal requires, as a mandatory ingredient, the kind of devotion of resources, personnel and techniques that can be accomplished only through whole-hearted legislative commitment. . . .

    b. Proposal for defense if mental disease impairs
capacity to such an extent that the defendant cannot
"justly be held responsible."

We have also pondered the suggestion that the jury be instructed that the defendant lacks criminal responsibility if the jury finds that the defendant's mental disease impairs his capacity or controls to such an extent that he cannot "justly be held responsible."

This was the view of a British commission, adapted and proposed in 1955 by Professor Wechsler, the distinguished Reporter for the ALI's Model Penal Code, and sustained by some, albeit a minority, of the members of the ALI's Council. In the ALI, the contrary view prevailed because of a concern over presenting to the jury questions put primarily in the form of "justice."

The proposal is not to be condemned out of hand as a suggestion that the jury be informed of an absolute prerogative that it can only exercise by flatly disregarding the applicable rule of law. It is rather a suggestion that the jury be informed of the matters the law contemplates it will take into account in arriving at the community judgment concerning a composite of factors.

However, there is a substantial concern that an instruction overtly cast in terms of "justice" cannot feasibly be restricted to the ambit of what may properly be taken into account but will splash with unconfinable and malign consequences. The Government cautions that "explicit appeals to 'justice' will result in litigation of extraneous issues and will encourage improper arguments to the jury phrased solely in terms of 'sympathy' and 'prejudice.'"

Nor is this solely a prosecutor's concern. Mr. Flynn, counsel appointed to represent defendant, puts it that even though the jury is applying community concepts of blameworthiness "the jury should not be left at large, or asked to find out for itself what those concepts are."

The amicus submission of the Public Defender Service argues that it would be beneficial to focus the jury's attention on the moral and legal questions intertwined in the insanity defense. It expresses concern, however, over a blameworthiness instruction without more, saying "it may well be that the 'average' American condemns the mentally ill."

It would apparently accept an approach not unlike that proposed by the ALI Reporter, under which the justice standard is coupled with a direction to consider the individual's capacity to control his behavior. Mr. Dempsey's recommendation is of like import, with some simplification.[27] But the problem remains, whether, assuming justice calls for the exculpation and treatment of the mentally ill, that is more likely to be gained from a jury, with "average" notions of mental illness, which is explicitly set at large to convict or acquit persons with impaired mental capacity according to its concept of justice.

It is the sense of justice propounded by those charged with making and declaring the law—legislatures and courts—that lays down the rule that persons without substantial capacity to know or control the act shall be excused. The jury is concerned with applying the community understanding of this broad rule to particular lay and medical facts. Where the matter is unclear it naturally will call on its own sense of justice to help it determine the matter. There is wisdom in the view that a jury generally understands well enough that an instruction composed in flexible terms gives it sufficient latitude so that, without disregarding the instruction, it can provide that application of the instruction which harmonizes with its sense of justice. The ALI rule generally communicates that meaning. This is recognized even by those who might prefer a more explicit statement of the matter. It is one thing, however, to tolerate and even welcome the jury's sense of equity as a force that affects its application of instructions which state the legal rules that crystallize the requirements of justice as determined by the lawmakers of the community. It is quite another to set the jury at large, without such crystallization, to evolve its own legal rules and standards of justice. It would likely be counter-productive and contrary to the larger interest of justice to become so explicit—in an effort to hammer the point home to the very occasional jury that would otherwise be too rigid—that one puts serious strains on the normal operation of the system of criminal justice.

Taking all these considerations into account we conclude that the ALI rule as announced is not productive of injustice, and we decline to proclaim the broad "justly responsible" standard. . . .

Elements of the ALI rule adopted by this court

Though it provides a general uniformity, the ALI rule leaves room for variations. Thus, we have added an adjustment in the *McDonald*

---

27. He proposes an instruction with this crucial sentence: "It is up to you to decide whether defendant had such an abnormal mental condition, and if he did whether the impairment was substantial enough, and was so related to the commission of the crime, *that he ought not be held responsible.*" (Emphasis added.)

definition of mental disease, which we think fully compatible with both the spirit and text of the ALI rule. In the interest of good administration, we now undertake to set forth, with such precision as the subject will permit, other elements of the ALI rule as adopted by this court.

The two main components of the rule define (1) mental disease, (2) the consequences thereof that exculpate from responsibility.

a. Intermesh of components

The first component of our rule, derived from *McDonald*, defines mental disease or defect as an abnormal condition of the mind, and a condition which substantially (a) affects mental or emotional processes and (b) impairs behavioral controls. The second component, derived from the Model Penal Code, tells which defendant with a mental disease lacks criminal responsibility for particular conduct: It is the defendant who, as a result of this mental condition, at the time of such conduct, either (i) lacks substantial capacity to appreciate that his conduct is wrongful, or (ii) lacks substantial capacity to conform his conduct to the law.

The first component establishes eligibility for an instruction concerning the defense for a defendant who presents evidence that his abnormal condition of the mind has substantially impaired behavioral controls. The second component completes the instruction and defines the ultimate issue, of exculpation, in terms of whether his behavioral controls were not only substantially impaired but impaired to such an extent that he lacked substantial capacity to conform his conduct to the law.

b. The "result" of the mental disease

The rule contains a requirement of causality, as is clear from the term "result." Exculpation is established not by mental disease alone but only if "as a result" defendant lacks the substantial capacity required for responsibility. Presumably the mental disease of a kleptomaniac does not entail as a "result" a lack of capacity to conform to the law prohibiting rape.

c. At the time of the conduct

Under the ALI rule the issue is not whether defendant is so disoriented or void of controls that he is never able to conform to external demands, but whether he had that capacity at the time of the conduct. The question is not properly put in terms of whether he would have capacity to conform in some untypical restraining situation—as with an attendant or policeman at his elbow. The issue is whether he was able to conform in the unstructured condition of life in an open society, and whether the result of his abnormal mental condition was a lack of substantial internal controls. . . .

d. Capacity to appreciate wrongfulness of his conduct

As to the option of terminology noted in the ALI code, we adopt the formulation that exculpates a defendant whose mental condition is such that he lacks substantial capacity to appreciate the wrongfulness of his conduct. We prefer this on pragmatic grounds to "appreciate the criminality of his conduct" since the resulting jury instruction is more like that conventionally given to and applied by the jury. While such an instruction is of course subject to the objection that it lacks complete precision, it serves the objective of calling on the jury to provide a community judgment on a combination of factors. And since the possibility of analytical differences between the two formulations is insubstantial in fact in view of the control capacity test, we are usefully guided by the pragmatic considerations pertinent to jury instructions. . . .

e. Caveat paragraph

Section 4.01 of the Model Penal Code as promulgated by ALI contains in subsection (2) what has come to be known as the "caveat paragraph":

> (2) The terms "mental disease or defect" do not include an abnormality manifested only by repeated criminal or otherwise anti-social conduct.

The purpose of this provision was to exclude a defense for the so-called "psychopathic personality."

There has been a split in the Federal circuits concerning this provision. . . .

Our own approach is influenced by the fact that our rule already includes a definition of mental disease (from *McDonald*). Under that definition, as we have pointed out, the mere existence of "a long criminal record does not excuse crime." We do not require the caveat paragraph as an insurance against exculpation of the deliberate and persistent offender. Our *McDonald* rule guards against the danger of misunderstanding and injustice that might arise, say, from an expert's classification that reflects only a conception defining all criminality as reflective of mental illness. There must be testimony to show both that the defendant was suffering from an abnormal condition of the mind and that it substantially affected mental or emotional processes and substantially impaired behavioral controls.

In this context, our pragmatic approach is to adopt the caveat paragraph as a rule for application by the judge, to avoid miscarriage of justice, but not for inclusion in instructions to the jury.

The judge will be aware that the criminal and antisocial conduct of a person—on the street, in the home, in the ward—is necessarily material information for assessment by the psychiatrist. On the other hand, rarely if ever would a psychiatrist base a conclusion of mental disease solely on criminal and antisocial acts. Our pragmatic solution provides for reshaping the rule, for application by the court, as follows: The introduction or proffer of past criminal and antisocial actions is not admissible as evidence of mental disease unless accompanied by expert testimony, supported by a showing of the concordance of a responsible segment of professional opinion, that the particular characteristics of these actions constitute convincing evidence of an underlying mental disease that substantially impairs behavioral controls.

This formulation retains the paragraph as a "caveat" rather than an inexorable rule of law. It should serve to obviate distortions of the present state of knowledge that would constitute miscarriages of justice. Yet it leaves the door open—on shouldering the "convincing evidence" burden—to accommodate our general rule to developments that may lie ahead. It is the kind of imperfect, but not unfeasible, accommodation of the abstract and pragmatic that is often found to serve the administration of justice. . . .

The case is remanded for further consideration by the District Court in accordance with this opinion.

So Ordered.

United States Code, Title 18, §17
Insanity Defense†

(a) Affirmative defense.—It is an affirmative defense to a prosecution under any Federal statute, that, at the time of the commission of the acts constituting the offense, the defendant, as a result of a severe mental disease or defect, was unable to appreciate the nature and quality or the wrongfulness of his acts. Mental disease or defect does not otherwise constitute a defense.

(b) Burden of proof.—The defendant has the burden of proving the defense of insanity by clear and convincing evidence.

Questions

1. McNaghten *Test*. What does the *McNaghten* formulation of the insanity test require (quoted in *Parsons*)? Would Michael get a defense under this formulation?

---

†Editor's Note.—This statute was enacted in October of 1984, after John Hinckley was acquitted, by reason of insanity, for his attempt to assassinate President Reagan.

2. *Irresistible Impulse.* In what way does *Parsons* expand on the *McNaghten* insanity test? What are the reasons for the expansion? Would Michael get an insanity defense under the *Parsons'* expansion (sometimes called the irresistible impulse test)?

3. *Durham Product Test.* How is the "product" test, adopted by the United States Court of Appeals for the District of Columbia in *Durham,* different from the *McNaghten* and irresistible impulse formulations? Why did the *Durham* court move to such a formulation? Would Michael get a defense under the "product" test?

4. *ALI Test.* What is the ALI formulation of the insanity defense and how is it different from the product test? Why did the *Brawner* court overrule *Durham* in favor of the ALI formulation? How does the ALI formulation compare to the *McNaghten*-plus-irresistible-impulse test? Would Michael get a defense under the ALI formulation?

5. *"Justly Held Responsible" Formulation.* One of the formulations urged on the *Brawner* court (and the ALI) would give the defendant an insanity defense if his or her mental illness impairs the defendant's capacity to such an extent that the defendant cannot "justly be held responsible" for the conduct constituting the offense. How is this formulation different from the ALI formulation? Why would some people think that this formulation is not different in concept from the ALI formulation? Why did the *Brawner* court reject this formulation in favor of the ALI test?

6. *Federal Formulation.* How is the federal formulation similar and different from *McNaghten*? From the *McNaghten*-plus-irresistible-impulse test? From the ALI test? Would Michael get a defense under this formulation?

7. *Lay vs. Expert Judgment.* Under which of the formulations above does an expert (a psychiatrist, a psychologist, etc.) have the greatest influence on the outcome of the insanity determination? In which does he or she have the least, and what is that role? What arguments can you make for and against having the insanity defense depend upon a primarily expert judgment? For having it depend upon a primarily lay judgment?

Model Penal Code §§2.08(4) & (5)
Defense of Involuntary Intoxication

(4) Intoxication which (a) is not self-induced or (b) is pathological is an affirmative defense if by reason of such intoxication the actor at the time of his conduct lacks substantial capacity either to appreciate its criminality [wrongfulness] or to conform his conduct to the requirements of law.

(5) *Definitions.* In this Section unless a different meaning plainly is required:

(a) "intoxication" means a disturbance of mental or physical capacities resulting from the introduction of substances into the body;

(b) "self-induced intoxication" means intoxication caused by substances which the actor knowingly introduces into his body, the tendency of which to cause intoxication he knows or ought to know, unless he introduces them pursuant to medical advice or under such circumstances as would afford a defense to a charge of crime;

(c) "pathological intoxication" means intoxication grossly excessive in degree, given the amount of the intoxicant, to which the actor does not know he is susceptible.

Questions

1. *Involuntary Intoxication as the Cause of the Offense.* In State v. Mriglot, 15 Wash. App. 446, 550 P.2d 17 (1976), defendant requested a jury instruction that would give an excuse if he were found "involuntarily *under the influence* or *affected* by the use of liquor or drugs." Should the court have accepted this proposed instruction? Assume the evidence is that Mriglot would not have committed the offense if he had not been involuntarily intoxicated. Should he get a defense?

2. *Blameworthiness Judgment.* Does the Model Penal Code's involuntary intoxication defense call for the jury to make a normative judgment as to whether the actor reasonably could have been expected to have avoided the violation? If so, what is the mechanism by which it invites the jury make this determination?

3. *Involuntary Intoxication vs. Insanity.* How are the defenses of involuntary intoxication and insanity similar and different? Which formulation of the insanity defense is most like the jury instruction proposed by the defendant in *Mriglot*? Which insanity formulation is most like the Model Penal Code's involuntary intoxication defense? Would one expect a jurisdiction's involuntary intoxication defense to be analogous to the jurisdiction's insanity formulation?

State v. Rodriques
Problem Case

Defendant was indicted on November 20, 1979, on three counts of sodomy in the first degree and one count of rape in the first degree.

His victims were all young girls, whom he would lure into secluded areas. He filed a notice of intention to rely on the defense of mental disease, disorder or defect [and moved for a judgment of acquittal on that basis]. [Defendant was initially declared incompetent to stand trial.]

For [a] year and a half, State psychiatrist Dr. Morgan treated defendant at Kaneohe, Hawaii State Hospital, and on June 25, 1982, the defendant was brought back into court. The defendant was presented as fit to proceed, so the court renewed hearings on the motion for the judgment of acquittal. On August 27, 1982, the judge granted the motion, and this appeal followed. . . .

The defendant in the case at hand introduced testimony from five psychiatrists to rebut the presumption of sanity. There was no contention that this was not sufficient to rebut the presumption. Accordingly, the burden of proof shifted to the State to prove, beyond a reasonable doubt, that appellant was sane at the time of the offenses.

The testimony introduced by the defense addressed the fact that under HRS §704-408, a defendant will be relieved of criminal responsibility if at the time of the alleged conduct the defendant suffered from a mental disease, disorder, or defect which substantially impaired his capacity to appreciate the wrongfulness of his conduct or to conform his conduct to the requirements of the law. In support of his motion for acquittal, the defendant raised the defense that at the time of the offense he was suffering from multiple personality syndrome, which should exclude his responsibility for his actions.

Multiple personality syndrome (MPS) is a disorder where there are within one individual, two or more distinct personalities, each of which is dominant at a particular time. Each individual personality is complex and integrated with its own behavior pattern and the personality that is dominant at any particular time determines the individual's behavior. Often there is amnesia on the part of one personality for the existence of the other.

The defense of MPS was raised in connection with HRS §704-408 because one personality often cannot control the actions of another personality. . . .

A summary of the testimony of all the psychiatrists reveals that: Defendant had anywhere from one to three personalities; *A* could appreciate the wrongfulness of his acts and conform his behavior to the requirement of the law, but could not control *B*; *B* could understand the wrongfulness of his conduct but could or could not (depending on whose testimony was more persuasive) control his behavior to the requirements of the law; and *C* did not care whether what he did was right or wrong or about the consequences of his conduct. Dr. Khaw, theorizing there was one personality, testified *A* committed the acts; four doctors theorizing there were two personalities, testified *B* committed the acts; and Dr. Morgan testified that *C* executed the crimes.

Questions

1. *Liability for A, B, and/or C?* Under which insanity formulations, if any, might Personality *A* get an insanity defense? Personality *B*? Personality *C*? Should Rodriques get an insanity defense? Does it matter which Personality was "active" when the offenses were committed? Does it matter which Personality is "active" at the time of trial? Which personality would go to prison?

2. *Multiple Personalities and the Insanity Defense.* Should the fact that someone has multiple personalities itself be grounds for an insanity defense? If so, why? Does current law, in any of the current formulations, admit the possibility that an actor might have more than one "personality"?

3. *Actors and their "Personalities."* What do the experts mean when they refer to Rodriques's "personalities"? Is an actor's "personality" something different from himself? Is an actor responsible for the "personality" that he has? Does the law, in any of the current insanity formulations, admit the possibility that an actor is not responsible for his own personality? Reconsider these questions after you have finished Section 16.5, Problematic Excuses.

Jones v. United States
Supreme Court of the United States
463 U.S. 354, 103 S. Ct. 3043, 77 L. Ed. 2d 694 (1983)

Justice POWELL delivered the opinion of the Court.

The question presented is whether petitioner, who was committed to a mental hospital upon being acquitted of a criminal offense by reason of insanity, must be released because he has been hospitalized for a period longer than he might have served in prison had he been convicted.

I

In the District of Columbia a criminal defendant may be acquitted by reason of insanity if his insanity is "affirmatively established by a preponderance of the evidence." If he successfully invokes the insanity defense, he is committed to a mental hospital. 24-301(d)(1).[2] The statute provides several ways of obtaining release. Within 50 days of commitment the acquittee is entitled to a judicial hearing to determine his eligibility for release, at which he has the burden of proving by a preponderance of the evidence that he is no longer mentally ill or dangerous. §24-301(d)(2). If he fails to meet this burden at the 50-day hearing, the committed acquittee subsequently may be released, with court approval, upon certification of his recovery by the hospital chief of service. §24-301(e). Alternatively, the acquittee is entitled to a judicial hearing every six months at which he may establish by a preponderance of the evidence that he is entitled to release. §24-301(k).**

Independent of its provision for the commitment of insanity acquittees, the District of Columbia also has adopted a civil-commitment procedure, under which an individual may be committed upon clear and convincing proof by the Government that he is mentally ill and likely to injure himself or others. The individual may demand a jury in the civil-commitment proceeding. Once committed, a patient may be released at any time upon certification of recovery by the hospital chief of service. Alternatively, the patient is entitled after the first 90 days, and subsequently at 6-month intervals, to request a judicial hearing at which he may gain his release by proving by a preponderance of the evidence that he is no longer mentally ill or dangerous.

II

On September 19, 1975, petitioner was arrested for attempting to steal a jacket from a department store. The next day he was arraigned in the District of Columbia Superior Court on a charge of attempted petit larceny, a misdemeanor punishable by a maximum prison sentence of one year. [The trial court ordered a competency hearing but found the defendant competent to stand trial.] Petitioner subsequently de-

---

2. Section 24-301(d)(1) provides:

If any person tried upon an indictment or information for an offense raises the defense of insanity and is acquitted solely on the ground that he was insane at the time of its commission, he shall be committed to a hospital for the mentally ill until such time as he is eligible for release pursuant to this subsection or subsection (e) of this section.

Under this provision, automatic commitment is permissible only if the defendant himself raised the insanity defense.

**Editor's Note.—The Model Penal Code provisions on commitment after an insanity acquittal are contained in Model Penal Code §4.08, which is reproduced in the Appendix.

cided to plead not guilty by reason of insanity. The Government did not contest the plea, and it entered into a stipulation of facts with petitioner. On March 12, 1976, the Superior Court found petitioner not guilty by reason of insanity and committed him to St. Elizabeth's pursuant to 24-301(d)(1).

On May 25, 1976, the court held the 50-day hearing required by 24-301(d)(2)(A). A psychologist from St. Elizabeth's testified on behalf of the Government that, in the opinion of the staff, petitioner continued to suffer from paranoid schizophrenia and that "because his illness is still quite active, he is still a danger to himself and to others." Petitioner's counsel conducted a brief cross-examination, and presented no evidence. The court then found that "the defendant-patient is mentally ill and as a result of his mental illness, at this time, he constitutes a danger to himself or others." Petitioner was returned to St. Elizabeth's. [A] second release hearing was held on February 22, 1977. By that date petitioner had been hospitalized for more than one year, the maximum period he could have spent in prison if he had been convicted. On this basis he demanded that he be released unconditionally or recommitted pursuant to the civil-commitment standards in 21-545(b), including a jury trial and proof by clear and convincing evidence, of his mental illness and dangerousness. The Superior Court denied petitioner's request for a civil-commitment hearing, reaffirmed the findings made at the May 25, 1976, hearing, and continued petitioner's commitment to St. Elizabeth's.

[The Court summarizes lower court actions that culminated in a Court of Appeals decision rejecting Jones's equal protection claim.]

We granted certiorari, 454 U.S. 1141 (1982), and now affirm.

III

It is clear that "commitment for any purpose constitutes a significant deprivation of liberty that requires due process protection." Therefore, a State must have "a constitutionally adequate purpose for the confinement." . . . [Petitioner contends that his] trial was not a constitutionally adequate hearing to justify an indefinite commitment.

Petitioner's argument rests principally on Addington v. Texas, in which the Court held that the Due Process Clause requires the Government in a civil-commitment proceeding to demonstrate by clear and convincing evidence that the individual is mentally ill and dangerous. Petitioner contends that these due process standards were not met in his case because the judgment of not guilty by reason of insanity did not constitute a finding of present mental illness and dangerousness and because it was established only by a preponderance of the evidence. Petitioner then concludes that the Government's only conceivably legitimate justification for automatic commitment is to insure that insanity acquittees do not escape confinement entirely, and that this interest can justify commitment at most for a period equal to the maximum prison sentence the acquittee could have received if convicted. Because petitioner has been hospitalized for longer than the one year he might have served in prison, he asserts that he should be released unconditionally or recommitted under the District's civil-commitment procedures.

A

We turn first to the question whether the finding of insanity at the criminal trial is sufficiently probative of mental illness and dangerousness to justify commitment. A verdict of not guilty by reason of insanity establishes two facts: (i) the defendant committed an act that constitutes a criminal offense, and (ii) he committed the act because of mental illness. Congress has determined that these findings constitute an adequate basis for hospitalizing the acquittee as a dangerous and mentally ill person. We cannot say that it was unreasonable and therefore unconstitutional for Congress to make this determination. The fact that a person has been found, beyond a reasonable doubt, to have committed a criminal act certainly indicates dangerousness.[12] Indeed, this concrete evidence generally may be at least as persuasive as any predictions about dangerousness that might be made in a civil-commitment proceeding. We do not agree with petitioner's suggestion that the requisite dangerousness is not established by proof that a person committed a nonviolent crime against property. This Court never has held that "violence," however that term might be defined, is a prerequisite for a constitutional commitment.

Nor can we say that it was unreasonable for Congress to determine that the insanity acquittal supports an inference of continuing mental illness. It comports with common sense to conclude that someone whose mental illness was sufficient to lead him to commit a criminal act is likely to remain ill and in need of treatment. The precise evidentiary force of the insanity acquittal, of course, may vary from case to case, but the Due Process Clause does not require Congress to make classifications that fit every individual with the same degree of relevance. Because a hearing is provided within 50 days of the commitment, there is assurance

---

12. The proof beyond a reasonable doubt that the acquittee committed a criminal act distinguishes this case from Jackson v. Indiana, 406 U.S. 715 (1972), in which the Court held that a person found incompetent to stand trial could not be committed indefinitely solely on the basis of the finding of incompetency. In *Jackson* there never was any affirmative proof that the accused had committed criminal acts or otherwise was dangerous.

that every acquittee has prompt opportunity to obtain release if he has recovered.

Petitioner also argues that, whatever the evidentiary value of the insanity acquittal, the Government lacks a legitimate reason for committing insanity acquittees automatically because it can introduce the insanity acquittal as evidence in a subsequent civil proceeding. This argument fails to consider the Government's strong interest in avoiding the need to conduct a *de novo* commitment hearing following every insanity acquittal—a hearing at which a jury trial may be demanded, and at which the Government bears the burden of proof by clear and convincing evidence. Instead of focusing on the critical question whether the acquittee has recovered, the new proceeding likely would have to relitigate much of the criminal trial. These problems accent the Government's important interest in automatic commitment. We therefore conclude that a finding of not guilty by reason of insanity is a sufficient foundation for commitment of an insanity acquittee for the purposes of treatment and the protection of society.

B

Petitioner next contends that his indefinite commitment is unconstitutional because the proof of his insanity was based only on a preponderance of the evidence, as compared to *Addington*'s civil-commitment requirement of proof by clear and convincing evidence. In equating these situations, petitioner ignores important differences between the class of potential civil-commitment candidates and the class of insanity acquittees that justify differing standards of proof. The *Addington* Court expressed particular concern that members of the public could be confined on the basis of "some abnormal behavior which might be perceived by some as symptomatic of a mental or emotional disorder, but which is in fact within a range of conduct that is generally acceptable." In view of this concern, the Court deemed it inappropriate to ask the individual "to share equally with society the risk of error." But since automatic commitment under §24-301(d)(1) follows only if the *acquittee himself* advances insanity as a defense and proves that his criminal act was a product of his mental illness, there is good reason for diminished concern as to the risk of error. More important, the proof that he committed a criminal act as a result of mental illness eliminates the risk that he is being committed for mere "idiosyncratic behavior." A criminal act by definition is not "within a range of conduct that is generally acceptable."

We therefore conclude that concerns critical to our decision in *Addington* are diminished or absent in the case of insanity acquittees. Accordingly, there is no reason for adopting the same standard of proof in both cases. "[D]ue process is flexible and calls for such procedural protections as the particular situation demands." Morrissey v. Brewer, 408 U.S. 471, 481 (1972). The preponderance of the evidence standard comports with due process for commitment of insanity acquittees.

C

The remaining question is whether petitioner nonetheless is entitled to his release because he has been hospitalized for a period longer than he could have been incarcerated if convicted. The Due Process Clause "requires that the nature and duration of commitment bear some reasonable relation to the purpose for which the individual is committed." Jackson v. Indiana, 406 U.S. 715, 738 (1972). The purpose of commitment following an insanity acquittal, like that of civil commitment, is to treat the individual's mental illness and protect him and society from his potential dangerousness. The committed acquittee is entitled to release when he has recovered his sanity or is no longer dangerous. And because it is impossible to predict how long it will take for any given individual to recover—or indeed whether he ever will recover—Congress has chosen, as it has with respect to civil commitment, to leave the length of commitment indeterminate, subject to periodic review of the patient's suitability for release.

In light of the congressional purposes underlying commitment of insanity acquittees, we think petitioner clearly errs in contending that an acquittee's hypothetical maximum sentence provides the constitutional limit for his commitment. A particular sentence of incarceration is chosen to reflect society's view of the proper response to commission of a particular criminal offense, based on a variety of considerations such as retribution, deterrence, and rehabilitation. The State may punish a person convicted of a crime even if satisfied that he is unlikely to commit further crimes.

Different considerations underlie commitment of an insanity acquittee. As he was not convicted, he may not be punished. His confinement rests on his continuing illness and dangerousness. Thus, under the District of Columbia statute, no matter how serious the act committed by the acquittee, he may be released within 50 days of his acquittal if he has recovered. In contrast, one who committed a less serious act may be confined for a longer period if he remains ill and dangerous. There simply is no necessary correlation between severity of the offense and length of time necessary for recovery. The length of the acquittee's hypothetical criminal sentence therefore is irrelevant to the purposes of his commitment.

IV

We hold that when a criminal defendant establishes by a preponderance of the evidence that he is not guilty of a crime by reason of insanity, the Constitution permits the Government, on the basis of the insanity judgment, to confine him to a mental institution until such time as he has regained his sanity or is no longer a danger to himself or society. . . .

The judgment of the District of Columbia Court of Appeals is Affirmed.

[Justice BRENNAN, with whom Justice MARSHALL and Justice BLACKMUN join, dissents:

I cannot agree with the Court that petitioner in this case has any less interest in procedural protections during the commitment process than [other persons subject to civil commitment], and I cannot agree that the risks of error which an indefinite commitment following an insanity acquittal entails are sufficiently diminished to justify relieving the Government of the responsibilities defined in *Addington*. . . . The maximum sentence for attempted petit larceny in the District of Columbia is one year. Beyond that period, petitioner should not have been kept in involuntary confinement unless he had been committed under the standards of *Addington* and *O'Connor*. . . . I would therefore reverse the judgment of the District of Columbia Court of Appeals.]

[Justice STEVENS also dissents:

The character of the conduct that causes a person to be incarcerated in an institution is relevant to the length of his permissible detention. In my opinion, a plea of not guilty by reason of insanity, like a plea of guilty, may provide a sufficient basis for confinement for the period fixed by the legislature as punishment for the acknowledged conduct, provided of course that the acquittee is given a fair opportunity to prove that he has recovered from his illness. But surely if he is to be confined for a longer period, the State must shoulder the burden of proving by clear and convincing evidence that such additional confinement is appropriate. . . .]

Questions

1. *Civil Commitment After a Successful Insanity Defense.* Assume the commitment procedures described in *Jones* are typical. If a defendant is successful in gaining an insanity defense, can the defendant automatically be civilly committed? Are normal civil commitment standards applied? Of what relevance, if any, is the defendant's prior offense for which he or she receives an insanity defense? Under what procedures and standards can an insanity acquittee be maintained under civil commitment once committed?

2. *Criminal vs. Civil Commitment.* What is the justification for civil commitment and how is it different from the justification for criminal

conviction and commitment? What does this difference in justification mean for the conditions of commitment? For example, could a person held under civil commitment argue that the conditions must be nonpunitive? What does the difference in justification mean for the terms of continued commitment? For example, could a person held under civil commitment argue that the grounds for commitment must be regularly reviewed? Could a person under criminal commitment make the same claim?

3. *Civil Commitment For a Period Longer than the Maximum Criminal Term.* What was defendant Jones's argument for why his commitment should not extend beyond the maximum term that he would have served if criminally convicted? What counterarguments can you make?

4. *Dangerousness as Grounds for Criminal Commitment.* Do your answers to Question 3, above, mean that dangerousness should not be used as a basis for criminal commitment? If an offender's sentence of incarceration is made longer because of the offender's dangerousness, should the offender be subject to civil commitment conditions and procedures during the extra, "dangerousness" portion of the sentence? Should the conditions be nonpunitive? Should continued confinement depend upon evidence of continuing dangerousness?

SECTION 16.3   DURESS, IMMATURITY, AND THE VOLUNTARY ACT REQUIREMENT

The insanity and involuntary intoxication defenses are just two of the disability excuses that may give an actor a defense even for admittedly wrongful conduct. Immaturity and duress also can have such an exculpatory effect, as can a host of other conditions that can destroy or reduce the voluntariness of an actor's conduct and make the actor eligible for a defense for failure to satisfy the voluntary act requirement.

Arthur's Adventure

Arthur, who just turned 18 years old, is a shy, 5' 10" overweight boy who lives with his mother in Winituck, Delaware. He has never been good at sports, or anything else involving people, but is an astonishingly successful writer of romance novels. He has never traveled outside his small town but he sets his stories in exciting locations around the world by using his imagination and reading travel books. His writing has just won him the Romance Writers' Guild's "Sweet Tear" Award, for the best newcomer in the business, and he is headed for his first trip out of Winituck, on a train to Philadelphia, where he is to receive his award at a Guild banquet dinner.

The Guild has reserved a room for Arthur at a local hotel. Feeling excited about his adventure, Arthur decides to experience the subway on his way to the banquet. In his black and pink formals, he stands out among the other passengers waiting for the train and is a target of ridicule by some local eleven-year-old boys. "Where you goin', fat boy?" asks one of the boys. Arthur stares down at the white knuckles on his folded hands. Perhaps they will leave him alone if he doesn't respond. "I'm talkin' to you, blimpo!" the boy insists. Perhaps he can just stand up slowly and walk away, Arthur thinks. "I think fat boy is scared, and he hasn't even met my friend Bob," the boy says to the others. He pulls a one-inch pen knife from his pocket and shows it to Arthur. "Meet Bob," he says. Arthur's eyes tear up, bringing howls of laughter from the boys. "Bob wants to take us to the movies but he's got no money. He wants you to go over to that newsstand, take the money from the register when the old man isn't looking, and bring it here." Arthur is shaking visibly but walks to the newsstand. He sees the boys watching him. Still shaking, he leans across the counter and takes the bills from the register. At that moment the old man turns and grabs Arthur by the sleeve. Arthur pulls loose and pulls the old man off balance as he does. He runs toward the stairs and throws the money at the boys as he passes, knocking down several people as he runs. He reaches the exit turnstile and tries to jump over, but gets only inches off the ground. A few minutes later, a police officer arrives to pull Arthur off the turnstile, where he has become stuck.

Between sobs, Arthur tells his story. The officer is sympathetic but the old man and one of the persons knocked down on the stairs are seriously injured. Arthur is charged with two counts of bodily injury and one count of theft. Does he have a defense?

State v. Toscano
Supreme Court of New Jersey
74 N.J. 421, 378 A.2d 755 (1977)

PASHMAN, J.

Defendant Joseph Toscano was convicted of conspiring to obtain money by false pretenses in violation of N.J.S.A. 2A:98-1. Although admitting that he had aided in the preparation of a fraudulent insurance claim by making out a false medical report, he argued that he had acted under duress. The trial judge ruled that the threatened harm was not sufficiently imminent to justify charging the jury on the defense of duress. After the jury returned a verdict of guilty, the defendant was fined $500. The Appellate Division affirmed the conviction. It stressed that defendant had ample opportunity between the time of the threat and the commission of the allegedly coerced act to report the matter to the police or to avoid participation in the conspiracy altogether. [I]t also concluded that defendant failed to satisfy the threshold condition that the threatened harm be "present, imminent and impending.". . .

On April 20, 1972, the Essex County Grand Jury returned a 48-count indictment alleging that eleven named defendants and two unindicted co-conspirators had defrauded various insurance companies by staging accidents in public places and obtaining payments in settlement of fictitious injuries. The First Count of the indictment alleged a single conspiracy involving twelve different "staged" accidents over a span of almost three years. . . .

Dr. Joseph Toscano, a chiropractor, was named as a defendant in the First Count and in two counts alleging a conspiracy to defraud the Kemper Insurance Company (Kemper). [Michael Hanaway, an unindicted co-conspirator who acted as the victim in a number of these staged accidents, testified that defendant was drawn into this scheme largely by happenstance. One of the doctors usually used to provide fraudulent medical reports had raised the suspicions of an insurance company claims adjuster. Confirmation of the need for treatment for the false injury was needed from a doctor not previously involved in the scheme. William Leonardo first called the defendant because William's brother knew the defendant as his doctor and a friend. William made several calls to the defendant, demanding that he help in the scheme. Each time defendant cut the conversation short by falsely claiming that he was with other people at the time and could not talk.]

The third and final call occurred on Friday evening. Leonardo was "boisterous and loud," repeating, "You're going to make this bill out for me." Then he said: "Remember, you just moved into a place that has a very dark entrance and you leave there with your wife. . . . You and your wife are going to jump at shadows when you leave that dark entrance." Leonardo sounded "vicious" and "desperate" and defendant felt that he "just had to do it" to protect himself and his wife. He thought about calling the police, but failed to do so in the hope that "it would go away and wouldn't bother me any more."

In accordance with Leonardo's instructions, defendant left a form in his mailbox on Saturday morning for Leonardo to fill in with the necessary information about the fictitious injuries. It was returned that evening and defendant completed it. On Sunday morning he met Hanaway at a prearranged spot and delivered a medical bill and the completed medical report. He received no compensation for his services, either in the form of cash from William Leonardo or forgiven gambling debts from Richard Leonardo. He heard nothing more from Leonardo after that Sunday.

Shortly thereafter, still frightened by the entire episode, defendant moved to a new address and had his telephone number changed to an unlisted number in an effort to avoid future contacts with Leonardo. He also applied for a gun permit but was unsuccessful. His superior at his daytime job with the Newark Housing Authority confirmed that the quality of defendant's work dropped so markedly that he was forced to question defendant about his attitude. After some conversation, defendant explained that he had been upset by threats against him and his wife. He also revealed the threats to a co-worker at the Newark Housing Authority.

After defendant testified, the trial judge granted the State's motion to exclude any further testimony in connection with defendant's claim of duress, and announced his decision not to charge the jury on that defense. He based his ruling on two decisions by the former Court of Errors and Appeals, . . . which referred to the common law rule that a successful claim of duress required a showing of a "present, imminent and impending" threat of harm. As he interpreted these decisions, the defendant could not satisfy this standard by establishing his own subjective estimate of the immediacy of the harm. Rather, the defendant was obliged to prove its immediacy by an objective standard which included a reasonable explanation of why he did not report the threats to the police. Since Toscano's only excuse for failing to make such a report was his doubts that the police would be willing or able to protect him, the court ruled that his subjective fears were irrelevant. . . .

Since New Jersey has no applicable statute defining the defense of duress, we are guided only by common law principles which conform to the purposes of our criminal justice system and reflect contemporary notions of justice and fairness.

At common law the defense of duress was recognized only when the alleged coercion involved a use or threat of harm which is "present, imminent and pending" and "of such a nature as to induce a well grounded apprehension of death or serious bodily harm if the act is not done."

It was commonly said that duress does not excuse the killing of an innocent person even if the accused acted in response to immediate threats. Aside from this exception, however, duress was permitted as a defense to prosecution for a range of serious offenses, [such as treason, kidnapping, and many lesser crimes, such as robbery, breaking and entering with intent to steal, forgery, and perjury].

To excuse a crime, the threatened injury must induce "such a fear as a man of ordinary fortitude and courage might justly yield to." Although there are scattered suggestions in early cases that only a fear of death meets this test, an apprehension of immediate serious bodily harm has been considered sufficient to excuse capitulation to threats. Thus, the courts have assumed as a matter of law that neither threats of slight injury nor threats of destruction to property are coercive enough to overcome the will of a person of ordinary courage. A "generalized fear of retaliation" by an accomplice, unrelated to any specific threat, is also insufficient.

More commonly, the defense of duress has not been allowed because of the lack of immediate danger to the threatened person. When the alleged source of coercion is a threat of "future" harm, courts have generally found that the defendant had a duty to escape from the control of the threatening person or to seek assistance from law enforcement authorities.

Assuming a "present, imminent and impending" danger, however, there is no requirement that the threatened person be the accused. Although not explicitly resolved by the early cases, recent decisions have assumed that concern for the well-being of another, particularly a near relative, can support a defense of duress if the other requirements are satisfied.

The insistence under the common law on a danger of immediate force causing death or serious bodily injury may be ascribed to its origins in early cases dealing with treason, to the proclivities of a "tougher-minded age," or simply to judicial fears of perjury and fabrication of baseless defenses. We do not discount the latter concern as a reason for caution in modifying this accepted rule, but we are concerned by its obvious shortcomings and potential for injustice. Under some circumstances, the commission of a minor criminal offense should be excusable even if the coercive agent does not use or threaten force which is likely to result in death or "serious" bodily injury. Similarly, it is possible that authorities might not be able to prevent a threat of future harm from eventually being carried out. . . . Warnings of future injury or death will be all the more powerful if the prospective victim is another person, such as a spouse or child, whose safety means more to the threatened person than his own well-being. Finally, as the drafters of the Model Penal Code observed, "long and wasting pressure may break down resistance more effectively than a threat of immediate destruction." §2.09, Comment at 8 (Tent. Draft No. 10, 1960).

Commentators have expressed dissatisfaction with the common law standard of duress. Stephen viewed the defense as a threat to the deterrent function of the criminal law, and argued that "it is at the moment when temptation is strongest that the law should speak most clearly and emphatically to the contrary." Stephen, 2 History of the Criminal Law in England 107 (1883). A modern refinement of this position is that the defense should be designed to encourage persons to act against their self-interest if a substantial percentage of persons in such a situation would do so. This standard would limit its applicability to relatively minor crimes and exclude virtually all serious crimes unless committed under threat of imminent death.

Others have been more skeptical about the deterrent effects of a strict rule. As the Alabama Supreme Court observed in an early case:

> That persons have exposed themselves to imminent peril and death for their fellow man, and that there are instances where innocent persons have submitted to murderous assaults, and suffered death, rather than take life, is well established; but such self-sacrifice emanated from other motives than the fear of legal punishment.

Building on this premise, some commentators have advocated a flexible rule which would allow a jury to consider whether the accused actually lost his capacity to act in accordance with "his own desire, or motivation, or will" under the pressure of real or imagined forces. The inquiry here would focus on the weaknesses and strengths of a particular defendant, and his subjective reaction to unlawful demands. Thus, the "standard of heroism" of the common law would give way, not to a "reasonable person" standard, but to a set of expectations based on the defendant's character and situation.

The drafters of the Model Penal Code and the New Jersey Penal Code sought to steer a middle course between these two positions by focusing on whether the standard imposed upon the accused was one with which "normal members of the community will be *able* to comply. . . ." They stated:

> . . . law is ineffective in the deepest sense, indeed it is hypocritical, if it imposes on the actor who has the misfortune to confront a dilemmatic choice, a standard that his judges are not prepared to affirm that they should and could comply with if their turn to face the problem should arise. Condemnation in such case is bound to be an ineffective threat; what is, however, more significant is that it is divorced from any moral base and is injust. Where it would be both "personally and socially debilitating" to accept the actor's cowardice as a defense, it would be equally debilitating to demand that heroism be the standard of legality. [Quoting Hart, The Aims of the Criminal Law, 23 Law & Contemp. Prob. 401, 414 and n.31 (1958).]

Thus, they proposed that a court limit its consideration of an accused's "situation" to "stark, tangible factors which differentiate the actor from another, like his size or strength or age or health," excluding matters of temperament. They substantially departed from the existing statutory and common law limitations requiring that the result be death or serious bodily harm, that the threat be immediate and aimed at the accused, or that the crime committed be a noncapital offense. While these factors would be given evidential weight, the failure to satisfy one or more of these conditions would not justify the trial judge's withholding the defense from the jury.

Both the Prosecutor and the Attorney General substantially approve of the modifications suggested by the drafters of the model codes. However, they would allow the issue to be submitted to the jury only where the trial judge has made a threshold determination that the harm threatened was "imminent." . . .

For reasons suggested above, a *per se* rule based on immediate injury may exclude valid claims of duress by persons for whom resistance to threats or resort to official protection was not realistic. While we are hesitant to approve a rule which would reward citizens who fail to make such efforts, we are not persuaded that capitulation to unlawful demands is excusable only when there is a "gun at the head" of the defendant. We believe that the better course is to leave the issue to the jury with appropriate instructions from the judge.

Although they are not entirely identical, under both [the Model Penal Code and the proposed New Jersey Penal Code] defendant would have had his claim of duress submitted to the jury.[12] Defendant's testimony provided a factual basis for a finding that Leonardo threatened him and his wife with physical violence if he refused to assist in the fraudulent scheme. Moreover, a jury might have found from other testimony adduced at trial that Leonardo's threats induced a reasonable fear in the defendant. Since he asserted that he agreed to complete the false documents only because of this apprehension, the requisite elements of the defense were established. Under the model code provisions, it would have been solely for the jury to determine whether a "person of reasonable firmness in his situation" would have failed to seek police assistance or refused to cooperate, or whether such a person would have been, unlike defendant, able to resist.

Exercising our authority to revise the common law, we have decided to adopt this approach as the law of New Jersey. Henceforth, duress shall be a defense to a crime other than murder if the defendant engaged in conduct because he was coerced to do so by the use of, or threat to use, unlawful force against his person or the person of another, which a person of reasonable firmness in his situation would have been unable to resist. . . .

We recognize that in other instances where the initial burden of producing evidence in support of an affirmative defense has been placed on the defendant, the burden of disproving the defense beyond a reasonable doubt has remained with the State. In this case, however,

---

12. The most significant difference between the two provisions is the treatment of duress as a defense to murder. The Model Penal Code permits it as an affirmative defense, while the New Jersey Penal Code allows it only to reduce a crime from murder to manslaughter. . . .

we think it more appropriate as a matter of public policy to follow the practice utilized in insanity cases and to require the defendant to prove the existence of duress by a preponderance of the evidence.

The peculiar nature of duress, which focuses on the reasonableness of the accused's fear and his actual ability to resist unlawful demands, is not completely offset by the "person of reasonable firmness" standard. While the idiosyncrasies of an individual's temperament cannot excuse an inability to withstand such demands, his attributes (age, health, etc.) are part of the "situation" which the jury is admonished to consider. We think that the admittedly open-ended nature of this standard, with the possibility for abuse and uneven treatment, justifies placing the onus on the defendant to convince the jury. In this respect, we adhere to the more traditional approach.

Defendant's conviction of conspiracy to obtain money by false pretenses is hereby reversed and remanded for a new trial.

Model Penal Code §2.09
Duress

(1) It is an affirmative defense that the actor engaged in the conduct charged to constitute an offense because he was coerced to do so by the use of, or a threat to use, unlawful force against his person or the person of another, which a person of reasonable firmness in his situation would have been unable to resist.

(2) The defense provided by this Section is unavailable if the actor recklessly placed himself in a situation in which it was probable that he would be subjected to duress. The defense is also unavailable if he was negligent in placing himself in such a situation, whenever negligence suffices to establish culpability for the offense charged.

(3) It is not a defense that a woman acted on the command of her husband, unless she acted under such coercion as would establish a defense under this Section. [The presumption that a woman, acting in the presence of her husband, is coerced is abolished.]

(4) When the conduct of the actor would otherwise be justifiable under Section 3.02, this Section does not preclude such defense.

Questions

1. *Duress Defense for Arthur?* Would Arthur get a duress defense under the common law, as described in *Toscano*? Is Arthur likely to get

a duress defense under the Model Penal Code? What arguments can the prosecution make that he ought not get a defense? What arguments can defense counsel make that he should?

2. *Limitations on Duress.* Many jurisdictions follow the common law rule in barring a duress defense for an offense involving the infliction of serious bodily injury. (For an interesting discussion and defense of the limitation, see Abbot v. The Queen, [1976] 3 All E.R. 140 (Privy Council).) If the actor was coerced to commit the offense and a person of reasonable firmness would have been unable to resist, on what grounds can it be said that the actor is sufficiently blameworthy to deserve criminal condemnation? Model Penal Code §2.09 rejects this limitation, but it keeps another common law limitation. Implicit in the terms of the section is the common law requirement that the actor be coerced *by another person* to commit the offense. Why not a defense if the coercion is from natural forces? Why should the source of the coercion matter if it is shown that the person of reasonable firmness would have been unable to resist? Recall Dudley and Stephens, from Section 15.2, who killed the cabin boy to avoid starving while adrift in a life boat. It is likely that their killing of an innocent nonaggressor would never be deemed justified. Would they, however, have an excuse, under the duress defense of §2.09?

3. *Duress vs. Insanity.* Both duress and insanity exculpate an actor for admittedly wrongful conduct, but insanity seems to focus on internal causes of the actor's nonresponsibility for his conduct (mental illness) while duress seems to focus on external causes (coercion). What are the other similarities and differences between the two defenses? Do they each call for the jury to make a normative judgment as to whether the actor reasonably could have been expected to have avoided the violation? If so, how do the defenses differ in the mechanisms by which they invite the jury to make this determination?

Model Penal Code §4.10
Immaturity Excluding Criminal Convictions; Transfer of Proceedings to Juvenile Court

(1) A person shall not be tried for or convicted of an offense if:

(a) at the time of the conduct charged to constitute the offense he was less than sixteen years of age [, in which case the Juvenile Court shall have exclusive jurisdiction††]; or

---

††The bracketed words are unnecessary if the Juvenile Court Act so provides or is amended accordingly.

(b) at the time of the conduct charged to constitute the offense he was sixteen or seventeen years of age, unless:

(i) the Juvenile Court has no jurisdiction over him, or,

(ii) the Juvenile Court has entered an order waiving jurisdiction and consenting to the institution of criminal proceedings against him.

(2) No court shall have jurisdiction to try or convict a person of an offense if criminal proceedings against him are barred by Subsection (1) of this Section. When it appears that a person charged with the commission of an offense may be of such an age that criminal proceedings may be barred under Subsection (1) of this Section, the Court shall hold a hearing thereon, and the burden shall be on the prosecution to establish to the satisfaction of the Court that the criminal proceeding is not barred upon such grounds. If the Court determines that the proceeding is barred, custody of the person charged shall be surrendered to the Juvenile Court, and the case, including all papers and processes relating thereto, shall be transferred.

Questions

1. *Youth as a Presumption of Immaturity.* Nothing in the Model Penal Code immaturity defense, or that of many jurisdictions, requires any assessment of the actor's actual immaturity. Why doesn't it? Why do you think that it conclusively presumes immaturity when an actor is under 16? Who decides whether a 17-year-old can be held responsible for his or her offense? Can we tell from the statute whether the criteria for this decision is the actor's immaturity or some other factor? Do you think that some 15-year-olds are sufficiently mature to be held responsible for an offense they commit? Some 17-year-olds?

2. *Conclusive vs. Rebuttable Presumptions.* The common law rule, and that of many American jurisdictions, provides a defense to an immature actor by creating a rebuttable presumption of immaturity if the actor is an adolescent (10 to 14 at common law). Whether he is judged sufficiently mature will be a function of his intellectual and psychological capacities. See authorities cited at 2 P. Robinson, Criminal Law Defenses §175 (1984). In this form, the immaturity defense looks more similar to other disability excuses. What are the advantages and disadvantages of the conclusive and the rebuttable presumption?

3. *Overage Immaturity.* Can an actor over the age of the immaturity defense (under either a conclusive or rebuttable formulation) get an immaturity defense if he or she has the maturity of a typical person well under the age of maturity? Could Arthur get a defense under

either the common law or the Model Penal Code formulation of the immaturity defense?

Hypnotizing Bunny

Bunny shares a cell with Lane, who is larger and more aggressive. They have developed a close relationship in which Lane is dominant. The relationship is built in part upon Lane's frequent sessions hypnotizing Bunny. The sessions began as simple entertainment, as a means of killing time, but have taken on considerable importance. Lane followed the instructions in a book that he had ordered through the mail and found that he could indeed put Bunny into a hypnotic trance. He sometimes demonstrates his ability to other inmates by having Bunny cut himself. He also has Bunny climb up on the stairway railing and attempt to jump over, grabbing him each time before he jumps. Because Bunny works in the superintendent's office, Lane decides he can put his power to good use by having Bunny steal keys and help him escape. Bunny steals the keys, as Lane directs him to do under hypnosis, but both are caught just after they leave the prison grounds.

Bunny claims an excuse under the involuntary act defense on grounds that his theft and escape were the product of a hypnotic suggestion by Lane. The testimony of the expert witnesses is conflicting. All agree that Bunny was hypnotized and that Lane apparently did give Bunny the hypnotic suggestions that he claims. Bunny's expert testifies that Bunny would not have stolen the keys or escaped from prison but for Lane's hypnotic suggestion. The State's witness testifies that the hypnotic suggestion may have created some mild motivation toward performing as requested—Bunny would have felt very anxious for a time if he had not complied—but that such was only a minor influence on Bunny's conduct in stealing the keys and escaping. Should Bunny get a defense?

Automatism: Nature of the Defense
G. Williams, Textbook on Criminal Law 608-611 (1979)

The most prominent instances of mental disorder . . . not amounting to insanity are those that are sometimes called "involuntary acts" but now more frequently go by the name of automatism, or, more fully, non-insane automatism.***

***Editor's Note.—This usage is common in English criminal law, which is Williams's subject. American courts and commentators still use the "involuntary act" label.

Does Automatism Mean That The Behavior is Virtually Mindless?

Yes in medical usage, but the legal meaning has developed far beyond that. The term "automatism" is used medically only in connection with epilepsy, and in its proper medical sense it is rare even in that disease. Although attacks of *grand mal* very occasionally result in violence, this is usually not because the sufferer is a complete automaton but because of confusion or delusion or a rage response. On the lips of lawyers, however, "automatism" has come to express any abnormal state of consciousness (whether confusion, delusion or dissociation) that is regarded as incompatible with the existence of *mens rea*,[†††] while not amounting to insanity. It would better be called "impaired consciousness," but the orthodox expression can be used if we bear in mind that it does not mean what it says.

Automatism is sometimes regarded as being incompatible not only with the mental element in crime but with the notion of an act. If it were a matter of pure theory this could be characterized as an unnecessary refinement, but the "act" doctrine has the advantage of enabling automatism to be a defense to the charge of an offence of strict liability.

The main instances of automatism are: sleepwalking, concussion, some cases of epilepsy, hypoglycemia, and dissociative states.

(a) *Sleep-walking*. It has happened from time to time that a person has killed or wounded another with whom he is asleep in bed, or while walking in his sleep or immediately upon rousing from sleep and while still in a state of semi-consciousness. Such a person is acquitted of murder or wounding, but there is no need to base the acquittal upon the absence of an "act." Clearly the defendant has killed or wounded; it would be a perversion of language to say otherwise; but he is acquitted for lack of a mental element. Some degree of normality of consciousness is essential for the legal notions of intention, recklessness and knowledge.

The position is not altogether simple, because the acts of a sleep-walker are in a sense purposive. The sleep-walker does not proceed as the cartoonists imagine him, with eyes tightly closed and arms outstretched. His eyes are open and he appears to be in perfect control. He will open a door and turn a corner, walk downstairs, open a drawer, take out a carving-knife, and return to the bedroom where his wife is asleep. But after waking up he will not remember his bloody deed. Although his acts have a certain purpose (indeed, he may have an understandable reason for killing his wife), it is the purpose of a dream-state. He is not acting with his normal conscious mind.

The commonest precipitant of sleep-walking or other behavior during sleep or semi-sleep is dissociation, but it is also attributed to

---

[†††]Editor's Note.—Williams uses "*mens rea*" in this passage in its broad sense, i.e., to include the absence of excuses.

hypoglycemia and nocturnal epilepsy. Sometimes dissociation results from brain disease, but more normally it is a hysterical symptom. The dissociated sleep-walker may act out a subconscious desire, but is not aware of it; and subconscious desire does not engage criminal responsibility. (There is, of course, a grave danger of the defence being feigned.) . . .

(b) *Concussion.* This is temporary damage to the brain resulting from a blow, and may produce a confusional state. It is accepted as justifying an ordinary acquittal.

(c) *Epilepsy*, though not classified as a psychosis, is certainly a disease of the brain. It does not predispose to criminal conduct, but it does to accidents, if uncontrolled by drugs. A driver will be incapacitated not only by a grand mal attack (the epileptic fit in the usual sense) but by petit mal epilepsy in which his mind simply fails to function for a few seconds. Also, the sufferer may in rare instances perform complicated acts in a somnambulist condition (the psychomotor attack), and these may unintentionally cause injury. . . . In the postictal period a patient may be confused and belligerent. . . .

The legal distinction between impairment of consciousness and impairment of self-control is a fine one. An epileptic may sometimes commit an act of violence in the "twilight" (confusional) state following a seizure; and here his mental condition would be regarded as incompatible with notions of *mens rea*. But the epileptic seizure is frequently preceded by extreme irritability which may cause the patient to commit an act of violence on the smallest provocation. Clearly, both acts have a pathological cause. It is hardly possible to frame a rule of law to distinguish the irritable but possibly controllable person from a person who loses all self-control because of abnormal electrical discharges in his brain; but the judge may distinguish between the two when it comes to disposal.

(d) *Hypoglycemia.* This condition, a deficiency of blood-sugar, can both impair the consciousness and induce an aggressive outburst. It may come about as the result of fasting followed by the consumption of alcohol, or when a diabetic takes an overdose of insulin or subjects himself to unusual fatigue or lack of food. Deficiency of insulin produces the opposite condition, hyperglycemia, excess of blood-sugar, which can also be caused by alcohol. This can have somewhat similar symptoms.

Model Penal Code §§2.01(1) & (2)
Requirement of Voluntary Act

(1) A person is not guilty of an offense unless his liability is based on conduct which includes a voluntary act or the omission to perform an act of which he is physically capable.

(2) The following are not voluntary acts within the meaning of this Section:
   (a) a reflex or convulsion;
   (b) a bodily movement during unconsciousness or sleep;
   (c) conduct during hypnosis or resulting from hypnotic suggestion;
   (d) a bodily movement that otherwise is not a product of the effort or determination of the actor, either conscious or habitual.

Questions

1. *"Involuntary" Conduct.* Presumably there can be little question that criminal liability should not be imposed upon an actor whose conduct is truly *in*voluntary, as in "not a product of the effort or determination of the actor" (Model Penal Code §2.01(2)(d)). There seems little reason to disagree with the Model Penal Code's treatment of such cases as per se grounds for exculpation. No elaborate inquiry need be made if the conduct is unconnected with the actor's exercise of will; there is no basis for a finding of blameworthiness. If Williams is correct, however, somnambulism and a host of other conditions can produce a wide range of disorders that stretch across the spectrum of volition and consciousness. If the disability simply impairs volition should it similarly be presumed to exculpate? Assume a somnambulistic state (or other disability) impairs an actor's ability to control his conduct or to appreciate what it is that he does. Might there be some instances where an excuse might be inappropriate? In other words, might an actor with impaired volition or cognition nonetheless be blameworthy?

2. *Voluntary Act Requirement vs. Excuse Defenses.* Assume a somnambulistic state (or other disability) impairs an actor's ability to control his conduct or to appreciate what it is that he does. Is this actor different, for purposes of exculpation, from an actor who suffers the same degree and type of dysfunction from mental illness? From involuntary intoxication? Does an actor get the benefit of these defenses if he or she suffers *some impairment*, or must the actor show that the degree of impairment is such that the actor could not reasonably have been expected to have avoided the violation?

3. *A Defense for Bunny?* Will Bunny get a defense under the Model Penal Code? In your view, should he? If the same degree of coercion to commit the theft and to escape came from threats of harm from Lane, would he get a duress defense under the Model Penal Code? If the same degree of compulsion to commit the thefts and escape came from claustrophobia, would he have a defense under the Model Penal Code?

SECTION 16.4 MISTAKE EXCUSES

Sophie's Stand

Sophie is upset at the recent practice of "pro-life" groups in heckling women who enter the local Woman's Center, where abortions are performed. As an active member of a "pro-choice" group, she has joined in counter-demonstrations but is increasingly persuaded that they are ineffective at deterring or countering what she sees as unfair harassment. Because she is a law student, she is asked at a recent planning meeting of her group to investigate other methods for minimizing the effect of the pro-life picketing. All present agree that any course of action that they take as a group should not be unlawful. While visiting the scene of the demonstrations, Sophie notices that the only access to the Center for a large group is along the street from the park where the pro-life people now assemble their group. If pro-choice forces congregated on both sidewalks at some point on the street, the pro-life demonstrators would have to switch to much longer and more narrow routes, which would both delay their arrival at the Center and force them to break into small groups that might not be quite as emotionally charged as the large excited groups that have done the harassing.

Sophie reviews applicable law and concludes that the planned action would not be unlawful because the pro-life demonstrators would never be touched or detained in any way, they would have another means of access to where they wished to go, and the sidewalk-blocking would last only a short time and therefore would not interfere with normal public usage. Her group likes her idea but asks that she check with officials to be sure that such congregation on the sidewalks would not be unlawful. In response to Sophie's inquiry, the local police advise against the proposed plan or any other such confrontational activity. When Sophie presses for a formal legal opinion, the police refer her to the State Attorney's Office, pointing out that they are police officers, not lawyers. They repeat their advice against this or any other confrontation. The State Attorney's Office responds to Sophie's inquiry by noting their long-standing policy against giving prior official interpretations of state law. Providing such legal advisory service, they note, would be impossible with their current legal staff, which is barely able to keep up with current court cases. Sophie reports her efforts to her group, together with her own research and her legal opinion that the planned conduct would not be a violation of law. The group accepts her recommendation.

The next day the pro-choice supporters congregate on the sidewalk in the path of the pro-life demonstrators. No contact is made. The pro-life marchers split up and take other routes to the Center. All members of Sophie's group are arrested for "Obstructing a Public Passageway," a county ordinance that does expressly criminalize their conduct. It turns out that her law school's library collection, where she did her research, does not include county ordinances. Does Sophie have a defense? Do the members of her group have a defense?

United States v. Anthony
United States Circuit Court, Northern District of New York
24 F. Cas. 829 (no. 14,459) (1873)

The defendant [Susan B. Anthony], a female, was indicted for a violation of the 19th section of the act of May 31st. 1870 (16 Stat. 144). . . . The trial took place before Hunt, Circuit Justice, and a jury. There was no dispute that the defendant had voted for a representative in the Congress of the United States at an election therefor, in Rochester, Monroe county, New York, and that, under the constitution and laws of the state of New York, none but males were authorized to vote at an election for members of the most numerous branch of the state legislature, and that the defendant possessed all the qualifications entitling a person to vote at such election, except that she was not a male.

HUNT, Circuit Justice, after argument had been heard on the legal questions involved, ruled as follows:

The defendant is indicted under the act of Congress of May 31st, 1870, for having voted for a representative in Congress, in November, 1872. Among other things, that act makes it an offence for any person knowingly to vote for such representative without having a lawful right to vote. It is charged that the defendant thus voted, she not having a right to vote, because she is a woman. The defendant insists that she has a right to vote; and that the provision of the constitution of this state, limiting the right to vote to persons of the male sex, is in violation of the Fourteenth Amendment of the Constitution of the United States, and is void. . . .

If she believed she had a right to vote, and voted in reliance upon that belief, does that relieve her from the penalty? It is argued, that the knowledge referred to in the act relates to her knowledge of the illegality of the act, and not to the act of voting; for, it is said, that she must know that she voted. Two principles apply here: First, ignorance of the law excuses no one, second, every person is presumed to understand and to intend the necessary effects of his own acts. Miss Anthony knew that she was a woman, and that the constitution of this state prohibits her from voting. She intended to violate that provision—intended to test it, perhaps, but, certainly, intended to violate it. The necessary effect of her act was to violate it, and this she is presumed to have intended. There was no ignorance of any fact, but, all the facts being known, she undertook to settle a principle in her own person. She takes the risk, and she cannot escape the consequences. . . .

[T]he counsel for the defendant requested the court to submit the case to the jury on the question of intent, and with the following instructions: (1) If the defendant, at the time of the voting, believed that she had a right to vote, and voted in good faith in that belief, she is not guilty of the offence charged. (2) In determining the question whether the defendant did or did not believe that she had a right to vote, the jury may take into consideration, as bearing upon that question, the advice which she received from the counsel to whom she applied, and, also, the fact, that the inspectors of the election considered the question and came to the conclusion that she had a right to vote. (3) The jury have a right to find a general verdict of guilty or not guilty, as they shall believe that the defendant has or has not committed the offence described in the statute.

The Court declined to submit the case to the jury, on any question, and directed the jury to find a verdict of guilty. A request, by the defendant's counsel, that the jury be polled, was denied by The Court, and a verdict of guilty was recorded. . . .

The defendant was thereupon sentenced to pay a fine of $100 and the costs of the prosecution.

United States v. Barker
United States v. Martinez
United States Court of Appeals, District of Columbia Circuit
546 F.2d 940 (1976)

WILKEY, Circuit Judge:

Two of the "footsoldiers" of the Watergate affair, Bernard Barker and Eugenio Martinez, are with us again. They haven't been promoted, they are still footsoldiers. They come before us this time to challenge their convictions under 18 U.S.C. §241, for their parts in the 1971 burglary of the office of Dr. Lewis J. Fielding.

Facts

During the summer of 1971, following the publication of the now famous "Pentagon Papers," a decision was made to establish a unit within the White House to investigate leaks of classified information. This "Room 16" unit, composed of Egil Krogh, David Young, G. Gordon Liddy, and E. Howard Hunt—and under the general supervision of John Ehrlichman—determined, or was instructed, to obtain all possible information on Daniel Ellsberg, the source of the Pentagon Papers leak. After Ellsberg's psychiatrist, Dr. Fielding, refused to be interviewed by FBI agents, the unit decided to obtain copies of Ellsberg's medical records through a covert operation.

Hunt had been a career agent in the CIA before his employment by the White House. One of his assignments was as a supervising agent for the CIA in connection with the Bay of Pigs invasion, and, as "Eduardo," he was well known and respected in Miami's Cuban-American community. A fact destined to be of considerable importance later, he had been Bernard Barker's immediate supervisor in that operation. When the "Room 16" unit determined that it would be best if the actual entry into Dr. Fielding's office were made by individuals not in the employ of the White House, Hunt recommended enlisting the assistance of some of his former associates in Miami.

Hunt had previously reestablished contact with Barker in Miami in late April 1971, and he met Martinez at the same time. He gave Barker an unlisted White House number where he could be reached by phone and wrote to Barker on White House stationery. On one occasion Barker met with Hunt in the Executive Office Building. By August 1971 Hunt returned to Miami and informed Barker that he was working for an organization at the White House level with greater jurisdiction than the FBI and the CIA. He asked Barker if he would become "operational" again and help conduct a surreptitious entry to obtain national security information on a "traitor to this country who was passing . . . classified information to the Soviet Embassy." He stated further that "the man in question . . . was being considered as a possible Soviet agent himself."

Barker agreed to take part in the operation and to recruit two additional people. He contacted Martinez and Felipe deDiego. Barker conveyed to Martinez the same information Hunt had given him, and Martinez agreed to participate. Like Barker, Martinez had begun working as a covert agent for the CIA after Castro came to power in Cuba. Although Barker's formal relationship with the CIA had ended in 1966, Martinez was still on CIA retainer when he was contacted.

Both testified at trial that they had no reason to question Hunt's credentials. He clearly worked for the White House and had a well known background with the CIA. During the entire time they worked for the CIA, neither Barker nor Martinez was ever shown any credentials by their superiors. Not once did they receive written instructions to engage in the operations they were ordered to perform. Nevertheless, they testified, their understanding was always that those operations had been authorized by the Government of the United States. That they did not receive more detail on the purpose of the Fielding operation or its target was not surprising to them; Hunt's instructions and actions were in complete accord with what their previous experience had taught them to expect. They were trained agents, accustomed to rely on the discretion of their superiors and to operate entirely on a "need-to-know" basis.

On 2 September 1971 Hunt and Liddy met Barker, Martinez, and deDiego at a hotel in Beverly Hills, California. Hunt informed the defendants that they were to enter an office, search for a particular file, photograph it, and replace it. The following day the group met again. Hunt showed Barker and Martinez identification papers and disguises he had obtained from the CIA. That evening the defendants entered Dr. Fielding's office. Contrary to plan, it was necessary for them to use force to effect the break-in. As instructed in this event, the defendants spilled pills on the floor to make it appear the break-in had been a search for drugs. No file with the name Ellsberg was found.

The next day Barker and Martinez returned to Miami. The only funds they received from Hunt in connection with the entry of Dr. Fielding's office were reimbursement for their living expenses, the cost of travel, and $100.00 for lost income.

On 7 March 1974 the defendants were indicted under 18 U.S.C. §241, along with Ehrlichman, Liddy, and deDiego for conspiring to violate the Fourth Amendment rights of Dr. Fielding by unlawfully entering and searching his office. On 7 May 1974 the defendants filed a Motion for Discovery and Inspection with an accompanying memorandum outlining, *inter alia*, their proposed defense of absence of *mens rea* due to a mistake of fact mixed with law attributable to their reasonable reliance on apparent authority. On 24 May 1974, in a memorandum order, the District Court rejected the defendants' position on the ground that "a mistake of law is no defense."

On 12 July 1974 the jury returned verdicts of guilty against both Barker and Martinez. . . .

The Defense Of Good Faith, Reasonable Reliance On
Apparent Authority

    A.

The primary ground upon which defendants Barker and Martinez rest their appeal is the refusal of the District Court to allow them a defense based upon their good faith, reasonable reliance on Hunt's apparent authority. They characterize this defense as a mistake of fact "coupled with" a mistake of law which negated the *mens rea* required for a violation of section 241. "The mistake of fact was the belief that

Hunt was a duly authorized government agent; the mistake of law was that Hunt possessed the legal prerequisites to conduct a search—either probable cause or a warrant."

It is a fundamental tenet of criminal law that an honest mistake of fact negatives criminal intent, when a defendant's acts would be lawful if the facts were as he supposed them to be. A mistake of law, on the other hand, generally will not excuse the commission of an offense. A defendant's error as to his *authority* to engage in particular activity, if based upon a mistaken view of legal requirements (or ignorance thereof), is a mistake of *law*. Typically, the fact that he relied upon the erroneous advice of another is not an exculpatory circumstance. He is still deemed to have acted with a culpable state of mind.****

Thus at first blush the trial judge's rejection of the defense proffered by the defendants—both in his pre-trial order and in his instruction to the jury—seems legally sound. He advised the jury that if the defendants honestly believed a *valid warrant* had been obtained, this would constitute a mistake of *fact* which would render them innocent of a conspiracy to conduct a search in violation of the Fourth Amendment. If, in contrast, they simply believed, despite the absence of a warrant, that for reasons of national security or superior authority the break-in was legal, such a mistake of *law* would not excuse their acts.

B.

With all due deference to the trial judge, I must conclude that both charges were in fact incorrect, and that this error must be faced by the court on this appeal. . . .

It is readily apparent that few courts would countenance an instruction to a jury—even assuming a criminal prosecution were brought against government agents in such a situation—which advised that since the mistake in acting on an invalid warrant was one of *law*, it would not excuse the agent's unlawful search. It is neither fair nor practical to hold such officials to a standard of care exceeding that exercised by a judge. Moreover, although the basic policy behind the mistake of law doctrine is that, at their peril, all men should know and obey the law, in certain situations there is an overriding societal interest in having individuals rely on the authoritative pronouncements of officials whose decisions we wish to see respected.

For this reason, a number of exceptions to the mistake of law doctrine have developed where its application would be peculiarly un-

---

****Editor's Note.—Is the Court using the terms *mens rea* and *culpable state of mind* in the broad sense (to mean general blameworthiness), or in the narrow sense (to mean the state of mind required by the offense definition)? See Section 7.1 (Determining Culpability Requirements).

just or counter-productive. Their recognition in a particular case should give the defendant a defense similar to one based upon mistake of fact, I submit, with one important difference. His mistake should avail him only if it is *objectively reasonable* under the circumstances. The mistake of a government agent in relying on a magistrate's approval of a search can be considered virtually *per se* reasonable. . . . Similarly, if a private person is summoned by a police officer to assist in effecting an unlawful arrest, his reliance on the officer's authority to make the arrest may be considered reasonable as a matter of law. The citizen is under a legal obligation to respond to a proper summons and is in no position to second-guess the officer's determination that an arrest is proper. Indeed, it is society's hope in recognizing the reasonableness of a citizen's mistake in this situation to encourage unhesitating compliance with a police officer's call.

Other situations in which a government official enlists the aid of a private citizen to help him perform a governmental task are not so obviously reasonable on their face. If the official does not *order* the citizen to assist him, but simply asks for such assistance, the citizen is not under a legal compulsion to comply. Also, if the circumstances do not require immediate action, the citizen may have time to question the lawfulness of the planned endeavor. Nevertheless, the public policy of encouraging citizens to respond ungrudgingly to the request of officials for help in the performance of their duties remains quite strong. Moreover, the gap (both real and perceived) between a private citizen and a government official with regard to their ability and authority to judge the lawfulness of a particular governmental activity is great. It would appear to serve both justice and public policy in a situation where an individual acted at the behest of a government official to allow the individual a defense based upon his reliance on the official's authority—*if* he can show that his reliance was *objectively reasonable* under the particular circumstances of his case.

C.

. . . Although the defendants characterized their mistake as to Hunt's authority as one of fact, rather than law, they requested an instruction which substantially coincides with my view of the proper test:

> [I]f you find that a defendant believed he was acting out of a good faith reliance upon the apparent authority of another to authorize his actions, that is a defense to the charge in Count 1, provided you find that such a mistake by a defendant was made honestly, sincerely, innocently and was a reasonable mistake to make based upon the facts as that defendant perceived them.

The District Court refused this instruction, regardless whether denominated a mistake of fact or an exception to the doctrine of mistake of law, and advised the jury simply that a mistake as to the legality of an unlawful search was no excuse.

It is clear from the above discussion of the search innocently conducted under an invalid warrant that the court's instruction did not state the law, and that a mistake as to the legality of an unlawful search may sometimes be an excuse. The trial judge can justify such an instruction in this context only if there is no legal possibility of equating the reliance of Barker and Martinez on Hunt's apparent authority with the reliance of a police officer on a judicial warrant subsequently held invalid. And this will be true *if and only* if Barker and Martinez could not show *both* (1) *facts* justifying their reasonable reliance on Hunt's apparent authority and (2) a *legal theory* on which to base a reasonable belief that Hunt possessed such authority.

Barker and Martinez meet the test as to *facts*. There was abundant evidence in the case from which the jury could have found that the defendants honestly and reasonably believed they were engaged in a top-secret national security operation lawfully authorized by a government intelligence agency. . . .

Barker and Martinez likewise meet the test as to the *legal theory* on which Hunt could have possessed such authority. That the President had the authority to confer upon a group of aides in the White House "more authority than the FBI or CIA," was in 1971 and is now by no means inconceivable as a matter of law. I certainly do not assert that the President here actually did so act, nor do we in this case need to decide the question of Executive authority to conduct warrantless searches pertaining to foreign agents . . . .

. . . I do think that defendants Barker and Martinez were entitled to act in objective good faith on the facts known to them in regard to Hunt's position and implicitly on the validity of a legal theory, still to be disproved, which has been vigorously espoused by President and Attorney General for the last forty years. I think it plain that a citizen should have a legal defense to a criminal charge arising out of an unlawful arrest or search which he has aided in the reasonable belief that the individual who solicited his assistance was a duly authorized officer of the law. It was error for the trial court to bar this defense in the admission of evidence and instructions to the jury, and the convictions must accordingly be

Reversed. . . .

LEVENTHAL, Circuit Judge (dissenting):

. . . Whatever equities may pertain to the case of these defendants of Cuban origin, who claim that their actions reflect their patriotism, were taken into account when the trial judge limited their sentence to a modest probation. Their quest for complete exculpation does not entitle them, in my view, to a ruling that the trial judge was mistaken as to the pertinent principles of law.

My opinion explaining why I dissent from the reversals contemplated by Judges Wilkey and Merhige, is cast in the conventional form of opinions that present first a statement of the facts, then an orderly discussion of the legal principles more or less seriatim. This case also calls, I think, for an opening exclamation of puzzlement and wonder. Is this judicial novelty, a bold injection of mistake of law as a valid defense to criminal liability, really being wrought in a case where defendants are charged with combining to violate civil and constitutional rights? Can this extension be justified where there was a deliberate forcible entry, indeed a burglary, into the office of a doctor who was in no way suspected of any illegality or even impropriety, with the force compounded by subterfuge, dark of night, and the derring-do of "salting" the office with nuggets to create suspicion that the deed was done by addicts looking for narcotics?

Judge Wilkey begins to cast his spell by describing Barker and Martinez as "footsoldiers" here in court again. Of course, they are here this time for an offense that took place the year before the notorious 1972 Watergate entry that led them to enter pleas of guilty to burglary. Every violation of civil rights depends not only on those who initiate, often unhappily with an official orientation of sorts, but also on those whose active effort is necessary to bring the project to fruition. To the extent appellants are deemed worthy of sympathy, that has been provided by the probation. To give them not only sympathy but exoneration, and absolution, is to stand the law upside down, in my view, and to sack legal principle instead of relying on the elements of humane administration that are available to buffer any grinding edge of law. That this tolerance of unlawful official action is a defense available for selective undermining of civil rights laws leads me to shake my head both in wonder and despair. . . .

The ultimate point is that appellant's mistake of law, whether or not it is classified as reasonable, does not negative legal responsibility, but at best provides a reason for clemency on the ground that the strict rules of law bind too tight for the overall public good. Any such clemency is not to be obtained by tinkering with the rules of responsibility but must be provided by those elements of the system of justice that are authorized by law to adjust for hardship and to provide amelioration. We should refuse to cut away and weaken the core standards for behavior provided by the criminal law. Softening the standards of conduct rather than ameliorating their application serves only to undermine the behavioral incentives the law was enacted to provide. It opens, and encourages citizens to find, paths of avoidance instead of rewarding the seeking of compliance with the law's requirements. The criminal law cannot "vary legal norms with the individual's capacity to meet the standards they prescribe, absent a disability that is both gross and verifiable, such as the mental disease or defect that may establish irresponsibility. The most that it is feasible to do with lesser disabilities is to accord them proper weight in sentencing."[59]

The sentence performed its proper function here. Our system is structured to provide intervention points that serve to mitigate the inequitable impact of general laws while avoiding the massive step of reformulating the law's requirements to meet the special facts of one hard case. Prosecutors can choose not to prosecute, for they are expected to use their "good sense . . . conscience and circumspection" to ameliorate the hardship of rules of law. Juries can choose not to convict if they feel conviction is unjustified, even though they are not instructed that they possess such dispensing power. In this case, Barker and Martinez were allowed to testify at length about the reasons motivating their involvement in the Fielding operation. This was an exercise of discretion by the judge that gave elbow room to both defendants and jury.

In sentencing Barker and Martinez after they were convicted to only three years probation, the trial judge made a subjective evaluation of the defendants' conduct in light of the goals of the criminal law. Barker and Martinez's patriotic motives, good intentions, and prior experience with the CIA and Hunt must all have influenced the sentence imposed. The trial judge exercised his sentencing power to distinguish, in terms of degree of moral guilt, between appellants Barker and Martinez and codefendant Ehrlichman. But sympathy for defendants, or the possibility that their mistake might be considered "reasonable" given their unique circumstances, must not override a pragmatic view of what the law requires of persons taking this kind of action. I come back—again and again, in my mind—to the stark fact that we are dealing with a breaking and entering in the dead of night, both surreptitious and forcible, and a violation of civil rights statutes. This is simply light years away from the kinds of situations where the law has gingerly carved out exceptions permitting reasonable mistake of law as a defense. . . . I dissent.

Model Penal Code §§2.04(3) & (4)
Ignorance or Mistake of Law Defense

(3) A belief that conduct does not legally constitute an offense is a defense to a prosecution for that offense based upon such conduct when:

---

59. A.L.I. Model Penal Code §2.09, Comment (Tent. Draft No. 10, 1960), at 6.

(a) the statute or other enactment defining the offense is not known to the actor and has not been published or otherwise reasonably made available prior to the conduct alleged; or

(b) he acts in reasonable reliance upon an official statement of the law, afterward determined to be invalid or erroneous, contained in (i) a statute or other enactment; (ii) a judicial decision, opinion or judgment; (iii) an administrative order or grant of permission; or (iv) an official interpretation of the public officer or body charged by law with responsibility for the interpretation, administration or enforcement of the law defining the offense.

(4) The defendant must prove a defense arising under Subsection (3) of this Section by a preponderance of evidence.

N.J. Stat. Ann §2C:2-4(c)(3)
Ignorance or Mistake

A belief that conduct does not legally constitute an offense is a defense to a prosecution for that offense based upon such conduct when: . . .

(3) The actor . . . diligently pursues all means available to ascertain the meaning and application of the offense to his conduct and honestly and in good faith concludes his conduct is not an offense in circumstances in which a law-abiding and prudent person would also so conclude.

The defendant must prove a defense arising under [this] subsection by clear and convincing evidence.

Questions

1. *Mistake of Law Negating an Element vs. General Excuse.* As we know from Section 7.3, the modern view allows a mistake of law as a defense if it negates an offense element, but knowledge of criminality is rarely an offense element. Older federal cases, and even some more recent cases, sometimes reject mistake of law as a defense even if the mistake negates an offense element, as in *Woods* case in Section 7.3. Assume that the offenses charged in *Anthony* and in *Barker & Martinez* did not require knowledge of criminality of the conduct. Do circumstances exist in those cases to suggest that a mistake defense nonetheless is appropriate?

2. *Mistake of Law Excuse.* What arguments can you make against

recognizing a general excuse for a reasonable mistake of law? What arguments does Judge Leventhal make in dissent in *Barker & Martinez*? What arguments can you make in favor of such a defense?

3. *Mistake of Law Under the Model Penal Code.* What is the difference between the mistake of law defense given in Model Penal Code §2.04(1) and that given in §2.04(3) & (4)? Would Susan B. Anthony have a defense under the Model Penal Code? Would Barker and Martinez? Would Sophie? Would the members of Sophie's group who blocked the sidewalk? In your view, should each of these defendants have an excuse defense?

4. *"Due Diligence" Mistake of Law Excuse.* Which of the defendants noted above would have a defense under the New Jersey "due diligence" excuse? Susan B. Anthony? Barker and Martinez? Sophie? The members of Sophie's pro-choice group? What arguments can you make for and against such a defense?

SECTION 16.5   PROBLEMATIC EXCUSES

Who Is Edward Drum?

When he is 6 years old, Edward Drum's parents join an "experimental community" of 25 people who live together in an old warehouse. They lead an unconventional life, try to avoid society's rules, and impose no rules or restrictions on their children. Edward and his older brothers begin to follow a pied piper of the community's children, a man named Donald ("Toad") Starr. Toad fawns over Edward in particular. As if courting him, he gives Edward presents and is extremely attentive. When Edward's parents break up, Edward is 8. He and his two older brothers move in with Toad, who has moved to an old bus in a field several miles from the community. Toad becomes sexually active with Edward and his two older brothers. Physical force is rarely used; generally the boys are psychologically pressured and occasionally denied food until they cooperate. Because of Toad's sexual preference for younger boys, he concentrates his sexual and emotional attention on Edward. The older boys eventually break with Toad and go on their own but Edward remains. Toad preaches a radical form of child rearing, in which sexual relations between children and adults is a good thing.

By age 16, Edward has long since lost the need for Toad's coaching to participate in sexual activities. He helps Toad kidnap a 13-year-old boy named My Lon. My is sexually abused by Toad and, at Toad's request, by Edward, during which Toad watches and takes video movies. Over the next two years, My comes to participate in these sexual activities without coaching, as Edward had come to do several years before. Two years after My is kidnapped, Toad conceives a plan to kidnap a young girl who he will impregnate (he believes this is possible as young as 8 or 9) and will have her become "the perfect mother" as she raises a child under his radical theory of parenting. Edward and My help Toad kidnap a 3-year-old girl named Betsey Wynn. For eight months, the four live out of a converted bread truck. Toad, Edward, and My take turns abusing Betsey.

On February 23, 1988, in Sacramento, California, a suspicious shopper opens the back door of a truck parked in the shopping mall's parking lot. She finds My lying with Betsey, both naked from the waist down. The police are notified. They arrest Toad and Edward when they return to the truck. Toad is charged with 121 counts of kidnapping, false imprisonment, lewd conduct, sodomy, rape, oral copulation, and assault. Edward is charged with 93 similar counts, and My with 23. Psychiatrists hired by defense counsels find no mental illness in any of the three defendants.[††††]

R. Delgado, Ascription of Criminal States of Mind: Toward a Defense Theory for the Coercively Persuaded ("Brainwashed") Defendant
63 Minn. L. Rev. 1, 1-11 (1978)

Coercive persuasion, or thought reform,[1] has been extensively described by psychologists and psychiatrists in field studies of prisoners of war, victims of Chinese "revolutionary universities," captives of outlaw or extremist groups, and members of religious cults. In more controlled settings, behavioral scientists have explored the contributions that isolation, physiological depletion, assertions of authority, guilt manipulation, peer pressure, and cognitive dissonance, can have in bringing about

---

[††††]Editor's Note.—The facts of this hypothetical are loosely based on the case of Luis Reynaldo (Tree Frog) Johnson and Alex Cabarga. See San Francisco Chronicle, August 5, 1984, at 9. Both were found guilty of the offenses charged and received sentences of 527 years and 208 years in prison, respectively. However, Cabarga's sentence was later reduced to 25 years on the recommendation of the District Attorney, making Cabarga eligible for parole within five years. At sentencing the court explained, "The court agrees that Mr. Cabarga is a tragic figure and comes from a tragic background." See San Francisco Examiner, April 25, 1989, at 39.

1. "Coercive persuasion" and "thought reform" are terms for a forcible indoctrination process designed to induce the subject to abandon existing political, religious, or social beliefs in favor of a rigid system imposed by the indoctrinator. This process is popularly referred to as "brainwashing," although scientists generally avoid use of this latter term because of a widespread public emotional response and misuse of the term, and because by glib repetition in many contexts it has lost all semblance of its original narrow meaning.

behavioral compliance and attitudinal change. Despite some disagreement over the theoretical model that best explains such changes, it is generally agreed that certain elements or themes are centrally involved in instances of coercive persuasion. These include:

(1) isolation of the victim and total control over his environment;
(2) control of all channels of information and communication;
(3) physiological debilitation by means of inadequate diet, insufficient sleep, and poor sanitation;
(4) assignment of meaningless tasks, such as repetitious copying of written material;
(5) manipulation of guilt and anxiety;
(6) threats of annihilation by seemingly all-powerful captors, who insist that the victim's sole chance for survival lies in identifying with them;
(7) degradation of and assaults on the pre-existing self;
(8) peer pressure, often applied through ritual "struggle sessions";
(9) required performance of symbolic acts of self-betrayal, betrayal of group norms, and confession;
(10) alternation of harshness and leniency.

Acting alone, none of these forces is likely to prove irresistible to a person of ordinary resolve, particularly if he is aware that an attempt is under way to influence him. Rather, it is the concentration of multiple forces, both physical and psychological, intensively applied over a short period of time, that gives coercive persuasion its peculiar power. Many authorities, including the drafters of a Department of Defense report prepared in response to evidence of widespread collaboration by American prisoners of war (POW) during the Korean conflict, have concluded that a determined captor, possessing total control over the life and environment of a captive, can produce behavioral and attitudinal change in even the most strongly resistant individual.[16] . . .

---

16. These conclusions, largely based on field studies and interviews, are further supported by the results of what appears to be the sole consciously designed experiment testing the ability of multiple coercive forces to elicit desired behavior changes. During the Vietnam War, the United States Air Force and Navy developed a survival training program for senior military officers, particularly pilots, who were exposed to the highest degree of risk of capture and interrogation by the North Vietnamese. The aim was to strengthen their resistance to coercive persuasion techniques in order to safeguard tactical military secrets for the longest possible time. . . . Despite introductory lectures forewarning them of the experiences they would undergo and reassuring them that neither they nor their families would be in any real physical danger, "a very remarkably high percentage, as high as twenty-five percent of these experienced . . . senior officers" confessed and divulged the "secrets" they had been told to conceal. Some even revealed genuine military secrets. Eventually the program was redesigned to make it "less realistic" because participants were experiencing psychiatric symptoms and developing fear of, instead of resistance to, the techniques employed. This study contributed to a decision by the Department of Defense not to court-martial returning POW collaborators after

[C]ommentators who have considered the problem of the coercively persuaded defendant have concluded, largely on an analysis of the Patricia Hearst case, that no legal defense is available to such an individual. If they are correct, their conclusion is a troubling one, for it means denying a defense to a class of defendants who are, by ordinary moral intuitions, often more victims than perpetrators.

Consider a hypothetical individual captured by an outlaw gang and subjected to lengthy thought reform techniques, beginning with threats and terror, and continuing with isolation, starvation, sleep deprivation, and guilt manipulation carried out by seemingly all-powerful captors. At various intervals in the process, that individual's captors demand that he perform criminal acts for their benefit. Under traditional criminal defense theories, exculpation would be available for those crimes the victim commits during the initial stages of captivity, when classic duress and coercion exist, but not during the latter stages, when such overt coercion no longer is necessary for the captors to maintain control. Such a result is surely wrong. The breakdown of the victim's identity and will in the latter stages of the coercive persuasion process destroys the very mechanisms by which he might have offered resistance. Thus, acquiescence is rendered more certain than in the early stages when simple duress is applied. A person under direct threats of death will rarely cling to even deeply held beliefs. Rarer still is the individual who can resist protracted, unremitting, coercive thought reform techniques.

Consideration of theories traditionally believed to justify punishment also suggests that coercive persuasion should be taken into account in assessing a defendant's criminal guilt. . . . Past experience demonstrates that most such victims, once removed from the coercive environment, soon lose their inculcated responses and return to their former modes of thinking and acting. This return often is accompanied by expressions of anger, in which the former captive accuses his captors of the "rape" of his mind and personality. Punishment of such individuals does little to promote the rationales of the criminal justice system.

If punishment of the coercively persuaded defendant conflicts with both basic intuitions and the justifications advanced for invocation of criminal punishment, yet cannot be avoided under any existing defense theory, it becomes necessary to fashion a new theory of defense. Occam's razor[41] dictates that any such new defense should constitute, insofar as is possible, a logical extension of existing concepts of act,

---

the Vietnamese conflict, except for those who had participated in the most egregious acts of complicity. In fact no such prosecutions were recorded.

41. Attributed to William of Occam, the principle—that entities should not be multiplied beyond necessity—urges that the simplest possible rule or theory be adopted that is consistent with the facts or phenomena to be explained. See, e.g., B. Russell, A History of Western Philosophy 472 (Essandess paperback ed. 1945).

intent, and blame. The actus reus of defendants who have undergone coercive persuasion is undisputed, they apparently are neither insane, coerced, nor acting under diminished capacity, and yet they seem less than fully responsible for their acts. This is so because the coercively persuaded defendant's choice to act criminally was not freely made and, indeed, appears to be not his choice at all. Traditional *mens rea* analysis has inquired only whether a defendant who committed an allegedly criminal act possessed the requisite state of criminal mind at the time of the act. In the case of the coercively persuaded defendant, it is appropriate to ask also whether the intent the actor possessed can properly be said to be his own.

The victim of thought reform typically commits criminal acts fully aware of their wrongfulness. He acts consciously, even enthusiastically, and without overt coercion. Yet, in an important sense, the guilty mind with which he acts is not his own. Rather, his mental state is more appropriately ascribed to the captors who instilled it in him for their own purposes. . . .

United States v. Alexander
United States Court of Appeals, District of Columbia Circuit
as amended, 471 F.2d 923 (1973)

[The Court divided on several of the issues raised by this appeal. Chief Judge Bazelon was in the majority on all issues except the issue that is of interest here: "Whether the trial judge erred in instructing the jury with respect to defendant Murdock's 'rotten social background.' " Judge Bazelon's dissenting opinion appears before that of the majority.]

BAZELON, Chief Judge:

Part I: The Trial

The Evidence Presented At Trial

Five United States Marine Lieutenants—Ellsworth Kramer, Thaddeus Lesnick, William King, Frank Marasco, and Daniel LeGear—attended a dinner at the Marine Corps Base in Quantico, Virginia, on the evening of June 4, 1968, in celebration of their near-completion of basic officers' training. After dinner, they drove to Washington, arriving about midnight, still wearing their formal dress white uniforms. They stopped for about an hour-and-a-half at a nightclub, where they each had a drink. They were well-behaved and "conducted themselves like gentlemen." At the nightclub they met Barbara Kelly, a good friend of

Lieutenant Kramer. They accompanied her to her apartment, which she shared with another young woman, and visited there with the two women until about 2:40 AM. When the five Marines departed, Miss Kelly accompanied them, intending to return to the nightclub to meet another friend. Along the way, they decided to stop at a hamburger shop to get some coffee and sandwiches before the trip back to Quantico. The six of them entered the shop, stood by the take-out counter, and ordered their food. They noticed three Negro males sitting at the other end of the counter. As described by Lieutenant Kramer, "[T]heir hair was in Afro-bush cut, wearing medallions, jersey knit shirts, sport jackets. . . . [T]hey were what I consider in eccentric dress." The three men were Alexander, Murdock, and Cornelius Frazier. The critical events which subsequently took place in the restaurant were described by the four survivors of the Marine group and by Murdock and Frazier. Alexander chose not to take the stand.

According to the prosecution witnesses, Lieutenant Kramer realized that appellant Alexander was staring at him, and he returned the stare. "[I]t was on the order of a Mexican stand-off type thing where you just keep staring at one another for an indefinite period of time." No words were exchanged between the two men, and Lieutenant Kramer soon turned and faced the counter. Shortly thereafter Frazier, Murdock, and Alexander got up from where they were sitting and walked to the door behind the Marines. Murdock and Frazier left the shop, but Alexander stopped in the doorway. He tapped Lieutenant Kramer on the shoulder. When the Marine turned around, Alexander poked his uniform name tag and said, "You want to talk about it more? You want to come outside and talk about it more?" When Lieutenant Kramer replied, "Yes, I am ready to come out" or "Yes, I guess so," Alexander added, "I am going to make you a Little Red Ridinghood." At this point, Lieutenant King stepped up beside Lieutenant Kramer and made a remark variously reported by the prosecution witnesses as "What you God-damn niggers want?", "What do you want, you nigger?", "What do you want, dirty nigger bastard?", and "Get out of here nigger." Thereupon Alexander abruptly drew a long-barrelled .38 caliber revolver, cocked it, and pointed it at the group or directly into Lieutenant King's chest, saying, "I will show you what I want," or "This is what I want."

The Marines possessed no weapons whatsoever and, according to their testimony, were not advancing toward Alexander. As they stood there, shocked at the sight of the gun, Murdock reentered the shop at Alexander's left and rear, and drew a short-barrelled .38 caliber revolver. A series of shots suddenly rang out, and the Marines and Miss Kelly fell or dived to the floor. None attempted to retaliate because they all were taking cover and trying to get out of the line of fire. Alexander and Murdock withdrew from the shop, but one of them stuck his arm back into the shop and attempted—unsuccessfully—to fire his weapon several times more. Only Lieutenant Kramer attempted to identify this man, and he said it was Murdock.

Lieutenants King and Lesnick were mortally wounded in the fusillade; they died within minutes. Lieutenant Kramer was wounded in the head, but he remained conscious, as did Miss Kelly, who had been shot in the hip. Only Lieutenants LeGear and Marasco were not hit.

Alexander, Murdock, and Frazier fled to Alexander's automobile and drove off rapidly in the wrong direction on a one-way street. Alexander was driving, and as the car drove off, Murdock fired three more shots from the window of the car, at the door of the hamburger shop, and at people in the street. A nearby scout car raced after the fleeing car and stopped them within a few blocks. Two revolvers were recovered from the front floorboard of Alexander's automobile. . . .

Part II: The Hearing on Criminal Responsibility

. . . [I]n the charge to the jury [at a bifurcated insanity trial for Murdock], the court used language that seemed to tell the jury to disregard a portion of the evidence that was critical to Murdock's theory of the case.

The court has concluded, for the reasons set forth in Judge McGowan's separate opinion, that the record does not call for reversal [because of the jury charge]. Because the author of this opinion is persuaded that there is substantial merit [to defendant Murdock's claim], the author's views are set forth below. . . .

Instructions to the Jury

I turn . . . to what I regard as a serious error in the jury charge on the issue of criminal responsibility. In order to put the problem in perspective, it will be necessary to review the testimony in some detail.

1. Murdock relied primarily on the testimony of Dr. Williams, a board-certified psychiatrist, and professor at Howard University Medical School. Dr. Williams had examined Murdock on two occasions during his confinement in St. Elizabeth's Hospital [for psychiatric evaluation upon his plea of insanity]. According to the testimony of Dr. Williams, Murdock was strongly delusional, though not hallucinating or psychotic; he was greatly preoccupied with the unfair treatment of Negroes in this country, and the idea that racial war was inevitable. He showed compulsiveness in his behavior, emotional immaturity, and some psychopathic traits. Since his emotional difficulties were closely tied to his sense of racial oppression, it is probable that when the Marine in the Little Tavern called him a "black bastard" Murdock had an irresistible

impulse to shoot.[94] His emotional disorder had its roots in his childhood, in the Watts section of Los Angeles; particularly important was the fact that his father had deserted his mother, and he grew up in a large family with little money and little love or attention.

Dr. Williams stated firmly that in his view Murdock was suffering from an abnormal mental condition that substantially impaired his behavior controls. But he stated just as firmly that the condition did not amount to a mental illness:

> My idea of mental illness is that an individual is out of touch with reality. He has auditory hallucinations, he has delusions, he has mannerisms that set him off as a different individual. He withdraws from society. And his behavior as such is tremendously bizarre. This is what I call, what they would call at Johns Hopkins, a major psychosis and a form of mental illness. . . . I look on [Murdock's condition] as psychoneurosis, but not, as such, a form of mental illness. It is not a psychotic reaction, which I consider a mental illness. It is an emotional response, an emotional illness. Not a mental illness in that it is psychotic.

This court has made it perfectly plain that for purposes of the insanity defense, "mental illness" is a legal term of art. A criminal defendant's responsibility cannot turn on the label attached to his condition. The insanity defense is neither expanded nor contracted by changing fashions in psychiatric terminology. In particular, mental illness for our purposes is not limited to psychosis; it includes any "abnor-

---

94. There is some support for this view in the testimony of Dr. Pugh, the St. Elizabeth's psychiatrist who testified for the government. Dr. Pugh found no recognized psychiatric disease, but he found "predisposing factors," and could not deny the possibility that Murdock's behavior controls were impaired by an abnormal mental condition:

> Whether he was under any irresistible compulsion, as I say, that is something that can't be scientifically answered. . . . As far as his personality is concerned, both by history and by psychological testing, he is a person who overreacts to the possibility of physical threat and is likely to defend himself against physical threats that are not as great as he sees them being. There are predisposing factors. But I don't think that any of them can be said to constitute a compulsion or some kind of a disabling of his willpower or decisionmaking capacity.

Only Dr. Marland, the independent psychiatrist appointed at the government's request, rejected with assurance the possibility that Murdock's behavior controls were impaired by an abnormal mental condition. Dr. Marland examined Murdock on two occasions in the D.C. Jail, after he had been released from the Hospital. He found that Murdock had some neurotic symptoms, but he regarded them as no more incapacitating than a headache or a digestive disturbance. As for the impact of Murdock's childhood experiences:

> Every man is influenced to some degree by his background and he is influenced by his background and general personality traits. But influenced to the degree where he was unable to make a decision as to what he would do, this I do not believe.

mal condition of the mind that substantially affects mental or emotional processes and substantially impairs behavior controls."

Defense counsel was thus confronted with a serious dilemma, arising from the fact that "mental illness" meant one thing to his witness, and another to the law. It was clear that the law would permit a jury to find mental illness on the basis of Dr. Williams's testimony about Murdock's "abnormal condition." In practice, however, a jury might well be reluctant to look beyond the doctor's statement that the condition did not amount to mental illness as he understood the term.

Counsel's strategy was to bypass the troublesome term "mental illness," and invite the jury to focus directly on the legal definition of that term. He conceded to the jury that Murdock "did not have a mental disease in the classic sense," i.e., he did not have a psychosis. But, counsel argued, the expert testimony showed that at the critical moment Murdock did not have control of his conduct, and the reason for that lack of control was a deepseated emotional disorder that was rooted in his "rotten social background."[100] Accordingly, he asked the trial court to omit the term "mental disease or defect" from the jury instructions. I think his proposal was ingenious; the trial court might well have framed a suitable instruction asking the jury to consider whether Murdock's act was the product, not of "mental illness," but of an "abnormal condition of the mind that substantially affects mental or emotional processes and substantially impairs behavior controls."

While the trial court denied the requested instruction, we cannot say that ruling was error. The judge carefully instructed the jury to resolve the question of mental illness in accordance with its legal definition; he told them they were not bound by medical conclusions as to what is or is not a mental disease, and he told them to ignore defense counsel's concession that Murdock was without mental disease. In this

---

100. In the language of the closing argument of Murdock's counsel:

Dr. Williams premised his conclusion on the fact that this man had had what we might call a rotten social background. Now we know that most people survive rotten social backgrounds. But most people are not now here at this time on trial. The question is whether the rotten social background was a causative factor and prevented his keeping controls at that critical moment.

At the critical moment when he stepped back in the Little Tavern restaurant and he was faced with five whites, with all of his social background, with all of his concepts, rightly or wrongly, as to whether white people were the bogeymen that he considered them to be, the question at this moment is whether he can control himself. That is the only question. Now you can expand it out, but the only question is not the question of how you label what he had. If you label it mental disease or not. But the real question is whether he had control of himself. Now you have got to take the trip back through his lifetime with him and look at the effect that his lifetime had on him at that moment and determine whether he could control himself or not.

respect the instructions conform to the requirements set forth in our cases.

But the judge injected into the instructions a special note of caution, in response to the testimony and argument presented in this case. He told the jury:

> We are not concerned with a question of whether or not a man had a rotten social background. We are concerned with the question of his criminal responsibility. That is to say, whether he had an abnormal condition of the mind that affected his emotional and behavioral processes at the time of the offense.

Defense counsel had objected to that instruction before it was given, because his theory of the case was that Murdock had an abnormal mental condition caused in part by his "rotten social background." The trial court overruled his objection, deeming the instruction necessary to counteract what he saw as an attempt by defense counsel to appeal to the jurors on the basis of sympathy, or passion, or prejudice.

It may well be that the trial judge was motivated by a reasonable fear that the jury would reach its decision on the basis not of the law but of sympathy for the victims of a racist society. Nevertheless, I think that the quoted instruction was reversible error. It had the effect of telling the jury to disregard the testimony relating to Murdock's social and economic background and to consider only the testimony framed in terms of "illness." Such an instruction is contrary to law, and it clearly undermined Murdock's approach to the insanity defense in this case. For Murdock's strategy had two parts: First, he sought to convince the jury to disregard Dr. Williams' finding of no "mental illness," and then he sought to persuade them to find mental illness in the legal sense of the term. The jury could hardly consider the issue of mental illness without considering Murdock's background, in view of the fact that all the witnesses traced such disabilities as they found at least in part to his background.

No matter what the trial judge intended, his instruction may have deprived Murdock of a fair trial on the issue of responsibility. But even if that instruction had not been offered, Murdock could argue that he was denied a fair opportunity to present his particular responsibility defense—a defense not clearly grounded on any medically recognized "mental disease or defect." While the language of our responsibility test theoretically leaves room for such a defense, our experience reveals that in practice it imposes illogical constraints on the flow of information to the jury and also on the breadth of the jury's inquiry. Our test demands an "abnormal condition of the mind," and that term carries implications that may mislead counsel, the court, and the jury.

McDonald defined mental illness for purposes of the responsibility defense as an abnormal condition of the mind that "substantially affects mental or emotional processes and substantially impairs behavior controls." The thrust of Murdock's defense was that the environment in which he was raised—his "rotten social background"—conditioned him to respond to certain stimuli in a manner most of us would consider flagrantly inappropriate. Because of his early conditioning, he argued, he was denied any meaningful choice when the racial insult triggered the explosion in the restaurant. He asked the jury to conclude that his "rotten social background," and the resulting impairment of mental or emotional processes and behavior controls, ruled his violent reaction in the same manner that the behavior of a paranoid schizophrenic may be ruled by his "mental condition." Whether this impairment amounted to an "abnormal condition of the mind" is, in my opinion, at best an academic question. But the consequences we predicate on the answer may be very meaningful indeed. We have never said that an exculpatory mental illness must be reflected in some organic or pathological condition. Nor have we enshrined psychosis as a prerequisite of the defense. But our experience has made it clear that the terms we use—"mental disease or defect" and "abnormal condition of the mind"—carry a distinct flavor of pathology. And they deflect attention from the crucial, functional question—did the defendant lack the ability to make any meaningful choice of action—to an artificial and misleading excursion into the thicket of psychiatric diagnosis and nomenclature.

It does not necessarily follow, however, that we should push the responsibility defense to its logical limits and abandon all of the trappings of the medical or disease model. However illogical and disingenuous, that model arguably serves important interests. Primarily, by offering a rationale for detention of persons who are found not guilty by reason of "insanity," it offers us shelter from a downpour of troublesome questions. If we were to facilitate Murdock's defense, as logic and morality would seem to command, so that a jury might acquit him because of his "rotten social background" rather than any treatable mental illness, the community would have to decide what to do with him.

If acquitted because he lacked responsibility, Murdock would automatically have been committed to St. Elizabeth's Hospital for further examination. He could then obtain an unconditional release only upon the certification of the hospital superintendent "(1) that such person has recovered his sanity, (2) that, in the opinion of the superintendent, such person will not in the reasonable future be dangerous to himself or others. . . ." Plainly, the Hospital would find it difficult to justify holding Murdock on the grounds that he was insane in any conventional sense. None of the psychiatrists who testified at trial, including those from St. Elizabeth's, suggested that his "sanity" had ever been lost.

Nevertheless, Murdock may well be dangerous. We have no carefully-crafted technique for resolving the complex of legal, moral, and political questions concealed in the determination of dangerousness. Regrettably, those questions are now decided, at least in the first instance, by psychiatrists. We can only speculate on the outcome of their inquiry. . . .

[W]e sacrifice a great deal by discouraging Murdock's responsibility defense. If we could remove the practical impediments to the free flow of information we might begin to learn something about the causes of crime. We might discover, for example, that there is a significant causal relationship between violent criminal behavior and a "rotten social background." That realization would require us to consider, for example, whether income redistribution and social reconstruction are indispensable first steps toward solving the problem of violent crime.

. . . It is a critical responsibility of courts, legislatures and commentators to undertake a purposive analysis of the responsibility defense, instead of merely paying it lip-service in deference to its historical significance and our "liberal" consciences. Under each of the prevailing tests of criminal responsibility, the operation of the defense has been haphazard, perfunctory, and virtually inexplicable. If we cannot overcome the irrational operation of the defense, we may have no honest choice but to abandon it and hold all persons criminally responsible for their action.

McGOWAN, Circuit Judge:

The tragic and senseless events giving rise to these appeals are a recurring byproduct of a society which, unable as yet to eliminate explosive racial tensions, appears equally paralyzed to deny easy access to guns. Cultural infantilism of this kind inevitably exacts a high price, which in this instance was paid by the two young officers who were killed. The ultimate responsibility for their deaths reaches far beyond these appellants.

As courts, however, we administer a system of justice which is limited in its reach. We deal only with those formally accused under laws which define criminal accountability narrowly. Our function on these appeals is to determine whether appellants had a fair opportunity to defend themselves, and were tried and sentenced according to law. . . .

Judge Bazelon . . . finds reversal to be compelled by reason of a statement made to the jury by the court in the course of its instructions. The bare words used are not a faulty statement of the law. They remind the jury that the issue before them for decision is not one of the shortcomings of society generally, but rather that of appellant Murdock's criminal responsibility for the illegal acts of which he had earlier been found guilty; and, the court added in the next breath, that issue turns on "whether [appellant] had an abnormal condition of the mind that affected his emotional and behavioral processes at the time of the offense." This last is, of course, an unexceptionable statement of what we have declared to be the law in this jurisdiction. . . .

[Affirmed.]

Questions

1. *Edward Drum and My Lon.* Does Edward Drum, now 19, have a defense under the Model Penal Code? Explain why or why not for each of the possibilities (self-defense, lesser evils, insanity, duress, immaturity, or other)? Does My Lon have a defense under the Code? Should either Edward Drum or My Lon have a defense, in your view? Does one have a better claim to a defense than the other?

2. *Prisoners of War and Radical Environmentalists.* When the "brainwashed" actor that Delgado describes (such as a prisoner of war) commits an offense in furtherance of his induced belief system, after brainwashing is complete, will he qualify for a defense under the Model Penal Code? Assume an actor is coercively indoctrinated (using techniques used on POWs) to believe that protection of the environment is more important than any single human life and, because of this belief, he assassinates the president of a chemical company that he thinks is ruining the environment. Will this actor have a defense under the Model Penal Code? Review each of the possibilities. Should either the POW or the radical environmentalist have a defense, in your view?

3. *"Rotten Social Background."* The defendant in *Alexander* argues, in part, that his social environment during his childhood shaped his value system, that he is not responsible for creating this environment or for its effects on him, and that the offense charged is in large part a result of these effects of his rotten social background. Judge Bazelon agrees that this issue should have been presented to the jury. What are the arguments against this view? How is Alexander's situation different from and how is it similar to that of Edward Drum and My Lon? How is it different from and similar to that of prisoners of war and the coercively-induced radical environmentalist? What facts in each case make the case more or less appealing for exculpation?

4. Alexander *and the* Durham *"Product" Test.* Recall that Judge Bazelon was the author of the *Durham* case (see the insanity discussion in Section 16.2), which was overruled by the court in *Brawner,* the year before *Alexander.* Does this suggest another reason why the majority might have rejected a "rotten social background" defense for Alexander?

People v. Kimura
"A 'Cultural Defense' at Issue in Trial"

Los Angeles—When 32-year-old Fumiko Kimura decided to kill herself—decided to walk into the icy cold Pacific Ocean to escape her humiliation and shame—she was essentially alone. She had no close friends, no job and a second husband who had just admitted he'd been cheating on her for three years. When she walked into the ocean one blustery January day, she did it quietly, clutching her two beloved children to her breast, trying to escape without bothering anyone. It was the way she would have done it in Japan.

Seven months later, as she sits in a Los Angeles women's jail awaiting trial on charges of first-degree murder, Kimura, ironically, is alone no longer.

Suddenly—too late—she has "friends." She has a husband who visits her every day. She receives hundreds of letters from strangers in Japan and around the United States. She has become a symbol to the Los Angeles Japanese-American and immigrant community, a challenge for attorneys and a cause celebre in the Japanese press.

But she does not have what she wants most, her children.

After 15 minutes of gulping down salt water and holding her children's heads under water, Kimura was pulled out by two college students. She survived. Her children, four-year-old son Kazutaka and six-month-old daughter Yuri, did not.

If she goes to trial Oct. 21, as scheduled, Kimura will face the death penalty. But attorneys for both sides are trying to reach an agreement that would prevent the case from reaching trial.

Kimura's case raises the issue of whether one's cultural background can be used as a defense for having committed acts that may be typical in the homeland but illegal in the United States. In Los Angeles, where the influx of several hundred thousand Asians during the last ten years has brought their numbers to 15 percent of the city's population, the problem is especially acute.

No one doubts that Kimura, despondent over her marriage, was doing what she thought best. Oyako-shinju, or parent-child suicide, occurs about once a day in Japan and is considered honorable, although not legal. A parent who survives usually is put on probation or given a light sentence.

A parent who left the children behind would be fiercely criticized. Not only would leaving the children put a burden on someone else or force the children to fend for themselves, but it would strap them with a legacy of shame and possibly discrimination for having had a parent who committed suicide.

But if the American judicial system were to make allowances for all the foreign practices brought here by immigrants, were to allow ignorance to be an excuse, the "cultural defense" would become a buzzword for chaos and crime, say some opponents of the concept.

But in Kimura's case, the cultural influence cannot be ignored. The problem is how much weight to give it.

"It's not the same situation as when a woman kills her kids because she's tired of having them around," said Deputy District Attorney Lauren Weis. "The jury must decide: Is she a criminal who is a danger to society, to herself, to other kids in the future?"

"The cultural aspect comes into it, but there are so many different cultures here, you can't really start letting people off for that sort of thing," she said. "Kimura was living in America. She can't forget that."

Weis, who noted that she had not heard of another oyako-shinju case in the United States, said she was not eager to try Kimura and would be willing to enter into plea-bargaining. She is waiting for proof that Kimura was mentally unstable at the time of the suicide attempt.

If there was nothing mentally wrong with Kimura, Weis said, the state cannot afford to go easy on her.

"We'd be saying to everyone of Japanese culture that it's OK to go out and kill your children, when it's not," she said. "I want a good psychiatric report that we can hang our hat on."

Kimura stands charged of first-degree murder with the special circumstances of multiple deaths. If special circumstances are proved, the state could seek the death penalty.

If defense attorneys can prove that Kimura was mentally disturbed, however, the charge could be reduced to manslaughter—which implies that there was no intent to commit murder—the special circumstances would be thrown out, and the death penalty would be out of range.

The jury could seek a sentence as light as several years' probation and psychiatric treatment.

Los Angeles attorney Ben Takahashi, who has written about the case for a Japanese newspaper, said a similar story would not be big news—"maybe five or six lines"—in Japan. "Any punishment would be light," he said, "because everyone would understand why the parent had committed oyako-shinju."

Questions

1. *The Cultural Defense in* Kimura. How is the *Kimura* case similar and different from the cases described earlier in this Section? Does it present a stronger or weaker case for exculpation than each of the other cases?

2. *The Abnormality of the Indoctrination Circumstances.* Some people seem more sympathetic to the more "abnormal" of the situations of claimed coercively-induced value systems. Thus, the POW case seems most sympathetic, followed by the Edward Drum and My Lon kind of situation, with least sympathy for Kimura (abnormal in this country) and then Alexander. What is at the root of these distinctions? What is it exactly that people with these views may be focusing on? How many people would qualify for a defense if limited to the POW type of situations? How many if limited to cases like Edward Drum and My Lon? How many if Alexander?

3. *The Breadth and Duration of the Indoctrination Circumstances.* The prisoners of war and the coercively-induced radical environmentalist can show considerable force and deprivation as the means by which they were indoctrinated. Alexander cannot show such concentrated abuse, at least not calculated to make him hold a certain set of beliefs, but his "indoctrination" might well be seen as being more powerful in its ultimate effect because it arose from his entire environment during every day of life, he would argue, not just the concentrated efforts of indoctrinators at a particular point in his life. Edward Drum and My Lon can make the same claim, perhaps to a lesser extent. Is it the coerciveness of the indoctrination, its duration, the age or vulnerability of the subject at its outset, the actor's escapability from it, or something else that makes these cases seem somewhat different from one another? How does the cultural defense offered in the *Kimura* case come out under your analysis?

4. *Factors Other than the Indoctrination Circumstances.* Are there factors other than the circumstances of the indoctrination that you would want to focus on in deciding whether to give a defense to the "brainwashed" defendant? Does it matter how close the induced value system is to his or her previous value system? Does it matter whether the subject repudiates the induced value system after the offense? Does it matter whether the value system is itself abnormal compared to the values of the society in general? (Ought it be compared to the subject's old society or new society, in *Kimura?*)

5. *Sympathy vs. Defense.* No jurisdiction has ever recognized a "brainwashing" defense or any other defense for a coercively-induced value system. The law conclusively presumes that each of us is accountable for our own values and beliefs. On the other hand, many people feel some sympathy for a defense for some of the people in some of the "brainwashing" situations. Given the apparent sympathy for such defendants, what explanation might you give, if any, for the complete absence of a defense of any dimension in any jurisdiction? (In People v. Kimura, No. A-09133 (L.A. Super. Ct. 1985), the defendant, pursuant to a plea agreement, pled no contest to two counts of voluntary manslaughter. She was sentenced to time served. Her probation included a condition of mandatory psychiatric counseling.)

Chapter 17. NONEXCULPATORY DEFENSES

SECTION 17.1 THE NATURE OF NONEXCULPATORY DEFENSES

In 1981 the actor robs, rapes, and beats an old woman. The crime goes unsolved until 1987 when he is identified and arrested. Although he has committed the offense, caused the harm sought to be prevented by the statute, and has no claim that his conduct is justified or excused, the actor nonetheless may have a defense. The statute of limitations may bar his conviction for robbery, rape, and assault, despite his clear blameworthiness, because foregoing the convictions is said to further other public interests, more important than imposing liability on deserving offenders. *Farnsworth* gives another example.

Farnsworth v. Zerbst, Warden
United States Court of Appeals, Fifth Circuit
98 F.2d 541 (1938)

SIBLEY, Circuit Judge.

On the original hearing before us the petitioner-appellant was not represented by counsel, indeed had filed no brief. On this motion for rehearing we welcome the able brief of counsel in his behalf and have given it full consideration. His summary of the [point] mainly relied on is this: . . . That if the indictment . . . is defective in that the co-conspirators named are Japanese diplomats immune to any conspiracy indictment, Farnsworth is entitled to discharge. . . .

The indictment is sufficient to support the sentence. . . . By this record it appears that there was a conspiracy between Farnsworth and two named Japanese, and others unknown, to violate 50 U.S.C.A. Sec. 32 by communicating, delivering and transmitting to a foreign government, Japan, documents, code and signal books, and writings relating to the national defense to be used to the advantage of Japan and the injury to the United States; and in furtherance thereof and to effect its object Farnsworth went on stated days to four stated places in Washington City. This is an offense under 50 U.S.C.A. Sec. 34. Section 32 forbids the doing of or attempting to do the things it names relating to the national defense. Section 34 punishes the conspiring of two or more persons to do them if any one of such persons "does any act to effect the object of the conspiracy." . . .

The bill of Particulars furnished by the District Attorney admits that the Japanese persons named in the indictment were "the representatives, officers and agents of the Imperial Japanese Government." The motion to quash, which was overruled on demurrer, states that one was a Commander in the Japanese navy, and the other registered in our Department of State as Assistant Naval Attache of the Japanese Government. We may assume it proven that they were such. It is thereupon argued that they have diplomatic immunity from prosecution, and could not be co-conspirators with Farnsworth so as to constitute a criminal conspiracy. . . . The Constitution does not declare that diplomatic persons cannot join in crimes against the United States, or that they cannot be punished for them. Indeed Art. 3, Sec. 2, Par. 1, U.S.C.A. Const. art. 3, §2, cl. 1, expressly extends the judicial power to "all Cases affecting Ambassadors, other public Ministers and Consuls." The inviolability of the persons and goods of foreign ambassadors and other ministers and their servants rests not on the Constitution, but the law of nations. Our statutes, made to protect them, make express reference to the law of nations. Diplomatic persons may well be treated with peculiar consideration and their reputations as well as their persons carefully guarded, but more out of diplomacy than because in law they can do no wrong. If such persons in the United States join with a citizen of the United States in a conspiracy to commit a crime, though it be conceded that the foreign diplomat would not be indicted in the District Court, or even that he could not be, his immunity will not excuse the local citizen. At least two persons must join in an unlawful enterprise to constitute it a conspiracy. The statute expressly so says. But both need not be prosecuted, or prosecutable. . . . The rule that the acquittal of all save one of alleged conspirators resulted in the acquittal of all applies to acquittals on the merits. The reason of it is that such judgments prove that there was in fact no criminal agreement among two or more persons. . . . An American citizen ought not to be excused in a case like this because he conspired with a foreign diplomat. Yet further, it seems that only one of the named co-conspirators could claim diplomatic character. Diplomats get their immunity by being received as such. The naval commander may have entered without asking any leave or status different from other aliens. On his Japanese vessel he would of course be safe from arrest under a federal warrant but there is nothing in his status to sanctify a conspiracy with him to violate the laws of the United States.

Farnsworth has no right to liberty because of the quality of his named co-conspirators. . . .

The motion for rehearing is denied.

Notes on the Nature of Nonexculpatory Defenses

Examples of nonexculpatory defenses "Nonexculpatory defenses," as they may be called, include not only statute of limitation and diplomatic immunity, but also judicial, legislative, and executive immunities, immunity after compelled testimony or pursuant to a plea agreement, and incompetency to stand trial. Each of these forms of immunity furthers an important societal interest, respectively: reciprocal protection of our diplomats abroad, protection of governmental officials from personal liability arising from their official duties, the need to compel incriminating testimony from some offenders to successfully prosecute others, and the avoidance of the costs and risks of trials through inducement of plea agreements. The last defense, incompetency, is based primarily on concerns of fairness to the defendant. It prohibits trial unless the defendant has "an adequate ability to consult with his lawyer and to understand the proceedings against him."

Constitutional defenses Overriding nonexculpatory public policy interests also serve as the basis for many constitutional defenses. The double jeopardy clause of the fifth amendment, for example, may foreclose the trial of even a blameworthy and convictable offender, by barring the state from making repeated attempts to convict him. Notions of procedural fairness are said to demand that the state not subject a defendant to the embarrassment, expense, and ordeal of trial more than once nor compel him to live in a continuing state of anxiety and insecurity. Dismissals based on the operation of the exclusionary rule or upon prosecutorial misconduct also may be nonexculpatory in nature, especially if the dismissals are unrelated to the reliability of the evidence of the fact-finding process. The public policies served by nonexculpatory defenses may be as broad as protecting all members of society from unlawful searches, or they may focus on assuring fairness in the treatment of individual defendants.

Distinguished from justifications The balancing of competing interests that underlie nonexculpatory defenses should be distinguished from the balancing that occurs in justification defenses. In the latter, the harm done by defendant's act is weighed against the harm avoided or the benefit gained from that conduct. The actor whose conduct causes no *net* societal harm or evil is given a justification defense. In nonexculpatory defenses, the defendant's conduct neither creates a societal benefit nor avoids a societal harm; the defendant may well be fully blameworthy. The societal benefit from the defense arises not from the actor's conduct, but from foregoing his conviction. Thus, the defendant escapes liability despite his or her blameworthiness.

Detrimental effects of nonexculpatory defenses It should be clear that the criminal justice system incurs a cost each time a nonexculpatory defense is permitted. Permitting such defenses undermines the purposes for which criminal liability is imposed. Acquitting culpable offenders, who admittedly have caused the harm or evil prohibited by the criminal law, undercuts the aims of special and general deterrence. The offender's acquittal shows others (and himself) that it is possible to culpably violate the criminal law without suffering the threatened sanctions. In addition, the criminal justice system is deprived of authority to incapacitate or rehabilitate such offenders, thereby increasing the likelihood of future offenses. Finally, utilitarian concerns aside, nonexculpatory defenses permit blameworthy offenders to escape the punishment they deserve.

Minimizing the detrimental effects Reforms to the current system could reduce the detrimental effects of nonexculpatory defenses, without abolishing the defenses. For example, while permitting an acquittal, the system nonetheless could make clear its condemnation of the conduct and the actor. A special verdict of "guilty but not punishable" might do this. Certainly, the verdict of "not guilty" exacerbates the detrimental effects of nonexculpatory acquittals, for it misleads the public into thinking that no wrong was done.[1] Minimizing the detrimental effects of nonexculpatory acquittals depends in part upon public awareness of the special nature of nonexculpatory defenses, yet at present there seems little public appreciation that nonexculpatory defenses are different and still less awareness of which defenses are of this sort.

Less strict adherence to legality principle The special nature of nonexculpatory defenses also suggests that less strict adherence to the legality principle might be in order. Recall that the legality principle is meant to assure, among other things, that an actor has the opportunity for notice of the rules governing liability.[2] Such potential for notice is desirable because an actor cannot conform his conduct to the requirements of law if those requirements are not made available to him. In the case of nonexculpatory defenses, where the conduct may be deplored and sought to be deterred, vagueness and ambiguity in the defenses may serve the useful purpose of deterring undesirable conduct. This deterrence must be distinguished from the undesirable "chilling effect" of vague offense definitions. Here, the prohibited conduct is

---

1. It is an advantage, in this respect, that most nonexculpatory defenses are determined by the judge before trial. But see the entrapment defense discussed later in this chapter.
2. See Chapter 5 (The Legality Principle).

clearly defined; only the limits of the nonexculpatory defense are vague. Thus, the immune foreign embassy attache may behave himself if he is unsure whether he is covered by diplomatic immunity. The corrupt congressman may decline to exercise improper influence if he is not sure whether his legislative immunity extends to such impropriety.[3] One can argue that such offenders have little grounds to complain of the vagueness or ambiguity of the defense or to insist on a favorable construction, for they had notice that their conduct is prohibited.

Mistake as to nonexculpatory defense For these same reasons, there seems little reason to provide a defense to an actor who calculates his or her conduct to take advantage of a nonexculpatory defense but who is mistaken, even reasonably mistaken, as to the conditions of the defense. The better rule provides that an actor who acts under a belief that he has a nonexculpatory defense acts at his peril. If the requirements for the defense in fact are not satisfied—the attache is not immune, legislative immunity does not extend to the contemplated crime, or the statute of limitations in fact has not fully run—then the public policy interests that normally would support the defense are not served and no defense ought to be permitted.

Resisting aggressor with nonexculpatory defense Defensive force justifications generally give an actor a right to resist physical aggression against his or her person and to interfere when aggression is directed against another person or against one's property. But this right should, and in many instances does, in current law depend upon whether the aggressor's conduct is lawful or unlawful. If the aggression is not unlawful, as with an officer making a lawful arrest, generally there is no right to resist or interfere.[4] When the aggressor's conduct is not unlawful because he has a nonexculpatory defense, however, resistance and interference should be permitted, even encouraged. The immune diplomat may escape conviction for an unjustified and unexcused attack, but it hardly follows that the victim is bound to submit or the observer to acquiesce.

Collateral consequences of conviction Conviction for a criminal offense typically risks not only punishment, as through imprisonment, fine, or probation, but also risks a host of other civil disabilities. An offender may lose many of his basic rights and privileges: citizenship; employment opportunities in licensed and unlicensed occupations; the capacity to litigate, to testify, and to serve as a juror or as a court-appointed fiduciary; voting, parental, and marital rights; and the rights to hold public office, to carry a firearm, to inherit, and to receive insurance, pension, and workmen's compensation benefits. The of-

---

3. In contrast, it remains important that the law clearly defines for legislators what is and is not improper influence.
4. See Section 15.4 (Defensive Force).

fender also may incur forfeiture, civil restraint and injunction, civil liability, and civil commitment. Further, the conviction may be used to impeach an offender in a subsequent trial where the offender is a witness or a defendant-witness, and to aggravate the sentence for a subsequent offense.

Collateral consequences of nonexculpatory acquittal Given the disfavored nature of nonexculpatory defenses, some of these collateral consequences might appropriately be retained, if the acquittal derives from a nonexculpatory defense. Even if the offender is not to be punished for his past violation, ought not society be able to protect itself from new violations? Some precedent exists for this. The criminal diplomat can be expelled from the country. The incompetent defendant can be incarcerated until his trial is possible. Collateral consequences are retained frequently where an offender is pardoned. In most cases, however, offenders acquitted under a nonexculpatory defense escape all penalties and disabilities. Assume a guilty defendant's case is dismissed because of police or prosecutorial misconduct. Presumably it has been concluded that allowing such an offender to escape the primary consequences of conviction—the condemnation of conviction and the restraint of imprisonment or supervision—is an acceptable cost of furthering the important societal interest in deterring such official misconduct. But is it equally clear that the interest in deterring such official misconduct also outweighs the benefits of all collateral consequences that might have attached to the conviction? Should the corrupt official be able to keep his public office? Should the child molester retain his license to drive a school bus? Should the rapist be permitted to escape sentencing as a repeat offender after a subsequent rape? Should the con-man escape impeachment as a prosecution witness in a subsequent capital offense trial?

Competing interests in collateral consequences The nonexculpatory acquittee may be by all standards blameworthy, and there may be nothing in his character or conduct to suggest that he deserves to escape conviction. It is the *societal* interests that justify an acquittal under a nonexculpatory defense. As society may choose to adopt a nonexculpatory defense because of the balance of competing societal interests, so may it properly modify or limit the defense or its consequences as it sees fit. Thus, a nonexculpatory defense might result in exemption from custodial or supervisory sanctions yet might permit the imposition of collateral consequences that are, on balance, too important to society's protection to be ignored. In other words, the public policy nature of nonexculpatory defenses means that the scope and effect of the defense ought to be a matter of balancing the competing societal interests. Because the interests supporting a nonexculpatory defense are enough to permit the offender to escape conviction itself, it does not follow that the interests necessarily support the offender escaping all collateral consequences that might accompany conviction. Collateral consequences often can provide the most critical protections for society, sometimes with modest infringement of an offender's interests.

Identifying nonexculpatory dismissals The greatest practical hurdle to maintaining collateral consequences is in identifying cases of nonexculpatory acquittals of blameworthy offenders. Many nonexculpatory defenses bar prosecution, thus no authoritative determination of blameworthiness is readily available. Double jeopardy, diplomatic immunity, and incompetency by their terms bar trial of the defendant. Other nonexculpatory defenses, such as the statute of limitations and the immunities (judicial, legislative, executive, testimonial, and plea bargaining) often are litigated before trial. The difficulty can be solved easily enough through a change in procedural rules. If the prosecution intends to seek the imposition of some of the collateral consequences of conviction despite a nonexculpatory dismissal, determination of the nonexculpatory defense could be delayed until after a determination of guilt. Alternatively, the issues of blameworthiness could be litigated at a proceeding concerning the imposition of the collateral consequences. Whether the additional expenditure of resources would be worth the effort may depend upon how great a threat the defendant would continue to present if no collateral consequences were imposed.[5]

Questions

1. *Nonexculpatory Defenses.* The court in *Farnsworth* distinguishes the co-conspirators' defense of diplomatic immunity from what it calls "acquittals on the merits." How are the two different? What kind of defenses would constitute an "acquittal on the merits"? Would they include defenses such as: mistake negating an offense element? renunciation of attempt? lesser evils? insanity?

2. *Nonexculpatory vs. Justification Defenses.* Justification defenses seem similar to nonexculpatory defenses in that they forego liability of an actor who satisfies the elements of an offense in order to further a greater societal interest. Is not that what is being done with most nonexculpatory defenses? If they are different, how are they different?

3. *Practical Implications.* Why does it matter whether a defense is a nonexculpatory defense or something else? Give some examples of a situation in which a case might come out differently depending upon

---

5. Of course, if imposition of collateral consequences are contemplated, an actor must be given the opportunity to rely instead upon an exculpatory defense if such is available to him.

whether an actor (not necessarily the defendant) had a nonexculpatory defense instead of a justification or an excuse defense?

SECTION 17.2 ENTRAPMENT

Where a police officer or agent has some hand in having an actor commit an offense, the actor may be entitled to an entrapment defense. The United States is one of the few countries in the world that recognizes such a defense and, within the United States, jurisdictions disagree over how the defense should be formulated. The apparent terms of the disagreement concern how much the defense should focus on the *police* conduct and how much it should focus on the effect of the police conduct on the *defendant*. The answer to these questions may depend on what it is that we seek to achieve in recognizing an entrapment defense.

JJ's Out

JJ has a string of arrests and convictions for various drug offenses. Recently out of prison, he is anxious to get back into the drug business because the money is so good. He decides to work for another dealer while he reestablishes his connections. Garrett, an undercover narcotics agent, hears about JJ and works out a plan to catch him dealing. He approaches JJ and after some preliminary conversation asks him if he wants a job. JJ replies, "Sounds good, but I don't even know you. How do I know you're not a cop?" Garrett assures JJ that he is not a cop and invites him to a party the following evening. For the party, Garrett hires JJ's ex-girlfriend, a prostitute, who left JJ after his last arrest. Garrett hopes that the party and the ex-girlfriend will remind JJ of the "good life" and that he will then be willing to take the risk of working with Garrett. On instructions from Garrett, JJ's ex-girlfriend has intercourse with JJ and tells him that if he starts working for Garrett, they can get back together again. At the end of the night, JJ agrees to work for Garrett.

Garrett arranges for JJ to deliver eight ounces of cocaine the following day. At the delivery point, JJ is arrested by narcotics officers. He is charged with possession of cocaine with intent to distribute. He offers an entrapment defense. Will he get it?

Del. Code Ann. Title 11, §432
Entrapment as Affirmative Defense; Defense Unavailable in Certain Situations

(a) In any prosecution for an offense, it is an affirmative defense that the accused engaged in the proscribed conduct because he was induced by a law-enforcement official or his agent who is acting in the knowing cooperation with such an official to engage in the proscribed conduct constituting such conduct which is a crime when such person is not otherwise disposed to do so. The defense of entrapment as defined by this Criminal Code concedes the commission of the act charged but claims that it should not be punished because of the wrongdoing of the officer [who] originates the idea of the crime and then induces the other person to engage in conduct constituting such a crime when the other person is not otherwise disposed to do so.

(b) The defense afforded by subsection (a) of this section is unavailable when causing or threatening physical injury is an element of the offense charged and the prosecution is based on conduct causing or threatening such injury to a person other than the person perpetrating the entrapment.

Harrison v. State
Supreme Court of Delaware
442 A.2d 1377 (1982) (en banc)

McNEILLY, Justice (for the majority):

This appeal requires the Court to interpret and apply the Delaware Entrapment Statute, 11 Del. C. §432, as revised in 1974.

The defendant, Winifred Harrison, was convicted after trial by jury and sentenced on charges relating to her employment as a prison guard at the Smyrna Correctional Institution. The appeal is based upon the Trial Court's refusal to set aside the jury verdict and hold that entrapment had occurred as a matter of law.

I

The defendant was indicted on two counts of each of the following offenses: Receiving a Bribe; Delivery of a Non-Narcotic Schedule I

Controlled Substance; Conspiracy Second Degree; Official Misconduct; and Promoting Prison Contraband.

The defendant was a 32-year-old woman, married, with one child, who did not drink, smoke, use drugs, or have a criminal record. At the time of the incidents in question, defendant had been employed at the prison for approximately two months.

The State Police were concerned about contraband, particularly drugs, being brought into the Smyrna Institution; a special police task force had been formed. This was a long-standing problem, pre-existing the defendant's employment by many years.

A prisoner, John Barlow, was concerned about the drug problem because he was a "long-termer." He wished to make the prison a better place in which to live and to ingratiate himself with the authorities. Shortly after the employment of the defendant, at a meeting with the police lieutenant involved in the task force, Barlow volunteered that, while he had no first-hand knowledge as to the identity of any guard bringing drugs into the prison, he would approach guards he had heard were doing so, and attempt to have them bring in drugs for him. At that time, Barlow named the defendant as one of the guards he would approach. Barlow testified that he singled out the defendant for the reason that the defendant was bringing food into the prison which was technical contraband and, therefore, a violation of prison rules and 11 Del. C. §1256.

The plan of the police was for Barlow to give a guard the telephone number of his outside drug contact named Dennis, who, in fact, was the police lieutenant with the task force. Then, under the plan, when a guard called Dennis at Barlow's request, a meeting time and place would be arranged and Dennis would give the guard two ounces of marijuana to deliver to Barlow in the prison together with $100 for the guard's services.

Barlow approached the defendant and first suggested the subject of smuggling marijuana into the prison for him. He testified that defendant agreed to bring the drug into the prison for him after deliberating for only an hour or two, and that there was no pressure or threat of physical or emotional harm exerted upon her. According to the defendant's version of how she was recruited into the scheme, Barlow approached her two or three times a week for a month, begging her to bring in drugs, but she rejected all of his pleas. Defendant related that Barlow would give her the telephone number of his contact on the outside to call, and she would lose it or tear it up, and he would write it out and give it to her again and again. The defendant further testified that she did not inform prison authorities of Barlow's behavior because she knew from experience that he could be punished severely and because he told her the second time she brought the drug into the prison for Barlow that, since he had promised it to other prisoners, she had to do it again for him or else he would be beaten up by the others for not delivering the drugs as promised.

The police lieutenant (Dennis) testified that, after the defendant telephoned him twice, three meetings were arranged: one at a public rest stop on a main highway near Smyrna; another at a restaurant on the same highway; and the third at the defendant's home near Smyrna. The officer stated that the defendant appeared nervous and on each occasion was given the opportunity to withdraw, but that she declined each time, stating that she wished to go through with the delivery. The lieutenant added that on two such occasions (separated by about a month) defendant received two ounces of marijuana and $100, delivered the drug to Barlow in the prison,[2] and he, in turn, returned the drug to the police. The police officer testified that at no point did he exert force or pressure of any kind upon the defendant. . . .

III

The defendant contests the denial of her motion [to set aside the jury's verdict] on three grounds: 1) that she was entrapped as a matter of law; 2) that she was denied due process of law through a conviction based upon overreaching and outrageous police conduct; and 3) that there was no evidence to show that she was predisposed to commit the crimes charged. . . .

IV

. . . The defendant bases her position that she was entrapped as a matter of law upon a series of "objective test" cases standing for the proposition that entrapment exists as a matter of law where government agents furnish contraband to a defendant, who, in turn, sells it to another government agent or other third person.

We find, however, that especially by virtue of §432 this Court does not have the discretion, exercised in the "objective test" cases, to apply "a 'chancellor's foot' veto over law enforcement practices of which" we may not approve. . . .

By the explicit language of §432, the legislative intent is made clear and unambiguous: Entrapment is a defense where there exists "wrongdoing of the officer [who] originates the idea of the crime and then induces the other person to engage in conduct constituting such

---

2. The defendant devised the procedure for delivery to Barlow: She took the drugs into the Correctional Institution, and hid them under a heater in the guard's bathroom. Thereafter, she informed Barlow and unlocked the door so that he could retrieve them.

a crime when the other person is not otherwise disposed to do so." Thus, the test for entrapment under the statute requires us to focus on the predisposition of the defendant and on the conduct of the government agents. . . . [W]e believe that the entrapment defense of §432 is a factual question which is strictly within the province of the jury, which must be proved by defendant under a preponderance of the evidence standard. In light of the language of §432 and the general principles set forth above, we hold that the circumstances at Bar do not amount to entrapment as a matter of law. Accordingly, the Trial Court was correct in denying the defendant's motion to set aside the verdict on that ground.

V

There remain defendant's second and third arguments to consider. We deal first with the latter.

Defendant maintains that there was no evidence to show that she was predisposed to commit the offenses charged. Defendant relies on *West*, [stating the Third Circuit Rule] in support of her claim that "the relevant predisposition" is the attitude of an accused "just before the government agent enlisted [her] participation in the venture." The evidence at trial showed that defendant brought food into the prison and gave it to inmates on numerous occasions. Under prison rules, food brought into the compound from outside is technically contraband. Applying the Third Circuit rule for establishing predisposition, defendant can fairly be said to have been predisposed to violate a prison rule and a statute forbidding the introduction of contraband into a prison. We recognize, however, that defendant's conduct in giving inmates left-over portions of her lunch is a slim reed upon which to find predisposition and rest her convictions for the offenses charged, and an insufficient one as a matter of law.

The Third Circuit test for predisposition is a useful tool for determining an accused's proclivity toward commission of a criminal act. Certainly a defendant's conduct "just before a government agent enlisted his participation in the venture" is relevant to a determination of a defendant's predisposition. However, we are disturbed by a test which confines the scope of focus wholly on the issue of predisposition to the time period "just before" the police solicited defendant to participate in the criminal scheme. The application of the rule in *West* would provide an entrapment defense to every individual who establishes an unblemished personal record prior to being approached to commit a crime. Furthermore, it is often the case that "the sole proof of predisposition consists of evidence as to what the defendant did on the occasion in question, in response to the overtures of the government agents." Hence, we believe that the interval between the solicitation and the actual commission of the offense is highly significant on the question of predisposition because it is within that time period that an accused may exhibit manifestations of his propensity for a specific crime which might not appear were it not for the State's initial enlistment of the defendant's participation.

Thus, we hold that the point of reference for ascertaining the predisposition of a defendant to commit a particular crime is the time period extending from just before the State's solicitation to just before the defendant's commission of the crime.

Under this test, we find that defendant was predisposed to commit the crimes charged. Defendant was approached by Barlow to secure and deliver drugs to him. By her own admission, without pressure or threat, defendant agreed to participate in the scheme. As planned, defendant called Officer Williams ("Dennis") and scheduled a meeting. Although nervous, she agreed to smuggle drugs into the prison even though she was twice given the opportunity to withdraw from the arrangement by Officer Williams. At the second and third meetings, defendant was more relaxed about the transactions. No pressure or force was exerted upon her to continue with the plan, yet she smuggled the drugs into the prison and accepted the bribes on two occasions separated by almost a month. Defendant conceded that she knew it was wrong to smuggle the marijuana into the institution yet she persisted in continuing the plan. Such evidence was sufficient to indicate that the defendant was predisposed to violate the law before she actually committed the offenses.

VI

Our inquiry does not end here. Pursuant to §432 and the apparent majority position of the United States Supreme Court, we must address the character of the State's inducement. If it was, as the defendant alleges, so outrageous and overreaching as to violate the right to due process, or if the police conduct was "intolerable" and went "beyond that necessary to sustain an entrapment defense," then her conviction cannot stand, notwithstanding our finding that she was predisposed to violate the law. . . .

While the exact boundaries for permissible and impermissible government conduct within the bounds of due process in the context of entrapment have not yet been set by the United States Supreme Court, we do not believe that the conduct of the police in the instant case rises to the level of a due process violation. The defendant was given the opportunity to withdraw on several occasions. The record is devoid of evidence of overbearing, pressure, threat or force exerted upon defendant to secure her cooperation. The police merely presented her with an opportunity for crime which she seized.

Courts must look to the nature of the crime and the means available to law enforcement officials to combat it in deciding whether police conduct violates due process. Illicit trafficking in narcotics presents special problems of proof, detection and danger for law enforcement personnel. Many times the only way for police to combat such crime is to set up an operation similar to the one *sub judice*. This is especially so when the setting for the drug trafficking is a State prison. To hold that the conduct of the State Police in this matter was overreaching and injurious to defendant's due process right would be to deprive our law enforcement officers of an effective tool for stamping out crime, and we decline to do so.

Invocation of an "entrapment" defense conjures up notions of tricky policemen trying to prey upon the needs and weaknesses of people and to persuade innocent citizens to commit crimes, when the police ought to be spending their time catching real criminals. We certainly agree that the police should not buy crimes and, if that were all there were to this case, it should be reversed.

Here, however, contraband, including drugs, was getting into the prison and the job of the police was to stop it. When the police gave defendant an opportunity to smuggle in drugs, she took it, did it twice (for a price) and got caught.

Since it is undisputed that the police originated the idea, inducement was the critical issue at trial. That is a factual question (was defendant persuaded by the police to do what she did?) and the jury, after hearing all of the facts, concluded that defendant was not induced to do what she was not otherwise disposed to do.

Certainly there was plenty of evidence from which the jury could conclude that defendant was not "induced": She was not under police observation during the times she took the contraband into the prison, she figured out how to do that and, significantly, she also worked out the scheme for delivering the drugs to Barlow within the prison. She (admittedly) had ample opportunity to back out, not only from the beginning but also while she acted alone, taking the drugs into the prison and making delivery. And she did all of that, not once, but twice, some three weeks apart. To the extent that "pre-disposition" is significant, completion of the first delivery at least shows that defendant was disposed to do it again.

The case presents a hard question in the administration of justice. There surely are limits to which the police may go and at which even good faith efforts to enforce the law (and protect society) transmutes into an entrapment which, as a matter of law, violates due process. But here, it should be noted, the offenses which were basic to defendant's criminal conduct ("promoting prison contraband . . . [by] . . . knowingly and unlawfully . . . [introducing] contraband into a detention facility," 11 Del.C. §1256, and the delivery of a "controlled substance," 16 Del.C. §4752, (marijuana)) involved her conduct while she was completely free from contemporaneous police persuasion. Factually, as the jury found, there was no "inducement" at that time. In the instant case, then, the State Police did not transgress the boundaries of permissible police practice in violation of due process.

Accordingly, the Superior Court's denial of the defendant's motion to set aside the jury's verdict of guilty is hereby

Affirmed.

QUILLEN, Justice, dissenting:

I confess shock at the absence of a clear federal constitutional restriction on the material inducement that a law enforcement officer or his agent can offer to another to get the other to commit a crime. While some of the same considerations are present, the question of a constitutional restriction is necessarily entirely separate from any legislative or common law intent as to the defense of entrapment. The independence arises necessarily from the language of the Fourteenth Amendment, "nor shall any State deprive any person of life, liberty, or property, without due process of law." The United States Supreme Court has said:

> Judicial review of that guaranty of the Fourteenth Amendment inescapably imposes upon this Court an exercise of judgment upon the whole course of the proceedings in order to ascertain whether they offend those canons of decency and fairness which express the notions of justice of English-speaking peoples even toward those charged with the most heinous offenses.

That is a different question than the question of legislative intent in the defense of entrapment.

I recognize that abuse is rampant in defense claims of entrapment. I also recognize that the recent, well publicized, despicable conduct of certain public officials in the ABSCAM cases has made entrapment-related defenses particularly unpopular nationally. Nor can I disagree with the majority here as to our particular statutory defense of entrapment. The history of the statute and the placing of the burden of proof on the defendant in the affirmative defense classification demonstrate the factual nature of the inquiry into the origin, inducement and disposition issues.

But I would have thought, given the frailty of mankind, that one difference between our society and totalitarian societies would be a constitutional recognition that government should not have the power to extend limitless temptation to make the average citizen a criminal, subject, at the State's discretion, to the loss of liberty and property.[4] We have enough crime without giving the State unlimited power to buy more. In other societies, particularly the Soviet Union, government sponsored corruption and related selective law enforcement are used as a means to perpetuate State subjugation of the citizenry. Under such a system everyone becomes subject to prosecution at the whim of the State. Failure to clearly recognize a similar potential evil in State sponsored crime in the entrapment context, in my opinion, is a glaring void in our constitutional case law. There is something fundamental at stake. . . .

In the instant case, I would reserve jurisdiction and remand the case to the Trial Judge to conduct a due process hearing and to make the necessary findings of fact and rulings of law. Thus, I would require a due process focus by the Trial Judge before rendering appellate judgment. By this separate opinion, I do not intend to suggest what the result of that focus would or should be in this case.

Model Penal Code §2.13
Entrapment

(1) A public law enforcement official or a person acting in cooperation with such an official perpetrates an entrapment if for the purpose of obtaining evidence of the commission of an offense, he induces or encourages another person to engage in conduct constituting such offense by either:

(a) making knowingly false representations designed to induce the belief that such conduct is not prohibited; or

(b) employing methods of persuasion or inducement which create a substantial risk that such an offense will be committed by persons other than those who are ready to commit it.

(2) Except as provided in Subsection (3) of this Section, a person prosecuted for an offense shall be acquitted if he proves by a preponderance of evidence that his conduct occurred in response to an entrap-

---

4. It is not a complete answer, in my opinion, to say that people should not commit crimes. Besides normal human sinfulness in face of monetary reward, there can be weakness due to numerous pressing variables such as illness in the family, overwhelming educational expenses or, in the case of a prison guard, limited salary and limited opportunity for advancement in a difficult work environment. These factors do not justify crime but, absent justification, it should not be the State that preys on the citizen's weakness.

ment. The issue of entrapment shall be tried by the Court in the absence of the jury.

(3) The defense afforded by this Section is unavailable when causing or threatening bodily injury is an element of the offense charged and the prosecution is based on conduct causing or threatening such injury to a person other than the person perpetrating the entrapment.

Questions

1. *Entrapment vs. Due Process Defense.* In Part VI of the majority opinion in *Harrison* and in the dissenting opinion, the court recognizes the existence of a constitutional defense for outrageous and overreaching police conduct, under the due process clause, which is related to but different from entrapment. How is this defense similar to and how is it different from the entrapment defense under the Delaware statute?

2. *Objective and Subjective Formulations of Entrapment.* How is the entrapment defense in the Delaware Code different from the entrapment defense in the Model Penal Code? These two kinds of formulations have been described as "subjective" and "objective" formulations. Which statute is which, and why might they have been given these labels?

3. *JJ's Liability.* Would JJ have a defense under the Delaware formulation? Under the Model Penal Code formulation?

United States v. Perl
United States Court of Appeals, Fourth Circuit
584 F.2d 1316 (1978)

WINTER, Circuit Judge:

William R. Perl was convicted of willfully attempting to damage property utilized by foreign officials in violation of 18 U.S.C. §970, of unlawfully receiving a firearm purchased outside the State of Maryland in violation of 18 U.S.C. §922(a)(3), and of conspiring with unknown persons to commit these crimes in violation of 18 U.S.C. §371. He was fined $12,000, given a two-year suspended sentence, and placed on three years' supervised probation. On appeal he urges a number of grounds of reversal, principally that the district court erroneously declined to give an entrapment instruction . . . and that it prejudicially confused the jury by its instructions on the conspiracy count. We agree that there was reversible error in the conspiracy conviction. . . . We therefore reverse defendant's conviction on the conspiracy count and award him a new trial. As to defendant's other contentions, however, we find no error and therefore affirm his conviction on both substantive counts.

The defendant, Dr. William R. Perl, has long been active in Jewish affairs, both in Europe and in this country, and, as a survivor of the Nazi persecutions, he has been particularly concerned about the welfare of Jews living in the Soviet Union. Among the organizations in which he has been active is the Jewish Defense League (JDL). He was a founder of the Washington, D.C., chapter of that organization and, at the time that the events material to the instant case commenced, was serving as its president. Both he and the Washington Chapter have a reputation for non-violence.

Sometime in 1973, an Israeli expatriate named Reuven Lev-tov attended a meeting of the Washington Chapter of the JDL held at the home of Dr. Perl. By all accounts, Reuven Lev-tov was and is a shadowy and intriguing figure. After ten years in the Israeli Navy, where he was a member of its elite "special forces," Lev-tov joined the Israeli foreign service and was assigned duty at the Israeli embassy in Washington as chauffeur and apparent bodyguard to the ambassador. In 1965, he married an American citizen and shortly thereafter was dismissed from service at the Israeli Embassy. In 1968, he returned to Israel for a three-year period before settling permanently in this country in 1971. He subsequently became a specialist in electrolysis, maintaining an office in Washington, D.C. Recently, he renounced his Israeli citizenship, after having become an American citizen some ten years earlier.

At trial, Lev-tov testified that by 1973 he had come to feel bad about acts of terrorism perpetrated in the name of various Jewish causes and became determined to take some action to combat its spread. To this end, he conceived a plan to induce a leading Jewish figure to join him in committing some violent act. Before the commission of the act, however, it was Lev-tov's intention to turn his accomplice over to the authorities. He apparently chose as his victim Dr. Perl and, with this plan in mind, attended the 1973 JDL meeting at Dr. Perl's home.

At the conclusion of this meeting, Lev-tov managed to engage Dr. Perl in private conversation. Lev-tov made known his own concern for the plight of Soviet Jews and his availability to help carry out any act of violence suitable to Dr. Perl. Dr. Perl gave Lev-tov no encouragement, stating, according to Lev-tov, that "we don't do things like that here in Washington."

Nothing more occurred until the spring of 1976, by which time Dr. Perl had developed Parkinson's Disease and was under constant medication. On April 10, 1976, Dr. Perl and Lev-tov met at a motel in the Maryland suburbs and agreed that an appropriate form of protest would be to shoot out the windows of the apartments of two Soviet officials living in Prince George's County, Maryland. It was agreed that

CHAPTER 17   NONEXCULPATORY DEFENSES   621

Lev-tov would do the actual shooting and that Dr. Perl would publicize the event and announce that it was the responsibility of the JDL. At a subsequent meeting, it was agreed that Dr. Perl would also supply the weapon and ammunition. Dr. Perl then took steps to obtain a rifle from JDL sources in New York. He was successful in these efforts and, on May 6, turned the weapon over to Lev-tov, and, on May 7, the ammunition to fire it. May 23, a Sunday, was fixed as the date for the shooting.

On May 19, Lev-tov went to the Israeli Embassy, there telling an official that he had been asked to shoot out the windows of two apartments belonging to Soviet officials. He was advised to contact "the authorities." However, before Lev-tov could make such contact he was approached at his office by two FBI agents who had been alerted to the situation by an attache at the Israeli Embassy. Lev-tov made a detailed statement to the agents concerning his association with Dr. Perl, and it was agreed that Lev-tov would continue with the plan. He was instructed to wear a body recorder at his next meeting with Dr. Perl, which was to take place on May 22. The recording was later introduced as evidence against Dr. Perl at trial. On May 23, the planned shooting was carried out with a weapon and blanks provided by the FBI.

On June 29, 1976, Dr. Perl was indicted for his role in the incident. Trial was held in November, 1976. Dr. Perl was convicted on three of the four counts on which he was charged, and this appeal followed.

Dr. Perl freely admits that he participated in the plan to shoot out the windows of the Soviet officials and that he provided Lev-tov a weapon for this purpose. At trial, his only defense was that he was entrapped by Lev-tov and that, therefore, no criminal liability should attach. In keeping with this theory of the case, the defense proposed three alternative entrapment instructions to the district court. The trial court rejected all three, instructing the jury flatly that "entrapment is not a defense in this case."

On appeal, defendant . . . contends that government involvement in the scheme to entrap should not be treated as a necessary element in the federal defense of entrapment and urges us to adopt this as the law of this circuit. . . . We do not agree with [the] contention.

The cases are legion which either hold directly or state as dictum that "[e]ntrapment cannot result from the inducements of a private citizen but must be the product of conduct by governmental agents."*

---

*Editor's Note.—For example, State v. Jackson, 243 N.C. 216, 90 S.E.2d 507, 510 (1955), concludes:

> It would be unconscionable and contrary to public policy and good morals to punish a man for the commission of an offense of which he would not have been guilty, in thought or deed, and would not have committed, if he had not been entrapped into committing the crime by officers or agents of the state or government, which is prosecuting him. On the other hand, to hold that entrapment is a defense under such circumstances when the inducement comes from a third party unconnected with the State, would gravely imperil the proper enforce-

On numerous occasions this court, without ever directly so holding, has clearly expressed its view that federal law does not recognize the defense of private entrapment.

Despite this vast array of precedent, defendant urges us to recognize a private-entrapment defense. Under defendant's theory, no showing of government involvement in the scheme to entrap need be made if there otherwise exists evidence that defendant was "induced to commit a crime he had no predisposition to commit solely and exclusively in order to have him handed over to the authorities." Defendant's Proposed Instruction No. 23. . . . In view of [the] longstanding and authoritative interpretation of legislative intent [requiring *government* entrapment], we hold that a defendant, in order to assert the defense of entrapment in a federal prosecution, must produce evidence of government involvement in the scheme to entrap. We therefore affirm the district court's rejection of defendant's private entrapment instruction.[3] . . .

Affirmed In Part; Reversed In Part; New Trial Awarded.

Questions

1. *Entrapment and Excuse Defenses.* How is the entrapment defense similar to an excuse defense, such as duress? How is it different? Which of the two kinds of entrapment formulations is most like an excuse defense? How is that formulation different from an excuse? The early federal entrapment cases spoke of the subjective formulation as if it were an excuse. Recall the *Durham* "product" test for insanity, overruled

---

ment of the criminal law. For instance, if two defendants committed burglary, and one could satisfy the jury that he was entrapped into committing the crime by his codefendant, he would go scot free.

3. By government involvement, we mean involvement of federal, state or local law enforcement officials or their agents. We do not mean involvement by agents of a foreign government. One of defendant's three proposed entrapment instructions provided that the "defense of entrapment is open to the defendant . . . if [Lev-tov] was at [the time of entrapment] working on behalf of the Israeli government, if the Israeli government intended to turn Dr. Perl over to American law enforcement authorities." As we view it, the principal purpose of the entrapment defense as it has developed in the federal courts is to deter official misconduct in the investigation of criminal activity. As we have elsewhere said: "The defense of entrapment rests on the premise that the purpose of *law enforcement* is the prevention, not the manufacture, of crime." This purpose would no more be served by extending the doctrine to include entrapment by foreign agents than it would be by extending the defense to include entrapment by private citizens. The district court, in our view, correctly rejected defendant's proposed instruction on foreign entrapment.

by the U.S. Court of Appeals for the D.C. Circuit in *Brawner*, discussed in Section 16.2. Would the subjective formulation of the entrapment defense qualify as an excuse under the *Durham* theory of excuse, which required only a "but for" causal connection between the disability and the offense?

2. *Private and Foreign Entrapment.* As the *Perl* case illustrates, a defense of private entrapment generally is rejected (as is a defense of entrapment by an agent of a foreign government, see footnote 3). What, if anything, does this say about whether entrapment is an excuse?

3. *Entrapment and Nonexculpatory Defenses.* What arguments can you make that entrapment is a nonexculpatory defense? If it is a nonexculpatory defense, what are the competing societal interests that give rise to the defense? Which of the two major formulations of the defense is likely to be more effective at deterring improper police conduct? Which of the two formulations is likely to let more blameworthy offenders go free?

V/CHANGING NOTIONS OF CRIME

The interaction between the criminal law and social norms is complex. As norms change, so should the criminal law. Recent waves of reform of sexual offense formulations reflect this dynamic. Many believe that influence should travel in the other direction as well, that the criminal law should change social norms where needed. Presumably this occurs where the legislature is enlightened by other than general public sentiment. In a democracy, this second dynamic is more tenuous, in part because legislatures generally are representative of the communities that they represent and, therefore, are not inclined to get too far ahead of their constituents' views.

Also limiting the law's ability to shape societal norms are the practical limits of the criminal law's power. To change public views, the law must communicate clearly with the community, yet the average person knows little of what law books say and the message of the law often is scrambled when conveyed through news reports of its application in individual cases. The law's ability to shape community views also is limited by its moral credibility with the community. For example, if the law is seen to punish persons who do not deserve it and to fail to punish persons who do deserve it, it may not be viewed as a persuasive source of moral authority.

Some sexual offense reforms not only reflect changing norms but attempt to change norms further. They are calculated to make people think differently about what is and is not acceptable conduct. Hate crimes serve the same dual function. Their advent may reflect both increased sensitivity to the dangers of intolerance and an attempt to create still greater public awareness.

A third motivation for criminal law reform is neither keeping up with changing social norms nor attempts to change social norms, but rather a practical response to changing crime patterns. Both sexual offense reforms and hate crime legislation may be driven in part by legislative perception that such victimization is increasing. But RICO legislation is premised almost exclusively on the need to combat a form of harmful activity not deterred by previous law. The criminalization of racketeer influenced and corrupt organizations represents a form of liability dramatically different from the traditional, a form calculated specifically to make feasible the prosecution of organized crime figures who have been able to escape liability under conventional offenses.

Chapter 18. SEXUAL OFFENSES

Bob and Linda

Steve and Bob, both over six feet tall and powerfully built, are teammates on the football team and good friends. After a game, Steve and Bob's locker room chatter turns to Linda. Bob and Linda have been dating ever since Linda broke up with Steve. Bob explains how very much he likes Linda. Steve agrees, Linda was great to date and a lot of fun. "Great in bed, isn't she?" Steve says. Bob looks sheepish and does not respond. Steve laughs. "So you haven't been to bed with her. I'm not surprised. Linda is a real nice girl. I had to push her into it a little the first time but she really loved it and never gave me a rest after that." Bob winces inside. He doesn't like thinking about Steve and Linda together and he isn't the type to push.

Bob is serious about Linda and that night plans to suggest that they move in together. He picks up Linda at her apartment. They have a quick bite to eat, go to a movie, and then to Bob's apartment where they talk for several hours. Bob tells Linda of his feelings for her and asks whether she would like it if they moved in together next week. Linda says she would like that, and Bob is thrilled. They hug and kiss and Bob begins fondling Linda, who responds by caressing Bob. They both slide to a reclining position on the couch, with Bob on top. Bob begins to unbutton Linda's blouse. "Let's make love," he says. Linda keeps hugging and caressing Bob but whispers in his ear, "That's a nice idea, but I don't know if we should. Why don't we wait until next week?" Bob whispers back, "I love you so much. I just can't wait." He undoes his own pants and takes them off. Linda continues to rub his back from a reclining position as he does so. Bob then pulls Linda's dress up and pulls her underpants down and off. "I'm not sure that this is a good idea, Bob," Linda says. "Let's wait till next week." Bob lies on Linda and has intercourse with her. Linda lies still and does not move. When Bob gets off her, Linda stands up, puts her underpants on, and says in a quiet voice, "I really didn't want to do that now, Bob. Why couldn't you have waited till next week?" Bob is surprised to see that Linda is angry with him. "I'm sorry. I thought you really wanted to." "You thought wrong," says Linda with obvious irritation. "I guess I just got carried away," Bob responds, afraid that he has hurt Linda. "I'm sorry. I promise it won't happen again." "I'm not sure that I want to have to worry about that," Linda responds. "I have to think more about whether we should move in together." She insists that Bob drive her home immediately.

Bob is heartbroken. He is angry with himself for not paying more attention to Linda's feelings and hopes that she will give him another chance to show that he loves her very much and wouldn't intentionally hurt her in any way. He feels worse when Linda stops by the following day to tell him that she has decided not to move in with him. He sees Linda in classes during the next few weeks, but she declines his invitations to go out. Three weeks after their date, police knock at Bob's door, and take him into custody. He learns at the police station that Linda has accused him of rape. Is he criminally liable?

Model Penal Code §213.1
Rape and Related Offenses

(1) *Rape.* A male who has sexual intercourse* with a female not his wife is guilty of rape if:

(a) he compels her to submit by force or by threat of imminent death, serious bodily injury, extreme pain or kidnapping, to be inflicted on anyone; or

(b) he has substantially impaired her power to appraise or control her conduct by administering or employing without her knowledge drugs, intoxicants or other means for the purpose of preventing resistance; or

(c) the female is unconscious; or

(d) the female is less than 10 years old.

Rape is a felony of the second degree unless (i) in the course thereof the actor inflicts serious bodily injury upon anyone, or (ii) the victim was not a voluntary social companion of the actor upon the occasion of the crime and had not previously permitted him sexual liberties, in which cases the offense is a felony of the first degree.

---

*Editor's Note.—Model Penal Code §213.0(2) provides: " 'Sexual intercourse' includes intercourse per os or per anum, with some penetration however slight; emission is not required."

CHAPTER 18 SEXUAL OFFENSES   629

(2) *Gross Sexual Imposition.* A male who has sexual intercourse with a female not his wife commits a felony of the third degree if:

(a) he compels her to submit by any threat that would prevent resistance by a woman of ordinary resolution; or

(b) he knows that she suffers from a mental disease or defect which renders her incapable of appraising the nature of her conduct; or

(c) he knows that she is unaware that a sexual act is being committed upon her or that she submits because she mistakenly supposes that he is her husband.

Questions

1. *Resistance.* At one time it was required that the victim of a rape must "resist to the utmost" if the attacker is to be held liable. That requirement generally has been abandoned; at most, only "reasonable resistance" is required. Did Bob use force to compel intercourse with Linda? Did Linda offer reasonable resistance? Some modern statutes expressly provide that the victim need not have resisted. See, e.g., Mich. Pen. Code §750.5201.

2. *The Threat Requirement.* The Model Penal Code criminalizes intercourse that is compelled by force or a threat to cause certain serious harms, §213.1(1)(a) (rape), or that is compelled by "any threat that would prevent resistance by a woman of ordinary resolution," §213.1(2)(a) (gross sexual imposition). Thus the victim need not resist at all, and perhaps thereby invite additional harm, if the threat is such that we would not expect her to resist. The standard here is not terribly precise: It asks what the woman of ordinary resolution would have done. On the other hand, such an objective standard is not unusual in criminal law. Recall that the definitions of negligence and recklessness, §2.02(2)(c) & (d), and the extreme emotional disturbance mitigation in homicide, §210.3(1)(b), use similarly general language designed to adopt an objective standard of sorts. Additionally, such a standard is used in defining the coercion sufficient to provide an actor a duress defense: a threat to use force "which a person of reasonable firmness in his situation would have been unable to resist," §2.09(1). As with all objective standards, a certain vagueness exists. It will not always be clear what constitutes a "threat that would prevent resistance by a woman of ordinary resolution." Might it be gross sexual imposition to induce intercourse by threatening to refuse a visa to the victim to visit her dying elderly parents? Might it be gross sexual imposition to induce

intercourse by refusing to sell the victim a family heirloom that her parents once owned?

3. *Individualize the Objective Standard of an Adequate Threat?* The objective standard used in the Model Penal Code—a "threat that would prevent resistance by a woman of ordinary resolution"—does differ from other objective standards in the Code in that the phrase "in the actor's situation" is missing. We saw that this phrase was the central means by which the objective standard was individualized. Thus the mildly retarded defendant, who is more susceptible to intimidation than the average person, might gain a duress defense where a nonretarded defendant in the same situation would not. In the context of resistance to rape, should we take account of the differences in a victim's "situation" in judging whether the threat is sufficient for liability? Should it matter, for example, that the victim is mildly retarded and significantly overestimates the seriousness of the threat or that the victim recently had been raped?

Is the issue here different from the other uses of objective standards because it is not the criminal liability of the victim that is at issue but rather liability of the attacker? That is, might we want to take account of the victim's "situation" if we were judging the blameworthiness of the victim's conduct but not if we are judging the blameworthiness of the actor's conduct? Would it matter in judging Bob's liability if, unknown to him, Linda had been raped previously and, because of that experience, reacted to the situation in a way different from that in which the ordinary woman would have?

4. *Threats Other Than of Violence.* Some jurisdictions require that the defendant use or threaten violence to gain compliance. E.g., Ill. Crim Code §12-13(1). The Model Penal Code aggravates the grade of the violation for threats of serious injury—this is the difference between rape and gross sexual imposition under the Code—but does not require a threat of violence for criminal liability. Any kind of threat will support liability under the Code if it is sufficiently coercive, "any threat that would prevent resistance by a woman of ordinary resolution." Thus, it might be rape ("gross sexual imposition" under the Code's terminology) for an employer to compel intercourse by threatening to fire an employee if she does not have intercourse. Assume that a state drops both a requirement of a threat of violence, as Illinois has, and a requirement that the coercion be of a given kind or amount, as the Model Penal Code has. That is, it defines criminal sexual conduct to require simply that "force or coercion is used to accomplish the sexual penetration." Mich. Pen. Code §750.520d(1)(b). Does this mean that any amount of coercion is sufficient? What arguments can one make for and against criminalizing sexual conduct upon any amount of coercion?

5. *Coercion vs. Bargain.* The Model Penal Code drafters express concern that a broad definition of an adequate threat would create a

danger of "extending the prospect of criminal sanctions into the shadow area between coercion and bargain."

> To take an extreme example, the man who "threatens" to withhold an expensive present unless his girlfriend permits his advances is plainly not a fit subject for punishment under the law of rape.

Model Penal Code §213.1 comment 312 (1980). To account for this potential overcriminalization, the Code limits the offense in several respects. As noted above, the threat must meet an objective standard: It must be such as would prevent resistance "by a woman of ordinary resolution." The drafters explain:

> The concept . . . achieves the essential purpose of eliminating cases of intimidation by threat of remote or trivial harm. Thus, for example, the policeman who persuades a woman to submit to intercourse rather than to accept a parking ticket may be guilty of some minor abuse of office, but he should not be subject to felony sanctions for gross sexual imposition. Similarly, a man who threatens to destroy an inexpensive object unless its owner agrees to sexual relations should not be guilty of this offense. These results are entirely appropriate, for it is virtually impossible to find genuine coercion in such situations. The absence of coercion arises not from the nature of the threat but simply from its triviality. In each of the hypotheticals, the male may make the plausible assumption that the woman's acquiescence has as much to do with his own attractiveness as with the prospect of threatened harm. In terms of blameworthiness and of dangerousness to society, he is not comparable to the male who compels submission by some threat generally sufficient to overcome the resistance of a woman of ordinary resolution.

Id. at 313. The drafters also note that, the statutory requirement of "compels to submit" is intended to require that submission result from coercion rather than bargain. The commentary explains:

> This inquiry into the essential character of the threat is distinct from, though complementary to, the requirement that it achieve a gravity sufficient to "prevent resistance by a woman of ordinary resolution." Thus, if a wealthy man were to threaten to withdraw financial support from his unemployed girlfriend, it is at least arguable under the circumstances that he is making a threat "that would prevent resistance by a woman of ordinary resolution." The reason why this case is excluded from liability . . . is not the gravity of the harm threatened—it may be quite substantial—but its essential character as part of a process of bargain. He is not guilty of compulsion overwhelming the will of his victim but only of offering her an unattractive choice to avoid some unwanted alternative.

Id. at 314.

Assume that Linda wants very much to move in with Bob and agrees to intercourse only because she is afraid that, if she does not, Bob will change his mind about moving in together. Is her consent invalid and is Bob then criminally liable for the resulting intercourse? Assume that Linda works for Bob and, while Bob has never said anything that suggests it, that Linda is afraid that if she does not agree to sleep with Bob she will not get the promotion that several people in the office are competing for. Is Bob criminally liable for the resulting intercourse? Assume that employer Bob presses Linda to sleep with him but does not say what will happen if she does not agree. Because Linda fears losing her job if she does not, she agrees. Is Bob criminally liable for the resulting intercourse?

6. *Why Require Coercion?* Why have a threat or coercion requirement at all? It is true that other offenses, such as robbery, have a threat requirement, and require threats of a certain seriousness. See, e.g., Model Penal Code §222.1(1). But typically this serves a grading function. Theft (taking property without consent) is an offense, under Model Penal Code §223.2(1), and making a threat of violence is an offense, under Model Penal Code §211.3. Robbery serves only to aggravate the grade of the violation when property is taken under a threat of violence. Why is not the same true for unconsented-to intercourse? Why not aggravate the grade of the violation where achieved through use or threat of violence or other improper coercion, but nonetheless criminalize unconsented-to intercourse even in the absence of such coercion? Consider the following provisions:

> *Third Degree Sexual Assault.* Whoever has sexual intercourse with a person without the consent of that person is guilty of a Class D felony.
> *Consent.* "Consent," as used in this section, means words or overt actions by a person who is competent to give informed consent indicating a freely given agreement to have sexual intercourse. . . .

Wis. Stat. Ann. §940.225(3) & (4). Did Linda consent to intercourse, under the Wisconsin definition of consent? Is Bob liable for Third Degree Sexual Assault under the Wisconsin statute? Should he be?

7. *Bargain vs. Coercion under the Without-Consent Formulation.* What does the Wisconsin statute mean by "a *freely given* agreement to have sexual intercourse"? If the victim agreed by words and overt actions, could the defendant nonetheless be liable if the victim was *induced* to agree? Could the inducement be in the form of either coercion or bargain? Where the wealthy man induces agreement to intercourse by threatening to withdraw financial support from his unemployed girlfriend, is her agreement "freely given" under the Wisconsin statute? What position, if any, has the Wisconsin statute taken in distinguishing unlawful *coercion* from permissible *bargain*?

8. *The Model Penal Code and the Without-Consent Formulation.* The Model Penal Code drafters consider and expressly reject the use of nonconsent in place of coercion:

> [O]veremphasis on non-consent can be troublesome. . . . Evidentiary considerations aside, consent appears to be a conceptually simple issue. Either the female assented to intercourse, or she did not. Searching for consent in a particular case, however, may reveal depths of ambiguity and contradiction that are scarcely suspected when the question is put in the abstract. Often the woman's attitude may be deeply ambivalent. She may not want intercourse, may fear it, or may desire it but feel compelled to say "no." Her confusion at the time of the act may later resolve into non-consent. Some have expressed the fear that a woman who subconsciously wanted to have sexual intercourse will later feel guilty and "cry rape." It seems plain, on the other hand, that a barrage of conflicting emotions at the time of the assault does not necessarily imply the victim's consent, although it may lead to misperception by the actor. Further ambiguity may be introduced by the fact that the woman may appear to consent because she is frozen by fear and panic, or because she quite rationally decides to "consent" rather than risk being killed or injured.
>
> The point, in any event, is that inquiry into the victim's subjective state of mind and the attacker's perceptions of her state of mind often will not yield a clear answer. The deceptively simple notion of consent may obscure a tangled mesh of psychological complexity, ambiguous communication, and unconscious restructuring of the event by the participants. Courts have not been oblivious to this difficulty, but in attempting to resolve it they have often placed disproportionate emphasis upon objective manifestations of non-consent by the woman. It seems plain that some courts have gone too far in this direction, although it is equally plain that one can go too far in the opposite direction.

Model Penal Code §213.1 comment 302-303 (1980). Are the drafters concerned that the "complexity" of the situation means that the victim will not know whether she herself has consented or that the defendant will not know whether she (the victim) has consented? Which is relevant to the defendant's criminal liability? If it is the latter, what is the effect of such complexity on proof that the defendant had the required culpability as to nonconsent?

9. *Culpability as to Coercion or Nonconsent.* If Linda in fact was not consenting to intercourse, would it matter if Bob thought that she was consenting? Assume a defendant improperly coerces a victim but does not realize that he is doing so. The victim does not consent but the defendant mistakenly believes that she does. Is the defendant liable? Such mistakes may not be an unusual situation if the feminist literature is correct that men and women often see different things in the same conduct and may mean different things by the same conduct.

[A] gender gap in sexual communications exists. Men and women frequently misinterpret the intent of various dating behaviors and erotic play engaged in by their opposite-sexed partners. . . . The man of "reasonable prudence and intelligence" in our society may not actively seek overt consent because he may assume that a nonconsenting woman will make her lack of consent known. A reasonable woman, however, may perceive certain behavior as indicating that the man plans to have sex with her whether she consents or not, although the man may not have meant to communicate such an intent.

Robin D. Wiener, Shifting the Communication Burden: A Meaningful Consent Standard in Rape, 6 Harv. Woman's L.J. 143, 147-148 (1983).

If the normal rules of criminal liability are applied to sexual offenses, liability will be imposed only if an actor is found to have been culpable as to applying coercion or as to the victim's lack of consent. Model Penal Code §2.02(3) presumably requires that the actor be at least reckless as to coercing the victim and as to whether his coercion is such as "would prevent resistance by a woman of ordinary resolution." That is, he must disregard a substantial risk that his conduct would have this effect. If it were an offense to have intercourse without the victim's consent, as it is in Wisconsin, and culpability were required as to Linda's lack of consent, would an actor be liable for the offense in ambiguous situations? Would Bob be liable for the offense if recklessness were required as to lack of consent? If a culpability requirement protects defendants from liability in situations where consent is ambiguous, is this an argument in favor of substituting lack of consent for coercion as the central element in sexual assault?

10. *Ambiguous Acquittals.* If mistake as to consent can provide a defense to rape, presumably some defendants will be acquitted of rape (or have charges dismissed or not be charged) although the victim did not in fact consent to the intercourse. What difficulties can you see arising in such situations? What, if anything, could be done to avoid or reduce these difficulties?

11. *Defining and Grading "Rape."* The Model Penal Code uses the term "rape" to apply only to cases where intercourse is compelled by "force or by threat of imminent death, serious bodily injury, extreme pain or kidnapping." Compulsion by lesser threats is punished at a reduced grade, as "gross sexual imposition." By using a term other than "rape," does the Code devalue the seriousness of the offense? Might the Code gain greater deterrence of the lesser offense by referring to these violations as "rape" as well? Might it also gain greater deterrence by punishing these offenses at the same level as the cases of more forceful compulsion? (If criminalization were extended to all instances of unconsented-to intercourse, not just those of compulsion or coercion, might there be greater deterrence if the term "rape" were applied here as well, and the offense were

graded the same as the cases of forceful compulsion?) What arguments can one make for distinguishing these different kinds of violations both in grade and in label?

Model Penal Code §213.1 Comment 8(c) (1980)
The Spousal Exclusion

The traditional explanation for legal incapacity to rape one's own wife is that the marriage constitutes a blanket consent to sexual intimacy which the woman may revoke only by dissolving the marital relationship. Alternately, the exclusion is treated as a logical derivation from the ancient definition of rape as "unlawful" carnal knowledge without consent: Intercourse between husband and wife is not unlawful but in fact is sanctioned by law. Neither of these rationalizations is entirely satisfactory. The former is essentially fictive, for there is no reason why agreement to enter a relation of intimacy necessarily means consent to intercourse on demand. The latter explanation simply begs the question.

The historic basis of the spousal exclusion probably lies not in statements of this sort but in the older conception of the wife as chattel. At a minimum, she was relegated to subordinate status in the marriage relationship, under oath to love, honor, and obey and therefore obliged to do the husband's bidding. Perhaps this grounding in an older view of the role of women explains why the spousal exclusion, so long an accepted feature of the law of rape, has recently come under attack. Extension of criminal sanctions to reach coercive relations between husband and wife is a common feature of feminist proposals for reforming the law of rape, and appears to have been accepted in a number of recent revisions. This activity should prompt a fresh look at the advisability of the spousal exclusion.

Today, it is certainly not true that marriage results in legal abrogation of the woman's autonomy over her own person. Just as a woman may agree to date but withhold consent for intercourse, so she may marry without surrendering to sex on demand. If on occasion she refuses, the husband has no right to compel her to submit. If he does so by force or physical menace, he may be guilty of assault and subject to a range of penalties dependent on the gravity of harm threatened or caused. Liability for rape is another matter. Rape may consist of wholly non-violent conduct, but where force is used, rape carries sanctions more severe than those authorized for assault. The existence of a prior and continuing relation of intimacy, whether formalized by ceremony or achieved by long practice, is not irrelevant to the concerns of the law of rape. Explication of this conclusion requires a look at the various kinds of conduct that may be punished as rape or a related offense.

First, marriage or equivalent relationship, while not amounting to a legal waiver of the woman's right to say "no," does imply a kind of generalized consent that distinguishes some versions of the crime of rape from parallel behavior by a husband. The relationship itself creates a presumption of consent, valid until revoked. At a minimum, therefore, husbands must be exempt from those categories of liability based not on force or coercion but on a presumed incapacity of the woman to consent. . . .

The major context of which those who would abandon the spousal exclusion are thinking, however, is the situation of rape by force or threat. The problem with abandoning the immunity in many such situations is that the law of rape, if applied to spouses, would thrust the prospect of criminal sanctions into the ongoing process of adjustment in the marital relationship. Section 213.1, for example, defines as gross sexual imposition intercourse coerced "by any threat that would prevent resistance by a woman of ordinary resolution." It may well be that a woman of ordinary resolution would be prevented from resisting by her husband's threat of this sort within the marital relationship is no doubt unattractive, but it is a risky business for the law to intervene by threatening criminal sanctions. Retaining the spousal exclusion avoids this unwarranted intrusion of the penal law into the life of the family.

Finally, there is the case of intercourse coerced by force or threat of physical harm. Here the law already authorizes a penalty for assault. If the actor causes serious bodily injury, the punishment is quite severe. The issue is whether the still more drastic sanctions of rape should apply. The answer depends on whether the injury caused by forcible intercourse by a husband is equivalent to that inflicted by someone else. The gravity of the crime of forcible rape derives not merely from its violent character but also from its achievement of a particularly degrading kind of unwanted intimacy. Where the attacker stands in an ongoing relation of sexual intimacy, that evil, as distinct from the force used to compel submission, may well be thought qualitatively different. The character of the voluntary association of husband and wife, in other words, may be thought to affect the nature of the harm involved in unwanted intercourse. That, in any event, is the conclusion long endorsed by the law of rape and carried forward in the Model Code provision.

Questions

1. *Spousal Exclusion.* Consider an alternative assessment of the seriousness of marital rape as compared to stranger rape:

> [W]ife rape can be as terrifying and life-threatening to the victim as stranger rape. In addition, it often evokes a powerful sense of betrayal, deep disillusionment, and total isolation. Women often receive very poor treatment by friends, relatives, and professional services when they are raped by strangers. This isolation can be even more extreme for victims of wife rape. And just as they are more likely to be blamed, they are more likely to blame themselves.
>
> Much more is at stake for a victim of wife rape than for a woman who is raped by a stranger. When a woman has been raped by her husband she cannot seek comfort and safety at home. She can decide to leave the marriage or to live with what happened. Either choice can be devastating. Leaving involves all the trauma and readjustment of divorce, economically, socially, and psychologically. . . . However, staying usually means being raped again, often repeatedly. [W]ife rape occurred more than once in 69 percent of the marriages [in which any wife rape had occurred], and in 31 percent of them it occurred more than 20 times. Since the victim of wife rape "accepted" it the first time, why not the second, and the third, and so on? We have seen how this happens with wives who are beaten. Being raped or beaten by a husband is likely to progressively lower a wife's sense of self-worth as the abuse continues. And the lower the self-esteem, the more difficult it is to stop the abuse or leave the marriage. A vicious cycle is set in motion that can lead a wife to suicide or madness.

Diana E. H. Russell, Rape in Marriage 198-199 (1982). What arguments can one make in support of the spousal exclusion? Do they apply equally to all offenses for which the exclusion is available (rape, gross sexual imposition, corruption of minors and seduction (text quoted below), sexual assault, indecent exposure)? What arguments can one make against the exclusion?

2. *"Living as Man and Wife."* The Code extends the spousal exclusion to cases where the man and woman are "living as man and wife, regardless of the legal status of their relationship." Model Penal Code §213.6(2). Do the arguments offered to support the spousal exemption also support this extension? Assume Bob knew Linda was not agreeing to intercourse. If Linda and Bob had moved in with each other a year ago, would the reasons offered in support of the spousal exemption apply to their situation? What if Linda and Bob have been living together for a week? What if they have separate apartments but sleep together each night at one or the other?

3. *Date Rape vs. Stranger Rape.* Recall that Model Penal Code §213.1(1) provides:

> Rape is a felony of the second degree unless (i) in the course thereof the actor inflicts serious bodily injury upon anyone, or (ii) the victim was not a voluntary social companion of the actor upon the occasion of the crime and had not previously permitted him sexual liberties, in which cases the offense is a felony of the first degree.

What arguments can you make in support of the "voluntary social companion" grading reduction? If a jurisdiction were to drop the spousal exclusion, should it also do away with the "voluntary social companion" grading reduction? If so, should it reduce stranger rape to a second degree felony or increase date rape to a first degree felony? (For comparison purposes, murder is a first degree felony; manslaughter is a second degree felony. Model Penal Code §§210.2(2) & 210.3(2).) If Bob used force to have intercourse with Linda but did not cause any physical injury, should he be liable for a first degree felony or a second degree felony?

Model Penal Code §213.3
Corruption of Minors and Seduction

(1) *Offense Defined.* A male who has sexual intercourse with a female not his wife, or any person who engages in deviate sexual intercourse or causes another to engage in deviate sexual intercourse, is guilty of an offense if:

(a) the other person is less than [16] years old and the actor is at least [4] years older than the other person; or

(b) the other person is less than 21 years old and the actor is his guardian or otherwise responsible for general supervision of his welfare; or

(c) the other person is in custody of law or detained in a hospital or other institution and the actor has supervisory or disciplinary authority over him; or

(d) the other person is a female who is induced to participate by a promise of marriage which the actor does not mean to perform.

(2) *Grading.* An offense under paragraph (a) of Subsection (1) is a felony of the third degree. Otherwise an offense under this section is a misdemeanor.

Model Penal Code §213.6(3)
Sexually Promiscuous Complainants

It is a defense to prosecution under Section 213.3 . . . for the actor to prove by a preponderance of the evidence that the alleged victim had, prior to the time of the offense charged, engaged promiscuously in sexual relations with others.

Model Penal Code §213.3 Comment 2 (1980)
Statutory Rape

Subsection (1)(a) is derived from the traditional coverage of consensual relations with underage females by the criminal law. The common law was supplemented by an early statute that included intercourse with a female under the age of 10 within the offense of rape. By the time the Model Code was drafted, American statutes had both raised the so-called "age of consent" in most instances and had also elaborated upon the common law by creating several grades of statutory rape. . . .

The first major issue under this provision is the specification of 16 as the age of consent. . . .

In the case of consensual vaginal intercourse between a male and an underage female, even a passing familiarity with contemporary American society makes it difficult to believe that girls of much higher ages than 16 are, as a class, so naive or immature as to be deemed incapable of giving effective consent. They are likely to be reasonably well informed on the subject of sex, and it blinks reality to assume that a girl of 17 or 18 will play a purely passive or dependant role in such affairs. The chief significance of punishing consensual relations with a late adolescent lies not in redressing victimization of an immature person but rather in vindicating community standards of ethically acceptable behavior. The Model Code forgoes any such attempt to legislate private morality. . . . Subsection (1)(a) encloses the figure in brackets in order to indicate that reasonable legislators might differ as to the precise age limit. The Model Code, however, strongly endorses a fairly low age that avoids imposition of felony sanctions for intercourse with a female who is physically mature and likely to be functioning as an independent adult in matters of sexuality. . . .

Once the age of the victim has been selected . . . the remaining questions concern the relevance of prior sexual conduct by the underage participant and the relevance of the age of the actor. These issues are closely related. The problem to which they are both relevant concerns the adolescent . . . who might be held liable to prosecution as an adult for consensual intercourse with an adolescent of like age. The result of a criminal law with such coverage is an extravagant use of penal sanctions to inhibit sexual experimentation among contemporaries. Worse still, criminal penalties are assigned to only one of two participants in consensual activity. The perception of unwisdom compounded by unfairness is especially acute when the underage person has a history of similar sexual activity. In such circumstances, the underage party may be expected to have played an active or at least knowledgeable role in encouraging intercourse. In short, the sexually experienced adolescent, whether male or female, may be regarded as an exception to the generality that persons of tender age are likely to be so inexperienced and naive that even consensual intercourse amounts to an imposition meriting criminal sanctions.

Some statutes in effect when the Model Code was drafted tried to solve part of this problem by reaching consensual relations with an adolescent female only if she were "innocent and virtuous" or "of previous chaste character." Some courts interpreted such a language to bar liability of the male if the female had previously lost her virginity. Other courts recognized that a woman once fallen and now reformed might be chaste within the meaning of such statutes. A minority of jurisdictions focused on the female's reputation for sexual morality rather than on specific acts of unchastity.

. . . The Model Code rejects a focus upon prior chastity, upon "innocence" and "virtue," and upon previous good reputation as proper elements of the offense. Virtually all modern revision efforts follow this position.

On the other hand, the Code does recognize the relevance of a history of sexual promiscuity by the underage party to the alleged offenses. Section 213.6(3) provides a defense [for prior promiscuity of the victim]. The basic purpose of the defense is to exclude from the coverage of Section 213.3(1)(a) those cases where the underage person has a sufficient history of sexual relations with others so as to negate the inference of imposition upon youth that is otherwise established by the statutory language. . . .

Neither of these solutions is entirely satisfactory, for each permits imposition of criminal sanctions upon a youth who engages in sexual relations with a willing contemporary. Girls commonly date older boys, and to some extent boys date older girls. Sexual experimentation among social contemporaries in such a context hardly seems the kind of wrong at which the law of statutory rape is aimed. . . . It will be rare that the comparably aged actor who obtains the consent of an underage person to sexual conduct included within Section 213.3 will be an experienced exploiter of immaturity. The more likely case is that both parties will be willing participants and that the assignment of culpability only to one will be perceived as unfair.

Section 213.3 therefore adopted the innovation that the actor must be at least four years older than the underage participant in order for Subsection (1)(a) to be violated. The Reporters favored a five-year differential, but the lesser figure was chosen to reflect the prevailing pattern of secondary education. High school commonly encompasses four grades, and it seems at least harsh and unreasonable to subject a school age romancer of either sex to felony sanctions for mutually consensual behavior with a person whom society regards as a fit associate in a common educational and social endeavor. The age is bracketed, however, to indicate that the precise differential is one on which reasonable people may disagree. The principle that some age differential should be chosen nevertheless seems clear. . . .

Questions

1. *Immorality or Ineffective Consent?* On what grounds do the Model Penal Code drafters justify statutory rape, as an enforcement of community standards of morality or upon a theory of lack of meaningful consent by adolescents or upon another theory? Note that the offense excludes intercourse between members of a married couple. If ineffective consent is the root of the offense, why should marriage matter? (Why would the state permit such a marriage?) Are community standards less offended if intercourse with an underage female occurs within a marriage?

2. *Prior Promiscuity in Statutory Rape.* Why do the drafters think that prior promiscuity of a victim is relevant to a defendant's liability for intercourse with her? Assume Bob, 20, has consensual intercourse with Linda, almost 16. Should Linda's prior intercourse with Steve provide a defense to Bob for statutory rape? Would it matter if Linda had had intercourse with five other males? What exactly is the harm or evil contemplated by the offense of statutory rape?

3. *Prior Intercourse in Forcible Rape.* Recall that forcible intercourse is graded as a first degree felony if the victim is not a voluntary social companion and "had not previously permitted him sexual liberties" but otherwise is a second degree felony. Model Penal Code §213.1(1). What arguments could one make in support of this grading difference? What arguments against it? If a jurisdiction were to drop the prior promiscuity defense to statutory rape, should it also drop the prior intercourse grading factor in forcible rape?

4. *Autonomy, Privacy, and Respect.* Consider the following view of statutory rape:

Feminists charge that [statutory rape laws] are harmful to women on both a practical and an ideological level. First, as an effort to control the sexual activities of young women, statutory rape laws are an unwarranted governmental intrusion into their lives and an oppressive restriction upon their freedom of action. . . . In the language of rights analysis, statutory rape laws violate the female's right to privacy and her right to be as free sexually as her male counterpart.

Feminists' second common objection to statutory rape laws is ideological. Gender-based statutory rape laws reinforce the sexual stereotype of men as aggressors and women as passive victims. The laws perpetuate the double standard of sexual morality. For males, sex is an accomplishment; they gain something through intercourse. For women, sex entails giving something up. Further, for the myth of male sexual accomplishment to exist, some females must give in. The double standard divides females into two classes—virgins and whores, "good girls" whose chastity should be protected and "bad girls" who may be exploited with impunity. Even if young women need more protection from sexual coercion and exploitation than the laws against forcible rape and incest provide, many feminists nevertheless oppose gender-based laws. They argue that males and females should be protected equally and that gender-based laws stigmatize women as weaker than men. In terms of rights theory, gender-based statutory rape laws violate the right of all women to be treated equally to men.

Although these two objections to statutory rape laws are analytically distinct, they nonetheless are related. Ideology affects people's lives, and daily life can limit and reshape ideology. The restrictive aspects of statutory rape laws are particularly objectionable because they exalt female chastity and treat women as lacking in sexual autonomy. This view of women both provides a reason (although a false and pernicious one) for state restrictions upon young women's sexual freedom and reinforces damaging stereotypes. At the same time, the laws imply that young men do not need the protection that they afford. This implication reinforces the ideology that sex is okay for young men; it also means that some women will have to be available to have sex with them.

The state restricts the young woman's sexual behavior for reasons related to sexist notions of what makes females valuable. The state does not merely restrict the young woman's freedom; it also treats her sexuality as a thing that has a value of its own and must be guarded. By refusing to grant women autonomy and by protecting them in ways that men are not protected, the state treats women's bodies—and therefore women themselves—as objects. Men are treated differently. Their bodies are regarded as a part of them, subject to their free control. . . .

Frances Olsen, Statutory Rape: A Feminist Critique of Rights Analysis, 63 Texas L. Rev. 387, 390 (1984). What kind of statutory rape offense, if any, would one adopt to reflect Olsen's views?

5. *Seduction.* What arguments can one make for and against a special provision to criminalize intercourse procured by a false promise of marriage (seduction), as in Model Penal Code §213.3(1)(d)?

Model Penal Code §213.6(1)
Mistake as to Age

Whenever in this Article the criminality of conduct depends on a child's being below the age of 10, it is no defense that the actor did not know the child's age, or reasonably believed the child to be older than 10. When criminality depends on the child's being below a critical age other than 10, it is a defense for the actor to prove by a preponderance of the evidence that he reasonably believed the child to be above the critical age.

Model Penal Code §213.6 Comment 2 (1980)
Mistake as to Age

As a general proposition, one would expect that honest and reasonable mistake as to the critical element of an offense would negate liability. The common law generally so provided, but there were some exceptions. Traditionally, statutory rape has been a strict liability offense, and mistake as to the age of an underage participant has been accorded no defensive significance. At one time, this rule obtained in virtually every American jurisdiction, and it continues today in a large number of states.

Disallowance of mistake as to age probably relates to the common-law definition of rape as including consensual intercourse with a girl less than 10 years old. Focus on so young an age made strict liability tolerable, for no credible error regarding the age of a child in fact less than 10 years old would render the actor's conduct anything less than a dramatic departure from societal norms. Furthermore, this fact achieved particular significance under the older conception of *mens rea* as something approaching a general criminal disposition. The law looked not so much for a specified mental attitude with respect to proscribed conduct but rather for evidence of a guilty mind. The articulation of this point of view in the doctrines of lesser legal wrong and lesser moral wrong provided that mistake would be disallowed as a defense where, had the facts been as the actor believed them to be, his conduct still would have been illegal or wrongful.[6] As one commentator

---

6. See, e.g., Regina v. Prince, L.R., 2 Cr. Cas. Res. 154 (1875). In that case, defendant was convicted of taking a girl under the age of 16 from possession of her father, even though he reasonably believed that she was older. A defense of mistake was disallowed,

expressed the common-law notion, exculpation for mistake "rests ultimately on the defendant's being able to say that he has observed the community ethic. . . ." The actor who is mistaken as to the age of a child under 10 can make no such claim, for no credible error of perception would be sufficient to recharacterize a child of such tender years as an appropriate subject of sexual gratification.

Of course, it is debatable whether the rule of strict liability is satisfactory even in this circumstance. Wherever the line is drawn between licit and illicit behavior, the actor who reasonably believes in the existence of facts that, if true, would render his conduct non-criminal has substantial claim for exculpation. Even if society chooses to set the age of consent very low, the actor who reasonably believes that his partner is above that age lacks culpability with respect to the factor deemed critical to liability. Punishing him anyway simply because his intended conduct would have been immoral under the facts as he supposed them to be postulates a relation between criminality and immorality that is inaccurate on both descriptive and normative grounds. The penal law does not try to enforce all aspects of community morality, and any thoroughgoing attempt to do so would extend the prospect of criminal sanctions far into the sphere of individual liberty and create a regime too demanding for all save the best among us.

But whatever the merits of strict liability with respect to an age of 10 or 12, the traditional disallowance of mistake in the law of statutory rape has been rendered intolerable by legislative extension of the age of consent to 16, 17, or 18. A girl of 15 may appear to be 18 or even older. A man who engages in consensual intercourse in the reasonable belief that his partner has reached her eighteenth birthday evidences no abnormality, no willingness to take advantage of immaturity, no propensity to corruption of minors. In short, he has demonstrated neither intent nor inclination to violate any of the interests that the law of statutory rape seeks to protect. At most, he has disregarded religious precept or social convention. In terms of mental culpability, his conduct is indistinguishable from that of any other person who engages in fornication. Whether he should be punished at all depends on a judgment about continuing fornication as a criminal offense, but at least he should not be subject to felony sanctions for statutory rape.

The Model Code effects a compromise between the traditional rule disallowing mistake in the law of statutory rape and a general policy against strict liability crimes. Without Section 213.6(1), the normal operation of the Model Code culpability structure would apply a *mens rea* of recklessness to the age element in statutory rape. . . . Section 213.6(1) provides, however, that it is no defense to liability for rape or

---

inter alia on the ground that his removal of an unmarried girl from the lawful custody of her parents would have been wrongful even had she been as old as he believed. . . .

deviate sexual intercourse that the actor reasonably believed the child to be older than 10. It was thought that strict liability would be acceptable for offenses based on such extreme youth and that in any event any proposed change on this point would encounter political resistance. Section 213.6(1) further provides, however, that the actor may defend in cases where the age is set higher than 10 by proving that he "reasonably believed" his sexual partner to be above the specified age. The phrase "reasonably believed" is defined in Section 1.13(16) supra to establish a minimum culpability of negligence. The defendant must establish both the fact and reasonableness of his mistake by a preponderance of the evidence. This rule places a heavier burden on the defendant than is generally provided by the Model Code, both as a matter of substantive standards of culpability and as an allocation of the procedural incidents of proof. It was thought, however, that this much effect could validly be given to the fact that, even crediting the actor's claim of mistake, his conduct would nevertheless amount to a conscious disregard of community standards. Furthermore, shifting the burden of persuasion to the defendant meets the usual prosecutorial objection that it would be virtually impossible in many cases to disprove beyond a reasonable doubt that the actor was mistaken as to the other's age.

This compromise solution has proved extremely influential. . . . The result is that today a majority of American jurisdictions have abandoned the traditional rule of strict liability for the upper age limit giving rise to liability of the partner for consensual intercourse. . . .

Questions

1. *Culpability as to Under 10.* What persons would escape liability if the Code required negligence as to the female being under age 10 (second degree felony), rather than the strict liability that it does impose? Would such a person be held liable for the lesser form of statutory rape under §213.3(1)(a) (third degree felony)? What are the arguments, if any, for insisting upon a second degree felony rather than a third degree felony for a 16-year-old or a 26- or 56-year-old who reasonably believes his consenting partner is 15 rather than 10?

2. *Culpability as to Under 16.* If recklessness were required as to the female being under 16 for the lesser form of statutory rape (third degree felony), what persons, if any, would escape liability that would not escape if the current negligence requirement were in place? What is different about the statutory rape context that justifies deviating from the normal rule that at least recklessness is required as to an offense element?

Model Penal Code §213.1 Comment 8(a) (1980)
Limitation of Liability to Males for Offenses Against Females

Traditionally, the law of rape punished only male aggression against females. The Model Code continues this limitation. . . .

[A large number of recent revisions define] the entire range of criminal conduct without reference to the actor's gender. This abrogation of the historic limitation of liability to males is also a feature of many feminist proposals for reforming the law of rape.

The Model Penal Code was drafted at a time when the social climate was such that the limitation of rape to male aggression was hardly questioned. This is not to say that the possibility of male attacks upon males or female attacks upon males or females was ignored. Rather, the significance of the difference between these cases on the one hand and the case of a male attack upon a female on the other was largely perceived as one of grading. [Editor's Note.—The commentary then details the way in which conduct by females analogous to rape or gross sexual imposition would be an offense, albeit at a lower grade, under the deviate sexual intercourse, sexual assault, aggravated assault, and assault offenses of the Code, which are drafted in gender-neutral terms.]

If the Model Penal Code were being redrafted today, it might well be that preserving these [grading] differences would not be thought to outweigh the advantages of describing the entire offense of rape in gender-neutral terms. [T]he advantage of gender neutrality in this respect seems primarily to be symbolic. Elimination of gender specificity may help to abrogate certain sex stereotypes that our society is appropriately beginning to address, as illustrated by the movement for the equal rights amendment, by recent state and federal legislation, and by judicial decisions at the state and federal level. On the other hand, to the extent that the purpose of gender neutrality is actually to adapt the law of rape to punish female aggression, it seems addressed principally to a hypothetical. Physical strength, role conception, and the mechanics of intercourse make sexual aggression an overwhelmingly male phenomenon. It is doubtful that female sexual aggression occurs with any frequency or that most cases would be reported even if it did occur.

Of course, coercive intercourse by females is possible, especially where threats are used to demand performance. In such cases, the issue is whether the harm accomplished by female aggression is sufficiently similar to that which occurs in the usual context to warrant punishment under the law of rape. This is a fairly close question with arguments on both sides. On the one hand, the male who is forced to engage in intercourse is denied freedom of choice in much the same way as the female victim of rape. On the other hand, the potential consequences of coercive intimacy do not seem so grave. For one thing there is no prospect of unwanted pregnancy. And however devalued virginity has become for the modern woman, it is difficult to believe that its loss constitutes a comparable injury to the male.

The problem of male aggression against males and female aggression against females also presents close questions. The penalties that are authorized by the Model Code for such conduct are high, though not at the first-degree felony level. Economy in the use of the most severe sanctions of the criminal law suggests that perhaps the punishment of rape as a first-degree felony should be limited to those cases where public outcry is likely to be the greatest, where the harm to the victim is likely to be perceived as the most severe, both by the victim and by society, and where the frequency of the offense has caused the greatest public apprehension. It can be expected, in other words, that very few cases will arise under a gender-neutral statute where the sentences authorized by Section 213.2 or Section 213.3 will be perceived as inadequate or where assault penalties will not suffice. Moreover, the criminalization of seduction of young boys and male adolescents by older females seems neither to be the serious problem of the other forms of sexual conduct, absent force, nor likely to have the same adverse effects on the victim. It is for these reasons, in any event, that the Model Code is not drafted in gender-neutral terms.

Questions

1. *Gender-Based Definitions of Statutory Rape.* Recall that gender limitations are used in both the rape and the statutory rape provisions of the Code. How are the arguments for and against gender limitations different for forcible rape than for statutory rape? In Michael M. v. Sonoma County Superior Court, 450 U.S. 464 (1980), the constitutionality of a gender-based statutory rape law was challenged on Equal Protection grounds. A plurality upheld the statute:

> The justification for the statute offered by the State, and by the Supreme Court of California, is that the legislature sought to prevent illegitimate teenage pregnancies. . . .
> We need not be medical doctors to discern that young men and women are not similarly situated with respect to the problems and the risks of sexual intercourse. Only women become pregnant, and they suffer disproportionately the profound physical, emotional, and psychological consequences of sexual activity. The statute at issue here protects women

from sexual intercourse at an age when those consequences are particularly severe.

Id. at 471-472. The dissent argued, among other things:

> Until very recently, no California court or commentator had suggested that the purpose of California's statutory rape law was to protect young women from the risk of pregnancy. Indeed, the historical development of §261.5 demonstrates that the law was initially enacted on the premise that young women, in contrast to young men, were to be deemed legally incapable of consenting to an act of sexual intercourse. Because their chastity was considered particularly precious, those young women were felt to be uniquely in need of the State's protection. In contrast, young men were assumed to be capable of making such decisions for themselves; the law therefore did not offer them special protection.
>
> It is perhaps because the gender classification in California's statutory rape law was initially designed to further these outmoded sexual stereotypes, rather than to reduce the incidence of teenage pregnancies, that the State has been unable to demonstrate a substantial relationship between the classification and its newly asserted goal. But whatever the reason, the State has not shown that Cal. Penal Code §261.5 is any more effective than a gender-neutral law would be in deterring minor females from engaging in sexual intercourse. . . .

Id. at 494-496 (Brennan, J., dissenting).

2. *Male Victims.* One aspect of gender-based statutes is their application only to female victims. What are the arguments for and against the claim that there is less harm where an underage male has consensual intercourse than when an underage female does? What are the arguments for and against the claim that there is less harm where a male is forcibly raped than where a female is?

3. *Female Offenders.* Another, distinct aspect of gender-based sexual offenses is their application only to male offenders. What arguments can one make for and against the claim that females who have intercourse with minors are less blameworthy than males who do the same? What arguments can one make for and against the claim that females who compel unconsented-to intercourse are less blameworthy?

4. *Another View of Rape, Statutory Rape, and Gender-Based Sexual Offenses.* Catherine MacKinnon has this view on the laws of rape and statutory rape:

> The law of rape divides women into spheres of consent according to indices of relationship to men. Which category of presumed consent a woman is in depends upon who she is relative to a man who wants her, not what she says or does. These categories tell men whom they can legally fuck, who is open season and who is off limits, not how to listen to women. The paradigm categories are the virginal daughter and other young girls, with whom all sex is proscribed, and the whorelike wives and

prostitutes, with whom no sex is proscribed. Daughters may not consent; wives and prostitutes are assumed to, and cannot but. Actual consent or nonconsent, far less actual desire, is comparatively irrelevant. If rape laws existed to enforce women's control over access to their sexuality, as the consent defense implies, no would mean no, marital rape would not be a widespread exception, and it would not be effectively legal to rape a prostitute.

All women are divided into parallel provinces, their actual consent counting to the degree that they diverge from the paradigm case in their category. Virtuous women, like young girls, are consenting, virginal, rapable. Unvirtuous women, like wives and prostitutes, are consenting, whores, unrapable. The age line under which girls are presumed disabled from consenting to sex, whenever they say, rationalizes a condition of sexual coercion which women never outgrow. One day they cannot say yes, and the next day they cannot say no. The law takes the most aggravated case for female powerlessness based on gender and age combined and, by formally prohibiting all sex as rape, makes consent irrelevant on the basis of an assumption of powerlessness. This defines those above the age line as powerful, whether they actually have power to consent or not. The vulnerability girls share with boys—age—dissipates with time. The vulnerability girls share with women—gender—does not. As with protective labor laws for women only, dividing and protecting the most vulnerable becomes a device for not protecting everyone who needs it, and also may function to target those singled out for special protection for special abuse. Such protection has not prevented high rates of sexual abuse of children and may contribute to eroticizing young girls as forbidden.

As to adult women, to the extent an accused knows a woman and they have sex, her consent is inferred. The exemption for rape in marriage is consistent with the assumption underlying most adjudications of forcible rape: To the extent the parties relate, it was not really rape, it was personal. As marital exemptions erode, preclusions for cohabitants and voluntary social companions may expand. As a matter of fact, for this purpose one can be acquainted with an accused by friendship or by meeting him for the first time at a bar or a party or by hitchhiking. In this light, the partial erosion of the marital rape exemption looks less like a change in the equation between women's experience of sexual violation and men's experience of intimacy, and more like a legal adjustment to the social fact that acceptable heterosexual sex is increasingly not limited to the legal family. So although the rape law may not now always assume that the woman consented simply because the parties are legally one, indices of closeness, of relationship ranging from nodding acquaintance to living together, still contraindicate rape. In marital rape cases, courts look for even greater atrocities than usual to undermine their assumption that if sex happened, she wanted it.

Catherine MacKinnon, "Rape: On Coercion and Consent," in Toward a Feminist Theory of the State 175-176 (1989). Under this view, how should the Model Penal Code sexual offenses be modified?

Model Penal Code §213.2 Comment 2 (1980)
Decriminalization of Deviate Sexual Intercourse Between Consenting Adults

Section 213.2 of the Model Code makes a fundamental departure from prior law in excepting from criminal sanctions deviate sexual intercourse† between consenting adults. This policy applies to the various styles of sexual intimacy between man and wife and to sexual relations between unmarried persons, regardless of gender. . . . Under the Model Code deviate sexual intercourse is not criminal where both participants consent, where each is of sufficient age and mental capacity to render consent effective, and where they conduct their relations in private and create no public nuisance. . . .

. . . Because ordinary genital copulation is not possible between persons of the same gender, homosexual relations typically involve some sort of deviate sexual intercourse as that term is defined [by the Code]. The popular aversion to such conduct arises not so much from the physical characteristics of sexuality as from the fact of sexual gratification with a person of one's own gender. This type of sexual preference constitutes a far more dramatic contravention of societal norms and prevailing moral attitudes than is involved in [consensual sodomy between a man and a woman]. Continued criminal punishment of homosexual relations may be advocated on the ground that such conduct threatens the moral fabric of society by undermining the viability of the family or on the supposition that permitting such behavior between consenting adults leads inevitably to the corruption of youth. Arguments of the former sort raise the broad issue of the proper relation of the criminal law to community morality—a matter that is discussed more fully below. The view that activity between consenting adults should be proscribed in order to protect young persons flounders on the absence of either empirical data or reasoned analysis to suggest that one leads to the other. Perhaps more important than either of these factors is the simple truth that homosexuality excites widespread and often violent emotional hostility. Its manifestation in sexual conduct is viewed by many persons with a deep antipathy. The origin of this reaction is as much aesthetic as moral, and its force is not diminished by the difficulty of specifying exactly what harm is occasioned thereby. The conviction that homosexual conduct is "bad" quickly translates into the conclusion that it

---

†Editor's Note.—Model Penal Code §213.0(3) provides: " 'Deviate sexual intercourse' means sexual intercourse per os or per anum between human beings who are not husband and wife, and any form of sexual intercourse with an animal."

therefore should be punished, and there is a corresponding fear that removing criminal sanctions would amount to implied endorsement of a kind of behavior that majoritarian sentiment finds abhorrent.

While these concerns may be dispositive to some, the Model Code takes the view that private homosexual conduct between consenting adults should not be punished as a crime. In part, this conclusion stems from uncertainty about the morality of such conduct. Without delving into the question of the causes of homosexuality, one can identify at least three ways of looking at the phenomenon. First, of course, it may be regarded as a sin. Most orthodox theologies take this position, though there are increasing challenges to this view even from sources within organized religion.

Second, homosexuality may be viewed as a disease. There are two lines of thought in the disease model of homosexuality. Some theorists have posited that homosexuality is a pathological condition, the result of abnormal genetic or hormonal influences. . . . On the other hand, many scientists today have adopted a psychological theory of homosexuality, thus viewing it as an emotional or mental disorder. . . .

The third view of homosexuality is that it is neither a sin nor an abnormality but only a difference. The notion here is that homosexual conduct is simply a matter of personal preference and devoid of any normative content whatever. This is the position of the gay rights movement, and it may be gaining support in the community at large.

No doubt this statement of three distinct points of view is simplistic. They are not cleanly different as described above but exist in an infinite variety of graduations and emphases. To the extent, however, that these positions may be taken as paradigms of broadly differing attitudes toward the subject, they suggest an important point. Only one of the three conceptions—i.e., the view that homosexual conduct is a sin—provides an appropriate starting point for imposition of penal sanctions. No principle is more broadly accepted than that the criminal law, involving as it does both punishment and condemnation, should be concerned with conduct that is morally reprehensible or culpable. To the extent that it seems inappropriate to regard homosexual relations as blameworthy—that is, as representative of moral failing by the actor—the essential premise for assigning criminal punishment is vitiated. Of course, many in the community view homosexual conduct as morally reprehensible, but it is equally clear that many do not. Given the absence of harm to the secular interests of the community occasioned by atypical sexuality between consenting adults, the problematical nature of the underlying ethical issue should suggest the need for caution in continuing criminal proscription of this kind of behavior.

. . . Even if one starts from the proposition that homosexual conduct is a moral default for which the actor may justifiably be condemned, there are still sufficient reasons to withhold penal sanctions. The criminal law cannot encompass all behavior that the average citizen may regard as immoral or deviate. In every field of activity the ethical precepts of the community set standards higher than the law can expediently enforce. Verbal cruelty, lying, racial and religious biases in private relationships, and the kiss that betrays a marriage are but a few examples of reprehensible conduct that no sensible legislator would make into a crime. Some of the reasons why the penal law must stop well short of encompassing all immoral conduct are eminently practical. Economic resources are finite. The amount of money that may be spent on law enforcement is limited by the wealth of the community and by the competing demands of other social interests. It seems sensible, therefore, that the criminal justice system should concentrate on repressing murder, robbery, rape, theft, and other crimes that directly threaten security of person and property. Authorization of penalties for consensual sodomy suggests not only that such conduct is wrongful, but also that it is sufficiently important to warrant diversion of resources from other areas. Furthermore, any genuine effort to enforce such prohibitions will be extremely costly and difficult. Private sexual behavior between consenting adults has no victim. There is no one who can be counted on to complain to the police or to provide evidence against suspected offenders. The resulting difficulty of identifying and convicting violators usually leads police to forego any attempt to enforce laws against consensual sodomy except in the rare case that happens to come to their attention. Cases that do surface commonly involve violence, corruption of minors, public solicitation, or some other aggravating factor that would continue to be punished under the Model Code. To the extent, however, that laws against deviate sexual behavior are enforced against private conduct between consenting adults, the result is episodic and capricious selection of an infinitesimal fraction of offenders for severe punishment. This invitation to arbitrary enforcement not only offends notions of fairness and horizontal equity, but it also creates unwarranted opportunity for private blackmail and official extortion. There is also the point that the methods available to the police for enforcing such laws involve tactics which are often unseemly and which, by their very nature, stretch the limits of constitutionality. Moreover, these costs may be incurred without gaining any corresponding benefit, for there is every reason to believe that continued criminal proscription of private sexual relations would prove largely ineffective to deter or inhibit such conduct. . . .

Questions

1. *Decriminalize Immorality?* Assume that a majority of the community clearly agreed that consensual sodomy was immoral. What arguments would remain to support decriminalization nonetheless?

2. *Morality Enforcement.* Are criminal codes generally used for morality enforcement? What provisions of the Model Penal Code might be viewed as enforcing community morality norms? What arguments can one make in support of using criminal codes to prohibit conduct that the community finds morally offensive but otherwise does not harm members of the community? What arguments against?

3. *Immorality vs. Injury.* If appropriate civil health and safety measures were drafted and enforced, should the criminal law prohibit: (a) prostitution conducted in private? (b) the dissemination and private use of cocaine? (c) the private handling and display of dead bodies? (d) the dissemination and private use of detailed drawings depicting children engaging in sexual acts? (e) bigamy? (f) incest between consenting adults? (g) bestiality? How would the arguments for and against decriminalization of each of these acts be different from the arguments for and against the decriminalization of consensual sodomy?

Chapter 19. RACKETEER INFLUENCED AND CORRUPT ORGANIZATIONS (RICO)

Statement of Findings and Purpose
Organized Crime Control Act of 1970
84 Stat. 922-923

The Congress finds that (1) organized crime in the United States is a highly sophisticated, diversified, and widespread activity that annually drains billions of dollars from America's economy by unlawful conduct and the illegal use of force, fraud, and corruption; (2) organized crime derives a major portion of its power through money obtained from such illegal endeavors as syndicated gambling, loan sharking, the theft and fencing of property, the importation and distribution of narcotics and other dangerous drugs, and other forms of social exploitation; (3) this money and power are increasingly used to infiltrate and corrupt legitimate business and labor unions and to subvert and corrupt our democratic processes; (4) organized crime activities in the United States weaken the stability of the Nation's economic system, harm innocent investors and competing organizations, interfere with free competition, seriously burden interstate and foreign commerce, threaten the domestic security, and undermine the general welfare of the Nation and its citizens; and (5) organized crime continues to grow because of defects in the evidence-gathering process of the law inhibiting the development of the legally admissible evidence necessary to bring criminal and other sanctions or remedies to bear on the unlawful activities of those engaged in organized crime and because the sanctions and remedies available to the Government are unnecessarily limited in scope and impact.

18 U.S.C. §§1961-1962
Racketeer Influenced and Corrupt Organization Act

Section 1961. Definitions

As used in this chapter—
(1) "racketeering activity" means (A) any act or threat involving murder, kidnaping, gambling, arson, robbery, bribery, extortion, dealing in obscene matter, or dealing in narcotic or other dangerous drugs, which is chargeable under State law and punishable by imprisonment for more than one year; (B) any act which is indictable under any of the following provisions of title 18, United States Code: [list of 42 sections relating to a variety of specific offenses]; (C) any act which is indictable under title 29, United States Code, section 186 (dealing with restrictions on payments and loans to labor organizations); or section 501(c) (relating to embezzlement from union funds); (D) any offense involving fraud connected with a case under title 11, fraud in the sale of securities, or the felonious manufacture, importation, receiving, concealment, buying, selling, or otherwise dealing narcotic or other dangerous drugs, punishable under any law of the United States; or (E) any act which is indictable under the Currency and Foreign Transactions Reporting Act; . . .
(3) "person" includes any individual or entity capable of holding a legal or beneficial interest in property;
(4) "enterprise" includes any individual, partnership, corporation, association, or other legal entity, and any union or group of individuals associated in fact although not a legal entity;
(5) "pattern of racketeering activity" requires at least two acts of racketeering activity, one of which occurred after the effective date of this chapter and the last of which occurred within ten years (excluding any period of imprisonment) after the commission of a prior act of racketeering activity; . . .

Section 1962. Prohibited activities

(a) It shall be unlawful for any person who has received any income derived, directly or indirectly, from a pattern of racketeering activity or through collection of an unlawful debt in which such person has participated as a principal within the meaning of section 2, title 18, United States Code, to use or invest, directly or indirectly, any part of such income, or the proceeds of such income, in acquisition of any interest in, or the establishment or operation of, any enterprise which is engaged in, or the activities of which affect, interstate or foreign commerce.

(b) It shall be unlawful for any person through a pattern of racketeering activity or through collection of an unlawful debt to acquire or maintain, directly or indirectly, any interest in or control of any enterprise which is engaged in, or the activities of which affect, interstate or foreign commerce.

(c) It shall be unlawful for any person employed by or associated with any enterprise engaged in, or the activities of which affect, interstate or foreign commerce, to conduct or participate, directly or indirectly, in the conduct of such enterprise's affairs through a pattern of racketeering activity or collection of unlawful debt.

(d) It shall be unlawful for any person to conspire to violate any of the provisions of subsections (a), (b), or (c) of this section.

United States v. Masters, Corbitt, and Keating
United States Court of Appeals, Seventh Circuit
924 F.2d 1362 (1991)

POSNER, Circuit Judge

Alan Masters and James Keating were charged in 1988 with, among other things, having "conduct[ed an] . . . enterprise's affairs through a pattern of racketeering activity" in violation of 18 U.S.C. §1962(c), and (along with Michael Corbitt) of having conspired to do so, in violation of §1962(d); both are, of course, provisions of the RICO (Racketeer Influenced and Corrupt Organizations) statute. The statute provides that "enterprise" includes "any individual, partnership, corporation, association, or other legal entity, and any union or group of individuals associated in fact although not a legal entity." §1961(4). The statutory term "pattern of racketeering activity" "requires at least two acts of racketeering activity," §1961(5), defined as violations of various federal and state statutes. The jury found Masters and Keating guilty on both counts and Corbitt guilty on the conspiracy count—the only one he had been charged with, because the statute of limitations had expired on his substantive violations. The judge gave Masters and Keating consecutive prison sentences of 20 and 20, and 20 and 15, years, respectively, and Corbitt 20 years. The judge also fined Masters $250,000 on the conspiracy count and ordered all three defendants to forfeit criminal proceeds of $42,000. These are all pre-Sentencing Guidelines sentences. There were other counts in the indictment besides the two RICO counts, but the jury acquitted the defendants on those counts.

There is no challenge to the jury instructions, so we must construe the facts as favorably to the prosecution as the trial record and the jury verdict permit. The facts are a lurid mixture of corruption and murder in a west suburban Chicago setting. Masters was a lawyer, Keating a lieutenant in the Cook County Sheriff's Police Department who commanded the vice squad and later the criminal investigative unit, and Corbitt the chief of police of Willow Springs. The RICO enterprise, as the government conceives it, was an informal association among the three defendants and three other entities (so a total of six in all): Masters' law firm (a professional corporation of which he was the sole shareholder and which employed another lawyer) and the two police departments. Between 1970 and June 1982, when Corbitt lost his job as chief of police of Willow Springs, Masters bribed Corbitt to refer persons arrested, ticketed, or investigated by the Willow Springs Police Department to Masters for legal assistance. Masters had similar kickback schemes with other police officers in the area. Keating entered the picture in 1972, two years after Corbitt. Between then and August 1984 Masters was the middleman in a scheme in which illegal bookmakers in Cicero, Illinois bribed Keating and officers under Keating's command to leave them alone.

In 1981 Masters discovered that his wife, Dianne, was having an affair. He asked a friend in the Cook County Sheriff's Police Department who would be in charge of any investigation arising out of events at Masters' home, and was disappointed when told that it would not be Keating. In January 1982 Dianne Masters hired a lawyer to file for a divorce. She let it be known that she hoped to obtain custody of her and Masters' four-year-old daughter. Masters hired a former police officer, Ted Nykaza, to install recording equipment in the Masters household for the purpose of eavesdropping on telephone conversations between Dianne and her paramour. Listening, with Nykaza and a Cook County Sheriff's Police sergeant, to one of the recorded conversations, Masters thought he heard Dianne and her paramour reminisce about the paramour's inserting a wine bottle into Dianne's vagina as part of their sex play. Masters exploded with anger and declared that he would have Dianne killed. Later he told a friend that he would ask Keating to kill her. Keating offered a former Cook County Sheriff's Police officer $25,000 to kill Dianne on Masters' behalf, explaining that Corbitt was unwilling to do the killing himself but had agreed to dispose of the body.

Dianne Masters disappeared in the early morning of March 19, 1982. Her body was recovered from the trunk of her car nine months later when the car was discovered submerged in a canal near Willow Springs. She had been beaten and shot. Probably Corbitt had driven the car into the canal, though the jury's findings on this point are ambiguous. In the following months Keating used his position in the

Cook County Sheriff's Police Department to obstruct the investigation of Dianne Masters' disappearance. Masters collected the proceeds of a $100,000 policy on Dianne's life. No one was ever charged with the murder.

The jury found that Masters had planned and solicited the murder of Dianne, that Keating had aided and abetted Masters' planning and solicitation, that Keating had obstructed the investigation, that (subject to our earlier qualification) Corbitt had sunk the car in the canal, and that all three defendants had agreed to conceal their actions relating to Dianne's murder indefinitely.

There is no question that the jury found, on sufficient and indeed abundant evidence, that defendants Masters and Keating committed, and all three defendants conspired to commit, two or more criminal acts that constitute "racketeering activity" within the meaning of the RICO statute. There were many distinct acts of bribery, criminal solicitation, and other crimes that come within the broad statutory definition of racketeering activity. The questions relate to the statutory requirements of "enterprise" and of "pattern." The alleged enterprise is an informal consortium of a law firm and two police departments with the three individuals who are the defendants. The defendants argue that a RICO enterprise, unless it is a legal entity such as an individual, a partnership, or a corporation, can only be a "union or group of *individuals*" (emphasis added), which Masters' law firm, the Willow Springs Police Department, and the Cook County Sheriff's Police Department are not. The argument has repeatedly and we think correctly been rejected, illustrative decisions being United States v. Feldman, 853 F.2d 648, 655 (9th Cir. 1988), and United States v. Perholtz, 268 U.S. App. D.C. 347, 842 F.2d 343, 352-53 (D.C. Cir. 1988) (per curiam). The statute says "'enterprise' includes"—not "'enterprise' means." The point of the definition is to make clear that it need not be a formal enterprise; "associated in fact" will do. Surely if three individuals can constitute a RICO enterprise, as no one doubts, then the larger association that consists of them plus entities that they control can be a RICO enterprise too. Otherwise while three criminal gangs would each be a RICO enterprise, a loose-knit merger of the three, in which each retained its separate identity, would not be, because it would not be an association of individuals. That would make no sense.

The next question is whether the acts of this enterprise formed a pattern. That rarely is a problem with a criminal enterprise, as distinct from a lawful enterprise that commits occasional criminal acts. The business of a criminal enterprise is crime. The crimes form a pattern defined by the purposes of the enterprise. United States v. Pungitore, 910 F.2d 1084, 1104 (3d Cir. 1990); United States v. Angiulo, 897 F.2d 1169, 1180 (1st Cir. 1990); United States v. Indelicato, 865 F.2d 1370, 1383 (2d Cir. 1989) (en banc) ("two racketeering acts that are not directly related to each other may nevertheless be related indirectly because each is related to the RICO enterprise"). The main purpose of the enterprise in this case was to bring under Masters' influence (for a price of course) the principal police agencies operating in his area of activity. He used this influence to obtain law business and to protect his clients. Like many a small businessman, legal and illegal, he did not make a rigid division between his business and his personal affairs. So when his wife's adultery and projected divorce brought about a personal crisis that he believed could best be resolved through murder, it was natural for him to "hire" his own criminal enterprise to help with the job. If it could protect bookmakers, maybe it could protect a murderer.

A criminal enterprise is more, not less, dangerous if it is versatile, flexible, diverse in its objectives and capabilities. Versatility, flexibility, and diversity are not inconsistent with pattern. The systematic corruption of law enforcement in the west Chicago suburbs brought about by the Masters enterprise could be used for a variety of purposes without destroying the integrity, the rationale, of the enterprise. The acts of a criminal enterprise within the scope of the enterprise's evolving objectives form pattern enough to satisfy the requirements of the RICO statute.

The most difficult issue relating to enterprise and pattern in this case is whether the two are separate. If the "enterprise" is just a name for the crimes the defendants committed, or for their agreement to commit these crimes that was charged separately in the conspiracy count, then it would not be an enterprise within the meaning of the statute. United States v. Turkette, 452 U.S. 576, 583, 69 L. Ed. 2d 246, 101 S. Ct. 2524 (1981); United States v. Neapolitan, 791 F.2d 489, 500 (7th Cir. 1986). Otherwise two statutory elements—enterprise and pattern—would be collapsed into one. The jury was properly instructed, however, that it had to find that the informal enterprise consisting of the three defendants and the three organizations that they controlled or manipulated existed as an organization with a structure and goals separate from the predicate acts themselves, and we cannot say that the jury's finding that it had such existence was without rational support in the record. The strongest evidence is the handling of the problem of dealing with Dianne Masters. When that problem arose, a loose-knit but effective criminal organization was in place ready to respond effectively by planning and carrying out a detection-proof crime that would have been beyond the capacities of the individual defendants acting either singly or without the aid of their organizations.

Criminal enterprises have less structure than legal ones. For formal relationships created by contract and rule they substitute informal relationships based on kinship and friendship. It would be ironic if the

RICO statute, aimed primarily at criminal enterprises such as the Mafia and its many petty imitators, was more effective against legal enterprises because the latter have a more perspicuous, articulated structure.

Despite the admitted elusiveness of the statutory terms, well illustrated by the preceding discussion, we do not agree with the defendants that, as applied to their activities, the statute is unconstitutionally vague. Provided the statutes criminalizing the predicate acts are not unconstitutionally vague—and no one argues they are—the defendants are on adequate notice that they are committing crimes, and the fact that they may not be aware of the extent of their criminality and consequent exposure to punishment is a detail (the original conception of RICO as a sentence-enhancement provision is pertinent here). So at least Fort Wayne Books, Inc. v. Indiana, 489 U.S. 46, 58, 103 L. Ed. 2d 34, 109 S. Ct. 916 (1989), appears to hold, although a narrower reading is proposed in United States v. Pungitore, supra, 910 F.2d at 1103 n.15. But forget *Fort Wayne Books* and the decision in this case must still be the same. The interpretive problems and resulting vagueness that afflict the RICO statute come from its application to lawful enterprises that commit occasional criminal acts. The miniature suburban mafia that the facts of this case disclose is within the statute's core. . . .

Affirmed in part, vacated in part, and remanded.

Questions

1. *The Requirements of RICO Liability.* For each subsection of 18 U.S.C. §1962, what is the specific *conduct* that is prohibited? What constitutes the "pattern of racketeering activity" in *Masters*? What constitutes the "enterprise" in *Masters*? Is there a difference between the "pattern of racketeering activity" and the "enterprise"? Can the enterprise be established simply by showing the pattern of racketeering activity? Must the acts constituting the pattern of racketeering activity be *in furtherance of* the enterprise (as is typically required in complicity and conspiracy) or just *performed by* the enterprise? Was the killing of Masters' wife in furtherance of or performed by the enterprise?

2. *RICO vs. Traditional Forms of Group Criminality.* Why did Congress feel a need to create RICO? That is, in what respect were existing criminal laws inadequate? Could Masters and his co-conspirators have been held liable for criminal offenses of similar seriousness without RICO? Could a person be held liable under RICO even if the person is not liable as a principal or an accomplice to any one of the underlying offenses constituting the "pattern of racketeering activity"? Could a

person be liable as an accomplice to one of these underlying offenses, yet not be liable under the RICO statute?

Gerard Lynch, RICO: The Crime of Being a Criminal
87 Colum. L. Rev. 661, 920, 932-953 (1987)

The Transaction-Based Model of Crime

Fundamental to our traditional law of crimes, criminal procedure and evidence is a conception of crime that is transaction-bound. Synthesizers of the common-law tradition tell us that the core of any definition of crime is a particular act or omission. That act or omission is conceived as taking place in an instant of time so precise that it can be associated with a particular mental state of intention, awareness of risk, or neglect of due care. The verbs that form the heart of the definitions of particular offenses ("takes and carries away," "engages in sexual intercourse," "damages by starting a fire," "sells a controlled substance") typically refer to single rather than repeated actions, completed in a brief span of time. Where the verbs in penal statutes instead refer to causing a particular result ("causes the death of another human being," "causes serious physical injury")—a process that can extend over a period of time—the focus of inquiry into a defendant's culpability must nevertheless be a specific, momentary act or omission. Even the crime of conspiracy, which in practice may permit an examination of an extended course of conduct by one or more individuals, does so in the guise of using that course of conduct as evidence from which to infer that a particular act of "agreement" occurred, presumably at a specific, if not precisely ascertainable, moment in time.

The focus on particular events in defining crimes is not merely a linguistic convention. The requirement that criminal punishment be based on a specific act has deep roots. The very nature of criminal punishment, as distinct from other uses of the compulsive power of the state (such as mandatory treatment for physical or mental illness), requires that a person not be punished for bad character, tendency to commit crime, or even a specifically formulated intention to commit some particular prohibited act. Before the state can deprive a citizen of liberty in a *punitive* way, the individual must manifest that character or tendency by the commission of some concrete prohibited act. In significant part, the purpose of this limitation is the protection of an individual from punishment for thoughts or traits not yet exemplified by actual harmful conduct. But the moral basis of the focus on particular acts extends beyond this problem. Even for those accused of committing what is unquestionably a concrete, particular offense, we are careful to guard against the possibility that a defendant may be convicted and punished for bad character rather than for the particular act charged. The insistence on incident-based liability thus has important consequences for our rules of procedure and evidence.

Since the crime with which a defendant is charged took place at a particular moment in time, the relevance of a defendant's actions prior to that moment is always problematic; some tendency to support an inference about what the defendant did or what he thought at the moment of the crime is always necessary for such a prior act or event to matter. We are particularly concerned about the relevance of prior actions which themselves constitute crimes. Because we fear that a jury will "irrationally" conclude that a person who has committed prior crimes will be guilty of the offense for which he stands accused on a particular occasion, or will dismiss the very question of his present guilt in favor of a condemnation of his general bad character, evidence of prior crimes—as well as evidence of general bad character or criminal associations—is usually excluded from evidence. Such information is admissible only where its particular relevance to the specific act charged greatly outweighs the "prejudice" it occasions by distracting the jury from the only question properly before it—the defendant's actions in the particular incident being examined. For similar reasons, charges that a defendant is guilty of more than one offense, or that two or more defendants are guilty of joint crimes, may only be tried together where the charges are so closely related that it would be manifestly inefficient to have separate trials. Where joint trials of different alleged offenses or offenders are permitted, we are—in theory at least—careful to guard against the danger that evidence relevant to one crime will unfairly "spill over" into what ought to be clinically pure evaluation of the evidence concerning another. A criminal trial thus tends to focus on a particular incident or transaction.

Both the procedural and substantive manifestations of the model of crime based on specific incidents or acts are indeed associated with a particular conception of the individual as a moral actor. The careful elaborations in our penal codes of the precise nature of the prohibited acts, and the equally careful calibrations of the degree of blameworthiness to be attributed to different prohibited acts, seem to presuppose actors with a free will to avoid the prohibited conduct, who can fairly be apportioned different degrees of guilt or punishment based on the nature of the conduct in which they have chosen to engage. Indeed, our rules of procedure seem to carry this notion of moral freedom even further. The individual is implicitly conceived not only as free in principle to act in accordance with or in violation of defined norms, but also as free in any given moment to make choices at odds with any consistent character that may be deduced from his prior acts. To infer that a defendant committed the particular offense for which he is being tried from the fact that he has previously committed other crimes of a generally similar nature—or, worse still, other crimes of an entirely different nature—is not only unfair, but inconsistent with a fundamental supposition that criminal behavior is punishable because it represents a free choice at a particular moment in time to commit an immoral act.

Indeed, the power of this model of the individual is so strong that some proponents of the "just deserts" model of punishment have argued that the focus on the individual incident rather than on the character of the offender should be extended even into the sentencing process. On this view, a defendant's past conduct or overall character would have no relevance at all in determining an appropriate sentence, giving especially concrete content to the idea of punishing the crime and not the criminal. At this point, however, our tradition until recently has balked, and the sentencing decision has been seen, within limits set by a vague principle of proportionality and by concrete maximum sentences devised by legislatures in correlation to the seriousness of particular offenses, as including appropriate attention to treatment and incapacitation goals based in part on the general character of the offender. The prevalence of legislative proposals for less discretionary, more conduct-based sentencing systems may suggest that the retributive view of crime may be weakening even the citadel of sentencing discretion.

The Enterprise Offense

RICO prosecutions of criminal enterprises present a serious challenge to the substantive and procedural implications of this transaction-based model of crime. . . .

Section 1962(c) . . . makes it a crime to "conduct or participate, directly or indirectly, in the conduct" of the affairs of any "enterprise . . . through a pattern of racketeering activity."[92] The very words of the statute reveal an intent to prohibit not any particular, time-bound action, but a course of conduct extending over a potentially lengthy period of time. Although the predicate acts of racketeering are conventional crimes, defined in terms of specific conduct, the actual RICO violation is not identifiable by the physical contours of a particular action or effect. Rather, the defining characteristic of the "pattern of racketeering" is the relationship of certain conduct to other conduct

---

92. 18 U.S.C. §1962(c) (1982).

and to the "enterprise" which itself is an abstract construct of certain interpersonal relationships. Whether or not this definition is vague in the technical legal sense of the work, the level of abstraction in the definition permits the offense to cover a wide variety of conduct for which ordinary language does not supply a single common term.

RICO is such an oddity among penal statutes that its exponents frequently claim that it is not really a criminal statute at all, arguing that "RICO is a remedial, as opposed to substantive, statute" because "[t]he provisions of section 1962 do not create 'new crimes' but serve as the prerequisites for the invocation of increased sanctions for conduct which is proscribed elsewhere in both federal and state criminal codes." But this claim is misleading. In formal terms, RICO is plainly a criminal statute; each of its provisions, including section 1962(c), defines a certain cluster of behaviors as a new crime. . . .

The distinction between remedial and substantive statutes is not merely formal or rhetorical; it has serious procedural and substantive consequences. [The author reviews the prosecutorial procedural advantages of RICO with regard to joinder, statutes of limitations, venue, and the rules of evidence, including the introduction in evidence of prior offenses and associations with other criminals.]

All of these procedural consequences stem from the fact that violation of section 1962(c) is defined as a single crime, and our procedural system, for reasons alluded to above, attaches considerable importance to the concept of a crime as a unified event, distinct from other crimes. If RICO's effects are principally remedial, in the sense that the statute's importance lies not in the prohibition of certain conduct, but in the procedural and sentencing consequences of committing conduct already defined as criminal, it accomplishes most of those effects precisely by the fact that it is indeed, in formal terms, a substantive criminal statute.

In substance, as well as in form, section 1962(c) defines a substantive crime. The RICO offense is *not* reducible to the predicate acts of racketeering. If the jury determines beyond a reasonable doubt that the defendant committed those acts, it still must find an additional element before it can convict: that the predicate acts were committed in the conduct of the affairs of an enterprise. . . .

The arguments made by appellants in *Turkette* and *Elliott* illustrate the importance of the enterprise element. In each case, the defendants' legal and factual claims were that the government had, at best, shown that various individuals had committed various distinct crimes. In effect, they were asserting the factual accuracy and legal necessity of applying a transactional view of crime to their various antisocial acts. The courts rejected this argument, however, holding the sum of its parts—that, at least on the facts of those cases, it was legitimate to hold the defendants guilty not only of a series of separate criminal transactions, but of entering into a relationship, exemplified by a course of conduct over a periods of years, that itself was criminal. It is the operation of the *criminal enterprise* through criminal acts, not merely the commission of the acts themselves, that constitutes the crime of RICO.

But whether or not a group of individuals, who, in various combinations, committed a series of predicate offenses, constituted an enterprise, and whether each of the defendants was part of that enterprise, are not always questions of historical fact. Where a criminal group has a sufficiently tangible organization, it may be possible to confirm the existence of enterprise, and to identify someone as a "member." But one need not be a "member" of an organization to participate in the conduct of its affairs, and, of course, not all illicit enterprises are so conveniently structured. As is often true with the "agreement" that is the *actus reus* of conspiracy, the jury is not necessarily being asked to decide whether a particular event occurred. Rather, it is being asked to impose a conceptual construct on the events that it finds took place. What the jury is being asked to decide is whether the defendant's acts should be treated as evidence of a commitment to a criminal association.

Such a commitment is not, in any conventional sense, an "act." The jury's task is to access in a global way the nature of the defendant's involvement in a network of criminal activities and associations, to determine whether the total picture of the defendant's criminal career permits the judgment that he has become part of an underworld of "enterprise." If character can be defined as the residue of a series of moral decisions, the jury in a very real sense is being asked to make a judgment on the defendant's character.

In making such a judgment, the jury is entitled to rely not only on evidence of the defendant's own crimes, but also on evidence of the crimes of those with whom he is alleged to have thrown in his lot. Such evidence is excluded from the transaction-model trial, precisely because it may distract the jury from its responsibility of deciding what the evidence shows about a particular act. In an illicit-enterprise RICO trial, it is admitted, precisely because the jury is asked to make a judgment not only about what discrete acts the defendant committed at particular moments in time, and what his intention was with respect to each act at those moments, but also about how those acts fit into his entire moral life: Were they parts of a pattern? Were they committed as part of his association with a subculture of crime?

RICO illicit association cases thus pose both a substantive and a procedural challenge to the transaction-bases model of criminal law. Substantively, the standard legal texts tell us that a distinct act or omission is the core event constituting a crime, and academic analyses of penal codes, including ones that in some ways radically attack the Anglo-American consensus, are principally concerned with articulating the precise circumstances in which specified acts should be subject to condemnation as crimes. The distinctive nature of criminal punishment, we are told, is that it represents a societal response to and judgment upon particular moral actions, rather than a person's character, status, or intentions. The RICO illicit association cases, in contrast, demand a more global judgment about a defendant's character and loyalties. To be found guilty, it is not enough that the defendant has committed specific criminal acts; those acts must be part of an ongoing commitment to the values of a criminal organization.

Our procedural and evidentiary rules support the substantive values of the transaction-based model of crime by rigorously focusing the trial process on information that bears indirectly on demonstrating what happened, in the physical world and in the defendant's consciousness, during the particular transaction under examination. RICO trials, however, permit a much wider exploration of the context of the particular predicate acts, both in the defendant's history, and within the institutions and communities of which he is a part.

Questions

1. *RICO as a New Breed of Offense.* Is RICO different in form from traditional criminal offenses? If so, how is it different and what advantages or dangers may flow from this?

2. *RICO, Character, and Dangerousness.* Why does the criminal law generally hesitate to punish an actor's character? Is the criminal law's concern for punishing character related to its concern for punishing mere status, as we saw in Robinson v. California? Does RICO punish an actor's "character" rather than the actor's acts? Is the act requirement satisfied in a prosecution for RICO? Is an actor's "character," as Lynch uses the term, different from his dangerousness? Is an offender's liability and punishment commonly increased if the offender is dangerous? Should it be?

3. *RICO Use Beyond Organized Crime.* Does anything in the requirements for RICO liability limit its use to organized crime? The Organized Crime Control Act of 1970, which created criminal RICO liability, also created a right of private plaintiffs to use the RICO statutes to bring civil actions for damages. 18 U.S.C. §1964(c). Plaintiffs were slow to use civil RICO, but the potential for recovering treble damages and attorneys' fees brought an increasing number of suits. Today, a sizable number of civil RICO plaintiffs use the statute to resolve ordinary commercial disputes arising between reputable business firms. As you

can imagine, this use of the statute is relatively controversial within the business community. The *NOW* case represents a further extension of the statute's use.

National Organization for Women, Inc. v. Scheidler
Supreme Court of the United States
—U.S.—, 114 S. Ct. 798, 127 L. Ed. 2d 99 (1994)

Chief Justice REHNQUIST delivered the opinion of the Court.

We are required once again to interpret the provisions of the Racketeer Influenced and Corrupt Organizations (RICO) chapter of the Organized Crime Control Act of 1970 (OCCA), Pub. L. 91-452, Title IX, 84 Stat. 941, as amended, 18 U.S.C. §§1961-1968 (1988 ed. and Supp. IV). Section 1962(c) prohibits any person associated with an enterprise from conducting its affairs through a pattern of racketeering activity. We granted certiorari to determine whether RICO requires proof that either the racketeering enterprise or the predicate acts of racketeering were motivated by an economic purpose. We hold that RICO requires no such economic motive.

Petitioner National Organization For Women, Inc. (NOW) is a national nonprofit organization that supports the legal availability of abortion; petitioners Delaware Women's Health Organization, Inc. (DWHO) and Summit Women's Health Organization, Inc. (SWHO) are health care centers that perform abortions and other medical procedures. Respondents are a coalition of antiabortion groups called the Pro-Life Action Network (PLAN), Joseph Scheidler and other individuals and organizations that oppose legal abortion, and a medical laboratory that formerly provided services to the two petitioner health care centers.

Petitioners sued respondents in the United States District Court for the Northern District of Illinois, alleging violations of the Sherman Act, 26 Stat. 209, as amended, 15 U.S.C. §1 et seq., and RICO's §§1962(a), (c), and (d), as well as several pendent state-law claims stemming from the activities of antiabortion protesters at the clinics. According to respondent Scheidler's congressional testimony, these protesters aim to shut down the clinics and persuade women not to have abortions. See, e. g., Abortion Clinic Violence, Oversight Hearings before the Subcommittee on Civil and Constitutional Rights of the House Committee on the Judiciary, 99th Cong., 1st and 2d Sess., 55 (1987) (statement of Joseph M. Scheidler, Executive Director, Pro-Life Action League). Petitioners sought injunctive relief, along with treble damages,

CHAPTER 19 RACKETEER AND CORRUPT ORGANIZATIONS   669

costs, and attorneys' fees. They later amended their complaint, and pursuant to local rules, filed a "RICO Case Statement" that further detailed the enterprise, the pattern of racketeering, the victims of the racketeering activity, and the participants involved.

The amended complaint alleged that respondents were members of a nationwide conspiracy to shut down abortion clinics through a pattern of racketeering activity including extortion in violation of the Hobbs Act, 18 U.S.C. §1951. Section 1951(b)(2) defines extortion as "the obtaining of property from another, with his consent, induced by wrongful use of actual or threatened force, violence, or fear, or under color of official right." Petitioners alleged that respondents conspired to use threatened or actual force, violence or fear to induce clinic employees, doctors, and patients to give up their jobs, give up their economic right to practice medicine, and give up their right to obtain medical services at the clinics. Petitioners claimed that this conspiracy "has injured the business and/or property interests of the [petitioners]." According to the amended complaint, PLAN constitutes the alleged racketeering "enterprise" for purposes of §1962(c).

The District Court dismissed the case pursuant to Federal Rule of Civil Procedure 12(b)(6). Citing Eastern Railroad Presidents Conference v. Noerr Motor Freight, Inc., 365 U.S. 127 (1961), it held that since the activities alleged "involved political opponents, not commercial competitors, and political objectives, not marketplace goals," the Sherman Act did not apply. It dismissed petitioners' RICO claims under §1962(a) because the "income" alleged by petitioners consisted of voluntary donations from persons opposed to abortion which "in no way were derived from the pattern of racketeering alleged in the complaint." The District Court then concluded that petitioners failed to state a claim under §1962(c) since "an economic motive requirement exists to the extent that some profit-generating purpose must be alleged in order to state a RICO claim." Finally, it dismissed petitioners' RICO conspiracy claim under §1962(d) since petitioners' other RICO claims could not stand.

The Court of Appeals affirmed. As to the RICO counts, it agreed with the District Court that the voluntary contributions received by respondents did not constitute income derived from racketeering activities for purposes of §1962(a). It adopted the analysis of the Court of Appeals for the Second Circuit in United States v. Ivic, 700 F.2d 51 (CA2 1983), which found an "economic motive" requirement implicit in the "enterprise" element of the offense. The Court of Appeals determined that "non-economic crimes committed in furtherance of non-economic motives are not within the ambit of RICO." Consequently, petitioners failed to state a claim under §1962(c). The Court of Appeals also affirmed dismissal of the RICO conspiracy claim under §1962(d).

We granted certiorari, 508 U.S.—(1993), to resolve a conflict among the courts of appeals on the putative economic motive requirement of 18 U.S.C. §1962(c) and (d). . . .

We [address] the question of whether the racketeering enterprise or the racketeering predicate acts must be accompanied by an underlying economic motive. Section 1962(c) makes it unlawful "for any person employed by or associated with any enterprise engaged in, or the activities of which affect, interstate or foreign commerce, to conduct or participate, directly or indirectly, in the conduct of such enterprise's affairs through a pattern of racketeering activity or collection of unlawful debt." Section 1961(1) defines "pattern of racketeering activity" to include conduct that is "chargeable" or "indictable" under a host of state and federal laws. RICO broadly defines "enterprise" in §1961(4) to "include any individual, partnership, corporation, association, or other legal entity, and any union or group of individuals associated in fact although not a legal entity." Nowhere in either §1962(c), or in the RICO definitions in §1961, is there any indication that an economic motive is required.

The phrase "any enterprise engaged in, or the activities of which affect, interstate or foreign commerce" comes the closest of any language in subsection (c) to suggesting a need for an economic motive. Arguably an enterprise engaged in interstate or foreign commerce would have a profit-seeking motive, but the language in §1962(c) does not stop there; it includes enterprises whose activities "affect" interstate or foreign commerce. Webster's Third New International Dictionary 35 (1969) defines "affect" as "to have a detrimental influence on—used especially in the phrase *affecting commerce*." An enterprise surely can have a detrimental influence on interstate or foreign commerce without having its own profit-seeking motives.

The Court of Appeals thought that the use of the term "enterprise" in §§1962(a) and (b), where it is arguably more tied in with economic motivation, should be applied to restrict the breadth of use of that term in §1962(c). Respondents agree, and point to our comment in Sedima, S. P. R. L. v. Imrex Co., 473 U.S. 479, 489 (1985), regarding the term "violation," that "we should not lightly infer that Congress intended the term [violation] to have wholly different meanings in neighboring subsections."

We do not believe that the usage of the term "enterprise" in subsections (a) and (b) leads to the inference that an economic motive is required in subsection (c). The term "enterprise" in subsections (a) and (b) plays a different role in the structure of those subsections than it does in subsection (c). Section 1962(a) provides that it "shall be unlawful for any person who has received any income derived, directly or indirectly, from a pattern of racketeering activity . . . to use or invest, directly or indirectly, any part of such income, or the proceeds of such income, in acquisition of any interest in, or the establishment or operation of, any enterprise which is engaged in, or the activities of which affect, interstate or foreign commerce." Correspondingly, §1962(b) states that it "shall be unlawful for any person through a pattern of racketeering activity or through collection of an unlawful debt to acquire or maintain, directly or indirectly, any interest in or control of any enterprise which is engaged in, or the activities of which affect, interstate or foreign commerce." The "enterprise" referred to in subsections (a) and (b) is thus something acquired through the use of illegal activities or by money obtained from illegal activities. The enterprise in these subsections is the victim of unlawful activity and may very well be a "profit-seeking" entity that represents a property interest and may be acquired. But the statutory language in subsections (a) and (b) does not mandate that the enterprise be a "profit-seeking" entity; it simply requires that the enterprise be an entity that was acquired through illegal activity or the money generated from illegal activity.

By contrast, the "enterprise" in subsection (c) connotes generally the vehicle through which the unlawful pattern of racketeering activity is committed, rather than the victim of that activity. Subsection (c) makes it unlawful for "any person employed by or associated with any enterprise . . . to conduct or participate . . . in the conduct of such enterprise's affairs through a pattern of racketeering activity. . . ." Consequently, since the enterprise in subsection (c) is not being acquired, it need not have a property interest that can be acquired nor an economic motive for engaging in illegal activity; it need only be an association in fact that engages in a pattern of racketeering activity.[5] Nothing in subsections (a) and (b) directs us to a contrary conclusion.

The Court of Appeals also relied on the reasoning of United States v. Bagaric, 706 F.2d 42 (CA2), cert. denied, 464 U.S. 840 (1983), to support its conclusion that subsection (c) requires an economic motive. In upholding the dismissal of a RICO claim against a political terrorist group, the *Bagaric* court relied in part on the congressional statement of findings which prefaces RICO and refers to the activities of groups that " 'drain[s] billions of dollars from America's economy by unlawful conduct and the illegal use of force, fraud, and corruption.' " 706 F.2d, at 57, n.13 (quoting OCCA, 84 Stat. 922). The Court of Appeals for the Second Circuit decided that the sort of activity thus condemned required an economic motive.

We do not think this is so. Respondents and the two courts of

---

5. One commentator uses the terms "prize," "instrument," "victim," and "perpetrator" to describe the four separate roles the enterprise may play in section 1962. See Blakey, The RICO Civil Fraud Action in Context: Reflections on Bennett v. Berg, 58 Notre Dame L. Rev. 237, 307-325 (1982).

appeals, we think, overlook the fact that predicate acts, such as the alleged extortion, may not benefit the protestors financially but still may drain money from the economy by harming businesses such as the clinics which are petitioners in this case.

We also think that the quoted statement of congressional findings is a rather thin reed upon which to base a requirement of economic motive neither expressed nor, we think, fairly implied in the operative sections of the Act. As we said in H. J. Inc. v. Northwestern Bell Telephone Co., 492 U.S. 229, 248 (1989), "the occasion for Congress' action was the perceived need to combat organized crime. But Congress for cogent reasons chose to enact a more general statute, one which, although it had organized crime as its focus, was not limited in application to organized crime."

In United States v. Turkette, 452 U.S. 576 (1981), we faced the analogous question of whether "enterprise" as used in §1961(4) should be confined to "legitimate" enterprises. Looking to the statutory language, we found that "there is no restriction upon the associations embraced by the definition: an enterprise includes any union or group of individuals associated in fact." Accordingly, we resolved that §1961(4)'s definition of enterprise "appears to include both legitimate and illegitimate enterprises within its scope; it no more excludes criminal enterprises than it does legitimate ones." We noted that Congress could easily have narrowed the sweep of the term "enterprise" by inserting a single word, "legitimate." Instead, Congress did nothing to indicate that "enterprise" should exclude those entities whose sole purpose was criminal.

The parallel to the present case is apparent. Congress has not, either in the definitional section or in the operative language, required that an "enterprise" in §1962(c) have an economic motive.

The Court of Appeals also found persuasive guidelines for RICO prosecutions issued by the Department of Justice in 1981. The guidelines provided that a RICO indictment should not charge an association as an enterprise, unless the association exists " 'for the purpose of maintaining operations directed toward an *economic* goal. . . .' " The Second Circuit, in United States v. Ivic, supra, believed these guidelines were entitled to deference under administrative law principles. See 700 F.2d, at 64. Whatever may be the appropriate deference afforded to such internal rules, for our purposes we need note only that the Department of Justice amended its guidelines in 1984. The amended guidelines provide that an association-in-fact enterprise must be "directed toward an economic *or other identifiable goal.*" U.S. Dept. of Justice, United States Attorney's Manual §9-110.360 (Mar. 9, 1984) (emphasis added).

Both parties rely on legislative history to support their positions. We believe the statutory language is unambiguous, and find in the parties' submissions respecting legislative history no such "clearly expressed legislative intent to the contrary" that would warrant a different construction. Respondents finally argue that the result here should be controlled by the rule of lenity in criminal cases. But the rule of lenity applies only when an ambiguity is present; "it is not used to beget one. . . . The rule comes into operation at the end of the process of construing what Congress has expressed, not at the beginning as an overriding consideration of being lenient to wrongdoers." *Turkette,* supra, at 587-588, n.10. We simply do not think there is an ambiguity here which would suffice to invoke the rule of lenity. "The fact that RICO has been applied in situations not expressly anticipated by Congress does not demonstrate ambiguity. It demonstrates breadth." *Sedima,* 473 U.S., at 499.[6]

We therefore hold that petitioners may maintain this action if respondents conducted the enterprise through a pattern of racketeering activity. The questions of whether the respondents committed the requisite predicate acts, and whether the commission of these acts fell into a pattern, are not before us. We hold only that RICO contains no economic motive requirement.

The judgment of the Court of Appeals is accordingly Reversed.

Questions

1. *Intended Reach of RICO.* Does a reading of the "Statement of Findings and Purpose" of RICO, quoted at the beginning of this chapter, suggest that Congress intended RICO to apply to the anti-abortion protestors in *NOW?* What is the Supreme Court's view of the "Statement of Findings and Purposes"?

2. *Economic Motive.* Does anything in the body of the RICO statute require an economic motive? Does an "economic motive" exist in the more traditional use of RICO against organized crime members? Under the traditional use, does each offense typically have an economic motive,

---

6. Several of the respondents, and several *amici* argue that application of RICO to anti-abortion protesters could chill legitimate expression protected by the First Amendment. However, the question presented for review asked simply whether the Court should create an unwritten requirement limiting RICO to cases where either the enterprise or racketeering activity has an overriding economic motive. None of the respondents made a constitutional argument as to the proper construction of RICO in the Court of Appeals, and their constitutional argument here is directed almost entirely to the nature of their activities, rather than to the construction of RICO. We therefore decline to address the First Amendment question argued by respondents and the *amici.*

or the enterprise itself? Did Masters have an economic motive for having his wife killed? Did the "enterprise" in *Masters* that did the killing operate for an economic motive?

    3. *Use of RICO for Prosecution of Persons Other than Organized Crime Members. NOW* suggests that RICO can be used to prosecute persons other than those involved in organized crime. What are the limits on the kind of cases for which RICO can be used? Could it be used against a corporation that systematically bribes governmental officials to get better government contracts? Could it be used against antiwar or anti-draft protestors who destroy Selective Service records, throw vials of blood on the Pentagon, and harass military recruiters who come to college campuses? Could it be used against labor unions whose members sometimes yell threats of violence against those who cross their picket line?

Chapter 20. HATE CRIMES

Many states have recently enacted so-called "hate crimes," which make it a more serious offense to commit a crime against a victim because the victim is a member of a certain group. The Wisconsin statute below is typical.

Recurring Nightmare of Hate Crimes
National Journal, Dec. 15, 1990, v. 22, no. 50, p. 3045

. . . Late last summer, Amber Jefferson, a 15-year-old high school cheerleader in Orange County, Calif., almost lost her life because of the fact that she has one white and one black parent. Four attackers, allegedly all white, beat her with a baseball bat and split her face open with a shard of plate glass. Surgery to fix the wounds took 10 hours. It will be two years before she regains muscle control in her face.

In Kentucky this September, assailants beat a young gay man with a tire iron, locked him in a car trunk with a bunch of snapping turtles and then tried to set the car on fire. He was left with severe brain damage.

In the Pacific Northwest, a study by the Northwest Coalition Against Malicious Harassment found that hate crimes motivated by a reaction against the race, religion or sexual orientation of the victim rose 20 percent last year. There were 149 assaults, two cross-burnings and a murder in the region.

Los Angeles County reported 378 hate crimes last year, with a marked increase in assaults against blacks, Hispanics, Jews and Arabs. In Maryland, from 1986-89, assaults, arson, cross-burnings and threats prompted by the victim's race or religion more than doubled, to 686. . . .

Anti-Semitic attacks erupt regularly, even at such supposedly progressive, enlightened institutions as the University of Wisconsin (Madison), where a Jewish student center has been pelted with rocks and bottles and where Jewish fraternities and sororities have been vandalized. Counselors at a Madison Jewish camp discovered that the brake linings had been cut on a bus used to transport children—fortunately before the bus was used. A Madison synagogue, after repeated anti-Semitic incidents, was kept under armed guard for some time. . . .

Wisconsin Criminal Code §939.645
Crimes Committed Against Certain People or Property*

(1) If a person does all of the following, the penalties for the underlying crime are increased as provided in sub. (2):

(a) Commits a crime under chs. 939 to 948.

(b) Intentionally selects the person against whom the crime under par. (a) is committed or selects the property which is damaged or otherwise affected by the crime under par. (a) because of the race, religion, color, disability, sexual orientation, national origin or ancestry of that person or the owner or occupant of that property.

(2) (a) If the crime committed under sub. (1) is ordinarily a misdemeanor other than a Class A misdemeanor, the revised maximum fine is $10,000 and the revised maximum period of imprisonment is one year in the county jail.

(b) If the crime committed under sub. (1) is ordinarily a Class A misdemeanor, the penalty increase under this section changes the status of the crime to a felony and the revised maximum fine is $10,000 and the revised maximum period of imprisonment is two years.

(c) If the crime committed under sub. (1) is a felony, the maximum fine prescribed by law for the crime may be increased by not more than $5,000 and the maximum period of imprisonment prescribed by law for the crime may be increased by not more than five years.

(3) This section provides for the enhancement of the penalties applicable for the underlying crime. The court shall direct that the trier of fact find a special verdict as to all of the issues specified in sub. (1).

---

*Editor's Note.—This is the Wisconsin statute in force at the time of the *Mitchell* case reproduced below. It has been modified slightly since then. Like many other state statutes of this sort, it is based in part on the model statute of the Anti-Defamation League of B'nai B'rith (ADL). See ADL Law Report: Hate Crimes Statutes: A 1991 Status Report 4 (1991).

(4) This section does not apply to any crime if proof of race, religion, color, disability, sexual orientation, national origin or ancestry is required for a conviction for that crime.

State v. Mitchell
Supreme Court of Wisconsin
485 N.W.2d 807 (1992)

HEFFERNAN, Chief Justice. . . .

The sole issue before the court is the constitutionality of sec. 939.645, the "hate crimes" statute. Mitchell asserts that the statute on its face violates: (1) his right of free speech guaranteed by the First Amendment and (2) his right to due process and equal protection of the laws guaranteed by the Fourteenth Amendment. We hold that the statute violates the First Amendment and is thus unconstitutional.

The facts are not in dispute. On October 7, 1989, a group of young black men and boys gathered at an apartment complex in Kenosha. Todd Mitchell, nineteen at the time, was one of the older members of the group. Some of the group were at one point discussing a scene from the movie "Mississippi Burning" where a white man beat a young black boy who was praying.

Approximately ten members of the group moved outdoors, still talking about the movie. Mitchell asked the group: "Do you all feel hyped up to move on some white people?" A short time later, Gregory Reddick, a fourteen-year-old white male, approached the apartment complex. Reddick said nothing to the group, and merely walked by on the other side of the street. Mitchell then said "you all want to fuck somebody up? There goes a white boy; go get him." Mitchell then counted to three and pointed the group in Reddick's direction.

The group ran towards Reddick, knocked him to the ground, beat him severely, and stole his "British Knights" tennis shoes. The police found Reddick unconscious a short while later. He remained in a coma for four days in the hospital, and the record indicates he suffered extensive injuries and possibly permanent brain damage.

Mitchell was convicted of aggravated battery, party to a crime. The jury separately found that Mitchell intentionally selected Reddick as the battery victim because of Reddick's race. The aggravated battery conviction carried a maximum sentence of two years. Because the jury found that Mitchell selected Reddick because of his race, sec. 939.645(2)(c) increased the potential maximum sentence for aggravated battery to seven years. The trial court sentenced Mitchell to four years for the aggravated battery.

After the circuit court denied Mitchell's request for a post conviction relief, Mitchell appealed the judgments of conviction and the sentence to the court of appeals, focusing on the constitutionality of the hate crimes statute. On June 5, 1991, the court of appeals affirmed the circuit court's judgments, concluding that Mitchell waived any equal protection and that the statute was neither vague nor overbroad. We granted Mitchell's petition for review on the constitutionality of the hate crimes statute, and now reverse.

This case presents an issue which has spawned a growing debate in this country: the constitutionality of legislation that seeks to address hate crimes. . . . Individuals and organizations traditionally allied behind the same agenda have separated on the issue of the legitimacy of hate crimes statutes. As one commentator noted:

> [T]he debate over these laws is occurring not merely between traditional allies, but between one side and itself. Moreover, whenever either viewpoint prevails, whether in the legislature, the courts, or even in a purely academic argument, its proponents do not seem to be very happy about it. They can see very well their opponents point of view, and in fact, largely agree with it. It is as if everyone involved in the debate over the permissibility and desirability of ethnic intimidation laws were actually on *both* sides at once.

Susan Gellman, 39 U.C.L.A. L. Rev. at 334 (emphasis in original).

The hate crimes statute violates the First Amendment directly by punishing what the legislature has deemed to be offensive thought and violates the First Amendment indirectly by chilling free speech.

The First Amendment of the United States Constitution states bluntly: "Congress shall make no law . . . abridging the freedom of speech." The First Amendment protects not only speech but thought as well. "[A]t the heart of the First Amendment is the notion that an individual should be free to believe as he will, and that in a free society one's beliefs should be shaped by his mind and his conscience, rather than coerced by the state." Even more fundamentally, the Constitution protects all speech and thought, regardless of how offensive it may be. "[I]f there is a bedrock principle underlying the First Amendment, it is that the government may not prohibit the expression of an idea simply because society finds the idea itself offensive or disagreeable." . . .

Without doubt the hate crimes statute punishes bigoted thought. The state asserts that the statute punishes only the "conduct" of intentional selection of a victim. We disagree. Selection of a victim is an element of the underlying offense, part of the defendant's "intent" in committing the crime. The state punishes the "because of" aspect of the defendant's selection, the *reason* the defendant selected the victim, the *motive* behind the selection.

. . . Because all of the crimes under chs. 393 to 948 are already punishable, all that remains is an additional punishment for the defendant's motive in selecting the victim. The punishment of the defendant's bigoted motive by the hate crimes statute directly implicates and encroaches upon First Amendment rights.

While the statute does not specifically phrase the "because of . . . race, religion, color, [etc.]" element in terms of bias or prejudice, it is clear from the history of antibias statutes, detailed above, that sec. 939.645, Stats., is expressly aimed at the bigoted bias of the actor. Merely because the statute refers in a literal sense to the intentional "conduct" of selecting, does not mean the court must turn a blind eye to the intent or practical effect of the law—punishment of offensive motive or thought. The conduct of "selecting" is not akin to the conduct of assaulting, burglarizing, murdering and other criminal conduct. It cannot be objectively established. Rather, an examination of the intentional "selection" of a victim necessarily requires a subjective examination of the actor's motive or reason for singling out the particular person against whom he or she commits a crime.

In this case, Todd Mitchell selected Gregory Reddick because Reddick is white. Mitchell is black. The circumstantial evidence relied upon to prove that Mitchell selected Reddick because Reddick is white included Mitchell's speech—"Do you all feel hyped up to move on some white people?"—and his recent discussion with other black youths of a racially charged scene from the movie "Mississippi Burning." This evidence was used not merely to show the intentional selection of the victim, but was used to prove Mitchell's bigoted bias. The physical assault of Reddick is the same whether he was attacked because of his skin color or because he was wearing "British Knight" tennis shoes. Mitchell's bigoted motivation for selecting Reddick, his thought which impelled him to act, is the reason that his punishment was enhanced. In Mitchell's case, that motivation was apparently a hatred of whites.

The statute commendably is designed to punish—and thereby deter—racism and other objectionable biases, but deplorably unconstitutionally infringes upon free speech. The state would justify its transgression against the constitutional right of freedom of speech and thought because its motive is a good one, but the magnitude of the proposed incursion against the constitutional right of all of us should no more be diminished for that good motive than should a crime be enhanced by a separate penalty because of a criminal's bad motive.

. . . The hate crimes statute enhances the punishment of bigoted criminals because they are bigoted. The statute is directed solely at the subjective motivation of the actor—his or her prejudice. Punishment of one's thought, however repugnant the thought, is unconstitutional. . . .

Finally, we consider the argument advanced by the *amici curiae*

ADL, et. al., and embraced by the dissent that an analogy exists between the hate crimes statute and antidiscrimination laws, and that the numerous United States Supreme Court decisions upholding antidiscrimination laws lend support to the hate crimes statute. We disagree.

Discrimination and bigotry are not the same thing. Under antidiscrimination statutes, it is the discriminatory act which is prohibited. Under the hate crimes statute, the "selection" which is punished is not an act, it is a mental process. In this case the act was the battery of Reddick; what was punished by the hate crimes statute was Mitchell's reason for selecting Reddick, his discriminatory motive. . . .

In the wake of the Los Angeles riots sparked by the acquittal of four white police officers accused of illegally beating black motorist Rodney King, it is increasingly evident that racial antagonism and violence are as prevalent now as they ever have been. Indeed, added to the statistical compilation of bias related crimes could be the vicious beating of white truck driver Reginald Denny by black rioters, horrifyingly captur[ed] on film by a news helicopter. As disgraceful and deplorable as these and other hate crimes are, the personal prejudices of the attackers are protected by the First Amendment. The Constitution may not embrace or encourage bigoted and hateful thoughts, but it surely protects them.

Because we wholeheartedly agree with the motivation of the legislature in its desire to suppress hate crimes, it is with great regret that we hold the hate crimes statute unconstitutional—and only because we believe that the greater evil is suppression of freedom of speech for all of us.

The decision of the court of appeals is reversed and the cause remanded to the circuit court for resentencing on the aggravation battery conviction.

Shirley S. ABRAHAMSON, Justice (dissenting). . . .

Section 939.645 addresses only those crimes committed "because of" the victim's "race, religion, color, disability, sexual orientation, national origin or ancestry." It does not punish all crimes committed by persons who have expressed bigoted beliefs. An individual may commit a criminal act. That same individual may possess or express bigoted beliefs. These two facts standing alone, however, do not subject that individual to punishment under sec. 939.645.

In my mind, it is the tight nexus between the selection of the victim and the underlying crime that saves this statute. The state must prove beyond a reasonable doubt both that the defendant committed the underlying crime and that the defendant intentionally selected the victim because of characteristics protected under the statute. To prove intentional selection of the victim, the state cannot use evidence that the defendant has bigoted beliefs or has made bigoted statements unrelated to the particular crime. Evidence of a person's traits or beliefs would not be permissible for the purpose of proving the person acted in conformity therewith on a particular occasion. The statute requires the state to show evidence of bigotry relating directly to the defendant's intentional selection of this particular victim upon whom to commit the charged crime. The state must directly link the defendant's bigotry to the invidiously discriminatory selection of the victim and to the commission of the underlying crime.

Interpreted in this way, I believe the Wisconsin statute ties discriminatory selection of a victim to conduct already punishable by state law in a manner sufficient to prevent erosion of First Amendment protection of bigoted speech and ideas.

Read narrowly as the legislature intended, this statute is a prohibition on conduct, not on belief or expression. The statute does nothing more than assign consequences to invidiously discriminatory acts. . . .

For the reasons set forth, I dissent.

BABLITCH, Justice (dissenting).

> everywhere the crosses are burning,
> sharp-shooting goose-steppers around every corner,
> there are snipers in the schools . . .
> (I know you don't believe this.
> You think this is nothing
> but faddish exaggeration. But they
> are not shooting at you.)

Lorna Dee CERVANTES.

The law in question is not a "hate speech" law.

Nor is it really a "hate crimes" law as it has been somewhat inappropriately named.

It is a law against discrimination—discrimination in the selection of a crime victim.

Today the majority decides that the same Constitution which does not protect discrimination in the marketplace does protect discrimination that takes place during the commission of a crime. Numerous federal and state laws exist which prohibit discrimination in the selection of who is to be hired, or fired, or promoted. No one seriously (at least until today) questions their constitutionality. Yet the majority today gives constitutional protection to discrimination in the selection of who is to be the victim of a crime. Both sets of laws involve discrimination, both involve victims, both involve action "because of" the victim's status. . . .

These are laws against discrimination, pure and simple. Dictionaries do not disagree on the meaning of the term discrimination: to distinguish, to differentiate, to act on the basis of prejudice. Laws forbidding discrimination in the marketplace and laws forbidding discrimination in criminal activity have a common denominator: They are triggered when a person acts "because of" the victim's protected status. These exact words appear in most, if not all antidiscrimination laws. These exact words appear in the laws before us today.

Yet the majority says one is constitutional, one is not. I submit it is pure sophistry to distinguish the two. In its efforts to protect speech, the majority's constitutional pen gets too close to the trees and fails to see the forest.

The majority rationalizes their conclusion by insisting that this statute punishes bigoted thought. Not so. The statute does not impede or punish the right of persons to have bigoted thoughts or to express themselves in a bigoted fashion or otherwise, regarding the race, religion, or other status of a person. It does attempt to limit the effects of bigotry. What the statute does punish is acting upon those thoughts. It punishes the act of discriminatory selection plus criminal conduct, not the thought or expression of bigotry. The Constitution allows a person to have bigoted thoughts and to express them, but it does not allow a person to act on them. The majority says otherwise. I disagree.

I conclude the statute in question is neither vague nor overbroad, nor does it offend equal protection. Accordingly, I dissent. . . .

Questions

1. *Criminalizing Intention and Motive.* Is a "hate crime," like the crime defined in the Wisconsin statute, different in a fundamental way from other criminal offenses that we have examined? Why does the *Mitchell* court think that this kind of crime is different?

2. *Motive as an Offense Element.* Webster's Dictionary defines "motive" as "something (as a need or desire) that causes a person to act." It frequently is said that "motive is irrelevant to criminal liability." It is what the actor does and the actor's awareness of the nature of the conduct that matters, not the actor's motive for acting. Hate crimes are criticized in part because they are said to violate this rule against looking at motive. Is it true that an actor's motivation generally is irrelevant to liability in modern codes? Review the definition of "purpose" in Model Penal Code §2.02(2)(a). Is motive a sentence enhancement when murder is punished more severely when committed "for pecuniary gain"? See, e.g., Model Penal Code §210.6(3)(g).

3. *Hate Crimes and RICO.* Is the gravamen of the offense the actor's despicable motive and what that motive tells us about the kind of person he or she is, or is it something else? Does the answer depend on how

the "hate crime" is formulated? One of the concerns expressed about RICO is its tendency to punish bad character rather than bad acts. Can one make the same claim about hate crimes?

4. *Hate as a Crime.* Assume an actor assaults another because he hates that person. Should his liability be greater because of his hate motivation? Why or why not? Is his conduct more condemnable or more dangerous than the same conduct with a different motivation? Why do hate crime statutes punish hatred of a group but not hatred of an individual? And, if the hate motivation is the essence of the offense, why should it be limited to hate for *particular* classes of persons? If the rationale of the offense is to criminalize and punish something other than simply the hate motivation, what could that other rationale be?

5. *Which Groups?* If there is justification for increasing punishment for hatred of a group, which groups are to be given this special treatment? Is it just those groups that historically have been victimized? (Could one argue, for example, that only crimes against members of such groups tend to intimidate or terrorize persons other than the immediate victim? Should the offense be applicable to nonminorities, as it was in *Mitchell*? Why or why not?

6. *Constitutional Challenges.* How might one alter the Wisconsin statute to avoid the difficulties that the Wisconsin Supreme Court seems concerned about? Would your alternative formulation of the Wisconsin statute look to the actor's motive? Would it limit the offense to certain classes of victims? Some courts have found statutes like Wisconsin's to be unconstitutional, as did the Wisconsin Supreme Court in *Mitchell.* See, e.g., State v. Wyant, 597 N.E.2d 450 (Ohio 1992). In R.A.V. v. St. Paul, 112 S. Ct. 2538 (1992), the United States Supreme Court struck down a statute that criminalized certain forms of expression; in that case the defendants burned a cross. But more recently such statutes have been upheld against constitutional challenge. *Mitchell* was reversed on appeal to the United States Supreme Court, in Wisconsin v. Mitchell, —U.S.—, 113 S. Ct. 2194, 124 L. Ed. 2d 436 (1993), and *Wyant* was vacated, 113 S. Ct. 2954 (1993). The Court held that statutes like Wisconsin's merely regulate nonexpressive conduct.

7. *Crimes of Group Terror.* How is the following statute similar and different from the Wisconsin statute?

> Causing or Risking Group Intimidation or Terror.
>
> Any person who commits an offense and, by such conduct, purposely or recklessly causes or hopes to cause intimidation or terror in a group of persons who identify with the victim through race, religion, gender, sexual preference, [or other group self-identification], shall be liable for an offense under this section. If the person purposely causes or hopes to cause such intimidation or terror, the offense is a [fourth degree

felony]. If the person recklessly causes such intimidation or terror, the offense is a [second degree misdemeanor].[17]

Hate Crimes: Crimes of Motive, Character, or Group Terror?, 1992/93 Annual Survey of American Law 605, 615. Could this offense be subject to First Amendment challenge? What cases, if any, included within the prohibition of the Wisconsin statute would not be included within this statute? What cases, if any, would be included within this statute but not Wisconsin's?

---

17. Offense grades are included not to propose the particular grades; different statutory grades have different meanings in different jurisdictions. The point, rather, is to show that purpose and recklessness as to causing intimidation or terror in the group might be graded differently.

VI/A FINAL OVERVIEW

Chapter 21. FUNCTIONS OF CRIMINAL LAW

We may think of criminal law doctrine as having the single function of imposing punishment but, in reality, it has three related but distinct functions. It must define and announce to the general public the conduct that is prohibited (or required) by the criminal law. It must tell judges and juries how to decide whether a violation of these rules of conduct is an appropriate basis for criminal liability. And, finally, it must determine the general amount of liability and punishment to be imposed, the grade of liability. More on these functions in a moment. As will become evident, each of these functions calls for a different set of legal rules, each of a different sort.

Your Basement Burglar

You are awakened by an unfamiliar sound from the basement garage of your rowhouse. As you sit up in bed, the handgun in your hall closet comes to mind; then you remember Earl Miller, a neighbor down the row who shot and killed a night burglar in his garage last year. The prosecutor said Earl had no right to kill the burglar. Earl's attorney claimed that Earl had the right and that even if Earl didn't—although he was sure Earl did—Earl honestly and reasonably believed he had the right. Earl was tried and acquitted. You aren't sure what that means for you. Can you or can't you lawfully shoot a burglar in your basement garage?

You grab your gun from the hall closet and head down to the first floor. The light switch is at the head of the basement stairs. You open the door quietly, flip the switch, and draw back into the dark hall. The sound of steps are followed by the shattering of glass, a muffled scream, and silence. On descending the stairs, you find the intruder standing by the back door. You quickly aim, squeeze . . . blam! After recovering from the recoil of the handgun, you realize that you missed the intruder.

You are about to squeeze off another round but it occurs to you that the intruder is motionless. A closer look shows him to be unconscious, hanging from the back door with his arm through the door's broken window. Blood is pouring from a cut in his neck.

You believe you can stop the bleeding by applying pressure but you don't really want to help the man: After all, you think he might have intended to steal from you. And on top of that, the gushing blood and mess make you wince. Should you help him? Must you? You aren't sure. You remember a newspaper story about a motorist who stood and watched another motorist bleed to death after their cars collided. The prosecutor claimed that the motorist could have and should have stopped the bleeding, but he stood and watched . . . which is exactly what you are doing now. The motorist's attorney claimed that he had no legal duty to act and, in any case, was dazed from the accident. The man was tried and acquitted. What does that mean for you? If you can, must you help the intruder? Will you be a criminal if you just stand and do nothing?

You wish you weren't thinking so clearly. Perhaps it would have been better to have fallen down the stairs and been dazed. Not a good time to be making jokes, you conclude.

Would it have been legal for you to have shot the burglar in your basement? Are you criminally liable for not helping?

Notes on the Functions of Criminal Law Doctrine

Rule articulation, liability, and grading As noted above, criminal law doctrine has three primary functions. First, it must define the conduct that is prohibited (or required) by the criminal law. Such "rules of conduct," as they have been called, provide ex ante direction to the members of the community as to the conduct that must be avoided (or that must be performed) upon pain of criminal sanction. This may be termed the *rule articulation function* of the doctrine. Where a violation of the rules of conduct occurs, the criminal law must take on another role. It must decide whether the violation is sufficiently blameworthy to merit criminal liability. This second function, setting the minimum conditions for *liability*, is part of the adjudication process. It assesses ex post whether an actor who violates a rule of conduct is culpable for the violation and therefore ought to be held criminally liable for it.[1]

---

1. For a general discussion, see Paul H. Robinson, Rules of Conduct and Principles of Adjudication, 57 U. Chi. L. Rev. 729 (1990). The distinction between rules of conduct and principles of adjudication is well-known in legal philosophy. It was most recently

Finally, where liability is to be imposed, criminal law doctrine must assess the relative seriousness of the violation and blameworthiness of the offender in order to determine the amount of punishment, in general terms, that is appropriate. While the first step in the adjudication process expresses a simple yes or no decision as to whether the minimum conditions for liability are satisfied, this second step, the *grading* function, expresses a judgment of degree.

Functions cut across doctrinal distinctions These three functions—rule articulation, liability, and grading—are the primary functions of criminal law doctrine, but they are not reflected in the current doctrinal structure. Some elements of offenses serve one function while other elements serve other functions. Nor are the different functions reflected in the traditional distinctions between offense elements, actus reus and mens rea, or objective and culpability elements. Similarly, some defenses serve one function while other defenses serve other functions. To give a sense of which doctrines serve which functions requires a review of most aspects of the doctrine.

Rule articulation doctrines As a group, the rule articulation doctrines define the criminal law's rules of conduct. The rules state both prohibitions and requirements:

> No person shall take, exercise control over, or transfer property of another without consent of the owner.

Presumably, your basement burglar was in the process of violating this prohibition, as well as one that prohibits entry without consent. The law's prohibitions concern not only conduct under certain circumstances—"without consent of the owner," "property of another"—but also conduct that creates a certain risk.

> No person shall engage in conduct that creates a risk of death to another person.

Thus, much of the criminal law's rule articulation function is performed by the conduct and circumstance elements of offenses.

Duties and omissions The law not only prohibits some conduct but also affirmatively requires other conduct.

> All legal custodians of a child must protect the child's health and safety.

Or,

> All persons over the age of 18 must register with the Selective Service System.

---

reintroduced into criminal law debate by Mier Dan-Cohen, Decision Rules and Conduct Rules: On Acoustic Separation in Criminal Law, 97 Harv. L. Rev. 625 (1984).

You may have a similar legal duty to save the life of the helpless bleeding burglar. The law creates many duties and punishes the failure to perform them. The law's statement of legal duties, then, serves part of the law's rule articulation function.

Secondary prohibitions In addition to these "primary violations" are what may be called "secondary violations." Secondary violations are not independent prohibitions but rather prohibitions defined by reference to the primary rules. Not only are persons bound to avoid conduct that would be a primary prohibition, but also:

> No person shall engage in conduct that assists another person in conduct that would be a violation [of the rules of conduct].
> No person shall attempt to engage in conduct that would constitute a violation [of the rules of conduct].[2]

Thus, additional aspects of the criminal law's rule articulation function are performed by the conduct and circumstance elements of such secondary prohibitions as complicity and inchoate offenses.

Criminalization culpability elements Not all rule articulation doctrines are objective elements, like conduct and circumstance elements. Some mens rea requirements serve to define the rules of conduct. That is, they are necessary elements in describing the conduct that the criminal law prohibits. In the general attempt offense, for example, the conduct and circumstance elements of the offense provide some statement of the prohibition but standing alone these objective elements do not fully define the prohibited conduct. The requirement that the conduct constitute a "substantial step toward commission of an offense," which is common in modern attempt definitions,[3] is inadequate in itself to define the conduct that is prohibited. As a purely objective matter, some conduct may constitute a "substantial step toward commission of an offense" but in fact may be entirely innocent and acceptable conduct and is not meant to be prohibited. Your shooting the target in your basement may not be an offense. Such conduct becomes unacceptable and a societal harm only when accompanied by an intention to violate the substantive rules of conduct. That is, your shooting is potentially criminal only because you intended to shoot another person. Lighting one's pipe is not a violation of the rules of conduct, unless it is a step in a plan to ignite a neighbor's haystack. Giving a young girl a ride is not a violation of the rules of conduct, unless it is done with the intention of sexually assaulting her. Thus, to describe the minimum requirements of prohibited conduct, the definition of a criminal at-

---

2. Nor may one conspire with or solicit another to engage in conduct that would constitute a violation of the rules of conduct.

3. See Model Penal Code §5.01(1)(c).

tempt must include a state of mind requirement—the intention to engage in conduct that would constitute a rule violation.

Criminalization offense modifications Also serving the rule articulation function are miscellaneous doctrines outside of offense definitions. These doctrines, such as the consent defense, further modify or refine the conduct rules. While the rules prohibit conduct that risks causing bodily harm, an exception to the prohibition is admitted where the victim consents to a risk of minor injury or where the risk arises from participation in a lawful sporting event.[4]

Justification defenses Taken together, these rule articulation doctrines give a complete account of what a person must not do or must do in order to obey the criminal law. They are not, however, a complete statement of the rules of conduct. The law recognizes that in some instances a greater harm can be avoided or a greater good can be achieved by allowing a person to violate a prohibition. Burning another person's property is a violation but it is to be tolerated (even encouraged) if the burning acts as a firebreak to save a town. Striking another person without consent is a violation but such is to be tolerated if done by a police officer if necessary to overcome resistance to a lawful arrest. These doctrines of justification are permissive only; they tell persons when they will be permitted to violate a rule of conduct.[5] While your attempt to shoot another person normally would be illegal, it may be justified if it serves to protect yourself and your house.

Confusion in rules of conduct The rules of lawful conduct frequently are unclear even to actors who are intelligent, thoughtful, and informed. Can you lawfully shoot the intruding burglar? Does the law require that you aid the helpless burglar? In the situation described above, the actor knows the disposition of a recently litigated case closely analogous to each dilemma confronted, and seeks to use that outcome to guide his own conduct; yet he is still unable to discern the applicable legal rules. Such uncertainty is not uncommon in our current system. Frequently, neither existing statements of the law nor our process of public adjudication effectively communicate the rules that define lawful conduct. Unfortunately, current criminal law doctrine does a poor job at one of its most important functions: telling people what they can, must, and must not do, under threat of criminal sanction.

Need for clear rules Our condemnation and punishment of criminal law violators, as distinguished from civil violators, rests upon an

---

4. See, e.g., Model Penal Code §2.11 (consent is a defense to conduct which causes or threatens bodily injury when the injury and conduct consented to are not serious or are reasonably foreseeable hazards of participation in an athletic contest or sport which is a lawful activity).

5. For a further discussion of the doctrines of justification and their relation to the doctrines of criminalization, see Robinson, Rules, supra note 1, at 740-742.

assumption that a criminal violation entails some consciousness of wrongdoing or at least a gross deviation from a clearly defined standard of conduct. But how can such an assumption be sustained if the demands of the law are unclear? How can we condemn and punish violations of the rules of conduct if the rules are not and cannot reasonably be known by the general public? One also may wonder how effective the criminal law can be in deterring criminal conduct if the law's demands are unclear.[6]

Doctrines of liability The liability function of criminal law doctrine arises from the special condemnatory nature of criminal law, which requires that inadvertent and unavoidable violations not be punished. If the actor's conduct is blameless, liability ought not be imposed, even though the actor may well have caused the harm or evil described by the rules of conduct.[7] Further, the moral base of the criminal law is such that liability properly is reserved for violations of sufficient seriousness committed with sufficient culpability to justify the condemnation of criminal liability.

Offense culpability elements To assure this minimum level of culpability, the law requires proof of an actor's culpability as to each rule articulation element of an offense.[8] Thus, the "burglar" in your basement is liable for burglary only if he knew it was another's house that he was entering without permission. If, because all of the rowhouses are identical and he just moved in next door, he had entered your garage honestly believing it to be his own, his trespass might be a violation of the rules of conduct but might not be a sufficiently culpable violation to merit criminal liability. Generally, at least recklessness as to each such objective element is required. Thus, an actor must be aware of a substantial risk that his conduct may cause another's death or obstruct a highway or that the property he is taking belongs to another. This preference for recklessness as the normal minimum culpability required is expressed by provisions like Model Penal Code's, which "read in" recklessness whenever an offense definition is silent on the required culpability as to an offense element.[9]

Culpability offense modifications Some of the requirements for assuring an actor's blameworthiness are not contained in the offense definition. The de minimis defense, for example, bars liability if the

---

6. For a discussion of the reasons for the law's failure in clearly communicating rules of conduct to the public, see Paul H. Robinson, A Functional Analysis of Criminal Law: Rule Articulation, Liability, and Grading, 88 Nw. U.L. Rev. 857 (1994); Paul H. Robinson, Are Criminal Codes Irrelevant?, 68 S. Cal. L. Rev. — (1994) (in press).

7. As the Model Penal Code suggests: "The general purposes of the provisions governing the definition of offenses are: . . . to safeguard conduct that is without fault from condemnation as criminal." Model Penal Code §1.02 (1985).

8. See Model Penal Code §2.02(1).

9. See Model Penal Code §2.02(3).

actor's conduct caused the harm or evil prohibited by the offense "only to an extent too trivial to warrant the condemnation of conviction."[10] Other defenses, such as renunciation, similarly refine the normal blameworthiness requirements for inchoate offenses. (Renunciation undercuts the blame that otherwise would apply if the actor did not voluntarily renounce his intention to violate a rule of conduct.)

Voluntariness doctrines In addition, the minimum requirements of liability are set by such doctrines as the voluntariness requirement in commission offenses, the capacity requirement for omission liability, and the requirement in possession offenses that the actor know of the possession for a period of time sufficient to terminate his possession. These requirements are designed to assure that the actor could have avoided the violation. Only if this is true can the actor be blamed for not avoiding it. Thus, the motorist who failed to help the accident victim might have been acquitted because his dazed condition made it impossible for him to help.

Culpability elements vs. voluntariness The culpable state of mind requirements in offense definitions serve a purpose similar to these doctrines, although they function in a slightly different way. We assume, from past experience, that most conduct is voluntary, most omitted conduct was possible, and most possession knowing. It is the unusual case, frequently where the actor suffers some disability, where an assumption of voluntariness, capacity to act, or knowledge of possession is not warranted. In contrast, it is common that an actor may be unaware of some characteristic or circumstance of his or her conduct, that is, may not have the culpability required by an offense definition. People frequently make mistakes and inadvertently create risks. It is these common possibilities for nonculpable violations that the culpability requirements are designed to exclude.

Doctrines of excuse The general excuse defenses—such as insanity, immaturity, involuntary intoxication, and duress—serve a function analogous to the voluntariness doctrines noted above. While our assumptions of sanity, maturity, sobriety, and absence of coercion normally are correct, in the unusual case an actor may suffer a disability—insanity, immaturity, intoxication, and coercion—and its effects may be such that he or she cannot reasonably be expected to have avoided the violation. The mistake excuses also are of this category but their excusing conditions operate in a different way.

Doctrines of grading The doctrines containing the rules of conduct plus those that establish the minimum requirements for liability provide the starting point for the grading function. The rule articulation doctrines contain many of the most important factors in assessing the

---

10. Model Penal Code §2.12(2).

degree of punishment an actor deserves, for they define the harm or evil of the offense. Assessing the relative seriousness of an offense requires an assessment of the relative value of the full range of interests protected by the criminal law. Human safety is more valuable than the safety of property; intercourse with a nine-year-old is a more egregious wrong than intercourse with a sixteen-year-old; etc. Criminal law theorists have only recently attempted to formulate principles for determining the relative seriousness of violations.

Culpability level In addition to the harm or evil of an offense, an actor's deserved punishment will depend upon his level of culpability. Culpability greater than the minimum required for liability frequently increases the actor's deserved punishment. Purposely causing a death is more culpable than recklessly doing the same, which is more culpable than negligently doing so. Thus, those culpability elements of offense definitions that require more than the minimum required for liability serve a grading function by distinguishing the case of greater culpability from the case of minimum culpability.

Result and causation requirements Result elements and causation requirements also serve a grading function. Most codes have a provision like the Model Penal Code's attempt offense, which provides in part:

> A person is guilty of an attempt to commit a crime if . . . when causing a particular result is an element of the crime, [he] does or omits to do anything with the purpose of causing or with the belief that it will cause such result without further conduct on his part; . . .[11]

Thus, where the elements of an offense definition are not satisfied only because of the absence of a required result, or the result is not attributable to the actor because of the absence of an adequate causal connection, the actor will always be liable for an offense, specifically an attempt, even if the code defines no other lesser included offense.[12] Your shooting at the person in the basement may be an offense even though your bad aim causes you to miss him.

Result vs. conduct and circumstances Note that result elements are objective elements, like conduct and circumstance elements, but they are not necessary to define the prohibited conduct. It is an actor's conduct, and not its results, that the criminal law prohibits; it is only the actor's conduct that the law can influence. The law may claim to prohibit a particular result but what it means by that is to direct actors not to engage in conduct that would bring about (or risk bringing about) that result. An actual resulting harm may make the violation more serious, most people would argue, but the fortuity of whether the

---

11. Model Penal Code §5.01(1)(b).
12. Not everyone would agree that results ought to increase an actor's punishment. See Chapter 8 (Inchoate Offenses).

result actually occurs does not alter the nature of the conduct that constitutes the violation. The conduct remains objectionable notwithstanding the happenstance that the result does not occur.[13] If you had wounded or killed the person in your basement, your potential liability would be higher than otherwise, but even your miss may subject you to liability, as noted above. Result elements, then, are like many culpability elements in this regard; they serve to aggravate an actor's blameworthiness and thus liability. Given the role of the causation requirement, in defining the relation between an actor's conduct and a result that will give rise to an actor's accountability for the result, the causation requirement is similarly part of the doctrines serving the grading function, not the criminalization function. Like the requirement of a result, the causation rules determine when an actor's liability is to be aggravated because the actor is accountable for a harmful result and therefore more blameworthy.

Special grading doctrines Special grading provisions also are recognized, including both doctrines of aggravation—such as the doctrines of felony murder and abandoned and malignant heart murder[14]—and doctrines of mitigation—such as the doctrines of provocation and extreme emotional disturbance.[15] These doctrines are drafted as offense elements but their actual effect is one of grading; their effect is to increase or decrease an actor's liability by shifting liability to a greater or lesser offense. Other special grading provisions are explicitly defined as grading provisions and vary the degree of liability within the same offense definition, such as varying the seriousness of a theft with the value of the property taken. In other words, like the rule articulation and liability functions, the grading function of criminal law doctrine is implemented through doctrines of many different sorts.

Cumulative nature of functions In determining which doctrines perform which function, the previous discussion groups the doctrines as if a doctrine served exclusively one function or another. In fact, the interrelation of the doctrines is slightly more complex than this. A complete description of the minimum requirements for liability requires not only reference to the doctrines serving the liability function

---

13. In some instances, however, as when less serious harms are only risked, the societal harm of the conduct may be too small to justify criminal condemnation. Conduct creating a low risk of a less serious harm may fall below the line of minimum seriousness required for adequate blameworthiness, unless the harm actually occurs. See the discussion of de minimis violations in Chapter 1.

14. See, e.g., Cal. Penal Code §188 (West 1988) (abandoned and malignant heart murder); Pa. Stat. Ann. tit. 18, §2502(b) (Purdon 1973) (felony murder); N.Y. Penal Law §125.25(3) (McKinney 1987) (felony murder).

15. See, e.g., Pa. Stat. Ann. tit. 18, §2503(a) (Purdon 1973) (provocation); N.Y. Penal Law §§125.20(2), 125.25(1)(a), 125.27(2)(a) (McKinney 1987) (extreme emotional disturbance).

but also the doctrines serving the rule articulation function. In other words, one prerequisite of liability is violation of the rules of conduct. Similarly, the criminal law's grading function cannot be performed by reference to the doctrines of grading alone. The doctrines of liability define the minimum grade in each instance. Thus, the doctrines might best be thought of as having cumulative functions as the law's inquiry moves from rule articulation to liability to grading. Their interrelation might be described as:

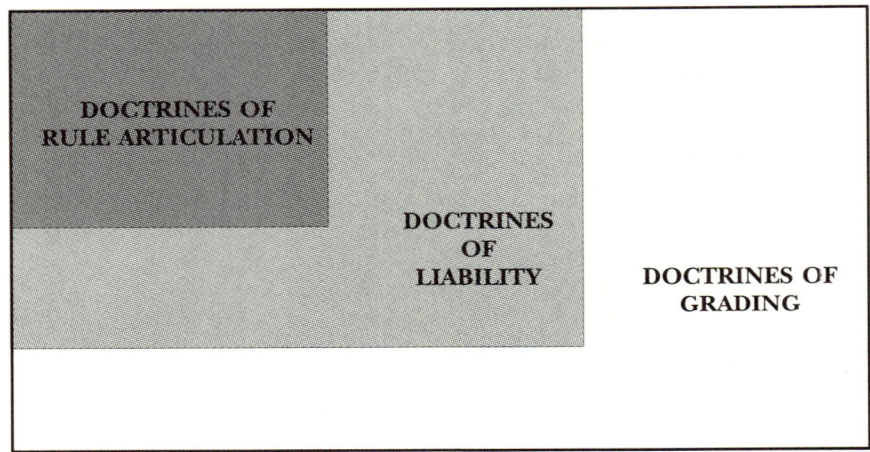

Communicative vs. adjudicative function Current criminal law doctrine sometimes performs poorly in its three primary functions and this frequently is caused by the failure of the doctrine to distinguish the functions. For example, the criminal law frequently fails to communicate clear rules of conduct because it fails to distinguish its communicative from its adjudicative function. The failure derives in part from the ambiguity of acquittals and dismissals. Does the acquittal of the neighbor who shot the burglar mean that shooting burglars is lawful, that such a shooting is permitted by the rules of conduct? Or, does the acquittal mean that such killing is not permitted but that the neighbor's mistake on the issue, given the difficult circumstances, was not blameworthy? The general "not guilty" acquittal does not tell us; thus, the case serves only to blur the rule of conduct not to reinforce it. Similarly, does the acquittal of the motorist who let the accident victim bleed to death mean that there is no legal duty to help the motorist? Or, given his particular (perhaps dazed) condition and his particular (perhaps decreased) abilities, does the acquittal mean that he cannot be fairly blamed for failure to perform what was his duty? Again, the general "not guilty" acquittal alone, without explanation, only serves to raise questions about the rule of conduct.

Danger of undercutting rules of conduct Instead of restating, reinforcing, and refining society's rules of conduct, acquittals at public trials (as well as dismissals by courts and publicly-reported decisions not to prosecute) frequently serve only to create ambiguity and confusion regarding those rules. Does the failure to condemn and punish follow from the propriety of the actor's conduct, or from the actor's blamelessness for admittedly improper conduct? Only a system that distinguishes a no-violation-of-the-rules-of-conduct acquittal from a blameless-violation acquittal can avoid this ambiguity and resurrect the educational value of our public adjudication system.

Making formulation sensitive to function The failure to distinguish between these kinds of functions—articulating and communicating rules of conduct, and adjudicating a violation of those rules (the liability and grading functions)—creates another kind of difficulty: The doctrines may be ineffectively formulated to serve their function. For example, rules of conduct need to communicate a legal standard that can be understood, remembered, and applied by the general public. To be effective, the rules of conduct must be simple, based on objective criteria with easily communicable and comprehensible standards. The doctrines embodying the principles of adjudication, on the other hand, must take account of the complex and varied situational factors relevant to an actor's blameworthiness, as well as the capacities and characteristics of the particular actor. The principles also must incorporate or at least mirror the community's expectations of the actor. In other words they must use subjective criteria and rely upon more individualized, judgmental, and normative standards.

Use of ineffective drafting form Unfortunately, rules of conduct are frequently drafted in a form that is more appropriate for a principle of adjudication, entailing broad and open-ended inquiries or detailed and complex rules. Many people consequently cannot discern the rules of conduct. And many people who think they know the answers will be wrong. Can one lawfully shoot a basement burglar? Must one help him when he is bleeding and helpless? The rules governing the justification of force in the defense of one's property or premises and the rules defining one's affirmative duties to act are notoriously complex.[16] In other instances, principles of adjudication are drafted in a form that

---

16. The lawfulness of your use of force against the burglar might require use of Model Penal Code §§3.04, 3.05, and 3.06, perhaps part of 3.07, each of which runs for more than a page of detail. See Chapter 15 (Justifications). Understanding one's duties to act affirmatively requires an understanding of all of civil law. These civil duties, together with duties created by criminal law, may give rise to liability under the terms set out in Model Penal Code §2.01(1) & (3). See Chapter 13 (Omission Liability).

may be appropriate for a rule of conduct but that does not accommodate the complex and multi-faceted analyses that determine an actor's blameworthiness for violating a rule of conduct.[17]

---

17. For a discussion of how doctrine may be drafted to more effectively perform its function, see Robinson, Functional Analysis, supra note 6, Robinson, Codes Irrelevant?, supra note 6.

APPENDIX: MODEL PENAL CODE

Model Penal Code Table of Contents

PART I. GENERAL PROVISIONS
Article 1. Preliminary

Section
- 1.01 Title and Effective Date
- 1.02 Purposes; Principles of Construction
- 1.03 Territorial Applicability
- 1.04 Classes of Crimes; Violations
- 1.05 All Offenses Defined by Statute; Application of General Provisions of the Code
- 1.06 Time Limitations
- 1.07 Method of Prosecution When Conduct Constitutes More Than One Offense
- 1.08 When Prosecution Barred by Former Prosecution for the Same Offense
- 1.09 When Prosecution Barred by Former Prosecution for Different Offense
- 1.10 Former Prosecution in Another Jurisdiction; When a Bar
- 1.11 Former Prosecution Before Court Lacking Jurisdiction or When Fraudulently Procured by the Defendant
- 1.12 Proof Beyond a Reasonable Doubt; Affirmative Defenses; Burden of Proving Fact When Not an Element of an Offense; Presumptions
- 1.13 General Definitions

Article 2. General Principles of Liability

Section
- 2.01 Requirement of Voluntary Act; Omission as Basis of Liability; Possession as an Act
- 2.02 General Requirements of Culpability
- 2.03 Causal Relationship Between Conduct and Result; Divergence Between Result Designed or Contemplated and Actual Result or Between Probable and Actual Result

2.04	Ignorance or Mistake
2.05	When Culpability Requirements Are Inapplicable to Violations and to Offenses Defined by Other Statutes; Effect of Absolute Liability in Reducing Grade of Offense to Violation
2.06	Liability for Conduct of Another; Complicity
2.07	Liability of Corporations, Unincorporated Associations and Persons Acting, or Under a Duty to Act, in Their Behalf
2.08	Intoxication
2.09	Duress
2.10	Military Orders
2.11	Consent
2.12	De Minimis Infractions
2.13	Entrapment

Article 3. General Principles of Justification

Section

3.01	Justification an Affirmative Defense; Civil Remedies Unaffected
3.02	Justification Generally: Choice of Evils
3.03	Execution of Public Duty
3.04	Use of Force in Self-Protection
3.05	Use of Force for the Protection of Other Persons
3.06	Use of Force for Protection of Property
3.07	Use of Force in Law Enforcement
3.08	Use of Force by Persons with Special Responsibility for Care, Discipline or Safety of Others
3.09	Mistake of Law as to Unlawfulness of Force of Legality of Arrest; Reckless or Negligent Use of Otherwise Justifiable Force; Reckless or Negligent Injury or Risk of Injury to Innocent Persons
3.10	Justification in Property Crimes
3.11	Definitions

Article 4. Responsibility

Section

4.01	Mental Disease or Defect Excluding Responsibility
4.02	Evidence of Mental Disease or Defect Admissible When Relevant to Element of the Offense; [Mental Disease or Defect Impairing Capacity as Ground for Mitigation of Punishment in Capital Cases]
4.03	Mental Disease or Defect Excluding Responsibility Is Affirmative Defense; Requirement of Notice; Form of Verdict and Judgment When Finding of Irresponsibility Is Made
4.04	Mental Disease or Defect Excluding Fitness to Proceed
4.05	Psychiatric Examination of Defendant with Respect to Mental Disease or Defect
4.06	Determination of Fitness to Proceed; Effect of Finding of Unfitness; Proceedings if Fitness Is Regaining; [Post-Commitment Hearing]
4.07	Determination of Irresponsibility on Basis of Report; Access to Defendant by Psychiatrist of His Own Choice; Form of Expert Testimony When Issue of Responsibility Is Tried

APPENDIX: MODEL PENAL CODE

4.08 Legal Effect of Acquittal on the Ground of Mental Disease or Defect Excluding Responsibility; Commitment; Release or Discharge
4.09 Statements for Purposes of Examination or Treatment Inadmissible Except on Issue of Mental Condition
4.10 Immaturity Excluding Criminal Convictions; Transfer of Proceedings to Juvenile Court

Article 5. Inchoate Crimes

Section
5.01 Criminal Attempt
5.02 Criminal Solicitation
5.03 Criminal Conspiracy
5.04 Incapacity, Irresponsibility or Immunity of Party to Solicitation or Conspiracy
5.05 Grading of Criminal Attempt, Solicitation and Conspiracy; Mitigation in Cases of Lesser Danger; Multiple Convictions Barred
5.06 Possessing Instruments of Crime; Weapons
5.07 Prohibited Offensive Weapons

Article 6. Authorized Disposition of Offenders

Section
6.01 Degrees of Felonies
6.02 Sentence in Accordance with Code; Authorized Dispositions
6.03 Fines
6.04 Penalties Against Corporations and Unincorporated Association; Forfeiture of Corporate Charter or Revocation of Certificate Authorizing Foreign Corporation to Do Business in the State
6.05 Young Adult Offenders [omitted]
6.06 Sentence of Imprisonment for Felony; Ordinary Terms
6.07 Sentence of Imprisonment for Felony; Extended Terms
6.08 Sentence of Imprisonment for Misdemeanors and Petty Misdemeanors; Ordinary Terms
6.09 Sentence of Imprisonment for Misdemeanors and Petty Misdemeanors; Extended Terms
6.10 First Release of All Offenders on Parole; Sentence of Imprisonment Includes Separate Parole Term; Length of Parole Term; Length of Recommitment and Re-parole After Revocation of Parole; Final Unconditional Release [omitted]
6.11 Place of Imprisonment [omitted]
6.12 Reduction of Conviction by Court to Lesser Degree of Felony or to Misdemeanor
6.13 Civil Commitment in Lieu of Prosecution or of Sentence

Article 7. Authority of Court in Sentencing

Section
7.01 Criteria for Withholding Sentence of Imprisonment and for Placing Defendant on Probation [omitted]

7.02	Criteria for Imposing Fines [omitted]
7.03	Criteria for Sentence of Extended Term of Imprisonment; Felonies
7.04	Criteria for Sentence of Extended Term of Imprisonment; Misdemeanors and Petty Misdemeanors
7.05	Former Conviction in Another Jurisdiction; Definition and Proof of Conviction; Sentence Taking into Account Admitted Crimes Bars Subsequent Conviction for Such Crimes
7.06	Multiple Sentences; Concurrent and Consecutive Terms
7.07	Procedure on Sentence; Pre-sentence Investigation and Report; Remand for Psychiatric Examination; Transmission of Records to Department of Correction [omitted]
7.08	Commitment for Observation; Sentence of Imprisonment for Felony Deemed Tentative for Period of One Year; Re-sentence on Petition of Commissioner of Correction [omitted]
7.09	Credit for Time of Detention Prior to Sentence; Credit for Imprisonment Under Earlier Sentence for Same Crime [omitted]

PART II. DEFINITION OF SPECIFIC CRIMES

Offenses Involving Danger to the Person

Article 210. Criminal Homicide

Section

210.0	Definitions
210.1	Criminal Homicide
210.2	Murder
210.3	Manslaughter
210.4	Negligent Homicide
210.5	Causing or Aiding Suicide
210.6	Sentence of Death for Murder; Further Proceedings to Determine Sentence

Article 211. Assault; Reckless Endangering; Threats

Section

211.0	Definitions
211.1	Assault
211.2	Recklessly Endangering Another Person
211.3	Terroristic Threats

Article 212. Kidnapping and Related Offenses; Coercion

Section

212.0	Definitions
212.1	Kidnapping
212.2	Felonious Restraint
212.3	False Imprisonment

212.4 Interference with Custody
212.5 Criminal Coercion

Article 213. Sexual Offenses
Section
213.0 Definitions
213.1 Rape and Related Offenses
213.2 Deviate Sexual Intercourse by Force or Imposition
213.3 Corruption of Minors and Seduction
213.4 Sexual Assault
213.5 Indecent Exposure
213.6 Provisions Generally Applicable to Article 213

Offenses Against Property
Article 220. Arson, Criminal Mischief, and Other Property Destruction
Section
220.1 Arson and Related Offenses
220.2 Causing or Risking Catastrophe
220.3 Criminal Mischief

Article 221. Burglary and Other Criminal Intrusion
Section
221.0 Definitions
221.1 Burglary
221.2 Criminal Trespass

Article 222. Robbery
Section
222.1 Robbery

Article 223. Theft and Related Offenses
Section
223.0 Definitions
223.1 Consolidation of Theft Offenses; Grading; Provisions Applicable to Theft Generally
223.2 Theft by Unlawful Taking or Disposition
223.3 Theft by Deception
223.4 Theft by Extortion
223.5 Theft of Property Lost, Mislaid, or Delivered by Mistake
223.6 Receiving Stolen Property
223.7 Theft of Services

223.8   Theft by Failure to Make Required Disposition of Funds Received
223.9   Unauthorized Use of Automobiles and Other Vehicles

Article 224. Forgery and Fraudulent Practices

Section
224.0   Definitions
224.1   Forgery
224.2   Simulating Objects of Antiquity, Rarity, Etc.
224.3   Fraudulent Destruction, Removal or Concealment of Recordable Instruments
224.4   Tampering with Records
224.5   Bad Checks [omitted]
224.6   Credit Cards [omitted]
224.7   Deceptive Business Practices
224.8   Commercial Bribery and Breach of Duty to Act Disinterestedly [omitted]
224.9   Rigging Publicly Exhibited Contest [omitted]
224.10 Defrauding Secured Creditors [omitted]
224.11 Fraud in Insolvency [omitted]
224.12 Receiving Deposits in a Failing Financial Institution [omitted]
224.13 Misapplication of Entrusted Property and Property of Government or Financial Institution [omitted]
224.14 Securing Execution of Documents by Deception [omitted]

Offenses Against the Family

Article 230. Offenses Against the Family

Section
230.1   Bigamy and Polygamy
230.2   Incest
230.3   Abortion
230.4   Endangering Welfare of Children
230.5   Persistent Nonsupport

Offenses Against Public Administration

Article 240. Bribery and Corrupt Influence

Section
240.0   Definitions [omitted]
240.1   Bribery in Official and Political Matters
240.2   Threats and Other Improper Influence in Official and Political Matters
240.3   Compensation for Past Official Action
240.4   Retaliation for Past Official Action
240.5   Gifts to Public Servants by Persons Subject to Their Jurisdiction [omitted]
240.6   Compensating Public Servant for Assisting Private Interests in Relation to Matters Before Him [omitted]
240.7   Selling Political Endorsement; Special Influence [omitted]

Article 241. Perjury and Other Falsification in Official Matters
Section
241.0 Definitions
241.1 Perjury
241.2 False Swearing
241.3 Unsworn Falsification to Authorities
241.4 False Alarms to Agencies of Public Safety
241.5 False Reports to Law Enforcement Authorities
241.6 Tampering with Witnesses and Informants; Retaliation Against Them [omitted]
241.7 Tampering with or Fabricating Physical Evidence [omitted]
241.8 Tampering with Public Records or Information
241.9 Impersonating a Public Servant

Article 242. Obstructing Governmental Operations; Escapes
Section
242.0 Definitions
242.1 Obstructing Administration of Law or Other Governmental Function [omitted]
242.2 Resisting Arrest or Other Law Enforcement
242.3 Hindering Apprehension or Prosecution
242.4 Aiding Consummation of Crime
242.5 Compounding
242.6 Escape
242.7 Implements for Escape; Other Contraband
242.8 Bail Jumping; Default in Required Appearance

Article 243. Abuse of Office
Section
243.0 Definitions
243.1 Official Oppression
243.2 Speculating or Wagering on Official Action or Information

Offenses Against Public Order and Decency
Article 250. Riot, Disorderly Conduct, and Related Offenses
Section
250.1 Riot; Failure to Disperse
250.2 Disorderly Conduct
250.3 False Public Alarms
250.4 Harassment
250.5 Public Drunkenness; Drug Incapacitation
250.6 Loitering or Prowling
250.7 Obstructing Highways and Other Public Passages
250.8 Disrupting Meetings and Processions
250.9 Desecration of Venerated Objects

250.10 Abuse of Corpse
250.11 Cruelty to Animals
250.12 Violation of Privacy

Article 251. Public Indecency

Section
251.2 Prostitution and Related Offenses
251.3 Loitering to Solicit Deviate Sexual Relations
251.4 Obscenity

[PART III. TREATMENT AND CORRECTION and PART IV. ORGANIZATION OF CORRECTION are omitted]

Selected Provisions of the Model Penal Code
[Copyright © 1962 by The American Law Institute.]

PART I. GENERAL PROVISIONS

Article 1. Preliminary

Section 1.01. Title and Effective Date.

(1) This Act is called the Penal and Correctional Code and may be cited as P.C.C. It shall become effective on _____ .

(2) Except as provided in Subsections (3) and (4) of this Section, the Code does not apply to offenses committed prior to its effective date and prosecutions for such offenses shall be governed by the prior law, which is continued in effect for that purpose, as if this Code were not in force. For the purposes of this Section, an offense was committed prior to the effective date of the Code if any of the elements of the offense occurred prior thereto.

(3) In any case pending on or after the effective date of the Code, involving an offense committed prior to such date:

   (a) procedural provisions of the Code shall govern, insofar as they are justly applicable and their application does not introduce confusion or delay;

   (b) provisions of the Code according a defense or mitigation shall apply, with the consent of the defendant;

   (c) the Court, with the consent of the defendant, may impose sentence under the provisions of the Code applicable to the offense and the offender.

(4) Provisions of the Code governing the treatment and the release or discharge of prisoners, probationers and parolees shall apply to persons under sentence for offenses committed prior to the effective date of the Code, except that the minimum or maximum period of their detention or supervision shall in no case be increased.

Section 1.02. Purposes; Principles of Construction.

(1) The general purposes of the provisions governing the definition of offenses are:

   (a) to forbid and prevent conduct that unjustifiably and inexcusably inflicts or threatens substantial harm to individual or public interests;

   (b) to subject to public control persons whose conduct indicates that they are disposed to commit crimes;

   (c) to safeguard conduct that is without fault from condemnation as criminal;

(d) to give fair warning of the nature of the conduct declared to constitute an offense;

(e) to differentiate on reasonable grounds between serious and minor offenses.

(2) The general purposes of the provisions governing the sentencing and treatment of offenders are:

(a) to prevent the commission of offenses;

(b) to promote the correction and rehabilitation of offenders;

(c) to safeguard offenders against excessive, disproportionate or arbitrary punishment;

(d) to give fair warning of the nature of the sentences that may be imposed on conviction of an offense;

(e) to differentiate among offenders with a view to a just individualization in their treatment;

(f) to define, coordinate and harmonize the powers, duties and functions of the courts and of administrative officers and agencies responsible for dealing with offenders;

(g) to advance the use of generally accepted scientific methods and knowledge in the sentencing and treatment of offenders;

(h) to integrate responsibility for the administration of the correctional system in a State Department of Correction [or other single department or agency].

(3) The provisions of the Code shall be construed according to the fair import of their terms but when the language is susceptible of differing constructions it shall be interpreted to further the general purposes stated in this Section and the special purposes of the particular provision involved. The discretionary powers conferred by the Code shall be exercised in accordance with the criteria stated in the Code and, insofar as such criteria are not decisive, to further the general purposes stated in this Section.

Section 1.03. Territorial Applicability.

(1) Except as otherwise provided in this Section, a person may be convicted under the law of this State of an offense committed by his own conduct or the conduct of another for which he is legally accountable if:

(a) either the conduct which is an element of the offense or the result which is such an element occurs within this State; or

(b) conduct occurring outside the State is sufficient under the law of this State to constitute an attempt to commit an offense within the State; or

(c) conduct occurring outside the State is sufficient under the law of this State to constitute a conspiracy to commit an offense within the State and an overt act in furtherance of such conspiracy occurs within the State; or

(d) conduct occurring within the State establishes complicity in the commission of, or an attempt, solicitation or conspiracy to commit, an offense in another jurisdiction which also is an offense under the law of this State; or

(e) the offense consists of the omission to perform a legal duty imposed by the law of the State with respect to domicile, residence or a relationship to a person, thing or transaction in the State; or

(f) the offense is based on a statute of this State which expressly prohibits conduct outside the State, when the conduct bears a reasonable relation to a legitimate interest of this State and the actor knows or should know that his conduct is likely to affect that interest.

(2) Subsection (1)(a) does not apply when either causing a specified result or a purpose to cause or danger of causing such a result is an element of an offense and the result occurs or is designed or likely to occur only in another jurisdiction where the conduct charged would not constitute an offense, unless a legislative purpose plainly appears to declare the conduct criminal regardless of the place of the result.

(3) Subsection (1)(a) does not apply when causing a particular result is an element of an offense and the result is caused by conduct occurring outside the State which would not constitute an offense if the result had occurred there, unless the actor purposely or knowingly caused the result within the State.

(4) When the offense is homicide, either the death of the victim or the bodily impact causing death constitutes a "result," within the meaning of Subsection (1) (a) and if the body of a homicide victim is found within the State, it is presumed that such result occurred within the State.

(5) This State includes the land and water and the air space above such land and water with respect to which the State has legislative jurisdiction.

Section 1.04. Classes of Crimes; Violations.

(1) An offense defined by this Code or by any other statute of this State, for which a sentence of [death or of] imprisonment is authorized, constitutes a crime. Crimes are classified as felonies, misdemeanors or petty misdemeanors.

(2) A crime is a felony if it is so designated in this Code or if persons convicted thereof may be sentenced [to death or] to imprisonment for a term which, apart from an extended term, is in excess of one year.

(3) A crime is a misdemeanor if it is so designated in this Code or in a statute other than this Code enacted subsequent thereto.

(4) A crime is a petty misdemeanor if it is so designated in this Code or in a statute other than this Code enacted subsequent thereto or if it is defined by a statute other than this Code which now provides that persons convicted thereof may be sentenced to imprisonment for a term of which the maximum is less than one year.

(5) An offense defined by this Code or by any other statute of this

State constitutes a violation if it is so designated in this Code or in the law defining the offense or if no other sentence than a fine, or fine and forfeiture or other civil penalty is authorized upon conviction or if it is defined by a statute other than this Code which now provides that the offense shall not constitute a crime. A violation does not constitute a crime and conviction of a violation shall not give rise to any disability or legal disadvantage based on conviction of a criminal offense.

(6) Any offense declared by law to constitute a crime, without specification of the grade thereof or of the sentence authorized upon conviction, is a misdemeanor.

(7) An offense defined by any statute of this State other than this Code shall be classified as provided in this Section and the sentence that may be imposed upon conviction thereof shall hereafter be governed by this Code.

Section 1.05. All Offenses Defined by Statute; Application of General Provisions of the Code.

(1) No conduct constitutes an offense unless it is a crime or violation under this Code or another statute of this State.

(2) The provisions of Part I of the Code are applicable to offenses defined by other statutes, unless the Code otherwise provides.

(3) This Section does not affect the power of a court to punish for contempt or to employ any sanction authorized by law for the enforcement of an order or a civil judgment or decree.

Section 1.06. Time Limitations.

(1) A prosecution for murder may be commenced at any time.

(2) Except as otherwise provided in this Section, prosecutions for other offenses are subject to the following periods of limitation:

   (a) a prosecution for a felony of the first degree must be commenced within six years after it is committed;

   (b) a prosecution for any other felony must be commenced within three years after it is committed;

   (c) a prosecution for a misdemeanor must be commenced within two years after it is committed;

   (d) a prosecution for a petty misdemeanor or a violation must be commenced within six months after it is committed.

(3) If the period prescribed in Subsection (2) has expired, a prosecution may nevertheless be commenced for:

   (a) any offense a material element of which is either fraud or a breach of fiduciary obligation within one year after discovery of the offense by an aggrieved party or by a person who has legal duty to represent an aggrieved party and who is himself not a party to the offense, but in no case shall this provision extend the period of limitation otherwise applicable by more than three years; and

(b) any offense based upon misconduct in office by a public officer or employee at any time when the defendant is in public office or employment or within two years thereafter, but in no case shall this provision extend the period of limitation otherwise applicable by more than three years.

(4) An offense is committed either when every element occurs, or, if a legislative purpose to prohibit a continuing course of conduct plainly appears, at the time when the course of conduct or the defendant's complicity therein is terminated. Time starts to run on the day after the offense is committed.

(5) A prosecution is commenced either when an indictment is found [or an information filed] or when a warrant or other process is issued, provided that such warrant or process is executed without unreasonable delay.

(6) The period of limitation does not run:

(a) during any time when the accused is continuously absent from the State or has no reasonably ascertainable place of abode or work within the State, but in no case shall this provision extend the period of limitation otherwise applicable by more than three years; or

(b) during any time when a prosecution against the accused for the same conduct is pending in this State.

Section 1.07. Method of Prosecution When Conduct Constitutes More Than One Offense.

(1) Prosecution for Multiple Offenses; Limitation on Convictions. When the same conduct of a defendant may establish the commission of more than one offense, the defendant may be prosecuted for each such offense. He may not, however, be convicted of more than one offense if:

(a) one offense is included in the other, as defined in Subsection (4) of this Section; or

(b) one offense consists only of a conspiracy or other form of preparation to commit the other; or

(c) inconsistent findings of fact are required to establish the commission of the offenses; or

(d) the offenses differ only in that one is defined to prohibit a designated kind of conduct generally and the other to prohibit a specific instance of such conduct; or

(e) the offense is defined as a continuing course of conduct and the defendant's course of conduct was uninterrupted, unless the law provides that specific periods of such conduct constitute separate offenses.

(2) Limitation on Separate Trials for Multiple Offenses. Except as provided in Subsection (3) of this Section, a defendant shall not be subject to separate trials for multiple offenses based on the same conduct or arising from the same criminal episode, if such offenses are

known to the appropriate prosecuting officer at the time of the commencement of the first trial and are within the jurisdiction of a single court.

(3) Authority of Court to Order Separate Trials. When a defendant is charged with two or more offenses based on the same conduct or arising from the same criminal episode, the Court, on application of the prosecuting attorney or of the defendant, may order any such charge to be tried separately, if it is satisfied that justice so requires.

(4) Conviction of Included Offense Permitted. A defendant may be convicted of an offense included in an offense charged in the indictment [or the information]. An offense is so included when:

(a) it is established by proof of the same or less than all the facts required to establish the commission of the offense charged; or

(b) it consists of an attempt or solicitation to commit the offense charged or to commit an offense otherwise included therein; or

(c) it differs from the offense charged only in the respect that a less serious injury or risk of injury to the same person, property or public interest or a lesser kind of culpability suffices to establish its commission.

(5) Submission of Included Offense to Jury. The Court shall not be obligated to charge the jury with respect to an included offense unless there is a rational basis for a verdict acquitting the defendant of the offense charged and convicting him of the included offense.

Section 1.08. When Prosecution Barred by Former Prosecution for the Same Offense.

When a prosecution is for a violation of the same provision of the statutes and is based upon the same facts as a former prosecution, it is barred by such former prosecution under the following circumstances:

(1) The former prosecution resulted in an acquittal. There is an acquittal if the prosecution resulted in a finding of not guilty by the trier of fact or in a determination that there was insufficient evidence to warrant a conviction. A finding of guilty of a lesser included offense is an acquittal of the greater inclusive offense, although the conviction is subsequently set aside.

(2) The former prosecution was terminated, after the information had been filed or the indictment found, by a final order or judgment for the defendant, which has not been set aside, reversed, or vacated and which necessarily required a determination inconsistent with a fact or a legal proposition that must be established for conviction of the offense.

(3) The former prosecution resulted in a conviction. There is a conviction if the prosecution resulted in a judgment of conviction which has not been reversed or vacated, a verdict of guilty which has not been set aside and which is capable of supporting

a judgment, or a plea of guilty accepted by the Court. In the latter two cases failure to enter judgment must be for a reason other than a motion of the defendant.

(4) The former prosecution was improperly terminated. Except as provided in this Subsection, there is an improper termination of a prosecution if the termination is for reasons not amounting to an acquittal, and it takes place after the first witness is sworn but before verdict. Termination under any of the following circumstances is not improper:

(a) The defendant consents to the termination or waives, by motion to dismiss or otherwise, his right to object to the termination.

(b) The trial court finds that the termination is necessary because:

(1) it is physically impossible to proceed with the trial in conformity with law; or

(2) there is a legal defect in the proceedings which would make any judgment entered upon a verdict reversible as a matter of law; or

(3) prejudicial conduct, in or outside the courtroom, makes it impossible to proceed with the trial without injustice to either the defendant or the State; or

(4) the jury is unable to agree upon a verdict; or

(5) false statements of a juror on voir dire prevent a fair trial.

Section 1.09. When Prosecution Barred by Former Prosecution for Different Offense.

Although a prosecution is for a violation of a different provision of the statutes than a former prosecution or is based on different facts, it is barred by such former prosecution under the following circumstances:

(1) The former prosecution resulted in an acquittal or in a conviction as defined in Section 1.08 and the subsequent prosecution is for:

(a) any offense of which the defendant could have been convicted on the first prosecution; or

(b) any offense for which the defendant should have been tried on the first prosecution under Section 1.07, unless the Court ordered a separate trial of the charge of such offense; or

(c) the same conduct, unless (i) the offense of which the defendant was formerly convicted or acquitted and the offense for which he is subsequently prosecuted each requires proof of a fact not required by the other and the law defining each of such offenses is intended to prevent a substantially different harm or evil, or (ii) the second offense was not consummated when the former trial began.

(2) The former prosecution was terminated, after the information was filed or the indictment found, by an acquittal or by a final

order or judgment for the defendant which has not been set aside, reversed or vacated and which acquittal, final order or judgment necessarily required a determination inconsistent with a fact which must be established for conviction of the second offense.

(3) The former prosecution was improperly terminated, as improper termination is defined in Section 1.08, and the subsequent prosecution is for an offense of which the defendant could have been convicted had the former prosecution not been improperly terminated.

Section 1.10. Former Prosecution in Another
Jurisdiction: When a Bar.

When conduct constitutes an offense within the concurrent jurisdiction of this State and of the United States or another State, a prosecution in any such other jurisdiction is a bar to a subsequent prosecution in this State under the following circumstances:

(1) The first prosecution resulted in an acquittal or in a conviction as defined in Section 1.08 and the subsequent prosecution is based on the same conduct, unless (a) the offense of which the defendant was formerly convicted or acquitted and the offense for which he is subsequently prosecuted each requires proof of a fact not required by the other and the law defining each of such offenses is intended to prevent a substantially different harm or evil or (b) the second offense was not consummated when the former trial began; or

(2) The former prosecution was terminated, after the information was filed or the indictment found, by an acquittal or by a final order or judgment for the defendant which has not been set aside, reversed or vacated and which acquittal, final order or judgment necessarily required a determination inconsistent with a fact which must be established for conviction of the offense of which the defendant is subsequently prosecuted.

Section 1.11. Former Prosecution Before Court
Lacking Jurisdiction or When Fraudulently Procured
by the Defendant.

A prosecution is not a bar within the meaning of Sections 1.08, 1.09 and 1.10 under any of the following circumstances:

(1) The former prosecution was before a court which lacked jurisdiction over the defendant or the offense; or

(2) The former prosecution was procured by the defendant without the knowledge of the appropriate prosecuting officer and with the purpose of avoiding the sentence which might otherwise be imposed; or

(3) The former prosecution resulted in a judgment of conviction

which was held invalid in a subsequent proceeding on a writ of habeas corpus, coram nobis or similar process.

Section 1.12. Proof Beyond a Reasonable Doubt; Affirmative Defenses; Burden of Proving Fact When Not an Element of an Offense; Presumptions.

(1) No person may be convicted of an offense unless each element of such offense is proved beyond a reasonable doubt. In the absence of such proof, the innocence of the defendant is assumed.

(2) Subsection (1) of this Section does not:

   (a) require the disproof of an affirmative defense unless and until there is evidence supporting such defense; or

   (b) apply to any defense which the Code or another statute plainly requires the defendant to prove by a preponderance of evidence.

(3) A ground of defense is affirmative, within the meaning of Subsection (2)(a) of this Section, when:

   (a) it arises under a section of the Code which so provides; or

   (b) it relates to an offense defined by a statute other than the Code and such statute so provides; or

   (c) it involves a matter of excuse or justification peculiarly within the knowledge of the defendant on which he can fairly be required to adduce supporting evidence.

(4) When the application of the Code depends upon the finding of a fact which is not an element of an offense, unless the Code otherwise provides:

   (a) the burden of proving the fact is on the prosecution or defendant, depending on whose interest or contention will be furthered if the finding should be made; and

   (b) the fact must be proved to the satisfaction of the Court or jury, as the case may be.

(5) When the Code establishes a presumption with respect to any fact which is an element of an offense, it has the following consequences:

   (a) when there is evidence of the facts which give rise to the presumption, the issue of the existence of the presumed fact must be submitted to the jury, unless the Court is satisfied that the evidence as a whole clearly negatives the presumed fact; and

   (b) when the issue of the existence of the presumed fact is submitted to the jury, the Court shall charge that while the presumed fact must, on all the evidence, be proved beyond a reasonable doubt, the law declares that the jury may regard the facts giving rise to the presumption as sufficient evidence of the presumed fact.

(6) A presumption not established by the Code or inconsistent with it has the consequences otherwise accorded it by law.

Section 1.13. General Definitions.

In this Code, unless a different meaning plainly is required:

(1) "statute" includes the Constitution and a local law or ordinance of a political subdivision of the State;

(2) "act" or "action" means a bodily movement whether voluntary or involuntary;

(3) "voluntary" has the meaning specified in Section 2.01;

(4) "omission" means a failure to act;

(5) "conduct" means an action or omission and its accompanying state of mind, or, where relevant, a series of acts and omissions;

(6) "actor" includes, where relevant, a person guilty of an omission;

(7) "acted" includes, where relevant, "omitted to act";

(8) "person," "he" and "actor" include any natural person and, where relevant, a corporation or an unincorporated association;

(9) "element of an offense" means (i) such conduct or (ii) such attendant circumstances or (iii) such a result of conduct as

  (a) is included in the description of the forbidden conduct in the definition of the offense; or

  (b) establishes the required kind of culpability; or

  (c) negatives an excuse or justification for such conduct; or

  (d) negatives a defense under the statute of limitations; or

  (e) establishes jurisdiction or venue;

(10) "material element of an offense" means an element that does not relate exclusively to the statute of limitations, jurisdiction, venue or to any other matter similarly unconnected with (i) the harm or evil, incident to conduct, sought to be prevented by the law defining the offense, or (ii) the existence of a justification or excuse for such conduct;

(11) "purposely" has the meaning specified in Section 2.02 and equivalent terms such as "with purpose," "designed" or "with design" have the same meaning;

(12) "intentionally" or "with intent" means purposely;

(13) "knowingly" has the meaning specified in Section 2.02 and equivalent terms such as "knowing" or "with knowledge" have the same meaning;

(14) "recklessly" has the meaning specified in Section 2.02 and equivalent terms such as "recklessness" or "with recklessness" have the same meaning;

(15) "negligently" has the meaning specified in Section 2.02 and equivalent terms such as "negligence" or "with negligence" have the same meaning;

(16) "reasonably believes" or "reasonable belief" designates a belief which the actor is not reckless or negligent in holding.

Article 2. General Principles of Liability.

Section 2.01. Requirement of Voluntary Act; Omission as Basis of Liability; Possession as an Act.

(1) A person is not guilty of an offense unless his liability is based on conduct which includes a voluntary act or the omission to perform an act of which he is physically capable.

(2) The following are not voluntary acts within the meaning of this Section:

(a) a reflex or convulsion;

(b) a bodily movement during unconsciousness or sleep;

(c) conduct during hypnosis or resulting from hypnotic suggestion;

(d) a bodily movement that otherwise is not a product of the effort or determination of the actor, either conscious or habitual.

(3) Liability for the commission of an offense may not be based on an omission unaccompanied by action unless:

(a) the omission is expressly made sufficient by the law defining the offense; or

(b) a duty to perform the omitted act is otherwise imposed by law.

(4) Possession is an act, within the meaning of this Section, if the possessor knowingly procured or received the thing possessed or was aware of his control thereof for a sufficient period to have been able to terminate his possession.

Section 2.02. General Requirements of Culpability.

(1) Minimum Requirements of Culpability. Except as provided in Section 2.05, a person is not guilty of an offense unless he acted purposely, knowingly, recklessly or negligently, as the law may require, with respect to each material element of the offense.

(2) Kinds of Culpability Defined.

(a) Purposely. A person acts purposely with respect to a material element of an offense when:

(i) if the element involves the nature of his conduct or a result thereof, it is his conscious object to engage in conduct of that nature or to cause such a result; and

(ii) if the element involves the attendant circumstances, he is aware of the existence of such circumstances or he believes or hopes that they exist.

(b) Knowingly. A person acts knowingly with respect to a material element of an offense when:

(i) if the element involves the nature of his conduct or the attendant circumstances, he is aware that his conduct is of that nature or that such circumstances exist; and

(ii) if the element involves a result of his conduct, he is aware that it is practically certain that his conduct will cause such a result.

(c) Recklessly. A person acts recklessly with respect to a material element of an offense when he consciously disregards a substantial and unjustifiable risk that the material element exists or will result from his conduct. The risk must be of such a nature and degree that, considering the nature and purpose of the actor's conduct and the circumstances known to him, its disregard involves a gross deviation from the standard of conduct that a law-abiding person would observe in the actor's situation.

(d) Negligently. A person acts negligently with respect to a material element of an offense when he should be aware of a substantial and unjustifiable risk that the material element exists or will result from his conduct. The risk must be of such a nature and degree that the actor's failure to perceive it, considering the nature and purpose of his conduct and the circumstances known to him, involves a gross deviation from the standard of care that a reasonable person would observe in the actor's situation.

(3) Culpability Required Unless Otherwise Provided. When the culpability sufficient to establish a material element of an offense is not prescribed by law, such element is established if a person acts purposely, knowingly or recklessly with respect thereto.

(4) Prescribed Culpability Requirement Applies to All Material Elements. When the law defining an offense prescribes the kind of culpability that is sufficient for the commission of an offense, without distinguishing among the material elements thereof, such provision shall apply to all the material elements of the offense, unless a contrary purpose plainly appears.

(5) Substitutes for Negligence, Recklessness and Knowledge. When the law provides that negligence suffices to establish an element of an offense, such element also is established if a person acts purposely, knowingly or recklessly. When recklessness suffices to establish an element, such element also is established if a person acts purposely or knowingly. When acting knowingly suffices to establish an element, such element also is established if a person acts purposely.

(6) Requirement of Purpose Satisfied if Purpose Is Conditional. When a particular purpose is an element of an offense, the element is established although such purpose is conditional, unless the condition negatives the harm or evil sought to be prevented by the law defining the offense.

(7) Requirement of Knowledge Satisfied by Knowledge of High Probability. When knowledge of the existence of a particular fact is an element of an offense, such knowledge is established if a person is aware of a high probability of its existence, unless he actually believes that it does not exist.

(8) Requirement of Wilfulness Satisfied by Acting Knowingly. A requirement that an offense be committed wilfully is satisfied if a person acts knowingly with respect to the material elements of the offense, unless a purpose to impose further requirements appears.

(9) Culpability as to Illegality of Conduct. Neither knowledge nor recklessness or negligence as to whether conduct constitutes an offense or as to the existence, meaning or application of the law determining the elements of an offense is an element of such offense, unless the definition of the offense or the Code so provides.

(10) Culpability as Determinant of Grade of Offense. When the grade or degree of an offense depends on whether the offense is committed purposely, knowingly, recklessly or negligently, its grade or degree shall be the lowest for which the determinative kind of culpability is established with respect to any material element of the offense.

Section 2.03. Causal Relationship Between Conduct and Result; Divergence Between Result Designed or Contemplated and Actual Result or Between Probable and Actual Result.

(1) Conduct is the cause of a result when:

(a) it is an antecedent but for which the result in question would not have occurred; and

(b) the relationship between the conduct and result satisfies any additional causal requirements imposed by the Code or by the law defining the offense.

(2) When purposely or knowingly causing a particular result is an element of an offense, the element is not established if the actual result is not within the purpose or the contemplation of the actor unless:

(a) the actual result differs from that designed or contemplated, as the case may be, only in the respect that a different person or different property is injured or affected or that the injury or harm designed or contemplated would have been more serious or more extensive than that caused; or

(b) the actual result involves the same kind of injury or harm as that designed or contemplated and is not too remote or accidental in its occurrence to have a [just] bearing on the actor's liability or on the gravity of his offense.

(3) When recklessly or negligently causing a particular result is an element of an offense, the element is not established if the actual result is not within the risk of which the actor is aware or, in the case of negligence, of which he should be aware unless:

(a) the actual result differs from the probable result only in the respect that a different person or different property is injured or affected or that the probable injury or harm would have been more serious or more extensive than that caused; or

(b) the actual result involves the same kind of injury or harm as the probable result and is not too remote or accidental in its occurrence to have a [just] bearing on the actor's liability or on the gravity of his offense.

(4) When causing a particular result is a material element of an offense for which absolute liability is imposed by law, the element is not established unless the actual result is a probable consequence of the actor's conduct.

Section 2.04. Ignorance or Mistake.

(1) Ignorance or mistake as to a matter of fact or law is a defense if:
    (a) the ignorance or mistake negatives the purpose, knowledge, belief, recklessness or negligence required to establish a material element of the offense; or
    (b) the law provides that the state of mind established by such ignorance or mistake constitutes a defense.

(2) Although ignorance or mistake would otherwise afford a defense to the offense charged, the defense is not available if the defendant would be guilty of another offense had the situation been as he supposed. In such case, however, the ignorance or mistake of the defendant shall reduce the grade and degree of the offense of which he may be convicted to those of the offense of which he would be guilty had the situation been as he supposed.

(3) A belief that conduct does not legally constitute an offense is a defense to a prosecution for that offense based upon such conduct when:
    (a) the statute or other enactment defining the offense is not known to the actor and has not been published or otherwise reasonably made available prior to the conduct alleged; or
    (b) he acts in reasonable reliance upon an official statement of the law, afterward determined to be invalid or erroneous, contained in (i) a statute or other enactment; (ii) a judicial decision, opinion or judgment; (iii) an administrative order or grant of permission; or (iv) an official interpretation of the public officer or body charged by law with responsibility for the interpretation, administration or enforcement of the law defining the offense.

(4) The defendant must prove a defense arising under Subsection (3) of this Section by a preponderance of evidence.

Section 2.05. When Culpability Requirements Are
Inapplicable to Violations and to Offenses Defined
by Other Statutes; Effect of Absolute Liability in
Reducing Grade of Offense to Violation.

(1) The requirements of culpability prescribed by Sections 2.01 and 2.02 do not apply to:
    (a) offenses which constitute violations, unless the requirement involved is included in the definition of the offense or the Court

determines that its application is consistent with effective enforcement of the law defining the offense; or

(b) offenses defined by statutes other than the Code, insofar as a legislative purpose to impose absolute liability for such offenses or with respect to any material element thereof plainly appears.

(2) Notwithstanding any other provision of existing law and unless a subsequent statute otherwise provides:

(a) when absolute liability is imposed with respect to any material element of an offense defined by a statute other than the Code and a conviction is based upon such liability, the offense constitutes a violation; and

(b) although absolute liability is imposed by law with respect to one or more of the material elements of an offense defined by a statute other than the Code, the culpable commission of the offense may be charged and proved, in which event negligence with respect to such elements constitutes sufficient culpability and the classification of the offense and the sentence that may be imposed therefor upon conviction are determined by Section 1.04 and Article 6 of the Code.

Section 2.06. Liability for Conduct of Another; Complicity.

(1) A person is guilty of an offense if it is committed by his own conduct or by the conduct of another person for which he is legally accountable, or both.

(2) A person is legally accountable for the conduct of another person when:

(a) acting with the kind of culpability that is sufficient for the commission of the offense, he causes an innocent or irresponsible person to engage in such conduct; or

(b) he is made accountable for the conduct of such other person by the Code or by the law defining the offense; or

(c) he is an accomplice of such other person in the commission of the offense.

(3) A person is an accomplice of another person in the commission of an offense if:

(a) with the purpose of promoting or facilitating the commission of the offense, he

(i) solicits such other person to commit it; or

(ii) aids or agrees or attempts to aid such other person in planning or committing it; or

(iii) having a legal duty to prevent the commission of the offense, fails to make proper effort so to do; or

(b) his conduct is expressly declared by law to establish his complicity.

(4) When causing a particular result is an element of an offense,

an accomplice in the conduct causing such result is an accomplice in the commission of that offense, if he acts with the kind of culpability, if any, with respect to that result that is sufficient for the commission of the offense.

(5) A person who is legally incapable of committing a particular offense himself may be guilty thereof if it is committed by the conduct of another person for which he is legally accountable, unless such liability is inconsistent with the purpose of the provision establishing his incapacity.

(6) Unless otherwise provided by the Code or by the law defining the offense, a person is not an accomplice in an offense committed by another person if:

   (a) he is a victim of that offense; or

   (b) the offense is so defined that his conduct is inevitably incident to its commission; or

   (c) he terminates his complicity prior to the commission of the offense and

      (i) wholly deprives it of effectiveness in the commission of the offense; or

      (ii) gives timely warning to the law enforcement authorities or otherwise makes proper effort to prevent the commission of the offense.

(7) An accomplice may be convicted on proof of the commission of the offense and of his complicity therein, though the person claimed to have committed the offense has not been prosecuted or convicted or has been convicted of a different offense or degree of offense or has an immunity to prosecution or conviction or has been acquitted.

Section 2.07. Liability of Corporations,
Unincorporated Associations and Persons Acting, or
Under a Duty to Act, in Their Behalf.

(1) A corporation may be convicted of the commission of an offense if:

   (a) the offense is a violation or the offense is defined by a statute other than the Code in which a legislative purpose to impose liability on corporations plainly appears and the conduct is performed by an agent of the corporation acting in behalf of the corporation within the scope of his office or employment, except that if the law defining the offense designates the agents for whose conduct the corporation is accountable or the circumstances under which it is accountable, such provisions shall apply; or

   (b) the offense consists of an omission to discharge a specific duty of affirmative performance imposed on corporations by law; or

   (c) the commission of the offense was authorized, requested, commanded, performed or recklessly tolerated by the board of directors or by a high managerial agent acting in behalf of the corporation within the scope of his office or employment.

(2) When absolute liability is imposed for the commission of an offense, a legislative purpose to impose liability on a corporation shall be assumed, unless the contrary plainly appears.

(3) An unincorporated association may be convicted of the commission of an offense if:

(a) the offense is defined by a statute other than the Code which expressly provides for the liability of such an association and the conduct is performed by an agent of the association acting in behalf of the association within the scope of his office or employment, except that if the law defining the offense designates the agents for whose conduct the association is accountable or the circumstances under which it is accountable, such provisions shall apply; or

(b) the offense consists of an omission to discharge a specific duty of affirmative performance imposed on associations by law.

(4) As used in this Section:

(a) "corporation" does not include an entity organized as or by a governmental agency for the execution of a governmental program;

(b) "agent" means any director, officer, servant, employee or other person authorized to act in behalf of the corporation or association and, in the case of an unincorporated association, a member of such association;

(c) "high managerial agent" means an officer of a corporation or an unincorporated association, or, in the case of a partnership, a partner, or any other agent of a corporation or association having duties of such responsibility that his conduct may fairly be assumed to represent the policy of the corporation or association.

(5) In any prosecution of a corporation or an unincorporated association for the commission of an offense included within the terms of Subsection (1)(a) or Subsection (3)(a) of this Section, other than an offense for which absolute liability has been imposed, it shall be a defense if the defendant proves by a preponderance of evidence that the high managerial agent having supervisory responsibility over the subject matter of the offense employed due diligence to prevent its commission. This paragraph shall not apply if it is plainly inconsistent with the legislative purpose in defining the particular offense.

(6) (a) A person is legally accountable for any conduct he performs or causes to be performed in the name of the corporation or an unincorporated association or in its behalf to the same extent as if it were performed in his own name or behalf.

(b) Whenever a duty to act is imposed by law upon a corporation or an unincorporated association, any agent of the corporation or association having primary responsibility for the discharge of the duty is legally accountable for a reckless omission to perform the required act to the same extent as if the duty were imposed by law directly upon himself.

(c) When a person is convicted of an offense by reason of his legal accountability for the conduct of a corporation or an unincorporated association, he is subject to the sentence authorized by law when a natural person is convicted of an offense of the grade and the degree involved.

Section 2.08. Intoxication.

(1) Except as provided in Subsection (4) of this Section, intoxication of the actor is not a defense unless it negatives an element of the offense.

(2) When recklessness establishes an element of the offense, if the actor, due to self-induced intoxication, is unaware of a risk of which he would have been aware had he been sober, such unawareness is immaterial.

(3) Intoxication does not, in itself, constitute mental disease within the meaning of Section 4.01.

(4) Intoxication which (a) is not self-induced or (b) is pathological is an affirmative defense if by reason of such intoxication the actor at the time of his conduct lacks substantial capacity either to appreciate its criminality [wrongfulness] or to conform his conduct to the requirements of law.

(5) Definitions. In this Section unless a different meaning plainly is required:

(a) "intoxication" means a disturbance of mental or physical capacities resulting from the introduction of substances into the body;

(b) "self-induced intoxication" means intoxication caused by substances which the actor knowingly introduces into his body, the tendency of which to cause intoxication he knows or ought to know, unless he introduces them pursuant to medical advice or under such circumstances as would afford a defense to a charge of crime;

(c) "pathological intoxication" means intoxication grossly excessive in degree, given the amount of the intoxicant, to which the actor does not know he is susceptible.

Section 2.09. Duress.

(1) It is an affirmative defense that the actor engaged in the conduct charged to constitute an offense because he was coerced to do so by the use of, or a threat to use, unlawful force against his person or the person of another, which a person of reasonable firmness in his situation would have been unable to resist.

(2) The defense provided by this Section is unavailable if the actor recklessly placed himself in a situation in which it was probable that he

would be subjected to duress. The defense is also unavailable if he was negligent in placing himself in such a situation, whenever negligence suffices to establish culpability for the offense charged.

(3) It is not a defense that a woman acted on the command of her husband, unless she acted under such coercion as would establish a defense under this Section. [The presumption that a woman, acting in the presence of her husband, is coerced is abolished.]

(4) When the conduct of the actor would otherwise be justifiable under Section 3.02, this Section does not preclude such defense.

Section 2.10. Military Orders.

It is an affirmative defense that the actor, in engaging in the conduct charged to constitute an offense, does no more than execute an order of his superior in the armed services which he does not know to be unlawful.

Section 2.11. Consent.

(1) In General. The consent of the victim to conduct charged to constitute an offense or to the result thereof is a defense if such consent negatives an element of the offense or precludes the infliction of the harm or evil sought to be prevented by the law defining the offense.

(2) Consent to Bodily Injury. When conduct is charged to constitute an offense because it causes or threatens bodily injury, consent to such conduct or to the infliction of such injury is a defense if:

    (a) the bodily injury consented to or threatened by the conduct consented to is not serious; or

    (b) the conduct and the injury are reasonably foreseeable hazards of joint participation in a lawful athletic contest or competitive sport or other concerted activity not forbidden by law; or

    (c) the consent establishes a justification for the conduct under Article 3 of the Code.

(3) Ineffective Consent. Unless otherwise provided by the Code or by the law defining the offense, assent does not constitute consent if:

    (a) it is given by a person who is legally incompetent to authorize the conduct charged to constitute the offense; or

    (b) it is given by a person who by reason of youth, mental disease or defect or intoxication is manifestly unable or known by the actor to be unable to make a reasonable judgment as to the nature or harmfulness of the conduct charged to constitute the offense; or

    (c) it is given by a person whose improvident consent is sought to be prevented by the law defining the offense; or

    (d) it is induced by force, duress or deception of a kind sought to be prevented by the law defining the offense.

Section 2.12. De Minimis Infractions.

The Court shall dismiss a prosecution if, having regard to the nature of the conduct charged to constitute an offense and the nature of the attendant circumstances, it finds that the defendant's conduct:

(1) was within a customary license or tolerance, neither expressly negatived by the person whose interest was infringed nor inconsistent with the purpose of the law defining the offense; or

(2) did not actually cause or threaten the harm or evil sought to be prevented by the law defining the offense or did so only to an extent too trivial to warrant the condemnation of conviction; or

(3) presents such other extenuations that it cannot reasonably be regarded as envisaged by the legislature in forbidding the offense. The Court shall not dismiss a prosecution under Subsection (3) of this Section without filing a written statement of its reasons.

Section 2.13. Entrapment.

(1) A public law enforcement official or a person acting in cooperation with such an official perpetrates an entrapment if for the purpose of obtaining evidence of the commission of an offense, he induces or encourages another person to engage in conduct constituting such offense by either:

(a) making knowingly false representations designed to induce the belief that such conduct is not prohibited; or

(b) employing methods of persuasion or inducement which create a substantial risk that such an offense will be committed by persons other than those who are ready to commit it.

(2) Except as provided in Subsection (3) of this Section, a person prosecuted for an offense shall be acquitted if he proves by a preponderance of evidence that his conduct occurred in response to an entrapment. The issue of entrapment shall be tried by the Court in the absence of the jury.

(3) The defense afforded by this Section is unavailable when causing or threatening bodily injury is an element of the offense charged and the prosecution is based on conduct causing or threatening such injury to a person other than the person perpetrating the entrapment.

Article 3. General Principles of Justification.

Section 3.01. Justification an Affirmative Defense; Civil Remedies Unaffected.

(1) In any prosecution based on conduct which is justifiable under this Article, justification is an affirmative defense.

(2) The fact that conduct is justifiable under this Article does not abolish or impair any remedy for such conduct which is available in any civil action.

Section 3.02. Justification Generally: Choice of Evils.

(1) Conduct which the actor believes to be necessary to avoid a harm or evil to himself or to another is justifiable, provided that:

    (a) the harm or evil sought to be avoided by such conduct is greater than that sought to be prevented by the law defining the offense charged; and

    (b) neither the Code nor other law defining the offense provides exceptions or defenses dealing with the specific situation involved; and

    (c) a legislative purpose to exclude the justification claimed does not otherwise plainly appear.

(2) When the actor was reckless or negligent in bringing about the situation requiring a choice of harms or evils or in appraising the necessity for his conduct, the justification afforded by this Section is unavailable in a prosecution for any offense for which recklessness or negligence, as the case may be, suffices to establish culpability.

Section 3.03. Execution of Public Duty.

(1) Except as provided in Subsection (2) of this Section, conduct is justifiable when it is required or authorized by:

    (a) the law defining the duties or functions of a public officer or the assistance to be rendered to such officer in the performance of his duties; or

    (b) the law governing the execution of legal process; or

    (c) the judgment or order of a competent court or tribunal; or

    (d) the law governing the armed services or the lawful conduct of war; or

    (e) any other provision of law imposing a public duty.

(2) The other sections of this Article apply to:

    (a) the use of force upon or toward the person of another for any of the purposes dealt with in such sections; and

    (b) the use of deadly force for any purpose, unless the use of such force is otherwise expressly authorized by law or occurs in the lawful conduct of war.

(3) The justification afforded by Subsection (1) of this Section applies:

    (a) when the actor believes his conduct to be required or authorized by the judgment or direction of a competent court or tribunal or in the lawful execution of legal process, notwithstanding lack of jurisdiction of the court or defect in the legal process; and

(b) when the actor believes his conduct to be required or authorized to assist a public officer in the performance of his duties, notwithstanding that the officer exceeded his legal authority.

Section 3.04. Use of Force in Self-Protection.

(1) Use of Force Justifiable for Protection of the Person. Subject to the provisions of this Section and of Section 3.09, the use of force upon or toward another person is justifiable when the actor believes that such force is immediately necessary for the purpose of protecting himself against the use of unlawful force by such other person on the present occasion.

(2) Limitations on Justifying Necessity for Use of Force.

(a) The use of force is not justifiable under this Section:

(i) to resist an arrest which the actor knows is being made by a peace officer, although the arrest is unlawful; or

(ii) to resist force used by the occupier or possessor of property or by another person on his behalf, where the actor knows that the person using the force is doing so under a claim of right to protect the property, except that this limitation shall not apply if:

(1) the actor is a public officer acting in the performance of his duties or a person lawfully assisting him therein or a person making or assisting in a lawful arrest; or

(2) the actor has been unlawfully dispossessed of the property and is making a re-entry or recaption justified by Section 3.06; or

(3) the actor believes that such force is necessary to protect himself against death or serious bodily harm.

(b) The use of deadly force is not justifiable under this Section unless the actor believes that such force is necessary to protect himself against death, serious bodily harm, kidnapping or sexual intercourse compelled by force or threat; nor is it justifiable if:

(i) the actor, with the purpose of causing death or serious bodily harm, provoked the use of force against himself in the same encounter; or

(ii) the actor knows that he can avoid the necessity of using such force with complete safety by retreating or by surrendering possession of a thing to a person asserting a claim of right thereto or by complying with a demand that he abstain from any action which he has no duty to take, except that:

(1) the actor is not obliged to retreat from his dwelling or place of work, unless he was the initial aggressor or is assailed in his place of work by another person whose place of work the actor knows it to be; and

(2) a public officer justified in using force in the perfor-

mance of his duties or a person justified in using force in his assistance or a person justified in using force in making an arrest or preventing an escape is not obliged to desist from efforts to perform such duty, effect such arrest or prevent such escape because of resistance or threatened resistance by or on behalf of the person against whom such action is directed.

(c) Except as required by paragraphs (a) and (b) of this Subsection, a person employing protective force may estimate the necessity thereof under the circumstances as he believes them to be when the force is used, without retreating, surrendering possession, doing any other act which he has no legal duty to do or abstaining from any lawful action.

(3) Use of Confinement as Protective Force. The justification afforded by this Section extends to the use of confinement as protective force only if the actor takes all reasonable measures to terminate the confinement as soon as he knows that he safely can, unless the person confined has been arrested on a charge of crime.

Section 3.05. Use of Force for the Protection of Other Persons.

(1) Subject to the provisions of this Section and of Section 3.09, the use of force upon or toward the person of another is justifiable to protect a third person when:

(a) the actor would be justified under Section 3.04 in using such force to protect himself against the injury he believes to be threatened to the person whom he seeks to protect; and

(b) under the circumstances as the actor believes them to be, the person whom he seeks to protect would be justified in using such protective force; and

(c) the actor believes that his intervention is necessary for the protection of such other person.

(2) Notwithstanding Subsection (1) of this Section:

(a) when the actor would be obliged under Section 3.04 to retreat, to surrender the possession of a thing or to comply with a demand before using force in self-protection, he is not obliged to do so before using force for the protection of another person, unless he knows that he can thereby secure the complete safety of such other person; and

(b) when the person whom the actor seeks to protect would be obliged under Section 3.04 to retreat, to surrender the possession of a thing or to comply with a demand if he knew that he could obtain complete safety by so doing, the actor is obliged to try to cause him to do so before using force in his protection if the actor knows that he can obtain complete safety in that way; and

(c) neither the actor nor the person whom he seeks to protect is obliged to retreat when in the other's dwelling or place of work to any greater extent than in his own.

Section 3.06. Use of Force for the Protection of Property.

(1) Use of Force Justifiable for Protection of Property. Subject to the provisions of this Section and of Section 3.09, the use of force upon or toward the person of another is justifiable when the actor believes that such force is immediately necessary:

(a) to prevent or terminate an unlawful entry or other trespass upon land or a trespass against or the unlawful carrying away of tangible, movable property, provided that such land or movable property is, or is believed by the actor to be, in his possession or in the possession of another person for whose protection he acts; or

(b) to effect an entry or re-entry upon land or to retake tangible movable property, provided that the actor believes that he or the person by whose authority he acts or a person from whom he or such other person derives title was unlawfully dispossessed of such land or movable property and is entitled to possession, and provided, further, that:

(i) the force is used immediately or on fresh pursuit after such dispossession; or

(ii) the actor believes that the person against whom he uses force has no claim of right to the possession of the property and, in the case of land, the circumstances, as the actor believes them to be, are of such urgency that it would be an exceptional hardship to postpone the entry or re-entry until a court order is obtained.

(2) Meaning of Possession. For the purposes of Subsection (1) of this Section:

(a) a person who has parted with the custody of property to another who refuses to restore it to him is no longer in possession, unless the property is movable and was and still is located on land in his possession;

(b) a person who has been dispossessed of land does not regain possession thereof merely by setting foot thereon;

(c) a person who has a license to use or occupy real property is deemed to be in possession thereof except against the licensor acting under claim of right.

(3) Limitations on Justifiable Use of Force.

(a) Request to Desist. The use of force is justifiable under this Section only if the actor first requests the person against whom such force is used to desist from his interference with the property, unless the actor believes that:

(i) such request would be useless; or

APPENDIX: MODEL PENAL CODE 731

(ii) it would be dangerous to himself or another person to make the request; or

(iii) substantial harm will be done to the physical condition of the property which is sought to be protected before the request can effectively be made.

(b) Exclusion of Trespasser. The use of force to prevent or terminate a trespass is not justifiable under this Section if the actor knows that the exclusion of the trespasser will expose him to substantial danger of serious bodily harm.

(c) Resistance of Lawful Re-entry or Recaption. The use of force to prevent an entry or re-entry upon land or the recaption of movable property is not justifiable under this Section, although the actor believes that such re-entry or recaption is unlawful, if:

(i) the re-entry or recaption is made by or on behalf of a person who was actually dispossessed of the property; and

(ii) it is otherwise justifiable under paragraph (1)(b) of this Section.

(d) Use of Deadly Force. The use of deadly force is not justifiable under this Section unless the actor believes that:

(i) the person against whom the force is used is attempting to dispossess him of his dwelling otherwise than under a claim of right to its possession; or

(ii) the person against whom the force is used is attempting to commit or consummate arson, burglary, robbery or other felonious theft or property destruction and either:

(1) has employed or threatened deadly force against or in the presence of the actor; or

(2) the use of force other than deadly force to prevent the commission or the consummation of the crime would expose the actor or another in his presence to substantial danger of serious bodily harm.

(4) Use of Confinement as Protective Force. The justification afforded by this Section extends to the use of confinement as protective force only if the actor takes all reasonable measures to terminate the confinement as soon as he knows that he can do so with safety to the property, unless the person confined has been arrested on a charge of crime.

(5) Use of Device to Protect Property. The justification afforded by this Section extends to the use of a device for the purpose of protecting property only if:

(a) the device is not designed to cause or known to create a substantial risk of causing death or serious bodily harm; and

(b) the use of the particular device to protect the property from entry or trespass is reasonable under the circumstances, as the actor believes them to be; and

(c) the device is one customarily used for such a purpose or reasonable care is taken to make known to probable intruders the fact that it is used.

(6) Use of Force to Pass Wrongful Obstructor. The use of force to pass a person whom the actor believe to be purposely or knowingly and unjustifiably obstructing the actor from going to a place to which he may lawfully go is justifiable, provided that:

(a) the actor believes that the person against whom he uses force has no claim of right to obstruct the actor; and

(b) the actor is not being obstructed from entry or movement on land which he knows to be in the possession or custody of the person obstructing him, or in the possession or custody of another person by whose authority the obstructor acts, unless the circumstances, as the actor believes them to be, are of such urgency that it would not be reasonable to postpone the entry or movement on such land until a court order is obtained; and

(c) the force used is not greater than would be justifiable if the person obstructing the actor were using force against him to prevent his passage.

Section 3.07. Use of Force in Law Enforcement.

(1) Use of Force Justifiable to Effect an Arrest. Subject to the provisions of this Section and of Section 3.09, the use of force upon or toward the person of another is justifiable when the actor is making or assisting in making an arrest and the actor believes that such force is immediately necessary to effect a lawful arrest.

(2) Limitations on the Use of Force.

(a) The use of force is not justifiable under this Section unless:

(i) the actor makes known the purpose of the arrest or believes that it is otherwise known by or cannot reasonably be made known to the person to be arrested; and

(ii) when the arrest is made under a warrant, the warrant is valid or believed by the actor to be valid.

(b) The use of deadly force is not justifiable under this Section unless:

(i) the arrest is for a felony; and

(ii) the person effecting the arrest is authorized to act as a peace officer or is assisting a person whom he believes to be authorized to act as a peace officer; and

(iii) the actor believes that the force employed creates no substantial risk of injury to innocent persons; and

(iv) the actor believes that:

(1) the crime for which the arrest is made involved conduct including the use or threatened use of deadly force; or

(2) there is a substantial risk that the person to be arrested will cause death or serious bodily harm if his apprehension is delayed.

(3) Use of Force to Prevent Escape from Custody. The use of force to prevent the escape of an arrested person from custody is justifiable when the force could justifiably have been employed to effect the arrest under which the person is in custody, except that a guard or other person authorized to act as a peace officer is justified in using any force, including deadly force, which he believes to be immediately necessary to prevent the escape of a person from a jail, prison, or other institution for the detention of persons charged with or convicted of a crime.

(4) Use of Force by Private Person Assisting an Unlawful Arrest.

(a) A private person who is summoned by a peace officer to assist in effecting an unlawful arrest, is justified in using any force which he would be justified in using if the arrest were lawful, provided that he does not believe the arrest is unlawful.

(b) A private person who assists another private person in effecting an unlawful arrest, or who, not being summoned, assists a peace officer in effecting an unlawful arrest, is justified in using any force which he would be justified in using if the arrest were lawful, provided that (i) he believes the arrest is lawful, and (ii) the arrest would be lawful if the facts were as he believes them to be.

(5) Use of Force to Prevent Suicide or the Commission of a Crime.

(a) The use of force upon or toward the person of another is justifiable when the actor believes that such force is immediately necessary to prevent such other person from committing suicide, inflicting serious bodily harm upon himself, committing or consummating the commission of a crime involving or threatening bodily harm, damage to or loss of property or a breach of the peace, except that:

(i) any limitations imposed by the other provisions of this Article on the justifiable use of force in self-protection, for the protection of others, the protection of property, the effectuation of an arrest or the prevention of an escape from custody shall apply notwithstanding the criminality of the conduct against which such force is used; and

(ii) the use of deadly force is not in any event justifiable under this Subsection unless:

(1) the actor believes that there is a substantial risk that the person whom he seeks to prevent from committing a crime will cause death or serious bodily harm to another unless the commission or the consummation of the crime is prevented and that the use of such force presents no substantial risk of injury to innocent persons; or

(2) the actor believes that the use of such force is necessary to suppress a riot or mutiny after the rioters or mutineers have

been ordered to disperse and warned, in any particular manner that the law may require, that such force will be used if they do not obey.

(b) The justification afforded by this Subsection extends to the use of confinement as preventive force only if the actor takes all reasonable measures to terminate the confinement as soon as he knows that he safely can, unless the person confined has been arrested on a charge of crime.

Section 3.08. Use of Force by Persons with Special Responsibility for Care, Discipline or Safety of Others.

The use of force upon or toward the person of another is justifiable if:

(1) the actor is the parent or guardian or other person similarly responsible for the general care and supervision of a minor or a person acting at the request of such parent, guardian or other responsible person and:

(a) the force is used for the purpose of safeguarding or promoting the welfare of the minor, including the prevention or punishment of his misconduct; and

(b) the force used is not designed to cause or known to create a substantial risk of causing death, serious bodily harm, disfigurement, extreme pain or mental distress or gross degradation; or

(2) the actor is a teacher or a person otherwise entrusted with the care or supervision for a special purpose of a minor and:

(a) the actor believes that the force used is necessary to further such special purpose, including the maintenance of reasonable discipline in a school, class or other group, and that the use of such force is consistent with the welfare of the minor; and

(b) the degree of force, if it had been used by the parent or guardian of the minor, would not be unjustifiable under Subsection (1)(b) of this Section; or

(3) the actor is the guardian or other person similarly responsible for the general care and supervision of an incompetent person; and:

(a) the force is used for the purpose of safeguarding or promoting the welfare of the incompetent person, including the prevention of his misconduct, or, when such incompetent person is in a hospital or other institution for his care and custody, for the maintenance of reasonable discipline in such institution; and

(b) the force used is not designed to cause or known to create a substantial risk of causing death, serious bodily harm, disfigurement, extreme or unnecessary pain, mental distress, or humiliation; or

(4) the actor is a doctor or other therapist or a person assisting him at his direction, and:

(a) the force is used for the purpose of administering a recognized form of treatment which the actor believes to be adapted to promoting the physical or mental health of the patient; and

(b) the treatment is administered with the consent of the patient or, if the patient is a minor or an incompetent person, with the consent of his parent or guardian or other person legally competent to consent in his behalf, or the treatment is administered in an emergency when the actor believes that no one competent to consent can be consulted and that a reasonable person, wishing to safeguard the welfare of the patient, would consent; or

(5) the actor is a warden or other authorized official of a correctional institution, and:

(a) he believes that the force used is necessary for the purpose of enforcing the lawful rules or procedures of the institution, unless his belief in the lawfulness of the rule or procedure sought to be enforced is erroneous and his error is due to ignorance or mistake as to the provisions of the Code, any other provision of the criminal law or the law governing the administration of the institution; and

(b) the nature or degree of force used is not forbidden by Article 303 or 304 of the Code; and

(c) if deadly force is used, its use is otherwise justifiable under this Article; or

(6) the actor is a person responsible for the safety of a vessel or an aircraft or a person acting at his direction, and

(a) he believes that the force used is necessary to prevent interference with the operation of the vessel or aircraft or obstruction of the execution of a lawful order, unless his belief in the lawfulness of the order is erroneous and his error is due to ignorance or mistake as to the law defining his authority; and

(b) if deadly force is used, its use is otherwise justifiable under this Article; or

(7) the actor is a person who is authorized or required by law to maintain order or decorum in a vehicle, train or other carrier or in a place where others are assembled, and:

(a) he believes that the force used is necessary for such purpose; and

(b) the force used is not designed to cause or known to create a substantial risk of causing death, bodily harm, or extreme mental distress.

Section 3.09. Mistake of Law as to Unlawfulness of Force or Legality of Arrest; Reckless or Negligent Use of Otherwise Justifiable Force; Reckless or Negligent Injury or Risk of Injury to Innocent Persons.

(1) The justification afforded by Sections 3.04 to 3.07, inclusive, is unavailable when:

(a) the actor's belief in the unlawfulness of the force or conduct against which he employs protective force or his belief in the lawfulness of an arrest which he endeavors to effect by force is erroneous; and

(b) his error is due to ignorance or mistake as to the provisions of the Code, any other provision of the criminal law or the law governing the legality of an arrest or search.

(2) When the actor believes that the use of force upon or toward the person of another is necessary for any of the purposes for which such belief would establish a justification under Sections 3.03 to 3.08 but the actor is reckless or negligent in having such belief or in acquiring or failing to acquire any knowledge or belief which is material to the justiciability of his use of force, the justification afforded by those Sections is unavailable in a prosecution for an offense for which recklessness or negligence, as the case may be, suffices to establish culpability.

(3) When the actor is justified under Sections 3.03 to 3.08 in using force upon or toward the person of another but he recklessly or negligently injures or creates a risk of injury to innocent persons, the justification afforded by those Sections is unavailable in a prosecution for such recklessness or negligence towards innocent persons.

Section 3.10. Justification in Property Crimes.

Conduct involving the appropriation, seizure or destruction of, damage to, intrusion on or interference with property is justifiable under circumstances which would establish a defense of privilege in a civil action based thereon, unless:

(1) the Code or the law defining the offense deals with the specific situation involved; or

(2) a legislative purpose to exclude the justification claimed otherwise plainly appears.

Section 3.11. Definitions.

In this Article, unless a different meaning plainly is required:

(1) "unlawful force" means force, including confinement, which is employed without the consent of the person against whom it is directed and the employment of which constitutes an offense or actionable tort or would constitute such offense or tort except for a defense (such as the absence of intent, negligence, or mental capacity; duress; youth; or diplomatic status) not amounting to a privilege to use the force. Assent constitutes consent, within the meaning of this Section, whether or not it otherwise is legally effective, except assent to the infliction of death or serious bodily harm.

(2) "deadly force" means force which the actor uses with the purpose of causing or which he knows to create a substantial risk of causing death or serious bodily harm. Purposely firing a firearm in the direction of another person or at a vehicle in which another person is believed to be constitutes deadly force. A threat to cause

death or serious bodily harm, by the production of a weapon or otherwise, so long as the actor's purpose is limited to creating an apprehension that he will use deadly force if necessary, does not constitute deadly force;

(3) "dwelling" means any building or structure, though movable or temporary, or a portion thereof, which is for the time being the actor's home or place of lodging.

Article 4. Responsibility.

Section 4.01. Mental Disease or Defect Excluding Responsibility.

(1) A person is not responsible for criminal conduct if at the time of such conduct as a result of mental disease or defect he lacks substantial capacity either to appreciate the criminality [wrongfulness] of his conduct or to conform his conduct to the requirements of law.

(2) As used in this Article, the terms "mental disease or defect" do not include an abnormality manifested only by repeated criminal or otherwise anti-social conduct.

Section 4.02. Evidence of Mental Disease or Defect Admissible When Relevant to Element of the Offense; [Mental Disease or Defect Impairing Capacity as Ground for Mitigation of Punishment in Capital Cases].

(1) Evidence that the defendant suffered from a mental disease or defect is admissible whenever it is relevant to prove that the defendant did or did not have a state of mind which is an element of the offense.

[(2) Whenever the jury or the Court is authorized to determine or to recommend whether or not the defendant shall be sentenced to death or imprisonment upon conviction, evidence that the capacity of the defendant to appreciate the criminality [wrongfulness] of his conduct or to conform his conduct to the requirements of law was impaired as a result of mental disease or defect is admissible in favor of sentence of imprisonment.]

Section 4.03. Mental Disease or Defect Excluding Responsibility Is Affirmative Defense; Requirement of Notice; Form of Verdict and Judgment When Finding of Irresponsibility Is Made.

(1) Mental disease or defect excluding responsibility is an affirmative defense.

(2) Evidence of mental disease or defect excluding responsibility is not admissible unless the defendant, at the time of entering his plea of not guilty or within ten days thereafter or at such later time as the

Court may for good cause permit, files a written notice of his purpose to rely on such defense.

(3) When the defendant is acquitted on the ground of mental disease or defect excluding responsibility, the verdict and the judgment shall so state.

Section 4.04. Mental Disease or Defect Excluding Fitness to Proceed.

No person who as a result of mental disease or defect lacks capacity to understand the proceedings against him or to assist in his own defense shall be tried, convicted or sentenced for the commission of an offense so long as such incapacity endures.

Section 4.05. Psychiatric Examination of Defendant with Respect to Mental Disease or Defect.

(1) Whenever the defendant has filed a notice of intention to rely on the defense of mental disease or defect excluding responsibility, or there is reason to doubt his fitness to proceed, or reason to believe that mental disease or defect of the defendant will otherwise become an issue in the cause, the Court shall appoint at least one qualified psychiatrist or shall request the Superintendent of the Hospital to designate at least one qualified psychiatrist, which designation may be or include himself, to examine and report upon the mental condition of the defendant. The Court may order the defendant to be committed to a hospital or other suitable facility for the purpose of the examination for a period of not exceeding sixty days or such longer period as the Court determines to be necessary for the purpose and may direct that a qualified psychiatrist retained by the defendant be permitted to witness and participate in the examination.

(2) In such examination any method may be employed which is accepted by the medical profession for the examination of those alleged to be suffering from mental disease or defect.

(3) The report of the examination shall include the following:

    (a) a description of the nature of the examination;

    (b) a diagnosis of the mental condition of the defendant;

    (c) if the defendant suffers from a mental disease or defect, an opinion as to his capacity to understand the proceedings against him and to assist in his own defense;

    (d) when a notice of intention to rely on the defense of irresponsibility has been filed, an opinion as to the extent, if any, to which the capacity of the defendant to appreciate the criminality [wrongfulness] of his conduct or to conform his conduct to the requirements of law was impaired at the time of the criminal conduct charged; and

    (e) when directed by the Court, an opinion as to the capacity of the defendant to have a particular state of mind which is an element of the offense charged.

If the examination cannot be conducted by reason of the unwillingness of the defendant to participate therein, the report shall so state and shall include, if possible, an opinion as to whether such unwillingness of the defendant was the result of mental disease or defect.

The report of the examination shall be filed [in triplicate] with the clerk of the Court, who shall cause copies to be delivered to the district attorney and to counsel for the defendant.

Section 4.06. Determination of Fitness to Proceed;
Effect of Finding of Unfitness; Proceedings if Fitness
is Regained; [Post-Commitment Hearing].

(1) When the defendant's fitness to proceed is drawn in question, the issue shall be determined by the Court. If neither the prosecuting attorney nor counsel for the defendant contests the finding of the report filed pursuant to Section 4.05, the Court may make the determination on the basis of such report. If the finding is contested, the Court shall hold a hearing on the issue. If the report is received in evidence upon such hearing, the party who contests the finding thereof shall have the right to summon and to cross-examine the psychiatrists who joined in the report and to offer evidence upon the issue.

(2) If the Court determines that the defendant lacks fitness to proceed, the proceeding against him shall be suspended, except as provided in Subsection (3) [Subsections (3) and (4)] of this Section, and the Court shall commit him to the custody of the Commissioner of Mental Hygiene [Public Health or Correction] to be placed in an appropriate institution of the Department of Mental Hygiene [Public Health or Correction] for so long as such unfitness shall endure. When the Court, on its own motion or upon the application of the Commissioner of Mental Hygiene [Public Health or Correction] or the prosecuting attorney, determines, after a hearing if a hearing is requested, that the defendant has regained fitness to proceed, the proceeding shall be resumed. If, however, the Court is of the view that so much time has elapsed since the commitment of the defendant that it would be unjust to resume the criminal proceeding, the Court may dismiss the charge and may order the defendant to be discharged or, subject to the law governing the civil commitment of persons suffering from mental disease or defect, order the defendant to be committed to an appropriate institution of the Department of Mental Hygiene [Public Health].

(3) The fact that the defendant's unfit to proceed does not preclude any legal objection to the prosecution which is susceptible of fair determination prior to trial and without the personal participation of the defendant. [Alternative: (3) At any time within ninety days after commitment as provided in Subsection (2) of this Section, or at any later time

with permission of the Court granted for good cause, the defendant or his counsel or the Commissioner of Mental Hygiene [Public Health or Correction] may apply for a special post-commitment hearing. If the application is made by or on behalf of a defendant not represented by counsel, he shall be afforded a reasonable opportunity to obtain counsel, and if he lacks funds to do so, counsel shall be assigned by the Court. The application shall be granted only if the counsel for the defendant satisfies the Court by affidavit or otherwise that as an attorney he has reasonable grounds for a good faith belief that his client has, on the facts and the law, a defense to the charge other than mental disease or defect excluding responsibility.]

[(4) If the motion for a special post-commitment hearing is granted, the hearing shall be by the Court without a jury. No evidence shall be offered at the hearing by either party on the issue of mental disease or defect as a defense to, or in mitigation of, the crime charged. After hearing, the Court may in an appropriate case quash the indictment or other charge, or find it to be defective or insufficient, or determine that it is not proved beyond a reasonable doubt by the evidence, or otherwise terminate the proceedings on the evidence or the law. In any such case, unless all defects in the proceedings are promptly cured, the Court shall terminate the commitment ordered under Subsection (2) of this Section and order the defendant to be discharged or, subject to the law governing the civil commitment of persons suffering from mental disease or defect, order the defendant to be committed to an appropriate institution of the Department of Mental Hygiene [Public Health].]

> Section 4.07. Determination of Irresponsibility on
> Basis of Report; Access to Defendant by Psychiatrist
> of His Own Choice; Form of Expert Testimony When
> Issue of Responsibility Is Tried.

(1) If the report filed pursuant to Section 4.05 finds that the defendant at the time of the criminal conduct charged suffered from a mental disease or defect which substantially impaired his capacity to appreciate the criminality [wrongfulness] of his conduct or to conform his conduct to the requirements of law, and the Court, after a hearing if a hearing is requested by the prosecuting attorney or the defendant, is satisfied that such impairment was sufficient to exclude responsibility, the Court on motion of the defendant shall enter judgment of acquittal on the ground of mental disease or defect excluding responsibility.

(2) When, notwithstanding the report filed pursuant to Section 4.05, the defendant wishes to be examined by a qualified psychiatrist or other examiner of his own choice, such examiner shall be permitted to have reasonable access to the defendant for the purposes of such examination.

(3) Upon the trial, the psychiatrists who reported pursuant to

Section 4.05 may be called as witnesses by the prosecution, the defendant or the Court. If the issue is being tried before a jury, the jury may be informed that the psychiatrists were designated by the Court or by the Superintendent of the _____ Hospital at the request of the Court, as the case may be. If called by the Court, the witness shall be subject to cross-examination by the prosecution and by the defendant. Both the prosecution and the defendant may summon any other qualified psychiatrist or other expert to testify, but no one who has not examined the defendant shall be competent to testify to an expert opinion with respect to the mental condition or responsibility of the defendant, as distinguished from the validity of the procedure followed by, or the general scientific propositions stated by, another witness.

(4) When a psychiatrist or other expert who has examined the defendant testifies concerning his mental condition, he shall be permitted to make a statement as to the nature of his examination, his diagnosis of the mental condition of the defendant at the time of the commission of the offense charged and his opinion as to the extent, if any, to which the capacity of the defendant to appreciate the criminality [wrongfulness] of his conduct or to conform his conduct to the requirements of law or to have a particular state of mind which is an element of the offense charged was impaired as a result of mental disease or defect at that time. He shall be permitted to make any explanation reasonably serving to clarify his diagnosis and opinion and may be cross-examined as to any matter bearing on his competency or credibility or the validity of his diagnosis or opinion.

Section 4.08. Legal Effect of Acquittal on the Ground of Mental Disease or Defect Excluding Responsibility; Commitment; Release or Discharge.

(1) When a defendant is acquitted on the ground of mental disease or defect excluding responsibility, the Court shall order him to be committed to the custody of the Commissioner of Mental Hygiene [Public Health] to be placed in an appropriate institution for custody, care and treatment.

(2) If the Commissioner of Mental Hygiene [Public Health] is of the view that a person committed to his custody, pursuant to paragraph (1) of this Section, may be discharged or released on condition without danger to himself or to others, he shall make application for the discharge or release of such person in a report to the Court by which such person was committed and shall transmit a copy of such application and report to the prosecuting attorney of the county [parish] from which the defendant was committed. The Court shall thereupon appoint at least two qualified psychiatrists to examine such person and to report within sixty days, or such longer period as the Court determines to be necessary for the purpose, their opinion as to his mental condition. To

facilitate such examination and the proceedings thereon, the Court may cause such person to be confined in any institution located near the place where the Court sits, which may hereafter be designated by the Commissioner of Mental Hygiene [Public Health] as suitable for the temporary detention of irresponsible persons.

(3) If the Court is satisfied by the report filed pursuant to paragraph (2) of this Section and such testimony of the reporting psychiatrists as the Court deems necessary that the committed person may be discharged or released on condition without danger to himself or others, the Court shall order his discharge or his release on such conditions as the Court determines to be necessary. If the Court is not so satisfied, it shall promptly order a hearing to determine whether such person may safely be discharged or released. Any such hearing shall be deemed a civil proceeding and the burden shall be upon the committed person to prove that he may safely be discharged or released. According to the determination of the Court upon the hearing, the committed person shall thereupon be discharged or released on such conditions as the Court determines to be necessary, or shall be recommitted to the custody of the Commissioner of Mental Hygiene [Public Health], subject to discharge or release only in accordance with the procedure prescribed above for a first hearing.

(4) If, within [five] years after the conditional release of a committed person, the Court shall determine, after hearing evidence, that the conditions of release have not been fulfilled and that for the safety of such person or for the safety of others his conditional release should be revoked, the Court shall forthwith order him to be recommitted to the Commissioner of Mental Hygiene [Public Health], subject to discharge or release only in accordance with the procedure prescribed above for a first hearing.

(5) A committed person may make application for his discharge or release to the Court by which he was committed, and the procedure to be followed upon such application shall be the same as that prescribed above in the case of an application by the Commissioner of Mental Hygiene [Public Health]. However, no such application by a committed person need be considered until he has been confined for a period of not less than [six months] from the date of the order of commitment, and if the determination of the Court be adverse to the application, such person shall not be permitted to file a further application until [one year] has elapsed from the date of any preceding hearing on an application for his release or discharge.

Section 4.09. Statements for Purposes of Examination
or Treatment Inadmissible Except on Issue of Mental
Condition.

A statement made by a person subjected to psychiatric examination or treatment pursuant to Sections 4.05, 4.06 or 4.08 for the purposes of such examination or treatment shall not be admissible in evidence against him in any criminal proceeding on any issue other than that of his mental condition but it shall be admissible upon that issue, whether or not it would otherwise be deemed a privileged communication [, unless such statement constitutes an admission of guilt of the crime charged].

Section 4.10. Immaturity Excluding Criminal Convictions; Transfer of Proceedings to Juvenile Court.

(1) A person shall not be tried for or convicted of an offense if:
    (a) at the time of the conduct charged to constitute the offense he was less than sixteen years of age [, in which case the Juvenile Court shall have exclusive jurisdiction*]; or
    (b) at the time of the conduct charged to constitute the offense he was sixteen or seventeen years of age, unless:
        (i) the Juvenile Court has no jurisdiction over him, or,
        (ii) the Juvenile Court has entered an order waiving jurisdiction and consenting to the institution of criminal proceedings against him.

(2) No court shall have jurisdiction to try or convict a person of an offense if criminal proceedings against him are barred by Subsection (1) of this Section. When it appears that a person charged with the commission of an offense may be of such an age that criminal proceedings may be barred under Subsection (1) of this Section, the Court shall hold a hearing thereon, and the burden shall be on the prosecution to establish to the satisfaction of the Court that the criminal proceeding is not barred upon such grounds. If the Court determines that the proceeding is barred, custody of the person charged shall be surrendered to the Juvenile Court, and the case, including all papers and processes relating thereto, shall be transferred.

Article 5. Inchoate Crimes.

Section 5.01. Criminal Attempt.

(1) Definition of Attempt. A person is guilty of an attempt to commit a crime if, acting with the kind of culpability otherwise required for commission of the crime, he:
    (a) purposely engages in conduct which would constitute the crime if the attendant circumstances were as he believes them to be; or
    (b) when causing a particular result is an element of the crime,

---

*The bracketed words are unnecessary if the Juvenile Court Act so provides or is amended accordingly.

does or omits to do anything with the purpose of causing or with the belief that it will cause such result without further conduct on his part; or

(c) purposely does or omits to do anything which, under the circumstances as he believes them to be, is an act or omission constituting a substantial step in a course of conduct planned to culminate in his commission of the crime.

(2) Conduct Which May Be Held Substantial Step Under Subsection (1)(c). Conduct shall not be held to constitute a substantial step under Subsection (1)(c) of this Section unless it is strongly corroborative of the actor's criminal purpose. Without negativing the sufficiency of other conduct, the following, if strongly corroborative of the actor's criminal purpose, shall not be held insufficient as a matter of law:

(a) lying in wait, searching for or following the contemplated victim of the crime;

(b) enticing or seeking to entice the contemplated victim of the crime to go to the place contemplated for its commission;

(c) reconnoitering the place contemplated for the commission of the crime;

(d) unlawful entry of a structure, vehicle or enclosure in which it is contemplated that the crime will be committed;

(e) possession of materials to be employed in the commission of the crime, which are specially designed for such unlawful use or which can serve no lawful purpose of the actor under the circumstances;

(f) possession, collection or fabrication of materials to be employed in the commission of the crime, at or near the place contemplated for its commission, where such possession, collection or fabrication serves no lawful purpose of the actor under the circumstances;

(g) soliciting an innocent agent to engage in conduct constituting an element of the crime.

(3) Conduct Designed to Aid Another in Commission of a Crime. A person who engages in conduct designed to aid another to commit a crime which would establish his complicity under Section 2.06 if the crime were committed by such other person, is guilty of an attempt to commit the crime, although the crime is not committed or attempted by such other person.

(4) Renunciation of Criminal Purpose. When the actor's conduct would otherwise constitute an attempt under Subsection (1)(b) or (1)(c) of this Section, it is an affirmative defense that he abandoned his effort to commit the crime or otherwise prevented its commission, under circumstances manifesting a complete and voluntary renunciation of his criminal purpose. The establishment of such defense does not, however, affect the liability of an accomplice who did not join in such abandonment or prevention. Within the meaning of this Article,

renunciation of criminal purpose is not voluntary if it is motivated, in whole or in part, by circumstances, not present or apparent at the inception of the actor's course of conduct, which increase the probability of detection or apprehension or which make more difficult the accomplishment of the criminal purpose. Renunciation is not complete if it is motivated by a decision to postpone the criminal conduct until a more advantageous time or to transfer the criminal effort to another but similar objective or victim.

Section 5.02. Criminal Solicitation.

(1) Definition of Solicitation. A person is guilty of solicitation to commit a crime if with the purpose of promoting or facilitating its commission he commands, encourages or requests another person to engage in specific conduct which would constitute such crime or an attempt to commit such crime or which would establish his complicity in its commission or attempted commission.

(2) Uncommunicated Solicitation. It is immaterial under Subsection (1) of this Section that the actor fails to communicate with the person he solicits to commit a crime if his conduct was designed to effect such communication.

(3) Renunciation of Criminal Purpose. It is an affirmative defense that the actor, after soliciting another person to commit a crime, persuaded him not to do so or otherwise prevented the commission of the crime, under circumstances manifesting a complete and voluntary renunciation of his criminal purpose.

Section 5.03. Criminal Conspiracy.

(1) Definition of Conspiracy. A person is guilty of conspiracy with another person or persons to commit a crime if with the purpose of promoting or facilitating its commission he:

    (a) agrees with such other person or persons that they or one or more of them will engage in conduct which constitutes such crime or an attempt or solicitation to commit such crime; or

    (b) agrees to aid such other person or persons in the planning or commission of such crime or of an attempt or solicitation to commit such crime.

(2) Scope of Conspiratorial Relationship. If a person guilty of conspiracy, as defined by Subsection (1) of this Section, knows that a person with whom he conspires to commit a crime has conspired with another person or persons to commit the same crime, he is guilty of conspiring with such other person or persons, whether or not he knows their identity, to commit such crime.

(3) Conspiracy With Multiple Criminal Objectives. If a person conspires to commit a number of crimes, he is guilty of only one conspiracy

so long as such multiple crimes are the object of the same agreement or continuous conspiratorial relationship.

(4) Joinder and Venue in Conspiracy Prosecutions.

(a) Subject to the provisions of paragraph (b) of this Subsection, two or more persons charged with criminal conspiracy may be prosecuted jointly if:

(i) they are charged with conspiring with one another; or

(ii) the conspiracies alleged, whether they have the same or different parties, are so related that they constitute different aspects of a scheme of organized criminal conduct.

(b) In any joint prosecution under paragraph (a) of this Subsection:

(i) no defendant shall be charged with a conspiracy in any county [parish or district] other than one in which he entered into such conspiracy or in which an overt act pursuant to such conspiracy was done by him or by a person with whom he conspired; and

(ii) neither the liability of any defendant nor the admissibility against him of evidence of acts or declarations of another shall be enlarged by such joinder; and

(iii) the Court shall order a severance or take a special verdict as to any defendant who so requests, if it deems it necessary or appropriate to promote the fair determination of his guilt or innocence, and shall take any other proper measures to protect the fairness of the trial.

(5) Overt Act. No person may be convicted of conspiracy to commit a crime, other than a felony of the first or second degree, unless an overt act in pursuance of such conspiracy is alleged and proved to have been done by him or by a person with whom he conspired.

(6) Renunciation of Criminal Purpose. It is an affirmative defense that the actor, after conspiring to commit a crime, thwarted the success of the conspiracy, under circumstances manifesting a complete and voluntary renunciation of his criminal purpose.

(7) Duration of Conspiracy. For purposes of Section 1.06(4):

(a) conspiracy is a continuing course of conduct which terminates when the crime or crimes which are its object are committed or the agreement that they be committed is abandoned by the defendant and by those with whom he conspired; and

(b) such abandonment is presumed if neither the defendant nor anyone with whom he conspired does any overt act in pursuance of the conspiracy during the applicable period of limitation; and

(c) if an individual abandons the agreement, the conspiracy is terminated as to him only if and when he advises those with whom he conspired of his abandonment or he informs the law enforcement authorities of the existence of the conspiracy and of his participation therein.

Section 5.04. Incapacity, Irresponsibility or Immunity
of Party to Solicitation or Conspiracy.

(1) Except as provided in Subsection (2) of this Section, it is immaterial to the liability of a person who solicits or conspires with another to commit a crime that:

    (a) he or the person who he solicits or with whom he conspires does not occupy a particular position or have a particular characteristic which is an element of such crime, if he believes that one of them does; or

    (b) the person whom he solicits or with whom he conspires is irresponsible or has an immunity to prosecution or conviction for the commission of the crime.

(2) It is a defense to a charge of solicitation or conspiracy to commit a crime that if the criminal object were achieved, the actor would not be guilty of a crime under the law defining the offense or as an accomplice under Section 2.06(5) or 2.06(6)(a) or (b).

Section 5.05. Grading of Criminal Attempt,
Solicitation and Conspiracy; Mitigation in Cases of
Lesser Danger; Multiple Convictions Barred.

(1) Grading. Except as otherwise provided in this Section, attempt, solicitation and conspiracy are crimes of the same grade and degree as the most serious offense which is attempted or solicited or is an object of the conspiracy. An attempt, solicitation or conspiracy to commit a [capital crime or a] felony of the first degree is a felony of the second degree.

(2) Mitigation. If the particular conduct charged to constitute a criminal attempt, solicitation or conspiracy is so inherently unlikely to result or culminate in the commission of a crime that neither such conduct nor the actor presents a public danger warranting the grading of such offense under this Section, the Court shall exercise its power under Section 6.12 to enter judgment and impose sentence for a crime of lower grade or degree or, in extreme cases, may dismiss the prosecution.

(3) Multiple Convictions. A person may not be convicted of more than one offense defined by this Article for conduct designed to commit or to culminate in the commission of the same crime.

Section 5.06. Possessing Instruments of Crime;
Weapons.

(1) Criminal Instruments Generally. A person commits a misdemeanor if he possesses any instrument of crime with purpose to employ it criminally. "Instrument of crime" means:

    (a) anything specially made or specially adapted for criminal use; or

(b) anything commonly used for criminal purposes and possessed by the actor under circumstances which do not negative unlawful purpose.

(2) Presumption of Criminal Purpose from Possession of Weapon. If a person possesses a firearm or other weapon on or about his person, in a vehicle occupied by him, or otherwise readily available for use, it is presumed that he had the purpose to employ it criminally, unless:

(a) the weapon is possessed in the actor's home or place of business;

(b) the actor is licensed or otherwise authorized by law to possess such weapon; or

(c) the weapon is of a type commonly used in lawful sport.

"Weapon" means anything readily capable of lethal use and possessed under circumstances not manifestly appropriate for lawful uses which it may have; the term includes a firearm which is not loaded or lacks a clip or other component to render it immediately operable, and components which can readily be assembled into a weapon.

(3) Presumptions as to Possession of Criminal Instruments in Automobiles. Where a weapon or other instrument of crime is found in an automobile, it shall be presumed to be in the possession of the occupant if there is but one. If there is more than one occupant, it shall be presumed to be in the possession of all, except under the following circumstances:

(a) where it is found upon the person of one of the occupants;

(b) where the automobile is not a stolen one and the weapon or instrument is found out of view in a glove compartment, car trunk, or other enclosed customary depository, in which case it shall be presumed to be in the possession of the occupant or occupants who own or have authority to operate the automobile;

(c) in the case of a taxicab, a weapon or instrument found in the passengers' portion of the vehicle shall be presumed to be in the possession of all the passengers, if there are any, and, if not, in the possession of the driver.

Section 5.07. Prohibited Offensive Weapons.

A person commits a misdemeanor if, except as authorized by law, he makes, repairs, sells, or otherwise deals in, uses, or possesses any offensive weapon. "Offensive weapon" means any bomb, machine gun, sawed-off shotgun, firearm specially made or specially adapted for concealment or silent discharge, any blackjack, sandbag, metal knuckles, dagger, or other implement for the infliction of serious bodily injury which serves no common lawful purpose. It is a defense under this Section for the defendant to prove by a preponderance of evidence that he possessed or dealt with the weapon solely as a curio or in a dramatic performance, or that he possessed it briefly in consequence of having found it or taken it from an aggressor, or under circumstances similarly negativing any purpose or likelihood that the weapon would be used unlawfully. The presumptions provided in Section 5.06(3) are applicable to prosecutions under this Section.

Article 6. Authorized Disposition of Offenders.

Section 6.01. Degrees of Felonies.

(1) Felonies defined by this Code are classified, for the purpose of sentence, into three degrees, as follows:
    (a) felonies of the first degree;
    (b) felonies of the second degree;
    (c) felonies of the third degree. A felony is of the first or second degree when it is so designated by the Code. A crime declared to be a felony, without specification of degree, is of the third degree.

(2) Notwithstanding any other provision of law, a felony defined by any statute of this State other than this Code shall constitute for the purpose of sentence a felony of the third degree.

Section 6.02. Sentence in Accordance with Code; Authorized Dispositions.

(1) No person convicted of an offense shall be sentenced otherwise than in accordance with this Article.

[(2) The Court shall sentence a person who has been convicted of murder to death or imprisonment, in accordance with Section 210.6.]

(3) Except as provided in Subsection (2) of this Section and subject to the applicable provisions of the Code, the Court may suspend the imposition of sentence on a person who has been convicted of a crime, may order him to be committed in lieu of sentence, in accordance with Section 6.13, or may sentence him as follows:
    (a) to pay a fine authorized by Section 6.03; or
    (b) to be placed on probation [, and, in the case of a person convicted of a felony or misdemeanor to imprisonment for a term fixed by the Court not exceeding thirty days to be served as a condition of probation]; or
    (c) to imprisonment for a term authorized by Sections 6.05, 6.06, 6.07, 6.08, 6.09, or 7.06; or
    (d) to fine and probation or fine and imprisonment, but not to probation and imprisonment [, except as authorized in paragraph (b) of this Subsection].

(4) The Court may suspend the imposition of sentence on a person who has been convicted of a violation or may sentence him to pay a fine authorized by Section 6.03.

(5) This Article does not deprive the Court of any authority con-

ferred by law to decree a forfeiture of property, suspend or cancel a license, remove a person from office, or impose any other civil penalty. Such a judgment or order may be included in the sentence.

Section 6.03. Fines.

A person who has been convicted of an offense may be sentenced to pay a fine not exceeding:

(1) $10,000, when the conviction is of a felony of the first or second degree;

(2) $5,000, when the conviction is of a felony of the third degree;

(3) $1,000, when the conviction is of a misdemeanor;

(4) $500, when the conviction is of a petty misdemeanor or a violation;

(5) any higher amount equal to double the pecuniary gain derived from the offense by the offender;

(6) any higher amount specifically authorized by statute.

Section 6.04. Penalties Against Corporations and Unincorporated Association; Forfeiture of Corporate Charter or Revocation of Certificate Authorizing Foreign Corporation to Do Business in the State.

(1) The Court may suspend the sentence of a corporation or an unincorporated association which has been convicted of an offense or may sentence it to pay a fine authorized by Section 6.03.

(2) (a) The [prosecuting attorney] is authorized to institute civil proceedings in the appropriate court of general jurisdiction to forfeit the charter of a corporation organized under the laws of this State or to revoke the certificate authorizing a foreign corporation to conduct business in this State. The Court may order the charter forfeited or the certificate revoked upon finding (i) that the board of directors or a high managerial agent acting in behalf of the corporation has, in conducting the corporation's affairs, purposely engaged in a persistent course of criminal conduct and (ii) that for the prevention of future criminal conduct of the same character, the public interest requires the charter of the corporation to be forfeited and the corporation to be dissolved or the certificate to be revoked.

(b) When a corporation is convicted of a crime or a high managerial agent of a corporation, as defined in Section 2.07, is convicted of a crime committed in the conduct of the affairs of the corporation, the Court, in sentencing the corporation or the agent, may direct the [prosecuting attorney] to institute proceedings authorized by paragraph (a) of this Subsection.

(c) The proceedings authorized by paragraph (a) of this Subsection shall be conducted in accordance with the procedures authorized by law for the involuntary dissolution of a corporation or the revocation of the certificate authorizing a foreign corporation to conduct business in this State. Such proceedings shall be deemed additional to any other proceedings authorized by law for the purpose of forfeiting the charter of a corporation or revoking the certificate of a foreign corporation.

Section 6.05. Young Adult Offenders.

[omitted]

Section 6.06. Sentence of Imprisonment for Felony; Ordinary Terms.

A person who has been convicted of a felony may be sentenced to imprisonment, as follows:

(1) in the case of a felony of the first degree, for a term the minimum of which shall be fixed by the Court at not less than one year nor more than ten years, and the maximum of which shall be life imprisonment;

(2) in the case of a felony of the second degree, for a term the minimum of which shall be fixed by the Court at not less than one year nor more than three years, and the maximum of which shall be ten years;

(3) in the case of a felony of the third degree, for a term the minimum of which shall be fixed by the Court at not less than one year nor more than two years, and the maximum of which shall be five years.

Alternative Section 6.06. Sentence of Imprisonment for Felony; Ordinary Terms.

A person who has been convicted of a felony may be sentenced to imprisonment, as follows:

(1) in the case of a felony of the first degree, for a term the minimum of which shall be fixed by the Court at not less than one year nor more than ten years, and the maximum at not more than twenty years or at life imprisonment;

(2) in the case of a felony of the second degree, for a term the minimum of which shall be fixed by the Court at not less than one year nor more than three years, and the maximum at not more than ten years;

(3) in the case of a felony of the third degree, for a term the minimum of which shall be fixed by the Court at not less than one year nor more than two years, and the maximum at not more than five years. No sentence shall be imposed under this Section of which the minimum is longer than one-half the maximum, or, when the maximum is life imprisonment, longer than ten years.

Section 6.07. Sentence of Imprisonment for Felony;
Extended Terms.

In the cases designated in Section 7.03, a person who has been convicted of a felony may be sentenced to an extended term of imprisonment, as follows:

(1) in the case of a felony of the first degree, for a term the minimum of which shall be fixed by the Court at not less than five years nor more than ten years, and the maximum of which shall be life imprisonment;

(2) in the case of a felony of the second degree, for a term the minimum of which shall be fixed by the Court at not less than one year nor more than five years, and the maximum of which shall be fixed by the Court at not less than ten years nor more than twenty years;

(3) in the case of a felony of the third degree, for a term the minimum of which shall be fixed by the Court at not less than one year nor more than three years, and the maximum of which shall be fixed by the Court at not less than five years nor more than ten years.

Section 6.08. Sentence of Imprisonment for
Misdemeanors and Petty Misdemeanors; Ordinary
Terms.

A person who has been convicted of a misdemeanor or a petty misdemeanor may be sentenced to imprisonment for a definite term which shall be fixed by the Court and shall not exceed one year in the case of a misdemeanor or thirty days in the case of a petty misdemeanor.

Section 6.09. Sentence of Imprisonment for
Misdemeanors and Petty Misdemeanors;
Extended Terms.

(1) In the cases designated in Section 7.04, a person who has been convicted of a misdemeanor or a petty misdemeanor may be sentenced to an extended term of imprisonment, as follows:

(a) in the case of a misdemeanor, for a term the minimum of which shall be fixed by the Court at not more than one year and the maximum of which shall be three years;

(b) in the case of a petty misdemeanor, for a term the minimum of which shall be fixed by the Court at not more than six months and the maximum of which shall be two years.

(2) No such sentence for an extended term shall be imposed unless:

(a) the Director of Correction has certified that there is an institution in the Department of Correction, or in a county, city [or other appropriate political subdivision of the State] which is appropriate for the detention and correctional treatment of such misdemeanants or petty misdemeanants, and that such institution is available to receive such commitments; and

(b) the [Board of Parole] [Parole Administrator] has certified that the Board of Parole is able to visit such institution and to assume responsibility for the release of such prisoners on parole and for their parole supervision.

Section 6.10. First Release of All Offenders on Parole; Sentence of Imprisonment Includes Separate Parole Term; Length of Parole Term; Length of Recommitment and Re-parole After Revocation of Parole; Final Unconditional Release.

[omitted]

Section 6.11. Place of imprisonment.

[omitted]

Section 6.12. Reduction of Conviction by Court to Lesser Degree of Felony or to Misdemeanor.

If, when a person has been convicted of a felony, the Court, having regard to the nature and circumstances of the crime and to the history and character of the defendant, is of the view that it would be unduly harsh to sentence the offender in accordance with the Code, the Court may enter judgment of conviction for a lesser degree of felony or for a misdemeanor and impose sentence accordingly.

Section 6.13. Civil Commitment in Lieu of Prosecution or of Sentence.

(1) When a person prosecuted for a [felony of the third degree,] misdemeanor or petty misdemeanor is a chronic alcoholic, narcotic addict [or prostitute] or person suffering from mental abnormality and the Court is authorized by law to order the civil commitment of such person to a hospital or other institution for medical, psychiatric or other rehabilitative treatment, the Court may order such commitment and dismiss the prosecution. The order of commitment may be made after conviction, in which event the Court may set aside the verdict or judgment of conviction and dismiss the prosecution.

(2) The Court shall not make an order under Subsection (1) of this Section unless it is of the view that it will substantially further the rehabilitation of the defendant and will not jeopardize the protection of the public.

Article 7. Authority of Court in Sentencing.

Section 7.01. Criteria for Withholding Sentence of Imprisonment and for Placing Defendant on Probation.

[omitted]

Section 7.02. Criteria for Imposing Fines.

[omitted]

Section 7.03. Criteria for Sentence of Extended Term of Imprisonment; Felonies.

The Court may sentence a person who has been convicted of a felony to an extended term of imprisonment if it finds one or more of the grounds specified in this Section. The finding of the Court shall be incorporated in the record.

(1) The defendant is a persistent offender whose commitment for an extended term is necessary for protection of the public. The Court shall not make such a finding unless the defendant is over twenty-one years of age and has previously been convicted of two felonies or of one felony and two misdemeanors, committed at different times when he was over [insert Juvenile Court age] years of age.

(2) The defendant is a professional criminal whose commitment for an extended term is necessary for protection of the public. The Court shall not make such a finding unless the defendant is over twenty-one years of age and:

(a) the circumstances of the crime show that the defendant has knowingly devoted himself to criminal activity as a major source of livelihood; or

(b) the defendant has substantial income or resources not explained to be derived from a source other than criminal activity.

(3) The defendant is a dangerous, mentally abnormal person whose commitment for an extended term is necessary for protection of the public. The Court shall not make such a finding unless the defendant has been subjected to a psychiatric examination resulting in the conclusions that his mental condition is gravely abnormal; that his criminal conduct has been characterized by a pattern of repetitive or compulsive behavior or by persistent aggressive behavior with heedless indifference to consequences; and that such condition makes him a serious danger to others.

(4) The defendant is a multiple offender whose criminality was so extensive that a sentence of imprisonment for an extended term is warranted. The Court shall not make such a finding unless:

(a) the defendant is being sentenced for two or more felonies, or is already under sentence of imprisonment for felony, and the

APPENDIX: MODEL PENAL CODE 755

sentences of imprisonment involved will run concurrently under Section 7.06; or

(b) the defendant admits in open court the commission of one or more other felonies and asks that they be taken into account when he is sentenced; and

(c) the longest sentences of imprisonment authorized for each of the defendant's crimes, including admitted crimes taken into account, if made to run consecutively would exceed in length the minimum and maximum of the extended term imposed.

Section 7.04. Criteria for Sentence of Extended Term of Imprisonment; Misdemeanors and Petty Misdemeanors.

The Court may sentence a person who has been convicted of a misdemeanor or petty misdemeanor to an extended term of imprisonment if it finds one or more of the grounds specified in this Section. The finding of the Court shall be incorporated in the record.

(1) The defendant is a persistent offender whose commitment for an extended term is necessary for protection of the public. The Court shall not make such a finding unless the defendant has previously been convicted of two crimes, committed at different times when he was over [insert Juvenile Court age] years of age.

(2) The defendant is a professional criminal whose commitment for an extended term is necessary for protection of the public. The Court shall not make such a finding unless:

(a) the circumstances of the crime show that the defendant has knowingly devoted himself to criminal activity as a major source of livelihood; or

(b) the defendant has substantial income or resources not explained to be derived from a source other than criminal activity.

(3) The defendant is a chronic alcoholic, narcotic addict, prostitute or person of abnormal mental condition who requires rehabilitative treatment for a substantial period of time. The Court shall not make such a finding unless, with respect to the particular category to which the defendant belongs, the Director of Correction has certified that there is a specialized institution or facility which is satisfactory for the rehabilitative treatment of such persons and which otherwise meets the requirements of Section 6.09, Subsection (2).

(4) The defendant is a multiple offender whose criminality was so extensive that a sentence of imprisonment for an extended term is warranted. The Court shall not make such a finding unless:

(a) the defendant is being sentenced for a number of misdemeanors or petty misdemeanors or is already under sentence of imprisonment for crime of such grades, or admits in open court the commission of one or more such crimes and asks that they be taken into account when he is sentenced; and

(b) maximum fixed sentences of imprisonment for each of the defendant's crimes, including admitted crimes taken into account, if made to run consecutively, would exceed in length the maximum period of the extended term imposed.

Section 7.05. Former Conviction in Another
Jurisdiction; Definition and Proof of Conviction;
Sentence Taking Into Account Admitted Crimes Bars
Subsequent Conviction for Such Crimes.

(1) For purposes of paragraph (1) of Section 7.03 or 7.04, a conviction of the commission of a crime in another jurisdiction shall constitute a previous conviction. Such conviction shall be deemed to have been of a felony if sentence of death or of imprisonment in excess of one year was authorized under the law of such other jurisdiction, of a misdemeanor if sentence of imprisonment in excess of thirty days but not in excess of a year was authorized and of a petty misdemeanor if sentence of imprisonment for not more than thirty days was authorized.

(2) An adjudication by a court of competent jurisdiction that the defendant committed a crime constitutes a conviction for purposes of Sections 7.03 to 7.05 inclusive, although sentence or the execution thereof was suspended, provided that the time to appeal has expired and that the defendant was not pardoned on the ground of innocence.

(3) Prior conviction may be proved by any evidence, including fingerprint records made in connection with arrest, conviction or imprisonment, that reasonably satisfies the Court that the defendant was convicted.

(4) When the defendant has asked that other crimes admitted in open court be taken into account when he is sentenced and the Court has not rejected such request, the sentence shall bar the prosecution or conviction of the defendant in this State for any such admitted crime.

Section 7.06. Multiple Sentences; Concurrent and
Consecutive Terms.

(1) Sentences of Imprisonment for More Than One Crime. When multiple sentences of imprisonment are imposed on a defendant for more than one crime, including a crime for which a previous suspended sentence or sentence of probation has been revoked, such multiple sentences shall run concurrently or consecutively as the Court determines at the time of sentence, except that:

(a) a definite and an indefinite term shall run concurrently and both sentences shall be satisfied by service of the indefinite term; and

(b) the aggregate of consecutive definite terms shall not exceed one year; and

(c) the aggregate of consecutive indefinite terms shall not exceed in minimum or maximum length the longest extended term authorized for the highest grade and degree of crime for which any of the sentences was imposed; and

(d) not more than one sentence for an extended term shall be imposed.

(2) Sentences of Imprisonment Imposed at Different Times. When a defendant who has previously been sentenced to imprisonment is subsequently sentenced to another term for a crime committed prior to the former sentence, other than a crime committed while in custody:

(a) the multiple sentences imposed shall so far as possible conform to Subsection (1) of this Section; and

(b) whether the Court determines that the terms shall run concurrently or consecutively, the defendant shall be credited with time served in imprisonment on the prior sentence in determining the permissible aggregate length of the term or terms remaining to be served; and

(c) when a new sentence is imposed on a prisoner who is on parole, the balance of the parole term on the former sentence shall be deemed to run during the period of the new imprisonment.

(3) Sentence of Imprisonment for Crime Committed While on Parole. When a defendant is sentenced to imprisonment for a crime committed while on parole in this State, such term of imprisonment and any period of re-imprisonment that the Board of Parole may require the defendant to serve upon the revocation of his parole shall run concurrently, unless the Court orders them to run consecutively.

(4) Multiple Sentences of Imprisonment in Other Cases. Except as otherwise provided in this Section, multiple terms of imprisonment shall run concurrently or consecutively as the Court determines when the second or subsequent sentence is imposed.

(5) Calculation of Concurrent and Consecutive Terms of Imprisonment.

(a) When indefinite terms run concurrently, the shorter minimum terms merge in and are satisfied by serving the longest minimum term and the shorter maximum terms merge in and are satisfied by discharge of the longest maximum term.

(b) When indefinite terms run consecutively, the minimum terms are added to arrive at an aggregate minimum to be served equal to the sum of all minimum terms and the maximum terms are added to arrive at an aggregate maximum equal to the sum of all maximum terms.

(c) When a definite and an indefinite term run consecutively, the period of the definite term is added to both the minimum and maximum of the indefinite term and both sentences are satisfied by serving the indefinite term.

(6) Suspension of Sentence or Probation and Imprisonment; Multiple Terms of Suspension and Probation. When a defendant is sentenced for more than one offense or a defendant already under sentence is sentenced for another offense committed prior to the former sentence:

(a) the Court shall not sentence to probation a defendant who is under sentence of imprisonment [with more than thirty days to run] or impose a sentence of probation and a sentence of imprisonment [, except as authorized by Section 6.02(3)(b)]; and

(b) multiple periods of suspension or probation shall run concurrently from the date of the first such disposition; and

(c) when a sentence of imprisonment is imposed for an indefinite term, the service of such sentence shall satisfy a suspended sentence on another count or a prior suspended sentence or sentence to probation; and

(d) when a sentence of imprisonment is imposed for a definite term, the period of a suspended sentence on another count or a prior suspended sentence or sentence to probation shall run during the period of such imprisonment.

(7) Offense Committed While Under Suspension of Sentence or Probation. When a defendant is convicted of an offense committed while under suspension of sentence or on probation and such suspension or probation is not revoked:

(a) if the defendant is sentenced to imprisonment for an indefinite term, the service of such sentence shall satisfy the prior suspended sentence or sentence to probation; and

(b) if the defendant is sentenced to imprisonment for a definite term, the period of the suspension or probation shall not run during the period of such imprisonment; and

(c) if sentence is suspended or the defendant is sentenced to probation, the period of such suspension or probation shall run concurrently with or consecutively to the remainder of the prior periods, as the Court determines at the time of sentence.

Section 7.07. Procedure on Sentence; Pre-sentence Investigation and Report; Remand for Psychiatric Examination; Transmission of Records to Department of Correction.

[omitted]

Section 7.08. Commitment for Observation; Sentence of Imprisonment for Felony Deemed Tentative for Period of One Year; Re-sentence on Petition of Commissioner of Correction.

[omitted]

Section 7.09. Credit for Time of Detention Prior to Sentence; Credit for Imprisonment Under Earlier Sentence for the Same Crime.

[omitted]

APPENDIX: MODEL PENAL CODE

PART II. DEFINITION OF SPECIFIC CRIMES

Offenses Involving Danger to the Person.

Article 210. Criminal Homicide.

Section 210.0. Definitions.

In Articles 210-213, unless a different meaning plainly is required:

(1) "human being" means a person who has been born and is alive;

(2) "bodily injury" means physical pain, illness or any impairment of physical condition;

(3) "serious bodily injury" means bodily injury which creates a substantial risk of death or which causes serious, permanent disfigurement, or protracted loss or impairment of the function of any bodily member or organ;

(4) "deadly weapon" means any firearm, or other weapon, device, instrument, material or substance, whether animate or inanimate, which in the manner it is used or is intended to be used is known to be capable of producing death or serious bodily injury.

Section 210.1. Criminal Homicide.

(1) A person is guilty of criminal homicide if he purposely, knowingly, recklessly or negligently causes the death of another human being.

(2) Criminal homicide is murder, manslaughter or negligent homicide.

Section 210.2. Murder.

(1) Except as provided in Section 210.3(1)(b), criminal homicide constitutes murder when:

(a) it is committed purposely or knowingly; or

(b) it is committed recklessly under circumstances manifesting extreme indifference to the value of human life. Such recklessness and indifference are presumed if the actor is engaged or is an accomplice in the commission of, or an attempt to commit, or flight after committing or attempting to commit robbery, rape or deviate sexual intercourse by force or threat of force, arson, burglary, kidnapping or felonious escape.

(2) Murder is a felony of the first degree [but a person convicted of murder may be sentenced to death, as provided in Section 210.6].

Section 210.3. Manslaughter.

(1) Criminal homicide constitutes manslaughter when:

(a) it is committed recklessly; or

(b) a homicide which would otherwise be murder is committed under the influence of extreme mental or emotional disturbance for which there is reasonable explanation or excuse. The reasonableness of such explanation or excuse shall be determined from the viewpoint of a person in the actor's situation under the circumstances as he believes them to be.

(2) Manslaughter is a felony of the second degree.

Section 210.4. Negligent Homicide.

(1) Criminal homicide constitutes negligent homicide when it is committed negligently.

(2) Negligent homicide is a felony of the third degree.

Section 210.5. Causing or Aiding Suicide.

(1) Causing Suicide as Criminal Homicide. A person may be convicted of criminal homicide for causing another to commit suicide only if he purposely causes such suicide by force, duress or deception.

(2) Aiding or Soliciting Suicide as an Independent Offense. A person who purposely aids or solicits another to commit suicide is guilty of a felony of the second degree if his conduct causes such suicide or an attempted suicide, and otherwise of a misdemeanor.

[Section 210.6. Sentence of Death for Murder;
Further Proceedings to Determine Sentence.]

(1) Death Sentence Excluded. When a defendant is found guilty of murder, the Court shall impose sentence for a felony of the first degree if it is satisfied that:

(a) none of the aggravating circumstances enumerated in Subsection (3) of this Section was established by the evidence at the trial or will be established if further proceedings are initiated under Subsection (2) of this Section; or

(b) substantial mitigating circumstances, established by the evidence at the trial, call for leniency; or

(c) the defendant, with the consent of the prosecuting attorney and the approval of the Court, pleaded guilty to murder as a felony of the first degree; or

(d) the defendant was under 18 years of age at the time of the commission of the crime; or

(e) the defendant's physical or mental condition calls for leniency; or

(f) although the evidence suffices to sustain the verdict, it does not foreclose all doubt respecting the defendant's guilt.

(2) Determination by Court or by Court and Jury. Unless the Court imposes sentence under Subsection (1) of this Section, it shall conduct a separate proceeding to determine whether the defendant should be

sentenced for a felony of the first degree or sentenced to death. The proceeding shall be conducted before the Court alone if the defendant was convicted by a Court sitting without a jury or upon his plea of guilty or if the prosecuting attorney and the defendant waive a jury with respect to sentence. In other cases it shall be conducted before the Court sitting with the jury which determined the defendant's guilt or, if the Court for good cause shown discharges that jury, with a new jury empaneled for the purpose.

In the proceeding, evidence may be presented as to any matter that the Court deems relevant to sentence, including but not limited to the nature and circumstances of the crime, the defendant's character, background, history, mental and physical condition and any of the aggravating or mitigating circumstances enumerated in Subsections (3) and (4) of this Section. Any such evidence, not legally privileged, which the Court deems to have probative force, may be received, regardless of its admissibility under the exclusionary rules of evidence, provided that the defendant's counsel is accorded a fair opportunity to rebut such evidence. The prosecuting attorney and the defendant or his counsel shall be permitted to present argument for or against sentence of death.

The determination whether sentence of death shall be imposed shall be in the discretion of the Court, except that when the proceeding is conducted before the Court sitting with a jury, the Court shall not impose sentence of death unless it submits to the jury the issue whether the defendant should be sentenced to death or to imprisonment and the jury returns a verdict that the sentence should be death. If the jury is unable to reach a unanimous verdict, the Court shall dismiss the jury and impose sentence for a felony of the first degree.

The Court, in exercising its discretion as to sentence, and the jury, in determining upon its verdict, shall take into account the aggravating and mitigating circumstances enumerated in Subsections (3) and (4) and any other facts that it deems relevant, but it shall not impose or recommend sentence of death unless it finds one of the aggravating circumstances enumerated in Subsection (3) and further finds that there are no mitigating circumstances sufficiently substantial to call for leniency. When the issue is submitted to the jury, the Court shall so instruct and also shall inform the jury of the nature of the sentence of imprisonment that may be imposed, including its implication with respect to possible release upon parole, if the jury verdict is against sentence of death.

Alternative formulation of Subsection (2):

(2) Determination by Court. Unless the Court imposes sentence under Subsection (1) of this Section, it shall conduct a separate proceeding to determine whether the defendant should be sentenced for a felony of the first degree or sentenced to death. In the proceeding, the Court, in accordance with Section 7.07, shall consider the report of the pre-sentence investigation and, if a psychiatric examination has been

ordered, the report of such examination. In addition, evidence may be presented as to any matter that the Court deems relevant to sentence, including but not limited to the nature and circumstances of the crime, the defendant's character, background, history, mental and physical condition and any of the aggravating or mitigating circumstances enumerated in Subsections (3) and (4) of this Section. Any such evidence, not legally privileged, which the Court deems to have probative force, may be received, regardless of its admissibility under the exclusionary rules of evidence, provided that the defendant's counsel is accorded a fair opportunity to rebut such evidence. The prosecuting attorney and the defendant or his counsel shall be permitted to present argument for or against sentence of death.

The determination whether sentence of death shall be imposed shall be in the discretion of the Court. In exercising such discretion, the Court shall take into account the aggravating and mitigating circumstances enumerated in Subsections (3) and (4) and any other facts that it deems relevant but shall not impose sentence of death unless it finds one of the aggravating circumstances enumerated in Subsection (3) and further finds that there are no mitigating circumstances sufficiently substantial to call for leniency.

(3) Aggravating Circumstances.

(a) The murder was committed by a convict under sentence of imprisonment.

(b) The defendant was previously convicted of another murder or of a felony involving the use or threat of violence to the person.

(c) At the time the murder was committed the defendant also committed another murder.

(d) The defendant knowingly created a great risk of death to many persons.

(e) The murder was committed while the defendant was engaged or was an accomplice in the commission of, or an attempt to commit, or flight after committing or attempting to commit robbery, rape or deviate sexual intercourse by force or threat of force, arson, burglary or kidnapping.

(f) The murder was committed for the purpose of avoiding or preventing a lawful arrest or effecting an escape from lawful custody.

(g) The murder was committed for pecuniary gain.

(h) The murder was especially heinous, atrocious or cruel, manifesting exceptional depravity.

(4) Mitigating Circumstances.

(a) The defendant has no significant history of prior criminal activity.

(b) The murder was committed while the defendant was under the influence of extreme mental or emotional disturbance.

(c) The victim was a participant in the defendant's homicidal conduct or consented to the homicidal act.

(d) The murder was committed under circumstances which the defendant believed to provide a moral justification or extenuation for his conduct.

(e) The defendant was an accomplice in a murder committed by another person and his participation in the homicidal act was relatively minor.

(f) The defendant acted under duress or under the domination of another person.

(g) At the time of the murder, the capacity of the defendant to appreciate the criminality [wrongfulness] of his conduct or to conform his conduct to the requirements of law was impaired as a result of mental disease or defect or intoxication.

(h) The youth of the defendant at the time of the crime.

Article 211. Assault; Reckless Endangering; Threats.

Section 211.0. Definitions.

In this Article, the definitions given in Section 210.0 apply unless a different meaning plainly is required.

Section 211.1. Assault.

(1) Simple Assault. A person is guilty of assault if he:

(a) attempts to cause or purposely, knowingly or recklessly causes bodily injury to another; or

(b) negligently causes bodily injury to another with a deadly weapon; or

(c) attempts by physical menace to put another in fear of imminent serious bodily injury. Simple assault is a misdemeanor unless committed in a fight or scuffle entered into by mutual consent, in which case it is a petty misdemeanor.

(2) Aggravated Assault. A person is guilty of aggravated assault if he:

(a) attempts to cause serious bodily injury to another, or causes such injury purposely, knowingly or recklessly under circumstances manifesting extreme indifference to the value of human life; or

(b) attempts to cause or purposely or knowingly causes bodily injury to another with a deadly weapon. Aggravated assault under paragraph (a) is a felony of the second degree; aggravated assault under paragraph (b) is a felony of the third degree.

Section 211.2. Recklessly Endangering Another Person.

A person commits a misdemeanor if he recklessly engages in conduct which places or may place another person in danger of death or serious bodily injury. Recklessness and danger shall be presumed where a person knowingly points a firearm at or in the direction of another, whether or not the actor believed the firearm to be loaded.

Section 211.3. Terroristic Threats.

A person is guilty of a felony of the third degree if he threatens to commit any crime of violence with purpose to terrorize another or to cause evacuation of a building, place of assembly, or facility of public transportation, or otherwise to cause serious public inconvenience, or in reckless disregard of the risk of causing such terror or inconvenience.

Article 212. Kidnapping and Related Offenses; Coercion.

Section 212.0. Definitions.

In this Article, the definitions given in Section 210.0 apply unless a different meaning plainly is required.

Section 212.1. Kidnapping.

A person is guilty of kidnapping if he unlawfully removes another from his place of residence or business, or a substantial distance from the vicinity where he is found, or if he unlawfully confines another for a substantial period in a place of isolation, with any of the following purposes:
    (a) to hold for ransom or reward, or as a shield or hostage; or
    (b) to facilitate commission of any felony or flight thereafter; or
    (c) to inflict bodily injury on or to terrorize the victim or another; or
    (d) to interfere with the performance of any governmental or political function.
Kidnapping is a felony of the first degree unless the actor voluntarily releases the victim alive and in a safe place prior to trial, in which case it is a felony of the second degree. A removal or confinement is unlawful within the meaning of this Section if it is accomplished by force, threat or deception, or, in the case of a person who is under the age of 14 or incompetent, if it is accomplished without the consent of a parent, guardian or other person responsible for general supervision of his welfare.

Section 212.2. Felonious Restraint.

A person commits a felony of the third degree if he knowingly:
    (a) restrains another unlawfully in circumstances exposing him to risk of serious bodily injury; or
    (b) holds another in a condition of involuntary servitude.

Section 212.3. False Imprisonment.

A person commits a misdemeanor if he knowingly restrains another unlawfully so as to interfere substantially with his liberty.

Section 212.4. Interference with Custody.

(1) Custody of Children. A person commits an offense if he knowingly or recklessly takes or entices any child under the age of 18 from the custody of its parent, guardian or other lawful custodian, when he has no privilege to do so. It is an affirmative defense that:

(a) the actor believed that his action was necessary to preserve the child from danger to its welfare; or

(b) the child, being at the time not less than 14 years old, as taken away at its own instigation without enticement and without purpose to commit a criminal offense with or against the child. Proof that the child was below the critical age gives rise to a presumption that the actor knew the child's age or acted in reckless disregard thereof. The offense is a misdemeanor unless the actor, not being a parent or person in equivalent relation to the child, acted with knowledge that his conduct would cause serious alarm for the child's safety, or in reckless disregard of a likelihood of causing such alarm, in which case the offense is a felony of the third degree.

(2) Custody of Committed Persons. A person is guilty of a misdemeanor if he knowingly or recklessly takes or entices any committed person away from lawful custody when he is not privileged to do so. "Committed person" means, in addition to anyone committed under judicial warrant, any orphan, neglected or delinquent child, mentally defective or insane person, or other dependent or incompetent person entrusted to another's custody by or through a recognized social agency or otherwise by authority of law.

Section 212.5. Criminal Coercion.

(1) Offense Defined. A person is guilty of criminal coercion if, with purpose unlawfully to restrict another's freedom of action to his detriment, he threatens to:

(a) commit any criminal offense; or

(b) accuse anyone of a criminal offense; or

(c) expose any secret tending to subject any person to hatred, contempt or ridicule, or to impair his credit or business repute; or

d) take or withhold action as an official, or cause an official to take or withhold action.

It is an affirmative defense to prosecution based on paragraphs (b), (c) or (d) that the actor believed the accusation or secret to be true or the proposed official action justified and that his purpose was limited to compelling the other to behave in a way reasonably related to the circumstances which were the subject of the accusation, exposure or proposed official action, as by desisting from further misbehavior, making good a wrong done, refraining from taking any action or responsibility for which the actor believes the other disqualified.

(2) Grading. Criminal coercion is a misdemeanor unless the threat is to commit a felony or the actor's purpose is felonious, in which cases the offense is a felony of the third degree.

Article 213. Sexual Offenses.

Section 213.0 Definitions.

In this Article, unless a different meaning plainly is required:
(1) the definitions given in Section 210.0 apply;
(2) "Sexual intercourse" includes intercourse per os or per anum, with some penetration however slight; emission is not required;
(3) "Deviate sexual intercourse" means sexual intercourse per os or per anum between human beings who are not husband and wife, and any form of sexual intercourse with an animal.

Section 213.1. Rape and Related Offenses.

(1) Rape. A male who has sexual intercourse with a female not his wife is guilty of rape if:
(a) he compels her to submit by force or by threat of imminent death, serious bodily injury, extreme pain or kidnapping, to be inflicted on anyone; or
(b) he has substantially impaired her power to appraise or control her conduct by administering or employing without her knowledge drugs, intoxicants or other means for the purpose of preventing resistance; or
(c) the female is unconscious; or
(d) the female is less than ten years old. Rape is a felony of the second degree unless (i) in the course thereof the actor inflicts serious bodily injury upon anyone, or (ii) the victim was not a voluntary social companion of the actor upon the occasion of the crime and had not previously permitted him sexual liberties, in which cases the offense is a felony of the first degree.

(2) Gross Sexual Imposition. A male who has sexual intercourse with a female not his wife commits a felony of the third degree if:
(a) he compels her to submit by any threat that would prevent resistance by a woman of ordinary resolution; or
(b) he knows that she suffers from a mental disease or defect which renders her incapable of appraising the nature of her conduct; or
(c) he knows that she is unaware that a sexual act is being

APPENDIX: MODEL PENAL CODE

committed upon her or that she submits because she mistakenly supposes that he is her husband.

Section 213.2. Deviate Sexual Intercourse by Force or Imposition.

(1) By Force or Its Equivalent. A person who engages in deviate sexual intercourse with another person, or who causes another to engage in deviate sexual intercourse, commits a felony of the second degree if:

    (a) he compels the other person to participate by force or by threat of imminent death, serious bodily injury, extreme pain or kidnapping, to be inflicted on anyone; or

    (b) he has substantially impaired the other person's power to appraise or control his conduct, by administering or employing without the knowledge of the other person drugs, intoxicants or other means for the purpose of preventing resistance; or

    (c) the other person is unconscious; or

    (d) the other person is less than ten years old.

(2) By Other Imposition. A person who engages in deviate sexual intercourse with another person, or who causes another to engage in deviate sexual intercourse, commits a felony of the third degree if:

    (a) he compels the other person to participate by any threat that would prevent resistance by a person of ordinary resolution; or

    (b) he knows that the other person suffers from a mental disease or defect which renders him incapable of appraising the nature of his conduct; or

    (c) he knows that the other person submits because he is unaware that a sexual act is being committed upon him.

Section 213.3. Corruption of Minors and Seduction.

(1) Offense Defined. A male who has sexual intercourse with a female not his wife, or any person who engages in deviate sexual intercourse or causes another to engage in deviate sexual intercourse, is guilty of an offense if:

    (a) the other person is less than [16] years old and the actor is at least [4] years older than the other person; or

    (b) the other person is less than 21 years old and the actor is his guardian or otherwise responsible for general supervision of his welfare; or

    (c) the other person is in custody of law or detained in a hospital or other institution and the actor has supervisory or disciplinary authority over him; or

    (d) the other person is a female who is induced to participate by a promise of marriage which the actor does not mean to perform.

(2) Grading. An offense under paragraph (a) of Subsection () is

a felony of the third degree. Otherwise an offense under this section is a misdemeanor.

Section 213.4. Sexual Assault.

A person who has sexual contact with another not his spouse, or causes such other to have sexual contact with him, is guilty of sexual assault, a misdemeanor, if:
    (1) he knows that the contact is offensive to the other person; or
    (2) he knows that the other person suffers from a mental disease or defect which renders him or her incapable of appraising the nature of his or her conduct; or
    (3) he knows that the other person is unaware that a sexual act is being committed; or
    (4) the other person is less than ten years old; or
    (5) he has substantially impaired the other person's power to appraise or control his or her conduct, by administering or employing without the other's knowledge drugs, intoxicants or other means for the purpose of preventing resistance; or
    (6) the other person is less than [16] years old and the actor is at least [4] years older than the other person; or
    (7) the other person is less than 21 years old and the actor is his guardian or otherwise responsible for general supervision of his welfare; or
    (8) the other person is in custody of law or detained in a hospital or other institution and the actor has supervisory or disciplinary authority over him. Sexual contact is any touching of the sexual or other intimate parts of the person for the purpose of arousing or gratifying sexual desire.

Section 213.5. Indecent Exposure.

A person commits a misdemeanor if, for the purpose of arousing or gratifying sexual desire of himself or of any person other than his spouse, he exposes his genitals under circumstances in which he knows his conduct is likely to cause affront or alarm.

Section 213.6. Provisions Generally Applicable to
Article 213.

(1) Mistake as to Age. Whenever in this Article the criminality of conduct depends on a child's being below the age of ten, it is no defense that the actor did not know the child's age, or reasonably believed the child to be older than ten. When criminality depends on the child's being below a critical age other than ten, it is a defense for the actor to prove by a preponderance of the evidence that he reasonably believed the child to be above the critical age.

(2) Spouse Relationships. Whenever in this Article the definition

of an offense excludes conduct with a spouse, the exclusion shall be deemed to extend to persons living as man and wife, regardless of the legal status of their relationship. The exclusion shall be inoperative as respects spouses living apart under a decree of judicial separation. Where the definition of an offense excludes conduct with a spouse or conduct by a woman, this shall not preclude conviction of a spouse or woman as accomplice in a sexual act which he or she causes another person, not within the exclusion, to perform.

(3) Sexually Promiscuous Complainants. It is a defense to prosecution under Section 213.3 and paragraphs (6), (7) and (8) of Section 213.4 for the actor to prove by a preponderance of the evidence that the alleged victim had, prior to the time of the offense charged, engaged promiscuously in sexual relations with others.

(4) Prompt Complaint. No prosecution may be instituted or maintained under this Article unless the alleged offense was brought to the notice of public authority within [3] months of its occurrence or, where the alleged victim was less than [16] years old or otherwise incompetent to make complaint, within [3] months after a parent, guardian or other competent person specially interested in the victim learns of the offense.

(5) Testimony of Complainants. No person shall be convicted of any felony under this Article upon the uncorroborated testimony of the alleged victim. Corroboration may be circumstantial. In any prosecution before a jury for an offense under this Article, the jury shall be instructed to evaluate the testimony of a victim or complaining witness with special care in view of the emotional involvement of the witness and the difficulty of determining the truth with respect to alleged sexual activities carried out in private.

Offenses Against Property.

Article 220. Arson, Criminal Mischief, and Other Property Destruction.

Section 220.1. Arson and Related Offenses.

(1) Arson. A person is guilty of arson, a felony of the second degree, if he starts a fire or causes an explosion with the purpose of:
    (a) destroying a building or occupied structure of another; or
    (b) destroying or damaging any property, whether his own or another's, to collect insurance for such loss. It shall be an affirmative defense to prosecution under this paragraph that the actor's conduct did not recklessly endanger any building or occupied structure of another or place any other person in danger of death or bodily injury.

(2) Reckless Burning or Exploding. A person commits a felony of

the third degree if he purposely starts a fire or causes an explosion, whether on his own property or another's, and thereby recklessly:

(a) places another person in danger of death or bodily injury; or

(b) places a building or occupied structure of another in danger of damage or destruction.

(3) Failure to Control or Report Dangerous Fire. A person who knows that a fire is endangering life or a substantial amount of property of another and fails to take reasonable measures to put out or control the fire, when he can do so without substantial risk to himself, or to give a prompt fire alarm, commits a misdemeanor if:

(a) he knows that he is under an official, contractual, or other legal duty to prevent or combat the fire; or

(b) the fire was started, albeit lawfully, by him or with his assent, or on property in his custody or control.

(4) Definitions. "Occupied structure" means any structure, vehicle or place adapted for overnight accommodation of persons, or for carrying on business therein, whether or not a person is actually present. Property is that of another, for the purposes of this Section, if anyone other than the actor has a possessory or proprietary interest therein. If a building or structure is divided into separately occupied units, any unit not occupied by the actor is an occupied structure of another.

Section 220.2. Causing or Risking Catastrophe.

(1) Causing Catastrophe. A person who causes a catastrophe by explosion, fire, flood, avalanche, collapse of building, release of poison gas, radioactive material or other harmful or destructive force or substance, or by any other means of causing potentially widespread injury or damage, commits a felony of the second degree if he does so purposely or knowingly, or a felony of the third degree if he does so recklessly.

(2) Risking Catastrophe. A person is guilty of a misdemeanor if he recklessly creates a risk of catastrophe in the employment of fire, explosives or other dangerous means listed in Subsection (1).

(3) Failure to Prevent Catastrophe. A person who knowingly or recklessly fails to take reasonable measures to prevent or mitigate a catastrophe commits a misdemeanor if:

(a) he knows that he is under an official, contractual or other legal duty to take such measures; or

(b) he did or assented to the act causing or threatening the catastrophe.

Section 220.3. Criminal Mischief.

(1) Offense Defined. A person is guilty of criminal mischief if he:

(a) damages tangible property of another purposely, recklessly, or by negligence in the employment of fire, explosives, or other dangerous means listed in Section 220.2(1); or

(b) purposely or recklessly tampers with tangible property of another so as to endanger person or property; or

(c) purposely or recklessly causes another to suffer pecuniary loss by deception or threat.

(2) Grading. Criminal mischief is a felony of the third degree if the actor purposely causes pecuniary loss in excess of $5,000, or a substantial interruption or impairment of public communication, transportation, supply of water, gas or power, or other public service. It is a misdemeanor if the actor purposely causes pecuniary loss in excess of $100, or a petty misdemeanor if he purposely or recklessly causes pecuniary loss in excess of $25. Otherwise criminal mischief is a violation.

Article 221. Burglary and Other Criminal Intrusion.

Section 221.0. Definitions.

In this Article, unless a different meaning plainly is required:

(1) "occupied structure" means any structure, vehicle or place adapted for overnight accommodation of persons, or for carrying on business therein, whether or not a person is actually present.

(2) "night" means the period between thirty minutes past sunset and thirty minutes before sunrise.

Section 221.1. Burglary.

(1) Burglary Defined. A person is guilty of burglary if he enters a building or occupied structure, or separately secured or occupied portion thereof, with purpose to commit a crime therein, unless the premises are at the time open to the public or the actor is licensed or privileged to enter. It is an affirmative defense to prosecution for burglary that the building or structure was abandoned.

(2) Grading. Burglary is a felony of the second degree if it is perpetrated in the dwelling of another at night, or if, in the course of committing the offense, the actor:

(a) purposely, knowingly or recklessly inflicts or attempts to inflict bodily injury on anyone; or

(b) is armed with explosives or a deadly weapon. Otherwise, burglary is a felony of the third degree. An act shall be deemed "in the course of committing" an offense if it occurs in an attempt to commit the offense or in flight after the attempt or commission.

(3) Multiple Convictions. A person may not be convicted both for burglary and for the offense which it was his purpose to commit after the burglarious entry or for an attempt to commit that offense, unless the additional offense constitutes a felony of the first or second degree.

Section 221.2. Criminal Trespass.

(1) Buildings and Occupied Structures. A person commits an offense if, knowing that he is not licensed or privileged to do so, he enters or surreptitiously remains in any building or occupied structure, or separately secured or occupied portion thereof. An offense under this Subsection is a misdemeanor if it is committed in a dwelling at night. Otherwise it is a petty misdemeanor.

(2) Defiant Trespasser. A person commits an offense if, knowing that he is not licensed or privileged to do so, he enters or remains in any place as to which notice against trespass is given by:

(a) actual communication to the actor; or

(b) posting in a manner prescribed by law or reasonably likely to come to the attention of intruders; or

(c) fencing or other enclosure manifestly designed to exclude intruders. An offense under this Subsection constitutes a petty misdemeanor if the offender defies an order to leave personally communicated to him by the owner of the premises or other authorized person. Otherwise it is a violation.

(3) Defenses. It is an affirmative defense to prosecution under this Section that:

(a) a building or occupied structure involved in an offense under Subsection (1) was abandoned; or

(b) the premises were at the time open to members of the public and the actor complied with all lawful conditions imposed on access to or remaining in the premises; or

(c) the actor reasonably believed that the owner of the premises, or other person empowered to license access thereto, would have licensed him to enter or remain.

Article 222. Robbery.

Section 222.1. Robbery.

(1) Robbery Defined. A person is guilty of robbery if, in the course of committing a theft, he:

(a) inflicts serious bodily injury upon another; or

(b) threatens another with or purposely puts him in fear of immediate serious bodily injury; or

(c) commits or threatens immediately to commit any felony of the first or second degree. An act shall be deemed "in the course of committing a theft" if it occurs in an attempt to commit theft or in flight after the attempt or commission.

(2) Grading. Robbery is a felony of the second degree, except that it is a felony of the first degree if in the course of committing the theft

the actor attempts to kill anyone, or purposely inflicts or attempts to inflict serious bodily injury.

Article 223. Theft and Related Offenses.

Section 223.0. Definitions.

In this Article, unless a different meaning plainly is required:
  (1) "deprive" means:
    (a) to withhold property of another permanently or for so extended a period as to appropriate a major portion of its economic value, or with intent to restore only upon payment of reward or other compensation; or
    (b) to dispose of the property so as to make it unlikely that the owner will recover it.
  (2) "financial institution" means a bank, insurance company, credit union, building and loan association, investment trust or other organization held out to the public as a place of deposit of funds or medium of savings or collective investment.
  (3) "government" means the United States, any State, county, municipality, or other political unit, or any department, agency or subdivision of any of the foregoing, or any corporation or other association carrying out the functions of government.
  (4) "movable property" means property the location of which can be changed, including things growing on, affixed to, or found in land, and documents although the rights represented thereby have no physical location. "Immovable property" is all other property.
  (5) "obtain" means:
    (a) in relation to property, to bring about a transfer or purported transfer of a legal interest in the property, whether to the obtainer or another; or
    (b) in relation to labor or service, to secure performance thereof.
  (6) "property" means anything of value, including real estate, tangible and intangible personal property, contract rights, chooses-in-action and other interests in or claims to wealth, admission or transportation tickets, captured or domestic animals, food and drink, electric or other power.
  (7) "property of another" includes property in which any person other than the actor has an interest which the actor is not privileged to infringe, regardless of the fact that the actor also has an interest in the property and regardless of the fact that the other person might be precluded from civil recovery because the property was used in an unlawful transaction or was subject to forfeiture as contraband. Property in possession of the actor shall not be deemed property of

another who has only a security interest therein, even if legal title is in the creditor pursuant to a conditional sales contract or other security agreement.

Section 223.1. Consolidation of Theft Offenses;
Grading; Provisions Applicable to Theft Generally.

(1) Consolidation of Theft Offenses. Conduct denominated theft in this Article constitutes a single offense. An accusation of theft may be supported by evidence that it was committed in any manner that would be theft under this Article, notwithstanding the specification of a different manner in the indictment or information, subject only to the power of the Court to ensure fair trial by granting a continuance or other appropriate relief where the conduct of the defense would be prejudiced by lack of fair notice or by surprise.

(2) Grading of Theft Offenses.

(a) Theft constitutes a felony of the third degree if the amount involved exceeds $500, or if the property stolen is a firearm, automobile, airplane, motorcycle, motorboat, or other motor-propelled vehicle, or in the case of theft by receiving stolen property, if the receiver is in the business of buying or selling stolen property.

(b) Theft not within the preceding paragraph constitutes a misdemeanor, except that if the property was not taken from the person or by threat, or in breach of a fiduciary obligation, and the actor proves by a preponderance of the evidence that the amount involved was less than $50, the offense constitutes a petty misdemeanor.

(c) The amount involved in a theft shall be deemed to be the highest value, by any reasonable standard, of the property or services which the actor stole or attempted to steal. Amounts involved in thefts committed pursuant to one scheme or course of conduct, whether from the same person or several persons, may be aggregated in determining the grade of the offense.

(3) Claim of Right. It is an affirmative defense to prosecution for theft that the actor:

(a) was unaware that the property or service was that of another; or

(b) acted under an honest claim of right to the property or service involved o that he had a right to acquire or dispose of it as he did; or

(c) took property exposed for sale, intending to purchase and pay for it promptly, or reasonably believing that the owner, if present, would have consented.

(4) Theft from Spouse. It is no defense that theft was from the actor's spouse, except that misappropriation of household and personal effects, or other property normally accessible to both spouses, is theft only if it occurs after the parties have ceased living together.

Section 223.2. Theft by Unlawful Taking or Disposition.

(1) Movable Property. A person is guilty of theft if he unlawfully takes, or exercises unlawful control over, movable property of another with purpose to deprive him thereof.

(2) Immovable Property. A person is guilty of theft if he unlawfully transfers immovable property of another or any interest therein with purpose to benefit himself or another not entitled thereto.

Section 223.3. Theft by Deception.

A person is guilty of theft if he purposely obtains property of another by deception. A person deceives if he purposely:

(1) creates or reinforces a false impression, including false impressions as to law, vale, intention or other state of mind; but deception as to a person's intention to perform a promise shall not be inferred from the fact alone that he did not subsequently perform the promise; or

(2) prevents another from acquiring information which would affect his judgment of a transaction; or

(3) fails to correct a false impression which the deceiver previously created or reinforced, or which the deceiver knows to be influencing another to whom he stands in a fiduciary or confidential relationship; or

(4) fails to disclose a known lien, adverse claim or other legal impediment to the enjoyment of property which he transfers or encumbers in consideration for the property obtained, whether such impediment is or is not valid, or is or is not a matter of official record.

The term "deceive" does not, however, include falsity as to matters having no pecuniary significance, or puffing by statements unlikely to deceive ordinary persons in the group addressed.

Section 223.4. Theft by Extortion.

A person is guilty of theft if he purposely obtains property of another by threatening to:

(1) inflict bodily injury on anyone or commit any other criminal offense; or

(2) accuse anyone of a criminal offense; or

(3) expose any secret tending to subject any person to hatred, contempt or ridicule, or to impair his credit or business repute; or

(4) take or withhold action as an official, or cause an official to take or withhold action; or

(5) bring about or continue a strike, boycott or other collective unofficial action, if the property is not demanded or received for the benefit of the group in whose interest the actor purports to act; or

(6) testify or provide information or withhold testimony or information with respect to another's legal claim or defense; or

(7) inflict any other harm which would not benefit the actor. It is an affirmative defense to prosecution based on paragraphs (2), (3) or (4) that the property obtained by threat of accusation, exposure, lawsuit or other invocation of official action was honestly claimed as restitution or indemnification for harm done in the circumstances to which such accusation, exposure, lawsuit or other official action relates, or as compensation for property or lawful services.

Section 223.5. Theft of Property Lost, Mislaid, or Delivered by Mistake.

A person who comes into control of property of another that he knows to have been lost, mislaid, or delivered under a mistake as to the nature or amount of the property or the identity of the recipient is guilty of theft if, with purpose to deprive the owner thereof, he fails to take reasonable measures to restore the property to a person entitled to have it.

Section 223.6. Receiving Stolen Property.

(1) Receiving. A person is guilty of theft if he purposely receives, retains, or disposes of movable property of another knowing that it has been stolen, or believing that it has probably been stolen, unless the property is received, retained, or disposed with purpose to restore it to the owner. "Receiving" means acquiring possession, control or title, or lending on the security of the property.

(2) Presumption of Knowledge. The requisite knowledge or belief is presumed in the case of a dealer who:

(a) is found in possession or control of property stolen from two or more persons on separate occasions; or

(b) has received stolen property in another transaction within the year preceding the transaction charged; or

(c) being a dealer in property of the sort received, acquires it for a consideration which he knows is far below its reasonable value.

"Dealer" means a person in the business of buying or selling goods including a pawnbroker.

Section 223.7. Theft of Services.

(1) A person is guilty of theft is he purposely obtains services which he knows are available only for compensation, by deception or threat, or by false token or other means to avoid payment for the service. "Services" includes labor, professional service, transportation, telephone or other public service, accommodation in hotels, restaurants or elsewhere, admission to exhibitions, use of vehicles or other movable property. Where compensation for service is ordinarily paid immediately upon the render-

ing of such service, as in the case of hotels and restaurants, refusal to pay or absconding without payment or offer to pay gives rise to a presumption that the service was obtained by deception as to intention to pay.

(2) A person commits theft if, having control over the disposition of services of others, to which he is not entitled, he knowingly diverts such services to his own benefit or to the benefit of another not entitled thereto.

Section 223.8. Theft by Failure to Make Required Disposition of Funds Received.

A person who purposely obtains property upon agreement, or subject to a known legal obligation, to make specified payment or other disposition, whether from such property or its proceeds or from his own property to be reserved in equivalent amount, is guilty of theft if he deals with the property obtained as his own and fails to make the required payment or disposition. The foregoing applies notwithstanding that it may be impossible to identify particular property as belonging to the victim at the time of the actor's failure to make the required payment or disposition. An officer or employee of the government or of a financial institution is presumed: (i) to know any legal obligation relevant to his criminal liability under this Section, and (ii) to have dealt with the property as his own if he fails to pay or account upon lawful demand, or if an audit reveals a shortage or falsification of accounts.

Section 223.9. Unauthorized Use of Automobiles and Other Vehicles.

A person commits a misdemeanor if he operates another's automobile, airplane, motorcycle, motorboat, or other motor-propelled vehicle without consent of the owner. It is an affirmative defense to prosecution under this Section that the actor reasonably believed that the owner would have consented to the operation had he known of it.

Article 224. Forgery and Fraudulent Practices.

Section 224.0. Definitions.

In this Article, the definitions given in Section 223.0 apply unless a different meaning plainly is required.

Section 224.1. Forgery.

(1) Definition. A person is guilty of forgery if, with purpose to defraud or injure anyone, or with knowledge that he is facilitating a fraud or injury to be perpetrated by anyone, the actor:

(a) alters any writing of another without his authority; or

(b) makes, completes, executes, authenticates, issues or transfers any writing so that it purports to be the act of another who did not authorize that act, or to have been executed at a time or place or in a numbered sequence other than was in fact the case, or to be a copy of an original when no such original existed; or

(c) utters any writing which he knows to be forged in a manner specified in paragraphs (a) or (b). "Writing" includes printing or any other method of recording information, money, coins, tokens, stamps, seals, credit cards, badges, trade-marks, and other symbols of value, right, privilege, or identification.

(2) Grading. Forgery is a felony of the second degree if the writing is or purports to be part of an issue of money, securities, postage or revenue stamps, or other instruments issued by the government, or part of an issue of stock, bonds or other instruments representing interests in or claims against any property or enterprise. Forgery is a felony of the third degree if the writing is or purports to be a will, deed, contract, release, commercial instrument, or other document evidencing, creating, transferring, altering, terminating, or otherwise affecting legal relations. Otherwise forgery is a misdemeanor.

Section 224.2. Simulating Objects of Antiquity, Rarity, Etc.

A person commits a misdemeanor if, with purpose to defraud anyone or with knowledge that he is facilitating a fraud to be perpetrated by anyone, he makes, alters or utters any object so that it appears to have value because of antiquity, rarity, source, or authorship which it does not possess.

Section 224.3. Fraudulent Destruction, Removal or Concealment of Recordable Instruments.

A person commits a felony of the third degree if, with purpose to deceive or injure anyone, he destroys, removes or conceals any will, deed, mortgage, security instrument or other writing for which the law provides public recording.

Section 224.4. Tampering with Records.

A person commits a misdemeanor if, knowing that he has no privilege to do so, he falsifies, destroys, removes or conceals any writing or record, with purpose to deceive or injure anyone or to conceal any wrongdoing.

Section 224.5. Bad Checks.

[omitted]

Section 224.6. Credit Cards.

[omitted]

Section 224.7. Deceptive Business Practices.

A person commits a misdemeanor if in the course of business he:

(1) uses or possesses for use a false weight or measure, or any other device for falsely determining or recording any quality or quantity; or

(2) sells, offers or exposes for sale, or delivers less than the represented quantity of any commodity or service; or

(3) takes or attempts to take more than the represented quantity of any commodity or service when as buyer he furnishes the weight or measure; or

(4) sells, offers or exposes for sale adulterated or mislabeled commodities. "Adulterated" means varying from the standard of composition or quality prescribed by or pursuant to any statute providing criminal penalties for such variance, or set by established commercial usage. "Mislabeled" means varying from the standard of truth or disclosure in labeling prescribed by or pursuant to any statute providing criminal penalties for such variance, or set by established commercial usage; or

(5) makes a false or misleading statement in any advertisement addressed to the public or to a substantial segment thereof for the purpose of promoting the purchase or sale of property or services; or

(6) makes a false or misleading written statement for the purpose of obtaining property or credit; or

(7) makes a false or misleading written statement for the purpose of promoting the sale of securities, or omits information required by law to be disclosed in written documents relating to securities. It is an affirmative defense to prosecution under this Section if the defendant proves by a preponderance of the evidence that his conduct was not knowingly or recklessly deceptive.

Section 224.8. Commercial Bribery and Breach of Duty to Act Disinterestedly.

[omitted]

Section 224.9. Rigging Publicly Exhibited Contest.

[omitted]

Section 224.10. Defrauding Secured Creditors.

[omitted]

Section 224.11. Fraud in Insolvency.

[omitted]

Section 224.12. Receiving Deposits in a Failing Financial Institution.

[omitted]

Section 224.13. Misapplication of Entrusted Property and Property of Government or Financial Institution.

[omitted]

Section 224.14. Securing Execution of Documents by Deception.

[omitted]

Offenses Against the Family.

Article 230. Offenses Against the Family.

Section 230.1. Bigamy and Polygamy.

(1) Bigamy. A married person is guilty of bigamy, a misdemeanor, if he contracts or purports to contract another marriage, unless at the time of the subsequent marriage:
    (a) the actor believes that the prior spouse is dead; or
    (b) the actor and the prior spouse have been living apart for five consecutive years throughout which the prior spouse was not known by the actor to be alive; or
    (c) a Court has entered a judgment purporting to terminate or annul any prior disqualifying marriage, and the actor does not know that judgment to be invalid; or
    (d) the actor reasonably believes that he is legally eligible to remarry.

(2) Polygamy. A person is guilty of polygamy, a felony of the third degree, if he marries or cohabits with more than one spouse at a time in purported exercise of the right of plural marriage. The offense is a continuing one until all cohabitation and claim of marriage with more than one spouse terminates. This Section does not apply to parties to a polygamous marriage, lawful in the country of which they are residents or nationals, while they are in transit through or temporarily visiting this State.

(3) Other Party to Bigamous or Polygamous Marriage. A person is guilty of bigamy or polygamy, as the case may be, if he contracts or purports to contract marriage with another knowing that the other is thereby committing bigamy or polygamy.

Section 230.2. Incest.

A person is guilty of incest, a felony of the third degree, if he knowingly marries or cohabits or has sexual intercourse with an ancestor or descendant, a brother or sister of the whole or half blood [or an uncle, aunt, nephew or niece of the whole blood]. "Cohabit" means to live together under the representation or appearance of being married. The relationships referred to herein include blood relationships without regard to legitimacy, and relationship of parent and child by adoption.

Section 230.3. Abortion.

(1) Unjustified Abortion. A person who purposely and unjustifiably terminates the pregnancy of another otherwise than by a live birth commits a felony of the third degree or, where the pregnancy has continued beyond the twenty-sixth week, a felony of the second degree.

(2) Justifiable Abortion. A licensed physician is justified in terminating a pregnancy if he believes there is substantial risk that continuance of the pregnancy would gravely impair the physical or mental health of the mother or that the child would be born with grave physical or mental defect, or that the pregnancy resulted from rape, incest, or other felonious intercourse. All illicit intercourse with a girl below the age of 16 shall be deemed felonious for purposes of this Subsection. Justifiable abortions shall be performed only in a licensed hospital except in case of emergency when hospital facilities are unavailable. [Additional exceptions from the requirement of hospitalization may be incorporated here to take account of situations in sparsely settled areas where hospitals are not generally accessible.]

(3) Physicians' Certificates; Presumption from Non-Compliance. No abortion shall be performed unless two physicians, one of whom may be the person performing the abortion, shall have certified in writing the circumstances which they believe to justify the abortion. Such certificate shall be submitted before the abortion to the hospital where it is to be performed and, in the case of abortion following felonious intercourse, to the prosecuting attorney or the police. Failure to comply with any of the requirements of this Subsection gives rise to a presumption that the abortion was unjustified.

(4) Self-Abortion. A woman whose pregnancy has continued beyond the twenty-sixth week commits a felony of the third degree if she purposely terminates her own pregnancy otherwise than by a live birth, or if she uses instruments, drugs or violence upon herself for that purpose. Except as justified under Subsection (2), a person who induces or knowingly aids a woman to use instruments, drugs or violence upon herself for the purpose of terminating her pregnancy otherwise than by a live birth commits a felony of the third degree whether or not the pregnancy has continued beyond the twenty-sixth week.

(5) Pretended Abortion. A person commits a felony of the third degree if, representing that it is his purpose to perform an abortion, he does an act adapted to cause abortion in a pregnant woman although the woman is in fact not pregnant, or the actor does not believe she is. A person charged with unjustified abortion under Subsection (1) or

an attempt to commit that offense may be convicted thereof upon proof of conduct prohibited by this Subsection.

(6) Distribution of Abortifacients. A person who sells, offers to sell, possesses with intent to sell, advertises, or displays for sale anything specially designed to terminate a pregnancy, or held out by the actor as useful for that purpose, commits a misdemeanor, unless:

 (a) the sale, offer or display is to a physician or druggist or to an intermediary in a chain of distribution to physicians or druggists; or

 (b) the sale is made upon prescription or order of a physician; or

 (c) the possession is with intent to sell as authorized in paragraphs (a) and (b); or

 (d) the advertising is addressed to persons named in paragraph (a) and confined to trade or professional channels not likely to reach the general public.

(7) Section Inapplicable to Prevention of Pregnancy. Nothing in this Section shall be deemed applicable to the prescription, administration or distribution of drugs or other substances for avoiding pregnancy, whether by preventing implantation of a fertilized ovum or by any other method that operates before, at or immediately after fertilization.

Section 230.4. Endangering Welfare of Children.

A parent, guardian, or other person supervising the welfare of a child under 18 commits a misdemeanor if he knowingly endangers the child's welfare by violating a duty of care, protection or support.

Section 230.5. Persistent Non-Support.

A person commits a misdemeanor if he persistently fails to provide support which he can provide and which he knows he is legally obliged to provide to a spouse, child or other dependent.

Offenses Against Public Administration.

Article 240. Bribery and Corrupt Influence.

Section 240.0. Definitions.

[omitted]

Section 240.1. Bribery in Official and Political Matters.

A person is guilty of bribery, a felony of the third degree, if he offers, confers or agrees to confer upon another, or solicits, accepts or agrees to accept from another:

 (1) any pecuniary benefit as consideration for the recipient's decision, opinion, recommendation, vote or other exercise of discretion as a public servant, party official or voter; or

 (2) any benefit as consideration for the recipient's decision, vote,

recommendation or other exercise of official discretion in a judicial or administrative proceeding; or

(3) any benefit as consideration for a violation of a known legal duty as public servant or party official. It is no defense to prosecution under this Section that a person whom the actor sought to influence was not qualified to act in the desired way whether because he had not yet assumed office, or lacked jurisdiction, or for any other reason.

Section 240.2. Threats and Other Improper Influence in Official and Political Matters.

(1) Offenses Defined. A person commits an offense if he:

(a) threatens unlawful harm to any person with purpose to influence his decision, opinion, recommendation, vote or other exercise of discretion as a public servant, party official or voter; or

(b) threatens harm to any public servant with purpose to influence his decision, opinion, recommendation, vote or other exercise of discretion in a judicial or administrative proceeding; or

(c) threatens harm to any public servant or party official with purpose to influence him to violate his known legal duty; or

(d) privately addresses to any public servant who has or will have an official discretion in a judicial or administrative proceeding any representation, entreaty, argument or other communication with purpose to influence the outcome on the basis of considerations other than those authorized by law. It is no defense to prosecution under this Section that a person whom the actor sought to influence was not qualified to act in the desired way, whether because he had not yet assumed office, or lacked jurisdiction, or for any other reason.

(2) Grading. An offense under this Section is a misdemeanor unless the actor threatened to commit a crime or made a threat with purpose to influence a judicial or administrative proceeding, in which cases the offense is a felony of the third degree.

Section 240.3. Compensation for Past Official Action.

A person commits a misdemeanor if he solicits, accepts or agrees to accept any pecuniary benefit as compensation for having, as public servant, given a decision, opinion, recommendation or vote favorable to another, or for having otherwise exercised a discretion in his favor, or for having violated his duty. A person commits a misdemeanor if he offers, confers or agrees to confer compensation acceptance of which is prohibited by this Section.

Section 240.4. Retaliation for Past Official Action.

A person commits a misdemeanor if he harms another by any unlawful act in retaliation for anything lawfully done by the latter in the capacity of public servant.

Section 240.5. Gifts to Public Servants by Persons Subject to Their Jurisdiction.

[omitted]

Section 240.6. Compensating Public Servant for Assisting Private Interests in Relation to Matters Before Him.

[omitted]

Section 240.7. Selling Political Endorsement; Special Influence.

[omitted]

Article 241. Perjury and Other Falsification in Official Matters.

Section 241.0. Definitions.

In this Article, unless a different meaning plainly is required:
    (1) the definitions given in Section 240.0 apply; and
    (2) "statement" means any representation, but includes a representation of opinion, belief or other state of mind only if the representation clearly relates to state of mind apart from or in addition to any facts which are the subject of the representation.

Section 241.1. Perjury.

(1) Offense Defined. A person is guilty of perjury, a felony of the third degree, if in any official proceeding he makes a false statement under oath or equivalent affirmation, or swears or affirms the truth of a statement previously made, when the statement is material and he does not believe it to be true.

(2) Materiality. Falsification is material, regardless of the admissibility of the statement under rules of evidence, if it could have affected the course or outcome of the proceeding. It is no defense that the declarant mistakenly believed the falsification to be immaterial. Whether a falsification is material in a given factual situation is a question of law.

(3) Irregularities No Defense. It is not a defense to prosecution under this Section that the oath or affirmation was administered or taken in an irregular manner or that the declarant was not competent to make the statement. A document purporting to be made upon oath or affirmation at any time when the actor presents it as being so verified shall be deemed to have been duly sworn or affirmed.

(4) Retraction. No person shall be guilty of an offense under this Section if he retracted the falsification in the course of the proceeding in which it was made before it became manifest that the falsification

was or would be exposed and before the falsification substantially affected the proceeding.

(5) Inconsistent Statements. Where the defendant made inconsistent statements under oath or equivalent affirmation, both having been made within the period of the statute of limitations, the prosecution may proceed by setting forth the inconsistent statements in a single count alleging in the alternative that one or the other was false and not believed by the defendant. In such case it shall not be necessary for the prosecution to prove which statement was false but only that one or the other was false and not believed by the defendant to be true.

(6) Corroboration. No person shall be convicted of an offense under this Section where proof of falsity rests solely upon contradiction by testimony of a single person other than the defendant.

Section 241.2. False Swearing.

(1) False Swearing in Official Matters. A person who makes a false statement under oath or equivalent affirmation, or swears or affirms the truth of such a statement previously made, when he does not believe the statement to be true, is guilty of a misdemeanor if:

(a) the falsification occurs in an official proceeding; or

(b) the falsification is intended to mislead a public servant in performing his official function.

(2) Other False Swearing. A person who makes a false statement under oath or equivalent affirmation, or swears or affirms the truth of such a statement previously made, when he does not believe the statement to be true, is guilty of a petty misdemeanor, if the statement is one which is required by law to be sworn or affirmed before a notary or other person authorized to administer oaths.

(3) Perjury Provisions Applicable. Subsections (3) to (6) of Section 241.1 apply to the present Section.

Section 241.3. Unsworn Falsification to Authorities.

(1) In General. A person commits a misdemeanor if, with purpose to mislead a public servant in performing his official function, he:

(a) makes any written false statement which he does not believe to be true; or

(b) purposely creates a false impression in a written application for any pecuniary or other benefit, by omitting information necessary to prevent statements therein from being misleading; or

(c) submits or invites reliance on any writing which he knows to be forged, altered or otherwise lacking in authenticity; or

(d) submits or invites reliance on any sample, specimen, map, boundary-mark, or other object which he knows to be false.

(2) Statements "Under Penalty." A person commits a petty misdemeanor if he makes a written false statement which he does not believe

to be true, on or pursuant to a form bearing notice, authorized by law, to the effect that false statements made therein are punishable.

(3) Perjury Provisions Applicable. Subsections (3) to (6) of Section 241.1 apply to the present Section.

Section 241.4. False Alarms to Agencies of Public Safety.

A person who knowingly causes a false alarm of fire or other emergency to be transmitted to or within any organization, official or volunteer, for dealing with emergencies involving danger to life or property commits a misdemeanor.

Section 241.5. False Reports to Law Enforcement Authorities.

(1) Falsely Incriminating Another. A person who knowingly gives false information to any law enforcement officer with purpose to implicate another commits a misdemeanor.

(2) Fictitious Reports. A person commits a petty misdemeanor if he:
    (a) reports to law enforcement authorities an offense or other incident within their concern knowing that it did not occur; or
    (b) pretends to furnish such authorities with information relating to an offense or incident when he knows he has no information relating to such offense or incident.

Section 241.6. Tampering With Witnesses and Informants; Retaliation Against Them.

[omitted]

Section 241.7. Tampering with or Fabricating Physical Evidence.

[omitted]

Section 241.8. Tampering With Public Records or Information.

(1) Offense Defined. A person commits an offense if he:
    (a) knowingly makes a false entry in, or false alteration of, any record, document or thing belonging to, or received or kept by, the government for information or record, or required by law to be kept by others for information of the government; or
    (b) makes, presents or uses any record, document or thing knowing it to be false, and with purpose that it be taken as a genuine part of information or records referred to in paragraph (a); or
    (c) purposely and unlawfully destroys, conceals, removes or other-

wise impairs the verity or availability of any such record, document or thing.

(2) Grading. An offense under this Section is a misdemeanor unless the actor's purpose is to defraud or injure anyone, in which case the offense is a felony of the third degree.

Section 241.9. Impersonating a Public Servant.

A person commits a misdemeanor if he falsely pretends to hold a position in the public service with purpose to induce another to submit to such pretended official authority or otherwise to act in reliance upon that pretense to his prejudice.

Article 242. Obstructing governmental operations; escapes.

Section 242.0. Definitions.

In this Article, unless another meaning plainly is required, the definitions given in Section 240.0 apply.

Section 242.1. Obstructing Administration of Law or Other Governmental Function.

[omitted]

Section 242.2. Resisting Arrest or Other Law Enforcement.

A person commits a misdemeanor if, for the purpose of preventing a public servant from effecting a lawful arrest or discharging any other duty, the person creates a substantial risk of bodily injury to the public servant or anyone else, or employs means justifying or requiring substantial force to overcome the resistance.

Section 242.3. Hindering Apprehension or Prosecution.

A person commits an offense if, with purpose to hinder the apprehension, prosecution, conviction or punishment of another for crime, he:
    (1) harbors or conceals the other; or
    (2) provides or aids in providing a weapon, transportation, disguise or other means of avoiding apprehension or effecting escape; or
    (3) conceals or destroys evidence of the crime, or tampers with a witness, informant, document or other source of information, regardless of its admissibility in evidence; or

(4) warns the other of impending discovery or apprehension, except that this paragraph does not apply to a warning given in connection with an effort to bring another into compliance with law; or

(5) volunteers false information to a law enforcement officer. The offense is a felony of the third degree if the conduct which the actor knows has been charged or is liable to be charged against the person aided would constitute a felony of the first or second degree. Otherwise it is a misdemeanor.

Section 242.4. Aiding Consummation of Crime.

A person commits an offense if he purposely aids another to accomplish an unlawful object of a crime, as by safeguarding the proceeds thereof or converting the proceeds into negotiable funds. The offense is a felony of the third degree if the principal offense was a felony of the first or second degree. Otherwise it is a misdemeanor.

Section 242.5. Compounding.

A person commits a misdemeanor if he accepts or agrees to accept any pecuniary benefit in consideration of refraining from reporting to law enforcement authorities the commission or suspected commission of any offense or information relating to an offense. It is an affirmative defense to prosecution under this Section that the pecuniary benefit did not exceed an amount which the actor believed to be due as restitution or indemnification for harm caused by the offense.

Section 242.6. Escape.

(1) Escape. A person commits an offense if he unlawfully removes himself from official detention or fails to return to official detention following temporary leave granted for a specific purpose or limited period. "Official detention" means arrest, detention in any facility for custody of persons under charge or conviction of crime or alleged or found to be delinquent, detention for extradition or deportation, or any other detention for law enforcement purposes; but "official detention" does not include supervision of probation or parole, or constraint incidental to release on bail.

(2) Permitting or Facilitating Escape. A public servant concerned in detention commits an offense if he knowingly or recklessly permits an escape. Any person who knowingly causes or facilitates an escape commits an offense.

(3) Effect of Legal Irregularity in Detention. Irregularity in bringing about or maintaining detention, or lack of jurisdiction of the committing or detaining authority, shall not be a defense to prosecution under this Section if the escape is from a prison or other custodial facility or from detention pursuant to commitment by official proceedings. In the case of other detentions, irregularity or lack of jurisdiction shall be a defense only if:

(a) the escape involved no substantial risk of harm to the person or property of anyone other than the detainee; or

(b) the detaining authority did not act in good faith under color of law.

(4) Grading of Offenses. An offense under this Section is a felony of the third degree where:

(a) the actor was under arrest for or detained on a charge of felony or following conviction of crime; or

(b) the actor employs force, threat, deadly weapon or other dangerous instrumentality to effect the escape; or

(c) a public servant concerned in detention of persons convicted of crime purposely facilitates or permits an escape from a detention facility.

Otherwise an offense under this Section is a misdemeanor.

Section 242.7. Implements for Escape; Other Contraband.

(1) Escape Implements. A person commits a misdemeanor if he unlawfully introduces within a detention facility, or unlawfully provides an inmate with, any weapon, tool or other thing which may be useful for escape. An inmate commits a misdemeanor if he unlawfully procures, makes, or otherwise provides himself with, or has in his possession, any such implement of escape. "Unlawfully" means surreptitiously or contrary to law, regulation or order of the detaining authority.

(2) Other Contraband. A person commits a petty misdemeanor if he provides an inmate with anything which the actor knows it is unlawful for the inmate to possess.

Section 242.8. Bail Jumping; Default in Required Appearance.

A person set at liberty by court order, with or without bail, upon condition that he will subsequently appear at a specified time and place, commits a misdemeanor if, without lawful excuse, he fails to appear at that time and place. The offense constitutes a felony of the third degree where the required appearance was to answer to a charge of felony, or for disposition of any such charge, and the actor took flight or went into hiding to avoid apprehension, trial or punishment. This Section does not apply to obligations to appear incident to release under suspended sentence or on probation or parole.

Article 243. Abuse of Office.

Section 243.0. Definitions.

In this Article, unless a different meaning plainly is required, the definitions given in Section 240.0 apply.

Section 243.1. Official Oppression.

A person acting or purporting to act in an official capacity or taking advantage of such actual or purported capacity commits a misdemeanor if, knowing that his conduct is illegal, he:

(a) subjects another to arrest, detention, search, seizure, mistreatment, dispossession, assessment, lien or other infringement of personal or property rights; or

(b) denies or impedes another in the exercise or enjoyment of any right, privilege, power or immunity.

Section 243.2. Speculating or Wagering on Official
Action or Information.

A public servant commits a misdemeanor if, in contemplation of official action by himself or by a governmental unit with which he is associated, or in reliance on information to which he has access in his official capacity and which has not been made public, he:

(1) acquires a pecuniary interest in any property, transaction or enterprise which may be affected by such information or official action; or

(2) speculates or wagers on the basis of such information or official action; or

(3) aids another to do any of the foregoing.

Offenses Against Public Order and Decency.

Article 250. Riot, Disorderly Conduct, and Related Offenses.

Section 250.1. Riot; Failure to Disperse.

(1) Riot. A person is guilty of riot, a felony of the third degree, if he participates with [two] or more others in a course of disorderly conduct:

(a) with purpose to commit or facilitate the commission of a felony or misdemeanor;

(b) with purpose to prevent or coerce official action; or

(c) when the actor or any other participant to the knowledge of the actor uses or plans to use a firearm or other deadly weapon.

(2) Failure of Disorderly Persons to Disperse Upon Official Order. Where [three] or more persons are participating in a course of disorderly conduct likely to cause substantial harm or serious inconvenience, annoyance or alarm, a peace officer or other public servant engaged in executing or enforcing the law may order the participants and others in the immediate vicinity to disperse. A person who refuses or knowingly fails to obey such an order commits a misdemeanor.

Section 250.2. Disorderly Conduct.

(1) Offense Defined. A person is guilty of disorderly conduct if, with purpose to cause public inconvenience, annoyance or alarm, or recklessly creating a risk thereof, he:

(a) engages in fighting or threatening, or in violent or tumultuous behavior; or

(b) makes unreasonable noise or offensively coarse utterance, gesture or display, or addresses abusive language to any person present; or

(c) creates a hazardous or physically offensive condition by any act which serves no legitimate purpose of the actor.

"Public" means affecting or likely to affect persons in a place to which the public or a substantial group has access; among the places included are highways, transport facilities, schools, prisons, apartment houses, places of business or amusement, or any neighborhood.

(2) Grading. An offense under this section is a petty misdemeanor if the actor's purpose is to cause substantial harm or serious inconvenience, or if he persists in disorderly conduct after reasonable warning or request to desist. Otherwise disorderly conduct is a violation.

Section 250.3. False Public Alarms.

A person is guilty of a misdemeanor if he initiates or circulates a report or warning of an impending bombing or other crime or catastrophe, knowing that the report or warning is false or baseless and that it is likely to cause evacuation of a building, place of assembly, or facility of public transport, or to cause public inconvenience or alarm.

Section 250.4. Harassment.

A person commits a petty misdemeanor if, with purpose to harass another, he:

(1) makes a telephone call without purpose of legitimate communication; or

(2) insults, taunts or challenges another in a manner likely to provoke violent or disorderly response; or

(3) makes repeated communications anonymously or at extremely inconvenient hours, or in offensively coarse language; or

(4) subjects another to an offensive touching; or

(5) engages in any other course of alarming conduct serving no legitimate purpose of the actor.

Section 250.5. Public Drunkenness; Drug Incapacitation.

A person is guilty of an offense if he appears in any public place manifestly under the influence of alcohol, narcotics or other drug, not therapeutically administered, to the degree that he may endanger himself or other persons or property, or annoy persons in his vicinity. An offense under this Section constitutes a petty misdemeanor if the actor has been convicted hereunder twice before within a period of one year. Otherwise the offense constitutes a violation.

Section 250.6. Loitering or Prowling.

A person commits a violation if he loiters or prowls in a place, at a time, or in a manner not usual for law-abiding individuals under circumstances that warrant alarm for the safety of persons or property in the vicinity. Among the circumstances which may be considered in determining whether such alarm is warranted is the fact that the actor takes flight upon appearance of a peace officer, refuses to identify himself, or manifestly endeavors to conceal himself or any object. Unless flight by the actor or other circumstance makes it impracticable, a peace officer shall prior to any arrest for an offense under this Section afford the actor an opportunity to dispel any alarm which would otherwise be warranted, by requesting him to identify himself and explain his presence and conduct. No person shall be convicted of an offense under this Section if the peace officer did not comply with the preceding sentence, or if it appears at trial that the explanation given by the actor was true and, if believed by the peace officer at the time, would have dispelled the alarm.

Section 250.7. Obstructing Highways and Other Public Passages.

(1) A person, who, having no legal privilege to do so, purposely or recklessly obstructs any highway or other public passage, whether alone or with others, commits a violation, or, in case he persists after warning by a law officer, a petty misdemeanor. "Obstructs" means renders impassable without unreasonable inconvenience or hazard. No person shall be deemed guilty of recklessly obstructing in violation of this Subsection solely because of a gathering of persons to hear him speak or otherwise communicate, or solely because of being a member of such a gathering.

(2) A person in a gathering commits a violation if he refuses to obey a reasonable official request or order to move:

    (a) to prevent obstruction of a highway or other public passage; or

    (b) to maintain public safety by dispersing those gathered in dangerous proximity to a fire or other hazard.

An order to move, addressed to a person whose speech or other lawful behavior attracts an obstructing audience, shall not be deemed reasonable if the obstruction can be readily remedied by police control of the size or location of the gathering.

Section 250.8. Disrupting Meetings and Processions.

A person commits a misdemeanor if, with purpose to prevent or disrupt a lawful meeting, procession or gathering, he does any act tending to obstruct or interfere with it physically, or makes any utterance, gesture or display designed to outrage the sensibilies of the group.

Section 250.9. Desecration of Venerated Objects.

A person commits a misdemeanor if he purposely desecrates any public monument or structure, or place of worship or burial, or if he purposely desecrates the national flag or any other object of veneration by the public or a substantial segment thereof in any public place. "Desecrate" means defacing, damaging, polluting or otherwise physically mistreating in a way that the actor knows will outrage the sensibilities of persons likely to observe or discover his action.

Section 250.10. Abuse of Corpse.

Except as authorized by law, a person who treats a corpse in a way that he knows would outrage ordinary family sensibilities commits a misdemeanor.

Section 250.11. Cruelty to Animals.

A person commits a misdemeanor if he purposely or recklessly:

(1) subjects any animal to cruel mistreatment; or

(2) subjects any animal in his custody to cruel neglect; or

(3) kills or injures any animal belonging to another without legal privilege or consent of the owner.

Subsections (1) and (2) shall not be deemed applicable to accepted veterinary practices and activities carried on for scientific research.

Section 250.12. Violation of Privacy.

(1) Unlawful Eavesdropping or Surveillance. A person commits a misdemeanor if, except as authorized by law, he:

(a) trespasses on property with purpose to subject anyone to eavesdropping or other surveillance in a private place; or

(b) installs in any private place, without the consent of the person or persons entitled to privacy there, any device for observing, photographing, recording, amplifying or broadcasting sounds or events in such place, or uses any such unauthorized installation; or

(c) installs or uses outside a private place any device for hearing, recording, amplifying or broadcasting sounds originating in such place which would not ordinarily be audible or comprehensible outside, without the consent of the person or persons entitled to privacy there.

"Private place" means a place where one may reasonably expect to be safe from casual or hostile intrusion or surveillance, but does not include a place to which the public or a substantial group thereof has access.

(2) Other Breach of Privacy of Messages. A person commits a misdemeanor if, except as authorized by law, he:

(a) intercepts without the consent of the sender or receiver a message by telephone, telegraph, letter or other means of communicating privately; but this paragraph does not extend to (i) overhearing of messages through a regularly installed instrument on a telephone party line or on an extension, or (ii) interception by the telephone company or subscriber incident to enforcement of regulations limiting use of the facilities or incident to other normal operation and use; or

(b) divulges without the consent of the sender or receiver the existence or contents of any such message if the actor knows that the message was illegally intercepted, or if he learned of the message in the course of employment with an agency engaged in transmitting it.

Article 251. Public Indecency.

Section 251.1. Open Lewdness.

A person commits a petty misdemeanor if he does any lewd act which he knows is likely to be observed by others who would be affronted or alarmed.

Section 251.2. Prostitution and Related Offenses.

(1) Prostitution. A person is guilty of prostitution, a petty misdemeanor, if he or she:

(a) is an inmate of a house of prostitution or otherwise engages in sexual activity as a business; or

(b) loiters in or within view of any public place for the purpose of being hired to engage in sexual activity.

"Sexual activity" includes homosexual and other deviate sexual relations. A "house of prostitution" is any place where prostitution or promotion of prostitution is regularly carried on by one person under the control, management or supervision of another. An "inmate" is a person who engages in prostitution in or through the agency of a house of prostitution. "Public place" means any place to which the public or any substantial group thereof has access.

(2) Promoting Prostitution. A person who knowingly promotes prostitution of another commits a misdemeanor or felony as provided in Subsection (3). The following acts shall, without limitation of the foregoing, constitute promoting prostitution:

(a) owning, controlling, managing, supervising or otherwise keeping, alone or in association with others, a house of prostitution or a prostitution business; or

(b) procuring an inmate for a house of prostitution or a place in a house of prostitution for one who would be an inmate; or

(c) encouraging, inducing, or otherwise purposely causing another to become or remain a prostitute; or

(d) soliciting a person to patronize a prostitute; or

(e) procuring a prostitute for a patron; or

(f) transporting a person into or within this state with purpose to promote that person's engaging in prostitution, or procuring or paying for transportation with that purpose; or

(g) leasing or otherwise permitting a place controlled by the actor, alone or in association with others, to be regularly used for prostitution or the promotion of prostitution, or failure to make reasonable effort to abate such use by ejecting the tenant, notifying law enforcement authorities, or other legally available means; or

(h) soliciting, receiving, or agreeing to receive any benefit for doing or agreeing to do anything forbidden by this Subsection.

(3) Grading of Offenses Under Subsection (2). An offense under Subsection (2) constitutes a felony of the third degree if:

(a) the offense falls within paragraph (a), (b) or (c) of Subsection (2); or

(b) the actor compels another to engage in or promote prostitution; or

(c) the actor promotes prostitution of a child under 16, whether or not he is aware of the child's age; or

(d) the actor promotes prostitution of his wife, child, ward or any person for whose care, protection or support he is responsible. Otherwise the offense is a misdemeanor.

(4) Presumption from Living off Prostitutes. A person, other than the prostitute or the prostitute's minor child or other legal dependent incapable of self-support, who is supported in whole or substantial part by the proceeds of prostitution is presumed to be knowingly promoting prostitution in violation of Subsection (2).

(5) Patronizing Prostitutes. A person commits a violation if he hires a prostitute to engage in sexual activity with him, or if he enters or remains in a house of prostitution for the purpose of engaging in sexual activity.

(6) Evidence. On the issue whether a place is a house of prostitution the following shall be admissible evidence: its general repute; the repute of the persons who reside in or frequent the place; the frequency, timing and duration of visits by non-residents. Testimony of a person against his spouse shall be admissible to prove offenses under this Section.

Section 251.3. Loitering to Solicit Deviate Sexual Relations.

A person is guilty of a petty misdemeanor if he loiters in or near any public place for the purpose of soliciting or being solicited to engage in deviate sexual relations.

Section 251.4. Obscenity.

(1) Obscene Defined. Material is obscene if, considered as a whole, its predominant appeal is to prurient interest, that is, a shameful or morbid interest, in nudity, sex or excretion, and if in addition it goes substantially beyond customary limits of candor in describing or representing such matters. Predominant appeal shall be judged with reference to ordinary adults unless it appears from the character of the material or the circumstances of its dissemination to be designed for children or other specially susceptible audience. Undeveloped photographs, molds, printing plates, and the like, shall be deemed obscene notwithstanding that processing or other acts may be required to make the obscenity patent or to disseminate it.

(2) Offenses. Subject to the affirmative defense provided in Subsection (3), a person commits a misdemeanor if he knowingly or recklessly:

    (a) sells, delivers or provides, or offers or agrees to sell, deliver or provide, any obscene writing, picture, record or other representation or embodiment of the obscene; or

    (b) presents or directs an obscene play, dance or performance, or participates in that portion thereof which makes it obscene; or

    (c) publishes, exhibits or otherwise makes available any obscene material; or

    (d) possesses any obscene material for purposes of sale or other commercial dissemination; or

    (e) sells, advertises or otherwise commercially disseminates material, whether or not obscene, by representing or suggesting that it is obscene.

A person who disseminates or possesses obscene material in the course of his business is presumed to do so knowingly or recklessly.

(3) Justifiable and Non-Commercial Private Dissemination. It is an affirmative defense to prosecution under this Section that dissemination was restricted to:

    (a) institutions or persons having scientific, educational, governmental or other similar justification for possessing obscene material; or

    (b) non-commercial dissemination to personal associates of the actor.

(4) Evidence; Adjudication of Obscenity. In any prosecution under this Section evidence shall be admissible to show:

    (a) the character of the audience for which the material was designed or to which it was directed;

    (b) what the predominant appeal of the material would be for ordinary adults or any special audience to which it was directed, and what effect, if any, it would probably have on conduct of such people;

(c) artistic, literary, scientific, educational or other merits of the material;

(d) the degree of public acceptance of the material in the United States;

(e) appeal to prurient interest, or absence thereof, in advertising or other promotion of the material; and

(f) the good repute of the author, creator, publisher or other person from whom the material originated.

Expert testimony and testimony of the author, creator, publisher or other person from whom the material originated, relating to factors entering into the determination of the issue of obscenity, shall be admissible. The Court shall dismiss a prosecution for obscenity if it is satisfied that the material is not obscene.

TABLE OF CASES

Abbot v. The Queen, 570
Ackerly, State v., 228
Ackridge, State v., 104
Adelson, State v., 425-427
Alexander, United States v., 591-599
Allen, Ulster County v., 166-172
Amecca, Commonwealth v., 239
Angiulo, United States v., 659
Anonymous, People v., 384-386
Anthony, United States v., 577-578
Archbold v. State, 299-302
Arnold's Case, 16 How. State Tr. 764, 539
Audette, State v., 228
Austin v. United States, 111

Backun v. United States, 358-361
Bad Heart Bull, State v., 491
Bagaric, United States v., 671
Bailey v. Commonwealth, 373-377
Baker v. State, 130
Balint, United States v., 216
Barker, United States v., 578-585
Beardsley, People v., 417
Bedder v. Director of Public Prosecutions, 105
Bellingham's Case, 539
Bennett v. Commonwealth, 244
Bess, State v., 515
Boswell v. State, 542
Braveman v. United States, 322 n.4
Brawner, United States v., 109-113, 543-551
Brown v. Commonwealth, 164
Bruno, United States v., 323
Buttrey, State v., 211-218

Calder v. Bull, 119-120
Calley, United States v., 517-519
Christy Pontiac - GMC, Inc., State v., 440-444
City of v. ──────────. *See* name of defendant
Cogan, Regina v., 380-383

Cogdon, King v., 109
Coleman, People v., 380 n.*
Collins, Regina v., 279
Collins v. Commonwealth, 376
Commonwealth v. ──────────. *See* name of defendant
Crimmins, United States v., 305, 306, 308, 310 n.64

Davis v. United States, 150
Delawder v. Commonwealth, 377
Director of Public Prosecutions v. ──────────. *See* name of defendant
Dorsey, State v., 467-469
Dotterweich, United States v., 216, 431, 432, 434, 436
Dudley and Stephens, The Queen v., 459-463
Durham v. United States, 544
Dusenbery v. Commonwealth, 376

Eastern Railroad Presidents Conference v. Noerr Motor Freight, Inc., 669
Everett, United States v., 281 n.*

Falcone, United States v., 359, 360
Farnsworth v. Zerbst, Warden, 603-605
Faulkner, Regina v., 184
Feldman, United States v., 659
Feola, United States v., 304-308, 310
Fisher v. United States, 112
Fort Wayne Books, Inc. v. Indiana, 661
Freed, United States v., 217

Garner, Tennessee v., 474-480
Gebardi v. United States, 312-315
Gibson, People v., 266 n.*
Goetz, People v., 502-510
Gounagias, State v., 97, 101

799

Gray, United States v., 139-140
Green, State v., 463
Griffith, State v., 483 n.†
Grimes, State v., 494 n.3
Grunewald v. United States, 325 n.15

Harrison v. State, 611-618
Henderson v. State, 235
Hilton Hotels Corp., United States v., 446
H.J. Inc v. Northwestern Bell Telephone Co., 672
Hopple, State v., 78
Hopt v. Utah, 111
Humphreys, Regina v., 383

Indelicato, United States v., 659
In re ──────. See name of party
International Minerals & Chemical Corp., United States v., 217
Ivic, United States v., 669, 672

Jackson, State v., 621 n.*
Jackson v. Indiana, 558 n.12, 560
Jackson v. Virginia, 157-165
Jaffe, People v., 280, 282, 284
Jones v. Commonwealth, 243-245
Jones v. United States, 415-418, 555-561

Kelly, State v., 511-517
Kimball, People v., 330-337
Kimura, People v., 600-601, 602
King v. ──────. See name of defendant
King v. United States, 544
Kline v. Moyer and Albert, 239
Kotteakos v. United States, 323

Lafferty, State v., 155, 156
Lambert v. California, 216
Laseter v. State, 221-226
Lassiter, State v., 242
Leak, Regina v., 380, 383
Leary v. United States, 171
Leland v. Oregon, 150, 151
Lester, United States v., 316-318
Levin, Commonwealth v., 238

Mack, United States v., 310
Maestas, State v., 273-274
Majewski, Director of Public Prosecutions v., 343, 397-404
Malone, Commonwealth v., 81-84
Martinez, United States v., 578-585

Masters, Corbitt, and Keating, United States v., 657-661
McDonald v. United States, 111
McFarland v. American Sugar Rfg. Co., 154
McNaughten's Case, 539
McPherson, Regina v., 279
Means, State v., 494
Means v. Solem, 469
Melnyczenko, Commonwealth v., 268 n.*
Mentry, People v., 115-116
Michael M. v. Sonoma County Superior Court, 647
Mitchell, State v., 677-682, 683
Mitchell, Wisconsin v., 683
Monell v. New York City Dept of Social Services, 479
Morgan, Regina v., 381, 382
Morissette v. United States, 546
Morrissey v. Brewer, 560
Mriglot, State v., 532 n.12, 553
Mullaney v. Wilbur, 149, 151, 154, 160, 168

National Organization for Women, Inc. v. Scheidler, 668-673
Neapolitan, United States v., 660

Ott, State v., 97-107

Papachristou v. City of Jacksonville, 120-126
Park, United States v., 430-437
Parsons v. State, 538-543
Patterson v. New York, 148-156, 160
Peaslee, Commonwealth v., 264 n.87
People v. ──────. See name of defendant
Perholtz, United States v., 659
Perl, United States v., 619-622
Pierson, People v., 202
Pinkerton v. United States, 322 n.1
Powell, State v., 514 n.9
Powell v. Texas, 216, 256-260
Prince, Regina v., 178-181, 184, 643 n.6
Pungitore, United States v., 661, 659

Queen v. ──────. See name of defendant

R.A.V. v. St. Paul, 683
Regina v. ──────. See name of defendant
Reynolds v. State, 224
Richards, People v., 464
Ring, Regina v., 280
Rivera v. Delaware, 151

TABLE OF STATUTES

Model Penal Code	
§1.02	692 n.7
§1.02(1)	45, 131 n.*
§1.02(1)(c)	28 n.12
§1.02(3)	131
§1.03(1)(a)	190 n.26
§1.03(2)	190 n.26
§1.04	211
§1.04(5)	26 n.5, 445
§1.05(1)	119
§1.06	59 n.8
§1.06(7)	370
§1.07(1)(b)	302-303
§1.12	147-148
§1.12(1)	114
§1.12(5)	84, 172
§1.13	189 n.23, 191, 193
§1.13(2)	191 n.27, 251, 261
§1.13(5)	191 n.27
§1.13(9)	183
§1.13(9)(a)	73
§1.13(16)	511, 533 n.14, 645
§2.01	211
§2.01(1)	250, 261, 414, 574, 697 n.16
§2.01(1)(c)	446
§2.01(2)	574
§2.01(2)(a)	411, 412
§2.01(2)(d)	575
§2.01(3)	250 n.1, 261, 414, 418, 697 n.16
§2.01(4)	261, 262
§2.02	211
§2.02 comment 2, at 124 (Tentative Draft No. 4, 1955)	188 n.18
§2.02 comment 2, at 233 (1985)	190 n.25
§2.02 comment 3, at 125 (Tent Draft No. 4, 1955)	196 n.37
§2.02 comment 4, at 242 (1985)	206
§2.02 comment 6, at 129 (Tentative Draft No. 4, 1955)	195 n.34
§2.02(1)	73, 114, 183, 185, 186, 260, 692 n.8
§2.02(2)	73, 78, 79, 80, 274
§2.02(2)(a)	682
§2.02(2)(c)	55 n.2, 76 n.3, 196 n.36, 629
§2.02(2)(d)	76 n.3, 533 n.14
§2.02(3)	27 n.9, 183, 186, 187, 196, 197, 198 n.44, 378, 634, 692 n.9
§2.02(4)	183, 187, 191, 195, 196, 197, 198 n.44
§2.02(5)	74, 188 n.21
§2.02(6)	74
§2.02(7)	74, 196 n.36
§2.02(9)	229, 288 n.2
§2.02(10)	198 n.42
§2.03	190 n.26, 245, 418
§2.03(2)	247, 248
§2.03(2)(a)	390, 391
§2.03(2)(b)	248
§2.03(3)	247
§2.03(3)(a)	390, 391
§2.04(1)	157, 186 n.11, 220, 587
§2.04(2) (Tentative Draft No. 4, 1955)	393
§2.04(2) comment 2, at 137 (Tentative Draft No. 4, 1955)	345 n.7
§2.04(2)	345 n.7, 349 n.22, 391, 392, 393
§2.04(3)	585, 587
§2.04(3)(a) (Tenative Draft No.1)	367
§2.04(3)(b) (Tenative Draft No.1)	367
§2.04(4) (Tenative Draft No.1)	367
§2.04(4) comment, at 34 (Tenative Draft No.1)	367
§2.04(4)	585, 587
§2.05	186, 211
§2.05(2)	27 n.10
§2.06	364 n.*
§2.06(1)-(2)(a)	377
§2.06(1)-(4)	354-355
§2.06(2)(a)	345 n.5, 378
§2.06(3)	260, 345 n.4
§2.06(3)(a)	320 n.3, 328
§2.06(3)(a)(ii)	298, 320 n.2, 358
§2.06(3)(b)(previously numbered §2.04(3)(b)) (in Tentative Draft No. 1)	361
§2.06(5)	315, 386
§2.06(6)	315
§2.06(6)(a) & (b)	386
§2.06(6)(c)	338
§2.06(7)	371, 386

803

804   Table of Statutes

Statute	Page
§2.07 comment, at 332, 335-338 (1985)	446
§2.07(1)-(5)	444
§2.07(1)(a)	445
§2.07(1)(b)	445
§2.07(5)	446
§2.07(6)	430
§2.07(6)(a)	437
§2.07(6)(b)	438
§2.08(1)	396
§2.08(2)	56 n.3, 396
§2.08(4)	28 n.11, 58 n.6, 534 n.15, 552
§2.08(5)	528 n.3, 552
§2.08(5)(b)	396
§2.09	28 n.11, 58 n.7, 157, 569
§2.09, comment (Tentative Draft No. 10, 1960)	585 n.59
§2.09, comment, at 8 (Tentative Draft No. 10, 1960)	566
§2.09(1)	411, 533 n.13, 629
§2.09(2)	411
§2.10	520, 531 n.10
§2.11	691 n.4
§2.11(1)	26 n.7
§2.11(1)(a)	26 n.6
§2.11(2)	27 n.8
§2.11(3)	26 n.7
§2.12	138 n.19
§2.12(2)	26 n.3, 131, 693 n.13
§2.12(3)	131
§2.13	618
§3.01(1)	500
§3.02	28 n.11, 58 n.5, 467, 469, 470, 523
§3.02(1)	459
§3.02(1)(a)	411, 455
§3.02(2)	411
§3.03	471
§3.04 comment, at 14-15 (Tentative Draft No. 8, 1958)	514 n.8
§3.04	58 n.4, 483, 508, 509, 514 n.8, 697 n.16
§3.04(1)	378, 469
§3.04(2)(b)	508
§3.04(2)(b)(ii)(2)	378
§3.05	485, 697 n.16
§3.05(1)	469
§3.06	485, 697 n.16
§3.07 comment 3, at 56 (Tentative Draft No. 8, 1958)	478
§3.07	28 n.11, 697 n.16
§3.07(1)	378
§3.07(1)-(3)	480
§3.07(5)	481
§3.08	472
§3.09	499
§3.10	488
§3.11	488
§3.11(1)	498, 501
§4.01	28 n.11, 543
§4.01 comment 3 (1985)	534 n.16
§4.01(1)	378, 528 n.4, 534 n.15, 543
§4.01(2)	529 n.5
§4.02(1)	113, 114
§4.02(2)	378
§4.08	556 n.**
§4.10	28 n.11, 570
§5.01	284, 358
§5.01 comment, at 38-48 (Tentative Draft No. 10, 1960)	263
§5.01 comment, at 297 (1985)	277
§5.01 comment (1985)	334
§5.01(1)	260, 268-269, 285, 292, 328
§5.01(1)(a)	288, 522 n.1, 524
§5.01(1)(b)	190 n.26, 694 n.11
§5.01(2)	269
§5.01(2)(c)	268 n.*, 690 n.3
§5.01(3)	298, 328, 386
§5.01(4) comment, at 69-73 (Tentative Draft No. 10, 1960)	335
§5.01(4)	157, 333, 337
§5.02	327
§5.02 comment 3, at 371 n.23 (1985)	327
§5.02(3)	337
§5.03 comment at 107 (Tentative Draft No. 10, 1960)	365
§5.03 comment 2, at 113 (Tenative Draft No. 10, 1962)	370
§5.03 comment, at 407-44 (1985)	308
§5.03(1)	260, 302, 311, 319
§5.03(1)(a)	324 n.10
§5.03(2)	324 n.9
§5.03(3)	323 n.5
§5.03(5)	302, 320
§5.03(6)	338
§5.03(7)	324 n.12
§5.03(7)(b)	325 n.14
§5.03(7)(c)	325 n.13
§5.04	315
§5.04(1)	320, 390
§5.05(2)	289
§5.05(3)	303
§5.06(1)	261
§210.0	70
§210.0(3)	55 n.1
§210.1	70
§210.1(1)	247, 418
§210.2	71, 198 n.41
§210.2 comment 6 (1980)	84
§210.2(1)(a)	247
§210.2(1)(b)	84, 87, 172, 173
§210.2(2)	390, 638
§210.3	71, 85, 198 n.41
§210.3 comment, at 48 (Tentative Draft No. 919)	102
§210.3(1)(b)	629
§210.3(2)	638
§210.4	71, 85, 196 n.38, 198 n.41
§210.5	71
§210.5(1)	187 n.16
§210.6	88
§210.6(1)	88-89
§210.6(2)	89-90

Table of Statutes

§210.6(3)	90-91		*United States Code*	
§210.6(3)(e)	87	15 U.S.C. §1 seq.		668
§210.6(3)(g)	682	18 U.S.C. §2		312
§211.1(1)(b)	196 n.38, 198 n.43	§17		551
§211.1(2)	55 n.1	§37		313
§211.2	312	§111		304, 305, 308
§211.3	632	§115		139
§212.1	192 n.30	§115(a)		139
§212.1(d)	390	§241		578, 580
§213.0(2)	628 n.*	§371		304, 305, 306, 619
§213.0(3)	650 n.†	§550		360
§213.1	628	§922(a)(3)		619
§213.1 comment (1980)	633	§970		619
§213.1 comment 8(a) (1980)	646	§1111		140
§213.1 comment 8(c) (1980)	635	§1112		140
§213.1 comment, at 312 (1980)	631	§1114		140
§213.1(1)	638, 641	§1201		62 n.15
§213.1(1)(a)	192 n.29, 629	§1202		62 n.15
§213.1(1)(d)	27 n.10	§1951		669
§213.1(2)(a)	629	§1951(b)(2)		669
§213.2	647	§1961		656, 670
§213.2 comment 2 (1980)	650	§1961(1)		670
§213.3	638, 640, 641, 647	§1961(4)		657, 670
§213.3 comment 2 (1980)	639	§1961(5)		657
§213.3(1)(a)	27 n.10, 393, 640, 641, 645	§1961-1968		668
§213.3(1)(b)	393	§1962		656, 661
§213.3(1)(d)	642	§1962(a)		668, 669, 670, 671
§213.4	291	§1962(b)		670, 671
§213.5	186 n.14	§1962(c)		657, 664, 665, 668, 669, 670, 671, 672
§213.6 comment 2 (1980)	643			
§213.6(1) comment (1980)	27 n.10	§1962(d)		657, 668, 669, 670
§213.6(1)	27 n.10, 643, 644, 645	§1964(c)		667
§213.6(2)	637	§2403(b)		479
§213.6(3)	639, 640	28 U.S.C. §2254		163, 491
§220.1(1)(a)	327	42 U.S.C. §1983		475
§220.3	410	50 U.S.C. §32		603
§220.3(1)(a)	410	§34		604
§220.3(1)(b)	188 n.19			
§221.1	195 n.35			
§222.1(1)	632		**Alabama**	
§223.2(1)	632			
§223.3	312		*Code*	
§223.3(a)	191 n.28	§13A-4-2(d)		297
§224.4	182 n.*			
§230.2	393			
§250.4(2)	196 n.40		**Alaska**	
§250.7	192 n.31			
§250.11	188 n.20		*Statutes*	
§250.12 (Tentative Draft No. 13, 1961)	347	§11.31.100(a)		221
		§11.31.100(d)		297
§432	613, 614, 615	§11.41.300(a)(1)(C)		221
		§11.41.410(a)(1)		221, 224
UNITED STATES		§11.81.610(b)		189 n.22, 221
		§11.81.900(a)(2)-(4)		189 n.22
Federal				
Constitution			**Arizona**	
Art. I §9	119			
§10	119		*Revised Statutes*	
Art. 3, §2, cl. 1	604	§13-1001(C)		297

Arkansas

Code Annotated
§41-703   297

California

Penal Code
§4	136 n.13
§182	297
§187	65
§188	65, 695 n.14
§189	66
§192	66
§261.5	648, 649

Colorado

Revised Statutes
§18-2-101(4)-(8)   297

Delaware

Code Annotated
tit.11, §432	611
§1256	612, 617
tit.16, §4752	617

Florida

Statutes
§777.04(4)   297

Georgia

Code Annotated
§16-4-6   297

Hawaii

Revised Statutes
§21-545(b)	557
§24-301(d)(1)	556, 557, 559
§24-301(e)	556
§24-301(k)	556
§24-301(2)(A)	557
§702-230 comment (1976)	405 n.50
§704-408	554

Idaho

Code
§18-306   297

Illinois

Revised Statutes
ch. 38, §8-4(c)	297
ch. 720, §12-13(1)	630

Indiana

Acts
P.L. 148, §24   299 n.1

Code
§35-1-111-1	299, 300, 301
§35-1-111-1 (Ind. Ann. Stat. §10-1101 [1956 Repl.])	300

Kansas

Statutes Annotated
§21-3302(3)   297

Kentucky

Revised Statutes
§501.070(2)	345 n.7
§506.010(4)	297

Louisiana

Revised Statutes Annotated
§14:27(D)   297

Maine

Revised Statutes Annotated
tit. 17-A, §152(4)   297

Massachusetts

General Laws Annotated
ch. 274, §6   297

Table of Statutes

Michigan

Compiled Laws Annotated
§750.92	297
§750.5201	629
§750.520d(1)(b)	630

Minnesota

Statutes
§609.055	442
§609.17, subd. 4	297
§609.52	442
§609.52, subd. 2	441
§609.625	442
§609.625, subd. 1	441

Missouri

Revised Statutes
§564.016(8)	297

Nevada

Revised Statutes
§193.330	297

New Hampshire

Revised Statutes Annotated
ch. 162-H, §1	468
§275:52	427
§626:1, I	426
§626:2,II(d)	368
§626:8	363, 365, 367, 368, 369
§626:8, I	367
§626:8, II(c)	365, 367
§626:8, II(d)	366
§626:8, III	365, 366
§626:8, III(a)	367, 368
§626:8, III(b)	368
§626:8, IV	365, 366, 367, 368, 369
§627:3	468
§630:3, I	366
§635:2	468

New Jersey

Revised Statutes
§2A:98-1	563
§2C:2-4(c)(3)	586
§2C:3-4	514
§2C:3-4(a)	513
§2C:3-4(b)(2)	513
§2C:11-5	76 n.2

New Mexico

Statutes Annotated
§30-28-1	297

New York

Penal Law
§35.05(a)	468
§35.15	508, 509
§35.15(1)	506
§35.15(2)	506
§110.05	297
§115.00	362
§125	67
§125.10	67
§125.15	67
§125.20	67
§125.20(2)	149 n.†, 695 n.14
§125.25	68, 148
§125.25(1)(a)	695 n.15
§125.25(3)	695 n.15
§125.27	69
§125.27(2)(a)	695 n.15
§265.01	504
§265.02	504
§265.15(3)	167 n.1
§265.15(3)(a)	167 n.1
§265.15(3)(c)	167 n.1
§265.20	167 n.1

North Carolina

General Statutes
§14-2.4	297

North Dakota

Century Code
§12.01-05-12	502
§12.1-05-03	500
§12.1-05-04	500
§12.1-05-07	501
§12.1-05-08	501
§12.1-05-12	501
§12.1-06-03	297

Ohio

Revised Code Annotated
§2923.02(E)	297

Oklahoma

Statutes Annotated
tit. 21, §42 — 297

Oregon

Revised Statutes
§63.115	97
§161.025(1)(d)	213
§161.055(2)	215
§161.085	213
§161.095	213
§161.095(2)	213
§161.105	213
§161.105(1)(b)	213
§161.115	213
§161.115(2)	213
§161.405(2)	297
§161.435(2)	297
§161.450(2)	297
§163.135(1)	105
§482.290	215
§482.560	212, 213, 214, 215, 216
§487.560(1)	215
§487.560(2)	212, 218
§487.560(2)(b)	215, 217
§487.560(3)(a)	215
§487.560(3)(b)	215
§487.560(3)(c)	215
§487.560(3)(d)	215

Pennsylvania

Statutes Annotated
tit. 18, §2502(b)	695 n.14
§2503(a)	695 n.15
§2504	418
§2804	414

Rhode Island

General Laws
§11-56-1 — 424

Proposed Criminal Code
§11A-2-4 — 391

South Dakota

Codified Laws Annotated
§22-4-1	297
§22-10-4	491

Tennessee

Code Annotated
§39-1-507	345 n.3, 345 n.6
§40-7-108	475

Texas

Penal Code Annotated
tit. 4, §15.01(c)	297
§15.02(d)	297
§15.03(d)	297
art. 477	256

Utah

Code Annotated
§76-4-101(1)	274
§76-4-102	297
§76-5-202(1)	273

Vermont

Laws, 1933
§8602 — 227

Statutes Annotated
tit. 13, §9(2) — 297

Virginia

Code
§18.2-22 — 297

Washington

Revised Code
§9.48.060	202
§9.48.150	202
§9A.28.020(3)	297

West Virginia

Code
§61-2-7 (b)	345 n.7
§61-11-8	297

Wisconsin

Statutes Annotated
§939.30	297
§939.32(1)	297
§939.645	676, 677, 679, 680

Table of Statutes

§939.645(2)(c)	677		**Virgin Islands**	
§940.34(1)	424			
§940.34(2)	424		*Code Annotated*	
§940.225(3)	632	tit. 14, §331		297
§940.225(4)	632			

United States Trust Territory

England

Trust Territory Code

Criminal Appeal Act 1968

tit. 11, §4   297   §33(2)   383

American Samoa

Criminal Justice Act 1967

§8   398

Code Annotated

§46.3404   297

New Zealand

Puerto Rico

Crimes Act of 1961

Laws Annotated   §169(1)   107

tit. 33, §3122   297   §169(2)   107

INDEX

Aaron, hypothetical with, 409-410
Abandoned and malignant heart murder, functional analysis of, 695
Abandonment, *see* Conspiracy
Abnormal step test, in attempt, 266
Abortion protesters, hypothetical with, 576-577
Abortion protesters, use of RICO against, 668-673
Abuse of corpse, hypothetical with, 130-131, 140
Accidental Kidnapping hypothetical, 389-390
Acker Motan, hypothetical with, 525-526, 536
Acme market, president of, 430-437
Act requirement, *see also* Voluntary act requirement
    generally, 250-262
    being addicted to narcotics, 253-256
    being intoxicated in public, 256-260
    liability for thoughts alone, 260
    Model Penal Code provision, 250-251
    necessity of having an, 251-253
    omission liability and, 261
    possession and, 261-262
    voluntariness requirement vs., 260-261
Actus non facit reum nisi mens sit rea, 180
Adrift at sea, killing to prevent starvation while, 459-463
AIDS research, hypothetical with, 458-459
Amber, hypothetical with, 72-73, 80
Ambiguity in statute, 131-132
Ambiguous acquittal, effect on functioning of criminal law, 696
American Civil Liberties Union (ACLU), 92
Amnesty International, 91
Amsterdam, Anthony, 125
Analogy, principle of, 132
Anna, hypothetical with, 182-183, 199
Ansel, hypothetical with, 389-390
Anthony, Susan B., 577-578
Appeals, 15-16
Arkin, hypothetical with, 389-390
Arraignment 12-13
Arrest, 3-4, 18-19

Arthur's Adventure hypothetical, 562-563, 569-570
Ashworth, Andrew, 448
Attempt, *see also* Inchoate offenses
    generally, 262-277
    abnormal step test, 266
    culpability requirements of, 270-277
    dangerous proximity doctrine, 264
    elevation of culpability requirement, 270-272, 275-277
    functional analysis of, 690
    impossibility, *see* Impossibility defense
    indispensable element test, 264-265
    inherently unlikely, 288-289
    last proximate test, 263
    Model Penal Code provision, 268-269
    no elevation of culpability requirement, 273-274
    objective requirements of, 262-269
    physical proximity doctrine, 263
    probable desistance test, 265-266
    proximity tests vs. substantial step test, 269
    purpose requirement, functional analysis of, 690-691
    renunciation, *see* Renunciation defense
    requirements of, summary chart, 287
    res ipsa loquitur test, 266-267
    space-age smuggling, 290
    substantial step, 267-268
    to create a risk, 276-277
Attie Winter, hypothetical with, 372-373
Automatism, non-insane, *see* Voluntary act requirement
Axis war criminals, criminal prosecution of, 126-129

Babies and Ditches hypothetical, 72-73
Bad temper, 108
Bank Robbery with a Sub hypothetical, 320-321
Baseball bat, hypothetical with killing with a, 537-538
Basement Burglar hypothetical, 687-688, 691, 697

811

812　　　　　　　　　　　　　　　　　　　　　　　　　　　　　　　　　　　Index

Battered woman's syndrome, 511-517
Beating Moles hypothetical, 109
Beccaria, Cesare, 91
Bedau, Hugo A., 91
Benine, hypothetical with, 31-32, 44
Bertie Graham, hypothetical with, 270
Betsey Wynn, hypothetical with, 587-588
Bib Tries to Help hypothetical, 353-354
Biker's Break hypothetical, 520-521
Blackstone, William, 61 n.11, 91
Bo, hypothetical with, 411-412
Bob and Linda hypothetical, 627-628
Bob (in culpability requirements hypothetical), 182-183, 199
Bob (in sexual offenses hypothetical), 627-628
Bob Turner (in liability of corporations hypothetical), 438-439
Bongo Sam, hypothetical with, 326, 327-328
Bongo Sam Blows It hypothetical, 326, 327-328
Booking, 4
Box, hypothetical with, 53-54, 55, 58
Brainwashing, 588-591, 599
Braithwaite, John, 449
Brock, hypothetical with, 250
Brother Constin, hypothetical with, 23-24
Brother's Brawl hypothetical, 525-536
Bubblegum, hypothetical with, 23-24
Buff, hypothetical with, 395-396, 408
Bunny, hypothetical with, 572, 575
Burden of persuasion
　generally, 145-147, 157
　constitutional limitations on shifting, 148-156
　constitutionalization of, 157
Burden of pleading, 143-144, 156
Burden of production
　generally, 144-145, 146-147
　constitutionalization of, 157-166
　failure to satisfy, 166
Burden of proof, *see also* Burden of pleading, Burden of production, Burden of persuasion, Presumptions
　generally, 143-174
　death penalty, 95
　Model Penal Code provision, 147-148
Burke, hypothetical with, 458, 469
Burt Richards, hypothetical with, 429-430, 437-438

Cabarga, Alex, 588 n.††††
Calley, Lieutenant, 517-519
Capacity requirement, *see* Omission liability
Carrie, hypothetical with, 72-73, 80
Cat in the Box hypothetical, 250
Causation, *see also* Factual cause requirement, Proximate cause requirement
　generally, 229-248

"but for" cause requirement, *see* Factual cause requirement
causing crime by an innocent and, 379
combined effect of multiple causes, 235-236
factual cause requirement, 231-234
functional analysis of requirements, 694
imputation and, 234-235
Model Penal Code provision, 245-248
multiple causes, 234-237
proposed Rhode Island provision, 231
proximate cause requirement, 233, 248
serial vs. intersecting causes, 236-237
simultaneous causes, 231, 243-245
volitional conduct of anther, 237-243
Causing crime by an innocent, *see also* Complicity
　generally, 372-379
　complicity vs., 379
　defenses to, *see* Defenses to imputation of another's conduct
　in causation, 379
　liability for justified killing by police, 373-377
　Model Penal Code provision, 377
　objective requirements, summery chart, 378
　rationale in modern codes, 379
Causing the conditions of one's own defense
　generally, 408-412
　choice of evils, 411
　duress, 411
　involuntary conduct, 412
Celia, hypothetical with, 391-392
Central Intelligence Agency (CIA), 579-580
CG-PLA at the UN hypothetical, 118
Charging decision, 5-7
Chester Turner, hypothetical with, 438-439
Choice of evils, *see* Lesser evils defense
Chucky Backs Out hypothetical, 379-380
Chucky the wheeze, hypothetical with, 379-380
Circumstance elements, functional analysis of, 694
Civil commitment
　after insanity acquittal, 555-562
　criminal commitment vs., 561-562
　dangerousness as grounds for, 562
　for a period longer than maximum criminal term, 562
Claustrophobia, failure to satisfy voluntary act requirement, 575
Cocker, hypothetical with, 326, 327-328
Coercive persuasion, *see* Problematic excuses
Cogden, Jeanne, hypothetical with, 109
Cogden, Pat, hypothetical with, 109
Collapse at Kalahoo No. 3 hypothetical, 429-430
Command Group of the Popular Liberation Army (CG-PLA), hypothetical with, 118

Index

Common law, 60-62
Common law offenses, abolition of, 119
Common thief, 122
Complaint, 7-8
Complicity, *see also* Causing crime by an innocent
   attempt to assist, 358
   causing crime by an innocent vs., 379
   conspiracy as, 322
   culpability as to circumstance, 369-370
   culpability as to result, 369
   culpability requirements, 358-370
   culpability requirements, summary chart, 370-371
   defenses to, *see* Defenses to imputation of another's conduct
   elevation of culpability requirements, 363-371
   functional analysis of, 690
   grading of, 371-372
   in rape of one's own wife, 380-383
   knowing vs. purposeful assistance, 358-363
   Model Penal Code provision, 354-355
   Model Penal Code tentative draft provision, 361-362
   objective requirements of, 355-358
   objective requirements, summary chart, 370-371
   objective vs. subjective views of criminality, 358
   purposeful vs. knowing assistance, 362
   requirement of "on proof of commission of the offence," 370-371
   requirements of, 353-372
   termination defense, *see* Termination of complicity
   United States Sentencing Commission guidelines, 371-372
Concurrence requirement
   generally, 79-80
   transaction analysis and, 79
Concussion, as failure to satisfy voluntary act requirement, 574
Condemnation, 28
Conduct elements, functional analysis of, 694
Conran, hypothetical with, 96-97, 108
Consent defense, 26-27, 28
Consent implicit in sporting events, functional analysis of, 691
Conspiracy, *see also* Termination of complicity, Renunciation defense
   generally, 298-326
   abandonment presumed, 325
   agreement requirement and impossibility, 303
   as an aggravation for group criminality, 299-303
   as attempt, 328
   bilateral agreement, 299-302
   "chains" and "wheels," 323-324
   collateral consequences of, 320-326
   culpability requirements, 304-312
   culpability requirements, summary chart, 319-320
   defenses to, Model Penal Code provisions, 315-316
   disagreement over multiple offense limitations, 312
   duration of, 324, 326
   elevation of culpability requirements, 308-311
   exemption of conduct inevitably incident to offense, 315
   exemption of victim, 315
   for persons exempted from substantive offense, 312-319
   gender difference in exempting participants, 319
   Model Penal Code provision, 302
   multiple objectives, 322-323, 326
   no elevation of circumstance element, 304-308
   objective requirements, summary chart, 319-320
   Pinkerton doctrine, 322
   prosecution for multiple offenses, 302-303
   scope of, 324, 326
   unconvictable co-conspirator, 319
   unilateral vs. bilateral agreement requirement, 303
   withdrawal from, 325
Convictions, 18-19
Convulsion, as failure to satisfy voluntary act requirement, 575
Corporate criminality, *see* Corporate officials, liability of, Corporations, liability of
Corporate officials, liability of
   generally, 429-438
   Model Penal Code provision, 430
Corporations, liability of
   generally, 438-452
   "due diligence" defense, 445-446
   for participation in fraud, 440-444
   Model Penal Code commentary, 446-448
   Model Penal Code provision, 444-445
   moral condemnation of nonhumans, 451
   "reactive corporate fault," 448-451
Corruption of minors, *see* Sexual offenses
Crays Go to Church hypothetical, 329-330
Crime, *see also* Hate crimes, RICO, Sexual offenses
   changing notions of, generally, 625-626
Crimes committed, 18-19
Crimes reported, 1-2, 18-19
Criminal code
   format of modern, 63-64
   special part vs. general part, 55
Criminal commitment
   civil commitment vs., 561-562
   dangerousness as grounds for, 562
Criminal facilitation, 362

Criminal justice process
  overview, 1-16
  overview chart, 17
Criminal law
  functional analysis of, *see* Functional analysis of criminal law
  overview, 685-698
  sources of, 60-64
  structure of, 53-60
Criminal mischief, Model Penal Code provision, 410
Criminal-civil distinction, 23-30
Criminal-civil similarities, 25
Criminalization culpability elements, *see* Functional analysis of criminal law
Criminalization offense modifications, *see* Functional analysis of criminal law
Culpability
  generally, 27, 72-81, 179-219
  applying stated culpability to all elements, 195-197
  as to conduct, 194-195
  as to illegality of conduct, 229
  asymmetry in definition of "purposely," 189
  confusion as to culpability as to conduct, 188-189
  determining requirements, generally, 177-199
  failure to define "recklessly and "negligenty" with respect to conduct, 188
  minimum requirements, generally, 199-219
  mistake and, *see* Mistake negating an offense element
  read in by general provisions, 186-187
  read in when none stated, 183, 197-198
  requirements defined, 73-74
  stated requirement applies to all elements, 183
  voluntariness vs., functional analysis of, 693
Culpability level, functional analyses of, 694
Cultural defense, *see* Problematic excuses

Dad, hypothetical with, 200, 205, 219
Dan-Cohen, Mier, 688 n.1
Dangerous proximity doctrine, in attempt, 264
Dangerousness, as grounds for civil commitment, 562
Darley, John, 43 n.9
Daughter's Mustard hypothetical, 31-32
Deadly force
  constitutionality of use to stop fleeing felon, 474-480
  defined, 488
Death penalty
  generally, 44, 88-96
  aggravating circumstances, 90
  arguments for and against, 91-95
  mitigating circumstances, 90-91
  Model Penal Code provision, 88-91, 485
  North Dakota provision, 500-501
Defense of property, *see also* Defensive force justifications
  Model Penal Code formulation, 485-488
  proportionality requirement, 488-490
Defenses, general, *see also* Justifications, Excuses, Nonexculpatory defenses
  criminalization vs. general, 57
  doctrines of, 56
  excuse, *see* Excuses
  failure of proof, 56-57
  offense modification, 57
Defense to imputation of another's conduct
  generally, 379-388
  retaining statutory exemption despite complicity, 384-386
  Model Penal Code provision, 386
  unconvictable perpetrator defense, 386-387
  loss of statutory exemption through complicity, 380-383
  exempted person defense, 387
Defensive force justifications, *see also* Justifications
  generally, 482-497
  defending against unlawful force, 456
  defense of others, Model Penal Code provision, 485
  defense of property, Model Penal Code provision, 485-488
  justification of property crimes, Model Penal Code provision, 488
  Model Penal Code provisions, 483-488
  North Dakota provisions, 500-501
  unlawful force as triggering conditions, 490-497
Deffi, hypothetical with, 497-498, 499-500, 501-502
Delgado, Richard, 588
De minimis defense, 25-26, 28-29, 131, 138
Dennis White, hypothetical with, 379-380, 387
Denny, Reginald, 275-276, 680
Deportation, 30
DeSaco, hypothetical with, 320-321, 326
Deterrence
  general, 36-37
  death penalty and general, 94-95
  individual, 37
Deviant sexual intercourse, *see* Sexual offenses
Disability excuses
  disability as "but for" cause of excusing condition, 532-533
  disability as distinguishing among excuses, 535

Index

disability requirement, 528-529
excusing conditions, 529
ignorance of criminality or wrongfulness of act, 530
ignorance of nature of act, 530
impairment of control, 531
involuntary act, 529-530
mistake excuses vs., 527-528
presumed satisfaction of objective standard, 534
specific rules for specific disabilities, 535
Disorderly loitering, 121
Distributive principles
conflict among, 40-41
for liability and punishment, generally, 31-52
hybrid, 45-51
Divergence between intended and actual result, *see also* Inculpatory mistake
generally, 389-391
inculpatory mistake vs., 391, 393
Model Penal Code provision, 390
proposed Rhode Island code, 391
Docker's Box hypothetical, 470-471
Doctor or the therapist, public authority justification for, 473
Drafting errors, recognition of, 132-133
Dressler, Joshua, 107
Due process defense vs. entrapment, 619
Dunn, hypothetical with, 329-330, 338-339
Dunning's Deal hypothetical, 414
Duress defense
generally, 562-570
functional analysis of, 693
insanity defense vs., 570
limitations on, 570
Model Penal Code provision, 569
Duty requirement, *see* Omission liability
Dwelling, defined, 488

Earl Miller, hypothetical with, 687-688
Earl Single, hypothetical with, 429-430, 437-438
Ed Begley, hypothetical with, 23-24
Ed Duffy, hypothetical with, 391-392
Ed Motan, hypothetical with, 525-526, 536
Ed Raymond, hypothetical with, 130-131
Edward Drum, hypothetical with, 587-588, 599
Egg Hunt hypothetical, 372-373
Ejusdem generis, 133
Element analysis, 185
Ellsberg, Daniel, 579-580
Emily, hypothetical with, 391-392
Entrapment defense
generally, 610-624
as nonexculpatory defense, 623
Delaware formulation, 611
due process defense vs., 619

excuse defenses and, 622-623
Model Penal Code formulation, 618-619
objective vs. subjective formulation, 611-618, 619
private entrapper, 619-623
Epilepsy, as failure to satisfy voluntary act requirement, 574
Escape from prison to avoid homosexual assault, 463-467
Escape, hypnotism defense for, 572
Escort service, hypothetical with, 414
Evergreen Greenbacks hypothetical, 438-439
Evocation requirement, *see* Public authority justifications
Excuses
generally, 27-28, 29, 58
common requirements of, 527
disability requirement, 528-529
disability, *see* Disability excuses
entrapment defense and, 622-623
excusing conditions, 529
justifications vs., 526
mistake as to an excuse, 535
mistake excuses, *see* Mistake excuses
nature of, 525-536
objective limitations on, 533-534
rational for recognizing, 526-527
voluntary act requirement vs., 575
Excusing conditions, 529-531
Ex post facto laws, prohibition against, 119-120
Expressio unius, 134
Extreme emotional disturbance
generally, 97-107, 157
individualization of reasonable person, standard for, 108
mental illness negating an element, 114
Model Penal Code formulation, 101-102
Oregon formulation, 102-104
reasonable person standard, 101-107
Extreme indifference to value of human life, 87-88

Factual cause requirement, *see also* Causation
generally, 231-234
simultaneous causes and, 245
Fair import, rule of, 136, 140
Fairness, violations of, 35-36
Fear of the Daggers hypothetical, 53-54
Fear, Pain, and Bubble Gum hypothetical, 23-25
Federal criminal code reform, 63
Federal Criminal Law, National Commission for Reform of, 63 n.19, 500 n.††
Felony murder
generally, 84-87, 88
functional analysis of, 695
Field hockey stick, hypothetical with, 109

816   Index

Firebreak to stop forest fire, hypothetical with, 409-410, 520-521
First appearance, 8-10
Fisse, Brent, 449
Fletcher, George P., 29-30, 294, 490 n.**
Food for Thought hypothetical, 395-396
Foote, Caleb, 124
Frankie, hypothetical with, 482-483, 496-497
Fraternity pledging, hypothetical with, 23-24
Fraudulent insurance claim, duress defense for, 563-569
Frear, hypothetical with, 329-330, 338-339
Fri, hypothetical with, 298-299, 311-312
Functional analysis of criminal law
　generally, 687-698
　communicative vs. adjudicative function, 696
　criminalization culpability elements, 690-691
　criminalization offense modification, 691
　culpability elements vs. voluntariness, 693
　culpability level, 694
　culpability offense modifications, 692-693
　cumulative nature of functions, 695-696
　doctrines of excuse, 693
　doctrines of grading, 693-695
　duties and omissions, 689-690
　grading, 688-689, 697
　justifications, 691
　liability assignment, 688-689, 692-693, 697
　making statutory formulations sensitive to function, 697-698
　offense culpability element, 692
　result and causation requirements, 694
　result vs. conduct and circumstance, 694-695
　rule articulation function, 688-692, 697
　rule articulation function, danger of undercutting, 697
　rules of conduct, 688-692, 697
　secondary prohibition, 690
　voluntariness doctrines, 693

Gainer, Ronald, 63 nn.19 & 21
Garden Center Supply, Inc., hypothetical with, 438-439
Garrett, hypothetical with, 610
Geets, hypothetical with, 72-73, 80
Gellman, Susan, 678
General defenses, see Justifications, Excuses, Nonexculpatory defenses, generally, 453-454
Genovese, Catherine, 418-421
Gestapo, 127
Glueck, Sheldon, 23 n.1
Golden daggers, hypothetical with, 53-54
Gorilla drug, hypothetical with, 525-526
Grading, doctrines of, see Functional analysis of criminal law

Grall, Jane, 185 n.9
Grand jury, 11-12
Greenawalt, Kent, 32
Gross sexual imposition, see Rape, Sexual offenses

Hague Convention, Fourth, 127
Hall, Jerome, 138 n.118
Handler, hypothetical with, 320-321, 326
Hans, hypothetical with, 298-299, 311-312
Harrington, Mrs., hypothetical with, 414
Hart, H.L.A., 30
Hate crimes
　generally, 675-684
　constitutional challenge to, 677-682, 683
　crimes of group terror, 683-684
　criminalizing motive, 682
　incidents of, 675-676
　RICO and, 682-683
　Wisconsin provision, 676-677
Headshop sale of cigarettes, as complicity, 363
Heart medication, substitution for, 270
Heat of passion, mitigation in homicide, 101, 157
Hegel, G.W.F., 33
Henry, hypothetical with, 458
Homicide
　generally, 65-116
　diminished capacity, see Mental illness negating an offense element
　doctrines of aggravation, 81-88
　doctrines of mitigation, 96-116
　extreme emotional disturbance, see Extreme emotional disturbance
　heat of passion, 101, 157
　mental illness negating an offense element, see Mental illness negating an offense element
　provocation, 30, 97-107
　statutes, 65-71
Hybrid distributive principles
　amount v. method, 50-51
　combined, 48-50
　priorities, 47-48
Hypnotism as a defense, 572, 575
Hypnotizing Bunny hypothetical, 572
Hypoglycemia, as failure to satisfy voluntary act requirement, 574

Ian, hypothetical with, 200
Ike, hypothetical with, 23-24
Immaturity defense
　generally, 570-572
　conclusive vs. rebuttable presumptions, 571
　functional analysis of, 693

Index

Model Penal Code provision, 570-571
overage, by an actor who is, 571-572
youth as presumption of immaturity, 571
Impeachment, 30
Impossibility defense
   generally, 277-291
   defense in modern criminal codes, 287-288
   due to mistake as to offense attempted, 287-288, 290-291
   factual, examples of, 281
   factual vs. legal, 279-284, 285
   imaginary offenses and, 288
   legal, examples of, 280-281
   legality and, 288
   Model Penal Code provision, 285
Impossible Incest hypothetical, 391-392
Imputation, *see also* Voluntary intoxication negating offense element, Causing the conditions of one's own defense, Complicity
   codified forms of, 347
   criticisms of, 343-344
   desert vs. utilitarian dispute, 350-351
   of culpability element because of voluntary intoxication, as immoral and unethical, 397-404
   of culpability elements, 56, 346-347
   of objective elements, 55-56, 345-346
   of offense elements, generally, 343-352
   theories of, 347-350
Incapacitation
   generally, 37
   death penalty and, 93-94
Inchoate offenses
   generally, 249-250, 292-298
   arguments for insignificance of resulting harm, 292-294
   arguments for the significance of resulting harm, 294-296
   Model Penal Code exception for first degree felony, 297
   Model Penal Code provision, 292
   rejection of Model Penal Code position, 297
Incompetent person, public authority justification for persons responsible for, 472-473
Inculpatory mistake
   generally, 391-394
   divergence between intended and actual result vs., 391, 393
   imputation between offenses of different grades, 393
   Model Penal Code provision, 392
Indian Penal Code, 422-424
Indispensable element approach, in attempt, 264-265
Information, 12

Insanity defense, *see also* Mental illness negating an offense element
   generally, 536-552, 553-555
   ALI test, 543, 548-551, 552
   ALI test, caveat paragraph, 550
   civil commitment after insanity acquittal, 555-562
   control prong, 538-543
   duress defense vs., 570
   Durham product test, 552
   Durham product test and rotten social background defense, 599
   federal formulation, 551, 552
   functional analysis of, 693
   involuntary intoxication vs., 536-537, 553
   irresistible impulse test, 552
   "justly held responsible" formulation, 547-548, 552
   lay vs. expert judgment, 552
   McNaughten test, 551
   Model Penal Code provision, 543
   multiple personalities and, 553-555
   personality of actor, 555
   product test, 552
   product test, need to depart from, 544-546
   proposal to abolish, 546-567
   sociopath excluded, 550-551
Interpretation of criminal statutes
   generally, 130-141
   Model Penal Code provision, 131
Intimate parts, as defined for sexual assault, 291
Intoxication, *see* Voluntary intoxication negating an offense element, Involuntary intoxication
Investigation
   post-arrest, 4-5
   pre-arrest, 2-3
Involuntary act defense, *see* Voluntary act requirement
Involuntary intoxication
   generally, 552-553
   functional analysis of, 693
   insanity vs., 536-537, 553
   Model Penal Code provision, 552-553
Iota, hypothetical with, 31-32, 44
Iva, hypothetical with, 270

Jackson, Justice Robert H., 126, 129 n.*
Jake (in culpablility hypothetical), 182-183, 199
Jake (in unknowingly justified actor hypothetical), 520-521, 523-524
Jake Sets a Record hypothetical, 182-183
Japanese, cultural defense for, 600-602
Jefferson, Thomas, 91
JJ's Out hypothetical, 610, 619
Jote, hypothetical with, 525-526
Judge's family, 139-141

Justification, generally, *see also* Lesser evils defense
  objective theory of, 522, 524
  subjective theory of, 523, 524
  unknowingly justified actor, *see* Unknowingly justified actor
Justifications, *see also* Lesser evils defense, Defensive force defense, Public authority justifications, Mistake as to a justification
  generally, 27-29, 57, 455-524
  balancing competing harms, 455-456
  causing the conditions of, 412
  defending against unlawful force, 456
  defensive force justifications, *see* Defensive force justifications
  excuses vs., 526
  functional analysis of, 691
  furthering public interest, 457
  lesser evils defense, *see* Lesser evils defense
  nature of, 455-458
  necessity requirement, 457-458
  nonexculpatory defenses vs., 605-606, 609
  property crimes, Model Penal Code provision, 488
  proportionality requirement, 458
  proportionality requirement, constitutionalization of, 482
  public authority justifications, *see* Public Authority justifications
  resisting, 412
  triggering conditions, 457
Justificatory proposes vs. distributive principles, 39-40

Kadish, Sanford, 62 n.14
Kalahoo mine, hypothetical with, 429-430
Kant, Immanuel, 33, 91
Kidnapping, accidental, hypothetical with, 389-390
King, Rodney, 275-276, 680
Knapp, Kay, 61 n.10
Knowledge
  generally, 75
  defined, 73
Krule, hypothetical with, 320-321, 326

Lane, hypothetical with, 572
Last proximate act, in attempt, 263
Later controls the earlier, statutory interpretation rule, 134
Law enforcement authority
  generally, 477-482
  constitutionality of use of deadly force in stopping fleeing felon, 474-480
  constitutionalization of the proportionality requirement, 482
  Model Penal Code provision, 480-481

Law school, difficulties of first year, hypothetical with, 395-396
Legality principle, generally, 61-62, 117-142
Lenity, rule of, *see* Strict construction, rule of
Lesser evils defense, *see also* Justifications
  generally, 455, 458-470
  balancing competing harms, 455-456
  imminent threat vs. immediately necessary conduct, 467
  legislative preemption, 467-469
  Model Penal Code provision, 459
  necessity defense, 44
  necessity requirement, 467
  proportionality requirement, 467
  superiority of more specific justification defense, 469
Lester, hypothetical with, 96-97, 108
Liability assignment, *see* Functional analysis of criminal law
Liability assignment vs. sentencing, 59
Libya, hypothetical with, 118
Liddy, Gordon, 579-580
Life-saving Break-in hypothetical, 458-459
Linda, hypothetical with 627-628
Livingston, 422
Locke, John, 91
Logan, Mr., hypothetical with, 482-483, 496-497
Lynch, Gerard, 662

Macaulay, T. B., 422-424
MacKinnon, Catherine, 649
Malice, defined, 65-66
Malignant heart murder, 87-88
Mandatory presumption, 169
Mann Act, 312-315, 318
Manny the Master hypothetical, 230-231, 233
Mansfield, John H., 293
Marsden, hypothetical with, 262, 269
Mens rea
  early notions of, 184
  significance of, 184
Mental illness negating an offense element, *see also* Insanity defense
  homicide, 109-114
  Model Penal Code provision, 113-114
Mentes reae, 184-185
Meurtre, 81
Michael's Madness hypothetical, 537-538
Military authority justification, 517-520
Military orders, Model Penal Code provision, 520
Mind transport, hypothetical with, 290
Mississippi Burning, hate crime attack after viewing, 677
Mistake as to consent, 221-225
Mistake as to justification
  generally, 497-520

Index

819

battered woman's syndrome as relevant to, 511-517
culpable mistake, 511
individualizing the objective standard of reasonableness of, 511-517
military orders, 517-520
Model Penal Code provision, 499
Model Penal Code's individualized objective standard, 511
North Dakota provisions, 500-501
objective standard in deciding reasonableness of, 502-511
reasonableness of, 502-511
Mistake excuses, *see also* Mistake as to a justification
generally, 576-587
defense of good faith reliance on apparent authority, 580-585
due diligence defense, New Jersey provision, 586
excusing condition, 531
mistake as to an excuse, 535
mistake negating an element vs., 586
Model Penal Code approach, 587
reliance upon official misstatement, 577-585
reliance upon official misstatement, Model Penal Code provision, 585-586
unavailable law defense, Model Penal Code provision, 585-586
Mistake negating an offense element
generally, 219-229
mistake excuse vs., 586
mistake of law, 227-229
Model Penal Code provision, 220
terminology, 226
Modafi, Ahmed, hypothetical with, 118, 129
Model Penal Code, history of, 62-63
Modern criminal codes, 62
Moral authority of the law, 43
Moral condemnation
generally, 25
as deterrence, 42-43
Moral guilt and social judgment, 33-35
Moro's Mistake hypothetical, 497-498, 499-500, 501-502
Morris, hypothetical with, 320-321, 326
Morris, Norval, 41 n.4, 109 n.*
Morse, hypothetical with, 329-330, 338-339
Motan brothers, hypothetical with, 525-526
Motive
criminalizing, 682
defined, 682
Muscle, hypothetical with, 353-354
My Lai massacre, 517
My Lon, hypothetical with, 587-588, 599

NAACP Legal Defense and Education Fund, 92
National Commission on Reform of Federal Criminal Law, 63 n.19, 500 n.††
Necessity defense, *see* Lesser evils defense
Necessity requirement, *see* Justifications
Negligence
generally, 76-77, 200-207
defined, 74, 80
individualizing the reasonable person standard of, 206
omission and, 207
reasons for punishing, 204-205
Nonexculpatory defenses, *see also* Entrapment
generally, 58-59, 603-624
collateral consequences of conviction, 607-608
collateral consequences of nonexculpatory acquittal, 608
constitutional defenses, 605
detrimental effects of, 606
difficulty in identifying dismissals from, 609
diplomatic immunity, 603-605
justifications vs., 605-606, 609
less strict adherence to legality principle for, 606-607
mistake as to, 607
resisting aggressor with, 607
Norm reinforcement, 37

Objective elements
generally, 190-195, 199
combining conduct and circumstance elements, 192
combining conduct and result elements, 192
defining conduct element, 193-194
distinction between circumstance and result elements, 194
distinguishing from one another, 190
Obstructing a public passageway by pro-life protesters, 576-577
Occam's razor, 590
Offense analysis, 185
Offense definitions, 54-55
Offense modification defenses, 57
Olsen, Frances, 642
Omission liability
generally, 413-428
capacity requirement, 425-428
capacity requirement, functional analysis of, 693
duty requirement, 418
duty requirement, functional analysis of, 689-690
duty to assist, Rhode Island provision, 424
duty to assist, Wisconsin provision, 424-425

Omission liability (continued)
  duty to stranger, 418-421
  functional analysis of, 689-690
  general duty statutes and bootstrapping, 425
  negligence and, 77-78
Order and safety on vehicle, public authority justification for person to maintain, 473-474
Overview chart, criminal justice process, 16-17
Oyako-Shinju (parent-child suicide), 600-601

Pacer (George Brook), hypothetical with, 470-471, 474
Parent, Dale, 60 n.10
Parent or guardian, public authority justification for, 472
Patton, General George S., 374
Penal plethysmograph, 44 n.*
Penne, hypothetical with, 31-32, 44
Pentagon Papers, 578-579
Permissive inference, 168-169
Pet, hypothetical with, 53-54, 55, 58
Peter the pig, hypothetical with, 395-396
Phinimin, hypothetical with, 326, 327-328
Physical proximity doctrine, in attempt, 263
Pinkerton doctrine, in conspiracy, 322
Plain meaning rule, 132
Plan to Kill hypothetical, 262-263
Pop, hypothetical with, 372-373
Possession
  defined as an act, 261-262
  liability for, 261-262
Post-conviction remedies, 16
Pot Boils hypothetical, 96-97
Predictions of future criminality, 44
Preliminary hearing, 10-11
Premeditation, in murder, 81-84, 87
Presumption
  conclusive vs. reputable for immaturity, 571
  constitutional limitations on, 166-174
  Model Penal Code provision, 172
Pre-trial motion, 13
Primary prohibitions, functional analysis of, 689
Prior criminal record, 44
Prisoners of war, 599
Privileged force, 501-502
Probable desistance test, in attempt, 265-266
Problematic excuses
  generally, 587-602
  brainwashing, 588-591
  coercive persuasion, 588-591
  cultural defense, 600-602
  cultural defense, factors other than indoctrination circumstances, 602
  cultural defense, indoctrination circumstances, 602
  sympathy vs. defense, 602
Pro-life groups, protests by, hypothetical with, 576-577
Proportionality requirement, *see also* Justifications
  use of deadly force in protection of property, 488-490
Propping Up Ed hypothetical, 130-131
Prosecutor Baylor, hypothetical with, 230-231, 233
Prostitution, exemption of customer from liability for, 384-386
Provocation
  generally, 30, 97-107
  New Zealand formulation, 107
Prowling by auto, 121
Proximate cause requirement, *see also* Causation
  generally, 233
  Model Penal Code remoteness requirement, 248
Public authority justifications, *see also* Justifications, Law enforcement authority
  generally, 456-457, 470-482
  evocation requirement, 457
  execution of public duty, Model Penal Code provision, 471-472
  furthering public interest, 456-457
  military orders, Model Penal Code provision, 520
  persons with special responsibility, Model Penal Code provision, 472-474
  triggering conditions, 457
Punishment
  defined, 29
  moral justification for, 31-52
  unanimous support among justificatory purposes, for institution of, 39
Purpose
  generally, 75
  as a form of motive, 682
  conditional, 74
  defined, 73, 79

Quarantine for a contagious disease, 30

Racism
  death penalty and, 92
  individualization of objective standard and, 206-207
Radical environmentalists, 599
Ranger Yardley, hypothetical with, 520-521
Rape, *see also* Sexual offenses and related offenses, Model Penal Code provisions, 628-629

Index

coercion requirement, 632
coercion vs. bargain, 630-631
culpability as to coercion or nonconsent, 633-634
date rape vs. stranger rape, 638
grading of, 634-635
gross sexual imposition, Model Penal Code provision, 629
individualization of objective standard for determining adequate threat, 630
Model Penal Code commentary, 631
Model Penal Code provision, 628-629
prior intercourse, 641
rape of one's own wife, complicity in, 380-383
resistance requirement, 629
special exemption from, 380-383, 387
spousal exclusion, generally, 635-638
spousal exclusion, living as man and wife, 637
spousal exclusion, Model Penal Code commentary, 635-636
threat requirement, 629
threats other than of violence, 630
without-consent formulation, 632-633
Reasonable person standard, *see* Extream emotional disturbances, Negligence, Recklessness
Reception statutes, 61
Recklessness
generally 75-76
defined, 73-74, 80
individualizing the reasonable person standard for, 206
Red Brigade hijacking, 362-363
Reflex, as failure to satisfy voluntary act requirement, 575
Reform, 37-38
Refusing to help, 418-421
Rehabilitation, 37-38
Renunciation defense
generally, 328-339
functional analysis of, 692-693
grading inchoate offenses and, 339
Model Penal Code commentary, 334-335
of attempt, Model Penal Code provision, 337
of conspiracy, Model Penal Code provision, 338
of solicitation, Model Penal Code provision, 337-338
termination vs., 338-339
Res ipsa loquitur test, in attempt, 266-267
Restitution, 30
Result elements
conduct and circumstance elements vs., functional analysis of, 694-695
functional analysis of, 594
Retribution, in the death penalty and, 92-93

Retributive distribution of liability and punishment
generally, 33-36
death penalty and, 92-93
disutility of, 41-42
utility of, 42
Return of escaped passenger to hijackers, as complicity, 362-363
RICO (Racketeer Influenced and Corrupt Organizations)
generally, 655-674
as a transaction-based model of crime, 662-664
as an enterprise offense, 664-667
character and dangerousness, 667
crime of being a criminal, 662-667
economic motive, 673-674
enterprise requirement, 657-661
federal provision, 656-657
hate crimes and, 682-683
pattern of activity, 661
statement of findings and purpose of federal act, 655
traditional forms of group criminality vs., 661-662
use against abortion protesters, 668-673
use against persons other than organized crime, 667-668, 674
Risk creation, functional analysis of, 689
Robinson, Paul H., 43 n.9, 51, 185 n.9, 404, 688 n.1, 692 n.6, 698 n.17
Romance Writer's Guild's "Sweet Tear" award, hypothetical with, 562-563
Rosie's Homerun hypothetical, 482-483
Rotten social background defense, *see also* Problematic excuses
generally, 591-599
Durham product test and, 599
Rousseau, Jean-Jacques, 91
Rule articulation function, *see* Functional analysis of criminal law
Rules of conduct, *see* Functional analysis of criminal law
Russell, Diana E.H., 636
Russian poker, 82

Schulhofer, Steven, 292
Scope, *see* Conspiracy
Secondary prohibitions, functional analysis of, 690
Seduction, *see* Sexual offenses
Selective service office, hypothetical with, 326
Self defense, *see also* Defensive force defenses
Model Penal Code provision, 483-484
North Dakota provision, 500
Selling Death hypothetical, 298-299
Sentences imposed, 18-19
Sentencing, 14-15, 59-60

Sexual intercourse, defined, 628 n.*
Sexual offenses, *see also* Rape, Statutory rape
  generally, 627-653
  corruption of minors and seduction, sexually permiscuous complainants, Model Penal Code provision, 639
  corruption of minors, Model Penal Code provision, 648
  deviant sexual intercourse, decriminalization between consenting adults, Model Penal Code commentary, 650-652
  gender based, 647-649
  immorality vs. injury, 653
  limitation of liability to males, Model Penal Code commentary, 646-647
  mistake as to age, culpability as to under 16, 645
  mistake as to age, Model Penal Code provision, 643
  mistake as to age, culpability as to under 10, 645
  mistake as to age, Model Penal Code commentary, 643-645
  morality enforcement, 653
  rape, *see* Rape
  seduction, 642
  seduction, Model Penal Code provision, 648
  sexual assault by smelling feet, 290-291
  statutory rape, *see* Statutory rape
Sexual psychopath, commitment of, 30
Sharon, hypothetical with, 395-396, 408
Shifting right of justification, 496-497
Sitting on child as discipline, 115
Skopezine, hypothetical with, 525-526
Sleep-walking, 573-574, 575
Smelling feet, hypothetical with, 290-291
Smoke detectors, selling defective, hypothetical with, 298-299
Smuggler's Deceit hypothetical, 278-279
Snake, hypothetical with, 497-498
So, hypothetical with, 278-279, 290
Societal norms
  interaction with law, 43
  violations of, 35-36
Sodomy, 96-97
Solicitation
  generally, 298, 326-328
  as attempt, 328
  as complicity, 328
  Model Penal Code provision, 327
Somnambulism, 573-574, 575
Sophie's Stand hypothetical, 576-577
South Yemen, government of, 362-363
Southbury Training School, hypothetical with, 372-373
Southern Poverty Law Center, 92
Spano, hypothetical with, 482-483
Special controls the general, statutory interpretation rule, 134

Special responsibility, persons with, *see* Public authority justifications
Spoon, hypothetical with, 520-521, 523-524
Squeeze, hypothetical with, 230-231, 233-234
Status excuses, 531-532, *see also* Excuses
Statutory rape, *see also* Sexual offenses
  generally, 391-392
  autonomy privacy and respect, 641-642
  gender based definitions, 647-648
  immorality or ineffective consent, 641
  Model Penal Code commentary, 639-641
  prior promiscuity, 641
Steve, hypothetical with, 627-628
Strict construction, rule of, 135-136, 140
Strict liability
  generally, 207-219
  assumed from absence of culpability requirement, 186, 211-218
  burden of persuasion, 219
  criticisms of, 207-210
  Model Penal Code provision, 211
Substantial step, in attempt, 267-268
Sugar smuggling, hypothetical with, 278-279
Susan Rigg, hypothetical with, 353-354

Tampering with records, hypothetical with, 182
Teacher, public authority justification of, 472
Teppi, hypothetical with, 409-410, 411-412
Termination of complicity
  generally, 328-329, 338-339
  Model Penal Code provision, 338
Terrorists, fourth generation, 108
Theft, functional analysis of, 689
Theory, practical importance of, 60
Thought reform, *see* Problematic excuses
Threatening federal judge, 139-140
Tim, hypothetical with, 458
Time served in prison, 18-19
Tittle, C. R., 43 n.8
Toad (Donald Starr), hypothetical with, 587-588
Tonry, Michael, 60 n.10
Tony Bumonte, hypothetical with, 379-380, 387
Trading Corn for People hypothetical, 409-410
Tree Frog (Luis Reynoldo Johnson), 588 n.††††
Trial, 13-14
Triggering conditions, *see* Justifications
Trucker, Ella, hypothetical with, 130-131
Turo "The Hat," hypothetical with, 230-231, 233
Tyler, Tom, 43 n.8

Undercover police officer, 298-299, 387, 610
United Nations, 118

Index

United States Marines, killing of, 591-599
United States Sentencing Commission guidelines, complicity, 371-372
Unknowingly justified actor
  generally, 520-524
  assisting and resisting, 523
  current law, 521-522
  impossible attempt, 522-523, 524
  justificatory purpose vs. knowledge, 523
  objective theory of justification, 522, 524
  resisting and assisting, 524
  subjective theory of justification, 523, 524
Unlawful force
  as triggering condition for defensive force, 490-497
  defined, 501
  defined, Model Penal Code provision, 498
Utilitarianism, 36-39

Vagabond, 120
Vagrancy, 120-121
Vagueness in statutes, 131-132
Vengeance, 38
Violations vs. crimes, 26
Voluntariness requirement, *see* Voluntary act requirement
Voluntary act requirement *see also* Act requirement
  generally, 529-530, 572-575
  excuse defenses vs., 575
  functional analysis of, 693
  habitual conduct, 575
  Model Penal Code provision, 574-575
  not a product of effort or determination of actor, 575

Voluntary intoxication negating an offense element
  generally, 395-408
  causing the conditions of one's own defense, 406-407, 408
  culpability as to becoming intoxicated, 408
  Model Penal Code provision, 396-397
  proposal, 407
von Hirsch, Andrew, 41 n.5, 61 n.10

Walker, hypothetical with, 372-373, 377-378
War crimes, nazi, 126-129
Warden or other correctional official, public authority justification of, 473
Warehouse, unclean conditions in as basis for criminal liability, 430-437
Watergate affair, 578-585
Watson, Henry, 275
Watson, hypothetical with, 278-279, 285, 290
Welfare fraud, hypothetical with, 130-131
Who is Edward Drum? hypothetical, 587-588
Wiener, Robin D., 634
Williams, Damian, 275-276
Williams, Glanville, 101, 105-106, 279 n.*, 572
Withdrawal, *see* Conspiracy
Wootton, Barbara, 23 n.1, 41 n.3

Yamashita, Commanding General of the Japanese Army in the Philippine Islands, 428
Your Basement Burglar hypothetical, 687-688

Z-type spruce trees, hypothetical with, 438-439